Frommer's®

Japan

10th Edition

by Beth Reiber

with Janie Spencer

WILEY

Wiley Publishing, Inc.

Published by:

WILEY PUBLISHING, INC.

111 River St.
Hoboken, NJ 07030-5774

ISBN 978-0-470-54129-6 (paper);
ISBN 978-0-470-87785-2 (ebk);
ISBN 978-0-470-39297-3 (ebk);
ISBN 978-0-470-90877-8 (ebk)

Editor: Billy Fox
Production Editor: Michael Brumitt
Cartographer: Andrew Murphy
Photo Editor: Richard Fox
Production by Wiley Indianapolis Composition Services

Front cover photo: A sculpture of Komokuten, the Guardian King of the South, at the Todaiji Temple in Nara ©Michael Rutkowski
Back cover photo: A view of Mount Fuji from a tea plantation in Shizuoka Prefecture ©Naoaki Watanabe / Sebun Photo / Getty Images

For information on our other products and services or to obtain technical support, please contact our Customer Care Department within the U.S. at 877/762-2974, outside the U.S. at 317/572-3993 or fax 317/572-4002.

Wiley also publishes its books in a variety of electronic formats. Some content that appears in print may not be available in electronic formats.

Manufactured in the United States of America

5 4 3 2 1

CONTENTS

8 THE JAPAN ALPS — 265

9 KYOTO & NARA — 290

10 THE REST OF WESTERN HONSHU — 357

11 SHIKOKU — 478

12 KYUSHU — 497

LIST OF MAPS

To my parents, who, while I was growing up in Kansas, always encouraged me to look farther than my own backyard; to my sons, Matthias and Johannes, for providing a teenager's perspective on Japan and for putting up with my absences for as long as they can remember; and to Jack, for everything.
—Beth Reiber

To my husband and daughter, who have always had to contend with my other love, Japan.
—Janie Spencer

ACKNOWLEDGMENTS

I would like to thank some fine and very special people, without whose generous assistance and advice this book could never be as comprehensive as it is. A special arigato goes to Nori Akashi, Yuki Yamagishi, Naoko Marutani, and Zenbon Tei of the Japan National Tourist Organization for their support and behind-the-scenes guidance. I would also like to thank the following for their regional expertise and the assistance they extended during my travels: Katsunori Hirano, Hidekazu Nasuno, and Miyako Tanaka in Shizuoka Prefecture; Eri Yamada and Toshihiko Nasaka in Nagoya; Yoshihiro Katayama in Inuyama City; Ken Yokohama in Kyoto; Toyohisa Matsuda, Sigehiro Suzuki, Yoshikazu Kitaguchi, and Toyohiro Ishii in Ishi-kawa Prefecture; Orie Miyazawa and Satoru Ogawa in Mie Prefecture; Noriki Ueki in Mount Koya; Makoto Inaya in Okayama Prefecture; Takashi Suyama in Kagawa Prefecture; Yukie Kawai and Hisashi Harada in Ehime Prefecture; Shizue Ishibashi in Hokkaido Prefecture; and Takashi Kinjo, Kumiko Teruya, Kaori Kinjo, Takafumi Okudaira, and Tetsuya Asao in Oki-nawa. Debbie Howard gets kudos for her moral support, not to mention her years as a partner in crime researching Tokyo's nightlife, while Junko Matsuda gets a huge thanks for her tireless fact-checking skills and valuable knowledge of Tokyo. Finally, I'd also like to thank Tak Nagaoka at JNTO for encouraging me so many years ago to take on this mammoth project, which sent my life in a totally unexpected direction.
—Beth Reiber

The Japan National Tourist Office, in particular Yohko Scott and her colleagues at JNTO in Los Angeles, have my deep appreciation for their invaluable help. Credit belongs to the local tourist information offices all over Japan, where unsung heroes tirelessly answer questions. I am indebted to Kagoshima Prefecture's Akimitsu Baba and Moyuru Nagata and Oita Prefecture's Atsushi Miyazaki and Noriko Kishikawa for their kindness and knowledge of their regions. I'd like to extend my gratefulness to Satsuki Watanabe of Kagoshima Prefecture and Tomo Matsuo of Nagasaki Prefecture for years of making my job easier. For their support, I thank JAL Group's Haruya Kusakabe, Yap Sze Hunn, and Miho Takahashi. I appreciate the hospitality and knowl-edge of Ken Yokoyama. Thank you, Mr. Satoshi Ichitani, for 20 years of elegant assistance. For his wisdom, a special thanks belongs to Ignatius Cronin of Imperial Hotels. *Un grand merci* goes to Jacques and Chizuko Borie for their culinary insights. To Debbie Howard and Julia Nolet for their insider information and long friendship: many, many thanks.
—Janie Spencer

HOW TO CONTACT US

In researching this book, we discovered many wonderful places—hotels, restaurants, shops, and more. We're sure you'll find others. Please tell us about them, so we can share the information with your fellow travelers in upcoming editions. If you were disappointed with a recommendation, we'd love to know that, too. Please write to:

Frommer's Japan, 10th Edition
Wiley Publishing, Inc. • 111 River St. • Hoboken, NJ 07030-5774
frommersfeedback@wiley.com

AN ADDITIONAL NOTE

Please be advised that travel information is subject to change at any time—and this is especially true of prices. We therefore suggest that you write or call ahead for confirmation when making your travel plans. The authors, editors, and publisher cannot be held responsible for the experiences of readers while traveling. Your safety is important to us, however, so we encourage you to stay alert and be aware of your surroundings. Keep a close eye on cameras, purses, and wallets, all favorite targets of thieves and pickpockets.

ABOUT THE AUTHORS

Long before she could read, **Beth Reiber** spent hours pouring over her grandparents' latest *National Geographic* magazines. After living several years in Germany as a university student and freelance travel writer writing for major U.S. newspapers and in Tokyo as editor of *Far East Traveler,* she authored several Frommer's guides, including *Frommer's Tokyo* and *Frommer's Hong Kong.* She also contributes to *Frommer's Europe by Rail, Frommer's China,* and *Frommer's USA.* When not on the road, she resides in Lawrence, Kansas, with her two sons, a dog, and a cat.

Janie Spencer spent 10 years in Japan working for *Kyodo News Service* and *Tokyo Journal,* as well as freelancing for Asian-based and other newspapers and magazines. Her love of travel has led her to more than 40 countries, and she and her family live near Paris and in Hollywood.

FROMMER'S STAR RATINGS, ICONS & ABBREVIATIONS

Every hotel, restaurant, and attraction listing in this guide has been ranked for quality, value, service, amenities, and special features using a **star-rating system.** In country, state, and regional guides, we also rate towns and regions to help you narrow down your choices and budget your time accordingly. Hotels and restaurants are rated on a scale of zero (recommended) to three stars (exceptional). Attractions, shopping, nightlife, towns, and regions are rated according to the following scale. zero stars (recommended), one star (highly recommended), two stars (very highly recommended), and three stars (must-see).

In addition to the star-rating system, we also use **seven feature icons** that point you to the great deals, in-the-know advice, and unique experiences that separate travelers from tourists. Throughout the book, look for:

Finds	Special finds—those places only insiders know about
Fun Facts	Fun facts—details that make travelers more informed and their trips more fun
Kids	Best bets for kids and advice for the whole family
Moments	Special moments—those experiences that memories are made of
Overrated	Places or experiences not worth your time or money
Tips	Insider tips—great ways to save time and money
Value	Great values—where to get the best deals

The following **abbreviations** are used for credit cards:

AE	American Express	**DISC**	Discover	**V**	Visa
DC	Diners Club	**MC**	MasterCard		

TRAVEL RESOURCES AT FROMMERS.COM

Frommer's travel resources don't end with this guide. Frommer's website, **www.frommers.com**, has travel information on more than 4,000 destinations. We update features regularly, giving you access to the most current trip-planning information and the best airfare, lodging, and car-rental bargains. You can also listen to podcasts, connect with other Frommers.com members through our active-reader forums, share your travel photos, read blogs from guidebook editors and fellow travelers, and much more.

The Best of Japan

Long ago, Japanese ranked the three best of almost every natural wonder and attraction in their country: the three best gardens, the three best scenic spots, the three best waterfalls, even the three best bridges. But choosing the "best" of anything is inherently subjective, and decades—even centuries—have passed since some of the original "three best" were so designated. Still, lists can be useful for establishing priorities. To help you get the most out of your stay, I've compiled this list of what I consider the best Japan has to offer based on years of traveling through the country. From the weird to the wonderful, the profound to the profane, the obvious to the obscure, these recommendations should fire your imagination and launch you toward discoveries of your own.

1 THE BEST TRAVEL EXPERIENCES

- **Making a Pilgrimage to a Temple or Shrine:** From mountaintop shrines to neighborhood temples, Japan's religious structures rank among the nation's most popular attractions. Usually devoted to a particular deity, they're visited for specific reasons: Shopkeepers call on Fushimi-Inari Shrine outside Kyoto, dedicated to the goddess of rice and therefore prosperity, while couples wishing for a happy marriage head to Kyoto's Jishu Shrine, a shrine to the deity of love. Shrines and temples are also the sites for Japan's major festivals. See chapter 3, the regional chapters, and "The Best Temples & Shrines" section, below, for more on Japan's temples and shrines.

- **Taking a Communal Hot-Spring Bath:** No other people on earth bathe as enthusiastically, as frequently, and for such duration as Japanese. Their many hot-spring baths—thought to cure all sorts of ailments as well as simply make you feel good—range from elegant, Zen-like affairs to rustic outdoor baths with views of the countryside. No matter what the setup, you'll soon warm to the ritual of soaping up, rinsing off, and then soaking in near-scalding waters. Hot-spring spas are located almost everywhere in Japan, from Kyushu to Hokkaido; see the "Bathing" section under "Minding Your P's & Q's" in chapter 2, and the regional chapters for more information.

- **Participating in a Festival:** With Shintoism and Buddhism as its major religions, and temples and shrines virtually everywhere, Japan has multiple festivals every week. These celebrations, which range from huge processions of wheeled floats to those featuring horseback archery and ladder-top acrobatics, can be lots of fun; you may want to plan your trip around one (and book early for a hotel). See the "Japan Calendar of Events," in chapter 3, for a list of some of the most popular festivals.

- **Dining on Japanese Food:** There's more to Japanese cuisine than sushi, and part of what makes travel here so fascinating is the variety of national and regional dishes. Every prefecture, it seems, has its own style of noodles, its special vegetables, and its delicacies. If money is no object, order *kaiseki*, a complete meal of visual and culinary finesse. See "Eating & Drinking in Japan," in chapter 2; the "Where to Dine" sections in the regional chapters; and "The Best Culinary Experiences," later in this chapter, for more on Japanese food.

- **Viewing the Cherry Blossoms:** Nothing symbolizes the approach of spring so vividly to Japanese as the appearance of the cherry blossoms—and nothing so amazes visitors as the way Japanese gather under the blossoms to celebrate the season with food, drink, and dance. See the "Japan Calendar of Events," in chapter 3, for cherry blossom details.

- **Riding the Shinkansen Bullet Train:** Asia's fastest train whips you across the countryside at more than 290km (180 miles) an hour as you relax, see Japan's rural countryside, and dine on boxed meals filled with local specialties. See "Getting Around Japan," in chapter 3.

- **Staying in a Ryokan:** Japan's legendary service reigns supreme in a top-class *ryokan,* a traditional Japanese inn. You'll bathe in a Japanese tub or hot-spring bath, feast your eyes on lovely views past *shoji* screens, dine like a king in your *tatami* room, and sleep on a futon. See "Tips on Accommodations" in chapter 3 and the "Where to Stay" sections in the regional chapters for more on ryokan.

- **Shopping in a Department Store:** Japan's department stores are among the best in the world, offering everything from food to designer clothing to electronics to kimono and traditional crafts. Service also is among the best in the world: If you arrive when the store opens, staff will be lined up at the front door to bow as you enter. See the "Shopping" sections throughout this book.

- **Visiting a Local Market:** Tsukiji Fish Market, in Tokyo, is Japan's largest, but there are local seafood and produce markets virtually everywhere. Those in

Kyoto, Kanazawa, Takayama, Hakodate, and Okinawa are among my favorites. See the "Shopping" sections of the regional chapters for more information.

- **Attending a Kabuki Play:** Based on universal themes and designed to appeal to the masses, *kabuki* plays are extravaganzas of theatrical displays, costumes, and scenes—but mostly they're just plain fun. See "Japanese Arts in a Nutshell," in chapter 2, and the kabuki section of "Tokyo After Dark," in chapter 6.

- **Strolling Through Tokyo's Nightlife District:** Every major city in Japan has its own nightlife district, but probably none is more famous, more wicked, or more varied than Tokyo's Shinjuku, which offers everything from hole-in-the-wall bars to strip joints, dance clubs, and gay clubs. See "Tokyo After Dark," in chapter 6.

- **Seeing Mount Fuji:** It may not seem like much of an accomplishment to see Japan's most famous and tallest mountain, visible from about 150km (100 miles) away. But, the truth is, it's hardly ever visible, except during the winter months and rare occasions when the air is clear. Catching your first glimpse of the giant peak is truly breathtaking and something you'll never forget, whether you see it from aboard the Shinkansen, a Tokyo skyscraper, or a nearby national park. If you want to climb it (possible only in July–Aug), be prepared for a group experience—400,000 people climb Mount Fuji every summer. See "Climbing Mount Fuji," in chapter 7.

- **Spending a Few Days in Kyoto:** If you see only one city in Japan, Kyoto should be it. Japan's capital from 794 to 1868, Kyoto is one of Japan's finest ancient cities, boasting some of the country's best temples, Japanese-style inns, traditional restaurants, shops, and gardens. See chapter 9 for extensive information on the city.

- **Meiji Jingu Shrine** (Tokyo): Tokyo's most venerable and refined Shinto shrine honors Emperor Meiji and his empress with simple yet dignified architecture surrounded by a dense forest. This is a great refuge in the heart of the city. See p. 184.

- **Sensoji Temple** (Tokyo): The capital's oldest temple is also its liveliest. Throngs of visitors and stalls selling both traditional and kitschy items lend it a festival-like atmosphere. This is the most important temple to see in Tokyo. See p. 185.

- **Kotokuin Temple** (Kamakura): This temple is home to the Great Buddha, Japan's second-largest bronze image, which was cast in the 13th century and sits outdoors against a magnificent wooded backdrop. The Buddha's face has a wonderful expression of contentment, serenity, and compassion. See p. 232.

- **Hase Kannon Temple** (Kamakura): Although this temple is famous for its 9m-tall (30-ft.) Kannon of Mercy, the largest wooden image in Japan, it's most memorable for its thousands of small statues of Jizo, the guardian deity of children, donated by parents of miscarried, stillborn, or aborted children. It's a rather haunting vision. See p. 234.

- **Toshogu Shrine** (Nikko): Dedicated to Japan's most powerful shogun, Tokugawa Ieyasu, this World Heritage Site is the nation's most elaborate and opulent shrine, made with 2.4 million sheets of gold leaf. It's set in a forest of cedar in a national park. See p. 239.

- **Kiyomizu Temple** (Kyoto): One of Japan's best-known temples with a structure imitated by lesser temples around the country, Kiyomizu commands an exalted spot on a steep hill with a view over Kyoto. The pathway leading to the shrine is lined with pottery and souvenir shops, and the temple grounds have open-air pavilions, where you can drink beer or eat noodles. Don't neglect a visit to the smaller **Jishu Shrine** on its grounds—it's dedicated to the god of love. See p. 329.

- **Sanjusangendo Hall** (Kyoto): Japan's longest wooden building contains the spectacular sight of more than 1,000 life-size wood-carved statues, row upon row of the thousand-handed Kannon of Mercy. See p. 330.

- **Kinkakuji (Temple of the Golden Pavilion;** Kyoto): Constructed in the 14th century as a shogun's retirement villa, this three-story pavilion shimmers in gold leaf and is topped with a bronze phoenix; it's a beautiful sight when the sun shines and the sky's blue. See p. 331.

- **Todaiji Temple** (Nara): Japan's largest bronze Buddha sits in the largest wooden structure in the world, making it the top attraction in this former capital. While not as impressive as the Great Buddha's dramatic outdoor stage in Kamakura (see above), the sheer size of Todaiji Temple and its Buddha make this sight not to be missed if you're in the Kansai area. See p. 353.

- **Horyuji Temple** (Nara): Despite the fact that Todaiji Temple with its Great Buddha (see above) gets all the glory, true seekers of Buddhist art and history head to the sacred grounds of Horyuji Temple with its treasures and ancient buildings. See p. 354.

- **Ise Grand Shrines** (Ise): Although there's not much to see, these shrines are the most venerated Shinto shrines in all of Japan, and pilgrims have been flocking here for centuries. Amazingly, the Inner Shrine, which contains the Sacred Mirror, is razed and reconstructed on a new site every 20 years in accordance with strict rules governing purification in the Shinto religion. Follow the age-old route of former pilgrims after you visit the shrines, and stop for a meal in the nearby Okage Yokocho District. See p. 373.

- **Myoryuji Temple** (Kanazawa): This is a temple of a different kind, popularly known as Ninja-dera and fun to visit because of its hidden stairways, trick doors, traps, secret chambers, and other Feudal-Era devices meant to thwart enemy intruders. See p. 387.

- **Itsukushima Shrine** (Miyajima): The huge red *torii* (the traditional entry gate of a shrine), standing in the waters of the Seto Inland Sea, is one of the most photographed landmarks in Japan and signals the approach to this shrine. Built over the tidal flats on a gem of an island called Miyajima, it's considered one of Japan's most scenic spots. At night, the shrine is illuminated. See p. 473.

- **Kotohiragu Shrine** (Kotohira, on Shikoku): One of Japan's oldest and most popular shrines beckons at the top of 785 granite steps on the Yashima Plateau with great views of the Seto Inland Sea, but for most Japanese, it's the "I made it!" that counts. See p. 481.

- **Dazaifu Tenmangu Shrine** (Fukuoka): Established in 905 to deify the god of scholarship, this immensely popular shrine has a festive atmosphere and is popular with students wishing to pass school exams. The road leading to the shrine is lined with souvenir and craft shops; the Kyushu National Museum is an escalator ride away. See p. 501.

3 THE BEST GARDENS

- **Rikugien Garden** (Tokyo): It's not as centrally located as Tokyo's other gardens, but Rikugien stands out not only for its quintessentially Japanese setting but also because its vistas are unmarred by surrounding skyscrapers. Created in 1702 and later donated to the city by the founder of Mitsubishi, it boasts a strolling path around a pond complete with islets, teahouses, and arched bridges. See p. 190.

- **Sankeien Garden** (Yokohama): Historic villas, tea arbors, a farmhouse, a pagoda, and other authentic buildings, all set in a century-old landscaped garden with ponds and streams, make this one of the most interesting and picturesque gardens near the capital. See p. 247.

- **Ryoanji Temple** (Kyoto): Japan's most famous Zen rock garden, laid out at the end of the 15th century, consists of moss-covered boulders and raked pebbles enclosed by an earthen wall. It is said that it's impossible to see all 15 rocks from any vantage point; see if you can. Come early in the morning for some peaceful meditation and to beat the crowds. See p. 331.

- **Katsura Imperial Villa** (Kyoto): Designed by Japan's most famous gardener, Kobori Enshu, the garden surrounding this imperial villa is, in my view, Japan's most beautiful. A "strolling garden," its view changes with every step but is always complete, perfectly balanced, and in harmony. It's well worth the extra effort involved to see it. See p. 341.

- **Saihoji** (Kyoto): Popularly known as the Moss Temple, Saihoji boasts Japan's most famous moss garden, with more than 100 varieties spread around a pond and giving off an iridescent glow. It's especially beautiful after a rainfall. See p. 342.

- **Kenrokuen Garden** (Kanazawa): Considered by some to be Japan's grandest landscape garden (and rated one of the "three best"), Kenrokuen is also one of the largest. The garden took 150 years to complete and consists of ponds, streams, rocks, mounds, trees, grassy expanses, and footpaths. Best of all, no tall buildings detract from the views. After Katsura (see above), this is my top choice. See p. 383.

- **Koko-en** (Himeji): It isn't old (it was laid out in 1992), but this is a wonderful surprise package of nine small gardens, each one different but typical of gardens during the Edo Period, which lasted from 1603 to 1867. Upon seeing what can be accomplished with skill and money in little more than 18 years, some gardeners may turn green with envy. See p. 434.

- **Korakuen Garden** (Okayama): Rated one of Japan's three most beautiful gardens, Korakuen was completed in 1700 and incorporates the surrounding hills and Okayama Castle into its design. It's definitely worth a visit if you're in the vicinity, though personally, I like Kenrokuen (see above) more. See p. 438.

- **Ritsurin Garden** (Takamatsu): Dating from the 17th century, this former private retreat of the ruling Matsudaira clan is an exquisite strolling garden that incorporates Mount Shiun in its landscaping and boasts 1,400 pine trees and 350 cherry trees. Stop for tea in the Feudal-Era teahouse and contemplate the view at leisure. See p. 479.

- **Sengan-en** (Kagoshima): Laid out more than 300 years ago by the Shimadzu clan, this summer retreat with a 25-room villa was known for its poem-composing parties, held beside a rivulet that still exists. After touring the garden and villa, be sure to visit the nearby museum with relics belonging to the Shimadzu family. This garden is one of my favorites. See p. 537.

4 THE BEST CASTLES, PALACES & VILLAS

- **Tamozawa Imperial Villa** (Nikko): Comprised of a 1632 villa and an 1899 expansion, this 106-room villa was the home of a prince who later became emperor. You can learn about traditional Japanese architectural details and lifestyles of the aristocracy on self-guided tours, and unlike Japan's other imperial villas, it does not require a reservation. See p. 240.

- **Matsumoto Castle** (Matsumoto): Popularly known as the Crow Castle due to its black color, this small castle boasts the oldest *donjon* (keep) in Japan (more than 400 years old). A moon-viewing room was added in 1635, and exhibited inside the castle is a superb collection of Japanese matchlocks and samurai armor dating from the mid–16th century through the Edo Period. Volunteer guides stand ready for personal tours. See p. 268.

- **Nijo Castle** (Kyoto): One of the few castles built by the mighty Tokugawa shogunate as a residence rather than for defense, Nijo Castle is where the shogun stayed whenever he was in Kyoto. It's famous for its nightingale (creaking) floorboards that warned of enemy intruders. The castle is considered the quintessence of Momoyama architecture. See p. 327.

- **Kyoto Imperial Palace** (Kyoto): Home to Japan's imperial family from the 14th to the 19th centuries, this palace is praised for its Heian design and graceful garden. Good news for travelers: Guided tours of the palace are free. See p. 326.

- **Katsura Imperial Villa** (Kyoto): Built in the 1600s by a brother of the emperor, this villa and garden are considered to be among the best—if not the best—in traditional architecture and landscape gardening. More than anyplace else, the villa illustrates the life of refinement enjoyed by 17th-century nobility, when leisurely pursuits included such activities as moon viewing. See p. 341.

- **Himeji Castle** (Himeji): Said to resemble a white heron poised in flight over the plains, this is quite simply Japan's most beautiful castle. With its extensive gates, moats, turrets, and maze of passageways, this UNESCO World Heritage Site has survived virtually intact since feudal times. If you see only one castle in Japan, make this the one. See p. 433.

- **Matsue Castle** (Matsue): This 17th-century castle features a five-story donjon with samurai gear and artifacts belonging to the ruling Matsudaira clan, with many Edo-Era attractions just outside its moat. See p. 453.

- **Matsuyama Castle** (Matsuyama): Occupying a hill above the city, this 400-year-old fortress boasts good views over Matsuyama from its three-story donjon as well as a collection of armor and swords of the Matsudaira clan. See p. 489.

- **Kumamoto Castle** (Kumamoto): Although a ferroconcrete reconstruction not nearly as huge as the original, this massive castle is still an impressive sight, especially at night when it's illuminated. It's famous for its curved walls, which made invasion virtually impossible. The interior houses a museum with palanquins, armor, swords, and other artifacts of the former ruling clans. See p. 527.

- **Shuri Castle** (Okinawa Island): One of nine historic structures in Okinawa that collectively make up a World Heritage Site, this castle with Chinese and Japanese influences was the center of the Ryukyu Kingdom, which thrived for about 500 years. See p. 561.

5 THE BEST MUSEUMS

- **Edo-Tokyo Museum** (Tokyo): Housed in a high-tech modern building, this ambitious museum chronicles the fascinating and somewhat tumultuous history of Tokyo (known as Edo during the Feudal Era) with models, replicas, artifacts, and dioramas. Volunteers stand ready to give free guided tours in English. See p. 180.

- **Tokyo National Museum** (Tokyo): Even professed museumphobes should make a point of visiting the National Museum, the largest repository of Japanese arts in the world. Lacquerware, china, kimono, samurai armor, swords, woodblock prints, religious art, and more are on display, making this the best place in Japan to view Japanese antiques and decorative objects. If you visit only one museum in Japan, this should be it. See p. 186.

- **Hakone Open-Air Museum** (Chokoku-no-Mori, Hakone): Beautifully landscaped grounds and spectacular scenery showcase approximately 400 20th-century sculptures, from Giacomo and Rodin to Henry Moore. Here, too, is the Picasso Pavilion, housing 200 of the artist's works. See p. 254.

- **Japan Ukiyo-e Museum** (Matsumoto): One of the best woodblock-print museums in Japan, this museum displays the largest collection of prints in the world on a rotating basis. A must-see in Matsumoto. See p. 269.

- **Hida Folk Village** (Takayama): Picturesquely situated around a pond with flowers, more than 30 shingled and thatched farmhouses—many transported from the surrounding Japan Alps—are filled with farm implements and objects of daily life, providing fascinating insight into the life and times of the extended families that once inhabited them. See p. 278.
- **Museum Meiji Mura** (Nagoya): This open-air architectural museum is an absolute treasure, with more than 60 original buildings and structures dating from the Meiji Period situated on 100 hectares (250 acres) that are beautifully landscaped on the shore of a lake. Western-style homes, churches, a kabuki theater, a bathhouse, a prison, a brewery, and much more are open for viewing and filled with furniture and household items. Mail a postcard from an authentic post office, buy candy from an old candy store, and drink tea in the lobby of the original Imperial Hotel, which was designed by Frank Lloyd Wright. See p. 365.
- **Ishikawa Prefectural Museum for Traditional Products and Crafts** (Kanazawa): Kanazawa is famous for its handcrafted items, including gold leaf, umbrellas, stringed instruments, Buddhist altars, pottery, and more. English-language explanations and an audio guide explain how they're made. See p. 384.

- **Disaster Reduction Museum** (Kobe): You can't tell by its name, but this excellent museum is devoted to Kobe's 1995 earthquake, with films, dioramas, and exhibits detailing the city's destruction and rebirth. See p. 421.
- **Ohara Museum of Art** (Kurashiki): Founded in 1930, this museum just keeps getting bigger and better, with works by both Western and Japanese greats spread throughout several buildings. Its location in the picturesque Kurashiki historic district is a bonus. See p. 446.
- **Adachi Museum** (Matsue): This museum near Matsue combines two of my passions—art and gardens—making it a winner. Japanese modern art is the focus indoors, while the perfectly landscaped garden—one of Japan's best—comes into view through framed windows, making it part of the art in a very surreal way. See p. 456.
- **Peace Memorial Museum** (Hiroshima): Japan's most thought-provoking museum contains exhibits examining Hiroshima's militaristic past, the events leading up to the explosion of the world's first atomic bomb, the city's terrible destruction, and its active antinuclear movement. See p. 464.
- **Benesse Art Site Naoshima** (Takamatsu): This is not a single museum, but rather an island in the Seto Inland Sea that's devoted to cutting-edge art, with two museums (both designed by Tadao Ando) and interactive art installations in traditional Japanese buildings. There's no other place in Japan quite like this. See p. 482.

6 THE BEST NATIONAL PARKS

- **Nikko National Park:** This 80,000-hectare (200,000-acre) national park centers on the sumptuous Toshogu Shrine with its mausoleum for Tokugawa Ieyasu, majestic cedars, and lakeside resorts. See p. 236.

- **Fuji-Hakone-Izu National Park:** Boasting magnificent Mount Fuji at its core, this popular weekend getaway beckons vacationing Tokyoites with its many hot-spring spas, stunning close-up views of Mount Fuji, sparkling lakes, historic attractions relating to the famous Feudal-Era Tokaido Highway, and coastal areas of Izu Peninsula. One of the best ways to see Hakone is via a circular route that involves travel on a two-car mountain streetcar, a cable car, a ropeway, and a boat; the delightful journey offers wonderful scenery and interesting sights along the way. See p. 251.

- **Japan Alps (Chubu Sangaku) National Park:** Encompassing Honshu's most impressive mountain ranges and the site of the 1998 Winter Olympics, this national park offers skiing and hiking as well as unique villages worth a visit in their own right. See p. 265.

- **Ise-Shima National Park:** Boasting a rugged seascape of capes, inlets, and islets, this park is the birthplace of cultivated pearls. It's famous for its bays dotted with pearl-cultivating oyster rafts, its female divers, a pearl museum, plus a top-notch aquarium and the Ise Grand Shrines, Japan's most venerable shrines. Two theme parks are also located here. See p. 372.

- **Seto-Naikai (Inland Sea) National Park:** Covering 650 sq. km (251 sq. miles) of water, islands, islets, and coastline, this sea park stretches from Kobe in the east to Beppu in the west. It's studded with numerous islands of all sizes, the most famous of which is Miyajima, home of the Itsukushima Shrine. Cruises ply the waters of the Seto Inland Sea, as do regular ferries sailing between Honshu, Shikoku, and Kyushu. The adventuresome can even cycle across the Seto Inland Sea via the Shimanami Kaido route linking Honshu with Shikoku (see "The Best Outdoor Adventures," below). See p. 472.

- **Unzen-Amakusa National Park:** At western Kyushu's high-altitude national park, you can climb Mount Fugen (1,360m/4,462 ft. above sea level), relax in a hot-spring bath, and take a walk through the Hells, the park's extra-steamy sulfur springs. See p. 521.

- **Iriomote National Park:** Japan's southernmost national park includes Iriomote Island, 80% of which is blanketed with subtropical forest and mangroves, as well as coral reefs and coastline. Part of the Okinawan island chain, it's a mecca for nature enthusiasts and scuba divers alike. See p. 570.

- **Towada-Hachimantai National Park:** Tohoku's most popular park beckons with scenic lakes, rustic hot-spring spas, hiking, and skiing. See p. 585.

- **Shikotsu-Toya National Park:** This 987-sq.-km (381-sq.-mile) park in eastern Hokkaido encompasses lakes, volcanoes, and famous hot-spring resorts such as Noboribetsu. See p. 612.

- **Daisetsuzan National Park:** The largest of Japan's 28 national parks—and some say Hokkaido's most beautiful—Daisetsuzan boasts three volcanic chains, fir- and birch-covered hillsides, impressive Sounkyo Gorge, and plenty of skiing and hiking opportunities. See p. 618.

- **Akan National Park:** Popular for hiking, skiing, canoeing, and fishing, Akan National Park in Hokkaido is characterized by dense forests of subarctic primeval trees and caldera lakes, the most famous of which are Kussharo, one of Japan's largest mountain lakes, and Mashu, considered one of Japan's least-spoiled lakes and one of the world's clearest. See p. 622.

7 THE BEST OF OLD JAPAN

- **Splurging on a Night in a Ryokan:** If you can afford to, splurge on at least 1 night in one of the country's best *ryokan,* where the service is impeccable, the *kaiseki* meals are out of this world, and glorious views outside your *tatami* room are of miniature landscaped gardens. You'll be pampered in a manner befitting an emperor; many of the nation's oldest ryokan were indeed born to serve members of the imperial court and feudal lords as they traveled Japan's highways. See "Tips on Accommodations," in chapter 3; the "Where to Stay" sections in the regional chapters; and "The Best Traditional Ryokan," below.

- **Attending a Sumo Match:** There's nothing quite like watching two monstrous sumo wrestlers square off, bluff, and grapple as they attempt to throw each other on the ground or out of the ring. Matches are great cultural events, but even if you can't attend one, you can watch them on TV during one of six annual 15-day tournaments. For more information, see "Spectator Sports," in chapter 6, and "Sumo," in chapter 2.

- **Strolling Through a Japanese Garden:** Most of Japan's famous gardens are relics of the Edo Period, when the shogun, *daimyo* (feudal lords), imperial family, and even samurai and Buddhist priests developed private gardens for their own viewing pleasure. Each step in a strolling garden brings a new view to die for. See "The Best Gardens," earlier in this chapter, and the attractions sections in the regional chapters to see which are heaven on earth.

- **Attending a Traditional Tea Ceremony:** Developed in the 16th century as a means to achieve inner harmony with nature, the highly ritualized ceremony is carried out in teahouses throughout the country, including those set in Japan's many parks and gardens. Several Tokyo hotels offer English-language instruction in the tea ceremony, but my favorite locale is Gyokusen-en in Kanazawa. See p. 188 and 384.

- **Getting a Shiatsu Massage:** Shiatsu, or pressure-point massage, is available in virtually all first-class accommodations in Japan and at most moderately priced ones as well. After a hard day of work or sightseeing, nothing beats a relaxing massage in the privacy of your room.

- **Relaxing at a Hot-Spring Resort:** No country in the world boasts more natural hot springs than Japan, which has 19,500 different springs. Hot-spring spas are found in virtually all regions of the country and feature everything from hot-sand baths to open-air baths. See the regional chapters for more information.

- **Spending a Day in Asakusa** (Tokyo): Asakusa is the best place to experience Tokyo's old downtown, with its popular Sensoji Temple, Nakamise shopping lane with crafts and kitsch, and casual traditional restaurants. As in days of yore, arrive by boat on the Sumida River. See chapter 6.

- **Exploring Kyoto's Higashiyama-ku District:** Kyoto's eastern sector is a lovely combination of wooded hills, temples, shrines, museums, shops, and traditional restaurants, making it one of the best neighborhoods in Japan for a stroll. See "Walking Tour 1: A Stroll Through Higashiyama-ku," in chapter 9.

- **Watching Cormorant Fishing:** Every night in summer, wooden boats gaily decorated with paper lanterns will take you out on rivers outside Nagoya for an up-close look at cormorant fishing. The birds, maneuvered by fishermen in traditional garb, have tight collars around their necks to prevent them from swallowing their catch. Drinking and dining on board contribute to the festive air. See p. 365.

- **Walking to Kobo Daishi's Mausoleum on Mount Koya:** Ever since the 9th century, when Buddhist leader Kobo Daishi was laid to rest at Okunoin on Mount Koya, his faithful followers have followed him to their graves—and now tomb after tomb lines a 1.5km (1-mile) pathway to Daishi's mausoleum. Cypress trees, moss-covered stone lanterns, and thousands upon thousands of tombs make this the most impressive graveyard stroll in Japan, especially at night. See "Exploring Mount Koya," in chapter 10.

8 THE BEST OF MODERN JAPAN

- **Visiting Tsukiji Fish Market:** One of the largest wholesale fish markets in the world, this indoor market bustles with activity from about 3am on as frozen tuna is unloaded from boats, auctions are held, and vendors sell octopus, fish, squid, and everything else from the sea that's edible to the city's restaurants. Be sure to bring your camera. See p. 186.

- **Attending a Baseball Game:** After sumo, baseball is Japan's most popular spectator sport. Watching a game with a stadium full of avid fans can be quite fun and can shed new light on America's favorite pastime. See p. 206 and the "Take Me Out to the Ballgame" box, on p. 502.

- **Seeing Tokyo from the TMG:** On the 45th floor of the Tokyo Metropolitan Government Office (TMG), designed by well-known architect Tange Kenzo, an observatory offers a bird's-eye view of Shinjuku's cluster of skyscrapers, the never-ending metropolis, and, on fine winter days, Mount Fuji. Best of all, it's free. See p. 195.

- **Hanging Out in Harajuku:** Nothing beats Sunday in Harajuku, where you can begin the day leisurely with brunch and then stroll the promenade of Omotesando Dori, shop the area's many boutiques, take in a museum and perhaps a flea market, and then relax over drinks at a sidewalk cafe and watch the never-ending parade of humanity. See "Walking Tour 2: In the Heart of Trendy Tokyo, A Stroll Through Harajuku & Aoyama," in chapter 6.

- **Shopping for Japanese Designer Clothes:** Japanese designer clothing is often outrageous, occasionally practical, but mostly just fun. Department stores and designer boutiques in Aoyama are the places to try on the styles if you have both the money and the figure for them. See "Shopping," in chapter 6.

- **Spending an Evening in an Entertainment District:** A spin through one of Japan's famous nightlife districts, such as **Shinjuku** or **Roppongi** in Tokyo or **Dotombori** in Osaka, is a colorful way to rub elbows with the natives as you explore narrow streets with their whirls of neon, tiny hole-in-the-wall bars and restaurants, and all-night amusement spots. See "Tokyo After Dark," in chapter 6, and "Osaka After Dark," in chapter 10.

- **Seeing Fish Eye-to-Eye in an Aquarium** (Nagoya, Toba, Osaka, Kagoshima, Beppu, Okinawa): Because Japan is surrounded by sea, it's no surprise that it has more than its share of aquariums, many with innovative displays that put you eye-to-eye with the creatures of the deep. My favorite is the one in Osaka. See p. 363, 377, 403, 538, 553, and 562.

9 THE BEST OUTDOOR ADVENTURES

- **Climbing Mount Fuji:** Okay, so climbing Japan's tallest—3,766m-high (12,355 ft.)—and most famous mountain is not the solitary, athletic pursuit you may have envisioned—but with 400,000 people climbing it annually, it's a great, culturally enriching group activity. Many opt to climb through the night with a flashlight and then cheer the sunrise from the top of the mountain. See "Climbing Mount Fuji," in chapter 7.

- **Hiking the Old Nakasendo Highway:** Back in the days of the shogun, feudal lords were required to return to Edo (now Tokyo) every other year, traveling designated highways. Nakasendo was one of these highways, and an 8km (5-mile) stretch through a valley still exists between the old post towns of **Magome** and **Tsumago.** It's a beautiful walk, and the towns are historic relics. See p. 274.

- **Skiing in Honshu & Hokkaido:** Host of two winter Olympics (in Sapporo in 1972 and Nagano in 1998) and riddled with mountain chains, Japan is a great destination for skiing, the most popular winter sport in the country, and for snowboarding. The Japan Alps in Central Honshu and the mountains of Tohoku and Hokkaido are popular destinations. See chapters 8, 14, and 15.

- **Cycling:** Hard to believe, but you can bike between Shikoku island and Hiroshima Prefecture via the 70km (43-mile) Shimanami Kaido route, which actually comprises seven bridges and six islands in the Seto Inland Sea and follows a well-maintained, dedicated biking path. See "Cycling the Shimanami Kaido," in chapter 11, and "Exploring Sights of the Seto Inland Sea," in chapter 10. Another favorite: Cycling through the historic, rural Kibiji District in Okayama Prefecture on a path that takes you past paddies, ancient burial grounds, temples, and shrines. See p. 492.

- **Shooting the Kumagawa Rapids:** You can glide down one of Japan's most rapid rivers in a long, traditional wooden boat, powered by men with poles. See "Shooting the Kumagawa Rapids," under "Kumamoto," in chapter 12.

- **Fishing:** Most foreigners laugh when they see Japanese fishing spots—a stocked pool in the middle of Tokyo or a cement-banked river, lined elbow to elbow with fishermen. For more sporting conditions, head to Lake Akan in Hokkaido's **Akan National Park,** where you can fish for rainbow trout or white spotted char. See "Akanko Spa & Akan National Park," in chapter 15.

- **Scuba Diving and Snorkeling:** Okinawa, an archipelago of 160 subtropical islands, is blessed with coral reefs, schools of manta rays, and operators offering excursions for all levels, not to mention some of the best dive spots in the world. Favorites include the Kerama Islands and Iriomote. See chapter 13.

10 THE BEST TRADITIONAL RYOKAN

- **Hiiragiya Ryokan** (Kyoto; © 075/ 221-1136): If ever there was an example of the quintessential *ryokan,* Hiiragiya is it. Located in the heart of old Kyoto, it's the ultimate in *tatami* luxury: a dignified enclave of polished wood and rooms with antique furnishings overlooking private gardens. Six generations of the same family have provided impeccable service and hospitality here since 1861. See p. 304.

- **Tawaraya** (Kyoto; ℂ 075/211-5566): This venerable inn has been owned and operated by the same family since it opened in the first decade of the 1700s; it's now in its 11th generation of innkeepers. Located in old Kyoto, its guest list reads like a who's who of visitors to Japan, including Leonard Bernstein, the king of Sweden, Alfred Hitchcock, and Saul Bellow. See p. 305.

- **Ryokan Kurashiki** (Kurashiki; ℂ 086/422-0730): Located right beside the willow-lined canal of Kurashiki's famous historic district, this ryokan occupies an old mansion and three 250-year-old converted warehouses, yet it contains only five elegant suites, each with a tatami living room and sleeping quarters with Western-style beds. See p. 448.

- **Iwaso Ryokan** (Miyajima; ℂ 0829/44-2233): The setting here is as romantic as any you'll find in Japan. If you can afford it, stay in one of the ryokan's 80-year-old cottages, where you'll have a view of maples and a gurgling brook on one of Japan's most scenic and famous islands. If staying here doesn't make you feel like a samurai or a geisha, nothing will. See p. 475.

- **Hakusuikan Ryokan** (Ibusuki; ℂ 0993/22-3131): I'm usually partial to historic Japanese inns, but this sprawling complex right on the coast, with manicured lawns dotted by pine trees, offers an assortment of accommodations (the oldest building is 45 years old), along with one of the best hot-spring spas I've ever seen, modeled after a public bath of the Edo Era, as well as a museum filled with antiques. See p. 547.

11 THE BEST WESTERN-STYLE HOTELS

- **Park Hyatt Tokyo** (ℂ 800/233-1234 in the U.S. and Canada): Occupying the 39th to 52nd floors of a skyscraper designed by Tange Kenzo, this gorgeous property offers stunning views of the city, one of Tokyo's hottest restaurants, rooms you could live in, and legendary service. No wonder it was the hotel featured in *Lost in Translation*. See p. 130.

- **The Ritz-Carlton, Tokyo** (ℂ 800/241-3333 in the U.S.): Occupying the lofty reaches of Tokyo's tallest building, this luxury property in Tokyo Midtown ranks as one of Japan's best hotels, with Tokyo's largest rooms and coolest bathrooms (the two sinks and counters are at opposite ends, making them perfect for couples). It cocoons guests from the mad whirl of central Tokyo, yet Roppongi's hopping nightlife is just outside its doors. See p. 132.

- **Four Seasons Hotel Tokyo at Chinzan-So** (ℂ 800/819-5053): Surrounded by a lush, 7-hectare (17-acre) garden, this top-rated hotel is a wonderful respite in one of the world's most crowded cities, with its impeccable service and a terrific spa and health club. See p. 132.

- **Nikko Kanaya Hotel** (Nikko; ℂ 0288/54-0001): Dating from the 19th century, this rambling, old-fashioned hotel combines the rustic charm of a European country lodge with design elements of old Japan—and it's just a 15-minute walk from Toshogu Shrine. See p. 241.

- **The Fujiya Hotel** (Hakone; ℂ 0460/82-2211): Established in 1878 and nestled on a wooded hillside, the Fujiya is one of Japan's oldest, grandest, and most majestic Western-style hotels. Resembling a *ryokan* from the outside, it boasts a comfortable interior of detailed woodwork, old-fashioned antiques-filled guest rooms, and a delightful 1930s dining hall. It also offers indoor/outdoor pools, extensive landscaping, and hot-spring baths. A stay here makes you feel like you've traveled not just to Hakone but to another century. See p. 257.

- **Shima Kanko Hotel Bay Suites** (Ise-Shima; ✆ 0599/43-2111): Its secluded setting on a hill overlooking a bay, hushed atmosphere, attentive service, and Zen-like decor make this 50-suite property seem more like a Japanese inn than a hotel. Enjoy the stunning views from the rooftop garden or from the privacy of your own bath or balcony. See p. 380.

- **The Westin Miyako** (Kyoto; ✆ 800/937-8461 in the U.S. and Canada): First built in 1890 but completely remodeled, this smartly appointed hotel sprawls across more than 6.4 hectares (16 acres) of hilltop on the eastern edge of town near many famous temples. Good views, a free shuttle service from the train station, indoor/outdoor swimming pools, and a Japanese garden

make this a winner. There's even an annex with Japanese-style rooms as well. See p. 311.

- **Nara Hotel** (Nara; ✆ 0742/26-3300): From far away, this 1909 building just a short walk from Nara Park resembles a palace. Rooms in the main building have high ceilings, antique light fixtures, and old-fashioned decor. See p. 355.

- **Unzen Kanko Hotel** (Unzen; ✆ 0957/73-3263): This rustic mountain lodge of ivy-covered wood and stone was built in 1935 to cater to foreigners in search of Mount Unzen's cooler climate. It offers a casual and relaxed atmosphere, hot-spring baths, and comfortable, old-fashioned rooms not far from the Hells. See p. 524.

- **Towada Hotel** (Lake Towada; ✆ 0176/75-1122): This Japanese-temple-meets-Western-lodge property occupies a secluded wooded hill overlooking Lake Towada. Its oldest wing, built in 1938, was crafted by shrine and temple carpenters. It offers both Japanese- and Western-style rooms, all facing the lake. See p. 591.

12 THE BEST AFFORDABLE JAPANESE-STYLE PLACES TO STAY

- **Homeikan** (Tokyo; ✆ 03/3811-1181): Although it's a bit far from Tokyo's main attractions, this is my top pick for an affordable, authentic Japanese inn in the capital. Rooms do not have private bathrooms, but pluses include a Japanese garden, nice public baths, and detailed *tatami* rooms adorned with traditional architectural features. Meals (optional) are served in your room. Another great plus: The owner speaks English. See p. 144.

- **Arai Ryokan** (Shuzenji; ✆ 0558/72-2007): Fifteen historic structures, all

registered as national cultural assets and situated around a river-fed pond, comprise this sprawling *ryokan,* in business since 1872. See p. 263.

- **Ryokan Fujioto** (Tsumago; ✆ 0264/57-3009): This 100-year-old inn is nestled back from the main street of Tsumago, a delightful village on the Edo-Era Nakasendo Highway. Meals feature local specialties, and the father-daughter team running it speaks perfect English. See p. 275.

- **Antique Inn Sumiyoshi** (Takayama; ✆ 0577/32-0228): Located in the heart of Takayama on the banks of the Miyagawa River, this 90-year-old former silkworm factory features an *irori* (open-hearth fireplace) in the high-ceilinged communal room, antiques and painted screens throughout, and simple but delightfully old-fashioned tatami rooms overlooking the river. See p. 281.

- **Minshuku in Shirakawago's Ogimachi:** Nestled in a narrow valley of the Japan Alps, Ogimachi is a small village of paddies, flowers, irrigation canals, and 200-year-old thatched farmhouses, about two dozen of which offer simple tatami accommodations and meals featuring local cuisine. This is a great, inexpensive escape. See "Rural Shirakawa-go & Ogimachi" in chapter 8.

- **Temple Accommodations on Mount Koya:** If your vision of Japan includes temples, towering cypress trees, shaven-headed monks, and religious chanting at the crack of dawn, head for the religious sanctuary atop Mount Koya, where some 50 Buddhist temples offer tatami accommodations—some with garden views—and two vegetarian meals a day. See "The Temples of Mount Koya" in chapter 10.

- **Miyajima Morinoyado** (Miyajima; ⓒ **0829/44-0430**): This public people's lodge, on picturesque Miyajima, is modern yet traditional and would easily cost four times as much if it were privately owned. See p. 475.

- **Tsuru-no-yu Onsen** (Nyuto Onsen; ⓒ **0187/46-2139**): This rustic inn, with a history stretching back to the Edo Period, thatched-roof building, and outdoor hot-spring baths, is as close as you can get to time travel. To really save money, opt for the self-cooking wing and prepare your own meals. See p. 588.

13 THE BEST CULINARY EXPERIENCES

- **Experiencing a Kaiseki Feast:** The ultimate in Japanese cuisine, *kaiseki* is a feast for the senses and spirit. Consisting of a variety of exquisitely prepared and arranged dishes, a kaiseki meal is a multicourse event to be savored slowly. Both the ingredients and the dishes they comprise are chosen with great care to complement the season. There are hundreds of exceptional kaiseki restaurants in Japan, from old-world traditional to sleek modern; a standout is **Kagetsu** in Nagasaki. Traditional *ryokan* also serve kaiseki. See p. 518 as well as "Eating & Drinking In Japan," chapter 2.

- **Spending an Evening in a Robatayaki:** Harking back to the olden days when Japanese cooked over an open fireplace, a *robatayaki* is a convivial place for a meal and drinks. One of the most famous is **Inakaya** in Tokyo, where diners sit at a counter; on the other side are two cooks, grills, and mountains of food. You'll love the drama of this place. See p. 170 as well as "Eating & Drinking in Japan," in chapter 2.

- **Dining on Western Food in Modern Settings:** Japan has no lack of great Western food, and some of the best places to dine are its first-class hotels. The **New York Grill,** on the 52nd floor of the Park Hyatt in Tokyo, epitomizes the best of the West with its sophisticated setting, great views, great food, and great jazz. See p. 162.

- **Buying Prepared Meals at a Department Store:** The basement floors of department stores are almost always devoted to foodstuffs, including takeout foods. Shopping for your meal is a fun experience: Hawkers yell their wares, samples are set out for you to nibble, and you can choose anything from tempura and sushi to boxed meals. See chapter 6, the regional chapters, and "Eating & Drinking in Japan," in chapter 2.

- **Slurping Noodles in a Noodle Shop:** You're supposed to slurp when eating Japanese noodles, which are prepared in almost as many different ways as there are regions. Noodle shops range from stand-up counters to traditional restaurants; one of my favorites is **Raitei** in Kamakura. See p. 235 as well as "Eating & Drinking in Japan," in chapter 2, and the "Where to Dine" sections in regional chapters.

- **Rubbing Elbows in a Izakaya:** Izakaya are pubs in Japan—usually tiny affairs with just a counter, serving up skewered grilled chicken, fish, and other fare. They're good places to meet the natives and are inexpensive as well. You'll find them in every nightlife district in the country. See the regional chapters and also "Eating & Drinking in Japan," in chapter 2.

14 THE BEST DESTINATIONS FOR SERIOUS SHOPPERS

- **For Everything:** Japanese department stores are microcosms of practically everything Japan produces, from the food halls in the basement to the departments selling clothing, accessories, office supplies, souvenirs, pottery, household goods, and cameras, to rooftop garden centers. What's more, service is great and purchases are beautifully wrapped. You'll be spoiled for life. See "Shopping" in chapter 6.

- **For Designer Fashions:** Tokyo's **Shibuya District** has the most designer boutiques in town, while **Aoyama** boasts main shops for all the big-name designers, including Issey Miyake and Comme des Garçons. Department stores also carry big-name designers; their annual summer sales are mob scenes. See "Shopping," in chapter 6.

- **For Souvenirs:** Japanese are avid souvenir shoppers when they travel, so souvenirs are sold literally everywhere, even near shrines and temples. **Nakamise Dori,** a pedestrian lane leading to Tokyo's Sensoji Temple, is one of Japan's most colorful places to shop for paper umbrellas, toys, and other souvenirs. The two best places for one-stop

memento shopping are the **Oriental Bazaar** (p. 211) in Tokyo and the **Kyoto Handicraft Center** (p. 345), both of which offer several floors of everything from fans to woodblock prints.

- **For Traditional Crafts:** Japan treasures its artisans so highly that it designates the best as National Living Treasures. Tokyo's **Japan Traditional Craft Center** (p. 211) offers a varied inventory of everything from knives and baskets to lacquerware, but there are many renowned shops in Kyoto and Kanazawa as well. Department stores also offer an excellent collection of traditional crafts. See "Shopping," in chapter 6, and the shopping sections for Kyoto in chapter 9 and Kanazawa on p. 387.

- **For Antiques & Curios:** Flea markets are great for browsing; you'll see everything from used kimono to Edo-Era teapots for sale. Japan's largest and one of its oldest monthly markets is held the 21st of each month at **Toji Temple** in Kyoto. (A lesser flea market is held there the first Sun of each month.) **Tokyo** also has great weekend markets. See chapters 6 and 9.

- **For Electronics:** Looking for that perfect digital camera, MP3 player, calculator, or rice cooker? Then join everyone else in the country by going to one of the nation's two largest electronics and electrical-appliance districts. In Tokyo, it's **Akihabara,** where open-fronted shops beckon up to 50,000 weekday shoppers with whirring fans, blaring radios, and sales pitches. In Osaka, head to **Den Den Town.** Be sure to comparison-shop and bargain. See "Shopping," in chapters 6 and 10.

- **For Local Specialties:** Many prefecture capitals have a government-owned exhibition hall where local products are displayed for sale. Often called a *kanko bussankan,* the hall may have everything from locally produced pottery to folk toys and foodstuffs. Cities with kanko bussankan include **Kanazawa, Okayama, Matsuyama,** and **Kumamoto.** See chapters 10, 11, and 12.

- **For Porcelain & Pottery:** Porcelain and pottery are produced seemingly everywhere in Japan. Some of the more famous centers include **Nagoya,** home to Noritake, Japan's largest chinaware company; **Kanazawa,** known for its Kutani pottery with its distinctive colorful glaze; **Matsuyama,** famous for its Tobe pottery (white porcelain with cobalt-blue designs); and **Kagoshima,** with its Satsuma pottery, which comes in white (used by the upper class in feudal Japan) and black (used by the common people). See chapters 10, 11, and 12.

Japan in Depth

Hardly a day goes by that you don't hear something about Japan, whether the subject is trade, travel, food, the arts, Japanese products, karaoke, or *anime*. Yet Japan remains something of an enigma to people in the Western world. What best describes this Asian nation? Is it the giant producer of cars and an entire array of sleek electronic goods that compete favorably with the best in the West? Or is it still the land of geisha and bonsai, the punctilious tea ceremony, and the delicate art of flower arrangement? Has it become, in its outlook and popular culture, a country more Western than Asian? Or has it retained its unique ancient traditions while forging a central place in the contemporary post-industrialized world?

In fact, Japan is an intricate blend of East and West. Its cities may look Westernized—often disappointingly so—but beyond first impressions, there's very little about this Asian nation that could lull you into thinking you're in the West. Yet Japan also differs greatly from its Asian neighbors. Although it borrowed much from China in its early development, including Buddhism and its writing system, the island nation remained steadfastly isolated from the rest of the world throughout much of its history, usually deliberately so. Until World War II, it had never been successfully invaded; and for more than 200 years, while the West was stirring with the awakenings of democracy and industrialism, Japan completely closed its doors to the outside world and remained a tightly structured feudalistic society with almost no outside influence.

It's been only 140-some years since Japanese opened their doors, embracing Western products wholeheartedly, yet at the same time altering them and making them unquestionably their own. Thus, that modern high-rise may look Western, but it may contain a rustic-looking restaurant with open charcoal grills, corporate offices, a pachinko parlor, a high-tech bar with surreal city views, a McDonald's, an acupuncture clinic, a computer showroom, and a rooftop shrine. Your pizza may come with octopus, beer gardens are likely to be fitted with AstroTurf, and "parsley" refers to unmarried women older than 25 (because parsley is what's left on a plate). City police patrol on bicycles; garbage collectors attack their job with the vigor of a well-trained army; and white-gloved elevator operators, working in some of the world's swankiest department stores, bow and thank you as you exit.

Because of this unique synthesis of East and West into a culture that is distinctly Japanese, Japan is not easy for Westerners to comprehend. Discovering it is like peeling an onion—you uncover one layer only to discover more layers underneath. Thus, no matter how long you stay in Japan, you never stop learning something new about it—and to me that constant discovery is one of the most fascinating aspects of being here.

In any case, with a population of about 127 million, a history stretching back thousands of years, the world's longest-reigning monarchy, and unique forms of culture, art, food, etiquette, and religion, Japan merits more than this short chapter can deliver. I urge you to delve deeper by seeking out my recommendations in "Japan in Popular Culture: Books & Film," later in this chapter.

1 LOOKING BACK AT JAPAN

ANCIENT HISTORY (CA. 30,000 B.C.–A.D. 710) According to mythology, Japan's history began when the sun goddess, Amaterasu, sent one of her descendants down to the island of Kyushu to unify the people of Japan. Unification, however, was not realized until a few generations later when Jimmu, the great-grandson of the goddess's emissary, succeeded in bringing all of the country under his rule. Because of his divine descent, Jimmu became emperor in 660 B.C. (the date is mythical), thus establishing the line from which all of Japan's emperors are said to derive. However mysterious the origin of this imperial dynasty, it is acknowledged as the longest reigning such family in the world.

Legend begins to give way to fact only in the 4th century A.D., when a family by the name of Yamato succeeded in expanding its kingdom throughout much of the country. At the core of the unification achieved by the Yamato family was the Shinto religion. Indigenous to Japan, **Shintoism** is marked by the worship of natural things—mountains, trees, stars, rivers, seas, fire, animals, even vegetables—as the embodiment of *kami* (gods) and of the spirits of ancestors. It is also marked by belief in the emperor's divinity. Along with Buddhism, Shintoism is still a driving belief in Japanese life.

Although the exact origin of Japanese people is unknown, we know Japan was once connected to the Asian mainland by a land bridge, and the territory of Japan was occupied as early as 30,000 B.C. From about 10,000 B.C. to 400 B.C., hunter-gatherers, called Jomon, thrived in small communities primarily in central Honshu; they're best known for their hand-formed pottery decorated with cord patterns. The Jomon Period was followed by the Yayoi Period, which was marked by metalworking, the pottery wheel, and the mastering of irrigated rice cultivation. The Yayoi Period lasted until about A.D. 300, after which the Yamato family unified the state for the first time and set up their court in what is now Nara Prefecture. Yamato (present-day Japan) began turning cultural feelers toward its great neighbor to the west, China.

In the 6th century, **Buddhism,** which originated in India, was brought to Japan via China and Korea, followed by the importation of Chinese cultural and scholarly knowledge—including art, architecture, and the use of Chinese written characters. In 604, the prince regent Shotoku, greatly influenced by the teachings of Buddhism and Confucianism and still a beloved figure today, drafted a document calling for political reforms and a constitutional government. By 607, he was sending Japanese scholars to China to study Buddhism, and he started building Buddhist temples. The most famous is **Horyuji Temple** near Nara, said to be the oldest existing wooden structure in the world. He also built **Shitennoji Temple** in what is now Osaka.

THE NARA PERIOD (710–84) Before the 700s, the site of Japan's capital changed every time a new emperor came to the throne. In 710, however, a permanent capital was established at Nara. Although it remained the capital for only 74 years, seven successive emperors ruled from Nara. The period was graced with the expansion of Buddhism and flourishing temple construction throughout the country. Buddhism also inspired the arts, including Buddhist sculpture, metal casting, painting, and lacquerware. It was during this time that Emperor Shomu, the most devout Buddhist among the Nara emperors, ordered the casting of a huge bronze statue of Buddha to be erected in Nara. Known as the Daibutsu, it remains Nara's biggest attraction.

THE HEIAN PERIOD (794–1192) In 794, the capital was moved to Heiankyo (present-day Kyoto), and following the example of cities in China, Kyoto was laid out in a grid pattern with broad roads and canals. Heiankyo means "capital of peace and tranquillity," and the Heian Period was a glorious time for aristocratic families, a time of luxury and prosperity during which court life reached new artistic heights. Moon viewing became popular. Chinese characters were blended with a new Japanese writing system, allowing for the first time the flowering of Japanese literature and poetry. The life of the times was captured in the works of two women: Sei Shonagon, who wrote a collection of impressions of her life at court known as the *Pillow Book;* and Murasaki Shikibu, who wrote the world's first major novel, *The Tale of Genji.*

Because the nobles were completely engrossed in their luxurious lifestyles, however, they failed to notice the growth of military clans in the provinces. The two most powerful warrior clans were the Taira (also called Heike) and the Minamoto (also called Genji), whose fierce civil wars tore the nation apart until a young warrior, Minamoto Yoritomo, established supremacy. (In Japan, a person's family name—here, Minamoto—comes first, followed by the given name; I have followed this order throughout this book.)

THE KAMAKURA PERIOD (1192–1333) Wishing to set up rule far away from Kyoto, Minamoto Yoritomo established his capital in a remote and easily defended fishing village called Kamakura, not far from today's Tokyo. In becoming the nation's first shogun, or military dictator, Minamoto Yoritomo laid the groundwork for 700 years of military governments—in which the power of the country passed from the aristocratic court into the hands of the warrior class—until the imperial court was restored in 1868.

The Kamakura Period is perhaps best known for the unrivaled ascendancy of the warrior caste, or **samurai.** Ruled by a rigid honor code, samurai were bound in loyalty to their feudal lord, and they became the only caste allowed to carry two swords. They were expected to give up their lives for their lord without hesitation, and if they failed in their duty, they could regain their honor only by committing ritualistic suicide, or *seppuku.* Spurning the soft life led by court nobles, samurai embraced a spartan lifestyle. When **Zen Buddhism,** with its tenets of mental and physical discipline, was introduced into Japan from China in the 1190s, it appealed greatly to the samurai. Weapons and armor achieved new heights in artistry, while *Bushido,* the way of the warrior, contributed to the spirit of national unity.

In 1274, Mongolian forces under Kublai Khan made an unsuccessful attempt to invade Japan. They returned in 1281 with a larger fleet, but a typhoon destroyed it. Regarding the cyclone as a gift from the gods, Japanese called it *kamikaze,* meaning "divine wind," which took on a different significance at the end of World War II when Japanese pilots flew suicide missions in an attempt to turn the tide of war.

THE MUROMACHI & AZUCHI-MOMOYAMA PERIODS (1336–1603) After the fall of the Kamakura shogunate, a new feudal government was set up at Muromachi in Kyoto. The next 200 years, however, were marred by bloody civil wars as *daimyo* (feudal lords) staked out their fiefdoms. Similar to the barons of Europe, the daimyo owned tracts of land, had complete rule over the people who lived on them, and had an army of retainers, the samurai, who fought his enemies. This period of civil wars is called Sengoku-Jidai, or **Age of the Warring States.**

Yet these centuries of strife also saw a blossoming of art and culture. Kyoto witnessed the construction of the extravagant

Golden and Silver pavilions as well as the artistic arrangement of Ryoanji Temple's famous rock garden. Noh drama, the tea ceremony, flower arranging, and landscape gardening became the passions of the upper class. At the end of the 16th century, a number of castles were built on mountaintops to demonstrate the strength of the daimyo, guard their fiefdoms, and defend themselves against the firearms introduced by the Portuguese.

In the second half of the 16th century, a brilliant military strategist by the name of Oda Nobunaga almost succeeded in ending the civil wars. Upon Oda's assassination by one of his own retainers, one of his best generals, Toyotomi Hideyoshi, took up the campaign, built magnificent Osaka Castle, and crushed rebellion to unify Japan. Oda and Toyotomi's successive rules are known as the **Azuchi-Momoyama Period,** after the names of their castles.

THE EDO PERIOD (1603–1867)

Upon Toyotomi's death (1598), power was seized by Tokugawa Ieyasu, a statesman so shrewd and skillful in eliminating enemies that his heirs would continue to rule Japan for the next 250 years. After defeating his greatest rival in the famous battle of Sekigahara, Tokugawa set up a shogunate government in 1603 in Edo (present-day Tokyo), leaving the emperor intact but virtually powerless in Kyoto. In 1615, the Tokugawa government assured its supremacy by getting rid of Toyotomi's descendants in a fierce battle at Osaka Castle that destroyed the castle and annihilated the Toyotomi clan.

Meanwhile, European influence in Japan was spreading. The first contact with the Western world had occurred in 1543, when Portuguese merchants (with firearms) arrived, followed by Christian missionaries. St. Francis Xavier landed in Kyushu in 1549, remaining for 2 years and converting thousands of Japanese; by 1580, there were perhaps as many as

150,000 Japanese Christians. Although Japan's rulers at first welcomed foreigners and trade (three Kyushu daimyo even went so far as to send emissaries to Rome, where they were received by the pope), they gradually became alarmed by the Christian missionary influence. Hearing of the Catholic Church's power in Rome and fearing the expansionist policies of European nations, Toyotomi banned Christianity in the late 1500s. In 1597, 26 Japanese and European Christians were crucified in Nagasaki.

The Tokugawa shogunate intensified the campaign against Christians in 1639 when it closed all ports to foreign trade. Adopting a policy of **total isolation,** the shogunate forbade foreigners from landing in Japan and Japanese from leaving; even Japanese who had been living abroad in overseas trading posts were never allowed to return. The only exception was in Nagasaki, home to a colony of tightly controlled Chinese merchants and a handful of Dutch confined to a tiny island trading post.

Thus began an amazing 215-year period in Japanese history during which Japan was closed to the rest of the world. It was a time of political stability at the expense of personal freedom, as all aspects of life were strictly controlled by the Tokugawa government. Japanese society was divided into four distinct **classes:** samurai, farmers, craftspeople, and merchants. Class determined everything in daily life, from where a person could live to what he was allowed to wear or eat. Samurai led the most exalted social position, and it was probably during the Tokugawa Period that the samurai class reached the zenith of its glory. At the bottom of the social ladder were the merchants, but as they prospered under the peaceful regime, new forms of entertainment arose to occupy their time. Kabuki drama and woodblock prints became the rage, while stoneware and porcelain, silk brocade for kimono, and lacquerware improved in quality. In fact, it was probably the shogunate's rigid policies that actually fostered the arts. Because anything new was considered dangerous and quickly suppressed, Japanese were forced to retreat inward, focusing their energies in the arts and perfecting handicrafts down to the minutest detail whether it was swords, kimono, or lacquered boxes. Only Japan's many festivals and pilgrimages to designated religious sites offered relief from harsh and restrictive social mores.

To ensure that no daimyo in the distant provinces would become too powerful and a threat to the shogun's power, the Tokugawa government ordered each daimyo to leave his family in Edo as permanent residents (effectively as hostages) and required the lord to spend a prescribed number of months in Edo every year or two. Inns and townships sprang up along Japan's major highways to accommodate the elaborate processions of palanquins, samurai, and footmen traveling back and forth between Edo and the provinces. In expending so much time and money traveling back and forth and maintaining elaborate residences both in the provinces and in Edo, the daimyo had no resources left with which to wage a rebellion.

Yet even though the Tokugawa government took such extreme measures to ensure its supremacy, by the mid–19th century it was clear that the feudal system was outdated and economic power had shifted into the hands of the merchants. Many samurai families were impoverished, and discontent with the shogunate became widespread.

In 1853, American Commodore Matthew C. Perry sailed to Japan, seeking to gain trading rights. He left unsuccessful, but returning a year later he forced the Shogun to sign an agreement despite the disapproval of the emperor, thus ending Japan's 2 centuries of isolation. In 1867, powerful families toppled the Tokugawa

regime and restored the emperor as ruler, thus bringing the Feudal Era to a close.

MEIJI PERIOD THROUGH WORLD WAR II (1868–1945)

In 1868, Emperor Meiji moved his imperial government from Kyoto to Edo, renamed it Tokyo (Eastern Capital), and designated it the official national capital. During the next few decades, known as the **Meiji Restoration,** Japan rapidly progressed from a feudal agricultural society of samurai and peasants to an industrial nation. The samurai were stripped of their power and no longer allowed to carry swords, thus ending a privileged way of life begun almost 700 years earlier in Kamakura. A prime minister and a cabinet were appointed, a constitution was drafted, and a parliament (called the Diet) was elected. With the enthusiastic support of Emperor Meiji, the latest in Western technological know-how was imported, including railway and postal systems, along with specialists and advisers: Between 1881 and 1898, about 10,000 Westerners were retained by the Japanese government to help modernize the country.

Meanwhile, Japan made incursions into neighboring lands. In 1894 to 1895, it fought and won a war against China; in 1904 to 1905, it attacked and defeated Russia; and in 1910, it annexed Korea. After militarists gained control of the government in the 1930s, these expansionist policies continued; Manchuria was annexed, and Japan went to war with China again in 1937. On the other side of the world, as **World War II** flared in Europe, Japan formed a military alliance (Axis) with Germany and Italy and attacked French Indochina.

After several years of tense diplomatic confrontations between Japan and America, Japanese extremists decided to attack Pearl Harbor in the hope that by striking first they could prevent U.S. mobilization. On December 7, 1941, Japan bombed

Pearl Harbor, entering World War II against the United States. Although Japan went on to conquer Hong Kong, Singapore, Burma, Malaysia, the Philippines, the Dutch East Indies, and Guam, the tide eventually turned, and American bombers reduced every major Japanese city to rubble with the exception of historic Kyoto. On August 6, 1945, the United States dropped the world's first atomic bomb over Hiroshima, followed on August 9 by a second over Nagasaki. Japan submitted to unconditional surrender on August 14, with Emperor Hirohito's radio broadcast telling his people the time had come for "enduring the unendurable and suffering what is insufferable." American and other **Allied occupation** forces arrived and remained until 1952. For the first time in history, Japan had suffered defeat by a foreign power; the country had never before been invaded or occupied by a foreign nation.

MODERN JAPAN (1946–PRESENT)

The experience of World War II had a profound effect on the Japanese, yet they emerged from their defeat and began to rebuild. In 1946, under the guidance of the Allied military authority headed by U.S. Gen. Douglas MacArthur, they adopted a democratic constitution renouncing war and the use of force to settle international disputes and divesting the emperor of divinity. A parliamentary system of government was set up, and 1947 witnessed the first general elections for the National Diet, the government's legislative body. After its founding in 1955, the **Liberal Democratic Party (LDP)** remained the undisputed majority party for decades, giving Japan the political stability it needed to grow economically and compete in world markets.

To the younger generation, the occupation was less a painful burden to be suffered than an opportunity to remake their country, with American encouragement, into a modern, peace-loving, and democratic state. A relationship developed between Japanese and their American occupiers. In the early 1950s, as the Cold War between the United States and the Communist world erupted in hostilities in Korea, that relationship grew into a firm alliance, strengthened by a security treaty. In 1952, the occupation ended, and Japan joined the United Nations as an independent country.

Avoiding involvement in foreign conflicts as outlined by its constitution, Japanese concentrated on economic recovery. Through a series of policies favoring domestic industries and shielding Japan from foreign competition, they achieved **rapid economic growth.** In 1964, Tokyo hosted the Summer Olympic Games, showing the world that the nation had transformed itself into a formidable industrialized power. Incomes doubled during the 1960s, and a 1967 government study found that 90% of Japanese considered themselves middle class. By the 1980s, Japan was by far the richest industrialized nation in Asia and the envy of its neighbors, who strove to emulate Japan's success. Sony was a household word around the globe; books flooded the international market touting the economic secrets of Japan, Inc. After all, Japan seemed to have it all: a good economy, political stability, safe streets, and great schools. As the yen soared, Japanese traveled abroad as never before, and Japanese companies gained international attention as they gobbled up real estate in foreign lands and purchased works of art at unheard-of prices.

Meanwhile, a snowballing trade surplus had created friction between Japan and the United States, its chief trading partner. In the 1980s, as Japanese auto sales in the United States soared and foreign sales in Japan continued to be restricted, disagreements between Tokyo and Washington heated up. In 1989, Emperor Hirohito died of cancer at age 87, bringing the 63-year Showa Era to an end and ushering in the **Heisei Period** under Akihito, the

125th emperor, who proclaimed the new "Era of Peace" (Heisei).

In the early 1990s, shadows of financial doubt began to spread over the Land of the Rising Sun, with alarming reports of bad bank loans, inflated stock prices, and overextended corporate investment abroad. In 1992, **recession** hit Japan, bursting the economic bubble and plunging the country into its worst recession since World War II. The Nikkei (the Japanese version of the American Dow) fell a gut-churning 63% from its 1989 peak, and, over the next decade, bankruptcies reached an all-time high and unemployment climbed to its highest level since World War II. Meanwhile, the Liberal Democratic Party, which had held power uninterruptedly for nearly 4 decades, suffered a huge loss of public confidence after its top officials were accused of participating in a series of political and financial scandals. But a revolving door of prime ministers (many of whom also became implicated in scandals) throughout the 1990s failed to revive the economy or alleviate voters' growing fears of financial doom.

Public confidence was further eroded in 1995, first by a major earthquake in Kobe that killed more than 6,000 people and proved that Japan's cities were not as safe as the government had maintained. Then an attack by an obscure religious sect that released the deadly nerve gas sarin on Tokyo's subway system during rush hour killed 12 people and sickened thousands. But the worst blow was in 2001, when a knife-wielding man fatally stabbed eight children in an elementary school in Osaka Prefecture. For many Japanese, it seemed that the very core of their society had begun to crumble.

In April 2001, after yet another prime minister resigned due to scandal, Koizumi Junichiro took the political helm. Although a member of the LPD, the long-haired, 59-year-old Koizumi, who enjoyed popularity usually reserved for rock stars, had long been considered something of a maverick, battling against the long-established power brokers of the LPD. Following the September 2001 terrorist attacks in the U.S., Koizumi quickly showed allegiance by pushing through an antiterrorism bill that allowed noncombat support in Afghanistan, followed by a pledge of foreign aid to American reconstruction efforts in Iraq. Koizumi's greatest domestic achievements were policies that nudged Japan's slow climb out of recession, including those that cut the number of bad bank loans in half and laid groundwork for the privatization of Japan's post office, which does far more than sell stamps and deliver mail. Tokyo real estate prices, which had fallen as much as 70% from their 1991 peak, rose for the first time in 2004, spurring investors to return. By 2008, a slew of international luxury hotels had muscled their way into the Tokyo market, while new urban-renewal projects had reshaped the Tokyo skyline.

On the international front, Japan's most immediate worry continued to be its neighbor, North Korea, which lobbed its first missile over Japan in 1998, declared in 2002 that it had never halted its nuclear-weapons program despite a 1994 nuclear accord, and in 2008 launched its first satellite rocket over Japan. In 2002, North Korea admitted that it had abducted 13 young Japanese in the '70s and '80s to teach its spies the Japanese language and customs. Five of the abductees were subsequently repatriated back to Japan; North Korea maintains the others died of natural causes.

In 1999, Japan, which did not have a legally recognized national flag nor an anthem, adopted a World War II hymn, *Kimigayo,* as its national anthem and declared the traditional Japanese sun flag, a red disk in a field of white, its official flag. But any overt displays of Japanese nationalism have always spurred criticism from Asian neighbors, who maintain that despite an official apology in 1995 for wartime aggression, Japan has never truly shown remorse for invading and occupying its neighbors. Prime ministers and other officials have repeatedly outraged fellow Asians with visits to Tokyo's Yasukuni Shrine, vilified by critics for honoring Japanese war dead, including those executed for wartime atrocities. Relations became further strained in 2005, when Japan's Education Ministry approved revised history textbooks that glossed over Japan's war crimes, sparking outrage in China and South Korea that erupted into anti-Japanese street riots. In 2007, an international furor arose when Abe Shinzo, who had replaced Koizumi as prime minister, claimed that no evidence existed of women being forced to work in Asian brothels established by Japanese military during World War II. Abe, who at 52 was Japan's youngest postwar premier, lasted only a year; his two successors fared little better.

Although Japan, whose foremost trading partner had shifted from the United States to China, seemed to be on the economic mend by the mid-2000s, the 2008 global financial meltdown hijacked its recovery by causing a downward spiral in foreign trade as demand for Japanese cars, electronics, and other exports dropped dramatically around the world. Sony, Toyota, Panasonic, Sharp, and other major companies were forced to dramatically curtail production and close plants, causing thousands of workers to lose their jobs. By mid-2009 the jobless rate was 5.7%, its highest postwar level. Many of the newly unemployed, forced from company-sponsored housing or unable to pay rent, joined the ranks of the homeless, estimated in 2009 at about 15,800. In 2010, grim news about two world-famous Japanese companies added to a growing sense of gloom: Japan Airlines, declaring bankruptcy, accepted a bailout and agreed to axe 15,600 jobs; Toyota, facing growing criticism about defective accelerator and brake pedals in many of its models, issued a global recall of more than 8.5 million vehicles.

Meanwhile, discontent with the status quo played a major role in Japan's 2008 national elections, when the left-of-center Democratic Party of Japan defeated the conservative Liberal Democratic Party, which had ruled for all but 10 months for the past 50-some years. Under the helm of the new prime minister, Hatoyama Yukio, the DPJ vowed to reshape the Japanese economy by shifting priorities supporting Japan, Inc., to policies focusing on people, including cash handouts to families, support for farmers and fishermen, and tax cuts.

2 JAPAN TODAY

I'll splurge every couple of years for that perfect Issey Miyake outfit (it travels so well!), but all my friends know I'm a cheapskate at heart. That's why I consider the economic recession that hit Japan in 1992—while bad news for those who lost their jobs, including many politicians—the beginning of a new Japan for frugal travelers. In contrast to the heady days of the 1980s bubble economy, when only designer goods would do and expense accounts seemed unlimited, today's Japan is a bargain-hunter's delight. Thanks to recession fallout, we have 100 Yen stores, shops selling used designer wear, buffets virtually everywhere, inexpensive set lunches in even the toniest of restaurants, and virtually every prefecture trying to figure out how to lure more international travelers. There are deals across the country only for foreigners, including regional rail passes and plane tickets. For the

Fun Facts — The Magical World of Vending Machines

One of the things that usually surprises visitors to Japan is the number of vending machines in the country, estimated to be more than 5.5 million—one for every 20 people. They're virtually everywhere—in train stations, in front of shops, on the back streets of residential neighborhoods. Most will take bills and give back change. Many have almost nonsensical English-language promotional lines on them, such as ENJOY REFRESHING TIME. Some will even talk to you.

And what can you buy in these vending machines? First, there are the obvious items—drinks and snacks, including hot or cold coffee in a can. But if you're on your way to someone's house, you might be able to pick up a bouquet of flowers from a machine. Your camera is out of batteries? You may be able to find those, too. Vending machines outside post offices sell stamps and postcards, while those in business hotels sell razors, cup noodles, beer, and even underwear.

In the not-too-distant past, things were also sold from sidewalk vending machines that would have met with instant protest in other countries around the world. Cigarettes and beer were available on almost every corner, where even children could buy them if they wanted to; nowadays, however, shoppers must first insert a computer-readable card certifying they're at least 20 years old. I remember a vending machine in my Tokyo neighborhood: By day, it was blank, with no sign as to what was inside; at night, however, the thing would light up, and on display were pornographic comics. Nowadays, pornographic vending machines are very rare, not for moral reasons, but because of the Internet.

Still, if it's available in Japan, it's probably in a vending machine somewhere.

cheapskate, there's never been a better time to visit Japan than now.

Not that I'm heartless about the challenges facing the Japan of today. Despite the ushering in of a new government in 2009 that promises to cut government waste, boost disposable household income, and reverse almost 20 years of deflation, Japan faces mind-boggling financial, social, and political obstacles. Certainly one of Japan's biggest concerns is its declining birthrate coupled with one of the most rapidly aging populations in the world. About 22% of its population is 65 and older; by 2055, that number is expected to double. Meanwhile, Japan's ratio of children aged 14 and younger is believed to the lowest in the world, accounting for only 13.5% of the population. This will undoubtedly lead to a shortage of labor, severely straining the country's resources for tax revenues, pensions, and healthcare.

Meanwhile, bankruptcies and corporate mergers have forever altered the relationship between Japanese workers and their employers, with lifelong employment with the same company no longer a given. Homelessness is now so common that it no longer draws stares, even in the swank Ginza District. Crime, once almost unheard of, is on the rise, especially theft. My former Tokyo landlady fears burglary so much that she refuses to open her doors to strangers.

On the other hand, crime, though undeniably on the increase, is still negligible when compared to levels in the United States, and Japan remains one of the safest countries in the world. Although it's true I'm more careful than I used to be—I guard my purse in crowded subways, I avoid parks after dark—for Americans such precautions seem merely self-evident. But while I'm vigilant about theft and purse snatching, I never worry about personal safety. Violent crime—especially against strangers—remains virtually unheard of in Japan.

In any case, the attributes that drew me to Japan in the first place and keep me coming back remain strongly in place: the country's unexpected physical beauty, its safety, and its unique cuisine, customs, and culture. Japan is much the same as when I first came here, humming with energy, crowded beyond belief in its major cities, and filled with acts of human kindness. But I also like the ways Japan has changed. I like that a greater influx of foreign visitors, coupled with a young generation of less inhibited Japanese, has forever altered the social landscape. Japan is more accessible than it has ever been, and in many ways it's also more fun. Whereas in the 1980s Japan was best known as an economic powerhouse, today it's known also for its cool pop culture, from *anime* and *manga* to fashion and food. It's still the land of the geisha, but it's also the land of Hello Kitty.

3 JAPANESE ARTS IN A NUTSHELL

TRADITIONAL THEATER

KABUKI   Probably Japan's best-known traditional theater art, *kabuki* is also one of the country's most popular forms of entertainment. Visit a performance and it's easy to see why—kabuki is fun! The plays are dramatic, the costumes are gorgeous, the stage settings are often fantastic, and the themes are universal—love, revenge, and the conflict between duty and personal feelings. Probably one of the reasons kabuki is so popular even today is that it developed centuries ago as a form of entertainment for the common people in feudal Japan, particularly the merchants. And one of kabuki's interesting aspects is that all roles—even those depicting women—are portrayed by men.

Kabuki has changed little in the past 100-some years. Altogether there are more than 300 kabuki plays, all written before the 20th century. Kabuki stages almost always revolve and have an aisle that extends from the stage to the back of the spectator theater. For a Westerner, one of the more arresting things about a kabuki performance is the audience itself. Because this has always been entertainment for the masses, the audience can get quite lively with yells, guffaws, shouts of approval, and laughter. In fact, old woodcuts of cross-eyed men apparently stemmed from kabuki—when things got a little too rowdy, actors would stamp their feet and strike a cross-eyed pose in an attempt to gain the audience's attention.

Of course, you won't be able to understand what's being said. Indeed, because much of kabuki drama dates from the 18th century, even Japanese sometimes have difficulty understanding the language. But it doesn't matter, though some theaters have English-language programs and earphones that describe the plots in minute detail. The best place to enjoy kabuki is Tokyo, where performances are held throughout much of the year.

NOH   Whereas *kabuki* developed as a form of entertainment for the masses, Noh was a much more traditional and aristocratic form of theater. Most of Japan's shogun were patrons of Noh; during the

Sumo (Fun Facts)

The Japanese form of wrestling known as **sumo** began perhaps as long as 1,500 years ago and was immensely popular by the 6th century. Today it's still popular, with the best wrestlers revered as national heroes, much as baseball or basketball players are in the United States. Often taller than 1.8m (6 ft.) and weighing well over 136 kilograms (300 lb.), sumo wrestlers follow a rigorous training period, which usually begins when they're in their teens and includes eating special foods to gain weight. Unmarried wrestlers even live together at their training schools, called sumo stables.

A sumo match takes place on a sandy-floored ring less than 4.5m (15 ft.) in diameter. Wrestlers dress much as they did during the Edo Period—their hair in a samurai-style topknot, an ornamental belt/loincloth around their huge girths. Before each bout, the two contestants scatter salt in the ring to purify it from the last bout's loss; they also squat and then raise each leg, stamping it into the ground to crush, symbolically, any evil spirits. They then squat down and face each other, glaring to psych each other out. Once they rush each other, each wrestler's object is to either eject his opponent from the ring or cause him to touch the ground with any part of his body other than his feet. This is accomplished by shoving, slapping, tripping, throwing, and even carrying the opponent, but punching with a closed fist and kicking are not allowed. Altogether, there are 48 holds and throws, and sumo fans know all of them.

Most bouts are very short, lasting only 30 seconds or so. The highest-ranking players are called *yokozuna*, or grand champions; in 1993, a Hawaiian named Akebono was promoted to the highest rank, the first non-Japanese ever to be so honored. Nowadays foreign-born sumo wrestlers are common, though their numbers are restricted by the Japan Sumo Association.

There are six 15-day sumo tournaments in Japan every year: Three are held in Tokyo (Jan, May, and Sept); the others are held in Osaka (Mar), Nagoya (July), and Fukuoka (Nov). Each wrestler in the tournament faces a new opponent every day; the winner of the tournament is the wrestler who maintains the best overall record.

If you'd like to attend a sumo match while you're in Tokyo, see the "Spectator Sports" section of chapter 6. Tournament matches are also widely covered on television.

Edo Period, it became the exclusive entertainment of the samurai class. In contrast to kabuki's extroverted liveliness, Noh is very calculated, slow, and restrained. The oldest form of theater in Japan, it has changed very little in the past 600 years, making it the oldest theater art in the world. The language is so archaic that Japanese cannot understand it at all, which explains in part why Noh does not have the popularity that kabuki does.

As in kabuki, all Noh performers are men, with the principal characters consisting mostly of ghosts or spirits, who illuminate foibles of human nature or tragic-heroic events. Performers often wear masks. Spoken parts are chanted by a chorus of about eight;

music is provided by a Noh orchestra that consists of several drums and a flute.

Because the action is slow, watching an entire evening can be quite tedious unless you are particularly interested in Noh dance and music. In addition, most Noh plays do not have English translations. You may want to drop in for just a short while. In between Noh plays, short comic reliefs, called *kyogen,* usually make fun of life in the 1600s, depicting the lives of lazy husbands, conniving servants, and other characters with universal appeal.

BUNRAKU *Bunraku* is traditional Japanese puppet theater. But contrary to what you might expect, bunraku is for adults, and themes center on love and revenge, sacrifice and suicide. Many dramas now adapted for *kabuki* were first written for the bunraku stage.

Popular in Japan since the 17th century—at times even more popular than kabuki—bunraku is fascinating to watch because the puppeteers are right onstage with their puppets. Dressed in black, they're wonderfully skilled in making the puppets seem like living beings. Usually, there are three puppeteers for each puppet, which is about three-fourths human size: One puppeteer is responsible for movement of the puppet's head, as well as for the expression on its face, and for the movement of the right arm and hand; another puppeteer operates the puppet's left arm and hand; while the third moves the legs. Although at first the puppeteers are somewhat distracting, after a while you forget they're there as the puppets assume personalities of their own. The narrator, who tells the story and speaks the various parts, is an important figure in the drama. The narrator is accompanied by a traditional three-stringed Japanese instrument called a *shamisen.* By all means, try to see bunraku. The most famous presentations are at the Osaka Bunraku Theater, but there are performances in Tokyo and other major cities as well.

THE TEA CEREMONY

Tea was brought to Japan from China more than 1,000 years ago. It first became popular among Buddhist priests as a means of staying awake during long hours of meditation; gradually, its use filtered down among the upper classes, and in the 16th century, the tea ceremony was perfected by a merchant named Sen-no-Rikyu. Using the principles of Zen and the spiritual discipline of the samurai, the tea ceremony became a highly stylized ritual, with detailed rules on how tea should be prepared, served, and drunk. The simplicity of movement and tranquillity of setting are meant to free the mind from the banality of everyday life and to allow the spirit to enjoy peace. In a way, it is a form of spiritual therapy.

The tea ceremony, *cha-no-yu,* is still practiced in Japan today and is regarded as a form of disciplinary training for mental composure and for etiquette and manners. In Kyoto, I once met a fellow guest in an inexpensive Japanese inn who asked whether she could serve me Japanese tea and a sweet after breakfast. She apologized for her ineptitude, saying she was only a mere apprentice of tea. When I asked how long she'd been studying cha-no-yu, she replied 7 years. That may seem like a long time, but the study of the tea ceremony includes related subjects, including the craftsmanship of tea vessels and implements, the design and construction of the teahouse, the landscaping of gardens, and literature related to the tea ceremony.

Several of Japan's more famous landscape gardens have teahouses on their grounds where you can sit on *tatami,* drink the frothy green tea (called *maccha*), eat sweets (meant to counteract the bitter taste of the tea), and contemplate the view. Traditionally, teahouses are quite small, with space for five or fewer people, and with two entrances: one for the host and the other for guests, so small that they must crawl through it to enter. In the center of the room is a small brazier for the teapot along with utensils needed for the making of tea—tea bowl, tea caddy, bamboo whisk, and bamboo spoon. Tea etiquette requires that guests compliment the host on the excellent flavor of the tea and on the beauty of the tea implements, which of course change with the seasons and are often valuable art objects.

Although several first-class hotels in Tokyo hold tea ceremonies in special tea-ceremony rooms (see chapter 6 for more information), nothing beats the atmosphere of a landscaped Japanese garden, many of which serve tea.

FLORAL & LANDSCAPE ARTS

IKEBANA Whereas a Westerner is likely to put a bunch of flowers into a vase and be done with it, Japanese consider the arrangement of flowers an art in itself. Most young girls have at least some training in flower arranging, known as *ikebana.* First popularized among aristocrats during the Heian Period (A.D. 794–1192) and spreading to the common people in the 14th to 16th centuries, traditional ikebana, in its simplest form, is supposed to represent heaven, man, and earth; it's considered a truly Japanese art without outside influences. As important as the arrangement itself is the vase chosen to display it. Department store galleries sometimes have ikebana exhibitions, as do shrines; otherwise, check with the local tourist office.

GARDENS Nothing is left to chance in a Japanese landscape garden: The shapes of hills and trees, the placement of rocks and waterfalls—everything is skillfully arranged in a faithful reproduction of nature. To Westerners, it may seem a bit strange to arrange nature to look like nature; but to Japanese, even nature can be improved upon to make it more pleasing through

the best possible use of limited space. Japanese are masters at this, as a visit to any of their famous gardens will testify.

In fact, Japanese have been sculpting gardens for more than 1,000 years. At first, gardens were designed for walking and boating, with ponds, artificial islands, and pavilions. As with almost everything else in Japanese life, however, Zen Buddhism exerted an influence, making gardens simpler and attempting to create the illusion of boundless space within a small area. To the Buddhist, a garden was not for merriment but for contemplation—an uncluttered and simple landscape on which to rest the eyes. Japanese gardens often use the principle of "borrowed landscape"—that is, the incorporation of surrounding mountains and landscape into the overall design and impact of the garden.

Basically, there are three styles of Japanese gardens. One style, called *tsukiyama,* uses ponds, hills, and streams to depict nature in miniature. Another style, known as the *karesansui,* uses stones and raked sand in place of water and is often seen at Zen Buddhist temples; it was developed during the Muromachi Period as a representation of Zen spiritualism. The third style, called *chaniwa,* emerged with the tea ceremony; built around a teahouse with an eye toward simplicity and tranquillity, such a garden will often feature stone lanterns, a stone basin filled with water, or water flowing through a bamboo pipe.

Famous gardens in Japan include Kenrokuen Park in Kanazawa, Korakuen Park in Okayama, Ritsurin Park in Takamatsu, and the grounds of the Adachi Museum. Kyoto alone has about 50 gardens, including the famous Zen rock gardens at Daitokuji and Ryoanji temples, the gardens at both the Golden and Silver pavilions, and those at Heian Shrine, Nijo Castle, and the Katsura Imperial Villa.

4 SHRINES & TEMPLES: RELIGION IN JAPAN

The main religions in Japan are Shintoism and Buddhism, and many Japanese consider themselves believers in both. Most Japanese, for example, will marry in a Shinto ceremony, but when they die, they'll have a Buddhist funeral.

A native religion of Japan, **Shintoism** is the worship of ancestors and national heroes, as well as of all natural things, both animate and inanimate. These natural things are thought to embody gods and can be anyone or anything—mountains, trees, the moon, stars, rivers, seas, fires, rocks, and animals. Shintoism also embraces much of Confucianism, which entered Japan in the 5th century and stressed the importance of family and loyalty. There are no scriptures in Shintoism, nor any ordained code of morals or ethics.

The place of worship in Shintoism is called a *jinja,* or shrine. The most obvious sign of a shrine is its *torii,* an entrance gate, usually of wood, consisting of two tall poles topped with either one or two crossbeams. Another feature common to shrines is a water trough with communal cups, where the Japanese will wash their hands and sometimes rinse out their mouths. Purification and cleanliness are important in Shintoism because they show respect to the gods. At the shrine, worshipers will throw a few coins into a money box, clap their hands twice to get the gods' attention, and then bow their heads and pray for whatever they wish—good health, protection, the safe delivery of a child, or a prosperous year.

Founded in India in the 6th to 5th centuries B.C., **Buddhism** came to Japan in the 6th century A.D. via China and Korea, bringing with it the concept of eternal life. By the end of the 6th century, Buddhism had gained such popularity that the prince regent Shotoku, one of Japan's most remarkable historical figures, declared Buddhism the state religion and based many of his governmental policies on its tenets. Another important Buddhist leader to emerge was a priest called Kukai, known posthumously as Kobo Daishi. After studying Buddhism in China in the early 800s, he returned and built temples throughout Japan, including the famous 88 temples on Shikoku island and those on Mount Koya, which continue to attract millions of pilgrims today.

Of the various Buddhist sects in Japan today, Zen Buddhism is probably the most well known in the West. Considered the most Japanese form of Buddhism, Zen is the practice of meditation and a strictly disciplined lifestyle to rid yourself of desire so that you can achieve enlightenment. There are no rites in Zen Buddhism, no dogmas, no theological conceptions of divinity. You do not analyze rationally, but rather know things intuitively. The strict and simple lifestyle of Zen appealed greatly to Japan's samurai warrior class, and many of Japan's arts, including the tea ceremony, arose from the practice of Zen.

Whereas Shintoists have shrines, Buddhists have temples, called *otera.* Instead of torii, temples will often have an entrance gate with a raised doorsill and heavy doors. Temples may also have a cemetery on their grounds (which Shinto shrines never have) as well as a pagoda.

5 EATING & DRINKING IN JAPAN

Whenever I leave Japan, it's the food I miss the most. Sure, there are sushi bars and other Japanese specialty restaurants in many major cities around the world, but they don't offer nearly the variety available in Japan (and often they aren't nearly as

> **(Tips) Taxes**
>
> Keep in mind that first-class restaurants will also add a 10% to 15% service charge, as do most hotel restaurants.

good). For just as America has more to offer than hamburgers and steaks and England more than fish and chips, Japan has more than just sushi and *teppanyaki*. For both the gourmet and the uninitiated, Japan is a treasure-trove of culinary surprises and a foodie's delight.

JAPANESE CUISINE

Altogether, there are more than a dozen different and distinct types of Japanese cuisine, plus countless regional specialties. A good deal of what you eat may be completely new to you as well as completely unidentifiable. Sometimes Japanese themselves don't even know what they're eating, so varied and so wide is the range of available edibles. The rule is simply to enjoy, and enjoyment begins even before you raise your chopsticks to your mouth.

To the Japanese, **presentation** of food is as important as the food itself, and dishes are designed to appeal not only to the palate but to the eye. In contrast to the American way of piling as much food as possible onto a single plate, Japanese use lots of small plates, each arranged artfully with bite-size morsels of food. After you've seen what can be done with maple leaves, flowers, bits of bamboo, and even pebbles to enhance the appearance of food, your relationship with what you eat may change forever. If there's such a thing as designer cuisine, Japan is its home.

Below are explanations of some of the most common types of Japanese cuisine. Generally, only one type of cuisine is served in a given restaurant—for example, only raw seafood is served in a sushi bar, whereas tempura is featured at a tempura counter. There are exceptions to this, especially in

regards to raw fish, which is served as an appetizer in many restaurants, and set meals, which contain a variety of dishes. In addition, Japanese restaurants in hotels may offer a great variety, and some Japanese drinking establishments (called *izakaya* or *nomiya*) offer a wide range of foods from soups to sushi to skewered pieces of chicken known as *yakitori*.

For a quick rundown of individual dishes, see the food terms in chapter 18.

FUGU Known as blowfish, puffer fish, or globefish in English, *fugu* is one of the most exotic and adventurous foods in Japan: If it's not prepared properly, it means almost certain death for the consumer. Every year a few dozen people are hospitalized from fugu poisoning and a handful die, usually fishermen who tried preparing it at home. The fugu's ovaries and intestines are deadly and must be entirely removed without puncturing them. So why eat fugu if it can kill you? Well, for one thing, it's delicious; for another, fugu chefs are strictly licensed by the government and are greatly skilled in preparing fugu dishes. Ways to order it include *fugu-sashi* (raw), when it's sliced paper thin and dipped into soy sauce with bitter orange and chives; in *fugu-chiri* (stew) cooked with vegetables at your table; and as *fugu-zosui* (rice porridge). The season for fresh fugu is October or November through March, but some restaurants serve it throughout the year.

KAISEKI The king of Japanese cuisine, *kaiseki* is the epitome of delicately and exquisitely arranged food, the ultimate in Japanese aesthetic appeal. It's also among the most expensive meals you can eat and can cost ¥25,000 or more per person; some restaurants, however, do offer more affordable mini-kaiseki courses. In addition, the better Japanese inns serve kaiseki, a reason for their high cost. Kaiseki, which is not a specific dish but rather a complete meal, is expensive because much time and skill are involved in preparing each of the many dishes, with the ingredients cooked to preserve natural flavors. Even the plates are chosen with great care to enhance the color, texture, and shape of each piece of food.

Kaiseki cuisine is based on the four seasons, with the selection of ingredients and their presentation dependent on the time of the year. In fact, so strongly does a kaiseki preparation convey the mood of a particular season, the kaiseki gourmet could tell what season it is just by looking at a meal.

A kaiseki meal is usually a lengthy affair with various dishes appearing in set order. First come the appetizer, clear broth, and one uncooked dish. These are followed by boiled, broiled, fried, steamed, heated, and vinegary dishes and finally by another soup, rice, pickled vegetables, and fruit. Although meals vary greatly depending upon the region and what's fresh, common dishes include some type of sashimi, tempura, cooked seasonal fish, and bite-size pieces of various vegetables. Because kaiseki is always a set meal, there's no problem in ordering. Let your budget be your guide.

KUSHIAGE Kushiage foods are breaded and deep-fried on skewers and include chicken, beef, seafood, and lots of seasonal vegetables (snow peas, green pepper, gingko nuts, lotus root, and the like). They're served with a slice of lemon and usually a specialty sauce. The result is delicious, and I highly recommend trying it. You'll find it at shops called *kushiage-ya* (*ya* means "shop"), which are often open only at night. Ordering the set meal is easiest,

and what you get is often determined by both the chef and the season.

OKONOMIYAKI *Okonomiyaki,* which originated in Osaka after World War II and literally means "as you like it," is often referred to as Japanese pizza. To me, it's more like a pancake to which meat or fish, shredded cabbage, and vegetables are added, topped with Worcestershire sauce. Because it's a popular offering of street vendors, restaurants specializing in this type of cuisine are very reasonably priced. At some places the cook makes it for you, but at other places it's do-it-yourself, which can be quite fun if you're with a group. *Yakisoba* (fried Chinese noodles with cabbage) is also usually offered at okonomiyaki restaurants.

RICE As in other Asian countries, rice has been a Japanese staple for about 2,000 years. In fact, rice is so important to the Japanese diet that *gohan* means both "rice" and "meal." There are no problems here—everyone is familiar with rice. The difference, however, is that in Japan it's quite sticky, making it easier to pick up with chopsticks. It's also just plain white rice—no salt, no butter, no soy sauce (it's thought to be rather uncouth to dump a lot of sauces in your rice)—though trendy restaurants may sprinkle rice bowls with black sesame seeds, plum powder, or other seasoning. In the old days, not everyone could afford the expensive white kind, which was grown primarily to pay taxes or rent to the feudal lord; peasants had to be satisfied with a mixture of brown rice, millet, and greens. Today, some Japanese still eat rice three times a day, although they're now just as apt to have bread and coffee for breakfast. Restaurants specializing in organic foods often offer *genmai* (unpolished brown rice).

ROBATAYAKI *Robatayaki* refers to restaurants in which seafood and vegetables are cooked over an open charcoal grill. In the olden days, an *robata* (open fireplace) in the middle of an old Japanese house was the center of activity for cooking, eating, socializing, and simply keeping warm. Therefore, today's robatayaki restaurants are like nostalgia trips back into Japan's past and are often decorated in rustic farmhouse style with the staff dressed in traditional clothing. Robatayaki restaurants—mostly open only in the evening—are popular among office workers for both eating and drinking.

There's no special menu in a robatayaki restaurant—rather, it includes just about everything eaten in Japan. The difference is that most of the food will be grilled. Favorites of mine include *ginnan* (gingko nuts), asparagus wrapped in bacon, *piman* (a type of green pepper), mushrooms (various kinds), *jagabataa* (potatoes), and just about any kind of fish. You can usually get skewers of beef or chicken as well as *nikujaga* (a stew of meat and potatoes)—delicious during cold winter months. Because ordering is often a la carte, you'll just have to look and point.

SASHIMI & SUSHI It's estimated that the average Japanese eats 38 kilograms (84 lb.) of seafood a year—that's six times the average American consumption. Although this seafood may be served in any number of ways from grilled to boiled, a great deal of it is eaten raw.

Sashimi is simply raw seafood, usually served as an appetizer and eaten alone (that is, without rice). If you've never eaten it, a good choice to start out with is *maguro*, or lean tuna, which doesn't taste fishy at all and is so delicate in texture that it almost melts in your mouth. The way to eat sashimi is to first put *wasabi* (pungent green horseradish) into a small dish of soy sauce and then dip the raw fish in the sauce using your chopsticks (some purists maintain that wasabi and soy sauce shouldn't be mixed, but that's what my Japanese friends do).

Sushi, which is raw fish with vinegared rice, comes in many varieties. The best known is *nigiri-zushi:* raw fish, seafood, or vegetables placed on top of vinegared rice with just a touch of wasabi. It's also dipped in soy sauce. Use chopsticks or your fingers to eat sushi; remember you're supposed to eat each piece in one bite—quite a mouthful, but about the only way to keep it from falling apart. Another trick is to turn it upside down when you dip it in the sauce, to keep the rice from crumbling.

Also popular is *maki-zushi,* which consists of seafood, vegetables, or pickles rolled with rice inside a sheet of *nori* seaweed. *Inari-zushi* is vinegared rice and chopped vegetables inside a pouch of fried tofu bean curd.

Typical sushi includes *maguro* (tuna), *hirame* (flounder), *tai* (sea bream), *ika* (squid), *tako* (octopus), *ebi* (shrimp), *anago* (sea eel), and *tamago* (omelet). Ordering is easy because you usually sit at a counter where you can see all the food in a refrigerated glass case in front of you. You also get to see the sushi chefs at work. The typical meal begins with sashimi and is followed by sushi, but if you don't want to order separately, there are always various *seto* (set meals or courses). Pickled ginger is part of any sushi meal.

By the way, the least expensive sushi is *chirashi,* which is a selection of fish, seafood, and usually tamago on a large shallow bowl of rice. Because you get more rice, those of you with bigger appetites may want to order chirashi. Another way to enjoy sushi without spending a fortune is at a *kaiten* sushi shop, in which plates of sushi circulate on a conveyor belt on the counter—customers reach for the dishes they want and pay for the number of dishes they take.

SHABU-SHABU & SUKIYAKI Until the Meji Restoration beginning in 1868, which brought foreigners to Japan, Japanese could think of nothing as disgusting as eating the flesh of animals (fish was okay). Meat was considered unclean by Buddhists, and consuming it was banned by the emperor way back in the 7th century. Imagine the horror of Japanese when they discovered that Western "barbarians" ate bloody meat! It wasn't until Emperor Meiji himself announced his intention to eat meat that Japanese accepted the idea. Today, Japanese have become skilled in preparing a number of beef dishes.

Sukiyaki is among Japan's best-known beef dishes and is one many Westerners seem to prefer. Whenever I'm invited to a Japanese home, this is the meal most often served. Like fondue, it's cooked at the table.

Sukiyaki is thinly sliced beef cooked in a broth of soy sauce, stock, and sake along with scallions, spinach, mushrooms, tofu, bamboo shoots, and other vegetables. All diners serve themselves from the simmering pot and then dip their morsels into their own bowl of raw egg. You can skip the raw egg if you want (most Westerners do), but it adds to the taste and also cools the food down enough so that it doesn't burn.

Shabu-shabu is also prepared at your table and consists of thinly sliced beef cooked in a broth with vegetables in a kind of Japanese fondue. (It's named for the swishing sound the beef supposedly makes when cooking.) The main difference between the two dishes is the broth: Whereas in sukiyaki it consists of stock flavored with soy sauce and sake and is slightly sweet, in shabu-shabu it's relatively clear and has little taste of its own. The pots used are also different.

Using their chopsticks, *shabu* diners submerge pieces of meat in the watery broth until they're cooked. This usually takes only a few seconds. Vegetables are left in longer to swim around until fished out. For dipping, there's either sesame sauce with diced green onions or a more bitter fish stock sauce. Restaurants serving sukiyaki usually serve shabu-shabu as well,

and they're usually happy to show you the right way to prepare and eat it.

SHOJIN RYORI **Shojin Ryori** is the ultimate vegetarian meal, created centuries ago to serve the needs of Zen Buddhist priests and pilgrims. Dishes may include *yudofu* (simmered tofu) and an array of local vegetables. Kyoto is the best place to experience this type of cuisine.

SOBA & UDON NOODLES Japanese love eating noodles, but I suspect at least part of the fascination stems from the way they eat them—they slurp, sucking in the noodles with gravity-defying speed. What's more, slurping noodles is considered proper etiquette. Fearing it would stick with me forever, however, slurping is a technique I've never quite mastered.

There are many different kinds of noodles, and it seems like almost every region of Japan has its own special style or kind—some are eaten plain, some in combination with other foods such as shrimp tempura, some served hot, some served cold. *Soba,* made from unbleached buckwheat flour and enjoyed for its nutty flavor and high nutritional value, is eaten hot *(kake-soba)* or cold *(zaru-soba)*. *Udon* is a thick white wheat noodle originally from Osaka; it's usually served hot. *Somen* is a fine white noodle eaten cold in the summer and dunked in a cold sauce. Establishments serving noodles range from stand-up eateries to more refined noodle restaurants with *tatami* seating. Regardless of where you eat them, noodles are among the least expensive dishes in Japan.

TEMPURA Today a well-known Japanese food, tempura was actually introduced by the Portuguese in the 16th century. Tempura is fish and vegetables coated in a batter of egg, water, and wheat flour and then deep-fried; it's served piping hot. To eat it, dip it in a sauce of soy, fish stock, *daikon* (radish), and grated ginger; in some restaurants, only some salt, powdered green tea, or a lemon wedge is provided as an accompaniment. Various tempura specialties may include *nasu* (eggplant), *shiitake* (mushroom), *satsumaimo* (sweet potato), *shishito* (small green pepper), *renkon* (sliced lotus root), *ebi* (shrimp), *ika* (squid), *shisho* (lemon-mint leaf), and many kinds of fish. Again, the easiest thing to do is to order the *teishoku* (set meal).

TEPPANYAKI A *teppanyaki* restaurant is a Japanese steakhouse. As in the famous Benihana restaurants in many U.S. cities, the chef slices, dices, and cooks your meal of tenderloin or sirloin steak and vegetables on a smooth, hot grill right in front of you—though with much less fanfare than his U.S. counterpart. Because beef is relatively new in Japanese cooking, some people categorize teppanyaki restaurants as "Western." However, I consider this style of cooking and presentation special enough to be referred to as Japanese. Teppanyaki restaurants also tend to be expensive, simply because of the price of beef in Japan, with Kobe beef the most prized.

TOFU Originally from China, tofu, or bean curd, is made from soy milk. It has little flavor of its own and is served cold in summer and *yudofu* (boiled) in winter. A byproduct of tofu is *yuba,* thin sheets rich in protein.

TONKATSU *Tonkatsu* is the Japanese word for "pork cutlet," made by dredging pork in wheat flour, moistening it with egg and water, dipping it in bread crumbs, and deep-frying it in vegetable oil. Because tonkatsu restaurants are generally inexpensive, they're popular with office workers and families. It's easiest to order the *teishoku,* which usually features either the *hirekatsu* (pork filet) or the *rosukatsu* (pork loin). In any case, tonkatsu is served on a bed of shredded cabbage, and one or two different sauces will be at your table, a Worcestershire sauce and perhaps a specialty sauce. If you order the teishoku, it will come with rice, miso soup, and pickled vegetables.

Pork cutlet served on a bowl of rice is *katsudon.*

UNAGI I'll bet that if you eat *unagi* without knowing what it is, you'll find it very tasty—and you'll probably be very surprised to find out you've just eaten eel. Popular as a health food because of its rich protein and high vitamin A content, eel is supposed to help you fight fatigue during hot summer months but is eaten year-round. *Kabayaki* (broiled eel) is prepared by grilling filet strips over a charcoal fire; the eel is repeatedly dipped in a sweetened barbecue soy sauce while cooking. A favorite way to eat broiled eel is on top of rice, in which case it's called *unaju* or *unagi donburi.* Do yourself a favor and try it.

YAKITORI *Yakitori* is chunks of chicken or chicken parts basted in a sweet soy sauce and grilled over a charcoal fire on thin skewers. Places that specialize in yakitori (*yakitori-ya,* often identifiable by a red paper lantern outside the front door) are technically not restaurants but drinking establishments; they usually don't open until 5 or 6pm. Most yakitori-ya are popular with workers as inexpensive places to drink, eat, and be merry.

The cheapest way to dine on yakitori is to order a set course, which will often include various parts of the chicken including the skin, heart, and liver. If this isn't entirely to your taste, you may wish to order a la carte, which is more expensive but gets you exactly what you want. In addition to chicken, other skewered, charcoaled delicacies are usually offered (called *kushi-yaki*). If you're ordering by the stick, you might want to try *sasami* (chicken breast), *tsukune* (chicken meatballs), *piman* (green peppers), *negima* (chicken and leeks), *shiitake* (mushrooms), or *ginnan* (gingko nuts).

OTHER CUISINES During your travels you might also run into these types of Japanese cuisine: ***Kamameshi*** is a rice casserole served in individual-size cast-iron pots with different toppings that might include seafood, meat, or vegetables. ***Donburi*** is also a rice dish, topped with tempura, eggs, and meat such as chicken or pork. ***Nabe,*** a stew cooked in an earthenware pot at your table, consists of chicken, sliced beef, pork, or seafood; noodles; and vegetables. ***Oden*** is a broth with fish cakes, tofu, eggs, and vegetables, served with hot mustard. If a restaurant advertises that it specializes in ***Kyodo-Ryori,*** it serves local specialties for which the region is famous and is often very rustic in decor. A more recent trend is **crossover fusion cuisine**—creative dishes inspired by ingredients from both sides of the Pacific. Upmarket *izakaya* may also serve nouvelle dishes.

Although technically considered Chinese fast-food restaurants, **ramen shops** are a big part of dining in Japan. Serving what I consider to be generic Chinese noodles, soups, and other dishes, ramen shops can be found everywhere; they're easily recognizable by red signs and often pictures of various dishes displayed right by the front door. Many are stand-up affairs—just a high counter to rest your bowl on. In addition to *ramen* (noodle and vegetable soup), you can also get such things as *yakisoba* (fried noodles) or—my favorite—*gyoza* (fried pork dumplings). What these places lack in atmosphere is made up for in price: Dishes average less than ¥700, making them some of the cheapest places in Japan for a meal.

DRINKS

All Japanese restaurants serve complimentary **green tea** with meals. If that's too weak, you might want to try **sake** (also known as *nihonshu*), an alcoholic beverage made from rice and served either hot or cold. It goes well with most forms of Japanese cuisine. Produced since about the 3rd century, sake varies by region, production method, alcoholic content, color, aroma, and taste. There are more than 1,800 sake brewers in Japan producing about 10,000

varieties. Miyabi is a prized classic sake; other brands are Gekkeikan, Koshinokanbai, Hakutsuru (meaning White Crane), and Ozeki. A good place to try a good variety of sake is at a Japanese-style pub, an *izakaya*.

Japanese **beer** is also very popular. The biggest sellers are Kirin, Sapporo, Asahi, and Suntory, with each brand offering a bewildering variety of brews. They enjoyed exclusive brewing rights until deregulation in the 1990s opened the gates to competition; now microbreweries are found everywhere in Japan. Businessmen are fond of **whiskey,** which they usually drink with ice and water. Popular in recent years is ***shochu,*** a clear, distilled spirit usually made from rice but sometimes from wheat, sweet potatoes, barley, or sugar cane. It used to be considered a drink of the lower classes, but sales have increased so much that it's threatening the sake and whiskey businesses. A clear liquid comparable, perhaps, to vodka, it can be consumed straight but is often combined with soda water in a drink called *chuhai*. My personal favorite is *ume-shu,* a plum-flavored shochu. But watch out—the stuff can be deadly. **Wine,** usually available only at restaurants serving Western food, has gained in popularity in recent years, with both domestic and imported brands available. Although **cocktails** are available in dance clubs, hotel lounges, and fancier bars at rather inflated prices, most Japanese stick with beer, wine, sake, shochu, or whiskey.

TIPS ON DINING IN JAPAN
Restaurant Essentials

ORDERING The biggest problem facing the hungry foreigner in Japan is ordering a meal in a restaurant without an English-language menu. This book alleviates the problem to some extent by recommending sample dishes and giving prices for restaurants throughout Japan; we've also noted which restaurants offer English-language menus.

One aid to simplified ordering is the use of plastic food models in glass display cases either outside or just inside the front door of many restaurants, especially those in tourist areas and department stores. Sushi, tempura, daily specials, spaghetti—they're all there in mouthwatering plastic replicas along with corresponding prices. Simply decide what you want and point it out to staff.

Unfortunately, not all restaurants in Japan have plastic display cases, especially the more exclusive or traditional ones. In fact, you'd be missing a lot of Japan's best cuisine if you restrict yourself to eating only at places with displays. If there's no display from which to choose, the best thing to do is see whether the Japanese-language menu has photos or to look at what people around you are eating and order what looks best. Or, order the *teishoku,* or daily special meal (also called "set course" or simply "course," especially in restaurants serving Western food); these fixed-price meals consist of a main dish and several side dishes, including soup, rice, and Japanese pickles. Although most restaurants have set courses for dinner as well, lunch is the usual time for the teishoku, generally from 11 or 11:30am to 1:30 or 2pm.

In any case, once you've decided what you want to eat, flag down a waiter or waitress; they will not hover around your table waiting for you to order but come only when summoned. In most restaurants there are no assigned servers to certain tables; rather, servers are multitaskers, so don't be shy about stopping any who pass by.

HOURS In larger cities, most restaurants are open from about 11am to 10 or 11pm. Of course, some establishments close earlier at 9pm, while others stay open past midnight; the majority close for a few hours in the afternoon (2–5pm). In big cities like Tokyo or Osaka, try to avoid the lunchtime rush from noon to 1pm. In rural areas and small towns, restaurants tend to close early, often by 7:30 or 8pm. Traditional Japanese restaurants hang a *noren* (split curtain) over the front door to signify they're open.

Another thing to keep in mind is that the closing time posted for most restaurants is exactly that—everyone is expected to pay his or her bill and leave. A general rule of thumb is that the last order is taken at least a half-hour before closing time, sometimes an hour or more for *kaiseki* restaurants (staff will usually alert you they're taking last orders). To be on the safe side, try to arrive at least an hour before closing time so you have time to relax and enjoy your meal.

Etiquette

UPON ARRIVAL As soon as you're seated in a Japanese restaurant (that is, a restaurant serving Japanese food), you'll be given a wet towel, which will be steaming hot in winter or pleasantly cool in summer. Called an *oshibori,* it's for wiping your hands. In all but the fancy restaurants, men can get away with wiping their faces as well, but women are not supposed to (I ignore this if it's hot and humid outside). Sadly, some cheaper Japanese restaurants now resort to a paper towel wrapped in plastic, which isn't nearly the same. Oshibori are generally not provided in Western restaurants.

CHOPSTICKS The next thing you'll probably be confronted with is chopsticks (though knives and forks are used in restaurants serving Western food). The proper way to use a pair is to place the first chopstick between the base of the thumb and the top of the ring finger (this chopstick remains stationary) and the second one between the top of the thumb and the middle and index fingers. (This second chopstick is the one you move to pick up food.)

The best way to learn to use chopsticks is to have a Japanese person show you how.

It's not difficult, but if you find it impossible, some restaurants might have a fork as well. How proficiently foreigners handle chopsticks is a matter of great curiosity for Japanese, and they're surprised if you know how to use them; even if you were to live in Japan for 20 years, you would never stop receiving compliments on how talented you are with chopsticks.

CHOPSTICK ETIQUETTE If you're taking something from a communal bowl or tray, you're supposed to turn your chopsticks upside down and use the part that hasn't been in your mouth; after transferring the food to your plate, you turn the chopsticks back to their proper position. The exception is *shabu-shabu* and sukiyaki.

Never point at someone with your chopsticks, and never stick them down vertically into your bowl of rice and leave them there, and never pass anything from your chopsticks to another person's chopsticks—both actions have origins relating to funerary rites but are now mostly considered bad manners.

EATING SOUP & NOODLES You don't use a spoon with Japanese soup. Rather, you'll pick up the bowl and drink from it, using your chopsticks to fish out larger pieces of food. You should also pick up a bowl of rice to eat it. It's considered good taste to slurp with gusto, especially if you're eating hot noodles. Noodle shops in Japan are always well orchestrated with slurps and smacks.

DRINKING Women should hold their glass or cup with both hands, but men do not. If you're drinking in Japan, the main thing to remember is that you never pour your own glass. Bottles of beer are so large that people often share one. The rule is that in turn, one person pours for everyone else in the group, so be sure to hold up your glass when someone is pouring for you. As the night progresses Japanese get sloppy about this rule. It took me awhile

to figure this out, but if no one notices your empty glass, the best thing to do is to pour everyone else a drink so that someone will pour yours. If someone wants to pour you a drink and your glass is full, the proper thing to do is to take a few gulps so that he or she can fill your glass. Because each person is continually filling everyone else's glass, you never know exactly how much you've had to drink, which (depending on how you look at it) is either very good or very bad. If you really don't want more to drink, leave your glass full and refuse refills.

PAYING THE BILL If you go out with a group of friends (not as a visiting guest of honor and not with business associates), it's customary to split the dinner bill equally, even if you all ordered different things. Even foreigners living in Japan adopt the practice of splitting the bill; it certainly makes figuring everyone's share easier, especially since **there's no tipping in Japan.** But it can be hard on frugal diners on a budget. If you're with friends who do wish to pay for only what they ate, tell the cashier you want to pay *"betsu, betsu."*

OTHER TIPS It's considered bad manners to walk down the street eating or drinking (except at a festival). You'll notice that if a Japanese buys a drink from a vending machine, he'll stand there, gulp it down, and throw away the container before going on. To the chagrin of their elders, young Japanese sometimes ignore this rule.

How to Eat Without Spending a Fortune

During your first few days in Japan—particularly if you're in Tokyo—money will seem to flow from your pockets like water. In fact, money has a tendency to disappear so quickly that many people become convinced they must have lost some of it somehow. At this point, almost everyone panics (I've seen it happen again and again), but with time they slowly realize that because prices are markedly different here (steeper), a bit of readjustment in thinking and habits is necessary. Coffee, for example, is something of a luxury, and some Japanese are astonished at the thought of drinking four cups a day. Here are some tips for getting the most for your yen.

BREAKFAST Buffet breakfasts are popular at Japanese hotels and can be an inexpensive way to eat your fill. Otherwise, coffee shops offer what's called "morning service" until 10 or 11am; it generally consists of a cup of coffee, a small salad, a boiled egg, and the thickest slice of toast you've ever seen for about ¥650. That's a real bargain when you consider that just one cup of coffee can cost ¥250 to ¥500. (Except at most hotel breakfast buffets, there's no such thing as the bottomless cup in Japan.) There are many coffee-shop chains in Japan, including Doutour, Pronto, and the ever-expanding Starbucks (854 in Japan at last count).

SET LUNCHES **Eat your biggest meal at lunch.** Many restaurants serving Japanese food offer a daily set lunch, or *teishoku,* at a fraction of what their set dinners might be. Usually ranging in price from ¥800 to ¥2,000, they're generally available from about 11am to around 2pm. A Japanese teishoku will include the main course (such as tempura, grilled fish, or the specialty of the house), soup, pickled vegetables, rice, and tea, while the set menu in a Western-style restaurant (often called set lunch) usually consists of a main dish, salad, bread, and coffee.

CHEAP EATS Inexpensive restaurants can be found in department stores (often one whole floor will be devoted to various kinds of restaurants, most with plastic-food displays), underground shopping arcades, nightlife districts, and in and around train and subway stations. Some of

the cheapest establishments for a night out on the town are *yakitori-ya, izakaya* (Japanese pubs), **noodle** and **ramen shops, coffee shops** (which often offer inexpensive pastries and sandwiches), and **conveyor-belt sushi restaurants** where you reach out and take the plates that interest you. Restaurants serving *gyudon* (beef bowl) are also cheap, with Yoshinoya the largest chain. Japan also has American **fast-food chains,** such as McDonald's (where Big Macs cost about ¥320) and KFC, as well as Japanese chains—Freshness Burger and First Kitchen, among them—that sell hamburgers.

Ethnic restaurants, particularly those serving Indian, Korean, Chinese, Italian, and other cuisines, are plentiful and usually inexpensive. **Hotel restaurants** can also be good bargains for inexpensive set lunches or buffets (called *viking* in Japanese), while inexpensive drinking places are good bets for dinner.

Street-side stalls, called *yatai,* are also good sources of inexpensive meals. These restaurants-on-wheels sell a variety of foods, including *oden* (fish cakes), *yakitori* (skewered barbecued chicken), and *yakisoba* (fried noodles), as well as sake and beer. They appear mostly at night, lighted by a single lantern or a string of lights, and most have a counter with stools as well, protected in winter by a wall of tarp. These can be great, cozy places for rubbing elbows with the locals. Fukuoka, in Kyushu, is famous for its yatai, but you may find them also near other cities' nightlife districts. Sadly, traditional pushcarts are being replaced by motorized vans, which are not nearly as romantic and do not offer seating.

PREPARED FOODS You can save even more money by avoiding restaurants altogether. There are all kinds of prepared foods you can buy; some are even complete meals, perfect for picnics in a park or right in your hotel room.

Perhaps the best known is the *obento,* or box lunch, commonly sold on express trains, on train-station platforms, in food sections of department stores, and at counter windows of tiny shops throughout Japan. In fact, the obento served by vendors on trains and at train stations are an inexpensive way to sample regional cuisine since they often include food typical of the region you're passing through. Costing between ¥800 and ¥1,500, the basic obento contains a piece of meat (generally fish or chicken), various side dishes, rice, and pickled vegetables. Sushi boxed lunches are also readily available.

My favorite place to shop for prepared foods is **department stores.** Located in basements, these enormous food and produce sections hark back to Japanese markets of yore, with vendors yelling out their wares and crowds of housewives deciding on the evening's dinner. Different counters specialize in different items—tempura, *yakitori,* eel, Japanese pickles, cooked fish, sushi (sometimes made by robots!), salads, vegetables, and desserts. Almost the entire spectrum of Japanese cuisine is available, as are numerous samples. There are also counters selling obento box meals. In any case, you can eat for less than ¥1,200, and there's nothing like milling with Japanese housewives to make you feel like one of the locals. Though not as colorful, **24-hour convenience stores** and grocery stores also sell packaged foods like sandwiches and obento.

6 MINDING YOUR P'S & Q'S

As an island nation with few natural resources, Japan's 127 million people are its greatest asset. Hardworking, honest, and proud about performing every task well no matter how insignificant it may seem, Japanese are well known for their politeness and helpfulness to strangers. Indeed, hardly anyone returns from a trip to Japan without stories of extraordinary kindnesses extended by Japanese.

With almost 99% of its population consisting of ethnic Japanese, Japan is one of the most homogeneous nations in the world. That—coupled with Japan's actual physical isolation as an island nation—has more than anything else led to a feeling among Japanese that they belong to a single huge tribe different from any other people on earth, and that all people can basically be divided into two categories: Japanese and non-Japanese. You'll often hear a Japanese preface a statement or opinion with the words "We Japanese," implying that all Japanese think alike.

While in the West the attainment of "happiness" is the elusive goal for a full and rewarding life, in Japan, it's satisfactory performance of **duty.** From the time they are born, Japanese are instilled with a sense of duty that extends toward parents, spouses, bosses, co-workers, neighbors, and society as a whole. In a nation as crowded as Japan, consideration of others is essential, and consideration of the group always wins out over the desire of the individual. In fact, I have had Japanese tell me they consider individuality synonymous with selfishness and a complete disregard for the feelings of others.

MEETING THE JAPANESE PEOPLE

On a personal level, Japanese are among the most likable people in the world. They are kind, thoughtful, and adept in perceiving another person's needs. Japanese have an unerring eye for pure beauty, whether it be food, architecture, or landscaped gardens; it's impossible to visit Japan and not have some of the Japanese appreciation of beauty rub off.

ⓘ Tips **The Home-Visit System**

Recognizing the difficulty foreigners may face in meeting Japanese people, a half-dozen or so cities offer a **Home Visit,** allowing overseas visitors the chance to visit an English-speaking Japanese family in their home for a few hours. Not only does such an encounter bring you in direct contact with Japanese, it also offers a glimpse into their lifestyle. You can even request that a family member share your occupation, though such requests are, of course, sometimes impossible to fulfill. The program doesn't cost anything, but it does take some preparation. You must make arrangements in advance, which differs from city to city and can range from 1 day in advance to 2 weeks in advance, by calling or applying in person at the local administrative authority or private organization (which is sometimes the local tourist office) that handles the city's home-visit program. After contacting a local family, the office will inform you of the family and the time to visit. Most visits take place for a few hours in the evening (dinner is not served). You should bring a small gift such as flowers, fruit, or a small souvenir from your hometown. Before your visit, you may be asked to appear in person at the application office to obtain detailed directions; or the office may call with the directions. Note that application offices may be closed on weekends and holidays. Here are a few contact numbers for cities participating in the Home-Visit System: **Narita** (ⓒ 0476/24-3232 or 24-3198; you can also apply in person at the Tourist Information Center in Terminal 2 at Narita airport), **Nagoya** (ⓒ 052/581-5689), **Kyoto** (ⓒ 075/752-3511), **Osaka** (ⓒ 06/6345-2189), **Kobe** (ⓒ 078/303-1010), **Kurashiki** (ⓒ 086/475-0543), **Hiroshima** (ⓒ 082/247-9715), **Fukuoka** (ⓒ 092/733-2220), and **Kumamoto** (ⓒ 096/359-2121). For information, contact local tourist information offices.

If you're invited to Japan by an organization or business, you'll receive the royal treatment and will most likely be wined and dined so wonderfully and thoroughly that you'll never want to leave. If you go to Japan on your own as an ordinary tourist, however, chances are that your experiences will be much different. Except for those who have lived or traveled abroad, few Japanese have had much contact with foreigners. In fact, even in Tokyo, there are some Japanese who have never spoken to a foreigner and would be quite embarrassed and uncomfortable if confronted with the possibility. And even though most of them have studied English, few Japanese have had the opportunity to use the language and cannot (or are too shy to) communicate in it. So don't be surprised if you find the empty seat beside you on the subway the last one to be occupied—most Japanese are deathly afraid you'll ask them a question they won't understand.

In many respects, therefore, it's much harder to meet the locals in Japan than in many other countries. Japanese are simply much shyer than Americans. Although they will sometimes approach you to ask whether they might practice English with you, for the most part you're left pretty much on your own unless you make the first move.

Probably the easiest way to meet Japanese is to go where they play—namely, the country's countless **bars,** including those that serve *yakitori* (skewered chicken).

Usually small affairs, each with perhaps just a counter and some tables, they're often filled with both younger and older Japanese, many of whom are regulars. As the evening wears on, you'll encounter Japanese who do want to speak to you if they understand English, and other slightly inebriated Japanese who will speak to you even if they don't. If you're open to them, such chance encounters may prove to be the highlight of your trip or, at the very least, an evening of just plain fun.

My co-worker Janie, who traveled around Japan with her then-3-year-old daughter, found that **traveling with children** opened up opportunities like a magic key. Other children talked freely to her child (they never seemed to have a language barrier), while Janie was able to talk to parents about their children. Complete strangers she met on a train even invited her and her daughter home; in contrast, some Japanese people she has known for years have never invited her home, preferring instead to meet at coffee shops or restaurants.

Another good way to meet Japanese people is to stay in a *minshuku,* an inexpensive lodging in a private home (see "Tips on Accommodations" in chapter 3). Also, national newspapers and local English-language newsletters list **international club activities;** you may be able to hook up with, say, a hiking or skiing group composed of both Japanese and international members.

Finally, you can meet locals and learn about destinations at the same time through **Goodwill Guides,** a national organization of volunteers (mostly retirees, housewives, and students) who donate their time to guide you around their city free of charge (you pay their travel expenses, admission fees to sights, and meals). There are Goodwill Guides in cities throughout Japan, including Fukuoka, Kumamoto, Beppu, Kagoshima, Takamatsu, Matsuyama, Hiroshima, Himeji, Kurashiki, Matsue, Kobe, Osaka, Kyoto, Nara, Kanazawa, Matsumoto, Nagoya, Tokyo, Yokohama, Kamakura, Hakone, Nikko, and Matsushima. Reservations for a guide must be made in advance—usually a week or more. For information, including contact information, ask for the pamphlet "Goodwill Guide Groups of Japan Welcome You," at Tourist Information Centers in Tokyo or Narita and Kansai international airports; or go to JNTO's website at **www.jnto.go.jp**, and click "Essential Info" (under "Arrange Your Travel"), and then "Guide Services."

ETIQUETTE

Much of Japan's system of etiquette and manners stems from its feudal days, when the social hierarchy dictated how a person spoke, sat, bowed, ate, walked, and lived. Failure to comply with the rules would bring severe punishment, even death. Many Japanese have literally lost their heads for committing social blunders.

Of course, nowadays it's quite different, although Japanese still attach much importance to proper behavior. As a foreigner, however, you can get away with a lot. After all, you're just a "barbarian" and, as such, can be forgiven for not knowing the rules. There are two cardinal sins, however, you should never commit: One is you should **never wear your shoes into a Japanese home, traditional inn, temple, or any room with *tatami;*** the other is that you should **never wash with soap inside a communal Japanese bathtub.** Except for these two horrors, you will probably be forgiven any other social blunders (such as standing with your arms folded or your hands in your pockets).

As a sensitive traveler, however, you should try to familiarize yourself with the basics of Japanese social etiquette. Japanese are very appreciative of foreigners who take the time to learn about their country and are quite patient in helping you. Remember, if you do commit a faux pas, apologize profusely and smile.

Most forms of behavior and etiquette in Japan developed to allow relationships to be as frictionless as possible—a pretty good idea in a country as crowded as Japan. Japanese don't like confrontations, and fights are extremely rare. Japanese are very good at covering almost all unpleasantness with a smile. Foreigners find the smile hard to read; a smiling Japanese face can mean happiness, sadness, embarrassment, or even anger. My first lesson in such physiognomic inscrutability happened on a subway in Tokyo, where I saw a middle-aged Japanese woman who was about to board the subway brutally knocked out of the way by a Japanese man rushing off the train. She almost lost her balance, but she gave a little laugh, smiled, and got on the train. A few minutes later, as the train was speeding through a tunnel, I stole a look at her and was able to read her true feelings on her face. Lost in her thoughts, she knitted her brow in consternation and looked most upset and unhappy. The smile had been a put-on.

Another aspect of Japanese behavior that sometimes causes difficulty for foreigners, especially in business negotiations, is **the reluctance of Japanese to say no when they mean no.** Many consider such directness poor manners. As a result, they're much more apt to say your request is very difficult, or they'll simply beat around the bush without giving a definite answer. At this point, you're expected to let the subject drop. Showing impatience, anger, or aggressiveness rarely gets you anywhere; apologizing sometimes does. And if someone does give in to your request, you can't thank him enough.

If you're invited to a Japanese home, you should know that it's both a rarity and an honor. Most Japanese consider their homes too small and humble for entertaining guests, which is why there are so many restaurants, coffee shops, and bars. **If you're invited to a home, don't show up empty-handed.** Bring a small gift such as candy, fruit, flowers, or perhaps a souvenir from your hometown. Alcohol is also appreciated. And if someone does extend you a favor, be sure to thank him again the next time you see him—even if it's a year later.

Don't blow your nose in public if you can help it, and never at the dinner table. It's considered most disgusting. On the other hand, even though Japanese are very hygienic, they're not at all averse to spitting on the sidewalk. And, even more peculiar, the men urinate when and where they want, usually against a tree or a wall and most often after a night of carousing in the bars.

This being a man's society, men will walk in and out of doors and elevators before women, and in subways, they will sit down while women stand. Some Japanese men who have had contact with the Western world (particularly hotel staff) will make a gallant show of allowing a Western woman to step out of the elevator first. For the sake of women living in Japan, thank them warmly.

BOWING The main form of greeting in Japan is the bow rather than the handshake. Although at first glance it may seem simple enough, the bow—together with its implications—is actually quite complicated. The depth of the bow and the number of seconds devoted to performing it, as well as the total number of bows, depend on who you are, to whom you're bowing, and how he's bowing back. In addition to bowing in greeting, Japanese also bow upon departing and to express gratitude. The proper form for a bow is to bend from the waist with a straight back and to keep your arms at your sides if you're a man or clasped in front of you if you're a woman, but if you're a foreigner, a simple nod of the head is enough. Knowing foreigners shake hands, a Japanese may extend his hand, although he probably won't be able to stop himself from giving a little bow as well. (I've even seen Japanese bow when talking on the telephone.) Although I've occasionally witnessed Japanese businessmen shaking hands among themselves, the practice is still quite rare. Kimono-clad hostesses of a high-end traditional Japanese inn will often kneel on *tatami* and bow to the ground as they send you off on your journey.

VISITING CARD   You're a nonentity in Japan if you don't have a visiting card, called a **meishi.** Everyone—from housewives to bank presidents—carries meishi to give out during introductions. If you're trying to conduct business in Japan, you'll be regarded suspiciously—even as a phony—if you don't have business cards. Meishi are very useful business tools for Japanese. Likewise, a meishi can be used as an introduction to a third party—a Japanese may give you his meishi, scribble something on it, and tell you to present it to his cousin who owns a restaurant in Fukuoka. *Voilà*—the cousin will treat you like a royal guest.

As a tourist, you don't have to have business cards, but it certainly doesn't hurt, and Japanese people will be greatly impressed by your preparedness. The card should have your address and occupation on it; you might even consider having your meishi made in Japan, with *katakana* (Japanese syllabic script) written on the reverse side.

Needless to say, there's a proper way to present a meishi. Turn it so that the other person can read it (that is, upside-down to you) and present it with both hands and a slight bow. If you are of equal status, you exchange meishi simultaneously; otherwise, the lower person on the totem pole presents the meishi first and delivers it underneath the card being received, to show deference. Afterward, don't simply put the meishi away. Rather, it's customary for both of you to study the meishi for a moment and, if possible, to comment on it (such as, "You're from Kyoto? My brother lived in Kyoto!" or "Sony! What a famous company!"). If you're at a business meeting, you should place the card in front of you on the table.

SHOES   Nothing is so distasteful to Japanese as the soles of shoes. Therefore, you should take off your shoes before entering a home, a Japanese-style inn, a temple, and even some museums and restaurants. Usually, there will be plastic slippers at the entryway for you to slip on, but whenever you encounter *tatami,* you should take off even these slippers—only bare feet or socks are allowed to tread upon tatami.

Restrooms present another set of slippers. If you're in a home or a Japanese inn, you'll notice another pair of slippers—again plastic or rubber—sitting right inside the restroom door. Step out of the hallway plastic shoes and into the bathroom slippers, and wear these the entire time you're in the restroom. When you're finished, change back into the hallway slippers. If you forget this last changeover, you'll regret it—nothing is as embarrassing as walking into a room wearing toilet slippers and not realizing what you've done until you see the mixed looks of horror and mirth on the faces of Japanese people.

BATHING   On my very first trip to Japan, I was certain I would never enter a Japanese bath. I was under the misconception that men and women bathed together, and I couldn't imagine getting into a tub with a group of smiling and bowing Japanese men. I needn't have worried—in almost all circumstances, bathing is gender segregated. There are some exceptions, primarily at outdoor hot-spring spas in the countryside, but the women who go to these are usually grandmothers who couldn't care less. Young Japanese women wouldn't dream of jumping into a tub with a group of male strangers.

Japanese baths are delightful—I'm addicted to them. You'll find them at Japanese-style inns, at *onsen* (hot-spring spas), and at *sento* (neighborhood baths); not everyone has his or her own bath in Japan. Sometimes they're elaborate affairs with indoor and outdoor tubs, and sometimes they're nothing more than a tiny tub. Public baths have long been regarded as social centers for Japanese—friends and co-workers will visit hot-spring resorts together; neighbors exchange gossip at the neighborhood bath. Sadly, neighborhood baths have been in great decline over the past decades, as more and more Japanese acquire private baths. Hot-spring spas, however, remain hugely popular.

In any case, whether large or small, the procedure at all Japanese baths is the same. After completely disrobing in the changing room and putting your clothes in either a locker or a basket, hold a washcloth (provided free or available for sale at the bathhouse) in front of you so that it covers your vital parts and walk into the bathing area. There you'll find plastic basins and stools (sometimes they're still made of wood), and faucets along the wall. Sit on the stool in front of a faucet and repeatedly fill your basin with water (or use the hand-held faucet if available), splashing water all over you. If there's no hot water from the faucet, it's acceptable to dip your basin into the hot bath, but your washcloth should never touch the tub water. Rinsing yourself thoroughly is not only proper onsen manners; it also acclimatizes your body to the bath's hot temperature so you don't suffer a heart attack. While some Japanese just throw a bit of water over themselves, others soap down completely—and I mean completely—and then rinse away all traces of soap before getting into the tub. At any rate, only when you feel squeaky-clean should you enter the tub.

As in a Jacuzzi, everyone uses the same bath water. For that reason, you should never wash yourself in the tub, never put your washcloth into the bath (place it on your head or lay it beside the bath), and never pull the plug when you're done. After you bathe is when you scrub your body and wash your hair. I have never seen a group of people wash themselves so thoroughly as the Japanese, from their ears to their toes. All sento provide shampoo and body soap, along with interesting products provided free by companies hoping to rope in new customers, but in small public baths you might have to provide your own.

Your first attempt at a Japanese bath may be painful—simply too scalding for comfort. It helps if you ease in gently and then sit perfectly still. You'll notice all tension and muscle stiffness ebbing away, a decidedly relaxing way to end the day. The Japanese are so fond of baths that many take them nightly, especially in winter when a hot bath keeps them toasty warm for hours. At an onsen, where hot-spring waters are considered curative, Japanese will bathe both at night and again in the morning, often making several trips between the faucet and the tubs and being careful not to rinse off the curative waters when they're done. With time, you'll probably become addicted, too. *Note:* Because tattoos in Japan have long been associated with *yakuza* (Japanese mafia), many public baths do not admit people with tattoos. However, if your tattoo is discreet and you're at, say, a small Japanese inn, you probably won't have any problems.

7 DEALING WITH THE LANGUAGE BARRIER

Without a doubt, the hardest part of traveling in Japan is the language barrier. Suddenly you find yourself transported to a crowded land of 127 million people where you can neither speak nor read the language. To make matters worse, many Japanese cannot speak English. And outside big cities and major tourist sites, menus, signs at train stations, and shop names are often in Japanese only.

However, millions of foreign visitors before you who didn't speak a word of Japanese have traveled throughout Japan on their own with great success. Much of the anxiety travelers experience elsewhere is eliminated in Japan because the country is safe and the people are kind and helpful to foreigners. In addition, the country has done a mammoth job during the past decade updating street signs, subway directions, and addresses in Roman letters, especially in Tokyo, Osaka, Kyoto, and other destinations popular with tourists. There are local **tourist information offices,** called *kanko annaijo,* in almost all cities and towns, usually at train stations. While not all staff speak English, they can provide maps, point out directions, and help with hotel reservations.

In addition, the **Japan National Tourist Organization (JNTO)** does a super job publishing helpful brochures, leaflets, and maps, including a nifty booklet called *The Tourist's Language Handbook.* It contains sentences in English and their Japanese equivalents for almost every activity, from asking directions, to shopping, to ordering in a restaurant, to staying in a Japanese inn. Pick up a copy at a Tourist Information Center in Tokyo or at Narita or Kansai airports. Otherwise, a glossary of common phrases and words appears in chapter 18 of this book. For more in-depth coverage, there are many language books geared toward travelers, including *Japanese for Travelers* by Scott Rutherford (Tuttle, 2009), with useful phrases and travel tips. It also doesn't hurt to be armed with a small pocket dictionary.

If you need to ask directions of strangers in Japan, your best bet is to **ask younger people.** They have all studied English in school and are most likely to be able to help you. Japanese businessmen also often know some English. And as strange as it sounds,

if you're having problems communicating with someone, **write it down** so he or she can read it. The emphasis in schools is on written rather than oral English (many English teachers can't speak English themselves), so Japanese who can't understand a word you say may know all the subtleties of syntax and English grammar. If you still have problems communicating, you can always call the **Tourist Information Center** (✆ **03/3201-3331**) to help with translation.

If you're heading out for a particular restaurant, shop, or sight, have your destination written down in Japanese by someone at your hotel. If you get lost along the way, look for one of the police boxes, called *koban,* found in virtually every neighborhood. They have maps of particular districts and can pinpoint exactly where you want to go if you have the address with you.

THE WRITTEN LANGUAGE No one knows the exact origins of the Japanese language, but we do know it existed only in spoken form until the 6th century. That's when the Japanese borrowed the Chinese pictorial characters, called *kanji,* and used them to develop their own form of written language. Later, two phonetic alphabet systems, *hiragana* and *katakana,* were added to kanji to form the existing Japanese writing system. Thus, Chinese and Japanese use some of the same pictographs, but otherwise there's no similarity between the languages; while they may be able to recognize parts of each other's written language, the Chinese and Japanese cannot communicate verbally.

The Japanese written language—a combination of kanji, hiragana, and katakana—is probably one of the most difficult in the modern world. As for the spoken language, there are many levels of speech and forms of expression relating to a person's social status and sex. Even nonverbal communication is a vital part of understanding Japanese, because what isn't said is often more important than what is. It's little wonder that St. Francis Xavier, a Jesuit missionary who came to Japan in the 16th century, wrote that Japanese was an invention of the devil designed to thwart the spread of Christianity. And yet, astoundingly, adult literacy in Japan is estimated to be 99%.

A note on establishment names: Many hotels and restaurants in Japan now have signs in *romaji* (Roman, or English-language, characters) in addition to their Japanese-character signs. For those that don't, take heart—chapter 17 contains the Japanese-character names of establishments recommended in this book that have signs in Japanese only.

OTHER HELPFUL TIPS   It's worth noting that Japanese nouns do not have plural forms; thus, for example, *ryokan,* a Japanese-style inn, can be both singular and plural, as can kimono. Plural sense is indicated by context.

In addition, the Japanese custom is to list the family name first followed by the given name. That is the format I have followed in this book (with the exception of a few celebrities known outside of Japan), but note that many things printed in English—business cards, city brochures, and so on—increasingly follow the Western custom of listing the family name last.

And finally, you may find yourself confused because of suffixes attached to Japanese place names. For example, *dori* can mean street, avenue, or road; and sometimes it's attached to a street name with a hyphen, while at other times it stands alone. Thus, you may see Chuo-dori, Chuo Dori, or even Chuo-dori Avenue on English-language maps and street signs, but they're all one and the same street.

Likewise, *dera* means "temple" and is often included at the end of the name, as in Kiyomizudera, which may be translated into English as Kiyomizu Temple; *jo* means "castle" and may appear at the end of a castle's name, as in Nijojo, or it may be left off and appear as Nijo Castle.

WRITTEN ENGLISH IN JAPAN   English-language words are quite fashionable in Japanese advertising, with the result that you'll often see them on shop signs, posters, shopping bags, and T-shirts. However, the words are often wonderfully misspelled or are used in such unusual contexts that you can only guess at the original intent. What, for example, can possibly be the meaning behind TODAY BIRDS, TOMORROW MEN, which appeared below a picture of birds on a shopping bag? I have treasured ashtrays that read THE YOUNG BOY GRASPED HER HEART FIRMLY and LET'S TRIP IN HOKKAIDO. In Okayama, I saw a shop whose name was a stern admonition to customers to GROW UP, while in Gifu you can only surmise at the pleasures to be had at HOTEL JOYBOX. A staff member of the Hokkaido Tourist Association whose business card identified him working for the PROPAGANDA SECTION was probably more truthful than most. And imagine my consternation upon stepping onto a bathroom scale that called itself the BEAUTY-CHECKER. But the best sign I've seen was at Narita Airport, where each check-in counter displayed a notice advising passengers they would have to pay a service-facility charge at THE TIME OF CHECK-IN FOR YOUR FRIGHT. I explained the cause of my amusement to the person behind the counter, and when I came back 2 weeks later, I was almost disappointed to find that all signs had been corrected. That's Japanese efficiency.

8 JAPAN IN POPULAR CULTURE: BOOKS & FILM

Japanese publisher **Kodansha International** (www.kodansha-intl.com) has probably published more books on Japan in English—including Japanese-language textbooks—than any other company. Available at major bookstores in Japan, they are also available at www.amazon.com.

HISTORY The definitive work of Japan's history through the ages is *Japan: The Story of a Nation* (Alfred A. Knopf, 1991) by Edwin O. Reischauer, a former U.S. ambassador to Japan. Ivan Morris's *The World of the Shining Prince: Court Life in Ancient Japan* (Kodansha Globe, 1994) highlights the golden age of the imperial court through diaries and literature of the Heian Period (794–1192), while *Everyday Life in Traditional Japan* (Tuttle, 2000) details the daily lives of samurai, farmers, craftsmen, merchants, courtiers, and outcasts during the Edo Period.

For personal accounts of Japan in ages past, there's no better anthology than Donald Keene's *Travelers of a Hundred Ages: The Japanese as Revealed Through 1,000 Years of Diaries* (Holt, 1989). Written by Japanese from all walks of life, the journals provide fascinating insight into the hidden worlds of imperial courts, Buddhist monasteries, isolated country inns, and more. Lafcadio Hearn, a prolific writer about things Japanese, describes life in Japan around the turn of the 20th century in *Writings from Japan* (Penguin, 1985), while Isabella Bird, an Englishwoman who traveled in Japan in the 1870s, writes a vivid account of rural Japanese life in *Unbeaten Tracks in Japan* (Cornell University Library, 2009). *Autobiography of a Geisha* (Columbia University Press, 2003), first published in 1957, is Masuda Sayo's account of being sold to a geisha house as a child, working

at a hot-spring spa, and living under harsh conditions during and after World War II.

SOCIETY Reischauer's *The Japanese Today: Change and Continuity* (Belknap Press, 1995) offers a unique perspective on the historical events that have shaped and influenced Japanese behavior and the role of the individual in Japanese society. A classic description of Japanese and their culture is found in Ruth Benedict's brilliant *The Chrysanthemum and the Sword: Patterns of Japanese Culture* (Mariner Books, 2006), first published in the 1940s but reprinted many times since. Debunking theories that have long shaped the outside world's views of Japan (many of which are espoused by the books above) is *Japan: A Reinterpretation* (Pantheon, 1997) by former *International Herald Tribune* Tokyo bureau chief Patrick Smith, who gives a spirited reinterpretation of Japan's economic miracle and demise; and Alex Kerr's *Dogs and Demons: Tales From the Dark Side of Modern Japan* (Hill and Wang, 2001), who writes a scathing, controversial indictment of a country he loves but says was ruined by corrupt bureaucracy. Jake Adelstein, a former Tokyo crime reporter, writes a gripping account of his run-in with Japanese mafia and the threat on his life in *Tokyo Vice: An American Reporter on the Police Beat in Japan* (Pantheon, 2009).

A more entertaining look at the Japanese psyche is provided by English translations of Japanese articles that never made it into the *Japan Times* in *Tabloid Tokyo: 101 Tales of Sex, Crime, and the Bizarre from Japan's Wild Weeklies* (Kodansha, 2005), edited by Mark Schreiber, and its sequel, *Tabloid Tokyo 2* (Kodansha, 2007).

CULTURE & THE ARTS For a cultural overview in one book, see *Introduction to*

Japanese Culture, edited by Daniel Sosnoski (Tuttle, 1996), which covers major festivals, the tea ceremony, flower arranging, kabuki, sumo, Japanese board games, Buddhism, kanji, and much more. Elizabeth Kiritani's *Vanishing Japan: Traditions, Crafts & Culture* (Tuttle, 1995) covers a wide spectrum of traditional Japanese crafts and professions that were once a part of daily life, from potato vendors, shoe shiners, and *tatami* makers to Japanese umbrellas and handmade paper, many of which are fast disappearing in today's Japan.

The Japan Travel Bureau puts out nifty pocket-size illustrated booklets on things Japanese, including *A Look into Japan, Living Japanese Style, Eating in Japan, Festivals of Japan,* and *Japanese Family & Culture,* which covers everything from marriage in Japan to problems with mothers-in-law and explanations of why Dad gets home so late. My favorite is *Salaryman in Japan* (JTB, 1987), which describes the private and working lives of Japan's army of white-collar workers who receive set salaries.

And while some might argue it's not art, there's no denying the power *manga* (Japanese comics) has over Japanese readers. The best primers on manga history and its various genres are Paul Gravett's *Manga: 60 Years of Japanese Comics* (Collins Design, 2004) and, though dated, Frederik L. Schodt and Tezuka Osamu's *Manga! Manga!: The World of Japanese Comics* (Kodansha, 1988), with a follow-up provided in Schodt's *Dreamland Japan: Writings on Modern Manga* (Stone Bridge Press, 1996). Likewise, travelers new to Japanese animation should check out *Anime from Akira to Howl's Moving Castle* by Susan J. Napier (Palgrave Macmillan, 2005).

CONTEMPORARY CHRONICLES For contemporary experiences of foreigners in Japan, there's the inimitable Dave Barry, who describes his whirlwind trip to the Land of the Rising Sun in the comical *Dave Barry Does Japan* (Random House, 1992) and solves such puzzling mysteries as why Japanese cars sell successfully (they're made of steel!). A delightful account of Japanese and their customs is given by the irrepressible George Mikes in *The Land of the Rising Yen* (Penguin, 1973). *Traveler's Tales Guides: Japan* (Traveler's Tales, 1999) relates the firsthand experiences of Dave Barry, Pico Iyer, and other writers who tackle such issues as sand bathing and Washlet toilets. A book seemingly from another era is *Geisha* (Vintage, 2000) by Liza C. Dalby, which describes her year living as a geisha in Kyoto as part of a research project. *The Japan Journals: 1947–2004* (Stone Bridge Press, 2004) by film scholar Donald Richie provides personal insight to Japan's transformation from a postwar nation to a cultural and economic powerhouse.

FICTION Whenever I travel in Japan, I especially enjoy reading fictional accounts of the country; they help put me in tune with my surroundings and increase my awareness and perception. The world's first major novel was written by a Japanese woman, Murasaki Shikibu, whose classic, *The Tale of Genji* (Knopf, 1978), dating from the 11th century, describes the aristocratic life of Prince Genji.

Tokyo bookstores have entire sections dedicated to English-language translations of Japan's best-known modern and contemporary authors, including Mishima Yukio, Soseki Natsume, Abe Kobo, Tanizaki Junichiro, and Nobel Prize winners Kawabata Yasunari and Oe Kenzaburo. An overview of Japanese classical literature from the earliest times to the mid–19th century is provided in *Anthology of Japanese Literature* (Grove Press, 1988), edited by Donald Keene. Likewise, *The Showa Anthology: Modern Japanese Short Stories* (Kodansha, 1992), edited by Van C. Gessel and Tomone Matsumoto, covers works by Abe Kobe, Mishima Yukio, Kawabata Yasunari, Oe Kenzaburo, and others written between

1929 and 1984, while *Modern Japanese Stories: An Anthology* (Tuttle, 1962), edited by Ivan Morris, introduces short stories by some of Japan's top modern writers, including Mori Ogai, Tanizaki Junichiro, Kawabata Yasunari, and Mishima Yukio.

For novels, you might read Mishima's *The Sea of Fertility* (Knopf), a collection of four separate works, the last of which, *The Decay of the Angel,* was delivered to his publisher on the day of his suicide; or *The Sound of Waves* (Knopf, 1956), about young love in a Japanese fishing village. Other famous works by Japanese authors include Soseki Natsume's first novel, *I am a Cat* (Tuttle, 1972), which describes the foibles of upper-middle-class Japanese during the Meiji Era through the eyes of a cat; and his later novel, *Kokoro* (Regnery Gateway Co., 1985), as well as Kawabata Yasunari's *Snow Country* (Knopf, 1956), translated by Edward G. Seidensticker. Although not well known in the West, Enchi Fumiko wrote an absorbing novel about women in an upper-class, late-19th-century family in *The Waiting Years* (Kodansha, 2002), first published in 1957. Tanizaki Junichiro's *Makioka Sisters* (Vintage, 1995) is an epic tale of four Japanese sisters during the turbulent 1940s and 1950s.

Oe Kenzaburo gained international recognition when he became the second Japanese to win the Nobel Prize for literature in 1994. One of his best-known novels is *Nip the Buds, Shoot the Kids* (Grove Press, 1996), a disturbing tale of a group of reform-school boys in the waning days of World War II. *A Personal Matter* (Grove Press, 1968) is about a man in search of himself after the birth of a handicapped son. *Hiroshima Notes* (Grove/Atlantic, 1996), featuring personal accounts of atomic bomb survivors, is a moving commentary on the meaning of the Hiroshima bombing.

Favorite writers of Japan's baby-boom generation include Murakami Ryu, who burst onto the literary scene with *Almost Transparent Blue* (Kodansha, 1977), and later captured the undercurrent of decadent urban life in his best-selling *Coin Locker Babies* (Kodansha, 1995). He wrote a shocking exposé of Tokyo's sex industry, *In the Miso Soup* (Kodansha, 2003). Murakami Haruki's writings include *Dance Dance Dance* (Kodansha, 1994); *Hard-Boiled Wonderland and the End of the World* (Vintage, 1993); *The Wind-Up Bird Chronicle* (Knopf, 1997); *South of the Border, West of the Sun* (Knopf, 1999); and *Norwegian Wood* (Vintage, 2000), a coming-of-age story set during the 1969 student movement in Japan. His *After the Quake: Stories* (Knopf, 2002) centers on fictional characters in the months after the 1995 Kobe earthquake.

For works of fiction about Japan by Western writers, most Westerners are familiar with James Clavell's *Shogun* (Dell, 1975), a fictional account based on the lives of Englishman William Adams and military leader Tokugawa Ieyasu around 1600. The best-selling *Memoirs of a Geisha* (Knopf, 1997), by Arthur Golden and also a movie, is the fictional autobiography of a fisherman's daughter sold to a geisha house, later becoming one of Kyoto's most celebrated geisha of the 1930s.

For fictional yet personal contemporary accounts of what it's like for Westerners living in Japan, entertaining novels include *Ransom* (Vintage, 1985) by Jay McInerney and *Pictures from the Water Trade* (Harper & Row, 1986) by John D. Morley. Pico Iyer taps into the mysterious juxtaposition of the old Japan vs. the new in *The Lady and the Monk: Four Seasons in Kyoto* (Knopf, 1991). *Audrey Hepburn's Neck* (Simon & Schuster, 1996) is Alan Brown's poignant portrait of Japan's mishmash of Western and Japanese culture, as seen through the eyes of a confused young Japanese comic illustrator. Mystery fans should read Sujata Massey's 10 novels following the adventures of Japanese-American Rei Shimura; her *Girl in a Box*

(HarperCollins, 2006), follows Rei's cross-cultural escapades as she works undercover in a Japanese department store.

FILMS

The classic samurai film is probably Kurosawa Akira's *The Seven Samurai* (1954), remade into the western *The Magnificent Seven*. Other films by what some consider to be Japan's greatest filmmaker include *Rashomon* (1951), about a murder and a rape and that raises as many questions as it answers about human nature; *Kagemusha* (1980), about warlords battling for control at the end of feudal Japan; and *Ran* (1985), an epic drama set in 16th-century Japan and based on Shakespeare's *King Lear*. For a look at Japan's mountain people in the 1880s, nothing can beat Kinoshita Keisuke's *Ballad of Narayama* (1958), with its unsentimental portrait of an elderly woman who goes off into the snowy countryside to die, as was the custom of her people.

Director Oshima Nagisa created a stir in the film world with *In the Realm of the Senses* (1976), a story of obsessive love so graphic and erotic it remains censored in Japan. Juzo Itami, a famous Japanese director who purportedly leapt to his death in Tokyo in 1997 (the circumstances are mysterious), is remembered for his humorous satires on Japanese life, including *Tampopo* (1985), about sex and food and a Japanese woman who achieves success with a noodle shop; *The Funeral* (1984), which takes a comic look at death in Japan, including the surviving family's helplessness when it comes to arranging the complex rituals of the Buddhist ceremony; and *A Taxing Woman* (1987), about a female tax auditor.

Love and Pop (1998), by director Anno Hideaki, best known for *anime* films, is a low-budget film based on a novel by Murakami Ryu about "compensated dating," in which teenage girls are paid to go out with older businessmen. Another film dealing with this phenomenon rarely covered in the Western press is Harada Masato's *Bounce Ko Gals* (1998), which presents a shocking but heartfelt story of sexual exploitation and loss of innocence.

A commentary on Japan's economic woes on a personal level is *Tokyo Sonata* (2008), directed Kurosawa Kiyoshi, about a father who loses his job but is too ashamed to tell his family and thus pretends he's going to work every day. *Departures* (2008) is Takita Yojiro's moving Academy Award–winning film (for best foreign film) about a musician who takes a job preparing corpses and eventually comes to see it as a deeply rewarding profession.

Probably the most internationally well-known film shot in Tokyo in recent years is Sophia Coppola's *Lost in Translation* (2003), in which two lost characters take solace in each other's company as they drift through an incomprehensible—and at times hilarious—Tokyo, while *The Harimaya Bridge* (2009), by Aaron Woolfolk, is a moving story about a man whose hatred for Japanese (his father died in a Japanese POW camp) slowly dissolves when he travels to Kochi to pick up his dead son's belongings.

One of Japan's most famous animated films is Miyazaki Hayao's *Spirited Away* (2001), about a young girl who must call upon her inner strength to save herself and her family.

3

Planning Your Trip to Japan

From experience, I know that the two biggest concerns for visitors to Japan are the language barrier and the high cost of living. To help alleviate fears about the first, I've provided a glossary of useful words and phrases (see chapter 18), given the Japanese characters for establishments that do not have English-language signs so you can recognize their names (see chapter 17), outlined tips for dealing with the language barrier (see "Dealing with the Language Barrier" in chapter 2), given brief instructions on how to reach most of the places I recommend, made suggestions for ordering in restaurants without English-language menus, and provided prices for everything from subway rides to admission to museums.

As for costs, probably everyone has heard horror stories about Japan's high prices. Ever since the dramatic fall of the dollar against the yen in the 1980s and 1990s, Tokyo and Osaka have been two of the world's most expensive cities, with food and lodging costing as much as in New York or London, maybe more. But after Japan's economic bubble burst in the early 1990s, something happened that would have been unthinkable during the heady spending days of the 1980s: Japanese became bargain conscious. There are now inexpensive French bistros, secondhand clothing stores, 100-yen shops, and budget hotels.

Still, it's difficult not to suffer an initial shock from Japan's high prices, which will seem especially exorbitant if you insist on living and eating exactly as you do back home. The secret is to live and eat as Japanese do. This book will help you do exactly that, with descriptions of eateries and Japanese-style inns that cater to the native population. By following this book's advice and exercising a little caution on your own, you should be able to cut down on needless expenses and learn even more about Japan in the process. While you may never find Japan cheap, you will find it richly rewarding for all the reasons you chose Japan as a destination in the first place.

Despite the difficulties inherent in visiting any foreign country, I think you'll find Japan very easy to navigate. There are many more signs in English now than there were even just a decade ago. And Japan remains one of the safest countries in the world; in general, you don't have to worry about muggers, pickpockets, or crooks. In fact, I sometimes feel downright coddled in Japan. Everything runs like clockwork: Trains are on time, public telephones work, and the service—whether in hotels, restaurants, or department stores—ranks among the best in the world. I know if I get truly lost, someone will help me and will probably even go out of his or her way to do so. Japanese are honest and extremely helpful toward foreign visitors. Indeed, it's the people themselves who make traveling in Japan such a delight.

This chapter will help you with the what, when, where, and how of travel to Japan— from what documents you need (only passports for most nationalities) to how to get around easily and economically (you'll want to purchase a Japan Rail Pass *before* going to Japan). For additional help in planning your trip and for more on-the-ground resources in Japan, please see "Fast Facts," on p. 628.

Because Japan stretches in an arc from northeast to southwest at about the same latitudes as Maine and Florida, you can travel in the country virtually any time of year. Winters in southern Kyushu and Okinawa are mild, while summers in northern Hokkaido are cool. There are, however, peak seasons to avoid, including April 29 to May 5, mid-July through August, and New Year's.

CLIMATE   Most of Japan's islands lie in a temperate seasonal wind zone similar to that of the East Coast of the United States, which means there are four distinct seasons. Japanese are very proud of their seasons and place much more emphasis on them than people do in the West. Kimono, dishes and bowls used for *kaiseki,* and even *noh* plays change with the season. Certain foods are eaten during certain times of the year, such as eel in summer and *fugu* (blowfish) in winter. Almost all haiku have seasonal references. The cherry blossom signals the beginning of spring, and most festivals are tied to seasonal rites. Even urban dwellers note the seasons; almost as though on cue, businessmen will change virtually overnight from their winter to summer attire.

Summer, which begins in June, is heralded by the rainy season, which lasts from about mid-June to mid-July (there's no rainy season in Hokkaido). Although it doesn't rain every day, it does rain a lot, sometimes quite heavily, making umbrellas imperative. After the rain stops, it turns unbearably hot and uncomfortably humid throughout the country, with the exception of Hokkaido, mountaintop resorts such as Hakone, and the Japan Alps. You'll be more comfortable in light cottons, though you should bring a light jacket for unexpected cool evenings or air-conditioned rooms. You should also pack sunscreen and a hat (Japanese women are also fond of parasols).

The period from the end of August to September is **typhoon season,** although the majority of storms stay out at sea and generally vent their fury on land only in thunderstorms.

Autumn, lasting through November, is one of the best times to visit Japan. The days are pleasant and slightly cool, and the changing red and scarlet of leaves contrast brilliantly with the deep blue skies. There are many chrysanthemum shows in Japan at this time, popular maple-viewing spots, and many autumn festivals. Bring a warm jacket.

Winter, lasting from December to March, is marked by snow in much of Japan, especially in the mountain ranges where the skiing is superb. Many tourists also flock to hot-spring resorts during this time. The climate is generally dry, and on the Pacific coast the skies are often blue. Tokyo doesn't get much snow, though it can be crisp, cold, and wet. Northern Japan's weather, in Tohoku and Hokkaido, can be quite severe, while southern Japan, especially Kyushu and Okinawa, enjoys generally mild, warm weather. Wherever you are, you'd be wise to bring warm clothing throughout the winter months.

Spring arrives with a magnificent fanfare of plum and cherry blossoms in March and April, an exquisite time when all of Japan is ablaze in whites and pinks. The **cherry-blossom season** starts in southern Kyushu in mid-March and reaches Hokkaido in early May. The blossoms themselves last only a few days, symbolizing to Japanese the fragile nature of beauty and of life itself. Other flowers also bloom through May or June, including azaleas and irises. During spring, numerous festivals throughout Japan celebrate the rebirth of nature.

	Jan	Feb	Mar	Apr	May	June	July	Aug	Sept	Oct	Nov	Dec
Temp. (°F)	42	45	50	61	69	71	78	81	76	68	57	48
Temp. (°C)	5	7	10	16	21	22	26	27	24	20	14	9
Days of Rain	4.3	6.1	8.9	10	9.6	12.1	10	8.2	10.9	8.9	6.4	3.8

BUSY SEASONS   Japanese have a passion for travel, and they generally travel at the same time, resulting in jampacked trains and hotels. The worst times to travel are around **New Year's,** from the end of December to January 4; **Golden Week,** from April 29 to May 5; and during the **Obon Festival,** about a week in mid-August. Avoid traveling on these dates at all costs, since all long-distance trains, domestic airlines, and most accommodations are booked solid and prices are higher. The weekends before and after these holidays are also likely to be crowded or booked. Exceptions are major cities like Tokyo or Osaka—since the major exodus is back to hometowns or the countryside, metropolises can be downright blissful during major holidays such as Golden Week, especially since most restaurants and municipal and national museums do not close.

Another busy time is during the **school summer vacation,** from around July 19 or 20 through August. It's best to reserve train seats and book accommodations during this time in advance. In addition, you can expect destinations to be packed during major festivals, so if one of these is high on your list, be sure to make plans well in advance.

HOLIDAYS   National holidays are January 1 (New Year's Day), second Monday in January (Coming-of-Age Day), February 11 (National Foundation Day), March 20 (Vernal Equinox Day), April 29 (Showa Day, after the late Emperor Showa), May 3 (Constitution Memorial Day), May 4 (Greenery Day), May 5 (Children's Day), third Monday in July (Maritime Day), third Monday in September (Respect-for-the-Aged Day), September 23 (Autumn Equinox Day), second Monday in October (Health Sports Day), November 3 (Culture Day), November 23 (Labor Thanksgiving Day), and December 23 (Emperor's Birthday).

When a national holiday falls on a Sunday, the following Monday becomes a holiday. Although government offices and some businesses are closed on public holidays, restaurants and most stores remain open. The exception is during the New Year's celebration, January 1 through January 3 or 4, when virtually all restaurants, public and private offices, stores, and even ATMs close; during that time, you'll have to dine in hotels.

All museums close for New Year's for 1 to 4 days, but most major museums remain open for the other holidays. If a public holiday falls on a Monday (when most museums are closed), many museums will remain open but will close instead the following day, Tuesday. Note, however, that privately owned museums, such as art museums or special-interest museums, generally close on public holidays. To avoid disappointment, be sure to phone ahead if you plan to visit a museum on a holiday or the day following it.

FESTIVALS   With Shintoism and Buddhism the major religions in Japan, it seems as though there's a *matsuri* (festival) going on somewhere in the country almost every day, especially in summer. Every major shrine and temple has at least one annual festival. Such festivals are always free, though admission may be charged for special exhibitions such as flower shows. There are also a number of national holidays observed throughout the country with events and festivals, as well as annual seasonal events like cormorant fishing and cherry-blossom viewing.

The larger, better-known festivals are exciting to attend but do take some advance planning since hotel rooms may be booked 6 months in advance. If you haven't made prior arrangements, you may want to let the following schedule be your guide in avoiding certain cities on certain days.

A note on festival dates: If you plan your trip around a certain festival, be sure to double-check the exact dates with the Japan National Tourist Organization since these dates can change. In Japan, stop by a TIC office in Tokyo or at Narita or Kansai airports for a monthly leaflet called "Calendar Events," which lists major festivals in Tokyo and the rest of Japan. You can also try calling the local tourist office of the city hosting the festival (though staff may not speak much English) or checking JNTO and local websites for information (see regional chapters).

JAPAN CALENDAR OF EVENTS

JANUARY

New Year's Day is the most important national holiday in Japan. Because this is a time when Japanese are with their families and because virtually all businesses, restaurants, museums, and shops close down, it's not a particularly rewarding time of the year for foreign visitors. Best bets are shrines and temples, where Japanese come in their best kimono or dress to pray for good health and happiness in the coming year. January 1.

Tamaseseri (Ball-Catching Festival), Hakozakigu Shrine, Fukuoka. The main attraction here is a struggle between two groups of men, dressed only in loincloths, who try to capture a sacred wooden ball. The winning team is supposed to have good luck the entire year. January 3.

Dezomeshiki (New Year's Parade of Firemen), Tokyo Big Sight, Odaiba, Tokyo. Agile firemen dressed in Edo-Era costumes prove their worth with acrobatic stunts atop tall bamboo ladders in this parade. January 6.

Usokae (Bullfinch Exchange Festival), Dazaifu Tenmangu Shrine, outside Fukuoka. The object here is to pass wooden bullfinches from person to person, hopefully ending up with the golden bullfinch, thought to bring good luck. A giant fire is lit in the evening to drive away evil spirits. January 7.

Coming-of-Age Day, a national holiday. This day honors young people who have reached the age of 20, when they can vote, drink alcohol, and assume other responsibilities. On this day, they visit shrines throughout the country to pray for their future, with many women dressed in kimono. In Tokyo, the most popular shrine is Meiji Shrine near Harajuku Station. Second Monday in January.

Toka Ebisu Festival, Imamiya Ebisu Shrine, Osaka. Ebisu is considered the patron saint of business and good fortune, so this is the time when businesspeople pray for a successful year. The highlight of the festival is a parade of women dressed in colorful kimono and carried through the streets in palanquins (covered litters). Stalls sell good-luck charms. January 9 to January 11.

Ame-Ichi (Candy Fair), Matsumoto. Formerly a salt fair, this lively festival has featured traditional candy for the past century. Second weekend in January.

Toh-shiya, Kyoto. This traditional Japanese archery contest is held in the back corridor of Japan's longest wooden structure, Sanjusangendo Hall. Sunday closest to January 15.

Yamayaki (Grass Fire Ceremony), Nara. As evening approaches, Wakakusayama Hill is set ablaze and fireworks are displayed. The celebration marks a time more than 1,000 years ago when a dispute over the boundary of two major temples in Nara was settled peacefully. Fourth Sunday in January.

Sounkyo Ice Festival, Sounkyo Onsen. Ice sculptures, ice slides, frozen waterfalls lit in various colors, and evening fireworks are the highlights of this small-town festival. Mid-January to Mid-March.

FEBRUARY

Oyster Festival, Matsushima. Matsushima is famous for its oysters, and this is the time they're considered to be at their best. Oysters are given out free at booths set up at the seaside park along the bay. First Sunday in February.

Setsubun (Bean-Throwing Festival), at leading temples throughout Japan. According to the lunar calendar, this is the last day of winter; people throng to temples to participate in the traditional ceremony of throwing beans to drive away imaginary devils, yelling, "Evil go out, good luck come in." February 3 or 4.

Lantern Festival, Kasuga Shrine, Nara. A beautiful sight in which more than 3,000 stone and bronze lanterns are lit from 6:30 to 9pm. February 3 and August 14 and 15.

Snow Festival, Odori Park, and Susukino, in Sapporo. This famous 7-day Sapporo festival features huge, elaborate statues and figurines carved in snow and ice. Competitors come from around the world. Second week in February.

Saidaiji Eyo, Saidaiji Kannon-in Temple, Okayama. Thousands of loincloth-clad men grapple for sacred wooden sticks tossed by priests. Third Saturday of February at midnight.

MARCH

Omizutori (Water-Drawing Festival), Todaiji Temple, Nara. This festival includes a solemn evening rite in which young ascetics brandish large burning torches and draw circles of fire. The biggest ceremony takes place on the night of March 12; on the next day, the ceremony of drawing water is held to the accompaniment of ancient Japanese music. March 1 to March 14.

Hinamatsuri (Doll Festival), observed throughout Japan. It's held in honor of young girls to wish them a future of happiness. In homes where there are girls, dolls dressed in ancient costumes representing the emperor, empress, and dignitaries are set up on a tier of shelves along with miniature household articles. Many hotels also display dolls in their lobbies. March 3.

Tokyo International Anime Fair, Tokyo Big Sight, Odaiba (www.tokyoanime.jp). One of the world's largest Japanese animation events draws more than 100 production companies, TV and film agencies, toy and game software companies, publishers, and other *anime*-related companies. Usually last weekend in March.

APRIL

Kanamara Matsuri, Kanayama Shrine, Kawasaki (just outside Tokyo). This festival extols the joys of sex and fertility (and more recently, raises awareness about AIDS), featuring a parade of giant phalluses, some carried by transvestites. You'll definitely get some unusual photographs here. First Sunday in April.

Buddha's Birthday (also called Hana Matsuri, or Floral Festival), observed nationwide. Ceremonies are held at all Buddhist temples. April 8.

Kamakura Matsuri, Tsurugaoka Hachimangu Shrine, Kamakura. This festival honors heroes from the past, including Minamoto Yoritomo, who made Kamakura his shogunate capital back in 1192. Highlights include horseback archery (truly spectacular to watch), a parade of portable shrines, and sacred dances. Second to third Sunday of April.

Takayama Spring Festival, Takayama. Supposedly dating from the 15th century, this festival is one of Japan's grandest with a dozen huge, gorgeous floats that are wheeled through the village streets. April 14 and 15.

Gumonji-do (Firewalking Ceremonies), Miyajima. Walking on live coals is meant to show devotion and to pray for purification and protection from illness and disaster. Daishoin Temple. April 15 and November 15.

Yayoi Matsuri, Futarasan Shrine, Nikko. Yayoi Matsuri features a parade of floats embellished with artificial cherry blossoms and paper lanterns. April 16 and 17.

Golden Week is a major holiday period throughout Japan, when many Japanese offices and businesses close down and families go on vacation. It's a crowded time to travel; reservations are a must. April 29 to May 5.

MAY

Hakata Dontaku Port Festival, Fukuoka. Citizens, dressed as deities, parade through the streets clapping wooden rice paddles. May 3 and 4.

Children's Day is a national holiday honoring all children, especially boys. The most common sight throughout Japan is colorful streamers of carp—which symbolize perseverance and strength—flying from poles. May 5.

Takigi Noh Performances, Kofukuji Temple, Nara. These *noh* plays are presented outdoors after dark under the blaze of torches. May 11 and 12.

Kanda Festival, Kanda Myojin Shrine, Tokyo. This festival, which commemorates Tokugawa Ieyasu's famous victory at Sekigahara in 1600, began during the Feudal Period as the only time townspeople could enter the shogun's castle and parade before him. Today this major Tokyo festival features a parade of dozens of portable shrines carried through the district, plus geisha dances and a tea ceremony. Held in odd-numbered years (with a smaller festival held in even years) on the Saturday and Sunday closest to May 15.

Aoi Matsuri (Hollyhock Festival), Shimogamo and Kamigamo Shrines, Kyoto. This is one of Kyoto's biggest events, a colorful parade with 500 participants wearing ancient costumes to commemorate the days when the imperial procession visited the city's shrines. May 15.

Kobe Matsuri, Kobe. This relatively new festival celebrates Kobe's international past with fireworks at Kobe Port, street markets, and a parade on Flower Road with participants wearing native costumes. Mid-May.

Shunki Reitaisai (Grand Spring Festival), Nikko. Commemorating the day in 1617 when Tokugawa Ieyasu's remains were brought to his mausoleum in Nikko, this festival re-creates that drama with more than 1,000 armor-clad people escorting three palanquins through the streets. May 17 and 18.

Sanja Matsuri, Asakusa Shrine, Tokyo. Tokyo's most celebrated festival features about 100 portable shrines carried through the district on the shoulders of men and women in traditional garb. Third Sunday and preceding Friday and Saturday of May.

Mifune Matsuri, Arashiyama, on the Oigawa River outside Kyoto, is when the days of the Heian Period (during which the imperial family used to take pleasure rides on the river) are reenacted by some 20 boats and people in costume. Third Sunday in May.

JUNE

Takigi Noh Performances, Kyoto. Evening performances of *noh* are presented on an open-air stage at the Heian Shrine. June 1 and 2.

Hyakumangoku Matsuri (One Million Goku Festival), Kanazawa. Celebrating Kanazawa's production of one million *goku* of rice (1 goku is about 150kg/330 lb.), this extravaganza features folk songs and traditional dancing in the streets, illuminated paper lanterns floating downriver, public tea ceremonies, geisha performances, and—the highlight—a parade that winds through the city in reenactment of Lord Maeda Toshiie's triumphant arrival in Kanazawa on June 14, 1583, with lion dances, ladder-top acrobatics by firemen, and a torch-lit outdoor *noh* performance. June 8 to June 14.

Sanno Festival, Hie Shrine, Tokyo. This Edo Period festival, one of Tokyo's largest, features the usual portable shrines, transported through the busy streets of the Akasaka District. June 10 to June 16.

Otaue Rice-Planting Festival, Sumiyoshi Taisha Shrine, Osaka. In hopes of a successful harvest, young girls in traditional farmers' costumes transplant rice seedlings in the shrine's rice paddy to the sound of traditional music and songs. June 14.

Ukai (Cormorant Fishing), Nagara River near Gifu and Kiso River in Inuyama (near Nagoya). Visitors board small wooden boats after dark to watch cormorants dive into the water to catch *ayu,* a kind of trout. Generally end of May to October.

JULY

Tanabata Matsuri (Star Festival), celebrated throughout Japan. According to myth, the two stars Vega and Altair, representing a weaver and a shepherd, are allowed to meet once a year on this day. If the skies are cloudy, however, the celestial pair cannot meet and must wait another year. Celebrations differ from town to town, but in addition to parades and food/souvenir stalls, look for bamboo branches with colorful strips of paper bearing children's wishes. July 7.

Hozuki Ichi (Ground-Cherry Pod Fair), Tokyo. This colorful affair at Sensoji Temple in Asakusa features hundreds of stalls selling ground-cherry pods and colorful wind bells. July 9 and 10.

Yamakasa, Fukuoka. Just before the crack of dawn, seven teams dressed in loincloths and *happi* coats (short, colorful, kimono-like jackets) race through town, bearing 1-ton floats on their shoulders. In addition, elaborately decorated, 9m-tall (30-ft.) floats designed by Hakata doll masters are on display throughout town. July 15.

Gion Matsuri, Kyoto. One of the most famous festivals in Japan, this dates back to the 9th century, when the head priest at Yasaka Shrine organized a procession to ask the gods' assistance in a plague raging in the city. Although celebrations continue throughout the month, the highlight is on the 17th, when more than 30 spectacular wheeled floats wind their way through the city streets to the accompaniment of music and dances. Many visitors plan their trip to Japan around this event. July 16 and 17.

Obon Festival, nationwide. This festival commemorates the dead who, according to Buddhist belief, revisit the world during this period. Many Japanese return to their hometowns for religious rites, especially if a family member has died recently. As one Japanese whose grandmother had died a few months before told me, "I have to go back to my hometown—it's my grandmother's first Obon." Mid-July or mid-August, depending on the region.

Tenjin Matsuri, Temmangu Shrine, Osaka. One of Japan's biggest festivals, this dates from the 10th century when the people of Osaka visited Temmangu Shrine to pray for protection against diseases prevalent during the long, hot summer. They would take pieces of paper cut in the form of human beings and, while the Shinto priest said prayers, would rub the paper over themselves in ritual cleansing. Afterward, the pieces of paper were taken by boat to the mouth of the river and disposed of. Today, events are reenacted with a procession of more than 100 sacred boats making their way downriver, followed by a fireworks display. There's also a parade of some 3,000 people in traditional costume. July 24 and 25.

Kangensai Music Festival, Itsukushima Shrine, Miyajima. There are classical court music and *Bugaku* dancing, and three barges carry portable shrines, priests, and musicians across the bay along with a flotilla of other boats. Because this festival takes place according to the lunar calendar, the actual date changes each year. Late July or early August.

Hanabi Taikai (Fireworks Display), Tokyo. This is Tokyo's largest summer celebration, and everyone sits on blankets along the banks of the Sumida River near Asakusa to see the show. It's great fun! Last Saturday of July.

Fuji Rock Festival, Naeba Ski Resort, Niigata. Japan's biggest outdoor rock festival, with an impressive lineup of international acts in a beautiful mountain setting. Last weekend in July.

AUGUST

Oshiro Matsuri, Himeji. This celebration is famous for its *noh* dramas lit by bonfire and performed on a special stage on the Himeji Castle grounds, as well as a procession from the castle to the city center with participants dressed as feudal lords and ladies in traditional costume. First Friday and Saturday of August.

Peace Ceremony, Peace Memorial Park, Hiroshima. This ceremony is held annually in memory of those who died in the atomic bomb blast of August 6, 1945. In the evening, thousands of lit lanterns are set adrift on the Ota River in a plea for world peace. A similar ceremony is held on August 9 in Nagasaki. August 6.

Tanabata Matsuri, Sendai. Sendai holds its Star Festival 1 month later than the rest of Japan. It's the country's largest, and the entire town is decorated with colored paper streamers. August 6 to August 8.

Matsuyama Festival, Matsuyama. Jubilant festivities include dances, fireworks, a parade, and a night fair. August 11 to August 13.

Takamatsu Festival, Takamatsu. About 6,000 people participate in a dance procession that threads its way along Chuo Dori Avenue; anyone can join in. Food stalls are set up in Chuo Park, and there's also a fireworks display. August 12 to August 14.

Toronagashi and Fireworks Display, Matsushima. A fireworks display is followed by the setting adrift on the bay of about 5,000 small boats with lanterns, which are meant to console the souls of the dead; another 3,000 lanterns are lit on islets in the bay. Evening of August 15.

Yamaga Lantern Festival, Kumamoto. Women dressed in *yukata* dance through town with illuminated paper lanterns on their heads, and there's also a fireworks display. August 15 and 16.

Daimonji Bonfire, Mount Nyoiga-dake, Kyoto. A huge bonfire in the shape of the Chinese character *dai,* which means "large," and other motifs are lit near mountain peaks; it's the highlight of the Obon Festival (see July, above). August 16.

Eisa Festival, Okinawa Island. Dance teams compete in lively folk performances to the accompaniment of drums, three-stringed *sanshin,* and other instruments. Late August.

SEPTEMBER

Yabusame, Tsurugaoka Hachimangu Shrine, Kamakura. Archery performed on horseback recalls the days of the samurai. September 16.

OCTOBER

Okunchi Festival, Suwa Shrine, Nagasaki. This 370-year-old festival, one of Kyushu's best, illustrates the influence of Nagasaki's Chinese population through the centuries. Highlights include a parade of floats and dragon dances. October 7 to October 9.

Marimo Matsuri, Lake Akan, Hokkaido. This festival is put on by the native Ainu population to celebrate *marimo* (a spherical weed found in Lake Akan) and includes a pine torch parade and fireworks. Early October.

Takayama Matsuri (Autumn Festival), Takayama. As in the festival held here in April, huge floats are paraded through the streets. October 9 and 10.

Nagoya Festival, Nagoya. Nagoya's biggest event commemorates three of its heroes—Tokugawa Ieyasu, Toyotomi Hideyoshi, and Oda Nobunaga—in a parade that goes from City Hall to Sakae and includes nine floats with

mechanical puppets, marching bands, and a traditional orchestra. Second weekend in October.

Naha Tug of War, Naha, Okinawa. Anyone can join in this tug of war with the world's largest rope (186m/619 ft.), once held to welcome Chinese ambassadors. Second Sunday in October.

Nada no Kenka Matsuri (Nada Fighting Festival), Matsubara Hachiman Shrine, Himeji. Men shouldering portable shrines jostle each other as they attempt to show their skill in balancing their heavy burdens. October 14 and 15.

Doburoku Matsuri, Ogimachi, Shirakawago. This village festival honors unrefined sake, said to represent the spirit of God, with a parade, an evening lion dance, and plenty of eating and drinking. October 14 to October 19.

Nikko Toshogu Shrine Festival, Nikko. A parade of warriors in early-17th-century dress are accompanied by spear-carriers, gun-carriers, flag-bearers, Shinto priests, pages, court musicians, and dancers as they escort a sacred portable shrine. October 17.

Jidai Matsuri (Festival of the Ages), Kyoto. Another of Kyoto's grand festivals, this one began in 1894 to commemorate the founding of the city in 794. It features a procession of more than 2,000 people dressed in ancient costumes representing different epochs of Kyoto's 1,200-year history, who march from the Imperial Palace to Heian Shrine. October 22.

NOVEMBER

Ohara Matsuri, Kagoshima. About 15,000 people parade through the town in cotton *yukata,* dancing to the tune of local folk songs. A sort of Japanese Mardi Gras, this event attracts several hundred thousand spectators each year. November 2 and 3.

Daimyo Gyoretsu (Feudal Lord Procession), Yumoto Onsen, Hakone. The old Tokaido Highway that used to link Kyoto and Tokyo comes alive again with a faithful reproduction of a feudal lord's procession in the olden days. November 3.

Shichi-go-san (Children's Shrine-Visiting Day), held throughout Japan. Shichi-go-san literally means "seven-five-three" and refers to children of these ages who are dressed in their kimono best and taken to shrines by their elders to express thanks and pray for their future. November 15.

Tori-no-Ichi (Rake Fair), Otori Shrine, Tokyo. This fair in Asakusa features stalls selling rakes lavishly decorated with paper and cloth, which are thought to bring good luck and fortune. Based on the lunar calendar, the date changes each year. Mid-November.

DECEMBER

Gishi-sai, Sengakuji Station, Tokyo. This memorial service honors 47 *ronin* (masterless samurai) who avenged their master's death by killing his rival and parading his head; for their act, all were ordered to commit suicide. Forty-seven men dressed as the ronin travel to Sengakuji Temple (the site of their and their master's burial) with the enemy's head to place on their master's grave. December 14.

Kasuga Wakamiya On-Matsuri, Kasuga Shrine, Nara. This festival features court music with traditional dance and a parade of people dressed as courtiers, retainers, and wrestlers of long ago. December 15 to December 18.

Hagoita-Ichi (Battledore Fair), Sensoji Temple, Tokyo. Popular since Japan's feudal days, this Asakusa festival features decorated paddles of all types and sizes. Most have designs of kabuki actors—images made by pasting together padded silk and brocade—and make great souvenirs and gifts. December 17 to December 19.

New Year's Eve. At midnight, many temples ring huge bells 108 times to signal the end of the old year and the beginning of the new. Families visit temples and shrines throughout Japan to pray for the coming year. December 31.

2 ENTRY REQUIREMENTS

PASSPORTS

For most tourists, including those from the United States, Canada, Australia, New Zealand, and the United Kingdom, the only document necessary to enter Japan is a passport. For information on how to get a passport, see "Passports" in chapter 16.

ENTRY REQUIREMENTS

Americans, Australians, and **New Zealanders** traveling to Japan as tourists for a stay of 90 days or less need only a valid passport to gain entry into the country. **Canadians** don't need a visa for stays of up to 3 months, and **United Kingdom** and **Irish citizens** can stay up to 6 months without a visa.

ENTRY PROCEDURES Since November 2007, all foreigners arriving in Japan are fingerprinted and photographed to prevent terrorists from entering Japan. Exceptions include children 15 and younger, diplomats, and some permanent residents of Japan.

CUSTOMS

If you're 20 or older, you can bring duty-free into Japan up to 400 non-Japanese

ⓘ Tips Passport Savvy

Safeguard your passport in an inconspicuous place and keep a photocopy of your passport's information page in your luggage. If you lose your passport, visit your nearest consulate as soon as possible for a replacement (see "Embassies & Consulates" on p. 629). **Note:** All foreigners must present their passports for bank transactions and for photocopying when checking into lodging facilities. In addition, foreigners are required to carry with them at all times either their passports or, for those who have been granted longer stays, their alien registration cards. Police generally do not stop foreigners, but if you're caught without an ID, you'll be taken to local police headquarters. It happened to me once and, believe me, I can think of better ways to spend an hour and a half than explaining in detail who I am, what I am doing in Japan, where I live, and what I plan to do for the rest of my life. I even had to write a statement explaining why I rushed out that day without my passport, apologizing and promising never to do such a thoughtless thing again. The policemen were polite and were simply doing their duty.

cigarettes; three bottles (760cc each) of alcohol; and 2 ounces of perfume. You can also bring in goods for personal use that were purchased abroad whose total market value is less than ¥200,000.

What You Can Take Home from Japan

For information on what you're allowed to bring home, contact one of the following agencies:

U.S. Citizens: U.S. Customs & Border Protection (CBP), 1300 Pennsylvania Ave., NW, Washington, DC 20229 (ⓒ **877/ 287-8667**; www.cbp.gov).

Canadian Citizens: Canada Border Services Agency (ⓒ **800/461-9999** or 204/ 983-3500; www.cbsa-asfc.gc.ca).

U.K. Citizens: HM Customs & Excise (ⓒ **0845/010-9000,** or 020/8929-0152 from outside the U.K.; www.hmce.gov.uk).

Australian Citizens: Australian Customs Service (ⓒ **1300/363-263;** www. customs.gov.au).

New Zealand Citizens: New Zealand Customs, The Customhouse, 17–21 Whitmore St., Box 2218, Wellington (ⓒ **04/473-6099** or 0800/428-786; www. customs.govt.nz).

MEDICAL REQUIREMENTS

Unless you're arriving from an area known to be suffering from an epidemic (particularly cholera or yellow fever), inoculations or vaccinations are not required for entry into Japan. Note, however, that at the time of going to press, all arriving passengers are requested to fill out a questionnaire regarding symptoms of the H1N1 influenza such as fever or coughing. In addition, the temperature of all arriving passengers is taken upon entering the Customs area; if you have a fever, you may be quarantined as a protection against H1N1 or avian flu.

3 GETTING THERE

BY PLANE

Japan has three international airports. Outside Tokyo is **Narita International Airport (NRT),** where you'll want to land if your main business is in the capital, the surrounding region, or at points north or east such as Hokkaido. Another international airport, **Kansai International Airport (KIX)** outside Osaka, is convenient if your destination is Osaka, Kobe, Nara, Kyoto, or western or southern Japan; it is also convenient for domestic air travel within Japan, since most domestic flights out of Tokyo depart from Haneda Airport, necessitating an airport transfer if you arrive at Narita International Airport. In between Narita and Kansai airports, outside Nagoya, is the **Central Japan International Airport (NGO),** nicknamed Centrair, which offers the advantage of slick airport facilities (including hot-spring baths!) and easy access to Nagoya, the Shinkansen bullet train, Japan Alps, and beyond.

Because the flight to Tokyo is such a long one (about 12 hr. from Los Angeles or London and 13½ hr. from Chicago or New York), you may wish to splurge for a roomier seat and upgraded service, including special counters for check-in, private lounges at the airport, and better meals, though these come with a price. You should also consider a mileage program, because you'll earn lots of miles going to Japan.

Japan's major carriers are **Japan Airlines (JAL)** and **All Nippon Airways (ANA).** JAL, Japan's flagship and largest domestic carrier, offers more international flights to Japan than any other airline, flying nonstop to Tokyo from Honolulu, Kona, Los Angeles, San Francisco, Chicago, New York, and Vancouver. JAL also serves other countries worldwide, including flights from London, Sydney, and Auckland to Tokyo. ANA offers daily nonstop service from New York, Washington, D.C., Chicago, Seattle, Los Angeles, San Francisco, Honolulu, Toronto, Vancouver, and London.

One advantage to flying with JAL or ANA to Japan is that you can purchase your Japan Rail Pass through them. In addition, flying to Japan with JAL (or another Oneworld fare partner such as American Airlines) or ANA (or a Star Alliance member such as United Airlines) means you are then eligible for deep discounts on domestic flights within Japan.

See "Getting Around Japan," below, for more on rail passes and domestic flights. For websites for these airlines, as well as other airlines that fly to Japan, see "Airline & Hotel Websites," p. 634.

Long-Haul Flights: How to Stay Comfortable

- Your choice of airline and airplane will definitely affect your legroom. Find the best seats at **www.seatguru.com** and **www.airlinequality.com**.
- Emergency exit seats and bulkhead seats typically have the most legroom. Emergency exit seats are usually left unassigned until the day of a flight (to ensure that someone able-bodied fills the seats); it's worth getting to the ticket counter early to snag one of these spots for a long flight. Many passengers find that bulkhead seating (the row facing the wall at the front of the cabin) offers more legroom, but keep in mind that bulkhead seats have no storage space on the floor in front of you.
- To have two seats for yourself in a three-seat row, try for an aisle seat in a center section toward the back of coach. If you're traveling with a companion, book an aisle and a window seat, as middle seats are usually booked last; in

> ## (Tips) Coping with Jet Lag
>
> A major consideration for visitors flying to Japan, especially on long flights from North America, is jet lag. Flying west has slightly less effect than flying east, which means you'll have a harder time recovering from your flight from Japan back to North America. Here are some tips for combating jet lag:
>
> - **Reset your watch** to your destination time before you board the plane.
> - **Drink lots of water** before, during, and after your flight. Avoid alcohol and caffeine.
> - **Exercise and sleep well** for a few days before your trip.
> - If you have trouble sleeping on planes, **fly eastward on morning flights.**
> - **Daylight** is the key to resetting your body clock. At the website for **Outside In** (www.bodyclock.com), you can get a customized plan of when to seek and avoid light. Upon reaching Japan, put in a normal day.

the event that a third passenger is assigned the middle seat, he or she will probably be more than happy to trade for a window or an aisle.

- Ask about entertainment options. Many airlines offer seat-back video systems where you get to choose your movies or play video games—but only on some of their planes.
- To sleep, avoid the last row of any section or the row in front of an emergency exit, as these seats are the least likely to recline. Avoid seats near highly trafficked toilet areas. Avoid seats in the back of many jets—these can be narrower than those in the rest of coach. Or reserve a window seat, so you can rest your head and avoid being bumped in the aisle.

- Get up, walk around, and stretch every 60 to 90 minutes to keep your blood flowing. This helps avoid deep-vein thrombosis, or "economy-class syndrome." If you have heart disease or another condition that puts you at high risk, ask your physician whether you should wear compression stockings, take anticoagulants, or take some other measure. Symptoms of deep vein thrombosis include leg pain or swelling, or even shortness of breath.
- If you're flying with kids, don't forget to carry on toys, books, pacifiers, and snacks and chewing gum to help them relieve ear pressure buildup during ascent and descent.

4 GETTING AROUND JAPAN

Japan has an extensive transport system, the most convenient segment of which is the nation's excellent rail service. You can also travel by plane (good for long-distance hauls but expensive unless you plan ahead), bus (the cheapest mode of travel), ferry, and car.

BY TRAIN

The most efficient way to travel around most of Japan is by train. Whether you're being whisked through the countryside aboard the famous Shinkansen bullet train or are winding your way up a wooded mountainside in an electric streetcar, trains

> **(Tips) Travel Tip**
>
> In the following chapters, to help you reach the hotels, restaurants, and sights recommended in this book, I've included the nearest train or subway station or bus or streetcar stop, followed in parentheses by the approximate number of minutes it takes to walk from the station or bus stop to your destination.

in Japan are punctual, comfortable, safe, and clean. All trains except local commuters have washrooms, toilets, and drinking water. Bullet trains even have telephones and carts selling food and drinks. And because train stations are usually located in the heart of the city next to the city bus terminal or a subway station, arriving in a city by train is usually the most convenient method. Furthermore, most train stations in Japan's major cities and resort areas have tourist offices. The staff may not speak English, but they usually have maps or brochures in English and can point you in the direction of your hotel. Train stations also may have a counter where hotel reservations can be made free of charge. Most of Japan's passenger trains are run by six companies (such as JR East and JR Kyushu) that make up the **Japan Railways (JR) Group.** There are also private regional companies, like **Kintetsu (Kinki Nippon Railway)** operating around Osaka, Kyoto, Nagoya, and Ise and **Odakyu Electric Railway** operating from Tokyo to Hakone.

SHINKANSEN (BULLET TRAIN) The Shinkansen is probably Japan's best-known train. With a front car that resembles a space rocket, the Shinkansen hurtles along at a maximum speed of 300kmph (187 mph) through the countryside on its own special tracks.

There are five basic Shinkansen routes in Japan, plus some offshoots. The most widely used line for tourists is the **Tokaido Shinkansen,** which runs from Tokyo and Shinagawa stations west to such cities as Nagoya, Kyoto, and Osaka. The **Sanyo**

Shinkansen extends westward from Osaka through Kobe, Himeji, Okayama, and Hiroshima before reaching its final destination in Hakata/Fukuoka on the island of Kyushu. Only *Nozomi Super Express* Shinkansen, the fastest and most frequent trains, cover the entire 1,179km (730 miles) between Tokyo and Hakata. The *Hikari* makes more stops than the Nozomi; the *Kodama* stops at every station. Frustratingly, the *Nozomi* is not covered by the Japan Rail Pass (see "Japan Rail Pass," below), so rail-pass travelers wishing to go the entire distance must take the Hikari or Kodama and transfer in Osaka or Okayama. Trains run so frequently—as often as four times an hour during peak times not including the *Nozomi*—that it's almost like catching the local subway.

The **Tohoku Shinkansen Line** runs north from Tokyo and Ueno stations to Sendai, Morioka, Kakunodate, and Hachinohe (some trains require reservations), with branches extending to Shinjo and Akita. By 2011, the Akita branch will extend farther north all the way to Aomori, with future plans calling for a new Hokkaido Shinkansen to extend all the way to Sapporo by 2013. The **Joetsu Shinkansen** connects Tokyo and Ueno stations with Niigata on the Japan Sea coast, while the **Nagano Shinkansen,** completed in time for the 1998 Winter Olympics, connects Tokyo and Ueno stations with Nagano in the Japan Alps. The newest line is the **Kyushu Shinkansen,** which currently runs between Shin-Yatsuhiro and Kagoshima but will extend all the way from Kagoshima to Hakata by 2011.

Shinkansen running along these lines usually offer two or more kinds of service—trains that stop only at major cities (like the *Nozomi* on the Tokaido-Sanyo Line) and trains that make more stops and are therefore slightly slower. ***Note:*** If your destination is a smaller city on the Shinkansen line, make sure the train you take stops there. As a plus, each stop is announced in English through a loudspeaker and a digital signboard in each car.

REGULAR SERVICE In addition to bullet trains, there are also two types of long-distance trains that operate on regular tracks. The **limited-express trains,** or LEX *(Tokkyu),* branch off the Shinkansen system and are the fastest after the bullet trains, often traveling scenic routes, while the **express trains** *(Kyuko)* are slightly slower and make more stops. Slower still are **rapid express trains** *(Shin-Kaisoku)* and the even slower **rapid trains** *(Kaisoku).* To serve the everyday needs of Japan's commuting population, **local trains** *(Futsu)* stop at all stations.

For long distances, say, between Tokyo and Sapporo, JR operates overnight **sleeper trains** *(Shindai-sha),* which offer compartments and berths.

INFORMATION For the most comprehensive site covering rail travel in Japan, go to **www.japanrailpass.net**, which also provides links to the websites of all six JR Group companies, gives fares and timetables for long-distance JR trains (including the Shinkansen), displays maps of Tokyo and Shinjuku stations, and contains information on rail passes. I also like **www.hyperdia.com** and **www.jorudan.co.jp**, both of which give routes (including transfers), fares, and timetables for trains and planes in Japan.

In Japan, stop by the **Tourist Information Center** in downtown Tokyo or at the international airports in Narita or Osaka (see chapters 5 and 10 for locations and open hours) for the invaluable *Railway Timetable,* published in English and providing train schedules for the Shinkansen and limited express JR lines throughout Japan. To be on the safe side, I also stop by the train information desk or the tourist information desk as soon as I arrive in a city to check on train schedules onward to my next destination. Another good resource is the **JR East InfoLine** (✆ **050/2016-1603;** www.jreast.co.jp/e), available daily 10am to 6pm to answer questions about train schedules, fares, how to buy tickets, and more.

TRAIN DISTANCES & TRAVELING TIME Japan is much longer than most people imagine. Its four main islands, measured from the northeast to the southwest, cover roughly the distance from Boston to Atlanta. Thank goodness for the Shinkansen bullet train! In addition, transportation can be slow in mountainous regions, especially if you're on a local train.

The chart below measures the distances and traveling times from Tokyo to principal Japanese cities. Traveling times do not include the time needed for transferring and are calculated for the fastest trains available, excluding the *Nozomi* Shinkansen because most tourists to Japan use the JR Rail Pass, which is not valid on the *Nozomi.*

TRAIN FARES & RESERVATIONS Ticket prices are based on the type of train (Shinkansen bullet trains are the most expensive), the distance traveled, whether your seat is reserved, and the season, with slightly higher prices (usually a ¥200 surcharge) during peak seasons (Golden Week, July 21–Aug 31, Dec 25–Jan 10, and Mar 21–Apr 5). Children (ages 6–11) pay half fare, while up to two children 5 and younger travel free if they do not require a separate seat. I've included train prices from Tokyo for many destinations covered in this book (see individual cities for more information). Unless stated otherwise, prices in this guide are for adults for **nonreserved seats** on the fastest train available (except the *Nozomi*) during regular season. You can

City	Distance (Miles)	Travel Time
Beppu*	763	7 hr.
Fukuoka (Hakata Station)*	730	6 hr.
Hakodate*	549	6 hr. 10 min.
Hiroshima*	554	4 hr. 50 min.
Kagoshima*	927	9 hr.
Kamakura	32	53 min.
Kanazawa*	386	4 hr. 30 min.
Kobe (Shin-Kobe Station)	366	3 hr. 20 min.
Kumamoto*	804	9 hr.
Kyoto	319	2 hr. 36 min.
Matsue*	578	5 hr. 45 min.
Matsumoto	146	2 hr. 30 min.
Matsuyama*	589	7 hr.
Nagasaki*	826	8 hr. 30 min.
Nagoya	227	1 hr. 55 min.
Narita Airport	49	1 hr.
Nikko	93	1 hr. 59 min.
Okayama	455	3 hr. 52 min.
Osaka (Shin-Osaka Station)	343	2 hr. 54 min.
Sapporo*	746	10 hr.
Takamatsu*	500	5 hr. 10 min.
Takayama*	331	4 hr.
Toba*	303	3 hr. 40 min.
Yokohama	18	30 min.

* Destination requires a change of trains.

buy JR tickets and obtain information about JR trains traveling throughout Japan at any Japan Railways station (in Tokyo this includes major stations along the Yamanote Line, which loops around Tokyo). If you wish to purchase a ticket using a credit card, go to a Ticket Reservation Office *(Midori-no-madoguchi)* at any major JR station.

No matter which train you ride, be sure to hang onto your ticket—you'll be required to give it up at the end of your trip as you exit through the gate.

SEAT RESERVATIONS You can reserve seats for the Shinkansen, as well as for limited-express and express trains (but not for slower rapid or local trains, which are on a first-come, first-served basis) at any major Japan Railways station in Japan. Reserved seats cost slightly more than unreserved seats (¥300–¥510 for the Shinkansen and express trains). The larger stations have a special reservation counter called **Midori-no-madoguchi (Ticket Reservation Office)** or View Plaza (Travel Service Center), easily recognizable by their green signs with RESERVATION TICKETS written on them. If you're at a JR station with no special reservation office, you can reserve your seats at one of the regular ticket windows. You can also purchase and reserve seats at several travel agents,

(Value) **Japan Rail Pass**

You can save quite a bit by purchasing a rail pass, even if you only plan to travel a little. How economical is a Japan Rail Pass? If you were to buy a round-trip reserved-seat ticket on the Shinkansen from Tokyo to Kyoto, it would cost ¥26,440, which is almost as much as a week's ordinary rail pass. Thus, if you plan to see more than just Tokyo and Kyoto, it pays to use a rail pass, *which you must buy outside Japan* (some regional rail passes, however, described below, can be purchased in Japan if you're a tourist).

With a Rail Pass, you can make seat reservations for free, which otherwise costs up to ¥510 per ride on the Shinkansen. Another advantage to a rail pass is that it offers a 10% discount or more off room rates at more than 50 JR Hotel Group hotels, including the Hotel Granvia in Kyoto, Okayama, and Hiroshima; the JR Tower Hotel Nikko Sapporo; Hotel Kurashiki; Nara Hote; JR Kyushu Hotel Fukuoka; JR Kyushu Hotel Kumamoto; JR Kyushu Hotel Nagasaki; and ANA Hotel Clement Takamatsu. A Japan Rail Pass booklet, which comes with your purchase of a rail pass, lists member hotels (or go to www.jrhotelgroup.com).

including the giant **Japan Travel Bureau (JTB),** which has offices all over Japan. Finally, **JR East** (serving the area around Tokyo and north through Tohoku) offers Internet reservation for its trains at http://jreast-shinkansen-reservation.eki-net.com; unfortunately, the reservation system does not apply to lines run by other JR companies, including the popular Tokaido/Sanyo Shinkansen to Kyoto and beyond.

It's a good idea to reserve your seats for your entire trip through Japan as soon as you know your itinerary if you'll be traveling during peak times; however, you can only reserve 1 month in advance. If it's not peak season, you'll probably be okay using a more flexible approach to traveling—all trains also have nonreserved cars that fill up on a first-come, first-seated basis. You can also reserve seats on the day of travel up to departure time. I hardly ever reserve a seat when it's not peak season, preferring instead the flexibility of being able to hop on the next available train (or, sometimes I reserve a seat just before boarding). If you want to sit in the nonsmoking car of the Shinkansen bullet train, ask for the

kinensha, though nowadays most trains are completely smoke free.

TIPS FOR SAVING MONEY If your ticket is for travel covering more than 100km (62 miles), you can make as many stopovers en route as you wish as long as you complete your trip within the period of the ticket's validity. Tickets for 100 to 200km (62–124 miles) are valid for 2 days, with 1 day added for each additional 200km. Note, too, that stopovers are granted only for trips that are not between major urban areas, such as Tokyo, Yokohama, Osaka, Nagoya, Kyoto, Kobe, Hiroshima, Kitakyushyu, Fukuoka, Sendai, or Sapporo. In addition, stopovers are not permitted when traveling by express and limited express. Ask about stopovers when purchasing your ticket.

You can also save money by purchasing a round-trip ticket for long distances. A round-trip ticket by train on distances exceeding 600km (373 miles) one-way costs 20% less than two one-way tickets.

If you don't qualify for a Japan Rail Pass (see below), the **Seishun 18 (Seishun ju-hachi kippu)** is a 5-day rail pass for

¥11,500 for travel anywhere in Japan as long as you use JR local and rapid trains (that is, no Shinkansen, limited express, or express trains), making it a good bet for day excursions in the countryside, albeit very slow ones (the trip from Tokyo to Kyoto would take 9 hr. and requires three or more changes of trains, compared to 2 hr. 20 min. on the Shinkansen). The biggest drawback, however, is that it's available only during Japan's three major school holidays: spring break (Mar 1–Apr 10); summer break (July 20–Sept 10); and winter break (Dec 10–Jan 10). You can use it on 5 consecutive days or on any 5 days within the school break period; people traveling together can share the five rides (for example, two people can travel for 2 days and one person can travel for 1 day).

There are also regional tickets good for sightseeing. The **Hakone Free Pass,** for example, offered by Odakyu railways (www.odakyu.jp/english), includes round-trip transportation from Tokyo and unlimited travel in Hakone for a specific number of days. The **Hokkaido Furii Pasu** (www.jrhokkaido.co.jp) valid for 7 days of JR train and bus travel in Hokkaido, costs ¥25,500, though some restrictions apply. There are also special passes for seniors (Full Moon Pass, valid for married couples with a combined total age of 88) and for two or three women age 30 and over traveling as a group (Nice Midi Pass). If you qualify, the Japan Rail Pass, however, is a better deal than these alternatives.

JAPAN RAIL PASS   The Japan Rail Pass is without a doubt the most convenient and most economical way to travel around Japan. With the rail pass, you don't have to worry about buying individual tickets, and you can reserve your seats on all JR trains for free. The rail pass entitles you to unlimited travel on all JR train lines including the Shinkansen (except, regrettably, the *Nozomi Super Express*), as well as on most JR buses and the JR ferry to Miyajima.

There are several types of rail passes available; make your decision based on your length of stay in Japan and the cities you intend to visit. You might even find it best to combine several passes to cover your travels in Japan, such as a 1-week standard pass for longer journeys, say, to Kyushu, plus a regional pass just for Kyushu. Online pass information is available at **www.japanrailpass.net**.

THE STANDARD PASS   If you wish to travel throughout Japan, your best bet is to purchase the standard Japan Rail Pass. It's available for ordinary coach class and for the first-class Green Car and is available for travel lasting 1, 2, or 3 weeks. Rates for the ordinary pass (as of Jan 2010) are ¥28,300 for 7 days, ¥45,100 for 14 days, and ¥57,700 for 21 days. Rates for the Green Car are ¥37,800, ¥61,200, and ¥79,600 respectively. Children (ages 6–11) pay half fare. Personally, I have never traveled in the first-class Green Car in Japan and don't consider it necessary. However, during peak travel times (New Year's, Golden Week, and Obon in mid-Aug), you may find it easier to reserve a seat in the first-class Green Car, which you can get by paying a surcharge in addition to showing your ordinary pass.

BEFORE YOU LEAVE HOME   The standard Japan Rail Pass is available only to foreigners visiting Japan as tourists and *can be purchased only outside Japan.* It's available from most travel agents, including **Kintetsu International** (✆ **800/422-3481;** www.kintetsu.com) and **JTB USA** (✆ **800/235-3523;** www.jtbusa.com). If you're flying **Japan Airlines** (**JAL;** ✆ **800/525-3663;** www.ar.jal.com/en) or **All Nippon Airways** (**ANA;** ✆ **800/235-9262;** www.ana.co.jp), you can also purchase a rail pass from them. A full list of authorized travel agents is available at **www.japanrailpass.net**.

Upon purchasing your pass, you'll be issued a voucher (called an **Exchange Order**), which you'll then exchange for the real pass after your arrival in Japan. Note that once you purchase your Exchange Order, you have 3 months until you must exchange it in Japan for the pass itself. When obtaining your actual pass, you must then specify the date you wish to start using the pass within a 1-month period.

ONCE YOU'VE ARRIVED In Japan, you can exchange your voucher for a Japan Rail Pass at more than 40 JR stations that have Japan Rail Pass exchange offices, at which time you must present your passport and specify the date you wish to begin using the pass; most offices are open daily from 10am to 6 or 7pm, some even longer.

At both Narita Airport (daily 6:30am– 9:45pm) and Kansai International Airport (daily 6:30am–9:45pm), you can pick up Japan Rail Passes at either the Travel Service Center or the Ticket Office. Other Travel Service Centers or Ticket Offices, all located in JR train stations, include those at Tokyo (daily 5:30am–10:45pm), Ueno, Shinjuku, Ikebukuro, Shibuya, and Shinagawa stations in Tokyo; Kyoto Station; Shin-Osaka and Osaka stations; and Sapporo, Hakodate, Nagoya, Kanazawa, Okayama, Matsue, Hiroshima, Taka-matsu, Matsuyama, Hakata, Nagasaki, Kumamoto, and Kagoshima Chuo stations. Stations and their open hours are listed in a pamphlet you'll receive with your voucher.

REGIONAL PASSES FOR FOREIGN VISITORS In addition to the standard Japan Rail Pass above, there are regional JR rail passes available for ordinary coach class that are convenient for travel in eastern or western Honshu, Kyushu, or Hokkaido. They can be purchased before arriving in Japan from the same vendors that sell the standard pass. All but the Kintetsu Rail Pass can also be purchased inside Japan, usually only within the area covered by the pass but also at Narita airport for some passes. These regional passes

are available only to foreign visitors and require that you present your passport to verify your status as a "temporary visitor"; you may also be asked to show your plane ticket. Only one pass per region per visit to Japan is allowed.

If you're arriving by plane at the Kansai Airport outside Osaka and intend to remain in western Honshu, you may opt for one of two different **JR-West Passes** (www.westjr.co.jp/english), available at Kansai Airport, Osaka JR station, and other locations. The **Kansai Area Pass,** which can be used for travel between Osaka, Kyoto, Kobe, Nara, Himeji, and other destinations in the Kansai area, is available as a 1-day pass for ¥2,000, 2-day pass for ¥4,000, 3-day pass for ¥5,000, or 4-day pass for ¥6,000. Travel is restricted to JR rapid and local trains, as well as unreserved seating in limited express trains that operate only between Kansai Airport, Shin-Osaka, and Kyoto (that is, Shinkansen are not included in the pass). Children pay half-price for all passes. The other JR-West Pass available is the **Sanyo Area Pass,** which covers a larger area, allows travel via Shinkansen (including the superfast *Nozomi*) and JR local trains from Osaka as far as Hakata (in the city of Fukuoka on Kyushu), and includes Hiroshima, Okayama, Kurashiki, Himeji, and Kobe. It's available for 4 days for ¥20,000 and for 8 days for ¥30,000.

There are also a couple other non-JR passes available for Kansai. The **Kansai Thru Pass** (www.surutto.com) is valid on city subways, private railways (*not* JR trains), and buses throughout the Kansai area. Available only to tourists, it costs ¥3,800 for a 2-day pass and ¥5,000 for 3 days and is sold at Kansai International Airport and Tourist Information Centers in Osaka and Nara. Or, if you plan to spend a few days traveling farther afield between Nagoya, Osaka, Kyoto, and Ise-Shima, you can save money by purchasing a **Kintetsu Rail Pass** (www.kintetsu.co.jp), which covers travel throughout the region on Kintetsu's private lines. Available only for foreigners, it must be purchased before arriving in Japan at Kintetsu offices or authorized travel agencies. It costs ¥3,500 and includes 5 days of unlimited travel (but only 3 trips on limited express trains). For ¥5,700, you can purchase the Kintetsu Rail Pass Wide, which adds a trip from Centrair or Kansai Airport, Mie Kotsu buses, and discount coupons for sightseeing spots.

Though not as popular as western Honshu, eastern Honshu also offers its own **JR-East Pass** (www.jreast.co.jp), which includes travel from Tokyo to Nagano in the Japan Alps and throughout the Tohoku District, including Sendai, Kakunodate, and Aomori via Shinkansen and local JR lines. Passes for travel in ordinary coach cars are available for 5 days for ¥20,000 and 10 days for ¥32,000; a 4-day flexible pass (valid for any 4 consecutive or non-consecutive days within a month) costs ¥20,000. Green Car passes are also available. Passes are available at Narita airport and JR stations in Tokyo, including Tokyo, Shinagawa, and Shinjuku, as well as online at http://jreast-shinkansen-reservation.eki-net.com.

If your travels are limited to the island of Kyushu, consider the **JR-Kyushu Rail Pass** (www.jrkyushu.co.jp), valid for 3 days for ¥13,000 (¥7,000 for northern Kyushu only) and for 5 days for ¥16,000 and available for purchase at Narita Airport and at Hakata, Nagasaki, Kumamoto, Kagoshima Chuo, and Beppu JR stations. Likewise, there's a **Hokkaido Rail Pass** (www.jrhokkaido.co.jp) valid for 3 days of travel for ¥15,000 or 5 days (or 4 flexible days within a 10-day period) for ¥19,500, sold at Narita Airport and Hakodate and Sapporo JR stations.

BY PLANE

Because it takes the better part of a day and night to travel by train from Tokyo down to southern Kyushu or up to northern Hokkaido, you may find it faster—not

to mention cheaper if you buy your ticket in advance (see below)—to fly at least one stretch of your journey in Japan. You could, for example, fly internationally into Osaka and then onward to Fukuoka on Kyushu, from where you can take a leisurely 2 weeks to travel by train through Kyushu and Honshu before returning to Osaka. I don't, however, advise flying short distances—say, from Tokyo to Osaka—simply because the time spent getting to and from airports is longer than the time spent traveling by Shinkansen.

Almost all domestic flights from Tokyo leave from the much more conveniently located **Haneda Airport.** If you're already in Tokyo, you can easily reach Haneda Airport via Airport Limousine Bus, monorail from Hamamatsucho Station on the Yamanote Line, or the Keikyu Line from Shinagawa. If you're arriving on an international flight at Narita Airport, therefore, make sure you know whether a connection to a domestic flight is at Narita or requires a transfer to Haneda Airport via the Airport Limousine Bus (see chapter 5 for details).

Two major domestic airlines are **Japan Airlines (JAL; ℂ 0570/025-071** in Japan; www.jal.co.jp) and **All Nippon Airways (ANA; ℂ 0570/029-709** in Japan; www. ana.co.jp). Regular fares with these two companies are generally the same no matter which airline you fly domestically and are more expensive for peak season including New Year's, Golden Week, and summer vacation. However, bargains do exist. Some flights early in the day or late at night may be cheaper than flights during peak time; there are also discounts for seniors 65 and over. Your best bet on snagging a discount, however, is to purchase your ticket in advance. ANA's *Tabiwari* and JAL's *Sakitoku* are discount fares on reservations made 28 days in advance, while the Super Tabiwari and Super Saitoku give deep discounts on tickets purchased 45 days in advance. Regular one-way fares from Tokyo to Naha, Okinawa, for example, are ¥40,900 but go as low as ¥12,800 for a Super Tabiwari or Super Saitoku on selected flights. There are also slight discounts on tickets booked 3 to 7 days before departure and on round-trip fares.

Otherwise, there are small regional airlines that generally offer fares that are cheaper than the standard full fare charged by JAL or ANA. These include **Skymark** (© 03/3433-7670 in Tokyo, or 092/736-3131 in Fukuoka; www.skymark.co.jp), operating out of Fukuoka; **Skynet Asia Airways** (© 0120/737-283 toll-free; www.skynetasia.co.jp), connecting Nagasaki, Kumamoto, and Kagoshima with Tokyo and Okinawa; and **Air Do** (© 0120/0570-333 toll-free), out of Sapporo.

For information on fares from Tokyo to major cities throughout Japan, see individual city listings in this guide. Tickets can be purchased directly through the airline or at a travel agent such as **Japan Travel Bureau (JTB),** which has offices virtually everywhere in Japan.

SPECIAL DOMESTIC FARES FOR FOREIGNERS Purchasing domestic tickets in advance in connection with your international flight is by far the most economical way to go. JAL's "Oneworld Yokoso/Visit Japan Fare" ticket, purchased in conjunction with a flight to Japan with JAL or one of its Oneworld fare partners (such as American Airlines) and sold only outside Japan, provides discount fares of ¥10,000 per flight for domestic travel to 42 cities in Japan served by JAL and its two subsidiaries, JAL Express and Japan Transocean Air (JTA).

Visitors flying other airlines into Japan can take advantage of JAL's "Welcome to Japan Fare," which provides discounts on JAL's domestic flights regardless of which international airline is used to reach Japan. Also sold only outside Japan, this costs ¥13,650 per flight, with a minimum of two flights required.

ANA offers a similar program, with its Star Alliance Japan Airpass ticket costing ¥11,000 per flight if you fly ANA or one of its Star Alliance partners such as United Airlines; if you fly another airline, its Visit Japan Fare is ¥13,000 per ticket. Note that there are blackout dates for all these fares, mostly in mid-March, during summer vacation (mid-July through Aug), and New Year's, and that fares exclude airport taxes and insurance. You should first purchase your international ticket and then contact JAL or ANA to purchase and book your Japan domestic tickets.

If you plant to visit at least two Okinawan islands in addition to Okinawa Island, you can save money by purchasing an Okinawa Island Pass, valid on five specific routes within the Okinawan island chain, including flights from Naha to Kume or Ishigaki, on Japan Transocean Air (a subsidiary of JAL). A minimum of two flights, at ¥9,000 each, is required, and tickets must be purchased from JAL before arriving in Japan. For more information, contact your nearest JAL office.

BY BUS

Buses often go where trains don't and thus may be the only way for you to get to the more remote areas of Japan, such as Shirakawa-go in the Japan Alps. In Hokkaido, Tohoku, Kyushu, and other places, buses are used extensively.

Some intercity buses require you to make reservations or purchase your ticket in advance at the ticket counter at the bus terminal. For others (especially local buses), when you board a bus you'll generally find a ticket machine by the entry door. Take a ticket, which is number-coded with a digital board displayed at the front of the bus. The board shows the various fares, which increase with the distance traveled. You pay when you get off.

In addition to serving the remote areas of the country, **long-distance buses** (called *chokyori basu*) also operate between major cities in Japan and offer the cheapest mode of transportation. Although **Japan Railways** operates almost a dozen bus routes eligible for JR Rail Pass coverage, the majority of buses are run by private companies (most of which do not have English-language websites). Some long-distance buses travel during the night and offer reclining seats and toilets, thus saving passengers the price of a night's lodging. Long-distance buses departing from **Tokyo Station,** for example, cost ¥4,200 to ¥8,600 for Kyoto or Osaka, depending on the company and time of day, and ¥12,060 for Hiroshima. Long-distance bus tickets can be purchased at View Plazas at major JR stations (for JR buses), at travel agencies such as JTB, or at bus terminals.

For more information on local and long-distance bus service, refer to individual cities covered in this guide, contact the **Tourist Information Center** in Tokyo (see "Visitor Information" in chapter 5) or the local tourist office, or check the websites www.bus.or.jp, www.jrbuskanto.co.jp, and http://willerexpress.com.

BY CAR

With the exception, perhaps, of Izu Peninsula, the Tohoku region, and Hokkaido, driving is not recommended for visitors wishing to tour Japan. Driving is British style (on the left side of the road), which may be hard for those not used to it; traffic can be horrendous; and driving isn't even economical. Not only is gas expensive, but all of Japan's expressways charge high tolls—the one-way toll from Tokyo to Kyoto is almost the same price as a ticket to Kyoto on the Shinkansen. And whereas the Shinkansen takes only 3 hours to get to Kyoto, driving can take about 8 hours. In addition, you may encounter few signs in English in remote areas. Driving in cities is even worse: Streets are often hardly wide enough for a rickshaw, let alone a car, and many roads don't have sidewalks so

you have to dodge people, bicycles, and telephone poles. Free parking is hard to find, and garages are expensive. Except in remote areas, it just doesn't make sense to drive.

If you're undeterred, a good roundup of more than 800 car-rental agencies in Japan, including those located at airports and train stations, is provided at **www2. tocoo.jp**, where you can make reservations, see pictures and descriptions of rental cars, and review your knowledge of international traffic signs. Otherwise, major car-rental companies in Japan include **Toyota Rent-A-Car** (✆ 03/5954-8020 in Tokyo, or 0800/7000-815 toll-free; www.rent.toyota.co.jp); **Nippon Rent-A-Car Service** (✆ 03/3485-7196 for the English Service Desk; www.nipponrentacar.co.jp), **Nissan Rent-A-Car** (✆ 0120/00-4123 toll-free), and **Avis** (✆ 0120/31-1911 toll-free; www.avis-japan.com). In Hokkaido, Kyushu, and some other areas, there is also **JR Eki Rent-A-Car,** located beside JR train stations and offering 20% discounts on train fares booked in conjunction with car rentals; you can reserve these cars at any JR Travel Service Center (located in train stations) anywhere in Japan.

Rates vary, but the average cost for 24 hours with unlimited mileage is about ¥10,500 for a subcompact including insurance but not gas; in some tourist areas, such as Hokkaido, rates are more expensive in peak season.

If you do intend to drive in Japan, you'll need either an **international** or a **Japanese driving license.** Remember, cars are driven on the left side of the road, and signs on all major highways are written in both Japanese and English. It is against the law to drink alcohol and drive, and you must wear seat belts at all times. Be sure to purchase a bilingual map, as back roads often have names of towns written in Japanese only. Recommended is the *Shobunsha Road Atlas Japan,* available in bookstores that sell English-language books; it also contains maps of major cities, including Tokyo, Sapporo, Hiroshima, and others.

BREAKDOWNS & ASSISTANCE The **Japan Automobile Federation (JAF;** www.jaf.or.jp) is one of several road service providers maintaining emergency telephone boxes along Japan's major arteries to assist drivers whose cars have broken down or drivers who need help. Calls from these telephones are free and will connect you to JAF's operation center at your request. English is spoken.

BY FERRY

Because Japan is an island nation, an extensive ferry network links the string of islands. Although travel by ferry takes longer, it's also cheaper and can be a pleasant, relaxing experience. For example, you can take a ferry from Osaka to Beppu (on Kyushu), with fares starting at ¥8,800 for the 11-hour trip. Unfortunately, information in English is hard to come by. Contact the **Tourist Information Center** (see "Visitor Information" in chapter 5) for details concerning routes, prices, schedules, and telephone numbers of the various ferry companies.

5 MONEY & COSTS

The Value of Yen vs. Other Popular Currencies

Yen	US$	Can$	UK£	Euro (€)	Aus$	NZ$
100	$1.11	C$1.19	0.71£	0.81€	A$1.28	NZ$1.62

Frommer's lists exact prices in the local currency. The currency conversions listed above were correct at press time but can fluctuate widely; if I could advise you accurately on the future exchange rate, I'd be too rich to be a guidebook writer. Consult a currency-exchange website such as **www.xe.com** to check up-to-the-minute rates.

CURRENCY The currency in Japan is called the *yen,* symbolized by ¥. Coins come in denominations of ¥1, ¥5, ¥10, ¥50, ¥100, and ¥500. Bills come in denominations of ¥1,000, ¥2,000, ¥5,000, and ¥10,000, though ¥2,000 notes are rarely seen. You'll find that all coins get used (though it's hard to get rid of ¥1 coins). Keep plenty of change handy for riding local transportation such as buses or streetcars. Although change machines are virtually everywhere, even on buses where you can change larger coins and ¥1,000 bills, you'll find it faster to have the exact amount on hand.

Some people like to arrive in a foreign country with that country's currency already on hand, but I do not find it necessary for Japan. **Narita, Kansai,** and **Nagoya international airports** all have exchange counters for all incoming international flights that offer better exchange rates than what you'd get abroad, as well as ATMs. I usually change enough money to last several days.

Personal checks are not used in Japan. Most Japanese pay with either credit cards or cash—and because the country overall has such a low crime rate, you can feel safe walking around with money (though of course you should always exercise caution). The only time you really need to be alert to possible pickpockets in Japan is when you're riding a crowded subway during rush hour or walking in heavily visited areas of Tokyo and other large cities.

In any case, although the bulk of your expenses—hotels, train tickets, major purchases, meals in tourist-oriented restaurants—can be paid for with credit cards,

What Things Cost in Tokyo	Japanese Yen
Narita Express from airport to Tokyo Station	2,940
Metro subway ride from Ginza to Asakusa	1.90
Local telephone call (per 1 min.)	0.10
Double room at the Peninsula Tokyo (deluxe)	60,000
Double room at Courtyard by Marriott Tokyo Ginza (moderate)	30,000
Double room at Asia Center of Japan (inexpensive)	12,390
Lunch for one at Ginza Daimasu (moderate)	2,100
Lunch for one at Limapuluh (inexpensive)	1,050
Dinner for one, without drinks, at New York Grill (deluxe)	11,000
Dinner for one, without drinks, at Waentei-Kikko (moderate)	6,825
Dinner for one, without drinks, at Gonpachi (inexpensive)	3,500
Glass of beer	600
Coca-Cola	300
Cup of coffee	400
Admission to the Tokyo National Museum	600

you'll want to bring traveler's checks for those times when you might not have easy access to an ATM for cash withdrawals.

ATMS The best way to get cash away from home is from an ATM (automated teller machine). Because most bank ATMs in Japan accept only cards issued by Japanese banks, your best bet for obtaining cash is at **7-Eleven** convenience stores, which are found throughout Japan, are often open 24 hours, and have ATMs that accept foreign bank cards operating on the **Cirrus** (www.mastercard.com) and **PLUS** (www.visa.com) systems, as well as American Express.

Another good bet is at one of 21,000 **post offices,** which also have ATMs accepting foreign bank cards operating on the Cirrus and PLUS systems. Although major post offices, usually located near main train stations, have long open hours for ATMs (generally 7am–11pm weekdays and 9am–7 or 9pm on weekends), small post offices may have only limited hours for ATMs (depending on the post office,

that may be until 6 or 7pm weekdays and until 5pm on weekends).

Other places with ATMs that might accept foreign-issued cards include Citibank and large department stores in major cities. Note that there is no public American Express office in Japan.

Be sure you know your four-digit personal identification number (PIN) and your daily withdrawal limit before leaving home. Also keep in mind that many banks impose a fee every time a card is used at a different bank's ATM, and that fee can be higher for international transactions than for domestic ones. In addition, the bank from which you withdraw cash may charge its own fee. For international withdrawal fees, ask your bank.

CREDIT CARDS Credit cards are a safe way to carry money, provide a convenient record of all your expenses, and generally offer relatively good exchange rates. You can withdraw cash advances from your credit cards at banks or ATMs, provided you know your four-digit PIN. Keep in mind that you'll pay interest from the moment of your withdrawal, even if you pay your monthly bills on time. Also, note that many banks assess a 1% to 3% "transaction fee" on all charges you incur abroad (whether you're using the local currency or your native currency).

The most readily accepted cards are **MasterCard** (also called Eurocard), **Visa,** and the Japanese credit card **JCB** (Japan Credit Bank); many tourist-oriented facilities also accept **American Express** and **Diners Club.** Shops and restaurants accepting credit and charge cards will usually post which cards they accept at the door or near the cash register. However, some establishments may be reluctant to accept cards for small purchases and inexpensive meals, so inquire beforehand. In addition, note that the vast majority of Japan's smaller and least-expensive businesses, including many restaurants, noodle shops, fast-food joints, ma-and-pa establishments, and the cheapest accommodations, do not accept credit cards.

TRAVELER'S CHECKS While traveler's checks are something of an anachronism now that ATMs have come onto the scene, they're still useful for Japan, where ATMs for foreign-issued cards are limited primarily to 7-Eleven convenience stores and post offices. Traveler's checks fetch a better exchange rate than cash and also offer protection in case of theft (be sure to keep a record of the traveler's checks' serial numbers separate from your checks in the event that they are stolen or lost). Note, however, that in some very remote areas, even banks won't cash them. Before taking off for small towns, therefore, be sure you have enough cash.

EXCHANGING MONEY All banks in Japan displaying an AUTHORIZED FOREIGN EXCHANGE sign can exchange currency and traveler's checks, with exchange rates usually displayed at the appropriate foreign-exchange counter. **Banks** are generally open Monday through Friday from 9am to 3pm, though business hours for exchanging foreign currency usually don't begin until 10:30 or 11am (be prepared for a long wait; you'll be asked to sit down as your order is processed). More convenient—and quicker—are **Travelex** (www.travelex.com) foreign-exchange kiosks, with locations in several cities in Japan, including Tokyo, Kyoto, Nagoya, Osaka, and Sapporo.

If you need to exchange money outside banking hours, inquire at your **hotel.** Likewise, large **department stores** also offer exchange services and are often open until 7:30 or 8pm. Note, however, that hotels and department stores may charge a handling fee, offer a slightly less favorable exchange rate, and require a passport for all transactions.

6 HEALTH

STAYING HEALTHY

It's safe to drink tap water and eat to your heart's content everywhere in Japan (pregnant women, however, are advised to avoid eating raw fish or taking hot baths). Although Japan had nine cases of mad cow disease after its first confirmed case in 2001, all slaughtered cows must now be checked for the disease before the meat is authorized for consumption. To prevent the spread of avian and H1N1 flu, all incoming passengers are monitored upon arrival at Narita Airport for fever; those with a higher than normal temperature may be quarantined. To be on the safe side, therefore, you may opt for an influenza vaccine before departing from home.

Otherwise, you don't need any inoculations to enter Japan. *Note:* **Prescriptions** can be filled at Japanese pharmacies only if

Healthy Travels to You

The following government websites offer up-to-date health-related travel advice.
- **Australia:** www.smartraveller.gov.au/tips/travelwell.html
- **Canada:** www.hc-sc.gc.ca/index-eng.php
- **U.K.:** www.nhs.uk/healthcareabroad/pages/healthcareabroad.aspx
- **U.S.:** www.cdc.gov/travel

they're issued by a Japanese doctor. To avoid hassle, bring more prescription medications than you think you'll need, clearly labeled in their original vials, and be sure to pack them in your carry-on luggage. But to be safe, bring copies of your prescriptions with you, including generic names of medicines in case a local pharmacist is unfamiliar with the brand name. Over-the-counter items are easy to obtain, though name brands are likely to be different from back home, some ingredients allowed elsewhere may be forbidden in Japan, and prices are likely to be higher.

What to Do If You Get Sick Away from Home

If you get sick, contact the concierge at your hotel—some upper-range hotels, especially in Tokyo, have in-house doctors or clinics (see individual hotel listings in each chapter). Otherwise, your concierge, consulate, and sometimes even the local tourist office can provide a list of area doctors who speak English (see p. 124 for embassy contact information). You can also contact the **International Association for Medical Assistance to Travellers** (*©* **716/754-4883,** or 416/652-0137 in Canada; www.iamat.org), an organization that lists many local English-speaking doctors and also posts the latest developments in global outbreaks. Otherwise, if you can't find a doctor who can help you right away, try the local hospital. Many have walk-in-clinics for cases that are not life-threatening. Doctors and hospitals generally do not accept credit cards and require immediate cash payment for health services.

You'll find a list of **emergency numbers** in "Fast Facts."

PLANNING YOUR TRIP TO JAPAN

3

SAFETY

7 SAFETY

One of the greatest delights of traveling in Japan is that the country is safe and the people are honest. When a friend of mine forgot her purse in a public restroom in Osaka, someone turned it in to the police station complete with money, digital camera, and passport. In all the years I've lived and worked in Japan, I've never had even one fearful encounter, and I never hesitate to walk anywhere any time of the night or day. If you lose something, say on a subway or in a park, chances are good that you'll get it back.

That being said, crime—especially pickpocketing—is on the increase, and there are precautions you should always take when traveling: Stay alert and be aware of your immediate surroundings. Be especially careful with cameras, purses, and wallets in congested areas like Narita airport, subways, department stores, or tourist attractions (like the retail district around Tokyo's Tsukiji Market). Some Japanese caution women against walking through parks alone at night.

8 SPECIALIZED TRAVEL RESOURCES

In addition to the destination-specific resources listed below, please visit Frommers.com for additional specialized travel resources.

GAY & LESBIAN TRAVELERS

While there are many gay and lesbian establishments in Tokyo (concentrated mostly in Shinjuku's Ni-chome district; see chapter 6), the gay community in Japan is not a vocal one, and in any case, local information in English is hard to come by. A useful website for gay club listings is **www.utopia-asia.com/tipsjapn. htm**, where you can also order the *Utopia Guide to Japan,* which covers the gay and lesbian scene in 27 cities in Japan.

TRAVELERS WITH DISABILITIES

For those with disabilities, traveling can be a nightmare in Japan, especially in Tokyo and other large metropolises. City sidewalks can be so jampacked that getting around on crutches or in a wheelchair is exceedingly difficult; some busy thoroughfares can be crossed only via pedestrian bridges.

Most major train and subway stations now have elevators, but they can be difficult to locate. Otherwise, smaller stations, especially in rural areas, may be accessible only by stairs or escalators, though in recent years some have been equipped with powered seat lifts. While some buses are now no-step conveyances for easy access, subway and train compartments are difficult for solo wheelchair travelers to navigate on their own due to a gap or slight height difference between the coaches and platforms. In theory you can ask a station attendant to help you board, though you might have to wait if he's busy; you can also request an attendant at your

destination to help you disembark. Although trains and buses have seating for passengers with disabilities—called "Priority Seats" and located in the first and last compartments of the train—subways can be so crowded that there's barely room to move. Moreover, Priority Seats are almost always occupied by commuters, so unless you look visibly handicapped, no one is likely to offer you a seat.

As for accommodations, only 10% of the nation's hotels have barrier-free rooms (called a "universal" room in Japan and used primarily by seniors), mostly in the expensive category. Only a scant 1% of Japanese inns have such rooms. Lower-priced accommodations may also lack elevators.

Restaurants can also be difficult to navigate, with raised doorsills, crowded dining areas, and tiny bathrooms that cannot accommodate wheelchairs. Best bets for ramps and easily accessible bathrooms include restaurants in department stores and upper-end hotels. Even Japanese homes are not very accessible, since the main floor is always raised about a foot above the entrance-hall floor.

For information on traveling with a wheelchair, including limited information on a handful of sights and hotels offering facilities for travelers with disabilities, visit the **Accessible Japan** website at **www. tesco-premium.co.jp/aj.**

When it comes to **facilities for the blind,** Japan has a very advanced system. At subway stations and on many major sidewalks in large cities, raised dots and lines on the ground guide blind people at intersections and to subway platforms. In some cities, streetlights chime a theme when the signal turns green east-west, and chime another for north-south. Even Japanese yen notes are identified by a slightly raised circle—the ¥1,000 note has one circle in a corner, while the ¥10,000 note has two. Many elevators have floors indicated in Braille, and some hotels identify rooms in Braille.

FAMILY TRAVEL

Japanese are very fond of children, which makes traveling in Japan with kids a delight. All social reserve seems to be waived for children. Taking along some small and easy-to-carry gifts (such as colorful stickers) for your kids to give to other children is a great icebreaker.

Safety also makes Japan a good destination for families. Still, plan your itinerary with care. To avoid crowds, visit tourist sights on weekdays. Never travel on city transportation during rush hour or on trains during popular public holidays. And remember that with all the stairways and crowded sidewalks, strollers are less practical than baby backpacks.

Children 6 to 11 years old are generally charged half-price for everything from temple admission to train tickets, while children 5 and under are often admitted free. Tourist spots in Japan almost always have a table or counter with a stamp and inkpad so that visitors can commemorate their trip; you might wish to give your children a small notebook so they can collect imprints of every attraction they visit. There are many attractions throughout Japan geared just toward kids, including sophisticated theme parks. And what teenager could resist Japan's pop culture, fashion, and fads?

Although it's not advertised, many hotels and *ryokan* (Japanese-style inns) give discounts to young children (up to 5 or 9 years of age) or allow them to stay for free, but only if they sleep with you and do not require an extra bed. Ryokan may also give discounts for meals. At budget chain Tokyo Inn, for example, children 5 and under stay free, while those 6 to 10 are charged an extra ¥1,050 per night. In any case, it's advisable to ask in advance. Many upper-range hotels in major cities like Tokyo and Osaka provide babysitting services, although they are prohibitively expensive. Expect to fork over a minimum of ¥5,000 for 2 hours of freedom.

As for food, the transition from kid-favorite spaghetti to *udon* noodles is easy, and udon and *soba* shops are inexpensive and ubiquitous. In addition, most family-style restaurants, especially those in department stores, offer a special children's meal that often includes a small toy or souvenir. For those real emergencies, Western fast-food places such as McDonald's and KFC are seemingly everywhere in Japan.

To locate those accommodations, restaurants, and attractions that are particularly kid-friendly, see the "Kids" icon throughout this guide. For a suggested itinerary in Japan with kids, see chapter 4.

SENIOR TRAVEL

More and more attractions are offering **free admission** or **discounts** to seniors 65 or 70 and over (be sure to have your passport handy). However, discounts may not be posted, so be sure to ask. Seniors also receive discounts on domestic plane fares.

Older visitors to Japan should be aware that there are many stairs to navigate in metropolitan areas, particularly in subway and train stations and even on pedestrian overpasses.

STUDENT TRAVEL

Students sometimes receive discounts at museums, though occasionally discounts are available only to students enrolled in Japanese schools. Furthermore, discounted prices are often not displayed in English. Your best bet is to bring along an **International Student Identity Card (ISIC)** together with your university student ID and show them both at ticket windows. For information on the ISIC card and where and how to obtain one, check the website www.isic.org.

9 SPECIAL-INTEREST TRIPS & ESCORTED TOURS

SPECIAL-INTEREST TRIPS

If your primary interest lies with *ikebana* (Japanese flower arranging), the tea ceremony, or other cultural pursuits, Tokyo and Kyoto are your best bets for finding instruction in English. For short introductions, **Sunrise Tours** (www.jtb-sunrise-tours.jp) offers the chance to experience the tea ceremony on 2- or 3-hour tours in both Tokyo and Kyoto, along with other cultural pursuits such as making sushi or writing calligraphy. Tokyo-based **H.I.S. Experience Japan** (www.hisexperience.jp) offers a wide range of hands-on activities, including a samurai sword class featuring a sword fight demonstration by instructors and a lesson covering the basic movements; a visit to a sumo stable followed by a typical sumo meal; a *taiko* drumming or *shamisen* course; a kimono workshop; a survival Japanese-language class; and cooking classes that cover sushi, *soba,* and traditional Japanese food.

In Tokyo, there are several **ikebana schools** offering one-time or ongoing instruction in English (see p. 188 for more information). In Kyoto, the **Women's Association of Kyoto** (www.wakjapan.com) offers short, one-time classes on the tea ceremony, flower arranging, origami, Japanese calligraphy, Japanese cooking, and other cultural activities. The tourist offices in both Tokyo and Kyoto have information on temples that provide *zazen* (sitting meditation) in English.

You won't become fluent in Japanese in a week or two, but for longer stays there are language schools in major cities across Japan that cater to both the beginner and the intermediate. Check the classified sections of city magazines, like *Metropolis* in Tokyo, for lists of language schools.

Outside Tokyo and Kyoto, local international centers in larger cities, founded to promote multicultural harmony and to assist foreigners living in their communities, are good resources for cultural activities and events. The **Nagoya International Center** (www.nic-nagoya.or.jp), for example, offers seven levels of Japanese instruction, from conversation for beginners to writing kanji, at reasonable prices. In Kanazawa, the **Ishikawa International Lounge** (www.ifie.or.jp) schedules cultural events and classes that might cover origami, calligraphy, the tea ceremony, Japanese flower arranging, Japanese folk dancing, Japanese cooking, and Japanese language; classes themselves are free, but materials for the class cost extra. Other cities with similar institutions, all offering Japanese language classes and sometimes cultural classes as well, include the **International House, Osaka** (www.ih-osaka.or.jp), Kobe's **Hyogo International Association** (www.hyogo-ip.or.jp/en), the **Okayama Prefectural International Exchange Foundation** (www.opief.or.jp/english), and the **Hiroshima International Center** (www.hiroshima-ic.or.jp). See individual cities in this guide for more information.

ESCORTED GENERAL-INTEREST TOURS

Escorted tours are structured group tours, with a group leader. The price usually includes everything from airfare to hotels, meals, tours, admission costs, and local transportation. They take you to the maximum number of sights in the minimum amount of time with the least amount of hassle. On the downside, you'll have little opportunity for serendipitous interactions with locals. Tours can be jampacked with activities, leaving little room for individual sightseeing, whim, or adventure—plus they often focus on heavily touristed sites, missing out on lesser-known gems.

That said, lots of tour companies offer group trips to Japan, including **General Tours** (☏ 800/221-2216; www.general tours.com), which offers tours to major tourist destinations in Japan. **JTB USA** (☏ 800/235-3523; www.jtbusa.com) offers tours that may highlight anything from Japanese cuisine to art. **Esprit Travel & Tours** (☏ 800/377-7481; www.esprit travel.com) specializes in small-group walking, hiking, and cultural tours that cover such interests as textile arts, Japanese gardens, and the old Tokaido Road. If you want someone else to take care of logistics but don't like group tours, **Artisans of Leisure** (☏ 800/214-8144; www.artisans ofleisure.com) provides luxury tours with

private gu
interests.
(☏ 0117
tours.com
both kno
the beate
more abo
ery Tou
Gauntner (☏ 415/3/66-1999;
sake-world.com).

For more ideas on escorted tours departing from North America, go to **www.japantravelinfo.com**; for tours departing from England, go to **www.seejapan.co.uk**. For more information on escorted tours, including questions to ask before booking your trip, see www.frommers.com/planning.

10 STAYING CONNECTED

TELEPHONES

To call Japan:

1. Dial the international access code: 011 from the U.S.; 00 from the U.K., Ireland, or New Zealand; or 0011 from Australia.
2. Dial the country code for Japan (81).
3. Dial the city code (3 for Tokyo, 6 for Osaka; for other area codes, check the listings for each city in this guide) and then the number.

Domestic calls: If you're making a long-distance domestic phone call, all telephone area codes for all Japanese cities begin with a zero (03 for Tokyo, 06 for Osaka).

Despite the proliferation of cellphones, you can still find public telephones in telephone booths on the sidewalk, in or near train stations, in hotel lobbies, restaurants and coffee shops, and even on the bullet train (the latter require a prepaid card; see below). A local call costs ¥10 for each minute; a warning chime will alert you to insert more coins or you'll be disconnected. I usually insert two or three coins so that I won't have to worry about

being disconnected; ¥10 coins that aren't used are returned at the end of the call. Most public phones accept both ¥10 and ¥100 coins. The latter is convenient for long-distance calls, but no change is given for unused minutes. All gray ISDN telephones are equipped for international calls and have dataports for Internet access.

If you think you'll be making a lot of domestic calls from public phones and don't want to deal with coins, purchase a magnetic **prepaid telephone card.** These are available in a value of ¥1,000 and are sold at vending machines (sometimes located right beside telephones), station kiosks, and convenience stores. Green and gray telephones accept telephone cards. In fact, many nowadays accept telephone cards exclusively. Insert the card into the slot. On the gray ISDN telephones, there's a second slot for a second telephone card, which is convenient if the first one is almost used up or if you think you'll be talking a long time. Domestic long-distance calls are cheaper at night, on weekends, and on national holidays for calls of distances more than 60km (37 miles).

nbers: Numbers begin-
20 or **0088** are toll-free.
-800 number in the U.S. from
not toll-free but costs the same as
ternational call.

To make international calls from Japan:
For a collect call or to place an operator-
assisted call through KDDI, dial the international telephone operator at ✆ **0051.** From
a public telephone, look for a specially
marked INTERNATIONAL AND DOMESTIC
CARD/COIN TELEPHONE. Although many of
the specially marked green or gray telephones, the most common public telephone,
accept both coins and magnetic telephone
cards for domestic calls, most do not accept
magnetic cards for direct overseas calls (due
to illegal usage of telephone cards), especially
in big cities, except for those in a few key
facilities such as the airport and some hotels.
You'll therefore either have to use coins, or
purchase a special prepaid international telephone card that works like telephone cards
issued by U.S. telephone companies. That is,
an access number must first be dialed, followed by a secret telephone number, and
then the number you wish to dial. Such
cards are often sold from vending machines
next to telephone booths in hotels or in
convenience stores such as Sunkus, Circle K,
Family Mart, or Lawson. There are numerous such cards (with instructions in English),
including the rechargeable **Brastel Smart
Phonecard** (✆ **0120/659-543;** www.brastel.
com), which charges ¥49 to ¥54 per minute
from a pay phone to a land line in the U.S.
or U.K.; or the **KDDI Super World Card**
(✆ **0057;** www.kddi.com), which gives
approximately 21 minutes of weekday talk
time to the U.S. on its ¥1,000 card. Some
hotels have special phones equipped to
accept credit cards.

International rates vary according to
when you call, which telephone company
you use, and what type of service you use.
Direct-dial service is cheaper than opera-
tor-assisted calls. The cheapest time to call
is between 11pm and 8am Japan time,

while the most expensive time is weekdays
from 8am to 7pm.

If you're not using a prepaid card (which
has its own set of instructions and access
numbers), to make a direct-dial international
call, you must first dial one of the international access codes offered by the various
telephone companies—**001** (KDDI), **0033**
(NTT Communications), or **0061** (Softbank Telecom)—followed by **010** and then
the country code. The country code for the
United States and Canada is **1;** for the
United Kingdom, it's **44;** for Australia, it's
61; and for New Zealand, it's **64.** Next you
dial the area code and number. For example,
if you wanted to call the British Embassy in
Washington, D.C., using KDDI you would
dial 001-010-1-202-588-6500. If you're
dialing from your hotel room, you must first
dial for an outside line, usually 0.

If you wish to be connected with an
operator in your home country, you can
do so from green international telephones
by dialing ✆ **0039** followed by the country code. (For the United States, dial
✆ **0039-111.**) These calls can be used for
collect calls or credit card calls. Some
hotels and other public places are equipped
with special phones that will link you to
your home operator with the push of a
button, with instructions in English.

If you have a U.S. calling card, ask your
phone company for the direct access number from Japan that will link you directly
to the United States. If you have AT&T,
for example, dial ✆ **00539-111** to place
calls using KDDI or ✆ **00665-5111** to
use Softbank Telecom.

CELLPHONES

The three letters that define much of the
world's wireless capabilities are GSM
(Global System for Mobiles). Unfortunately, Japan uses a system that is incom-
patible with GSM, and foreigners are not
allowed to buy cellphones in Japan. You
can, however, use your **own mobile phone
number** in Japan by bringing your own
SIM card from home and inserting it into

Tips **Over & Out**

If you're traveling with a buddy, consider bringing along walkie-talkies. They're cheaper than phones, could be a lifesaver if you get separated, and make it easier to rendezvous, especially in big cities.

a handset rented from **Softbank Global Rental** or **NTT DoCoMo.** It only works, however, if your home service provider has a roaming agreement with Softbank or NTT. For more information, contact your mobile phone company, NTT DoCoMo (http://roaming.nttdocomo.co.jp), or Softbank Global Rental (www.softbank-rental.jp), where you can also find out about rental costs and rental locations and make online reservations. Another option is to bring your own mobile phone and rent a SIM card from Softbank.

Otherwise, if you want to have a telephone number before arriving in Japan, consider renting a phone before leaving home. North Americans can rent one from **InTouch USA** (✆ 800/872-7626; www.intouchglobal.com) or **Roadpost** (✆ 888/290-1606; www.roadpost.com).

You can also rent a phone in Japan. If you're in Japan for only a few days and are staying in an upper-class hotel, most convenient but most expensive is to rent a mobile phone from your hotel. A check of several hotels in Tokyo turned up rental fees ranging from ¥600 to ¥1,200 per day (the more expensive the hotel, the more expensive the rental). I suggest, therefore, that you rent a phone at Narita Airport. Lots of companies maintain counters at both terminals, including NTT DoCoMo and Softbank Global Rental (see above), as well as **G-Call** (www.g-call.com/e), **Telecom Square** (www.telecom square.co.jp/en), and **PuPuRu** (www. pupuru.com/en), which have the extra convenience of easy pickup and drop-off and offer online reservations. Most rentals start at ¥525 per day, though bargains are often offered online or on-site. Charges for domes-

tic and international calls vary, but incoming calls are usually free.

For travelers staying in Japan a week or longer, **Go Mobile** (www.gomobile.co.jp) offers 1-week, 2-week, and 30-day rentals, including a limited number of free local calls. A 1-week rental costs ¥2,995 and includes 15 minutes of free local calls. Phones are shipped to an address in Japan (such as your hotel) and returned via a prepaid, pre-addressed envelope.

INTERNET/E-MAIL
Without Your Own Computer
Many hotels in Japan, especially medium-range and business hotels, have computers in their lobbies, either coin operated (usually ¥100 for 10 min.) or for free. Otherwise, cybercafes can be found in most cities, though they're often nonexistent in small towns. I've listed cybercafes for many destinations when I could find them (see individual chapters), but more may have opened by the time you travel. Ask local tourist offices for updated locations.

With Your Own Computer
With the exception of some budget hotels, virtually all hotels in Japan's major cities provide Internet access in their guest rooms (see individual hotel listings for each city). While most provide high-speed connections, more and more are going **Wi-Fi** (wireless fidelity). I'm also happy to report that more and more are also offering Internet connections for free. Otherwise, expect to pay anywhere from ¥500 to ¥1,050 on average per day. For Japan's electric requirements, see "Fast Facts."

11 TIPS ON ACCOMMODATIONS

Accommodations available in Japan range from Japanese-style inns to large Western-style hotels, in all price categories. Although you can travel throughout Japan without making reservations beforehand, it's essential to book in advance if you're traveling during peak travel seasons and is recommended at other times (see "When to Go," earlier in this chapter, for peak travel times). If you arrive in a town without reservations, most local tourist offices—generally located in or near the main train station—will find accommodations for you at no extra charge. Note that in popular resort areas, most accommodations raise their rates during peak times. Some also charge more on weekends.

A note on reservations: When making reservations at Japanese-style accommodations and small business hotels, it's usually best if the call is conducted in Japanese or by fax or e-mail if available, as written English is always easier for most Japanese to understand. First-class hotels, however, always have English-speaking staff, as do many of the Japanese inns recommended in this guide.

A note about taxes and service charges: A 5% consumption tax is included in all hotel rates, including those given in this book. Furthermore, upper-end hotels and some moderately priced hotels also add a 10% to 15% service charge to their published rates, while expensive *ryokan* will add a 10% to 20% service charge. No service charge is levied at business hotels, pensions, and *minshuku* (accommodations in a private home) for the simple reason that no services are provided. In resort areas with hot-spring spas, an *onsen* (spa) tax of ¥150 is added per night. Tokyo levies its own local hotel tax (¥100–¥200 per person per night). Unless otherwise stated, the prices given in this guide include all

consumption taxes and service charge, but not onsen or local hotel tax.

JAPANESE-STYLE INNS

Although an overnight stay in a *ryokan* (traditional Japanese inn) can be astoundingly expensive, it's worth the splurge at least once during your stay. Nothing quite conveys the simplicity and beauty—indeed the very atmosphere—of old Japan more than these inns with their gleaming polished wood, *tatami* floors, rice-paper sliding doors, and meticulously pruned gardens. Personalized service by kimono-clad hostesses and exquisitely prepared *kaiseki* meals are the trademarks of such inns, some of which are of ancient vintage. Indeed, staying in one is like taking a trip back in time.

If you want to experience a Japanese-style inn but can't afford the prices of a full-service ryokan, a number of alternatives are described below. Although they don't offer the same personalized service, beautiful setting, or memorable cuisine, they do offer the chance to sleep on a futon in a simple tatami room and, in some cases, eat Japanese meals.

RYOKAN Ryokan developed during the Edo Period, when *daimyo* (feudal lords) were required to travel to and from Edo (present-day Tokyo) every 2 years. They always traveled with a full entourage including members of their family, retainers, and servants. The best ryokan, of course, were reserved for the daimyo and members of the imperial family. Some of these exist today, passed down from generation to generation.

Traditionally, ryokan are small, only one or two stories high, contain about 10 to 30 rooms, and are made of wood with a tile roof. Most guests arrive at their ryokan around 3 or 4pm. The entrance is often through a gate and small garden; upon entering, you're met by a bowing woman in a kimono. Take off your shoes, slide on the proffered plastic slippers, and follow your hostess down the long wooden corridors until you reach the sliding door of your room. After taking off your slippers, step into your tatami room, almost void of furniture except for a low table in the middle of the room, floor cushions, an antique scroll hanging in a *tokonoma* (alcove), and a simple flower arrangement. Best of all is the view past rice-paper sliding screens of a Japanese landscaped garden with bonsai, stone lanterns, and a meandering pond filled with carp. Notice there's no bed in the room.

Almost immediately, your hostess serves you welcoming hot tea and a sweet at your low table so you can sit there for a while, recuperate from your travels, and appreciate the view, the peace, and the solitude. Next comes your hot bath, either in your own room (if you have one) or in the communal bath. Because many ryokan are clustered around onsen, many offer the additional luxury of bathing in thermal baths, including outdoor baths. (For bathing, be sure to follow the procedure outlined in "Minding Your P's & Q's" in chapter 2—soaping and rinsing *before* getting into the tub.) After bathing and soaking away all travel fatigue, aches, and pains, change into your *yukata,* a cotton kimono provided by the ryokan. You can wear your yukata throughout the ryokan, even to its restaurant (in Western-style hotels, however, never wear a yukata outside your room unless you're going to its public bath).

When you return to your room, you'll find the maid ready to serve your *kaiseki* dinner, an elaborate spread that is the highlight of a ryokan stay. It generally consists of locally grown vegetables, sashimi (raw fish), grilled or baked fish, tempura, and various regional specialties, all spread out on many tiny plates; the menu is determined by the chef. Admire how each dish is in itself a delicate piece of artwork; it all looks too wonderful to eat, but finally hunger takes over. If you want, you can order sake or beer to accompany your meal (but you'll pay extra for drinks).

After you've finished eating, your maid will return to clear away the dishes and to lay out your bed. The bed is really a futon, a kind of two-layered mattress with quilts, and is laid out on the tatami floor. The next morning, the maid will wake you, put away the futon, and serve a breakfast of fish, pickled vegetables, soup, dried seaweed, rice, and other dishes. Feeling rested, well fed, and pampered, you're then ready to pack your bags and pay your bill. Your hostess sees you off at the front gate, smiling and bowing as you set off for the rest of your travels.

Such is life at a good ryokan. Sadly, the number of upper-class ryokan diminishes each year. Unable to compete with more profitable high-rise hotels, many ryokan in Japan have closed down, especially in large cities; very few remain in such cities as Tokyo and Osaka. If you want to stay in a Japanese inn, it's best to do so in Kyoto, smaller towns like Takayama, or at a hot-spring spa.

In addition, although ideally a ryokan is an old wooden structure that once served traveling daimyo or was perhaps the home of a wealthy merchant, many today—especially those in hot-spring resort areas—are actually modern concrete affairs with as many as 100 or more rooms, with meals served in communal dining rooms. What they lack in intimacy and personal service, however, is made up for with cheaper prices and such amenities as modern bathing facilities and perhaps a bar and outdoor recreational facilities. Most guest rooms are fitted with a TV, a telephone, a safe for locking up valuables, and a cotton yukata, as well as such amenities as soap, shampoo, a razor, a toothbrush, and toothpaste.

Rates in a ryokan are always per person rather than per room and include breakfast, dinner, and often service and tax. Thus, while rates may seem high, they're actually competitively priced compared to what you'd pay for a hotel room and comparable meals in a restaurant. Although rates can vary from ¥9,000 to an astonishing ¥150,000 per person, the average cost is generally ¥12,000 to ¥20,000. Even within a single ryokan the rates can vary greatly, depending on the room you choose, the dinner courses you select, and the number of people in your room. If you're paying the highest rate, you can be certain you're getting the best room, the best view of the garden or perhaps even your own private garden, and a much more elaborate meal than lower-paying guests. All the rates for ryokan in this book are based on double occupancy; if there are more than two of you in one room, you can generally count on a slightly lower per-person rate; small children who sleep in the same bed as their parents often receive a discount as well. Although most Japanese would never dream of checking into an exclusive ryokan solo, lone travelers may be able to secure a room if it's not peak season.

Although I heartily recommend you try spending at least 1 night in a ryokan, there are a number of **disadvantages** to this style of accommodations. The most obvious problem is that you may find it uncomfortable sitting on the floor. And because the futon is put away during the day, there's no place to lie down for an afternoon nap or rest, except on the hard, tatami-covered floor. In addition, some of the older ryokan, though quaint, are bitterly cold in the winter and—though increasingly rare—may have only Japanese-style toilets (see "Toilets" in chapter 16). As for breakfast, you might find it difficult to swallow raw egg, rice, and seaweed in the morning. (I've even been served grilled grasshopper—quite crunchy.) Sometimes you can get a Western-style breakfast if you order it the night before, but more often than not the fried or scrambled eggs will arrive cold, leading you to suspect they were cooked right after you ordered them.

A ryokan is also quite rigid in its **schedule.** You're expected to arrive sometime between 3 and 5pm, take your bath, and then eat at around 6 or 7pm. Breakfast is served early, usually by 8am, and checkout is by 10am. That means you can't sleep in, and because the maid is continually coming in and out, you have a lot less privacy than you would in a hotel.

Another drawback of the ryokan is that some will not take you. They simply do not want to deal with the problems inherent in accepting a foreign guest, including the language barrier and differing customs. I've seen a number of beautiful old ryokan I'd like to include in this book, but I've been turned away at the door. Sadly, I've also lost ryokan that once accepted foreigners but now refuse to do so because of unacceptable behavior (such as climbing in the window at midnight). In any case, those recommended in the pages that follow do welcome Westerners.

You should always make a **reservation** if you want to stay in a first-class ryokan (and even in most medium-priced ones), because the chef has to shop for and prepare your meals. Ryokan staff members often do not look kindly upon unannounced strangers turning up on their doorstep (though I did this on a weekday trip to Nikko without any problems at all). You can make a reservation for a ryokan through any travel agency in Japan or by contacting a ryokan directly. You may be required to pay a deposit. For more information on ryokan in Japan, including destinations not covered in this guide, pick up the *Japan Ryokan Guide* at one of the Tourist Information Centers in Japan, which lists some 1,300 members of the **Japan Ryokan Association** (© 03/3231-5310); or go online at **www.ryokan.or.jp**.

(Tips) **Roller Bag Etiquette**

I love my roller bag, but under no circumstances should you roll a bag on tatami or on old wooden floors of Japanese inns.

Another useful resource is **Japanese Guest Houses** (www.japaneseguesthouses.com), with more than 600 member high-end and moderately priced Japanese inns.

JAPANESE INN GROUP If you want the experience of staying in a Japanese-style room but cannot afford the extravagance of a ryokan, you might consider staying in one of the participating members of the Japanese Inn Group—an organization of more than 80 Japanese-style inns and hotels throughout Japan offering inexpensive lodging and catering largely to foreigners. Although you may balk at the idea of staying at a place filled mainly with foreigners, keep in mind that some inexpensive Japanese-style inns are not accustomed to guests from abroad and may be quite reluctant to take you in. I have covered many Japanese Inn Group members in this book over the years and have found the owners for the most part to be an exceptional group of friendly people eager to offer foreigners the chance to experience life on tatami and futons. In many cases, these are good places in which to exchange information with other world travelers and are popular with both young people and families.

Although many of the group members call themselves ryokan, they are not ryokan in the true sense of the word, because they do not offer the trademark personalized service and only rarely the beautiful setting common to ryokan. However, they do offer simple tatami rooms that generally come with TVs and air conditioners; most have towels and cotton yukata. Some offer Western-style rooms as well, and/or rooms with private bathrooms. Facilities generally include a coin-operated washer and dryer, a public bath, and sometimes a computer for checking e-mail. The average cost of a 1-night stay is about ¥5,000 to ¥6,000 per person, without meals. Breakfast is usually available if you pay extra; dinner is also sometimes available.

You can view member inns at **www.japaneseinngroup.com**. Or, upon your arrival in Tokyo, head to the Tourist Information Center for the free pamphlet called *Japanese Inn Group*. Make reservations directly with the inn in which you wish to stay (most have faxes and e-mail). In some cases, you'll be asked to pay a deposit (most accept American Express, MasterCard, and Visa). Many member inns belong to the Welcome Inn Group as well (see "Finding a Hotel or Inn," below), which means you can also make reservations through one of the methods described there.

MINSHUKU Technically, a *minshuku* is inexpensive Japanese-style lodging in a private home—the Japanese version of a bed-and-breakfast. Usually located in tourist areas, rural settings, or small towns, minshuku can range from thatched farmhouses and rickety old wooden buildings to modern concrete structures. Because minshuku are family-run affairs, there's no personal service, which means you may be expected to lay out your own futon at night, stow it away in the morning, and tidy up your room. Most also do not supply a towel or *yukata,* nor do they have rooms with a private bathroom. There is, however, a public bathroom, and meals, included in the rates, are served in a communal dining room. Because minshuku cater primarily to domestic travelers, they're often excellent places to meet Japanese. Keep in mind, however, that many minshuku owners have day jobs, so it's important for guests to be punctual for meals and checkout.

Officially, what differentiates a ryokan from a minshuku is the level of service and corresponding price, but the differences are sometimes very slight. I've stayed in cheap ryokan providing almost no service and in minshuku too large and modern to be considered private homes. The average per-person cost for 1 night in a minshuku, including two meals, is generally ¥7,000 to ¥9,000 with two meals.

Reservations for minshuku should be made directly with the establishment. Or, contact the **Minshuku Network Japan** (© **0120/07-6556;** www.minshuku.jp) for a reservation in one of its 3,000 members throughout Japan.

KOKUMIN SHUKUSHA & QKAMURA

A *kokumin shukusha* can be translated as a people's lodge—public lodging found primarily in or around national parks and resort and vacation areas. Established by the government (though some are privately managed), there are more than 300 of these facilities throughout Japan. Catering largely to Japanese school groups and families, they offer basic, Japanese-style rooms at an average daily rate of about ¥8,000 to ¥9,000 per person, including two meals. Because they're usually full during the summer, peak seasons, holidays, and weekends, reservations are a must and can be made directly at the facility or through a travel agency; many are also in the *Directory of Welcome Inns* (see "Finding a Hotel or Inn," below). There are also 36 National Park Resort Villages (nicknamed Qkamura; www.qkamura. or.jp) located exclusively in national parks and popular with families. The drawback for many of these lodges is that because they're often located in national parks and scenic spots, the best way to reach them is by car.

SHUKUBO These are lodgings in a Buddhist temple, similar to inexpensive ryokan, except they're attached to temples and serve vegetarian food. There's usually an early morning service at 6am, which you're welcome—in some *shukubo,* required—to join. Probably the best place to experience life in a temple is at Mount Koya (see chapter 10). Prices at shukubo generally range from about ¥7,000 to ¥15,000 per person, including two meals.

WESTERN-STYLE ACCOMMODATIONS

Western-style lodgings range from luxurious first-class hotels to inexpensive ones catering primarily to Japanese businessmen.

When selecting and reserving your hotel room, contact the hotel directly to inquire about rates, even if a North American toll-free 800 number is provided; sometimes there are special deals, such as weekend or honeymoon packages, that central reservation desks are not aware of. Special rates are also often available only through the hotel's website. In any case, always ask what kinds of rooms are available. Almost all hotels in Japan offer a wide range of rooms at various prices, with room size the overwhelming factor in pricing. Other aspects that often have a bearing on rates include bed size, floor height (higher floors are more expensive), and in-room amenities. Rooms with views—whether of the sea or a castle—are also generally more expensive. In Japan, a **twin room** refers to a room with twin beds, and a **double room** refers to one with a double (or larger) bed; most hotels charge more for a twin room, but others charge more for doubles. Because Japanese couples generally prefer twin beds, doubles are often in short supply, especially in business hotels. A **Hollywood twin** means two twin beds pushed together side by side.

Note: For the sake of convenience, the "double" rates for hotels listed in this book refer to two people in one room and include both twin and double beds.

Some of the upper-priced hotels also offer executive floors, which are generally on the highest floors and may offer such perks as a private lounge with separate check-in, more in-room amenities, complimentary breakfast and evening cocktails, extended checkout time, and privileges that can include free use of the health club. At just a few thousand yen more than regular rates, these can be quite economical.

When making your reservation, therefore, inquire about the differences in room categories and rates and what they entail. Once you decide on the type of room you want, ask for the best in that category. For example, if you want a standard room, and deluxe rooms start on the 14th floor, ask for a standard on the 13th floor, which may give better views than standards on the 10th. In addition, be specific about the kind of room you want, whether it's a nonsmoking room, a room with a view of Mount Fuji, or a room with Internet connections for your laptop.

Be sure to give your approximate time of arrival, especially if it's after 6pm, when they might give your room away. Check-in ranges from about 1 or 2pm in first-class hotels to 3 or 4pm for business hotels. Checkout is generally about 10am for business hotels and 11am or noon for upper-range hotels. In any case, it's perfectly acceptable to leave luggage with the front desk or bell captain if you arrive early or want to sightsee after checking out.

HOTELS Both first-class and midpriced hotels in Japan are known for excellent service and cleanliness. The first-class hotels in the larger cities can compete with the best hotels in the world and offer a **wide range of services,** from health clubs and

aesthetic spas with massage services to business centers and top-class restaurants and shopping arcades. Unfortunately, health clubs and swimming pools usually cost extra—anywhere from ¥1,050 to an outrageous ¥5,000 per single use. In addition, outdoor pools are generally open only in July and August. Rooms come with such **standard features** as a minibar, bilingual cable TV with pay movies and English-language channels like CNN or BBC, high-speed Internet or wireless connections (usually at a charge at expensive hotels but often free in less expensive ones), clock, a radio, *yukata,* a hot-water pot and tea (and occasionally coffee, though you usually have to pay extra for it), a hair dryer, and a private bathroom with a tub/shower combination. (Because Japanese are used to soaping down and rinsing off before bathing, it would be rare to find tubs without showers; similarly, showers without tubs are practically nonexistent in this nation of bathers.) Virtually all hotels nowadays also have "Washlet" toilets, which are combination toilets and spray bidets with a controllable range of speeds and temperatures. Because they're accustomed to foreigners, most hotels in this category employ an English-speaking staff and offer nonsmoking floors or rooms. Services provided include room service, same-day laundry and dry cleaning, and English-language newspapers such as the *Japan Times* delivered free to your room. Note that in medium-range hotels, same-day laundry service is not available Sundays and holidays and you must turn in your laundry by 10am to receive it by 5pm that day.

The most expensive hotels in Japan are in Tokyo and Osaka, where you'll pay at least ¥32,000 for a double or twin room in a first-class hotel and ¥16,000 to ¥32,000 for the same in a midpriced hotel. Outside the major cities, rooms for two people

(Value) Tips for Saving on Your Hotel Room

Although Japanese hotels traditionally remained pretty loyal to their published **rack rates,** which are always available at the front desk, the recession has opened possibilities for bargains.

- **Always ask politely whether there's a room less expensive than the first one offered.** Because there are usually many categories, ask what the difference is, say, between a standard twin and a superior twin. If there are two of you, ask whether a double or a twin room is cheaper. Find out the hotel's policy on children—do children stay free in the room or is there a special rate?
- **Contact the hotel directly.** In addition to calling a hotel's toll-free number, call the hotel directly to see where you can get the best deal.
- **Check the Internet.** Check to see whether discounts or special promotions are offered; some hotels offer discounts exclusively through the Internet. For websites of hotel chains, see "Airline & Hotel Websites" in chapter 16.
- **Ask about promotions and special plans.** Hotels frequently offer special "plans," including "Spring Plans," "Ladies' Plans," and even "Shopping Plans" that provide cheaper rates and services.
- **Remember the law of supply and demand.** Resort hotels are more crowded and therefore more expensive on weekends and during peak travel periods such as Golden Week. Discounts, therefore, are often available for midweek and off-season stays. Business hotels, on the other hand, are sometimes cheaper on weekends.
- **Ask about hotel membership plans.** Some chain business hotels offer hotel memberships with discounts on meals and free stays after a certain number of nights. Others, such as the New Otani, Okura, and the Imperial in Tokyo, allow free use of the hotel swimming pool simply if you become a member at no extra charge. Ask the concierge or front desk.

range from about ¥20,000 to ¥30,000 for first-class hotels and ¥10,000 to ¥20,000 for midpriced hotels.

Although some internationally known high-end chains have a presence in Japan, including Four Seasons, Hyatt, and Ritz-Carlton, Japanese chains naturally dominate, including New Otani, Okura, Nikko, and JAL Hotels (associated with Japan Airlines), Prince, and the Japan Railways Group, which provides discounts to those with a Japan Rail Pass.

In addition to the recommendations in this guide, you can also check out the 400-

some members of the Japan Hotel Association listed in the brochure *Hotels in Japan* available from the Tourist Information Centers in Japan or online at **www.j-hotel. or.jp**. For websites of individual hotel chains, see "Airline & Hotel Websites" in chapter 16.

BUSINESS HOTELS Catering traditionally to traveling Japanese businessmen, a "business hotel" is a no-frills establishment with tiny, sparsely furnished rooms, most of them singles but usually with some twin and maybe double rooms also available. Primarily just places to crash for the night, these rooms usually have everything you need, but in miniature form—minuscule bathroom, tiny bathtub/shower, small bed (or beds), empty fridge, and barely enough space to unpack your bags. If you're a large person, you may have trouble sleeping in a place like this. There are no bellhops, no room service, and sometimes not even a lobby or coffee shop, although usually there are vending machines selling beer, soda, cigarettes, and snacks. Most business hotels have non-smoking rooms, but a few still do not. The advantages of staying in business hotels are price—starting as low as ¥6,000 or ¥7,000 for a single—and location—usually near major train and subway stations. Check-in is usually not until 3 or 4pm, and check-out is usually at 10am; you can leave your bags at the front desk.

As for business-hotel chains, I'm partial to the Tokyo Inn chain, which boasts more than 160 locations around Japan and always employs female managers. They offer minuscule rooms outfitted with about everything you need, including free Internet access, and have raised the bar in business-hotel amenities by adding lobby computers with free Internet access, free domestic calls from lobby phones (but limited to 3 min.), usually free Japanese breakfast, and sometimes free nightly in-room movies (often in English). Other chains to look for are Tokyu Hotels, including its budget Tokyu Inns, all with specially designed Ladies Rooms with female-oriented toiletries and amenities, Washington Hotels, the Sunroute Hotel Chain, and newcomer Super Hotel with the lowest rates around.

PENSIONS Pensions are like *minshuku,* except that accommodations are Western-style with beds instead of futons, and the two meals served are usually Western. Often managed by a young couple or a young staff, they cater to young Japanese

and are most often located in ski resorts and in the countryside, sometimes making access a problem. Averaging 10 guest rooms, many seem especially geared to young Japanese women and are thus done up in rather feminine-looking decor with lots of pinks and flower prints. In recent years, *Wa-fu* Pensions (with Japanese-style rooms) have also made an appearance. The average cost is ¥8,000 per person per night, including two meals.

YOUTH HOSTELS There are some 350 youth hostels in Japan, most of them privately run and operating in locations ranging from temples to concrete blocks. There's no age limit (though children 3 and younger may not be accepted), and although most of them require a youth hostel membership card, they let foreigners stay without one at no extra charge or for ¥600 extra per night (after 6 nights you automatically become a YH member). Youth hostels are reasonable, averaging about ¥3,000 per day without meals, and can be reserved in advance. However, there are usually quite a few restrictions, such as a 9 or 10pm curfew, a lights-out policy shortly thereafter, an early breakfast time, and closed times through the day, generally from about 10am to 3pm. In addition, rooms generally have many bunk beds or futons, affording little privacy. On the other hand, they're certainly the cheapest accommodations in Japan.

Because youth hostels are often inconveniently located, I have included only one, in Tokyo, but if you plan on staying almost exclusively in hostels, pick up a pamphlet called "Youth Hostel Map of Japan," available at the **Tourist Information Centers** in Japan, or check www.jyh.or.jp. For youth hostel membership in the U.S., contact **Hostelling International USA** (© 301/495-1240; www.hiusa.org).

CAPSULE HOTELS Capsule hotels, which became popular in the early 1980s, are used primarily by Japanese businessmen who have spent an evening out drinking and missed the last train home—costing about ¥4,000 per person, a capsule hotel is sometimes cheaper than a taxi to the suburbs. Units are small—no larger than a coffin and consisting of a bed, a private TV, an alarm clock, and a radio—and are usually stacked two deep in rows down a corridor; the only thing separating you from your probably inebriated neighbor is a curtain. A cotton kimono and a locker are provided, and bathrooms and toilets are communal. Most capsule hotels do not accept women, but those that do have separate facilities.

LOVE HOTELS Finally, a word about Japan's so-called "love hotels." Usually found close to entertainment districts and along major highways, such hotels do not provide sexual services themselves; rather, they offer rooms for rent by the hour to couples. You'll know that you've wandered into a love-hotel district when you notice hourly rates posted near the front door, though gaudy structures shaped like ocean liners or castles are also a dead giveaway. Because many of them have reasonable overnight rates as well, I have friends who, finding themselves out too late and too far from home, have checked into love hotels, solo.

FINDING A HOTEL OR INN

If all my recommendations for a certain city are fully booked, or if you're traveling to destinations not covered in this guide, there are several ways to find alternative accommodations.

SURFING FOR HOTELS In addition to well-known booking sites like Travelocity, Expedia, Orbitz, and Hotels.com, you should also check Asia-specific sites like Asiatravel.com, Asia-hotels.com, and agoda. com. Of course, you'll also want to check all the websites mentioned earlier, such as

www.j-hotel.or.jp for members of the Japan Hotel Association, as well as the websites of Japanese and foreign hotel chains listed in chapter 16.

For budget accommodations, go to hostelworld.com, as well **Rakuten Travel** (𝄞 **050/2017-8977;** www.travel.rakuten. co.jp/en), Japan's largest reservations company for budget and moderately priced accommodations. At the top of my list for budget accommodations are also members of **Welcome Inns** (www.itcj.jp), operated in cooperation with the Japan National Tourism Organization (JNTO) and International Tourism Center of Japan (ITCJ). Some 700 modestly priced accommodations, including business hotels and Japanese-style inns, are members of Welcome Inn, with rates no more than ¥8,000 for a single and ¥13,000 for a double. There's no fee for the service, but you must sign up for membership and guarantee your reservation with a credit card. Applications should be made about 2 weeks before desired check-in dates.

In any case, it's always a good idea to **get a confirmation number** and **make a printout** of any online booking transaction.

FINDING A ROOM WHEN YOU'RE IN JAPAN In addition to booking Welcome Inns via the Internet (see above), you can also book a room by visiting one of the three Tourist Information Centers in Japan—at Narita Airport (in the arrivals lobbies of terminals 1 and 2; see p. 109); near Yurakucho Station in the heart of Tokyo (p. 111); and at Osaka's Kansai International Airport (p. 394), as well as Kyoto Tourist Information in Kyoto Station (p. 293). Reservations are accepted at the Narita TIC daily from 8am to 7:30pm; at the Tokyo TIC daily from 9 to 11:30am and 1 to 4:30pm; in Kyoto daily from 10am to 12:30pm and 2 to 5:30pm (closed the 2nd and 4th Tues of every month); and at the Kansai TIC daily

8:30am to 8pm April to October and 9am to 8:30pm November to March.

High-end hotels and *ryokan* can be booked through travel agencies in Japan, including the ubiquitous Japan Travel Bureau.

Finally, if you arrive at your destination without accommodations, most major train stations contain a tourist information office or a hotel and ryokan reservation counter where you can book a room. Although policies may differ from office to office, you generally don't have to pay a fee for their services, but you usually do have to pay a percentage of your overnight charge as a deposit. The disadvantage is that you don't see the locale beforehand, and if there's space left at a ryokan even in peak tourist season, there may be a reason for it. Although these offices can be a real lifesaver in a pinch and in most cases may be able to recommend quite reasonable and pleasant places in which to stay, it pays to plan in advance.

Suggested Japan Itineraries

Japan, with its rich culture and varied geography, has much to offer the curious visitor, not only in and around the major cities but in many of the outlying regions as well. If you want to see *everything*, you should plan on spending at least a year in Japan. More likely, your time will be limited to a week or two, so you'll have to be selective; this section will help you decide on an itinerary.

If you're in Japan for several weeks, you can fashion a personalized tour by combining several of these suggested itineraries, along with recommended routes provided in the chapters for the Japan Alps (chapter 8) and Kyushu (chapter 12). But regardless of what itinerary you plan, I am adamant about one thing: *Kyoto is a must.* It served as the nation's capital for more than 1,000 years and has more temples, shrines, and historic sights than any other Japanese city.

---

1 THE REGIONS IN BRIEF

Separated from mainland China and Korea by the Sea of Japan, the nation of Japan stretches in an arc about 2,900km (1,800 miles) long from northeast to southwest, yet it is only 403km (250 miles) wide at its broadest point. Japan consists primarily of four main islands—**Honshu, Hokkaido, Shikoku,** and **Kyushu.** Surrounding these large islands are more than 6,000 smaller, mostly uninhabited islands and islets. Far to the southwest are the **Okinawan islands,** perhaps best known for the fierce fighting that took place there during World War II and for their continued (and controversial) use as an American military base. If you were to superimpose Japan's four main islands onto a map of the United States, they would stretch all the way from Boston to Atlanta, which should give you an idea of the diversity of Japan's climate, flora, and scenery—Hokkaido in the north is subarctic, while Kyushu is subtropical. Honshu, Japan's most populous island and home to Tokyo, Kyoto, and Osaka, is connected to the other three islands by tunnel or bridge, which means you can travel to all four islands by train.

As much as 70% of Japan consists of **mountains.** They are found on all four main islands and most are volcanic in origin. Altogether, there are some 265 **volcanoes,** more than 30 of them still considered active. Mount Fuji (on Honshu), dormant since 1707, is Japan's highest and most famous volcano, while Mount Aso (on Kyushu) boasts the largest caldera in the world. Because of its volcanic origins, earthquakes have plagued Japan throughout its history. In the 20th century, the two most destructive earthquakes were the 1923 Great Kanto Earthquake, which killed more than 100,000 people in the Tokyo area, and the 1995 Great Hanshin Earthquake, which claimed more than 6,000 lives in Kobe.

Japan is divided into 47 regional divisions, or **prefectures.** Each prefecture has its own prefectural capital and is comparable to the U.S. state or the British county, though

prefectures vary greatly in size (greater Tokyo is one prefecture; all of Hokkaido is another). Japan's total landmass is slightly smaller than California in area, yet Japan has 41% the population of the United States. And because three-fourths of Japan is mountainous and therefore uninhabitable, its people are concentrated primarily in only 10% of the country's landmass, with the rest of the area devoted to agriculture. In other words, imagine 41% of the U.S. population living in California—primarily in San Diego County—and you get an idea of how crowded Japan is. For this island nation—isolated physically from the rest of the world, struck repeatedly through the centuries by earthquakes, fires, and typhoons, and possessed of only limited space for harmonious living—geography and topography have played major roles both in determining its development and in shaping its culture, customs, and arts.

HONSHU

Of the four main islands, Honshu is the largest and most populated. Because it's also the most important historically and culturally, it's where most visitors spend the bulk of their time.

Kanto District

Located in east-central Honshu and comprising metropolitan **Tokyo** and six prefectures, this district is characterized by the Kanto Plain, the largest flatland in Japan. Although development of the district didn't begin in earnest until the establishment of the shogunate government in Edo (present-day Tokyo) in 1603, Tokyo and surrounding giants such as **Yokohama** make this the most densely populated region in Japan.

Kansai District

Also called the Kinki District and encompassing seven prefectures, this is Japan's most historic region. **Nara** and **Kyoto**—two of Japan's ancient capitals—are here, as are two of Japan's most important port cities, **Kobe** and **Osaka.** Since the 1994 opening of Kansai International Airport outside Osaka, many foreign visitors opt to bypass Tokyo altogether in favor of Kansai's many historic spots, including **Mount Koya** with its many temples, **Himeji** with what I consider to be Japan's most beautiful castle, **Ise-Shima National Park** with Japan's most revered Shinto shrine, Nara with its Great Buddha and temples, and, of course, Kyoto, the former capital for more than 1,000 years with so many temples, imperial villas, and gardens that it ranks as Japan's foremost tourist destination.

Chubu District

The Chubu District lies between Tokyo and Kyoto and straddles central Honshu from the Pacific Ocean to the Japan Sea, encompassing nine prefectures. **Nagoya,** Japan's fourth-largest city and home to an international airport nicknamed Centrair, is Chubu's most important city and a gateway to its other destinations. The district features mountain ranges (including the **Japan Alps,** see below), volcanoes (including **Mount Fuji**), large rivers, and coastal regions on both sides of the island. It's popular for skiing and hiking, for quaint mountain villages such as **Takayama** and **Shirakawa-go,** and for tourist attractions that include the open-air Museum Meiji Mura (near Nagoya), the castle in **Matsumoto,** and Kenrokuen Garden in **Kanazawa,** considered one of Japan's finest.

The Japan Alps

Spreading over central Honshu in the Chubu District, the Japan Alps are among Japan's most famous mountain ranges, especially since hosting the 1998 XVIII Winter Olympics in **Nagano. Chubu-Sangaku National Park** (also called the Japan Alps National Park) contains some of the nation's most beautiful mountain scenery and the country's best skiing, while destinations like **Takayama** and **Shirakawa-go** boast quaint historic districts and thatched-roof farmhouses.

Ise-Shima

Shima Peninsula, in Mie Prefecture, juts into the Seto Inland Sea and is famous for **Ise-Shima National Park,** noted for its coastal scenery and Ise Jingu Shrines. **Toba,** birthplace of the cultured pearl, is popular for its Mikimoto Pearl Island and the Toba Aquarium. Shima Peninsula also boasts two theme parks, one fashioned after Japan's Warring States Era and the other an amusement park with a Spanish theme.

Chugoku District

Honshu's western district has five prefectures and is divided by the Chugoku Mountain Range. Industrial giants such as **Hiroshima** and **Okayama** lead as the major cities, drawing tourists with reconstructed castles, Korakuen Garden, and the sobering Peace Memorial Park in Hiroshima, dedicated to victims of the world's first atomic bomb. **Kurashiki** is a must for its photogenic, historic warehouse district, while **Miyajima,** part of the Seto-Naikai (Inland Sea) National Park, is considered one of Japan's most beautiful islands.

Tohoku District

Northeastern Honshu, with **Sendai** as its regional center, encompasses six prefectures. Known as the Tohoku District, it isn't nearly as developed as the central and southern districts of Honshu, due in large part to its rugged, mountainous terrain and harsh climate. **Matsushima,** about halfway up the coast between Tokyo and the northern tip of Honshu, is the district's major tourist destination; with its pine-clad islets dotting the bay, it's considered one of Japan's most scenic spots. **Kakunodate,** located inland, is a former castle town offering preserved samurai houses and, during cherry-blossom season, a stunning show of pink flowers to travelers willing to take a road less traveled. **Towada-Hachimantai National Park,** which extends over three prefectures, boasts scenic lakes, rustic hot-spring spas, hiking, and skiing.

HOKKAIDO

Japan's second-largest island, Hokkaido lies to the north of Honshu and is regarded as the country's last frontier with its wide-open pastures, evergreen forests, mountains, gorges, crystal-clear lakes, and wildlife, much of it preserved in national parks. Originally occupied by the indigenous Ainu, it was colonized by Japanese settlers mostly after the Meiji Restoration in 1868. Today it's home to 5.7 million people, 1.9 million of whom live in **Sapporo.** With a landmass that accounts for 22% of Japan's total area, Hokkaido has the nation's lowest population density: about 4.5% of the total population. That, together with the island's cold, severe winters but mild summers, and its unspoiled natural beauty make this island a nature lover's paradise.

SHIKOKU

Shikoku, the smallest of the four main islands, is off the beaten path for many foreign visitors. It's famous for its 88 Buddhist temples founded by one of Japan's most interesting historical figures, the Buddhist priest Kukai, known posthumously as Kobo Daishi. Other major attractions are Ritsurin Park in **Takamatsu,** Matsuyama Castle in **Matsuyama,** and **Dogo Spa,** one of Japan's oldest hot-spring spas. For active travelers, the

Shimanami Kaido route offers 70 scenic km (43 miles) of dedicated biking trails that connect Shikoku with Hiroshima Prefecture via six islands and a series of bridges in the Seto Inland Sea.

KYUSHU

The southernmost of the four main islands, Kyushu boasts a mild subtropical climate, active volcanoes, and hot-spring spas. Because it's the closest major island to Korea and China, Kyushu served as a gateway to the continental mainland throughout much of Japan's history, later becoming the springboard for both traders and Christian missionaries from the West. **Fukuoka,** Kyushu's largest city, serves as the rail gateway from Honshu, dispersing travelers to hot springs in **Beppu, Unzen,** and **Ibusuki** and to such major attractions as Kumamoto Castle in **Kumamoto** and Sengan-en Garden in **Kagoshima.** **Nagasaki,** victim of the world's second atomic bomb, is one of Japan's most cosmopolitan cities.

OKINAWA

Okinawa is comprised of 160 islands stretching 400km (248 miles) north to south and 1,000km (620 miles) east to west. Part of the Ryukyu Island chain, Okinawa developed its own languages, culture, cuisine, and architecture under the Ryukyu Kingdom, which traded extensively with both Japan and China before being annexed to Japan after the 1868 Meiji Restoration. **Okinawa Island,** the largest Ryukyu island, is home to **Naha** (Okinawa Prefecture's capital), large U.S. military bases, war memorials, and natural attractions, including white sandy beaches and coral reefs popular with divers and snorkelers. Other popular destinations include the laid-back, mostly rural **Kume Island** and **Iriomote Island,** 80% of it protected in state and national parks and boasting dense forests, mangroves, and pristine beaches.

2 JAPAN IN 1 WEEK

This trip takes you to Japan's highlights, from fast-paced Tokyo to the quiet temples of Kyoto, along with a couple of other worthwhile destinations. It's designed for first-timers, so if you've already been to Japan and seen all the must-sees, refer to the other itineraries to create your own 1-week itinerary.

Day ❶: Arrive in Tokyo

After your arrival at Narita Airport, head to your Tokyo hotel (about a 2-hr. trip). Recuperate from your flight, settle in, and get a feel for the city, take a walk through a nearby neighborhood and top off the day with a meal in a traditional restaurant. Stay up as late as you can to adjust to the new time zone.

Day ❷: Exploring Tokyo

Because of the difference in time zones, you'll probably be wide awake in the wee hours of the morning, so get up and head for **Tsukiji Fish Market.** After a breakfast of fresh sushi, head to **Hama Rikyu,** one of Tokyo's oldest Japanese gardens (open at 9am), from which you can board a ferry for a cruise up the Sumida River to **Asakusa,** where you can visit **Sensoji Temple** and shop for souvenirs along **Nakamise Dori.** Afterward, see the **Tokyo National Museum,** the world's finest repository of Japanese art and crafts. Toward evening, head to Ginza for a stroll through a department store, and then try to attend a *kabuki* play. See chapter 6.

Day ❸: More of Tokyo

Visit the **Edo-Tokyo Museum** for a colorful portrayal of the city's tumultuous history, followed by a stroll through **Akihabara,** with store after store offering the latest computers, cellphones, cameras, and more. Next, go to Harajuku to see **Meiji Shrine,** Tokyo's most popular shrine, followed by shopping at **Oriental Bazaar,** great for Japanese souvenirs. End the day with eye-popping views from the 45th-floor observatory in Shinjuku's **Tokyo Metropolitan Government Office,** followed by a stroll through Japan's most

notorious and craziest nightlife district, **Kabuki-cho.** See chapter 6.

Day ❹: Hakone ★★★

Take an early train to Hakone Yumoto, gateway to the wonderful **Fuji-Hakone-Izu National Park** (if possible, leave your luggage at Odawara or Hakone Yumoto Station and travel overnight only with a small bag). Here you can travel through some of Japan's most scenic countryside via a circuitous route that includes a three-car streetcar, a cable car, ropeway, and a boat, while seeing such sights as the wonderful **Hakone Open-Air Museum** and, if you're lucky, the elusive Mount Fuji. Be sure to schedule some time for a dip in a hot-spring bath, and spend the night in the **Fujiya Hotel,** one of my favorites in all of Japan, or in a Japanese inn. See chapter 7.

Day ❺: Hakone to Kyoto

Complete your trip through Hakone, returning to pick up your luggage and then transferring in Odawara for the 3-hour Shinkansen bullet train to **Kyoto.** End the day with a stroll through Kyoto's central shopping area, topped with a stroll through the **Pontocho nightlife area.** Spend the night in one of Kyoto's many Japanese-style inns. See chapter 9.

Days ❻ & ❼: Exploring Kyoto ★★★

Start Day 6 with a self-guided walk through eastern Kyoto, seeing **Sanjusan-gendo Hall** with its 1,001 wooden statues, **Kiyomizu Temple,** and **Heian Shrine** with its garden, followed by shopping at the **Kyoto Handicraft Center.**

On Day 7, visit Kyoto's other main attractions—**Nijo Castle,** former home of the shogun; **Kyoto Imperial Palace; Ryoanji Temple** with its famous Zen rock garden; and the **Golden Pavilion.** In the evening, head for **Gion,** Japan's most famous geisha quarters, followed by an evening performance at **Gion Corner** with its cultural demonstrations. See chapter 9.

3 JAPAN IN 2 WEEKS

This is something of a whirlwind trip, but it allows you to take in some of the best that Honshu has to offer. If you have 1 or 2 extra days, you might wish to devote more time to Kyoto or head over to Kyushu (see chapter 12).

Days ❶, ❷ & ❸: Tokyo

Hit Tokyo's highlights as outlined above in "Japan in 1 Week."

Day ❹: Nikko ★★★

An excellent choice for a day trip is **Nikko,** famous for its sumptuous mausoleum of Tokugawa Ieyasu, Japan's most famous shogun, set in a forest of majestic cedars. See chapter 7.

Day ❺: Takayama & the Japan Alps ★★★

Early in the morning, take the Shinkansen to Nagoya (about 2 hr.) and then a 3-hour train ride to **Takayama** in the Japan Alps (if you don't have a rail pass, there are also direct buses from Tokyo's Shinjuku Station). Explore the picturesque, narrow streets of this old castle town and its many interesting museums and merchants' homes. Since Takayama has more traditional Japanese inns than hotels, this is the perfect place to experience *tatami* living,

with accommodations available at various price ranges. See chapter 8.

Day ❻: Exploring Takayama

Start your day with a stroll through the **Miyagawa Morning Market** on the bank of a river. Of the many small museums and attractions in Takayama, must-sees include the **Hida Folk Village** with its rural architecture, old **merchant homes** open to the public, and the **Hirata Folk Art Museum** filled with items used in daily life during the Edo Period (1603–1867). Also not to be missed is the **Historical Government House,** the only regional administrative building from the shogun era still in existence. See chapter 8.

Day ❼: Overnight in Shirakawa-go

Take a 1-hour bus ride to Shirakawa-go, where you'll find the village of **Ogimachi,** a UNESCO World Cultural and Natural Heritage Site with thatch-roofed houses. Several farmhouses are open to the public

WEEK 1
- **1-3** Tokyo
- **4** Nikko
- **5** Takayama & the Japan Alps
- **6** Exploring Takayama
- **7** Overnight in Shirakawa-go

WEEK 2
- **8-9** Kanazawa
- **10** Mount Koya
- **11-13** Kyoto
- **14** Hiroshima

SUGGESTED JAPAN ITINERARIES

4

JAPAN IN 2 WEEKS

as museums, but your reason for coming here is to actually spend the night in one. See chapter 8.

Days ⓼ & ⓽: Kanazawa ★★

Take the bus 1¼ hours (available only mid-Mar to Nov) or return to Takayama for the train onward to **Kanazawa,** famous for its artisans and crafts. It also boasts one of my favorite gardens in Japan, **Kenrokuen,** several fine art museums, well-preserved former geisha and samurai districts, and Myoryuji Temple (known as the Ninja Temple). See chapter 10.

Day ⓾: Mount Koya ★★★

Take an early morning train to Osaka, transferring there for a train and cable car

to **Mount Koya.** Japan's most sacred religious site, Mount Koya is achingly beautiful with more than 115 Buddhist temples spread through the forests. Be sure to take both a day and a nighttime stroll past towering cypress trees and countless tombs and memorial tablets to **Okunoin,** the burial ground of Kobo Daishi, one of Japan's most revered Buddhist priests. Spend the night in a temple, dining on vegetarian food. See chapter 10.

Days ⓫, ⓬ & ⓭: Kyoto ★★★

After a vegetarian breakfast and perhaps an early morning Buddhist service, return to Osaka and take the train to Kyoto, where you'll spend the next few days as outlined above in "Japan in 1 Week." If time permits, include an excursion to **Nara,** an ancient capital even older than Kyoto. Most of Nara's historic buildings and temples, including **Todaiji Temple** with its **Great Buddha,** are enclosed within an expansive park that is also home to free-roaming deer. For more sightseeing ideas, see chapter 9.

Day ⓮: Hiroshima ★★

Take a bullet train bound for Hiroshima. En route, make a stopover in **Himeji** to see **Himeji Castle,** easily the most impressive castle in Japan. In Hiroshima, you'll want to head to **Peace Memorial Park** with its sobering memorials and museum that does an impressive job of detailing events surrounding the explosion of the atomic bomb. See chapter 10.

4 JAPAN FOR FAMILIES

There is no end to family entertainment in Japan. To keep your children's interest and preserve your sanity, this itinerary includes temples, shrines, museums, and castles for culture and a little education, along with a healthy dose of Japanese pop culture, from theme parks to sophisticated game arcades. Of course, you'll want to tailor your itinerary to fit your children's ages and interests; just be sure to schedule a lot of downtime so you don't burn out on sensory overload. This tour has you arrive in Tokyo and depart from Osaka.

Days ❶, ❷ & ❸: Exploring Tokyo

Don't plan anything strenuous the first day, but do walk around to absorb your new environment and to help adjust your body clocks. To help get your bearings and introduce your kids to Tokyo's magnitude, head for Shinjuku's 45th-floor **observatory** in the Tokyo Metropolitan Government Office for eye-popping views. Then take the Yamanote Line directly to popular Ueno Park, where you'll want to visit the **National Museum of Nature and Science** with its dinosaurs, Japanese mummy, and hands-on discovery room, followed, perhaps, with a stroll through **Ueno Zoo.**

The next day it's a tossup between the **Edo-Tokyo Museum,** where older kids can learn about Tokyo's tumultuous history, and the smaller **Fukagawa Edo Museum,** a charming re-creation of a 19th-century neighborhood that appeals especially to young children. **Harajuku,** with its teen fashions, Sunday street scene, and hordes of teeny-boppers is a must for young adults, while little ones may be happier at the **National Children's Castle,** a huge complex with everything from music and art rooms to a rooftop playground. See chapter 6.

Day ❹: Nakasendo Highway ★★

Take the bullet train 2 hours to Nagoya and change there for a train to Nakatsugawa, where you'll board a bus for the short ride to Magome. This is the start of the old **Nakasendo Highway,** once traversed by feudal lords and samurai. After a 3-hour hike through woods along a rushing river, you'll find yourself in the quaint village of **Tsumago,** where you'll sleep in a traditional inn. My 14-year-old son declared this hike the highlight of his Japan trip. See chapter 8.

Days ❺, ❻ & ❼: Exploring Kyoto ★★★

In Kyoto you'll want to limit yourselves to only the highlights: **Kiyomizu Temple** is one of Kyoto's most famous temples, with plenty of food stalls and activities to keep little ones interested (be sure to have them

- **1-3** Exploring Tokyo
- **4** Nakasendo Highway
- **5-7** Exploring Kyoto
- **8** Nara
- **9-10** Hiroshima
- **11-12** Beppu
- **13-14** Osaka

RUSSIA

HOKKAIDO

NORTH KOREA

SOUTH KOREA

Sea of Japan

HONSHU

PACIFIC OCEAN

Korea Strait

Kyoto
Hiroshima
Kokura
Beppu
SHIKOKU
Osaka
Nara
Tokyo

KYUSHU

0   200 mi
0   200 km

walk the distance between the two stones at Jishu Shrine). **Nijo Castle** is a painless introduction to the world of the shogun. And be sure the darlings walk down **Nishiki-Koji Dori** for an up-close look at the octopus, fish, and everything else Japanese eat. But probably the biggest hit with young children is **Toei Kyoto Studio Park/Movie Land,** an actual working studio for Edo-Era film productions, along with a ninja show, haunted house, and other attractions. Teenagers may also want to take in the **Kyoto International Manga Museum,** the largest *manga* museum in the world. See chapter 9.

Day **8**: Nara ★★

Although your children may not care that **Nara** is even older than Kyoto and served as the nation's capital for 74 years, they'll be intrigued by **Nara Park,** where deer (considered divine messengers) roam free. They might also be impressed by the **Great Buddha,** Japan's largest bronze Buddha. See if they can crawl through a tiny passageway behind the Buddha—and supposedly attain enlightenment. Back in Kyoto, good evening diversions for older kids include a stroll through **Gion,** where they might catch a glimpse of a geisha, and **Gion Corner,** where they'll be exposed to traditional cultural pursuits, including *Bunraku* (Japanese puppetry). See chapter 9.

Days ❾ & ❿: Hiroshima ★★

Take a bullet train bound for Hiroshima. En route, make a stopover in **Himeji** to see **Himeji Castle,** easily the most impressive castle in Japan. In Hiroshima, if you have teenagers, they're old enough for **Peace Memorial Park,** where they'll learn about the horrors of war, particularly the devastation caused by an atomic bomb (pictures are too graphic for younger children). If time permits, **Miyajima** is also a good destination, not only for the ferry ride and the free-roaming deer but also for the trails through the woods, its swimming beaches, and cable car. See chapter 10.

Days ⓫ & ⓬: Beppu ★★

If you can stand another theme park, **Space World,** a few minutes' walk from Kokura Station, offers diversions for kids of all ages with the usual roller coasters and amusement rides based on space travel.

From Kokura Station, it's another 1½-hour train ride to **Beppu,** the king of hot-spring resorts in Kyushu. There's probably no child who wouldn't be fascinated by the **Hells,** a series of thermal wonders ranging from red, bubbling waters to hot springs that house crocodiles (you might not be impressed, but your kids will be). They'll also like the wild monkey refuge on Mount **Takasaki** and the nearby **Umitamago** aquarium. But the highlight for everyone will undoubtedly be **Aqua-Beat,** an indoor water park. Your kids will like the splash rides and wave pool; you'll like unwinding in its outdoor hot spring. See chapter 12.

Days ⓭ & ⓮: Osaka

It's a 4-hour train trip from Beppu to Osaka (not including a transfer in Kokura). Or, depart Beppu on the night of Day 12 by ferry for an overnight trip to Osaka. There's more than enough in Osaka to keep families entertained, including the **Floating Garden Observatory** with its surreal views, **Osaka Castle** (a remake, but impressive nonetheless), the **Osaka Museum of History,** and **Osaka Aquarium** (bigger and better than Beppu's). It's also a trip at **Sega Amusement Theme Park,** the reigning king of amusement arcades. Teenagers will also want to take in **Den Den Town,** Osaka's electronics shopping street, and **America-Mura,** where young Osakans shop for American and other hip fashions. But if you want to end your trip with a bang, take your kids to **Universal Studios Japan.** It's almost a carbon copy of its U.S. counterpart, and most attractions are dubbed in Japanese, but do your kids really care? See chapter 10.

5 NORTHERN JAPAN IN 2 WEEKS

Tohoku and Hokkaido are usually ignored by travelers. Though it's true that the country's most significant historic treasures lie in the southern regions, Northern Japan, where the emphasis is on natural wonders and hot-spring spas, offers a more relaxed vacation for those who have already seen the country's must-sees.

Day ❶: Arrive in Tokyo

Spend the night in Tokyo; if you wish to spend a few days in the capital sightseeing, refer to the itineraries earlier.

Days ❷ & ❸: Akan National Park ★★

Fly from Tokyo's Haneda Airport 1½ hours to Kushiro Airport, where you should stop by the small tourist office for

WEEK 1
1 Arrive in Tokyo
2-3 Akan National Park
4-5 Sapporo
6 Noboribetsu Spa
7 Hakodate Port Town

WEEK 2
8-9 Lake Towada
10-11 Back in Time in Nyuto Onsen
12 Kakunodate Castle Town
13 Matsushima
14 Back to Tokyo

a pamphlet on tours of **Kushiro Marshland National Park;** you may be able to join one that day. Otherwise, take the bus (1 hr. and 20 min.) to Akanko Onsen. Take a boat cruise of **Lake Akan,** famous for its *marimo,* a spongelike ball of duckweed, and tour the marimo museum. Visit **Ainu Kotan Village** with its shops and traditional Ainu dancing. Outdoor pursuits include hiking, canoeing, and fishing (including ice fishing in winter). See chapter 15.

Days 4 & 5: Sapporo
Board an early morning **sightseeing bus** for a tour of **Akan National Park** and its natural wonders, and then board a train

Bihoro Station for the 3-hour ride to Sapporo. Capital of Hokkaido Prefecture and the island's largest city, Sapporo is an easygoing city that's a snap to navigate. Highlights include **Nopporo Forest Park,** where you can visit the **Historical Museum of Hokkaido** and see vintage homes and buildings at the **Historical Village of Hokkaido.** Be sure to dine at the **Sapporo Bier Garten** on the grounds of the old Sapporo brewery. See chapter 15.

Day 6: Noboribetsu Spa
En route to Noboribetsu, stop off at the **Poroto Kotan and Ainu Museum** in Shiraoi with its impressive collection of indigenous Ainu artifacts. In **Noboribetsu**

Onsen, known for its curative hot springs, hike through **Hell Valley** for a view of the bubbling hot water that has made Noboribetsu famous, and then experience its magic at the Dai-ichi Takimotokan hot-spring baths. See chapter 15.

Day ❼: Hakodate Port Town ★

Take the train 2 hours to Hakodate. Wander the **waterfront warehouse district** and historic **Motomachi,** a picturesque neighborhood of steep slopes and turn-of-the-20th-century clapboard homes and other buildings, relics of when Hakodate opened as one of Japan's first international ports following 2 centuries of isolation. In the evening, take a cable car to the top of **Mount Hakodate,** renowned for its night view of Hakodate. See chapter 15.

Days ❽ & ❾: Lake Towada

Visit Hakodate's **morning market** (famous for its hairy crabs) and then board a train for the 2-hour ride to Aomori Station, where you'll transfer for the 3-hour bus ride to Lake Towada. Take a **boat cruise** of the lake and visit **Towada Jinja Shrine,** but the highlight of a stay here is a hike along the **Oirase Stream,** a coursing river shaded by trees and marked by huge boulders. See chapter 14.

Days ❿ & ⓫: Back in Time at Nyuto Onsen

There's a sightseeing bus that departs Lake Towada every morning mid-April through October, arriving at Tazawako Station 7 hours later, where you then board a local bus for **Nyuto Onsen,** a secluded valley of hot springs and rustic inns. It's a good base from which to explore the many wonders of the Towada-Hachimantai National Park, including skiing in winter and hiking, biking, and swimming in summer. For the ultimate *ryokan* experience, spend the night in **Tsuru-no-yu Onsen,** a rustic and remote Japanese inn with outdoor baths. See chapter 14.

Day ⓬: Kakunodate Castle Town ★

Only one stop away from Tazawako Station on the Shinkansen is **Kakunodate,** a small and relatively unspoiled castle town famous for its samurai district and cherry trees. Be sure to see the **Aoyagi Samurai Manor,** a compound of traditional buildings packed with Edo Period memorabilia. Spend the night here or return to Nyuto Onsen. See chapter 14.

Day ⓭: Matsushima ★

Take the Shinkansen to Sendai (about 1½ hr.) and then board a sightseeing boat for a 50-minute trip to **Matsushima,** famous for its scenic coastline of pine-studded islets. Visit the venerable **Zuiganji Temple,** northern Japan's most famous Zen temple; **Entsuin Temple,** with its nice gardens and restaurant serving Buddhist vegetarian cuisine; and a museum or two. See chapter 14.

Day ⓮: Back to Tokyo

Return to Sendai and take the Shinkansen south to Tokyo.

Settling into Tokyo

To the uninitiated, Tokyo may seem like a whirlwind of traffic and people, so confusing that visitors might think they have somehow landed on another planet. Little wonder first-time visitors are almost invariably disappointed. They come expecting an exotic Asian city, but instead they find a city Westernized and modernized to the point of ugliness, much of it a drab concrete jungle of unimaginative buildings clustered so close together that there's hardly room in which to breathe.

Simply stated, Tokyo is a crush of humanity. Its subways are often packed, its sidewalks are crowded, its streets are congested, and its air is filled with noise, pollution, and what can only be called mystery smells. Approximately 12.5 million people live in its 2,100 sq. km (811 sq. miles), many of them in bedroom towns from which they have to commute to work for an average of 2 to 3 hours every day. No matter where you go in Tokyo, you're never alone. After you've been here for a while, Paris, London, and even New York will seem deserted.

Crowds and urban ugliness, however, are what you'll see only if you don't bother to look beneath the surface. For Tokyo is alluring in its own way; and if you open yourself to it, you'll find a city unlike any other in the world, humming with energy and vitality. People rush around here with such purpose, such determination, it's hard not to feel that you're in the midst of something important, that you're witnessing history in the making.

A LOOK AT THE PAST Though today the nation's capital, Tokyo is a relative newcomer to the pages of Japanese history. For centuries it was nothing more than a rather unimportant village called Edo,

which means simply "mouth of the estuary." In 1603, Edo was catapulted into the limelight when the new shogun, Tokugawa Ieyasu, made the sleepy village the seat of his government. He expanded Edo Castle, making it the largest and most impressive castle in the land, and surrounded it with an ingenious system of moats that radiated from the castle in a great swirl, giving him easy access to the sea and an upper hand in thwarting enemy attack.

The town developed quickly, due largely to the shogun's decree requiring all *daimyo* (feudal lords) to permanently leave their families in Edo, a shrewd move to thwart insurrection in the provinces. There were as many as 270 daimyo in Japan in the 17th century, all of whom maintained several mansions in Edo, complete with elaborate compounds and expansive gardens. The daimyo's trusted samurai soon accounted for more than half of Edo's population, and the merchant class expanded as well. By 1787 the population had grown to 1.3 million, making Edo—even then—one of the largest cities in the world.

When the Tokugawas were overthrown in 1868, the Japanese emperor was restored to power and moved the capital from Kyoto to Edo, now renamed Tokyo (Eastern Capital). Japan's Feudal Era—and its isolation from the rest of the world—was over. As the capital city, Tokyo was the hardest hit in this new era of modernization, with fashion, architecture, food, and even people imported from the West. West was best, and things Japanese were forgotten or ignored.

It didn't help that Tokyo was almost totally destroyed twice in the first half of the 20th century: In 1923, a massive earthquake measuring 7.9 on the Richter scale destroyed more than a third of the city and claimed more than 100,000 lives; disaster struck again in 1945, toward the end of World War II when Allied incendiary bombs laid more than half the city to waste and killed another 100,000 people.

TOKYO TODAY Perhaps that's why most visitors are disappointed with Tokyo: It has almost nothing of historical importance to match Kyoto or Kamakura. So put your notions of quaint Japan out of your mind and plunge headfirst into the 21st century, because that's what Tokyo is all about. In fact, in the past few years, skyscrapers and new developments have been mushrooming faster than you can say shiitake, some of them the most ambitious land projects Japan has ever seen.

As the financial nerve center of Japan, Tokyo has long set the pace for what happens in the rest of Asia. The city is the reigning capital of Asian pop art and kitsch, fads, fashions, and trends.

But even though the city has a fast-paced, somewhat zany side, it also has a quieter and often overlooked side that makes the city both lovable and livable. Although formidable at first glance, Tokyo is nothing more than a series of small towns and neighborhoods clustered together, each with its own atmosphere, narrow, winding streets, mom-and-pop shops, fruit stands, and stores. Look for the details, and you'll notice carefully pruned bonsai adorning the sidewalks; old women in kimono shuffling down the streets; traditional wooden houses tucked between massive apartment complexes; everywhere, neatness and order. Peer inside those concrete high-rises, and you're apt to find Japanese restaurants that are perfect replicas of wood-beamed farmhouses side by side with cocktail bars that epitomize high-tech avant-garde.

I love Tokyo. Despite its daily frustrations, Tokyo is exhilarating, often exciting, and unceasingly interesting. Best of all, it's one of the world's safest metropolises, with the lowest theft rate of any large city on the planet. Although common sense dictates I avoid public parks after dark when I'm out alone and watch my purse in crowded subways, I otherwise walk without fear anywhere and anytime in Tokyo, day or night. The city's safety is best illustrated by what an American friend living in Tokyo was told when her daughter started first grade in a Japanese school: Parents were to refrain from walking their children to or from school, allowing, instead, the children to walk on their own.

Perhaps the only thing in Tokyo you have to watch out for are those Japanese businessmen who've had too much to drink. Reserve thrown off, they might want to practice their English on you.

1 ORIENTATION

ARRIVING
By Plane
There are two airports serving Tokyo, but most likely you'll arrive at **Narita International Airport** (NRT), 66km (41 miles) outside Tokyo. If you're arriving in Tokyo from elsewhere in Japan, your flight will probably land at **Haneda Airport** (HND), used primarily for domestic flights.

FACILITIES AT NARITA AIRPORT   Narita International Airport (© **0476/34-8000;** www.narita-airport.jp) consists of two terminals, Terminal 1 and 2. Arrival lobbies in both terminals have ATMs and counters for money exchange, open daily 6:30am to 11pm (change enough money here to last several days, as the exchange rate is the same as in town, the process is speedy, and facilities in town are somewhat limited). Both are connected to all ground transportation into Tokyo.

A **Tourist Information Center (TIC),** managed by the Japan National Tourist Organization, is located in the arrival lobbies of both Terminal 1 (© **0476/30-3383**) and Terminal 2 (© **0476/34-5877**). The TIC offers free maps and pamphlets and can direct you to your hotel or inn. Both are open daily 8am to 8pm; if you don't yet have a hotel room and want one at a modest price, you can make reservations here free of charge until 7:30pm.

If you've purchased a Japan Rail Pass, you can turn in your voucher at one of the **Japan Railways (JR) View Plazas** (Travel Service Centers) or ticket office, located in both Terminal 1 and Terminal 2 and open daily 6:30am to 9:45pm. Other facilities at both terminals include post offices, medical clinics, shower rooms, day rooms for napping, children's playrooms, luggage storage and lockers, cellular phone rentals, and coin-operated computers with Internet capabilities (¥100 for 10 min.).

GETTING TO TOKYO FROM NARITA AIRPORT Jumping into a **taxi** is the easiest way to get to Tokyo, but it's also prohibitively expensive—and may not even be the quickest if you happen to hit rush hour. Expect to spend around ¥19,000 to ¥21,000 for a 1½- to 2-hour taxi ride to central Tokyo.

BY BUS The most popular and stress-free way to get from Narita to Tokyo is via the **Airport Limousine Bus** (© **03/3665-7220;** www.limousinebus.co.jp), which picks up passengers and their luggage from just outside the arrival lobbies of Terminals 1 and 2 and delivers them to downtown hotels. This is the best mode of transportation if you have heavy baggage or are staying at one of the 40 or so major hotels served by the bus. Buses depart for the various hotels generally once an hour, and it can take almost 2 hours to reach a hotel in Shinjuku. Buses also travel to both Tokyo and Shinjuku stations, Haneda Airport, and the **Tokyo City Air Terminal (TCAT)** in downtown Tokyo, with more frequent departures (up to four times an hour in peak times). If your hotel is not served by limousine bus, take it to the hotel or station nearest your destination. In addition to taxis, TCAT, Shinjuku Station, and Tokyo Station are also served by public transportation; TCAT is connected to the subway Hanzomon Line via moving walkways and escalators; Shinjuku and Tokyo stations are hubs for subway lines and commuter trains, but if it's your first trip to Japan, you might want to avoid these big, crowded stations.

Check with the staff at the Airport Limousine Bus counter in the arrival lobbies to inquire which bus stops nearest your hotel and its departure time. The fare to most destinations is ¥3,000. Children 6 to 12 are charged half fare; those 5 and under ride free.

BY TRAIN The quickest way to reach Tokyo is by train, with several options available. Trains depart directly from the airport's two underground stations, called Narita Airport Station (which is in Terminal 1) and Airport Terminal 2 Station.

The JR **Narita Express (NEX;** © **03/3423-0111;** www.jreast.co.jp) is the fastest way to reach Tokyo Station, Shinagawa, Shibuya, Shinjuku, and Yokohama, with departures approximately once an hour, or twice an hour during peak hours. The hour-long trip to Tokyo Station costs ¥2,940 one-way. At Tokyo Station, the train splits, with the front cars going to Shibuya, Shinjuku, and Ikebukuro, and rear cars going to Shinagawa (cost to these stations: ¥3,110). Note, however, that if you have a validated JR Rail Pass, you can ride the NEX free (as mentioned above, you must first validate your rail pass at the JR View Plaza, also called the JR Travel Service Center, located in both terminals). *Note:* Seats are sometimes sold out in advance, especially during peak travel times. If you want

> ### (Tips) Saving on Transportation
>
> If you're going to be traveling around Tokyo by public transportation (and who doesn't?), you can save money by purchasing both a NEX and Suica card for ¥3,500, which includes the Narita Express into Tokyo plus ¥2,000 worth of travel in Tokyo. The discount ticket, available only at Narita Airport to foreign visitors, can be purchased at JR East Travel Service Centers in the basement of both terminals. Likewise, there's an Airport Limousine and Metro Pass combination ticket that includes one Airport Limousine trip to or from the airport plus 1 day of unlimited rides on Metro subways for ¥3,100. This ticket is available at Airport Limousine counters at the airport, TCAT, and Shinjuku Station West Exit, and Tokyo Metro Pass offices around town. Finally, there are also 1- and 2-day Metro passes available only in the arrival lobbies of both terminals at Narita for ¥600 and ¥980 respectively. For more information on the Suica and 1-day Metro cards, see "Getting Around," later in this chapter.

to reserve a seat for your return trip to Narita Airport—and I strongly recommend it—you can do so at the NEX counter or at any of Tokyo's major JR stations. Plan to arrive at Narita 2 hours before your plane's departure.

If the NEX is sold out and you're still determined to use your rail pass, you can take the slower **JR Airport Liner,** which will get you to Tokyo Station in 80 minutes. Without a rail pass, this rapid train will cost you ¥1,280.

An alternative is the privately owned **Keisei Skyliner** train (© **03/3831-0131;** www.keisei.co.jp), which departs directly from both Narita Airport Station (Terminal 1) and Airport Terminal 2 Station and travels to Ueno Station in Tokyo in about 1 hour, with a stop at Nippori Station on the way. You'll find Keisei Skyliner counters in the arrival lobbies of both terminals. Trains depart about every 40 minutes between 7:52am and 10pm, with the fare from Narita Airport to Ueno Station in Tokyo ¥1,920 one-way. Travelers on a budget can take one of Keisei's slower limited express trains to Ueno Station, with fares starting at ¥1,000 for the 71-minute trip. (*Note:* In late 2010, the faster New Skyliner will open for business, cutting the connection between the airport and Ueno station down to 36 min.) At Keisei Ueno Station, where you'll find a **Tokyo Tourist Information Center** (daily 9:30am–6:30pm), you can take either the subway or JR Yamanote Line to other parts of Tokyo. There are also plenty of taxis.

GETTING TO HANEDA AIRPORT If you're connecting to a domestic flight, you may need to transfer to Haneda Airport. The **Airport Limousine Bus** makes runs between Narita Airport and Haneda Airport that cost ¥3,000. The trip takes about 75 minutes.

GETTING FROM HANEDA AIRPORT INTO CENTRAL TOKYO If you're arriving at **Haneda Airport,** also called Tokyo International Airport (© **03/5757-8111;** www.tokyo-airport-bldg.co.jp), located near the center of Tokyo and used mainly for domestic flights, you can take the **Airport Limousine Bus** to Shinjuku Station, Tokyo Station, the Tokyo City Air Terminal (TCAT) in downtown Tokyo, and hotels in Shinjuku, Ikebukuro, Shibuya, and Akasaka. Fares run ¥900 to ¥1,200. Locals, however, are more likely to take the **monorail** from Haneda Airport 15 minutes to Hamamatsucho Station (fare: ¥470), or the **Keikyu Line** 19 minutes to Shinagawa (fare: ¥400). Both Hamamatsucho and Shinagawa connect to the very useful Yamanote Line, which travels to major stations,

including Tokyo and Shinjuku stations. Be sure to stop by the **Tokyo Tourist Informa-**
tion Center (© 03/5757-9345) in Haneda Airport, open daily 9am to 10pm.

By Land or Sea

BY TRAIN   If you're traveling to Tokyo from elsewhere in Japan, you'll most likely
arrive via Shinkansen bullet train at Tokyo, Ueno, or Shinagawa stations (avoid Tokyo
Station if you can; it's very big and confusing). All are well served by trains (including
the useful JR Yamanote Line), subways, and taxis.

BY BUS   Long-distance bus service from Hiroshima, Nagoya, Osaka, Kyoto, and other
major cities delivers passengers to Tokyo and Shinjuku stations, both of which are connected to the rest of the city via subway and commuter train, including the JR Yamanote
Line, which loops around the city.

BY FERRY   There are no international ferry services to Tokyo, but domestic long-distance ferries arrive at Ariake Ferry Terminal, located on an artificial island adjacent to
Odaiba in Tokyo Bay; the nearest station is Kokusai-Tenjijo-Seimon. Cruise lines usually
dock at Harumi Terminal.

VISITOR INFORMATION

The **Tourist Information Center (TIC),** 2–10–1 Yurakucho (© **03/3201-3331**), is
located on the 10th floor of a rather obscure office building called Kotsu Kaikan Building
next to the JR Yurakucho Station (look for its circular top). Assuming you're able to find
them, the TIC staff can answer all your questions regarding Tokyo and Japan, can give
you a map of the city plus various sightseeing materials, and will even book inexpensive
hotels for you around the country, charging no fee for the service. They're courteous and
efficient; I cannot recommend them highly enough. Maintained by the Japan National
Tourist Organization, the TIC also has information on the rest of Japan, including pamphlets and brochures on major cities and attractions. Be sure to stop here if you plan to
visit other destinations, because information in English may not be available at the destination itself. The TIC is open daily from 9am to 5pm. Other TIC offices are located in
the arrival lobbies of terminals 1 and 2 at Narita Airport, open daily from 8am to 8pm.

There's also the new **TIC TOKYO,** facing the Nihombashi exit of Tokyo Station at
1–8–1 Marunouchi (© **03/5220-7055**; www.tictokyo.jp). Open daily 10am to 7pm, it
dispenses information on traveling throughout Japan and books accommodations, tours,
and even air tickets.

Another great source of information is the **Tokyo Tourist Information Center,** operated by the Tokyo Metropolitan Government and located on the first floor of the Tokyo
Metropolitan Government (TMG) Building No. 1, 2–8–1 Nishi-Shinjuku (© **03/5321-
3077**; www.tourism.metro.tokyo.jp; station: Tochomae or Shinjuku); you'll probably
want to come here anyway for TMG's great free observation floor. The center dispenses
pamphlets, its own city map (which is a great complement to the one issued by TIC),
and handy one-page detailed maps of various city districts, from Ueno to Roppongi. It's
open daily 9:30am to 6:30pm. Other city-run information counters are at Keisei Ueno
Station (© **03/3836-3471**; Station: Ueno), open daily 9:30am to 6:30pm; and Haneda
Airport (© **03/5757-9345**), open daily 9am to 10pm.

TOURIST PUBLICATIONS   Be sure to pick up *Event Calendar* at the TIC, a monthly
leaflet listing festivals, antiques and crafts fairs, and other events throughout the metropolitan area. Of the many free giveaways available at the TICs, restaurants, bars, bookstores, hotels, and other establishments visitors and expats are likely to frequent, the best

is the weekly *Metropolis* (www.metropolis.co.jp), with features on Tokyo, club listings, and restaurant and movie reviews. Look also for the free *Japanzine* (www.seekjapan.jp/japanzine) and *att.Japan* (www.att-japan.net). Weekly entertainment sections on theater, films, and special events are published in the English-language newspapers, appearing on Friday in the *Japan Times* and on Thursday in the *Daily Yomiuri*.

CITY LAYOUT

Your most frustrating moments in Tokyo will probably occur when you find that you're totally lost. Maybe it will be in a subway or train station, when all you see are signs in Japanese, or on a street somewhere as you search for a museum, restaurant, or bar. At any rate, accept it here and now: You *will* get lost if you are at all adventurous and strike out on your own. It's inevitable. But take comfort in the fact that Japanese get lost, too—even taxi drivers! And don't forget that most of the hotel and restaurant listings in this book have the number of minutes (in parentheses) it takes to walk there from the nearest station; if you take note, you'll at least know the radius from the station to your destination. It's wise, too, to always allow extra time to find your way around.

Tokyo, situated at one end of Tokyo Bay and spreading across the Kanto Plain, still retains some of its Edo Period features. If you look at a map, you'll find a large green oasis in the middle of the city, site of the Imperial Palace and its grounds. Surrounding it is the castle moat; a bit farther out are remnants of another circular moat built by the Tokugawa shogun. The JR Yamanote Line forms another loop around the inner city; most of Tokyo's major hotels, nightlife districts, and attractions are near or inside this oblong loop.

For administrative purposes, Tokyo is broken down into **23 wards**, known as *ku*. Its business districts of Marunouchi and Hibiya, for example, are in Chiyoda-ku, while Ginza is part of Chuo-ku (Central Ward). These two ku are the historic hearts of Tokyo, for it was here that the city had its humble beginnings.

MAIN STREETS & ARTERIES   One difficulty in finding your way around Tokyo is that hardly any streets are named. Think about what that means: some 12 million people living in a huge metropolis of nameless streets. Granted, major thoroughfares and some well-known streets in areas such as Ginza and Shinjuku received names after World War II at the insistence of American occupation forces, and a few more have been labeled or given nicknames that only the locals know, but for the most part, Tokyo's address system is based on a complicated number scheme that must make the postal worker's job here a nightmare. To make matters worse, most streets in Tokyo zigzag—an arrangement apparently left over from olden days, to confuse potential attacking enemies. Now they confuse Tokyoites and visitors alike.

Among Tokyo's most important named streets are **Meiji Dori,** which follows the loop of the Yamanote Line and runs from Minato-ku in the south through Ebisu, Shibuya, Harajuku, Shinjuku, and Ikebukuro in the north; **Yasukuni Dori** and **Shinjuku Dori,** which cut across the heart of the city from Shinjuku to Chiyoda-ku; and **Sotobori Dori, Chuo Dori, Harumi Dori,** and **Showa Dori,** which pass through Ginza. Other major thoroughfares are named after the districts they're in, such as **Roppongi Dori** in Roppongi and **Aoyama Dori** in Aoyama (*dori* means avenue or street, as does *michi*).

Intersections in Tokyo are called a crossing; it seems every district has a famous crossing. **Ginza 4-chome Crossing** is the intersection of Chuo Dori and Harumi Dori. **Roppongi Crossing** is the intersection of Roppongi Dori and Gaien-Higashi Dori.

ADDRESSES Because streets did not have names when Japan's postal system was established, the country has a unique address system. A typical Tokyo address might read 6–4–21 Ginza, Chuo-ku, which is the address of the Ginza Nikko Hotel. Chuo-ku is the name of the ward. Wards are further divided into named districts, in this case Ginza. Ginza itself is broken down into *chome* (numbered subsections), the first number in the series, here 6–chome. The second number (4 in the example) refers to a smaller area within the *chome*—usually an entire block, sometimes larger. Thus, houses on one side of the street will usually have a different middle number from houses on the other side. The last number, in this case 21, refers to the actual building. Although it seems reasonable to assume that next to a no. 21 building will be a no. 22, that's not always the case; buildings were assigned numbers as they were constructed, not according to location.

Addresses are usually, but not always, posted on buildings beside doors, on telephone poles, and at major intersection traffic lights, but sometimes they are written in kanji only. One frustrating trend is that new, modern buildings omit posting any address whatsoever on their facades, perhaps in the belief that no one understands the address system anyway.

FINDING YOUR WAY AROUND If you're traveling by subway or JR train, the first thing you should do upon exiting your compartment is to look for **yellow signs** posted on every platform that tell you which exit to take for particular buildings, attractions, and *chome.* At Roppongi Station, for example, you'll find yellow signboards that tell you the exit to take for Roppongi Hills, which will at least get you pointed in the right direction once you emerge from the station. Stations also have maps of the areas either inside the station or at the exit; these are your best plan of attack when trying to find a particular address.

As you walk around Tokyo, you will also notice **maps** posted beside sidewalks giving a breakdown of the postal number system for the area (look for a white circle with an "i" in the middle). The first time I tried to use one, I stopped one Japanese, then another, and asked them to point out on the map where a particular address was. They both studied the map and pointed out the direction. Both turned out to be wrong. Not very encouraging, but if you learn how to read these maps, they're invaluable. Nowadays, many of them include landmarks translated in English.

Another invaluable source of information is the numerous **police boxes,** called *koban,* located in every neighborhood throughout the city. Police officers have area maps and are very helpful (helping lost souls seems to occupy much of their time). You should also never hesitate to ask a Japanese the way, but be sure to ask more than one. You'll be amazed at the conflicting directions you'll receive. Apparently, Japanese would rather hazard a guess than impolitely shrug their shoulders and leave you standing there. The best thing to do is ask directions of several Japanese and then follow the majority opinion. You can also duck into a shop and ask someone where a nearby address is, although in my experience employees do not even know the address of their own store. However, they may have a map of the area.

MAPS Before setting out on your own, arm yourself with a few maps. Maps are so much a part of life in Tokyo that they're often included in shop or restaurant advertisements or brochures, on business cards, and even in private party invitations. Even though I've spent years in Tokyo, I rarely venture forth without a map. The Tourist Information Center issues a *Tourist Map of Tokyo,* which includes a subway map. Better, in my opinion, are the free maps given away by the Tokyo Metropolitan Government, which range

from a city map to detailed maps of Tokyo's many districts (such as Shinjuku). Armed with these maps, you should be able to locate at least the general vicinity of every place mentioned in this chapter and the next. Hotels also sometimes distribute their own maps. In short, never pass up a free map.

For more detailed maps, head for **Tower Books, Kinokuniya,** or one of the other bookstores with an English-language section (see "Shopping from A to Z" in chapter 6). My own personal favorite is Shobunsha's *Bilingual Map of Tokyo,* listing *chome* and *chome* subsections for major areas; the waterproof compact folded map can be carried in a purse or backpack. If you plan to write a guidebook, consider the *Bilingual Atlas of Tokyo* by Tokyo Chizu Publishing Company or Kodansha International's *Tokyo City Atlas,* both of which cover all 23 of Tokyo's wards with specific postal maps, provide both Japanese and English-language place names, rail and subway maps, and an index to important buildings, museums, and other places of interest.

TOKYO'S NEIGHBORHOODS IN BRIEF

Taken as a whole, Tokyo seems formidable and unconquerable. It's best, therefore, to think of it as nothing more than a series of villages scrunched together, much like the pieces of a jigsaw puzzle. Holding the pieces together, so to speak, is the **Yamanote Line,** a commuter train loop around central Tokyo that passes through such important stations as Yurakucho, Tokyo, Ueno, Ikebukuro, Shinjuku, Harajuku, Shibuya, and Shinagawa. Since 2001, several districts have witnessed massive redevelopment, including Shinagawa, both sides of Tokyo Station, and Roppongi.

Marunouchi   Bounded by the Imperial Palace to the west and Tokyo Station to the east, Marunouchi is one of Tokyo's oldest business districts but has undergone a massive revival since the turn of this century. It's home to office buildings, swanky hotels, and wide avenues like the fashionable, tree-lined **Marunouchi Naka Dori,** home to international designer boutiques from Armani and Burberry to Tiffany.

Hibiya   This is not only the business heart of Tokyo, but its spiritual heart as well. This is where the Tokugawa shogun built his magnificent castle and was thus the center of old Edo. Today, Hibiya, in Chiyoda-ku, is no less important as the home of the **Imperial Palace,** built on the ruins of Edo Castle and the residence of Japan's 125th emperor. Bordering the palace is the wonderful East Garden and Hibiya Park, both open free to the public.

Ginza   Ginza is the swankiest and most expensive **shopping area** in all Japan. When the country opened to foreign trade in the 1860s, following 2 centuries of self-imposed seclusion, it was here that Western imports and adopted Western architecture were first displayed. Today, Ginza is where you'll find a multitude of department stores, international name-brand boutiques, exclusive restaurants, hotels, art galleries, and drinking establishments.

Tsukiji   Located only two subway stops from Ginza, Tsukiji was born from reclaimed land during the Tokugawa shogunate; its name, in fact, means "reclaimed land." Today it's famous for the **Tsukiji Fish Market,** one of the largest wholesale fish markets in the world. Nearby is Hama Rikyu Garden, one of Tokyo's most famous gardens.

Akihabara Two stops north of Tokyo Station on the Yamanote Line, Akihabara has long been Japan's foremost shopping destination for electronic and electrical appliances, with hundreds of shops offering a look at the latest in gadgets and gizmos, including Yodobashi Camera, Japan's largest appliance store. In recent years, Akihabara has also become a mecca for *otaku* (geek) culture, home of *anime* and *manga* stores and the **Tokyo Anime Center.** This is a fascinating area for a stroll, even if you aren't interested in buying anything. About a 12-minute walk to the west is **Kanda,** with many stores specializing in new and used books.

Asakusa In the northeastern part of central Tokyo, Asakusa and areas to its north served as the pleasure quarters for old Edo. Today it's known throughout Japan as the site of the famous **Sensoji Temple,** one of Tokyo's top and oldest attractions. It also has a wealth of tiny shops selling traditional Japanese crafts. When Tokyoites talk about old *shitamachi* (downtown), they are referring to the traditional homes and tiny narrow streets of the Asakusa and Ueno areas.

Ueno Located just west of Asakusa, on the northern edge of the JR Yamanote Line loop, Ueno is also part of the city's old downtown. Ueno boasts **Ueno Park,** a huge green space comprising a zoo and several acclaimed museums, including the **Tokyo National Museum,** which houses the largest collection of Japanese art and antiquities in the world. Ueno Station serves as a stop for major train lines heading north and eastward, including some lines of the Shinkansen bullet train. Under the train tracks of the JR Yamanote Line loop is the spirited **Ameya Yokocho,** a thriving market for food, clothing, and accessories.

Shinjuku Originating as a post town in 1698 to serve the needs of feudal lords and their retainers traveling between Edo and the provinces, Shinjuku was hardly touched by the 1923 Great Kanto Earthquake, making it an attractive alternative for businesses wishing to relocate following the destruction. In 1971, Japan's first skyscraper was erected with the opening of the Keio Plaza Hotel in western Shinjuku, setting a dramatic precedent for things to come. Today more than a dozen skyscrapers, including several hotels, dot the Shinjuku skyline, and with the opening of the **Tokyo Metropolitan Government Office (TMG)** in 1991 (with a tourist office and a great free observation floor), Shinjuku's transformation into the capital's upstart business district was complete. Separating eastern and western Shinjuku is **Shinjuku Station,** the nation's busiest commuter station, located on the western end of the Yamanote Line loop. Surrounding the station is a bustling shopping district, particularly the huge **Takashimaya Shinjuku** complex and the many discount electronics stores. Shinjuku is also known for its nightlife, especially in **Kabuki-cho,** one of Japan's most famous—and naughtiest—amusement centers; and in **Shinjuku 2–chome,** Tokyo's premier gay nightlife district. An oasis in the middle of Shinjuku madness is **Shinjuku Gyoen Park,** a beautiful garden for strolling.

Ikebukuro Located north of Shinjuku on the Yamanote Line loop, Ikebukuro is the working person's Tokyo, less refined and a bit rougher around the edges. Ikebukuro is where you'll find **Seibu** and **Tobu,** two of the country's largest department stores, as well as the **Japan Traditional Craft Center**

with its beautifully crafted traditional items. The **Sunshine City Building,** one of Tokyo's tallest skyscrapers, is home to a huge indoor shopping center.

Harajuku The mecca of Tokyo's younger generation, Harajuku swarms throughout the week with teenagers in search of fashion and fun. **Takeshita Dori** is a narrow pedestrian lane packed elbow to elbow with young people looking for the latest in inexpensive clothing; at its center is Harajuku Daiso, a ¥100 discount shop. Harajuku is also home to one of Japan's major attractions, the **Meiji Jingu Shrine,** built in 1920 to deify Emperor and Empress Meiji; and to the small but delightful **Ukiyo-e Ota Memorial Museum of Art,** with its woodblock prints. Another draw is the **Oriental Bazaar,** Tokyo's best shop for products and souvenirs of Japan. Linking Harajuku with Aoyama (below) is **Omotesando Dori,** a fashionable tree-lined avenue flanked by trendy shops, restaurants, and sidewalk cafes, making it a premier promenade for people-watching.

Aoyama While Harajuku is for Tokyo's teeny-boppers, nearby chic Aoyama is its playground for trendsetting yuppies, boasting sophisticated restaurants, pricey boutiques, and more cutting-edge designer-fashion outlets than anywhere else in the city. It's located on the eastern end of **Omotesando Dori** (and an easy walk from Harajuku), centered on Aoyama Dori. The upscale **Omotesando Hills** shopping center on Omotesando Dori stretches from Harajuku to Aoyama.

Shibuya Located on the southwestern edge of the Yamanote Line loop, Shibuya serves as a vibrant nightlife and shopping area for the young. More subdued than Shinjuku, more down-to-earth than Harajuku, and less cosmopolitan than Roppongi, it's home to more than a dozen department stores specializing in everything from designer clothing to housewares and CDs. Don't miss the light change at Shibuya Crossing, reportedly Japan's busiest intersection, with its hordes of pedestrians, neon, and five video billboards that have earned it the nickname "Times Square of Tokyo" (and a spot in the movie *Lost in Translation*).

Ebisu One station south of Shibuya on the JR Yamanote Line, Ebisu was a minor player in Tokyo's shopping and nightlife league until the 1995 debut of **Yebisu Garden Place,** a smart-looking complex of apartments, concert halls, two museums, restaurants, a department store, and a first-class hotel, all connected to Ebisu Station via moving walkway. The vicinity east of Ebisu Station, once a sleepy residential and low-key shopping district, is now a small but thriving nightlife mecca popular with ex-pats who find Roppongi too crass or commercial.

Roppongi Tokyo's best-known nightlife district for young Japanese and foreigners, Roppongi has more bars and nightclubs than any other district outside Shinjuku, as well as a multitude of restaurants serving international cuisines. It's anchored by two new developments: the eye-popping, 11-hectare (28-acre) **Roppongi Hills,** Tokyo's largest urban development housing 230 shops and restaurants, a first-class hotel, a garden, apartments, offices, a cinema complex, and Tokyo's highest art museum, on the 53rd floor of Mori Tower; and the 10-hectare (25-acre) **Tokyo Midtown,** which boasts Tokyo's tallest building, a luxury hotel, medical center, 130 restaurants and fashion boutiques, apartments, offices, a garden, and art museum.

Akasaka Close to Japan's seat of government and home to several large hotels and a small nightlife district, Akasaka caters mostly to businessmen and bureaucrats, making it of little interest to tourists. It does, however, boast some good restaurants; in recent years, so many Koreans have opened restaurants and other establishments here that it has been dubbed "Little Korea."

Shinagawa Once an important post station on the old Tokaido Highway, Shinagawa remains an important crossroads due to **Shinagawa Station,** a stop on the Shinkansen bullet train route and on the southern end of the Yamanote Line loop. Home to several major hotels, it also witnessed a major blossoming of office construction in recent years, making it a serious rival to Shinjuku's business district.

Odaiba This is Tokyo's newest district, constructed from reclaimed land in Tokyo Bay. Connected to the mainland by the **Rainbow Bridge** (famous for its chameleon colors after nightfall), the Yurikamome Line monorail, the Rinkai Line, and a vehicular harbor tunnel, Odaiba is home to hotels, Japan's largest convention space, several shopping complexes (including the fancy Venus Fort), the **Museum of Maritime Science,** the **National Museum of Emerging Science and Innovation,** a hot-spring public bath that hearkens back to the Edo Era, a monolithic Ferris wheel, and **Megaweb,** a huge multimedia car amusement and exhibition center sponsored by Toyota. For young Japanese, it's one of Tokyo's hottest date spots.

2 GETTING AROUND

The first rule of getting around Tokyo: It will always take longer than you think. For short-term visitors, calculating travel times in Tokyo is a tricky business. Taking a taxi is expensive and involves the probability of getting stuck interminably in traffic, with the meter ticking away. Taking the subway is usually more efficient, even though it's more complicated and harder on your feet: Choosing which route to take isn't always clear, and transfers between lines are sometimes quite a hike in themselves. If I'm going from one end of Tokyo to the other by subway, I usually allow anywhere from 30 to 60 minutes, depending on the number of transfers and the walking distance to my final destination. If you don't have to change trains, you can travel from one end of central Tokyo to the other in about 30 minutes or less. In any case, travel times to destinations within each line are posted on platform pillars, along with diagrams showing which train compartments are best for making quick transfers between lines.

Your best bet for getting around Tokyo is to take the subway or a Japan Railways (JR) commuter train such as the Yamanote Line to the station nearest your destination. From there you can either walk, using a map and asking directions along the way, or take a taxi.

BY PUBLIC TRANSPORTATION

Each mode of transportation in Tokyo—subway (with two different companies), JR train (such as the Yamanote Line), and bus—has its own fare system and therefore requires a new ticket each time you transfer from one mode of transport to another. If you're going to be in Tokyo for a few days, it's much more convenient to purchase a **Suica,** a contactless card issued by JR East that automatically deducts fares and can be used on virtually all modes of transportation, including JR trains (excluding the Shinkansen), private railways (such as the Rinkai Line to Odaiba or Minato Mirai Line to Yokohama), subways, and buses. It can even be used for purchases at designated vending machines, convenience stores, and fast-food outlets that display the Suica sign. First-time buyers must purchase the Suica from vending machines for ¥2,000, which includes a ¥500 deposit. The Suica is rechargeable, at amounts ranging from ¥1,000 to ¥10,000. Note, however, that when you return your Suica to get your deposit back, you must be sure that the card is depleted, or you'll be charged a ¥210 handling fee for any remaining stored balance on the card. A similar card to the Suica is the **Pasmo** (also available from vending machines), which can also be used on various modes of transportation throughout Tokyo. Although there are other options available, including 1-day cards and metro-only cards, the Suica and the Pasmo are by far my favorites.

If you think you're going to be traveling a lot by public transportation on any given day, consider purchasing a **Tokyo Free Kippu** (Tokyo Round Tour Ticket), which, despite its name, costs ¥1,580, but does allow unlimited travel for 1 day on all subways, JR trains, and Toei buses within Tokyo's 23 wards. It's available at all JR stations with a *midori-no-madoguchi* (reservation ticket office) or View Plaza (Travel Service Center), and most Metro subway stations.

Avoid taking the subway or JR train during the weekday morning **rush hour,** from 8 to 9am—the stories you've heard about commuters packed into trains like sardines are all true. There are even "platform pushers," men who push people into compartments so that the doors can close. If you want to witness Tokyo at its craziest, go to Shinjuku Station at 8:30am—but go by taxi unless you want to experience the crowding firsthand. Most lines provide women-only compartments weekdays until 9:30am.

Finally, please note that all cellphones should be switched to silent mode (called "manner mode" in Japanese) on public conveyances.

By Subway

To get around Tokyo on your own, it's imperative to learn how to ride its subways. Fortunately, the Tokyo Metro system (which uses a symbol "M" vaguely reminiscent of McDonald's famous arches) is efficient, modern, clean, and easy to use; in fact, I think it's one of the most user-friendly systems on the planet. All station names are written in English. Many cars also display the next station in English on digital signs above their doors and announce stops in English.

Altogether, there are 13 underground subway lines crisscrossing the city, operated by two companies: Tokyo Metro (the bigger of the two) and Toei (which operates four lines). Each line is color-coded. The Ginza Line, for example, is orange, which means that all its trains and signs are orange. If you're transferring to the Ginza Line from another line, follow the orange signs and circles to the Ginza Line platform. Each line is also assigned a letter (usually its initial), so that Ginza has the letter "G" and Hibiya the letter "H." Additionally, each station along each line is assigned a number in chronological order beginning with the first station (Asakusa Station, for example, is G19, the 19th stop from Shibuya on the Ginza Line), so you always know how many stops to your destination. Before boarding, however, make sure the train is going in the right direction—signs at each station show both the previous and the next stop, so you can double-check you're heading in the right direction. Tokyo's newest line, Toei's Oedo Line, makes

a zigzag loop around the city and is useful for traveling between Roppongi and Shinjuku;
be aware, however, that it's buried deep underground and that platforms take a while to
reach, despite escalators.

Whereas it used to be a matter of skill to know exactly which train compartment to
board if making transfers down the line, diagrams at each station (usually on a pillar at
the entrance to each platform) show which end of the train and compartment is most
useful for connections. There are also signs that show exactly how many minutes it takes
to reach every destination on that line.

Remember, once you reach your destination, look for the yellow signs on station
platforms designating which exit to take for major buildings, museums, and addresses. If
you're confused about which exit to take, ask someone at the window near the ticket gate.
Taking the right exit can make a world of difference, especially in Shinjuku, where there
are some 60 station exits.

TICKETS Vending machines at all subway stations sell tickets; fares begin at ¥160 for
the shortest distance and increase according to how far you're traveling. Children 6 to 11
pay half fare; children 5 and under ride free. Vending machines give change, even for a
¥10,000 note. **To purchase your ticket,** insert money into the vending machine until
the fare buttons light up, and then push the amount for the ticket you want. Your ticket
and change will drop onto a little platform at the bottom of the machine.

Before purchasing your ticket, you first have to figure out your **fare.** Fares are posted
on a large subway map above the vending machines, but they're generally in Japanese
only; major stations also post a smaller map listing fares in English, but you may have to
search for it. An alternative is to look at the subway map contained in the "Tourist Map
of Tokyo" issued by TIC—it lists stations in both Japanese and English. When you know
what the Japanese characters look like, you may be able to locate your station and the
corresponding fare. If you still don't know the fare, just buy a basic-fare ticket for ¥160.
When you exit at your destination, look for the **fare adjustment machine;** insert your
ticket to find out how much more you owe, or look for a subway employee at the ticket
window to tell you how much extra you owe. In any case, be sure to hang onto your
ticket, as you must give it up at the end of your journey. Since buying individual tickets
is a hassle (and vending machines are unfortunately not as user-friendly as the subway
system is), I suggest buying either a Suica or Pasmo card (see above).

HOURS Most subways run from about 5am to midnight, although the times of the
first and last trains depend on the line, the station, and whether it's a weekday or a weekend. Schedules are posted in the stations, and throughout most of the day, trains run
every 3 to 5 minutes.

For more information on tickets, passes, and lines for the subway, as well as a detailed
subway map and brochure, stop by **Metro Information desks** located at Ginza, Shinjuku, Omotesando, and other major stations in Tokyo. Or check the website **www.
tokyometro.jp/global.en.** Staff at the Metro's Customer Relations Center (© **03/3941-
2004**) speak Japanese only. Information on **Toei Subway** is available at **www.kotsu.
metro.tokyo.jp/english.**

By JR Train

In addition to subway lines, electric commuter trains operated by the **East Japan Railways Company (JR)** run aboveground throughout greater Tokyo. These are also color-
coded, with fares beginning at ¥130. Buy your ticket from vending machines just as you

Transfers on the Subway & Train

You can transfer between most subway lines without buying another ticket, and you can transfer between JR train lines on one ticket. However, your ticket or prepaid card does not allow a transfer between Tokyo's two subway companies (Metro and Toei), JR train lines, and private train lines connecting Tokyo with outlying destinations such as Nikko. You usually don't have to worry about this, though, because if you exit through a wicket and have to give up your ticket, you'll know you have to buy another one.

The general rule is that if your final destination and fare are posted above the ticket vending machines, you can travel all the way to your destination with only one ticket. But don't worry about this too much; the ticket collector will set you straight if you've miscalculated. Note, however, that if you pay too much for your ticket, the portion of the fare that's left unused is not refundable—so, again, the easiest thing to do if in doubt is to buy the cheapest fare. Even better, buy a Suica.

would for the subway, but more convenient is the Suica. Otherwise, if you think you'll be traveling a lot by JR lines on any given day, consider purchasing a **1-Day Tokunai Pass,** which allows unlimited travel for ¥730.

The **Yamanote Line** (green-colored coaches) is the best-known and most convenient JR line. It makes an oblong loop around the city, stopping at 29 stations along the way, all of them announced in English and with digital signboards in each compartment. In fact, you may want to take the Yamanote Line and stay on it for a roundup view of Tokyo; the entire trip takes about an hour, passing such stations as Shinjuku, Tokyo, Akihabara, Ueno, Harajuku, and Shibuya on the way.

Another convenient JR line is the orange-colored **Chuo Line;** it cuts across Tokyo between Shinjuku and Tokyo stations, with both express (which doesn't make as many stops) and local trains available. The yellow-colored **Sobu Line** runs between Shinjuku and Akihabara and beyond to Chiba. Other JR lines serve outlying districts for the metropolis's commuting public, including Yokohama and Kamakura. Because the Yamanote, Chuo, and Sobu lines are rarely identified by their specific names at major stations, look for signs that say JR LINES.

For more information on JR lines and tickets, stop by one of JR's **Information Centers** at Tokyo Station, Ueno, Shinjuku, Shibuya, or Shinagawa or call the English-language **JR East Infoline** at ✆ **050/2016-1603** daily from 10am to 6pm. You can also check its website at **www.jreast.co.jp/e.**

By Bus

Buses are not as easy to use as trains or subways unless you know their route, because only the end destination is written on the bus and routes listed at bus stops are usually not in English. In addition, many bus drivers don't speak English. Buses are sometimes convenient for short distances, however. If you're feeling adventurous, board the bus at the front and drop the exact fare (usually ¥200) into the box. If you don't have the exact amount, fare boxes accept coins or bills; your change minus the fare will come out below. Suica and Pasmo cards are also accepted. A signboard at the front of the bus displays the next stop, usually in English. When you wish to get off, press one of the buttons on the railing near the door or the seats. You can pick up an excellent Toei bus map showing all major routes at one of the Tokyo Tourist Information Centers operated by the Tokyo Metropolitan Government (see "Visitor Information," earlier). Or check the Toei website at **www.kotsu.metro.tokyo.jp/english**.

An exception to the city buses above is Toei's **Tokyo Shitamachi Bus,** a user-friendly sightseeing bus that follows a fixed route to seven major sightseeing spots. Departing from the Marunouchi north exit of Tokyo Station, buses stop at Nihombashi's Mitsukoshi Department Store, Akihabara with its many *anime* and electronics stores, Ueno Park, Kappabashi-dougugai Dori with its many kitchen stores, and Asakusa before terminating at Ryogoku Station with the Edo-Tokyo Museum. Buses travel in both directions at 30-minute intervals daily between 9am and 6:30pm. The fare is ¥200 each time you board (you can use a Suica card); or purchase a 1-day Toei bus pass for ¥500. For information about the Tokyo Shitamachi Bus, including a schedule and map, stop by the Tokyo Tourist Information Center in Shinjuku or Ueno.

By Taxi

Taxis are shamefully expensive in Tokyo. **Fares** start at ¥710 for the first 2km (1¼ miles) and increase ¥90 for each additional 288m (950 ft.) or 40 seconds of waiting time. There are also smaller, more compact taxis for a maximum of four persons that charge slightly less, but they are fewer in number. Fares are posted on the back of the front passenger seat. If you're like me, you probably won't shop around—you'll gratefully jump into the first taxi that stops. Note that from 10pm to 5am, an extra 30% is added to your fare. Perhaps as an admission of how expensive taxis are, fares can also be paid by all major credit cards, though some companies require a minimum fare of ¥5,000.

With the exception of some major thoroughfares in the downtown area, you can hail a taxi from any street or go to a taxi stand or a major hotel. A red light above the dashboard shows if a taxi is free to pick up a passenger; a yellow light indicates that the taxi is occupied. ***Note:*** Be sure to stand clear of the back left door—it swings open automatically. Likewise, it shuts automatically once you're in. Taxi drivers are quite perturbed if you try to maneuver the door yourself. The law requires that back-seat passengers wear seat belts.

Unless you're going to a well-known landmark or hotel, it's best to have your destination written out in Japanese, since most taxi drivers don't speak English. But even that may not help. Tokyo is so complicated that taxi drivers may not know a certain area, although many now have navigation systems. If a driver doesn't understand where you're going, he may refuse to take you.

There are so many taxis cruising Tokyo that you can hail one easily on most thoroughfares—except when you need it most: when it's raining, or just after 1am on weekends, after all subways and trains have stopped. To call a major taxi company for a pickup, try **Nihon Kotsu** (✆ **03/5755-2336**) for an English-speaking operator or **Kokusai** (✆ **03/3505-6001;** Japanese only). Note, however, that you'll be required to pay extra (usually not more than ¥400 for an immediate pickup). I have rarely telephoned for a taxi—as in the movies, one usually cruises by just when I raise my hand.

Fast Facts Tokyo

If you can't find answers to your questions here, check "Fast Facts: Japan," in chapter 16. If you still can't find an answer, call the **Tourist Information Center** (℡ 03/3201-3331) daily from 9am to 5pm; the city-run **Tokyo Tourist Information Center** (℡ 03/5321-3077) daily from 9:30am to 6:30pm; or the **TIC TOKYO** (℡ 03/5220-7055) daily from 10am to 7pm. Another good source is the **Foreign Residents' Advisory Center** (℡ 03/5320-7744), which can answer questions on a wide range of topics from problems of daily life and emergency numbers to Japanese customs, Monday through Friday from 9:30am to noon and 1 to 5pm. Finally, if you're staying in a first-class hotel, another valuable resource is the concierge or guest-relations desk, where the staff can tell you how to reach your destination, answer general questions, and even make restaurant reservations.

American Express There is no public American Express office in Japan.

Area Code The area code for Tokyo is 3 if calling from abroad and 03 if calling from within Japan. For details on calling Tokyo from outside Japan, see "Staying Connected" in chapter 3.

Babysitters Most major hotels can arrange babysitting services, but expect to pay a minimum of ¥5,000 for 2 hours. Some hotels have day-care centers for young children, though they are no less expensive. See individual hotel listings or "Family-Friendly Hotels" later in this chapter.

Business Hours See "Fast Facts: Japan" in chapter 16.

Currency Exchange See "Money & Costs," p. 74.

Drugstores There are no 24-hour drugstores *(kusuri-ya)* in Tokyo, but ubiquitous 24-hour convenience stores such as 7-Eleven, Lawson, and Family Mart carry things like aspirin. If you're looking for specific pharmaceuticals, a good bet is the **American Pharmacy,** in the basement of the Marunouchi Building, 2–4–1 Marunouchi, Chiyoda-ku (℡ 03/5220-7716; Mon–Fri 9am–9pm, Sat 10am–9pm, and Sun and holidays 10am–8pm), which has many of the same over-the-counter drugs you can find at home (many of them imported from the United States) and can fill American prescriptions—but note that you *must first visit a doctor in Japan* before foreign prescriptions can be filled, so it's best to bring an ample supply of any prescription medication with you.

Embassies & Consulates Visa or passport sections of most embassies are open only at certain times during the day, so it's best to call in advance.

U.S. Embassy: 1–10–5 Akasaka, Minato-ku, near Toranomon subway station (℡ 03/3224-5000; http://japan.usembassy.gov; consular section open Mon–Fri 8:30am–noon and Mon–Tues and Thurs–Fri 2–4pm; phone inquiries Mon–Fri 8:30am–1pm and 2–5:30pm).

Canadian Embassy: 7–3–38 Akasaka, Minato-ku, near Aoyama-Itchome Station (℡ 03/5412-6200; www.international.gc.ca/missions/japan-japon/menu-eng.asp; consular section open Mon–Fri 9:30–11:30am; embassy open Mon–Fri 9am–12:30pm and 1:30–5:30pm).

British Embassy: 1 Ichibancho, Chiyoda-ku, near Hanzomon Station (℡ 03/5211-1100; http://ukinjapan.fco.gov.uk/en; Mon–Fri 9am–12:30pm and 2–5:30pm; consulate inquiries Mon–Fri 9:15am–2:15pm).

Irish Embassy: Ireland House, 2–10–7 Kojimachi, Chiyoda-ku, near Hanzomon Station, exit 3 (☎ **03/3263-0695;** www.irishembassy.jp; Mon–Fri 10am–12:30pm and 2–4pm).

Australian Embassy: 2–1–14 Mita, Minato-ku, near Azabu-Juban Station, exit 2 (☎ **03/5232-4111;** www.australia.or.jp; consular section open Mon–Fri 9am–5:30pm; embassy open Mon–Fri 9am–12:30pm and 1:30–5pm).

New Zealand Embassy: 20–40 Kamiyama-cho, Shibuya-ku, a 15-minute walk from Shibuya Station (☎ **03/3467-2271;** www.nzembassy.com/japan; Mon–Fri 9am–5:30pm; call for consular hours).

Emergencies The national emergency numbers are ☎ **110** for **police** and ☎ **119** for **ambulance** and **fire** (ambulances are free in Japan unless you request a specific hospital). You do not need to insert any money into public telephones to call these numbers. However, if you use a green public telephone, it's necessary to push a red button before dialing. If you call from a gray public telephone or one that accepts only prepaid cards, you won't see a red button; in that case simply lift the receiver and dial.

Holidays See "When to Go," in chapter 3.

Hospitals Large hospitals in Japan are open only a limited number of hours (designated hospitals remain open for emergencies, however, and an ambulance will automatically take you there). Otherwise, you can make appointments at these hospital clinics to see a doctor: the **International Catholic Hospital (Seibo Byoin),** 2–5–1 Naka-Ochiai, Shinjuku-ku, near Mejiro Station on the Yamanote Line (☎ **03/3951-1111;** http://catholic-toshima.web9.jp/english/seibohospital.html; clinic hours Mon–Sat 8–11am; closed third Sat each month; walk-ins accepted); **St. Luke's International Hospital (Seiroka Byoin),** 9–1 Akashi-cho, Chuo-ku, near Tsukiji Station on the Hibiya Line (☎ **03/3541-5151;** www.luke.or.jp/eng; Mon–Fri 8:30–11am; appointment necessary for some treatments); and **Japan Red Cross Medical Center (Nihon Sekijujisha Iryo Center),** 4–1–22 Hiroo, Shibuya-ku (☎ **03/3400-1311;** www.med.jrc.or.jp/en; Mon–Fri 8:30–11am; walk-ins only), whose closest subway stations are Roppongi, Hiroo, and Shibuya—from there, you should take a taxi.

Many first-class hotels offer medical facilities or an in-house doctor. Both your embassy and the **AMDA International Medical Information Center** (☎ **03/5285-8088;** www.amdainternational.com; Mon–Fri 9am–5pm) can refer you to medical professionals who speak English.

The following clinics have some English-speaking staff and are popular with foreigners living in Tokyo: **Tokyo Midtown Medical Center,** an affiliate of Johns Hopkins and located on the sixth floor of Midtown Tower, 9–7–1 Akasaka, Minato-ku, near Roppongi Station (☎ **03/5413-7911;** www.tokyomidtown-mc.jp; open Mon–Fri 10:30am–1pm; accepts walk-ins, appointments, and emergencies); the **International Clinic,** 1–5–9 Azabudai, Minato-ku, within walking distance of Roppongi or Azabu-Juban stations (☎ **03/3582-2646;** open Mon–Fri 9am–noon and 2–5pm, Sat 9am–noon; walk-ins only); and **Tokyo Medical & Surgical Clinic,** 3–4–30 Shiba-koen, Minato-ku, near Kamiyacho, Onarimon, or Shiba-koen stations and across from Tokyo Tower (☎ **03/3436-3028;** www.tmsc.jp; open Mon–Fri 9–11:30am and 2–4:30pm, Sat 9am–noon; appointments only).

At the Tokyo Medical & Surgical Clinic, above, is the **Tokyo Clinic Dental Office** (✆ **03/3431-4225;** open Mon–Thurs 9am–6pm and Sat 9am–5pm). Just a 3-minute walk away is the **United Dental Office,** 2–3–8 Azabudai, Minato-ku (✆ **03/5570-4334;** www.uniteddentaloffice.com; open Mon–Tues and Thurs–Sat 9am–1pm and 2–6pm). Tokyo Midtown Medical Center (above) also has a **Dental Clinic;** call ✆ **03/5413-7912** for an appointment.

Internet Access   A good place to set up a temporary office is at the sophisticated **Gran Cyber Café Bagus,** on the 12th floor of the Roi Building, 5–5–1 Roppongi (✆ **03/5786-2280;** station: Roppongi). Open 24 hours, it offers individual cubicles with prices that depend on the chair you select: ¥500 for the first hour for a straight-back chair, ¥530 for a recliner, and ¥600 for a massage chair. Unsurprisingly, given Tokyo's high taxi prices, it also offers a "night pack" in a reclining chair, available for a maximum of 6 hours between 11pm to 8am for ¥1,450, as well as— brace yourself—booths for couples. You have to wonder how many people actually work. Ladies take note: There's a section just for you. Another 24-hour Gran Cyber Café Bagus is located in Shibuya, on the seventh floor of the HMV music store at 24–1 Udagawacho (✆ **03/5456-8922**).

A few places offer free Internet access, though waits can be long: **Marunouchi Café,** located on the tree-lined Marunouchi Naka Dori avenue in the Shin Tokyo Building, 3–3–1 Marunouchi (✆ **03/3212-5025;** stations: Marunouchi or Tokyo), with six computers available Monday to Friday 8am to 9pm and Saturday and Sunday 11am to 8pm (you'll need to show a photo ID, such as a passport); and the **Apple Store,** Ginza, 3–5–12 Ginza (✆ **03/5159-8200;** station: Ginza), with approximately five Macs on the fourth floor available daily from 10am to 9pm.

Although expensive, **FedEx Kinko's** has more than 30 locations throughout Tokyo, including one at Tokyo Station at the Yaesu north exit (✆ **03/3213-1811**). Most Kinko's are open 24 hours and charge ¥210 per 10 minutes of computer time.

Lost Property   For lost credit cards, see "Fast Facts: Japan" in chapter 16. I If you've lost something in a taxi, have someone who speaks Japanese contact the **Tokyo Taxi Center,** 7–3–3 Minamisuma, Koto-ku (✆ **03/3648-0300**). For JR trains, go to the nearest stationmaster's office (usually near the exit) or call the **JR East Infoline** (✆ **050/2016-1603**). For items lost in the **subway,** go to the nearest subway station; after 1 day, lost items are kept at Ueno Station's Lost and Found Center (✆ **03/3834-5577**) for 3 to 4 days.

Eventually, every unclaimed item in Tokyo ends up at the Central Lost and Found Office of the **Metropolitan Police Board,** 1–9–11 Koraku, Bunkyo-ku (✆ **03/3814-4151;** Mon–Fri 8:30am–5:15pm; station: Iidabashi).

Luggage Storage & Lockers   At Narita International Airport, delivery service counters will send luggage to your hotel the next day (or from your hotel to the airport) for about ¥1,690 to ¥2,000 per bag. Coin-operated lockers are located at all major JR stations, such as Tokyo, Shinjuku, and Ueno, as well as at most subway stations. Lockers cost ¥300 to ¥600 per day, depending on the size.

Mail   If your hotel cannot mail letters for you, ask the concierge where the nearest post office is. Although all post offices are open Monday through Friday from 9am to 5pm, major post offices in each ward remain open to 7pm. The **Shibuya Central**

Post Office, 1–12–13 Shibuya (☎ **03/5469-9907;** station: Shibuya), has longer business hours than most: Monday through Friday 9am to 9pm; and Saturday, Sunday, and holidays 9am to 7pm. An after-hours counter remains open through-out the night for mail and packages, making it the only 24-hour post office in town. *Note:* The Central Post Office, built in 1931 near Tokyo Station, is closed for major renovation until approximately 2012.

For English-language postal information, call ☎ **03/3560-1139** Monday through Friday between 9:30am and 4:30pm or check the website **www.post. japanpost.jp/english**. Also see "Mail" under "Fast Facts: Japan," in chapter 16.

Police   The national emergency telephone number is ☎ **110**. The Metropolitan Police Department also maintains a telephone counseling service for foreigners at ☎ **03/3501-0110** Monday through Friday from 8:30am to 5:15pm.

Safety   Tokyo is one of the safest cities in the world. However, crime is on the increase, and there are precautions you should always take when traveling: Stay alert and be aware of your immediate surroundings. Be especially careful with cameras, purses, and wallets, particularly in crowded subways, department stores, or tourist attractions (such as the retail district around Tsukiji Fish Market), espe-cially because pickpocketing has been on the rise. Some Japanese also caution women against walking through parks alone at night.

Smoking   The legal age for purchasing tobacco products and smoking in Japan is 20. Smoking is banned in Tokyo's public areas, including train and subway sta-tions and office buildings. In most wards (city districts), nonsmoking ordinances ban smoking on sidewalks but allow it in marked "Smokers Corner" areas, usually near train stations. Many restaurants have nonsmoking sections, though bars do not. Virtually all hotels offer nonsmoking rooms nowadays, including business hotels. Japanese-style inns, however, usually do not (though some are entirely nonsmoking facilities).

Taxes   In addition to the national 5% consumption tax, which is already included in the price of goods and services, Tokyo levies a local hotel tax on rooms costing ¥10,000 and up per person per night: ¥100 per person per night on rooms cost-ing ¥10,000 to ¥14,999; ¥200 per person per night on rooms of ¥15,000 and up.

Telephones   For information on how to make calls or where to rent mobile phones in Japan, see "Staying Connected" in chapter 3. For directory assistance in Tokyo, dial ☎ **104.**

Toilets   If you need a restroom in Tokyo, your best bets are train and subway stations, big hotels, department stores, and fast-food chains such as McDonald's. For an explanation on using Japanese toilets, see "Fast Facts: Japan" in chapter 16.

Visitor Information   See "Fast Facts: Japan" in chapter 16.

SETTLING INTO TOKYO

5

WHERE TO STAY

3 WHERE TO STAY

Tokyo has no old, grand hotels in the tradition of Hong Kong's Peninsula or Bangkok's Oriental; it has hardly any old hotels, period. But what the city's hotels may lack in quaintness or old grandeur is more than made up for by excellent service—for which Japanese are legendary—as well as cleanliness and efficiency. Be prepared, however, for

(Tips) **Mapping out Tokyo's Hotels**

Once you've chosen a hotel or inn that appeals to you, you can locate it using the following neighborhood maps:

small rooms. Space is at a premium in Tokyo, so with the exception of some of the upper-range hotels, rooms seem to come in only three sizes: small, minuscule, and barely adequate.

Unfortunately, Tokyo also doesn't have many first-class *ryokan,* or Japanese-style inns. I suggest, therefore, that you wait for your travels around the country to experience a first-rate ryokan. Otherwise, there are moderate and inexpensive Japanese-style inns in Tokyo. In fact, if you're traveling on a tight budget, a simple Japanese-style inn is often the cheapest way to go, though don't expect much in the way of service or amenities. In addition, most of the upper-bracket hotels offer at least a few Japanese-style rooms, with *tatami* mats, a Japanese bathtub (deeper and narrower than the Western version), and a futon. Although these rooms tend to be expensive, they're usually large enough for four people.

For more on available types of accommodations, see "Tips on Accommodations" in chapter 3.

PRICE CATEGORIES   The recommended hotels that follow are arranged first according to price, then by location. After all, because attractions are spread throughout the city, and Tokyo's public transportation service is fast and efficient (I've provided nearest subway or train stations for each listing)—and as this is one of the most expensive hotel cities in the world—the overriding factor in selecting accommodations will likely be cost. I've divided Tokyo's hotels into price categories based upon two people per night, including tax: **Very Expensive** hotels charge ¥50,000 and above, **Expensive** hotels charge ¥32,000 to ¥50,000, **Moderate** hotels offer rooms for ¥16,000 to ¥32,000, and **Inexpensive** accommodations offer rooms for less than ¥16,000.

Unless otherwise indicated, units have private bathrooms. Note, too, that in Japan, a **twin room** refers to a room with two twin beds, while a **double room** refers to a room with one double bed. For convenience's sake, however, the "double" rates for hotels listed below refer to two people in one room and include both twin and double beds. Most hotels charge more for a twin room, but sometimes the opposite is the case. When making your reservation, therefore, inquire about the differences in rates and what they entail.

TAXES & SERVICE CHARGES   All hotel rates below include a 5% government **tax.** An additional local hotel tax will be added to bills that cost more than ¥10,000 per person per night. ¥100 is levied per person per night for rates between ¥10,000 and ¥14,999; rates of ¥15,000 and up are taxed at ¥200. Furthermore, upper-class hotels and

SETTLING INTO TOKYO

5

WHERE TO STAY

SETTLING INTO TOKYO

5

WHERE TO STAY

ACCOMMODATIONS ■
Asia Center of Japan **3**
Hotel New Otani **1**

NIGHTLIFE◆
Garden Lounge **1**
Hobgoblin Tokyo **10**
Sam & Dave **8**

DINING ◆
Aux Bacchanales **2, 11**
daidaiya **7**
Gyu-Kaku **4**
Hayashi **9**
Ninja **5**
Nobu Tokyo **12**
Sekishin Tei **1**
Ten-ichi **6**

most medium-range hotels add a **service charge** of 10% to 15% (cheaper establishments do not add a service charge, because no service is provided). Unless otherwise stated, prices for accommodations include all taxes and service charge.

RESERVATIONS   Although Tokyo doesn't suffer from a lack of hotel rooms during peak holidays (when most Japanese head for the hills and beaches), rooms may be in short supply at other times because of conventions and other events. If possible, avoid coming to Tokyo in mid-February unless you book well in advance; that's when university entrance exams bring aspiring high-school students and their parents flocking to the capital for a shot at one of the most prestigious universities in the country. And in summer, when most foreign tourists visit Japan, the cheaper accommodations are likely to fill up first.

It's always best, therefore, to make your hotel reservations in advance, especially if you're arriving in Japan after a long transoceanic flight and don't want the hassle of searching for a hotel room. See "Finding a Hotel or Inn" in chapter 3 for tips on securing rooms. If you arrive in Tokyo without reservations, stop by the **Tourist Information Center** (**TIC;** see "Visitor Information" earlier in this chapter), where its Welcome Inn Reservation Center will book an inexpensive room free of charge.

VERY EXPENSIVE
Near Ginza

The Peninsula Tokyo ★★★   Travelers who love the ornate lobby of Hong Kong's The Peninsula may experience culture shock here. While the lobby layouts are the same—dominated by a restaurant popular for people-watching—here the decor is Zen-like, and the emphasis is on the rooms. Rooms begin at 51 sq. m. (544 sq. ft.), with the most expensive facing the Imperial Palace and Hibiya Park, and amenities include bedside controls that light up with the slightest touch, gorgeous bathrooms with mood lighting (and tubs big enough for two), dryers just for nails, humidifiers, and mobile phones for use throughout the hotel. Add a fantastic location between the Imperial Palace and Ginza, gratis transportation via Rolls-Royce within a 2km (1¼-mile) radius, free iPod tours of the surrounding area, and the Peninsula Academy offering tours of Tsukiji Fish Market or classes for cooking and flower arranging, and it's clear this hotel is in a class all its own.

1–8–1 Yurakucho, Chiyoda-ku, Tokyo 100-0006. © **866/382 8388** in the U.S., or 03/6270-2888. Fax 03/6270-2000. www.peninsula.com. 314 units. ¥60,000–¥80,000 single or double; from ¥100,000 suite. Rates exclude all taxes and service charge. AE, DC, MC, V. Station: Yurakucho (3 min.); Hibiya (1 min.). **Amenities:** 5 restaurants; lounge; babysitting; concierge; health club and spa; indoor pool w/outdoor terrace; room service; smoke-free rooms. *In room:* A/C, TV/DVD/DVD library, CD player, fax/printer, hair dryer, minibar, Wi-Fi.

Shinjuku

Park Hyatt Tokyo ★★★   Located on the 39th to 52nd floors of Kenzo Tange's granite-and-glass Shinjuku Park Tower, the Park Hyatt is among the most gorgeous hotels in Japan, a perfect reflection of high-tech Tokyo. If you can afford it, stay here. Though it doesn't attract as much off-the-street foot traffic as Shinjuku's other hotels, the Park Hyatt's debut in *Lost in Translation* assures a steady stream of curious fans to its lounges and restaurants. Be sure to book early, therefore, for the 52nd-floor New York Grill, one of Tokyo's best restaurants. All rooms average at least 45 sq. m (484 sq. ft.) and have original artwork, stunning views (including Mount Fuji on clear days), bathrooms to die for with deep tubs and separate showers, walk-in closets, and even Japanese/English-language dictionaries. Although no longer the only high-in-the-sky luxury hotel, this property remains high on my short list of great places to stay.

3-7-1-2 Nishi-Shinjuku, Shinjuku-ku, Tokyo 163-1055. Ⓒ **800/233-1234** in the U.S. and Canada, or 03/5322-1234. Fax 03/5322-1288. www.tokyo.park.hyatt.com. 178 units. ¥69,300–¥87,780 single or double; from ¥167,000 suite. Rates exclude hotel tax. AE, DC, MC, V. Station: Shinjuku (13-min. walk or 5-min. free shuttle ride); Hatsudai on the Keio Line (7 min.); or Tochomae (8 min.). **Amenities:** 3 restaurants, including New York Grill (p. 162); 2 bars; lounge; babysitting; concierge; health club and spa; dramatic 20m (66-ft.) indoor swimming pool w/great views; room service; free shuttle service to Shinjuku Station up to 3 times an hour; smoke-free rooms. *In room:* A/C, TV/DVD, CD player/CD library, hair dryer, minibar, Wi-Fi.

Ebisu

Westin Tokyo ★★ (Value)   Set in the attractive Yebisu Garden Place (Tokyo's first planned community), it's still a hike from Ebisu Station, even with the aid of the elevated moving walkways. But the largely Japanese clientele (North Americans account for 25% of the guests) favors it for its European ambience, relaxed atmosphere, and Yebisu Garden Place with its restaurants and shopping. The spacious, high-ceilinged rooms blend luxurious 19th-century Biedermeier style with contemporary furnishings and Westin's trademark "Heavenly Beds." Rooms on higher floors cost more, with the best views considered those facing Tokyo Tower, though on clear days those facing west treat you to views of Mount Fuji. Executive Club rooms include Guest Office rooms (with printer/fax machines and office supplies), Workout Rooms (with exercise equipment), and a Ladies Floor with heightened security along with a yoga DVD and mat, jewelry box, vanity, humidifiers, female toiletries, and free espresso.

1-4-1 Mita, Meguro-ku, Tokyo 153-8580. Ⓒ **800/937-8461** in the U.S. and Canada, or 03/5423-7000. Fax 03/5423-7600. www.westin-tokyo.co.jp. 438 units. ¥65,100–¥68,250 single or double; from ¥73,500 Executive Club; from ¥157,500 suite. Rates exclude service charge and hotel tax. AE, DC, MC, V. Station: Ebisu (7 min. via Yebisu Sky Walk). **Amenities:** 5 restaurants; 2 bars; lounge; babysitting; concierge; executive-level rooms; exercise room (¥1,000; free for Starwood Preferred Guest and Executive Club members); access to nearby health club w/heated indoor pool and gym (¥4,000; ¥2,500 for Executive Club and Platinum members); room service; smoke-free rooms; spa. *In room:* A/C, TV/DVD, hair dryer, Internet (¥1,800 for 24 hr.), minibar.

Roppongi

Grand Hyatt Tokyo ★★★   Depending on the surrounding Roppongi Hills development with its 200-some shops and restaurants to act as a major draw, this ambitious hotel wows with a wide range of recreational and dining facilities, as well as technically advanced rooms that older hotels can only dream about. In contrast to sister Park Hyatt's subdued, sophisticated atmosphere that attracts bigwigs hoping to escape the limelight, the Grand Hyatt strives for a livelier clientele who relish being in the center of it all. Key cards inserted into elevators block public access to guest floors, and those seeking pampering can opt for the Grand Club floor. Rooms, starting at 42 sq. m (452 sq. ft.), feature Italian furnishings, large mahogany desks, blackout blinds, safes designed for laptops with plug ins for recharging, and duvet-covered beds with focused reading lights. One-quarter of each unit's space is taken up by a huge bathroom equipped with separate shower and tub areas and a small TV that swivels from the tub to the sink.

6-10-3 Roppongi, Minato-ku, Tokyo 106-0032. Ⓒ **800/233-1234** in the U.S. and Canada, or 03/4333-1234. Fax 03/4333-8123. www.tokyo.grand.hyatt.com. 389 units. ¥60,060–¥68,145 single; ¥65,835–¥73,920 double; from ¥77,385 Grand Club double; from ¥112,035 suite. Rates exclude hotel tax. AE, DC,

SETTLING INTO TOKYO

WHERE TO STAY

5

MC, V. Station: Roppongi (exit 1, 3 min.) or Azabu-Juban (exit A3, 5 min.). **Amenities:** 7 restaurants; 3 bars; babysitting; concierge (plus technology concierge to address your computer woes); executive-level rooms; health club w/20m (66-ft.) indoor pool and spa (¥4,200); room service; smoke-free rooms. *In room:* A/C, TV/DVD and DVD library, hair dryer, Internet, minibar.

The Ritz-Carlton, Tokyo ★★★   Of the several luxury hotels to come online the past few years, the Ritz-Carlton literally tops them all: It occupies the lofty upper reaches of Tokyo's tallest building, making it the highest hotel in a city that prides itself on sky-scraper hotels. The crowning glory of Roppongi's Midtown urban renewal project, it boasts Tokyo's largest rooms (starting at 52 sq. m/560 sq. ft.), its most expensive suite (¥2,100,000), and the city's highest ratio of nonsmoking rooms (80%). Rooms, from the 47th to 53rd floors, provide eye-popping views of Tokyo and come with everything you'd expect from a top-rated hotel, including king-size (the majority) or two double beds, wireless telephones you can take with you anywhere in the hotel, a safe with plug-ins to recharge laptops, a good working desk, and—great for couples—two large closets. Bathrooms, which account for a third of the room's space, are among the best I've seen in Japan.

Tokyo Midtown, 9–7–1 Akasaka, Minato-ku, Tokyo 107-6245. ✆ **800/241-3333** in the U.S. and Canada, or 03/3423-8000. Fax 03/3423-8001. www.ritzcarlton.com. 248 units. ¥68,250–¥71,400 single; ¥73,500–¥76,650 double; Grand Floor from ¥84,000 single, ¥94,500 double; from ¥115,500 suite. Rates exclude service charge and hotel tax. AE, DC, MC, V. Station: Roppongi or Nogizaka (3 min.). **Amenities:** 3 restaurants; bar; lounge; babysitting; concierge; executive-level rooms; health club w/20m (66-ft.) indoor lap pool and spa (free entrance to health club; spa entrance: ¥5,250); room service; smoke-free rooms. *In room:* A/C, TV/DVD, CD player, hair dryer, minibar, Wi-Fi.

Other Neighborhoods

Four Seasons Hotel Tokyo at Chinzan-So ★★★ (Finds) (Kids)   Although inconveniently located in northwest Tokyo (about a 15-min. taxi ride from Ikebukuro), the Four Seasons Tokyo is a superb hotel set in the luscious 6.8-hectare (17-acre), 100-year-old Chinzan-So Garden, making it extremely inviting after a bustling day in Tokyo. It also has what may be Tokyo's best spa, including a gorgeous glass-enclosed indoor pool surrounded by greenery with a glass ceiling that opens in summer and a Japanese hot-springs bath (the water is shipped in from Izu Peninsula). Its luxurious interiors make this one of the most beautiful European-style hotels in Japan, and because the hotel embraces the park, most rooms have peaceful garden views from their V-shaped bay windows (those that don't are cheaper, but the garden views are worth the splurge). Don't miss a stroll through the garden, which contains several charming, traditional Japanese restaurants; a pagoda; and stone monuments.

2–10–8 Sekiguchi, Bunkyo-ku, Tokyo 112-8667. ✆ **800/819-5053** in the U.S. and Canada, or 03/3943-2222. Fax 03/3943-2300. www.fourseasons.com/tokyo. 259 units. ¥52,500–¥57,750 single; ¥57,750–¥70,350 double; from ¥84,000 suite. Rates exclude service charge and hotel tax. AE, DC, MC, V. Station: Edogawabashi (exit 1a, a 10-min. walk along a cherry-tree-lined canal or a 2-min. ride). **Amenities:** 3 restaurants (plus 3 tenant restaurants in the garden); 2 lounges; babysitting; concierge; executive-level rooms; health club w/indoor pool and spa (fee: ¥4,200); room service; smoke-free rooms. *In room:* A/C, TV/DVD and DVD library, CD player, hair dryer, Internet, minibar, MP3 docking station.

EXPENSIVE
Ginza & Hibiya

Imperial Hotel ★★★ (Kids)   Located across from Hibiya Park, this is one of Tokyo's best-known hotels. Its history dates from 1890, when it opened at the request of the imperial family to house foreigners coming to Japan; it was rebuilt in 1922 by Frank

Family-Friendly Hotels

Four Seasons Hotel Tokyo at Chinzan-So (p. 132) If money is no object, little princes and princesses receive the royal treatment here, including child-size robes, children's menus, complimentary toiletries, and bedtime cookies and milk. And for those hard-to-please teenagers, there's even free use of TV video games.

Hotel New Otani (p. 134) This huge hotel has an outdoor swimming pool (which you can use free of charge by becoming a Hotel Club member), but best for parents is the babysitting room for children ages 1 month to 5 years. For a small fortune, you can even leave the darlings overnight.

Imperial Hotel (p. 132) This famous hotel makes it easier to bring the family along, with its day-care center for children ages 2 weeks to 6 years, its babysitting service, and an indoor pool, which you can use free of charge by becoming a member of the Imperial Club.

Ryokan Kamogawa (p. 143) Located in colorful Asakusa with its famous Sensoji Temple and small Hanayashiki amusement park, this Japanese inn offers *tatami* rooms large enough for up to six persons, plus a private family bath.

Shinagawa Prince (p. 142) Japan's largest hotel boasts a children's day-care center, cinema complex, amusement arcade, indoor and outdoor pools, aquarium, bowling alley, sports center, and much more.

Lloyd Wright, but the present hotel dates from 1970, with a 31-story tower added in 1983. Wright's legacy lives on in the hotel's Art Deco Old Imperial bar (p. 227) and Wright-inspired designs and furniture in public spaces. (Part of Wright's original structure survives as Meiji Mura, an architectural museum outside Nagoya.) A full range of facilities includes a children's day-care center. Rooms in the main building are quite large, while Tower rooms, slightly smaller, are higher up, have floor-to-ceiling windows, and offer fantastic views of either Imperial Palace grounds or, my preference, Ginza. All come with first-class amenities you'd expect, as well as such extras as a hands-free phone, safes with plug-ins for laptops, and one-touch bedside controls for lights, drapes, and music. *Tip:* Become a member of the Imperial Club (membership is free), and you can use the small pool and gym free.

1–1–1 Uchisaiwaicho, Chiyoda-ku, Tokyo 100-8558. ℂ **800/223-6800** in the U.S. and Canada, or 03/3504-1111. Fax 03/3581-9146. www.imperialhotel.co.jp/e/tokyo. 1,019 units. ¥33,600—¥57,750 single; ¥38,850–¥63,000 double; from ¥63,000 suite. Imperial Floor ¥45,150–¥63,000 single; ¥50,400–¥68,250 double. Rates exclude service charge and hotel tax. AE, DC, MC, V. Station: Hibiya (1 min.). **Amenities:** 13 restaurants, including Kamon, Ten-ichi, and the Imperial Viking Sal (p. 149, 152, and 153); 2 bars; 2 lounges; babysitting; children's day-care center for ages 2 weeks–6 years (¥5,250 for 2 hr.); concierge; executive-level rooms; exercise room (¥1,050; free for Imperial Club members); in-house doctor; 20th-floor indoor pool (¥1,050; free for Imperial Club members); post office; room service; sauna; smoke-free rooms; tea-ceremony room. *In room:* A/C, TV, hair dryer, Internet, minibar.

Marunouchi Hotel ★   A modern replacement of a 1924 hotel, this low-key lodging is in the heart of Tokyo's business district, and it is convenient to both train and plane travel. Occupying the top 11 floors of the Marunouchi Oazo glass high-rise, it exudes Zen-like solemnity, with bare wooden floors and *shoji*-like walls in a lobby that overlooks a rooftop garden. Key cards are required to access elevators to guest rooms, which are of standard size and decorated in warm browns. Small bathrooms have deep Japanese-style tubs with pillows for relaxing. Roomy deluxe twins have "Japanese corners," a *tatami* area with a low table (and a "leg well" for errant limbs). For the best view ask for a room facing Tokyo Station, where triple-pane glass allows you to watch bullet trains glide by. Though quite classy, the Marunouchi lacks in facilities and services, placing it more squarely in the business-hotel category.

1–6–3 Marunouchi, Chiyoda-ku, Tokyo 100-0005. ✆ **03/3217-1111.** Fax 03/3217-1115. www. marunouchi-hotel.co.jp. 205 units. ¥23,300–¥29,075 single; ¥31,385–¥52,375 double; ¥115,900 suite. AE, DC, MC, V. Station: Tokyo (1 min., via underground passageway) or Otemachi (2 min.). **Amenities:** 3 restaurants; bar; concierge; room service; smoke-free rooms. *In room:* A/C, TV, fridge, Internet.

Shinjuku

Hyatt Regency Tokyo ★   Located on Shinjuku's west side next to Shinjuku Chuo (Central) Park (popular with joggers), this least expensive and oldest of the Hyatt's three Tokyo properties celebrated its 25th anniversary in 2005 with renovated restaurants and rooms. Remaining is the hotel's impressive seven-story atrium lobby with three of the most massive chandeliers you're likely to see anywhere. Many foreigners (mostly American) pass through the hotel's doors, ably assisted by the excellent staff, which meets the Hyatt's usual high standards. However, since this hotel is popular with both business and leisure groups, those seeking a quieter, more personalized experience will want to book elsewhere. Rates are based on size; even the cheapest units are adequate, but they do face another building and don't receive much sunshine. If you can afford it, spring for a more expensive room on a high floor with bay windows overlooking the park (in winter, you might also have a view of Mount Fuji).

2–7–2 Nishi-Shinjuku, Shinjuku-ku, Tokyo 160-0023. ✆ **800/233-1234** in the U.S. and Canada, or 03/3348-1234. Fax 03/3344-5575. www.tokyo.regency.hyatt.com. 744 units. ¥32,270 single; ¥42,735–¥47,355 double. Regency Club from ¥49,665 single; ¥53,130 double. Rates exclude hotel tax. AE, DC, MC, V. Station: Tochomae (1 min.), Nishi-Shinjuku (3 min.), or Shinjuku (10-min. walk, or free 3-min. shuttle ride). **Amenities:** 6 restaurants; bar; concierge; executive-level rooms; health club w/indoor pool (¥2,000) and spa; room service; smoke-free rooms; free shuttle service to Shinjuku Station every 20 min. *In room:* A/C, TV, hair dryer, Internet, minibar.

Akasaka

Hotel New Otani ★★ (**Kids**)   Like a city unto itself, the New Otani is so big that two information desks are needed to assist lost souls searching for a particular restaurant or one of the shops in the meandering arcade. The hotel's most splendid feature is a 400-year-old Japanese garden that once belonged to a feudal lord, with 4 hectares (10 acres) of ponds, waterfalls, bridges, bamboo groves, and manicured bushes. Rooms in the main building are comfortable, with full-length windows to take advantage of city and garden views. Tower rooms, including "*fusui* healing" rooms with such extras as in-room humidifier and foot bath, offer the best views (on clear days, Mount Fuji). Since rates are the same no matter which way you face, be sure to request a room overlooking the garden. Parents appreciate the 24-hour Baby Room and the fact that the outdoor pool is free for those who become Hotel Club members (membership is free).

4-1 Kioi-cho, Chiyoda-ku, Tokyo 102-8578. ℂ **800/421-8795** in the U.S. and Canada, or 03/3265-1111. Fax 03/3221-2619. www.newotani.co.jp. 1,533 units. ¥31,500–¥34,650 single; ¥37,800–¥73,500 double; from ¥50,400 Executive House Zen; from ¥89,250 suite. Rates exclude service charge and hotel tax. AE, DC, MC, V. Station: Akasaka-mitsuke or Nagatacho (3 min.). **Amenities:** 38 restaurants and cafes, including Sekishin Tei (p. 175); 6 bars and lounges; art museum (free for hotel guests); children's day-care center for ages 1 month–5 years (¥6,300 for 2 hr.); concierge; executive-level rooms; small exercise room; health club w/indoor pool and spa (¥5,250); medical and dental clinics; outdoor pool (¥2,000; free for Hotel Club members); post office; room service; smoke-free rooms; tea-ceremony room; lighted outdoor tennis courts. *In room:* A/C, TV, hair dryer, Internet (fee: ¥1,260 for 24 hr.), minibar.

Hotel Okura ★★★   Located across from the U.S. Embassy and long considered one of Tokyo's most venerable hotels, the Okura is struggling to keep up with newer hotels in the city. Still, it remains a favorite home-away-from-home of visiting U.S. dignitaries, and the service is gracious and impeccable. Rich decor elegantly combines Japanese traditions with an old-fashioned Western spaciousness. The atmosphere is low-key, with none of the flashiness inherent in some newer hotels. All rooms are comfortable, with opaque windows designed to resemble *shoji* and gold colors offset by fuchsia or other bright-colored armchairs and pillows. My favorite rooms are in the main building facing the garden; some on the fifth floor here have balconies overlooking the garden and pool. Other rooms have views of a rooftop garden or Tokyo Tower, while "Grand Comfort rooms" on the 9th and 10th floors offer free entrance to the spa. *Tip:* Become a member of Okura Club International (membership is free) and you can use the health club and pools for free.

2-10-4 Toranomon, Minato-ku, Tokyo 105-0001. ℂ **800/526-2281** in the U.S. and Canada, or 03/3582-0111. Fax 03/3582-3707. www.okura.com/tokyo. 833 units. ¥36,750–¥44,100 single; ¥42,000–¥49,350 double; from ¥78,750 suite. Grand Comfort rooms ¥52,500 single; ¥66,150 double. Rates exclude service charge and hotel tax. AE, DC, MC, V. Station: Toranomon or Kamiyacho (5 min.). **Amenities:** 10 restaurants; 3 bars; children's day-care center (¥6,300 for 2 hr.); concierge; in-house dentist; health club w/ indoor 20m (66-ft.) pool (¥5,775) and spa; private museum showcasing Japanese art (free); packing and shipping service; pharmacy; nicely landscaped outdoor pool (¥2,100); post office; room service; free shuttle to the nearest subways (weekends only); smoke-free rooms; tea-ceremony room. *In room:* A/C, TV, hair dryer, Internet (¥1,500 for 1 day), minibar.

Near Shinagawa
Sheraton Miyako Hotel Tokyo ★★ (**Value**)   This hotel is one of my favorites in Tokyo, for its calm peacefulness as well as its small-luxury-hotel service. Because it's a bit off the beaten path, it has a quieter, more relaxed atmosphere than those found at more centrally located hotels, evident the moment you step into its lobby lounge with its gas-flame fireplace (winter only) on one end and the lush greenery of a garden on its other. It offers average-size rooms, with good bedside reading lamps and beds so comfortable you'd sneak them into your luggage if you could. The best rooms are on higher floors with huge floor-to-ceiling windows overlooking the hotel's own lush garden, a famed garden next door, or Tokyo Tower. This is a fine choice of hotel, despite its out-of-the-way location (mitigated by frequent complimentary shuttle service to Meguro Station).

1-1-50 Shirokanedai, Minato-ku, Tokyo 108-8640. ℂ **800/325-3535** in the U.S. and Canada, or 03/3447-3111. Fax 03/3447-3133. www.miyakohotels.ne.jp/tokyo. 495 units. ¥28,350–¥44,100 single; ¥31,500–¥47,250 double; from ¥74,550 suite. Rates exclude service charge and hotel tax. AE, DC, MC, V. Station: Shirokanedai (4 min.), Shirokane-Takanawa (5 min.), or free shuttle from Meguro Station. **Amenities:** 3 restaurants; bar; lounge; concierge; dental/medical clinics; health club w/25m (82-ft.) indoor heated pool and spa (¥735); room service; free shuttle service to Meguro Station every 15 min. and Shinagawa Station (mornings only); smoke-free rooms. *In room:* A/C, TV, hair dryer, Internet, minibar.

Shinjuku West

NISHI-SHINJUKU
6-CHOME

Ohme Kaido

Shinjuku
Nomura Bldg.

Yasuda Kasai
Kaijo Bldg.

L Tower
Bldg.

Shinjuku Dai-ichi
Seimei Bldg.

Shinjuku
Mitsui Bldg.

Odakyu HALC

Sumitomo
Bldg.

Shinjuku
Center Bldg.

Bus Terminal

NISHI-SHINJUKU   Chuo Dori
2-CHOME

Kogakuin
Univ.

Odakyu Dept.
Store

TMG

Shinjuku Post Office

Keio Dept.
Store

No. 11 Street

No. 10 Street

No. 9 Street

NISHI-SHINJUKU
1-CHOME

Shinjuku
Station

TMG

N.S. Bldg.

KDD Bldg.

ODAKYU LINE

YOYOGI

Koshu-Kaido   Dori

KEIO LINE

Railway
Subway
Tourist
Information

Odaiba

Hotel Nikko Tokyo ★★   This is the most un-Tokyo-like hotel in the city. Located on Odaiba in Tokyo Bay with its convention center, shopping malls, and sightseeing attractions, this grand lodging is surrounded by parks and sea. Billing itself as an "urban resort," it's especially popular with young well-to-do Japanese in search of an exotic weekend getaway. A curved facade assures waterfront views from most rooms, which have the added benefit of private balconies with two chairs. The most expensive rooms offer commanding views of Tokyo Bay, Rainbow Bridge, and the city skyline (impressive at night); the least expensive rooms face another hotel or the Maritime Museum and Haneda Airport across the bay. This is a great choice if you want to get away from the bustle of Tokyo, but the location can be a disadvantage; it's served only by the expensive monorail Yurikamome Line, the JR Saikyo Line to Shibuya, and the inconvenient Rinkai Line, which can be quite crowded on weekends.

1–9–1 Daiba, Minato-ku, Tokyo 135-8625. ℂ **800/645-5687** in the U.S. and Canada, or 03/5500-5500. Fax 03/5500-2525. www.hnt.co.jp. 453 units. ¥42,000–¥68,000 single or double; from ¥150,000 suite. Rates exclude hotel tax. AE, DC, MC, V. Station: Daiba (1 min.) or Tokyo Teleport Station (10 min., or free shuttle

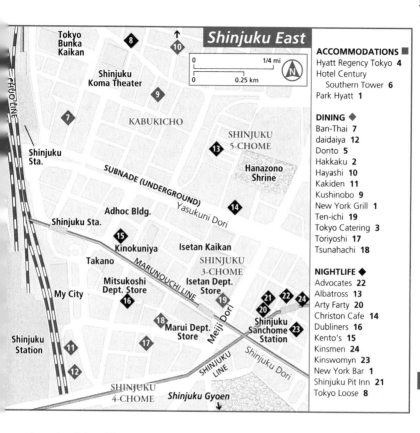

Shinjuku East

0 — 1/4 mi
0 — 0.25 km

Tokyo Bunka Kaikan **8**
10
Shinjuku Koma Theater
9
7
KABUKICHO
Shinjuku Sta.
SHINJUKU 5-CHOME
13
Hanazono Shrine
SUBNADE (UNDERGROUND)
Yasukuni Dori
Adhoc Bldg.
Shinjuku Sta.
14
15
Kinokuniya
Isetan Kaikan
Takano
SHINJUKU 3-CHOME
MARUNOUCHI LINE
Mitsukoshi Dept. Store
Isetan Dept. Store
My City
16
19
Meiji Dori
21 **22** **24**
20
18 Marui Dept. Store
Shinjuku Sanchome Station
23
17
SHINJUKU LINE
Shinjuku Dori
Shinjuku Station
11
12
SHINJUKU 4-CHOME
Shinjuku Gyoen
CHUO LINE

ACCOMMODATIONS ■
Hyatt Regency Tokyo **4**
Hotel Century Southern Tower **6**
Park Hyatt **1**

DINING ◆
Ban-Thai **7**
daidaiya **12**
Donto **5**
Hakkaku **2**
Hayashi **10**
Kakiden **11**
Kushinobo **9**
New York Grill **1**
Ten-ichi **19**
Tokyo Catering **3**
Toriyoshi **17**
Tsunahachi **18**

NIGHTLIFE ◆
Advocates **22**
Albatross **13**
Arty Farty **20**
Christon Cafe **14**
Dubliners **16**
Kento's **15**
Kinsmen **24**
Kinswomyn **23**
New York Bar **1**
Shinjuku Pit Inn **21**
Tokyo Loose **8**

SETTLING INTO TOKYO

5

WHERE TO STAY

bus to hotel). **Amenities:** 8 restaurants; bar; lounge; babysitting; concierge; room service; free shuttle service from Tokyo Teleport Station every 15 min.; smoke-free rooms; spa w/indoor pool linked to outdoor heated tub, Jacuzzi, and sun terrace overlooking Rainbow Bridge (¥3,150 the 1st day; thereafter ¥1,000). *In room:* A/C, TV, hair dryer, Internet (¥2,600 per stay), minibar.

MODERATE
Ginza & Hibiya
Courtyard by Marriott Tokyo Ginza Hotel ★   This small, classy, and personable hotel, located on Showa Dori behind the Ginza Matsuzakaya department store and within easy walking distance of shopping and nightlife, attracts a foreign clientele as high as 60%, thanks mainly to its association with Marriott. Primarily a business hotel, it has limited facilities—you are clearly paying for location here. Rooms are contemporary but small, including small windows (there's nothing to see anyway) and small bathrooms. Be sure to pick up the hotel's sightseeing leaflets at the concierge's desk, which give information on the city's top attractions, opening hours, and how to reach them from the hotel.

6–14–10 Ginza, Chuo-ku, Tokyo 104-0061. ℰ **888/321-2211** in the U.S. and Canada, or 03/3546-0111. Fax 03/3546-8990. www.marriott.com/tyocy. 206 units. ¥25,500 single; ¥30,000 double. AE, DC, MC, V. Station: Ginza (5 min.) or Higashi-Ginza (1 min.). **Amenities:** 2 restaurants; bar; lounge; concierge; executive-level rooms; exercise room; room service; smoke-free rooms. *In room:* A/C, TV, hair dryer, Internet (¥1,000 for 24 hr.), minibar.

Hotel Com's Ginza   Because of its great location, convenient to Ginza, Shimbashi, and Hibiya shopping and business centers, this attractive hotel caters mostly to business travelers, but tourists like it, too. The lobby, on the second floor, has a friendly staff and an exceptionally long front desk, which hopefully translates into quicker service. Rooms, from the 3rd to 11th floors, are tiny but pleasant, with the more expensive rooms sporting comfortable leather chairs, good-size desks, espresso machines, a TV with headphones, and duvet-covered beds (but no closets). Note that the cheapest rooms (also without closets) don't have desks or space to unpack, a good example of what ¥25,000 buys in Tokyo. I suggest asking for a room away from the highway overpass beside the hotel.

8–6–15 Ginza, Chuo-ku, Tokyo 104-0061. ℰ **03/3572-4131.** Fax 03/3572-4254. www.granvista.co.jp. 267 units. ¥14,500–¥21,500 single; ¥25,000–¥34,800 double. AE, DC, MC, V. Station: Shimbashi (2 min.). **Amenities:** 3 restaurants; bar; lounge; smoke-free rooms. *In room:* A/C, TV, hair dryer, Internet.

Hotel Gracery ★★ ⓥ**alue**   You can't beat the rates and prime Ginza location of this budget hotel, just off Chuo Dori behind Ginza Sapporo Lion. Part of a business hotel chain targeting downtown metropolises, it offers tiny rooms smartly decorated in beige and red, with duvet-covered beds, unit bathrooms, and clothes racks filling in for closets. Female travelers may opt for the Lady's Floor, which features wooden floors (in the belief that walking barefoot on wood makes one feel more relaxed) and amenities geared toward women (including cleansing cream, facial masks, and bath salts), while those looking for an upgrade can try the Executive Floor, with TVs that double as computers.

7–10–1 Ginza, Chuo-ku, Tokyo 104-0061. ℰ **03/6686-1000.** Fax 03/6858-1020. www.gracery-ginza.com. 270 units. ¥15,600–¥22,200 single; ¥22,200–¥24,200 double. AE, DC, MC, V. Station: Ginza (3 min.) or Shimbashi (7 min.). **Amenities:** Restaurant; smoke-free rooms. *In room:* A/C, TV, fridge, hair dryer, Internet.

Mitsui Garden Hotel Ginza Premier ★★ ⒻFinds   This chic hotel is a notch above older Ginza properties and a good choice for business travelers looking for stylish rooms with good views. Located at the edge of Ginza close to Shimbashi, it occupies the upper floors of an office building (reception is on the 16th floor), with guest rooms providing panoramic views of either Tokyo Bay or Ginza with its glittering night views. As with most business hotels, rooms are mostly singles, with both desks and love seats placed strategically at windows to take advantage of the hotel's best feature. Even bathrooms take advantage of the views, with those in single rooms boasting windows that look out past the bedroom toward the views beyond (the glass can be switched from transparent to opaque with the flip of a switch), while those in the most expensive double and twin rooms have windows that let you gaze upon Tokyo right from the tub.

8–13–1 Ginza, Chuo-ku, Tokyo 104-0061. ℰ **03/3543-1131.** Fax 03/3543-5531. www.gardenhotels.co.jp/eng/ginza.html. 361 units. ¥18,900–¥21,000 single; ¥25,200–¥34,650 double. Rates exclude hotel tax. AE, DC, MC, V. Station: Shimbasi (5 min.) or Ginza (7 min.). **Amenities:** Restaurant; bar; smoke-free rooms. *In room:* A/C, TV, fridge, hair dryer, Internet.

Park Hotel Tokyo ★★ ⒻFinds   Occupying the top 10 floors of the building it shares with international media organizations, this hotel is located downtown just a few minutes' walk from Ginza. Its lobby, decorated with large trees and dark woods in a theme

> ## ⓘ Tips   A Double or a Twin?
>
> For the sake of convenience, the price for two people in a room is listed as a "double" in this book. Japanese hotels, however, differentiate between rooms with a double bed or two twin beds, usually with different prices. Most hotels charge more for a twin room, but sometimes the opposite is true; if you're looking for a bargain, therefore, be sure to inquire about prices for both. Note, too, that hotels usually have more twin rooms than doubles, for the simple reason that Japanese couples, used to their own futon, traditionally prefer twin beds.

of "nature and health," is bathed in the natural sunlight afforded by its 10-story atrium topped with an opaque ceiling. Restaurants follow a natural-foods concept, using organic ingredients. The front desk is one of the most dramatic I've seen, backed by nothing but great views of Tokyo Tower and the city. Rooms are simply decorated, with original art; they also provide views, the best of which can be found on the 30th floor and above facing Hama Rikyu Garden and Tokyo Bay or facing Tokyo Tower (and Mount Fuji on clear winter days). The hotel even has a trained "pillow fitter," who can take your measurements and provide one made to fit, at no extra cost.

Shiodome Media Tower, 1-7-1 Higashi Shimbashi, Minato-ku, Tokyo 105-7227. ☎ **03/6252-1111.** Fax 03/6252-1001. www.parkhoteltokyo.com. 273 units. ¥21,000 single; ¥26,250–¥37,800 double. Rates exclude service charge and hotel tax. AE, DC, MC, V. Station: Shiodome (1 min.) or Shimbashi (8 min.). **Amenities:** 3 restaurants; bar; lounge; room service; smoke-free rooms. *In room:* A/C, TV, hair dryer, Internet, minibar.

Asakusa

Asakusa View Hotel   This upper-bracket, modern hotel in the Asakusa area looks out of place rising 28 stories above this famous district's older buildings. Still, it's a good place to stay if you want to be in Tokyo's old downtown but don't want to sacrifice any creature comforts. The medium-size guest rooms are pleasant, with contemporary furnishings and bay windows that let in plenty of sunshine (and smaller windows that can be opened, a rarity in Tokyo). Rooms facing the front (east) have views over the famous Sensoji Temple, but those on the top floor facing west have views of Mount Fuji on clear days (mostly in winter). In the Asakusa area, on Kokusai Dori.

3-17-1 Nishi-Asakusa, Taito-ku, Tokyo 111-8765. ☎ **03/3847-1111.** Fax 03/3842-2117. www.viewhotels. co.jp/asakusa. 337 units. ¥15,750–¥18,900 single; ¥31,500–¥34,650 double. Executive floor from ¥33,600 double. Rates exclude service charge and hotel tax. AE, DC, MC, V. Station: Tawaramachi (8 min.) or Tsukuba Express Asakusa (1 min.). **Amenities:** 4 restaurants; 2 bars; lounge; executive-level rooms; 20m (66-ft.) indoor pool w/retractable roof (¥3,150); room service; smoke-free rooms. *In room:* A/C, TV, hair dryer, Internet, minibar.

Hotel Sunroute Asakusa   Located on Kokusai Dori, this pleasant business hotel is a good choice for leisure travelers as well. Not only does it boast a good location near the sightseeing attractions of Asakusa, but it is also classier than most business hotels, with Miró reprints in the lobby and modern artwork in each guest room. Though small, the (mostly single) rooms come with all the comforts, with slightly larger beds and bathrooms than those found at most business hotels. Double rooms, however, are very small for two people, so you might want to spring for a more expensive twin-bedded room.

SETTLING INTO TOKYO

5

WHERE TO STAY

The hotel's one coffee shop, a chain called Jonathan's serving both Japanese and Western food, is open daily 24 hours, a huge plus if you're suffering from jet lag.

1–8–5 Kaminarimon, Taito-ku, Tokyo 111-0034. ☎ **03/3847-1511.** Fax 03/3847-1509. www.sunroute-asakusa.co.jp. 120 units. ¥10,500–¥11,550 single; ¥16,275–¥21,000 double. Rates exclude hotel tax. AE, DC, MC, V. Station: Tawaramachi (1 min.) or Asakusa (8 min.). **Amenities:** Restaurant; lobby computers w/ free Internet; smoke-free rooms. *In room:* A/C, TV, fridge, hair dryer, Internet.

Shinjuku

Hotel Century Southern Tower ★★★ ⒻFinds This chic, modern hotel is located just southwest of Shinjuku Station and just a footbridge away from the huge Takashimaya Shinjuku shopping complex. Because it occupies the top floors of a sleek white building, it seems far removed from the hustle and bustle of Shinjuku below. Its 20th-floor lobby (with free wireless access), is simple and uncluttered and boasts almost surreal views of Tokyo stretching in the distance. Ask for a room on a higher floor. Rooms facing east or south are considered best (and are therefore pricier), especially at night when neon is in full regalia. Rooms facing west have views of Shinjuku's skyscrapers and, on clear days (mostly in winter), of Mount Fuji. A playful touch: Maps in each room outline the important buildings visible from your room.

2–2–1 Yoyogi, Shibuya-ku, Tokyo 151-8583. ☎ **03/5354-0111.** Fax 03/5354-0100. www.southerntower.co.jp. 375 units. ¥18,480–¥20,790 single; ¥27,720–¥34,650 double. Rates exclude hotel tax. AE, DC, MC, V. Station: Shinjuku (south exit, 3 min.). **Amenities:** 3 restaurants; lounge; executive-level rooms; exercise room; smoke-free rooms. *In room:* A/C, TV, fridge, hair dryer, Internet.

Aoyama

Tokyu Stay Aoyama Premier ★★ ⒻFinds Finally, a Tokyo hotel chain that provides discounts for guests staying longer than a week, plus in-room extras road-weary travelers can appreciate. All Tokyu Stay hotels offer rooms with kitchenettes (complete with cooking and dining utensils) in all but the cheapest singles (which come instead with microwaves but no hot plates), as well as combination washer/dryers and plenty of storage space, but this Aoyama property is the cream of the crop, with a central location convenient to both Aoyama and Roppongi and high floors affording expansive city views. Of course, these advantages also come with a price (note that only singles and twins are available; that is, no rooms with double beds). Cheaper alternatives include **Tokyu Stay Shibuya Shin-Minamiguchi,** 3–26–21 Shibuya (☎ **03/5466-0109;** station: Shibuya) and **Tokyu Stay Higashi-Ginza,** with a colorful location near the Tsukiji Fish Market at 4–11–5 Tsukiji (☎ **03/5551-0109;** station: Tsukiji or Tsukijijo).

2–27–18 Minami-Aoyama, Minato-ku, Tokyo 107-0062. ☎ **03/3497-0109.** Fax 03/3497-1091. www.tokyustay.co.jp. 170 units. ¥14,000–¥16,500 single; ¥24,500–¥26,500 double. Rates exclude hotel tax. Rates include breakfast. Discounts for stays longer than 6 nights. AE, DC, MC, V. Station: Gaienmae (exit 1a, 2 min.). **Amenities:** Restaurant; smoke-free rooms. *In room:* A/C, TV/DVD, hair dryer, Internet, kitchenette (most rooms).

Roppongi

Hotel Ibis Once the only hotel in Roppongi, this is still as close as you can get to the night action of Roppongi, just a minute's walk away from Roppongi Crossing. It caters to both businessmen and couples who come to Roppongi's dance clubs and don't make (or don't want to make) the last subway home. The lobby is on the fifth floor, with the guest rooms above. Tiny but comfortable, the rooms feature modern furniture and windows that you can open—though with a freeway nearby, I'm not sure you'd want to. The cheapest doubles come with semi-double-size beds, just slightly wider than a single. On

SETTLING INTO TOKYO

5 WHERE TO STAY

ASAKUSA 3-CHOME

Railway
Subway
Tourist Info ⓘ

NISHI-ASAKUSA
3-CHOME

ASAKUSA 2-CHOME

Kototoi Dori

Hisago Dori

Kokusai Dori

1

HANAYASHIKI
AMUSEMENT
PARK

Asakusa
Shrine

Sensoji
Temple

Five-storied
Pagoda

Horizon
Gate

HANAKAWADO
2-CHOME

HANAKAWADO
1-CHOME

Umamichi Dori

Dempoin
Temple

9

Sushiya Dori

NISHI-ASAKUSA
2-CHOME

ASAKUSA 1-CHOME

Orange Dori

Chinyoko Dori

Nakamise Dori

Kannon Dori

Asakusa
Station

Matsuya
Dept.
Store

TOBU ASAKUSA
LINE

Edo Dori

SUMIDA PARK

Drum
■ Museum

2

Kaminarimon
Dori

4

5

10

6

11

12

3

KAMINARIMON 1-CHOME

Tarawamachi
Station

Asakusa
Information ⓘ
Center

Asakusa
Station

Ferry
Pier

7

Edo Dori

AZUMA BRIDGE

14 **14**

Asakusa Dori

GINZA LINE

ASAKUSA LINE

Asahi
Beer →
Tower

13

Asakusa
Station

KOMAGATA BRIDGE

Sumida River

METROPOLITAN EXPWY.

8

0   1/10 mile
0   100 meters

DINING ◆
Chinya **6**
Kamiya Bar **12**
Komagata Dojo **8**
La Ranarita Azumabashi **14**
Mugitoro **13**
Namiki Yabusoba **7**
Sansado **11**
Sometaro **2**
Waentei-Kikko **9**

ACCOMMODATIONS ■
Asakusa View Hotel **1**
Hotel Sunroute Asakusa **3**
Ryokan Kamogawa **5**
Ryokan Shigetsu **4**

NIGHTLIFE ◆
Sky Room **14**
Daimasu **10**

the 13th floor is a reasonably priced Italian restaurant, Sabatini (p. 166), with views of the city.

7-14-4 Roppongi, Minato-ku, Tokyo 106-0032. © **03/3403-4411.** Fax 03/3479-0609. www.ibis-hotel. com. 182 units. ¥13,382–¥16,023 single; ¥16,285–¥26,765 double. AE, DC, MC, V. Station: Roppongi (1 min.). **Amenities:** 2 restaurants; room service; lobby computers (¥500 for 25 min.); smoke-free rooms. *In room:* A/C, TV, hair dryer, Internet, minibar.

Shibuya

Shibuya Excel Hotel Tokyu ★★
Across from bustling Shibuya Station and connected by a footbridge and underground passage, this busy, modern hotel has an excellent location above Mark City shopping mall (reception is on the fifth floor). The hotel tries hard to appeal to everyone: For business travelers, "Excel" rooms offer use of a hallway computer free of charge; for female travelers, there are two women-only floors accessed by a special key and with special in-room amenities such as face cream and jewelry boxes. Rooms are available for visitors with disabilities, and 50% of all rooms are for nonsmokers. Ask for an upper-floor room facing Shinjuku (rooms run from the 7th to 24th floors); the night view is great.

1-12-2 Dogenzaka, Shibuya-ku, Tokyo 150-0043. © **800/428-6598** in the U.S., or 03/5457-0109. Fax 03/5457-0309. www.tokyuhotelsjapan.com. 408 units. ¥21,945–¥23,100 single; ¥28,875–¥34,650 double. Rates exclude hotel tax. AE, DC, MC, V. Station: Shibuya (1 min. by footbridge). **Amenities:** 3 restaurants, plus many more in Mark City mall; room service; lobby computers (¥100 for 10 min.); smoke-free rooms. *In room:* A/C, TV, hair dryer, Internet, minibar.

Shinagawa

Shinagawa Prince Hotel (Kids)
With four gleaming white buildings added at various stages (each with its own check-in), the Shinagawa Prince Hotel is a virtual city within a city, with more than a dozen food and beverage outlets, a 10-screen cinema complex, a small aquarium with dolphin shows, a sports center with nine indoor tennis courts, an 80-lane bowling center, an indoor golf practice center, a SEGA amusement/arcade-game center, indoor and outdoor pools, and a fitness center. Rooms and prices vary widely depending on which building you select. Assuming you can find it, be sure to have a drink or meal at the 39th-floor Top of Shinagawa; its views of Tokyo Bay and the city are among the best in town. With its many diversions, this hotel is like a resort getaway, but is too big and busy for my taste.

4-10-30 Takanawa, Minato-ku, Tokyo 108-8611. © **800/542-8686** in the U.S. or Canada, or 03/3440-1111. Fax 03/3441-7092. www.princehotelsjapan.com. 3,679 units. ¥9,300–¥20,500 single; ¥16,300–¥36,000 double. Rates exclude hotel tax. AE, DC, MC, V. Station: Shinagawa (2 min.). **Amenities:** 13 restaurants, including a 24-hr. Internet cafe; bar; children's day-care center (¥2,000–¥2,500 for 1 hr.); smoke-free rooms; sports and recreation center (various fees charged; ¥1,050 for indoor pool, ¥1,100 for outdoor pool). *In room:* A/C, TV, fridge, hair dryer, Internet (some rooms; ¥1,050 for 24 hr.).

Other Neighborhoods

The Hilltop Hotel (Yama-no-Ue Hotel) ★★ (Finds)
This is a delightfully old-fashioned, unpretentious hotel with character. Built in 1937 and boasting an Art Deco facade, it was once the favorite haunt of writers, including novelist Mishima Yukio. Avoid the cheaper, more boring rooms in the 1954 annex unless you spring for the higher-priced Art Septo rooms with their flower boxes outside the windows, black leather furnishings, LCD TV with CD player, and fancier bathrooms. Otherwise, rooms in the main building have such homey touches as fringed lampshades, doilies, cherry-wood furniture, velvet curtains, vanity tables, and old-fashioned heaters with intricate

Narita Stopover

An early departure out of Narita Airport? A late-night arrival? It might make sense to spend the night near the airport. Topping the list is the **Hilton Narita,** 456 Kosuge, Narita, Chiba 286-0127 (© **800/445-8667** in the U.S. and Canada, or 0476/33-1121; www.hilton.com), a 10-minute free shuttle ride from the airport and downtown rail stations. With a glass-enclosed garden and waterfall centered in its lobby, it's the only airport hotel that imparts an Asian flair. Facilities include three restaurants, a health club with gym and outdoor pool, and 548 good-size rooms with all the amenities you'd expect. Rates average ¥20,000 for one person and ¥24,000 to ¥29,000 for two.

The 500-room **Holiday Inn Tobu Narita,** 320–1 Tokko, Narita, Chiba 286-0106 (© **800/465-4329** in the U.S. and Canada, or 0476/32-1234; www.holidayinntobunarita.com), a 5-minute free shuttle ride from the airport, offers singles starting at ¥15,015 and twins at ¥23,100. Facilities include a coffee shop, Chinese restaurant, and health club with indoor pool and gym. A good budget choice is the 142-room downtown **Comfort Hotel Narita,** near the Keisei and JR Narita stations at 968 Hanazaki-cho (© **0476/24-6311;** www.choicehotels.com). Singles here begin at ¥5,800 and twins at ¥11,000, including breakfast.

If you have 3 hours to spare, consider an excursion to downtown **Narita** (10 min. by train from the airport; most airport hotels also offer shuttle buses), a quaint village with a winding, shop-lined street leading to Narita-san Temple, an impressive complex consisting of a main hall, several pagodas, and a nice park.

SETTLING INTO TOKYO

5

WHERE TO STAY

grillwork. Some twins even combine a *tatami* area and *shoji* with beds; the most expensive twin overlooks its own Japanese garden. Don't be surprised if the reception desk remembers you by name. Although the Hilltop is not as centrally located or up-to-date as other hotels, nearby Meiji University brings lots of liveliness to the area.

1–1 Surugadai, Kanda, Chiyoda-ku, Tokyo 101-0062. © **03/3293-2311.** Fax 03/3233-4567. www.yamanoue-hotel.co.jp. 74 units. ¥12,600–¥21,000 single; ¥23,100–¥33,600 double. Rates exclude service charge and hotel tax. AE, DC, MC, V. Station: Ochanomizu or Shin-Ochanomizu (8 min.) or Jimbocho (5 min.). **Amenities:** 7 restaurants; 3 bars; room service. *In room:* A/C, TV, hair dryer, Internet, minibar.

INEXPENSIVE

Asakusa

Ryokan Kamogawa ★ (**Kids**) If Shigetsu (see below) is full, this is a very good alternative. Established in 1948 by the present owner's parents and located just off Nakamise Dori, it's small and personable, with a coffee shop (and computer you can use for free) and *tatami* rooms with *shoji* screens. Four room sizes are available, with and without private bathrooms. The largest sleep four to six persons, making them a good choice for families, as is the family bath you can use privately (reserve in advance). Note that the inn is usually fully booked in April and December, so if you hope to stay here then, book far ahead.

1–30–10 Asakusa, Tokyo 111-0032. © **03/3843-2681.** Fax 03/3843-2683. www.f-kamogawa.jp. 13 units (8 with bathroom). ¥6,400 single without bathroom, ¥6,800–¥8,200 single with bathroom; ¥12,600–¥13,000 double without bathroom, ¥12,800–¥14,600 double with bathroom; ¥19,200 triple without bathroom, ¥21,300 triple with bathroom. Rates include coffee and toast. Japanese breakfast ¥1,000 extra; Japanese dinner ¥4,000 extra (reservations required). AE, DC, MC, V. Station: Asakusa (3 min.). **Amenities:** Coffee shop. *In room:* A/C, TV, fridge, hair dryer (in rooms with bathroom).

Ryokan Shigetsu ★ (Finds) Whenever a foreigner living in Tokyo, soon to host first-time visitors to Japan, asks me to recommend a reasonably priced *ryokan* in Tokyo, this is the one I most often suggest. It has a great location in Asakusa just off Nakamise Dori, a colorful, shop-lined pedestrian street leading to the famous Sensoji Temple—an area that gives you a feel for the older Japan. A member of the Japanese Inn Group, it represents the best of modern yet traditional Japanese design—simple yet elegant, with *shoji*, unadorned wood, and artwork throughout. Two public Japanese baths have views of the nearby five-story pagoda. There are eight Western-style rooms, but I prefer the 15 slightly more expensive *tatami* rooms, which include Japanese-style mirrors and comfortable chairs for those who don't like relaxing on the floor. This ryokan costs no more than a regular business hotel but has much more class. What a pity that the front-desk staff can be brusque.

1–31–11 Asakusa, Taito-ku, Tokyo 111-0032. © **03/3843-2345.** Fax 03/3843-2348. www.shigetsu.com. 23 units. ¥7,700–¥9,450 single; ¥14,700–¥16,800 double. Japanese or Western breakfast ¥1,300 extra. AE, DC, MC, V. Station: Asakusa (4 min.). **Amenities:** Restaurant; lobby computer w/free Internet access; smoke-free rooms. *In room:* A/C, TV, hair dryer, Internet, minibar.

Ueno

Annex Katsutaro ★★ (Finds) This thoroughly modern concrete *ryokan* is a standout for its simple yet chic designs, spotless Japanese-style rooms (all with bathroom), and location—right in the heart of Yanaka with its old-fashioned neighborhood and about a 20-minute walk northwest of Ueno Park (the Keisei Skyliner from Narita Airport stops at nearby Nippori Station). The English-speaking proprietor, Arakawa-san, distributes a free map of the area showing the best way to get around and offers free coffee in the lobby. If the ryokan is full, don't let management talk you into taking a room in its much older main Ryokan Katsutaro; it's not nearly as nice as the annex.

3–8–4 Yanaka, Taito-ku, Tokyo 110-0001. © **03/3828-2500.** Fax 03/3821-5400. www.katsutaro.com. 17 units. ¥6,300 single; ¥10,500–¥12,600 double; ¥14,700–¥16,800 triple. Continental breakfast ¥840 extra. MC, V. Station: Sendagi (2 min.) or Nippori (7 min.). **Amenities:** Lobby computers w/free Internet. *In room:* A/C, TV, fridge, hair dryer, Internet.

Homeikan ★★★ (Finds) Although not as conveniently located as the other *ryokan,* this lovely place is my number-one choice if you want to experience an authentic ryokan in a traditional neighborhood. It consists of three separate buildings acquired over the last century by the present owner's grandfather. Homeikan, the main building (Honkan), was purchased almost 100 years ago; today it is listed as a "Tangible Cultural Property," and is used mainly by groups of students and seniors. Across the street is Daimachi Bek-kan, built after World War II to serve as the family home. A beautiful 31-room property, it boasts a private Japanese garden with a pond, public baths (including one open 24 hr.), and wood-inlaid and pebbled hallways leading to nicely detailed *tatami* rooms adorned with such features as gnarled wood trim and sitting alcoves. This is where most foreigners are placed. If you opt for meals, they will be served in your room in true ryokan fashion. The third building, Morikawa Bekkan, about a 5-minute walk away, was built as an inn about 45 years ago and, with 35 rooms, is the largest. Owner Koike-san, who speaks

5

DINING ◆

Grill Fukushima **5**

Hard Rock
  Cafe Ueno **7**

Innsyoutei **4**

Izu'ei **8**

Kohmen **9**

Mantra **10**

Tokori **6**

ACCOMMODATIONS ■

Annex Katsutaro **1**

Homeikan **3**

Ryokan Sawanoya **2**

	Railway
	Railway (tunnel)
	Subway
(i)	Tourist Information

excellent English, points out that travelers who need the latest in creature comforts (including private bathrooms) should go elsewhere; those seeking a traditional ryokan experience, however, will not be disappointed.

5-10-5 Hongo, Bunkyo-ku, Tokyo 113-0033. ⓒ **03/3811-1181** or 3811-1187. Fax 03/3811-1764. www. homeikan.com. 89 units (none with bathroom). ¥6,825–¥7,350 single; ¥11,550–¥12,600 double; ¥14,175–¥15,750 triple. ¥525 more per person in peak season; ¥525 less per person in off season. Western- or Japanese-style breakfast ¥1,050; Japanese dinner ¥3,150; not available 1st night of stay). AE, DC, MC, V. Station: Hongo Sanchome (8 min.) or Kasuga (5 min.). *In room:* A/C, TV, minibar.

Ryokan Sawanoya ★ Although this family-run, smoke-free *ryokan,* open since 1949, looks relatively unexciting, it's delightfully located in a wonderful residential area of old Tokyo, northwest of Ueno Park and within walking distance of the park's attractions and Nezu Shrine. Upon your arrival, the owner, English-speaking Sawa-san, gives a short tour of the establishment before taking you to your *tatami* room; throughout the ryokan are written explanations to help the novice. The owner also gives you a map outlining places of interest in the vicinity. Several times a month, Sawa-san's son provides guests with a special treat—a traditional Japanese lion dance, free of charge. His daughter-in-law sometimes gives demonstrations of the tea ceremony. The nice public baths (which you can lock for privacy) have a view of a small garden, and there's free coffee and a computer in the lobby. This is a great place to stay thanks to Sawa-san's enthusiastic devotion to his neighborhood, which he readily imparts to his guests (he's even written a book about his years as an innkeeper). Highly recommended.

2-3-11 Yanaka, Taito-ku, Tokyo 110-0001. ⓒ **03/3822-2251.** Fax 03/3822-2252. www.sawanoya.com. 12 units (2 with bathroom). ¥5,040–¥5,355 single without bathroom; ¥9,450 double without bathroom, ¥10,080 double with bathroom; ¥12,915 triple without bathroom, ¥14,490 triple with bathroom. Breakfast of toast and fried eggs ¥315 extra, Japanese breakfast ¥945 extra. AE, MC, V. Closed Dec 29–Jan 3. Station: Nezu (exit 1, 7 min.). **Amenities:** 2 rental bikes (¥200 for 1 day); lobby computer w/free Internet access. *In room:* A/C, TV, hair dryer, Internet.

Shinjuku

Tokyo International Hostel (Value) This spotless hostel, operated by the Tokyo Metropolitan Government and situated in a high-rise, is definitely the best place to stay in its price range—it offers fantastic Tokyo views. Even the public baths boast good views (especially at night). All beds are dormitory style, with two, four, or five bunk beds to a room. Rooms are very pleasant, with big windows, and each bed has its own curtain for privacy. If there are vacancies, you can stay longer than the normal 6-day maximum. In summer, it's a good idea to reserve about 2 months in advance (reservations can be made up to 3 months in advance). The hostel is closed from 10am to 3pm and locked at 11pm (lights out also at 11pm).

1-1 Kagura-kashi, Shinjuku-ku, Tokyo 162-0823. ⓒ **03/3235-1107.** Fax 03/3264-4000. www.tokyo-ih.jp. 158 beds. ¥3,860 adult, ¥2,000 child. Breakfast ¥450; dinner ¥900. No youth-hostel card required; no age limit. AE, MC, V. Closed Dec 29–Jan 3. Station: Iidabashi (2 min.; take the West Exit from the JR station or the B2b subway exit). Reception is on the 18th floor of the Central Plaza Bldg. **Amenities:** Lobby computer (fee charged); communal kitchen. *In room:* A/C, no phone.

Roppongi & Akasaka

Arca Torre (Value) This smart-looking, 10-story property looks expensive from the outside but is actually a business hotel. It has a great location on Roppongi Dori, between Roppongi Crossing and Roppongi Hills, making it popular with both business types and tourists on a budget. Its (mostly single) rooms are small but cheerful, with flat-panel TVs and complimentary bottled water in the otherwise empty fridge. Rooms facing the back are quiet but face another building with glazed windows and are rather dark. If you opt for a room facing the front, spring for the more expensive rooms on higher floors above the freeway; otherwise, from the cheaper rooms on lower floors your view will be of cars and, at certain times of the day, traffic jams.

6–1–23 Roppongi, Minato-ku, Tokyo 106-0032. © 03/3404-5111. Fax 03/3404-5115. www.arktower. co.jp/arcatorre. 77 units. ¥11,550–¥13,650 single; ¥14,700–¥22,050 double. AE, DC, MC, V. Station: Roppongi (1 min.). **Amenities:** Restaurant; smoke-free rooms. In room: A/C, TV, fridge, hair dryer, Internet.

Asia Center of Japan (Asia Kaikan) ★ (Value) Great rates make this a top choice if you're looking for inexpensive Western-style accommodations in the center of town (it's wise to reserve months in advance). Everyone—from businessmen to students to travelers to foreigners teaching English—stays here; I know one teacher who lived here for years. Resembling a college dormitory, the Asia Center is popular with area office workers for its inexpensive cafeteria with outdoor seating. Accommodations are basic, with few frills, and in the singles you can almost reach out and touch all four walls. The cheapest doubles are actually single rooms with small, semi-double-size beds (not quite full size but larger than single/twin size). Avoid rooms on the ground floor—windows can open, and in Japan there are no screens. Tucked on a side street off Gaien-Higashi Dori not far from Aoyama Dori, the center is a 15-minute walk to the nightlife of Roppongi or Akasaka, one station away by subway.

8–10–32 Akasaka, Minato-ku, Tokyo 107-0052. © 03/3402-6111. Fax 03/3402-0738. www.asiacenter. or.jp. 173 units. ¥8,610–¥10,290 single; ¥12,390–¥18,690 double. AE, MC, V. Station: Aoyama-Itchome (exit 4, 5 min.) or Nogizaka (exit 3, 5 min.). **Amenities:** Restaurant; coin-op computer; smoke-free rooms. In room: A/C, TV, fridge, hair dryer, Internet.

Shinagawa

Toyoko Inn Shinagawa-Eki Takanawaguchi ★ (Value) I like this hotel chain for its clean, functional rooms, complimentary breakfast of coffee and pastries served in the lobby, free in-room Internet connections and free wireless access in the lobby (and for those who don't have their own laptops, free use of computers in the lobby), and complimentary movies (only occasionally in English). Rooms are all very small singles and doubles. Other convenient Tokyo locations of this popular chain include **Toyoko Inn Shinjuku Kabuki-cho,** 2–20–15 Kabuki-cho (© 03/5155-1045; station: Shinjuku) and **Toyoko Inn Ikebukuro Kita-guchi No. 1,** 2–50–5 Ikebukuro (© 03/5960-1045; station: Ikebukuro), both with single, double, and twin rooms at similar costs and with the same freebies.

4–23–2 Takanawa, Minato-ku, Tokyo 108-0074. © 03/3280-1045. Fax 03/3280-1046. www.toyoko-inn. com. 180 units. ¥7,140 single; ¥9,240 double. Rates include continental breakfast. AE, DC, MC, V. Station: Shinagawa (3 min.); from JR Station's Takanawa (west) exit, turn left. **Amenities:** Lobby computers w/free Wi-Fi; smoke-free rooms. In room: A/C, TV, fridge, hair dryer, Internet.

Ikebukuro

Kimi Ryokan ★ (Finds) This has long been a Tokyo favorite for inexpensive Japanese-style lodging. Spotlessly clean and with such Japanese touches as sliding screens, a cypress public bath, flower arrangements in public spaces, and traditional Japanese music playing softly in the hallways, it caters almost exclusively to foreigners (mostly 20-somethings) and is so popular there's sometimes a waiting list. A bulletin board and newsletter lists rental apartments and job opportunities (primarily teaching English); a lounge with cable TV is a favorite hangout and a good place to network with other travelers. Rooms are Japanese style, with the cheapest single the size of four and one-half *tatami* mats, and the larger double the size of six tatami mats (each tatami measures 1m×1.8m/3¼ ft.×6 ft.). Note that there's a 1am curfew.

2–36–8 Ikebukuro, Toshima-ku, Tokyo 171-0014. ℂ **03/3971-3766.** Fax 03/3987-1326. www.kimi-ryokan.jp. 38 units (none with bathroom). ¥4,500 single; ¥6,500–¥7,500 double; ¥10,000–¥12,000 triple. Prices exclude tax. No credit cards. Station: Ikebukuro (west exit, 7 min.). The police station (take the west exit from Ikebukuro Station and turn right) has maps that will guide you to Kimi; there's also an area map outside the station. *In room:* A/C, Wi-Fi (some rooms).

4 WHERE TO DINE

From stand-up noodle shops and pizzerias to exclusive *kaiseki* restaurants and sushi bars, there are at least 80,000 restaurants in Tokyo—which gives you some idea of how fond Japanese are of eating out. In a city where apartments are so small and cramped that entertaining at home is almost unheard of, restaurants serve as places for socializing, meeting friends, and wooing business associates—as well as great excuses for drinking a lot of beer, sake, and whiskey.

HOW TO DINE IN TOKYO WITHOUT SPENDING A FORTUNE   I know people in Tokyo who claim they haven't cooked in years—and they're not millionaires. They simply take advantage of one of the best deals in Tokyo—the fixed-price lunch, usually available from 11am to 2pm. Called a *teishoku* in a Japanese restaurant, a fixed-price meal is likely to include soup, a main dish such as tempura or whatever the restaurant specializes in, pickled vegetables, rice, and tea. In restaurants serving Western food, the fixed-price lunch is variously referred to as a set lunch, *seto coursu,* or simply *coursu,* and usually includes an appetizer, a main course with one or two side dishes, coffee or tea, and sometimes dessert. Even restaurants listed under **Very Expensive**—where you'd otherwise spend at least ¥13,000 or more per person for dinner, excluding drinks—and **Expensive**—where you can expect to pay ¥9,000 to ¥13,000 for dinner—usually offer set-lunch menus, allowing you to dine in style at very reasonable prices. To keep your costs down, therefore, try having your biggest meal at lunch, avoiding, if possible, the noon-to-1pm weekday crush when Tokyo's army of office workers flood area restaurants. Because Japanese tend to order fixed-price meals rather than a la carte, set dinners are also usually available (though they're not as cheap as set lunches). All-you-can-eat buffets (called *viking* in Japanese, probably because Japan's first buffet was in a restaurant called Viking in the Imperial Hotel), offered by many hotel restaurants, are also bargains for hearty appetites.

So many of Tokyo's good restaurants fall into the **Moderate** category that it's tempting to simply eat your way through the city—and the range of cuisines is so great you could eat something different at each meal. Dinner in this category will average ¥4,000 to ¥9,000, lunch likely half as much.

Many of Tokyo's most colorful, noisy, and popular restaurants fall into the **Inexpensive** category, where meals usually go for less than ¥4,000; indeed, many offer meals for less than ¥2,000 and lunches for ¥1,000 or less. The city's huge working population heads to these places to catch a quick lunch or to socialize with friends after hours. There are also many excellent yet inexpensive French bistros, Italian trattorie, and ethnic restaurants, particularly those serving Indian, Chinese, and other Asian cuisines. Hotel restaurants are good bargains for inexpensive set lunches and buffets. Finally, see "Tokyo After Dark," in chapter 6, for suggestions on inexpensive drinking places that serve food. And

Tips Mapping Out Tokyo's Restaurants

You can locate the restaurants reviewed below using the following neighborhood maps:

- To locate restaurants in **Akasaka,** p. 129.
- To locate restaurants in **Shinjuku,** p. 136.
- To locate restaurants in **Asakusa,** p. 141.
- To locate restaurants in **Ueno,** p. 145.
- To locate restaurants in **Hibiya** and **Ginza,** p. 150.
- To locate restaurants in **Harajuku,** p. 165.
- To locate restaurants in **Roppongi,** p. 171.

because I can cover only a limited number of cheap restaurants in each neighborhood, I also suggest you ask your concierge or hotel manager for recommendations; there might be a great little place just around the corner.

OTHER DINING NOTES   The restaurants listed below are organized first by neighborhood and then by price category. For information on Japanese food, see "Tips on Dining in Japan," in chapter 2.

Note that the 5% consumption tax is included in menu prices. However, many first-class restaurants, as well as hotel restaurants, will add a 10% to 15% service charge to the bill. Unless otherwise stated, the prices given below include the tax but not the service charge.

Note that restaurants that have no signs in English letters are preceded by a numbered icon, which is keyed to a list of **Japanese characters** in chapter 17.

Finally, keep in mind that the **last order** is taken at least 30 minutes before the restaurant's actual closing time, sometimes even an hour before closing at the more exclusive restaurants.

GINZA & HIBIYA
Very Expensive

In addition to the recommendations here, there's also a branch of **Inakaya,** 8–7–4 Ginza (© **03/3569-1708**), a *robatayaki* restaurant serving grilled foods (see p. 170 for a review).

Kamon ★★★ TEPPANYAKI   Kamon, which means "Gate of Celebration," has an interior that could be a statement on Tokyo itself—traditionally Japanese yet ever so high-tech. Located on the 17th floor of the Imperial Hotel, the restaurant offers seating at one of several large counters (some with views over Hibiya) centered around grills where expert chefs prepare excellent *teppanyaki* before your eyes according to your wishes. Japanese sirloin steaks or filets, cooked to succulent perfection, are available, as well as seafood ranging from fresh prawns and scallops to crabmeat and fish, and seasonal vegetables, served with traditional Japanese accompaniments. The service is, of course, imperial.

In the Imperial Hotel, 17th floor, 1-1-1 Uchisaiwai-cho. © **03/3539-8116.** www.imperialhotel.co.jp. Reservations recommended for dinner. Set dinners ¥13,650–¥31,500; set lunches ¥3,675–¥7,875. AE, DC, MC, V. Daily 11:30am–2:30pm and 5:30–9:30pm. Station: Hibiya (1 min.).

Ginza & Hibiya

ACCOMMODATIONS ■
Hotel Com's Ginza **4**
Courtyard by Marriott
 Tokyo Ginza Hotel **13**
Hotel Gracery **12**
Imperial Hotel **1**
Mitsui Garden
 Hotel Premier **7**
Park Hotel Tokyo **6**
The Peninsula Tokyo **16**

DINING ◆
Andy Shin's Hinomoto **19**
Aux Bacchanales **21**
Donto **17**
Ginza Daimasu **29**
Gonpachi **36**
The Imperial Viking Sal **1**
Inakaya **9**
Kamon **1**
Kihachi **28**
La Boheme **22, 36**
Manpuku **18**
Meal Muji **23**
Monsoon **36**
Ohmatsuya **27**
Ohmatsuya Kura **25**
Rangetsu **35**
Shabusen **30**
Ten-ichi **2, 24**
Tsukiji Sushi Sen **31**
Yakitori stands **15**
Zest Cantina **36**
Zipangu **5**

NIGHTLIFE ◆
300 Bar **3, 32**
Cotton Club **20**
Ginza Sapporo Lion **11**
Kabuki-za **34**
Kento's **10**
Lupin **26**
Old Imperial **1**
Shinbashi Enbujo Theater **33**
Show Dining Konparuza **8**
Takarazuka Gekijo **14**

Railway
Subway
Tourist Info ⓘ

HIBIYA PARK

HIBIYA LINE

Imperial Tower

KEIHIN-TOHOKU LINE

New Ginza Bldg.

Sotobori Dori

Soni Dori

Namiki Dori

Metropolitan (Shuto) Expressway

Nishi-Go-Bangai (West 5th St.)

Azuma Dori

0   1/10 mile
0   100 meters

Kihachi ★★ FUSION With a cool, crisp interior accented with Art Nouveau trimmings, this second-floor restaurant offers an interesting French-influenced menu that combines flavors of the West with Japanese and Asian ingredients, creations of its French-trained chef. Past choices on the English-language menu have included such starters as pan-fried foie gras or half-baked egg wrapped in smoked salmon and topped with carrot and crab; mains have included grilled sea bream with cumin and roasted vegetables or Japanese-flavored duck breast. The hardest part of dining here? Limiting yourself to one meal—you just might have to come back. To spare your wallet, consider dining in the first-floor cafe, which offers set lunches beginning at ¥2,000 and dinner entrees ranging from a fish of the day to grilled duck with *yuza* pepper and lemon.

2-2-6 Ginza. ✆ **03/3567-6281.** Reservations not required. Main dishes ¥2,000–¥3,000; set dinners ¥8,400–¥13,650; set lunches ¥3,675–¥6,300. AE, DC, MC, V. Daily 11:30am–2:30pm and 6–9:30pm (last order). Station: Yurakucho (5 min.). Near the Tourist Information Center and Printemps department store.

Ten-ichi ★ TEMPURA In this restaurant, located on Namiki Dori in the heart of Ginza's nightlife, you can sit at a counter and watch the chef prepare your meal. This is the main outlet of an 80-year-old restaurant chain that helped the tempura style of cooking gain worldwide recognition by serving important foreign customers. Today Ten-ichi still has one of the best reputations in town for serving the most delicately fried foods, along with its special sauce (or, if you prefer, you can dip the morsels in lemon juice with a pinch of salt).

Other Ten-ichi restaurants in Tokyo are in the Imperial Hotel's Tower basement (✆ **03/3503-1001;** station: Hibiya); Akasaka Tokyu Plaza (✆ **03/3581-2166;** station: Akasaka-mitsuke); and Isetan department store, 3–14–1 Shinjuku (✆ **03/5379-3039;** station: Shinjuku Sanchome).

6-6-5 Ginza. ✆ **03/3571-1949.** Reservations recommended for lunch, required for dinner. Set dinners ¥10,500–¥18,900; set lunches ¥8,400–¥12,600. AE, DC, MC, V. Daily 11:30am–9:30pm. Station: Ginza (3 min.). On Namiki Dori.

Moderate

① **Donto** ★★ (Finds) VARIED JAPANESE Located in Hibiya on Harumi Dori in the basement of an unlikely looking office building, this is a great place for lunch. Popular with the local working crowd (and therefore best avoided noon–1pm), it's pleasantly decorated in a rustic style with *shoji* screens, wooden floors, and an open kitchen. Take off your shoes at the entryway and put them into one of the wooden lockers. Choose what you want from the plastic display case by the front door, which shows various *teishoku* and set meals. Everything from noodles, sashimi, tempura, and *obento* to *kaiseki* is available. Unfortunately, the best deals are daily specials written in Japanese only; ask about them or look around at what others are eating.

There are other Donto restaurants at 2–6–1 Shimbashi (✆ **03/3501-0123;** station: Shimbashi) and on the 49th floor of the Sumitomo Building in Shinjuku (✆ **03/3344-6269;** station: Tochomae).

Yurakucho Denki Building. basement, 1-7-1 Yurakucho. ✆ **03/3201-3021.** Set dinners ¥3,500–¥4,500; set lunches ¥800–¥950. AE, DC, MC, V. Mon–Sat 11am–2pm and 5–11pm. Closed holidays. Station: Hibiya (1 min.). On Harumi Dori.

② **Ginza Daimasu** KAISEKI/OBENTO This 90-year-old restaurant has a simple, modern decor with Japanese touches. Experienced, kimono-clad waitresses serve artfully arranged set meals from the English-language menu. The *Fukiyose-zen obento*—many

---

Tips **A Note on Establishments with Japanese Signs**

Many establishments and attractions in Japan do not have signs in Roman (English-language) letters. Those that don't are indicated in this guide by an oval with a number that corresponds to a number in chapter 17 showing the Japanese equivalent. Thus, to find the Japanese *kanji*, or alphabet, for Rangetsu (below), refer to no. 4 in chapter 17.

---

delicate dishes served in three courses—includes beautiful tempura delicacies for ¥3,675. A plastic-food display in the front window will help you recognize the restaurant. Set lunches are served until 4pm.

6-9-6 Ginza. ℂ **03/3571-3584.** Reservations required for kaiseki meals costing more than ¥9,450. Kaiseki ¥5,250–¥12,600; obento ¥2,415–¥3,675; set lunches ¥2,100–¥2,940. AE, DC, MC, V. Daily 11:30am–8:30pm (last order). Station: Ginza (2 min.). Across from Matsuzakaya department store on Chuo Dori.

The Imperial Viking Sal ★ INTERNATIONAL   No, this has nothing to do with Scandinavian invaders; rather, *viking* is the Japanese word for "all-you-can-eat buffet." Although lots of Tokyo hotels now offer such spreads, this 17th-floor restaurant was the first and has been serving buffets for more than 50 years. It offers more than 40 mostly European and some international dishes, which vary according to seasonal food promotions spotlighting a country's cuisine, from Indonesian to Swiss. Views are of Ginza and Hibiya Park, and there's live jazz in the evenings. This restaurant has enjoyed great popularity for decades, making reservations a must.

In the Imperial Hotel, 17th floor, 1-1-1 Uchisaiwai-cho. ℂ **03/3504-1111.** www.imperialhotel.co.jp. Reservations strongly recommended. Buffet dinner ¥7,875; buffet lunch ¥5,250. AE, DC, MC, V. Daily 11:30am–2:30pm and 5:30–9:30pm. Station: Hibiya (1 min.).

(3) **Ohmatsuya** ★★ (Finds) JAPANESE GRILL   Enter this restaurant of a nondescript building and you're instantly back in time: After you're greeted by waitresses clad in traditional country clothing, you'll find yourself enveloped in an old farmhouse atmosphere. (Part of the decor is from a 17th-c. samurai house in northern Japan.) Even the style of cooking is traditional, as customers grill their own food over a hibachi. Sake, served in a length of bamboo, is drunk from bamboo cups. Dinner menus (in English) include such delicacies as grilled fish, skewered meat, and vegetables. This is a true find—and easy to find at that—just off Harumi Dori on West 5th Street. If this place is full, there's a nearby sister restaurant, **Ohmatsuya Kura,** 6-6-19 Ginza (ℂ **03/3574-4200**), with the same atmosphere and two set meals starting at ¥5,250; it's open Monday to Friday from 5 to 10pm.

5-6-13 Ginza, 7th floor. ℂ **03/3571-7053.** Reservations required. Set dinners ¥5,040–¥9,450, plus a ¥500 table charge. AE, DC, MC, V. Mon–Fri 5–10pm; Sat 5–9pm (last order). Closed holidays. Station: Ginza (3 min.). On W. 5th St.

(4) **Rangetsu** SUKIYAKI/SHABU-SHABU/KAISEKI/OBENTO   This well-known Ginza restaurant has been dishing out sukiyaki, *shabu-shabu, obento* (traditional box meals), and steaks since 1947. It uses only Matsuzaka beef (bought whole and carved up by the chefs), which ranges from costlier fine-marbled beef to cheaper cuts with thick marbling. There are also crab dishes (including a crab sukiyaki), *kaiseki,* sirloin steaks, and eel dishes. Especially good deals are the obento box meals (available day and night

(Kids) Family-Friendly Restaurants

Hard Rock Cafe (p. 174)   This internationally known establishment should pacify grumbling teenagers. They can munch on hamburgers, gaze at famous guitars and other rock-'n'-roll memorabilia and, most important, buy that Hard Rock Cafe T-shirt.

Kua' Aina (p. 168)   When your kids start asking for "real food," take them here for some of the best burgers in town.

Sometaro (p. 160)   This traditional restaurant specializes in Japanese-style pancakes filled with meat and vegetables and fried noodles that you cook yourself at your table, which might delight more adventuresome little eaters, especially because they get to pick their own ingredients.

Tokyo Catering (p. 164)   This inexpensive cafeteria won't break the bank, and with everything from sushi to noodles, offers enough to satisfy most diners. Your kids will be impressed, too, with the views from its location on the 32nd floor, but to really wow the little ones, take them also to the free observatory on the 45th floor.

and offering a variety of small dishes) and the set lunches served until 2:30pm. In the basement is a sake bar with more than 80 different varieties from all over Japan, which you can also order with your meal.

3–5–8 Ginza. ℂ **03/3567-1021.** Reservations recommended. Beef sukiyaki or shabu-shabu set meals from ¥8,000 for dinner, ¥2,500 for lunch; obento and mini-kaiseki ¥2,400–¥5,800. AE, DC, MC, V. Daily 11:30am–10pm. Station: Ginza (3 min.). On Chuo Dori across from the Matsuya department store.

Zipangu NOUVELLE JAPANESE   Just outside Ginza and located high in the sky—on the 47th floor of the Caretta Shiodome Building with shimmering views over Tokyo Bay—this contemporary Japanese restaurant offers set meals for lunch that are difficult to describe—the constantly changing presentations border on nouvelle Japanese cuisine, with international influences (luckily, there's an English-language menu). In the evenings, the stone-and-wood venue is more of a drinking bar, with an a la carte menu offering charcoal-grilled steak or salmon, *yakitori*, sashimi, and dishes that go well with wine. In any case, this is a great choice if you're visiting nearby Hama Rikyu Garden.

Caretta Shiodome, 1–8–1 Higashi-Shimbashi. ℂ **03/6215-8111.** Reservations required. Main dishes ¥1,460–¥4,536; set lunches ¥2,940–¥6,300. AE, DC, MC, V. Daily 11:30am–2:30pm and 5–10pm (last order). Station: Shiodome (2 min.) or Shimbashi (5 min.).

Inexpensive

In addition to the restaurants here, check out **Meal Muji,** 3–8–3 Marunouchi (ℂ **03/5208-8241**), a cafeteria on the second floor of the popular minimalist Muji clothing and housewares store, where you can load up on mostly salads and veggies daily from 11am to 8:30pm. There are also a number of restaurants on the eighth floor of **Matsuya Ginza department store** serving everything from French and Chinese food to sushi, tempura, noodles, and more. **Aux Bacchanales** (p. 177), a brasserie offering sandwiches, salads, and daily specials, has a branch at 6–3–2 Ginza (ℂ **03/3569-0202**).

Gonpachi (p. 173), at the G-Zone, 1–2–3 Ginza (☎ **03/5524-3641**), serves a variety of Japanese food.

For atmospheric dining, head to an arch underneath the elevated Yamanote railway tracks located about halfway between Harumi Dori and the Imperial Hotel Tower; it has a handful of tiny *yakitori* **stands,** each with a few tables and chairs. They cater to a rather boisterous working-class clientele, mainly men. The atmosphere, unsophisticated and dingy, harks back to prewar Japan, somewhat of an anomaly in the otherwise chic Ginza. Stalls are open from about 5pm to midnight Monday through Saturday.

Andy's Shin Hinomoto (Value) VARIED JAPANESE   Occupying its own arch underneath the Yamanote tracks, this Japanese-style pub is owned by Andy, a Brit, who buys all his seafood and vegetables fresh daily at Tsukiji Market. The upstairs is the place to be, with its arched ceiling and mixed foreign and Japanese crowd. If you don't have reservations, you'll be shunted into the less ambient downstairs, where you'll feel like a refugee in a fallout shelter as you sit elbow-to-elbow with local office workers at long tables under fluorescent lighting. Sashimi, grilled fish, tempura, sautéed vegetables, deep-fried chicken, tofu, salad, and much more are offered on the English-language menu.

2-4-4 Yurakucho. ☎ **03/3214-8021.** Reservations strongly recommended. Main dishes ¥500–¥1,600. No credit cards. Mon–Sat 5pm–midnight. Station: Yurakucho or Ginza (1 min.). Underneath the Yamanote elevated tracks, across from the Yurakucho Denki Building.

La Boheme ITALIAN   The food is passable, but what sets La Boheme apart is that it's open every day until 5am, making it a good bet for a late-night meal. I also like its huge, open kitchen in the middle of the room, surrounded by a U-shaped counter that provides a ringside view of the action. The pasta ranges from spaghetti with eggplant and tomato sauce to spaghetti Bolognese, along with Japanese-style versions like steamed breast of chicken with Japanese baby leek, spinach, and sesame oil.

You'll find other La Boheme restaurants at many popular spots around Tokyo, including Ginza at 1–2–3 Ginza (☎ **03/5524-3616**; station: Ginza); in Aoyama at 7–11–4 Minami Aoyama (☎ **03/3499-3377**; station: Omotesando), 6–2–2 Minami Aoyama (☎ **03/6418-4242**; station: Omotesando), and 3–6–25 Kita-Aoyama (☎ **03/5766-1666**; station: Gaienmae); in Harajuku at 5–8–5 Jingumae (☎ **03/5467-56661**; station: Meiji-Jingumae); in Roppongi at 4–11–13 Roppongi (☎ **03/3478-0222**; station: Roppongi); in Nishi Azabu at 2–25–18 Nishi Azabu (☎ **03/3407-1363**; station: Roppongi); in Shibuya at 1–6–8 Jinnan (☎ **03/3477-0481**; station: Shibuya); and on the fourth floor of Mediage on Odaiba (☎ **03/3599-4801**; station: Odaiba). All are open daily from 11:30am to 3:30am or later.

6-4-1 Ginza. ☎ **03/3572-5005.** www.boheme.jp. Pizza and pasta ¥550–¥1,480; set lunches ¥900–¥1,300. AE, DC, MC, V. Daily 11:30am–5am. Station: Hibiya (5 min.) or Ginza (10 min.). Behind Mosaic, on a corner.

Manpuku (Value) YAKITORI   This *yakitori* restaurant differs from the others under the Yamanote tracks in that it offers tables along a covered passageway where you can watch office workers bustling by. Decorated with old posters inside and out, it has a slight post–World War II retro feel; its sign even boasts RETRO DINING. Manpuku offers an English-language menu of yakitori, braised tofu with meat, noodles, and other pub grub. The food isn't the greatest, but prices are cheap and it's often packed.

2-4-1 Yurakucho. ☎ **03/3211-6001.** Main dishes ¥504–¥1,134; set lunches ¥810–¥1,449. No credit cards. 24 hr., except 1st and 3rd Sun when it's closed 1–6am. Station: Yurakucho or Hibiya (1 min.). On Harumi Dori, underneath the elevated Yamanote tracks btw. the Sony and Yurakucho Denki buildings.

⑤ **Shabusen** ★ Value SHABU-SHABU   With an improbable location on the second floor of a fashion department store just a stone's throw from Ginza 4–chome Crossing (the Harumi Dori–Chuo Dori intersection), this is a fun restaurant where you can cook your own sukiyaki or *shabu-shabu* in a boiling pot as you sit at a round counter or at your private table. It's also one of the few restaurants that caters to individual diners (shabu-shabu is usually shared by a group). Orders are shouted back and forth among the staff, service is rapid, and the place is lively. There's an English-language menu complete with cooking instructions, so it's user-friendly. The special shabu-shabu dinner for ¥4,147, with appetizer, tomato ("super dressing") salad, beef, vegetables, noodles or rice porridge, and dessert, is enough for most voracious appetites. You'll find a branch of Shabusen in the basement of the same building (✆ **03/3572-3806**).

Core Building. 2F, 5–8–20 Ginza. ✆ **03/3571-1717**. Set dinners ¥2,310–¥5,880; set lunches ¥1,155–¥3,150. AE, DC, MC, V. Daily 11am–10pm. Station: Ginza (1 min.). On Chuo Dori next to the Nissan Building.

⑥ **Tsukiji Sushi Sen** SUSHI   Too brightly lit and possessing as much charm as an interrogation room, this second-floor Ginza branch nevertheless offers fresh sushi at bargain prices, served at a counter or at tables overlooking busy Harumi Dori. Other dishes are also available on the English-language menu, including salads, tofu, grilled seafood, tempura, and sushi rolls. If you find yourself hungry in Ginza in the dead of night, this all-nighter is a good choice.

5–9–1 Ginza. ✆ **03/5537-2878**. Sushi a la carte ¥52–¥514; set lunches ¥892–¥945; set dinners ¥1,260–¥3,150. AE, MC, V. 24 hr. Station: Higashi Ginza or Ginza (2 min.). On the south side of Harumi Dori, btw. Chuo Dori and Showa Dori.

Zest Cantina TEX-MEX   You can probably find better Mexican restaurants at home, but this will do for a quick fix, especially once the margaritas kick in. It offers chicken and cheese burritos, shrimp enchiladas, tacos, and other Tex-Mex fare, as well as steaks, hamburgers, and very good salads in a rustic, cowboy-themed setting. This restaurant is actually one of four restaurants ensconced under a freeway in a nifty dining complex called **G-Zone**. Southeast Asian fare is offered in **Monsoon** (✆ **03/5524-3631**); pizza and pasta in Italian-themed **La Boheme** (✆ **03/5524-3616;** see above); and Japanese food in **Gonpachi** (✆ **03/5524-3641;** see p. 173 for a review). English-language menus, inexpensive food, friendly and polished staff, and late opening hours make these restaurants winners whether you're a Tokyo novice or a pro.

You'll find other Zest Cantinas in Shibuya at 1–6–8 Jinnan (✆ **03/5489-3332**); in Ebisu at 1–22–19 Ebisu (✆ **03/5475-6291**); and in Odaiba on the fourth floor of Mediage (✆ **03/3599-4803**).

1–2–3 Ginza. ✆ **03/5524-3621**. www.zest-cantina.jp. Main dishes ¥800–¥2,600; set lunches ¥900–¥2,200. AE, DC, MC, V. Daily 11:30am–5am. Station: Kyobashi (exit 3, 2 min.) or Ginza-Itchome (exit 7, 1 min.). On Chuo Dori, at the northern edge of Ginza.

NEAR TOKYO STATION

There's a **Kua' Aina** (p. 168) outlet selling burgers in the Marunouchi Building on the fifth floor, across from Tokyo Station at 2–4–1 Marunouchi (✆ **03/5220-2400**).

Moderate

Aux Amis Tokyo ★ FRENCH   This small, tony restaurant specializing in creative French cuisine is one of several on the top two floors of the Marunouchi Building (called

Maru Biru by locals), located on the west side of Tokyo Station. Sweeping views make it a dining hot spot (reserve one of the few coveted window seats), as do an extensive wine list and a changing French/Japanese menu that might include such entrees as roast lamb with shiitake mushrooms, pork filet in a red-wine sauce, and a fish of the day. It's also a great spot for lunch, but note that the rather bare dining room fails to absorb the constant chatter of this popular venue. Other restaurants on the two floors serve *shabu-shabu*, sushi, tempura, and *kaiseki*, as well as Italian, Thai, French, and Chinese cuisines. There are many more inexpensive eateries in the basement.

Marunouchi Building, 35th floor, 2-4-1 Marunouchi. Ⓒ **03/5220-4011**. Main dishes ¥2,940–¥5,114; set dinners ¥6,300–¥12,600; set lunches ¥2,940–¥7,140, plus a weekday lunch for ¥1,800. AE, DC, MC, V. Daily 11am–2:30pm and 5:30–11:30pm (last order). Station: Tokyo (Marunouchi exit, 2 min.).

TSUKIJI

As Tsukiji is home to the nation's largest wholesale fish market, it's not surprising that this area abounds in sushi and seafood restaurants. In addition to the recommendations here, don't neglect the many stalls in and around the market where you can eat everything from noodles to fresh sashimi.

Moderate

⑦ **Tentake** FUGU People who really know their *fugu,* or blowfish, will tell you that the proper time to eat it is October through March, when it's fresh. You can eat fugu year-round, however, and a good place to try this Japanese delicacy is Tentake, popular with the Tsukiji working crowd. An English-language menu lists dishes such as tempura fugu, along with complete fugu dinners with all the trimmings. Otherwise, if you want suggestions, try the *fugu-chiri* for ¥2,800, a do-it-yourself blowfish and vegetable stew in which you cook raw blowfish, cabbage, dandelion leaves, and tofu in a pot of boiling water in front of you; this was more than I could eat, but you can make a complete meal of it by ordering the Tsukiji course for ¥6,500, which adds tempura, yakitori, and other dishes. You can wash it all down with fugu sake. If someone in your party doesn't like fugu, I recommend the crab set menu for ¥4,090. And yes, that's fugu swimming in the fish tank. (For information on fugu, see "Tips on Dining in Japan," in chapter 2.)

6-16-6 Tsukiji. Ⓒ **03/3541-3881**. Fugu dishes ¥520–¥4,090; fugu set courses ¥4,800–¥13,500; set lunches ¥840–¥1,570. AE, MC, V. Daily 11:30am–9:30pm (last order). Station: Tsukiji (7 min.). From the Harumi Dori/Shinohashi intersection, walk on Harumi Dori in the opposite direction of Ginza; the restaurant is on the left in a modern building just before the Kachidoki-bashi Bridge.

Inexpensive

⑧ **Edogin** SUSHI There are two Edogin sushi restaurants in Tsukiji, both within walking distance of one another. Since they're close to the famous fish market, you can be sure that the fish will be fresh. There's nothing aesthetic about the main Edogin, first established about 80 years ago—the lights are bright, it's packed with the locals, and it's noisy and busy. It's particularly crowded during lunch- and dinnertime because the food is dependably good and plentiful. The menu is in Japanese only, but an illustrated menu outside displays some of the set meals, with most prices ¥3,700 or less. There are also sushi platters for ¥1,600 to ¥4,200. As an alternative, look at what the people around you are eating or, if it's lunchtime, order the *teishoku* (served until 2pm). The *nigiri-zushi teishoku* for ¥1,050 offers a variety of sushi, along with soup and pickled vegetables; if you're really hungry, a more plentiful nigiri-zushi teishoku is available for ¥1,470.

4–5–1 Tsukiji. ☏ **03/3543-4401.** Set meals ¥1,800–¥5,500; lunch teishoku ¥1,050–¥1,470. AE, DC, MC, V. Mon–Sat 11:30am–9:30pm; Sun and holidays 11:30am–9pm. Station: Tsukiji or Tsukijijo (3 min.). Located near the Harumi and Shinohashi Dori intersection behind McDonald's; anyone in the neighborhood can point you in the right direction.

⑨ **Sushi Dai** ★ SUSHI   Located right in the Tsukiji Fish Market, this sushi bar boasts some of the freshest fish in town (and often a long line of people queuing for one of the dozen seats; waits can be up to an hour). The easiest thing to do is order the *seto*, a set sushi course that usually comes with tuna, eel, shrimp, and other morsels, plus six rolls of tuna and rice in *onigiri* (seaweed). You won't get plates here—food is served directly on the raised counter in front of you.

Tsukiji Fish Market. ☏ **03/3547-6797.** Sushi a la carte ¥315–¥1,000; sushi seto ¥2,500–¥3,900. No credit cards. Mon–Sat 5am–2pm. Closed Wed if the market is closed, and on holidays. Station: Tsukijijo (2 min.) or Tsukiji (10 min.). Located in a row of barracks housing other restaurants and shops beside the covered market, in Building no. 6 in the 3rd alley (just past the mailbox); it's the 3rd shop on the right.

ASAKUSA
Moderate

⑩ **Chinya** ★ (**Value**) SHABU-SHABU/SUKIYAKI   Established in 1880, Chinya is an old sukiyaki restaurant with a new home in a seven-story building to the left of Kaminarimon Gate, adjacent to its own butcher shop. The entrance to this place is open-fronted; all you'll see is a man waiting to take your shoes and a hostess in a kimono ready to lead you to one of the *tatami*-floored dining areas above. Chinya offers very good *shabu-shabu* and sukiyaki set lunches for ¥4,300, available until 3pm and including an appetizer, miso soup, rice or noodles, and side dishes. Otherwise, dinner set meals of shabu-shabu or sukiyaki, including sashimi, rice, and soup, begin at ¥5,500 (reservations required). The English-language menu and an English-language pamphlet include instructions, making this a good bet for the sukiyaki/shabu-shabu novice.

1–3–4 Asakusa. ☏ **03/3841-0010.** www.chinya.co.jp. Reservations required for set dinners. Sukiyaki or shabu-shabu ¥3,200–¥8,100; set dinners ¥5,500–¥12,000; set lunch ¥4,300. AE, DC, MC, V. Mon–Sat noon–9pm; Sun and holidays 11:30am–9pm (last order 7pm). Station: Asakusa (1 min.). On Kaminarimon Dori; located to the left of the Kaminarimon Gate if you stand facing Asakusa Kannon Temple (look for the SUKIYAKI sign).

⑪ **Komagata Dojo** ★ (**Finds**) DOJO   This is a restaurant very much out of the Edo Period. Following a tradition spanning 200 years and now in its sixth generation of owners, this old-style dining hall specializes in *dojo*, a tiny, sardinelike river fish that translates as "loach." It's served in a variety of styles listed on an English-language menu, from grilled to stewed. Easiest is to order one of the set meals (described in Japanese only), which includes a popular *dojo nabe*, cooked on a charcoal burner in front of you (dojo nabe ordered a la carte costs ¥1,700). Otherwise, look around and order what someone else is eating. The dining area is a single large room of *tatami* mats, with ground-level boards serving as tables, and waitresses in traditional dress moving quietly about.

1–7–12 Komagata, Taito-ku. ☏ **03/3842-4001.** Reservations recommended for dinner. Dojo dishes ¥850–¥1,700; set dinners ¥2,450–¥7,300; set lunches ¥2,400–¥2,550. AE, DC, MC, V. Daily 11am–9pm. Station: Asakusa (3 min.). Walk south on Asakusa Dori (away from Kaminarimon Gate/Sensoji Temple); the restaurant—a large, old-fashioned wood house on a corner, with blue curtains at its door—is on the right side of the street, about a 5-min. walk from Kaminarimon Gate, past the MUFJ Bank.

La Ranarita Azumabashi ★ ITALIAN   The Asahi Beer Tower may not mean anything to you, but if I mention the building with the golden hops poised on top, you'll certainly know it when you see it (the building was designed by Philippe Starck). The

Asahi Beer Tower is the high-rise next to the golden hops, looking like . . . a foaming beer mug? On the top floor (in the foam), this Italian restaurant has soaring walls and great views of Asakusa. It's a perfect perch from which to watch barges on the river or the sun set over Asakusa as you dine on everything from pasta and grilled lamb with rosemary to fresh fish of the day prepared baked, grilled, or meunière. The set lunches include an antipasto, salad, a main dish, and coffee. If you want a ringside seat, make a reservation at least 3 days in advance, avoid weekends and holidays, or arrive just when they open.

Asahi Beer Tower (on the opposite side of the Sumida River from Sensoji Temple), 22nd floor, 1-23-1 Azumabashi. ℂ **03/5608-5277.** Reservations recommended on weekends. Pizza and pasta ¥1,300–¥1,800; main dishes ¥2,200–¥5,000; set lunches ¥1,800–¥4,800. AE, DC, MC, V. Mon–Sat 11:30am–2pm and 5–9pm; Sun and holidays 11:30am–3pm and 5–9pm (last order). Station: Asakusa (4 min.).

(12) **Mugitoro** YAM/KAISEKI Founded about 65 years ago but now housed in a new building, this restaurant specializes in *tororo-imo* (yam) *kaiseki* and has a wide following among middle-age Japanese women. Popular as a health food, the yams used here are imported from the mountains of Akita Prefecture and are featured in almost all the dishes. If you're on a budget or want a quick meal, come for the weekday lunch buffet offered until 1pm; it includes a main dish such as fish or beef, yam in some form, vegetable, soup, and rice—just deposit ¥1,000 into the pot on the table and help yourself.

2-2-4 Kaminarimon. ℂ **03/3842-1066.** Reservations recommended. Set dinners ¥5,250–¥10,500; set lunches weekends/holidays only ¥2,625–¥3,675. AE, DC, MC, V. Mon–Fri 11:30am–9pm; Sat–Sun and holidays 11am–9pm (last order). Station: Asakusa (2 min.). From Sensoji Temple, walk south (with your back to Kaminarimon Gate) until you reach the 1st big intersection with the stoplight. Komagata-bashi Bridge will be to your left; Mugitoro is beside the bridge on Edo Dori, next to a tiny temple.

(13) **Waentei-Kikko** ★★★ (Finds) KAISEKI Just southeast of Sensoji Temple, Waentei-Kikko is actually a tiny, traditional house tucked behind a tiny garden. Inside, it's like a farmhouse in the countryside with its flagstone entry, wooden rafters, and *tatami* seating. A warm and friendly husband-and-wife team manage it, but what makes this establishment especially compelling are the *shamisen* performances by the husband, Fukui Kodai, who plays with the fervor of a rock star, or by other staff members, as well as performances of other traditional Japanese music (performances are at 12:15, 1:30, 6:30, and 8pm). Of course, the food shines, too, with *obento* lunch boxes and *kaiseki* dinners that change with the seasons. Fugu kaiseki dinners, beginning at ¥9,975, are also available with advance reservations. This place is a true find.

2-2-13 Asakusa. ℂ **03/5828-8833.** www.waentei-kikko.com. Reservations recommended. Obento lunches ¥2,500 and ¥3,500; kaiseki dinners ¥6,825–¥14,175. AE, DC, MC, V. Thurs–Tues 11:30am–1:30pm and 5–8:30pm (last order). Station: Asakusa (5 min.). Walk on Nakamise Dori toward Sensoji Temple, turning right after the last shop; go past the 2 stone Buddhas and then turn right again at the tiny Benten-do Temple with the large bell; the restaurant is on the right side of the street across from the playground.

Inexpensive

Kamiya Bar VARIED JAPANESE/WESTERN This inexpensive restaurant, established in 1880 as the first Western bar in Japan, serves both Japanese and Western fare on its three floors. The first floor is the bar, popular with older, tobacco smoking Japanese men and famous for its *Denki Bran* (a concoction of brandy, gin, wine, vermouth, Curacao, and herbs). The second floor offers Western food of a sort (that is, the Japanese version of Western food), including fried chicken, smoked salmon, spaghetti, fried shrimp, and hamburger steak. The third floor serves Japanese food ranging from *udon* noodles and yakitori to tempura and sashimi. I personally prefer the third floor for both its food and its atmosphere. Although the menus are in Japanese only, extensive plastic-food display cases show set meals of Japanese food costing ¥1,500 to ¥3,500. This is a very casual restaurant, very much a place for older locals, and it can be quite noisy and crowded.

1–1–1 Asakusa. ℭ **03/3841-5400.** Main dishes ¥700–¥1,500. AE, DC, MC, V (2nd/3rd floors only). Wed–Mon 11:30am–9:30pm (last order). Station: Asakusa (1 min.). Located on Kaminarimon Dori in a plain, brown-tiled building btw. Kaminarimon Gate and the Sumida River.

⑭ **Namiki Yabusoba** ★ NOODLES Asakusa's best-known noodle shop, founded in 1913, offers plain buckwheat noodles in cold or hot broth as well as more substantial tempura with noodles, all listed on an English-language menu. Seating is at tables or on *tatami* mats, and it's a small place, so there's often a queue outside the front door and you won't be able to linger if people are waiting.

2–11–9 Kaminarimon. ℭ **03/3841-1340.** Dishes ¥700–¥1,700. No credit cards. Fri–Wed 11:30am–7:30pm. Station: Asakusa (2 min.). From Kaminarimon Gate, walk south (away from Sensoji Temple) 1 min.; Namiki is on the right side of the street, a brown building with bamboo trees, a small maple, and a stone lantern by the front door.

⑮ **Sansado** TEMPURA Located right beside Kaminarimon Gate, next to the Kurodaya paper shop, this simple tempura restaurant specializes in Edo-style tempura, fried in a light oil. On the first floor, seating is either at tables or on *tatami,* while the upstairs is more traditional with tatami-only seating; one room overlooks the temple gate. Sansado is run by an army of very able grandmotherly types, and since the menu is in Japanese only, they're more than happy to go outside with you to help you make a selection from the plastic display case.

1–2–2 Asakusa. ℭ **03/3841-3400.** Set meals ¥1,385–¥3,235. AE, DC, MC, V. Daily 11:30am–9pm (last order). Station: Asakusa (1 min.). East of Kaminarimon Gate, with entrances beside Kurodaya paper shop and on Kaminarimon Dori.

⑯ **Sometaro** ★ **Kids** OKONOMIYAKI/YAKISOBA This very atmospheric neighborhood restaurant specializes in *okonomiyaki,* a working-class meal that is basically a Japanese pancake filled with beef, pork, and vegetables, and prepared by the diners themselves as they sit on *tatami* at low tables inset with griddles. Realizing that some foreigners may be intimidated by having to cook an unfamiliar meal, this restaurant makes the process easier with an English-language menu complete with instructions. The busy but friendly staff can also help you get started. In addition to okonomiyaki, *yakisoba* (fried noodles) with meat or vegetables and other do-it-yourself dishes are available. This is a fun, convivial way to enjoy a meal, especially for kids who might like to try their own hand in cooking their meal (and selecting their own ingredients). Before entering the restaurant, be sure to deposit your shoes in the proffered plastic sacks by the door.

2–2–2 Nishi-Asakusa. ℭ **03/3844-9502.** Main dishes ¥588–¥880; set meals ¥1,575. No credit cards. Daily noon–10pm (last order). Station: Tawaramachi (2 min.) or Asakusa (5 min.). Just off Kokusai Dori, on the side street that runs btw. the Drum Museum and the police station, in the 2nd block on the right.

UENO
Expensive
Grill Fukushima ★ CLASSIC FRENCH Parent company Seiyoken opened one of Japan's first restaurants serving Western food in 1876. Its restaurant here, ensconced in a nondescript building dating from the 1950s, is nonetheless the classiest place to eat in Ueno Park, serving pricey but quite good French cuisine, with a relaxing view of greenery outside its large windows and classical music playing softly in the background. The a la

carte menu, in French and Japanese, includes seafood such as lobster in an orange sauce and meat dishes ranging from filet mignon in red-wine sauce to roast lamb, but most people order one of the many fixed-price meals. There's a varied selection of French wines as well as wines from Germany, California, and Australia. The Grill is located to the right as you enter the building and is not to be confused with the much cheaper utilitarian restaurant to the left.

In Ueno Park. ℂ **03/3821-2181.** Reservations not required. Main dishes ¥4,200–¥7,875; set dinners ¥10,500–¥18,900; set lunches ¥4,800–¥10,500. AE, DC, MC, V. Daily 11am–8pm (last order). Station: JR Ueno (6 min.). Btw. Kiyomizu Temple and Toshogu Shrine.

Moderate

⑰ **Innsyoutei** ★ KAISEKI/OBENTO   This traditional Japanese restaurant in Ueno Park has been a Tokyo landmark since 1875. Downstairs is a simple tearoom, but for a meal you'll be ushered upstairs to a dining room with tables overlooking trees or a private *tatami* room. For lunch it offers a variety of set meals (including a vegetarian meal), *obento,* and *kaiseki* meals from an English-language menu, while dinner features kaiseki and chicken sukiyaki. If you've never had kaiseki, this is a good choice, but it's also a convenient lunch spot after visiting Ueno Park's many museums.

In Ueno Park. ℂ **03/3821-8126.** Reservations recommended. Set dinners ¥5,300–¥10,500; set lunches ¥1,680–¥6,300. No credit cards. Daily 11am–4pm and 5–11pm (Sun to 10pm). Station: JR Ueno (6 min.). Btw. Grill Fukushima (see above) and the row of orange *torii* leading downhill.

⑱ **Izu'ei** EEL   Put aside all your prejudices about eels and head for this modern yet traditionally decorated multistoried restaurant with a 260-year history dating from the Edo Period and views of Shinobazu Pond. Since eels are grilled over charcoal, the Japanese place a lot of stock in the quality of the charcoal used, and this place boasts its own furnace in the mountains of Wakayama Prefecture, which is said to produce the best charcoal in Japan. *Unagi donburi* (rice topped with strips of eel), tempura, and sushi are available, as well as set meals. There's no English-language menu, but there is a display case outside, and the menu has some pictures.

2-12-22 Ueno. ℂ **03/3831-0954.** Reservations recommended. Main dishes ¥1,595–¥5,250; set meals ¥2,100–¥10,500. AE, DC, MC, V. Daily 11am–9:30pm (last order). Station: JR Ueno (3 min.). On Shinobazu Dori, across the street from Shinobazu Pond and the Shitamachi Museum, next to KFC.

Tokori KOREAN BARBECUE   One of three restaurants in a modern concrete building called Bamboo Garden (the other two restaurants serve Chinese and Japanese food), this friendly establishment offers Korean-style barbecued meats, which you grill yourself at your table, as well as salads, *kimchi* (spicy Korean cabbage), Korean-style pancakes, rice porridge, noodles, and soups from an English-language menu with photographs. Set lunches feature one-pot meals or grilled beef, along with side dishes of soup, salad, and kimchi.

1-52 Ueno Park. ℂ **03/5807-2255.** Main dishes ¥840–¥1,880; set lunches ¥1,000–¥2,200. AE, DC, MC, V. Daily 11am–11:30pm. Station: JR Ueno (2 min.). On a steep hillside across the street from JR Ueno Station's west side, in Ueno Park next to the Ueno Royal Museum.

Inexpensive

The **Hard Rock Cafe Ueno** (see p. 174 for a review), 7–1–1 Ueno (ℂ **03/5826-5821**), is located in JR Ueno Station, while **Kohmen** (p. 175), 4–8–8 Ueno (ℂ **03/5807-4535**), offers tasty ramen and *gyoza.*

Mantra INDIAN   Decorated in pink with etched mirrors and lots of brass, this tiny, spotless restaurant offers curries, tandoori, and halal food at inexpensive prices. A good way for lone diners to try a variety of dishes is the all-you-can-eat lunch buffet served from 11am to 4pm, or one of the meat or vegetarian *thali* (set meals). Another good choice for budget travelers: a set dinner for ¥2,395 that's all you can eat within 90 minutes; add ¥1,050 for all you can drink.

Nagafuji Building Annex, 3rd floor, 4–9–6 Ueno. ℭ **03/3835-0818.** Main dishes ¥890–¥1,680; set meals ¥1,980–¥3,300; lunch buffet ¥998 weekdays, ¥1,300 weekends and holidays. AE, DC, MC, V. Daily 11am–9:30pm (last order). Station: JR Ueno (2 min.). From the south end of Ueno Park, look for the modern Nagafuji Building on Chuo Dori; the annex is in the back, facing the north end of Ameyokocho shopping street.

SHINJUKU

In addition to the suggestions below, be sure to check out the restaurant floors of several buildings in Shinjuku, where you can find restaurants in all price categories serving a variety of Japanese and international cuisine, some with very good views. These include the 29th and 30th floors of the **N. S. Building** where, in addition to Hakkaku (described below), there are restaurants serving tempura, tonkatsu, teppanyaki, sushi, and Italian fare; the top four floors of the **Sumitomo Building** where, in addition to Donto (p. 152), you'll find more than 20 outlets offering everything from tempura to Chinese cuisine; and the 12th, 13th, and 14th floors of **Takashimaya Shinjuku** where there are restaurants serving sushi, eel, *tonkatsu,* noodles, tempura, hamburgers, and more.

Very Expensive

New York Grill ★★★ AMERICAN   On the 52nd floor of one of Tokyo's most exclusive hotels, the New York Grill has remained *the* place to dine ever since its 1994 opening; some swear it's the most sophisticated restaurant in all of Japan. Surrounded on four sides by glass, it features stunning views (especially at night), live jazz in the evenings, and a 1,600-bottle wine cellar (with an emphasis on California wines). The restaurant backs up its dramatic setting with generous portions of steaks, seafood, and other fare ranging from delectable roast duck to Australian veal chop, all prepared in an open kitchen with counter seating for close-up views of the action. Both the set lunch and the weekend and holiday brunches are among the city's best and most sumptuous—and are great options for those who don't want to pawn their belongings to eat dinner here. I wouldn't miss it.

Park Hyatt Tokyo, 52nd floor, 3–7–1–2 Nishi-Shinjuku. ℭ **03/5322-1234.** www.parkhyatttokyo.com. Reservations required. Main dishes ¥4,800–¥11,000; set lunches ¥5,200; set dinners ¥11,000–¥21,000; Sat–Sun and holiday brunch ¥6,600. AE, DC, MC, V. Daily 11:30am–2:30pm and 5:30–10:30pm. Station: Shinjuku (west exit, a 13-min. walk or a 5-min. free shuttle ride), Hatsudai on the Keio Line (7 min.), or Tochomae on the Oedo Line (8 min.).

Expensive

In addition to the listing here, there's a branch of the famous tempura restaurant **Ten-ichi** (p. 152) on the seventh floor of Isetan department store, 3–14–1 Shinjuku (ℭ **03/5379-3039**).

⑲ **Kakiden** ★★ KAISEKI   Although it's located on the eighth floor of a rather uninspiring building, Kakiden has a relaxing teahouse atmosphere with low chairs, *shoji* screens, bamboo trees, and soothing traditional Japanese music playing softly in the background. Sibling restaurant to one in Kyoto founded more than 260 years ago as a catering service for the elite, this *kaiseki* restaurant serves set meals that change with the seasons according to what's fresh and available. An English-language menu lists the set meals, but it's probably best to simply pick a meal to fit your budget. The set lunch is available until 3pm. Set dinners include box kaiseki starting at ¥5,250, mini-kaiseki for ¥8,400, and kaiseki courses ranging from ¥8,400 to ¥15,750. Some of the more common dishes here include fish, seasonal vegetables, eggs, sashimi, shrimp, and mushrooms, but don't worry if you can't identify everything—I've found that even the Japanese don't always know what they're eating.

3-37-11 Shinjuku, 8th floor. ℂ **03/3352-5121.** Reservations recommended for lunch. Set dinners ¥5,250–¥21,000; set lunches ¥4,200–¥6,300. AE, DC, MC, V. Daily 11am–9pm (last order). Station: Shinjuku (east exit, 1 min.). Next to Shinjuku Station's east side.

Moderate

In addition to the suggestions here, an excellent choice for nouvelle Japanese cuisine is **daidaiya** (p. 177), located next to the east exit of Shinjuku station on the third floor of the Nowa Building, 3–37–12 Shinjuku (ℂ **03/5362-7173**). In addition, **Kushinobo** (p. 172) is a kushikatsu restaurant at 1–10–5 Kabuki-cho (ℂ **03/3232-9744**).

⑳ **Ban-Thai** THAI   One of Tokyo's longest-running Thai restaurants and credited with introducing authentic Thai food to the Japanese, Ban-Thai prepares excellent Thai fare, with 90 mouthwatering items on the menu. My favorites are the cold and spicy meat salad, the chicken soup with coconut and lemon grass, and the pad Thai. Note that set dinners are available only for parties of two or more; also, portions are not large, so if you order several portions and add beer, your tab can really climb. Finally, the service is indifferent. Yet this place is packed every time I come here.

1-23-14 Kabuki-cho, 3rd floor. ℂ **03/3207-0068.** Reservations recommended. Main dishes ¥1,200–¥1,800; set dinners ¥2,500–¥6,000; set lunches ¥630–¥1,365. AE, DC, MC, V. Mon–Fri 11:30am–3pm and 5–11pm; Sat–Sun and holidays 11:30am–11pm (last order). Station: Shinjuku (east exit, 7 min.). In East Shinjuku in the seediest part of Kabuki-cho (don't worry, the interior is nicer than the exterior) on the west side of a neon-lit pedestrian street running from Yasukuni Dori (look for the red neon archway and 7-Eleven) to Koma Stadium, a Kabuki-cho landmark.

㉑ **Hayashi** ★★ Finds ROBATAYAKI   This restaurant specializes in Japanese set meals cooked over your own hibachi grill. It's small and cozy, with only five grills and a woman in kimono overseeing the cooking operations, taking over if customers seem the least bit hesitant. The rustic interior was imported intact from the mountain region of Takayama. Four set meals are offered (vegetarian meals are available on request). My ¥5,250 meal came with sashimi, *yakitori,* tofu steak, scallops cooked in their shells, shrimp, and vegetables, all grilled one after the other. Watch your alcohol intake—drinks can really add to your bill.

Jojoen Daini Shinjuku Building, 2-22-5 Kabuki-cho. ℂ **03/3209-5672.** Reservations recommended. Set dinners ¥4,200–¥7,350. AE, DC, MC, V. Mon–Sat 5–11:30pm. Closed holidays. Station: Shinjuku (east exit, 10 min.). On the northern edge of Kabuki-cho; you'll know you're getting close when you see Godzilla hanging from a building; the restaurant is just a bit farther to the north, on a corner.

㉒ **Tsunahachi** TEMPURA   Inside a small, old-fashioned brown building in the heart of fashionable East Shinjuku is the main branch of a restaurant that has been serving tempura since 1923. Now there are several dozen outlets in Japan, including one on the 13th floor of Takashimaya Shinjuku (ℂ **03/5361-1860**). The Shinjuku location is the largest outlet, with an open kitchen and counter plus table seating. Though it has an English-language menu, the easiest option is to order one of three set meals, the least expensive of which includes six pieces of tempura, including deep-fried shrimp, conger eel, seasonal fish, shrimp balls and vegetables, along with miso soup, Japanese pickles, and rice.

3–31–8 Shinjuku. ✆ **03/3352-1012.** Reservations recommended. Tempura a la carte ¥470–¥1,200; tempura set meals ¥1,995–¥3,990. AE, DC, V. Daily 11am–10pm. Station: Shinjuku Sanchome (2 min.) or Shinjuku (east exit, 5 min.). Off Shinjuku Dori on the side street that runs along the east side of Mitsukoshi department store.

Inexpensive

Toriyoshi (p. 168), 3–34–16 Shinjuku (✆ **03/3225-1922**), is a popular Japanese-style pub with inexpensive meals.

㉓ **Hakkaku ★** (Finds) VARIED JAPANESE/ROBATAYAKI   This lively, crowded establishment has a lot going for it: a corner location in a skyscraper with expansive views over Yoyogi Park, inexpensive dishes and meals on an English-language menu, and Kirin beer on tap. Its decor and food resemble those of a bar. During lunch only set meals are available; choose grilled fish, fried chicken, tempura, or from the display case. Dinner offers a wider range of possibilities, including sashimi, grilled fish, fried noodles, and salads. *Yakitori*, beginning at ¥399 per two skewers, includes asparagus wrapped in bacon and *tsukune* (chicken meatballs), two of my favorites. There's also a *robatayaki* counter, where you can point at various dishes, watch them be prepared on the open grill, and then receive them from a wooden paddle passed in your direction.

N. S. Building, 29th floor (be sure to take the dedicated Sky Restaurant elevator at the northeast corner of the building), 2–4–1 Nishi-Shinjuku. ✆ **03/3345-1848.** Main dishes ¥700–¥1,869; set lunches ¥780–¥850. AE, DC, MC, V. Daily 11am–2:30pm and 5–9:30pm (last order). Station: Tochomae (3 min.) or Shinjuku (west exit, 8 min.).

Tokyo Catering (Kids) VARIED JAPANESE   This is probably the cheapest place in town for a meal with a view. Located on the 32nd floor in the north tower of the Tokyo Metropolitan Government Office (TMG), which offers a free observation room on its 45th floor, this cafeteria is for public employees but is open to everyone. Choose your meal—which can include the likes of pork cutlet, fried fish, sushi, curry rice, or noodles—from the display case, where every item is identified by a number. You then purchase your selections from a vending machine and take your tickets to the cafeteria window. The cafeteria lacks charm, but if you can get a table by the window, you'll have a good view of Tokyo. On the same floor is also a cafe, open Monday to Friday from 10am to 5pm for drinks and dessert.

TMG, 32nd floor of North Tower (take the office elevator, not the elevator to the observatory), 2–8–1 Nishi-Shinjukuku. ✆ **03/5320-7510.** Set meals ¥580–¥660. No credit cards. Mon–Fri 11:15am–2pm and 5–7pm. Station: Tochomae (1 min.), Shinjuku (10 min.), or Nishi-Shinjuku (5 min.).

HARAJUKU & AOYAMA
Expensive

Casita ★★★ (Finds) PACIFIC RIM/FUSION   One of the reasons I'm a great fan of Casita is that I feel truly pampered here. Who wouldn't, with a staff that proffers flashlights to the aged among us who have difficulty reading menus in dim lighting, stands ready to carry out every whim, and, on chilly nights, tucks us under electric blankets so

SETTLING INTO TOKYO

5 WHERE TO DINE

ACCOMMODATIONS ■
Asia Center of Japan **6**
Tokyu Stay
Aoyama Premier **6**

DINING ◆
Casita **18**
Fonda de la Madrugada **1**
Harajuku Gyoza Lou **10**
Heirokuzushi **13**
Hiroba **14**
Kohmen **9**
Kua' Ana **19**
La Boheme **12,15, 21, 22**
Limapuluh **16**
Maisen **7**
Sabatini **5**
Toriyoshi **4**
Venire Venire **3**
Wolfgang Puck Express **2**
Yai Yai **8**
Yasaiya Mei **11**

NIGHTLIFE ◆
Blue Note **23**
Body & Soul **20**
Crocodile **17**
Velours **24**

we can enjoy after-dinner drinks on the deck before we head over to the massage chairs? Casita aims to please, carving its own niche in Tokyo's fiercely competitive market by creating a tropical, resortlike atmosphere bolstered by great service and a year-round outdoor deck that's heated in winter and covered when it rains. Of course, none of that matters if the food falls short, but Casita turns out dishes that border on awesome, whether it's the Caesar salad with serious shavings of Parmesan, the caramelized foie gras with balsamic sauce, the wrapped langoustines with *garam masala*–flavored béarnaise sauce, or the grilled Japanese beef sirloin with seasonal vegetables in a wasabi-flavored red-wine sauce. Who wouldn't be a fan?

La Porte Aoyama, 5th floor, 5–51–8 Jingumae. 📞 **03/5485-7353.** www.casita.jp. Reservations required. Main dishes ¥3,200–¥5,500; set dinners ¥8,400–¥12,600. AE, DC, MC, V. Daily 5–11pm (last order). Station: Omotesando (3 min.). Head toward Shibuya on Omotesando Dori; it will be on your right, buried in an unlikely looking building past Kinokuniya and the stoplight.

Sabatini ★ ITALIAN This restaurant, with its Italian furniture and tableware and strolling musicians, seems as if it has been moved intact from the Old World. In fact, the only thing to remind you that you're in Tokyo is your Japanese waiter. The Italian family that opened Sabatini (no relation to the Sabatini restaurant in Ginza) has had a restaurant in Rome for more than 50 years, and many of the ingredients—olive oil, ham, salami, tomato sauce, and Parmesan—are flown in fresh from Italy. The menu includes seafood, veal, steak, and lamb, from the traditional saltimbocca to grilled scampi. Naturally, there's a wide selection of Italian wines.

Suncrest Building, 2–13–5 Kita-Aoyama. 📞 **03/3402-3812.** Reservations recommended for dinner. Main dishes ¥3,990–¥7,770; set dinners ¥10,500–¥14,700; set lunches ¥2,310–¥6,090 (from ¥2,730 weekends and holidays). AE, DC, MC, V. Daily 11:30am–2:30pm and 5:30–10:30pm (last order). Station: Gaienmae (2 min.). On Aoyama Dori near Gaien-Nishi Dori.

Moderate

㉔ **Yasaiya Mei** ★ VARIED JAPANESE/VEGETARIAN If you like veggies, this restaurant specializing in fresh, seasonal vegetables is a must. For starters you might choose the green papaya *kimchi* or the Mei Special *bagna cauda,* which comes with a variety of vegetables—like eggplant, radish, and asparagus—plus a dipping sauce. Not to be missed is the wild plant tempura, which changes with the seasons; spring might feature young bamboo shoots, while autumn may include eggplant and water chestnuts. Although the emphasis here is clearly on things that grow in the ground, a few meat dishes are also available, such as grilled pork with mashed potatoes. Set lunches feature a vegetable curry or fish, along with an *obento* served in a charming box with drawers. Seating is either at the U-shaped open kitchen or a table (try to snag one beside the large windows overlooking the trees of Omotesando Dori). There's a branch in Roppongi Hills, on the fifth floor of Mori Tower in an area called West Walk (📞 **03/5775-2960;** station: Roppongi).

Omotesando Hills, 3rd floor, 4–12–10 Jingumae 📞 **03/5785-0606.** Reservations required. Main dishes ¥900–¥2,100; set dinners ¥5,800; set lunches ¥1,400–¥3,800. AE, DC, MC, V. Mon–Sat 11am–11pm; Sun 11am–10pm (last order). Station: Station: Meiji-Jingumae or Omotesando (4 min.). On Omotesando Dori.

Inexpensive

In addition to the choices below, consider **La Boheme** (p. 155) serving pizza and pasta, with locations at 7–11–4 Minami Aoyama (📞 **03/3499-3377**), 6–2–2 Minami Aoyama (📞 **03/6418-4242**), 3–6–25 Kita-Aoyama (📞 **03/5766-1666**), and on Omotesando

Dori at 5–8–5 Jingumae (© **03/5467-5666**). **Kohmen** (p. 175), 6–2–8 Jingumae
(© **03/5468-6344**), serves tasty ramen and *gyoza*.

Fonda de la Madrugada MEXICAN   Serving what is probably Tokyo's most authentic Mexican food, this dark basement restaurant has a cavernous main dining room, several small and cozy offshoots, and a strolling mariachi band, making it seem as if you're dining in a Mexican villa. Shrimp marinated in tequila, chicken mole, and soft tacos served with chicken, fish, beef, or pork are just some of the items on the trilingual (Japanese/Spanish/English) menu, along with the requisite Mexican beers, tequila shots and shooters, margaritas, rum and vodka cocktails, and wine from Mexico, Chile, and Argentina.

2–33–12 Jingumae. © **03/5410-6288.** Reservations required. Main dishes ¥1,050–¥3,045. AE, DC, MC, V. Sun–Thurs 5:30pm–2am; Fri–Sat 5pm–5am. Station: Meiji-Jingumae (10 min.). From the Meiji Dori/Omotesando intersection, walk north on Meiji Dori (toward Shinjuku); it will be on your right after the pedestrian overpass.

㉕ **Harajuku Gyoza Lou** ★ GYOZA   If you like *gyoza* (pork dumplings), you owe yourself a meal here. Unlike most greasy spoons that specialize in fast-food Chinese (and tend to be on the dingy side), this restaurant in the heart of Harajuku is hip yet unpretentious and draws a young crowd with its straightforward menu posted on the wall (an English-language menu is also available). Only four types of gyoza are offered: steamed *(sui-gyoza)* or fried *(yaki-gyoza),* and with or without garlic *(ninniku).* A few side dishes, such as cucumber, boiled cabbage with vinegar, sprouts with a spicy meat sauce, and rice, are available, as are beer and sake. A U-shaped counter encloses the open kitchen, which diners can watch as they chow down on the very good gyoza.

6–2–4 Jingumae. © **03/3406-4743.** Gyoza ¥290 for a plate of 6. No credit cards. Mon–Sat 11:30am–4:30am; Sun and holidays 11:30am–10:30pm (last order). Station: Meiji-Jingumae (3 min.) or Harajuku (5 min.). From the Meiji/Omotesando Dori intersection, walk on Omotesando Dori toward Aoyama and take the 3rd right (just before Kiddy Land); it's at the end of this alley, on the right.

㉖ **Heirokuzushi** SUSHI   Bright (a bit too bright), clean, and modern, this is one of those fast-food sushi bars where plates of food are conducted along a conveyor belt on the counter. Customers help themselves to whatever strikes their fancy. To figure your bill, the cashier counts the number of plates you took from the conveyor belt: green plates cost ¥136, blue ones ¥168, red ones ¥231, gold ones ¥398, and brown ones ¥504. You can order takeout; you might want to eat in nearby Yoyogi Park.

5–8–5 Jingumae. © **03/3498-3968.** Plates of sushi ¥136–¥504. No credit cards. Daily 11am–9pm. Station: Meiji-Jingumae (2 min.) or Omotesando (5 min.). On Omotesando Dori close to the Oriental Bazaar.

Hiroba JAPANESE HEALTH FOOD/VEGETARIAN   Located in the basement of the Crayon House, which specializes in Japanese children's books, this natural-food restaurant offers a buffet lunch of organic veggies, fish, brown rice, and other health foods. For dinner, an English-language menu offers varied fare, including seasonal fish grilled with herbs, tandoori chicken, and stir-fried pork with soy sauce and ginger. The dining hall is very simple (its atmosphere reminds me of a potluck supper in a church basement), and because of the upstairs bookstore, there are likely to be families here.

Crayon House, 3–8–15 Kita-Aoyama. © **03/3406-6409.** Lunch buffet ¥1,260; main dishes ¥840–¥1,890. No credit cards. Daily 11am–2pm and 5:30–10pm. Station: Omotesando (2 min.). Off Omotesando Dori on the side street to the right of the Hanae Mori Building.

Kua' Aina ★ (Kids) AMERICAN/HAMBURGERS/SANDWICHES   This Hawaiian import is one of the best burger chains in town. In fact, if you come at mealtime you'll probably have to wait for a table in one of the tiny upstairs dining rooms. Burgers come as third- and (whopping) half-pounders. There are also sandwiches ranging from BLTs with avocado to roast beef to tuna. A good fix for carnivores.

Branches can be found at 1–10–4 Shibuya (**© 03/3409-3200**; station: Shibuya), in the Marunouchi Building across from Tokyo Station at 2–4–1 Marunouchi (**© 03/5220-2400**; station: Tokyo), and in Aqua City on Odaiba (**© 03/3599-2800**; station: Daiba).

5-10-21 Minami Aoyama. **© 03/3407-8001.** Burgers and sandwiches ¥750–¥1,330. No credit cards. Mon–Sat 11am–1pm; Sun 11am–10pm. Station: Omotesando (2 min.). On Aoyama Dori (heading toward Shibuya), at its busy intersection with Kotto Dori.

Limapuluh ★★ (Finds) FUSION   Not far from the Omotesando Dori-Aoyama Dori intersection, this breezy restaurant with an outdoor terrace wins kudos for both its laid-back atmosphere and its fusion French-Asian cuisine at very reasonable prices. Set lunches offer a meat dish, fish, or pasta of the day, along with a salad, dessert, and drink (such as lychee juice). Offerings for dinner change often and are written in Japanese only on a blackboard but always include the day's pasta, pizza, and heartier fare. Join local hipsters for happy hour, available Monday to Friday from 5 to 7pm, with drinks starting at ¥500. In short, it's hard to imagine going wrong here. What you save on a meal can be spent at Issey Miyake's Pleats Please shop just a few steps away.

La Place, 3-13-21 Minami Aoyama. **© 03/3401-1193.** Main dishes ¥1,200–¥2,100; set lunches ¥1,050–¥1,800. AE, DC, MC, V. Daily 11am–11:30pm. Station: Omotesando (1 min.). Off Aoyama Dori in the direction of Gaienmae, almost immediately to the right and hidden in a small shopping complex centered around a plaza.

(27) **Maisen** ★ (Finds) TONKATSU   Extremely popular with the locals, this restaurant has been dishing out *tonkatsu* (deep-fried breaded pork cutlet) for more than 25 years and is especially known for its black pork, originally from China and prized for its sweet, intense flavor. But what makes this restaurant a real standout is that it occupies a former pre–World War II public bathhouse; its main dining hall was once the changing room and it sports a high ceiling and original architectural details. There's an English-language menu, but lunch specials (available until 4pm) are listed in Japanese only, though there are photos. It's easiest to order a set meal.

4-8-5 Jingumae. **© 03/3470-0071.** Set meals ¥1,420–¥2,995; set lunches ¥840–¥1,420. AE, DC, MC, V. Daily 11am–10pm (last order). Station: Omotesando (4 min.). Take the A2 exit and turn right on the side street btw. Ito Hospital and McDonald's (the one with HARAJUKU above it); take the 1st left and then an immediate right. It will be in the next block on the left.

(28) **Toriyoshi** VARIED JAPANESE/INTERNATIONAL   This upscale jazz bar is a popular dining spot as well, especially for its chicken specialties such as fried chicken wings and half a fried chicken. The English-language menu lists a variety of Japanese and Asian pub fare as well, including salads, *yakitori*, tofu (I love the black sesame tofu, called *kuroi gomadofu*), *kimchi,* and more. A good place for a convivial evening. There are more than a dozen branches in Tokyo, including 3–18–16 Minami Aoyama (**© 03/3403-7720**; station: Omotesando) and 3–34–16 Shinjuku (**© 03/3225-1922**; station: Shinjuku).

4-28-21 Jingumae. ✆ **03/3470-3901.** Main dishes ¥620–¥1,400. AE, DC, MC, V. Mon–Fri 5-11pm; Sat–Sun 4-11pm (last order). Station: Meiji-Jingumae (3 min.). From the Meiji Dori/Omotesando intersection, walk on Omotesando toward Aoyama and take the 1st left (there's a Wendy's here); Toriyoshi is down this street, on the right side beside a willow tree. Look for its VOICE signboard, a reference to the jazz vocals often aired here.

Venire Venire ITALIAN   You'll have to see for yourself how inexpensive doesn't necessarily mean drab. This tall-ceilinged trattoria, on the fifth floor of the Y.M. Square building in Harajuku, is light and airy, with a large outdoor terrace affording sweeping views over the surrounding rooftops (open Golden Week to Oct). It offers mostly pizzas and pastas, such as fettuccine with scampi or pizza topped with prosciutto and mozzarella, as well as a handful of main dishes, including grilled chicken or pork with rosemary. Lunch gives a choice of pizza, pasta, or a main dish such as fish, along with a trip through the appetizer and salad bar. There's a large selection of Italian wines.

Y.M. Square, 4-31-10 Jingumae. ✆ **03/5775-5333.** Pizza and pasta ¥1,300–¥2,200; main dishes ¥1,400–¥3,000; set lunch ¥1,680. AE, DC, MC, V. Mon–Fri 11:30am–3pm and 5-11pm; Sat 11:30am–4pm and 5-11pm; Sun and holidays 11:30am–4pm and 5-10:30pm. Station: Harajuku (1 min.). On Meiji Dori, just north of Gap and across from La Foret.

Wolfgang Puck Express AMERICAN   This is the most casual and least expensive of Puck's invasion of eateries in Japan. It concentrates on burgers, pizza, pasta, roast chicken, salads, and other fast foods. What I like about this location is that it's right at the top of Takeshita Dori (Harajuku's most popular shopping street) across from the station, and it's more stylish than other fast-food competitors that shall remain nameless. Fast service, pop music, and beer—what more could you ask for?

1-17-1 Jingumae. ✆ **03/5786-4690.** Main dishes ¥980–¥1,480; set lunches ¥650–¥1,780. AE, DC, MC, V. Daily 11am–11pm. Station: Harajuku (1 min.). Across the street from Harajuku Station's north exit, at the top of Takeshita Dori.

㉙ **Yai Yai** OKONOMIYAKI   Instead of having to cook your own *okonomiyaki,* all you have to do here is order, whereupon the young staff sets to work cooking your meal on a griddle in front of you. You choose your toppings—such as pork or scallops, together with vegetables such as green onions or *kimchi*—which are then added to the pancake-like base, cabbage, and egg. Fried noodles and *udon,* also cooked with a choice of toppings, are also available.

6-8-7 Jingumae. ✆ **03/3406-8181.** Okonomiyaki or fried noodles ¥980–¥1,490. AE, DC, MC, V. Mon–Fri 5pm–3am; Sat noon–3am; Sun and holidays noon–11pm. Station: Meiji-Jingumae (3 min.) or Harajuku (7 min.). From the Meiji Dori/Omotesando intersection, walk on Omotesando toward Aoyama and take the 2nd right; it will be on the left.

ROPPONGI

Because Roppongi is such a popular nighttime hangout for young Tokyoites and foreigners, it boasts a large number of both Japanese and Western restaurants. To find the location of any of the Roppongi addresses below, stop by the tiny police station on Roppongi Crossing (Roppongi's main intersection of Roppongi Dori and Gaien-Higashi Dori), where you'll find a map of the area. If you still don't know where to go, ask one of the policemen.

About a 10-minute walk west of Roppongi (via Roppongi Dori in the direction of Shibuya) is another popular nighttime area: **Nishi Azabu.** Once primarily a residential neighborhood, Nishi Azabu has slowly changed over the years as it began absorbing the overflow of Roppongi. It has restaurants and bars yet remains mellower and much less crowded than Roppongi. Between Roppongi Crossing and Nishi Azabu is **Roppongi Hills,** a sprawling urban development with many choices in dining. **Tokyo Midtown,** Tokyo's newest urban development and attracting huge crowds, also offers dining, but good luck in securing a seat.

Very Expensive

㉚ **Inakaya** ★★ ROBATAYAKI   Whenever I host first-time foreign visitors in Tokyo, I take them to this festive restaurant, and they've never been disappointed. Although tourist-oriented and overpriced, it's still great fun; the drama of the place alone is worth it. Customers sit at a long, U-shaped counter, on the other side of which are mountains of fresh vegetables, beef, and seafood. And in the middle of all that food, seated in front of a grill, are male chefs—ready to cook whatever you point to in the style of *robatayaki.* Orders are yelled out by your waiter and are repeated in unison by all the other waiters, resulting in ongoing, excited yelling. Sounds strange, I know, but actually it's a lot of fun. Food offerings may include yellowtail, red snapper, sole, scallops, king crab legs, giant shrimp, steak, meatballs, gingko nuts, potatoes, eggplant, and asparagus, all piled high in wicker baskets and ready for the grill. Although prices for individual dishes may not seem high, they quickly add up. Most meals here average around ¥15,000, including a ¥800 per person table charge.

Other branches are at 5–3–4 Roppongi (✆ **03/3408-5040**), open daily 5pm to 5am, and at 8–7–4 Ginza (✆ **03/3569-1708**), open daily 5 to 11pm, but only the one detailed here has an English-language menu.

4-10-11 Roppongi. ✆ **03/5775-1012.** www.roppongiinakaya.jp. Grilled vegetables ¥650–¥900; grilled seafood and meats ¥1,050–¥5,100. AE, DC, MC, V. Daily 5–10:30pm (last order). Station: Roppongi (2 min.). Off Gaien-Higashi Dori on a side street opposite Ibis Hotel; from Roppongi Crossing, walk on Gaien-Higashi Dori in the direction of Midtown and take the 2nd right.

Expensive

㉛ **Fukuzushi** ★★ SUSHI   This is one of Tokyo's classiest sushi bars, attracting a cosmopolitan crowd. Although it has a traditional entrance through a small courtyard with lighted lanterns and the sound of trickling water, the interior is slick and modern with bold colors of black and red. Some people swear it has the best sushi in Tokyo, although with 7,000 sushi bars in the city, I'd be hard-pressed to say which one is tops. Certainly, you can't go wrong here. Three different set lunches are available, featuring sushi, *chirashi-zushi* (assorted sashimi with rice), or eel as the main course. Dinners are more extensive, with the ¥8,400 set course consisting of salad, sashimi, steamed egg custard, grilled fish, sushi, miso soup, dessert, and coffee (set dinners require orders by a minimum of two people).

5-7-8 Roppongi. ✆ **03/3402-4116.** www.roppongifukuzushi.com. Reservations recommended, especially for dinner. Set dinners ¥6,300–¥8,400; set lunches ¥2,625–¥4,725. AE, DC, MC, V. Mon–Sat 11:30am–1:30pm and 5:30–10pm (last order); holidays 5:30–9pm. Closed 1 week in mid-Aug. Station: Roppongi (4 min.). From Roppongi Crossing, walk toward Tokyo Tower on Gaien-Higashi Dori, turning right after McDonald's, left in front of Hard Rock Cafe, and then right.

Tokyo Shiba Toufuya Ukai ★★★ Finds TOFU   It's hard to imagine you're in Tokyo when you enter the lush grounds of this exquisite restaurant. Indeed, though it's located at the foot of Tokyo Tower (about a 15-min. walk from Roppongi), it's a world

ACCOMMODATIONS ■
Arca Torre **26**
Asia Center of Japan **11**
Grand Hyatt Tokyo **9**
Hotel Ibis **20**
Hotel Okura **18**
The Ritz-Carlton Tokyo **13**

DINING ◆
Aux Bacchanales **17**
Erawan **38**
Fukuzushi **36**
Ganchan **10**
Gonpachi **2**
Gyu-Kaku **27**
Hard Rock Cafe **37**
Ichioku **16**
Inakaya **23, 35**
Kamakura **22**
Kitchen Five **3**
Kohmen **19**
Kushinobo **8**
La Boheme **1, 21**
La Colina **14**
Mado Lounge **6**
Roti Roppongi **7**
Tokyo Shiba
Toufuya Ukai **39**
Yasaiya Mei **5**

NIGHTLIFE ◆
A971 **15**
Agave **24**
Bauhaus **32**
Cavern Club **33**
El Café Latino **31**
Fiesta International
Karaoke Bar **12**
Gaspanic Bar **30**
Gaspanic
Club **29**
Geronimo **25**
Heartland **4**
Kento's **34**
Kingyo **28**

— Subway

apart from the bustling city, with a landscaped garden complete with ponds (and three full-time gardeners) and traditional Japanese structures that include a main building constructed with heavy beams and foot-thick lacquered pillars imported from a 200-year-old Takayama farmhouse. Yet despite its aristocratic atmosphere, this restaurant specializes in classic tofu cuisine, with set meals that change with the seasons and are described on an English-language menu. The least expensive set lunch, for example, may start with an egg custard, deep-fried tofu with sweet miso sauce, and assorted sashimi, followed by deep-fried simmered tofu, sushi topped with cooked eel along with deep-fried burdock root, tofu seasoned in soy milk, rice, and sweet red-bean soup with rice cake.

4-4-13 Shibakoen. © **03/3436-1028.** Reservations required. Set dinners ¥8,400–¥12,600; set lunches ¥5,500–¥6,500. AE, DC, MC, V. Daily 11am–10pm (last order 8pm). Station: Akabanebashi (5 min.). Behind Tokyo Tower, to the left.

Moderate

Yasaiya Mei (p. 166) specializes in fresh vegetables and is located in Roppongi Hills on the fifth floor of Mori Tower in an area called West Walk (© **03/5775-2960**).

Erawan ★★THAI   Perched 13 floors above the Roppongi madness and offering cool, aloof views on three sides (ask to be seated on the Tokyo Tower side), this restaurant is massive but well divided into intimate dining areas that create a pleasant Thai aura with dark gleaming woods, woodcarvings, plants, bamboo screens, and a smiling Thai staff. Although it has an a la carte menu, most economical is to opt for the dinner buffet (available until 9pm), which includes an appetizer, salad, and dessert bar, plus two main dishes such as stir-fried minced pork with basil wrapped in lettuce or steamed deep-fried chicken wrapped in pandamus leaves.

Roi Building, 13th floor, 5-5-1 Roppongi. © **03/3404-5741.** Main dishes ¥1,300–¥1,800; set dinner buffet ¥5,300. AE, DC, MC, V. Mon–Fri 5:30–11:30pm; Sat–Sun and holidays 4–10pm. Station: Roppongi (3 min.). From Roppongi Crossing, Erawan is on the right side of Gaien-Higashi Dori (the road leading to Tokyo Tower), just past McDonald's.

Kushinobo KUSHIKATSU   First opened in Osaka in 1950, this small and cozy restaurant specializing in *kushikatsu* (deep-fried skewers of food) is ensconced in Roppongi Hills. Every day it prepares more than 40 different kinds of meat, seafood, and vegetable kushikatsu, drawn from more than 100 in-house recipes. A progression of skewers are served one at a time until you say stop (if you like one especially well, you can ask for it again), along with the restaurant's own special tartar sauce, miso sauce, sweet-and-sour sauce, and other sauces for dipping. Most people average about 16 skewers, which cost about ¥4,500 including a side dish and dessert. By the way, this is the first restaurant I've seen that charges a 10% "night charge," levied to those entering after 10pm or departing after 11pm. Still, I really like kushikatsu and wish there were more restaurants serving it in Tokyo. There's a Kushinobo branch in Shinjuku, at 1–10–5 Kabuki-cho (© **03/3232-9744;** station: Shinjuku).

Roppongi Hills, 5th floor of West Walk, 6-10-1 Roppongi. © **03/5771-0094.** Set dinners ¥3,990–¥4,500; set lunches ¥1,575–¥4,500. AE, DC, MC, V. Mon–Fri 11am–11pm; Sat 11am–4am; Sun and holidays 11am–10pm (last order). Closed holidays. Station: Roppongi (Roppongi Hills exit, 2 min.).

La Colina ★ MEXICAN   Since Tokyo Midtown's 2007 opening, it's been abuzz with curious sightseers, most of whom seem more than willing to brave long lines for the privilege of dining in one of its posh restaurants. A marked contrast to its sister restaurant Fonda de la Madrugada in Harajuku (p. 167), this stylish restaurant with its modern decor, strolling musicians, and outdoor terrace offers more hope than most for securing a seat if you haven't made a reservation, simply because Mexican food remains unknown to many Japanese. In any case, the food is more creative and refined (and pricier) than at its sister restaurant, offering the likes of chicken crepe on *poblano* chili and pistachio sauce or lamb shank marinated in chili, garlic, and herbs. To be honest, I don't understand the fuss about Midtown; I like Roppongi Hills better, for both its architecture and its facilities.

Tokyo Midtown, Garden Terrace (shop D-0118), 1st floor, 9-7-4 Roppongi. 𝄐 **03/5413-0092.** Reservations strongly recommended. Main dishes ¥2,200–¥3,050; set dinners ¥6,830–¥8,930; set lunches ¥2,300–¥4,500. AE, DC, MC, V. Daily 11am–11pm (last order). Station: Roppongi (Oedo exit, 2 min.). From Roppongi Crossing, walk on Gaien-Higashi Dori to Midtown and then head to Garden Terrace.

Inexpensive

In addition to the recommendations below, **La Boheme** (p. 165), 2-25-18 Nishi Azabu (𝄐 **03/3407-1363**) and 4-11-13 Roppongi (𝄐 **03/3478-0222**), serves pizza and pasta. **Gyu-Kaku** (p. 178), 5-1-2 Roppongi (𝄐 **03/5414-5129**), is a Korean barbecue restaurant.

㉜ **Ganchan** ★ YAKITORI   This is one of my favorite *yakitori-ya*. Small and intimate, it's owned by a friendly and entertaining man who can't speak English worth a darn but keeps trying with the help of a worn-out Japanese-English dictionary he keeps behind the counter. His staff is young and fun-loving. There's an eclectic cassette collection—I never know whether to expect Japanese pop tunes or American oldies. Seating is along a single counter with room for only a dozen or so people. Though there's an English-language menu, it's easiest to order the *yakitori seto,* a set course that comes with salad and soup and eight skewers of such items as chicken, beef, meatballs, green peppers, and asparagus rolled with bacon. There's a table charge of ¥600 per person, but it includes an appetizer.

6-8-23 Roppongi. 𝄐 **03/3478-0092.** Yakitori skewers ¥315–¥735; yakitori set course ¥2,625. AE, MC, V. Daily 5:30pm–1:30am. Station: Roppongi (7 min.). From Roppongi Crossing, take the small street going downhill to the left of the Almond Coffee Shop; Ganchan is at the bottom of the hill on the right.

Gonpachi ★★ ⓥ𝐚𝐥𝐮𝐞 VARIED JAPANESE   Housed in a re-created *kura* (traditional Japanese warehouse) with a high ceiling, three-tiered seating, and a central, open kitchen, this is one of Tokyo's most imaginative inexpensive Japanese restaurants (it's said to have served as the inspiration for the restaurant scene in the movie *Kill Bill*). It offers a wide variety of dishes, including *yakitori* (such as duck breast with wasabi), fish (such as miso-glazed black cod), sushi (on the third floor), noodles, tempura, and more. From the outside, you'd expect this place to be much more exclusive than it is—and you probably will be excluded if you fail to make reservations for dinner.

There are branches of Gonpachi at the G-Zone, 1-2-3 Ginza (𝄐 **03/5524-3641;** station: Kyobashi or Ginza-Itchome); in Shibuya on the 14th floor of E-Space Tower, 3-6 Maruyama-cho (𝄐 **03/5784-2011;** station: Shibuya); and at Mediage on Odaiba (𝄐 **03/3599-4807;** station: Daiba), all open from 11:30am to 3:30am or later. However, they don't match the Nishi Azabu location's atmosphere.

1-13-11 Nishi Azabu. ✆ **03/5771-0170**. www.gonpachi.jp. Reservations recommended for dinner. Yakitori ¥300–¥1,500; main dishes ¥1,000–¥2,800; set meals ¥3,500–¥6,000; set lunches ¥950–¥1,100. AE, DC, MC, V. Daily 11:30am–5am. Station: Roppongi (10 min.). From Roppongi Crossing, walk toward Shibuya on Roppongi Dori. It will be on your right, at Gaien-Nishi Dori.

Hard Rock Cafe (Kids) AMERICAN   Hard Rock Cafe has more than half a dozen locations in Japan; this was the first. If you have disgruntled teenagers in tow, bring them to this world-famous hamburger joint dedicated to rock 'n' roll to ogle the memorabilia on the walls, chow down on burgers, and check out the T-shirts for sale. In addition to hamburgers, the menu includes salads, sandwiches, steak, barbecued ribs, barbecued chicken, fish of the day, fajitas, and a few Asian dishes. Be prepared: The music is loud.

A branch is located in JR Ueno Station at 7–1–1 Ueno (✆ **03/5826-5821**).

5-4-20 Roppongi. ✆ **03/3408-7018**. www.hardrockjapan.com. Main dishes ¥1,480–¥3,980. AE, DC, MC, V. Sun–Thurs 11:30am–2am; Fri–Sat 11:30am–4am. Station: Roppongi (3 min.). From Roppongi Crossing, walk on Gaien-Higashi Dori toward Tokyo Tower and take a right at McDonald's.

(33) **Ichioku** ★ JAPANESE ORIGINALS   This is one of my favorite restaurants in Roppongi for casual dining. It's a tiny, cozy place with only eight tables, and you fill out your order yourself using the English-language menu—complete with pictures—which is glued underneath the clear glass tabletop. The food, featuring organically grown vegetables, can best be called nouvelle Japanese, with original creations offered at very reasonable prices. About 25 dishes are available, including tuna and ginger sauté, mushroom sauté, shrimp spring rolls, Thai curry, asparagus salad, fried potatoes, sautéed eggplant, and a dish of grated radish and tiny fish. I personally like the tofu steak (fried tofu and flakes of dried fish) and the cheese *gyoza* (fried pork dumpling topped with melted cheese).

4-4-5 Roppongi. ✆ **03/3405-9891**. Main dishes ¥800–¥2,450. AE, DC, MC, V. Mon–Fri 11:30am–2pm and 6pm–12:30am; Sat 6pm–1am; holidays 5–11pm (last order). Station: Roppongi (4 min.). On a side street in the neighborhood behind the police station.

Kamakura YAKITORI   Much more refined than most *yakitori-ya*, this basement establishment is decorated with paper lanterns and sprigs of fake but cheerful spring blossoms, with traditional *koto* music playing softly in the background. The English-language menu lists yakitori set courses; a la carte sticks are skewered with shrimp, meatballs, gingko, squid, eggplant, or mushrooms.

4-10-11 Roppongi. ✆ **03/3405-4377**. Yakitori skewers ¥240–¥550; set dinners ¥2,300–¥4,300. AE, DC, MC, V. Mon–Sat 5–11pm. Station: Roppongi (2 min.). From Roppongi Crossing, walk on the right side of Gaien-Higashi Dori in the direction of Tokyo Midtown and take the 2nd right.

Kitchen Five ★ (Finds) MEDITERRANEAN/INTERNATIONAL   If it's true that love is the best spice for cooking, then perhaps that's why Yuko Kobayashi's 25-year-old, 18-seat restaurant is so popular. She goes to market every morning to fetch ingredients for a dozen main dishes, which may include stuffed eggplant, lasagna, moussaka, and other casseroles and curries and are spread on a counter along with their prices. Every year Kobayashi goes off to search for recipes in Sicily, South America, northern Africa, and other countries that feature garlic, tomatoes, and olive oil in their cuisine. The love for what she does shines in her eyes as she cooks, serves, and walks you through the menu of daily dishes displayed. ***A word of warning:*** The food is so delicious, it's tempting to over order. Highly recommended.

4-2-15 Nishi Azabu. ℭ **03/3409-8835.** Dishes ¥1,300-¥1,900. No credit cards. Tues–Sat 6–9:30pm (last
order). Closed holidays, Jan, Golden Week, and late July to early Sept. Station: Hiroo (7 min.) or Roppongi (15 min.). Opposite Gaien-Nishi Dori from the gas station, down a side street.

(34) Kohmen (Value) RAMEN   Famished in the wee hours of the morning but spent most of your cash carousing? Head to this quirky ramen restaurant, where black-clad staff move around the dark interior like ninjas, fish swim in a bird cage, and personal-size TVs at counters and tables broadcast Kohmen commercials, concerts, and movie previews. An English-language menu gives a good choice of various ramen noodles, from thick or thin to crispy, along with various broths and extra toppings ranging from grilled pork to fried leek. I'm crazy about the *kogashi-tantanmen,* a creamy sesame soup with hot chili and charcoal-grilled marinated pork. There are branches across the city, including those at 6–2–8 Jingumae in Harajuku (ℭ **03/5468-6344;** station: Harajuku); 1–9–5 Ebisu (ℭ **03/5475-0185;** station: Ebisu); and 4–8–8 Ueno (ℭ **03/5807-4535;** station: Ueno).

7-14-3 Roppongi. ℭ **03/6406-4565.** Ramen ¥730–¥1,080. No credit cards. Daily 11am–6am. Station: Roppongi (1 min.). From Roppongi Crossing, head away from Tokyo Tower on Gaien-Higashi Dori; it will be on the left, next to the Ibis Hotel.

Mado Lounge ★ ITALIAN/FRENCH   You have to pay the admission fee to the Mori Art Museum (p. 192) to dine here, but at 52 floors above the city, it's worth it for the views alone (the cutting-edge exhibitions are great, too). For lunch you'll choose one of the sets, which may include the likes of grilled chicken with tomato sauce or Japanese pork ragout served with *penne rigatte,* while dinner allows you to nibble on a range of tapas (like ratatouille with white beans), salads, pastas, pizzas, and main dishes ranging from Norwegian salmon to Japanese beef stewed in red wine. From 2:30 to 6:30pm there's a curry set for ¥1,200 along with various cakes. Note that on Friday and Saturday nights (usually from 8pm) there's live music or a guest DJ, with a cover charge averaging ¥3,500.

Mori Tower, 52nd floor, Roppongi Hills, 6–10–1 Roppongi. ℭ **03/3470-0052.** Main dishes ¥1,300–¥2,300; set lunches ¥1,200–¥2,400. AE, DC, MC, V. Wed–Mon 11am–midnight (last order). Station: Roppongi (Roppongi Hills exit, 2 min.).

Roti Roppongi ★ AMERICAN   A casual brasserie with both indoor (nonsmoking) and outdoor seating, Roti counts many expats among its loyal customers, due in part to its quiet, tucked-away location just a minute's walk from Roppongi Hills and also to its bilingual staff and modern American fare, which includes free-range rotisserie chicken, grilled steaks, burgers, serious Caesar salads, and many other delectable dishes too numerous to mention. More than 90 bottles of New World, Australian, and New Zealand wines, as well as American ales and Belgian microbrews, are offered.

6-6-9 Roppongi. ℭ **03/5785-3671.** www.roti.jpco.com. Main dishes ¥1,600–¥3,300; set lunches (Mon–Fri only) ¥1,500–¥2,000. AE, DC, MC, V. Mon–Fri 11:30am–2:30pm; Sat–Sun 11:30am–5pm; daily 6–11pm. Station: Roppongi (A1 exit, 1 min.). On a side street that parallels Roppongi Dori, a stone's throw from Roppongi Hills.

AKASAKA
Very Expensive
Sekishin Tei ★★ TEPPANYAKI   Nestled in the New Otani's 400-year-old garden (which is the reason this is the hotel's most popular restaurant), this glass-enclosed *teppanyaki* pavilion has an English-language menu for Kobe beef, fish, lobster, and

vegetables, cooked on a grill right in front of you. If you order a salad, try the soy sauce dressing; it's delicious. You'll eat surrounded by peaceful views, making this place a good lunchtime choice.

Hotel New Otani, 4–1 Kioi-cho, Chiyoda-ku. ☎ **03/3238-0024.** www.newotani.co.jp/en. Reservations required. Set dinners ¥15,750–¥29,400; set lunches ¥5,250–¥8,400. AE, DC, MC, V. Mon–Fri 11:30am–2pm; Sat–Sun and holidays 11:30am–3pm; daily 6–9pm. Station: Nagatacho or Akasaka-mitsuke (3 min.).

Expensive

In addition to the recommendations here, there's a branch of **Ten-ichi** (p. 152), specializing in tempura, in Akasaka Tokyu Plaza, 2–14–3 Nagata-cho (☎ **03/3581-2166**).

(35) **Hayashi** ★★★ (Finds) ROBATAYAKI/DONBURI   One of the most delightful old-time restaurants I've been to in Tokyo, this cozy, rustic-looking place serves home-style country cooking and specializes in grilled food that you prepare over your own square hibachi. There are only a handful of grills in this small restaurant, some of them surrounded by *tatami* mats and some by wooden stools or chairs. As the evening wears on, the one-room main dining area can get quite smoky, but that adds to the ambience. Other nice touches are the big gourds and memorabilia hanging about and the waiters in traditional baggy pants. Hayashi serves three set menus, which change with the seasons. The ¥6,300 meal—which will probably end up being closer to ¥8,000 by the time you add drinks and service charge—may include such items as sashimi and vegetables, chicken, scallops, and gingko nuts, which you grill yourself. At lunch, only *oyakodonburi* is served—literally, "parent and child," a simple rice dish topped with egg and chicken.

Sanno Kaikan Building, 4th floor, 2–14–1 Akasaka. ☎ **03/3582-4078.** Reservations required for dinner. Set dinners ¥6,300, ¥8,400, and ¥10,500; set lunches ¥900. AE, DC, MC, V. Mon–Fri 11:30am–2pm; Mon–Sat 5:30–11pm (last order 10pm). Closed holidays. Station: Akasaka (exit 2, 1 min.). Just south of Misuji Dori on the 4th floor of a nondescript, improbable-looking building.

Ninja ★ VARIED JAPANESE   At this themed restaurant, diners enter the secret world of the ninja as soon as they step inside the darkened entrance, where costumed waiters appear out of nowhere to lead the hungry through a labyrinth of twisting passageways to private dining nooks. A scroll unrolls to reveal an English-language menu listing various set dinner menus that may include *shabu-shabu*, as well as a la carte items such as sweet-and-sour pork with asparagus, sole baked with herbs in saffron sauce, and grilled tenderloin beef and foie gras wrapped in *yuba* (soymilk skin). A fun place for a meal, but book early to reserve a seat.

Akasaka Tokyu Plaza, 1st floor, 2–14–3 Nagata-cho. ☎ **03/5157-3936.** Reservations required. Main dishes ¥2,000–¥3,800; set dinners ¥7,777–¥20,000. AE, DC, MC, V. Mon–Sat 5pm–2am; Sun and holidays 5–11pm. Station: Akasaka-mitsuke (1 min.). In the candy cane–striped building, below the Akasaka Excel Tokyu Hotel.

Nobu Tokyo ★★★ NOUVELLE JAPANESE/FUSION   Sister restaurant to New York's Nobu (and now with 20 locations worldwide), this classy, modern establishment is the place to see and be seen—and you can count on being seen since the efficient, black-clad staff yells *"Irashaimase!"* ("Welcome!") the moment anyone is ushered into the large dining room. The food, beautifully presented and served one dish at a time, is a unique blend of Pacific Rim ingredients (not quite Japanese) with decidedly American/Latin influences. Sushi and sashimi are served, as well as sushi rolls such as California rolls (with avocado) and soft-shell-crab rolls. Other dishes include the roast fish of the day with jalapeño dressing, sake-roasted cod with *sansho* salsa, baby squid with ginger salsa, *wagyu* steak with a choice of sauce, and sautéed scallops with wasabi pepper sauce. If ordering is too much of a chore, you can leave your meal to the discretion of Chef Matsuhisa by ordering the *omakase,* a complete chef's-choice dinner starting at ¥12,000. Nobu has an unlikely location in an obscure office building, but the Hotel Okura across the street and the nearby U.S. Embassy assure it a steady stream of moneyed customers.

Toronomon Towers Office, 4-1-28 Toronomon. www.nobutokyo.com. **03/5733-0070.** Reservations recommended. Sushi and sashimi (per piece) ¥600–¥1,200; set dinners ¥12,000–¥25,000; set lunches ¥2,300–¥12,000. AE, DC, MC, V. Mon–Fri 11:30am–2pm; Mon–Sat 6–10pm; Sun and holidays 6–9:30pm (last order). Closed for lunch holidays. Station: Kamiyacho (6 min.) or Tameike Sanno (8 min.). Behind Hotel Okura.

Moderate

Aux Bacchanales FRENCH   This brasserie made a name for itself as the best people-watching sidewalk cafe in Harajuku, but then it abandoned teeny-bopper paradise for this grown-up location, where it does a booming trade with area business types. It still has the requisite sidewalk seating of sorts, on a back terrace of the Ark Hills complex, but the parade is not nearly as interesting. Inside it's a faithful brasserie replica, with booths, a tiled floor, and a long bar, making it equally popular for a drink after work. Lunch features specials written on a blackboard, along with such mainstays as croque-monsieur, quiche Lorraine, and hot dog Parisien (though it's hard to imagine there is such a thing), while dinner offers more substantial fare such as grilled scallops in a garlic butter sauce and stewed beef in red wine.

There's another location in Akasaka, in front of the Hotel New Otani at 4–1 Kioicho (𝄢 **03/5276-3422;** station: Akasaka-mitsuke or Nagatacho), as well as in Ginza at 6–3–2 Ginza (𝄢 **03/3569-0202;** station: Ginza or Hibiya).

Ark Hills, 1st floor, 1-12-33 Akasaka. 𝄢 **03/3582-2225.** www.auxbacchanales. Main dishes ¥1,980–¥3,700; set dinner ¥5,000; set lunches ¥950–¥1,900 (¥2,900 on weekends). AE, DC, MC, V. Mon–Sat 10am–11pm; Sun and holidays 11am–10pm. Closed 1 day a month (usually 2nd Sun). Station: Tameiko Sanno (3 min.) or Roppongi Itchome (2 min.). At the back of the Ark Mori Building, off Roppongi Dori.

daidaiya ★ **Finds** VARIED JAPANESE/NOUVELLE JAPANESE   Upon exiting the elevator, you'll be forgiven for confusedly thinking you've landed in a nightclub rather than a restaurant—daidaiya's dark, theatrical entrance is the first clue that this is not your ordinary Japanese restaurant. The dining room, a juxtaposition of modern and traditional with a slate stone floor, *shoji* screens, warm woods, and black furniture, is rather like the cuisine—a curious mix of traditional Japanese food and original nouvelle creations, all mouthwateringly good. Pop music or jazz plays in the background, and for dinner, gauzy sheets of fabric are hung from the ceiling to create tiny, tête-à-tête dining cubicles for couples. Tatami seating is also available, with views over Akasaka. An English-language seasonal menu lists such intriguing entrees as Japanese beef filet with foie gras and whole chicken leg deep-fried and then topped with a sweet sauce and served with risotto. Lunch sets, including *obento,* are equally satisfying. I love this place.

There's a branch located on the third floor of the Nowa Building, 3–37–12 Shinjuku (𝄢 **03/5362-7173;** station: Shinjuku).

Bellevie Akasaka Building, 9th floor, 3-1–6 Akasaka. 𝄢 **03/3588-5087.** www.chanto.com. Reservations recommended for dinner. Main dishes ¥1,500–¥3,500; set dinners ¥6,300–¥8,400; set lunches ¥1,300–¥3,500. AE, DC, MC, V. Mon–Sat 11:30am–2pm and 5pm–midnight; Sun 11:30am–3pm and 5–10pm (last order). Station: Akasaka-mitsuke (1 min., underneath the Bellevie Akasaka Building). Take the elevator from inside the Belle Vie Shopping Center.

Gyu-Kaku KOREAN BARBECUE   Akasaka is known for its Korean restaurants, but this one is easier than most with an English-language menu that describes each dish in almost encyclopedic detail. There are various kinds of meats—beef, pork, chicken—which you grill yourself on charcoal briquettes at your table, along with side dishes ranging from salad and *kimchi* to roasted garlic wrapped in foil. There are also platters for two diners beginning at ¥1,974, and on weeknights there's an all-you-can-eat buffet for ¥2,750; note that the whole table must order it and there's a time limit of 90 minutes. This is a fun, boisterous place, popular with groups of office workers and couples unwinding and letting loose. There's a branch in Roppongi, at 5–1–2 Roppongi (✆ **03/5414-5129;** station: Roppongi).

3–10–10 Akasaka. ✆ **03/5572-6129.** Meat dishes ¥514–¥1,029. AE, DC, MC, V. Daily 5pm–midnight. Station: Akasaka-mitsuke (2 min.). On Misuji Dori, on the 2nd floor above a pachinko parlor.

Exploring Tokyo

Tokyo hasn't fared very well over the centuries. Fires and earthquakes have taken their toll, old buildings have been torn down in the zeal of modernization, and World War II left most of the city in ruins. The Tokyo of today has very little remaining of historical significance. Save your historical sightseeing for places such as Kyoto, Nikko, and Kamakura, and consider Tokyo your introduction to the newest of the new in Japan, the showcase of the nation's accomplishments in the arts, technology, fashion, pop art, and design. It's also the best place in the world to take in Japan's performing arts, such as *kabuki,* and such diverse activities as the tea ceremony, flower arranging, and sumo. Tokyo also has more museums than any other city in Japan, as well as a wide range of other attractions, including parks, temples, and shrines. In Tokyo you can explore mammoth department stores, sample unlimited cuisines, walk around unique neighborhoods, revel in kitsch, and take advantage of glittering nightlife. There's so much to do in Tokyo that I can't imagine ever being bored—even for a minute.

SEEING THE CITY BY GUIDED TOUR
With the help of this book and a good map, you should be able to visit Tokyo's major attractions easily on your own. Should you be pressed for time, however, you might consider taking a group tour of Tokyo and its environs offered by the **Japan Travel Bureau (JTB; ℗ 03/5796-5454;** www.jtb-sunrisetours.jp) or **Japan Gray Line (℗ 03/3595-5939;** www.jgl.co.jp/inbound/index.htm). Day tours may include Tokyo Tower, the Imperial Palace and Ginza districts, Asakusa Sensoji Temple, Meiji Jingu Shrine, and a harbor or

river cruise. There are also specialized tours that take in local festivals, kabuki, Tsukiji Fish Market, Akihabara, sumo wrestling, or Tokyo's nightlife, as well as cultural-themed tours that allow participants to experience such activities as the tea ceremony, making sushi, or dressing up in a kimono. Be warned, however, that tours are very tourist-oriented, do not allow much time for exploration, and are more expensive than touring Tokyo on your own. Prices range from about ¥4,500 for a half-day tour to about ¥12,000 for a full-day tour including lunch. You can easily book tours through most hotels and travel agencies.

Although they cover less ground, 10 tours offered by the **Tokyo Metropolitan Government** concentrate on specific areas or themes, such as Japanese gardens, Asakusa, or Harajuku. Lasting 2 to 3 hours, they are conducted mostly on foot or utilize public transportation and vary in price from free (such as a walking tour of Shinjuku and the food floor of Isetan department store) to ¥3,540 (for tours of Ginza, Tsukiji Outer Market, Hama Rikyu Garden, and Odaiba), plus admission costs for the volunteer guides. Tours depart from the Tokyo Tourist Information Center in the TMG building in Shinjuku at 1pm Monday to Friday (excluding public holidays; some tours depart also at 10am). Preregistration 3 days in advance of the tour is required, and a minimum of one participant must be at least 20 years old. For more information, go to www.tourism.metro.tokyo.jp/english or contact the tourist office (see "Fast Facts: Tokyo" in chapter 5 for location and open hours).

Volunteer guides are also on hand at the Ueno Green Salon in Ueno Park every Wednesday, Friday, and Sunday for free 90-minute walking tours departing at 10:30am and 1:30pm; and at the Asakusa Information Center every Sunday for 1-hour tours departing at 11am and 2pm (for the location of the latter, see the walking tour of Asakusa beginning on p. 196). No registration is required. For more information, call (C) **03/3842-5566.**

Free guided tours are also offered through **www.tokyofreeguide.com,** staffed by volunteers. You're expected to pay for the guide's entrance to museums, meals, and transportation fees if applicable, but you get to choose what you'd like to see; because many of these volunteers work, weekends are the best days to book a tour.

One tour I especially like is a **boat trip on the Sumida River** ★★ between Hama Rikyu Garden and Asakusa. Commentary on the 40-minute trip is in both Japanese and English (be sure to pick up the English-language leaflet, too). You'll get descriptions of the 12 bridges you pass along the way and views of Tokyo you'd otherwise miss. Boats depart Hama Rikyu Garden hourly or more frequently between 10:35am and 4:15pm, with the fare to Asakusa costing ¥720 one-way. There are also other cruise routes, including those between Hinode Pier (closest station: Hinode, about a 1-min. walk) and Asakusa (fare: ¥760), Asakusa and Odaiba (fare: ¥1,520) and Hinode Pier and Odaiba (fare: ¥460). For more information, contact the **Tokyo Cruise Ship Co.** ((C) **0120-977311;** www.suijobus.co.jp).

Finally, for personalized, one-on-one tours of Tokyo, contact **Jun's Tokyo Discovery Tours,** managed by Tokyoite Junko Matsuda, which offers tailored sightseeing trips to Tsukiji, Asakusa, Yanaka, Harajuku, Aoyama, Shibuya, Shinjuku, and Kamakura, as well as shopping trips and special trips designed to fit your interests. Tours utilize public transportation and are especially useful if you wish to communicate with shopkeepers and the locals, want to learn more about what you're seeing, or are timid about finding your way on public transportation (if you wish, you'll be met at your hotel). The cost is ¥25,000 for 1 day (7 hr.) for up to four adults or a family. Reserve tours at least 3 days in advance (1 week preferred) by fax (03/5477-6022) or e-mail (me2@gb3.so-net.ne.jp), stating the desired tour date and what you'd like to see; messages can also be left at (C) **090/7734-0079** (if you're calling from abroad, drop the initial 0).

1 THE TOP ATTRACTIONS

There are two things to remember when planning your sightseeing itinerary: The city is huge, and it takes time to get from one end to the other. Plan your days so you cover Tokyo neighborhood by neighborhood, coordinating sightseeing with dinner and evening plans. The suggestions below will guide you to the most important attractions, but note that some attractions are closed 1 day of the week.

Edo-Tokyo Museum (Edo-Tokyo Hakubutsukan) ★★★ (Kids) The building housing this impressive museum is said to resemble a rice granary when viewed from afar, but to me it looks like a modern *torii,* the entrance gate to a shrine. This is the metropolitan government's ambitious attempt to present the history, art, disasters, science, culture, and architecture of Tokyo from its humble beginnings in 1590—when the first shogun, Tokugawa Ieyasu, made Edo (old Tokyo) the seat of his domain—to 1964, when Tokyo hosted the Olympics. All in all, the museum's great visual displays create a vivid

portrayal of Tokyo through the centuries. I wouldn't miss it. Plan on spending 2 hours here.

After purchasing your ticket and taking a series of escalators to the sixth floor, you'll enter the museum by walking over a replica of Nihombashi Bridge, the starting point for all roads leading out of old Edo. Exhibits covering the Edo Period portray the lives of the shoguns, merchants, craftsmen, and townspeople. The explanations are mostly in Japanese only, but there's plenty to look at, including a replica of an old kabuki theater, a model of a *daimyo's* (feudal lord's) mansion, portable floats used during festivals, maps and photographs of old Edo, and—perhaps most interesting—a row-house tenement where Edo commoners lived in cramped quarters measuring only 10 sq. m (108 sq. ft.). Other displays cover the Meiji Restoration, the Great Kanto Earthquake of 1923, and the bombing raids of World War II (Japan's own role as aggressor is disappointingly glossed over), with plenty of old-style conveyances—from a palanquin to a rickshaw—for kids to climb in and have parents take their picture.

If you wish, take advantage of a free museum tour offered by volunteers daily 10am to 3pm (last tour). Most tours last 1 to 2 hours, depending on the level of visitor interest, and are insightful for their explanations of the Japanese-only displays. However, tours are necessarily rushed and focus on particular displays; you may wish to tour the museum afterward on your own.

1-4-1 Yokoami, Sumida-ku. © **03/3626-9974.** www.edo-tokyo-museum.or.jp. Admission ¥600 adults, ¥480 college students, ¥300 seniors and junior-high/high-school students, free for children. Tues–Sun 9:30am–5:30pm (Sat to 7:30pm). Station: Ryogoku on the JR Sobu Line (West exit, 3 min.) and Oedo Line (exit A4, 1 min.). Tokyo Shitamachi Bus: Ryogoku Station.

The Imperial Palace (Kyokyo) ★   The Imperial Palace, home of the imperial family, is the heart and soul of Tokyo. Built on the very spot where Edo Castle used to stand during the days of the Tokugawa shogunate, it became the imperial home upon its completion in 1888 and is now the residence of Emperor Akihito, 125th emperor of Japan. Destroyed during air raids in 1945, the palace was rebuilt in 1968 using the principles of traditional Japanese architecture. But don't expect to get a good look at it; most of the palace grounds' 114 hectares (282 acres) are off-limits to the public, with the exception of 2 days a year when the royal family makes an appearance before the throngs: January 2 and December 23 (the emperor's birthday). Or, you can visit Imperial Palace grounds on free **guided tours** Monday through Friday at 10am and 1:30pm (1:30pm tour not available July 21–Aug 31), but you must register at least 1 day in advance (reservations are accepted up to 1 month in advance) by calling © **03/3213-1111** and then stopping by the Imperial Household Agency (located at the Sakashita-mon Gate, on the east side of the palace grounds) to show your passport number and provide nationality, name, age, gender, and home address. It's easier to book online at **http://sankan.kuna-icho.go.jp** at least 4 days before the tour. Tours, conducted in Japanese but with English-language audio guides, last about 75 minutes and lead past official buildings, the inner moat and historic fortifications, and Nijubashi Bridge. I recommend this tour only if you have seen Tokyo's other top attractions (and it doesn't come close to the more impressive imperial palace tours in Kyoto).

Otherwise, you'll have to console yourself with a camera shot of the palace from the southeast side of **Nijubashi Bridge,** where the moat and the palace turrets show above the trees. Most Japanese tourists make brief stops here to pay their respects. The wide moat, lined with cherry trees, is especially beautiful in the spring. You might even want to spend an hour strolling the 5km (3 miles) around the palace and moat. But the most

EXPLORING TOKYO

THE TOP ATTRACTIONS

6

To Disneyland →
Tokyo

WAKASU
GOLF CLUB →

KEIYO LINE

Asakusabashi

Port
of
Tokyo

Tokyo

JAPAN

Toyosu

Harumi Wharf

Kiyosumi Dori

HAMA RIKYU
GARDEN

Ferry
Terminal

ODAIBA

27

28

29

Tokyo Bay

i Tourist Info
Expressway
Monorail
Railway

24

Rainbow
Bridge

Hamamatsucho

Tamachi

Central
Wholesale
Market ■

Shinagawa

Daiichi-keihin Dori

Hara Museum
of Contemporary Art

SHINAGAWA-KU

Omachi

To Tokyo
International Airport →

Omori

TOKAIDO LINE

Shimoshinmei

Osaki

Shinagawa

MINATO-KU

26

ROPPONGI
HILLS

Roppongi Dori

NATIONAL PARK
FOR NATURE
STUDY

Sakurada Dori

Gotanda

Dami-keihin Doro

Meguro

Ebisu

Shibuya

MEGURO-KU

Kannana Dori

SHINKANSEN LINE

YOKOSUKA LINE

Frommer's Favorite Tokyo Experiences

Strolling Through Asakusa   Asakusa conveys the atmosphere of old Tokyo better than any other place in the city. Sensoji Temple is the city's oldest and most popular temple, and Nakamise Dori, the pedestrian lane leading to the temple, is lined with open-fronted stalls selling souvenirs and traditional Japanese goods.

Taking in the Early Morning Action at Tsukiji Fish Market   Get up early your first morning in Japan (you'll probably be wide awake with jet lag anyway) and head straight for the country's largest fish market, where you can watch the tuna auctions, browse through stalls of seafood, and sample the freshest sushi you'll ever have.

Spending an Evening in a Yakitori-ya   There's no better place to observe Tokyo's army of office workers at play than at a *yakitori-ya*, a drinking place that serves skewered foods and bar snacks. They're fun and noisy.

Watching a Kabuki Play   *Kabuki* has served as the most popular form of entertainment for the masses since the Edo Period. Observe the audience members as they yell their approval; watch the stage for gorgeous costumes, stunning stage settings, and easy-to-understand dramas of love, duty, and revenge.

Viewing the Treasures at the Tokyo National Museum   There's a feast for the eyes at the world's largest museum of Japanese art, packed with everything from samurai armor and lacquerware to kimono and woodblock prints. If you visit only one museum in Tokyo, this should be it. The surrounding Ueno Park contains other noteworthy attractions as well, including museums, a shrine, and a temple.

Hanging Out in Harajuku on Sunday   Start with brunch and then stroll Omotesando Dori for people-watching. Shop the area's boutiques, visit a couple of museums and the Meiji Shrine, or just sit back and take in all the action from a sidewalk cafe.

important thing to do in the palace's vicinity is visit its **East Garden (Higashi Gyoen),** where you'll find what's left of the central keep of old Edo Castle, the stone foundation; see "Parks & Gardens," later in this chapter.

Hibiya Dori Ave. Station: Nijubashi-mae (1 min.) or Hibiya (5 min.).

Meiji Jingu Shrine ★★   This is Tokyo's most venerable Shinto shrine, opened in 1920 in honor of Emperor and Empress Meiji, who were instrumental in opening Japan to the outside world more than 120 years ago. Japan's two largest *torii* (the traditional entry gate of a shrine), built of cypress more than 1,700 years old, give dramatic entrance to the grounds, once the estate of a *daimyo*. The shaded pathway is lined with trees, shrubs, and dense woods. In late May/June, the **Iris Garden** is in spectacular bloom (admission fee charged). About a 10-minute walk from the first torii, the shrine is a fine example of dignified and refined Shinto architecture. It's made of plain Japanese cypress

Seeing Sumo Nothing beats watching huge sumo wrestlers (most weigh well over 135kg/300 lb.) throw each other around. Matches are held in Tokyo in January, May, and September; catch one on TV if you can't make it in person.

Shopping the Department Stores Tokyo's department stores are huge, spotless, and filled with merchandise, some of which you never knew existed; many also have first-rate art galleries. Be there when the doors open in the morning and you can witness a sight you'll never see back home: employees lined up in a row, bowing to incoming customers.

Hunting for Bargains at Flea Markets You never know what treasure you might find at Tokyo's weekend outdoor flea markets, where vendors sell everything from used kimono to curios and antiques. Go early and be sure to bargain.

Browsing the Electronics and Anime Shops of Akihabara Even if you don't buy anything, it's great fun—and very educational—to see the latest in electronic gadgetry in Japan's largest electronics district, which offers many products unknown in Western markets. In recent years, shops specializing in *manga* (Japanese comic books) and *anime* have also opened, along with so-called "maid cafes."

Soaking in Hot-Spring Baths at Oedo-Onsen Monogatari This Edo-themed public bath features hot-spring waters pumped up from the deep outdoor tubs, massage, souvenirs, and restaurants, making this a standout for soaking away urban stress.

Taking a Spin Through Kabuki-cho Shinjuku's Kabuki-cho has the craziest nightlife in all of Tokyo, with countless strip joints, porn shops, restaurants, bars, and the greatest concentration of neon you're likely to see anywhere. It's a fascinating place for an evening stroll.

and topped with green-copper roofs. Meiji Jingu Shrine is the place to be on New Year's Eve, when more than two million people crowd onto the grounds to usher in the new year.

Meiji Shrine Inner Garden, 1–1 Kamizono-cho, Yoyogi, Shibuya-ku. ☎ 03/3379-5511. www.meijijingu. or.jp. Free admission. Daily sunrise–sunset (about 4:30pm in winter). Station: Harajuku (2 min.).

Sensoji Temple ★★★ Also popularly known as Asakusa Kannon, this is Tokyo's oldest and most popular temple, with a history dating from 628. That was when, according to popular lore, two brothers fishing in the nearby Sumida River netted the catch of their lives: a tiny golden statue of Kannon, the Buddhist goddess of mercy and happiness who is empowered with the ability to release humans from all suffering. Sensoji Temple was erected in her honor, and although the statue is housed here, it's never shown to the public. Still, through the centuries, worshipers have flocked here seeking favors of Kannon; and when Sensoji Temple burned down during a 1945 bombing raid, the present structure was rebuilt with donations from the Japanese people. (*Note:* Due to renovation, Sensoji Temple is under wraps until Dec 2010 but remains open to the public.)

Colorful **Nakamise Dori,** a pedestrian lane leading to the shrine, is lined with traditional shops and souvenir stands, while nearby **Demboin Garden** remains an insider's favorite as a peaceful oasis away from the bustling crowds. Asakusa is one of my favorite neighborhoods, and you can easily spend half a day here; see the walking tours later in this chapter for more on this fascinating part of old Tokyo.

2-3-1 Asakusa, Taito-ku. ✆ **03/3842-0181.** Free admission. Daily 6:30am–5pm. Station: Asakusa (2 min.). Tokyo Shitamachi Bus: Asakusa Kaminarimon.

Tokyo National Museum (Tokyo Kokuritsu Hakubutsukan) ★★★ The National Museum is not only the largest and oldest museum in Japan, it boasts the largest collection of Japanese art in the world. This is where you go to see antiques from Japan's past—old kimono, samurai armor, priceless swords, lacquerware, metalwork, pottery, scrolls, screens, *ukiyo-e* (woodblock prints), calligraphy, ceramics, archaeological finds, and more. Items are shown on a rotating basis with about 3,000 on display at any one time—so no matter how many times you visit the museum, you'll always see something new. There are also frequent special exhibitions. Schedule at least 2 hours to do the museum justice.

The museum comprises five buildings. The **Japanese Gallery (Honkan),** straight ahead as you enter the main gate, is the most important one, devoted to Japanese art. Here you'll view Japanese ceramics; Buddhist sculptures dating from about A.D. 538 to 1192; samurai armor, helmets, and decorative sword mountings; swords, which throughout Japanese history were considered to embody spirits all their own; textiles and kimono; lacquerware; ceramics; and paintings, calligraphy, ukiyo-e, and scrolls. Be sure to check out the museum shop in the basement; it sells reproductions from the museum's collections as well as traditional crafts by contemporary artists.

The **Heiseikan Gallery** is where you'll find archaeological relics of ancient Japan, including pottery and Haniwa clay burial figurines of the Jomon Period (10,000 B.C.– 1000 B.C.) and ornamental, keyhole-shaped tombs from the Yayoi Period (400 B.C.–A.D. 200). The **Gallery of Horyuji Treasures (Horyuji Homotsukan)** displays priceless Buddhist treasures from the Horyuji Temple in Nara, founded by Prince Shotoku in A.D. 607. Although the building's stark modernity (designed by Taniguchi Yoshio, who also designed the expansion of the New York Museum of Modern Art) seems odd for an exhibition of antiquities, the gallery's low lighting and simple architecture lend dramatic effect to the museum's priceless collection of bronze Buddhist statues, ceremonial *gigaku* masks used in ritual dances, lacquerware, and paintings. *Note:* The **Asian Gallery (Toyokan),** housing art and archaeological artifacts from everywhere in Asia outside Japan, is closed for renovation until 2012. Until its reopening, selections from China, Cambodia, India, Vietnam, Thailand, and elsewhere are on display at the **Hyokeikan,** built on the museum grounds in 1909 to commemorate the marriage of Emperor Taisho.

Ueno Park, Taito-ku. ✆ **03/3822-1111.** www.tnm.jp. Admission ¥600 adults, ¥400 college students, free for seniors and children. Special exhibits cost more. Tues–Sun 9:30am–5pm (enter by 4:30pm; Apr–Dec open to 8pm Fri during special exhibitions; Apr–Sept open to 6pm weekends and holidays). Closed Dec 28–Jan 1. Station: Ueno (10 min.). Tokyo Shitamachi Bus: Ueno Koen Yamashita/Ueno Station.

Tsukiji Fish Market ★★★ This huge wholesale fish market—the largest in Japan and one of the largest in the world—is a must for anyone who has never seen such a market in action. The action here starts early: At about 3am, boats begin arriving from the seas around Japan, from Africa, and even from America, with enough fish to satisfy the demands of a nation where seafood reigns supreme. To give you some idea of its enormity, this market handles almost all the seafood—about 450 kinds—consumed in Tokyo. The king is tuna, huge and frozen, unloaded from the docks, laid out on the ground, and numbered. Wholesalers walk up and down the rows, jotting down the numbers of the best-looking tuna, and by 5:30am, the tuna auctions are well underway. The entire auction of sea products takes place from about 4:40 to 6:30am, with auctions of vegetables at a corner of the market starting at 6:30am. The wholesalers then transfer what they've bought to their own stalls in the market, subsequently selling fish and produce to their regular customers, usually retail stores and restaurants.

Although it used to be possible to arrive before dawn and visit the entire market freely, an increasing number of tourists over the years has prompted authorities to close tuna auctions to visitors, except for a small viewing area open 5–6:15am (get there before 5am and expect to wait in line). Otherwise, I think it's just as fun to the visit the wholesale market area, held in a cavernous, hangarlike building, which means you can visit even on a dismal rainy morning. There's a lot going on—men in black rubber boots rushing wheelbarrows and forklifts through the aisles, hawkers shouting, knives chopping and slicing. Wander the aisles and you'll see things you never dreamed were edible. This is a good place to bring your camera, but note that no flash photography of auctions or the market is allowed. Also, the floors are wet, so leave your fancy shoes at the hotel. Finally, be mindful of the many forklifts and carts, and please don't touch the fish.

Tsukiji is also a good place to come if you want sushi for breakfast. Alongside the covered market are rows of barracklike buildings divided into sushi restaurants and shops related to the fish trade. In addition, in between the market and Tsukiji Station is the *Jogai* (Outer Market), a delightful district of tiny retail shops and stalls where you can buy the freshest seafood in town, plus dried fish and fish products, seaweed, vegetables, knives, and other cooking utensils. ***Warning:*** While walking through the Outer Market, my Japanese friend and I were warned several times by local shopkeepers to watch our purses, advice we didn't take lightly. Apparently, pickpockets have been at work here on unsuspecting tourists.

5-2-1 Tsukiji, Chuo-ku. ℂ **03/3542-1111.** www.tsukiji-market.or.jp. Free admission. Mon–Sat 5–11am (best time 5–9am). Closed some Wed, holidays, several days around New Year's, and 3 days in mid-Aug. Station: Tsukijishijo (exit A2, 2 min.) or Tsukiji (Honganji Temple exit, 10 min.).

2 IMMERSING YOURSELF IN JAPANESE CULTURE

Just walking down the street could be considered a cultural experience in Japan, but there are more concrete ways to learn more about this country's cultural life: The best is by participating in some of its time-honored rituals and traditions. For some background information on Japanese flower arranging, the tea ceremony, and other activities recommended below, see "Japanese Arts in a Nutshell," in chapter 2.

In addition to the recommendations below, JTB's **Sunrise Tours** (ℂ **03/5796-5454;** www.jtb-sunrisetours.jp) and **H.I.S. Experience Japan** (www.hisexperience.jp) offer a wide range of cultural activities, from Japanese cooking classes or visits to a sumo stable to those covering the tea ceremony. Prices range from ¥5,000 for a bonsai tour or survival Japanese-language class to ¥30,000 for a 4-hour Japanese traditional cooking class, including lunch.

IKEBANA   Instruction in *ikebana,* or Japanese flower arranging, is available at several schools in Tokyo, a few of which offer classes in English on a regular basis. (Note that you should call beforehand to enroll.) **Sogetsu Ikebana School,** 7–2–21 Akasaka (✆ **03/3408-1209** or 3408-1551; www.sogetsu.or.jp; station: Aoyama-Itchome, a 5-min. walk from exit 4), offers instruction in English on Monday from 10am to noon (closed in Aug). The cost of one lesson for first-time participants is ¥3,800, including flowers. The **Ohara Ikebana School,** 5–7–17 Minami Aoyama (✆ **03/5774-5097;** www.ohararyu.or.jp; station: Omotesando, 3-min. walk from exit B1), offers 2-hour instruction in English at 10am on Wednesday and 10am and 1:30pm on Thursday for ¥4,000 (no classes July 15–Sept 3); if you wish to observe the class but not participate, you can do so for ¥800.

If you wish to see ikebana, ask at the **Tourist Information Office** whether there are any special exhibitions. Department stores sometimes have special ikebana exhibitions in their galleries. Another place to look is **Yasukuni Shrine,** located on Yasukuni Dori northwest of the Imperial Palace (station: Ichigaya or Kudanshita). Dedicated to Japanese war dead, the shrine is also famous for ongoing ikebana exhibitions.

TEA CEREMONY   Several first-class hotels hold tea-ceremony demonstrations in special tea-ceremony rooms. Reservations are usually required, and because ceremonies are often booked by groups, you'll want to call in advance to see whether you can participate. **Seisei-an,** on the seventh floor of the Hotel New Otani, 4–1 Kioi-cho, Chiyoda-ku (✆ **03/3265-1111,** ext. 2443; station: Nagatacho or Akasaka-mitsuke, a 3-min. walk from both), holds 20-minute demonstrations Thursday through Saturday from 11am to 4pm. The cost is ¥1,050, including tea and sweets. **Chosho-an,** on the seventh floor of the Hotel Okura, 2–10–4 Toranomon, Minato-ku (✆ **03/3582-0111;** station: Toranomon or Kamiyacho, a 10-min. walk from both), gives 40-minute demonstrations anytime between 11am and noon and between 1 and 4pm Monday, Tuesday, and Thursday through Saturday except holidays. Appointments are required; the cost is ¥1,050 for tea and sweets. At **Toko-an,** on the fourth floor of the Imperial Hotel, 1–1–1 Uchisaiwaicho, Chiyoda-ku (✆ **03/3504-1111;** station: Hibiya, 1 min.), demonstrations are given from 10am to 4pm Monday through Saturday except holidays. Reservations are required. The fee is ¥1,500 for tea and sweets.

ACUPUNCTURE & SHIATSU   Although most Westerners have heard of acupuncture, they may not be familiar with *shiatsu* (Japanese pressure-point massage). Most first-class hotels in Japan offer shiatsu in the privacy of your room. There are acupuncture clinics everywhere in Tokyo, and the staff of your hotel may be able to tell you of one nearby. As it's not likely the clinic's staff will speak English, it might be a good idea to have the hotel guest relations officer not only make the reservation but specify the treatment you want. Otherwise, English is spoken at **Yamate Acupuncture Clinic,** second floor of the ULS Nakameguro Building, 1–3–3 Higashiyama, Meguro-ku (✆ **03/3792-8989;** station: Nakameguro, 6 min.), open Monday to Friday 9am to 8pm and Saturday 9am to 2pm. Specializing in athletic injuries, it charges ¥3,000 for a specific treatment or ¥5,000 for the whole body, plus a ¥1,000 initial fee. English is also spoken at **Tani Clinic,** third floor of the Taishoseimei Hibiya Building, 1–9–1 Yurakucho, Chiyoda-ku (✆ **03/3201-5675;** station: Hibiya, 1 min.), open Monday, Tuesday, Wednesday, and Friday 9am to noon and 2 to 5pm and Saturday 8:30am to noon and 2 to 4:30pm and charging

¥10,500 for the first visit, ¥6,300 for each subsequent visit. The **Shirokane Oriental Therapy Center,** 1–26–4 Shirokane, Minato-ku (☎ **03/5789-8222;** www.shirogane-s. com; station: Shirokane-Takanawa, 1 min.), offers 60-minute shiatsu for ¥7,350 and 90-minute massage and acupuncture treatments for ¥10,500.

PUBLIC BATHS   Tokyo has approximately 1,000 *sento* (public baths)—which may sound like a lot but is nothing compared to the 2,687 the city used to have in the 1970s. Easily recognizable by a tall chimney and shoe lockers just inside the door, a sento sells just about anything you might need at the bathhouse: soap, shampoo, towels, even underwear. Keep in mind, however, that people with tattoos are prohibited at many public and hot-spring baths, because tattoos are associated with the Japanese mafia. If your tattoo is discreet, however, or you're using a public bath in, say, a hotel, you probably won't experience any problems.

For a unique bathing experience, nothing beats a 3- or 4-hour respite at the **Ooedo-Onsen Monogatari,** 2–57 Aomi on Odaiba ((☎ **03/5500-1126;** www.ooedoonsen.jp; station: Telecom Center Station, 2 min.), which tapped mineral-rich hot-spring waters 1,380m (4,528 ft.) below ground to supply this re-created Edo-Era bathhouse village. After changing into a *yukata* (cotton kimono) and depositing your belongings in a locker (your key is bar-coded, so there's no need to carry any money), you'll stroll past souvenir shops and restaurants on your way to massage rooms, sand baths (extra fee charged), and *onsen* (hot-spring baths) complete with outdoor baths, Jacuzzi, steam baths, foot baths, and saunas. Because as many as 6,500 bathers pour into this facility on weekends, try to come on a weekday. Also, signs in English are virtually nonexistent, so observe gender before entering bathing areas (a hint: women's baths usually have pink or red curtains, men's blue). Open daily 11am to 9am the next day. Admission is ¥2,900 for adults and ¥1,600 for children 4 to 11, with reduced prices after 6pm.

ZAZEN   A few temples in the Tokyo vicinity occasionally offer sitting meditation with instruction in English. You should call in advance to make a reservation and arrive 30 minutes early for instructions. The **Toshoji International Zen Center,** 4–5–18 Yutaka-machi, Shinagawa-ku (☎ **03/3781-4235;** station: Togoshikoen, 5 min.), offers free *zazen* at 5am every morning (except Sun and holidays), as well as Zen training meetings Saturday from 6 to 8pm, including zazen, a lecture, and tea. Accommodations are also available to those who wish to stay for longer periods to practice Zen. **Sounin Temple,** 4–1–12 Higashi-Ueno, Taito-ku (☎ **03/3844-3711;** station: Ueno, 5 min.), holds zazen the second Saturday, Sunday, and Monday of each month from 7 to 8pm, followed by a talk and tea. ***Note:*** Newcomers should arrive by 6:20am for instruction on zazen.

3 PARKS & GARDENS

Although Japan's most famous gardens are not in Tokyo, most of the places listed below use traditional principles of landscaping, which gives visitors an idea of the scope and style of Japanese gardens. More information on parks and gardens is available at **www. tokyo-park.or.jp**.

East Garden (Higashi Gyoen) ★★   The 21 hectares (52 acres) of the formal Higashi Gyoen—once the main grounds of Edo Castle and located next to the Imperial Palace—are a wonderful respite in the middle of the city. Yet surprisingly, this garden is hardly ever crowded (except when cherry trees, azaleas, and other blossoms are in full bloom or at lunchtime when *obento*-eating office workers fill the benches). **Ninomaru** ★★★, my favorite part, is laid out in Japanese style with a pond, stepping-stones, and winding paths; it's particularly beautiful when the wisteria, azaleas, irises, and other flowers are at their peak. Near Ninomaru is the **Sannomaru Shozokan,** with free changing exhibitions of art treasures belonging to the imperial family.

On the highest spot of East Garden is the **Honmaru** (inner citadel), where Tokugawa's main castle once stood. Built in the first half of the 1600s, the castle was massive, surrounded by a series of whirling moats and guarded by 23 watchtowers and 99 gates around its 15km (10-mile) perimeter. At its center was Japan's tallest building at the time, the five-story castle keep, soaring 50m (168 ft.) above its foundations and offering an expansive view over Edo. This is where Tokugawa Ieyasu would have taken refuge, had his empire ever been seriously threatened. Although most of the castle was a glimmering white, the keep was black with a gold roof, which must have been quite a sight in old Edo as it towered above the rest of the city. All that remains today of the shogun's castle are a few towers, gates, stone walls, moats, and the stone foundations of the keep.

Free guided tours of the garden, run by volunteers, are given Saturday from 1 to 3pm. The meeting point is outside Tokyo Station's Marunouchi Central Exit. For more information, visit **www.freewalkingtour.org**.

1–1 Chiyoda, Chiyoda-ku. ⓒ **03/3213-1111.** Free admission. Tues–Thurs and Sat–Sun 9am–5pm (to 4:30pm Mar to mid-Apr and Sept–Oct; to 4pm Nov–Feb). You must enter 30 min. before closing. Closed Dec 23 and Dec 28–Jan 3; open other national holidays. Station: Otemachi, Takebashi, or Nijubashi-mae.

Hama Rikyu Garden (Overrated) Considered by some to be the best garden in Tokyo (but marred, in my opinion, by skyscrapers in Shiodome that detract from its charm; there ought to be a law), this urban oasis has origins stretching back 300 years, when it served as a retreat for a former feudal lord and as duck-hunting and falconry grounds for the Tokugawa shoguns. In 1871, possession of the garden passed to the imperial family, which used it to entertain such visiting dignitaries as Gen. Ulysses S. Grant. Come here to see how the upper classes enjoyed themselves during the Edo Period. The garden contains an inner tidal pool, spanned by three bridges draped with wisteria (views from the south end of the garden are the most picturesque). There are also other ponds; a refuge for ducks, herons, and migratory birds; a promenade along the bay lined with pine trees; a 300-year-old pine; moon-viewing pavilions; and teahouses (powdered green tea and a sweet will cost you ¥500). Plan on at least an hour's stroll to see everything, but the best reason for coming here is to board a ferry from the garden's pier bound for Asakusa, with departures every hour (or more often) between 10:35am and 4:15pm; the fare is ¥720 one-way.

1–1 Hamarikyuteien, Chuo-ku. ⓒ **03/3541-0200.** Admission ¥300 adults, ¥150 seniors, free for children 12 and under. Daily 9am–5pm. Station: Shiodome (exit 5, 5 min.) or Tsukiji-shjjo (7 min.).

Rikugien Garden ★★ (Finds) Though not as centrally located nor as easy to reach as Tokyo's other famous gardens, this one is a must for fans of traditional Japanese gardens and is probably my favorite. It was created in 1702 by a trusted confidante of the shogun, who began as a page and rose to the highest rank as a feudal lord. During the Meiji Era, the founder of Mitsubishi took it over for his second residence and later donated it to the city. What I like most about the garden is that it's dominated by a pond in its center, complete with islands and islets, viewing hills, and strolling paths around its perimeter, providing enchanting views. The garden is especially famous for its changing maple leaves in autumn. Since it takes some effort to reach, you'll probably want to enjoy at least an hour here.

Shinjuku Gyoen ★★ (**Kids**) Formerly the private estate of a feudal lord and then of the imperial family, this is considered one of the most important parks of the Meiji Era. It's wonderful for strolling because of the variety of its planted gardens; styles range from French and English to Japanese traditional. This place amazes me every time I come here. The park's 58 hectares (143 acres) make it one of the city's largest, and each bend in the pathway brings something completely different: Ponds and sculpted bushes give way to a promenade lined with sycamores that opens onto a rose garden. Cherry blossoms, azaleas, chrysanthemums, and other flowers provide splashes of color from spring through autumn. The Japanese garden, buried in the center, is exquisite; if you have time only for a quick look at traditional landscaping, you won't be disappointed here. There are also wide grassy expanses, popular for picnics and playing, and a greenhouse filled with tropical plants (closed for renovation until 2011). You could easily spend a half-day of leisure here, but for a quick fix of rejuvenation, 1½ hours will do.

11 Naitocho, Shinjuku-ku. © **03/3350-0151.** Admission ¥200 adults, ¥50 children. Tues–Sun 9am–4:30pm. Station: Shinjuku Gyoen-mae (2 min.) or Sendagaya (5 min.).

Ueno Park Ueno Park—on the northeast edge of the Yamanote Line—is one of the largest parks in Tokyo and one of the most popular places in the city for Japanese families on a day's outing. It's a cultural mecca with a number of attractions, including the prestigious Tokyo National Museum; the National Museum of Western Art; the delightful Shitamachi Museum with its displays of old Tokyo; Ueno Zoo; and Shinobazu Pond, a bird sanctuary. For a map of the Ueno area, see p. 145.

A landmark in the park is the small **Toshogu Shrine.** Erected in 1651, it's dedicated to Tokugawa Ieyasu, founder of the Tokugawa shogunate. Stop here to pay respects to the man who made Edo (present-day Tokyo) the seat of his government and thus elevated the small village to the most important city in the country. The pathway to the shrine is lined with massive stone lanterns, as well as 50 copper lanterns donated by *daimyo* (feudal lords) from all over Japan. The shrine itself is closed for renovations until 2014.

Also in the park is **Kiyomizu Kannon-do Temple,** completed in 1631 as a copy of the famous Kiyomizu Temple in Kyoto (but on a much less grand scale). It enshrines Kosodate Kannon, protector of childbearing and child-raising. Women hoping to become pregnant come here to ask for the goddess's blessing; those whose wishes have been fulfilled return to pray for their children's good health and protection. Many leave behind dolls as symbols of their children. Once a year, a requiem service is held for all the dolls at the temple, after which they are cremated.

The busiest time of the year at Ueno Park is April, during the **cherry-blossom season,** when people come en masse to celebrate the birth of the new season. It's not the spiritual communion with nature that you might think, however. On weekends and in the evenings during cherry-blossom time (which only lasts for a few days), havoc prevails as office workers break out of their winter shells. Entire companies converge on the park to sit under the cherry trees on plastic or cardboard, and everyone drinks sake and beer and gets drunk and rowdy, seemingly oblivious to the fragile pink blossoms shimmering above. At any rate, visiting Ueno Park during cherry-blossom season is an experience no one should miss. More than likely, you'll be invited to join one of the large groups—and by all means, do so.

Taito-ku. Free admission to the park; separate admissions to each of its attractions. Daily 24 hr. Station: Ueno (1 min.).

EXPLORING TOKYO

6

PARKS & GARDENS

4 MORE MUSEUMS

In addition to the museums listed below, Tokyo has a wealth of small museums specializing in everything from woodblock prints to architecture; for a more complete list of Tokyo museums, see *Frommer's Tokyo*. For details on the **Tokyo National Museum** and the **Edo-Tokyo Museum,** see p. 186 and 180.

Fukagawa Edo Museum (Fukagawa Edo Shiryokan) ★ **Kids**   This is the Tokyo of your dreams, the way it appears in all those samurai flicks on Japanese TV: a reproduction of a 19th-century neighborhood in Fukagawa, a prosperous community on the east bank of the Sumida River during the Edo Period. This delightful museum is located off Kiyosumi Dori on a pleasant tree-lined, shop-filled street called Fukagawa Shiryokan Dori. The museum's hangarlike interior contains 11 full-scale replicas of traditional houses, vegetable and rice shops, a fish store, two inns, a fire watchtower, and tenement homes, all arranged to resemble an actual neighborhood. There are lots of small touches and flourishes to make the community seem real and believable—a cat sleeping on a roof, a snail crawling up a fence, a dog relieving itself on a pole, birdsong, and a vendor shouting his wares. The village even changes with the seasons (with trees sprouting cherry blossoms in spring and threatened by thunderstorms in summer) and, every 45 minutes or so, undergoes a day's cycle from morning (roosters crow, lights brighten) to night (the sun sets, the retractable roof closes to make everything dark). Of Tokyo's museums, this one is probably the best for children; plan on spending about an hour here. Don't confuse this museum with the much larger Edo-Tokyo Museum, which traces the history of Tokyo. *Note:* Closed for renovations until August 2010.

1–3–28 Shirakawa, Koto-ku. ✆ **03/3630-8625.** Call for updated information on admission and open hours. Station: Kiyosumi-Shirakawa (3 min.).

Miraikan—National Museum of Emerging Science and Innovation (Nippon Kagaku Miraikan) ★★ **Kids**   Opened in 2001 on Odaiba, this fascinating educational museum provides hands-on exploration of the latest developments in cutting-edge science and technology, including interactions with robots, virtual-reality rides, and displays that suggest future applications such as noninvasive medical procedures and an environmentally friendly home. Everything from nanotechnology and genomes to space exploration is explained in detail; touch screens in English and a volunteer staff eager to assist in demonstrations and answer questions catapult this to one of the most user-friendly technology museums I've seen (avoid, however, weekends and school holidays, when it's packed with families). A great place to get your brain cells up and running whether you're 8 years old or 80, this museum deserves at least 3 hours.

2–41 Aomi, Koto-ku, Odaiba. ✆ **03/3570-9151.** www.miraikan.jst.go.jp. Admission ¥600 adults, ¥200 children. Wed–Mon 10am–5pm. Station: Telecom Center, on the Rinkai Line; or Fune-no-Kagakukan, on the Yurikamome Line (5 min. from either).

Mori Art Museum (Mori Bijutsukan) ★★   This is Tokyo's highest museum, on the 53rd floor of the Roppongi Hills Mori Tower. Opened in 2003, it features state-of-the-art galleries with 6m-tall (20-ft.) ceilings, controlled natural lighting, and great views of Tokyo. Innovative exhibitions of emerging and established artists from around the world are shown four times a year, with past shows centering on contemporary Asian, African, and Japanese art. Although the installations alone, ranging from paintings and fashion to architecture and design, are worth a visit, an extra incentive is the attached

Tokyo City View observatory, usually included in the museum admission and providing eye-popping views over Tokyo. Plan on at least 90 minutes up here.

Roppongi Hills Mori Tower, 6–10–1 Roppongi, Minato-ku. (✆ **03/5777-8600**. www.mori.art.museum. Admission varies according to the exhibit but averages ¥1,500 adults, ¥1,000 high-school and college students, and ¥500 children. Wed–Mon 10am–10pm; Tues 10am–5pm. Station: Roppongi (Roppongi Hills exit, 1 min.).

MOT or Museum of Contemporary Art, Tokyo (Tokyo-to Gendai Bijutsu-kan) ★ The MOT is inconveniently located but well worth the trek if you're a fan of the avant-garde (you'll pass the Fukagawa Edo Museum, described above, on the way, so you may wish to visit both). This modern structure of glass and steel, with a long corridor entrance that reminds me of railroad trestles, houses both permanent and temporary exhibits of Japanese and international postwar art in rooms whose sizes lend themselves to large installations. Although temporary exhibits, which occupy most of the museum space, have ranged from Southeast Asian art to a retrospective of Jasper Johns, the smaller permanent collection presents a chronological study of 40 years of contemporary art, beginning with anti-artistic trends and pop art in the 1960s and continuing with minimalism and cutting-edge contemporary works, with about 100 works displayed on a rotating basis. Included may be works by Andy Warhol, Gerhard Richter, Roy Lichtenstein, David Hockney, Frank Stella, Sandro Chia, Mark Rothko, and Julian Schnabel. Depending on the number of exhibits you visit, you'll spend anywhere from 1 to 2 hours here. There are two pleasant places to dine here, a restaurant and a cafe.

4–1–1 Miyoshi, Koto-ku. (✆ **03/5245-4111**. www.mot-art-museum.jp. Admission to permanent collection ¥500 adults, ¥400 college students, ¥250 high-school students and seniors, free for children; special exhibits cost more. Tues–Sun 10am–6pm. Station: Kiyosumi-Shirakawa (exit A3, 15 min.). On Fukagawa Shiroyokan-dori, just off Mitsume Dori.

The National Art Center, Tokyo ★ This national museum doesn't have a collection of its own. Rather, its purpose is to exhibit works organized by Japanese artists' associations, its own curators, and joint efforts by mass media companies and other art institutions. The range of changing exhibitions, therefore, can be staggering, with past exhibitions showing masterworks from the Rijksmuseum Amsterdam; fashion and architecture organized by the Museum of Contemporary Art, Los Angeles; works by Monet and Lalique; and a retrospective on Japanese government-sponsored art exhibitions held the past 100 years. Even the building itself—with an undulating, seductive facade of glass—attracts crowds with its Paul Bocuse restaurant, museum shop, and changing exhibitions by national artists' associations. This museum, the nearby Mori Art Museum, and Suntory Museum of Art, all within walking distance of one another, have been dubbed Art Triangle Roppongi.

7-22-2 Roppongi, Minato-ku. © 03/5777-8600. www.nact.jp. Admission ¥500–¥1,500 for most exhibitions. Wed–Mon 10am–6pm (Fri to 8pm). Station: Nogizakai (exit 6, 1 min.) or Roppongi (exit 4A or 7, 5 min.)

National Museum of Modern Art (Tokyo Kokuritsu Kindai Bijutsukan) ★★

This museum houses the largest collection of modern Japanese art under one roof, including both Japanese- and Western-style paintings, prints, watercolors, drawings, and sculpture, all dating from the Meiji Period through the 20th century. Names to look for include Munakata Shiko, Kuroda Seiki, and Yokoyama Taikan. A few works by Western artists, such as Picasso, Klee, and Kandinsky, are also on display as examples of Western artistic styles of the same period. Expect to spend about 1 hour here.

3 Kitanomaru Koen Park, Chiyoda-ku. © 03/3214-2561. www.momat.go.jp. Admission ¥420 adults, ¥130 college students, free for children; special exhibits cost more. Tues–Sun 10am–5pm (Fri to 8pm). Station: Takebashi (5 min.).

National Museum of Nature and Science (Kokuritsu Kagaku Hakubutsu-kan) ★ (Kids)

Japan's largest science museum covers everything from the evolution of life to Japanese inventions and technology, in expansive, imaginative displays, with plenty of exhibits geared toward children. A highlight is an entire arena of 100-some taxidermic animals from around the world, including a polar bear, camel, gorilla, tiger, and other creatures (some are animals that died at Ueno Zoo). Other highlights include a dinosaur display; a hands-on discovery room for children exploring sound, light, magnetism, and other scientific phenomena; re-created wood and marine habitats; a Japanese mummy from the Edo Period curled up in a burial jar; Hachiko (stuffed, on the second floor of the main building—there's a famous statue of this dog at Shibuya Station); and an extensive exhibition that allows visitors to stroll through some 4 billion years of evolutionary history. You'll want to spend about 2 hours here, more if you have children in tow or if you opt for the audio guide (¥200 extra), recommended since English-language explanations are limited.

Ueno Park, Taito-ku. © 03/5777-8600. www.kahaku.go.jp. Admission ¥600 adults, free for children. Tues–Sun 9am–5pm (Fri to 8pm). Station: Ueno (5 min.). Tokyo Shitamachi Bus: Ueno Koen Yamashita/Ueno Station.

The National Museum of Western Art (Kokuritsu Seiyo Bijutsukan) ★

Japan's only national museum dedicated to Western art is housed in a main building designed by Le Corbusier and in two more recent additions. It presents a chronological study of sculpture and art from the end of the Middle Ages through the 20th century, beginning with works by old masters, including Lucas Cranach the Elder, Rubens, El Greco, Murillo, and Tiepolo. French painters and Impressionists of the 19th and 20th centuries are well represented, including Delacroix, Monet (with a whole room devoted to his work), Manet, Renoir, Pissarro, Sisley, Courbet, Cézanne, and Gauguin. The museum's 20th-century collection includes works by Picasso, Ernst, Miró, Dubuffet, and Pollock. The museum is also famous for its 50-odd sculptures by Rodin, one of the largest collections in the world, encompassing most of his major works including *The Kiss, The Thinker, Balzac,* and *The Gates of Hell.* Plan on spending at least an hour here, though frequent—and ambitious—special exhibitions may entice you to linger longer.

Ueno Park, Taito-ku. ℭ **03/3828-5131.** www.nmwa.go.jp. Admission ¥420 adults, ¥130 college students, free for children 17 and under and seniors; special exhibits require separate admission fee. Free admission to permanent collection 2nd and 4th Sat of the month. Tues–Sun 9:30am–5pm (Fri to 8pm). Station: Ueno (4 min.). Tokyo Shitamachi Bus: Ueno Koen Yamashita/Ueno Station.

Ukiyo-e Ota Memorial Museum of Art (Ota Kinen Bijutsukan) ★ (Finds)

This great museum features the private *ukiyo-e* (woodblock print) collection of the late Ota Seizo, who early in life recognized the importance of ukiyo-e as an art form and dedicated himself to its preservation. Although the collection contains 12,000 prints, only 80 to 100 are displayed at any given time, in thematic exhibitions that change monthly and include English-language descriptions. The museum itself is small but delightful. You can tour it in about 30 minutes, and be sure to take a peek in the basement shop with its *furoshiki* (traditional wrapping cloth), handkerchiefs, and other items.

1-10-10 Jingumae, Shibuya-ku. ℭ **03/3403-0880.** www.ukiyoe-ota-muse.jp. Admission ¥700–¥1,000 adults, ¥500–¥700 high-school and college students, ¥200–¥400 junior-high students, free–¥200 children; price depends on the exhibit. Tues–Sun 10:30am–5:30pm (enter by 5pm). Closed from the 27th to end of each month. Station: Harajuku (2 min.) or Meiji-Jingumae (1 min.). Near the Omotesando Dori and Meiji Dori intersection, behind La Forêt.

Yushukan ★

Located on the grounds of Yasukuni Shrine, built in 1869 to commemorate some 2.5 million Japanese war dead, this war memorial museum chronicles the rise and fall of the samurai, Sino-Japanese War, Russo-Japanese War, and World Wars I and II, though English-language explanations are rather vague and Japan's military aggression in Asia is glossed over. Still, a fascinating 90 minutes can be spent here gazing at samurai armor, uniforms, tanks, guns, and artillery, as well as such thought-provoking displays as a human torpedo (a tiny submarine guided by one occupant and loaded with explosives) and a suicide attack plane. But the most chilling displays are the seemingly endless photographs of war dead, some of them young teenagers. In stark contrast to the somberness of the museum, temporary exhibits of beautiful *ikebana* (Japanese flower arrangements) and bonsai are often held on shrine grounds in rows of glass cases. The shrine is also famous for its cherry blossoms and for its Sunday flea market held from 6am to 3pm. Yasukuni Shrine is most well known, however, for the controversy that erupts every August 15 when World War II memorials are held and top government officials stop by, causing outrage among Japan's Asian neighbors.

Yasukuni Shrine, 3-1-1 Kudan-kita, Chiyoda-ku. ℭ **03/3261-8326.** www.yasukuni.or.jp. Admission ¥800 adults, ¥500 students, ¥300 junior-high and high-school students; ¥100 children. Daily 9am–5pm. Station: Kudanshita (3 min.); Ichigayaumae or Iidabashi (7 min.). On Yasukuni Dori.

5 SPECTACULAR CITY VIEWS

Tokyo Metropolitan Government Office (TMG) ★★★ (Kids)

Tokyo's city hall—designed by one of Japan's best-known architects, Kenzo Tange—is an impressive addition to the skyscrapers of west Shinjuku. The complex comprises three buildings—TMG no. 1, TMG no. 2, and the Metropolitan Assembly Building—and together they contain everything from Tokyo's Disaster Prevention Center to the governor's office. Most important for visitors is TMG no. 1, the tall building to the north that offers the best free view of Tokyo. This 48-story, 240m (787-ft.) structure, the tallest building in Shinjuku, boasts two observatories located on the 45th floors of both its north and south towers. Both observatories offer the same spectacular views—on clear winter days you can even see Mount Fuji—as well as a small souvenir shop and coffee shop (the North Tower also has a Hakuhinkan Toy Park, with fun souvenirs, but a large restaurant annoyingly takes up the entire east side of the observatory). In expensive Tokyo, this is one of the city's best bargains, and kids love it. On the first floor is a Tokyo Tourist Information Center, open daily 10am to 6:30pm.

2–8–1 Nishi-Shinjuku. ℰ **03/5321-1111.** Free admission. Daily 9:30am–10:30pm. Closed Dec 29–Jan 3. Station: Tochomae (1 min.), Shinjuku (10 min.), or Nishi-Shinjuku (5 min.).

Tokyo Tower ★ (Overrated) Japan's most famous observation tower was built in 1958 and was modeled after the slightly smaller Eiffel Tower in Paris. Lit up at night, this 330m (1,083-ft.) tower, a relay station for TV and radio stations, is a familiar and beloved landmark in the city's landscape; but with the construction of skyscrapers over the past few decades (including the TMG, above, with its free observatory), it has lost some of its appeal as an observation platform and seems more like a relic from the 1950s. With its tacky souvenir shops and assorted small-time attractions, this place is about as kitsch as kitsch can be.

The tower has two observatories: the main one at 149m (489 ft.) and the top observatory at 248m (814 ft.). The best time of year for viewing is said to be during Golden Week at the beginning of May. With many Tokyoites gone from the city and most factories and businesses closed down, the air at this time is thought to be the cleanest and clearest. There are several offbeat tourist attractions in the tower's base building, including a wax museum (where you can see the Beatles, a wax rendition of Leonardo's *Last Supper,* Hollywood stars, and a medieval torture chamber), a small aquarium, a museum of holography, a Guinness World Records Museum, and a trick art gallery, all with separate admission fees and appealing mainly to children.

4–2 Shiba Koen, Minato-ku. ℰ **03/3433-5111.** www.tokyotower.co.jp. Admission to both observatories ¥1,420 adults, ¥860 children. Daily 9am–10pm. Station: Onarimon or Kamiyacho (6 min.).

6 CITY STROLLS

WALKING TOUR 1	SEARCHING FOR OLD EDO, A WALKING TOUR OF ASAKUSA
START:	Hama Rikyu Garden (Shiodome Station) or Asakusa Station (exit 1 or 3).
FINISH:	Kappabashi Dori (Station: Tawaramachi).
TIME:	Allow approximately 5 hours, including the boat ride.
BEST TIMES:	Tuesday through Friday, when the crowds aren't as big, or Sunday, when you can join a free tour of Asakusa, but:
WORST TIMES:	Sunday, when the shops on Kappabashi Dori are closed.

If anything remains of old Tokyo, Asakusa is it. This is where you'll find narrow streets lined with small residential homes, women in kimono, Tokyo's oldest and most popular temple, and quaint shops selling boxwood combs, fans, kitchen knives, sweet pastries, and other products of yore. With its temple market, rickshaw drivers vying for the tourist trade, old-fashioned amusement park, traditional shops, and restaurants, Asakusa preserves the charm of old downtown Edo better than anyplace else in Tokyo. For many

EXPLORING TOKYO

6

WALKING TOUR 1: SEARCHING FOR OLD EDO

1 Hama Rikyu Garden
2 Asakusa Information Center
3 Kaminarimon Gate
4 Tokiwado Kaminari Okoshi
5 Nakamise Dori
6 Covered shopping arcades
7 Incense burner
8 Sensoji Temple
9 Asakusa Jinja Shrine
10 Hanayashiki
11 Kappabashi-dougugai Dori

older Japanese, a visit to Asakusa is like stepping back to the days of their childhood; for tourists, it provides a glimpse of the way things were.

Pleasure-seekers have been flocking to Asakusa for centuries. Originating as a temple town back in the 7th century, it grew in popularity during the Tokugawa regime as merchants became wealthy and entirely new forms of popular entertainment arose to cater to them. Theaters for *kabuki* and *bunraku* flourished in Asakusa, as did restaurants and shops. By 1840, Asakusa had become Edo's main entertainment district. In stark contrast to the solemnity surrounding places of worship in the West, Asakusa's temple market had a carnival atmosphere reminiscent of medieval Europe, complete with street performers and exotic animals. It retains some of that festive atmosphere even today.

The most dramatic way to arrive in Asakusa is by boat from Hama Rikyu Garden (see stop no. 1, below), just as people used to arrive in the olden days. If you want to forgo the boat ride, take the subway to Asakusa Station and start your tour from stop no. 2. Otherwise, head to:

❶ Hama Rikyu Garden

Located at the south end of Tokyo (Station: Shiodome, exit 5, then a 5-min. walk), this garden was laid out during the Edo Period in a style popular at the time, in which surrounding scenery was incorporated into its composition. Today, the only surrounding scenery you'll see is an overabundance of skyscrapers, but it does contain an inner tidal pool, bridges draped with wisteria, moon-viewing pavilions, and teahouses. (See p. 190 for more details.)

Boats depart the garden to make their way along the Sumida River every 30 to 60 minutes between 10:35am and 4:15pm, with the fare to Asakusa costing ¥720. Although much of what you see along the working river today is only concrete embankments, I like the trip because it affords a different perspective of Tokyo—barges making their way down the river, high-rise apartment buildings with laundry fluttering from balconies, warehouses, and superhighways. The boat passes under approximately a dozen bridges during the 40-minute trip, each one completely different. During cherry-blossom season, thousands of cherry trees lining the bank make the ride particularly memorable.

Upon your arrival in Asakusa, walk away from the boat pier a couple of blocks inland, where you'll soon see the colorful Kaminarimon Gate on your right. Across the street on your left is the:

❷ Asakusa Information Center

Located at 2–18–9 Kaminarimon (☎ 03/6280-6710), the center is open daily from 9:30am to 8pm but is staffed by English-speaking volunteers only from 10am to 5pm. Stop here to pick up a map of the area, use the restroom, and ask for directions to restaurants and sights. On Sundays, volunteers give free 1-hour guided tours of Asakusa at 11am and 2pm (arrive 10 min. earlier). Note the huge Seiko clock on the center's facade—every hour on the hour from 10am to 7pm, mechanical dolls reenact scenes from Asakusa's most famous festivals.

Then it's time to head across the street to the:

❸ Kaminarimon Gate

The gate is unmistakable with its bright red colors and 100-kilogram (220-lb.) lantern hanging in the middle. The statues inside the gate are the god of wind to the right and the god of thunder to the left, ready to protect the deity enshrined in the temple. The god of thunder is particularly fearsome: He supposedly has an insatiable appetite for navels.

To the left of the gate, on the corner, is:

❹ Tokiwado Kaminari Okoshi

This open-fronted confectionery has been selling *okoshi* (rice-based sweets) for 250 years and is popular with visiting Japanese buying gifts for the folks back home. It's open daily from 9am to 9pm.

Once past Kaminarimon Gate, you'll find yourself immediately on a pedestrian lane called:

❺ Nakamise Dori

The lane leads straight to the Sensoji Temple. *Nakamise* means "inside shops," and historical records show that vendors have sold wares here since the late 17th century. Today Nakamise Dori is lined on both sides with tiny stall after tiny stall, many owned by the same family for generations. If you're expecting austere religious artifacts, however, you're in for a surprise: sweets, shoes, barking toy dogs, *sembei* (Japanese crackers), bags, umbrellas, Japanese dolls, T-shirts, fans, masks, and traditional Japanese accessories are all sold. How about a brightly colored straight hairpin—and a black hairpiece to go with it? Or a temporary tattoo in the shape of a dragon? This is a great place to shop for souvenirs, gifts, and items you have no earthly need for—a little bit of unabashed consumerism on the way to spiritual purification.

TAKE A BREAK
If you're hungry for lunch, there are many possibilities in the neighborhood. **Chinya** (p. 158), 1–3–4 Asakusa, just west of Kaminarimon Gate on Kaminarimon Dori, has been serving sukiyaki and *shabu-shabu* since 1880. Northeast of Kaminarimon Gate is **Waentei-Kikko** (p. 159), 2–2–13 Asakusa, offering *obento* lunch boxes and *shamisen* performances. For Western food, head to the other side of the Sumida River, where on the 22nd floor of the Asahi Beer Tower is **La Ranarita Azumabashi** (p. 158), 1–23–1 Azumabashi, a moderately priced Italian restaurant with great views of Asakusa; and the utilitarian **Sky Room** (p. 227) with inexpensive beer, wine, and snacks.

Before reaching the end of Nakamise Dori, there are a couple of interesting side streets worth exploring. Just 2 blocks north of Kaminarimon Gate are two:

❻ Covered Shopping Arcades

Stretching to both the right and left of Nakamise Dori, these pedestrian-only covered lanes are typical of what you'll see everywhere in Japan—regular streets that became instant shopping centers by covering them with roofs and banning vehicular traffic. This is where locals come to shop, with stores selling clothing, household goods, souvenirs, and more.

Farther along Nakamise Dori is the second gate, which opens onto a square filled with pigeons and a large:

❼ Incense Burner

This is where worshipers "wash" themselves to ward off or help cure illness. If, for example, you have a sore throat, be sure to rub some of the smoke over your throat for good measure.

The building dominating the square is:

❽ Sensoji Temple

Sensoji is Tokyo's oldest temple. Founded in the 7th century and therefore already well established long before Tokugawa settled in Edo, Sensoji Temple is dedicated to Kannon, the Buddhist goddess of mercy, and is therefore popularly called the Asakusa Kannon Temple. According to legend, the temple was founded after two fishermen pulled a golden statue of Kannon from the sea. The sacred statue is still housed in the temple, carefully preserved inside three boxes; even though it's never on display, an estimated 20 million people flock to the temple annually to pay their respects.

Within the temple is a counter where you can buy your fortune by putting a 100-yen coin into a wooden box and shaking it until a long bamboo stick emerges from a small hole. The stick will have a Japanese number on it, which corresponds to one of the numbers on a set of drawers. Take the fortune, written in both English and Japanese, from the drawer that has your number. But don't expect the translation to clear things up; my fortune contained such cryptic messages as "Getting a beautiful lady at your home, you want to try all people know about this" and "Stop to start a trip." If you find that your fortune raises more questions than it answers or you simply don't like what it has to say, you can conveniently negate it by tying it to one of the wires provided for this purpose just outside the main hall.

If you walk around the temple to the right, on the northeast corner of the grounds is the small orange:

⑨ Asakusa Jinja Shrine

This shrine was built in 1649 by Iemitsu Tokugawa, the third Tokugawa shogun, to commemorate the two fishermen who found the statue of Kannon and their village chief. Its architectural style, called *Gongen-zukuri*, is the same as the style of Toshogu Shrine in Nikko. West of Sensoji Temple is a gardenlike area of lesser shrines and memorials, flowering bushes, and a stream filled with carp. The most picturesque photos of Sensoji Temple can be taken from here.

Farther west still is:

⑩ Hanayashiki

This is a small and corny amusement park that first opened in 1853 and still draws in the little ones. (See p. 204 for more details.)

Most of the area west of Sensoji Temple (the area to the left if you stand facing the front of the temple) is a small but interesting part of Asakusa popular among Tokyo's older working class. This is where several of Asakusa's old-fashioned pleasure houses remain, including bars, restaurants, strip shows, traditional Japanese vaudeville, and so-called "love hotels," which rent rooms by the hour.

If you keep walking west, past the Asakusa View Hotel, within 10 minutes you'll reach:

⑪ Kappabashi-dougugai Dori

This district, generally referred to as Kappabashi Dori, is Tokyo's wholesale district for restaurant items. Shop after shop sells pottery, chairs, tableware, cookware, lacquerware, rice cookers, *noren* (short curtains hung outside shops and restaurants to signify they are open), and everything else needed to run a restaurant. And yes, you can even buy those models of plastic food you've been drooling over in restaurant displays. Ice cream, pizza, sushi, mugs foaming with beer—they're all here, looking like the real thing. (Stores close about 5pm and are closed Sun.)

> **WINDING DOWN**
> The **Asakusa View Hotel,** on Kokusai Dori Avenue between Sensoji Temple and Kappabashi Dori, has several restaurants and bars. In the basement is the clubby **Ice House,** the hotel's main bar.

WALKING TOUR 2	**IN THE HEART OF TRENDY TOKYO, A STROLL THROUGH HARAJUKU & AOYAMA**

START:	Meiji Jingu Shrine (Station: Harajuku).
FINISH:	Aoyama (Station: Omotesando).
TIME:	Allow approximately 4 hours.
BEST TIMES:	The first Sunday of every month, when there's an antiques flea market at Togo Shrine.
WORST TIMES:	Monday, from the 27th to the end of every month (when the Ota Memorial Museum of Art is closed), and Thursday (when the Oriental Bazaar is closed).

Harajuku is one of my favorite neighborhoods in Tokyo, though I'm too old to really fit in. In fact, anyone over 25 is apt to feel ancient here, as this is Tokyo's most popular hangout for Japanese high-school and college students. The young come here to see and

1 Meiji Jingu Shrine
2 Takeshita Dori
3 Togo Shrine
4 La Forêt
5 Ukiyo-e Ota Memorial Museum of Art
6 Chicago
7 Condomania
8 Kiddy Land
9 Oriental Bazaar
10 Omotesando Hills
11 Hanae Mori Building
12 Issey Miyake
13 Comme des Garçons
14 Prada
15 Yohji Yamamoto

Railway
Subway
Take a Break stop

0   1/4 mi
0   0.25 km

be seen; you're sure to spot Japanese punks, girls decked out in the fashions of the moment, and young couples out on dates. I like Harajuku for its vibrancy, its sidewalk cafes, its street hawkers, and its trendy clothing boutiques. It's also the home of Tokyo's most important Shinto shrine, as well as a delightful woodblock-print museum and an excellent souvenir shop of traditional Japanese items. If you have teenagers in tow, you'll definitely want to make Harajuku a top priority.

Nearby is **Aoyama,** a yuppified version of Harajuku, where the upwardly mobile dine and shop for designer clothing. Connecting Harajuku and Aoyama is **Omotesando Dori,** a wide, tree-lined, European-style shopping boulevard that forms the heart of this area; its many sidewalk cafes make it a popular promenade for people-watching.

From Harajuku Station, take the south exit (the one closer to Shibuya) and turn right over the bridge, where you will immediately see the huge cypress *torii* marking the entrance to:

❶ Meiji Jingu Shrine

Dedicated to Emperor and Empress Meiji, Meiji Jingu Shrine (p. 184) opened in 1920 and remains the most venerable shrine in Tokyo. The shrine is surrounded by a dense forest of 365 different species totaling 120,000 trees, donated by people from all over Japan. If it's June, stop off at the Iris Garden, located halfway on the 10-minute tree-shaded path to the shrine.

> **TAKE A BREAK**
> If the hike to Meiji Shrine has made you thirsty, stop off at the rustic **Café Mori no Terrace** outdoor pavilion just inside the entryway to the shrine grounds. Open daily 9am to sunset, it offers coffee, beer, pastries, and ice cream. For something more substantial, wait until you get to Takeshita Dori (described below), where you'll find a **Wolfgang Puck Express,** 1–17–1 Jingumae, good for burgers and pizza (p. 169).

After visiting the shrine, retrace your steps to Harajuku Station. If it's Sunday, you'll see groups of teenagers—many bizarrely dressed—gathered on the bridge over the train tracks. They're all that's left of the masses of teens that used to congregate on nearby Yoyogi Dori back when it was closed to vehicular traffic on Sundays. Sadly, authorities decided to open Yoyogi

and Omotesando Dori streets to traffic, thereby putting an end to Tokyo's most happening Sunday scene.

At Harajuku Station, continue walking north beside the station to its north exit. Across the street from Harajuku Station's north exit is:

❷ Takeshita Dori

This pedestrian-only street is lined non-stop with stores that cater to teenagers. It's packed—especially on Sunday after-noons—with young people hunting for bargains on inexpensive clothing, shoes, music, sunglasses, jewelry, watches, cosmetics, and more. One shop worth point-ing out is **Harajuku Daiso** (© 5775-9641; daily 10am–9pm) on the left, one of many bargain variety stores to hit Japan after the recession. It offers four floors of kitchen-ware, tableware, cosmetics, office supplies, and more, most priced at ¥100.

After inching your way through the flow of humanity along this narrow lane, you'll eventually find yourself on a busy thoroughfare, Meiji Dori. If it's the first Sunday of the month, turn left (north) onto Meiji Dori; in a couple of minutes, on your left you'll see:

❸ Togo Shrine

Dedicated to Admiral Heihachiro Togo, who was in charge of the fleet that defeated the Russian navy in 1905 in the Russo-Japanese War, the shrine nowadays is most popular for its flea market held the first Sunday of every month to 2pm. Every-thing from old chests, dolls, porcelain, and kimono are for sale, spread out on a tree-shaded sidewalk that meanders around the shrine.

Head back south on Meiji Dori. To your right, just before the big intersection, is:

4 La Forêt

La Forêt is filled with trendy shoe and clothing boutiques. The less expensive boutiques tend to be on the lower floors; the more exclusive are higher up. (See "Shopping," later in this chapter, for details on many of the shops and department stores listed in this walking tour.)

Behind La Forêt is one of my favorite museums, the:

5 Ukiyo-e Ota Memorial Museum of Art

Located at 1–10–10 Jingumae, this museum features the private *ukiyo-e* (woodblock prints) collection of the late Ota Seizo. Exhibitions of the museum's 12,000 prints change monthly and are always worth checking out (p. 195).

Across Omotesando Dori is:

6 Chicago

This store specializes in used American clothing but also stocks hundreds of used and new kimono and *yukata* in the far back corner of its basement.

Near La Forêt is Harajuku's major intersection, Meiji Dori and Omotesando Dori. Here, at the intersection at 6–30–1 Jingumae, is one of Harajuku's more unusual shops:

7 Condomania

Condoms are for sale here in a wide range of sizes, colors, and styles, from glow-in-the-dark to scented. It's open daily 11am to 11pm.

Heading east on Omotesando Dori (away from Harajuku Station), you'll soon see, to your right:

8 Kiddy Land

Located at 6–1–9 Jingumae, this store sells gag gifts and a great deal more than just toys, including enough to amuse less discerning adults. You could spend an hour browsing here, but the store is so crowded with teenagers that you may end up rushing for the door.

Continue east on Omotesando Dori (where sidewalk vendors selling jewelry and ethnic accessories set up

shop on weekends); to your right will soon be Harajuku's most famous store:

9 Oriental Bazaar

Located at 5–9–13 Jingumae, this is Tokyo's best one-stop shopping spot for Japanese souvenirs. Four floors offer antiques, old and new kimono, Japanese paper products, fans, jewelry, woodblock prints, screens, chinaware, and much more at reasonable prices. I always stock up on gifts here for the folks back home.

On the other side of Omotesando Dori is the new:

10 Omotesando Hills

This posh commercial and residential shopping center, designed by Tadao Ando, houses upscale clothing and accessory shops, as well as restaurants. Unique is 36 **Hasegawa Sake Shop** (✆ 03/5785-0833), with selected offerings from sake breweries across Japan. Its stand-up bar allows you to sample sake for ¥300 a cup.

Back on Omotesando Dori and continuing east, you'll pass shops dedicated to the wares of Gucci, Armani, Louis Vuitton, and Tod's, but none have been here as long as the:

11 Hanae Mori Building

Near the end of Omotesando Dori to the right, it was designed in 1978 by Japanese architect Kenzo Tange (who also designed the TMG City Hall in Shinjuku). It houses the entire collection of Hanae Mori, from casual wear to evening wear.

TAKE A BREAK

Harajuku and Aoyama have more sidewalk cafes than any other part of Tokyo. Most conspicuous is the fancy **Anniversaire Café**, 3–5–30 Kita-Aoyama, across from the Hanae Mori Building (see no. 11, above). **Café hors et dans,** 4–11–6 Jingumae (✆ 03/5775-5433), just east of Omotesando Hills on Omotesando Dori, has a second-floor outdoor terrace. **Montoak,** next to Kiddy Land (see no. 8, above) at 6–1–9 Jingumae (✆ 03/5468-5928), is a hip (so hip it doesn't even bother to hang out a shop sign) multilevel bar/coffee shop with comfy chairs and a small second-floor balcony.

At the end of Omotesando Dori, where it connects with Aoyama Dori, is Omotesando Station. You can board the subway here, but fashionistas will want to cross Aoyama Dori and continue heading east, where there are a number of designer shops. First, on the left at 3–18–11 Minami-aoyama, is:

⑫ **Issey Miyake**

The clothes here are known for their richness in texture and fabrics.

To the right, at 5–2–1 Minami-Aoyama, is:

⑬ **Comme des Garçons**

Rei Kawakubo's designs for both men and women are showcased here.

Farther down the street, on the right at 5–2–6 Minami-Aoyama, is:

⑭ **Prada**

By far the most interesting design on the block, the building looks like a giant bug eye (to me, at least), with its dome structure comprising hundreds of glass bubbles.

Just past Prada, on the right at 5–3–6 Minami-Aoyama, is:

⑮ **Yohji Yamamoto**

As with all Yamamoto shops, this store has an interesting avant-garde interior.

Return to Aoyama Dori, where you'll find the Omotesando subway station.

WINDING DOWN

Between Comme des Garçons and Yohji Yamamoto is **Yoku Moku,** easy to find at 5–3–3 Minami-Aoyama (☎ **03/5485-3330**) with its bright blue exterior and terrace. It's famous for its pastries and desserts. For more sinful pleasures, head to **Berry Café,** 5–10–19 Minami-Aoyama (☎ **03/5774-7130**), on the left side of Aoyama Dori in the direction of Shibuya. Its berry-topped cakes have to be seen to be believed; even its plastic-food displays look good enough to eat.

---

7 ESPECIALLY FOR KIDS

In addition to its observatories, **Tokyo Tower** (p. 196) contains a few other attractions that might be worth a visit if you have children in tow, including a small **aquarium** and a **wax museum.** Other attractions listed earlier that are good for children include the **Edo-Tokyo Museum, Fukagawa Edo Museum, National Museum of Emerging Science and Innovation, National Museum of Nature and Science,** and the free **observatory** of the Tokyo Metropolitan Government Office.

Hanayashiki   Opened in 1853 while the shogun still reigned, this small and rather corny amusement park is Japan's oldest. It offers a small roller coaster, a kiddie Ferris wheel, a carousel, a haunted house, a 3-D theater, samurai and ninja shows, and other diversions that appeal to younger children. Note, however, that after paying admission, you must still buy tickets for each ride; tickets are ¥100 each, and most rides require three to four tickets.

2–28–1 Asakusa (northwest of Sensoji Temple), Taito-ku. ☎ **03/3842-8780.** www.hanayashiki.net. Admission ¥900 adults, ¥400 children 5–12 and seniors, free for children 4 and under. Daily 10am–6pm (to 5pm in winter). Station: Asakusa (5 min.). Tokyo Shitamachi Bus: Ueno Koen Yamashita/Ueno Station.

Joypolis Sega   Bored teenagers in tow, grumbling at yet another temple or shrine? Bring them to life at Tokyo's most sophisticated virtual amusement arcade, outfitted with the latest in video games and high-tech virtual-reality attractions, courtesy of Sega. Video games include bobsledding, snowboarding and car races, in which participants maneuver curves utilizing virtual-reality equipment, as well as numerous aeronautical battle games. There's also a 3-D attraction with seats that move with the action on the screen, several virtual-reality rides (sky diving, anyone?), a virtual aquarium, and much more. Most harmless are the Print Club machines, which will print your face on stickers with the background (Mount Fuji, perhaps?) of your choice. If you think your kids will want to try everything, buy them a passport for ¥3,500 for those 15 and older or ¥3,100 for those 7 to 14 (children 6 and younger get in free but are charged for attractions—note that some activities have height restrictions).

There's a smaller Sega on Dogenzaka slope in Shibuya at 2–6–16 Dogenzaka (✆ **03/5458-2201;** station: Shibuya, 2 min.), open daily 10am to midnight and offering arcade and virtual-reality games, but note that because this is in a nightlife area, children 15 and under aren't allowed after 6pm and children 17 and under aren't allowed after 8pm.

Tokyo Decks, 3rd floor, Odaiba. ✆ **03/5500-1801.** http://tokyo-joypolis.com. Admission ¥500 adults, ¥300 children; individual attractions an additional ¥300–¥600 each. Daily 10am–11pm. Station: Odaiba Kaihin Koen (2 min.).

National Children's Castle (Kodomo-no-Shiro) ★

Conceived by the Ministry of Health and Welfare to commemorate the International Year of the Child in 1979, the Children's Castle holds various activity rooms for children of all ages (though most are geared to elementary-age kids and younger). The third floor, designed for spontaneous and unstructured play, features a large climbing gym, building blocks, a playhouse, dolls, books, and a preteen corner with billiards, Foosball, and other age-appropriate games; there's also an art room staffed with instructors to help children with projects suitable for their ages. On the fourth floor is a music room with instruments the kids are invited to play, as well as a video room with private cubicles where visitors can make selections from a library of English-language and Japanese videos, including Disney films. On the roof is an outdoor playground complete with a wading pool (open summer only; ¥200 extra admission) and tricycles. Various programs are offered throughout the week, including puppet shows, fairy tales, live music performances, and origami presentations.

5–53–1 Jingumae, Shibuya-ku. ✆ **03/3797-5666.** www.kodomono-shiro.or.jp/english. Admission ¥500 adults, ¥400 children 3–17, free for children 2 and under. Tues–Fri 12:30–5:30pm; Sat–Sun and holidays (including school holidays) 10am–5:30pm. Station: Omotesando (exit B2, 8 min.) or Shibuya (10 min.). On Aoyama Dori btw. Omotesando and Shibuya stations.

Tokyo Disneyland & Tokyo DisneySea ★★★

Virtually a carbon copy of Disneyland back home, this one also boasts the Jungle Cruise, Pirates of the Caribbean, the Haunted Mansion, and Space Mountain. Other hot attractions include Toontown, a wacky theme park where Mickey and other Disney characters work and play; MicroAdventure, which features 3-D glasses and special effects; and Star Tours, a thrill adventure created by Disney and George Lucas.

Adjacent to Disneyland is **DisneySea,** a theme park based on ocean legends and myths. It offers seven distinct "ports of call," including the futuristic Port Discovery marina with its StormRider that flies straight into the eye of a storm; the Lost River Delta with its Indiana Jones Adventure; Mermaid Lagoon based on the film *The Little Mermaid;* the Arabian Coast, with its Sinbad's Seven Voyages boat ride; and the American Waterfront with its Tower of Terror. Because DisneySea is unique to Tokyo, I personally think this is the one to see; its installations are a class act.

1–1 Maihama, Urayasu-shi, Chiba. ✆ **047/310-0733.** www.tokyodisneyresort.co.jp. 1-day passport to either Disneyland or DisneySea, including entrance to and use of all attractions, ¥5,800 adults, ¥5,100 seniors, ¥5,000 children 12–17, ¥3,900 children 4–11, free for children 3 and under. Daily 8 or 9am to 10pm, with slightly shorter hours in winter. Station: Maihama Station on the JR Keiyo Line from Tokyo Station (1 min.).

Ueno Zoo   Founded in 1882, Japan's oldest zoo is small by today's standards but remains one of the most well-known zoos in Japan. A vivarium houses amphibians, fish, and reptiles, including snakes and crocodiles. Also of note is the five-storied pagoda dating from the Edo Era, along with a teahouse built 350 years ago to receive the shogun when visiting nearby Toshogu Shrine. Shinobazu Pond on the west end of the zoo serves as a sanctuary for wild cormorants and other birds. Personally, I can't help but feel sorry for some of the animals in their small spaces, but children will enjoy the Japanese macaques, polar and Hokkaido brown bears, California sea lions, penguins, gorillas, giraffes, zebras, elephants, hippos, deer, and tigers. Expect a minimum of 2 hours here.

Ueno Park, Taito-ku. © **03/3828-5171**. www.tokyo-zoo.net/english. Admission ¥600 adults, ¥300 seniors, ¥200 children 12–14, free for children 11 and under. Tues–Sun 9:30am–5pm (enter by 4pm). Closed some holidays. Station: Ueno (4 min.). Tokyo Shitamachi Bus: Ueno Koen Yamashita/Ueno Station.

8 SPECTATOR SPORTS

For information on current sporting events, ranging from kickboxing and pro wrestling to soccer, table tennis, martial arts, and golf classics, contact the Tourist Information Center or pick up a copy of the free weekly *Metropolis* magazine (www.metropolis.co.jp). Tickets for many events can be purchased at convenience stores like Lawson, Family Mart, and 7-Eleven.

BASEBALL   Japanese are so crazy about baseball, you'd think they invented the game. Actually, it was introduced to Japan by the United States way back in 1873. Today, it's as popular among Japanese as it is among Americans. Even the annual high-school playoffs keep everyone glued to the TV set.

As with other imports, Japanese have added their own modifications: Some of the playing fields are smaller (though newer ones tend to have American dimensions) and, borrowing from American football, each team has its own cheerleaders. There are several American players who have proved very popular with local fans; but according to the rules, no more than four foreigners may play on any one team. On the other hand, recent years have also seen an exodus of top Japanese players to Major League Baseball teams, including the hugely popular and successful Ichiro Suzuki, leadoff hitter and right fielder for the Seattle Mariners and the 2007 MLB All-Star MVP; and Hideki Matsui, a power-hitting designated hitter and 2009 World Series MVP with the New York Yankees (now with the Los Angeles Angels). In fact, Japanese fans have been so mesmerized by the Mariners and Yankees (whose games are broadcast on Japanese TV) that television ratings for Japanese games have fallen.

There are two professional leagues, the Central and the Pacific, which play from April to October and meet in the Japan Series. In Tokyo, the home teams are the **Yomiuri Giants,** who play at the Tokyo Dome (© **03/5800-9999;** station: Korakuen or Suidobashi), and the **Yakult Swallows,** who play at Jingu Stadium (© **03/3404-8999;** station: Gaienmae). Other teams playing in the vicinity of Tokyo are the **Chiba Lotte Marines,** who play at Chiba Marine Stadium in Chiba (© **043/296-8900**), and the **Yokohama BayStars,** who play in downtown Yokohama Stadium (© **045/661-1251**). Advance tickets go on sale Friday, 2 weeks before the game, and can be purchased at one of many **Ticket Pia** locations around town (such as the Sony Building in Ginza or Isetan department store annex in Shinjuku; ask your hotel concierge for the nearest one), except for the Giants, where tickets can be purchased only at Tokyo Dome. Prices for the Tokyo

Dome and Jingu Stadium range from ¥1,800 for an unreserved seat in the outfield to ¥6,000 for seats behind home plate. The Giants are so popular, however, that tickets are hard to come by.

SUMO   Sumo matches are held in Tokyo at the **Kokugikan,** 1–3–28 Yokoami, Sumida-ku (C **03/3622-1100;** www.sumo.or.jp; station: Ryogoku, then a 1-min. walk; Tokyo Shitamachi Bus: Ryogoku Station). Matches are held in January, May, and September for 15 consecutive days, beginning at around 9:30am and lasting until 6pm; the top wrestlers compete after 3:30pm. The best seats are ringside box seats, but they're snapped up by companies or the friends and families of sumo wrestlers. Usually available are balcony seats, which can be purchased at Ticket Pia and JTB travel agencies. You can also purchase tickets directly at the Kokugikan ticket office beginning at 9am every morning of the tournament. Prices range from about ¥2,100 for an unreserved seat (sold only on the day of the event at the stadium, with about 400 seats available) to ¥8,200 for a good reserved seat.

If you can't make it to a match, watching on TV is almost as good. Tournaments in Tokyo, as well as those that take place annually in Osaka, Nagoya, and Fukuoka, are broadcast on the NHK channel from 4 to 6pm daily during matches. For more information on sumo, see p. 27.

9 SHOPPING

It won't take you long to become convinced that shopping is the number-one pastime in Tokyo. Women, men, couples, and even entire families go on buying expeditions in their free time, making Sunday the most crowded shopping day of the week.

THE SHOPPING SCENE

BEST BUYS   Tokyo is the country's showcase for everything from the latest in camera, computer, or music equipment to original woodblock prints and designer fashions. Traditional Japanese crafts and souvenirs that make good buys include toys (both traditional and the latest in technical wizardry), kites, Japanese dolls, carp banners, swords, lacquerware, bamboo baskets, *ikebana* (flower arranging) accessories, ceramics, pottery, iron teakettles, chopsticks, fans, masks, knives, scissors, sake, incense, and silk and cotton kimono. And you don't have to spend a fortune: You can pick up handmade Japanese *washi* (paper products), such as umbrellas, lanterns, boxes, stationery, and other souvenirs, for a fraction of what they cost in import shops in the United States. In Harajuku, it's possible to buy a fully lined dress of the latest fashion craze for ¥8,000 or less, and I can't even count the number of pairs of fun, casual shoes I've bought in Tokyo for a mere ¥4,000. Used camera equipment can be purchased for a song, reproductions of famous woodblock prints make great inexpensive gifts, and many items—from pearls to electronic video and audio equipment—can be bought tax-free (see "Taxes," below).

Japan is famous for its electronics, but if you're buying new you can probably find these products just as cheaply, or even more cheaply, in the United States. If you want to shop for electronic products while you're in Tokyo, it pays to do some comparison shopping before you leave home so that you can spot a deal when you see one. On the other hand, one of the joys of shopping for electronics in Japan is discovering new, advanced models; you might decide you want that new Sony HD camcorder simply because it's the coolest thing you've ever seen, no matter what the price.

GREAT SHOPPING AREAS   Another enjoyable aspect of shopping in Tokyo is that specific areas are often devoted to certain goods, sold wholesale but also available to the individual shopper. **Kappabashi-dougugai Dori** (station: Tawaramachi), for example, is where you'll find shops specializing in kitchenware, while **Kanda** (station: Jimbocho) is known for its bookstores. **Akihabara** (station: Akihabara) is packed with stores selling the latest in electronics, as well as *anime*-related items. **Ginza** (station: Ginza) is the chic address for high-end international designer brands as well as art galleries. **Aoyama** (station: Omotesando) boasts the city's largest concentration of Japanese designer-clothing stores and an ever-increasing number of international names, while nearby **Harajuku** (stations: Harajuku, Meiji-Jingu-mae, or Omotesando) and **Shibuya** (station: Shibuya) are the places to go for youthful, fun, and inexpensive fashions.

SALES   Department stores have sales throughout the year, with bargains on everything from electronic goods and men's suits to golf clubs, toys, kitchenware, food, and lingerie; there are even sales for used wedding kimono. The most popular sales are for **designer clothing,** usually held twice a year in July and December or January, when you can pick up fantastic clothing at cut-rate prices—but be prepared for crowds. Sales are generally held on one of the top floors of the department store in what's usually labeled the "Exhibition Hall" or "Promotion Hall" in the store's English-language brochure. Stop by the store's information desk, usually located near the main entrance, for the brochure as well as fliers listing current sales promotions.

TAXES   A 5% consumption tax is included in the price of marked goods, but all major department stores and most tourist shops in Tokyo will refund the tax to foreign visitors if total purchases amount to more than ¥10,001 on that day. Exemptions include food, beverages, tobacco, pharmaceuticals, cosmetics, film, and batteries. When you've completed your shopping, take the purchased goods and receipts to the tax refund counter in the store. There are forms to fill out (you will need your passport). Upon completion, a record of your purchase is placed on the visa page of your passport, and you are given the tax refund on the spot. When you leave Japan, make sure you have your purchases with you (pack them in your carry-on); you may be asked by Customs to show them, though I've never been asked.

SHIPPING IT HOME   Many first-class hotels in Tokyo provide a packing and shipping service. In addition, most large department stores, as well as tourist shops such as the Oriental Bazaar and antiques shops, will ship your purchases overseas.

If you wish to ship packages yourself, the easiest method is to go to a post office and purchase an easy-to-assemble cardboard box, available in several sizes (along with the necessary tape). Keep in mind that packages mailed abroad cannot weigh more than 20 kilograms (about 44 lb.), and that only the larger international post offices accept packages to be mailed overseas (ask your hotel concierge for the closest one). Remember, too, that mailing packages from Japan is expensive (for details, see "Fast Facts," in chapter 5 and chapter 16).

SHOPPING FROM A TO Z
Antiques & Curios

In recent years, it has become a buyer-beware market in Japan, with fake antiques produced in China infiltrating the Japanese market. You shouldn't have any problems with the reputable dealers listed here, but if you're buying an expensive piece, be sure to ask whether there are any papers of authenticity.

In addition to the listings here, other places to look for antiques include the **Oriental** **Bazaar** (p. 211) and Tokyo's outdoor **flea markets** (see later in this section).

Antique Mall Ginza Japanese, European, and some American antiques, collectibles, and odds and ends crowd three floors of Tokyo's largest antiques mall, where you could spend hours browsing among furniture, jewelry, watches, porcelain, pottery, dolls, *netsuke,* scrolls, glassware, kimono, folk art, and much more. Open Thursday to Tuesday 11am to 7pm. 1–13–1 Ginza, Chuo-ku. ✆ **03/3535-2115.** www.antiques-jp.com. Station: Ginza-Itchome or Kyobashi (3 min.). Btw. Chuo Dori and Showa Dori.

Kurofune Antiques Finds Located in a large house in Roppongi, Kurofune is owned by American John Adair, who for more than 25 years has specialized in Japanese antique furniture in its original condition. The largest collection here is of mid- to top-quality pieces, but browsing is a delight even if you can't afford to buy; stock in addition to furniture includes hibachi, fabrics, prints, maps, lanterns, screens, folk art, and the country's largest collection of Japanese baskets. Open Monday to Saturday 10am to 6pm. Closed early April through Golden Week. 47-7-4 Roppongi, Minato-ku. ✆ **03/3479-1552.** www.kurofuneantiques.com. Station: Roppongi (5 min.). From Roppongi Crossing, walk away from Tokyo Tower on Gaien-Higashi Dori, take the diagonal street (Ryudocho-Bijitsukan-dori) to the left (across from Tokyo Midtown), and then take a right at 7-Eleven.

Arcades & Shopping Malls

UNDERGROUND ARCADES Underground shopping arcades are found around several of Tokyo's train and subway stations; the biggest are at **Tokyo Station** (the Yaesu side) and **Shinjuku Station** (the east side). They often have great sales and bargains on clothing, accessories, and electronics. My only complaint is that once you're in them, it sometimes seems as if you'll never find your way out again.

SHOPPING MALLS **Sunshine City** (station: Higashi Ikebukuro or Ikebukuro) is one of Tokyo's oldest shopping malls, with more than 200 shops and restaurants spread through several adjoining buildings. Its popularity, however, is now challenged by newer and grander shopping centers, including chic **Omotesando Hills** (station: Harajuku, Omotesando, or Meiji-Jingumae) with a varied mix of upscale boutiques and restaurants; **Roppongi Hills** (station: Roppongi), an urban renewal project with approximately 130 shops spread throughout several buildings and along tree-lined streets; and **Tokyo Midtown** (station: Roppongi) with its mix of tony shops, restaurants, and offices. In the harbor, on man-made island Odaiba (station: Odaiba Kaihin Koen), is **Palette Town,** an amusement/shopping center that contains the sophisticated, upscale Italian-themed **Venus Fort,** an indoor mall that evokes scenes from Italy with its store-fronted lanes, painted sky, fountains, plazas, and Italian name-brand boutiques. Nearby **Tokyo Decks** targets Japanese youths with its international goods, including imports from the United States, Europe, China, and Hong Kong; I especially like its Daiba 1-chome Syoutengai section (on the fourth floor of Tokyo Deck's "Seaside Mall" section), a remake of mid-1900s Japan, with crafts, food, and an old-fashioned games arcade, and the Daiba Little Hong Kong department with its Chinese accessories, souvenirs, and restaurants (on the sixth and seventh floors of the "Island Mall" section of Tokyo Decks).

Books

Yasukuni Dori in Jimbocho-Kanda (station: Jimbocho) is lined with bookstores selling both new and used books, with several dealing in English-language books. Remember, however, that English-language books are usually more expensive in Japan than back home. Still, no bibliophile should pass up this street. Stores are closed on Sunday; most are closed holidays as well. The largest English-language bookstore is **Kitazawa** (📞 **03/3263-0011**), on the second floor of Book House, boasting an overwhelming selection, including the most recently published novels, American and English-language classic literature, topical books ranging from history to politics, books on Japan, and antiquarian books. Nearby **Ohya Shobo** (📞 **03/3291-0062**), established in 1882, doesn't have any English-language books but it does claim to have the world's largest stock of 18th- and 19th-century Japanese illustrated books, woodblock prints, and maps, including maps from the Edo Period.

Kinokuniya This is one of Tokyo's best-known bookstores, with one of the city's largest selections of books and magazines in English—including books on Japan, dictionaries and textbooks for students of Japanese, and novels—on its sixth floor. Open daily 10am to 8pm; closed some Wednesdays. Takashimaya Annex, Takashimaya Times Sq. complex. 📞 03/5361-3301. Station: Shinjuku (south exit, 2 min.).

Maruzen This is Japan's oldest bookstore, founded in 1869 but now ensconced in the modern Oazo Building across from Tokyo Station's Marunouchi exit. Its English-language section, on the fourth floor, is huge and well laid out, with everything from dictionaries to travel guides to special-interest books on Japan. It also carries books on science, politics, and history, as well as magazines and paperbacks. If you're searching for a specific title, you'll probably want to come here first. Open daily 9am to 9pm. 1–6-4 Marunouchi. 📞 03/5288-8881. Station: Tokyo (1 min.). Take the Marunouchi exit from Tokyo Station and turn right (north); it's across the street.

Tower Records and Books My friends in Tokyo don't shop anywhere else for their books and magazines, as prices are usually lower here than elsewhere. The seventh floor is devoted to imported publications, with a good selection of English-language books, more than 3,000 different kinds of magazines, and—available via computer printout for a fee—more than 300 newspapers from around the world. Open daily 10am to 11pm. 1–22-14 Jinnan. 📞 03/3496-3661. Station: Shibuya (Hachiko exit, 5 min.).

Crafts & Traditional Japanese Products

If you want to shop for traditional Japanese folk crafts in a festival-like atmosphere, nothing beats **Nakamise Dori** (station: Asakusa), a pedestrian lane leading to Sensoji Temple in Asakusa. It's lined with stall after stall selling souvenirs galore, from wooden *geta* shoes and hairpins worn by geisha to T-shirts, fans, umbrellas, toy swords, and dolls. Most are open daily from 10am to 6pm; some may close 1 day a week.

Another good place to search for traditional crafts are **department stores,** which usually have sections devoted to ceramics, pottery, bambooware, flower-arranging accessories, and kimono.

Japan Sword Coming here is like visiting a museum. Established more than 100 years ago, this is the best-known sword shop in Tokyo, with a knowledgeable staff and an outstanding collection of fine swords, daggers, sword guards, fittings, and other sword accessories, as well as antique samurai armor. The place also sells copies and souvenir items of traditional swords at prices much lower than those of the very expensive historic swords. Note that antique and modern swords require permission to export, which takes about 2 weeks (the company can ship purchases to you), but you can take replicas with you—just be sure to pack them in checked bags. Open Monday to Friday 9:30am to 6pm, Saturday 9:30am to 5pm. Closed holidays. 3–8-1 Toranomon, Minato-ku. 📞 03/3434-4321. www.japansword.co.jp. Station: Toranomon (exit 2, 5 min.) or Kamiyacho (exit 3, 5 min.).

Established to distribute information on Japanese crafts and promote the country's artisans, this two-story center is a great introduction to both traditional and contemporary Japanese design, with explanations in English. It sells various top-quality crafts from all over Japan on a rotating basis, so there are always new items on hand. Crafts for sale may include lacquerware, ceramics, textiles, paper products, bamboo items, calligraphy brushes, fans, metalwork, knives, furniture, and sometimes even stone lanterns or Buddhist family altars. Prices are high, but rightfully so. Unfortunately, its location in out-of-the-way Ikebukuro makes a trip here feasible only if you have the time; otherwise, you're probably better off shopping in the crafts section of a department store. Open daily 11am to 7pm. 1st floor of Metropolitan Plaza Building, 1–11–1 Nishi-Ikebukuro. C 03/5954-6066. Station: Ikebukuro (1 min.).

Oriental Bazaar If you have time for only one souvenir shop in Tokyo, this should be it. This is the city's best-known and largest souvenir/crafts store, selling products at reasonable prices and offering four floors of souvenir and gift items, including cotton *yukata*, kimono (new and used), woodblock prints, paper products, fans, chopsticks, Imari chinaware, sake sets, Japanese dolls, pearls, books on Japan, and a large selection of antique furniture. This store will also ship things home for you. Open Friday to Wednesday 10am to 7pm. 5–9–13 Jingumae, Shibuya-ku. C 03/3400-3933. Station: Meiji-Jingumae (3 min.), Harajuku (4 min.), or Omotesando (5 min.). On Omotesando Dori in Harajuku; look for an Asian-looking facade of orange and green.

Sakai Kokodo Gallery This gallery claims to be the oldest woodblock print shop in Japan. It was first opened back in 1870 in the Kanda area of Tokyo by the present owner's great-grandfather; altogether four generations of the Sakai family have tended the store. It's a great place for original prints, as well as reproductions of great masters like Hiroshige. (If you're really a woodblock print fan, you'll want to visit the Sakai family's excellent **Japan Ukiyo-e Museum,** in the small town of Matsumoto in the Japan Alps.) Open daily 11am to 6pm. 1–2–14 Yurakucho, Chiyoda-ku (across from the Imperial Hotel's Tower). C 03/3591-4678. www.ukiyo-e.co.jp. Station: Hibiya (1 min.).

Department Stores

Japanese department stores are institutions in themselves. Usually enormous, well designed, and chock-full of merchandise, they have about everything you can imagine, including museums and art galleries, pet stores, rooftop playgrounds or greenhouses, travel agencies, restaurants, grocery markets, and flower shops. You could easily spend an entire day in a department store—eating, attending cultural exhibitions, planning your next vacation, having your neck massaged, and, well, shopping.

One of the most wonderful aspects of the Japanese department store is the **courteous service.** If you arrive at a store in the morning when it opens, you'll witness a daily rite: Lined up at the entrance are staff who bow in welcome. Some Japanese shoppers arrive just before opening time so as not to miss this favorite ritual. Sales clerks are everywhere, ready to help you. In some stores, you don't even have to go to the cash register once you've made your choice; just hand over the product, along with your money, to the sales clerk, who will return with your change, your purchase neatly wrapped, and an *"Arigato gozaimashita"* ("Thank you very much"). Many department stores will also ship your purchases home for you, send them to your hotel, or hold them until you're ready to leave the store. A day spent in a Japanese department store could spoil you for the rest of your life.

Many department stores include **boutiques** by such famous Japanese and international fashion designers as Issey Miyake, Rei Kawakubo (creator of Comme des Garçons), Hanae Mori, Takeo Kikuchi, Vivienne Westwood, and Paul Smith, as well as a department devoted to the kimono. Near the **kimono department** may also be the section devoted to **traditional crafts,** including *ikebana* vases, pottery, and lacquerware. Many famous **restaurants** maintain branches in department stores, but not to be missed is the basement (nicknamed a *depachika,* which is a combination *depa*—from department store—and *chika,* meaning basement), where you'll find one or two levels devoted to **foodstuffs:** fresh fish, produce, green tea, sake, prepared snacks and dinners, and delectable pastries. There are often free samples of food; if you're hungry, walking through the food department could do nicely for a snack.

To find out what's where, stop by the store's information booth located on the ground floor near the front entrance and ask for the floor-by-floor English-language pamphlet. Be sure, too, to ask about **sales** on the promotional floor—you never know what bargains you may chance upon.

Hours are generally daily from 10 or 10:30am to 8 or 9pm. Department stores used to close 1 day a week, but now they rarely close, or close irregularly on the same day of the week (say, on Tues) but in no apparent pattern. One month they may be closed the second and third Tuesday of the month, but the next month only the first or not at all. In any case, you can always find department stores that are open, even on Sundays and holidays (major shopping days in Japan).

Isetan With a history stretching 120 years and attracting more than 30 million customers a year, Isetan is a favorite among foreigners living in Tokyo. Now part of the Isetan-Mitsukoshi conglomerate, it has a good line of conservative work clothes, as well as contemporary and fashionable styles, including designer goods by Issey Miyake, Yohji Yamamoto, Hanae Mori, Comme des Garçons, Marc Jacobs, and Salvatore Ferragamo, as well as large dress sizes (on the second floor). It has a great kimono section along with all the traditional accessories (*obi,* shoes, purses). Its basement food hall is legendary, with its dessert and massive chocolate sections an especially illuminating commentary on Japan's obsession with food. An annex offers eight floors of men's clothing and accessories. Open daily 10am to 8pm. 3-14-1 Shinjuku, Shinjuku-ku. © **03/3352-1111.** Station: Shinjuku Sanchome (1 min.) or Shinjuku (east exit, 6 min.). On Shinjuku Dori, east of Shinjuku Station.

Matsuya Ginza This is one of my favorite department stores in Tokyo; if I were buying a wedding gift, Matsuya is one of the first places I'd look. It has a good selection of Japanese folk crafts items, kitchenware, kimono, and beautifully designed contemporary household goods, in addition to the usual designer clothes and accessories ("queen" sizes are on the sixth floor). I always make a point of stopping by the seventh floor's Design Collection, which displays items from around the world selected by the Japan Design Committee as examples of fine design, from the Alessi teapot to Braun razors. Two basement floors are devoted to food. Open daily 10am to 8pm. There's a branch in Asakusa at 1–41–1 Hanakawado (© **03/3842-1111;** daily 10am–7:30pm). 3–6–1 Ginza, Chuo-ku. © **03/3567-1211.** Station: Ginza (2 min.). On Chuo Dori, just a long block north of Ginza 4–chome Crossing.

Mitsukoshi This Nihombashi department store is one of Japan's oldest and grandest, founded in 1673 by the Mitsui family as a kimono store. In 1683, it became the first store in the world to deal only in cash sales; it was also one of the first stores in Japan to display goods on shelves rather than have merchants fetch bolts of cloth for each

customer, as was the custom of the time. Today, housed in a building dating from 1914,
it remains one of Tokyo's loveliest department stores, with a beautiful and stately Renaissance-style facade and an entrance guarded by two bronze lions, replicas of the lions in Trafalgar Square. The store carries many name-brand boutiques, from Chanel to Christian Dior. Its kimono, by the way, are still hot items. Open daily 10am to 8pm. Another branch, located at Ginza 4–chome Crossing (© **03/3562-1111;** open daily 10am–8pm), is popular with young shoppers. 1–4–1 Nihombashi Muromachi, Chuo-ku. © **03/3241-3311.** Station: Mitsukoshimae (1 min.).

Seibu   Once the nation's largest department store—and still one of the biggest—Seibu has 47 entrances, thousands of sales clerks, dozens of restaurants, 12 floors, 31 elevators, and more than 100,000 shoppers a day. Two basement floors are devoted to foodstuffs—you can buy everything from taco shells to octopus to seaweed there. Dishes are set out so you can nibble the food as you move along, and hawkers yelling out their wares give the place a marketlike atmosphere. Fast-food counters sell salads, grilled eel, chicken, sushi, and other ready-to-eat dishes. The rest of the floors offer clothing, furniture, art galleries, kitchenware, and a million other things. Loft, Seibu's department for household goods and interior design, and Wave, Seibu's CD department, occupy the top four floors of the main building. Many of the best Japanese and Western designers have boutiques here; it also carries large, tall, and petite sizes.

There's another Seibu in **Ginza** near the elevated tracks of the JR Yamanote Line (© **03/3286-0111;** open Mon–Wed 11:30am–8:30pm, Thurs–Fri 11:30am–9pm, Sat 11am–9pm, Sun 11am–8:30pm; station: Yurakucho). It specializes mostly in women's clothing and accessories, from casual to formal wear. Also look for Seibu in **Shibuya** at 21–1 Udagawacho (© **03/3462-0111;** open Sun–Wed 10am–8pm, Thurs–Sat 10am–9pm; station: Shibuya, Hachiko exit). Similar to the main store in Ikebukuro, this Seibu consists of two buildings connected by pedestrian skywalks, with lots of designer boutiques like Issey Miyake, Comme des Garçons, Tsumori Chisato, Vivienne Westwood, and Vivienne Tam. Nearby are Loft, with household goods, and Movida, a fashion department store with fun young fashions for waifs.

Open Monday to Saturday 10am to 9pm, Sunday 10am to 8pm. 1–28–1 Minami Ikebukuro, Toshima-ku. © **03/3981-0111.** Station: Ikebukuro (underneath the store).

Takashimaya   This department store has always provided stiff competition for Mitsukoshi, with a history just as long. It was founded as a kimono shop in Kyoto during the Edo Period and opened in Tokyo in 1933. Today it's one of the city's most attractive department stores, with a Renaissance-style building and gloved elevator operators whisking customers to eight floors of shopping and dining. Naturally, it features boutiques by such famous designers as Chanel, Louis Vuitton, Gucci, Issey Miyake, and more. Its sale of used kimono (look for advertisements in the *Japan Times*) draws huge crowds, even more than the usual 35,000 daily customers.

A branch, **Takashimaya Shinjuku,** 5–24–2 Sendaygaya, Shinjuku (© **03/53610111;** open daily 10am–8pm; station: Shinjuku), has been the number-one draw in Shinjuku since its 1996 opening. Much larger than Takashimaya's Nihombashi flagship, this huge complex boasts 10 floors of clothing and restaurants (lower floors target affluent seniors, while upper floors appeal to younger shoppers and families; petite and "queen-size" clothing are on the sixth floor). There's also Tokyu Hands with everything imaginable for the home hobbyist, and Kinokuniya bookstore with English-language books on the sixth floor. Open daily 10am to 8pm. 2–4–1 Nihombashi (on Chuo Dori Ave.), Chuo-ku. © **03/3211-4111.** Station: Nihombashi (1 min.).

6

SHOPPING

Wako   This is one of Ginza's smallest department stores but also one of its classiest, housed in one of the few area buildings that survived World War II. It was erected in 1932 by the Hattori family, founders of the Seiko watch company, and is famous for its distinctive clock tower, graceful curved facade, and innovative window displays. The store's ground floor carries a wide selection of Seiko watches and handbags, while the upper floors carry imported and domestic fashions and luxury items with prices to match. It caters to older, well-to-do customers; you won't find hordes of young Japanese girls shopping here. Open Monday to Saturday 10:30am to 6pm; closed holidays. 4–5–11 Ginza (at Ginza 4–chome Crossing), Chuo-ku. ℂ 03/3562-2111. Station: Ginza (1 min.).

Electronics/Anime

The largest concentration of electronics and electrical-appliance shops in Japan is in an area of Tokyo called **Akihabara,** also known simply as Akiba and centered around Chuo Dori (station: Akihabara). Although you can find good deals on video and audio equipment elsewhere (especially just west of Shinjuku Station, where Yodobashi dominates with several stores devoted to electronics), Akihabara is a must-see simply for its sheer volume. With hundreds of multilevel stores, shops, and stalls, Akihabara accounts for one-tenth of the nation's electronics and electrical-appliance sales. An estimated 50,000 shoppers come here on a weekday, 100,000 per day on a weekend. Even if you don't buy anything, it's great fun walking around. Most of the stores and stalls are open-fronted, and many are painted neon green and pink. Salespeople yell out their wares, trying to get customers to look at their cellular phones, computers, video equipment, digital cameras, MP3 players, TVs, calculators, watches, and rice cookers. This is the best place to see the latest models of everything electronic; it's an educational experience in itself.

If you do intend to buy, make sure you know what the item would cost back home. Or, you may be able to pick up something that's unavailable back home. Be sure to bargain and don't buy at the first place you hit. One woman I know who was looking for a portable music device bought it at the third shop she went to for ¥4,000 less than what was quoted to her at the first shop. Make sure, too, that whatever you purchase is made for export—that is, with instructions in English, an international warranty, and the proper electrical connectors. All the larger stores have duty-free floors where products are made for export, and most shops are open daily from about 10am to 8pm or later.

The largest store here is **Yodobashi Akiba,** just east of JR Akihabara Station at 1–1 Hanaoka-cho (ℂ 03/5209-1010; open daily 9:30am–10pm), which offers a staggering number of electronic-related goods such as cameras, computers, TVs, and rice cookers, but it also offers a slew of other leisure-related items like games and bicycles (some people fear this monolith will put independent Akiba shop owners out of business). Other reputable stores, with English-speaking staff and models for export, include **Laox,** 15–3 Soto-Kanda (ℂ 03/3255-5301), and **AKKY International,** 1–12–5 Soto-Kanda (ℂ 03/5207-5027), both on Chuo Dori (the latter store also with Japanese souvenirs in its basement). If you're serious about buying, check these stores first.

In recent years, Akihabara has also earned a reputation as *the* place to shop for *manga* (Japanese comic books and graphic novels), items related to *anime* (Japanese animation) and *cosplay* (short for "costume play," or dress-up clothes). Anime fans should make a point of stopping by the free **Tokyo Anime Center,** just north of the JR Akihabara Station on the fourth floor of UDX (ℂ 03/5298-1188; www.animecenter.jp; open Tues–Sun 11am–7pm), with an information desk, a merchandise shop, and a 3-D theater (admission charged for theater only).

One of the best anime/manga chain stores in Japan is **Mandarake,** with a shop in Akihabara about 4 minutes from JR Akihabara Station at 3–11–2 Soto-Kanda (📞 **03/3252-7007;** www.mandrake.co.jp; open daily noon–8pm). This sleek black building offers eight floors of both new and secondhand goods, including pop and vintage figurines, video games, manga, and posters. **Kotobukiya,** conveniently located across from JR Akihabara Station in the Radio Kaikan Building at 1–15–16 Soto-Kanda (📞 **03/5298-6300;** open daily 10am–8pm), sells stuffed anime characters, movie props, and figurines (some of them definitely X-rated). It's also worth popping into �37 **Don Quijote** on Chuo Dori at 4–3–3 Soto-Kanda (📞 **03/5298-5411;** www.donki.com; open daily 10am–5am), which has to be seen to appreciate its jumble of everyday goods too numerous to mention, including maid costumes and even a maid cafe (I don't even want to get into why these are so popular) on the fifth floor.

For more information on Akihabara, go to **www.akihabara-tour.com**. At press time, free 2-hour tours of Akihabara were offered two Saturdays a month at 1pm, but check the site for current schedules.

Cameras

You can purchase cameras at many duty-free shops, including those in Akihabara, but if you're serious about photographic equipment, make a trip to a shop dealing specifically in cameras, including Akihabara's **Yodobashi Akiba,** above. If a new camera is too formidable an expense, consider buying a used camera. New models come out so frequently that older models can be snapped up for next to nothing.

Bic Camera   This huge, eight-floor store near Ginza offers not only single-lens reflex, large and medium format, and digital cameras, but also computers, DVD and MP3 players, camcorders, watches, toys, and much more. Note, however, that it caters primarily to Japanese; English-speaking sales clerks are scarce, and export models are limited. Ask for the English-language brochure, and if you're buying sensitive equipment, make sure it will work outside Japan and comes with English-language instructions. Open daily 10am to 10pm. There's a branch in Shibuya at 1–24–12 Shibuya (📞 **03/5466-1111;** open daily 10am–8pm; station: Shibuya, 2 min.). 1–11–1 Yurakucho, Chiyoda-ku. 📞 **03/5221-1112.** Station: Yurakucho (1 min.).

�38 **Lemon**   Its name doesn't inspire confidence, but this company specializes in used and new cameras and lenses from around the world. On the eighth floor are both new and used Japanese and foreign cameras, including digital cameras and large-format models. Leica, Hasselblad, Rolleiflex, Canon, Pentax, and Nikon are just some of the brands available, along with watches and eyeglasses. A camera buff's paradise. Open Monday to Saturday 11am to 8pm, Sunday 11am to 5pm. 4–2–2 Ginza, Chuo-ku. 📞 **03/3567-3131.** Station: Ginza (1 min.). In a green glazed-brick building also housing the Ginza Methodist Church.

Yodobashi Camera   Shinjuku is the photographic equipment center for Tokyo, and this store, 1 block west of the station, is the biggest in the area. It ranks as one of the largest discount camera shops in the world (though the new Yodobashi in Akihabara, above, now surpasses it), with around 30,000 items in stock, and it reputedly sells approximately 500 to 600 cameras daily. Prices are marked, but you can bargain here. In addition to cameras, it sells watches, calculators, computers, and other electronic equipment, though if you're interested specifically in watches, clocks, audio/video equipment, games, and other wares, nearby branches specialize in all of these (ask the main shop for a map of shops in the area). Open daily 9:30am to 10pm. 1–11–1 Nishi-Shinjuku, Shinjuku-ku. 📞 **03/3346-1010.** Station: Shinjuku (west exit, 3 min.).

The **department stores** and **shopping malls** listed earlier are all good places to check out the latest trends. For inexpensive, basic clothing (think Japanese version of Gap), look for one of the 40 **Uniqlo** shops in Tokyo selling T-shirts, jeans, socks, shirts, and other clothing for the entire family. A convenient location is 5–7–7 Ginza, on Chuo Dori (*C* 03/5569-6781; station: Ginza). Another popular chain, selling cotton clothing in basic colors, is **Muji**, with its flagship located next to the Tourist Information Center at 3–8–3 Marunouchi (*C* 03/5208-8241; station: Yurakucho).

Otherwise, Harajuku and Shibuya are the places to go for hundreds of small shops selling inexpensive designer knockoffs, as well as fashion department stores—multistoried buildings filled with concessions of various designers and labels. The stores below are two of the best known and largest.

La Forêt This is not only the largest store in Harajuku but also one of the most fashionable, appealing mostly to teenage and 20-something shoppers. Young and upcoming Japanese designers are here as well as established names, in boutiques spread on several floors. There's so much to see—from pink frilly dresses to Goth—you can easily kill a few hours here. Open daily 11am to 8pm. 1–11–6 Jingumae, Shibuya-ku. *C* 03/3475-0411. Station: Meiji-Jingumae (1 min.) or Harajuku (3 min.). On Meiji Dori, just off Harajuku's main intersection of Omotesando Dori and Meiji Dori.

Parco A division of Seibu, Parco is actually two buildings clustered together and called Parco Part 1 and Part 3 (Part 2 recently closed). Parco Part 1 is the place to go for designer boutiques for men and women, with clothes by Japanese designers such as Yohji Yamamoto and Tsumori Chisato and foreign designers including Anna Sui and Vivienne Westwood, while Part 3 is devoted to casual, young fashions. Parco has two sales a year that you shouldn't miss if you're in town—one in January and one in July. Open daily 10am to 9pm. 15–1 Udagawacho, Shibuya-ku. *C* 03/3464-5111. Station: Shibuya (Hachiko exit, 4 min.)

Designer Boutiques

Ginza is home to international designer names, including Prada, Cartier, Chanel, Christian Dior, and Louis Vuitton. For top Japanese designers, the block between Omotesando Crossing and the Nezu Museum (currently undergoing renovation) in **Aoyama** (station: Omotesando) is the Rodeo Drive of Japan. Even if you can't buy here (steep prices for most pocketbooks), a stroll is de rigueur for clothes hounds and those interested in design. Most shops are open daily from 11am to 8pm.

Issey Miyake (*C* 03/3423-1408), on the left side as you walk from Aoyama Dori, offers two floors of cool, spacious displays of Miyake's interestingly structured designs for men and women. (His very popular Pleats Please line is around the corner on Aoyama Dori, 3–13–21 Minami Aoyama; *C* 03/5772-7750.) Across the street is **Comme des Garçons** (*C* 03/3406-3951), Rei Kawakubo's showcase for her daring—and constantly evolving—men's and women's designs. The goddess of Japanese fashion and one of the few females in the business when she started, Kawakubo has remained on the cutting edge of design for more than 2 decades. Of the many non-Japanese designers to have invaded this trendy neighborhood in recent years, none stands out as much as **Prada** (*C* 03/6418-0400), a bubble of convex/concave windows on the right side of the street. One of Japan's newer designers, **Tsumori Chisato**, has a shop on the left side of the street (*C* 03/3423-5170). Also worth seeking out is **Yohji Yamamoto** on the right (*C* 03/3409-6006), where Yamamoto's unique, classically wearable clothes are sparingly hung, flaunting the avant-garde interior space.

On the other side of Aoyama Dori, on Omotesando Dori, is **Hanae Mori** (© 03/3400-3301), the grande dame of Japanese design, with everything from separates and men's golf wear to haute couture and wedding gowns on display on three floors of a building designed by Japanese architect Kenzo Tange.

Flea Markets

Flea markets are good places to shop for antiques as well as for delightful junk. You can pick up secondhand kimono at very reasonable prices, as well as kitchenware, vases, cast-iron teapots, small chests, woodblock prints, dolls, household items, and odds and ends. (Don't expect to find any good buys in furniture.) The markets usually begin as early as dawn or 6am and last until 3 or 4pm or so, but go early if you want to pick up bargains. Bargaining is expected. Note that since most markets are outdoors, they tend to be canceled if it rains.

Togo Shrine, 1–5–3 Jingumae, on Meiji Dori in Harajuku (near Meiji-Jingumae and Harajuku stations), has a small antiques market on the first Sunday of every month from 6am to 2pm. It's great for used kimono and curios and is one of my favorites. For more information, see the walking tour of Harajuku and Aoyama earlier in this chapter.

Nogi Shrine, a 1-minute walk from Nogizaka Station at 8–11–27 Akasaka, has an antiques flea market from dawn to about 2pm the second Sunday of each month except November. It has a lovely setting; the shrine commemorates General Nogi and his wife, both of whom committed suicide on September 13, 1912, to follow the Meiji emperor into the afterlife. Their simple home and stable are on shrine grounds.

Hanazono Shrine, 5–17–3 Shinjuku, near the Yasukuni Dori/Meiji Dori intersection east of Shinjuku Station (a 5-min. walk from Shinjuku Sanchome Station), has a flea market every Sunday from dawn to about 2pm (except in May and Nov due to festivals).

Yasukuni Shrine, a 3-minute walk from Kudanshita Station at 3–1–1 Kudanshita, holds a flea market every Sunday from 6am to about 3pm on the long walkway to this very famous shrine (see earlier in this chapter for information on the shrine and its military museum).

The **Oedo Antique Fair,** held at 3–5–1 Marunouchi in the courtyard of the Tokyo International Forum beside Yurakucho Station, claims to be the largest outdoor antiques market in Japan (it has also taken away vendors from Tokyo's other flea markets). Held the first and third Sunday of the month from 9am to 5pm, it features Western antiques (at highly inflated prices), as well as Japanese glassware, furniture, ceramics, furniture, kimono, woodblock prints, and odds and ends. If you hit only one flea market, this should be it.

Finally, the closest thing Tokyo has to a permanent flea market is **Ameya Yokocho** (also referred to as Ameyoko, Ameyokocho, or Ameyacho), a narrow street near Ueno Park that runs along and underneath the elevated tracks of the JR Yamanote Line between Ueno and Okachimachi stations. There are about 400 stalls here selling discounted items ranging from vegetables and cosmetics to handbags, tennis shoes, watches, and casual clothes. The scene retains something of the *shitamachi* spirit of old Tokyo. Although housewives have been coming here for years, young Japanese recently discovered the market as a good bargain spot for fashions, accessories, and cosmetics. Some shops close on Wednesdays, but hours are usually daily from 10am to 7pm; early evening is the most crowded time. Don't even think of coming here on a holiday—it's a standstill pedestrian traffic jam.

Kimono

Chicago, on Omotesando Dori in Harajuku (© **03/3409-5017;** station: Meiji-Jingu-mae or Harajuku), is a good place for used kimono. It stocks hundreds of affordable used kimono, cotton *yukata* (casual kimono), and *obi* (sashes) back in the far left corner of the basement shop, past the used American clothes. It's open daily from 11am to 8pm. The nearby **Oriental Bazaar** (p. 211) also has a decent selection of new and used kimono at affordable prices, including elaborate wedding kimono. On weekends and holidays, there's a **secondhand kimono stand** on the corner of Meiji Dori and Omotesando Dori in Harajuku from 11am to 5pm, with very good prices.

In addition, department stores sell new kimono, notably **Takashimaya** and **Mitsuko-shi** in Nihombashi and **Isetan** in Shinjuku. They also hold sales for rental wedding kimono. Flea markets are also good for used kimono and yukata, particularly the antiques market at **Togo Shrine.**

Established in 1913, **Hayashi Kimono** (© **03/3501-4012**), in the International Arcade (near the Imperial Hotel under the elevated JR Yamamote train tracks; station: Hibiya), sells all manner of kimono, including antique kimono, yukata, and *tanzen* (the heavy winter overcoat that goes over the yukata), as well as used and antique kimono. If you're buying a gift for someone back home, this is a good place to start. Open daily from 10am to 7pm (to 6pm on Sun).

Kitchenware & Tableware

In addition to the department stores listed earlier, the best place to shop for items related to cooking and serving is **Kappabashi-dougugai Dori** (station: Tawaramachi), popularly known as Kappabashi; this is Japan's largest wholesale area for cookware. There are approximately 150 specialty stores here selling cookware, including sukiyaki pots, woks, lunch boxes, pots and pans, aprons, knives, china, lacquerware, rice cookers, plastic food (the kind you see in restaurant display cases), *noren* (Japanese curtains), and disposable wooden chopsticks in bulk. Although stores are wholesalers selling mainly to restaurants, you're welcome to browse and purchase as well. Stores are closed on Sunday but are otherwise open from about 10am to 5pm.

Pearls

Mikimoto, on Chuo Dori not far from Ginza 4-chome Crossing, past Wako department store (© **03/3535-54611;** station: Ginza), is Japan's most famous pearl shop. It was founded by Mikimoto Koichi, the first to produce a really good cultured pearl, in 1905. Open Thursday to Tuesday 11am to 7pm. Also, there's a Mikimoto branch (© **03/3591-5001**) in the **Imperial Hotel Arcade,** under the Imperial Hotel (station: Hibiya), where you'll also find **Asahi Shoten** (© **03/3503-2528**), with a good selection in the moderate price range; and **Uyeda Jeweller** (© **03/3503-2587**), with a wide selection of pearls in many price ranges.

10 TOKYO AFTER DARK

By day, Tokyo is arguably one of the least attractive cities in the world. Come dusk, however, Tokyo comes into its own. The drabness fades, the city blossoms into a profusion of giant neon lights and paper lanterns, and its streets fill with millions of overworked Japanese out to have a good time. If you ask me, Tokyo at night is one of the craziest cities in the world, a city that never gives up and never seems to sleep. Entertainment districts are as crowded at 3am as they are at 10pm, with many establishments open until the first subways start running after 5am. Whether it's jazz, reggae, gay bars, sex shows, dance clubs, mania, or madness that you're searching for, Tokyo has it all.

GETTING TO KNOW THE SCENE   Tokyo has several nightlife districts spread throughout the city, each with its own atmosphere, price range, and clientele. Most famous are probably **Kabuki-cho** in Shinjuku, and **Roppongi.** Before visiting any of the locales suggested below, be sure to just walk around one of these neighborhoods and absorb the atmosphere. The streets will be crowded, the neon lights will be overwhelming, and you never know what you might discover on your own.

Although there are many bars, dance clubs, and nightclubs packed with young Japanese of both sexes, nightlife in Japan for the older generations is still pretty much a man's domain, just as it has been for centuries. At the high end of this domain are the **geisha bars,** concentrated primarily in Kyoto. All Japanese cities, however, have so-called **hostess bars;** in Tokyo these are concentrated in Ginza, Roppongi, Shinjuku, and Akasaka. A woman will sit at your table, talk to you, pour your drinks, listen to your problems, and boost your ego. You buy her drinks as well, which is one reason the tab can be so high. Hostess bars in various forms have been a part of Japanese society for centuries. Most foreign visitors find the cost of visiting a hostess bar not worth the price, as hostesses usually speak Japanese only, but such places provide Japanese males with sympathetic ears and the chance to escape the world of both work and family. Men usually have their favorite hostess bar, often a small place with just enough room for regular customers. In the more exclusive hostess bars, only those customers with an introduction are allowed entrance.

The most popular nightlife spots are **drinking establishments,** where the vast majority of Japan's office workers, college students, and expatriates go for an evening out. These places include Western-style bars as well as Japanese-style watering holes, called *nomi-ya. Yakitori-ya,* restaurant-bars that serve yakitori and other snacks, are included in this group. Dancing and live-music venues are also hugely popular with young Tokyoites. At the low end of the spectrum are Tokyo's topless bars, strip shows, massage parlors, and porn shops, with the largest concentration of such places in Shinjuku's **Kabuki-cho District.**

In addition to the establishments listed below, be sure to check the restaurants listed in the inexpensive category under "Where to Dine" in chapter 5 for a relatively cheap night out on the town. Many places serve as both eateries and watering holes, especially yakitori-ya.

EXTRA CHARGES & TAXES   One more thing you should be aware of is the **"table charge"** imposed on customers by some bars (especially *nomiya*) and many cocktail lounges. Included in the table charge is usually a small appetizer—maybe nuts, chips, or a vegetable; for this reason, some locales call it an *otsumami,* or snack charge. At any rate, the charge is usually between ¥300 and ¥500 per person. Some establishments levy a table charge only after a certain time in the evening; others may add it only if you don't order food from the menu. If you're not sure and it matters to you, be sure to ask before you order anything. Remember, too, that there's a 5% consumption tax, though most menus already include it in their price. Some higher-end establishments, especially nightclubs, hostess bars, and dance clubs, will add a service charge ranging anywhere from 10% to 20%.

FINDING OUT WHAT'S ON   Keep an eye out for *Metropolis* (www.metropolis.co.jp), a free weekly that carries a nightlife section covering concerts, theaters, and events and is available at bars, restaurants, and other venues around town. The *Japan Times* and *Daily Yomiuri* also have entertainment sections.

GETTING TICKETS   If you're staying in a higher-end hotel, the concierge or guest-relations manager can usually get tickets for you. Otherwise, you can head to the theater or hall itself. An easier way is to go through one of many ticket services available such as **Ticket PIA,** which has outlets on the first floor of the Sony Building in Ginza, the Isetan department store annex in Shinjuku, and many other locations in Tokyo (ask your hotel concierge for the nearest one).

THE PERFORMING ARTS

For descriptions of Japanese traditional performance arts such as *kabuki* and *noh,* see "Japanese Arts in a Nutshell," in chapter 2. In addition to the performance art listings below, Tokyo also has occasional shows of more avant-garde or lesser-known performance art productions, including highly stylized Butoh dance performances from such companies as Sankai Juku and percussion demonstrations by Kodo drummers and other Japanese drum groups. See one of the publications listed above for complete listings.

KABUKI   One of Japan's most prestigious theaters for kabuki is **Kabuki-za,** 4–12–15 Ginza, which unfortunately closed for demolition in April 2010, with an expected resurrection in a new building in 2013. Although I lament the destruction of the handsome older structure influenced by 16th-century castle architecture, the new theater will undoubtedly incorporate the usual kabuki stage fittings, including a platform that can be raised above and lowered below the stage for dramatic appearances and disappearances of actors, a revolving stage, and a runway stage extending into the audience.

In any case, until the Kabuki-za's reopening, kabuki performances will be held at the nearby **Shinbashi Enbujo Theater,** 6–18–2 Ginza (© **03/3541-2600** or 5565-6000 for advance reservations; www.shochiku.co.jp/play/kabukiza/theater; station: Higashi-Ginza), as well as other venues in town. Shochiku, a major film and production company that also serves as Tokyo's chief kabuki production company, stages about eight or nine kabuki productions a year. Each production begins its run between the first and third of each month and runs about 25 days (there are no shows in Aug). Usually, two different programs are shown; matinees run from about 11 or 11:30am to 4pm, and evening performances run from about 4:30 or 5pm to about 9pm. It's considered perfectly okay to come for only part of a performance. Of course, you won't be able to understand what's being said, but that doesn't matter; the productions themselves are great entertainment. For an outline of the plot, you should rent **English-language earphones** for ¥650, plus a ¥1,000 refundable deposit—these provide a running commentary on the story, music, actors, stage properties, and other aspects of kabuki. Renting earphones will add immensely to your enjoyment of the play.

Tickets generally range from ¥2,500 to ¥17,000, depending on the program and seat location. Advance tickets can be purchased at the theater box office daily 10am to 6pm. You may also make advance reservations by phone (same-day bookings are not accepted). Otherwise, tickets for each day's performance are placed on sale 1 hour before the start of each performance.

Another venue for kabuki is the **National Theatre of Japan (Kokuritsu Gekijo),** 4–1 Hayabusacho, Chiyoda-ku (© **03/3230-3000;** www.ntj.jac.go.jp; station: Hanzomon, 6 min.). Kabuki is scheduled throughout the year except during February, May, August, and September, when *bunraku* (see below) is staged. Matinees usually begin at 11:30am or noon, and afternoon performances at 4:30pm. Most tickets range from about ¥1,500 to ¥8,500, with earphones available for ¥700 plus a ¥1,000 deposit. Tickets can be purchased at the box office (daily 10am–6pm), by phone, or online.

NOH   *Noh* is performed at a number of locations in Tokyo, but most famous is the **National Noh Theater (Kokuritsu Nohgakudo),** 4–18–1 Sendagaya, Shibuya-ku (© 03/3423-1331 or 3230-3000 for reservations; www.ntj.jac.go.jp; station: Sendagaya, 5 min.). Opened in 1983, it is dedicated to presenting classical noh and *kyogen,* with about three to five performances monthly. Tickets range from about ¥2,600 to ¥4,800 but are often sold out in advance. However, about 30 tickets are held back to be sold on the day of the performance. In addition, privately sponsored noh performances are also held here, for which the admission varies. Check the *Japan Times* or *Daily Yomiuri* for performance dates and times, or go to www.theatrenohgaku.org for information on noh performances being staged throughout Japan.

BUNRAKU   Although the main *bunraku* theater in Japan is in Osaka, the **National Theatre of Japan** (see above for information) stages about four bunraku plays a year (in Feb, May, Aug, and Sept). There are usually two to three performances daily, beginning at 11am, with tickets costing ¥1,500 to ¥6,500. Earphones with English-language explanations are available for ¥550, plus a ¥1,000 deposit.

TAKARAZUKA KAGEKIDAN   This world-famous, all-female troupe stages elaborate musical revues with dancing, singing, and gorgeous costumes. Performances range from Japanese versions of Broadway hits to original Japanese works based on local legends. The first Takarazuka troupe, formed in 1912 at a resort near Osaka, gained instant notoriety because all its performers were women, in contrast to the all-male kabuki. When I went to see this troupe perform, I was surprised to find that the audience also consisted almost exclusively of women; indeed, the troupe has an almost cultlike following.

Performances, with story synopses available in English, are generally held in March, April, July, August, November, December, and sometimes in June, at **Tokyo Takarazuka Gekijo,** 1–1–3 Yurakucho (© **03/5251-2001;** www.kageki.hankyu.co.jp/english; station: Hibiya, 1 min.). Tickets, available at the box office or through **Ticket Pia,** usually range about ¥3,500 to ¥11,000.

SHOW NIGHTCLUBS ★   For unique, casual entertainment, nothing beats an evening at an entertainment nightclub, featuring fast-paced dancing in intimate venues. Although the emcee may speak Japanese only, no translation is necessary for the stage productions, which center on easy-to-understand themes or include humorous antics. One of the oldest show nightclubs is **Kingyo,** 3–14–17 Roppongi (© **03/3478-3000;** www.kingyo.co.jp; station: Roppongi, 4 min.), which stages one of the most high-energy, visually charged acts I've seen—nonstop action of ascending and receding stages and stairs, fast-paced choreography, elaborate costumes, and loud music. There are a few female dancers, but most of the dancers are males assuming female parts, just like in kabuki. It's located in the Roppongi nightlife district near the Roppongi cemetery. (From Roppongi Crossing, walk toward Tokyo Tower on Gaien-Higashi Dori and take the second left; it's on the right.) Cover is ¥3,500 for shows at 7:30 and 10pm, with additional shows Friday and Saturday at 1:15am (closed Sun–Mon; reservations recommended). You are required to purchase one drink and one food item, and there's a 20% tax and service charge. Or, you can opt for admission packages that include a set meal and drinks beginning at ¥6,000.

I also like **Show Dining Konparuza,** 8–7–5 Ginza (© **03/6215-8593;** station: Ginza or Shimbashi), also with moving stages and with lively choreography by Makato-san, who also performs. Productions change twice a year, but there's always a traditional number with dancers dressed in kimono, along with performances that act out popular songs or movies. Doors open daily at 6pm, with the first show at 7:30pm. Cover charge is ¥3,000, plus a minimum of one drink and one food purchase. Alternatively, there's an all-you-can-drink set that includes three dishes and the cover charge for ¥5,800.

THE CLUB & MUSIC SCENE
The Major Entertainment Districts

GINZA   A chic and expensive shopping area by day, Ginza transforms itself into a dazzling entertainment district of restaurants, bars, and first-grade hostess bars at night. It's the most sophisticated of Tokyo's nightlife districts and is also one of the most expensive. Some of the Japanese businessmen you see out carousing in Ginza are paying by expense account; prices can be ridiculously high. Because I'm not wealthy, I prefer Shinjuku and Roppongi. However, because Ginza does have some fabulous restaurants and several hotels, I've included some reasonably priced recommendations for a drink in the area if you happen to find yourself here after dinner. The cheapest way to absorb the atmosphere in Ginza is simply to wander about, particularly around **Namiki Dori** and its side streets.

SHINJUKU   Northeast of Shinjuku Station is an area called **Kabuki-cho,** which undoubtedly has the craziest nightlife in all of Tokyo, with block after block of strip joints, massage parlors, pornography shops, peep shows, bars, restaurants, and, as the night wears on, lots of drunk revelers. A world of its own, it's sleazy, chaotic, crowded, vibrant, and fairly safe. Despite its name, Shinjuku's primary night hot spot has nothing to do with kabuki. At one time, there was a plan to bring some culture to the area by introducing a kabuki theater; the plan never materialized but the name stuck. Although Kabuki-cho used to be the domain of businessmen out on the town, nowadays young Japanese, including college-age men and women, have claimed parts of it as their own; the result is a growing number of inexpensive drinking and live-music venues well worth a visit.

To the east of Kabuki-cho, just west of Hanazono Shrine, is a smaller district called **Goruden Gai,** which is "Golden Guy" mispronounced. It's a warren of tiny alleyways leading past even tinier bars, each consisting of just a counter and a few chairs. Many of these closet-size bars are closed to outsiders, catering to regular customers, though others welcome strangers as well. Although many thought Goruden Gai would succumb to land-hungry developers in the 1980s, the economic recession brought a stay of execution and now Goruden Gai has experienced a revival, with more than 100 tiny drinking dens lining the tiny streets. Still, it occupies such expensive land that I still fear for the life of this tiny enclave, one of Tokyo's most fascinating.

Even farther east is **Shinjuku Ni-chome** (pronounced "*nee*-chomay"), officially recognized as the gay-bar district of Shinjuku. Its lively street scene of mostly gays and some straights of all ages (but mostly young) make this one of the most vibrant nightlife districts. It's here that I was once taken to a host bar featuring young men in crotchless pants. The clientele included both gay men and groups of young, giggling office girls. That place has since closed down, but Shinjuku is riddled with other spots bordering on the absurd.

The best thing to do in Shinjuku is to simply walk about. In the glow of neon light, you'll pass everything from smoke-filled restaurants to hawkers trying to get you to step

(Tips) **Mapping Out Tokyo's Nightlife**

Once you've chosen a nightlife spot that appeals to you, you can locate it using the following neighborhood maps:

- To locate bars and clubs in **Akasaka,** p. 128.
- To locate bars and clubs in **Shinjuku,** p. 136.
- To locate bars and clubs in **Asakusa,** p. 141.
- To locate bars and clubs in **Ginza and Hibiya,** p. 150.
- To locate bars and clubs in **Harajuku,** p. 165.
- To locate bars and clubs in **Roppongi,** p. 171.

inside so they can part you from your money. If you're looking for strip joints, topless or bottomless coffee shops, peep shows, or porn, I leave you to your own devices, but you certainly won't have any problems finding them. In Kabuki-cho alone there are an estimated 200 sex businesses in operation, including bathhouses where women are available for sex at a high price. Although prostitution is illegal in Japan, everyone seems to ignore what goes on behind closed doors. Just be sure you know what you're getting into; your bill may end up much higher than you bargained for.

A word of **warning** for women traveling alone: Forgo the experience of strolling around Kabuki-cho. The streets are crowded and therefore relatively safe, but you may not feel comfortable with so many inebriated men stumbling around. If there are two of you, however, go for it. I took my mother to Kabuki-cho for a spin around the neon, and we escaped relatively unscathed. You're also fine walking alone to any of my recommended restaurants.

ROPPONGI   To Tokyo's younger crowd, Roppongi is the city's most fashionable place to hang out. It's also a favorite with the foreign community, including models, business types, English-language teachers, and tourists staying in Roppongi's posh hotels. Roppongi has more than its fair share of live-music houses, restaurants, dance clubs, expatriate bars, and pubs. Some Tokyoites complain that Roppongi is too crowded, too crass, and too commercialized (and has too many foreigners). However, for the casual visitor, Roppongi offers an excellent opportunity to see what's new and hot in the capital city and is easy to navigate because nightlife activity is so concentrated. There is one huge **caveat,** however: Roppongi's concentration of foreigners has also attracted the unscrupulous, with reports of spiked drinks causing patrons to pass out, only to awaken hours later to find their credit cards missing or fraudulently charged for huge amounts. In other words, never leave your drinks unattended, and you're best off following the buddy system.

The center of Roppongi is **Roppongi Crossing** (the intersection of Roppongi Dori and Gaien-Higashi Dori), at the corner of which sits the Almond Coffee Shop (under renovation until Dec 2010). The shop has mediocre coffee and desserts at inflated prices, but the sidewalk in front is the number-one meeting spot in Roppongi.

If you need directions, there's a conveniently located *koban* (police box) catty-corner from the Almond Coffee Shop and next to a bank. It has a big outdoor map of the Roppongi area showing the address system, and someone is always there to help. The map on p. 171 will help you locate the Roppongi clubs and bars mentioned in this chapter.

If the buzz of Roppongi is too much, a quieter, saner alternative is neighboring **Nishi Azabu,** which has restaurants and bars catering to both Japanese and foreigners. The center of Nishi Azabu is the next big crossroads, Nishi-Azabu Crossing (the intersection of Roppongi Dori and Gaien-Nishi Dori). Nishi Azabu is about a 10-minute walk from Roppongi Station, past Roppongi Hills in the direction of Shibuya. **Roppongi Hills** is a massive urban development with many restaurants and some bars of its own, while the newest kid on the block, **Tokyo Midtown,** has brought gentrification—and an influx of affluent customers—to Roppongi's nightlife.

LIVE MUSIC

The live-music scene exploded in the 1990s and is now located throughout the metropolis. In addition to the dedicated venues below, several bars offer live music most nights of the week, including What the Dickens (see "The Bar Scene," below).

Bauhaus Since 1981, this small club has had the same great house band that plays mostly 1970s and 1980s British and American hard rock, including the music of Led Zeppelin, Queen, Jimi Hendrix, the Who, Aerosmith, the Eagles, Van Halen, Santana, Red Hot Chili Peppers, and others, with music beginning around 8pm. The band puts on quite a show—a bit raunchy at times but very polished. Open Monday to Saturday 7pm to 1am. Closed holidays. Reine Roppongi, 2nd floor, 5–3–4 Roppongi. © **03/3403-0092.** Cover ¥2,835. Station: Roppongi (3 min.). From Roppongi Crossing, walk toward Tokyo Tower on Gaien-Higashi Dori and turn right at McDonald's. It's ahead to the right of the parking lot.

Blue Note Tokyo's most expensive, elegant jazz venue is cousin to the famous Blue Note in New York. The musicians are top-notch; Sarah Vaughan, Tony Bennett, Chick Corea, David Sanborn, the Milt Jackson Quartet, and Tower of Power have all performed here. However, the 300-seat establishment follows the frustrating practice of selling tickets good for only one set. There are usually two sets nightly, generally at 7 and 9:30pm Monday to Saturday and 6:30 and 9pm Sunday and holidays. 6–3–16 Minami Aoyama. © **03/5485-0088.** www.bluenote.co.jp. Cover ¥7,350–¥8,400 for most performances, more for top names. Station: Omotesando (8 min.). Off Kotto Dori.

Cavern Club If you know your Beatles history, you'll know Cavern is the name of the Liverpool club where the Fab Four got their start. The Tokyo club features Beatles memorabilia and house bands performing Beatles music exclusively—and very convincingly at that. Extremely popular with both Japanese and foreigners, it's packed on weekends—expect long lines, or call to reserve a table. Hours are Monday to Saturday 6pm to 2:30am (music begins at 7:30pm), Sunday and holidays 6pm to midnight. 5–3–2 Roppongi. © **03/3405-5207.** Cover ¥1,890 for men, 1,575 for women, plus a 1-drink minimum and 10% service charge. Station: Roppongi (4 min.). Take the side street going downhill on the left side of Almond Coffee Shop and then take the 1st left; the club will be on the right.

Cotton Club This cool venue is the best proof yet that Marunouchi, which already boasts new skyscrapers, hotels, and designer shops, is on its way to becoming an urban destination. Taking its name from Harlem's legendary establishment and attracting well-heeled business types, this sophisticated supper club, ensconced on the second floor of an office building, offers a wide range of musical entertainment, from traditional and fusion jazz to salsa and modern Hawaiian music, performed by trios, quartets, bands, solo guitarists, and vocalists. Past performers include Rickie Lee Jones, Rita Coolidge, and the Duke Ellington Orchestra. There are usually two seatings, at 7 and 9:30pm (5 and 8pm Sun and holidays). 2–7–3 Marunouchi. © **03/3215-1555.** www.cottonclubjapan.co.jp. Cover

Crocodile   Popular with a young Japanese crowd, the eclectic Crocodile describes itself as a casual rock-'n'-roll club, with live bands ranging from rock and blues to jazz-fusion, reggae, soul, experimental, and even country and Hawaiian. It's a good place to check out new Japanese bands; on the fourth Friday of the month, the Tokyo Comedy Store (www.tokyocomedy.com) provides more than 2 hours of live stand-up and improv comedy in English. The club has an interesting interior and a good, laid-back atmosphere. Open daily 6pm to 2am; performances start around 8pm. 6-18-8 Jingumae. ℂ **03/3499-5205.** www.crocodile-live.jp. Cover ¥2,000–¥3,000, occasionally more for big acts. Station: Meiji-Jingumae or Shibuya (10 min.). On Meiji Dori halfway btw. Harajuku and Shibuya.

Kento's   Kento's was one of the first places to open when the wave of 1950s nostalgia hit Japan in the 1980s; it has even been credited with creating the craze. This is the place to come if you feel like bopping the night away to tunes of the 1950s and 1960s played by live bands. Although there's hardly room to dance, that doesn't stop the largely over-30 Japanese audience from twisting in the aisles as the night wears on. Hours are Monday to Saturday from 6pm to 2:30am, Sunday and holidays from 6pm to midnight. (Also at 8-2-1 Ginza, on the ninth floor, ℂ **03/3572-9161;** and in east Shinjuku at 3-18-4 Shinjuku, on the sixth floor, ℂ **03/3355-6477.**) Daini Reine Building, 5-3-1 Roppongi. ℂ **03/3401-5755.** www.kentos-tokyo.jp. Cover ¥1,890 for men, 1,575 for women, plus 10% service charge and 1-drink minimum. Station: Roppongi (4 min.). Take the side street going downhill on the left side of Almond Coffee Shop and then take the 1st left; the club is on the right.

Liquidroom   This is the most happening place in Ebisu (if not all of Tokyo) for live events, with concerts, well-known DJs, and stage events most nights of the week. Lots of groups kick off their world tours here, in a huge, cavernous room where the energy is so pervasive the floor vibrates. On the second floor is Time Out Café & Diner, open Monday to Friday noon to midnight or later, Saturday 1pm to 5am, and Sunday from 3 to 10pm. Liquidroom usually opens around 6pm, with live events from about 7 to 10pm or later. 3-16-6 Higashi. ℂ **03/5464-0800.** www.liquidroom.net. Cover ¥3,000–¥6,000, depending on the event. Station: Ebisu (3 min.). Take the west exit, cross Komazawa Dori, turn right, and then turn left at Meiji Dori; it will be almost immediately on your left.

New York Bar   This is one of Tokyo's most sophisticated venues, boasting Manhattan-style jazz and breathtaking views of glittering west Shinjuku. Unfortunately, it's also one of the city's smallest. Consider coming for dinner in the adjacent **New York Grill** (p. 162); it costs a small fortune, but you'll save the cost of the cover. Hours are daily from 5pm, with live music 8pm to midnight (from 7pm on Sun; open until 1am Thurs–Sat). Park Hyatt Hotel, 52nd floor, 3-7-1-2 Nishi-Shinjuku. ℂ **03/5322-1234.** www.tokyo.park. hyatt.com. Cover ¥2,000. Station: Shinjuku (13 min.), Hatsudai on the Keio Line (7 min.), or Tochomae (8 min.).

The Ruby Room   I've seen living rooms larger than this second-floor venue, home to local acts, open-mic Tuesdays (with a one-drink minimum), house and techno DJs, and other events. The crowd depends on the music, but since there's no room to move, people dance where they are. The band is close, close, close—any closer and you'd be in the drummer's lap. Open Monday, Tuesday, Friday, and Saturday from 7pm or later, depending on the event (some concerts get underway at midnight), until 5am. 2-25-17

Dogenzaka, Shibuya-ku. © **03/3780-3022.** www.rubyroomtokyo.com. Cover ¥1,500–¥2,000 Fri–Sat only, including 1 drink. Station: Shibuya (Hachiko exit, 4 min.). Walk on Dogenzaka to the Prime Building and Royal Host and take the 1st right; keep to the left at the Y intersection.

Shinjuku Pit Inn This is one of Tokyo's most famous and longest-running jazz, fusion, and blues clubs, featuring both Japanese and foreign musicians. There are two programs daily—from 2:30 to 5pm and from 7:30 or 8pm—making it a great place to stop for a bit of music in the middle of the day. 2-12-4 Shinjuku. © **03/3354-2024.** www.pit-inn.com. Cover, including 1 drink, ¥1,300 for the 2:30pm show (¥2,500 weekends and holidays), ¥3,000 for the evening shows. Station: Shinjuku Sanchome (3 min.). Northeast of the Shinjuku Dori/Meiji Dori intersection.

DANCE CLUBS

Discos lost popularity after their 1980s heyday, but with the rise of almost cult-figure DJs, dance clubs have witnessed resurgence, with Roppongi still boasting more clubs than anywhere else in the city. Sometimes the cover charge includes drinks, which makes for an inexpensive way to spend an evening. Keep in mind, however, that prices are usually higher on weekends and are sometimes higher for men than for women. Although clubs are required by law to close at midnight, many of them ignore the rule and stay open until dawn. Finally, you must be at least 20 years old (the legal drinking age in Japan) to enter most clubs.

In addition to the recommendations here, many bars bring in DJs and become mostly dance clubs later in the evening, including Gaspanic and Enjoy House; see "The Bar Scene," below.

Arty Farty One of Ni-chome's larger gay bars, this is also one of the best places to dance, due to a good sound system and music that ranges from house to hip-hop. Although it used to be strictly males only, it recently moved to a new location (across from the legendary Pit Inn jazz house) and threw open its doors to all. A fun climax to a pub-crawl in Shinjuku. It's open Sunday to Thursday 7pm to 3am, Friday and Saturday 7pm to 5am. 2-11-7 Shinjuku. © **03/5362-9720.** Station: Shinjuku Sanchome (3 min.). Northeast of the Shinjuku Dori/Meiji Dori intersection.

El Café Latino All the smooth Latin moves make their way to the tiny dance floor of this happening club. It's fun to watch, even if you don't know how to perform salsa, rumba, merengue, reggaeton (Latin reggae), or other Latin dances, but if you want to get in the groove, show up for one of the free 30-minute classes at 7pm on Tuesday, Thursday, and Friday. Open Tuesday to Thursday and Sunday 6pm to midnight, Friday and Saturday 6pm to 5am. 3-15-24 Roppongi. © **03/3402-8989.** www.elcafelatino.com. Cover (Fri–Sat only) ¥1,500, including 1 drink. Station: Roppongi (4 min.). From Roppongi Crossing, walk down Gaien-Higashi Dori in the direction of Tokyo Tower, turning left after passing McDonald's on your right, and then turning right at Gaspanic.

Sam & Dave This Osaka import is party central in Akasaka with its disco ball, palm trees, black interior, video screens, and events that range from swing night on Wednesdays to DJs on Fridays and Saturdays. Open daily 7pm to 5am. 4-3-6 Akasaka. © **03/3585-0325.** www.samanddave.org. Cover ¥1,000–¥2,000, depending on the event. Station: Akasaka (3 min.) or Akasaka-mitsuke (4 min.). On Hitotsugi Dori.

Tokyo Loose Young Tokyoites who work in Shinjuku come here after hours to hang out and to dance to trance, hip-hop, techno, soul, R&B, and house music spun by local DJs. Things don't get hopping until after midnight, and even when the sun comes up it's night at this small basement club that attracts a good mix of Japanese and foreigners, most in their twenties. Happy hour is until 11pm Monday to Thursday, when drinks cost ¥500. Open daily at 8pm, closing when the crowd thins out (about 10am on weekends). 2-37-3 Kabuki-cho. ☏ 03/3207-5677. www.tokyoloose.com. Cover (Fri–Sat only) ¥1,000, including 1 drink for men, 2 drinks for women. Station: Shinjuku (east exit, 10 min.). North of Koma Stadium, on Hanamichi Dori.

Velours   Every guest is a star, or at least, that's how every clubber is supposed to feel at this posh venue for adults, complete with imported French furniture and a 19th-century Baccarat chandelier. It all might ring a bit pretentious for some, but after the DJ gets things rolling and the drinks kick in, celebrity wannabes might find they're having fun just being who they are. Popular with foreigners and Japanese alike. Open Wednesday to Saturday from 9pm to 5am. 6-4-6 Minami Aoyama. ☏ 03/5778-4777. Cover ¥2,500 for men, ¥2,000 for women, including 1 drink. Station: Omotesando Roppongi (8 min.). Off Kotto Dori, near Blue Note (see above).

THE BAR SCENE

GINZA   If you're looking for a quiet place for a drink, you can't do better than ㊴ **Lupin** ★, 5–5–11 Ginza (☏ 03/3571-0750; station: Ginza, 2 min.), located in a tiny alley between Namiki and Ginza West 5th Street. This tiny basement bar first opened in 1928, and little has changed over the decades. Even the staff looks as if they've been here since it opened. Because no music is played, it's is a good place to come if you want to talk. Note that there's a ¥700 per person snack/table charge. The bar is closed Sunday and Monday. Another good bar is the **Old Imperial** in the Imperial Hotel (☏ 03/3539-8088; station: Hibiya, 1 min.); the bar is the hotel's tribute to its original architect, Frank Lloyd Wright, and is the only place in the hotel with some Wright originals, including an Art Deco terra-cotta wall and a mural. With its low lighting and comfortable chairs and tables that are copies of Wright originals, it has a clubby, masculine atmosphere. Try a Mount Fuji, the bar's own cocktail original.

Sapporo beer is the draw at **Ginza Sapporo Lion,** a large beer hall with a mock Gothic ceiling and kitschy decor, on Chuo Dori not far from Matsuzakaya department store (☏ 03/3571-2590; station: Ginza, 3 min.). A large display of plastic foods and an English-language menu help you choose from snacks ranging from *yakitori* to sausage and spaghetti. A younger crowd gathers at **300 Bar,** with two locations in Ginza at 8–3–12 Ginza (☏ 03/3571-8300) and 5–9–11 Ginza (☏ 03/3572-6300). These stand-up bars offer an assortment of drinks and appetizers, all priced at ¥315.

ASAKUSA   **Sky Room,** on the 22nd floor of the Asahi Beer Tower, across the Sumida River from Sensoji Temple and next to the building that looks like a mug of beer (☏ 03/5608-5277; station: Asakusa, 4 min.), is a great place for an inexpensive drink after an active day in historic Asakusa. A simple cafeteria-type place, it offers great views as well as different kinds of Asahi beer, wine, coffee, and other drinks, all priced at ¥600 or less. It can be crowded on weekends, and note that the last order is taken at 8:30pm. **Daimasu,** 1–2–8 Asakusa (☏ 03/5806-3811; station: Asakusa: 3 min.), is a sake bar offering more than 100 different kinds of sake and *shochu* by the glass. Or, purchase your own alcohol at the shop's adjoining liquor store and drink it at the sake bar for a ¥500 corkage fee.

SHINJUKU   Tiny **Albatross,** 1–1–7 Kabuki-cho (☏ 03/3203-3699; station: Shinjuku Sanchome, 7 min.), located up a narrow flight of stairs with room for only a handful of patrons, is typical of a multitude of miniature establishments that line the alleyways of Goruden Gai (see "The Major Entertainment Districts," earlier in this section). Also near

Hanazono Shrine, on the eighth floor of the Oriental Wave building on Yasukuni Dori, is one of weirdest theme bars I've seen in Tokyo, **Christon Café,** 5–17–13 Shinjuku (☎ 03/5287-2426; station: Shinjuku Sanchome, 5 min.). Decorated like a church with its stained-glass windows, vaulted ceiling, organ music, crosses, and a statue of Jesus, it's packed to the rafters despite the ¥300 cover charge. What to order? A bloody mary, of course. More down-to-earth is **Dubliners Irish Pub,** behind Mitsukoshi on the second floor above Lion, 3–28–9 Shinjuku (☎ 03/3352-6606; station: Shinjuku, 3 min.), which attracts a mixed Japanese/ex-pat crowd.

EBISU   Ebisu's most popular bar (especially with ex-pats) is **What the Dickens,** 1–13–3 Ebisu Nishi (☎ 03/3780-2088; station: Ebisu, west exit, 2 min.), which features free live bands nightly, English and Irish beer, and British pub grub. Take the side street that runs between Wendy's and KFC; the bar is at the end of the second block on the left on the fourth floor. It's closed on Monday. Personally, my favorite bar is the inimitable **Enjoy House,** 2–9–9 Ebisu Nishi (☎ 03/5489-1591; station: Ebisu, west exit, 3 min.), with its 1960s-reminiscent decor, efficient yet relaxed and funky staff, friendly atmosphere, and tiny dance floor. Everyone here seems high and happy; the place is aptly named. Closed on Monday.

ROPPONGI   **Gaspanic Bar,** 3–15–24 Roppongi (☎ 03/3405-0633; station: Roppongi, 3 min.), epitomizes Roppongi frenzy, attracting foreign and Japanese 20-somethings. The music is loud, and after midnight, this place can get so crowded that women have been known to dance on the countertops. Thursdays are especially crowded because all drinks go for only ¥400. From Roppongi Crossing, walk toward Tokyo Tower on Gaien-Higashi Dori, turning left at Family Mart. Nearby **Gaspanic Club,** on Gaien-Higashi Dori across from the Roi Building at 3–10–5 Roppongi (☎ 03/3402-7054), is open nightly for dancing. All offer the same Thursday and happy-hour drink specials. Large bouncers at all the doors serve as clues that these places can get rough.

I'm more partial to **Geronimo,** 7–14–10 Roppongi (☎ 03/3478-7449; station: Roppongi, 1 min.), on Roppongi Dori opposite Almond Coffee Shop. A tiny place with a bar in the middle and ex-pats practically two-deep everywhere else, it's the kind of place where people dance, drink way too much, and party till they can't party anymore. When the gong rings, it means someone is buying shots for everyone at the bar. I also like the more upscale **Heartland,** 6–10–1 Roppongi (☎ 03/5772-7600; station: Roppongi, 3 min.), on Roppongi Dori just past Roppongi Hills on the left. Attracting everyone from bankers to artistic types, it offers cocktails and its own Heartland microbrew and is packed with ex-pats on the prowl. **A971,** 9–7–2 Akasaka (☎ 03/5413-3210; station: Roppongi, 2 min.), attracts a well-heeled crowd due to its location in Tokyo Midtown and its contemporary cuisine.

Tequila fans gravitate to **Agave,** on Roppongi Dori at 7–15–10 Roppongi (☎ 03/3497-0229; station: Roppongi, 3 min.), a cellar bar boasting Japan's largest selection of tequila (more than 500 kinds), as well as cigars from the Dominican Republic, Nicaragua, Honduras, Mexico, and Jamaica. Closed on Sunday. And if you yearn for a chance in the spotlight, head to **Fiesta International Karaoke Bar,** 7–9–3 Roppongi (☎ 03/5410-3008; station: Roppongi, 3 min.), on the small diagonal street across from Tokyo Midtown. For ¥3,500 you get three drinks and all the songs you care to sing from the 10,000 English-language song menu. Closed on Sunday.

If your idea of a wild night is relaxing over a drink in a sophisticated lounge, head to the **Garden Lounge** at the Hotel New Otani (© **03/5226-0246**; station: Nagatacho or Akasaka-mitsuke, 3 min.) before sunset. The bonus here is a view of a 400-year-old Japanese landscape garden, complete with a waterfall, a pond, bridges, and manicured bushes. For a more casual setting, try **Hobgoblin Tokyo Brewery Pub and Restaurant,** 2–13–19 Akasaka (© **03/3585-3681**; station: Akasaka, exit 2, 2 min.), a British chain offering nine brews on tap, major sporting events from its satellite TVs, darts, and hearty pub meals.

GAY & LESBIAN BARS

Shinjuku Ni-chome (pronounced "*nee*-chomay"), southeast of the Yasukuni-Gyoen Dori intersection (station: Shinjuku Sanchome), is Tokyo's gay and lesbian quarter, with a lively street scene and countless establishments catering to a variety of age groups and preferences. The following are good starting points, but you'll find a lot more in the immediate area by exploring on your own. Attracting both gays and straights, **Advocates,** 2–18–1 Shinjuku (© **03/3358-3988**), is a crowded, small bar open to the street with a few sidewalk tables, making this a good vantage point from which to watch the street action. It's also a good place to network and find out about neighboring bars. **Kinsmen,** on the second floor at 2–18–5 Shinjuku (© **03/3354-4949**), welcomes customers of all persuasions. It's a pleasant oasis, small and civilized. It's closed on Monday. The casual, laid-back, women-only **Kinswomyn,** 2–15–10 Shinjuku (© **03/3354-8720**), attracts a regular clientele of mainly Japanese lesbians and has a friendly, welcoming atmosphere. It's closed on Tuesday.

7

Side Trips from Tokyo

If your stay in Tokyo is long enough, you should consider taking an excursion or two. **Kamakura** and **Nikko** rank as two of the most important historical sites in Japan, while the **Fuji-Hakone-Izu National Park** serves as a huge recreational playground for the residents of Tokyo. **Yokohama,** with its thriving port, waterfront development, and several museums and attractions, also makes an interesting day trip. For overnight stays, I heartily recommend **Hakone** or **Izu Peninsula,** both with *ryokan* (Japanese-style inns) where you'll be able to experience the atmosphere of old Japan.

Before departing Tokyo, stop by the **Tourist Information Center (TIC)** for pamphlets on Kamakura, Nikko, Hakone, and the Mount Fuji area, some of which give train schedules and other useful information; see "Visitor Information," in chapter 5, for the TIC location.

1 KAMAKURA, ANCIENT CAPITAL ★★★

51km (32 miles) S of Tokyo

If you take only one day trip outside Tokyo, it should be to Kamakura, especially if you're unable to include the ancient capitals of Kyoto and Nara in your travels. (If you are going to Kyoto and Nara, I would probably choose Nikko, below.) Kamakura is a delightful hamlet with no fewer than 65 Buddhist temples and 19 Shinto shrines spread throughout the town and surrounding wooded hills. Most of these were built centuries ago, when a warrior named Minamoto Yoritomo seized political power and established his shogunate government in Kamakura back in 1192. Wanting to set up his seat of government as far away as possible from what he considered to be the corrupt imperial court in Kyoto, Yoritomo selected Kamakura because it was easy to defend. The village is enclosed on three sides by wooded hills and on the fourth by the sea—a setting that lends a dramatic background to its many temples and shrines.

Although Kamakura remained the military and political center of the nation for a century and a half, the Minamoto clan was in power for only a short time. After Yoritomo's death, both of his sons were assassinated, one after the other, after taking up military rule. Power then passed to the family of Yoritomo's widow, the Hojo family, which ruled until 1333, when the emperor in Kyoto sent troops to crush the shogunate government. Unable to stop the invaders, 800 soldiers retired to the Hojo family temple at Toshoji, where they disemboweled themselves in ritualistic suicide known as *seppuku.*

Today Kamakura is a thriving seaside resort (pop. 173,500), with old wooden homes, temples, shrines, and wooded hills—a pleasant 1-day trip from Tokyo. (There's also a beach in Kamakura called Yuigahama Beach, but I find it unappealing; it's often strewn with litter and unbelievably crowded in summer. Skip it.)

ESSENTIALS
GETTING THERE Take the **JR Yokosuka Line** bound for Zushi, Kurihama, or Yokosuka; it departs every 10 to 15 minutes from Yokohama, Shinagawa, Shimbashi, and

Atami 6
Hakone 5
Kamakura 4
Mashiko 2
Mt. Fuji 8
Nikko 1
Shuzenji 7
Yokohama 3

Railway

Tokyo JR stations. The trip takes almost 1 hour from Tokyo Station and costs ¥890 to Kamakura Station. From Shinjuku, take the JR Shonan-Shinjuku Line 1 hour to Kamakura for the same price. Suica cards and Japan Rail Passes can be used for both lines.

VISITOR INFORMATION   In Kamakura, there's a **tourist information window** (🕿 **0467/22-3350;** www.city.kamakura.kanagawa.jp) inside Kamakura Station near the east (main) exit. You can pick up a map here and get directions to the village's most important sights and restaurants. It's open daily 9am to 5:30pm April to September, and 9am to 5pm October to March.

ORIENTATION & GETTING AROUND   Kamakura's major sights are clustered in two areas: **Kamakura Station,** the town's downtown with the tourist office, souvenir shops spread along Komachi Dori and Wakamiya Oji, restaurants, and Tsurugaoka Hachimangu Shrine; and **Hase,** with the Great Buddha and Hase Kannon Temple. You can travel between Kamakura Station and Hase Station via the **Enoden Line,** a wonderful small train, or you can walk the distance in about 20 minutes. Destinations are also easily reached by buses departing from Kamakura Station.

SEEING THE SIGHTS

AROUND KAMAKURA STATION   About a 12-minute walk from Kamakura Station, **Tsurugaoka Hachimangu Shrine** ★★★ (🕿 **0467/22-0315**) is the spiritual heart of Kamakura and one of its most popular attractions. It was built by Yoritomo and dedicated to Hachiman, the Shinto god of war who served as the clan deity of the Minamoto family. The pathway to the shrine is along Wakamiya Oji, a cherry tree–lined pedestrian lane that was also constructed by Yoritomo in the 1190s so that his oldest son's first visit to the family shrine could be accomplished in style with an elaborate procession. The lane stretches from the shrine all the way to Yuigahama Beach, with three massive *torii* gates set at intervals along the route to signal the approach to the shrine. On both sides of the pathway are souvenir and antiques shops selling lacquerware, pottery, and folk art (I suggest you return to Kamakura Station via Komachi Dori, a fun pedestrian shopping lane that parallels Wakamiya Oji to the west).

At the top of the stairs, which afford a panoramic view toward the sea, is the vermilion-colored shrine with its small shrine museum, not worth the ¥100 admission. However, you can get your fortune in English for ¥100 by shaking out a bamboo stick with a number on it and giving it to the attendant. You can also buy a charm to assure good luck in health, driving a car, business, or other ventures. Shrine grounds are always open, free to the public.

AROUND HASE STATION   To get to these attractions, you can go by bus, which departs from in front of Kamakura Station (take any bus from platform no. 1 or 6 to the Daibutsuen-mae stop). Or, for a more romantic adventure, you can go by the **JR Enoden Line,** a tiny train that putt-putts its way seemingly through backyards on its way from Kamakura Station to Hase and beyond. Since it's mostly only one track, trains have to take turns going in either direction. I suggest that you take the bus from Kamakura Station directly to the Great Buddha, walk to Hase Shrine, and then take the Enoden train back to Kamakura Station.

Probably Kamakura's most famous attraction is the **Great Buddha** ★★★ (🕿 **0467/ 22-0703**), called the Daibutsu in Japanese and located at **Kotokuin Temple.** Eleven meters (36 ft.) high and weighing 93 tons, it's the second-largest bronze image in Japan. The largest Buddha is in Nara, but in my opinion the Kamakura Daibutsu is much more

ATTRACTIONS ●
Great Buddha (Daibutsu) **4**
Hase Kannon Temple **6**
Tsurugaoka Hachimangu
  Shrine **1**

DINING ◆
Kaikoan **6**
Milano a Riccione **2**
Raitei **3**
Soetaro **5**

> ### (Tips) A Note on Japanese Symbols
>
> Many establishments and attractions in Japan do not have signs in Roman (Eng-lish-language) letters. Those that don't are indicated in this guide by an oval with a number that corresponds to a number in chapter 17 showing the Japanese symbols. Thus, to find the Japanese symbol for, say, Raitei (see below), refer to no. 40 in chapter 17.

impressive. For one thing, the Kamakura Buddha sits outside against a dramatic back-drop of wooded hills. Cast in 1252, the Kamakura Buddha was indeed once housed in a temple like the Nara Buddha, but a huge tidal wave destroyed the wooden structure—and the statue has sat under sun, snow, and stars ever since. I also prefer the face of the Kamakura Buddha; I find it more inspiring and divine, as though with its half-closed eyes and calm, serene face it's above the worries of the world. It seems to represent the plane above human suffering, the point at which birth and death, joy and sadness merge and become one. Open daily from 7am to 6pm (to 5:30pm Oct–Mar). Admission is ¥200 for adults and ¥150 for children. If you want, you can pay an extra ¥20 to go inside the statue—it's hollow—but there's usually a line and I find it claustrophobic.

About a 10-minute walk from the Daibutsu is **Hase Kannon Temple (Hasedera)** ★★★ (© **0467/22-6300;** www.hasedera.jp), located on a hill with a sweeping view of the sea. This is the home of an 11-headed gilt statue of Kannon, the goddess of mercy, housed in the Kannon-do (Kannon Hall). More than 9m (30 ft.) high and the tallest wooden image in Japan, it was made in the 8th century from a single piece of camphor wood. The legend surrounding this Kannon is quite remarkable. Supposedly, two wooden images were made from the wood of a huge camphor tree. One of the images was kept in Hase, not far from Nara, while the second was given a short ceremony and then tossed into the sea to find a home of its own. The image drifted about 500km (300 miles) eastward and washed up on shore but was thrown back in again when all who touched it became ill or incurred bad luck. Finally, the image reached Kamakura, where it gave the people no trouble. This was interpreted as a sign that the image was content with its surroundings, and Hase Kannon Temple was erected at its present site. Note how each face has a different expression, representing the Kannon's compassion for various kinds of human suffering. Also in the Kannon-do is a museum with religious treasures from the Kamakura, Heian, Muromachi, and Edo periods.

Another golden statue housed here is of **Amida,** a Buddha who promised rebirth in the Pure Land to the West to all who chanted his name. It was created by order of Yori-itomo Minamoto upon his 42nd birthday, considered an unlucky year for men. You'll find it housed in the Amida-do (Amida Hall) beside the Kannon-do to the right. Also of interest is the **Kyozo,** with rotating book racks containing sutras (if you give the book racks a spin, it's considered just as auspicious as reading the sutras; but alas, you can do so only on the 18th of each month). **Benten-kutsu Cave** contains many stone images, including one of Benzaiten (seated, with a lute and a money box in front). A sea goddess and patroness of music, art, and good fortune, she is the only female of Japan's Seven Lucky Gods. **Prospect Road** is a 10-minute hiking path featuring flowers in bloom and panoramic views.

As you climb the steps to the Kannon-do, you'll encounter statues of a different sort. All around you will be likenesses of **Jizo,** the guardian deity of children. Although parents originally came to Hase Temple to set up statues to represent their children in hopes the deity would protect and watch over them, through the years the purpose of the Jizo statues changed. Now they represent miscarried, stillborn, or aborted infants. The hundreds or so you see here will remain only a year before being burned or buried to make way for others. Some of the statues are fitted with hand-knitted caps, bibs, and sweaters; the effect is quite chilling.

Hase Temple is open daily 8am to 5pm (to 4:30pm Oct–Feb); admission is ¥300 for adults, ¥100 for children.

WHERE TO DINE

In addition to the suggestions below, a simple restaurant called **Kaikoan** at Hase Temple (described above) serves noodles, desserts, and drinks. After deciding what you want, purchase tickets from a vending machine. It offers a great view, making it a good place for a snack on a fine day, and is open daily from 10am to 4pm.

Milano a Riccione ITALIAN   This is the Japanese branch of a Milan restaurant known for its handmade pasta, seafood, and good selection of wines. Although located in a basement, it opens onto a subterranean courtyard, making it brighter and more cheerful than you would expect. There's an English-language seasonal menu, but the best bargain is the daily set lunch for ¥1,575, which includes an appetizer; a choice of pasta or pizza; and coffee, espresso, or tea. It's the quickest meal you can order, but for other choices dine here only if you aren't in a hurry, as care and time are devoted to the preparation of such meals as sautéed Nagoya cochin chicken with Gorgonzola or simmered whole fish. At dinnertime, a table charge of ¥315 is levied per person and set meals are available only for two or more diners.

2-12-30 Komachi. ⓒ **0467/24-5491.** Reservations required for lunch only. Pizza and pasta ¥1,260– ¥1,785; main dishes ¥1,785–¥2,572; set dinners ¥4,200–¥4,935; set lunches ¥1,575–¥2,730. AE, DC, MC, V. Thurs–Tues 11:30am–3pm and 5:30–9:30pm (last order). Station: Kamakura (6 min.). On the left side of Wakamiya Oji when walking from Kamakura Station to Tsurugaoka Hachimangu Shrine.

④ **Raitei** ★★★ ⓕ Finds NOODLES/OBENTO   Though it's a bit inconveniently located, this is the absolute winner for a meal in Kamakura. Visiting Raitei is as much fun as visiting the city's temples and shrines. The restaurant is situated in the hills on the edge of Kamakura, surrounded by verdant countryside, and the wonder is that it serves inexpensive *soba* (Japanese noodles) and *obento* (lunch boxes), as well as priestly *kaiseki* feasts. Take the stone steps on the right to the back entry, where you'll be given an English-language menu with such offerings as noodles with chicken, various obento, and kaiseki. The pottery used here comes from the restaurant's own kiln, and you'll sit on

---

ⓒ **Moments**   **A Special Stroll**

When you've finished your meal at Raitei, be sure to walk the loop through the garden past a bamboo grove, stone images, and a miniature shrine. The stroll takes about 20 minutes, unless you stop for a beer at the refreshment house, which has outdoor seating and a view of the countryside.

roughly hewn wood stools or on *tatami*. If you make a reservation in advance for kaiseki, you'll dine upstairs in your own private room in a refined traditional setting with great views. The house, once owned by a wealthy landowner, was moved to this site in 1929.

Takasago. ☎ **0467/32-5656.** Noodles ¥900–¥1,522; obento ¥3,675; soba set meals ¥2,625; kaiseki from ¥6,300. Entry fee ¥500, which counts toward the price of your meal. AE, DC. Daily 11am–sundown (about 7pm in summer). Bus: 4 from platform no. 6 at Kamakura Station or Daibutsuen-mae to Takasago stop (or a 15-min. taxi ride).

㊶ **Sometaro** ⓥalue OKONOMIYAKI   Located near the approach to Hase Temple, this small, second-floor restaurant offers do-it-yourself *okonomiyaki* (a kind of Japanese pancake; cooking instructions are available in English) stuffed with cabbage, bean sprouts, and a choice of a main ingredient like beef, pork, or shrimp. It also serves *yakisoba* (fried noodles) and *teppanyaki* (grilled steak, seafood, or vegetables), all from an English-language menu. The lone waitress is a bit gruff, but if you can ignore that, you'll enjoy the conviviality of dining here.

3-12-11 Hase. ☎ **0467/22-8694.** Reservations recommended for lunch. Main dishes ¥900. No credit cards. Thurs–Tues 11:30am–9pm (last order). Station: Hase (2 min.). On the slope leading to the entrance of Hase Temple, at the beginning on the left side.

2 SHOGUN COUNTRY: NIKKO ★★★

150km (93 miles) N of Tokyo

After the publication of James Clavell's novel *Shogun,* many people became familiar with Tokugawa Ieyasu, the powerful real-life shogun of the 1600s on whom Clavell's fictional shogun was based. Quashing all rebellions and unifying Japan under his leadership, Tokugawa established such a military stronghold that his heirs continued to rule Japan for the next 250 years without serious challenge.

If you'd like to join the millions of Japanese who through the centuries have paid homage to this great man, head north of Tokyo to Nikko, where **Toshogu Shrine** ★★★ was constructed in his honor in the 17th century and where Tokugawa's remains were entombed in a mausoleum. Nikko means "sunlight"—an apt description of the way the sun's rays play upon this sumptuous shrine of wood and gold leaf. In fact, nothing else in Japan matches Toshogu Shrine for its opulence. Nearby is another mausoleum containing Tokugawa's grandson, as well as a temple, a shrine, and a garden. Surrounding the sacred grounds, known collectively as Nikko Sannai and designated a World Heritage Site by UNESCO in 1999, are thousands of majestic cedar trees in the 80,000-hectare (200,000-acre) **Nikko National Park** ★★. Another worthwhile sight is the **Nikko Tamozawa Imperial Villa** ★★, built in 1899.

I've included a few recommendations for an overnight stay. Otherwise, you can see Nikko in a very full day. Plan on 4 to 5 hours for round-trip transportation, 2½ hours to see Toshogu Shrine and vicinity, and 1 hour to see the imperial villa.

ESSENTIALS

GETTING THERE   The easiest, fastest, and most luxurious way to get to Nikko is on the privately owned Tobu Line's Limited Express, called the **Spacia,** which departs every hour or more frequently from Tobu's Asakusa Station. The cost is ¥2,620 one-way for the 1-hour-and-50-minute trip on weekdays and ¥2,720 on weekends and holidays (most trains require a transfer at Shimo-Imaichi Station). All seats are reserved, which means

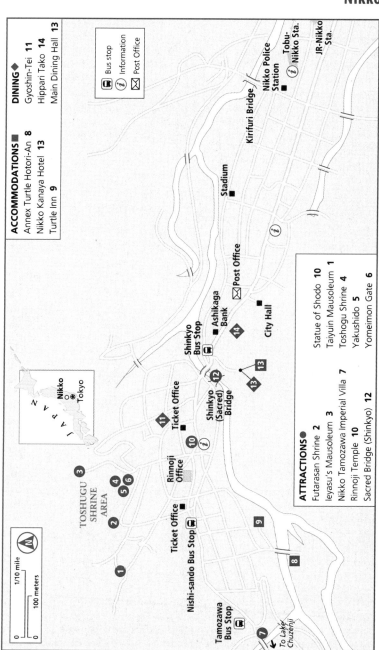

ACCOMMODATIONS ■
Annex Turtle Hotori-An **8**
Nikko Kanaya Hotel **13**
Turtle Inn **9**

DINING ◆
Gyoshin-Tei **11**
Hippari Tako **14**
Main Dining Hall **13**

Bus stop
Information
Post Office

TOSHUGU SHRINE AREA

ATTRACTIONS ●
Futarasan Shrine **2**
Ieyasu's Mausoleum **3**
Nikko Tamozawa Imperial Villa **7**
Rinnoji Temple **10**
Sacred Bridge (Shinkyo) **12**
Statue of Shodo **10**
Taiyuin Mausoleum **1**
Toshogu Shrine **4**
Yakushido **5**
Yomeimon Gate **6**

Nishi-sando Bus Stop
Ticket Office
Rinnoji Office
Ticket Office
Shinkyo (Sacred) Bridge
Shinkyo Bus Stop
Ashikaga Bank
Post Office
City Hall
Stadium
Kirifuri Bridge
Nikko Police Station
Tobu-Nikko Sta.
JR-Nikko Sta.
Tamozawa Bus Stop
To Lake Chuzenji

JAPAN Nikko Tokyo

1/10 mile
100 meters

you are guaranteed a seat; if you're traveling on a holiday or a summer weekend, you may wish to purchase and reserve your ticket in advance. Another plus is that there's usually an English-speaking hostess on board who passes out pamphlets on the area and can answer sightseeing questions about Nikko.

To save money, purchase Tobu's World Heritage Pass, which provides round-trip train travel between Asakusa and Nikko via Limited Express, unlimited bus travel in Nikko, and admission to Toshogu Shrine (excluding Ieyasu's mausoleum), Rinnoji Temple, and Futarasan Shrine. Cost of the pass, valid for 2 days and available only to foreign visitors, is ¥3,600 for adults, ¥3,200 for senior-high students, ¥3,000 for junior-high students, and ¥1,700 for children. You can purchase the pass online at www.tobu.co.jp/foreign or at the Tobu Sightseeing Service Center at Asakusa Station (© **03/3841-2871**), open daily 7:45am to 5pm.

Otherwise, you can reach Nikko on Tobu's slower **rapid train** from Asakusa, which costs ¥1,320 one-way and takes 2 hours and 10 minutes, with trains departing every hour or more frequently. There are no reserved seats, which means you might have to stand if trains are crowded.

If you have a Japan Rail Pass, take the Tohoku Shinkansen bullet train from Tokyo Station to Utsunomiya (there are departures every 20–40 min. and the trip takes about 55 min.), where you change for the JR train to Nikko (45 min., with departures every hour or less).

VISITOR INFORMATION　　Before leaving Tokyo, pick up the leaflet "Nikko" from the Tourist Information Center (TIC). It gives the train schedule for both the Tobu Line departing from Asakusa Station, and JR trains from Shinjuku. The TIC also has color brochures with maps of the Nikko area.

Nikko's Tobu and JR stations are located almost side by side in the village's downtown area. The **Nikko Tobu Station tourist information counter** (© **0288/53-4511;** www. nikko-jp.org), located inside Tobu Station, has staff who can give you a map, answer basic questions, and point you in the right direction. You can also make hotel and *ryokan* reservations here for ¥100. Open daily 8:30am to 5pm.

Another tourist office, the **Nikko Information Center** (© **0288/54-2496**), is located on the left side of the main road leading from the train station to Toshogu Shrine (next to Eneos gas station). It has English-speaking staff and lots of information in English, including information on public hot springs. Open daily from 9am to 5pm.

GETTING AROUND　　Toshogu Shrine and its mausoleum are on the edge of town, but you can walk from either the JR or Tobu train stations to the shrine in about half an hour. Head straight out the main exit, pass the bus stands, and then turn right. Signs in English point the way throughout town. Keep walking on this main road (you'll pass the Nikko Information Center about halfway down on the left side, as well as souvenir shops) until you come to a T intersection with a vermilion-colored bridge spanning a river (about a 15-min. walk from the train stations). The stone steps opposite lead up the hill into the woods and to Toshogu Shrine. If you'd rather go by bus from Tobu Station, get off at either the Shinkyo (a 7-min. ride) or Nishi Sando (a 10-min. ride) bus stop.

SEEING THE SIGHTS

ON THE WAY TO THE SHRINE　　The first indication that you're nearing the shrine is the vermilion-painted **Sacred Bridge (Shinkyo)** arching over the rushing Daiyagawa River. It was built in 1636 for visiting shogun and their emissaries. Across the road from the Sacred Bridge, steps lead uphill into a forest of cedar where, after a 5-minute walk, you'll see a statue of **Shodo,** a priest who founded Nikko 1,200 years ago when mountains were revered as gods. In the centuries that followed, Nikko became one of Japan's greatest mountain Buddhist retreats, with 500 subtemples spread through the area. Behind Shodo is the first major temple, Rinnoji Temple, where you can buy a **combination ticket** for ¥1,300 for adults, ¥450 for children; it allows entry to Rinnoji Temple and its garden, Toshogu Shrine, neighboring Futarasan Shrine, and the other Tokugawa mausoleum, Taiyuin. Once at Toshogu Shrine, you'll have to pay an extra ¥520 to see Ieyasu's tomb. Combination tickets sold at the entry to Toshogu Shrine already include Ieyasu's tomb. It doesn't really matter where you buy your combination ticket since you can always pay the extra fee to see sights not covered. A note for bus riders: If you take the bus to the Nishi Sando bus stop, the first place you'll come to is the Taiyuin Mausoleum, where you can also purchase a combination ticket.

Toshogu Shrine and the other sights in Nikko Sannai are open daily from 8am to 5pm April through October (to 4pm the rest of the year); you must enter at least 30 minutes before closing time.

RINNOJI TEMPLE   Rinnoji Temple (☏ **0288/54-0531**) was founded by the priest Shodo in the 8th century, long before the Toshogu clan came onto the scene. Here you can visit **Sanbutsudo Hall,** a large building that enshrines three 8.4m-high (28-ft.) gold-plated wooden images of Buddha, considered the "gods of Nikko"; today people pray here for world peace. Perhaps the best thing to see at Rinnoji Temple is **Shoyo-en Garden** (opposite Sanbutsudo Hall). Completed in 1815 and typical of Japanese landscaped gardens of the Edo Period, this small strolling garden provides a different vista with each turn of the path, making it seem much larger than it is. Your ticket also gains entrance to a small treasure house, where relics are displayed on a rotating basis.

TOSHOGU SHRINE ★★★   The most important and famous structure in Nikko is Toshogu Shrine (☏ **0288/54-0560**), built by Tokugawa's grandson (and third Tokugawa shogun), Tokugawa Iemitsu, as an act of devotion. It seems that no expense was too great in creating the monument: Some 15,000 artists and craftspeople were brought to Nikko from all over Japan, and after 2 years' work, they erected a group of buildings more elaborate and gorgeous than any other Japanese temple or shrine. Rich in colors and carvings, Toshogu Shrine is gilded with over two million sheets of gold leaf (they could cover an area of almost 2.4 hectares/6 acres). The mausoleum was completed in 1636, almost 20 years after Ieyasu's death, and was most certainly meant to impress anyone who saw it as a demonstration of the Tokugawa shogunate's wealth and power. The shrine is set in a grove of magnificent ancient **Japanese cedars** planted over a 20-year period during the 1600s by a feudal lord named Matsudaira Masatsuna. Some 13,000 of the original trees still stand, adding a sense of dignity to the mausoleum and shrine.

You enter Toshogu Shrine via a flight of stairs that passes under a huge stone *torii* gateway, one of the largest in Japan. On your left is a five-story, 35m-high (115-ft.) **pagoda.** Although normally pagodas are found only at temples, this pagoda is just one example of how Buddhism and Shintoism are combined at Toshogu Shrine. After climbing a second flight of stairs, turn left and you'll see the **Sacred Stable,** which houses a sacred white horse. Horses have long been dedicated to Shinto gods and are kept at shrines. Shrines also kept monkeys as well, since they were thought to protect horses from disease; look for the three monkeys carved above the stable door, fixed in the poses of "see no evil, hear no evil, speak no evil"—they're considered guardians of the sacred horse. Across from the stable is **Kami-Jinko,** famous for its carving by Kano Tanyu, who painted the images of the two elephants after reading about them but without seeing what they actually looked like.

The central showpiece of Nikko is **Yomeimon Gate,** popularly known as the Twilight Gate, implying that it could take you all day (until twilight) to see everything carved on it. Painted in red, blue, and green, and gilded and lacquered, this gate is carved with about 400 flowers, dragons, birds, and other animals. It's almost too much to take in at once and is very un-Japanese in its opulence, having more in common with Chinese architecture than with the usual austerity of most Japanese shrines.

You can visit the shrine's main sanctuary, **Hai-den,** comprising three halls: One was reserved for the Imperial family, one for the shogun, and one (the central hall) for conducting ceremonies. You can buy good-luck charms here that will guard against such misfortunes as traffic accidents, or that will ensure good health, success in business, easy childbirth, or other achievements in daily life. To the right of the main hall is the entrance to **Tokugawa Ieyasu's mausoleum.** If it's not already included in your combination ticket, admission is ¥520 extra. After the ticket counter, look for the carving of a sleeping cat above the door, dating from the Edo Period and famous today as a symbol of Nikko (you'll find many reproductions in area souvenir shops). Beyond that are 200 stone steps leading past cedars to Tokugawa's tomb. After the riotous colors of the shrine, the tomb seems surprisingly simple.

On the way out you'll pass **Yakushido,** famous for its dragon painting on the ceiling. A monk gives a brief explanation (in Japanese) and demonstrates how two sticks struck together produce an echo that supposedly resonates like a bell. Twelve statues here represent the Chinese zodiac calendar.

FUTARASAN SHRINE   Directly to the west of Toshogu Shrine is Futarasan Shrine (✆ **0288/54-0535**), the oldest building in the district (ca. 1617), which has a pleasant garden and is dedicated to the gods of mountains surrounding Nikko. You'll find miniature shrines dedicated to the god of fortune, god of happiness, god of trees, god of water, and god of good marriages. On the shrine's grounds is the so-called **ghost lantern,** enclosed in a small vermilion-colored wooden structure. According to legend, it used to come alive at night and sweep around Nikko in the form of a ghost. It apparently scared one guard so much that he struck it with his sword 70 times; the marks are still visible on the lamp's rim. Entrance to the miniature shrines and ghost lantern is ¥200 extra.

TAIYUIN MAUSOLEUM ★   Past Futarasan Shrine is **Taiyuin Mausoleum** (✆ **0288/53-1567**), the final resting place of Iemitsu, the third Tokugawa shogun (look for his statue). Completed in 1653, it's not nearly as large as Toshogu Shrine, but it's ornate and serenely elegant nevertheless. To show respect for the first shogun, Taiyuin's buildings face Toshogu Shrine. Tourists usually bypass this shrine, making it a pleasant last stop on your tour of Nikko Sannai.

NIKKO TAMOZAWA IMPERIAL VILLA (TAMOZAWA GOYOUTEI KINEN KOEN) ★★
If you haven't seen the Imperial villas of Kyoto (which require advance planning), this villa, at 8–27 Honcho (✆ **0288/53-6767**), is a great alternative. It's not as old, having been built in 1899 for Prince Yoshihito (who later became the Taisho emperor), and recently painstakingly restored so that it looks brand-new. It has the distinction of being the largest wooden Imperial villa of its era, with 106 rooms, 37 of which are open to the public. In addition, the central core of the villa is actually much older, constructed in 1632 by a feudal lord and brought to Nikko from Edo (present-day Tokyo). Altogether, three emperors and three princes used the villa between 1899 and 1947. A self-guided

tour of the villa provides insight into traditional Japanese architectural methods—from its 11 layers of paper-plastered walls to its nail-less wood framing—as well as the lifestyle of Japan's aristocracy. Be sure to wander the small outdoor garden. Admission is ¥500 for adults, half-price for children. Open Wednesday to Monday 9am to 4:30pm. It's about a 20-minute walk from Toshogu Shrine, or take the bus to Tamozawa stop.

WHERE TO STAY

If it's peak season (Golden Week, Aug, or Oct.) or a weekend, it's best to reserve a room in advance, which you can do by calling a lodging either directly or through a travel agency in Tokyo. Off-peak, you can make a reservation upon arrival at Nikko Tobu Station, either at the **tourist information counter** or at the **accommodations-reservation window** (☎ **0288/54-0864;** Mon–Fri 9am–5pm, Sat–Sun and holidays 8:25am–5:55pm), both of which are familiar with the area accommodations and will make all arrangements for you. Note that the charge for booking a room at either of these facilities is ¥100 per person.

Moderate

Nikko Kanaya Hotel ★★ (Finds) Founded in 1873, this distinguished-looking place on a hill above the Sacred Bridge is the most famous hotel in Nikko, combining the rustic heartiness of a European country lodge with elements of old Japan. The present complex, built in spurts over the past 137 years, has a rambling, delightfully old-fashioned atmosphere that fuses Western architecture with Japanese craftsmanship. Through the decades it has played host to a number of VIPs, from Charles Lindbergh to Indira Gandhi to Shirley MacLaine; Frank Lloyd Wright left a sketch for the bar fireplace, which was later built to his design. Even if you don't stay here, you might want to drop by for lunch (see review below). Pathways lead to the Daiyagawa River and several short hiking trails. All rooms are Western-style twins, with the differences in price based on room size, view (river view is best), and facilities. Some 10 rooms have been updated, but I prefer the older, simpler rooms because they have more character; some have antiques and claw-foot tubs. The best (and priciest) room in the house is the corner room in the 72-year-old wing where the emperor once stayed.

1300 Kami-Hatsuishi, Nikko City, Tochigi 321-1401. ☎ **0288/54-0001.** Fax 0288/53-2487. www.kanaya hotel.co.jp. 70 units. ¥15,015–¥46,200 single; ¥17,325–¥51,970 double. ¥3,465–¥4,620 extra Fri–Sat, and evening before national holidays; ¥5,775 extra in peak season. AE, DC, MC, V. Bus: From Nikko Tobu Station to the Shinkyo stop, a 5-min. ride. On foot: 20 min. from Tobu Station. **Amenities:** 3 restaurants, including the Main Dining Hall; bar; small outdoor heated pool (summer only); outdoor skating rink (in winter). *In room:* A/C, TV, minibar.

Inexpensive

Annex Turtle Hotori-An ★★ (Kids) Owned by the superfriendly family that runs Turtle Inn (see below), this is one of my favorite places to stay in Nikko. One dip in the hot-springs bath overlooking the Daiyagawa River (which you can lock for privacy) will tell you why, at night, you're lulled to sleep by the sound of the rushing waters. A simple but spotless modern structure (all nonsmoking), it's located in a nice rural setting on a quiet street with a few other houses; an adjoining park and playground provide plenty of space for kids to play. All its rooms except one are Japanese style. A plentiful Western-style breakfast costs ¥1,050 in the pleasant living area/dining room. For dinner, you can go to the nearby Turtle Inn (reservations must be made the day before; see below), or buy a pizza from the freezer and microwave it yourself. There's also a communal refrigerator where you can store food.

8–28 Takumi-cho, Nikko City, Tochigi 321-1433. © **0288/53-3663.** Fax 0288/53-3883. www.turtle-nikko. com. 11 units. ¥6,500 single; ¥12,400 double. ¥300 extra per person in peak season. Hot-spring tax ¥150 extra. Special rates for children. Winter discounts available. AE, MC, V. Bus: From Nikko Station to the Sogo Kaikan-mae stop, a 7-min. ride; then a 9-min. walk. **Amenities:** Hot-spring baths; computer w/free Internet at Turtle Inn. *In room:* A/C, TV.

Turtle Inn ★   This excellent, nonsmoking pension, a Japanese Inn Group member, is located within walking distance of Toshogu Shrine in a newer two-story house on a quiet side street beside the Daiyagawa River. The friendly owner, Mr. Fukuda, speaks English and is very helpful in planning a sightseeing itinerary. Rooms are bright and cheerful in both Japanese and Western styles; the five *tatami* rooms are without bathroom. Excellent Japanese dinners (served on local Mashiko pottery) are available for ¥2,100, as are Western breakfasts for ¥1,050. Dinner must be ordered the day before; note that it's not available on Sunday, Tuesday, and Thursday.

2–16 Takumi-cho, Nikko City, Tochigi 321-1433. © **0288/53-3168.** Fax 0288/53-3883. www.turtle-nikko. com. 10 units (3 with bathroom). ¥4,800 single without bathroom, ¥5,600 single with bathroom; ¥9,000 double without bathroom, ¥10,600 double with bathroom. ¥300 extra per person in peak season. Hot-spring tax ¥150 extra. Special rates for children. Winter discounts available. AE, MC, V. Bus: From Nikko Station to the Sogo Kaikan-mae stop, a 7-min. ride; then a 5-min. walk. **Amenities:** Hot-spring baths; computer w/free Internet. *In room:* A/C, TV, no phone.

WHERE TO DINE
Expensive
Main Dining Hall at Nikko Kanaya Hotel ★★ (Finds) CONTINENTAL   Even if you don't spend the night here, the Kanaya Hotel's quaint dining hall with its wood-carved pillars is one of the best places in town for lunch. Since it's beside the Sacred Bridge, only a 10-minute walk from Toshogu Shrine, you can easily combine it with your sightseeing tour. I suggest Nikko's specialty: locally caught rainbow trout available cooked three different ways. I always order mine cooked Kanaya style—covered with soy sauce, sugar, and sake; grilled; and served whole. The best bargain is the set lunch for ¥3,500, available until 3pm, which comes with soup, salad, a main dish such as trout, bread or rice, and dessert. Steak, lobster, salmon, chicken, and other Western fare are also listed on the English-language menu.

Nikko Kanaya Hotel, 1300 Kami-Hatsuishi. © **0288/54-0001.** Reservations recommended during peak season. Main dishes ¥2,900–¥9,240; set lunches from ¥3,500; set dinners ¥9,800. AE, DC, MC, V. Daily 11:30am–3pm and 6–8pm. Station: Nikko Tobu (20 min).

Moderate
Gyoshin-Tei ★★ VEGETARIAN/KAISEKI   This lovely Japanese restaurant, with a simple *tatami* room and a view of pines, moss, and bonsai, serves two kinds of set meals—*kaiseki* and Buddhist vegetarian cuisine—both of which change monthly and include the local specialty, *yuba,* a high-protein food made from soybeans and produced only in Kyoto and Nikko. Until 100 years ago, it could be eaten only by priests and members of the imperial family. Gyoshin-Tei is actually one of several restaurants in a parklike setting all under the same management and with the same open hours. **Meijino-Yakata** (closed Wed), occupying a stone house built 110 years ago as the private retreat of an American businessman, serves Western food such as grilled rainbow trout, veal cutlet, and steak. **Fujimoto** (closed Thurs), in a small stone cottage, serves French food created with Japanese ingredients and eaten with chopsticks. All restaurants offer a

set lunch for ¥3,150. The drawback: This place is harder to find than my other recommendations, but it's only a 4-minute walk northeast of Rinnoji Temple.

2339-1 Sannai. 𝄞 **0288/53-3751.** Reservations recommended. Vegetarian/kaiseki meals ¥3,990–
¥5,775; set lunches ¥3,150. AE, DC, MC, V. Fri–Wed 11am–7pm (from 11:30am in winter). Station: Nikko
Tobu (25 min.); or bus from Nikko Station to Shinkyo (then a 7-min. walk).

Inexpensive

㊷ **Hippari Tako** NOODLES   This tiny, three-table establishment is under the caring supervision of motherly Miki-san, who serves a limited selection of noodle dishes,
including ramen and stir-fried noodles with vegetables, as well as *onigiri* (rice balls),
vegetarian tempura, and *yakitori* (skewered barbecued chicken). There's an English-language menu, and the walls, covered with business cards and messages left by appreciative
guests from around the world, are testimony to both the tasty meals and Miki-san's warm
hospitality. A computer allows guests access to the Internet 30 minutes for free.

1011 Kami-Hatsuishi. 𝄞 **0288/53-2933.** Main dishes ¥650–¥850. No credit cards. Daily 11am–7pm (last
order). Station: Nikko Tobu (15 min.). On the left side of the main street leading from Toshogu Shrine, 1
min. before the Nikko Kanaya Hotel and the Sacred Bridge.

3 YOKOHAMA, CITY OF THE 21ST CENTURY

29km (18 miles) S of Tokyo

Few attractions in Yokohama warrant a visit if your time is limited. If you find yourself
in Tokyo for an extended period, however, Yokohama is a pleasant destination for an easy
day trip. Be sure to make time for wonderful Sankeien Garden; although a mere 90-some
years old, it ranks on my long list as one of the top gardens in Japan.

A rather new city in Japan's history books, Yokohama was nothing more than a tiny
fishing village when Commodore Perry arrived in the mid-1800s and demanded that
Japan open its doors to the world. The village was selected by the shogun as one of several
ports to be opened for international trade, transforming it from a backwater to Japan's
most important gateway. Yokohama subsequently grew by leaps and bounds and was a
pioneer when it came to Western goods and services, boasting Japan's first bakery (1860),
photo studio (1862), beer brewery (1869), cinema (1870), daily newspaper (1870),
public restroom (1871), and ice cream (1879).

Now Japan's second-largest city with a population of almost 3.6 million, Yokohama
remains the nation's largest international port and supports a large international community, with many foreigners residing in the section called the Bluff. Yokohama has an
especially large Chinese population and Japan's largest Chinatown, whose restaurants
serve as a mecca for hungry Tokyoites. Befitting a city known for its firsts, Yokohama
constructed Japan's first and largest urban development project more than a decade
ago—**Minato Mirai 21,** with a conference center, museums, hotels, shopping centers,
and restaurants. Hard to imagine that a mere 150 years ago, Yokohama was a village of
100 houses.

ESSENTIALS

GETTING THERE   Because many Yokohama residents work in Tokyo, it's as easy to get
to Yokohama as it is to get around Tokyo. Although Yokohama Station is the city's main
train station, I suggest taking a train from Tokyo that will take you farther to Sakuragicho,
Minato Mirai, or Motomachi Chukagai station, since most attractions are clustered here.

(However, if you're headed first to Sankeien Garden, you'll want to disembark at Yokohama Station and transfer to bus no. 8 at the east exit.) Best is the **Minato Mirai Line** (of the Tokyu-Toyoko private company), which departs from Shibuya and reaches Minato Mirai in about 30 minutes on the limited express. A one-way fare costs ¥440; an all-day Minato Mirai Line pass, including transportation from Shibuya and back, is worth the cost of ¥840. Alternatively, the **JR Keihin-Tohoku Line** travels through Ueno, Tokyo, Yurakucho, Shimbashi, and Shinagawa stations before continuing on to Sakuragicho, with the journey from Tokyo Station taking approximately 40 minutes and costing ¥540 one-way.

VISITOR INFORMATION   There are several Tourist Information Centers in Yokohama, but probably the most convenient and easiest to find is **Sakuragicho Station Tourist Information Center** (✆ 045/211-0111; daily 9am–7pm), located in a kiosk outside JR Sakuragicho Station in the direction of Minato Mirai and its Landmark Tower. The main office, the **Yokohama Convention & Visitors Bureau,** is located in the Sangyo Boeki Center (nicknamed Sambo Center), 2 Yamashita-cho, Naka-ku (✆ 045/641-4759; www.welcome.city.yokohama.jp; Mon–Fri 9am–5pm), close to the Silk Center and Yamashita Park. Both have excellent city maps and brochures.

Next door to the Convention & Visitors Bureau, in the Silk Center, is the **Kanagawa Prefectural Tourist Office** (✆ 045/681-0007; www.kanagawa-kankou.or.jp; Tues–Sun 10am–6pm), with information on Hakone and Kamakura, both in Kanagawa Prefecture.

GETTING AROUND   If you start your day in Yokohama at either Sakuragicho or Minato Mirai Station, you can visit the museums and attractions there and then walk onward to Yamashita Park via a waterfront promenade (about a 30-min. walk, with a stop, perhaps, at the Red Brick Warehouse shopping mall on the way). If you prefer not to walk, there's a red retro-looking tourist bus called the **Akai Kutsu** which makes the rounds of central Yokohama, including Sakuragicho Station, Minato Mirai, Yamashita Park, and Chinatown throughout the year, with departures every 20 to 30 minutes and costing ¥100 per ride (pick up a map and timetable at the Sakuragicho Station tourist office). To reach Sankeien Garden, take bus no. 8, which departs from Yokohama Station's east exit and passes Minato Mirai, Chinatown, and Yamashita Park on its way to the garden. If you end the day with a meal at Chinatown, you can catch the Minato Mirai Line back to Shibuya at nearby Motomachi Chukagai Station.

SEEING THE SIGHTS

MINATO MIRAI   There's no mistaking **Minato Mirai 21** (www.minatomirai21.com) when you see it—it looks like a vision of the future with its dramatic monolithic buildings. It boasts a huge state-of-the-art convention facility, three first-class hotels, Japan's tallest building, office buildings, two great museums, and an amusement park. It's all a bit too sterile for my taste, but its museums make a visit here worthwhile.

If you arrive at Sakuragicho Station, take the moving walkway that connects the station to the Landmark Tower in Minato Mirai in 5 minutes. Otherwise, the Minato Mirai Line will deposit you directly in the middle of the massive urban development.

There are several shopping malls in Minato Mirai, including Queen's Square, Yokohama World Porter's, Landmark Plaza, Jack Mall, and the restored Red Brick Warehouse, but the area's most conspicuous building is **Landmark Tower,** Japan's tallest building and also with Japan's highest observatory in a building. The fastest elevator in the world will whisk you up 270m (886 ft.) in about 40 seconds to the 69th floor, where there's an observation room called **Sky Garden** (✆ 045/222-5030; daily 10am–9pm, to 10pm

North Pier

0   1/4 mi
0   0.25 km

ATTRACTIONS ●
China Museum **10**
Landmark Tower **2**
Red Brick Warehouse **6**
Silk Museum **7**
Yamashita Park **8**
Yokohama Cosmo World **4**
Yokohama Doll Museum **11**
Yokohama Museum of Art **1**
Yokohama Port Museum **5**

Yokohama Sta. ⓘ
Sea Bass Terminal
SEASIDE PARK
Sea Bass Terminal
MINATO MIRAI LINE
Metropolitan Expressway
Minato Mirai Sta.
MINATO MIRAI
Center Pier
Sakuragicho Sta. ⓘ
South Pier
KEIHINKYUKO LINE
NOGEYAMA PARK & ZOO
Bashamichi Shopping Street
Kaigan Dori
Nihon Odori
Kannai Sta.
Yokohama Stadium
Main St ⓘ
Motomachi Chukagai Sta.
Sea Bass Terminal
NEGISHI LINE
CHINATOWN
Isezaki Mall Shopping Street
Ishikawacho Sta.
Motomachi Shopping Street
YAMATE-CHO (BLUFF AREA)
Italian Garden

- - - - Ferry/shuttles
━━━ Railway
━━━ Subway
ⓘ Tourist Info

DINING ◆
Beer Next **6**   Hard Rock Cafe **3**
Chinatown **9**   Kua 'Aina **6**
daidaiya **3**   Sirius Sky Lounge **2**

SIDE TRIPS FROM TOKYO

7

YOKOHAMA, CITY OF THE 21ST CENTURY

Sat). From here you can see the harbor with its container port and Yokohama Bay Bridge, as well as almost the entire city and even, on clear days in winter, Mount Fuji. However, its admission fees—¥1,000 for adults, ¥800 for seniors and high-school students, ¥500 for elementary and junior-high students, and ¥200 for children—make it too expensive in my book. Better is Landmark Tower's 70th-floor **Sirius Sky Lounge;** although there's a cover charge, its atmosphere is more relaxing (see below).

Maritime buffs should spend an hour checking out the **Yokohama Port Museum (Yokohama Minato Hakubutsukan),** 2–1–1 Minato Mirai (ⓒ 045/221-0280; www. nippon-maru.or.jp), which concentrates on Yokohama's history as a port, beginning with the arrival of Perry's "Black Ships." Other displays chart the evolution of ships from Japan and around the world from the 19th century to the present, with lots of models of everything from passenger ships to oil tankers and a full-scale simulator that lets you bring a cruise ship into Yokohama's port. Kids like the three telescopes connected to cameras placed around Yokohama and the captain's bridge with a steering wheel; sailing fans enjoy touring the 96m (315-ft.), four-masted *Nippon-Maru* moored nearby, built in 1930 as a sail-training ship for students of the merchant marines. Admission is ¥600 for adults and ¥300 for children. The museum is open Tuesday to Sunday 10am to 5pm.

The most important thing to see in Minato Mirai is the **Yokohama Museum of Art★**, 3–4–1 Minato Mirai (ⓒ 045/221-0300; www.yaf.or.jp/yma), which emphasizes 20th-century art by Western and Japanese artists in its ambitious goal to collect and display works reflecting the mutual influence of Europe and Japan on modern art since the opening of Yokohama's port in 1859. The light and airy building, designed by Kenzo Tange and Urtec Inc., features exhibits from its permanent collection—which includes works by Cézanne, Picasso, Matisse, Leger, Max Ernst, Dalí, and Japanese artists—that change three times a year (you can tour its four rooms in about 30 min.), as well as special exhibitions on loan from other museums. Open Friday through Wednesday from 10am to 6pm. Admission is ¥500 for adults, ¥300 for high-school and college students, and ¥100 for children. Special exhibitions cost more.

It would be hard to miss **Yokohama Cosmo World** (ⓒ 045/641-6591; www.senyo. co.jp/cosmo), an amusement park spread along both sides of a canal: it boasts one of the largest Ferris wheels in the world. Other diversions include a roller coaster that looks like it dives right into a pond (but vanishes instead into a tunnel), a haunted house, a simulation theater with seats that move with the action, kiddie rides, a games arcade, and much more. Admission is free but rides cost ¥300 to ¥700 apiece. The park is open daily 11am to 8pm in winter and 11am to 10pm in summer; closed most Thursdays (except in summer).

IN & AROUND YAMASHITA PARK   You can walk to Yamashita Park from Minato Mirai's Cosmo World in less than 30 minutes along a waterfront promenade. Along the way you'll pass the **Red Brick Warehouse (Aka Renga),** located in the Shinko-cho district of Minato Mirai (ⓒ 045/227-2002). This restored waterfront warehouse is home to dozens of shops selling crafts, furniture, housewares, clothing, and jewelry, as well as restaurants, with most shops open daily 11am to 8pm. If you don't want to walk, take the Minato Mirai Line to either Nihon Odori or Motomachi Chukagai Station, from which Yamashita Park is about a 5-minute walk.

Laid out after the huge 1923 earthquake that destroyed much of Tokyo and Yokohama, Yamashita Park is Japan's first seaside park, a pleasant place for a stroll along the waterfront where you have a view of the city's mighty harbor and Bay Bridge. Across the gingko-lined street from Yamashita Park are two worthwhile special-interest museums. At the west end (closest to Minato Mirai) is the Silk Center, where you'll find both the prefectural tourist office and the excellent **Silk Museum★★**, 1 Yamashita-cho, Naka-ku (ⓒ 045/641-0841; www.silkmuseum.or.jp; station: Nihon Odori). For many years after Japan opened its doors, silk was its major export, and most of it was shipped to the rest of the world from Yokohama, the nation's largest raw-silk market. In tribute to the role silk has played in Yokohama's history, this museum has displays showing the metamorphosis of the silkworm and the process by which silk is obtained from cocoons, all well documented in English; from April to October you can even observe live cocoons and silkworms at work (compared to the beauty they produce, silkworms are amazingly ugly). The museum also displays various kinds of silk fabrics, as well as gorgeous kimono and reproduction Japanese costumes from the Nara, Heian, and Edo periods. Don't miss this museum, which takes about 30 minutes to see; surprisingly, it's never crowded. Open Tuesday through Sunday from 9am to 4:30pm; admission is ¥500 for adults, ¥300 for seniors, ¥200 for students, and ¥100 for children.

At the opposite end of Yamashita Park is the **Yokohama Doll Museum,** 18 Yamashita-cho (ⓒ 045/671-9361; www.museum.or.jp/yokohama-doll-museum; station: Motomachi

Chukagai), which boasts a collection of approximately 13,000 dolls from 140 countries, with about 1,300 dolls on display. A trip through the museum begins with a collection of old Western dolls introduced to Japan when Yokohama opened as an international harbor, as well as Japanese dolls sent to the West. Exhibits that follow feature dolls from around the world dressed in their native costume, popular international figures of the past few decades (from Hello Kitty to R2-D2 of *Star Wars* fame), antique dolls (including those produced by such famous doll makers as Lenci and Jumeau), and Japanese dolls, from *hina* (elaborate dolls representing the empress and emperor, used for the March Hina Festival) to *kokeshi* (simple wooden dolls). Open daily 10am to 6:30pm; closed the third Monday of every month (except July–Aug and Dec). Admission is ¥500 for adults and ¥150 for children. Plan on spending about 30 minutes here.

Not far from Yamashita Park is **Chukagai,** Japan's largest Chinatown with hundreds of souvenir shops and restaurants; see "Where to Dine," below.

SANKEIEN GARDEN ★★★ In my opinion, **Sankeien Garden** (© 045/621-0634; www.sankeien.or.jp) is the best reason to visit Yokohama. Although not old itself, this lovely park contains more than a dozen historic buildings that were brought here from other parts of Japan, including Kyoto and Nara, all situated around streams and ponds and surrounded by Japanese-style landscape gardens. The park, divided into an Inner Garden and Outer Garden, was laid out in 1906 by Tomitaro Hara, a local millionaire who made his fortune exporting silk. As you wander along the gently winding pathways, you'll see a villa built in 1649 by the Tokugawa shogunate clan, tea arbors, a 500-year-old three-story pagoda, and a farmhouse built in 1750 without the use of nails. The gardens are well known for their blossoms of plums, cherries, wisteria, azaleas, irises, and waterlilies, but no matter what the season, the views here are beautiful.

Plan on at least 2 hours to see both gardens. Sankeien is open daily from 9am to 5pm (you must enter the Inner Garden by 4pm, the Outer Garden by 4:30pm). Admission is ¥500 for adults, ¥300 for seniors, and ¥200 for children. The easiest way to reach Sankeien Garden is by bus no. 8, which departs from platform no. 2 at Yokohama Station's east exit (near Sogo department store) and winds its way past Sakuragicho Station, past Chinatown (via Hon-cho Dori), and through Kannai before it reaches the Honmoku-Sankeien-mae bus stop 30 minutes later (the bus stop is announced in English).

WHERE TO DINE

CHINATOWN (CHUKAGAI)   Located in Yamashita-cho, a couple blocks inland from Yamashita Park and next to Motomachi Chukagai Station of the Minato Mirai Line, Chinatown has more than 500 restaurants and shops lining two main streets and dozens of offshoots. Tokyoites have long been coming to Yokohama just to dine; many of the restaurants have been owned by the same families for generations. Most serve Cantonese food and have plastic-food displays, English-language menus, or pictures of their dishes, so your best bet is to wander around and let your budget be your guide. Most dishes run ¥850 to ¥3,000, and set lunches go for ¥900 to ¥1,200. Larger restaurants accept credit cards; those that do display them on the front door. Most Chinatown restaurants are open from 11 or 11:30am to 9:30pm or later; some close Tuesday or Wednesday, but there are always other restaurants open.

While here, you might want to take a spin through the **China Museum (Yokohama Daisekai),** 97 Yamashita-cho (© 045/681-5588), an eight-story building with an interior that replicates Shanghai of the 1920s and 1930s (Shanghai and Yokohama are sister cities), with re-created street scenes, artisans producing traditional crafts, souvenir shops, and a food court with stalls offering dishes from around China, most priced less than ¥800. It's open Sunday to Thursday 10am to 9pm, and Friday and Saturday 10am to 10pm.

MINATO-MIRAI   For sophisticated surroundings or just a romantic evening cocktail, take the elevator up to the 70th floor of Landmark Tower, where you'll find the Yoko-hama Royal Park Hotel Nikko's **Sirius Sky Lounge** ★ (✆ **045/221-1111**), with stun-ning seaside views. It serves a buffet lunch for ¥3,500 daily from 11:30am to 2:30pm, which often centers on a changing, ethnic cuisine but also offers items like salmon, lamb, and pizza. After lunch, it's teatime until 5pm. From 5pm to 1am daily, Sirius is a cocktail lounge (no one 19 and under allowed) and levies a cover charge: ¥1,050 per person from 5 to 7pm and again from 11pm to 1am; ¥2,100 for live music from 7 to 11pm. It offers a small, a la carte dinner menu, as well as set dinners for ¥6,300 and ¥9,450.

Nearby, a good place for a drink or a hamburger is the local branch of the **Hard Rock Cafe,** located on the first floor of Queen's Square Yokohama Tower A (✆ **045/682-5626;** open daily 11am–11pm). Nearby, on the fourth and fifth floors of the Queen's Square Yokohama, is a branch of **daidaiya** (✆ **045/228-5035;** open daily 11am–3pm and 5–10:30pm). See p. 174 and 177 for reviews of these restaurants.

The 1911 renovated Red Brick Warehouse (see above) also has fast-food outlets, including a **Kua' Aina** burger shop (✆ **045/227-5300;** p. 168), but for something more substantial, head to the third floor for **Beer Next** (✆ **045/226-1961;** daily 11am–10pm [last order]), which strives admirably to create an international cuisine that goes down well with beer. Pizza, pasta, rotisserie roast chicken, and seared tuna with garlic oil and soy sauce are just some of the dishes offered; prices range from ¥1,470 to ¥2,310.

4 MOUNT FUJI ★★

100km (62 miles) SW of Tokyo

Mount Fuji, affectionately called "Fuji-san" by Japanese, has been revered since ancient times. Throughout the centuries, Japanese poets have written about it, painters have painted it, pilgrims have flocked to it, and more than a few people have died on it. Without a doubt, this mountain has been photographed more than anything else in Japan.

Mount Fuji is stunningly impressive. At 3,766m (12,355 ft.), it's the tallest mountain in Japan, towering far above anything else around it, a cone of almost perfectly sym-metrical proportions. Mount Fuji is majestic, grand, and awe-inspiring. To Japanese, it symbolizes the very spirit of their country. Though it's visible on clear days (mostly in winter) from as far as 150km (100 miles) away, Fuji-san, unfortunately, is almost always cloaked in clouds. If you catch a glimpse of this elusive mountain (which you can some-times do from the bullet train btw. Tokyo and Nagoya), consider yourself extremely lucky. Some of the best spots for views of Mount Fuji are **Hakone** and **Izu** (discussed later).

ESSENTIALS

There are four ascents to the summit of Mount Fuji (and four descents), each divided into 10 stations of unequal length, with most climbs starting at the Go-go-me, or the Fifth Station, about 1,400 to 2,400m (4,593–7,874 ft.) above sea level. From Tokyo, the **Kawaguchiko-Yoshidaguchi Trail** is the most popular and most easily accessible, as well as the least steep. The "official" climbing season is very short, only from July 1 to August

31. Climbers are discouraged from climbing outside the season, due to low temperatures, superstrong winds, and no emergency services. To beat the crowds—and I do mean crowds—try to schedule your climb on a weekday during the first 2 weeks of July, before the start of Japan's school vacation (around July 20).

GETTING THERE   The easiest way to reach the Kawaguchiko Fifth Station is by **bus** from Shinjuku Station. In July and August there are six buses daily that travel directly from Shinjuku Station to Kawaguchiko Trail's Fifth Station, costing ¥2,600 one-way and taking almost 2½ hours. Otherwise, there are also buses that go to Kawaguchiko Station in 1 hour and 45 minutes and cost ¥1,700 one-way; from Kawaguchiko Station there are buses onward to the Fifth Station, with this trip taking approximately 45 minutes and costing another ¥1,500 one-way or ¥2,000 round-trip. Buses, which depart a 2-minute walk from the west side of Shinjuku Station in front of the Yasuda Seimi no. 2 Building, require reservations, which you can make at the **Keio Highway Bus Reservation Center** (**Keio Kosoku Bus Yoyaku Center;** ℂ **03/5376-2222**) or a travel agency such as JTB. Less frequent **Fujikyu Buses** (ℂ **0555/72-5111**) depart from Tokyo Station's Yaesu south exit for Kawaguchiko Station for ¥1,700, but the trip takes an hour longer.

If you want to use your Japan Rail Pass, you can leave from Tokyo's Shinjuku Station via the **JR Chuo Line** to Otsuki, where you change to the **Fuji Kyuko Line** for Kawaguchiko Station. The entire trip takes about 3 hours. Note, however, that you must pay an extra ¥1,110 for the last leg of the journey, and from Kawaguchiko Station you must still take the 45-minute bus ride onward to the Fifth Station.

VISITOR INFORMATION   More information and train and bus schedules can be obtained from the **Tokyo Tourist Information Center** (see "Visitor Information," in chapter 5), including a leaflet called "Mount Fuji and Fuji Five Lakes." A good online source is Fujiyoshida City's website, **www.city.fujiyoshida.yamanashi.jp**, which carries information on the Kawaguchiko-Yoshidaguchi Trail, bus schedules from Tokyo, mountain huts, and other information. Finally, there's a tourist information office at Kawaguchiko Station (ℂ **0555/72-6700**), open daily 9am to 5pm during climbing season.

CLIMBING MOUNT FUJI

Mount Fuji is part of a larger national park called **Fuji-Hakone-Izu National Park.** Of the handful of trails leading to the top, most popular for Tokyoites is the **Kawaguchiko-Yoshidaguchi Trail,** which is divided into 10 different stages; the Fifth Station, located about 2,475m (8,120 ft.) up and served by bus, is the usual starting point. From here it takes about 6 hours to reach the summit and 3 hours for the descent.

PREPARING FOR YOUR CLIMB   Because of snow and inclement weather from fall to late spring, the best time to make an ascent is during the "official" climbing season from July to August. Keep in mind that this is not a solitary pursuit. Rather, more than 400,000 people climb Fuji-san every year, mostly in July and August and mostly on weekends—so if you plan on climbing Mount Fuji on a Saturday or a Sunday in summer, go to the end of the line, please.

You don't need climbing experience to ascend Mount Fuji (you'll see everyone from grandmothers to children making the pilgrimage), but you do need stamina and a good pair of walking shoes. The climb is possible in tennis shoes, but if the rocks are wet, they can get awfully slippery. You should also bring a light plastic raincoat (which you can buy at souvenir shops at the Fifth Station)—it often rains on the mountain—a sun hat, sunglasses, a bottle of water, a sweater for the evening, gloves, socks, tissues (for pay toilets, which may not have toilet paper), and a flashlight (or headlamp) if you plan on hiking

> ## (Fun Facts Mount Fuji or Bust
>
> The first documented case of someone scaling Mount Fuji is from the early 8th century. During the Edo Period, pilgrimages to the top were considered a purifying ritual, with strict rules governing dress and route. Women, thought to defile sacred places, were prohibited from climbing mountains until 1871.

at night. It gets very chilly on Mount Fuji at night. Even in August, the average temperature on the summit is 43°F (6°C). Finally, there are places to eat and rest on the way to the top, but prices are high, so carry as many snacks and liquids with you as you can.

Don't be disappointed when your bus deposits you at **Kawaguchiko Fifth Station,** where you'll be bombarded with souvenir shops, restaurants, and busloads of tourists; most of these tourists aren't climbing to the top. As soon as you get past them and the blaring loudspeakers, you'll find yourself on a steep rocky path, surrounded only by scrub brush and the hikers on the path below and above you. After a couple of hours, you'll probably find yourself above the roily clouds, which stretch in all directions. It will be as if you are on an island, barren and rocky, in the middle of an ocean.

Strategies for Climbing to the Top   The usual procedure for climbing Mount Fuji is to take a morning bus, start climbing in early afternoon, spend the night near the summit, get up early in the morning to climb the rest of the way to the top, and then watch the sun rise (about 4:30am) from atop Mount Fuji. (You can, of course, also wake up in time to see the sun rise and then continue climbing.) At the summit is a 1-hour hiking trail that circles the crater. Hikers then begin the descent, reaching the Fifth Station before noon. There are about 16 **mountain huts** along the Kawaguchiko Trail above the Fifth Station, but they're very primitive, providing only a futon and toilet facilities. Some have the capacity to house 500 hikers. The cost is ¥5,250 per person without meals, ¥7,350 with two meals. Some huts charge ¥1,000 extra for Friday or Saturday night. When I stayed in one of these huts, dinner consisted of dried fish, rice, miso soup, and pickled vegetables; breakfast was exactly the same. Still, unless you want to carry your own food, I'd opt for the meals. Note that most huts are open only in July and August; book as early as you can to ensure a place. I recommend **Seikanso** at the 6th stage (© 0555/24-6090; www.seikanso.jp), with flush toilets and open from July to mid-October; **Toyokan Hut** at the 7th Stage (© 0555/22-1040), or **Taishikan Hut** at the 8th Stage (© 0555/22-1947). Call the **Japanese Inn Union of Mount Fuji** at © 0555/22-1944 for more information.

In the past few decades, there's been a trend in which climbers arrive at the Fifth Station late in the evening and then climb to the top during the night with the aid of flashlights. After watching the sunrise, they then make their descent. That way, they don't have to spend the night in one of the huts. My days of walking up a mountain through the night, however, are far behind me.

Climbing Mount Fuji is definitely a unique experience, but there's a saying in Japan: "Everyone should climb Mount Fuji once; only a fool would climb it twice."

5 HAKONE ★★★

97km (60 miles) SW of Tokyo

Part of the **Fuji-Hakone-Izu National Park ★★**, Hakone is one of the closest and most popular destinations for residents of Tokyo. Beautiful Hakone has about everything a vacationer could wish for: hot-spring resorts, mountains, lakes, breathtaking views of Mount Fuji, and interesting historical sites. You can tour Hakone as a day trip if you leave early in the morning and limit your sightseeing to a few key attractions, but adding an overnight stay—complete with a soak in a hot-spring tub—is much more rewarding. If you can, travel on a weekday, when modes of transportation are less crowded and some hotels offer cheaper weekday rates.

ESSENTIALS

GETTING THERE & GETTING AROUND   Getting to and around Hakone is half the fun! An easy loop tour you can follow through Hakone includes various forms of unique transportation: Starting out by train from Tokyo, you switch to a three-car streetcar that zigzags up the mountain, then change to a cable car, and then to a smaller ropeway (aerial streetcar), and end your trip with a boat ride across Lake Ashi, stopping to see major attractions along the way. From Lake Ashi (that is, from the villages of Togendai, Hakone-machi, or Moto-Hakone), you can then board a bus bound for Odawara Station (an hour's ride), where you board the train back to Tokyo. These same buses also pass by all the recommendations listed below, which is useful if you wish to complete most of your sightseeing the first day before going to your hotel for the evening. A bus also runs directly between Togendai and Shinjuku in about 2 hours.

Odakyu operates the most convenient network of trains, buses, streetcars, cable cars, and boats to and around Hakone. The most economical and by far easiest way to see Hakone is with Odakyu's **Hakone Free Pass,** which, despite its name, isn't free but does give you a round-trip ticket on the express train from Shinjuku Station to Odawara or Hakone Yumoto and includes all modes of transportation in Hakone listed above and described below. The pass lets you avoid the hassle of buying individual tickets and gives nominal discounts on most Hakone attractions. A 2-day pass costs ¥5,000 and a 3-day pass is ¥5,500. Children pay ¥1,500 and ¥1,750 respectively.

The trip from Shinjuku to Odawara via Odakyu Express takes 90 minutes, with departures two to four times an hour. In Odawara, you then transfer to another train for a 15-minute trip to Hakone Yumoto; trains depart four times an hour. If time is of the essence or if you want to ensure a seat during peak season, reserve a seat on the faster and more luxurious **Odakyu Romance Car,** which travels from Shinjuku all the way to Hakone Yumoto in 1½ hours and costs an extra ¥870 one-way with a Hakone Pass.

If you have a **Japan Rail Pass,** you should take the Shinkansen bullet train first to Odawara (not all bullet trains stop here, so make sure yours does). From there, you can buy a 2-day Hakone Free Pass for ¥3,900 or a 3-day Pass for ¥4,400. Children pay ¥1,000 and ¥1,250 respectively.

All passes described above can be purchased at any station of the Odakyu Railway, including Shinjuku and Odawara. In Tokyo, the best place to purchase Hakone Free Pass tickets is at the **Odakyu Sightseeing Service Center,** located on the ground floor near the west exit of Odakyu Shinjuku Station (© **03/5321-7887;** www.odakyu.jp/english;

daily 8am–6pm), where you can obtain sightseeing information in English in addition to purchasing tickets.

VISITOR INFORMATION   Before leaving Tokyo, pick up the "Hakone and Kamakura" leaflet available from the Tourist Information Center; it provides transportation information for throughout the Hakone area. A color brochure called "Hakone National Park" includes sightseeing information and contains a map of the Hakone area. See "Visitor Information" in chapter 5 for TIC locations. The Odakyu Sightseeing Service Center, above, also has a wealth of information, including the useful *Timetable of Traffic in Hakone,* a booklet that lists the schedules for all forms of transportation in Hakone.

In Odawara, the **Odawara Tourist Information Center** (✆ **0465/33-1521;** daily 9am–5pm) is inside Odawara Station. In Hakone Yumoto, the **Yumoto Tourist Office** (✆ **0460/85-8911;** daily 9:30am–6pm Apr–Nov, to 5:30pm Dec–Mar) is across the street from Hakone Yumoto Station.

LUGGAGE   If you plan to return to Tokyo, I suggest you leave your luggage in storage at your Tokyo hotel or at Shinjuku Station and travel to Hakone with only an overnight bag. If you're traveling onward to, say, Kyoto, you can leave your bags at a check-in counter at Hakone Yumoto Station, open daily 8am to 10pm (a large bag costs ¥500 a day). Or, if you deliver your bags to the **Hakone Carry Service** (✆ **0460/86-4140**) at Hakone Yumoto Station between 8:30am and noon, it will transport your bags to your Hakone accommodations by 3pm. The next day, it can also pick up your bags at your hotel at 10am and deliver them to Yumoto Station by 1pm, where they will keep them until 7pm. The service costs ¥700 to ¥1,000 per bag, depending on the size and weight, and is available daily year-round.

EXPLORING HAKONE

STRATEGIES FOR SEEING HAKONE   If you plan on spending only a day in Hakone, you should leave Tokyo very early in the morning and plan on visiting only a few key attractions—I recommend the **Hakone Open-Air Museum, Owakudani Nature Trail,** and, if time permits, **Hakone Check Point** and/or **Narukawa Art Museum.** Keep in mind that most forms of transportation (like the ropeway), as well as museums, close at 5pm.

If you're spending the night—and I strongly urge that you do—you can arrange your itinerary in a more leisurely fashion and devote more time to Hakone's attractions. You may wish to travel only as far as your hotel the first day, stopping at sights along the way and in the vicinity. The next day you could continue with the rest of the circuit through Hakone. Or, you can opt to complete most of your sightseeing the first day, and then backtrack to your accommodations or reach it by bus from Togendai, Hakone-machi, or Moto-Hakone.

SCENIC RAILWAY TO GORA   Regardless of whether you travel via the Odakyu Romance Car or the ordinary Odakyu express, you'll end up at Hakone Yumoto Station. Here you'll transfer to the **Hakone Tozan Railway,** in operation since 1919. This delightful, mountain-climbing, three-car electric streetcar winds its way through forests and over streams and ravines as it travels upward to Gora, making several switchbacks along the way. The entire trip from Hakone Yumoto Station to Gora takes only 40 minutes, but the ride through the mountains is beautiful and this is my favorite part of the whole journey. The railway, which runs every 10 to 15 minutes, makes about a half-dozen stops before reaching Gora, including **Tonosawa** and **Miyanoshita,** two hot-spring spa resorts with a number of old *ryokan* and hotels. Some of the ryokan date back several centuries, to the days when they were on the main thoroughfare to Edo, called

LEGEND

- ⓘ Tourist Info
- ▪▪▪ Cable Car
- ▬▬ Mountain Tram
- ▬ ▬ Railway
- ▬·▬ Ropeway
- ─ ─ Sightseeing boat

ACCOMMODATIONS ■
Ashinoko Camp Mura **1**
Fuji-Hakone Guest House **2**
The Fujiya Hotel **7**
Ichinoyu **8**

DINING ◆
Bella Foresta **6**
Main Dining Room **7**
Owakudani Sky **3**

ATTRACTIONS ●
Hakone Kowakien
Yunessun **5**
Hakone Museum of Art **4**
Hakone Check Point **10**
Hakone Detached
Palace Garden **11**
Hakone Open-Air Museum **6**
Owakudani Nature Trail **3**
Tokaido Highway **12**

the old Tokaido Highway. Miyanoshita is the best place for lunch. See "Where to Stay" and "Where to Dine," later.

For relaxing hot-springs bathing en route, visit the thoroughly modern, sophisticated public bath called **Hakone Kowakien Yunessun** ★★ (© **0460/82-4126;** www.yunessun.com/english). To reach it, disembark from the Hakone Tozan Railway at Kowakudani, and then take a 15-minute taxi or bus ride (bus stop: Kowaki-en). This self-described "Hot Springs Amusement Park & Spa Resort" offers a variety of both indoor and outdoor family baths, which means you wear your bathing suit. In addition to indoor Turkish, Roman, and salt baths, there's also a children's play area with slides and a large outdoor area with a variety of small baths, including those mixed with healthy minerals and—I am not making this up—coffee, green tea, sake, and wine. For those who desire more traditional bathing, there's the Mori No Yu, with both indoor and outdoor baths separated for men and women (you don't wear your suit here). Most people who come stay 2 to 3 hours. Admission is ¥3,500 to Yunessun, ¥1,800 to Mori No Yu, or ¥4,000 to both; if you have a Hakone Free Pass, you'll pay ¥2,800, ¥1,400 or ¥3,200 respectively. Children pay half-fare. Upon admission, you'll be given a towel, robe, and wristband to pay for drinks and extras (rental suits are available), so you can leave all valuables in your assigned locker. Yunessun is open daily 9am to 7pm March to October, 9am to 6pm in November to February; Mori No Yu is open 9am to 9pm year-round.

The most important stop on the Hakone Tozan Railway is the next-to-the-last stop, Chokoku-no-Mori, where you'll find the famous **Hakone Open-Air Museum (Chokoku-no-Mori Bijutsukan)** ★★★ (© **0460/82-1161;** www.hakone-oam.or.jp), a minute's walk from the station. With the possible exception of views of Mount Fuji, this museum is, in my opinion, Hakone's number-one attraction. Using nature as a dramatic backdrop, it showcases sculpture primarily of the 20th century in a spectacular setting of glens, formal gardens, ponds, and meadows. There are 400 sculptures on display, both outdoors and in several buildings, with works by Carl Milles, Manzu Giacomo, Jean Dubuffet, Willem de Kooning, Barbara Hepworth, and Joan Miró, as well as more than 25 pieces by Henry Moore, shown on a rotating basis. The Picasso Pavilion contains works by Picasso from pastels to ceramics (it's one of the world's largest collections) and photographs of the artist's last 17 years of life taken by David Douglas Duncan. The Picture Gallery is devoted to changing exhibitions. Several installations geared toward children allow them to climb and play. I could spend all day here; barring that, count on staying at least 2 hours. Be sure to stop off at the "foot *onsen*" near the Picture Gallery, where you can immerse your tired feet in soothing, hot-spring water. The museum is open daily 9am to 5pm; admission is ¥1,600 adults, ¥1,100 university and high-school students and seniors, and ¥800 children. Your Hakone Free Pass gives you a ¥200 discount.

BY CABLE CAR TO SOUNZAN   Cable cars leave Gora every 20 minutes or so and arrive 9 minutes later at the end station of Sounzan, making several stops along the way as they travel steeply uphill. One of the stops is Koen-Kami, from which it's only a minute's walk to the **Hakone Museum of Art** (© **0460/82-2623;** www.moaart.or.jp/english/hakone). This five-room museum displays Japanese pottery and ceramics from the Jomon Period (around 4000–2000 B.C.) to the Edo Period, including terra-cotta *haniwa* burial figures, huge 16th-century Bizen jars, and Imari ware. What makes this place particularly rewarding are the bamboo grove and small but lovely moss garden, shaded by Japanese maples, with a teahouse where you can sample Japanese tea for ¥630. Open Friday through Wednesday from 9:30am to 4:30pm (to 4pm Dec–Mar); admission is

¥900 for adults, ¥700 for seniors, ¥400 for university and high-school students, and free for children. The Hakone Free Pass gives you a ¥200 discount. Plan on spending about a half-hour here, more if you opt for tea.

BY ROPEWAY TO TOGENDAI From Sounzan, you board a ropeway with gondolas for a 30-minute haul over a mountain to Togendai on the other side, which lies beside Lake Ashi, known as Lake Ashinoko in Japanese. Note that the ropeway stops running at around 5:15pm in summer and 4pm in winter.

Before reaching Togendai, however, get off at the first stop, Owakudani, the ropeway's highest point, to hike the 30-minute **Owakudani Nature Trail ★**. Owakudani means "Great Boiling Valley," and you'll soon understand how it got its name when you see (and smell) the sulfurous steam escaping from fissures in the rock, testimony to the volcanic activity still present here. Most Japanese commemorate their trip by buying boiled eggs cooked here in the boiling waters, available at the small hut midway along the trail.

ACROSS LAKE ASHI BY BOAT From Togendai you can take a pleasure boat across Lake Ashi, also referred to as "Lake Hakone" in some English-language brochures. Believe it or not, a couple of the boats plying the waters are replicas of a man-of-war pirate ship. It takes about half an hour to cross the lake to Hakone-machi (also called simply Hakone; *machi* means city) and Moto-Hakone, two resort towns right next to each other on the southern edge of the lake. This end of the lake affords the best view of Mount Fuji, one often depicted in tourist publications. Boats are in operation year-round (though they run less frequently in winter and not at all in stormy weather); the last boat departs around 5pm from the end of March to the end of November. Buses connect Togendai with Moto-Hakone, Odawara, and Shinjuku.

After the boat ride, if you're heading back to Tokyo, buses depart for Odawara near the boat piers in both Hakone-machi and Moto-Hakone. Otherwise, for more sightseeing, get off the boat in Hakone-machi, turn left, and walk about 5 minutes on the town's main road, following the signs and turning left to **Hakone Check Point (Hakone Sekisho) ★ (© 0460/83-6635)**, on a road lined with souvenir shops. This is a reconstructed guardhouse originally built in 1619 to serve as a checkpoint along the famous Tokaido Highway, which connected Edo (present-day Tokyo) with Kyoto. In feudal days, local lords, called *daimyo,* were required to spend alternate years in Edo; their wives were kept in Edo as virtual hostages to discourage the lords from planning rebellions while in their homelands. This was one of several points along the highway that guarded against the transport of guns, spies, and female travelers trying to flee Edo. Passes were necessary for travel, and although it was possible to sneak around it, male violators who were caught were promptly executed, while women suffered the indignity of having their heads shaven and then being given away to anyone who wanted them. Inside the reconstructed guardhouse, which was rebuilt on the site of the original checkpoint using traditional carpenter tools and architectural techniques of the Edo Period, you'll see life-size models reenacting scenes inside a checkpoint. A small museum has displays relating to the Edo Period, including items used for travel, samurai armor, and gruesome articles of torture. Open daily from 9am to 5pm (until 4:30pm Dec–Feb); admission is ¥500 for adults and ¥250 for children. Your Hakone Free Pass gives you a ¥100 discount. It shouldn't take more than 20 minutes to see everything.

Just beyond the Hakone Check Point, at the big parking lot with the traditional gate, is the **Hakone Detached Palace Garden (Onshi-Hakone-Koen),** which lies on a small promontory on Lake Ashi and has spectacular views of the lake and, in clear weather, Mount Fuji. Originally part of an imperial summer villa built in 1886, the garden is open to the public 24 hours and admission is free. It's a great place for wandering. On its grounds is the **Lakeside Observation Building** (daily 9am–4:30pm), with displays relating to Hakone Palace, destroyed by earthquakes.

If you take the northernmost exit from the garden, crossing a bridge, you'll see the neighboring resort town, **Moto-Hakone,** down the road. Across the highway and lined with ancient and mighty cedars is part of the old **Tokaido Highway** itself. During the Edo Period, more than 400 cedars were planted along this important road, which today stretches 2.5km (1½ miles) along the curve of Lake Ashi and makes for a pleasant stroll (unfortunately, a modern road has been built right beside the original one). Moto-Hakone is a 5-minute walk from the Detached Palace Garden.

In Moto-Hakone, **Narukawa Art Museum** ★★ (© **0460/83-6828;** www.narukawa museum.co.jp) is worthwhile and located just after you enter town, up the hill to the right when you reach the orange *torii* gate. It specializes in modern works of the *Nihonga* style of painting, developed during the Heian Period (794–1185) and sparser than Western paintings (which tend to fill in backgrounds and every inch of canvas). Large paintings and screens by contemporary Nihonga artists are on display, including works by Yamamoto Kyujin, Maki Susumu, Kayama Matazo, Hirayama Ikuo, and Hori Fumiko. Changing exhibitions feature younger up-and-coming artists, as well as glassware. I wouldn't miss it; views of Lake Ashi and Mount Fuji are a bonus. Open daily 9am to 5pm; admission is ¥1,200 for adults, ¥900 for high-school and university students, and ¥600 for children.

WHEN YOU'RE DONE SIGHTSEEING FOR THE DAY   Buses depart for Hakone Yumoto and Odawara from both Hakone-machi and Moto-Hakone two to four times an hour. Be sure to check the time of the last departure; generally it's around 8pm, but this can change with the season and the day of the week. (The bus also passes two of the accommodations recommended below, the Fujiya Hotel and Ichinoyu, as well as Yunessun hot-springs baths; another bus will take you to Fuji-Hakone Guest House.) Otherwise, the trip from Moto-Hakone takes approximately 30 minutes to Hakone Yumoto and 50 minutes to Odawara, where you can catch the Odakyu train back to Shinjuku or the Shinkansen bullet train onward toward Nagoya and Kyoto.

WHERE TO STAY

Japan's *ryokan* sprang into existence to accommodate the stately processions of daimyo and shogun as they traversed the roads between Edo and the rest of Japan. Many of these ryokan were built along the Tokaido Highway, and some of the oldest are found in Hakone. Most accommodations cost more during peak travel times like Golden Week, school holidays, New Year's, weekends and national holidays.

Ashinoko Camp Mura **Kids**   Since you're in a national park, you might be inclined to enjoy nature by roughing it in a cabin beside Lake Ashi, just a 10-minute walk from the ropeway to Sounzan and the boat to Hakone-machi. Operated by Kanagawa Prefecture and also with tent camping, it offers row and detached (more expensive and closer to the lake) cabins that sleep up to six persons, each with two bedrooms, a bathroom, a living room with cooking facilities and tableware, and a deck with picnic table. However, there is no supermarket in nearby Togendai, so you'll either want to bring your own food or dine at the camp's restaurant, which offers both Japanese and Western selections (reservations required for lunch and dinner). There's a hiking trail around the lake. A great place for kids. Open year-round.

164 Hakone-machi, Moto-Hakone, Kanagawa 250-0522. ℂ **0460/84-8279.** Fax 0460/84-6489. 36 units. **257**

Peak season ¥26,250 row cabin, ¥31,500 detached cabin; off season ¥15,750 row cabin, ¥21,000 detached cabin. No credit cards. Bus: Togendai, from Odawara (1 hr.) or Shinjuku (2 hr.), and then a 10-min. walk. **Amenities:** Restaurant; rental bikes; barbecue grills; hot-spring bath. *In room:* Kitchenette.

Fuji-Hakone Guest House   It's a bit isolated, but this Japanese Inn Group member offers inexpensive, spotlessly clean lodging in *tatami* rooms, all nonsmoking. A 20-some-year-old house, situated in tranquil surroundings set back from a tree-shaded road, is run by a man who speaks very good English and is happy to provide sightseeing information, including a map of the area with local restaurants. Some of the rooms face the Hakone mountain range. Pluses are the communal lounge area with fridge, microwave, TV and even a piano, and the outdoor hot-spring bath (for which there's an extra ¥500 charge).

912 Sengokuhara, Hakone, Kanagawa 250-0631. ℂ **0460/84-6577.** Fax 0460/84-6578. http://hakone. syuriken.jp/hakone. 14 units (none with bathroom). ¥5,250–¥6,300 single; ¥10,500–¥12,600 double; ¥15,750–¥16,800 triple. Peak season and weekends ¥1,000–¥2,000 extra. Minimum 2-night stay preferred. Western breakfast ¥840 extra. AE, DC, MC, V. Bus: Hakone Tozan (included in the Hakone Free Pass) from Togendai (15 min.) or from Odawara Station (50 min.) to the Senkyoro-mae stop (announced in English), and then a 1-min. walk. **Amenities:** Computer (¥100 for 30 min.); hot-spring bath; free Wi-Fi in lobby. *In room:* A/C, TV.

The Fujiya Hotel ★★★ (Finds)   The Fujiya, established in 1878, is quite simply the grandest, most majestic old hotel in Hakone; indeed, it might be the loveliest historic hotel in Japan. I love this hotel for its comfortably old-fashioned atmosphere, including such Asian touches as a Japanese-style roof and long wooden corridors with photographs of famous guests, from Einstein to Eisenhower. A landscaped garden out back, with a waterfall, pond, greenhouse, outdoor pool, and stunning views over the valley is great for strolls and meditation. There's also a small hotel museum and an indoor thermal pool and public hot-spring baths (hot-spring water is also piped in to each guest's bathroom). Even if you don't stay here, come for a meal or tea.

There are five separate buildings, all different and added on at various times in the hotel's long history, but management has been meticulous in retaining its historic traditions. Rooms are old-fashioned and spacious with high ceilings and antique furnishings. The most expensive rooms are the largest, but my favorites are those in the Flower Palace, which has an architectural style reminiscent of a Japanese temple and seems unchanged since its 1936 construction. Be sure to ask the front desk for the hotel's map of the surrounding village and leaflets describing how to reach sightseeing spots in Hakone from the hotel.

Note: A limited number of the least expensive rooms in the main building (dating from 1891) are available for foreigners at a special discounted rate, in dollars, based on the hotel's age. However, the special rate is not available on Saturday, the night before national holidays, during Golden Week, the month of August, or New Year's. And if these discounted rooms are sold out, you'll pay the regular rate.

359 Miyanoshita, Hakone-machi, Kanagawa-ken 250-0404. ℂ **0460/82-2211.** Fax 0460/82-2210. www. fujiyahotel.jp. 146 units. Special rates for foreigners (excluding tax and service charge): $131 single or double in 2010, $132 in 2011. Regular rates: ¥20,040–¥44,190 single or double; ¥5,670–¥13,860 extra on Sat, night before holiday, and peak travel times. AE, DC, MC, V. Station: Miyanoshita (Hakone Tozan Railway; 5 min.). Bus: From Odawara or Moto-Hakone to Miyanoshita Onsen stop (1 min.). **Amenities:** 3 restaurants (see "Where to Dine," below); bar; golf course; hot-spring baths; Jacuzzi; museum; indoor/outdoor pools; room service; sauna; Wi-Fi in lobby. *In room:* A/C, TV, hair dryer, minibar.

SIDE TRIPS FROM TOKYO

7

HAKONE

㊸ **Ichinoyu ★★** Located near Tonosawa Station (on the Hakone Tozan Line) next to a roaring river, this delightful, rambling wooden building stands on a tree-shaded winding road that follows the track of the old Tokaido Highway. Opened more than 380 years ago, Ichinoyu is now in its 15th generation of owners. It claims to be the oldest *ryokan* in the area and was once honored by the visit of a shogun during the Edo Period. Old artwork, wall hangings, and paintings decorate the place. The ryokan has only *tatami* rooms, the oldest dating from the Meiji Period, more than 100 years ago. My favorites are the Take, Kotobuki, and Matsue rooms, old-fashioned and consisting mainly of seasoned and weathered wood; they face the river and have private outdoor baths, also with views of the river. (Rooms with private *rotenburo,* or outdoor hot-spring baths, cost ¥3,000 extra.) Both the communal tubs and the tubs in the rooms are supplied with hot water from a natural spring. The price you pay depends on your room, the meals you select (served communally in a dining room), and the time of year you visit; rooms for single travelers are not available.

90 Tonosawa, Hakone-machi, Kanagawa-ken 250-0315. ✆ **0460/85-5331.** Fax 0460/85-5335. http:// english.ichinoyu.co.jp/honkan. 24 units (12 with bathroom). ¥8,400–¥15,225 per person including 2 meals. Higher rates on Sat, night before holiday, and peak travel times. AE, DC, MC, V. Station: Tonosawa (Hakone Tozan Railway; 6 min.). Bus: From Odawara or Moto-Hakone to Tonosawa bus stop (2 min.). **Amenities:** Hot-spring baths. *In room:* A/C, TV, fridge.

WHERE TO DINE

For casual dining, the Hakone Open-Air Museum has a pleasant restaurant, **Bella Foresta,** overlooking the park's fantastic scenery and offering a buffet lunch daily from 11am to 3:30pm for ¥1,980. Also sporting a view is the even less formal restaurant **Owakudani Sky,** on the third floor of the Owakudani Ropeway Station, serving curry rice, noodles, and other fare for less than ¥1,200.

Main Dining Room ★★ CONTINENTAL   Hakone's grandest, oldest hotel, conveniently located near a stop on the three-car Hakone Tozan Railway, is a memorable place for a good Western meal. The main dining hall, dating from 1930, is very bright and cheerful, with a high and intricately detailed ceiling, large windows with Japanese screens, a wooden floor, and white tablecloths. The views of the Hakone hills are impressive, and the service by the bow-tied waitstaff is attentive. For lunch you can have such dishes as crab curry, beef stew, fried prawn, rainbow trout, and sirloin steak. The excellent dinners, with seatings at 6 and 8pm, feature elaborate set courses or a la carte dishes ranging from scallops and grilled lamb to chicken, rainbow trout, and steak. Afterward, be sure to tour the landscaped garden.

In the Fujiya Hotel, 359 Miyanoshita. ✆ **0460/82-2211.** Reservations required for dinner. Main dishes ¥2,200– ¥7,500; set dinners ¥11,500–¥23,100; set lunches ¥5,000–¥12,000. AE, DC, MC, V. Daily noon–2pm (to 2:30pm weekends and holidays) and 6–8:30pm. Station: Miyanoshita on the Hakone Tozan Railway (5 min.).

6 IZU PENINSULA, TOKYO'S PLAYGROUND

Atami: 107km (66 miles) SW of Tokyo; Ito: 120km (75 miles) SW of Tokyo

Whenever Tokyoites want to spend a night or two at a hot-spring spa on the seashore, they head for Izu Peninsula. Jutting into the Pacific Ocean southwest of Tokyo, Izu boasts some fine beaches and a dramatic coastline marked in spots by high cliffs and tumbling surf. It also has a verdant, mountainous interior with quaint hot-spring resorts. However, even though the scenery is at times breathtaking and Izu offers a relaxing respite from bustling Tokyo, there's little of historical interest to lure a short-term visitor to Japan; make sure you've seen both Kamakura and Nikko before you consider coming here.

Keep in mind also that Izu's resorts are terribly crowded during the summer vacation period from mid-July to the end of August. If you do travel during the peak summer season, make accommodations reservations at least several months in advance. Otherwise, there are hotel, *ryokan,* and *minshuku* reservation offices in all of Izu's resort towns that will arrange accommodations for you. Be aware, however, that if a place has a room still open at the last minute in August, there's probably a reason for it—poor location, poor service, or unimaginative decor.

Before you leave Tokyo, be sure to pick up the leaflet "The Izu Peninsula" at the Tourist Information Center.

ATAMI

Atami means "hot sea." According to legend, once upon a time local fishermen, concerned about a geyser spewing forth into the sea and killing lots of fish and marine life, asked a Buddhist monk to intervene on their behalf and to pray for a solution to the problem. The prayers paid off when the geyser moved itself to the beach; not only was the marine life spared, but Atami was blessed with hot-spring water the townspeople could henceforth bathe in. It's rumored that Tokugawa Ieyasu (1543–1616), Japan's most famous shogun, was so enamored by the quality of Atami's hot-spring waters that he ordered barrels of it delivered to his castle in Edo (present-day Tokyo).

Today, Atami—with a population of 40,000—is a conglomeration of hotels, *ryokan,* restaurants, pachinko parlors, souvenir shops, and a sizable red-light district, spread along narrow, winding streets that hug steep mountain slopes around Atami Bay. Although I find the setting picturesque, the city itself isn't very interesting—in fact, its economy is severely depressed, and because it has none of the fancy shops and nightlife to attract a younger generation, mostly older Japanese vacation here, giving the town an old-fashioned, unpretentious atmosphere. In any case, this is the most easily accessible hot-spring seaside resort from Tokyo, and it has a wide beach flanked by a 1km (½-mile) boardwalk, a wonderful art museum, and several other attractions that make it popular even on just a day trip.

Essentials

GETTING THERE From Tokyo Station, it's 40 to 50 minutes by **Shinkansen bullet train;** be sure to check the schedule beforehand, as the Hikari bullet train stops at Atami only three times a day (though the slower Kodama bullet trains run more frequently). The fare is ¥3,570 for an unreserved seat. You can also take the **JR Odoriko** or **Super View Odoriko,** which travels from Tokyo Station to Atami in 1 hour and 15 or 20 minutes, with the fare ranging from ¥3,190 to ¥4,270, depending on the train. Slower is the local **JR Tokaido Line** for ¥1,890, which takes about 1 hour and 40 minutes.

VISITOR INFORMATION The **Atami Tourist Information Office** (adjacent to a coffee shop) is to the left as you exit the train station (✆ **0557/81-5297;** daily 9am–5:30pm; to 5pm Oct–Mar). No English is spoken, but English-language literature and a map are available, including the very useful "Atami Walking Guide." You'll also find information on Atami online at **www.atamispa.com.**

GETTING AROUND Buses serve major sightseeing attractions in Atami. If you're spending the day here, you might wish to purchase a 1-day ticket for the **YuYu Bus,**

which has two routes, both making circuitous trips through town and departing Atami Station every 35 minutes. You can leave and reboard as often as you wish or stay on for a tour of the city. The cost is ¥800 for adults and ¥400 for children.

Seeing the Sights

Atami's must-see is the **MOA Art Museum** ★, 26–2 Momoyama-cho (℃ **0557/84-2511;** www.moaart.or.jp), housed in a modern building atop a hill with sweeping views of Atami and the bay. It's a 5-minute bus ride from Atami Station on the YuYu Bus; or take a bus from platform 4 to the last stop (fare: ¥160). The museum's entrance is dramatic—a long escalator ride through a tunnel—but the museum itself concentrates on traditional Asian art, including woodblock prints by Hokusai, Hiroshige, and their contemporaries; Chinese ceramics; Japanese bronze religious art; and lacquerware. Although some 200 items from the 3,500-piece private collection are changed monthly, keep an eye out for a few things always on display: the Golden Tea Room (a remake of Toyotomi Hideyoshi's tearoom), a *noh* theater, and a tea-storage jar with a wisteria design by Edo artist Nonomura Ninsei, a National Treasure. Another National Treasure, displayed only in February of each year, is a gold-leaf screen of red and white plum blossoms by Ogata Korin, whose residence next door is also part of the museum. It takes about an hour to tour the museum, open Friday through Wednesday from 9:30am to 4:30pm; admission is ¥1,600 for adults, ¥1,200 for seniors, ¥800 for university and high-school students, free for children.

I also love ④④ **Kiunkaku,** 4–2 Showa-cho (℃ **0557/86-3101;** YuYu Bus: Kiunkaku stop), built in 1919 as the private villa of a shipping magnate, converted to a *ryokan* in 1947, and now open to the public. It's an eclectic mix of Japanese and Western architectural styles, with stained-glass windows, fireplaces, parquet floors, gaily painted European furniture, and *tatami* rooms, wrapped around a lovely inner garden. It was once a favorite haunt of famous Japanese writers (including Mishima Yukio); who wouldn't feel inspired here? Allow 30 minutes to tour the facilities, open Thursday to Tuesday from 9am to 5pm. Admission is ¥500 for adults, ¥300 for university and high-school students, and free for children.

Finally, if you're here on a Saturday or Sunday, try to catch the 11am dancing performance of the **Atami Geisha,** at Geigi Kenban (across from City Hall), 17–13 Chuo-cho (℃ **0557/81-3575;** YuYu Bus: Shiyakusho-mae). Although reservations are not required for the 30-minute show, I advise making one anyway to assure getting a seat, as these performances are very popular with the older generation. Stick around after the show; most of the geisha come out to greet the audience and you can ask to have your picture taken standing next to a performer. Admission, including tea and a Japanese sweet, is ¥1,300.

Where to Stay

④⑤ **Taikanso** ★★ Located on a pine-shaded mountain slope above the city, this beautiful *ryokan* was built in 1938 as the private villa of a steelworks owner and was named after his friend Yokoyama Taikan, a famous Japanese painter. Ten years later it was converted to a Japanese inn; since then, it's been expanded into several buildings connected by covered pathways and meandering streams, adhering to a Kyoto style of architecture popular in the 16th century. Various styles of rooms are available, with the most expensive (including the room where Taikan stayed) offering the best views, the most space, and the best meals (Western-style breakfasts available on request). Rooms are *tatami,* but beds can be installed upon request. The ultimate in luxury is the oldest unit, a three-room suite with a sitting alcove and cypress tub, where Queen Beatrix of the Netherlands stayed with her husband and three sons. Although all the rooms boast hot-spring water for the tubs, there are three public baths with open-air bathing, saunas, and Jacuzzis, as well as three private baths with outdoor baths and views over Atami (extra fee for these: ¥2,100). Be sure to wander the corridors and garden with its 300-year-old pines, stopping off at the footbaths on the third floor of the annex, where you can soak your feet, order drinks, and look out over the town.

7-1 Hayashigaoka-cho, Atami City, Shizuoka 413-0031. ☏ **0557/81-8137.** Fax 0557/83-5308. www. atami-taikanso.com. 44 units. ¥29,550–¥70,000 per person. Rates include 2 meals. ¥3,150–¥5,000 extra per person weekends, holidays, and peak season. AE, DC, MC, V. Take a taxi from Atami Station, a 4-min. ride. **Amenities:** 2 restaurants; coffee shop; nightclub; indoor/outdoor hot-spring baths; Jacuzzi; sauna. *In room:* A/C, TV, minibar, hair dryer, Internet.

Where to Dine

46 **Home Run Sushi** (Value) SUSHI For excellent sushi, head to this simple, 30-year-old, one-room restaurant near the waterfront with both counter and table seating. There's no English-language menu, but there are plastic-food displays of various sushi sets. I have no idea why this place is called Home Run—one of Japan's many mysteries.

5-1 Nagisacho. ☏ **0557/82-7300.** Sushi set meals ¥1,050–¥2,000. AE, DC, MC, V. Daily 11:45am–3pm and 5–10pm. A 10-min. walk from Atami Station, at the end of Ginza Dori St., on a corner to the left.

SHUZENJI

Whereas Atami, above, is popular for its seaside setting, Shuzenji Onsen is Izu Peninsula's most famous mountain spa. Nestled in a valley and straddling both sides of a river, it has a history stretching back more than 1,200 years, when one of Japan's most revered figures in Japanese Buddhism, Kobo Daishi, discovered a hot spring here and founded Shuzenji Temple. Today, Shuzenji, home to some 16,000 residents, is a small mountain village easily navigated on foot. Most people come for a night or two, staying in a *ryokan,* soaking in restorative hot-spring baths, strolling along the town's narrow streets to a few historic sights, and feasting on meals featuring local cuisine. Along with Shuzenji Temple, there are several historic sites tied to the Minamoto clan, who established a shogunate government in Kamakura in the 12th century (see "Kamakura, Ancient Capital," earlier in this chapter).

Essentials

GETTING THERE The rail gateway to Shuzenji is Mishima, a minor stop on the Shinkansen bullet train. The Hikari bullet train stops at Mishima about six times a day, though the slower Kodama bullet train stops more frequently; be sure to check the schedule beforehand. In any case, it takes 45 to 60 minutes by bullet train from Tokyo Station to Mishima, where you can then transfer to the **Izu-Hakone Railway's** Sunzu Line for the 30-minute ride onward to Shuzenji. The fare for the entire journey is ¥4,390 for a reserved seat. Alternatively, you can save money by taking the slower **JR Tokaido Line** from Tokyo to Mishima and then board the Izu Hakone Railway bound for Shuzenji; the fare for this is ¥2,710 and takes about 3 hours. If you're coming from Atami, take the JR Tokaido Line 12 minutes to Mishima for ¥320 and then transfer to the Izu-Hakone Railway for another ¥500.

You can also reach Shuzenji by Odakyu's **Tokai Bus** (☏ **0570/01-1255**) from Tokyo's Shinjuku Station. Travel time is 2 hours and 45 minutes, and the fare is ¥2,500 one-way or ¥4,500 round-trip. There are two departures daily (as of press time, at 9:15am and 6:35pm), and reservations are required.

VISITOR INFORMATION   The **Shuzenji Tourist Information Office** (☎ **0558/72-2501**) is located inside Shuzenji Station, to the right after exiting the ticket gate. There's no English-speaking staff, but you can pick up a pamphlet with a map. It's open daily 9am to 5pm.

GETTING AROUND   Shuzenji Spa (Shuzenji Onsen), with its *ryokan,* hot-spring baths, Shuzenji Temple, and other sights, is a 30-minute walk from Shuzenji Station, so you'll probably want to take the local bus. Buses depart Shuzenji Station approximately every 10 or 15 minutes from stop no. 1 bound for "Shuzenji Onsen," the last stop. The fare is ¥210. Once you're ensconced in your ryokan, you can walk everywhere. Signs in English direct you to major attractions.

Seeing the Sights

Shuzenji Spa spreads along the Katsura River. In the center of the spa town, in the river-bed, is **Tokko-no-yu,** the oldest hot spring in Izu. According to legend, in 807 Kobo Daishi saw a young boy washing his ill father in the cold water of Katsura River. Taking pity, Kobo Daishi struck a rock in the riverbed with a *tokko* (iron club), causing the rock to split open and release a hot spring that cured the sick father. Today, a pavilion along the river marks the historic spot.

After discovering Tokko-no-yu, Kobo Daishi founded **Shuzenji Temple** just steps away from the river on a small hill. Because of its associations with the great Buddhist leader, the temple flourished and a village sprang up around it. During the Kamakura Period (1185–1333), Shuzenji Temple was associated with two tragic events involving the Minamoto clan's bitter family feud. First, Minamoto Yoritomo, who established the Kamakura shogunate but feared that his younger brother Noriyori had ambitions to take over, had Noriyori imprisoned here in 1193. Noriyori, who had proved his bravery by acting as commander in chief in the defeat of the rival Heike clan, subsequently killed himself. Later, Yoritomo's son, Yoriie, the second Kamakura shogun, was assassinated in Shuzenji while enjoying his bath at nearby Hakoyu spa, reportedly from poison added to his bath water. The present temple building dates from 1883, when it was rebuilt following a mysterious fire. The Shuzenji Treasure House contains items relating to the temple, including the *tokko* said to have belonged to Kobo Daishi and Yoriie's death mask. You'll also find a statue of Dainichi Nyorai, given to the temple by Hojo Masako, Yoritomo's wife, in honor of her son Yoriie. Admission to the treasure house, open daily 8:30am to 4pm, is ¥300; temple grounds are open daily 6am to 5pm.

Across the river from Shuzenji Temple is **Hakoyu,** now a modern hot-spring public bath housed in an eye-catching tower. You can bathe in its tub made of *hinoki* cypress for ¥350. It's open daily from noon to 9pm.

Nearby is the **Bamboo Forest Path,** a pedestrian walkway through a bamboo grove, as well as **Shigetsuden,** the oldest wooden structure in Izu. Yoriie's mother, Masako, ordered construction of Shigetsuden to house several thousand rolls of Buddhist scriptures, donated to console the soul of her son Yoriie. Most of the scriptures are thought to have been sent later to Edo (present-day Tokyo) by order of the Tokugawa shogunate, though one roll is displayed at Shuzenji Temple's Treasure House. Beside Shigetsuden is **Minamoto Yoriie's Grave,** marked by a stone pillar erected in 1703 by Shuzenji Temple's head priest to mark the 500th anniversary of Yoriie's death. The eldest son of Yoritomo, Yoriie was only 18 when he became the second shogun and was placed under house arrest in Shuzenji after only 5 years of reign. He was 23 when murdered in his bath by assassins from Kamakura. Three stones behind the pillar mark the graves of Yoriie, his concubine, and their son.

A walking trail leads across the river to **Minamoto Noriyori's Grave.** Other hiking trails lead through the surrounding mountain scenery, including the 5km (3-mile) Okunoin Walking Trail leading to Okunoin, where Kobo Daishi is said to have practiced meditation as a youth.

Where to Stay
Expensive
47 **Yagyu-no-Sho** ★★★   This elegant sanctuary, surrounded by a wall and beautiful garden complete with streams, pond, mossy ground, and bamboo groves, sits on the edge of Shuzenji and feels like it's deep in the countryside. It was built some 40 years ago, a replica of the original Yagyu-no Sato in Nara, and offers 16 rooms, each one with a different atmosphere and unique architectural details from ceiling designs to door pulls. They range from standard rooms, located in the main building accessible by elevator and decorated with antiques, to villas with their own private garden and open-air bath. The inn's most popular room is Tsukikage, with its own balcony over a pond and open-air bath. Kyoto-style *kaiseki* meals, with local specialties and mountain vegetables, are served in your room, and the owner's wife speaks English. If you're looking for a pampered mountain retreat, this place fits the bill.

1116–6 Shuzenji Onsen, Izu-shi, Shizuoka 410-2416. (℃ **0558/72-4126.** Fax 0558/72-5212. www.yagyu-no-sho.com. 16 units. ¥40,050–¥68,400 per person. Rates include 2 meals. ¥2,100 extra per person Sat and nights before holidays. AE, MC, V. From the bus terminal, turn right and follow the main road; it will be on your right (7 min.). **Amenities:** Indoor/outdoor hot-spring baths. *In room:* A/C, TV, hair dryer, minibar.

Moderate
48 **Arai Ryokan** ★★   Open since 1872, this is one of Shuzenji's most acclaimed inns. It has welcomed many Japanese celebrities over the decades, from writers and artists to kabuki actors. It's located right in the center of the village, beside the river and just a stone's throw from Shuzenji Temple and the Bamboo Forest Path. Its 15 structures, all registered as national cultural assets and situated around a river-fed pond, include a delightful main building where you're served a welcome tea on an old-fashioned wooden veranda, a wooden covered bridge leading to rooms, and a 90-year-old public bath built in the style of Horyuji Temple in Nara without the use of nails. Rooms are spread through several buildings constructed during different times in the inn's long history, including standard rooms with and without private bathroom and more elaborate rooms that face the pond and Katsura River. Seasonal meals are served in your room. This inn is highly recommended for its nostalgic atmosphere.

970 Shuzenji Onsen, Izu-shi, Shizuoka 410-2416. (℃ **0558/72-2007.** Fax 0558/72-5119. www.arairyokan.net. 30 units (15 with bathroom; 12 with toilet only; 3 without bathroom). ¥22,000–¥70,000 per person. Rates exclude tax and service charge. Rates include 2 meals. AE, MC, V. From the bus terminal, turn right and follow the main road; it will be on your left, past Shuzenji Temple (3 min.). **Amenities:** Indoor/outdoor hot-spring baths; indoor hot-spring pool (open summer only); Internet in lobby. *In room:* A/C, TV, hair dryer, minibar.

Inexpensive
49 **Goyokan**   This family-run inn, in a warehouse-style building of black tiles topped with white mortar, opened about 20 years ago. Sandwiched between Shuzenzji's main road and the Katsura River, near the bus terminal, it offers simple but clean *tatami*

rooms, some with views of the river. *Note:* No dinner is served and no single accommodations are available.

765–2 Shuzenji Onsen, Izu-shi, Shizuoka 410-2416. ✆ **0558/72-2066.** Fax 0558/72-8212. www.goyokan. co.jp. 11 units (none with bathroom). ¥6,450 per person without breakfast; ¥7,500 per person with breakfast. Rates include tax. No credit cards. Across the street from the bus terminal, to the left (1 min.). **Amenities:** Indoor hot-spring baths. *In room:* A/C, TV, fridge, no phone.

Where to Dine

㊿ **Nanaban** (Value NOODLES   Nanaban is famous in Shuzenji for its buckwheat noodles, but you have to work a bit to release your meal's special aroma and flavors. Most popular is the Zendera Soba, which you prepare by grinding your own sesame seeds and then grating fresh wasabi root, all of which is added to your *soba* along with soy sauce (you can take any extra wasabi root home with you). Other soba and *udon* dishes are also available, including those with mountain vegetables and tempura. There's no English-language menu, but there's a plastic food display outside and the menu has pictures. After taking your shoes off at the entrance, you'll be seated at a low table with leg wells, surrounded by antiques and gleaming wood.

761–1-3 Shuzenji Onsen. ✆ **0558/72-0007.** Set meals ¥1,260–¥1,890. No credit cards. Fri–Wed 10am–4pm. Across the street from the bus terminal, to the left (1 min.); look for the statue of the raccoon dog and the bamboo fountain.

The Japan Alps

The several volcanic mountain ranges that lie in central Honshu together comprise **Japan Alps National Park (Chubu Sangaku Kokuritsu Koen)** ★★★. With the exception of Japan's tallest mountain, Mount Fuji (p. 248), all of Japan's loftiest mountains are in these ranges, making the Japan Alps a popular destination for hikers in summer and skiers in winter (Nagano, near Matsumoto, hosted the XVIII Winter Olympics in 1998). In addition, because some of the villages nestled in these mountains retain much of their traditional architecture, the Japan Alps provide a unique look at mountain life both past and present.

A GOOD STRATEGY FOR SEEING THE JAPAN ALPS Because towns and villages in this region are spread out—with lots of mountains in between—traveling isn't as fast in this part of the country as on Honshu's broad plains. Your best strategy for visiting all the destinations covered in this chapter is to start from Nagoya Station by taking the JR Shinano train in the morning to Nakatsugawa, where you can then board a bus for Magome and spend the day hiking to Tsumago. From Tsumago, it's only a short bus ride to Nagiso, where you can then reboard the Shinano train bound for Matsumoto. From Matsumoto, you'll travel by bus onward to Takayama and then on to Ogimachi (in Shirakawa-go). From there you can return to Takayama to catch the train to Nagoya, or take a bus onward to Kanazawa (see chapter 10 for information on Nagoya and Kanazawa).

1 MATSUMOTO, GATEWAY TO THE JAPAN ALPS ★

235km (146 miles) NW of Tokyo

Located in the middle of a wide plateau about 200m (660 ft.) above sea level and surrounded on all sides by mountain ranges, **Matsumoto** ★ boasts a fine feudal castle with the oldest existing *donjon* (keep) in Japan, as well as an outstanding woodblock-print museum. Although the city itself (pop. 230,000) is modern with little remaining from its castle days, it does boast approximately 100 *kura* (storehouses) scattered throughout town, built more than a century ago after a devastating fire destroyed much of the town. Some of the kura, made of earth and straw and then painted many times to protect valuables against future flames, have been renovated into shops, restaurants, and other establishments, especially on Nakamachi Street.

In any event, I find Matsumoto pleasant, the air fresh, and its people among the nicest I've encountered in Japan. Encircled by towering peaks, sparkling mountain lakes, and colorful wildflowers, Matsumoto also serves as the gateway to the hiking trails of Japan Alps National Park; most travelers heading to the more remote regions of the Japan Alps pass through here on their way.

GETTING THERE   **By Train**   The **JR Chuo Honsen Line** runs directly to Matsumoto from Tokyo's Shinjuku Station. Its *Limited Express Azusa,* departing every hour or so, reaches Matsumoto in about 2½ to 3 hours and costs ¥6,200 one-way for an unreserved seat. There's also a direct JR train from Nagoya, the *Limited Express Shinano,* which departs about every hour, takes about 2 hours, and costs ¥5,360 for an unreserved seat.

BY BUS   From Tokyo's Shinjuku Station's west exit, Keio Highway buses ((*C* **03/5376-2222**) depart for Matsumoto Bus Terminal (across from Matsumoto Station) approximately every hour, taking about 3¼ hours and costing ¥3,400. From Nagoya, the ride is 2½ hours and ¥3,460; from Osaka, the ride is 5½ hours and ¥5,710; from Takayama, the ride is 2¼ hours and ¥3,100.

VISITOR INFORMATION   Before departing Tokyo, pick up a sheet called "Nagano" at the **Tourist Information Center** (p. 111), or download it from JNTO's website at **www.jnto.go.jp**, under "Browse by Destinations." It provides information on buses and trains to Matsumoto, as well as information on sights in and around Matsumoto. It also recommends 2- to 4-hour hiking trips from **Kamikochi** ★, the Japan Alps' most popular destination for serious hikers.

In Matsumoto, you'll find **Matsumoto Tourist Information** ((*C* **0263/32-2814;** www.city.matsumoto.nagano.jp or http://welcome.city.matsumoto.nagano.jp; daily 9am–5:45pm) just across from the main wicket of Matsumoto Station. It has a good English-language map of the city, and its excellent English-speaking staff will also help with accommodations and can provide information on nearby destinations.

GETTING AROUND   You can **walk** to Matsumoto Castle, about 1.5km (1 mile) northeast of the station, in about 20 minutes, with signs in English pointing the way. Alternatively, **Town Sneaker Bus** is a dedicated tourist bus, with three routes departing from Matsumoto Station every 30 minutes and making circular routes to all city sights (most useful for the sights below is the Kita, or Northern, Course). It costs ¥190 each time you get off or ¥500 for an all-day pass (half-price for children). To visit the Japan Ukiyo-e Museum, however, you'll have to go by local **train** or **taxi.** Alternatively, free **bicycles** are available daily 8:30am to 5pm at various locations throughout town, including the Matsumoto City Museum next to Matsumoto Castle and the Kaichi Gakko Primary School. They're convenient for visiting sights not accessible by Sneaker Bus; ask the Matsumoto Tourist Information staff for details.

SEEING THE SIGHTS

In addition to the sights below, good places for strolling and shopping include the **Nakamachi** district in the heart of the city with its *kura,* restaurants, and shops selling Matsumoto furniture, crafts, and antiques; and **Nawate Dori,** a narrow pedestrian lane flanking the Metoba River where vendors sell fruit, vegetables, flowers, and souvenirs.

If you want to do some hiking, stop by the Matsumoto Tourist Information for the **"Kamikochi Guide Map,"** which contains a map and recommended hiking trails. It takes a little more than 2 hours via train and bus to reach Kamikochi; the fare is ¥2,400 one-way or ¥4,400 round-trip.

Unless otherwise noted, all directions below are from Matsumoto Station.

Matsumoto Castle ★★   Originally built in 1504 when Japan was in the throes of continuing and bloody civil wars, Matsumoto Castle is a fine specimen of a feudal castle with a 400-year-old *donjon* that's the oldest existing keep in the country. Surrounded by a moat with ducks and white swans and lined with willow and cherry trees, the outside walls of the donjon are black, earning the place the nickname of Karasu-jo, or Crow Castle. Although it appears to have five stories from the outside, it's actually a six-story structure, with a secret floor that may have hidden warriors. It's rather small as castles go, but English-speaking Goodwill Guides stand ready daily to provide free, 1-hour tours outlining the castle's history and architectural features. Take your shoes off at the entrance and walk in stocking feet over worn wooden floors and up steep and narrow steps until you finally reach the sixth floor, from which you have a nice view of the city. This would have served as the *daimyo's* (feudal lord's) headquarters in case of enemy attack, while the fifth floor, with views in all directions, was where the generals would have conferred during war. Although the Ishikawa clan rebuilt the castle in 1593 in anticipation of gun warfare (guns were introduced to Japan in 1543) with many arrow and gun slots and walls thick enough to withstand bullets, the castle was never attacked because the civil wars ended with the coming of the Edo Period (1603–1867). Nevertheless, guns were manufactured in Japan throughout the Edo Period, and on display inside the castle are approximately 370 matchlocks, armor, and other arms manufactured in Japan from 1543 to the late Edo Era, providing interesting insight into how the import was adapted for domestic use. With war no longer a threat, a moon-viewing room was added to the castle in 1635.

Included in your castle ticket is admission to the **Matsumoto City Museum** ★ (ⓒ **0263/32-0133**) next to the castle. This rather eclectic museum has displays relating to archaeology, history, Matsumoto's many festivals (including the summer Tanabata Festival and a fertility festival held in Sept featuring, well, phalluses), and folklore of the surrounding region, including samurai armor, an ornate palanquin, and farming equipment. You can tour both castle and museum in about 90 minutes.

4–1 Marunouchi. ⓒ **0263/32-2902.** Admission ¥600 adults, ¥300 children. Daily 8:30am–5pm. Town Sneaker Bus, Northern Course: Matsumotojo Kuromon (stop no. 6). To walk, take Agatanomori (also called Ekimae Dori), the main road leading away from the station, and turn left onto Honmachi Dori.

Former Kaichi School (Kaichi Gakko)   Japan's public school system was founded in 1872 (before that, Buddhist temples were the only source of education). In 1876, this handsome white mortar building of black tile topped by an octagonal turret opened its doors, making it one of the oldest Western-style schools still standing and a fine example of Meiji Era architecture. Serving as an elementary school for 90 years, it remains much as it was, with displays of books, games, desks, abacuses, and other educational items. Most fascinating are the photographs of former pupils (showing how many young girls came to school with young siblings strapped to their backs, as parents were hard at work) and the children's books dating from World War II, with offending passages blackened out by demand of Allied occupational forces after the war. Next to the school is an 1889 parsonage you can see for free. In any case, you can tour everything in about 30 minutes.

2–4–12 Kaichi. ⓒ **0263/32-5725.** Admission ¥300 adults, ¥150 children. Daily 8:30am–5pm. Closed Mon Dec–Feb. Town Sneaker Bus, Northern Course: Takajomachi (stop no. 8). Behind the castle, about a 7-min. walk north.

Matsumoto Timepiece Museum (Tokei Hakubutsukan) ★   I dropped by on a whim but was mesmerized by the pocket watches, sundials, mechanized clocks, early

> **(Tips) A Note on Japanese Characters**
>
> Many establishments and attractions in Japan do not have signs in Roman (English-language) letters. Those that don't are indicated in this guide by an oval with a number that corresponds to a number in chapter 17 showing the Japanese equivalent. Thus, to find the Japanese symbol for, say, the **Matsumoto Folkcraft Museum** (see below), refer to no. 51 in chapter 17.

alarm clocks, grandfather clocks, cuckoo clocks (both 18th-c. German and Japanese imitations), Edo-Era Japanese clocks, and hundreds of other timepieces, mostly of Japanese and European origin from the 18th to 20th centuries. Most amazing of all: Most of the 300 or so timepieces on display are actually wound and working. Expect to spend about 40 minutes here.

1-21-15 Chuo. ✆ **0263/36-0969.** Admission ¥300 adults, ¥150 children. Tues–Sun 9am–5pm. Town Sneaker Bus, Eastern Course: Tokei Hakubutsukan (stop no. 15). Btw. Matsumoto Station and Matsumoto Castle, a 10-min. walk from both.

More to See & Do

Japan Ukiyo-e Museum (Nihon Ukiyo-e Hakubutsukan) ★★★ (Finds)

Don't miss this ultramodern building housing the private collection of the Sakai family, quite simply one of the best museums of woodblock prints in Japan. With more than 100,000 prints, it's believed to be the largest collection of its kind in the world and includes representative masterpieces of all known Ukiyo-e artists. The exhibition changes every 3 months, with approximately 100 prints on display at any one time. A 15-minute slide show with English-language explanations introduces the current exhibition, and an English-language pamphlet describes the history of the collection and how woodblock prints are made. You'll want to spend at least 45 minutes here, longer if you browse the museum shop of reproduction and original prints.

2206–1 Koshiba, Shimadachi. ✆ **0263/47-4440.** www.ukiyo-e.co.jp/jum-e. Admission ¥1,050 adults, ¥530 children. Tues–Sun 10am–5pm. From platform 7 at Matsumoto Train Station, take the local Kamikochi Line 10 min. to Oniwa Station (¥170; JR Rail Pass not accepted) and then walk 15 min. (turn left out of the station, and then left at the T-intersection with the post office; after passing under the bridge, take the 3rd right at the small cemetery and continue straight on, past the underpass); or take a ¥1,500 10-min. taxi ride; or, better yet, come by bike (about 20 min. from Matsumoto Station).

Matsumoto City Museum of Art (Matsumoto-shi Bijutsukan)

This inviting museum showcases the talents of artists with connections to Matsumoto, including Kamijyo Shiuzan, who elevated calligraphy to an art, landscape artist Tamura Kazuo, and Kusama Yayoi, a female artist known for her exuberant colors and polka-dot modern art. Expect to spend about 30 minutes here.

4-2-22 Chuo. ✆ **0263/39-7400.** Admission ¥400 adults, ¥200 university and high-school students, free for children and seniors. Tues–Sun 9am–5pm. Town Sneaker Bus, Southern Course: Matsumoto-shi Bijutsukan (stop no. 30); or a 15-min. walk east of Matsumoto Station on Ekimae Dori.

(51) Matsumoto Folkcraft Museum (Matsumoto Mingei-kan) ★

Here's a museum worth visiting if you have an extra hour (including the bus ride). Housed in a *kura* built to store fish, it contains folk art made primarily of wood, glass, bamboo, and porcelain from Japan and other countries, with exhibits changed three times a year. On display may be items as diverse as combs from around the world to Japanese store signs designed during the Edo Period for people who couldn't read. Particularly beautiful are the wooden chests.

1313–1 Satoyamabe. ☏ **0263/33-1569.** Admission ¥300 adults, free for children 15 and younger. Tues–Sun 9am–5pm. About 15 min. by bus (¥290); from the bus terminal, take the platform 1 bus and get off at the Shimoganai Mingeikan Guchi.

WHERE TO STAY

Because Matsumoto is popular primarily with hikers used to roughing it along nature trails, accommodations are geared mainly toward convenience. Directions are from Matsumoto Station.

Expensive

Buena Vista ★   Matsumoto's biggest and fanciest hotel is a white gleaming structure popular for its conference and wedding facilities and with those attending the Saito Kinen Festival. Rooms range from very small singles and semi-doubles (cramped for two persons at ¥13,860–¥16,170, depending on the season) to top-floor premier rooms with updated furnishings and the best views of the mountains in the distance. Rates below reflect the seasons, with the highest prices in peak season (July 20–Sept 15) and the lowest in off season (Apr–June and Nov–Mar).

1–2–1 Honjo, Matsumoto, Nagano 390-0184. ☏ **0263/37-0111.** Fax 0263/37-0666. www.buena-vista. co.jp. 200 units. ¥9,240–¥11,550 single; ¥19,635–¥27,720 double. AE, DC, MC, V. Station: Matsumoto (7 min.). Turn right out of the station onto Shirakaba Dori; the hotel will be on a side street to the left. **Amenities:** 4 restaurants; 2 bars; lobby computers w/free Internet; room service; smoke-free rooms. *In room:* A/C, TV, fridge, hair dryer, Internet.

Moderate

Matsumoto Hotel Kagetsu ★ (**Value**)   This *ryokan,* in a newer building constructed in the style of a *kura* (storehouse) but with a history going back more than 100 years, imparts a pleasant, old-fashioned atmosphere with its antique wooden furnishings in public spaces. Both Western- and Japanese-style rooms are available, comfortably large for the price. For the best views, ask for one of the upper-floor rooms facing the castle and mountains. For a splurge, deluxe corner rooms boast more windows, larger sitting areas, and toilets separate from the bathrooms.

4–8–9 Ote, Matsumoto, Nagano 390-0874. ☏ **0263/32-0114.** Fax 0263/33-4775. www.mcci.or.jp/www/ kagetsu. 80 units. ¥7,350–¥10,500 per person. AE, DC, MC, V. Town Sneaker Bus, Northern Course: Agetsuchimachi (stop no. 10, 1 min.). **Amenities:** 2 restaurants; room service. *In room:* A/C, TV, Internet.

Matsumoto Tokyu Inn   Visible from the station, this practical and clean business hotel's main selling point is its convenient location, which probably accounts for rates that are a bit higher than you would expect in Matsumoto. The majority of rooms are singles and twins, all with semi-double-size beds with feather quilts and Swedish pillows (easier to sleep on, perhaps, than the Japanese bean variety). There are also six doubles and five deluxe twins, the latter with sofa, chairs, and a separate vanity area with its own sink. On clear days, higher-priced rooms facing west have views of the Japan Alps.

1–3–21 Fukashi, Matsumoto, Nagano 390-0185. ☏ **0263/36-0109.** Fax 0263/36-0883. www.tokyuhotels japan.com. 160 units. ¥8,500–¥11,500 single; ¥13,800–¥28,000 double. AE, DC, MC, V. Station: Matsumoto (3 min.). Across the street to the right. **Amenities:** Restaurant; bar; lobby computers w/free Internet; smoke-free rooms. *In room:* A/C, TV, Internet, minibar.

A Double or a Twin?

For the sake of convenience, the price for two people in a room is listed as a "double" in this book. Japanese hotels, however, differentiate between rooms with a double bed or two twin beds, usually with different prices. Although most hotels charge more for a twin room, sometimes the opposite is true; if you're looking for a bargain, therefore, be sure to inquire about prices for both. Note, too, that hotels usually have more twin rooms than doubles, for the simple reason that Japanese couples, used to their own futon, traditionally prefer twin beds.

Inexpensive

In addition to the more atmospheric choice below, there's the **Toyoko Inn Matsumoto Ekimae Honmachi,** at 2–1–23 Chuo (⌀ **0263/36-1045**), a 6-minute walk west of Matsumoto Station (take the small side street to the right of McDonald's; it's straight ahead). Charging ¥5,460 to ¥6,090 for a single and ¥8,190 for a double, it offers the budget chain's usual freebies, including computers with free Internet access in the lobby, complimentary breakfast, and free Internet access in the rooms.

⑤② **Marumo** ★★ (Finds) This is my top pick for accommodations that epitomize the old-fashioned atmosphere of Matsumoto during the Meiji Era. Located in the traditional district of Nakamachi and occupying a *kura* and traditional Japanese inn constructed after the great 1888 fire that destroyed much of Matsumoto, it boasts a diminutive but eye-catching entryway of polished woods and antiques, very narrow stairs and corridors leading to Japanese-style rooms, and a wonderful coffee shop that has changed little over the decades. Rooms are simple and without the usual creature comforts, but the location is great and the atmosphere is truly one of a kind. If you're searching for "traditional Japan," this is where you'll want to stay.

3-3-10 Chuo, Matsumoto, Nagano 390-0811. ⌀ **0263/32-0115.** www.avis/ne.jp/~marumo/index.html. 8 units, none with bathroom. ¥5,250 per person without breakfast; ¥6,300 per person with Japanese breakfast. Rates include service charge. No credit cards. Town Sneaker Bus, Eastern Course: Kurashikkukan (stop no. 17, 2 min.). Or a 15-min. walk from Matsumoto Station. **Amenities:** Coffee shop. *In room:* A/C, TV.

WHERE TO DINE

Matsumoto is famous for its buckwheat noodles, which are fairly thick with a hearty flavor and can be served hot or cold, with several kinds of dips and sauces. It is also known for its *basashi*—raw horse meat.

⑤③ **Kura** ★ (Finds) TEMPURA This restaurant occupies the ground floor of one of the largest *kura* in Matsumoto, built in the late Meiji Period and rare for its three stories (most *kura* are two-storied). Enter the dining room through the thick vaultlike door and sit at the dark-wood counter or at one of the tables. The restaurant is known for its delicious tempura, though it also offers sushi, *basashi*, and *kaiseki* on its English-language menu. Best values are set meals, and try to avoid peak mealtimes, when the overworked staff can be brusque.

1-10-22 Chuo. ⌀ **0263/33-6444.** Tempura and sushi set meals ¥945–¥2,100; kaiseki ¥3,675–¥5,250. AE, DC, MC, V. Thurs-Tues 11:30am–2pm and 5:30–10pm. Station: Matsumoto (5 min.). Walk down Koen Dori (the small side street to the left of McDonald's) and take the 1st left past the Parco department store; it's on the left.

⑤④ **Nomugi** ★ NOODLES There are only three tables in this well-known eatery popular with the locals, which means you may have to wait for a seat and can't dawdle over a meal. Its handmade buckwheat noodles are served until they run out, which is why the restaurant has a flexible closing time. You'll be given a sauce to pour into a cup; add green onion, wasabi, and *daikon* radish, and then dip your *soba* into the mix. At the end of your meal, make a soup from the soba water stock (served in a teapot) and the soba sauce. In winter, the soba is served with boiled toppings.

2–9–11 Chuo. ☎ **0263/36-3753.** Soba ¥1,100; half portion ¥700. No credit cards. Thurs–Mon 11:30am to around 2pm. Town Sneaker Bus, Northern Course: Kuranomachi Nakamachi (stop no. 16, 1 min.). Or a 13-min. walk from Matsumoto Station; walk down Koen Dori (the small side street to the left of McDonald's), turn left at Honmachi, then right at Nakamachi, and then take the 1st right; it's on the left.

55 **Shikimi** ★ (**Value** EEL/SUSHI   For inexpensive Japanese fare close to Matsumoto Station, try this place specializing in eel and sushi. An atmosphere of old Japan is evoked by its traditional tiled roof, cast-iron lanterns, and interior with wooden sliding doors, small *tatami* rooms, wooden counter, and paper lanterns. I recommend the *unagi donburi* (strips of eel on rice), which comes with soup and pickled vegetables. If sushi is more to your liking, try one of Shikimi's platters of assorted sushi, called *moriawase* (¥ 1,680–¥3,150), or sushi rolls starting at ¥630.

1–5–5 Chuo. ☎ **0263/35-3279** or 36-7716. Unagi donburi ¥1,780; set lunch (Mon–Fri only) ¥980. No credit cards. Mon–Fri 11:45am–3pm and 4:30–9:30pm; Sat–Sun 11:45am–9pm. Station: Matsumoto (3 min.). Take Koen Dori (left side of McDonald's) 1 block and turn left; it's on the corner on your left.

Sunny Place Cafe INTERNATIONAL   This combination cafe/bar is a good place for lunch, offering wraps (like an avocado-shrimp combo or a BLT), lunch specials, and a wide assortment of drinks, coffees, and teas, including Chinese and herbal teas and shakes. From 2:30pm onward it becomes more of a bar, with a Japanese-language menu offering pizzas, salads, pasta, and rice dishes.

2–6–1 Chuo. ☎ **0263/37-5517.** Wraps ¥730–¥780; set lunches ¥1,050. MC, V. Daily 11:30am–11pm. Station: Matsumoto (7 min.). Head east on Agatanomori (also called Ekimae Dori), the main road leading away from the station, and turn left onto Honmachi Dori; it's on the right, next to the post office.

Taiman ★★★ FRENCH   If you feel like treating yourself, this ivy-covered, rustic yet elegant restaurant with a view of a garden is an excellent choice. In business for 60 years and located just south of Matsumoto Castle, it offers wonderful French cuisine from a changing menu that might include grilled duck, whitefish in a shrimp cream sauce, scallops, lamb cutlet with pistachio, or grilled steak in a red-wine sauce. My ¥5,250 lunch—which included bread or rice, dessert, and coffee—started with a corn potage, followed by stuffed *ayu* (river fish) and then the main dish, lamb with cèpe mushrooms.

4–2–4 Ote. ☎ **0263/32-0882.** Reservations recommended. Main dishes ¥4,200–¥6,300; set lunches ¥5,250–¥9,450; set dinners ¥12,600–¥18,900. AE, DC, MC, V. Thurs–Tues 11:30am–2pm and 5–9pm (last order 8pm). Town Sneaker Bus, Northern Course: Hachijuni-ginkomae (stop no. 5, 2 min.). Or a 12-min. walk from Matsumoto Station; walk east on Agatanomori (also called Ekimae Dori) and turn left on Honmachi Dori; after the bridge, turn right at the 2nd stoplight where the NTT Building is.

2 THE NAKASENDO HIGHWAY

About 100km (60 miles) E of Nagoya; 88km (55 miles) SW of Matsumoto

If you're traveling between Nagoya and Matsumoto, you'll most likely pass through Kiso Valley in mountainous Nagano Prefecture. Formed by the Kiso River, the valley has always served as a natural passageway through the Japan Alps and was, in fact, one of two official roads linking Kyoto with Edo (Tokyo) back in the days of the Tokugawa shogunate (the other route was the Tokaido Hwy., which passes through Hakone). Known as the **Nakasendo Highway** ★★, it was the route of traveling *daimyo* and their entourages of samurai retainers journeying between Japan's two most important towns. To serve their needs, 11 post towns sprang up along the Nakasendo Highway in Kiso Valley. Back then, it took 3 days to travel through the valley.

Of the old post towns, ㊳ **Tsumago** ★★ and ㊲ **Magome** ★ are two that still survive, with many of the old buildings left intact. An 8km (5-mile) pathway skirting the Kiso River links the two villages, providing hikers with the experience of what it must have been like to travel the 400-year-old Nakasendo Highway back in the days of the shogun. You can visit the two picturesque villages and take the hike in a 1-day excursion from Nagoya or Matsumoto, but I've included an overnight recommendation in case you want to linger. When I took my son, then 14 years old, on this hike in 2009, he declared it the highlight of our 2-week trip in Japan.

ESSENTIALS

GETTING THERE Because neither Magome nor Tsumago is directly on a train line, you'll have to make the final journey by bus.

To reach **Magome,** take the **JR Shinano express train** (which connects Nagoya and Matsumoto and departs hourly) to Nakatsugawa Station. Trains from Nagoya take about 50 minutes and cost ¥2,430 for an unreserved seat. From Matsumoto, trains take about 75 minutes and cost ¥3,670. The 20-minute bus ride onward to Magome costs ¥540, with buses departing about once an hour.

Because of less frequent train and bus connections, it's harder to reach **Tsumago,** so be sure to check schedules beforehand. Take the **JR Shinano train** to Nagiso Station and then a 10-minute bus ride (¥300). A taxi ride between Tsumago and Nagiso costs about ¥1,400.

Note: Train and bus schedules do not always coincide and not all trains stop in Nagiso or Nakatsugawa, so be sure to plan ahead. Although it's the same JR Shinano train that travels to both Nagiso and Nakatsugawa, express trains stop at Nagiso much less frequently than in Nakatsugawa. Note also that buses between Nagiso and Tsumago are also less frequent than those running between Nakatsugawa and Magome, so inquire about bus schedules beforehand. The Matsumoto Station tourist office has information on bus schedules (see "Visitor Information," on p. 266).

VISITOR INFORMATION The best way to obtain information about Kiso Valley is to stop by the **Tourist Information Center** in Tokyo or Narita or Kansai international airports to pick up a leaflet called "Kiso Valley" (or download it from JNTO's website at www.jnto.go.jp by looking under "Browse by Destinations"), which provides a rough sketch of the 8km (5-mile) hiking path between Magome and Tsumago and gives some basic information about the villages; you can also stop by the tourist office in Matsumoto.

Otherwise, there's a tourist office in Tsumago (✆ **0264/57-3123;** open daily 8:30am–5pm) and one in Magome (✆ **0573-69-2336;** open daily 9am–5pm except in summer when it opens at 8:30am). No English is spoken, but they do have English-language pamphlets, bus and train schedules, and maps of the hiking trail.

TRAVELING BETWEEN TSUMAGO & MAGOME If you want to see the post towns of Tsumago and Magome but don't want to hike between the two (or wish to hike the trail, say, from Magome to Tsumago and then return to Magome), a **bus** travels between the two villages for ¥600, but service is infrequent so be sure to get the schedule beforehand.

Especially useful for hikers is a **luggage-transfer service** available between Magome and Tsumago on weekends and national holidays from mid-March to mid-November (offered daily during peak season, July 20–Aug 31). Luggage is accepted at either town's tourist office no later than 11:30am, at a charge of ¥500 per bag, and can be picked up at your destination's tourist office after your hike as early as 1pm, but must be picked up by 5pm. During other times of the year, your bags can be sent by taxi to either tourist office or your *ryokan* for ¥3,000 for one or more bags.

WALKING THE NAKASENDO HIGHWAY
BETWEEN TSUMAGO & MAGOME

Allow about 3 hours for the 8km (5-mile) hike between Tsumago and Magome. It doesn't matter which town you start from, though starting from Tsumago is easier if you have heavy luggage being sent via transfer service, as starting in Magome requires an 8-minute walk from the bus stop up a steep slope to the tourist office. I, however, like starting in Magome and ending up in Tsumago, which I consider the crown jewel of the hike.

In any case, the trail is mainly a footpath tracing the contours of the Kiso Valley and crisscrossing a rushing stream over a series of bridges. At times the trail follows a paved road and leads past interesting farming villages, as well as old signposts, watch-house ruins, and other historic remnants, with a short detour leading to two waterfalls, Odaki and Medaki. There are public toilets along the way. Because the trail goes up some steep inclines, wear your walking shoes. And have fun—this is a great walk!

TSUMAGO ★★ Tsumago, the second post town from the south, is the more beautiful and authentic of the two towns. Threatened with gradual decline and desertion after the train line was constructed in 1911, bypassing Tsumago, the town experienced decades of neglect—and that's probably what ultimately saved it. Having suffered almost no modernization in the rebuilding zeal of the 20th century, Tsumago was a perfect target for renovation and restoration in the early 1970s, and in a rare show of insight, electrical wires, TV antennas, and telephone poles were hidden from sight along the main road and strict building codes forbid changes to existing buildings. Thus, Tsumago looks much as it did back in the days of Edo. There are, of course, the ubiquitous souvenir shops, but many sell locally made crafts made of wood and bamboo, including sun hats made from shaved cypress, which started as a cottage industry in the Edo Era.

On the main street of Tsumago are three separate buildings, called collectively the **Nagiso-machi Museum** (© **0264/57-3322**) and open daily from 9am to 5pm for a ¥700 admission. The **Tsumagojuku Honjin** was an officially appointed inn that once served as a way station for the 30 or so *daimyo* who used the Nakasendo Highway to travel to and from Edo. Like all *honjin* (an inn designated as the resting place for daimyo), it's divided into two parts: a large, grand area for the feudal lord and his attendants, and a few smaller, simpler rooms for the Shimazaki family, which managed the inn.

Apparently, the Shimazaki family had plans drawn up to rebuild its inn in 1830. Renovation, however, didn't take place until 160 years later when an heir discovered the plans and gave them to the township, which rebuilt the inn according to the original plans using techniques dating from the period. You'd swear it's the original.

Across the lane is the **Waki-honjin Okuya** ★, the town's secondary inn, used by court nobles or by *daimyo* when the *honjin* was already occupied. The present house, a lovely traditional structure with a garden, dates from 1877 and was rebuilt with *hinoki* cypress trees, a fact that has a special significance for this region. For centuries, all the way

> ## (Fun Facts) Daimyo Paranoia
>
> *Daimyo* (feudal lords) almost never ate meals prepared by local innkeepers. Rather, feudal lords traveled with their own cooks, who shopped for provisions in the village and then prepared meals in the inn's kitchen. Even then the food was first tested by a taster before the daimyo himself ate, to make sure it wasn't poisoned.

through the Edo Period, wood in the Kiso Valley was as good as gold and was used instead of rice to pay taxes. Commoners, therefore, were prohibited from cutting down trees, and those who did so literally lost their heads. When the Meiji Period dawned and the ban was finally lifted, wealthy landowners were quick to rebuild in a statelier manner. Emperor Meiji himself visited the inn in 1880, and though a special tub and toilet were built just for the occasion, he stayed only 30 minutes. Upstairs is a secret room, used for important discussions.

Next door is the **Rekishi Shiryokan,** which serves as a local history museum with displays of lacquerware, porcelain, a model of how the Waki-honjin looked during the Edo Period, diagrams showing how trees were felled and transported from the steep mountainsides, and photographs of buildings in Tsumago before and after they were renovated.

MAGOME   The southernmost post town, Magome has old inns, restaurants, and shops selling beautiful basket work and wooden articles that line both sides of a steeply sloping, cobblestone road. It takes about 20 minutes to stroll through the town.

WHERE TO STAY & DINE

Both Tsumago and Magome have simple *minshuku* and *ryokan* (tourist offices in both towns can make reservations). I love staying at (58) **Ryokan Fujioto** ★★, Tsumago, Nagiso-machi 399-5302 (© **0264/57-3009;** fax 0264/57-2239; www.takenet.or. jp/~fujioto), set back from the main road of Tsumago and buffered from foot traffic by a nice Japanese garden. The 100-year-old inn offers nine *tatami* rooms (none with bathroom) for ¥11,050 per person, including two delicious meals but excluding tax (no credit cards accepted). What makes this place a standout is innkeeper Fujihara-san and his daughter Sayaka-san, both of whom speak excellent English, can provide information on the area, and visit with guests in the dining room, explaining all the unique dishes they serve. Even if you don't spend the night, you can sample the inn's local specialties for lunch, served from 10am to 2:30pm daily. An English-language menu with pictures offers broiled trout, carp sashimi, Shinshu beef cooked on magnolia leaf, noodles, and other fare, as well as set meals for ¥1,050 to ¥1,650. Both the inn and restaurant are closed mid-December through February.

In Magome, on the main street through town, (59) **Magome-Chaya,** Magome, Nakatsugawa-shi 4296 (© **0265/59-2038**), offers 13 simple Japanese-style rooms (none with bathroom) for ¥5,250 for a single and ¥8,190 for a double, without meals (Master-Card and Visa accepted but with a 5% surcharge). The inn's restaurant across the street offers noodles (¥800–¥1,000) and set meals (¥1,600–¥1,800) daily 11am to 3pm.

3 TAKAYAMA, LITTLE KYOTO OF THE MOUNTAINS ★★★

533km (331 miles) NW of Tokyo; 165km (103 miles) NE of Nagoya

Located in the Hida Mountains (part of the Japan Alps National Park), **Takayama** is surrounded by 3,000m (10,000-ft.) peaks, making the train or bus ride here breathtaking. The town, situated along a river on a wide plateau with a population of 95,000, was founded in the 16th century by Lord Kanamori, who selected the site because of the impregnable position afforded by the surrounding mountains. Modeled after Kyoto but also with strong ties to Edo (Tokyo), Takayama borrowed from both cultural centers in developing its own architecture, food, and crafts, all well preserved today thanks to centuries of isolation. With a rich supply of timber provided by surrounding forests, its carpenters were legendary, creating not only beautifully crafted traditional merchants' homes in Takayama but also the Imperial Palace and temples in Kyoto.

Today, Takayama boasts a delightful and elegant historic district, called **San-machi Suji**, with homes of classical design typical of 18th-century Hida. The streets are narrow and clean and are flanked on both sides by tiny canals of running water, which in centuries past were useful for fire prevention, washing clothes, and dumping winter snow, but which now give the town its distinct character. Rising from the canals are one- and two-story homes and shops of gleaming dark wood with overhanging roofs; latticed windows and slats of wood play games of light and shadow in the white of the sunshine. In the doorways of many shops, blue curtains flutter in the breeze.

With its quaint old character, great shopping (including a lively city market), and museums, Takayama is a town that invites exploration. As you walk down the streets, you'll also notice huge cedar balls hanging from the eaves in front of several shops, indicating one of Takayama's sake breweries. Altogether there are six of them in Takayama, most small affairs. Go inside, sample the sake, and watch the men stirring rice in large vats. There are also a surprising number of museums, most housed in traditional homes and filled with historical relics and antiques of Takayama's past.

ESSENTIALS

GETTING THERE   By Train   The easiest way to reach Takayama is by direct train from Nagoya, with about 10 departures daily for the 2¼-hour trip that costs ¥5,360 for an unreserved seat. There's also one direct train a day from Osaka via Kyoto, which takes about 4 hours and costs ¥7,560 for an unreserved seat.

BY BUS   Nohi buses (✆ 03/5376-2222; www.nouhibus.co.jp) depart Tokyo's Shinjuku Station four to six times daily spring through autumn, arriving in Takayama 5½ hours later and costing ¥6,500. Reservations are required. There are fewer departures in winter, when snowfall sometimes makes roads impassable. Nohi buses also depart from Kanazawa (✆ 076/234-0123) twice a day for Takayama, passing through Shirakawa-go on the way and costing ¥3,300 for the 2¼-hour trip. From Matsumoto, the **Highland Express Bus** (✆ 0263/35-7400) passes through mountain scenery on the 2-hour and 20-minute trip and costs ¥3,100.

VISITOR INFORMATION   Before departing Tokyo or Narita or Kansai airports, stop by the **Tourist Information Center** for the "Takayama and Shirakawa-go" leaflet (or download it from JNTO's website at www.jnto.go.jp), which contains maps and sightseeing information. In Takayama, the **tourist office** (✆ **0577/32-5328;** daily 8:30am–6:30pm, to 5pm Nov–Mar) is housed in a wooden booth just outside the main (east) exit of Takayama Station. You can pick up an English-language brochure with a map of the town showing the location of all museums and attractions. You can also use the tourist office's laptop for free Internet access, but you have to stand. A small **tourist counter** on Sanno-machi street is open daily 10am to 4pm. More information is available at **www. hida.jp/english.**

GETTING AROUND Takayama is one of Japan's easiest towns to navigate. Most of its attractions lie east of the train station in San-machi Suji and are easily reached from the station in about 10 to 15 minutes **on foot.** Throughout the town are English-language signs pointing directions to the many attractions; they're even embedded in sidewalks and streets.

To reach Hida Folk Village, Hida Takayama Museum of Art, or Teddy Bear Eco Village (see below), you'll have to go by **Takayama City Circle Bus (Sarubobo Bus),** which departs from in front of the train station twice an hour daily from 9am to 4pm. The fare is ¥600 for an all-day pass; a pass that includes admission to the Hida Folk Village costs ¥900. Better yet, ask at the tourist Information Center for the free **London Bus** (operated by the Museum of Art only for museum customers Apr–Oct), which departs from Takayama Station four times a day. From the museum it's about a 10-minute walk to the folk village.

Alternatively, lots of shops ringing the station rent bicycles, with most charging ¥1,200 or ¥1,300 for the day, including Daily convenience store right beside the station (✆ 0577/35-5377) and Hara Cycling (✆ 0577/32-1657) a few minutes' walk from the station on Kokubunji Dori. Note, however, that it's straight up a very long hill to Hida Folk Village, Hida Takayama Museum of Art, and Teddy Bear museum. Personally, I'd rather walk.

SEEING THE SIGHTS

Takayama's main attraction is its old merchants' houses (Furui-Machi-nami), which are clustered together in San-machi Suji on three narrow streets called **Ichino-machi, Nino-machi,** and **Sanno-machi.** Be sure to allow time to wander around. In addition to the district's many museums, there are also shops selling Takayama's specialties, including sake, yew woodcarvings, beautiful cypress furniture, and a unique lacquerware called *shunkei-nuri.*

Be sure, too, to visit the **Miyagawa Morning Market,** which stretches on the east bank of the Miyagawa River between Kajibashi and Yayoibashi bridges. Held every morning from 7am (6am in summer) to noon, it's very picturesque, with cloth-covered stalls selling fresh vegetables, flowers, pickled vegetables, locally made crafts, and toys. A smaller morning market is held in front of the Historical Government House (Takayama Jinya; see below).

And if you have more free time still, consider the **Higashiyama Hiking Course,** which leads past a string of 13 temples and five shrines nestled on a wooded hill on the east edge of town in an area called Higashiyama Teramachi. It also leads to Shiroyama Park, site of the Kanamori clan castle until it was torn down in 1695 by order of the Tokugawa shogunate. Parts of its stone foundations still remain. The hiking course stretches 3.5km (2¼ miles) end to end, but English-language signs are few and far between and the map provided by the tourist office is hopeless; you could consider getting lost part of the fun.

Note that the attractions listed below are closed during the New Year's holiday.

Hida Folk Village (Hida no Sato) ★★   This is an open-air museum of more than 30 old thatched and shingled farmhouses, sheds, and buildings, many of which were brought here from other parts of the region to illustrate how farmers and artisans used to live in the Hida Mountain range. The entire village is picturesque, with swans swimming in the central pond, green moss growing on the thatched roofs, and flowers blooming in season. Some of the houses have *gassho-zukuri*-style roofs, built steeply to withstand the region's heavy snowfalls; the tops of the roofs are said to resemble hands joined in prayer. All the structures, which range from 100 to 500 years old, are open to the public and are filled with furniture, old spindles and looms, utensils for cooking and dining, instruments used in the silk industry, farm tools, sleds, and straw boots and snow capes for winter. Be sure to ask for the free 20-minute English-language audio guide at the entrance, which describes the social life and architecture of the region.

Workshops set up in one corner of the village grounds demonstrate Takayama's well-known woodcarving, tie-dying, weaving, and lacquer-work industries; some of the artisans even live here. On weekends you can try your hand at sandal-making, weaving, and other crafts; class fees range from ¥500 to¥1,000. You'll want to spend about 1½ hours at the village, but if you're heading to Shirakawa-go, skip it; there's a similar, more accessible open-air museum there.

© **0577/34-4711.** Admission ¥700 adults, ¥200 children 15 and under. Daily 8:30am–5pm. Bus: City Circle Bus to Hida-no-Sato, or the free London Bus to the Hida Takayama Museum of Art (then a 10-min. walk). Or, a 30-min. walk southwest of the train station.

Merchants' Houses ★★★   In contrast to other castle towns during the Edo Period, Takayama was under the direct control of the Tokugawa government rather than a feudal lord, which meant its homes were built and owned by merchants and commoners rather than the samurai class that dominated other Japanese cities. Located side by side in San-machi Suji and both toured easily in less than 30 minutes, **Yoshijima-ke** or Yoshijima House (© **0577/32-0038**) and **Kusakabe Mingeikan** (© **0577/32-0072**) are merchants' mansions that once belonged to two of the richest families in Takayama. With its exposed attic, heavy crossbeams, sunken open-hearth fireplace, and sliding doors, Yoshijima House is a masterpiece of geometric design. It was built in 1907 as both the home and factory of the Yoshijima family, well-to-do brewers of sake. Notice how the beams and details of the home gleam, a state attained through decades of polishing as each generation of women did their share in bringing the wood to a luster. Yoshijima-ke is also famous for its lattices, typical of Takayama yet showing an elegance influenced by Kyoto. Its walls serve as an art gallery for the lithographs of female artist Shinoda Toko, one of my favorite Japanese artists (and a distant relative of present owner Yoshijima Tadao, who also uses the house for his other passion, jazz, heard softly in the back gallery).

The Kusakabe Mingeikan, built in 1879 for a merchant dealing in silk, lamp oil, and finance, is more refined and imposing. Its architectural style is considered unique to Hida but has many characteristics common during the Edo Period, including a two-story warehouse at the back of the house with open beams and an earthen floor, now filled with folk art and other items. On display, too, are personal items such as lacquerware and chests from Japan and imports from other countries, handed down through the generations and arranged just as they would have been in the 18th and 19th centuries. If you

have time for only one house, this one has more to see; free green tea and rice crackers
are served in the courtyard.

North end of Nino-machi St., Oshinmachi. Admission to either house ¥500 for adults, ¥300 for junior high and younger. Mar–Nov both daily 9am–5pm. Dec–Feb Yoshijima-ke Wed–Mon 9am–4:30pm; Kusakabe Mingeikan daily 9am–4pm. Station: Takayama (20 min.).

MORE MUSEUMS

Fujii Folk Craft Museum (Fujii Bijutsu Mingei-Kan) ★

This gallery in the heart of San-Machi Suji occupies a traditional merchant's storehouse; its entrance is a replica of an outer gate that once led to Takayama Castle. The eclectic collection from the Edo Period includes beautiful *tansu* (chests) inlaid with mother-of-pearl, sake cups, lacquerware, Imari and Kutani porcelain, tortoiseshell combs, ceremonial dolls, kimono, teakettles, paper lanterns, rice barrels, smoking utensils, matchlocks, swords, farming tools, spinning wheels, and more. Many items are identified in English, making this a very worthwhile museum; you can see it all in about 20 minutes.

Sanno-machi St., 69 Kamisanno-machi. ✆ **0577/35-3778.** Admission ¥700 adults, ¥350 children. Daily 9am–5pm. Station: Takayama (12 min.).

60 Hida Takayama Museum of Art (Hida Takayama Bijutsukan) ★★

Serious glass lovers will not want to miss this museum with its collection of mostly European antique and contemporary glassware from the 16th to the 20th centuries, including works by Tiffany, Lalique, and Gallé, as well as contemporary works by Japanese glassmakers like Fujita Kyohei. Several rooms are furnished in decorative and applied arts by masters such as Louis Majorelle, Mackintosh, and Vienna's Secessionist artists. Don't miss the museum shop with its Japanese and imported glassware and crafts; I also like the Mackintosh-inspired tearoom with outdoor terrace seating. Plan on spending about 45 minutes here.

1-124-1 Kamiokamoto-cho. ✆ **0577/35-3535.** www.htm-museum.co.jp. Admission ¥1,300 adults, ¥1,000 university and high-school students, ¥800 junior-high age and younger. Apr–Nov daily 9am–5pm; Dec–Mar Thurs–Mon 9am–5pm. Bus: City Circle Bus to Hida-no-Sato Shita, or take the free London Bus. Station: Takayama (20-min. southwest).

Hirata Folk Art Museum (Hirata Kinen-kan) ★★

Here you'll find what is probably Takayama's most varied and extensive collection of folk art. It vividly conveys what life was like during the Edo Period by displaying household utensils, crafts, and fine arts found in a typical middle-class home; the house itself, built in 1897 in traditional style with a sunken hearth and both living and working quarters, belonged to a candle-maker. Items are identified in English. On display are folk toys, coin boxes, mirrors, toiletry sets, *geta* sandals, spectacles, hair adornments, *shunkei* lacquerware, and paper and kerosene lamps; my favorite is the room outfitted with items used for travel, including guide maps, portable abacuses, compasses, a traveling pillow, a folding lantern, and even a folding hat. You'll probably spend 20 minutes here.

Ichino-machi St., 39 Kaminino-machi. ✆ **0577/33-1354.** Admission ¥300 adults, ¥150 junior-high age and younger. Daily 9am–5pm. Station: Takayama (10 min.).

Historical Government House (Takayama Jinya) ★★★

I highly recommend a visit here to anyone interested in Japanese history. The building served as the Tokugawa government's administrative building for 177 years (1692–1868). Of some 60 local government offices that were once spread throughout Japan, this is the only one still in existence. Resembling a miniature palace with its outer wall and an imposing entrance gate, the sprawling complex consists of both original buildings and reconstructions. In addition to administrative offices, chambers, and courts, the complex contained living quarters, a huge kitchen, an interrogation room with torture devices, and a 400-year-old rice granary, the oldest and biggest in Japan, where rice collected from farmers as a form of taxation was stored.

Making visits here especially educational are the free guided tours available in English, which last about 30 to 40 minutes and provide fascinating insight into administrative life during the Edo Period.

1–5 Hachi-ken-machi. *Ⓒ* **0577/32-0643.** Admission ¥420 for adults, free for high-school age and younger. Mar–Oct daily 8:45am–5pm; Nov–Feb daily 8:45am–4:30pm. Station: Takayama (10 min.).

Lacquerware Museum (Hida Takayama Shunkei Kaikan) This museum, which can be toured in 15 minutes, displays Takayama lacquerware, known for the transparency of its finish, which enhances the grain of the wood. Takayama lacquerware is admired all over Japan for its honey-colored sheen, which becomes lighter and more beautiful over time. The museum displays some 1,000 items dating from the 17th century to the present, including beautifully crafted trays, furniture, vases, rice containers, and lunch boxes; one exhibit explains the multistage production technique and tools of the craft. There's also a shop—and after seeing the time-consuming process to produce *shunkei* ware, you'll know why prices are high.

1–88 Kanda-cho. *Ⓒ* **0577/32-3373.** Admission ¥300 adults, ¥200 high-school and junior-high students, free for children. Summer daily 8:30am–5:30pm; winter daily 9am–5pm. Station: Takayama (15 min.).

�61 **Lion Dance Ceremony Exhibition Hall (Shishi-Kaikan)** More than 200 lion masks from all over Japan, used to perform the lion dance in Japanese festivals, are on display here, as well as Edo-Period screens, ceramics, scrolls, coins, samurai armor, and swords. Best, however, are the 15-minute performances given every half-hour by *karakuri* (automated dolls), which decorate many of Takayama's floats in its two festivals; they're capable of wonderful acrobatics.

53–1 Sakura-machi. *Ⓒ* **0577/32-0881.** Admission ¥600 adults, ¥400 junior-high age and younger. Summer daily 8:30am–5:30pm; winter daily 9am–5pm. A 1-min. walk from Takayama Festival Float Exhibition Hall (see below).

�62 **Showa Kan** ★ If you're a history or a kitsch buff, check out this eclectic museum packed with original items used in daily life during the Showa era (Showa refers to the reign of Emperor Hirohito, 1926–89), including posters, shop signs, bikes, washing machines, rice cookers, clocks, and more, most of it arranged in themed rooms. You can step inside a toyshop, photo studio, doctor's office, dry goods store (it's fun to see what was considered high-tech back then), schoolroom, beauty salon, movie theater, and other establishments, providing a unique perspective on how much Japan has changed in just a few short decades (you'll probably find yourself wishing more from the Showa era remained). After spending about 30 minutes here, be sure to take a look at the small museum shop selling replica tin toys and candies of yesteryear. You'll recognize the museum by the old vehicles and gas pump in the entranceway.

6 Shimoichino-machi. *Ⓒ* **0577/33-7836.** Admission ¥500 adults, ¥300 children. Daily 9am–6pm. Station: Takayama (10 min.); just off Kokubunji Dori.

Takayama Festival Float Exhibition Hall (Takayama Matsuri Yatai Kaikan) ★ This exhibition hall displays 4 of the 11 huge, elaborate floats used for Takayama's famous Takayama Matsuri (Autumn Festival). Dating mostly from the 17th century and colorfully decorated with carvings, hanging lanterns, and sometimes marionettes, floats are as high as 7m (23 ft.) and are mounted on wheels (it takes 20 people to pull them through the streets). Free 20-minute guided tours in English make the festival hall an interesting stop if you're unable to see the festival itself.

The admission price also allows entrance to **Sakurayama Nikko Kan** next door, which houses a replica of the Toshogu Shrine in Nikko (p. 239), built almost 100 years ago over a period of 15 years at ¹⁄₁₀th the scale. I was initially skeptical, but the 28 buildings—complete with computerized sunsets and sunrises—are works of art.

178 Sakura-machi. © **0577/32-5100.** Admission ¥820 adults, ¥510 high-school students, ¥410 junior-high age and younger. Summer daily 8:30am–5pm; winter daily 9am–4:30pm. In the precincts of Sakurayama Hachimangu Shrine, about a 10-min. walk north of San-machi Suji or a 25-min. walk from the train station.

Teddy Bear Eco Village (**Kids**) Kids of all ages might enjoy a 30-minute stopover here, where 1,000 bears from around the world are on display, including rare finds like a 1911 Steiff polar bear, a 1903 Steiff named Franz that once belonged to the Habsburg family, a Smokey the Bear, and a bear donated by Patagonia made entirely from excess fleece. Its cafe, with indoor and outdoor seating, offers organic coffee and teas, soy hot dogs, and a very good salad wrap with organic veggies.

3–829–4 Nishino-ishiki. © **0577/37-2525.** Admission ¥600 adults, ¥500 high-school students, ¥400 children. Daily 10am–6pm. Closed irregularly in winter. Bus: City Circle Bus to Hida-no-Sato Shita. Station: Takayama (20 min.); btw. Hida Folk Village and Hida Takayama Museum of Art.

WHERE TO STAY

There are as many *minshuku* and *ryokan* in Takayama as hotels, making it the perfect place to stay in a traditional inn. In fact, staying in a *tatami* room and sleeping on a futon is the best way to immerse yourself in the life of this small community.

You should be aware that in peak season—Golden Week (Apr 29–May 5), August, festival times in April and October, and New Year's—prices will be higher, generally between 10% and 20%, than prices given below.

Expensive

Best Western Hotel Takayama ★ Purists might decry the size of this chain hotel in such a historic town, but it does have a convenient location just a minute's walk from the train station and could be a lifesaver for those who do not like sleeping on the floor. Besides, at seven stories, it's not even the tallest building around, and its facade, with a replica Meiji-Era design, could be worse. Otherwise, its mostly twin rooms are fairly small and ordinary, though cheerful and bright; ask for a room on a higher floor facing east, where you have a view of mountains in the distance.

6–6 Hanasato-cho, Takayama, Gifu 506-0026. © **0577/37-2000.** Fax 0577/37-2005. www.bestwestern. com. 78 units. ¥11,000 single; ¥18,000–¥21,000 double. Rates include breakfast. AE, MC, V. Station: Takayama (1 min.). Walk straight out of the station for 1 block and turn left. **Amenities:** 2 restaurants; lounge; lobby computer w/free Internet; smoke-free rooms. *In room:* A/C, TV, fridge, hair dryer, Wi-Fi.

Moderate

⑥③ **Antique Inn Sumiyoshi** ★★★ (**Finds**) This calls itself a *ryokan*, but its price and homey atmosphere make it seem more like a *minshuku*. Built about 100 years ago by a well-known local carpenter to house a silkworm industry, it opened in 1950 as a ryokan and probably hasn't changed much since then. An open-hearth fireplace, samurai armor, and antiques fill the reception area, where you are invited to have tea or coffee, and on the second floor there's an outdoor deck facing the river. *Tatami* rooms are comfortable and old-fashioned, many with painted screens and antiques; request one facing the river, across which you have a view of the morning market. Rates are based on room type. Minami-san, the man running the ryokan, is a fourth-generation innkeeper and speaks English. In addition to Japanese and vegetarian dinners (order when making reservations), both Japanese and Western breakfasts are available.

21–4 Honmachi, Takayama, Gifu 506-0011. © **0577/32-0228.** Fax 0577/33-8916. www.sumiyoshi-ryokan. com. 8 units (1 with bathroom; 2 with sink/toilet). ¥6,300–¥9,450 per person. Dinner ¥3,150 extra; breakfast ¥1,050 extra. No credit cards. Station: Takayama (10 min. northeast). Across from historic San-machi Suji on the Miyagawa River. *In room:* A/C, TV, minibar, no phone.

Four Seasons (Value) Although this modern-looking building with an arched roof looks out of place in Takayama, the hotel is a good choice in terms of price. Catering to business travelers during the week and tourists on weekends, it has free coffee in the lobby. Avoid the cheaper rooms on the second and third floors, as these have glazed windows. Rooms on the fourth through sixth floors have views over the city (request a corner room), with those on the sixth floor decorated with wooden furniture and wooden floors (important for the allergy conscious; rooms on the second floor are also with wood floors). A large Japanese bath with Jacuzzi and sauna overlooking a small garden is a plus. (By the way, as you may have guessed by its rates, this place is not part of the famous Four Seasons hotel chain.)

1–1 Kanda-machi, Takayama, Gifu 506-0006. © **0577/36-0088.** Fax 0577/36-0080. 46 units. ¥6,900–¥7,500 single; ¥13,500–¥14,500 twin. AE, MC, V. Station: Takayama (10 min. northeast). **Amenities:** Restaurant; rental bikes (free); hot-spring indoor bath; lobby computer w/free Internet; sauna. *In room:* A/C, TV, fridge, hair dryer, Wi-Fi.

Yamakyu ★ This spotless *minshuku* has a reputation of offering the best meals in town in its price range, served in a communal dining room. Although it's a bit far from the station—about a 20-minute walk or a 5-minute taxi ride—it's located in a quiet residential area near Takayama's many temples and shrines (and Higashiyama Hiking Course; see p. 277) and is only a 10-minute walk or short bike ride to the historic district. Its hallways boast a good collection of folk art, antique clocks, glassware, and lamps; eaves above all guest-room doors give it a "village" atmosphere. In the mornings, free coffee is available from the small lobby lounge, where you have a view of a small courtyard garden. As with most *minshuku*, the Japanese-style rooms—nicely done with natural woods and artwork—are without private bathrooms, but the communal baths are large and include tiny outdoor tubs, one ceramic and one wood.

58 Tenshoji-machi, Takayama, Gifu 506-0832. © **0577/32-3756.** Fax 0577/35-2350. www.takayama-yamakyu. com. 20 units (all with toilet and sink only). ¥7,980 per person. Rates include 2 meals. No credit cards. Station: Takayama (20 min.). Walk straight up San-machi Suji. **Amenities:** Rental bikes (¥500 per day or ¥300 per half-day); lobby computer w/free Internet. *In room:* A/C, TV.

Inexpensive
Minshuku Sosuke ★ The entryway of this friendly *minshuku* is filled with country knickknacks and has an *irori* (open hearth) in the communal room, where you can warm yourself on chilly days and where guests (85% foreigners) gather to chat in the evening. Although the building housing the minshuku is 180 years old (moved here from a village) and some of the original atmosphere has been preserved, the inside has been remodeled, and all the *tatami* rooms, though simple, are clean and are nonsmoking. Note,

however, that some have skylights, and morning arrives awfully early in summer. Also, though it's not far from the station, it's in the opposite direction from the town center, making it less convenient for sightseeing. On the plus side, the owner, who speaks English, will pick you up from the station if he's not busy, and the Green Hotel across the street rents bicycles. Generous meals feature local specialties, with vegetarian choices available if requested in advance.

1–64 Okamoto-cho, Takayama, Gifu 506-0054. ℂ **0577/32-0818.** Fax 0577/33-5570. www.irori-sosuke. com. 13 units, none with bathroom. ¥5,040 per person. Japanese dinner ¥2,100–¥4,725 extra; Western or Japanese breakfast ¥735 extra. No credit cards. Station: Takayama (8 min. west). Turn right out of the station onto the main street and then take the 1st right (at the T intersection); it's past the bridge over the tracks, on the right side of the street across from the Green Hotel. **Amenities:** Lobby computer w/free Internet; smoke-free rooms. *In room:* A/C, TV, no phone.

Rickshaw Inn ★★ Ⓚ**ids** In a modern house in a central location, Rickshaw Inn (entirely nonsmoking) is welcoming, due in no small part to the friendly owner, Setoyama Eiko, a Takayama native who lived in the United States and speaks flawless English. A communal living room—with sofas, TV, newspapers, a table, and an adjoining kitchen with refrigerator, hot plate, microwave, and toaster—is a good place to relax with fellow guests. No dinner is served, but Eiko-san can recommend restaurants (ask for her map) and is knowledgeable about museums, crafts, and Takayama's history. Japanese- and Western-style rooms, with sinks or bathrooms, feature Asian artwork and batik shades to block out light. Some Japanese rooms are big enough for three or four people, but best for families or longer stays are the two suites with *tatami* sleeping areas and bathrooms: the Bamboo suite with a kitchenette, table, and chairs; and Sakura with a large living area complete with two sofas, large-screen TV, table, and chairs.

54 Suehiro-cho, Takayama, Gifu 506-0016. ℂ **0577/32-2890.** Fax 0577/32-2469. www.rickshawinn.com. 11 units, 8 with bathroom. ¥4,200 single without bathroom; ¥8,900–¥10,200 double without bathroom, ¥11,900 double with bathroom. Suites from ¥20,700 triple; ¥27,200 quad. Western breakfast ¥800 extra. MC, V. Station: Takayama (6 min. east), just off Kokubunji St. **Amenities:** Communal kitchen; smoke-free rooms. *In room:* A/C, TV, Internet, no phone.

Super Hotel Hida Takayama Ⓥ**alue** Super Hotel is a burgeoning chain offering super-cheap small rooms with few amenities. This one, near the train station and popular with business travelers, is in a modern—if rather stark—building. After checking in via automated machine, you'll pick up a *yukata* and your preferred pillow type from a shelf by the elevator. Other than its rates and location, the only bonus to staying here is its one hot-spring bath, which alternates open hours between the sexes. Note that you have to vacate your room from 10am to 3pm for cleaning.

4–76 Temmacho, Takayama, Gifu 506-0025. ℂ **0577/32-9000.** Fax 0577/32-9090. www.superhotel.co.jp. 77 units. ¥4,980 single; ¥6,980 double. Rates include Japanese breakfast. No credit cards. Station: Takayama (2 min.). Turn right out of the station onto the main street and take the 1st left. **Amenities:** Lobby computer w/free Internet. *In room:* A/C, TV, fridge, Internet, no phone.

WHERE TO DINE

Takayama has some local specialties you should try while you're here (they may well be served at your *ryokan* or *minshuku*). The best known is *hoba miso*, which is soybean paste mixed with dried scallions, ginger, and mushrooms and cooked on a dry magnolia leaf at your table above a small clay burner. *Sansai* are mountain vegetables, including edible ferns and other wild plants; and *ayu* is river fish, grilled with soy sauce or salt. Other favorite dishes include Takayama's own style of *soba* (buckwheat noodles), *mitarashi-dango* (grilled rice balls with soy sauce), and Hida beef.

In addition to the listings below, stop by ⑭ **Fujiya Hanaikada,** 46 Hanakawa-cho (📞 **0577/36-0339**), a 4-minute walk straight ahead from the station, on a corner to the left. Open Friday to Wednesday from 10am to 6pm, it serves traditional Japanese home-made sweets along with tea and coffee, but what makes this place memorable is its award-winning locally made cypress furniture.

Very Expensive

㊽ **Kakusho ★★★** (Finds) VEGETARIAN For a big splurge, dine at Kakusho, established 180 years ago and offering local vegetarian fare called *shojin-ryori,* typically served at Buddhist temples. Situated on the slope of a hill in the eastern part of the city, a 5-minute walk from San-machi Suji, this delightful restaurant serves meals either in small, private *tatami* rooms dating from the Edo Period or in a larger room from the Meiji Period that can be opened to the elements on three sides, all of which overlook a dreamy, mossy garden enclosed by a clay wall. The least expensive meals consist of various mountain vegetables, mushrooms, nuts, tofu, and other dishes; more dishes are added for the more expensive set meals. The owner speaks some English.

2–98 Babacho. 📞 **0577/32-0174.** Reservations required. Kaiseki shojin-ryori ¥10,000–¥20,000; set lunches ¥5,500. Prices exclude tax and service charge. No credit cards. Daily seatings at 11:30am and 2pm and 5:30–7:30pm (last order). Irregular closing days. Station: Takayama (15 min.). Just north off of San-machi and 1 block east of Kami-ichino-machi.

Moderate

Le Midi ★★ FRENCH This tiny, two-level restaurant with red-and-white checkered tablecloths and wood trim, imparts a European flair and delivers delicious food. Its specialty is Hida beef, available as sirloin steak, beef stew, or beef cheek simmered 6 hours in red wine. Even the humble hamburger steak, served on potatoes and with green beans, is quite a presentation. Other dishes include Hida pork, fish of the day, and duck breast.

2–2 Honmachi. 📞 **0577/36-6386.** Main courses ¥2,000–¥6,890; set dinners ¥4,800–¥12,000; set lunches ¥1,800–¥3,800. AE, DC, MC, V. Mon–Wed and Fri 11:30am–3pm and 6:30–9:30pm; Sat–Sun and holidays 11:30am–3:30pm and 5–9:30pm. Station: Takayama (9 min.). On Honmachi near Ikadabashi Bridge.

㊻ **Matsuki Sushi ★** SUSHI Takayama is a 90-minute drive from the ocean, but that's where this sushi purveyor shops daily. Seating is at the counter or at low tables with leg wells. An English-language brochure lists various set meals, including a Ninja Course that gives you eight *nigiri-zushi,* one hand-rolled sushi, assorted tempura, and crab miso soup. Or, leave it to chef Kazu and order the *omakase,* which comes with 12 sushi selections along with miso soup; two diners can even split this feast. Oddly, another specialty here is Hida beef—but thank goodness, it's grilled.

1–40 Sowa-cho. 📞 **089/1567-0077.** Set meals ¥2,980–¥4,980. AE, V. Tues–Sun 11am–2pm; daily 5:30–11:30pm. Station: Takayama (5 min.). Walk east on Kokubunji St. and turn left after passing Kokubunji Temple; it will be on the right.

㊼ **Suzuya ★★** LOCAL SPECIALTIES Darkly lit with traditional Takayama country decor, this restaurant specializing in Takayama cuisine is very popular. There's an English-language menu complete with photographs and explanations of each dish, including such local specialties as mountain vegetables, *hoba miso,* and Hida beef, as well as *shabu-shabu* and sukiyaki.

24 Hanakawa-cho. 📞 **0577/32-2484.** Set meals ¥1,260–¥4,200. AE, DC, MC, V. Wed–Mon 11am–3pm and 5–8pm (last order). Station: Takayama (6 min.). Just off Kokubunji St. to the right, halfway btw. the station and the Miyagawa River.

Agura ★★ (Finds) LOCAL SPECIALTIES/PIZZA   A converted rice *kura,* with a high-beamed ceiling, wooden floors, slabs of wood for tables, and locally crafted bentwood chairs makes for a lovely, airy setting, heightened by eclectic cuisine, hip waiters, and jazz. The English-language menu lists several salads (I especially like the "Agura Original Salad" with lettuce, shrimp, boiled egg, tomato, ham, tuna, and sprouts), three kinds of pizzas fired in a wood-burning stove, and food that goes down well with beer, including *edamame,* chicken marinated in miso, spring rolls with sweet chili sauce, and Hida beef and miso cooked on a "dead" (they meant to write "dried") Hoba leaf. Note that there's a ¥200-per-person snack charge.

4–7 Shinmeicho. ✆ **0577/37-2666.** Main dishes ¥680–¥1,500. AE, MC, V. Tues–Sun 6–11:30pm (last order). Station: Takayama (12 min.). Just south of Takayama City Memorial Hall; look for the green sign with the yellow seated Buddha.

(68) **Myogaya** VEGETARIAN   Just a minute's walk east of the train station, this tiny shop packed with books and some health foods offers a limited selection of homemade organic set meals from an English-language menu, including chicken or veggie curry and stir-fried rice, which come with miso soup and vegetables (takeout available). The friendly proprietress makes this a pleasant place to come even for just a drink, from organic coffee and tea to plum juice and wine made from organic grapes.

5–15 Hanasato-cho. ✆ **0577/32-0426.** Set meals ¥1,000–¥1,100. No credit cards. Wed–Sun 8–10:30am and 11:30am–3pm. Walk straight out of the station 1 block and turn right.

4 RURAL SHIRAKAWA-GO & OGIMACHI

555km (347 miles) NW of Tokyo

With its thatched-roof farmhouses, paddies trimmed with flower beds, roaring river, and pine-covered mountains rising on all sides, **Shirakawa-go** is one of the most picturesque regions in Japan. Unfortunately, it also has more than its fair share of tour buses (especially in May, Aug, and Oct), with about 1.8 million visitors annually. Still, because of its rather remote location, accessible only by car or bus, Shirakawa-go remains off the beaten path for most foreign tourists. A visit to this rural region could well be the highlight of your trip.

Although Shirakawa-go stretches about 39km (24 miles) beside the Shokawa River and covers 229 sq. km (88 sq. miles), mountains and forest account for 95% of the region, and Shirakawa-go's 1,800 residents and cultivated land are squeezed into a valley averaging less than 3km (2 miles) in width. Thus, land in Shirakawa-go for growing rice and other crops has always been scarce and valuable. As a result, farmhouses were built large enough to hold extended families, with as many as several dozen family members living under one roof. Because there wasn't enough land available for young couples to marry and build houses of their own, only the eldest son was allowed to marry; the other children were required to spend their lives living with their parents and helping with the farming. But even though younger children weren't allowed to marry, a man was allowed to choose a young woman, visit her in her parents' home, and father her children. The children then remained with the mother's family, becoming valuable members of the labor force.

Before the roads came to Shirakawa-go, winter always meant complete isolation as snow 2m (6 ft.) deep blanketed the entire region. *Irori* (open-hearth fireplaces) in the middle of a communal room were used for cooking, warmth, and light during the long winter months. The family lived, therefore, on the ground floor, while upper floors were used for silk cultivation and storage of utensils. Because of the heavy snowfall, thatched roofs were constructed at steep angles, known as *gassho-zukuri* in reference to the fact that the tops of the roofs look like hands joined in prayer. The steep angle also allowed rain to run off quickly, and the thatch (Japanese pampas grass) dried quickly in the sun, preventing decay. Remarkably, the massive homes were constructed without nails; rather, sturdy ropes held the framework together and helped withstand earthquakes. Because there were no chimneys, smoke from the irori simply rose into the levels above, helping to ward off insects in the thatch and to keep the ropes taut.

Today, there are about 115 thatched farmhouses, barns, and sheds in Shirakawa-go, most of them built about 200 to 300 years ago. The thatched roofs are about .6m (2 ft.) thick and last some 40 years. The old roofs are replaced in Shirakawa-go every April, when one to four roofs are changed on successive weekends. The entire process involves about 200 people, who can replace one roof in a couple of days.

Shirakawa-go's inhabitants live in several small villages. Of these, **Ogimachi** ★★★, declared a UNESCO World Cultural and Natural Heritage site in 1995, boasts the greatest concentration of thatched-roof buildings. With just 600 residents, it's a delightful hamlet of narrow lanes winding past thatched-roof farmhouses, which stand like island sentinels surrounded by paddies. Many of the farmhouses have been turned into *minshuku,* souvenir shops, restaurants, and museums, including an **open-air museum** that depicts life in the region before roads opened it to the rest of the world.

ESSENTIALS

GETTING THERE   The most common way to reach Ojimachi is by **bus** from Takayama, which takes about 1 hour and costs ¥2,400. There are usually seven departures from Takayama (✆ **0577/32-1688**) daily April through November, less frequently in winter (heavy winter snowfall sometimes renders the road impassable). From Kanazawa, a bus operates thrice daily mid-March through November; the fare is ¥1,800 for the 1¼-hour trip. In any case, buses arrive at a parking lot next to the Gassho Zukuri Minka-en open-air museum (see below); *minshuku* are located in the village on the other side of the river, reached via pedestrian suspension bridge.

VISITOR INFORMATION   There's a **tourist office** (✆ **05769/6-1013;** daily 8:30am–5pm) located next to the bus parking lot. You can pick up an English-language map, reserve a room in a *minshuku* if you have not already done so, and store luggage here for ¥300 if it won't fit in any of the adjacent lockers. There's a second tourist office across the river on the main road in the center of town, open daily 9am to 5pm.

GETTING AROUND   Your own two feet can do it best. You can **walk** from one end of the village to the other in about 15 minutes; English-language signs direct you to the various attractions.

SEEING THE SIGHTS IN & AROUND OGIMACHI

In addition to an open-air museum, several old farmhouses in Ogimachi are open to the public. *Note:* Because Ogimachi is so small, no addresses are given in this section. This is a very small village, basically just one main street and some side streets.

> ## (Moments) A View of Ogimachi
>
> For an overview (and the best vantage point for photographs) of the entire village, walk along the gently sloping road that leads from the north side of Ogimachi to the **Shiroyama Viewing Point** ★★. There's a souvenir shop/restaurant here, but the best thing to do is to turn left at the crest of the hill and walk to the hill's westernmost point (toward the river), where there are some secluded benches. From here, you'll have a marvelous view of the entire valley. If you're thirsty or hungry, go to the restaurant (also with an outdoor viewing point) to buy a drink or a snack and then take it with you to the lookout.

(69) **Doburoku Matsuri no Yakata (Festival Hall)**　This Festival Hall was erected in honor of the Doburoku Matsuri Festival held in Shirakawa-go every year from October 14 to October 19. Centering on locally produced, potent sake, the festival is held just outside the museum's grounds at Hachimanjinja Shrine. If you've never seen a Japanese festival, you might want to come here to see some of the costumes worn during the festival, sample the festive sake, and watch a 20-minute video of the yearly festivities and folk dancing.

(ᗒ **05769/6-1655.** Admission ¥300 adults, ¥100 junior-high and elementary students. Daily 9am–5pm. Closed Oct 13–16 and Dec–Mar.

Gassho Zukuri Minka-en ★★★　To see how rural people lived in centuries past, visit Shirakawa-go's top attraction, this open-air museum with 25 *gassho-zukuri* houses and sheds that were relocated mostly from Kazura village and restored here. Filled with the tools of everyday life and displays ranging from silk production to straw clothing, the buildings are picturesquely situated around ponds, paddies, flower beds, and streams, a photographer's dream. You can occasionally see artisans engage in traditional handicrafts here, and a DVD depicts rural life almost 50 years ago in Kazura, abandoned in 1967. You'll easily spend an hour here.

(ᗒ **05769/6-1231.** Admission ¥500 adults, ¥300 children 7–15. Apr–July and Sept–Nov daily 8:40am–5pm; Aug daily 8am–5:30pm; Dec–Mar Fri–Wed 9am–4pm (if Thurs is a holiday, it remains open but closes Wed instead). Beside the bus parking lot and tourist office.

(70) **Nagase Ke** ★★　Of several homes open to the public, this is my favorite. Built in 1890 using 150- to 200-year-old cypress and 300- to 400-year-old chestnut, the Nagase house is the largest home here, once housing 44 people (a few members of the Nagase family still live here). The enormous cross beam is 18m (59 ft.) long and the height of the house is more than 17m (55 ft.) high. A 15-minute video shows the 2001 rethatching in which 500 people took part, including 40 women involved just in cooking meals for the workers. Because the Nagase ancestors were the personal doctors of the powerful Maeda lords, the house contains gifts from the Maedas as well as medical tools. Like other homes, it also contains a family altar, this one 500 years old and adjoined to the house so it could be quickly removed in case of fire. Upstairs is a mezzanine where 17 laborers lived, while the next level displays various tools used for everything from making rope to making cloth; in this remote area, almost everything people used was homemade. The fourth floor, where silk production once took place, contains tools related to the business, including flat trays where the silk worms were bred.

THE JAPAN ALPS

8

RURAL SHIRAKAWA-GO & OGIMACHI

Ⓒ **05769/6-1047.** Admission ¥300 adults, ¥150 children. Daily 9am–5pm. Occasionally closed. Just north of the main street.

⑦ **Wada Ke** ★   This thatched-roof home is Ogimachi's finest—not surprising, as it belonged to the wealthy Wada family, which served as the region's top officials. Still occupied by the Wada family, the 300-year-old house boasts carved transoms, painted sliding doors, lacquerware passed down through generations, a family altar, and *tatami* rooms overlooking a private garden. Upstairs you can see how the heavy roof beams are held together using only rope (no nails were used), as well as containers once used in silkworm cultivation.

Ⓒ **05769/6-1058.** Admission ¥300 adults, ¥150 children. Daily 9am–5pm. Occasionally closed. Just north of the main street.

WHERE TO STAY

Because huge extended families living under one roof are a thing of the past, many residents of Ogimachi have turned their *gassho-zukuri* homes into *minshuku*. Staying in one gives you the unique chance to lodge in a thatched farmhouse with a family that might consist of grandparents, parents, and children. English is often limited to the basics of "bath," "breakfast," and "dinner," but smiles go a long way. Most likely, the family will drag out their family album with its pictures of winter snowfall and the momentous occasion when their thatched roof was repaired. What I like best about staying overnight is that most tourists (about 4,900 on average daily) are day-trippers, which means you have the village pretty much to yourself by late afternoon. Be sure to take both an evening and early morning stroll.

Most *minshuku* are fairly small, with about four to nine *tatami* rooms open to guests. Rooms are basic without bathroom or toilet, and you may be expected to roll out your own futon. Privacy may be limited, as only a flimsy sliding partition may separate you from the guest next door. All recommended minshuku below are in thatch-roofed homes; rates include breakfast and dinner (add ¥400 in winter for heating charges), and none accept credit cards or have private bathrooms. Check-in is at 3pm; checkout is 9am. The tourist office can make a reservation for you at these or any of the others around town.

Although all minshuku have public baths, I like soaking in the indoor and outdoor hot-spring baths at ⑦ **Shirakawa-go no Onsen** (Ⓒ 05769/6-0026). Open daily from 7am to 9:30pm, it charges ¥700 for adults and ¥200 for children, but ask your minshuku for a ¥200 discount coupon. If you didn't bring your own towel, you can buy or rent one here.

⑦ **Juemon** ★   Juemon is a favorite among foreigners traveling in Japan. This attractive *minshuku*, in a 270-year-old farmhouse, features a stone-ringed pond with flowering shrubs and a couple of benches where you can relax and enjoy the view. In addition, there's an *irori* in the dining room; don't be surprised if the outgoing 70-something Mrs. Sakai who runs this place serenades you during dinner with a *shamisen* and folk songs.

Shirakawa Mura, 1653 Ogimachi, Ono-gun, Gifu 501-5627. Ⓒ **05769/6-1053.** 6 units, none with bathroom. ¥8,400 per person. No credit cards. A 15-min. walk from the bus stop, on the south edge of Ogimachi past Doburoku Festival Hall.

⑦ **Koemon** ★★   This is my top choice for accommodations. English-speaking Otani Shoji is the fifth-generation innkeeper of this 200-year-old farmhouse, which became a *minshuku* 30 years ago and has been modernized with a heated floor, automatic sensor lights, communal Washlet toilets, and even dim switches to enhance the mood **289** around his *irori* fireplace, where you'll have your meals and watch a video during dinner showing the rethatching of the farmhouse. Rooms are spotless, with the best one facing a pond. If you have heavy luggage, you'll be happy to know that this one is closest to the bus terminal.

Shirakawa Mura, 456 Ogimachi, Ono-gun, Gifu 501-5627. *C* **05769/6-1446.** Fax 05769/6-1748. 4 units, none with bathroom. ¥8,400 per person. No credit cards. A 3-min. walk from the bus stop, just over the footbridge.

(75) **Shimizu**　On the edge of town, mercifully far from the tourist crowds and souvenir shops, this small *minshuku* is a good choice for travelers who desire more privacy than that afforded living with a family, as the owner, who speaks some English, lives in the house next door. There's a communal room with an *irori*, where you can serve yourself coffee and tea. Although you can stay here without opting for meals, note that dinner options in the village are minimal.

Shirakawa Mura, 2613 Ogimachi, Ono-gun, Gifu 501-5627. *C* **05769/6-1053.** Fax 05769/6-1924. www.shimizuinn.com. 3 units, none with bathroom. ¥8,400 per person with meals; ¥5,900 per person without meals. No credit cards. A 15-min. walk from the bus stop, on the south edge of Ogimachi past Doburoku Festival Hall.

WHERE TO DINE

(76) **Ochiudo** ★ (Finds) COFFEEHOUSE　With its small front porch overlooking a paddy and welcoming old-fashioned interior in a thatched house, this tea and coffee shop is a relaxing place for lunch or a snack. It's owned by charming Miyako-san (whose husband is from the Nagase family; see above), who lets you choose your own cup for tea or coffee and offers a yummy daily curry that veers from the usual (with, for example, asparagus), along with a few other healthy choices.

792 Ogimachi. *C* **090/5458-0418.** Curry ¥1,000. No credit cards. Daily 10am–5pm (6pm in summer). In the middle of the village, near the Kanda House.

Kyoto & Nara

If you go to only one place in all of Japan, **Kyoto** ★★★ should be it. Not only is it the most historically significant town in the nation, this former capital was also the only major Japanese city spared from the bombs of World War II. As such, it's rife with temples, shrines, imperial palaces, gardens, and *machiya* (traditional wooden houses). In nearby **Nara** ★★, another former capital—one even more ancient than Kyoto—are Japan's largest bronze Buddha and more historic temples.

No fewer than 17 UNESCO World Heritage Sites are located in Kyoto Prefecture, including Kiyomizu Temple, Kinkakuji, Ginkakuji, Ryoanji Temple, Nijo Castle, Kokedera (Saihoji), Toji Temple, and Byodoin Temple. Kyoto is also home to the nation's greatest concentration of craft artisans, making Kyoto famous for its shops dealing in textiles, dyed fabrics, pottery, bambooware, cutlery, fans, metalwork, umbrellas, and other goods. No wonder Kyoto boasts 20% of Japan's National Treasures.

As your Shinkansen bullet train glides toward Kyoto Station, however, your first reaction is likely to be great disappointment. There's Kyoto Tower looming in the foreground like some misplaced spaceship. Kyoto Station itself is strikingly modern and unabashedly high tech, looking as though it was airlifted straight from Tokyo. Modern buildings and hotels surround the station on all sides, making Kyoto look like any other Japanese town.

In other words, as Japan's seventh-largest city with a population of about 1.5 million people, Kyoto hasn't escaped the afflictions of the modern age. Yet it has always led a rather fragile existence, as a look at any of its temples and shrines will tell you. Made of wood, they've been destroyed through the years by man, fire, and earthquake and have been rebuilt countless times.

Come and explore; you'll soon understand why I consider Kyoto to be Japan's most romantic city despite modernization, because even though its architecture and relics are what put Kyoto on the sightseeing map, I've always felt that its scenes from daily life are what make the city exceptional. No one who comes to this country should miss the wealth of experiences this ancient capital has to offer.

A LOOK AT THE PAST Kyoto served as Japan's capital for more than 1,000 years, from 794 to the Meiji Restoration in 1868. Originally known as Heian-kyo, it was laid out in a grid pattern borrowed from the Chinese with streets running north, south, east, and west. Its first few hundred years—from about A.D. 800 to the 12th century—were perhaps its grandest, a time when culture blossomed and court nobility led luxurious and splendid lives dotted with poetry-composing parties and moon-gazing events. Buddhism flourished and temples were built. A number of learning institutions were set up for the sons and daughters of aristocratic families, and scholars were versed in both Japanese and Chinese.

Toward the end of the Heian Period, military clans began clashing for power as the samurai class grew more powerful, resulting in a series of civil wars that eventually pushed Japan into the Feudal Era of military government that lasted nearly 680 years—until 1868. The first shogun to rise to power was Minamoto Yoritomo, who set up his shogunate government in Kamakura. With the downfall of the

Kamakura government in 1336, however, Kyoto once again became the seat of power, home to both the imperial family and the shogun. The beginning of this era, known as the Muromachi and Azuchi-Momoyama periods, was marked by extravagant prosperity and luxury, expressed in such splendid shogun villas as Kyoto's Gold Pavilion and Silver Pavilion. Lacquerware, landscape paintings, and the art of metal engraving came into their own. Zen Buddhism was the rage, giving rise to such temples as Saihoji Temple and the Ryoanji rock garden. And, despite civil wars that rocked the nation in the 15th and 16th centuries and destroyed much of Kyoto, culture flourished. During these turbulent times, *noh* drama, the tea ceremony, flower arranging, and landscape gardening gradually took form.

Emerging as victor in the civil wars, Tokugawa Ieyasu established himself as shogun and set up his military rule in Edo (presently Tokyo) far to the east. For the next 250 years, Kyoto remained the capital in name only, and in 1868 (which marked the downfall of the shogunate and the restoration of the emperor to power), the capital was officially moved from Kyoto to Tokyo.

1 ORIENTATION

GETTING THERE

FROM KANSAI AIRPORT If you arrive in Japan at Kansai International Airport (KIX) outside Osaka, the **JR Haruka Super Express train** has direct service every 30 minutes to Kyoto Station. The trip takes approximately 75 minutes and costs ¥3,490 for a reserved seat (recommended during busy departure times or peak season) and ¥2,980 for a nonreserved seat, or you can ride free with your JR Rail Pass. A cheaper, though slower and less convenient, alternative is the JR Kanku Kaisoku, which departs every 30 minutes or so from Kansai Airport and arrives in Kyoto 1 hour and 40 minutes later, with a change at Osaka Station. It costs ¥1,830.

If you have lots of luggage, consider taking the **Kansai Airport Limousine Bus** (© **075/682-4400;** www.kate.co.jp) from Kansai Airport; buses depart every hour or less for the 1¾-hour trip to Kyoto Station and cost ¥2,300. More convenient but costlier is **Yasaka Kansai Airport Shuttle** (© **075/803-4800;** www.yasaka.jp/taxi/shuttle-e/service-e.html), which provides transportation from the Kansai airport to any hotel or home in Kyoto for ¥3,500, including one suitcase (a second suitcase costs ¥1,000); reservations for this are required 2 days in advance.

FROM ITAMI AIRPORT If you're arriving on a domestic flight at Itami Airport, the Airport Bus takes 1 hour to Kyoto Station and costs ¥1,280.

BY TRAIN FROM ELSEWHERE IN JAPAN Kyoto is a major stop on the Shinkansen bullet train; trip time from **Tokyo** is 2½ hours, with the fare for a nonreserved seat ¥12,710 one-way if you don't have a rail pass. Kyoto is only 20 minutes from Shin-Osaka Station in **Osaka,** but you may find it more convenient to take one of the local commuter lines that connect Kyoto directly with Osaka Station. From **Kobe,** you can reach Kyoto from Sannomiya and Motomachi stations on local JR trains. The strikingly modern **Kyoto Station,** which is like a city in itself with tourist offices, restaurants, a hotel, a department store, a shopping arcade, a theater, and stage events, is connected to the rest of the city by subway and bus.

Frommer's Favorite Kyoto Experiences

Spending a Night in a Ryokan Kyoto is one of the best places in Japan to experience the traditional inn, where you'll sleep on a futon in a *tatami* room and be treated to a beautifully presented multicourse *kaiseki* feast, perhaps with a view of your own private garden. Though expensive, it's the utmost in simple elegance and well worth the splurge.

Dining on a Tofu Vegetarian Meal in a Garden Setting *Shojin ryori*, vegetarian meals served at Buddhist temples, are one of Kyoto's specialties. There are a number of rustic restaurants with outdoor garden seating throughout Kyoto.

Visiting a Japanese Garden Kyoto has a wide range of traditional gardens, from austerely beautiful Zen rock gardens used by Buddhist priests for meditation to the miniature bonsai-like landscape gardens of the ruling classes.

Strolling Through Eastern Kyoto Temples, shrines, gardens, craft shops, traditional neighborhoods—these are highlights of a day spent walking through this historic part of Kyoto. You won't find a slice of old Japan like this in other Japanese cities.

Shopping for Traditional Crafts Traditional arts and crafts thrive in Kyoto, where skills are passed down from generation to generation. You'll find small specialty shops selling everything from fans to wooden combs.

Seeing How the Upper Class Lived Kyoto has more imperial palaces and villas than any other Japanese city. Walk through the shogun's digs at Nijo Castle and if you have time, visit the Kyoto Imperial Palace, Katsura Imperial Villa, or Shugakuin Imperial Villa with their splendid gardens.

Exploring Gion Kyoto's traditional pleasure quarter is fascinating for its austere architecture, hushed atmosphere, and the sight of heavily made-up geisha in traditional kimono hurrying to their evening appointments. Though touristy, Gion Corner is your best bet for observing performances of traditional dance, puppetry, and other cultural presentations.

Taking an Evening Stroll Through Pontocho A small, narrow pedestrian lane, Pontocho is lined with a dazzling collection of brightly lit hostess bars, restaurants, and drinking establishments. If it's a warm night, end the evening by sitting for a while along the banks of the nearby Kamo River, a popular spot for Kyoto's young couples.

BY BUS FROM TOKYO Lots of buses travel between Tokyo and Kyoto; reservations are necessary. **JR Highway buses** (✆ **03/3516-1950;** www.jrbuskanto.co.jp) depart from Tokyo Station's Yaesu South Exit four times daily (with a stop at Shinjuku Station), arriving at Kyoto Station approximately 8 hours later and costing ¥6,000. There are also three JR Dream Highway night buses (including one only for women) that depart Tokyo Station between 10 and 11:10pm, arriving in Kyoto early the next morning. The fare for

these is ¥8,180. Cheaper still are JR's Seishun Dream buses that depart Tokyo Station at
10pm and Shinjuku Station at 11:10pm, arriving at Kyoto at 5:41am and 7:21am
respectively and costing ¥5,000. Tickets can be purchased at any major JR station or a
travel agency like JTB. In addition, **Willer Express** (℡ **050/5805-0383;** www.willer
express.com) buses depart Tokyo and Shinjuku stations several times nightly, arriving at
Kyoto Station the next morning. The cost of these ranges from ¥4,200 to ¥8,600,
depending on the date and type of seat selected (reclining seats cost more); only online
reservations are accepted.

VISITOR INFORMATION

In addition to a **Kyoto City Tourist Information Office** (℡ 075/343-6656; daily 8am–
7pm) on the second floor of Kyoto Station serving Japanese visitors, there's also **Kyoto
Tourist Information** on the second floor near the ticket gate and Isetan department store
(℡ **075/344-3300**). Open daily 10am to 6pm (closed the second and fourth Tues of
every month), it provides English-language city and bus maps and sightseeing pamphlets,
including pamphlets for Kyoto Prefecture. You can also make reservations here for inexpensive lodging throughout Japan free of charge until 5:30pm. In addition, the **Kyoto
City Tourist Association Visitor Information,** located in front of Heian Shrine
(℡ 075/752-0227), is open daily from 8am to 5pm, while the **Tourist Information
Counter** at the Kyoto Handicraft Center (p. 345) is open daily from 10am to 7pm. Otherwise, you can find free English-language maps of Kyoto at any 7-Eleven or Starbucks.

ON THE WEB Kyoto city's website is **http://kaiwai.city.kyoto.jp/raku/modules/
english**. Kyoto Prefecture's website is **www.pref.kyoto.jp/visitkyoto/en**. I also like **www.
kyoto.travel**.

PUBLICATIONS A monthly tabloid distributed free at hotels and restaurants is the
Kyoto Visitor's Guide (www.kyotoguide.com), with maps, a calendar of events, and
information on sightseeing and shopping. *Kansai Scene* (www.kansaiscene.com) is a
monthly giveaway with information on nightlife, festivals, and other events in Kyoto,
Osaka, and Kobe.

CITY LAYOUT

Most of Kyoto's attractions and hotels are north of Kyoto Station (take the Central exit),
spreading like a fan toward the northeast and northwest. The **northern and eastern
edges** of the city contain the most famous temples. The heart of the city is in **central
Kyoto (Nakagyo-ku ward),** which boasts the largest concentration of restaurants, shops,
and bars and which radiates outward from the intersection of Kawaramachi Dori and
Shijo Dori. It includes a narrow street called Pontocho, a nightlife mecca that runs along
the western bank of the Kamo River. Across the Kamo River to the east is the ancient
geisha district of Gion.

FINDING AN ADDRESS Kyoto's streets are laid out in a grid pattern with named
streets (a rarity in Japan) and an address system that's actually quite easy to understand
once you get to know the directional terms. Streets north of Kyoto Station that run east-
west are numbered; for example, the *shi* of Shijo Dori means "Fourth Avenue." *Agaru*
means "to the north," *sagaru* means "to the south," *nishi-iru* means "to the west," and
higashi-iru means "to the east." Thus, an address that reads Shijo-agaru, Teramachi
Higashi-iru means "north of Fourth Avenue, east of Teramachi."

Many addresses also indicate which cross streets a building is near. Take the Hotel
Gimmond, for example: Its address is Takakura, Oike Dori, which tells you that the hotel

is near the intersection of Takakura Dori and Oike Dori. Complete addresses include the ward, or *ku,* such as Higashiyama-ku.

KYOTO'S NEIGHBORHOODS IN BRIEF

The following are Kyoto's main tourist areas; to locate them, see the "Kyoto" map on p. 298.

Around Kyoto Station   The southern ward of **Shimogyo-ku,** which stretches from Kyoto Station north to Shijo Dori Avenue, caters to tourists with its cluster of hotels and to commuters with its shops and restaurants. Kyoto Station, which caused quite a controversy when built because of its size, height, and futuristic appearance, is now this area's top attraction with Isetan department store, a shopping arcade, restaurants, and dramatic public spaces, including a rooftop plaza.

Central Kyoto   Nakagyo-ku, the central part of Kyoto west of the Kamo River and north of Shimogyo-ku, embraces Kyoto's main shopping and nightlife districts, with most of the action on **Kawaramachi Dori** and **Shijo Dori** and **Teramachi** and **Shinkyogoku** covered shopping arcades. Most of Kyoto's legendary craft stores are located here, along with numerous restaurants and bars. Home also to **Nijo Castle,** Nakagyo-ku has a number of exclusive *ryokan* tucked away in delightful neighborhoods typical of old Kyoto. But downtown is changing fast, as Kyoto's younger generation lays claim to new shopping and entertainment complexes, such as **Shin-Puh-Kan,** a renovated telephone company building on Karasuma Dori filled with shops and restaurants and an open stage for concerts, and **Kyoto International Manga Museum,** housed in a former elementary school. Nakagyo-ku is one of the most desirable places to stay in terms of convenience and atmosphere.

Pontocho, a narrow lane that parallels the Kamo River's western bank just a stone's throw from the Kawaramachi-Shijo Dori intersection, is Kyoto's most famous street for nightlife. It's lined with bars and restaurants that boast outdoor verandas extending over the Kamo River in summer. Paralleling Pontocho to the east is Kiyamachi, a narrow lane beside a canal lined with bars and restaurants popular with the young.

Eastern Kyoto   Eastern Kyoto is a great area for walking, shopping, and sightseeing. East of the Kamo River, the wards of **Higashiyama-ku** and **Sakyoku** boast a number of the city's most famous temples and shrines, as well as restaurants specializing in Kyoto cuisine and Buddhist vegetarian dishes, and shops selling local pottery and other crafts. **Gion,** Kyoto's most famous geisha entertainment district, is part of Higashiyama-ku. Customers are entertained in traditional wooden geisha houses that are not open to the public (you can only gain entry through introductions provided by someone who is already a customer)—but the area makes for a fascinating stroll.

Northern Kyoto   Embracing the **Kita-ku, Kamigyo-ku,** and **Ukyo-ku** wards, northern Kyoto is primarily residential but contains a number of Kyoto's top sights, including the Kyoto Imperial Palace, Kinkakuji (Temple of the Golden Pavilion), and Ryoanji Temple, site of Kyoto's most famous Zen rock garden.

2 GETTING AROUND

Kyoto is Japan's most visitor-friendly city, with lots of English-language signs and an easy-to-navigate transportation system.

BY PUBLIC TRANSPORTATION   Kyoto's subway and bus networks are efficient and quite easy to use. For more information, stop by the **Bus and Subway Information counter** in front of Kyoto Station to the right of the bus platforms (© **075/371-4474;** daily 7:30am–8pm) or check online at **www.city.kyoto.lg.jp/kotsu**. One of the best ways to explore Kyoto, however, is by foot.

BY SUBWAY   Kyoto has two subway lines, with stops announced in English. The older **Karasuma Line** runs north and south, from Takeda in the south to Kokusai Kaikan in the north, with stops at Kyoto Station and Imadegawa Station (convenient for visiting the Imperial Palace). The newer **Tozai Line** runs in a curve from east to west and is convenient for visiting Nijo Castle and Higashiyama-ku. The two lines intersect in central Kyoto at Karasuma Oike Station. Fares start at ¥210 (children pay half fare in Kyoto) and service runs from 5:30am to about 11:30pm. Although buses are generally more convenient (they usually get you closer to where you want to go), I sometimes opt for the subway even if I have to walk a bit, simply to avoid hassling with buses and their unknown stops.

BY BUS   The easiest way to get around Kyoto and to most of its attractions is by bus. Buses depart from Kyoto Station's Central (north/Karasuma) exit, with platforms clearly marked in English listing destinations. Both the Kyoto Tourist Information office (see "Visitor Information," above) and the Bus and Subway Information counter give out excellent maps showing major bus routes. Some of the buses loop around the city, while others go back and forth between two destinations. Most convenient for sightseeing is Raku bus no. 100 (some of which look like old-fashioned trolleys), which makes a run every 10 minutes from Kyoto Station to major attractions in east Kyoto, including the Kyoto National Museum, Gojo-zaka (the approach to Kiyomizu Temple), Gion, Heian Shrine, Nanzenji, and Ginkakuji. Raku bus no. 101 departs Kyoto Station for Nijo Castle and Kinkakuji, while Raku bus no. 102 cuts across north Kyoto and connects Ginkakuji and Kinkakuji.

The fare for traveling in central Kyoto is ¥220 for a single ride or ¥500 for a 1-day pass (good for all local buses; you can buy it on the bus). Board the bus at the rear entrance and pay when you get off. If the bus is traveling a **long distance** out to the suburbs, there will be a ticket machine right beside the back door—take the ticket and hold onto it. It has a number on it and will tell the bus driver when you got on and how much you owe. You can see for yourself how much you owe by looking for your number on a lighted panel at the front of the bus; the longer you stay on the bus, the higher the fare.

TRANSIT PASSES   If you think you'll be doing a lot of sightseeing in 1 or 2 days, it may pay to buy a pass. A city bus all-day pass costs ¥500. Passes for both buses and subways cost ¥1,200 for 1 day or ¥2,000 for 2 days and are available at subway stations or the Bus and Subway Information counter at Kyoto Station. Alternatively, such prepaid cards as the Traffica Kyoto Card, which give you a 10% discount, can be used for city buses and subways, and are available in values of ¥1,000 and ¥3,000. Because there is no time limit, they're convenient if you're staying in Kyoto for several days.

For journeys farther afield, the **Kansai Thru Pass** (**Surutto Kansai;** www.surutto. com) allows foreigners (you must show your passport) to ride subways, private railways (no JR trains), and buses throughout Kansai, including Osaka, Kyoto, Kobe, Nara, and Mount Koya, with a 2-day pass costing ¥3,800 and a 3-day pass costing ¥5,000. Children pay half-price. You would have to do quite a bit of traveling to make this worthwhile. It's available at the Kansai International Airport's Travel Desk (first floor international arrivals) or at the **Bus and Subway Information counter** in front of Kyoto Station.

BY TAXI   Taxis in Kyoto come in two different sizes with only slightly different fares. Small ones are ¥660 for the first 2km (1¼ miles), and large ones are ¥710. Taxis can be waved down or, in the city center, boarded at marked taxi stands or at hotels. **MK Taxi** (𝄢 **075/721-4141**) also offers individualized English-language guided tours.

BY BICYCLE   A popular way to get around Kyoto is by bike, made easy because there are few hills and because most streets are named. During peak season, you might even be faster on a bike than a bus. However, you do have to be on guard for vehicular traffic. **Kyoto Cycling Tour Project,** a 3-minute walk from the Central (north) Exit of Kyoto Station (turn left upon exiting the station and walk past the post office and APA Hotel; 𝄢 **075/354-3636;** www.kctp.net), open daily 9am to 7pm, rents bikes beginning at ¥1,000 a day, including a cycling map of the city. It also offers guided cycling tours.

(Fast Facts Kyoto

In addition to the information here, see "Fast Facts: Japan" in chapter 16. You can also make inquiries at one of the tourist offices (see "Visitor Information," above) or the **Kyoto City International Foundation** (𝄢 **075/752-3010;** www.kcif.or.jp), which provides information in English for people living in Japan and some tourist information. It's open Tuesday to Sunday from 9am to 9pm.

Area Code   If you're calling a Kyoto number from outside Kyoto but within Japan, the area code for Kyoto is 075. For calls within Kyoto, don't dial the area code. For details on calling Kyoto from outside Japan, see "Staying Connected," in chapter 3.

Climate   Kyoto is generally hotter and more humid than Tokyo in summer and colder than Tokyo in winter. For more information, see "When to Go," in chapter 3.

Currency Exchange   In addition to banks, places to exchange money after banks close are large department stores like Isetan, Takashimaya, and Daimaru, and the Kyoto Handicraft Center (p. 345). You can also exchange money at the World Currency Shop on the eighth floor of Kyoto Station (𝄢 **075/365-7750**), open Monday to Friday 11am to 5pm. When changing money, be sure to bring your passport. The most convenient ATMs accepting foreign credit cards are at Kyoto Central Post Office next to Kyoto Station (see "Mail," below) or at one of many 7-Eleven convenience stores in Kyoto.

Electricity   In both Kyoto and Nara it's 100 volts, 60 cycles, almost the same as in the United States (110 volts, 60 cycles); your two-pronged appliances should work, but they'll run a little slowly (there are no three-pronged plugs in Japan).

Hospitals Most hospitals are not equipped to handle emergencies 24 hours a day, but a system has been set up in which hospitals handle emergencies on a rotating basis. Hospitals in Kyoto include **Japan Baptist Hospital (Nihon Baputesuto Byoin),** north of Kikage, east of Shirakawa, Sakyo-ku (② 075/781-5191), **Kyoto University Hospital (Kyoto Daigaku Byoin),** Shogoin Kawahara-cho, Sakyo-ku (② 075/751-3111), and **Kyoto Municipal Hospital (Kyoto Shiritsu Byoin),** Gojo Dori Onmae, Nakagyo-ku (② 075/311-5311). There's also a **holiday emergency clinic** on Shichihonmatsu Street, north of Marutamachi (② 075/811-5072). For less urgent care, **Sakabe International Clinic,** Gokomachi, Nijo-sagaru, Nakagyo-ku (② 075/231-1624), has an English-speaking staff. In addition, the **Kyoto City International Foundation** (② 075/752-3010) has information on English-speaking doctors and dentists.

Internet Access **Media Café Popeye** has two locations in central Kyoto: next to the Kyoto Royal Hotel & Spa at Sanjo Kawaramachi (② **075/253-5300**) and just north of Shijo Dori and east of Teramachi, above a United Colors of Benetton shop (② **075/257-5512;** entrance around the back). Both are open 24 hours and charge ¥420 for 1 hour, with discounts for additional hours. There's an Internet cafe in the **Kyoto Handicraft Center** (p. 345), open daily 10am to 7pm and charging ¥400 for the first 30 minutes and ¥200 for every 30 minutes after that.

Lost Property If you leave something on the **Shinkansen bullet train,** you have to call the last stop of the train (regardless of where you got off). For trains terminating in Kyoto call ② 075/691-1000. Items lost at **Kyoto Station** are turned in to the lost-and-found office (② 075/371-0134), which is open daily 8am to 7:30pm. If you lost something along a street or outside, contact the nearest *koban* (police box). **Taxi Kyodo Center** (② 075/672-1110) handles lost and found for all taxi companies.

Luggage Storage & Lockers Kyoto Station has lockers for storing luggage beginning at ¥300 for 24 hours, including lockers large enough for big suitcases (¥600) on its south (Shinkansen) side.

Mail The **Kyoto Central Post Office,** located just west of Kyoto Station's Central (north) Exit (② **075/365-2471**), is open Monday to Friday 9am to 9pm, Saturday 9am to 7pm, Sunday and holidays 9am to 7pm. You can mail packages bound for international destinations here. To the south of the Central Post Office's main entrance is a counter offering 24-hour postal service; stamps for letters are also sold from vending machines. There are also ATMs here, where you can obtain currency Monday to Saturday from 5 minutes past midnight to 11:55pm, Sundays and holidays 5 minutes past midnight to 8pm, and consecutive holidays (for example, 3-day weekends) 7am to 8pm.

Police The national emergency telephone number is ② **110.**

3 WHERE TO STAY IN KYOTO

If you've never stayed in a *ryokan*, Kyoto is one of the best places to do so. With the exception of hot-spring resorts, Kyoto has more choices of ryokan in all price categories

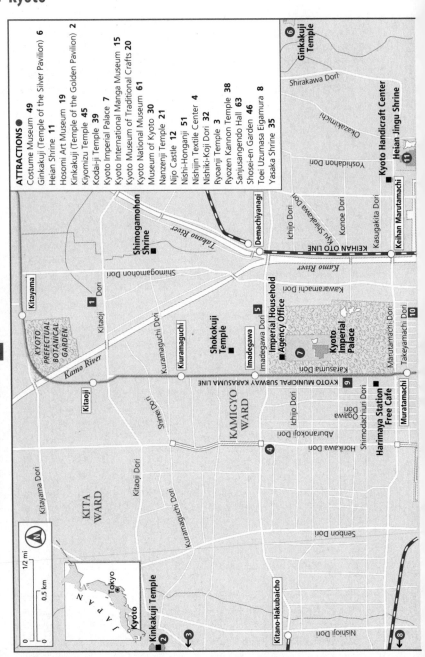

ATTRACTIONS ●

Costume Museum **49**
Ginkakuji (Temple of the Silver Pavilion) **6**
Heian Shrine **11**
Hosomi Art Museum **19**
Kinkakuji (Temple of the Golden Pavilion) **2**
Kiyomizu Temple **45**
Kodai-ji Temple **39**
Kyoto Imperial Palace **7**
Kyoto International Manga Museum **15**
Kyoto Museum of Traditional Crafts **20**
Kyoto National Museum **61**
Museum of Kyoto **30**
Nanzenji Temple **21**
Nijo Castle **12**
Nishi-Honganji **51**
Nishijin Textile Center **4**
Nishiki-Koji Dori **32**
Ryoanji Temple **3**
Ryozen Kannon Temple **38**
Sanjusangendo Hall **63**
Shosei-en Garden **46**
Toei Uzumasa Eigamura **8**
Yasaka Shrine **35**

ACCOMMODATIONS

ANA Hotel Kyoto **14**
APA Hotel Kyoto Ekimae **56**
APA Hotel Kyotoeki-
Horikawa Dori **55**
Aranvert Hotel Kyoto **41**
Budget Inn **53**
Hiiragiya Ryokan **27**
Hiraiwa Ryokan and Annex **44**
Hotel Alpha Kyoto **24**
Hotel Fujita Kyoto **18**
Hotel Gimmond **29**
Hotel Granvia Kyoto **57**
Hotel Hokke Club Kyoto **59**
Hotel Mystays Kyoto Shijo **31**
Hotel Nishiyama **16**
Hyatt Regency Kyoto **62**
Kinoe **37**
Koshokaikan **52**
Kyoto Central Inn **34**
Kyoto Gion Hotel **36**
Kyoto Hotel Okura **17**
Kyoto Kokusai Hotel **13**
Kyoto Royal Hotel & Spa **23**
Kyoto Tower Hote **60**
Kyoraku Ryokan **48**
Matsubaya Ryokan **47**
Nashinoki Inn **5**
New Miyako Hotel **58**
The Palace Side Hotel **9**
Rakucho **1**
Rihga Royal Hotel **54**
The Screen **10**
Seikoro Inn **43**
Shoho-In **40**
Sumiya **26**
Tawaraya **25**
Tour Club **50**
Toyoko Inn Gojo-
Karasuma **42**
Toyoko Inn Kyoto Shijo-
Karasuma **33**
The Westin Miyako **22**
Yoshikawa Inn **28**

A Note on Directions

For all hotel and restaurant listings in this chapter, directions provided are from Kyoto Station unless otherwise indicated. Numbers in parentheses after stations and bus stops refer to the time it takes to reach your destination on foot after alighting from public conveyance.

than any other city in Japan. Small, usually made of wood, and often situated in delightfully quaint neighborhoods, these ryokan can enrich your stay in Kyoto by putting you in direct touch with the city's traditional past. Remember that in upper- and midpriced ryokan, the room charge is per person, and though the prices may seem prohibitive at first glance, they do include two meals, tax, and usually the service charge. These meals are feasts, not unlike kaiseki meals you'd receive at a top restaurant where they could easily cost ¥10,000. Ryokan in the budget category, on the other hand, usually don't serve meals unless stated otherwise and often charge per room rather than per person, but they do provide the futon experience.

Be sure to make reservations in advance, particularly in spring when flowers bloom, in autumn for the changing of the leaves, during summer vacation from mid-July through August, and during major festivals (see "Japan Calendar of Events," in chapter 3). Some accommodations raise their rates during these times. In any case, accommodations are expensive in Kyoto, almost on par with Tokyo.

Because Kyoto is relatively small and has such good bus and subway systems, no matter where you stay you won't be too far away from the heart of the city. Most hotels and ryokan are concentrated around Kyoto Station (Shimogyo-ku Ward), in central Kyoto not far from the Kawaramachi-Shijo Dori intersection (Nakagyo-ku Ward), and east of the Kamo River (in the Higashiyama-ku and Sakyo-ku wards).

TAXES & SERVICE CHARGES   The 5% tax levied by hotels is included in room rates. Mid- and upper-range hotels also add a 10% to 15% service. Unless noted otherwise, all rates below include tax and service charge.

AROUND KYOTO STATION
Expensive
Hotel Granvia Kyoto ★★   Owned by the Japan Railways group (holders of a Japan Rail Pass get discounts), this hotel boasts Kyoto's most convenient location for travelers arriving by train: It's right atop the futuristic-looking Kyoto Station. Only a minute's walk from city buses and trains, it's a good base for exploring Kyoto, Nara, and beyond. The dimly lit hotel lobby is on the second floor, removed from the foot traffic of the station but still buzzing with activity. If you can, avoid the least expensive rooms—they have rather unexciting views of the station's glass roof. Otherwise, modern rooms on higher floors facing north have great Kyoto views. Hotel packages are available that include cooking classes, a visit to the inner sanctums of a Shinto shrine, or the opportunity to spend the evening with a geisha.

JR Kyoto Station, Central Exit, Karasuma Dori Shiokoji-sagaru, Shimogyo-ku, Kyoto 600-8216. ℂ **075/344-8888.** Fax 075/344-4400. www.granviakyoto.com. 535 units. ¥25,410–¥40,425 single or double. Granvia Floor ¥40,425–¥46,200 single or double. 15%–30% discount off Superior Twins for holders of Japan Rail Pass (check the website for blackout dates). AE, DC, MC, V. **Amenities:** 8 restaurants; bar; 2 lounges; lobby

A Double or a Twin?

For the sake of convenience, the price for two people in a room is listed as a "double" in this book. Japanese hotels, however, differentiate between rooms with a double bed or two twin beds, usually with different prices. Most hotels charge more for a twin room, but sometimes the opposite is true; if you're looking for a bargain, therefore, be sure to inquire about prices for both. Note, too, that hotels usually have more twin rooms than doubles, for the simple reason that Japanese couples, used to their own futon, traditionally prefer twin beds.

computers (¥100 for 10 min.); concierge; executive-level rooms; health club w/indoor pool, fitness gym, and sauna (fee: ¥1,050); room service; smoke-free rooms. *In room:* A/C, TV, hair dryer, Internet, minibar.

New Miyako Hotel   Sister hotel to the famous Westin Miyako in eastern Kyoto, this is a popular choice near Kyoto Station due to its location near the terminus of both the Shinkansen and Kintetsu trains. The city bus terminus, however, is a 5-minute walk away on the other side of Kyoto Station, and the hotel has the dubious honor of being Kyoto's largest. After passing through the utilitarian, almost spartan lobby, you'll reach rooms that vary in price according to floor and size, though the view is nothing special (children may like rooms facing the front, where they can see the Shinkansen trains arrive, though they're noisier). The cheapest twins are so small that couples may fight over who gets the lone luggage rack, while those in the classier (and pricier) south wing seem like a different hotel altogether, with tall ceilings, mock balconies, and upbeat colors. I like the rooftop summer beer garden with its all-you-can-eat buffet (those staying at the hotel get a discount).

17 Nishikujo-Inmachi, Minami-ku, Kyoto 601-8412. © **800/336-1136** in the U.S., or 075/661-7111. Fax 075/661-7135. www.miyakohotels.ne.jp/newmiyako. 986 units. ¥11,550–¥13,860 single; ¥23,100–¥38,115 double. AE, DC, MC, V. Across the street and to the right from Kyoto Station's south side (Hachijo exit). **Amenities:** 4 restaurants; bar; lounge; beer garden (summer only); lobby computers w/free Internet; room service; smoke-free rooms. *In room:* A/C, TV, fridge, hair dryer, Internet (south wing only).

Rihga Royal Hotel ★   This has been one of Kyoto's grand hotels since 1969. The building's aging exterior offers a modern rendition of traditional Japanese architecture with its railed ledges, but the lobby is rather confining and uninteresting, with a row of chairs near the checkout desk testimony to the sometimes long queues (the hotel is a popular choice for tour groups). Still, rooms are comfortable enough, with adequately sized standard rooms that feature *shoji* screens and window panels that close for darkness. The most expensive rooms, occupying the top two floors, have smart-looking Italian-style furnishings and better city views. Another plus is the frequent shuttle bus to Kyoto Station, though it delivers you to the south side of the station (city buses depart from the north side of Kyoto Station).

1 Taimatsu-cho, Shiokoji-sagaru, Higashi Horikawa, Shimogyo-ku, Kyoto 600 8237. © **075/341-1121.** Fax 075/341-3073. www.rihga.com/kyoto. 484 units. ¥17,325–¥25,410 single; ¥24,255–¥42,735 double. AE, DC, MC, V. Free shuttle bus 4 times an hour 7:30am–9pm from Kyoto Station's Hachijo exit (turn left and walk to the end of the parking lot, past McDonald's), or a 7-min. walk from Kyoto Station. **Amenities:** 7 restaurants; bar; lounge; concierge; executive-level rooms; indoor pool (fee: ¥1,050); sauna (men only; fee: ¥2,625); room service; complimentary shuttle to station; smoke-free rooms. *In room:* A/C, TV, hair dryer, Internet (fee: ¥1,050 for 24 hr.), minibar.

Moderate

APA Hotel Kyoto Ekimae   This smart-looking business hotel is a good choice for its location. Rooms, however, are very small (the cheapest singles are minuscule) but pleasantly decorated and, though close to the train tracks, are relatively quiet. Japanese-style rooms are also available. In short, stay here or at its sister hotel below only if this book's top choices are full, you want to stay close to the station, or if you don't plan on spending any quality time in your room.

Just a 2-minute walk farther west is APA Hotel Kyotoeki-Horikawa Dori, 1 Nishi Aburakojicho, Shiokoji, Aburakoji Dori, across the street from the Rihga Royal Hotel (© **075/341-6111**). It offers similarly miniature rooms (all with free Internet) at cheaper prices, beginning at ¥9,000 for a single, ¥12,000 for two in a semi-double (smaller than a full-size bed), 14,000 for a double, and ¥17,000 for a twin. The cheapest rooms face an inner courtyard (read: no sunshine), and you'll be climbing over your partner to get out of bed in the cheapest semi-double. Note that ¥500 per person is added to all APA hotels on Saturday and nights before public holidays; ¥1,000 to ¥2,000 per person is added in peak season.

806 Minami Fudodocho, Shiokoji-sagaru, Nishinotoin Dori, Shimogyo-ku, Kyoto 600-8234. © **075/365-4111.** Fax 075/365-8720. www.apahotel.com. 192 units. ¥9,500–¥10,000 single; ¥18,000–¥23,000 double. AE, MC, V. A 3-min. walk from Kyoto Station's north Central exit; turn left out of the station and walk btw. the post office and train station. **Amenities:** Restaurant; smoke-free rooms. *In room:* A/C, TV, fridge, hair dryer, Internet.

Aranvert Hotel Kyoto ★   Located about halfway between Kyoto Station and the central downtown area (about a 15-min. walk from both) and close to a subway station and bus stops, this hotel offers small but spotless rooms and, best of all, a public bath on the 13th floor with panoramic views. Be sure to ask for the hotel's hand-drawn map showing the location of nearby bus stops, an Internet cafe, and restaurants.

179 Higashi Kazariya-cho, Gojo Dori, Shimogyo-ku, Kyoto 600-8107. © **075/365-5111.** Fax 075/365-6800. www.aranvert.co.jp. 183 units. ¥9,817–¥12,127 single; ¥15,015–¥34,650 double. AE, DC, MC, V. Subway: Gojo (exit 2, 2 min.). On Gojo Dori, west of Karasuma Dori. **Amenities:** Restaurant; lounge; smoke-free rooms. *In room:* A/C, hair dryer, Internet, minibar.

Kyoto Tower Hotel   There's no problem finding this hotel, located under Kyoto Tower and in business since 1960. It doesn't have a lot to offer, other than convenient access and reasonable prices. Check-in is on the ground floor, and though there's a functional lobby on the eighth floor, it's doubtful you'll want to spend a lot of time here. Tiny guest rooms are long and narrow, with *shoji* screens. Only the higher-priced rooms afford a view of the station, but they tend to be noisy; the rest face other buildings.

Even cheaper prices are available at the nearby Kyoto Tower Hotel Annex, Shinmachi Dori, Shichijo-sagaru (© **075/343-3111**), and at the Kyoto Dai-Ni Tower Hotel, Higashinotoin Dori, Shichijo-sagaru (© **075/361-3261**), with singles starting at ¥6,500 and twins at ¥14,000. Both are within a 4-minute walk from the station. Staying at any of these three hotels gives you free admission to Kyoto Tower.

Karasuma Dori, Shichijo-sagaru, Shimogyo-ku, Kyoto 600-8216. © **075/361-3212.** Fax 075/343-5645. www.kyoto-tower.co.jp. 160 units. ¥10,000–¥14,500 single; ¥16,000–¥31,000 double. AE, DC, MC, V. A 1-min. walk from Kyoto Station's north Central exit, across the street. **Amenities:** 2 restaurants; bar; smoke-free rooms. *In room:* A/C, TV, fridge, hair dryer, Internet.

Inexpensive

Budget Inn ★★ (Finds)   Keiji-san and his wife, Hiromi-san, opened this hostelry in 2003 in a former apartment building with six tatami rooms for three to five persons (three of which are gilded in gold and have refrigerators) complete with balconies, plus two dormitory rooms that sleep up to five persons. The level of caring is impressive, with little maps of the neighborhood given to guests that show the location of restaurants, supermarkets, and more; tips dispensed on what's going on and how to spend rainy days; free coffee and tea in the communal kitchen; and the chance to try on a kimono. With its good location, English-speaking staff, and clean rooms, this place beats most other budget accommodations hands down, but too bad it doesn't have double rooms.

Luckily, Keiji offers an additional 13 rooms (including Japanese-style twins) and three dormitory rooms at his nearby **Tour Club,** 362 Momiji-cho, Kitakoji-agaru, Higashi-Nakasuji Dori (✆ **075/353-6968;** www.kyotojp.com), a 9-minute walk from the station. With similar facilities and amenities, it offers twin rooms from ¥7,770, triples from ¥8,880, quads from ¥1,720, and dormitory beds for ¥2,450.

295 Aburanokoji-cho, Aburanokoji, Shichijo-sagaru, Shimogyo-ku, Kyoto 600-8231. ✆/fax **075/344-1510.** www.budgetinnjp.com. 8 units. ¥10,980 triple; ¥12,980 quad; ¥2,500 dormitory bed. ¥150 extra for 1-night stays; discounts available for longer stays. No credit cards. A 6-min. walk from Kyoto Station's Central (north) exit; turn left on Shiokoji Dori and right at the Esso gas station. **Amenities:** Rental bikes (¥690 per day); lobby computer (¥100 per 20 min.); communal microwave. *In room:* A/C, TV, fridge, Wi-Fi, no phone.

Hiraiwa Ryokan and Annex   This *ryokan,* halfway between Kyoto Station and downtown, is one of the best-known and oldest members of the Japanese Inn Group. Although they speak limited English, the Hiraiwa family has been welcoming foreigners from all over the world since opening their doors in 1973. The tatami guest rooms, spread through the 95-year-old traditional main building and a newer annex, are spotless. Note that a Japanese breakfast, which includes *kamameshi* (rice casserole), miso soup, and tofu, must be ordered a day in advance, but you can have coffee and toast until 9am. Shower and bathing facilities are limited (you might opt for the neighborhood public bath and sauna just around the corner) and toilet stalls are unisex, affording little privacy for the shy. And because there's no lounge, there's no chance to meet other guests unless you pass them shuffling down the hall to the bathroom. If you're traveling with a group of friends and would like to hang out in a communal room, stay elsewhere.

314 Hayao-cho, Kaminoguchi-agaru, Ninomiyacho Dori, Shimogyo-ku, Kyoto 600-8114. ✆ **075/351-6748.** Fax 075/351-6969. www2.odn.ne.jp/hiraiwa. 18 units, none with bathroom. ¥4,200–¥5,250 single; ¥8,400–¥9,450 double. Japanese breakfast ¥1,050 extra. AE, MC, V. Bus: 17 or 205 (don't take the express 205) to Kawaramachi-Shomen (3rd stop) and then a 4-min. walk (look for the side street beside Tony Lama), or a 15-min. walk from Kyoto Station. **Amenities:** Lobby computer w/free 30-min. Internet access; communal fridge. *In room:* A/C, TV.

Hotel Hokke Club Kyoto   Popular with tourists thanks to its great location just opposite Kyoto Station and its reasonable rates, this chain hotel opened 90 years ago but underwent a much-needed renovation in 2000 and now offers clean and pleasantly decorated Western-style rooms, all with feather quilts and smallish bathrooms. Note that the cheapest singles and doubles don't have windows (which could drive the claustrophobic over the brink). Otherwise, other singles have only tiny glazed windows (but they do have semi-double-size beds), and the most expensive twins, large for this price category, face Kyoto Station.

Kyoto Eki-mae, Shomen Chuoguchi, Karasuma, Shimogyo-ku, Kyoto 600-8216. ✆ **075/361-1251.** Fax 075/361-1255. 188 units. ¥8,190–¥9,240 single; ¥9,870–¥15,750 double. AE, DC, MC, V. Across from Kyoto Station's Central exit. **Amenities:** 2 restaurants; free Internet; smoke-free rooms. *In room:* A/C, TV, fridge, hair dryer, Internet.

Kyoraku Ryokan ★★ Near the Matsubaya (see below), this pleasant and spotlessly clean member of the Japanese Inn Group offers nicely decorated rooms, some of which look over an inner courtyard garden. Though the English-speaking son is a fourth-generation innkeeper, the building housing this *ryokan* was erected in 2007 and has the bonus of an elevator. Guests can help themselves to free coffee and tea in the dining room. Rooms, including two that are Western style with private bathroom, are simple and spotless, with screened windows that open. Japanese breakfasts must be ordered the night before, and note that the ryokan locks its doors at 11pm. The higher rates below are for larger rooms.

231 Kogawa-cho, Shichijo-agaru, Akezu-dori, Shimogyo-ku, Kyoto 600-8149. ☎ **075/371-1260.** Fax 075/ 371-7161. www.ryokankyoraku.jp. 16 units, 9 with bathroom. ¥5,200–¥5,600 single without bathroom; ¥6,000–¥6,600 single with bathroom; ¥9,200–¥10,200 double without bathroom, ¥11,000–¥12,300 double with bathroom. AE, MC, V. A 9-min. walk north of Kyoto Station's Central exit; walk north on Karasuma Dori, turn right on Shichijo Dori, and then left. **Amenities:** Lobby computer w/free Internet; smoke-free rooms. *In room:* A/C, TV, no phone.

Matsubaya Ryokan ★★★ (Finds) A member of the Japanese Inn Group, this highly recommended nonsmoking *ryokan* just east of Higashi Honganji Temple is a great choice in this category. First opened in 1885 and completely rebuilt in 2008 using architectural details from the old inn, it's owned and managed by the friendly Hayashi family, representing the sixth generation of innkeepers. Fourteen rooms are Japanese style, with the best rooms overlooking a garden, while six Western-style rooms, all on the fifth floor, are actually apartments complete with kitchenettes, miniature balconies, free Internet, and free use of the washing machine. The comfortable lobby lounge is a good place to meet fellow travelers and chat with the Hayashis, who have made this ryokan the highlight of many a voyager's trip for many decades.

Higashinotoin Nishi, Kamijuzuyamachi Dori, Shimogyo-ku, Kyoto 600-8150. ☎ **075/351-3727.** Fax 075/ 351-3505. www.matsubayainn.com. 20 units (2 without bathroom). ¥4,200 single without bathroom, ¥6,510–¥9,030 single with bathroom; ¥7,770 double without bathroom, ¥12,180–¥15,120 double with bathroom. Reservations require a 1-night deposit. AE, MC, V. A 10-min. walk north of Kyoto Station's Central exit; walk north on Karasuma Dori and take the 3rd right after passing Shichijo Dori. **Amenities:** Lobby computer w/free Internet. *In room:* A/C, TV, fridge, Internet (in some), kitchenette (in some).

CENTRAL KYOTO
Very Expensive

Hiiragiya Ryokan ★★★ This exquisite *ryokan* is as fine an example of a traditional inn as you'll find in Japan. Situated in the heart of old Kyoto, it offers the ultimate in Japanese-style living, with a kind and accommodating staff that's helpful in initiating foreigners unfamiliar with Japan to the joys of a ryokan. If you're going to splurge just once in Japan, this is one of my top choices. Built in 1818 and an inn since 1861—Ms. Nishimura is the sixth-generation innkeeper—Hiiragiya is a haven of simple design that makes artful use of wood, bamboo, screens, and stones in its spacious, traditionally arranged rooms. Even the remote controls for the lights and curtains are cleverly concealed in specially made lacquered boxes shaped like gourds (invented by the present owner's great-grandfather). Rooms, each one unique, are also outfitted with art and antiques such as gold-painted folding screens or lacquered bathrooms, and most offer garden views and cypress baths. Even the least expensive room—a former tearoom only 4½ tatami-mats big, with a sink but no bathroom and a view of the garden—is good enough for me. A recent addition added seven new but elegant rooms. Dinners are exquisite multicourse kaiseki feasts served in your room; Western-style breakfasts are available upon request.

Nakahakusancho, Fuyacho, Anekoji-agaru, Nakagyo-ku, Kyoto 604-8094. ℂ **075/221-1136.** Fax 075/221-1139. www.hiiragiya.co.jp. 28 units, 23 with bathroom; 2 with toilet only. ¥30,000–¥90,000 per person. Rates include 2 meals but exclude tax. AE, DC, MC, V. Located on the corner of Fuyacho and Oike sts. Subway: Kyoto Shiyakusho-mae (4 min.) or Karasuma-Oike (7 min.). Bus: 4, 17, or 205 to Kyoto Shiyakusho-mae (5 min.). Taxi: 10 min. **Amenities:** Lobby computer w/free Internet. *In room:* A/C, TV, hair dryer, Internet (new addition only), minibar.

Sumiya ★★★   Like the other traditional Japanese inns listed here, the 100-year-old Sumiya has a great location in a typical Kyoto neighborhood just a few minutes' walk from bustling downtown. Offering excellent service amid simple yet elegant surroundings, including wooden corridors that wrap around courtyard gardens and several tearooms (a tea ceremony is performed after dinner on the 7th and 17th of each month), it has a variety of rooms, most with wooden tubs and some with wonderful views of tiny private gardens with outdoor benches and platforms for sitting. The oldest rooms employ a striking variety of different woods in their design (be sure to notice the Edo-Era designs on the sliding doors), while rooms in a 45-year-old addition may have sliding screen doors that open onto a private garden. Meals feature Kyoto kaiseki cuisine; Western breakfasts are also available.

Sanjo-sagaru, Fuyacho, Nakagyo-ku, Kyoto 604-8075. ℂ **075/221-2188.** Fax 075/221-2267. sumiyaryokan@par.odn.ne.jp. 23 units, 17 with bathroom. ¥35,000–¥65,000 per person, including 2 meals. AE, DC, MC, V. On Fuyacho Dori just south of Sanjo St. Subway: Kyoto Shiyakusho-mae (6 min.) or Karasuma-Oike (9 min.). Bus: 4, 5, 17, or 205 to Kawaramachi Sanjo (5 min.). Taxi: 10 min. *In room:* A/C, TV, hair dryer, Internet, minibar.

Tawaraya ★★   Across the street from the Hiiragiya (see above) is another distinguished, venerable old inn, owned and operated by the same family since it opened in the first decade of the 1700s (Mrs. Toshi Okazaki Satow is the 11th-generation innkeeper). Unfortunately, fire consumed the original building, so the oldest part of the *ryokan* now dates back a mere 220 years. This inn has had an impressive list of former guests, from Leonard Bernstein to Alfred Hitchcock. Saul Bellow wrote in the ryokan's guest book, "I found here what I had hoped to find in Japan—the human scale, tranquility, and beauty." With refined taste reigning supreme, each room is different and exquisitely appointed. Some, for example, have glass sliding doors opening onto a mossy garden of bamboo, stone lanterns, and manicured bushes, with cushions on a wooden veranda where you can sit and soak in the peacefulness.

Fuyacho, Oike-Sagaru, Nakagyo-ku, Kyoto 604-8094. ℂ **075/211-5566.** Fax 075/211-2204. 18 units. ¥42,263–¥84,525 per person, including 2 meals. AE, DC, MC, V. Subway: Kyoto Shiyakusho-mae (4 min.) or Karasuma-Oike (7 min.). Bus: 17 or 205 to Shiyakusho-mae (5 min.). Taxi: 10 min. *In room:* A/C, TV, hair dryer, minibar.

Yoshikawa Inn ★   Known for its tempura (see "Where to Dine in Kyoto," later in this chapter), this inn also offers tatami rooms, the best of which offer views of the largest garden I've seen in a downtown Kyoto *ryokan*. Built more than 100 years ago and opening as an inn a half-century ago, it offers the extra benefit of leg wells under the tables of its tatami rooms, making dining easier for foreigners not used to sitting on the floor. It offers the usual elegance you'd expect from an inn of this caliber, including a warm, hospitable staff.

Tominokoji Dori Oike-sagaru, Nakagyo-ku, Kyoto 604-8093. ℂ **075/211-5544.** Fax 075/211-6805. 8 units. From ¥32,400–¥66,000 per person, including 2 meals. AE, DC, MC, V. Subway: Karasuma Oike Station

(6 min.; on Tominokoji St. just south of Oike Dori). Taxi: 10 min. **Amenities:** Restaurant. *In room:* A/C, TV, hair dryer.

Expensive

ANA Hotel Kyoto (Zenniku Hotel Kyoto) ★★ Just across the street from Nijo Castle and offering rooms with castle views, this hotel has one of the most eye-catching lobby lounges in town, complete with a glass wall overlooking an impressive waterfall and tiny landscape garden, all to the accompaniment of *koto* music (a Japanese stringed instrument). Kimono-clad hostesses greeting guests as they enter the lobby are a welcoming touch. Rooms are attractive if a bit cramped, with roomy bathrooms and unusual extras like shoe dryers and dehumidifiers (both handy during the rainy season), and ion-free hair dryers and hairbrushes. None of the singles face the castle; double rooms that do—with floor-to-ceiling windows—start at ¥31,185 during the regular season. Other pluses: a rooftop beer garden in summer, and a complimentary shuttle bus four times an hour to and from Kyoto Station from 8am to 7:45pm (to 9:45pm in summer).

Nijojo-mae, Horikawa Dori, Nakagyo-ku, Kyoto 604-0055. (C) **800/993-3563** in the U.S. and Canada, or 075/231-1155. Fax 075/231-5333. www.ana-hkyoto.com. 298 units. ¥15,015 single; ¥24,255–¥33,495 double. 10%–15% extra per person Apr–May and Oct–Nov; ¥1,155 extra per person Sat and nights before holidays. AE, DC, MC, V. Subway: Nijojo-mae (1 min.). Free shuttle bus from Kyoto Station; or bus: 9, 50, or 101 to Nijojo-mae. **Amenities:** 5 restaurants, including Unkai (p. 317); bar; lounge; concierge; lobby computer w/free Internet; indoor pool and sauna (fee: ¥1,575); room service; smoke-free rooms. *In room:* A/C, TV, hair dryer, Internet, minibar.

Kyoto Hotel Okura ★★★ First built in 1888, one of Kyoto's oldest hotels underwent a complete metamorphosis in 1994 and is now the city's tallest building, with 17 floors. Its height caused a stir of protest by those who advocate stricter height restrictions; though I usually side with historical preservationists, I must admit that no finer building could have violated the skyline. Its modern facade hints at traditional Japanese lattice-work, while the spacious lobby, designed after the hotel's original 1920s ballroom, exudes a gracefully elegant old-world ambience. Restaurants on the top floor offer stunning views. Rooms, built around a central atrium, are the utmost in comfort and grandeur. The best views are of the Kamo River, especially from the most expensive rooms on upper floors that also take in the hills of Higashiyama-ku beyond the city. In short, luxurious accommodations, a great location in the heart of Kyoto, and a hospitable staff come together to make this an excellent choice. The only drawback is that the indoor pool and related facilities are open only from 7 to 10am (children 17 and under not allowed), after which they become a private club (if they're not crowded, you may get in—but it costs more).

Kawaramachi-Oike, Nakagyo-ku, Kyoto 604-8558. (C) **075/211-5111,** or 223-2333 for reservations. Fax 075/221-7770. www.kyotohotel.co.jp. 322 units. ¥21,945–¥24,255 single; ¥31,185–¥56,595 double; from ¥43,890 executive double. AE, DC, MC, V. Subway: Kyoto Shiyakusho-mae (1 min., below the hotel). Bus: 4, 17, or 205 to Shiyakusho-mae (2 min.). **Amenities:** 8 restaurants; 2 bars; lounge; children's day-care center (¥5,250 for 2 hr.); concierge; executive-level rooms; indoor pool w/Jacuzzi and sauna (fee: ¥2,100); room service; smoke-free rooms. *In room:* A/C, TV, hair dryer, Internet, minibar.

Kyoto Royal Hotel & Spa ★ The main reason to stay here? Location, location, location. In the heart of Kyoto on Kawaramachi Dori, this typical tourist hotel has a friendly staff and has been stylishly renovated to achieve a top-class atmosphere, yet it still can't compete with the facilities and grandeur of Kyoto's other top hotels. However, it's a convenient base for sightseeing and has an information desk to answer guest questions. Chic blonde-and-black furnished rooms feature focused bedside reading lamps, but they are otherwise fairly basic. Note that most single rooms and some doubles face an inner courtyard, which cuts down on noise but also on sunshine, while rooms that face the Kamo River have better views but are minuscule. Again, the best reason to stay here is location, though the spa might help you get over jet lag.

Sanjo-agaru Kawaramachi, Nakagyo-ku, Kyoto 604-8005. © **075/223-1234.** Fax 075/223-1702. www. ishinhotels.com. 355 units. ¥20,000 single; ¥30,000–¥40,000 double. AE, DC, MC, V. Subway: Kyoto Shi-yakusho-mae (2 min.). Bus: 4, 17, or 205 to Kawaramachi Sanjo (2 min.). **Amenities:** Coffee shop; bar; lounge; concierge; lobby computers w/free Internet; room service; smoke-free rooms; spa. *In room:* A/C, TV, hair dryer, Internet, minibar.

The Screen ★★   If you prefer small hotels and contemporary design, you might enjoy staying at this strikingly modern yet inviting hotel, complete with traditional touches that make it seem like a hybrid between a traditional *ryokan* and a boutique hotel. Each of its 13 rooms, by 13 different designers, has its own style. Two Japanese-style rooms, for example, have futons on raised tatami platforms along with black lac-quered furniture, while another has a playful forest motif and another yet is lined with sheer white curtains. Its location between the Imperial Palace and downtown, on a street lined with craft and antiques stores, is another plus, and I also like the Sky Lounge with its outdoor seating. There aren't many cool hotels like this one in Japan, and after staying in unimaginative rooms, you might be ready for a splurge here.

640–1 Shimogoryomae-cho, Nakagyoku, Nakagyo-ku, Kyoto 604-0995. © **075/252-1113.** Fax 075/252-1311. www.the-screen.jp. ¥27,000–¥45,000 single or double. Rates ¥10,000 higher on weekends and peak periods. AE, DC, MC, V. Subway: Karasuma Marutamachi (7 min.). Bus: 4, 17, or 205 to Kawaramachi Marutamachi (7 min.). South of Marutamachi Dori, on Teramachi Dori. **Amenities:** Restaurant; lounge; lobby computers w/free Internet; smoke-free rooms; spa. *In room:* A/C, TV/DVD, hair dryer, Internet, minibar, MP3 docking station.

Moderate

Hotel Alpha Kyoto   This small and unassuming but pleasant brick business hotel has a great, hidden location near the Kawaramachi-Shijo Dori intersection, and I have always found the staff accommodating. Most rooms, including singles, are outfitted with dou-ble-size beds, but because the cheapest singles face an inner courtyard and are fairly dark, it may be worthwhile to dish out the extra yen for a brighter room. My favorite rooms are those that overlook a quiet temple and Buddhist cemetery—a fitting view in a town that boasts so many religious structures. There are also three Japanese-style rooms with cedar tubs, and the handmade origami crane in each room is a nice touch. In short, this is a good choice if you like to be in the thick of things and are willing to sacrifice space and facilities to be there.

Kawaramachi, Sango-agaru, Nakagyo-ku, Kyoto 604-8006. © **075/241-2000.** Fax 075/211-0533. hotel-alpha@ joytel.co.jp. 119 units. ¥7,900–¥8,900 single; ¥12,400–¥18,100 double. AE, DC, MC, V. Subway: Kyoto Shi-yakusho-mae (2 min.). Bus: 4, 5, 17, or 205 to Kawaramachi Sanjo (1 min.). Just off Kawaramachi Dori not far from Sanjo Dori; entrance is on a side street called Aneyakoji Dori. **Amenities:** Restaurant; lobby computer w/free Internet; smoke-free rooms (single and twin only). *In room:* A/C, TV, fridge, hair dryer, Internet (in some).

Hotel Fujita Kyoto   Its downtown location right beside the Kamo River, on the former grounds of a baron's second home complete with a small landscape garden, is the best feature of this 40-year-old property, so if you can, splurge for a room facing the river with views of the Higashiyama Mountains in the distance. Rooms are rather average, though they do have *shoji* screens and window panels that can be slid shut for complete darkness.

Kamogawa Nijo-ohashi Tamoto, Nakagyo-ku, Kyoto 604-0902. © **075/222-1511.** Fax 075/222-1515. www.fujita-kyoto.com. 189 units. ¥10,395–¥19,635 single; ¥18,480–¥36,960 double. AE, DC, MC, V. Subway: Kyoto Shiyakusho-mae (3 min.). Bus: 4, 17, or 205 to Shiyakusho-mae (4 min.). Walk toward the Kamo River, past the Hotel Okura, and turn left. **Amenities:** 6 restaurants; bar; lounge; babysitting; room service; smoke-free rooms. *In room:* A/C, TV, fridge, hair dryer, Internet (in some).

Hotel Gimmond   This small hotel on Oike Dori was built some 30 years ago, but it achieves an even older ambience in its lobby with the clever use of antique-looking lighting and decor. Though the hotel calls itself a tourist hotel and offers mainly twins, its accommodations and lack of services and facilities place it squarely in the category of business hotel. Simple rooms are soundproof, but I still think those that face away from Oike Dori are quieter; ask for one on a higher floor. The cheapest rooms are quite small.

Takakura, Oike Dori, Nakagyo-ku, Kyoto 604-8105. © **075/221-4111.** Fax 075/221-8250. www.gimmond. co.jp. 140 units. ¥9,586–¥10,741 single; ¥16,170–¥20,790 double. AE, DC, MC, V. Subway: Karasuma-Oike (2 min.). **Amenities:** 2 restaurants; smoke-free rooms. *In room:* A/C, TV, fridge, hair dryer, Internet.

Kyoto Kokusai Hotel ★   I like this hotel across from Nijo Castle because it offers a few surprises you wouldn't expect in medium-range accommodations. Billing itself as a Western-style hotel with a Japanese atmosphere, it has a very nice lobby overlooking a pleasant, lush garden, which you can gaze upon from either the lobby tea lounge or restaurant, Azalea. Every Friday and Saturday evening at 7:30pm, the garden also serves as a stage for a free 15-minute dance presentation given by *maiko* (geisha apprentices), but arrive at 7pm with your camera so you can have your photo taken with a performer. Room rates are based on decor and amenities, with higher-priced rooms offering views of Nijo Castle (note, however, that only 50 twins and two doubles face the castle and that none of the singles do). All rooms are comfortable and are outfitted with *shoji* screens. Despite the hotel's name, which translates as the International Hotel, more than 90% of its guests are Japanese.

Nijojo-mae, Horikawa Dori, Nakagyo-ku, Kyoto 604-8502. © **075/222-1111.** Fax 075/231-9381. www. kyoto-kokusai.com. 274 units. ¥8,085–¥19,635 single; ¥16,170–¥38,115 double. AE, DC, MC, V. Subway: Nijojo-mae (2 min.). Bus: 9, 50, or 101 to Nijojo-mae (2 min.). Across from Nijo Castle. **Amenities:** 4 restaurants, including Azalea (p. 318); lounge; room service; smoke-free rooms. *In room:* A/C, TV, hair dryer, Internet (in some), minibar.

Hotel Mystays Kyoto Shijo ★   This tourist/business hotel is a step ahead of older competitors, offering stylish rooms with contemporary furnishings (like red lounge chairs in its single rooms) and black-and-white photos of Kyoto on the walls. Nagomi rooms, with their bamboo floors and low bed, have a traditional Japanese atmosphere, while rooms on the top floors have good city views.

52 Kasaboko-cho, Aburanokoji Higashi-iru, Shijo Dori, Shimogyo-ku, Kyoto 600-8494. © **075/283-3939.** Fax 075/283-3940. 224 units. ¥12,000 single; ¥18,000–¥25,500 double. Rates ¥1,000–¥6,000 higher in peak season. AE, DC, MC, V. Subway: Shijo (4 min.). Bus: 26 to shijo Nishinotoin (2 min.). On the north side of Shijo Dori, east of Aburanokoji. **Amenities:** Restaurant; room service; smoke-free rooms. *In room:* A/C, TV, fridge, hair dryer, Internet.

Hotel Nishiyama (Value)   Located just a few minutes' walk north of downtown Kyoto, this 40-year-old property has a traditional atmosphere, from the old lantern above its front door to the small courtyard garden just beyond the lobby. Although the building itself is fairly plain and nondescript, it has more soul than a chain hotel and offers mostly Japanese-style tatami rooms and four small Western-style twins. A public bath boasts views of a garden waterfall. Low rates make this a popular choice for school groups, but if you don't mind the youthful clientele this makes for a good choice for moderately priced Japanese-style accommodations in the heart of the city. Manager Mr. Nishiyama speaks English.

Gokomachi, Nijo-sagaru, Nakagyo-ku, Kyoto 604-0933. © **075/222-1166.** Fax 075/231-3558. www. ryokan-kyoto.com. 31 units, 27 with bathroom, 4 with toilet only. ¥6,000 single with toilet only, ¥9,000 single with bathroom; ¥12,500–¥16,000 double. Rates ¥1,000–¥3,000 higher in peak season. Japanese dinner ¥7,000 extra; Japanese or Western breakfast ¥1,500 extra. AE, DC, MC, V. Subway: Shiyakusho-mae (3 min.). Bus: 4, 17, or 205 to Shiyakusho-mae (3 min.). 2 blocks northwest of City Hall. **Amenities:** Lobby computer w/free Internet. *In room:* A/C, TV.

Inexpensive

Kyoto Central Inn   As the name implies, this inn is centrally located in the heart of the city, near the intersection of Shijo Dori and Kawaramachi Dori. It resembles a business hotel, but thanks to its great location, about 50% of its guests are tourists, with twins making up the vast majority of its rooms. However, rooms are worn and dated, with narrow corridors leading to tiny rooms. Because the main building is boxed in between higher buildings, rooms here are dark (and some don't even have windows), so you might want to pay slightly more for the annex (ask for a room on a high floor facing the back, where you might have a view over surrounding buildings). Clearly, the best things this aged hotel has going for it are its prices and its location. You even have to fetch your own tea from the lobby.

Shijo Kawaramachi, Nishi-iru, Shimogyo-ku, Kyoto 600-8002. © **075/211-1666.** Fax 075/241-2765. 149 units. ¥7,350–¥8,400 single; ¥11,550–¥13,650 double. AE, DC, MC, V. Bus: 4, 5, 17, or 205 to Shijo Kawaramachi (1 min.). **Amenities:** Lobby computer w/free Internet; smoke-free rooms. *In room:* A/C, TV, fridge, hair dryer.

The Palace Side Hotel ★ (Finds)   Budget-conscious travelers in the know have been flocking to this modest hotel with its contemporary lobby and cafe for more than 4 decades. Although its location just west of the Imperial Palace is not as convenient as my other inexpensive recommendations in central Kyoto, it's near a subway line and offers more facilities than most (joggers like running on palace grounds). Also impressive are the free Japanese-language lessons offered several evenings a week. With the exception of original artwork that graces half the rooms by artists who actually stayed in them, rooms (all nonsmoking) otherwise resemble those in a dormitory, small with just the basics of a desk too tiny for any serious work, windows that open, and old tiled bathrooms. The most expensive twins and doubles have kitchenettes.

Karasuma Shimodachiuri-agaru, Kamigyo-ku, Kyoto 602-8011. © **075/415-8887.** Fax 075/415-8889. www.palacesidehotel.co.jp. 120 units. ¥6,000–¥7,000 single; ¥9,000–¥11,800 double. Long-term rates available. AE, DC, MC, V. Subway: Marutamachi (exit 2, 3 min.). **Amenities:** Restaurant; bar; Thai massage room; rental bikes (free 1st hour, then ¥500 for 12 hr.); lobby computers w/free Internet; smoke-free rooms; communal kitchen. *In room:* A/C, TV, fridge, hair dryer.

Toyoko Inn Kyoto Shijo-Karasuma ★ (Value)   This popular budget chain has easy subway access from Kyoto Station, is located in the heart of downtown, and offers Toyoko Inn's usual free computers in the lobby, free domestic phone calls from lobby telephones, and tiny rooms with all the necessities. There's another in this chain, **Toyoko Inn Kyoto Gojo-Karasuma,** 393 Gojo-Karasuma-cho, on Karasuma Dori near Gojo Station (© **075/344-1045**), with similar amenities and slightly cheaper rates.

28 Naginataboko-cho, Shijo Dori, Karasuma-higashi-iru, Shimogyo-ku, Kyoto 600-8008. © **075/212-1045.** Fax 075/212-1049. www.toyoko-inn.com. 223 units. ¥6,720 single; ¥8,820 double. Rates include Japanese breakfast. AE, DC, MC, V. Subway: Shijo-Karasuma (1 min.). On Shijo Dori, west of Daimaru

department store. **Amenities:** Lobby computers w/free Internet; smoke-free rooms. *In room:* A/C, TV, fridge, hair dryer, Internet.

EASTERN KYOTO
Very Expensive

⑦ **Kinoe ★** This *ryokan* is different from my other high-end Japanese inn recommendations in that it's been in operation only half a century and occupies a modern, 14-year-old building. However, there may be room at this inn when more famous establishments are full, and it has an interesting location on the edge of the Gion geisha district. Under the able management of Ms. Chizuyo Miyata, it offers simple but elegant tatami rooms with all the traditional flourishes such as *shoji* screens, sliding paper doors, calligraphy in the *tokonoma* alcove, and a seating area beside the window. Meals, including Western breakfasts on request, are served in your room.

Higashioji, Yasuikado, Higashiyama-ku, Kyoto 605-0812. ✆ **075/561-1230.** Fax 075/561-8719. www.kinoe. co.jp. 13 units. ¥15,750 per person without meals; ¥26,200 per person including 2 meals. AE, DC, MC, V. On Higashioji Dori, south of Yasaka Shrine. Bus: 207 to Higashiyama Yasui (1 min.). Taxi: 10 min. *In room:* A/C, TV, hair dryer.

Seikoro Inn ★★★ (Finds) This *ryokan* just east of the Kamo River was established in 1831, with the present building dating from a century ago. After passing through a traditional front gate and small courtyard, you'll find yourself in one of the most charming entryways I've seen in Kyoto, which adjoins a cozy parlor replete with an eclectic mix of Japanese and Western antiques. The rooms, also decorated in antiques, are homey and comfortable; some open onto a garden with sliding doors and *shoji* screens. Rooms in an annex built just before the 1964 Olympics are high enough that you can see over the surrounding rooftops, but most of these don't have garden views so I prefer the ones in the oldest buildings. The nice public bath boasts a tub made of 400-year-old black pine, making it one of the inn's most treasured possessions. The English-speaking, sixth-generation innkeeper doesn't mind if you take your meals elsewhere, especially if you're here for a while. The staff is warm and welcoming and will prepare Western breakfasts on request. If you wish, you can dress up in an elaborate kimono (a 30-min. process) for ¥2,000 so you can take pictures.

Tonyamachi Dori, Gojo-sagaru, Higashiyama-ku, Kyoto 605-0907. ✆ **075/561-0771.** Fax 075/541-5481. www.seikoro.com. 22 units. ¥28,875 double room without meals; ¥28,875–¥57,750 per person including 2 meals. AE, DC, MC, V. Bus: 4, 17, or 205 to Kawaramachi Gojo and then a 5-min. walk; cross the bridge over the Kamo River and after Kawabata Dori take the 1st right. Keihan Electric Railway: GoJo Station (2 min.). **Amenities:** Parlor computer w/free Internet. *In room:* A/C, TV, hair dryer.

Expensive

Hyatt Regency Kyoto ★★★ Located in Higashiyama-ku near the Kyoto National Museum and Sanjusangendo Hall, this boutiquelike gem combines traditional art and materials with contemporary styles. Occupying the former residence of Emperor Goshirakawa, it also has a beautiful 850-year-old garden, complete with waterfall and pond, visible from restaurants and some of its rooms. Its spa, offering acupuncture, moxibustion, and shiatsu in addition to the usual aromatherapy, boasts more Asian treatments than any other hotel spa in Japan. Classy rooms blend Japanese aesthetics with technical know-how, from kimono-covered headboards and elegant teaware to large safes with electric hookups for laptops. For a splurge, eight deluxe rooms have tatami areas and Japanese-style tubs placed next to balconies, with views of the garden or National Museum. In short, you can't go wrong staying here. Rates below reflect the seasons.

644–2 Sanjusangendo-mawari, Higashiyama-ku, Kyoto 605-0941. ℂ 800/233-1234 in the U.S. and Canada, or 075/541-1234. Fax 075/541-2203. www.hyattregencykyoto.com. 189 units. ¥22,000–¥43,000 single or double; ¥63,000–¥84,000 deluxe rooms. AE, DC, MC, V. Bus: 100, 206, or 208 to Hakubutsukan Sanjusangendo (1 min.). **Amenities:** 3 restaurants, including Touzan (p. 323); 2 bars; babysitting; concierge; gym (free for hotel guests); room service; smoke-free rooms; spa (fee: ¥1,600); Wi-Fi (free, in lobby). *In room:* A/C, TV/DVD (free DVDs), hair dryer, Internet (¥1,575 per day), minibar.

The Westin Miyako ★★★ (Kids)   One Japan's best-known hotels, the Miyako opened in 1890 and boasts a guest list that reads like a who's who of visitors to Japan: Douglas Fairbanks, Queen Elizabeth II, Prince Charles and Princess Diana, Anwar el-Sadat, and Ted Kennedy. Even today, half of the guests staying here are foreigners. Still, you'd be hard-pressed to find evidence of that history today. Rather, this is one of Kyoto's most smartly appointed hotels, on par with the best of Tokyo's hotels. Its setting is as good as it gets: The hotel sprawls over more than 6.4 hectares (16 acres) of hilltop at the northeastern end of the city, close to some of Kyoto's most famous temples (and a subway station). There's a Japanese garden, and families appreciate the indoor and outdoor pools and a small playroom equipped with billiards, video games, and an activity corner just for toddlers.

Western-style rooms, which come with Westin's trademark Heavenly Beds and one-touch express service for everything from room service to messages, come in a variety of styles and prices, with the least expensive occupying the oldest wing and the best on the fifth floor with large terraces overlooking the valley. For those who wish to experience the pleasures of a traditional tatami room but with all the nearby conveniences of a first-rate hotel, the Japanese-style Kasui-en annex is a good bet for *ryokan* first-timers; built in 1959, it offers 20 modern, elegant rooms with views of the Japanese garden and cypress baths.

Keago, Sanjo, Higashiyama-ku, Kyoto 605-0052. ℂ 800/937-8461 in the U.S. and Canada, or 075/771-7111. Fax 075/751-2490. www.westinmiyako-kyoto.com. 501 units. ¥33,500–¥59,000 single or double; from ¥65,600 Executive Club floor; ¥53,000 double in Kasui-en. AE, DC, MC, V. Free shuttle every 30 min. from Kyoto Station's Hachijo exit (9am–6:30pm). Subway: Keage (2 min.). **Amenities:** 6 restaurants; bar; 2 lounges; babysitting; concierge; executive-level rooms; gym (free for hotel guests); 20m (66-ft.) indoor pool and shallow outdoor pool (fee: ¥500 for either); room service; sauna; smoke-free rooms; sun decks (available also for viewing the full moon); grass tennis court (¥5,250 per hour); wild-bird sanctuary and bird-watching trail; jogging trail. *In room:* A/C, TV, hair dryer, Internet (¥1,575 per 24 hr.), minibar.

Moderate

Kyoto Gion Hotel   This older, simple hotel has no frills but a great location in the heart of Gion, within easy walking distance of the city center, shops, nightlife, and the many sights in Higashiyama-ku. There's no view to speak of, but I prefer the rooms facing west, which have floor-to-ceiling windows overlooking the quaint tiled roofs of Gion (corner rooms are best). The single rooms are among the smallest I've seen (I'm not sure there's even room to unpack), and only twins are available for two people (no doubles). A plus is the rooftop beer garden, open in summer.

555 Minamigawa, Gion, Higashiyama-ku, Kyoto 605-0074. ℂ 075/551-2111. Fax 075/551-2200. www.apahotel.com. 154 units. ¥9,500–¥10,000 single; ¥17,000–¥25,000 double. ¥500 extra on Sat and day before holidays; ¥1,000–¥2,000 extra per person during high season. AE, DC, MC, V. Bus: 100 or 206 to Gion (2 min.). On Shijo Dori, west of Yasaka Shrine. **Amenities:** Restaurant; bar; beer garden; Starbucks; smoke-free rooms. *In room:* A/C, TV, fridge, hair dryer, Internet.

NORTHERN KYOTO
Inexpensive
Nashinoki Inn ★ (Kids)   In a quiet, peaceful neighborhood north of the Kyoto Imperial Palace, this *ryokan* has been run since 1970 by a warm and friendly elderly couple

Temple Lodgings

There's another inexpensive lodging option in Kyoto—in one of its temples. Note that payment is in cash only. **Shoho-In,** Omiya-Matsubara Nishi-iru, Shimogyu-ku (🕿 **090/8988-2998;** ask for Kato-san) offers three rooms for two or more persons beginning at ¥5,000 per person, including a large room for up to seven persons and a two-bedroom condo, complete with kitchen and its own entrance, for stays of a week or longer. No meals are served. Be sure to take a peek inside the small 200-year-old temple, famous for its thousand-year-old statue of Amida. To reach it, take bus no. 206 to Omiya Matsubara.

Koshokaikan, Horikawa Shichijo Kado, Shimogyu-ku (🕿 **075/361-7666**), offers nine dormitory-style tatami rooms without bathrooms on the large Koshoji Temple grounds. Rates start at ¥5,000 for one person and ¥9,400 for two. A Japanese restaurant in the same building is open Monday to Saturday from 9am to 6pm. No English is spoken, so it's best to have a Japanese speaker make reservations. It's a 13-minute walk northwest of Kyoto Station; from the Central exit, turn left on Shiokoji Dori and right on Horikawa Dori.

that speaks some English. Staying here is like living with a Japanese family, as the home looks very lived in and is filled with the personal belongings of a lifetime. Some of the tatami rooms, which feature touches such as vases, Japanese dolls, and pictures, are quite large and adequate for families. Western or Japanese breakfasts are served in your room.

Agaru Imadegawa Nashinoki Dori, Kamikyo-ku, Kyoto 602-0838. 🕿 **075/241-1543.** Fax 075/211-0854. www.nande.com/nashinoki. 6 units, none with bathroom. ¥5,700 single; ¥10,100 double. Breakfast ¥945–¥1,050 extra. No credit cards. Subway: Imadegawa Station (7 min. from exit 3); walk past Doshisha University and turn left at Yaomon coffee shop. **Amenities:** Bicycles (free); free guest computer. *In room:* A/C, TV, no phone.

Rakucho ★★ (Finds) This member of the Japanese Inn Group isn't as conveniently situated as most of the other inns listed above, but that shouldn't stop anyone from staying in this well-kept 70-year-old *ryokan,* managed by English-speaking Kimiko Urade and her son. All but one of the spotless tatami rooms, decorated with such traditional touches as scrolls, have views of a small peaceful garden. Entrance to the ryokan is through a well-tended tiny courtyard filled with plants. There's a kitchenette with two communal refrigerators, a toaster, microwave, and free instant coffee and tea.

67 Higashihangi-cho, Shimogamo, Sakyo-ku, Kyoto 606-0824. 🕿 **075/721-2174.** Fax 075/791-7202. www.rakucho-ryokan.com. 11 units, none with bathroom. ¥5,300 single; ¥8,400–¥9,240 double; ¥12,600 triple. AE, MC, V. Subway: Kitaoji Station (10 min.); walk east on Kitaoji Dori and turn left at the 5th traffic light. Bus: 205 to Furitsudaigaku-mae (2 min. to the north). **Amenities:** Lobby computer w/free Internet; communal kitchenette. *In room:* A/C, no phone.

4 WHERE TO DINE IN KYOTO

Kyoto cuisine, known as *Kyo-ryori,* is linked to Kyoto's long history and to seasonal foods produced in the surrounding region. Among the various types of Kyo-ryori available, most famous are probably the vegetarian dishes, which were created to serve the needs of Zen Buddhist priests and pilgrims making the rounds of Kyoto's many temples.

> **Tips** **A Note on Japanese Characters**
>
> Many hotels, restaurants, attractions, and other establishments in Japan do not
> have signs giving their names in Roman (English-language) letters. Chapter 17 in
> this book lists the Japanese equivalent for all such places described in this guide.
> Each set of characters representing an establishment name has a number in
> chapter 17 that corresponds to the number that appears inside the oval before
> the establishment's name in the text. Thus, to find the Japanese for, say, **Kaisen**
> **EkiBiru Ichiba** (see above), refer to no. 78 in chapter 17.

Called *shojin ryori,* these vegetarian set meals may include *yudofu* simmered in a pot at
your table, filmy sheets of *yuba* (soy milk curd), and an array of local vegetables. Kyoto
is also renowned for its own style of kaiseki called *Kyo-kaiseki,* originally conceived as a
meal to be taken before the tea ceremony but eventually becoming an elaborate feast
enjoyed by the capital's nobility with its blend of ceremonial court cuisine, Zen vegetarian food, and simple tea-ceremony dishes. Today, Kyoto abounds in restaurants serving
both vegetarian tofu dishes and kaiseki meals fit for an emperor (Kyoto's better *ryokan*
also serve kaiseki as the evening meal). Simpler restaurants specialize in *obanzai,* home-
style Kyoto cooking using traditional seasonal ingredients. Otherwise, any restaurant
advertising that it serves Kyo-ryori generally offers a variety of Kyoto specialties. For
more on kaiseki and other Japanese-style meals, see "Tips on Dining in Japan," beginning
on p. 36 in chapter 2.

Remember: Last orders are taken 30 to 60 minutes before the restaurant's actual closing time, even earlier for kaiseki restaurants (which often require a reservation). Bus
information to each restaurant is from Kyoto Station.

AROUND KYOTO STATION

In addition to the restaurants listed here, a good place for inexpensive dining is **Kyoto**
Station, which houses approximately 70 restaurants in underground arcades, at major
exits, at Isetan department store (there are more than 20 outlets here alone, mostly on
the 11th floor), and at Hotel Granvia. For fast, inexpensive sushi, try 78 **Kaisen Eki-**
Biru Ichiba (℗ **075/341-1001**), a conveyor-belt sushi shop in Kyoto Station open daily
11am to 10pm.

Moderate

The Kitchen Salvatore Cuomo ★★ **Finds** ITALIAN   This contemporary eatery
with an open kitchen, above Kyoto Station, has a good view toward the north, over
rooftops and temples to the hills in the distance. At night, with dimmed lights and an
elegant setting, it's a good place for a romantic meal. Its a la carte English-language menu
lists pastas, pizzas (like the Diavola with chicken, salami, red pepper, and mozzarella),
and main dishes such as the Italian grilled beef with balsamic vinegar sauce. Or, opt for
one of the set meals. Set lunches include a trip through an antipasto and a salad bar, along
with a choice of main dish.

There's a cheaper, more casual branch, **Pizza Salvatore Cuomo & Grill,** in the heart
of the nightlife district alongside the Kiyamachi canal (℗ **075/212-4965**), offering pizzas, pastas, and outdoor seating.

KYOTO & NARA

9

WHERE TO DINE IN KYOTO

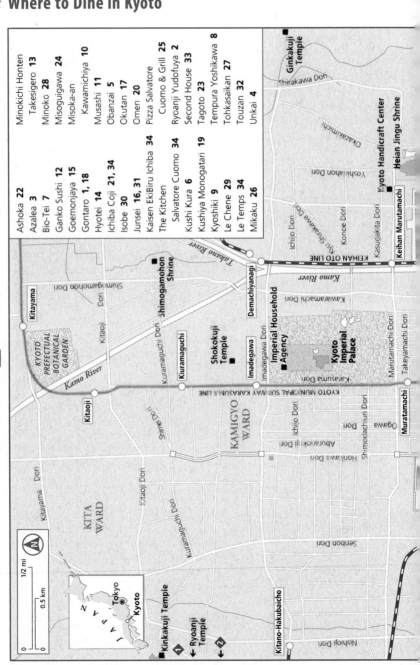

Ashoka **22**
Azalea **3**
Bio-Tei **7**
Ganko Sushi **12**
Goemonjaya **15**
Gontaro **1, 18**
Hyotei **14**
Ichiba Coji **21, 34**
Isobe **30**
Junsei **16, 31**
Kaisen EkiBiru Ichiba **34**
The Kitchen
  Salvatore Cuomo **34**
Kushi Kura **6**
Kushiya Monogatari **19**
Kyoshiki **9**
Le Chene **29**
Le Temps **34**
Mikaku **26**

Minokichi Honten
  Takesigero **13**
Minoko **28**
Misoguigawa **24**
Misoka-an
  Kawamichiya **10**
Musashi **11**
Obanzai **5**
Okutan **17**
Omen **20**
Pizza Salvatore
  Cuomo & Grill **25**
Ryoanji Yudofuya **2**
Second House **33**
Tagoto **23**
Tempura Yoshikawa **8**
Tohkasaikan **27**
Touzan **32**
Unkai **4**

10th floor, Isetan department store, Kyoto Station. ℂ **075/365-7765.** Reservations recommended. Main dishes ¥1,800–¥2,400; set dinners ¥3,800–¥6,800; set lunches ¥1,800–¥3,000. AE, DC, MC, V. Daily 11am–3pm and 5–10pm (last order).

Le Temps ★ INTERNATIONAL   Of Hotel Granvia's many dining choices, I like this bustling restaurant off the lobby the most for its casual setting and long hours. Its buffet offers a variety of tantalizing dishes, from Japanese noodles and stir-fries to French cuisine. Or, you can order from the menu, with dishes starting at ¥600.

2nd floor, Hotel Granvia, Kyoto Station. ℂ **075/342-5525.** Dinner buffet ¥4,300 weekdays, ¥4,900 weekends and holidays; lunch buffet ¥2,900 weekdays, ¥3,500 weekends and holidays. AE, DC, MC, V. Daily 6:30am–11:30pm (last order).

Inexpensive

⑦⑨ **Ichiba Coji** VARIED JAPANESE/INTERNATIONAL   This inexpensive beer hall offers a variety of snacks and dishes that go well with its long list of locally brewed beer and sake, as well as *shochu*, wine, and cocktails, listed on an English-language menu and on view in a display case. Sashimi, tofu dishes, grilled whitefish in a balsamic sauce, spareribs served with miso sauce, Vietnamese spring rolls, salads, *nabe* (one-pot meals cooked at your table), and more are offered, along with views north over the city from its ninth-floor perch.

There's another Ichiba Coji in the heart of central Kyoto in the Teramachi covered shopping arcade, in the basement of the Withyou Building (ℂ **075/252-2008**), with a hip, modern decor and set lunches priced from ¥980 to ¥1,980. It's open Monday to Friday 11:30am to 3pm and 5 to 10:15pm; Saturday and Sunday 11:30am to 10:15pm (last order).

9th floor, Isetan department store, Kyoto Station. ℂ **075/365-3388.** Dishes ¥670–¥3,990; set dinners ¥3,150–¥5,250. AE, DC, MC, V. Daily 11am–11pm. Above Kyoto Station.

Second House PASTA   Occupying a former bank with tall ceilings, a large nonsmoking section, and a young staff, this casual restaurant is part of a local chain offering a variety of Western and Asian pasta dishes, such as spaghetti with eggplant, tomato, and bacon; pasta with pork and *kimchi* (spicy cabbage); and spaghetti with mushrooms and baby clams. It also has quiche, lunch specials, and homemade cakes and pastries, listed on an English-language menu.

Higashi-Nakasuji Dori, Shijo-agaru. ℂ **075/342-2555.** Dishes ¥800–¥1,000. AE, DC, MC, V. Daily 10am–10pm (last order). A 7-min. walk north of Kyoto Station; from Kyoto Station's Central (north) exit, walk north on Karasuma Dori and turn left on Shichijo Dori (it will be on your right).

CENTRAL KYOTO

The heart of Kyoto's shopping, dining, and nightlife district is in Nakagyo-ku, especially on Kawaramachi and Shijo Dori and along the many side streets. In summer, restaurants on the west bank of the Kamo River erect large wooden outdoor platforms that extend over the water and offer open-air dining.

Very Expensive

⑧⓪ **Misoguigawa** ★★★ (Finds) FRENCH KAISEKI   Dining here could well be the culinary highlight of your trip. For more than 30 years—long before fusion cuisine burst onto the scene—this lovely and exclusive restaurant has been serving nouvelle French cuisine that utilizes the best of Japanese style and ingredients in what could be called French kaiseki. It's located on narrow Pontocho, which parallels the Kamo River and is one of Kyoto's most famous nightlife districts, in a century-old renovated wooden building that once belonged to a geisha. Dishes are the creations of owner/master-chef Teruo Inoue, who trained with a three-star Michelin chef and successfully blends the two cuisines into dishes that are arranged like a work of art and served on Japanese tableware.

Although four set meals are offered, the chef inquires about allergies and preferences and takes it from there, so no two meals are the same. The dining experience is enhanced by an English-speaking staff, who explain the ingredients of each dish as it's presented, and by an extensive wine list, culled from Inoue's annual visits to France. Seating options include an L-shaped counter with tatami seating and leg wells; an informal counter for customers who prefer to order a la carte dishes (written in French and changing regularly) while watching chefs at work; private tatami rooms; and my favorite, an outdoor summer veranda overlooking the river. Note that the L-shaped counter and veranda add a 10% service charge and private rooms add a 15% service charge, but no service charge is added for the a la carte counter. This is a great place for a splurge.

Sanjo-sagaru, Pontocho. (©) **075/221-2270.** www.misogui.jp. Reservations required. Set dinners ¥12,600–¥21,000; set lunches ¥4,725–¥10,500. AE, DC, MC, V. Tues–Sun 11:30am–1:30pm and 5:30–8:30pm (last order). Bus: 4, 5, 17, or 205 to Kawaramachi Sanjo (5 min.); on Pontocho, north of the playground.

Expensive

Kyoshiki ★ KAISEKI/KYO-RYORI This reasonably priced kaiseki restaurant, with a small garden in the back, was converted from a Meiji-Era private home more than 30 years ago. I recommend the *Hisago obento* for ¥3,150, offered for lunch on the English-language menu. It consists of a variety of seasonal foods served in individual dishes that stack neatly on top of one another to form a gourd; you take the bowls apart to eat. The atmosphere here is relaxed and comfortable, with both tatami and table seating.

Fuyacho Dori, Sanjo-agaru (just north of Sanjo Dori). (©) **075/221-4840.** Set meals ¥5,250–¥7,350; set lunches ¥3,150–¥5,200. AE, DC, MC, V. Tues–Sun 11:40am–2pm and 5–8pm (last order). Bus: 5 to Shijo-Fuyacho (1 min.). On Fuyacho Dori, just north of Sanjo Dori.

Tempura Yoshikawa ★★ TEMPURA If you're hungering for tempura, this restaurant has a sign in English and is easy to find. Located in an old-fashioned part of Kyoto that boasts a number of expensive *ryokan*, it's a tiny, intimate place with a traditional atmosphere. The tempura counter, where you can watch the chefs prepare delicate deep-fried morsels, seats only 12. Meals served in tatami rooms, with views of an expansive garden (lit at night), are more expensive.

Tominokoji Dori, Oike-sagaru. (©) **075/221-5544.** Reservations required. Set dinners ¥6,000–¥10,000; set lunches ¥3,000–¥4,000. AE, DC, MC, V. Mon–Sat 11am–2pm and 5–8:30pm (last order). Subway: Karasuma Oike Station (6 min.). On Tominokoji St. just south of Oike Dori.

Unkai ★ KAISEKI/SHABU-SHABU/VEGETARIAN A convenient place for a meal if you're visiting Nijo Castle (across the street), Unkai has a modern and refined decor, floor-to-ceiling windows overlooking greenery, and kimono-clad waitresses. The English-language menu has photos illustrating *shabu-shabu*, kaiseki, tempura, and *shojin ryori* (a vegetarian set meal typical of Kyoto). The ¥6,300 Tempura Kaiseki is the one most often recommended for foreigners and includes an appetizer, sashimi, grilled fish, tempura, miso soup, and rice.

ANA Hotel Kyoto, Nijojo-mae, Horikawa Dori. (©) **075/231-1155.** Set dinners ¥6,300–¥12,000; set lunches ¥3,300–¥4,650. AE, DC, MC, V. Daily 11:30am–2:30pm and 5–9:30pm. Subway: Nijojo-mae (1 min.). Bus: 9, 50, or 101 to Nijojo-mae. On Horikawa Dori, across from Nijo Castle.

Ashoka ★ INDIAN   One of Kyoto's most popular and longest-running Indian restaurants, in business more than 30 years, serves vegetarian and meat curries prepared by Indian chefs, including mutton, chicken, fish, vegetable, and shrimp selections, as well as tandoori. On weekdays, it offers an even cheaper set lunch than given below, only ¥950.

Kikusui Building, 3rd floor, Teramachi Dori. ✆ **075/241-1318.** Main dishes ¥1,500–¥2,400; set dinners ¥3,500–¥6,000; set lunches ¥1,250–¥2,100. AE, DC, MC, V. Daily 11am–3pm and 5–9pm (last order). Bus: 4, 5, 17, or 205 to Shijo Kawaramachi (1 min.). On the north side of Shijo Dori, to the right at the entrance of the Teramachi covered shopping arcade.

Azalea CONTINENTAL   Azalea is a pleasant place for a casual Western meal if you're visiting nearby Nijo Castle. Offering an English-language menu and a view of its small, Japanese landscaped garden, it has inexpensive set lunches that may include a pasta or risotto dish as the main course, along with a la carte selections like sandwiches and beef curry rice. Dinner entrees include salmon and steak. Obviously, at these prices you can't expect perfection, but the setting is nice and it's easy to find. Plus, every Friday and Saturday evening at 7:30pm the hotel garden serves as a stage for a free 15-minute dance presentation given by *maiko* (geisha apprentices); if you arrive at 7pm, you can even have someone snap a picture of you standing beside them.

Kyoto Kokusai Hotel, Nijojo-mae, Horikawa Dori. ✆ **075/222-1111.** Set dinners ¥3,000–¥8,000; set lunches ¥1,600–¥3,900. AE, DC, MC, V. Daily 11:30am–2:30pm and 5–9pm. Subway: Nijojo-mae (2 min.). Bus: 9, 50, or 101 to Nijojo-mae. On Horikawa Dori across from Nijo Castle's main entrance.

(81) **Kushi Kura** YAKITORI   Housed in a 100-year-old warehouse with heavy-beamed, dark-polished wood and whitewashed walls, this refined *kushiyaki* and *yakitori* restaurant serves specially raised chicken grilled over top-grade charcoal, with an English-language menu offering various set meals and a la carte selections. You can watch the action while you're comfortably seated at the counter with its leg wells. On weekdays, a lunch costing only ¥840 is also available. A large selection of sake (including the local Fushimi brew) adds to the great atmosphere here.

Takakura Dori, Oike-agaru. ✆ **075/213-2211.** Set dinners ¥1,600–¥4,800; set lunches ¥1,800–¥2,000. AE, DC, MC, V. Daily 11:30am–2pm and 5–10pm (last order). Subway: Karasuma-Oike (2 min.). Just north of Oike Dori on Takakura Dori.

(82) **Tagoto** (Value) KYO-RYORI/KAISEKI/OBENTO   Nestled in an inner courtyard off busy Shijo Dori and offering a peaceful retreat in the heart of downtown Kyoto, this restaurant has been serving a variety of Japanese dishes at moderate prices since 1868. The English-language menu includes Kyo-ryori set meals (including one with *yuba*, a low-calorie curd made from soy milk, for ¥4,300), seasonal kaiseki meals, mini-kaiseki meals, *obento* box meals, and *soba* noodles (available all day for ¥750–¥1,800).

Shijo-Kawaramachi, Nishi-iru, Kitagawa. ✆ **075/221-1811.** Set meals ¥3,700–¥12,600; set lunches ¥1,890–¥3,700. AE, DC, MC, V. Daily 11am–8:30pm. Bus: 4, 5, 17, or 205 to Shijo Kawaramachi (1 min.). The entrance is on Shijo Dori just west of Kawaramachi, east of Kyoto Central Inn (look for a narrow passageway to the back courtyard).

Inexpensive

In addition to the choices here, there's a branch of **Ichiba Coji** in the Teramachi covered shopping arcade (on the west side about halfway down), with a modern, hip decor and pub food that goes well with beer, sake, and spirits. There's also **Pizza Salvatore Cuomo & Grill,** in the heart of the nightlife district on Kiyamachi canal at 90 Nakajima-cho (✆ **075/212-4965**), offering pizzas for ¥1,500 to ¥2,000 and set pizza or pasta lunches for ¥1,000. With pleasant outdoor seating, it's open daily 11am to 4pm and 5 to **319** 10:30pm. See "Around Kyoto Station," above, for reviews.

83 Bio-Tei VEGETARIAN/HEALTH FOOD   If you're yearning for a healthy meal or vegetarian food, head to this very informal second-floor restaurant down the street from the Museum of Kyoto and catty-corner from the post office. Using organic, preservative-free ingredients, it serves only one thing at lunch: a great *teishoku* (fixed-price meal). Last time I was there it came with *genmae* (brown rice), salad, miso soup, pickles, and a curry-based tofu stew with potatoes and carrots. For dinner, a set meal and vegetarian a la carte dishes are offered from a Japanese-language menu. Seating is at sturdy wooden tables hewn from Japanese cypress, and meals are served on tableware from local kilns. As befits a health-food restaurant, smoking is not allowed.

Sanjo Dori Higashinotoin. ☎ 075/255-0086. Lunch teishoku ¥840; set dinner ¥1,260; dinner main courses ¥700–¥800. No credit cards. Tues–Fri 11:30am–2pm; Tues–Wed and Fri–Sat 5–8:30pm (last order). Closed holidays. Subway: Karasuma-Oike (exit 5, 3 min.). On the southwest corner of Sanjo-Higashinotoin intersection, on the 2nd floor.

84 Ganko Sushi SUSHI/VARIED JAPANESE   This popular, lively sushi restaurant offers the usual raw fish selections, as well as an extensive array of Japanese dishes such as grilled *yakitori, shabu-shabu,* tempura, tofu, noodles, and shrimp or crab dishes on an English-language menu. Behind the sushi counter is a fish tank with some rather large specimens swimming around happily until their numbers come up.

Kawaramachi-Sanjo, Higashi-iru. ☎ 075/255-1128. Sushi a la carte ¥180–¥680; set meals ¥1,150–¥2,980. AE, MC, V. Daily 11:30am–11pm. Subway: Kyoto Shiyakusho-mae (4 min.). Bus: 4, 17, or 205 to Kawaramachi Sanjo (2 min.). On Sanjo Dori, just west of the Kamo River (look for its logo of a face with glasses and a bandanna).

85 Gontaro NOODLES   This noodle shop has been serving its own handmade noodles for a mere 100-some years. A small place with a modern yet traditional interior and an English-language menu, it offers various noodle dishes of either *soba* (buckwheat) or *udon* (a thicker wheat noodle) with such toppings as tempura, as well as *donburi* (a rice casserole with tempura, *yakitori,* or other topping) and *nabe* (udon boiled in broth with seafood, chicken, and vegetables). Those with insatiable appetites can have it all with the Okimori set meal for ¥6,000, which comes with nabe, tempura, barbecue chicken, and noodles.

Fuyacho Dori, Shijo-agaru. ☎ 075/221-5810. Noodles ¥750–¥1,400; donburi ¥900–¥1,450; nabe ¥4,200. AE. Thurs–Tues 11am–10pm. Bus: 5 to Shijo-Fuyacho (1 min.). On the west side of Fuyacho Dori just north of Shijo Dori; look for a tiny recessed courtyard, white curtains, and a lone pine tree.

Kushiya Monogatari (Value) KUSHIYAKI   This is the first all-you-can-eat, do-it-yourself *kushiyaki* restaurant I've seen. After choosing skewers of chicken, beef, salmon, scallops, fish, mushrooms, onions, potatoes, and other meats and vegetables from refrigerated cases, you cook them yourself by dipping them in a paste, covering them with bread crumbs, and then deep-frying them at your table (there are English-language instructions to help you along). There's also rice, noodles, and a dessert and salad bar. Gluttony is restricted to 90 minutes, and you can add all-you-can-drink alcohol and soft drinks for an additional ¥1,050.

5th Floor, Sakizo Plaza Building, Shijo-agaru, Nishi-Fuyacho. ☎ 0120/194-948 (toll-free). All-you-can-eat kushiyaki ¥2,625. No credit cards. Daily 5–11pm. Bus: 5 to Shijo-Fuyacho (2 min.). On the north side of Shijo Dori west of Fuyacho Dori; look for the English-language billboard.

KYOTO & NARA

9

WHERE TO DINE IN KYOTO

Misoka-An Kawamichiya ★★ NOODLES Charming and delightful with a central courtyard and cubbyhole rooms, this tiny, 300-year-old noodle shop in a traditional merchant's home makes a great place for an inexpensive meal in the heart of traditional Kyoto. It offers hot or cold buckwheat noodles as well as noodles with such adornments as tempura and chicken and onions. Its specialty is a one-pot noodle dish prepared at your table called *hokoro*, which includes chicken, *yuba*, mushrooms, and vegetables for two. There's an English-language menu.

Fuyacho Dori, Sanjo-agaru. ✆ **075/221-2525**. Noodles ¥650–¥1,580; hokoro ¥8,000 for 2 people. AE, DC, MC, V. Fri–Wed 11am–8pm (last order). Bus: 5 to Shijo-Fuyacho (2 min.). On the west side of Fuyacho Dori just north of Sanjo Dori.

(86) **Musashi** (Value) SUSHI For a cheap meal of raw fish, this conveniently located restaurant can't be beat. Morsels of sushi ranging from tuna to octopus are served via a conveyor belt that moves plates along the counter; reach out and take whatever strikes your fancy. Sushi is priced at ¥137 a plate. Takeout sushi is also available from the sidewalk front counter.

On the northwest corner of the Kawaramachi-Sanjo intersection. ✆ **075/222-0634**. ¥137 per plate. AE, DC, MC, V. Daily 11am–10pm. Bus: 4, 5, 17, or 205 to Kawaramachi Sanjo (1 min.).

(87) **Obanzai** HEALTH FOOD/VEGETARIAN (Value) With a natural, all-wood interior, Obanzai offers an all-you-can-eat buffet using primarily organic vegetables. It's very much self-service here; you pay by depositing your money into a basket upon entering and you're expected to clear your table when you're done. The mostly seasonal dishes, including lots of vegetarian choices, may range from pumpkin soup and tofu croquettes to salads, steamed vegetables, and fish catch of the day. A healthy choice near Nijo Castle.

Koromonotana Dori, Oike-agaru. ✆ **075/223-6623**. Lunch buffet ¥840 weekdays, ¥1,050 weekends and holidays; dinner buffet ¥2,100. No credit cards. Daily 11:30am–2pm; Thurs–Tues 5–8:30pm (last orders). Subway: Karasuma-Oike (exit 2, 5 min.). On the east side of Koromonotana Dori, in the 2nd block north of Oike.

(88) **Omen** UDON A casual atmosphere and reasonably priced food make this tiny place popular. *Omen* (vegetable *udon*) is the specialty, and the house's traditional style is to serve the wheat noodles in a flat wooden bowl, the sauce in a pottery bowl, the vegetables delicately arranged (sushi style) on a handmade platter with a bowl of sesame seeds alongside. You dip and mix yourself, unlike at other udon shops where it all arrives like a stew swimming in one bowl. Tempura, sushi, lightly fried tofu, and *kamonasu dengaku* (fried eggplant topped with a rich miso sauce) are among the other dishes offered. Other branches are located just south of Ginkakuji (✆ **075/771-8994**; daily 11am–9pm), and on Pontocho (✆ **075/253-0377**; daily 11:30am–3pm and 5–10pm). There's also one in New York.

Gokomachi Dori, Shijo-agaru. ✆ **075/255-2125**. Main dishes ¥650–¥1,050; set meals ¥1,650–¥1,950; set lunches ¥2,300. MC, V. Fri–Wed 11:30am–3pm and 5–9:30pm. Subway: Shijo (5 min.). Bus: 4, 5, 17, or 205 to Shijo Kawaramachi (3 min.). On the east (right) side of Gokomachi Dori, just north of Shijo.

Tohkasaikan BEIJING CHINESE This Beijing-style Chinese restaurant popular with families started life as a Western restaurant. The old building features an ancient, manually operated elevator, lots of wood paneling, high ceilings, old-fashioned decor, and a friendly staff. From June to mid-September, you can sit outside on a wooden veranda over the Kamo River, one of the cheapest places along the river to do so. If it's winter or raining, consider sitting in the fifth-floor dining room, which has nice views of the city. The best views, however, are from the rooftop garden (in summer only), where you can order mugs of beer and dine on dishes from the extensive English-language menu, including sweet-and-sour pork, cooked shrimp with arrowroot, and chicken and green pepper. The service tends to be slow and I've had better Chinese food, but the atmosphere is great and is reminiscent of another era.

Nishizume, Shijo Ohashi. ☎ **075/221-1147.** Main dishes ¥1,470–¥2,630; set meals from ¥5,000 for 2 people. AE, DC, MC, V. Daily 11:30am–9pm (last order). Bus: 4, 5, 17, or 205 to Shijo Kawaramachi (2 min.). On Shijo Dori just west of the bridge spanning the Kamo River in a large yellow stone building.

EASTERN KYOTO
Expensive

(89) **Hyotei** ★★★ (Finds) KAISEKI/OBENTO   This 300-year-old restaurant first opened its doors as a teahouse to serve pilgrims and visitors on their way to Nanzenji Temple. Today it consists of two parts: one that offers expensive *Kyo-kaiseki*, which originated with the tea ceremony but is now associated with Kyoto cooking, and an annex offering seasonal obento lunch boxes. The kaiseki meals are served in separate tiny houses situated around a beautiful garden with a pond, maple trees, and bushes; the oldest house, which resembles a small teahouse, is more than 3 centuries old. You'll dine seated on a tatami floor in a private room, the food brought to you by kimono-clad women. The *bekkan* (annex), to the left of the kaiseki restaurant and with its own entrance, serves delicious *shokado bento* (lunch boxes), which change with the season and are served in a communal tatami room with views of a garden.

35 Kusakawa-cho, Nanzenji. ☎ **075/771-4116.** Reservations required for kaiseki, recommended for obento. Kaiseki lunches from ¥23,000, dinners from ¥27,000; obento ¥5,000. AE, DC, MC, V. Kaiseki daily 11am–7:30pm; shokado bento Fri–Wed noon–4pm; closed 2nd and 4th Tues of each month. Subway: Keage (5 min.). Bus: 5 or 100 to Dobutsuen-mae (3 min.). West of Shirakawa Dori Murin-an; look for a plain facade hidden behind a bamboo fence with a sign shaped like a gourd.

Le Chene FRENCH   Located on the edge of Maruyama Park and a good—though pricey—place to stop if you're walking from Kiyomizu Temple to Gion, this restaurant, housed in a building called (90) Chorakukan dating from the Meiji Period with elaborate woodwork and marble, is one of the few Western restaurants in eastern Kyoto. Ensconced in an elegant, drawing room–style hall, Le Chene serves only set meals. Alternatively, consider dropping by the adjoining cafe, a beautiful room reminiscent of European coffee shops, open daily 10am to 9:30pm; an afternoon tea, served from 1 to 5pm, costs ¥3,000.

In the southwest corner of Maruyama Park. ☎ **075/561-0001.** Set dinners ¥12,000–¥20,000; set lunches ¥4,000–¥9,000. No credit cards. Daily 11:30am–2pm and 5–8pm (last order). Bus: 100 or 206 to Gion (7 min.); after passing Yasaka Shrine, look to the right for a large stone-and-brick, Western-style building with a huge stone lantern in its driveway.

(91) **Mikaku** ★ JAPANESE STEAKHOUSE   Established almost a century ago, this restaurant on the second floor (with counter seating) and third floor (tatami rooms) of a modern building offers sukiyaki, *shabu-shabu*, oil-yaki (sliced beef cooked on an iron griddle and flavored with soy sauce, lemon, and Japanese radish), and *teppanyaki*, all made with high-grade Kobe beef.

Nawate Dori, Shijo-agaru, Gion. ☎ **075/525-1129.** Reservations recommended. Set meals ¥10,000–¥22,000. AE, DC, MC, V. Prices include service charge. Mon–Sat 11:30am–1pm and 5–9pm (last order). Bus: 100 or 206 to Gion (5 min.) or 4, 5, 17, or 205 to Shijo Kawaramachi (5 min.). From Shijo Dori, go 1 block north on Nawate Dori and take the 1st left.

Minokichi Honten Takesigero ★★ KYO-KAISEKI   One of Japan's best-known restaurants for Kyoto cuisine, Minokichi was founded in 1716 as one of eight restaurants licensed to serve freshwater fish and is now in its 10th generation of restaurateurs. With several branches in Japan, this flagship restaurant is an elegantly simple modern building, with tatami rooms reminiscent of those used in tea ceremonies, all with peaceful views of a graceful moss-and-bamboo garden. The specialty is *Kyo-kaiseki* (Kyoto-style kaiseki); the emphasis is on the appearance of the food, and great care is given to the selection and preparation of seasonal ingredients. Although the dishes themselves change, a kaiseki meal here always consists of 10 items: appetizer, raw fish, light soup, food cooked in delicate broth, steamed food, broiled food, deep-fried food, vinegared food, fruit, and green tea with a sweet.

Sanjo-agaru, Dobutsuen-mae Dori. ℃ **075/771-4185.** www.minokichi.co.jp/takeshigero. Reservations required. Kyo-kaiseki dinner ¥15,750–¥31,500; kaiseki lunch ¥7,350–¥15,750. AE, DC, MC, V. Daily 11:30am–2pm and 5–7:30pm (last order). Subway: Keage (10 min.). Bus: 5 or 100 to Dobutsuen-mae (5 min.). North of Sanjo Dori on the road to the Zoological Gardens.

(92) **Minoko** ★★★ KAISEKI/OBENTO   This former villa is an enclave of traditional Japan with a simple, austere exterior and an interior of winding wooden corridors, tatami rooms, and a garden. Opened nearly a century ago by the present owner's father, Minoko does its best to retain the spirit of the tea ceremony, specializing in an elaborate kind of kaiseki dinner called *cha-kaiseki,* usually served at tea-ceremony gatherings and utilizing seasonal ingredients that are beautifully arranged to please both the palate and the eye. If you come for dinner, when only kaiseki is served, you'll eat in a private tatami room. Lunch, which is served communally in a large tatami room with a view of a beautiful garden, is more economical and less formal but still draws on the tea ceremony for inspiration. The obento lunch box, for example, called *chabako-bento,* is named after the lacquered box it's served in, which is traditionally used to carry tea utensils to outdoor tea ceremonies. A *hiru-kaiseki,* or mini-kaiseki set meal, is also available at lunch.

480 Kiyoi-cho, Shimogawara-dori, Gion. ℃ **075/561-0328.** Reservations recommended for lunch, required for dinner. Kaiseki from ¥15,697; mini-kaiseki lunch ¥10,444; obento ¥4,000–¥5,200. Prices include service charge. AE, DC, MC, V. Daily 11:30am–2:30pm and 5–10pm (last order 8pm). Closed irregularly 3 days a month. Bus: 100 or 206 to Gion (3 min.). A short walk south of Yasaka Shrine.

Moderate

(93) **Isobe** KAISEKI/VARIED JAPANESE   A convenient place to stop for lunch if you're walking from Kiyomizu Temple to Gion, this modern, pleasant restaurant offers a nice view of Maruyama Park from its dining room and has an English-language menu with photos listing a variety of set meals featuring sashimi, tempura, and kaiseki.

Maruyama Park, Ikenohata. ℃ **075/561-2216.** Set meals ¥3,150–¥10,500. AE, DC, MC, V. Daily 11am–10pm. Bus: 100 or 206 to Gion (10 min.). On the southeastern edge of the park (if you're walking from Kiyomizu, take a right at the park entrance; if you're coming from Gion, walk past Yasaka Shrine and keep to the right); look for the outdoor red umbrella (up only in dry weather but also depicted on the sign).

(94) **Junsei** ★ TOFU/KAISEKI/OBENTO   Specializing in tofu, Junsei opened in 1961, but the grounds and garden were originally part of a medical school established in the 1830s during the shogun era. Although tourist oriented and popular with tour groups, the food is good and an English-language menu makes ordering easy. There are several buildings spread throughout the grounds, and what you want determines where you go; as soon as you arrive, you'll be given a menu and asked what you'll be eating. I chose the house special—a *yudofu* meal—and was directed to an older building with a

view of the garden and filled with antiques and tatami mats. My meal came with vegetable tempura and various tofu dishes, including fried tofu on a stick and yudofu boiled in
a pot at my table. Other set meals include kaiseki (by reservation only), *yuba, shabu-shabu,* or sukiyaki.

There's a branch, Kiyomizudera Junsei (© **075/541-7111**), located just off Kiyomizu-
zaka, the main slope leading to Kiyomizu Temple. Housed in a grand, 1914 former villa
with high ceilings, wainscoting, and stained-glass windows, it offers just three set tofu
meals priced ¥2,100 to ¥5,250 and is open daily 10:30am to 5pm (last order), closed
irregularly.

Nanzenjimon-mae, Sakyo-ku. © **075/761-2311.** www.to-fu.co.jp. Reservations required for kaiseki and
shabu-shabu. Yudofu meal ¥3,150; yuba kaiseki ¥6,300; shabu-shabu or sukiyaki ¥8,400; kaiseki ¥10,000–
¥20,000. AE, DC, MC, V. Daily 11am–8pm (last order). Subway: Keage (5 min.). Bus: 5 to Nanzenji-Eikando-
michi (7 min.). East of Shirakawa Dori on the road to Nanzenji Temple.

95 **Okutan** ★★★ Finds TOFU/VEGETARIAN   This is one of the oldest, most
authentic, and most delightful tofu restaurants in Kyoto. Founded about 350 years ago
as a vegetarian restaurant serving Buddhist monks, this thatched-roof wooden retreat in
a peaceful setting with pond and garden serves just two things: *yudofu* (a tofu set meal)
and a more traditional tofu meal originally from China. Okutan is very simple and rustic
with seating either in tatami rooms or outdoors on cushioned platforms, making it especially delightful in fine weather. Women dressed in traditional rural clothing bring your
food. The yudofu set meal, which changes slightly with the seasons, includes a pot of tofu
boiled at your table, fried tofu on a stick, vegetable tempura, yam soup, and pickled
vegetables. It's all highly recommended.

86–30 Fukuchi-cho, Nanzenji. © **075/771-8709.** Reservations recommended (but not accepted in peak
season). Yudofu set meal ¥3,150; traditional tofu meal ¥4,200. No credit cards. Fri and Mon–Wed 11am–
4pm; Sat–Sun and holidays 11am–4:30pm (last order). Bus: 5 to Nanzenji-Eikando-michi (6 min.). Just
north of Nanzenji Temple's main gate (the San Mon Gate).

Touzan ★★★ SUSHI/SUMIBIYAKI/KAISEKI   Next door to Sanjusangendo and
across the street from Kyoto National Museum, this eatery is convenient to sightseeing
but worth going out of your way for. Modeled after a traditional Kyoto home but with
innovative interior designs (such as pottery shards encased in glass serving as room divid-
ers), it offers views of a traditional rock garden (dramatically lit at night) and specializes
in charcoal-grilled foods. In addition to *sumibiyaki* (vegetables, fish, and meat grilled over
high-quality charcoal), it also serves *Kyo-kaiseki* and sushi (available in both the restaurant and a sushi counter). The *Shokado Bento,* available for lunch, comes with an appetizer, seasonal dishes like simmered prawn and lotus root, sashimi, rice, miso soup, and
other dishes for ¥4,300. A large selection of sake, including 13 local brands, serves as a
perfect complement to the meals, but if you have trouble choosing, the sake-tasting set
for ¥2,500 lets you sample four varieties.

Hyatt Regency Kyoto, 644–2 Sanjusangendo-mawari, Higashiyama-ku. © **075/541-1234.** Set dinners
¥6,000–¥13,000; set lunches ¥2,000–¥4,300. AE, DC, MC, V. Tues–Sun 11:30am–2:30pm and 5:30–10pm.
Bus: 100, 206, or 208 to Hakubutsukan Sanjusangendo (1 min.).

Inexpensive

96 **Goemonjaya** TOFU/TEMPURA/NOODLES   Convenient if you're visiting
Nanzenji, this typical Japanese restaurant specializes in tofu dishes and tempura. With
tatami seating, a miniature garden, and a carp-filled pond, it offers a *yudofu* set meal, a
shrimp or vegetarian tempura *teishoku,* and, in summer only, inexpensive noodle dishes

KYOTO & NARA

9

WHERE TO DINE IN KYOTO

ranging from ¥650 for *somen* (thin vermicelli served cold) to ¥800 for *zaru soba* (cold buckwheat noodles). You might also wish to try its desserts, including *mitarashi dango* (soy-flavored rice dumplings on a stick) and *zensai-mochi* (rice cake with black beans).

67 Kukasawa-cho, Nanzenji. ✆ **075/751-9638.** Set meals ¥1,800–¥2,800. No credit cards. Daily 11am–6pm (last order). Closed some Tues. Bus: 5 to Nanzenji-Eikando-michi (2 min.). Across the street from Yachiyo Inn on the road leading to Nanzenji Temple (look for a red lantern beside the road and a display case of plastic food); the restaurant is back off the main road past a smiling Buddha and a red paper umbrella (open only in dry weather).

NORTHERN KYOTO

In addition to the selection here, there's a branch of **Gontaro,** serving noodles, at Hinomiyashiki-cho 26 (✆ **075/463-1039**), with the same English-language menu as its main shop (p. 319). It's located about halfway down the street that runs between Ryoanji and Ginkakuji, on the west side; look for the red paper lantern. It's open Thursday to Tuesday from 11am to 10pm.

Inexpensive

Ryoanji Yudofuya ★★ Finds TOFU/VEGETARIAN If you're visiting Ryoanji Temple in northeastern Kyoto, there's no lovelier setting for a meal than this traditional restaurant, which calls itself the Ryoanji Seven Herb Tofu Restaurant in honor of the only thing it serves, *yudofu,* which is boiled tofu and vegetables topped with seven herbs. You can order it by itself, or as a set meal with side dishes. Entrance to the restaurant, situated beside the Kyoyoike Pond on temple grounds, is along a small path that takes you past a stream, a small pond, a grove of maple and pine, and moss-covered grounds, which are also what you look out on as you dine, seated on tatami. You'll know you're getting close to the restaurant when you hear the *thonk* of a bamboo trough fed by a stream, which fills and hits against stone as it empties. Note that if you wish to come here only for a beer after visiting the temple, you'll pay an extra ¥300 table charge in addition to ¥500 for the beer.

Ryoanji Temple. ✆ **075/462-4742.** Yudofu ¥1,500; yudofu vegetarian set meal ¥3,300. No credit cards. Daily 10am–5pm. Bus: 59 from Shijo Kawaramachi to Ryoanji-mae (2 min.), or 50 to Ritsumeikan Daigaku-mae (4 min.).

5 EXPLORING THE CITY

Because Kyoto has so many worthwhile sights, you must plan your itinerary carefully. Even the most avid sightseer can become jaded after days of visiting yet another temple or shrine, no matter how beautiful or peaceful, so be sure to temper your visits to cultural and historical sights with time spent simply walking around. Kyoto is a city best seen on foot; take time to explore small alleyways and curio shops, pausing from time to time to soak in the beauty and atmosphere. If you spend your days in Kyoto racing around in a taxi or a bus from one temple to another, the essence of this ancient capital and its charm may literally pass you by.

Before setting out, be sure to stop by **Kyoto City Tourist Information** at Kyoto Station (✆ **075/344-3300**) to get a detailed map of the city, a bus map, and the *Kyoto's Visitor's Guide* (which also contains maps).

Keep in mind, too, that you must enter Kyoto's museums, shrines, and temples at least a half-hour before closing time. Listings in this section and those that follow give numbers not only for buses departing from Kyoto Station but from elsewhere as well.

For a map of Kyoto's attractions, see p. 298.

As strange as it sounds, the biggest tourist draw around Kyoto Station is **Kyoto Station** itself. Japan's second-largest station building (after Nagoya) is a futuristic-looking building with soaring glass atriums, space-age music, escalators rising to a rooftop observatory, and open stages for free concerts and other events. In a bold move to attract young Japanese (who nowadays prefer to take their vacations in more exotic or trendier climes), it also has a shopping center selling everything from clothing to Kyoto souvenirs, the fashionable Isetan department store, and restaurants galore. I see more tourists photographing Kyoto Station than any other modern building in town.

Just a 10- and 5-minute walk (respectively) north of Kyoto Station are two massive temple compounds, **Nishi-Honganji** and **Higashi-Honganji.** They were once joined as one huge religious center called Honganji, but they split after a disagreement several centuries ago. Higashi-Honganji is Kyoto's largest wooden structure, while Nishi-Honganji, headquarters for 12 million Shin Buddhists, is an outstanding example of Buddhist architecture. A 2-minute walk east of Higashi-Honganji is its garden, **Shosei-en** (𝄞 075/371-2961). Once the private villa of Higashi-Honganji's abbot and designed in part by famous landscape architect Kobori Enshu in the 17th century, it features a pond and several buildings in a parklike setting. Although there are far more beautiful and grander gardens in Kyoto, it provides a nice respite if you're in the area. It's open daily 9am to 4pm, with a ¥500 "donation" expected.

For a personalized English-language tour that takes in Higashi-Honganji, a couple shrines, a former Geisha area, and back streets of Kyoto before ending near Kiyomizu Temple, join **Johnnie Hillwalker's Kyoto Walking** (𝄞 **81/75-622-6803;** http://web. kyoto-inet.or.jp/people/h-s-love) tour, held every Monday, Wednesday, and Friday from 10am to 3:15pm March through November (no walks on national holidays). Led by Hajime Hirooka, with 50 years guide experience, tours start from in front of Kyoto Station and cost ¥2,000 for adults, ¥1,000 for 13- to 15-year-olds, and free for children. No reservations are required; pick up his brochure at the tourist office.

Costume Museum   This one-room museum (above a clothing store for monks) is filled with an elaborate, quarter-size replica of the Spring Palace as immortalized by Murasaki Shikibu in *The Tale of Genji,* complete with scenes of ceremonies, rituals, and everyday court life depicted by dolls wearing gorgeous kimono and by miniature furniture and other objects of the Heian Period. The exhibit, including costumes, changes twice a year. In an adjoining room, life-size kimono and costumes can be donned for free, so be sure to bring your camera. You can see everything in about 15 minutes.

Izutsu Building, 5th floor, Shinhanayacho Dori, Horikawa Higashiiru (on the corner of Horikawa and Shinhanayacho sts. just northeast of Nishi-Honganji Temple). 𝄞 **075/342-5345.** www.iz2.or.jp/english. Admission ¥400 adults, ¥300 university and high-school students, ¥200 children 7–12, children 6 and under free. Mon–Sat 9am–5pm. Closed for exhibition change June and Dec. Bus: 9 or 28 to Nishi-Honganji-mae (2 min.), or a 15-min. walk north from Kyoto Station.

CENTRAL KYOTO

Much of Central Kyoto has been taken over by the 21st century, but there are a few interesting sites worth investigating.

If you've never been to a market in Japan, take a stroll down **Nishiki-Koji Dori,** a fish-and-produce market right in the heart of town. A covered pedestrian lane parallel to Shijo Dori to the north and stretching west from Teramachi Dori, Nishiki-Koji has been Kyoto's principal food market for more than 4 centuries. This is where the city's finest restaurants and inns buy their food; you'll find approximately 135 open-fronted shops

(Tips) Refreshment for Free

Across from the Imperial Palace is **Free Café Harimaya Station,** where you can help yourself to juice, coffee, and rice crackers—all absolutely free. It's sponsored by Harimaya Honten, a major confectionary company, whose president wants you to not only enjoy his crackers but also think about the state of the environment (pick up the English-language pamphlet in the cafe or go to www.harimaya honten.co.jp/pc to read his comments). It's open daily 10am to 7pm.

and stalls selling seasonal vegetables, fish, beans, seaweed, and pickled vegetables, as well as crafts and cooking supplies. Shops are open from the early morning hours until about 6pm; many close on either Wednesday or Sunday.

Kyoto Imperial Palace (Kyoto Gosho) ★★ This is where the imperial family lived from 1331 until 1868 when they moved to Tokyo. The palace was destroyed several times by fire but was always rebuilt in its original style; the present buildings date from 1855. Modestly furnished with delicate decorations, the palace shows the restful designs of the peaceful Heian Period, and the emperor's private garden is graceful. You can visit the palace only on a free, 1-hour guided tour in English, but fair warning: Tours are conducted quickly, leaving little time for dawdling or taking pictures. In addition, tours view buildings only from the outside, though they do impart interesting information on court life and palace architecture.

Kyotogyoen-nai, Karasuma-Imadegawa. ℂ 075/211-1215. Free admission. Tours in English Mon–Fri at 10am and 2pm; tours in Japanese 3rd Sat of every month and every Sat Mar–Apr and Oct–Nov. Closed national holidays. Permission must be obtained from the Imperial Household Agency Office (ℂ 075/211-1215), either online at http://sankan.kunaicho.go.jp/english at least 4 days in advance; or in person at palace grounds near the northeast corner, Mon–Fri 8:45am–noon and 1–5pm. Foreign visitors can apply in person in advance or on the day of the tour 20 min. before the tour starts (1-day advance application required for Sat tours), but tours can fill up (especially in spring and fall). You must be 18 or older (or accompanied by an adult) and you must present your passport. Subway: Karasuma Line to Imadegawa (exit 3); then turn left and walk south on Karasuma Dori (5 min.).

Kyoto International Manga Museum (Kids) The lofty goal of this new museum (with more 300,000 items the largest *manga* museum in the world) is to conduct research on the history and culture of manga and to preserve manga that has appeared through the ages, including historic materials produced since the Edo Period, popular contemporary Japanese works, foreign manga, animation, and other related topics. For most visitors, however, it provides an hour or so of fun, with changing exhibits of approximately 50,000 items on display at any one time. Housed in a former primary school built in 1869, it contains a very popular children's library with manga and picture books kids can enjoy, a memorial hall dedicated to the former elementary school, picture-story shows (popular before the days of TV) three times a day, a Wall of Manga with shelves upon shelves of thousands of manga you can peruse, and—my favorite—an archive that illustrates the long history of Japanese manga. On weekends, manga artists demonstrate their craft. Unfortunately, unless you can read Japanese or are a manga fanatic, you won't be able to take full advantage of this facility. But if you have children, they're likely to feel right at home.

(Moments) Cultural Immersion

If you're interested in learning firsthand about the tea ceremony, flower arranging, origami, Japanese calligraphy, Japanese cooking, and other cultural pursuits, you can do so with the help of the members of the **Women's Association of Kyoto (WAK Japan;** ✆ **075/212-9993;** www.wakjapan.com). Courses, conducted mostly in members' homes, run 55 minutes to 1¹/₂ hours and cost ¥3,500 to ¥7,800 per person depending on the class and the number of people, including pickup from your hotel. Reservations should be made 1 day in advance, if possible.

Karasuma Oike, Nakagyo-ku. ✆ **075/254-7414.** www.kyotomm.jp. Admission ¥500 adults, ¥300 junior-high and high-school students, ¥100 children. Thurs–Tues 10am–6pm. Subway: Karasuma-Oike (1 min.).

Museum of Kyoto (Kyoto Bunka Hakubutsukan) ★ Through video displays, slides, and even holograms, this museum presents Kyoto's 1,200-year history from prehistoric relics to contemporary arts and crafts. I particularly like the various architectural models depicting a local market, merchants' homes, and a wholesale store, but best of all is the vermilion-colored Heian Shrine model with its holographic display of construction workers. An annex, occupying a 1906 bank with its original main hall (complete with teller cages), houses special exhibits and events.

Unfortunately, explanations are in Japanese only, but the museum does offer free English-language guides every day from 10am to 5pm; personal tours last between 30 and 60 minutes depending on your interest (because guides are volunteers, it's a good idea to make a reservation for one). A special feature of the museum is its film library, which houses hundreds of Japanese classics from silent movies to films made up to 20 years ago (the Japanese movie industry was based in Kyoto for decades). Movies, in Japanese only and included in admission price of the museum, are shown twice a day Thursday through Sunday (at 1:30 and 5pm at last check, but confirm the time). Be sure to browse the Roji Temple Mercantile Street, a re-created merchant's quarters with shops selling crafts and souvenirs and restaurants serving typical Kyoto dishes.

At Sanjo and Takakura sts. ✆ **075/222-0888.** www.bunpaku.or.jp. Admission ¥500 adults, ¥400 students, free for children. Special exhibits cost more. Tues–Sun 10am–7:30pm. Subway: Karasuma-Oike (exit 5, 3 min.).

Nijo Castle (Nijojo) ★★★ The Tokugawa shogun's Kyoto home stands in stark contrast to most of Japan's other remaining castles, which were constructed purely for defense. Built by the first Tokugawa shogun, Ieyasu, in 1603, Nijo Castle, a UNESCO World Heritage Site, is considered the quintessence of Momoyama architecture, built almost entirely of Japanese cypress and boasting delicate transom woodcarvings and paintings by the Kano School on sliding doors. Unfortunately, no photos are allowed.

I prefer Nijo Castle to the Imperial Palace because you can explore its interior on your own. The main building, **Ninomaru Palace,** has 33 rooms, some 800 tatami mats, and an understated elegance, especially compared with castles being built in Europe at the same time. All the sliding doors on the outside walls of the castle can be removed in summer, permitting breezes to sweep through the building. Typical for Japan at the time, rooms were unfurnished, and the mattresses were stored in closets.

One of the castle's most intriguing features is its so-called **nightingale floors.** To protect the shogun from real or imagined enemies, the castle was protected by a moat

KYOTO & NARA 9 EXPLORING THE CITY

and stone walls. How deep the shogun's paranoia ran, however, is apparent by the installation of these special floorboards, which creaked when trod upon in the castle corridors. The nightingale floors were supplemented by hidden alcoves for bodyguards. Furthermore, only female attendants were allowed in the shogun's private living quarters. Ironically, it was from Nijo Castle that Emperor Meiji issued his 1868 decree abolishing the shogunate form of government.

Outside the castle is an extensive **garden,** designed by the renowned gardener Kobori Enshu, which is famous in its own right. The original grounds of the castle, however, were without trees—supposedly because the falling of leaves in autumn reminded the shogun and his tough samurai of life's transitory nature, making them terribly sad. Plan on spending 1½ hours here, especially if you decide to rent an audio guide for ¥500 extra, recommended because it describes the significance of what you're seeing.

On the corner of Horikawa Dori and Nijo Dori. ℭ **075/841-0096.** Admission ¥600 adults, ¥350 junior-high and high-school students, ¥200 children. Daily 8:45am–5pm (you must enter by 4pm). Closed Tues Dec–Jan and July–Aug. Subway: Nijojo-mae Station (1 min.). Bus: 9, 12, 50, or 101 to Nijojo-mae (1 min.).

Nishijin Textile Center (Nishijin-Ori Kaikan) ★ About a 10-minute walk west of the Imperial Palace is this museum dedicated to the weavers who for centuries produced elegant textiles for the imperial family and nobility. The history of Nishijin silk weaving began with the history of Kyoto itself back in 794; by the Edo Period, there were an estimated 5,000 weaving factories in the Nishijin District. Today, the district remains home to one of Japan's largest handmade weaving industries. The museum regularly holds weaving demonstrations at its ground-floor hand looms, which use the Jacquard system of perforated cards for weaving. One of the most interesting things to do here is attend the free **Kimono Fashion Show,** held six or seven times daily from 10am to 4pm, showcasing kimono that change with the seasons. Other activities—for which you need reservations—include dressing up in a kimono for ¥3,600, or as a *maiko* (geisha apprentice) or *geiko* (professional entertainer) for ¥10,000, as well as trying your own hand at producing a textile on a small loom (¥1,800), which you can then take home with you. There's also, naturally, a shop selling kimono, sashes, fabric, and other woven products and souvenirs.

On Horikawa Dori just south of Imadegawa Dori. ℭ **075/451-9231.** www.nishijin.or.jp. Free admission. Daily 9am–5pm. Subway: Imadegawa (8 min.). Bus: 9, 12, 59, 101, 102, 201, or 203 to Horikawa Imadegawa (2 min.).

EASTERN KYOTO

The eastern part of Kyoto, embracing the area of Higashiyama-ku with its Kiyomizu Temple and stretching up all the way to the Temple of the Silver Pavilion (Ginkakuji Temple), is probably the richest in terms of culture and charm. Although temples and gardens are the primary attractions, Higashiyama-ku also boasts several fine museums, forested hills and running streams, great shopping opportunities, and some of Kyoto's oldest and finest restaurants. I've included two **recommended strolls** through eastern Kyoto later in this chapter that will lead you to the region's best attractions as well as to some lesser-known sights that are worth a visit if you have the time.

Ginkakuji (The Temple of the Silver Pavilion) ★★ Ginkakuji, considered one of the more beautiful structures in Kyoto, was built in 1482 as a retirement villa for Shogun Ashikaga Yoshimasa, who intended to coat the structure with silver in imitation of the Golden Pavilion built by his grandfather. He died before this could be accomplished, however, so the Silver Pavilion is not silver at all but remains a simple, two-story

wood structure enshrining the goddess of mercy and Jizo, the guardian god of children.
Note the sand mound in the garden, shaped to resemble Mount Fuji, and the sand raked in the shape of waves, created to enhance the views during a full moon.

Ginkakuji-cho. ℭ **075/771-5725.** www.shokoku-ji.or.jp/english. Admission ¥500 adults, ¥300 junior-high and elementary students, younger children free. Mid-Mar to Nov daily 8:30am–5pm; Dec to mid-Mar daily 9am–4:30pm. Bus: 5, 17, 102, 203, or 204 to Ginkakuji-michi (10 min.); or 32 or 100 to Ginkakuji-mae (5 min.).

Heian Shrine ★★ Although it dates only from 1895, Kyoto's most famous shrine was built in commemoration of the 1,100th anniversary of the founding of Kyoto and is a replica of the first Imperial Palace, though on a less grand scale. It also deifies two of Japan's emperors: Emperor Kanmu, 50th emperor of Japan, who founded Heian-kyo in 794; and Emperor Komei, the 121st ruler of Japan, who ruled from 1831 to 1866. Although the orange, green, and white structure is interesting for its Heian-Era architectural style, the most important thing to see here is the 33-sq.-m (355-sq.-ft.) **Shinen Garden ★★★**, the entrance to which is on your left as you face the main hall. Typical of gardens constructed during the Meiji Era, it's famous for its weeping cherry trees in spring, its irises and waterlilies in summer, and its changing maple leaves in the fall. Don't miss it.

Nishi Tennocho, Okazaki. ℭ **075/761-0221.** www.heianjingu.or.jp. Free admission to grounds; Shinen Garden ¥600 adults, ¥300 children. Daily 8:30am–6pm (to 5pm Nov–Feb). Subway: Higashiyama (10 min.). Bus: 5, 32, 46, or 100 to Kyoto Kaikan Bijutsukan-mae (2 min.).

Hosomi Art Museum ★ This highly acclaimed private museum houses changing exhibits of Buddhist and Shinto art, primarily from temples and shrines in Kyoto and Nara, including Heian bronze mirrors, Buddhist paintings, lacquerware, tea-ceremony objects, scrolls, folding screens, and pottery. In contrast to the objects it contains, the building itself is starkly modern, complete with automatic doors that open and clang shut with the finality of a prison. The 30 minutes it takes to walk through are worthwhile; be sure to browse through the gift shop of finely crafted goods.

6-3 Saishoji-cho Okazaki. ℭ **075/752-5555.** www.emuseum.or.jp. Admission ¥1,000 adults, ¥800 students and children. Tues–Sun 10am–6pm. Subway: Higashiyama (exit 2, 7 min.). Bus: 31, 201, 202, 203, or 206 to Higashiyama-Nijo (3 min.). Catty-corner from the Kyoto Museum of Traditional Crafts (Fureaikan).

Kiyomizu Temple (Kiyomizudera) ★★★ This is Higashiyama-ku's most famous temple, known throughout Japan for the grand views afforded from its main hall. Founded in 798 and rebuilt in 1633 by the third Tokugawa shogun, Iemitsu, the temple occupies an exalted spot on Mount Otowa, with its main hall constructed over a cliff and featuring a large wooden veranda supported by 139 pillars, each 15m (49 ft.) high. The main hall is dedicated to the goddess of mercy and compassion, but most visitors come for the magnificence of its height and view, which are so well known to Japanese that the idiom "jumping from the veranda of Kiyomizu Temple" means that they're about to undertake some particularly bold or daring adventure. Kiyomizu's grounds are particularly spectacular (and crowded) in spring during cherry-blossom season and in fall during the turning of the maple leaves.

Also worth checking out are the three-story pagoda and Otowa Falls (known for the purity of its water; *kiyomizu* translates as "pure water"), but be sure not to spite the gods by neglecting to visit **Jishu Shrine ★★** (ℭ **075/541-2097**), a vermilion-colored Shinto shrine behind Kiyomizu's main hall that has long been considered the dwelling place of the god of love and matchmaking. Ask for the English-language pamphlet and be sure to take the ultimate test: On the shrine's grounds are two "love–fortune telling" stones placed 9m (30 ft.) apart; if you're able to walk from one to the other with your eyes closed, your desires for love will be granted.

1–294 Kiyomizu. ✆ **075/551-1234.** Admission ¥300 adults, ¥200 children 7–15, children 6 and under free. Daily 6am–6pm (until 6:30pm in summer); Jishu Shrine closes at 5pm. Bus: 100, 202, 206, or 207 to Gojo-zaka (10 min.).

Kodai-ji Temple ★ Located between Kiyomizu Temple and Yasaka Shrine, this temple was founded in 1605 by Toyotomi Hideyoshi's widow, popularly referred to as Nene, to commemorate her husband and to pacify his spirit. Shogun Tokugawa Ieyasu, who served under Toyotomi before becoming shogun, financed its construction. It contains lovely gardens laid out by Kobori Enshu, as well as teahouses designed by Sen no Rikyu, a famous 16th-century tea master. A memorial hall enshrines wooden images of Hideyoshi (to the left) and Nene. Nene, by the way, became a Buddhist nun after her husband's death, as was the custom of noblewomen at the time.

526 Shimogawara-cho, Kodai-ji. ✆ **075/561-9966.** Admission ¥600 adults, ¥250 children 17 and under. Daily 9am–4:30pm (until 4pm in winter). Bus: 100, 202, 206, or 207 to Higashiyama Yasui (5 min.).

Kyoto Museum of Traditional Crafts (Fureaikan) ★★ (Finds) Near Heian Shrine is this excellent museum dedicated to the many crafts that flourished during Kyoto's long reign as the imperial capital. Various displays and videos demonstrate the step-by-step production of crafts ranging from stone lanterns and fishing rods to textiles, paper fans, umbrellas, boxwood combs, lacquerware, Buddhist altars, and *noh* masks. The displays are fascinating, the crafts beautiful, and explanations are in English, making even a 30-minute stop here well worth the effort. Crafts are sold in the museum shop.

In the basement of the Miyako Messe (International Exhibition Hall; look for the bright orange installation outside), 9–1 Seishoji-cho, Okazaki. ✆ **075/762-2670.** www.miyakomesse.jp/fureaika. Free admission. Daily 9am–5pm. Subway: Higashiyama (7 min.). Bus: 5, 32, 46, or 100 to Kyoto Kaikan Bijutsukan-mae (2 min.), or 31, 201, 202, 203, or 206 to Higashiyama-Nijo.

Kyoto National Museum (Kokuritsu Hakubutsukan) ★★ This museum, housed in a French baroque–style building constructed in 1897, is under renovation until after 2013 and is therefore open only for special exhibitions held three or four times a year (check the website for a schedule or ask at the tourist office). Once renovations are complete, it will again feature exhibits highlighting magnificent art objects and treasures, many of which once belonged to Kyoto's many temples and the imperial court, including Japanese and Chinese ceramics, sculpture, Japanese paintings, clothing and kimono, lacquerware, and metalworks.

527 Chaya-machi (across the street from Sanjusangendo Hall). ✆ **075/541-1151.** www.kyohaku.go.jp. Special exhibition fees vary. Contact museum for exhibition dates and times. Bus: 100, 206, or 208 to Hakubutsukan Sanjusangendo-mae (1 min.).

Sanjusangendo Hall ★★★ Originally founded as Rengeoin Temple in 1164 and rebuilt in 1266, Sanjusangendo Hall has one of the most visually stunning sights I've seen in a Japanese temple: 1,001 wooden statues of the thousand-handed Kannon. Row upon row, these life-size figures, carved from Japanese cypress in the 12th and 13th centuries, make an impressive sight; in the middle is a large seated Kannon carved in 1254 by Tankei, a famous sculptor from the Kamakura Period. Don't expect to actually see a thousand arms on each statue; there are only 40, the idea being that each hand has the power to save 25 worlds. In front of the 1,001 Kannon are a row of 28 guardian deities; not only are they all National Treasures, but it's rare to find a whole set like this one still intact. In any case, to accommodate all these statues, the hall stretches almost 120m (400 ft.), making it the longest wooden building in Japan (no photography or videos are allowed in the building). Its length was too hard to ignore—in the corridor behind the statues, archery competitions have been held for centuries; standing here, you can easily imagine how hard it must be to hit a piece of sacred cloth attached to the wall at the opposite end.

Shichijo Dori. © **075/525-0033.** Admission ¥600 adults, ¥400 junior-high and high-school students, ¥300 children. Apr to mid-Nov daily 8am–5pm; mid-Nov to Mar daily 9am–4pm. Bus: 100, 206, or 208 to Hakubutsukan Sanjusangendo-mae (1 min.).

NORTHERN KYOTO

Two of Kyoto's most famous sights are in the northwestern corner of the city.

Kinkakuji (Temple of the Golden Pavilion) ★★★ One of Kyoto's best-known attractions—and the inspiration for the Temple of the Silver Pavilion (see above)—Kinkakuji was constructed in the 1390s as a retirement villa for Shogun Ashikaga Yoshimitsu and features a three-story pavilion covered in gold leaf with a roof topped by a bronze phoenix. Apparently, the retired shogun lived in shameless luxury while the rest of the nation suffered from famine, earthquakes, and plague. If you come here on a clear day, the Golden Pavilion shimmers against a blue sky, its reflection captured in the waters of a calm pond. However, this pavilion is not the original; in 1950, a disturbed student monk burned Kinkakuji to the ground (the story is told by author Mishima Yukio in his famous novel *The Temple of the Golden Pavilion*). The temple was rebuilt in 1955 and in 1987 was recovered in gold leaf, five times thicker than the original coating: You almost need sunglasses. Be sure to explore the surrounding **park** with its moss-covered grounds and teahouses.

1 Kinkakuji-cho. © **075/461-0013.** www.shokoku-ji.or.jp/english. Admission ¥400 adults, ¥300 children. Daily 9am–5pm. Bus: 12, 59, 101, 102, 204, or 205 to Kinkakuji-michi (3 min.).

Ryoanji Temple ★★★ About a 20-minute walk southwest of the Golden Pavilion is Ryoanji—home to what is probably the most famous **Zen rock garden** ★★★ in all of Japan—laid out at the end of the 15th century during the Muromachi Period. Fifteen rocks set in waves of raked white pebbles are surrounded on three sides by a clay wall and on the fourth by a wooden veranda, in an area that measures about 25m (80 ft.) long and 10m (30 ft.) wide. Sit down and contemplate what the artist was trying to communicate. The interpretation of the rocks is up to the individual. (Mountains above the clouds? Islands in the ocean?) My only objection to this peaceful place is that, unfortunately, it's not always peaceful—a loudspeaker on occasion extols the virtue of the garden, destroying any chance for peaceful meditation. If you get here early enough, you may be able to escape both the crowds and the noise.

After visiting the rock garden, be sure to take a walk around the temple grounds. There's a 1,000-year-old **pond,** on the rim of which sits a beautiful little restaurant, **Ryoanji Yudofuya** ★★ (p. 324), with tatami rooms and screens, where you can eat *yudofu* and enjoy the view. There's also a nice landscape garden, with moss so inviting you'll wish you could lie down and take a nap.

Goryoshita-cho. © **075/463-2216.** www.ryoanji.jp. Admission ¥500 adults, ¥300 children 14 and under. Mar–Nov daily 8am–5pm; Dec–Feb daily 8:30am–4:30pm. Bus: 59 to Ryoanji-mae (2 min.); or 12 or 50 to Ritsumeikan Daigaku-mae (4 min.).

Toei Kyoto Studio Park/Movie Land (Toei Uzumasa Eigamura) ★ (Kids) If
your kids are ready to mutiny because of yet another temple, get on their good side by
coming to this studio park, one of Japan's three major film companies and where most
of the samurai flicks are made. Don't expect the high-tech, polished glitz of American
theme parks—rather, this is a working studio where more than 200 TV and movie productions are filmed each year. Indoor and outdoor movie sets re-create the mood, setting,
and atmosphere of feudal and turn-of-the-20th-century Japan, complete with "villages"
lined with samurai houses and old-time shops. Stagehands carry around props, hammers,
and saws, and rework sets. You may even see a famous star walking around dressed in
samurai garb, or come upon a scene being filmed. There are, of course, other attractions,
including a museum tracing the history of the film industry, a 20-minute ninja show four
times a day Monday through Friday, a special-effects show, a haunted house, a games
arcade, and indoor rides and play areas for children (extra charges for haunted house and
rides). You can also have a photo taken of yourself decked out in a kimono or samurai
gear. *Note:* Back lots are open only on weekends when there is no filming, but kids will
prefer a weekday when there are ninja shows and filming. Come here only if you have a
lot of time (you'll probably spend a minimum of 2 hr. here), are a cinema buff, or have
youngsters in tow.

10 Higashi-Hachigaokacho, Uzumasa, Ukyo-ku. (℄) **075/864-7718.** www.toei-eigamura.com. Admission
¥2,200 adults, ¥1,300 junior-high and high-school students, ¥1,100 children. Daily 9am–5pm (9:30am–
4pm Dec–Feb). Closed Dec 26–Jan 1. Train: JR line to Uzumasa or Hanazono Station (13 min.) or Keifuku
Line to Uzumasa (5 min.). Bus: 75, 91, or 93 to Uzumasa Eigamuramichi (4 min.).

| WALKING TOUR 1 | A STROLL THROUGH HIGASHIYAMA-KU |

START:	Sanjusangendo Hall on Shichijo Dori a couple of blocks east of the Kamo River; to get there, walk 20 minutes from Kyoto Station or take bus no. 100, 206, or 208 to Hakubutsu-kan Sanjusangendo-mae.
FINISH:	Gion.
TIME:	Allow approximately 5 hours, including stops for shopping and museums.
BEST TIMES:	Weekdays, when temples and shops aren't as crowded.
WORST TIMES:	There is no worst day for this tour.

A stroll through Higashiyama-ku will take you to Kiyomizu Temple, one of Kyoto's most
famous sights, and other worthwhile attractions like Sanjusangendo Hall. It will also take
you through some of Kyoto's most charming neighborhoods, with plenty of shopping
opportunities en route.

Note: The second walk, "The Philosopher's Stroll" (see below), includes several attractions that could be combined with this walk if you don't have time for two walks. If you
continue walking north from Maruyama Park instead of heading west for Gion, for
example, you could take in Heian Shrine and the Kyoto Handicraft Center (covered at
the end of the second walk). In any case, because eastern Kyoto has some of the city's
most traditional and beautiful restaurants, be sure to read through the dining section to
decide beforehand where you want to eat lunch or dinner.

Before setting out, pick up the walking-tour leaflet "Kyoto Walks" at either the Tourist Information Center in Tokyo or Kyoto Tourist Information. It's useful for its maps of
four walks, but disregard its claim that you can walk from Kiyomizu Temple to Heian
Shrine in 50 minutes. I don't see how it's possible unless you run the entire way. I've

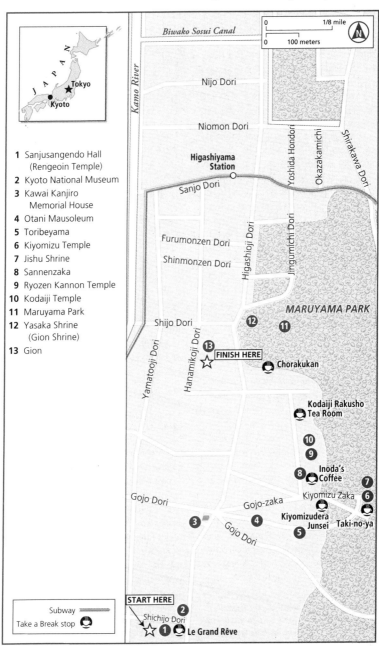

1 Sanjusangendo Hall
 (Rengeoin Temple)
2 Kyoto National Museum
3 Kawai Kanjiro
 Memorial House
4 Otani Mausoleum
5 Toribeyama
6 Kiyomizu Temple
7 Jishu Shrine
8 Sannenzaka
9 Ryozen Kannon Temple
10 Kodaiji Temple
11 Maruyama Park
12 Yasaka Shrine
 (Gion Shrine)
13 Gion

Biwako Sosui Canal

0   1/8 mile
0   100 meters

JAPAN
Tokyo
Kyoto

Kamo River

Nijo Dori

Niomon Dori

Yoshida Hondori

Okazakamichi

Shirakawa Dori

Higashiyama
Station

Sanjo Dori

Furumonzen Dori

Shinmonzen Dori

Higashioji Dori

Jingumichi Dori

MARUYAMA PARK

Shijo Dori

Yamatooji Dori

Hanamikoji Dori

12

11

13 FINISH HERE

Chorakukan

Kodaiji Rakusho
Tea Room

10

9

Inoda's
Coffee

8

7

Kiyomizu Zaka

6

Gojo Dori

Gojo-zaka

Kiyomizudera
Junsei

Taki-no-ya

3

4

5

Gojo Dori

Subway

Take a Break stop

START HERE

Shichijo Dori

1

2

Le Grand Rêve

KYOTO & NARA

9

WALKING TOUR 1: A STROLL THROUGH HIGASHIYAMA-KU

walked this route almost a dozen times, and it's always taken me the better part of a day—perhaps I'm slow, but it's a pace that I've found does justice to this wonderful area of Kyoto.

Start your stroll at:

❶ Sanjusangendo Hall

This hall dates from 1266 and is only about 15m (50 ft.) wide, but stretches almost 120m (400 ft.), making it the longest wooden building in Japan. However, it's not the building itself that impresses but what it contains—1,001 life-size images of the thousand-handed Kannon. Seeing so many of them—row upon row of gold figures, glowing in the dark hall—is stunning (unfortunately, no photographs or videos allowed). In the middle is a 3.3m-tall (11-ft.) seated figure of Kannon carved in 1254. At the back of the hall is a 117m (384-ft.) archery range where a competition is held every January 15. (See "Exploring the City," earlier in this chapter, for more information on this and other major sights described in this stroll.)

Across the street is the:

❷ Kyoto National Museum (Kokuritsu Hakubutsukan)

In 1889, the Meiji government, fearful that Japan's cultural objects were going the way of the samurai with the increasing import of Western ways and products, established three national museums—one in Tokyo, one in Nara, and this one in Kyoto, which serves as a repository for art objects and treasures that once belonged to Kyoto's temples and royal court. It's presently undergoing renovation, however, with an expected reopening of its permanent collection of ceramics, paintings, lacquerware, textiles, sculptures, and other precious objects after 2013. Until then, special exhibitions are mounted three to four times a year.

East of the Kyoto National Museum (toward the wooded hills) are Higashioji Dori and a stoplight; take a left and walk about 5 minutes until you come to the second stoplight, at a small intersection with a Sunkus convenience store. Turn left here, take the

first right down a narrow street, and to your right you'll soon see:

❸ Kawai Kanjiro Memorial House

Kawai Kanjiro Memorial House, Gojo-zaka (✆ **075/561-3585**), is the former home and studio of one of Japan's most well-known potters, Kawai Kanjiro (1890–1966). Inspired at a young age by Bernard Leach and one of the cofounders of the Japan Folk Crafts Museum in Tokyo, this versatile man handmade much of the furniture in this lovely home, which is a traditional Japanese house with an indoor open-pit fireplace and gleaming woodwork. Pottery, personal effects, and his outdoor clay kiln, built on a slope in the traditional Japanese method, are all on display, but this museum is worth seeing for the house alone, especially if you haven't had much opportunity to see the interiors of traditional Japanese homes. Admission is ¥900 for adults, ¥500 for students, and ¥300 for children. It's open Tuesday to Sunday from 10am to 5pm.

Take a right out of the museum, walk to the busy road with the overpass, and turn right. When you get to the big intersection, look catty-corner across the intersection to the left and you'll see a slope leading uphill between two big stone lanterns. This marks the entrance to the:

❹ Otani Mausoleum

It serves as a major mausoleum for members of Shin Buddhism (a Japanese religious sect). In addition to a memorial hall dedicated to victims of World War II, it holds many memorial services for deceased Shin Buddhists from throughout Japan. After passing through a two-story wooden gate, you should turn left and then right for:

❺ Toribeyama

Since ancient times it has served as a cremation site and burial ground, with more than 15,000 tombs spread along the slopes.

Follow the pathway uphill through the cemetery for about 10 minutes to the top, where you should then turn left and follow the painted white arrow in the street to the vermilion-colored tower gate, which marks the entrance to:

⓺ Kiyomizu Temple

This temple is the star attraction of this stroll. First founded in 798 and rebuilt in 1633 by the third Tokugawa shogun, Iemitsu, the temple occupies an exalted spot. The main hall is built over a cliff and features a large wooden veranda supported by 139 pillars, each 15m (50 ft.) high. Take in the view of Kyoto from its deck, but to fully appreciate the grandeur of the main hall with its pillars and dark wood, be sure to walk to the three-story pagoda, which offers the best view of the main hall, built without the use of a single nail. From the pagoda, descend the stone steps to Otowa Falls, where you'll see Japanese lined up to drink from the refreshing spring water. Kiyomizu's name, in fact, translates as "pure water." From here you'll also have the best view of the temple's impressive pillars.

TAKE A BREAK
On the grounds of Kiyomizu Temple, just beside Otowa Falls, is **Taki-no-ya** (☏ **075/561-5117**), an open-air pavilion where you can sit on tatami and enjoy noodles and a beer or flavored shaved ice from the English-language menu. This is a great place to stop (and now you know why this walk takes me all day). If you're lucky to be here in autumn, the fiery reds of the maple trees will set the countryside around you aflame. Open Friday through Wednesday from 10am to 5pm. Or, for something more substantial, wait until after your temple visit to dine on tofu at **Kiyomizu-dera Junsei**, located off Kiyomizu-zaka (see p. 322 for a complete review). On Sannenzaka (see below), keep your eyes peeled for **Inoda's Coffee** (☏ **075/532-5700**), where you'll have views of a Japanese-style garden along with pastries, sandwiches, and coffee. It's open daily 9am to 5pm.

Before departing Kiyomizu Temple, be sure to make a stop at the vermilion-colored Shinto shrine located behind the temple's main hall:

⓻ Jishu Shrine

This shrine is regarded as a dwelling place of the deity in charge of love and match-making. Ask for the English-language leaflet that gives its history. Throughout the grounds are English-language signs and descriptions telling about its various parts; for once, you're not left in the dark about the purpose of the various statues and memorials and what Japanese are doing as they make their rounds. It's very enriching. You can buy good-luck charms for everything from a happy marriage to easy delivery of a child to success in passing an examination. On the shrine's grounds are two stones placed about 9m (30 ft.) apart—if you're able to walk from one stone to the other with your eyes closed, you're supposedly guaranteed success in your love life. It sure doesn't hurt to try. There's also a place where you can write down your troubles on a piece of paper and then submerge it in a bucket of water, which supposedly will cause both the paper and your troubles to dissolve. If you failed the rock test, you might make a point of stopping here.

From Kiyomizu Temple, retrace your steps to the vermilion-colored entry tower gate you passed earlier. From here, on a downhill slope called Kiyomizu-zaka, you'll pass shop after shop selling sweets, pottery, fans, ties, hats, souvenirs, and curios. It's okay to go crazy shopping here, but remember that you're going to have to carry whatever you buy. After passing a couple of small shrines nestled in among the shops, you'll come to a split in the road and a small shrine on the right shaded by trees in front. Just beside this shrine are stone steps leading downhill (north) to a stone-cobbled street called:

⓼ Sannenzaka

The slope leads past lovely antiques stores, upscale craft shops, and restaurants and winds through neighborhoods of wooden buildings reminiscent of old Kyoto. Keep your eyes peeled for downhill stairs to the right leading to Maruyama Park; after you take these, the street will wind a bit as it goes downhill and eventually end at a T intersection. Take the stairs opposite the road to:

9 Ryozen Kannon Temple

This temple (𝒞 **075/561-2205**) has a 24m-high (80-ft.) white statue dedicated to unknown soldiers who died in World War II. Memorial services are conducted four times daily at a shrine that contains memorial tablets of the two million Japanese who perished during the war. There's also a Memorial Hall commemorating the more than 48,000 foreign soldiers who died on Japanese territory. Open daily from 8:45am to 4:20pm; because admission is ¥200, you may only want to take a peek at the statue. Just past Ryozen Kannon Temple, across the parking lot, is:

10 Kodaiji Temple

This temple was founded by the widow Nene in commemoration of her husband, Toyotomi Hideyoshi, who succeeded in unifying Japan at the end of the 16th century. In addition to teahouses and a memorial hall containing wooden images of the couple, there's a beautiful garden designed by master gardener Kobori Enshu. Don't miss it.

Exit Kodai-ji Temple via the main steps leading downhill and turn right, continuing north.

> ☕ **TAKE A BREAK**
> Past Kodai-ji Temple and just before the street ends at a pagoda with a crane on top, keep your eyes peeled for a teahouse on your right with a garden, which you can glimpse from the street through a gate. The ㊾ **Kodaiji Rakusho Tea Room,** 516 Washiochiyo (𝒞 **075/561-6892**), is a lovely place and one of my favorite tearooms in Kyoto. It has a 100-year-old miniature garden with a pond that's home to some of the largest and most colorful carp I've ever seen, some of which are 20 years old and winners of the many medals displayed in the back room. In summer, stop for *somen* (finely spun cold noodles), tea,

or traditional desserts, and refresh yourself with views of the small but beautiful garden from one of the tables or from the back tatami room. If you're a gardener, you'll probably want to give up the hobby after you've seen what's possible—but rarely achieved. Open from 9:30am to 5:30pm (until 6pm in summer); closed 1 day a week but, unfortunately, not a fixed day. For coffee or afternoon tea, there's a cafe in **Chorakukan,** a brick-and-stone Meiji-Era building at the southwest corner of Maruyama Park (described earlier; to the left as you enter the park).

Continuing on your stroll north, turn right at the pagoda with the crane and then take an immediate left, which marks the beginning of:

11 Maruyama Park

An unkempt field of shrubs and weeds until designated a public park in 1886, this is one of Kyoto's most popular outdoor respites, filled with ponds, pigeons, and gardens. In spring, it's one of the most popular spots for viewing cherry blossoms; to the left after you enter the park is one of the oldest, most famous cherry trees in Kyoto. Also farther west is:

12 Yasaka Shrine

Yasaka Shrine is also known as Gion Shrine because of its proximity to the Gion District. Its present buildings date from 1654; the stone *torii* (gates) on the south side are considered among the largest in Japan. But the reason most people come here is one of practicality—the shrine is dedicated to the gods of health and prosperity, two universal concerns. This shrine, free to the public and open 24 hours, is packed during the Gion Festival and on New Year's Eve.

Exit Yasaka Shrine to the west; this brings you to a busy street called Higashioji. Cross it and continue walking west on busy Shijo Dori, until you reach Hanamikoji Dori on your left. This is:

13 Gion

Gion is one of Japan's most famous nightlife districts. It's centered primarily on

Hanamikoji Dori, which translates as "Narrow Street for Flower Viewing." This is Kyoto's long-standing geisha district, an enclave of discreet, traditional, and almost solemn-looking wooden homes that reveal nothing of the gaiety that goes on inside— drinking, conversation, and business dealings with dancing, singing, and music provided by geisha and their apprentices, called *maiko*. If it's early evening, you might glimpse one of these women as she small-steps her way in *geta* (a traditional wooden shoe) to an evening appointment, elaborately made up and wearing a beautiful kimono. You might also wish to visit

Gion Corner on Hanamikoji Dori, which offers performances of dance, puppetry, and other traditional arts nightly; see "Kyoto After Dark," later in this chapter, for details.

> **WINDING DOWN**
> If all this sightseeing and shopping have made you thirsty, there are many restaurants and bars to the west across the Kamo River, on Pontocho, and near Shijo and Kawaramachi streets. See "Where to Dine in Kyoto" and "Kyoto After Dark" in this chapter for many suggestions in this area.

WALKING TOUR 2 THE PHILOSOPHER'S STROLL

START:	Ginkakuji, the Temple of the Silver Pavilion; from Kyoto Station, take bus no. 32 or 100 to Ginkakuji-mae stop or bus no. 5, 17, 102, 203, or 204 to Ginkakuji-michi stop.
FINISH:	Kyoto Handicraft Center, Marutamachi Dori.
TIME:	Allow about 5 hours, including stops along the way.
BEST TIMES:	Early on weekdays, when crowds aren't as thick.
WORST TIMES:	There is no worst time for this walk.

This stroll takes in the Temple of the Silver Pavilion as well as a couple of other temples, a museum dedicated to Kyoto's traditional crafts, Kyoto's most well-known shrine and its garden, and the best place in town for one-stop souvenir shopping. Linking the Silver Pavilion with the other sights is a canal lined by trees—a path known as the **Philosopher's Pathway.**

From the Ginkakuji-mae or Ginkakuji-michi bus stop, head east (toward the wooded hills) along the canal, and continue east when the canal veers to the (right) south, up the gentle slope to:

❶ Ginkakuji, the Temple of the Silver Pavilion

This World Heritage Site is the architectural jewel of this stroll. Contrary to its name, however, Ginkakuji isn't silver at all. It was built in 1482 as a retirement villa for Shogun Ashikaga Yoshimasa, who intended to coat the structure with silver in imitation of the Golden Pavilion built by his grandfather. However, he died before this could be accomplished, which is just as well—the wood of the Silver

Pavilion is spectacular just as it is. The entire complex is designed for enjoyment of the tea ceremony, moon viewing, and other aesthetic pursuits, with a beautiful garden of rippled sand, rocks, and moss. One of the small sandhills is in the image of Mount Fuji. It's easy to imagine the splendor, formality, and grandeur of the life of Japan's upper class as you wander the grounds here. Be sure to take the hillside pathway with its lookout point, dozens of different kinds of moss, and streams; you might be able to escape the crowds that sometimes overwhelm this attraction.

Head back to that narrow canal you saw on the way to the temple, heading south lined with cherry, willow, and maple trees and flanked by a small pathway. It's known as the:

❷ Philosopher's Pathway

The name Philosopher's Pathway refers to the fact that, throughout the ages, philosophers and priests have strolled this tranquil canal thinking deep thoughts. It's a particularly beautiful sight in spring during the cherry-blossom season. The pathway runs almost 1.6km (1 mile), allowing you to think your own deep thoughts.

TAKE A BREAK
Approximately 5 minutes down the Philosopher's Pathway, to the right, is **Café de Sagan** (℃ 075/751-7968), a coffee shop with an English-language menu listing sandwiches, desserts, beer, and juices. It's open Friday to Wednesday from 8am to 5pm, with views of the shaded path through its windows.

At the end of the Philosopher's Pathway (a 30-min. walk), near Nyakuoji Shrine, turn right and walk for a few minutes through a residential area until you reach a street with some traffic on it (and a wooden sign pointing toward Eikando and Nanzenji). Here you should turn left. After a couple of minutes, on the left, you'll come to:

❸ 98 Eikando Temple

Founded in 863, this temple (also known as **Zenrinji Temple;** ℃ 075/761-0007; www.eikando.or.jp) derives its popular name from the seventh head priest Eikan (1032–1111), who was loved by the people for attending to the impoverished sick and for planting plum trees as sources of medicine. The temple is famous for a small statue of the Amida Buddha with his head turned, looking back over his shoulder. According to popular lore, it was carved after Eikan, who while walking and reciting chants he believed would propel him toward rebirth, was so astonished to

see that the Amida Buddha had descended from the altar and was walking ahead of him that he stopped short in his tracks, whereupon the Buddha looked back over his shoulder and admonished, "Eikan, you are dawdling." How typically Zen. The Buddha facing backward is in the Amidado Hall. Otherwise, there isn't much to see unless it's autumn and the many maples here are at their most glorious. The temple's pagoda, up on a hillside, offers a view over the city. Open daily from 9am to 4pm (last entry); admission is ¥600, except in autumn when it's ¥1,000 and there's also night viewing.

A few minutes' walk farther south brings you to:

❹ Nanzenji Temple

Nanzenji Temple (℃ 075/771-0365; www.nanzenji.com) is a Rinzai Zen temple set amid a grove of spruce. One of Kyoto's best-known Zen temples, it was founded in 1293, though its present buildings date from the latter part of the 16th century during the Momoyama Period. Attached to the main hall is a Zen rock garden attributed to Kobori Enshu; it's sometimes called "Young Tigers Crossing the Water" because of the shape of one of the rocks, but the association is a bit of a stretch for me. In the building behind the main hall is a sliding door with a famous painting by Kano Tanyu of a tiger drinking water in a bamboo grove. Spread throughout the temple precincts are a dozen other lesser temples and buildings worth exploring if you have the time, including Nanzen-in, which was built about the same time as Nanzenji Temple and served as the emperor's vacation house whenever he visited the temple grounds. The temple is open daily from 8:40am to 5pm (to 4:30pm in winter); admission to the main hall is ¥500 and to Nanzen-in ¥300.

0   1/4 mi

0   0.25 km

1 Ginkakuji, the Temple of the Silver Pavilion
2 Philosophers' Pathway
3 Eikando Temple
4 Nanzenji Temple
5 Kyoto Museum of Traditional Crafts
6 Heian Shrine
7 Kyoto Handicraft Center

Higashioji Dori

Demachiyanagi Station

Imadegawa Dori

Kyoto University

Higashiichijo Dori

Shirakawa Dori

START HERE

☆

1

Yoshida Shrine

Okazaki Dori

Café de Sagan

Philosophers' Pathway

Canal

Konoe Dori

2

☆ FINISH HERE

7

Marutamachi Dori

6 **Heian Shrine**

Reisen Dori

Nijojo Dori

5

3

Lake Biwa Aquaduct

Goemonjaya

Okutan

Niomon Dori

Hyotei

Junsei

4

← **Higashiyama–Sanjo Station**

Keage ■ Station

Miyako ■ Hotel

Take a Break stop

TAKE A BREAK
Several traditional restaurants near Nanzenji reflect the settings of the temples themselves. **Okutan,** just north of Nanzenji and with a view of a peaceful pond, has been serving vegetarian tofu meals for 350 years. On the road leading west from Nanzenji are **Junsei,** serving tofu, obento lunch boxes, and kaiseki in a beautiful garden setting; **Goemonjaya,** which serves moderately priced set meals and noodles; and **Hyotei,** which opened more than 300 years ago to serve pilgrims to Nanzenji, offering obento lunches as well as expensive kaiseki. See "Where to Dine in Kyoto," earlier in this chapter, for details.

Head straight out (west) from Nanzenji until you see a body of water on your right, the Lake Biwa Aqueduct. Continue west on Niomon Dori (the water will be on your right) to the vermilion-colored bridge to your right, where you'll also see a vermilion-colored *torii.* Turn right here and continue straight ahead to Nijo Dori, where you turn left for one of my favorite museums (look for the bright orange installation outside), the:

❺ Kyoto Museum of Traditional Crafts (Fureaikan)

This basement museum displays all the Kyoto crafts you can think of, from combs, umbrellas, and fans to textiles, sweets, bambooware, and masks. English-language explanations and videos describe how the crafts are made (mostly by hand). The best news: The museum is free. For details, see p. 330.

Across the street to the north, it would be hard to miss:

❻ Heian Shrine

If orange and green are your favorite colors, you're going to love Heian Shrine, one of Kyoto's most famous. Although it was built as late as 1895 in commemoration of the 1,100th anniversary of the founding of Kyoto, Heian Shrine is a replica of the city's first administrative quarters, built in Kyoto in 794, giving you some idea of the architecture back then. The most important thing to see here is the **garden,** the entrance to which is on your left as you face the main hall. Typical of gardens constructed during the Meiji Era, it's famous for its weeping cherry trees in spring, its irises and waterlilies in summer, and its changing maple leaves in the fall. I love sitting on the bench on the wooden bridge topped by a phoenix; you'll probably want to dawdle here, too.

Take a right out of the shrine's main exit onto Reisen Dori and then take the next right, which after 5 minutes will bring you to the:

❼ Kyoto Handicraft Center

This center is located behind the shrine on its north side. It's the best place in Kyoto for one-stop shopping for souvenirs of Japan, including pearls, kimono and the less-formal *yukata,* fans, paper products, toys, and more; see p. 345 for complete information. You may want to take advantage of the free shuttle service the center provides to major hotels in Kyoto four times per afternoon; the last bus departs at 6pm. Otherwise, take bus no. 206 for Kyoto Station or 203 for downtown Kyoto.

6 IMPERIAL VILLAS & TEMPLES WITHIN EASY REACH OF KYOTO

If this is your first visit to Kyoto and you're here for only a couple days, you should concentrate on seeing sights in Kyoto itself. If, however, this is your second trip to Kyoto, you're here for an extended period of time, or you have a passion for traditional Japanese architecture or gardens, there are a number of worthwhile attractions in the region surrounding Kyoto. Foremost on my list is **Katsura Imperial Villa.**

Note: The Katsura Imperial Villa, **Shugakuin Imperial Villa,** and **Saihoji** (popularly called the Moss Temple) all require advance permission to visit. To see the Katsura Imperial Villa or Shugakuin Imperial Villa, which are free, you must apply for permission either online at **http://sankan.kunaicho.go.jp** at least 4 days before your intended visit; or go in person to the **Imperial Household Agency Office** (✆ **075/221-1215;** no English is spoken and no reservations are accepted by phone, but you can have a Japanese speaker call to see whether space is available), located on the northwest grounds of the **Kyoto Imperial Palace** near Inui Gomon Gate, a 5-minute walk from Imadegawa subway station. It's open Monday through Friday from 8:45am to noon and 1 to 5pm. In the off season, you may be able to make a reservation for a tour on the same day, though keep in mind that it takes an hour to reach Katsura Imperial Villa and 30 minutes to reach Shugakuin by taxi from the Imperial Household Agency Office. It's always better, therefore, to make a reservation a day or two in advance if applying in person; in spring and fall, try to make a reservation a week in advance. The time of your tour will be designated when you apply. Parties are limited to four persons, everyone must present their passports, and **participants must be at least 18 years old.** Tours are conducted in Japanese only, but an English-language video is shown.

Tours, which take place weekdays (except holidays) and the third Saturday of every month year-round, as well as on Saturdays in April, May, October, and November (even if they are national holidays), are given at Katsura Imperial Villa at 9am, 10am, 11am, 1:30pm, 2:30pm, and 3:30pm and at Shugakuin Imperial Villa at 9am, 10am, 11am, 1:30pm, and 3pm.

For tours of Saihoji, see below.

KATSURA IMPERIAL VILLA ★★★ About a 20-minute walk from Katsura Station on the Hankyu railway line, or a 30-minute bus ride from Kyoto Station (take bus no. 33 to the Katsura Rikyu-mae stop) and then an 8-minute walk, this villa is considered the jewel of traditional Japanese architecture and landscape gardening. It was built between 1620 and 1624 by Prince Toshihito, brother of the emperor, with construction continued by Toshihito's son. The garden, markedly influenced by Kobori Enshu, Japan's most famous garden designer, is a "stroll garden" in which each turn of the path brings an entirely new view.

The first thing you notice upon entering Katsura is its simplicity—the buildings were all made of natural materials, and careful attention was paid to the slopes of the roofs and to the grain, texture, and color of the various woods used. A pavilion for moon viewing, a hall for imperial visits, a teahouse, and other buildings are situated around a pond; as you walk along the pathway, you're treated to views that literally change with each step you take. Islets; stone lanterns; various scenes representing seashores, mountains, and hamlets; manicured trees; and bridges of stone, earth, or wood that arch gracefully over the water—everything is perfectly balanced. No matter where you stand, the view is complete and in harmony. Every detail was carefully planned down to the stones used in the path, the way the trees twist, and how scenes are reflected in the water. Little wonder the Katsura Imperial Villa has influenced architecture not only in Japan but around the world. Sadly, tours are much too hurried (they last only 1 hr.), and no photography is allowed.

SHUGAKUIN IMPERIAL VILLA ★★ Northeast of Kyoto, about a 40-minute bus ride from Kyoto Station (take bus no. 5 from Kyoto Station to the Shugakuin Rikyu-michi bus stop) and then a 15-minute walk, this villa was built in the mid-1600s as a

9

IMPERIAL VILLAS & TEMPLES WITHIN EASY REACH OF KYOTO

retirement retreat for Emperor Go-Mizunoo, who came to the throne at age 15 and suddenly abdicated 18 years later to become a monk, passing the throne to his daughter in 1629. Amazingly, though the villa was only 2 hours from the Imperial Palace, the emperor came here only on day trips; he never once spent the night. The 53-hectare (133-acre) grounds, among Kyoto's largest, are situated at the foot of Mount Hiei and are famous for the principle known as "borrowed landscape" in which the surrounding landscape is incorporated in the overall garden design. Grounds are divided into three levels (only two of which have compelling features): The **upper garden,** with its lake, islands, and waterfalls, is the most extensive of the three and offers grand views of the surrounding countryside from its hillside pavilion. The **middle garden,** built as a residence for the emperor's daughter, contains a villa with the famous "Shelves of Mist"; in keeping with the Japanese penchant for ranking the best three of everything, this is considered one of the three most beautiful shelves in Japan. The gardens are more spacious and natural than most Japanese-style gardens, which are often small and contrived. Tours, which take 1 hour and 15 minutes and cover about 3km (2 miles), allow ample time for photography.

SAIHOJI ★★   Popularly known as the **Moss Temple (Kokedera),** Saihoji was converted into a Zen temple in 1339 and is famous for its velvety-green moss garden spread underneath the trees. Altogether, there are more than 100 different varieties of moss throughout the grounds, with such popular names as "velvet moss," "water moss," and "snake-stomach moss." They give off an iridescent and mysterious glow that's best just after a rain; indeed, Kyoto's rainy season and high summer humidity create the perfect breeding ground for moss. Before being allowed to visit the grounds, you'll be ushered with other tour participants into a tatami room, where monks light incense, sound the bells, chant for our happiness and ancestry, and instruct participants to write their wishes on a tablet with a calligraphy brush. You can then walk on your own through the moss garden, which looks like it's straight out of a fairy tale and which circles a pond shaped in the Japanese word for heart, and linger as long as you wish; plan on a minimum of 1 hour here.

Note: Because the monks are afraid that huge numbers of visitors will trample the grounds of this UNESCO World Heritage Site to death, permission is needed to visit Saihoji, and you can obtain it only by writing to the temple at least 7 days in advance (applications up to 2 months in advance are accepted). You can write in English to Saihoji Temple, 56 Matsuo Kamigatani-cho, Nishikyo-ku, Kyoto 615-8286 (© **075/391-3631**), and give your name, your (hotel) address in Japan, your age, the number of people in your group, and the date you'd like to visit (plus second and third choices). Include a self-addressed return envelope; if you want it sent to a hotel in Japan the monks will send it to you free, but if you want it sent outside Japan to your home, include International Reply Coupons for return postage. The cost of the visit is a "donation" of at least ¥3,000 (no change given), payable when you arrive at the temple to pick up your ticket on the day of your tour. To reach Saihoji, take the Hankyu Line from Kawaramachi or Karasuma stations 10 minutes to Katsura and then the Arashiyama Line one stop to Kami-Katsura Station, from which it's a 15-minute walk. Or, take bus no. 73 from Kyoto Station or 63 from downtown Kyoto to the Kokedera-michi stop, but it takes longer.

BYODOIN TEMPLE ★★   Located in the town of Uji, about 18km (11 miles) southeast of Kyoto and a 15-minute ride by express JR train from Kyoto Station, Byodoin Temple (© **0774/21-2861**) is a good example of temple architecture of the Heian Period. Originally a villa, it was converted into a temple in 1053. Most famous is the main hall, known as **Phoenix Hall,** the only original building remaining. It has three wings, creating an image of the mythical bird of China, the phoenix; on the gable ends are two bronze phoenixes. On the temple grounds is a National Treasure: one of the most famous bells in Japan (there are no inscriptions on the bell, but it has reliefs of maidens and lions and is thought to contain Korean influences) as well as a monument to Minamoto Yorimasa, who took his own life here after being defeated by the rival Taira clan. Byodoin is best known to Japanese, however, for gracing the back of ¥10 coins. Byodoin is about a 10-minute walk from the Uji JR Station (there's a map of the town in front of the station). Admission to the grounds is ¥600 for adults, ¥400 for junior-high students, and ¥300 for children; ¥300 more for Phoenix Hall. Open daily 8:30am to 5:30pm (9am–4pm Dec–Feb).

FUSHIMI-INARI SHRINE ★ Just a 2-minute walk from the JR Inari Station (which is just two stops by local commuter train from Kyoto Station), Fushimi-Inari Shrine (© 075/641-7331) is one of Japan's most celebrated Shinto shrines. Founded in 711, it's dedicated to the goddess of rice (rice was collected as taxes during the shogun era) and has therefore long been popular with merchants, who come here to pray for success and prosperity. The 4km (2½-mile) pathway behind the shrine is lined with more than 10,000 red *torii,* presented by worshipers throughout the ages and by Japanese businesses. There are also stone foxes, which are considered messengers of the gods, usually with a key to the rice granary hanging from their mouths. It's a glorious, almost surreal, walk as you wind through the woods and the tunnel of vermilion-colored torii gates and then gradually climb a hill, where you'll have a good view of Kyoto. At several places along the path are small shops where you can sit down for a bowl of noodles or other refreshments. Admission is free, and the expansive grounds never close. The most popular times to visit are the first day of each month and New Year's, but I prefer weekdays when almost no one is there.

Note: Both Byodoin Temple and Fushimi-Inari Shrine are on the same JR line that continues to Nara. If you plan on spending the night in Nara, you could easily take in these two attractions on the way. Note, however, that the express train to Nara does not stop at JR Inari Station; for that you'll have to take a local train.

7 SHOPPING IN KYOTO

As the nation's capital for more than 1,000 years, Kyoto spawned a number of crafts and exquisite art forms that catered to the elaborate tastes of the imperial court and the upper classes. Kyoto today is still renowned for its **crafts,** including Nishijin textiles, Yuzen-dyed fabrics, Kyo pottery (pottery fired in Kyoto), fans, dolls, cutlery, gold-leaf work, umbrellas, paper lanterns, combs, *noh* masks, cloisonné, and lacquerware.

GREAT SHOPPING AREAS The majority of Kyoto's tiny specialty shops are situated in central Kyoto along Shijo Dori and in the area of Kawaramachi Dori. The square formed by **Kawaramachi Dori, Shijo Dori, Sanjo Dori,** and **Teramachi Dori** includes two covered shopping arcades and specialized shops selling lacquerware, combs and hairpins, knives and swords, tea and tea-ceremony implements, and more—including, of course, clothing and accessories.

If you're looking for antiques, woodblock prints, and art galleries, head toward **Shinmonzen Dori** and **Furumonzen Dori** in Gion, which parallel Shijo Dori to the north on the eastern side of the Kamo River, as well as **Teramachi Dori** north of Oike. You'll find pottery and souvenir shops in abundance on the roads leading to Kiyomizu Temple in **Higashiyama-ku.**

For clothing, accessories, and modern goods, Kyoto's many **department stores** are good bets. They're conveniently located near Kyoto Station or in central Kyoto near the Shijo-Kawaramachi intersection. In addition, there's a big underground shopping mall beneath Kyoto Station selling everything from clothing and shoes to stationery and local souvenirs.

CRAFTS & SPECIALTY SHOPS

(99) **Aritsugu**   The fact that this family-owned business is located at the Nishiki-Koji market is appropriate, as it sells hand-wrought knives and other handmade cooking implements, including sushi knives, bamboo steamers, pots, pans, and cookware used in the preparation of traditional Kyoto cuisine, as well as *ikebana* scissors. In business for 400 years, the shop counts the city's top chefs among its customers. Note that no credit cards are accepted. Open daily 9am to 5:30pm. Nishiki-Koji Dori, Gokomachi Nishi-iru, Nakagyo-ku. ℂ **075/221-1091.** Bus: 4, 5, 10, 11, 12, 17, 32, 46, 201, 203, 207, or 205 to Shijo Kawaramachi (5 min.). 1 block north of Shijo Dori on the north side of Nishiki-Koji Dori, west of Gokomachi.

(100) **Ippodo**   In business since 1717, this famous shop is a good place not only to buy high-quality Japanese green teas but to learn more about them. Pick up the shop's English-language brochure that explains the different varieties, from *matcha* to *sencha* to *genmaicha*, or sample them at the shop's hands-on tearoom, Kaboku, where you can experience brewing techniques for the different types of tea. Open Monday to Saturday 9am to 7; Saturday and holidays 9am to 6pm (Kaboku open daily 11am–5pm). Teramachi Dori, north of Nijo, Nakagyo-ku. ℂ **075/211-3421.** www.ippodo-tea.co.jp. Bus: 4, 10, 17, 32, 59, and 205 to Kyoto Shiyakushomae.

Kasagen   Kasagen has been making traditional *bangasa* (umbrellas) since 1861. They're more expensive than elsewhere but are of high quality and are made to last a lifetime. Open Monday, Tuesday, Thursday, and Friday 1 to 7pm; Saturday, Sunday, and holidays 10am to 7pm. 284 Gion-machi, Kitagawa. ℂ **075/561-2832.** Bus: 12, 46, 100, 201, 202, 203, 206, or 207 to Gion. On the north side of Shijo Dori, just west of Yasaka Shrine.

Kikuya   Kikuya has a good selection of used kimono, *haori* (short kimono-like jackets, traditionally worn by men), *geta,* and kimono accessories for both adults and children. Although they're not antiques as Kikuya advertises but secondhand, the goods here are beautiful and timeless. Everything is in good condition (Japanese wear kimono only for special occasions), but be sure to look thoroughly for any defects. No credit cards are accepted. Open Monday to Saturday 9am to 7pm. Closed holidays. On Manjuji Dori, east of Sakaimachi. ℂ **075/351-0033.** Take the Keihan Electric Line to Gojo (5 min.).

(101) **Kyoto Aburatorishi Senmontenzo**   I realize this is a bit odd, but this shop is dedicated to one of my favorite Japanese cosmetic products: face paper. Kyoto is famous for its face paper, long used by geisha and *maiko,* and this shop sells a bewildering choice of varieties, for everything from dry to troubled skin. I like it for blotting oily skin on hot, humid days. Daily 11am to 8:30pm. Kawaramachi, Shijo-agaru. ℂ **075/213-3322.** Bus: 4, 5, 10, 11, 12, 17, 32, 46, 201, 203, 207, or 205 to Shijo Kawaramachi. On the east side of Kawaramachi Dori, north of Shijo Dori; look for its sign with an elephant.

Kyoto Ceramics Center (Kyoto Tojiki Kaikan) This modern shop with a glass facade is operated by an association of Kyoto potters who display their wares of Kyo pottery (pottery fired locally). Approximately 10,000 items are on display, from sake cups and vases to bowls, plates, and chopstick rests. Daily 10am to 6pm. Higashioji Dori, Gojoagaru. *©* **075/541-1103.** Bus: 100 or 206 to Gojo-zaka (one of the approaches to Kiyomizu Temple). On Higashioji Dori, north of Gojo Dori.

Kyoto Handicraft Center For one-stop souvenir shopping, your best bet is Kyoto's largest craft, gift, and souvenir center. Five floors of merchandise contain almost everything Japanese imaginable: pearls, lacquerware, dolls, children's toys, kimono (including antique kimono), woodblock prints, pottery, paper products, swords, lanterns, silk and textile goods, painted scrolls, T-shirts, and jewelry boxes—and that's just for starters. You can even buy the socks worn with *geta* wooden shoes and the *obi* sashes worn with the kimono.

You can easily spend an hour or two here just wandering around; artisans also demonstrate their various crafts, including woodblock printing and the production of damascene. You can even try your own hand at 10 different craft activities, including woodblock prints, cloisonné, damascene, and more, with instruction provided. No reservations are necessary, but plan on at least an hour. Lessons run ¥1,890 to ¥3,990 and are a great way for older children to get creative while you shop. And if you spend more yen than you have in your wallet, you can exchange money here at a favorable rate. Other facilities include a tourist office on the ground floor, a buffet restaurant serving lunch daily from noon to 2pm for ¥1,575, and an Internet cafe charging ¥400 for the first half-hour of Internet use and ¥200 for each half-hour after that. Open daily from 10am to 7pm. Heian Jingu Kita, Marutamachi Dori, Sakyo-ku. *©* **075/761-8001.** Bus: 93, 201, 202, 203, 204, or 206 to Kumano-jinja-mae (3 min.). Free bus service from the center to major hotels throughout Kyoto at 1, 2:30, 4, and 6pm. Just north of Heian Shrine on Marutamachi Dori.

(102) **Miyawaki Baisen-an** This elegant, open-fronted shop has specialized in handmade fans since 1823, particularly fans characteristic of Kyoto. Prices range from ¥2,000 for a small tea-ceremony fan to ¥50,000 for the best that money can buy. Open daily 9am to 7pm (to 6pm in winter). 102 Tominokoji-nishi, Rokkaku-dori, Nakagyo-ku. *©* **075/221-0181.** Subway: Karasuma Oike (6 min.). On Rokkaku-dori just west of Tominokoji, across from a playground.

DEPARTMENT STORES

Department stores are good places to shop for Japanese items and souvenirs, including pottery, lacquerware, and kimono as well as clothing, foodstuff, and everyday items.

JR Kyoto Isetan, located in Kyoto Station (*©* **075/352-1111;** daily 10am–8pm), is Kyoto's most fashionable department store for young people, specializing in women's imported and domestic clothing.

In central Kyoto, **Daimaru,** on Shijo Dori west of Takakura (*©* **075/211-8111;** daily 10am–8pm), is Kyoto's largest department store, with everything from clothing to food to electronic goods spread on nine floors. Nearby are **Hankyu,** on the southeast corner of Shijo-Kawaramachi intersection (*©* **075/223-2288;** Mon–Wed 11am–8pm, Thurs–Sun 11am–9pm), with seven floors of fashion, housewares, and food; and **Takashimaya,** across the street at the southwest corner of the Shijo-Kawaramachi intersection (*©* **075/221-8811;** daily 10am–8pm), one of Japan's oldest and most respected department stores with a good selection of traditional crafts.

On the 21st of each month, a flea market is held at **Toji Temple** (© 075/691-3325), about a 15-minute walk southwest of Kyoto Station. Japan's largest flea market, it's also one of the oldest; its history stretches back more than 700 years, when pilgrims began flocking to Toji Temple to pay their respects to Kobo Daishi, who founded the Shingon sect of Buddhism. Today, Toji Temple, a World Heritage Site, is still a center for the Shingon sect, and its market (popularly known as Kobo-san) is a colorful affair with booths selling Japanese antiques, old kimono, ethnic goods, odds and ends, and many other items. Worshipers come to pray before a statue of Kobo Daishi and to have their wishes written on wooden slats by temple calligraphers. Even if you don't buy anything, the festive atmosphere of the market and booths makes a trip memorable. The largest Kobo-san markets take place in December and January. All markets at Toji are held from about 6am to 4pm. A smaller market, devoted entirely to Japanese antiques, is held at Toji Temple on the first Sunday of each month.

Commemorating the scholar and poet Sugawara Michizane, the **Tenjin-san market** held at **Kitano Tenmangu Shrine** (© 075/461-0005) the 25th of every month is a large market offering a little bit of everything—antiques, used clothing, ceramics, food—in a beautiful setting. It's open from about 8am to dusk, but go as early as you can. Kitano Shrine is on Imadegawa Dori between Nishi-oji and Senbon; take bus no. 10, 26, 101, 102, and 203 to the Kitano Tenmangu-mae stop.

Unlike the other temple markets, the **Chion-ji market** (© 075/691-3325), held the 15th of each month from 9am to 4pm, is devoted to handmade goods and crafts, including pottery and clothing. To reach it, take bus no. 17, 102, 201, 203, or 206 to Hyaku-manben at the Higashioji and Imadegawa intersection; **Chion-ji Temple** is just to the northeast.

On the first Sunday of every month (though sometimes the date changes), a flea market is held in front of **City Hall** from 10am to 4pm, with local citizens selling unwanted stuff, mostly clothing. Although you may not buy anything to take home with you, a stroll through the **Nishiki-Koji Dori market** is worthwhile just for the atmosphere. Kyoto's 400-year-old city produce market, this covered shopping arcade 1 block north of Shijo Dori in the heart of old Kyoto is lined with vendors selling fish, flowers, eggs, pickled vegetables, fruit, and takeout foods, as well as crafts. It's open from 10am to about 6pm; some shops close on either Wednesday or Sunday.

8 KYOTO AFTER DARK

Nothing beats a fine summer evening spent strolling the streets of Kyoto. From the geisha district of Gion to the bars and restaurants lining Pontocho, Kyoto is utterly charming and romantic at night. Begin with a walk along the banks of the Kamo River—it's a favorite place for young couples in love. In summer, restaurants stretching north and south of Shijo Dori along the river erect outdoor wooden platforms on stilts over the water.

There are many annual events and dances, including the very popular geisha dances held in June, the only time of year you can see traditional dances performed by all five of Kyoto's traditional geisha districts; Gion Odori dances in October featuring *geiko* and *maiko* (geisha and apprentice geisha in Kyoto) dressed in elaborate costume; and *kabuki* at the Minamiza Theater in December.

distributed free at tourist offices, hotels, and restaurants, which contains a calendar of events and performances for the month. ***Kansai Scene*** is also a monthly giveaway with information on nightlife, festivals, and events.

THE MAJOR NIGHTLIFE DISTRICTS
Gion ★★

A small neighborhood of plain wooden buildings in Higashiyama-ku on the eastern side of the Kamo River, Gion doesn't look anything like what you've probably come to expect from an urban Japanese nightlife district; in fact, there's little neon in sight. There's something almost austere and solemn about Kyoto's most famous geisha district, as though its raison d'être were infinitely more important and sacred than mere entertainment. Gion is a shrine to Kyoto's past, an era when geisha numbered in the thousands.

Contrary to popular Western misconceptions, geisha are not prostitutes. Rather, they're trained experts in the traditional arts, conversation, and coquettishness, and their primary role is to make men feel like kings when they're in the soothing enclave of the geisha house. There are now only a mere 200 geisha in Gion; after all, in today's high-tech world, few women are willing to undergo the years of rigorous training to learn how to conduct the tea ceremony, to play the *shamisen* (a three-stringed instrument), or to perform ancient court dances.

Gion is about a 5-minute walk from the Shijo-Kawaramachi intersection; to reach it, walk east on Shijo Dori and then take a right on Hanamikoji Dori. Its narrow streets are great for strolling; a good time to take a walk through the neighborhood is around dusk when geisha are on their way to their evening appointments. Perhaps you'll see one—or a *maiko* (a young woman training to be a geisha)—clattering in her high *geta* (wooden shoes). She'll be dressed in a brilliant kimono, her face a chalky white, and her hair adorned with hairpins and ornaments. From geisha houses, music and laughter lilt from behind paper screens, sounding all the more inviting because you can't enter. Don't take it personally; not even Japanese will venture inside without the proper introductions. There are, however, an increasing number of bars and restaurants in Gion that are open to outsiders; it's not hard to imagine that in another 100 years, Gion will look no different from Tokyo's Ginza.

Gion Corner   After strolling around Gion, visit Gion Corner, which stages special variety programs in the ancient cultural arts. You'll see short demonstrations of the tea ceremony, flower arrangement, *koto* (Japanese harp) music, *gagaku* (ancient court music and dance), *kyogen* (*noh* comic play), *kyomai* (Kyoto-style dance) performed by *maiko,* and *bunraku* (puppetry). The shows cater to tourists, and none of the individual performances beat a full-scale production of the real thing, but this is a convenient and quick introduction to the traditional forms of Japanese entertainment. If you wish, you can also partake in a 30-minute tea ceremony following each performance (available Mar–Nov). Be sure, too, to wander through the Maiko Gallery with its displays relating to maiko hairstyles and accessories. Performances are daily at 7pm and 8pm March through November (no performances Aug 16); December through February performances are only on Friday, Saturday, and holidays at 7pm. Reservations are not necessary, but arrive early (no credit cards accepted), or purchase in advance at most hotels or Gion Corner box office. Yasaka Hall, 570–2 Minamigawa, Gion. ℂ **075/561-1119.** www.kyoto-gion-corner. info. Tickets ¥3,150; ¥4,200 including tea ceremony. Bus: 12, 46, 100, 102, 202, 203, 206, or 207 to Gion (10 min.). Located on Hanamikoji Dori south of Shijo Dori.

Pontocho is a narrow alley that parallels the Kamo River's western bank, stretching from Shijo Dori north to Sanjo Dori. Once riddled with geisha houses and other members-only establishments, it is now lined with bars, clubs, restaurants, and hostess bars that fill every nook and cranny. Pontocho makes for a fascinating walk as you watch groups of Japanese enjoying themselves.

Another good place to look for nightlife is **Kiyamachi,** another small street that parallels Pontocho just to the west and runs beside a small canal.

THE CLUB & LIVE MUSIC SCENE

Hello Dolly   With an unlikely location on Pontocho, this dark, tiny club with velvet-upholstered chairs looks like a holdout from the '50s. It has live jazz Friday and Saturday, with classic jazz recordings the rest of the week. To find it, look for an album cover of Doris Day in the window; it's that kind of place. Open daily 6pm to 1am. East side of Pontocho. ℂ 075/241-1728. Live music cover ¥1,000–¥1,200 (Fri–Sat only), and 20% service charge. Bus: 4, 5, 10, 11, 12, 17, 32, 46, 59, 201, 203, 205, or 207 to Shijo Kawaramachi (3 min.).

Live Spot RAG   Depending on who's playing, the crowd at one of Kyoto's longest-standing live clubs, established in 1981, ranges from an older, more mellow audience to a younger, rowdier bunch. Mostly, however, it's a college-age crowd that comes here to listen to rock, jazz, acoustic, and fusion. Open nightly from 6pm to 2am (to 4:30am on weekends), with live music 7:30 to 10:30pm. Empire Building, 5th floor, Kiyamachi Dori, Sanjo Agaru. ℂ 075/241-0446. Live music cover ¥1,300–¥4,800 for most performances, plus a 1-drink, 1-dish minimum. Discounts for advance purchases and usually for students. Subway: Kyoto Shiyakusho-mae (3 min.). Bus: 4, 5, 10, 11, 17, 32, 59, or 205 to Kawaramachi Sanjo (2 min.). On the east side of Kiyamachi with its narrow canal, north of Sanjo Dori.

THE BAR SCENE

Ichiba Coji and **Kushi Kura** (both reviewed under "Where to Dine in Kyoto," earlier in this chapter) are also good spots to grab a drink.

The Hill of Tara   Live traditional Irish music is the main draw here Friday, Saturday, and Sunday evenings, but it's lively any day of the week at this popular pub. Happy hour is from 5 to 8pm daily, and the menu lists Irish stew, fish and chips, and other pub grub. Open Monday to Friday 5pm to midnight and Saturday and Sunday from noon to midnight. Oike Dori, Kawaramachi-higashiiru. ℂ 075/213-3330. www.thehilloftara.com. Subway: Kyoto Shiyakusho-mae (2 min.). Bus: 4, 10, 17, 32, 59, or 205 to Kyoto Shiyakusho-mae (3 min.). On Oike Dori just east of Kyoto Hotel Okura.

Man in the Moon   At last, a good place to wet your whistle at Kyoto Station, this small Irish pub offers seven beers on tap, 60 single-malt whiskeys, lunch specials, and sporting events shown on large TVs. Open Sunday to Thursday 11am to 2am, Friday and Saturday 11am to 4am. Kintetsu-Meitengai Miyakomich 31-1. ℂ 075/672-2522. www.maninthemoon.jp. Station: Kyoto (1 min.). Underneath the tracks on Kyoto Station's south (Shinkansen/Kintetsu) side, across from the New Miyako Hotel to the right.

McLoughlin's Irish Bar and Restaurant (Finds)   Congenial owners Taidg, a professional chef, and Mika, a composer and pianist, lend both their talents and humor to this great bar/restaurant, offering bar seating, tables with expansive views of Kyoto's temples and mountains, Guinness and Kilkenny on tap, live music most Friday nights, free Wi-Fi connection (and one computer you can use for free), and good food, including handmade pizza and vegan and vegetarian choices in addition to the usual Irish stew, bangers and mash, and other pub fare. Open Monday, Wednesday, and Thursday 6pm to 1am; Friday and Saturday 6pm to 4am; and Sunday 1pm to 1am. Empire Building, 8th floor, Kiyamachi Dori, Sanjo Agaru. ℂ **075/212-6339**. www.kyotoirish.com. Subway: Kyoto Shiyakusho-mae (3 min.). Bus: 4, 5, 10, 11, 17, 32, 59, or 205 to Kawaramachi Sanjo (2 min.). In the same building as Live Spot RAG, above.

Pig & Whistle Here's a traditional, noisy, and fun English-style pub where you can play darts, stand at the bar, or sit at a table with your mum. It attracts an older, mixed crowd of both foreigners and Japanese, including foreigners who are networking for employment or business opportunities. Happy hour is from 5 to 7pm nightly. Open daily 5pm to 2am (Fri–Sat to 5am). Shobi Building, 2nd floor, 115 Ohashi-cho, Ohashi, Higashi Iru, Sanjo Dori. ℂ **075/761-6022**. Subway: Sanjo Keihan (2 min.). Bus: 5, 10, 11, 12, or 59 to Sanjo Keihan-mae (2 min.) On the north side of Sanjo Dori, east of the Kamo River.

Rub-A-Dub This tiny basement bar, decorated like a beach shack with fake palm trees and a corrugated tin roof, has been Kyoto's premier reggae spot for more than 20 years, a laid-back place that plays all genres of Jamaican music. Open Monday to Thursday 7pm to 2am and Friday and Saturday 7pm to 5am. Tsujita Building, 115 Ishiyamachi, Kiyamachi-sagaru. ℂ **075/256-3122**. Bus: 4, 5, 10, 11, 17, 32, 59, or 205 to Kawaramachi Sanjo. On the east side of Kiyamachi Dori, south of Sanjo Dori.

9 A SIDE TRIP TO NARA ★★

42km (26 miles) S of Kyoto

In early Japanese history, the nation's capital was moved to a new site each time a new emperor came to the throne. In 710, however, the first permanent Japanese capital was set up at **Nara.** Not that it turned out to be so permanent: After only 74 years, the capital was moved first to Nagaoka and shortly thereafter to Kyoto, where it remained for more than 1,000 years. What's important about those 74 years, however, is that they witnessed the birth of Japan's arts, crafts, and literature, as Nara imported everything from religion to art and architecture from China. Even the city itself, laid out in a rectangular grid pattern, was modeled after Chinese concepts. It was during the Nara Period that Japan's first historical account, first mythological chronicle, and first poetry anthology (with 4,173 poems) were written. Buddhism also flourished, and Nara grew as the political and cultural center of the land with numerous temples, shrines, pagodas, and palaces.

Japanese flock to Nara because it gives them the feeling that they're communing with ancestors. Foreigners come here because Nara offers them a glimpse of a Japan that was. Remarkably enough, many of Nara's historic buildings and temples remain intact, and long ago someone had enough foresight to enclose many of these historical structures in the quiet and peaceful confines of a large and spacious park, which has the added attraction of free-roaming deer.

ESSENTIALS

GETTING THERE Nara is easily reached from Kyoto Station on two lines: the JR Nara Line and the Kintetsu Limited Express. If you have a Japan Rail Pass, you'll probably want to take the commuter **JR Nara Express,** which departs about four times an hour and takes 43 to 57 minutes depending on the train; if you don't have a pass, the trip costs ¥690 one-way. If speed or luxury is of the utmost importance, the deluxe **Kintetsu Special Limited Express** whisks you to Nara in 35 minutes, guarantees you a seat (all seats

Moments   Your Own Personal Guide

Nara YMCA Goodwill Guides will be glad to show you the sights in exchange for the chance to practice their English. A national organization of volunteers, Goodwill Guides range from students and housewives to retired people. Although a guide is often waiting at Kintetsu Station's tourist office to lead the first tourists who show up any day except Sunday, make reservations in advance if you want to be assured of having a guide by calling © **0742/45-5920** at least the day before to arrange a time. Guides are available daily from 9am to 5pm. There's no charge for these personal guides, but you are requested to pay their transportation to meet you, and I suggest you also pay for the guide's lunch (guides do not have to pay admission fares to attractions). Similar services are provided by **Nara Student Guides** by calling © **0742/26-4753** and by **Nara S.G.G. Club** at © **0742/22-5595.**

are reserved), and costs ¥1,110; departures are every 30 minutes (if it's peak season, it's a good idea to buy your ticket in advance). A slower **Kintetsu ordinary express** takes 45 minutes and costs ¥610.

You can also reach Nara from Osaka in about 30 to 50 minutes, depending on the train and the station from which you leave. The **Kintetsu Nara Line,** departing from Namba Station, takes 40 minutes and costs ¥540; **JR railways** departs from Osaka Station, takes 50 minutes, and costs ¥780.

VISITOR INFORMATION   There are tourist information offices at both **JR Nara Station** (© **0742/22-9821;** daily 9am–5pm) and **Kintetsu Nara Station** (© **0742/24-4858;** daily 9am–5pm). Both have good brochures and maps with useful information on how to get around Nara by foot and bus, as well as city magazine *Nara Explorer.* For more detailed information on Nara, visit the **Nara City Tourist Center,** 23–4 Kami-sanjo-cho (© **0742/22-3900;** daily 9am–9pm), located in the heart of the city on Sanjo Dori between both stations and about a 5-minute walk from each. Finally, there's **Sarusawa Information Center** (© **0742/26-1991;** daily 9am–5pm), located at Sarusawa-ike Pond, south of Nara Park and not far from Nara's many attractions. Websites with information on Nara include **www.city.nara.nara.jp**; **www.pref.nara.jp**; and **www.naraexplorer.jp**.

GETTING AROUND   If you take the Kintetsu Line, you'll arrive at **Kintetsu Nara Station;** if you take the JR train, you'll arrive at **JR Nara Station.** Both stations are about a 10-minute walk from each other and are within walking distance of Nara Park and its attractions. Kintetsu Station is slightly closer, about a 5-minute walk to the entrance of the park, while the JR Station is about a 10-minute walk to the park. Keep in mind, however, that Nara Park is quite large and its major attractions are far-flung; it takes about 20 minutes to walk from Kintetsu Nara Station to Todaiji Temple. Around the stations themselves is Nara's small downtown area, with Sanjo Dori serving as the main shopping street and running from JR Nara Station to Nara Park.

IF YOU'RE HEADING TO HORYUJI   If you plan to visit the Horyuji Temple area (see below), the cheapest and fastest way to get there is from JR Nara Station on the JR Kansai Yamatoji Line going in the direction of Namba (in Osaka); departures are every 10

KYOTO & NARA

9 A SIDE TRIP TO NARA

ATTRACTIONS ●
Horyuji Temple **1**
Kasuga Grand Shrine **13**
Kofukuji Temple **8**
Nara National Museum **9**
Shin-en **12**
Todaiji Temple **10**

ACCOMMODATIONS ■
Hotel Nikko Na-ra **2**
Kikusuiro **7**
Nara Hotel **6**
Seikan-so **4**

DINING ◆
Harishin **5**
Noh **11**
Trattoria Piano **3**

⊠ Post Office
Railway
ⓘ Tourist Info

Nara-Okuyama Driveway

Wakakusayama Hill

Mt. Mikasayama

Byakugoji Temple

NARA PARK

Manyo Botanical Gardens

Isuien Garden

Sagiike Pond

Araike Pond

Nara Prefectural Museum

Sarusawa-ike Pond

Nara Stadium

Machi–idono Dori

Kintetsu Nara Station

Nara City Tourist Center

Ichijo Dori

Route No. 24

JR Sakurai Line

JR/Kansai Line (Yamatoji Line)

Sanjo Dori

JR Nara Station

Noborioji Dori

Kintetsu Railway/Nara Line

Kintetsu Railway/Kashiwara Line

Akishino River

Unamabeike Pond

Minakamiike Pond

Ancient Mausoleums

Hokkeji Temple

To Kyoto

Saidaiji Temple

JAPAN

Tokyo

Nara

1/2 mi
0.5 km

minutes or so and bring you to Horyuji Station in 13 minutes (fare: ¥210). From there, you can either walk to the temple area in about 20 minutes or take a bus (fare: ¥170), which departs two to three times an hour from 10am. Alternatively, there's bus no. 97, an excursion line that runs between Kasuga Grand Shrine and Horyuji, passing Todaiji Temple and both train stations on the way, but it takes about an hour and costs ¥760 one-way, with seven departures daily. Obviously, because it takes quite a bit of time getting to and from Horyuji, you must limit your sightseeing to only the major attractions if you plan on visiting both Nara Park and Horyuji in 1 day.

SEEING THE SIGHTS

The best way to enjoy Nara is to arrive early in the morning before the first tour buses start pulling in. If you don't have much time, the most important sites to see are **Todaiji Temple, Kasuga Shrine,** and **Kofukuji Temple's Treasure House,** which you can view in about 3 hours. If you have more time, add **Horyuji Temple.** Or, take a stroll through **Naramachi,** Nara's most historic part of town and boasting many *machiya* (traditional wooden residences). Although a reproduction, **Koshi-no-ie** (✆ **0742/23-4820;** Tues–Sun 9am–5pm) displays common machiya features and is free; ask the tourist office for a Naramachi map.

Around Nara Park

With its ponds, grassy lawns, trees, and temples, Nara Park covers about 520 hectares (1,300 acres) and is home to more than 1,100 deer, which are considered divine messengers and are therefore allowed to roam freely through the park. The deer are generally quite friendly; throughout the park you can buy "deer cookies," which all but the shyest fawns will usually take right out of your hand. All of the below listings are within Nara Park.

Kofukuji Temple ★   As you walk east from either the JR or Kintetsu Station, this is the first temple you reach. It was established in 710 as the family temple of the Fujiwaras, the second-most powerful clan after the imperial family from the 8th to 12th centuries. At one time as many as 175 buildings were erected on the Kofukuji Temple grounds, giving it significant religious and political power up until the 16th century; through centuries of civil wars and fires, however, most of the structures were destroyed. Only a handful of buildings remain, but even these were rebuilt after the 13th century.

The **five-story pagoda,** first erected in 730, was burned down five times. The present pagoda dates from 1426 and is an exact replica of the original; at 50m (164 ft.) tall, it's the second-tallest pagoda in Japan (the tallest is at Toji Temple in Kyoto). Also of historical importance is the **Eastern Golden Hall (Tokondo),** originally constructed in 726 by Emperor Shomu to speed the recovery of the ailing Empress Gensho. Rebuilt in 1415, it houses several priceless images, including a bronze statue of Yakushi Nyorai, a Buddha believed to cure illnesses, which was installed by Emperor Shomu on behalf of his sick wife; a 12th-century wooden bodhisattva of wisdom, long worshiped by scholar monks and today by pupils hopeful of passing university entrance exams; and the 12 Heavenly Guards, wooden reliefs carved in the 12th century.

But the best thing to see here is the temple's **Treasure House (Kokuhokan)** ★★, which displays many statues and works of art originally contained in the temple's buildings, many of them National Treasures. Most famous are a statue of standing Ashura carved in the 8th century and a bronze head of Yakushi Nyorai, but my favorites are the six 12th-century carved wooden statues representing priests of the Kamakura Period with fascinating facial features that render them strikingly human.

© **0742/22-7755.** Admission to Treasure House ¥500 adults, ¥400 junior-high and high-school students, ¥150 elementary-school students; Eastern Golden Hall ¥300 adults, ¥200 junior-high and high-school students, ¥100 elementary-school students. Daily 9am–5pm.

Nara National Museum (Nara Kokuritsu Hakubutsukan) ★   To the east of Kofukuji, this museum opened in 1895 to house invaluable Buddhist art and archaeological relics and has since expanded into a second building, used for special exhibits. Many masterpieces formerly in Nara's temples are now housed here, including Buddhist sculptures from various periods in Japan's history; paintings, masks, scrolls, calligraphy; and archaeological objects obtained from temple ruins, tombs, and sutra mounds. Unfortunately, although items are identified in English, explanations of their historic significance are not. You'll spend 20 to 30 minutes here.

© **0742/22-7771.** www.narahaku.go.jp. Admission ¥500 adults, ¥250 high-school and college students, free for children and seniors. Special exhibits cost more. Tues–Sun 9:30am–5pm.

Todaiji Temple ★★★   Nara's premier attraction is Todaiji Temple and its **Great Buddha (Daibutsu),** Japan's largest bronze Buddha. When Emperor Shomu ordered construction of both the temple and Daibutsu in the mid-700s, he intended to make Todaiji the headquarters of all Buddhist temples in the land. As part of his plans for a Buddhist utopia, he commissioned work for this huge bronze statue of Buddha; it took eight castings to complete this remarkable work of art. At a height of more than 15m (50 ft.), the Daibutsu is made of 437 tons of bronze, 286 pounds of pure gold, 165 pounds of mercury, and 7 tons of vegetable wax. However, thanks to Japan's frequent natural calamities, the Buddha of today isn't quite what it used to be. In 855, in what must have been a whopper of an earthquake, the statue lost its head. It was repaired in 861, but alas, the huge wooden building housing the Buddha was burned twice during wars, melting the Buddha's head. The present head dates from 1692.

Be sure to walk in a circle around the Great Buddha to see it from all angles. Behind the statue is a model of how the Daibutsuden used to look, flanked by two massive pagodas. Behind the Great Buddha to the right is a huge wooden column with a small hole in it near the ground. According to popular belief, if you can manage to crawl through this opening, you'll be sure to reach enlightenment (seemingly a snap for children). You can also get your English-language fortune for ¥200 by shaking a bamboo canister until a wooden stick with a number comes out; the number corresponds to a piece of paper. Mine told me that though I will win, it will be of no use, an illness will be serious, and the person for whom I am waiting will not come. And the monk who gave me the fortune said mine was a good one!

The wooden structure housing the Great Buddha, called **Daibutsuden,** was also destroyed several times through the centuries; the present structure dates from 1709. Measuring 48m (160 ft.) tall, 57m (187 ft.) long, and 50m (165 ft.) wide, it's the largest wooden structure in the world—but is only two-thirds its original size. My architect sister, just completing a year's trip around the world with her family, declared the Daibutsuden among the most magnificent buildings she had ever seen.

© **0742/22-5511.** Admission ¥500 adults, ¥300 children. Mar daily 8am–5pm; Apr–Sept daily 7:30am–5:30pm; Oct daily 7:30am–5pm; Nov–Feb daily 8am–4:30pm.

Kasuga Grand (Taisha) Shrine ★   A stroll through the park will bring you to one of my favorite Shinto shrines in the Kyoto area. Originally the tutelary shrine of the powerful Fujiwara family, it was founded in 768 and, according to Shinto concepts of purity, was torn down and rebuilt every 20 years in its original form until 1863. As virtually all empresses hailed from the Fujiwara family, the shrine enjoyed a privileged status with the imperial family. Nestled in the midst of verdant woods, it's a shrine of vermilion-colored pillars and an astounding 3,000 stone and bronze lanterns. The most spectacular time to visit is mid-August or the beginning of February, when all 3,000 lanterns are lit. Here, too, you can pay ¥200 for an *omikuji,* a slip of paper on which your fortune is written in English. If the fortune is unfavorable, you can conveniently negate it by tying the piece of paper to the twig of a tree. Although admission to the grounds is free, admission is charged for the garden of Kasuga Grand Shrine, **Shin-en,** a botanical garden preserving about 300 varieties of native Japanese plants and famous for its wisteria (it's located to the left on the approach to the shrine), and to the **Homotsuden,** a treasure house displaying costumes, swords, and armor. Fork out the extra yen only if you have time and the interest.

© **0742/22-7788.** Free admission to grounds; Shin-en ¥500 adults, ¥250 children; Homotsuden ¥420 adults, ¥315 junior- and senior-high students, ¥210 children. Grounds daily 6:30am–6pm summer, 7am–4:30pm winter; Homotsuden and Shin-en Tues–Sun 9am–4pm.

THE HORYUJI TEMPLE AREA ★★★

Founded in 607 by Prince Shotoku as a center for Buddhism in Japan, **Horyuji Temple** ★★★ (© **0745/75-2555**) is one of Japan's most significant gems for historic architecture, art, and religion. It was from here that Buddhism blossomed and spread throughout the land. Today about 45 buildings remain, some of them dating from the end of the 7th century and comprising what are probably the oldest wooden structures in the world. Although they are the main reason people come here, it's the atmosphere of the compound itself that I love—serene, ancient, and a fitting tribute to Prince Shotoku, founder of Buddhism in Japan and much revered still today. Little wonder Horyuji was selected as Japan's first UNESCO World Cultural Heritage Site, in 1993 (for details on reaching Horyuji, see "Essentials," above).

At the western end of the grounds is the two-story, 17m-high (58-ft.) **Kondo,** or main hall, which is considered the oldest building at Horyuji Temple, erected sometime between the 6th and 8th centuries. It contains Buddhas commemorating Prince Shotoku's parents, protected by Japan's oldest set of four heavenly guardians (from the late 7th or early 8th c.). Next to the main hall is Japan's oldest **five-story pagoda,** dating from the foundation of the temple and considered the most important structure of Buddhist temples, as it is here that relics of the Buddha are enshrined; it contains four scenes from the life of Buddha. The **Gallery of Temple Treasures,** or Daihozoden, constructed in 1998, contains statues, tabernacles, and other works of art from the 7th and 8th centuries, many of them National Treasures. On the eastern precincts of Horyuji Temple is an octagonal building called **Yumedono Hall,** or the Hall of Visions, built in 739 as a sanctuary to pray for the repose of Prince Shotoku.

Admission to Kondo, Gallery of Temple Treasures, and Yumedono Hall is ¥1,000 for adults and ¥500 for children. The grounds are open daily from 8am to 5pm (to 4:30pm Nov 4–Feb 21).

Just behind Yumedono is ⑩ **Chuguji Temple** (© **0745/75-2106**), once part of a large nunnery built for members of the imperial family. It contains two outstanding National Treasures: The wooden statue of **Nyoirin Kannon Bosatsu,** dating from the 7th century, is noted for the serene and compassionate expression on her face. The **Tenjukoku Mandala,** the oldest piece of embroidery in Japan, was originally about 5m (16 ft.) long and was created by Shotoku's consort and her female companions after Shotoku's death at the age of 48. It shows scenes from the Land of Heavenly Longevity, where only those with good karma are invited by the Buddha in the afterlife and where Shotoku surely resides. Only a replica of the fragile embroidery is now on display. Open daily from 9am to 4:30pm (to 4pm Oct–Mar 20); admission is ¥400 for adults, ¥200 for children.

WHERE TO STAY

Although you can see Nara in a day trip from Kyoto or Osaka, I've included some recommendations for an overnight stay for more leisurely sightseeing. An extra incentive for staying overnight is provided from mid-July through September, when many of Nara's most important historic buildings, like Todaiji Temple, are lit at night, making for a romantic nighttime stroll.

Hotel Nikko Nara ★   This hotel next to the West exit of the JR Nara station is one of Nara's most convenient: Drop off your bags, hop on a rental bicycle to see the sights, and then soak away all cares in the hotel's large public baths. Rooms are comfortable, with fluffy quilted spreads and plenty of desk space. The best rooms are on the 9th and 10th floors with great views toward distant mountains and Nara's temples, especially beautiful when lit at night in summer.

8–1 Sanjo-hommachi, Nara 630-8122. ℂ **0742/35-8831**. Fax 0742/35-6868. www.jalhotels.com. 330 units. ¥12,000 single; ¥20,000–¥30,000 double. AE, DC, MC, V. Station: JR Nara (1 min.). **Amenities:** 4 restaurants; lounge; rental bikes (per day: ¥500 for regular bike, ¥1,500 for electric bike); lobby computer (¥100 for 10 min.); concierge; smoke-free rooms. In room: A/C, TV, fridge, hair dryer, Internet.

(104) **Kikusuiro ★★★**   You can't find a more beautiful example of a Japanese-style *ryokan* than this lovely 120-year-old inn, an imposing structure with an ornate Japanese-style roof, surrounded by a white wall, and designated a private cultural asset by the Ministry of Culture. Rooms, some of which face Ara-ike Pond, are outfitted with scrolls and antiques and are connected to one another with rambling wooden corridors. There's also a beautiful garden. The manager, Mr. Itoh, speaks English.

1130 Takahata-cho Bodaimachi, Nara 630-8301. ℂ **0742/23-2001**. Fax 0742/26-0025. 14 units, 8 with bathroom. ¥30,000–¥40,000 per person. Rates include 2 meals but exclude tax and service charge. AE, DC, MC, V. South of Nara Park's Kofukuji 5-story pagoda on Sanjo Dori (corner of Rte. 308 and 369). Station: Kintetsu Nara (10 min.) or JR Nara (15 min.). **Amenities:** 2 restaurants. In room: A/C, TV, minibar.

Nara Hotel ★★★ (Finds)   One of the most famous places to stay in Nara (and with a front-desk staff eager to please), the Nara Hotel sits like a palace atop a hill on the south edge of Nara Park. Built in 1909 in the Momoyama Period style of architecture and similar to Japan's other hotels built to accommodate foreigners who poured into the country following the Meiji Restoration, it's constructed as a Western-style hotel but has many Japanese features. You have your choice of accommodations in the old section of the hotel with its wide corridors, high ceilings, antique light fixtures, fireplaces (no longer in use), and comfortable old-fashioned decor, or in the new addition, which opened in 1984 and offers larger modern rooms and verandas overlooking woods or the old town. I prefer the atmosphere of the older rooms: Those facing the city are less expensive than those in the new wing, while deluxe twins have more amenities and views of a pond or park (*note:* only the newer wing has an elevator).

Nara-Koennai, Nara 630-8301. ℂ **0742/26-3300**. Fax 0742/23-5252. www.narahotel.co.jp. 129 units. ¥18,480 single; ¥28,875–¥57,750 double. 10% discount for holders of Japan Rail Pass. AE, DC, MC, V. An 8-min. taxi ride from the train station. **Amenities:** 2 restaurants; bar; lounge; room service. In room: A/C, TV, hair dryer, Internet, minibar.

Seikan-so ★ (Value) This is a lovely choice in inexpensive Japanese-style accommodations. It boasts a beautiful garden, complete with azalea bushes and manicured trees—the kind of garden usually found only at *ryokan* costing twice as much. Located in quaint Naramachi, a historic neighborhood about a 10-minute walk south of Nara Park, the traditional Japanese building dates from 1916 and wraps around the inner garden. Unfortunately, the rooms are beginning to show their age, but all is forgiven if you can get one of the four facing the garden—be sure to request one when making your reservation. The friendly owners speak English, and both a Japanese or Western breakfast is available.

29 Higashi-Kitsuji-cho, Nara 630-8327. ℂ **0742/22-2670.** Fax 0742/22-2670. seikanso@chive.ocn.ne.jp. 9 units, none with bathroom. ¥4,200 per person. Breakfast ¥473–¥735 extra. AE, MC, V. Loop bus 1 to Kitakyobate stop (1 min.). Station: Kintetsu Nara (12 min.) or JR Nara (25 min.). **Amenities:** Lobby computer w/free Internet. *In room:* A/C, TV, no phone.

WHERE TO DINE

(105) **Harishin ★★★ (Finds)** OBENTO Many tourists never see this lovely part of old Nara near Gangoji Temple, called Naramachi and consisting of narrow lanes and traditional wooden homes and shops. The restaurant itself is a 200-year-old house of ocher-colored walls and a wood-slat facade, and dining is on tatami with a view of a garden. Only an obento that changes with the season, the creation of chef-owner Nakagawa-san, is served (a mini-kaiseki meal is also available only in the evening for ¥4,000, but only if you make a reservation 2 days in advance). My obento included an aperitif wine, light tofu flavored with sesame, soup, rice, pickled vegetables, tempura, and various exquisitely prepared bite-size morsels of shrimp, chicken, potatoes wrapped in bacon, and scallops. A meal here is highly recommended.

15 Nakashinya-cho. ℂ **0742/22-2669.** Reservations required for kaiseki 2 days in advance. Obento ¥2,900. AE, DC, MC, V. Tues–Sun 11:30am–2:30pm and 6–8pm (last order); closed Tues if Mon is a national holiday. A 5-min. walk south of Sarusawa-ike Pond, on the road that leads south from the west edge of the pond (stop at the tourist office for directions).

Noh CONTINENTAL This looks like an unlikely place for a meal. Under management of the Nara Hotel and housed in the Nara Prefecture Public Hall, which looks like some kind of modern temple building at the east end of Nara Park, this restaurant would be rather ordinary if it weren't for one thing: a glass wall overlooking an expanse of lawn and manicured trees. It offers limited main courses like fried prawns with tartar sauce and lighter fare like spaghetti and curry rice from an English-language menu, as well as daily specials and a Japanese *teishoku* (set meal).

Nara Park. ℂ **0742/27-0620.** Main dishes ¥840–¥1,890; set meals ¥2,625–¥4,725; teishoku ¥1,575. AE, DC, MC, V. Tues–Sun 11am–5pm.

Trattoria Piano ITALIAN If you find yourself hungry near the station, try this restaurant in downtown Nara. Located on the second floor above a bar, it offers pastas, pizzas (both Napoli style and those with Japanese ingredients), as well as main dishes like veal scaloppini or grilled pork with lemon sauce, along with a fish of the day.

15–1 Hashimoto-cho. ℂ **0742/26-1837.** Pizza ¥1,480–¥1,680; main dishes ¥1,580–¥1,890. MC, V. Daily 11am–2:30pm and 5–10pm (Fri–Sat to 11pm). Station: JR Nara (8 min.) or Kintetsu Nara (3 min.), on the corner of Sanjo Dori and the Higashimuki covered shopping arcade.

The Rest of Western Honshu

In addition to Tokyo, Kyoto, and the Japan Alps (covered in previous chapters), the island of Honshu has numerous other towns and attractions in its western half that are well worth a visit. As the largest of Japan's islands and home to 80% of the country's population, Honshu is where most of the country's important historical events took place; you'll find many castles, gardens, temples, shrines, and other famous sights linked to the past here. Western Honshu's climate ranges from snowy winters in its mountain ranges to subtropical weather in the south. The middle of the island is traversed by Japan's longest river, the Shinano. With all this to offer, it's little wonder that many travelers to Japan never make it off this central island.

1 NAGOYA

366km (227 miles) W of Tokyo; 147km (92 miles) E of Kyoto; 186km (116 miles) E of Osaka

Nagoya was founded as a castle town almost 400 years ago on orders of Tokugawa Ieyasu, who considered its strategic position on the Tokaido Highway useful for controlling Osaka and other points west. Today, Nagoya is Japan's fourth-largest city with a population of 2.2 million—yet it's a place most foreigners never stop to see. True, it doesn't have the attractions of many of the nation's other cities (it was leveled during World War II), but it does have a castle originally built by the first Tokugawa shogun, as well as one of Japan's most important Shinto shrines. You can also stroll through an aquarium famous for its penguins and sea turtles, visit the world-famous Noritake chinaware display rooms, spend hours at a nearby open-air architectural museum (one of my favorites in Japan), and watch cormorant fishing in summer. Nagoya, capital of Aichi Prefecture, is also home to an international airport and has long served as the gateway to the Japan Alps (see chapter 8) and Ise-Shima National Park (covered later in this chapter).

ESSENTIALS

GETTING THERE **By Plane** Known officially as the Central Japan International Airport (NGO) but dubbed **Centrair** (© **0569/38-1195;** www.centrair.jp/en), this airport occupies a man-made island in Ise Bay about 35km (22 miles) outside Nagoya. It boasts two hotels; 130 shops and restaurants (including Japan's largest duty-free store); ATMs in the arrival lobby that accept foreign credit cards; coin-operated computers (¥100 for 10 min.); a health clinic; post office; and even hot-spring baths, Fu-no-Yu (© **0569/38-7070;** daily 8am–10pm), with views of planes landing and taking off. A Tourist Information Center (TIC; © **0569/38-1050;** daily 9am–7pm) is located past the arrivals hall, but little English is spoken.

Meitetsu trains (www.meitetsu.co.jp) connect Centrair with Nagoya Station in 40 minutes by regular train (¥850) or in 28 minutes by express (¥1,200). A taxi from Centrair to downtown Nagoya will run about ¥14,000 and take 50 minutes.

By JR Train   The fastest way to get to Nagoya from Tokyo is by Shinkansen bullet train, which takes approximately 2 hours from Tokyo Station to **JR Nagoya Station** and costs ¥10,070 for an unreserved seat. Nagoya is 40 minutes from Kyoto and about 1 hour from Shin-Osaka Station.

By Bus   From Shinjuku Station in Tokyo, the **JR Highway Bus** (© 03/3515-1950; www.jrbuskanto.co.jp) costs ¥5,100 one-way for the 6-hour trip, with several departures daily. From Kyoto, the Highway Bus costs ¥2,500 and takes 2¾ hours; from Osaka, the trip takes just over 3 hours and costs ¥2,900. **Willer Express** (© 050/5805-0383; http://willerexpress.com) buses depart Tokyo's Shinjuku Station approximately four times daily, arriving at Nagoya Station approximately 6 hours later. The cost of these range from ¥3,200 to ¥7,500 depending on the date and type of seat; only online reservations are accepted.

VISITOR INFORMATION   Before departing Tokyo or Narita or Kansai international airports, stop by the Tourist Information Center for the leaflet "Nagoya and Vicinity," which contains a city map and transportation and sightseeing information (you can also download it from the Japan National Tourist Organization's website at www.jnto.go.jp by looking under "Browse by Destinations"). In Nagoya Station, the **Nagoya Tourist Information Center** (**TIC;** © 052/541-4301; daily 9am–7pm) is in the central concourse (look for the "?" signs) and has maps and brochures. There's another Tourist Information Center downtown, in the basement of Oasis 21 (which looks like a space ship) on Hisaya Dori near Sakae Station (© 052/963-5252; daily 10am–8pm).

Another good source for information is the **Nagoya International Center,** an 8-minute walk from Nagoya Station's Central exit straight down Sakura Dori (or take the subway one stop to Kokusai Center Station), located on the third floor of the Nagoya International Center Building, 1–47–1 Nagono (© 052/581-0100; www.nic-nagoya.or.jp; Tues–Sun 9am–7pm; closed second Sun in Feb and Aug). It's one of Japan's best facilities for foreign visitors and residents, with an English-speaking staff, a lounge area with a TV featuring CNN newscasts, Internet access, and lots of information on the city, including the free monthly publications *Nagoya Calendar* and *Avenues.* The center also offers practical advice on living in Japan, from how to get a visa to which doctors speak English. On the fourth floor, you can apply to visit a Japanese family in their home in the local **Home-Visit System.** You must apply in person, with your passport, no later than 5pm the day before your intended visit. Call © 052/581-5689 for details; the earlier you reserve, the better your chances of finding a family.

For recorded English-language information on events, concerts, festivals, and the arts, call © 052/581-0400; or go to www.nic-nagoya.or.jp. You can check the city's website at www.ncvb.or.jp.

INTERNET ACCESS   The Nagoya International Center (see "Visitor Information," above) provides 15-minute Internet access for ¥100. Cheaper is **Media Popeye,** with two locations in downtown Nagoya: across from the TV Tower at 3–6–15 Nishiki (© 052/955-0059), and on the ninth floor of Become Sakae at 3–32–6 Sakae (© 052/242-8369). Both are open 24 hours and charge ¥250 for 1 hour.

MONEY/MAIL   Nagoya's Central Post Office (© 052/564-2106), located to the left of the Sakura exit of JR Nagoya Station, is open for mail and money exchange Monday to Friday 9am to 6pm. In addition to a counter open 24 hours for mail, it has ATMs open 12:05am to 11:55pm Monday through Saturday and 12:05am to 8pm on Sunday.

ATTRACTIONS ●
Atsuta Jinja Shrine **25**
Nagoya Castle **4**
Ninomaru Garden **5**
Noritake Garden **2**
Tokugawa Art Museum **7**
Toyota Commemorative
  Museum of Industry &
  Technology **1**

ACCOMMODATIONS ■
the b Nagoya **21**
Ekimae MontBlanc Hotel **8**
Meiryu Ryokan **24**
Nagoya Marriott
  Associa Hotel **14**
Petite Ryokan Ichifuji **6**
Sofitel The Cypress
  Nagoya **9**
Toyoko Inn Nagoya-eki
  Sakuradori-guchi
  Honkan **10**
Tokyo Dai-Ichi
  Hotel Nishiki **17**
Westin Nagoya Castle **3**

DINING ◆
Farmer's Restaurant
  Moku Moku **13**
The 59's Café & Diner **19**
Hard Rock Cafe **16**
Hourai-ken
  Matsuzakaya **22, 26**
Mikuni **14**
Soramame **11**
Tiger Cafe **15, 20**
Torigin Honten **18**
Yabaton **23**
Yamamoto-ya Honten **12**

THE REST OF WESTERN HONSHU

10

NAGOYA

> **(Tips) A Note on Directions**
>
> All directions in the listings below are from Nagoya Station unless otherwise noted; the time in parentheses indicates walking time from the subway or bus stop indicated.

ORIENTATION Almost completely destroyed during World War II, Nagoya was rebuilt with wide, straight streets, many of which are named.

The ultramodern, twin-towered **JR Nagoya Station,** with its many train lines (including the Shinkansen), soars more than 50 stories above the skyline and contains Takashimaya department store, Tokyu Hands, a Marriott hotel, many restaurants, and an observatory. Built in 1999, it has been recognized by Guinness World Records as being the world's largest building containing a railway station. Clustered nearby are the Meitetsu Bus Terminal, Meitetsu Nagoya Station, the city bus terminal (on the second floor of Matsuzakaya department floor), Kintetsu Station, and a subway station for the Sakuradori and Higashiyama lines, as well as many hotels and a huge underground shopping arcade that stretches 6km (3¾ miles) and includes about 600 shops.

Most of the city's attractions spread out east of Nagoya Station (the Central/Sakuradori exit), including **Sakae,** the city's downtown area, located two subway stops from Nagoya Station and with many shops, restaurants, bars, and department stores. Also in Sakae is **Hisaya Odori,** a wide boulevard that stretches north and south with a park and a TV tower in its green meridian. North of Hisaya Odori is **Nagoya Castle,** while south is **Atsuta Jingu Shrine.**

GETTING AROUND The fastest way to get around is via the city's eight-line **subway** system, which is simple to use because station names, written in both English and Japanese, are assigned both a letter (representing the line; H, for example, is for the Higashiyama Line) and a number (so you can count how many stops before your destination). There are also English-language announcements and digital signs in trains. Probably the most important line for tourists is the loop **Meijo Line,** which runs through Sakae underneath Hisaya Odori and takes you to both Nagoya Castle (Station: Shiyakusho) and Atsuta Jingu Shrine (Station: Jingu-Nishi), with a branch, the Meiko Line, terminating at Nagoya Port with its aquarium. If you take the Meijo Line in the opposite direction, you'll eventually end up at the—I like this—Ozone stop. Individual tickets for the subway are ¥200 to ¥320, depending on the distance.

The **Nagoya Sightseeing Route Bus** (called (106) **Me-guru** in Japanese) departs from platform 0 of the city bus terminal (on the second floor of Matsuzakaya department store, to the left after exiting Nagoya Station) and is convenient for traveling to the Toyota museum, Noritake Garden, Nagoya Castle, Tokugawa Art Museum, and Sakae. It costs ¥200 per trip or ¥500 for the Me-guru 1-Day (the pass also gives slight discounts to most sights). It operates from 9:30am to about 5pm, hourly Tuesday through Friday and twice an hour weekends and holidays.

For **city buses,** you'll pay a flat fare of ¥200. There's also the private **Meitetsu Bus Line** with a terminal located at Nagoya Station; for these buses, take a ticket and pay the exact fare according to the digital panel display at the front when you get off.

There are several **transportation passes** worth considering if you'll be traveling a lot within a single day. For subways, there's the **Ichinichi Jo-sha,** a 1-day pass for ¥740 that

> **Tips** **Regional Traveling at a Discount**
>
> If you plan to spend a few days traveling between Nagoya, Osaka, Kyoto, and Ise-Shima, you can save money by purchasing a **Kintetsu Rail Pass** (www.kintetsu.co.jp) that covers travel throughout the region on Kintetsu's private lines. Available only for foreigners, it must be purchased *before arriving in Japan* at Kintetsu offices or authorized travel agencies. It costs ¥3,500 for adults and ¥1,850 for children and includes 5 days of unlimited travel (but only three trips on limited express trains). For ¥5,700, you can purchase the Kintetsu Rail Pass Wide, which adds a trip from Centrair or Kansai Airport, Mie Kotsu buses, and discount coupons for sightseeing spots.

allows you to ride as much as you want for a full day; for ¥850 you can ride as much as you want on subways, city buses, and Me-guru sightseeing bus. On the weekends the **Eco Pass** for ¥600 allows unlimited rides on subways and buses. For more information, drop by a Transportation Bureau Service Center (at Nagoya, Sakae, Kanayama, and other major stations), call ℂ **052/522-0111,** or go to the website www.kotsu.city.nagoya.jp/english.

SEEING THE SIGHTS

⑩⑦ **Tie-Dyeing Museum (Arimatsu Narumi Shibori Kaikan)**   During the days of the shogun, Arimatsu was a small village on the old Tokaido Highway. Its inhabitants made a living producing *shibori* (tie-dyed cotton cloth), which they then sold as towels to passing travelers. Today, Arimatsu is a suburb of Nagoya on its southeastern edge, yet it still retains its historic core, with several buildings remaining from the Edo Period and more than 2,500 people still involved in this cottage industry. This small museum pays tribute to the painstaking tie-dying process; more than 100 patterns are possible, with a single kimono requiring between 50,000 and 200,000 handmade stitches and taking 4 to 6 months to complete. A short film tells the history of Arimatsu tie-dying and the lengthy process involved in the craft: engraving a pattern, transferring the pattern to the cloth, tying the cloth, dying it, and then taking the stitches out. Several women are usually on hand practicing their trade; a small shop sells their wares. If you want, you can experience tying a handkerchief (¥1,050; allow 1 hr.), a curtain or table center (¥2,100; allow 2 hr.), or an apron or T-shirt (¥3,150; allow 3 hr.). Your craft will be tie-dyed later and sent to you; reservations are required.

3008 Arimatsu, Midori-ku. ℂ 052/621-0111. www.shibori-kaikan.com. Admission ¥300 adults, ¥100 children. Thurs–Tues 9:30am–5pm. From Meitetsu Nagoya Station, take a local Meitetsu train (not express) 30 min. to Arimatsu Station, walk straight out of the station, turn left at the bottom of the stairs, and then turn left at the sign for HATTORI RESIDENCE; the museum will be on the right (5 min.).

Atsuta Jingu Shrine   Because it contains one of the emperor's Three Sacred Treasures, this is revered as one of the three most important shrines in Japan. Founded in the 2nd century and last rebuilt in 1955, it enshrines the Grass-Mowing Sword (Kusanagi-no-Tsurugi), which is one of the Imperial Regalia of the Emperor. The other two sacred treasures are the Sacred Mirror (in the Ise Grand Shrines; see p. 373) and the Jewels (in the Imperial Palace in Tokyo; see p. 181). According to legend, the Grass-Mowing Sword was presented to a prince named Yamato-Takeru, who used it during a campaign against

> ## Fun Facts   Born to Rule
>
> Three of Japan's greatest rulers—generals Oda Nobunaga and Toyotomi Hideyo-shi, as well as Shogun Tokugawa Ieyasu—were all born in Nagoya.

rebels in eastern Japan; the rebels set a field of grass on fire, and the prince used the sword to mow down the grass, thereby quelling the fire. (*Atsuta* means "hot field" in Japanese.) Actually, there isn't much to see of the shrine—the sword is never on public display—yet this remains one of Nagoya's top attractions (especially on New Year's), and Japanese make pilgrimages here to pay their respects, first purifying their hands or mouths with water, then throwing coins into the money box, clapping to gain the attention of the gods, and bowing as they pray. A Treasure Hall displays exhibits that change monthly of items donated through the ages by members of the Imperial family, shoguns, feudal lords, and common people, including furniture, household goods, and, thanks to the legend of the Kusanagi-no-Tsurugi, an impressive number of swords and daggers. Surrounded by stately, ancient cypress trees, the shrine provides a nice respite from city life.

1-1-1 Jingu, Atsuta-ku. *(C)* 052/671-4151. www.atsutajingu.or.jp. Free admission to the grounds; Trea-sure Hall ¥300 adults, ¥150 children. Grounds daily dawn–dusk; treasure house daily 9am–4:30pm (closed last Wed and the following day of every month). Station: Jingu-mae (3 min.) via the Meitetsu train line from Meitetsu Nagoya Station or Jingu-Nishi via subway (7 min.).

Nagoya Castle ★   Built for his ninth son by Tokugawa Ieyasu, the first Tokugawa shogun, Nagoya Castle was completed in 1612 and served as both a strategic stronghold on the Tokaido Highway and a residence for members of the Owari branch of the Tokugawa family for almost 250 years, until the Meiji Restoration ended their rule in 1868. A shrewd and calculating shogun, Tokugawa forced feudal lords throughout Japan to contribute to the castle's construction, thereby depleting their resources and making it harder for them to rebel. Although Nagoya Castle was largely destroyed in World War II (only three turrets and three gates escaped destruction), the main *donjon* and other struc-tures, rebuilt in 1959, are almost carbon copies of the original. Like most reconstructed castles in Japan, this replica is made of ferroconcrete, yet it's still impressive from afar. Inside, the 20m-high (66-ft.) donjon is thoroughly modern and even has an elevator up to the fifth floor, where you have fine views of Nagoya and beyond. The castle houses treasures that escaped the bombing during World War II, including beautiful paintings on sliding doors and screens that once adorned the castle's Honmaru Palace (destroyed during World War II but presently being rebuilt the traditional way without the use of nails, a painstaking process that will take 10 years). Also on display are flintlocks, swords, helmets, and exhibits relating to the castle's construction and what life was like during the Edo Period.

Atop the *donjon* roof are two **golden dolphins,** replicas of those that perished during World War II and long thought to protect the castle from dreaded fires. The dolphins each weigh about 1,190 kilograms (2,650 lb.) and are made of cast bronze covered with 18-karat-gold scales. Incidentally, the dolphin on the south end—the favored, warmer side—is considered female, while the one relegated to the colder northern side is male. Through the centuries, the dolphins' gold scales have been stolen three times.

East of the castle is **Ninomaru Garden,** laid out at the time of the castle's construc-tion, converted to a dry Japanese landscape garden in 1716 and today one of the few remaining castle gardens in Japan. Besides providing a beautiful setting, it served as an emergency shelter for the lord in case of enemy attack. Stop by the **Ninomaru Tea House**—it's said that if you drink tea here when it's made with a golden kettle (available only on Fri), 5 years will be added to your life. That should allow you ample time to linger, but otherwise you can tour the castle and grounds in less than 1½ hours.

1-1 Honmaru, Naka-ku. 🕻 **052/231-1700.** Admission ¥500 adults, free for junior high and younger. Daily 9am–4:30pm. Station: Shiyakusho (5 min.). Me-guru sightseeing bus: Osakajo (1 min.).

Noritake Garden ★★★   Nagoya has been a pottery and porcelain production center for centuries; today, the city and its vicinity manufacture 90% of Japan's total export chinaware. The largest chinaware company in Japan is Noritake, founded in 1904 and known the world over for its fine tableware. You can learn more about Noritake by spending about an hour at the site of its former factory, beginning with the Welcome Center's short film depicting the history of Noritake. At the Craft Center, you'll see displays explaining the manufacturing and decorating processes involved in making porcelain, as well as watch artisans, who, unlike at most modern-day factories where work is largely automated, do almost all their work by hand. The Noritake Museum is probably my favorite part of the complex, with its examples of all the Noritake chinaware ever produced (including a great Art Deco collection). At the Canvas hall, all you ever wanted to know about the role ceramics plays in everyday life—from Washlet toilets to computers—is presented in hands-on displays activated by your own ceramic microchip card. And of course, there are also shops, including those selling Noritake fine chinaware, tableware for everyday use, and an outlet store.

3-1-36 Noritake Shinmachi, Nishi-ku. 🕻 **052/561-7290.** Admission to Craft Center and museum ¥500 adults, ¥300 high-school students, free for children and seniors; free admission to the Welcome Center, Canvas, and shops. Tues–Sun 10am–5pm (you must enter the Craft Center by 4pm); shops open until 6pm. Subway: Kamejima (5 min.). Me-guru sightseeing bus: Noritake Garden (1 min.). A 15-min. walk north of Nagoya Station.

Port of Nagoya Public Aquarium ★★★ **Kids**   Young Japanese flock to Nagoya's port area on weekends, drawn by a small amusement park, a maritime museum, a shopping complex, and sightseeing boats. But the Public Aquarium, one of Japan's largest, is the major draw for kids of all ages. For the kids there's a touch tank with sea urchins, starfish, and other animals, and an IMAX theater with shows on the hour (included in the entry price). In addition to displays of marine life from the seas around Japan, the aquarium is best known for its penguin tank, which copies the environment of the Antarctic with artificial falling snow and cold temperatures to maintain the penguins' reproductive cycle; the loggerhead and green turtles with a sand beach to encourage them to lay eggs; and its Beluga whales, including the only baby Beluga born in a Japanese aquarium. Not to be missed are the Beluga training sessions, held apparently to keep the Belugas from getting bored. There are also dolphin performances, which you can watch either above or below the water's surface of the second-largest show pool in the world. Count on 3 hours here, including the IMAX.

1-3 Minato-machi, Minato-ku. 🕻 **052/654-7080.** Admission ¥2,000 adults, ¥1,000 children. Tues–Sun 9:30am–5:30pm (to 5pm Nov–Mar, to 8pm July 21–Aug). Station: Nagoyako (exit 3, 7 min.)

Tokugawa Art Museum ★★★ **Finds**   Located on the grounds of a former mansion owned by the Owari branch of the Tokugawa family—with the original entry gate and a guardhouse still intact—this worthwhile museum houses a changing display of documents, samurai armor, swords, matchlocks, helmets, pottery, lacquerware, *noh* costumes and masks, and paintings that once belonged to the Tokugawa family, including objects inherited from the first Tokugawa shogun, Ieyasu. There are also replicas of structures and items that once adorned Nagoya Castle, including decorative alcoves, a teahouse, and a noh stage. Of the museum's nine National Treasures, most famous is the 12th-century picture scrolls of *The Tale of Genji,* but they're displayed only 1 week a year at the end of November (check with the tourist office); otherwise, replicas are on display. Excellent English-language explanations throughout the museum put the displays in historical context. You can easily spend 90 minutes here and in the museum's garden, the Tokugawaen, with a pond, waterfalls, and strolling paths.

For an even more memorable experience, make reservations to dine at the classy **Garden Restaurant Tokugawaen** ★ (② 052/932-7887), overlooking the garden's pond and serving fusion Japanese-French cuisine. Although its wooden veranda and stone foundation give it a traditional atmosphere, candles and jazz music playing in the background lend it a contemporary edge. Only set meals are available, with lunches ranging from ¥3,800 to ¥5,000 and dinners starting at ¥7,000. It's open daily from 11am to 2pm and 5 to 10pm (last order).

1017 Tokugawa-cho, Higashi-ku. ② **052/935-6262.** www.tokugawa-art-museum.jp. Admission to art museum ¥1,200 adults, ¥1,000 seniors, ¥700 university and high-school students, ¥500 children; combination ticket to museum and garden ¥1,350, ¥1,150, ¥850, and ¥570 respectively. Tues–Sun 10am–5pm (garden 9:30am–5:30pm). Me-guru sightseeing bus: Tokugawaen (1 min.). Station: Ozone (exit 3, 10 min.).

Toyota Commemorative Museum of Industry and Technology ★★ (Kids)

This museum seems an odd marriage: It's devoted to both textile machinery and automobile production and technology. That's because the Toyota Group, founded by Toyoda Sakichi, the inventor of automatic looms, has a long history of producing both. Housed at the site where the Toyota Group had its beginnings, in an attractive brick building dating from the Taisho Period (1912–25), the museum displays approximately 90 looms and textile machinery, from wooden hand looms to air-jet looms that utilize computer graphics. The automobile pavilion provides a historical chronology of automobile production, beginning with a replica of the first Toyota car (1935), early assembly lines using manpower, and automated assembly lines using industrial robots for everything from engine mounting to painting. There's also a display of both old and new Toyota cars and four films of how Toyota makes its cars, including design. Frequent demonstrations of looms (they're loud!), auto-making equipment (including robotics), a Swiss 1898 steam engine, and a trumpet-playing robot make this a fun destination for adults and kids alike. There's also a children's hands-on discovery room. Expect to spend 90 minutes here, longer if you opt for the ¥200 audio guide.

4-1-35 Noritake Shinmachi, Nishi-ku. ② **052/551-6115.** www.tcmit.org. Admission ¥500 adults, ¥300 junior-high and high-school students, ¥200 children, free for seniors. Tues–Sun 9:30am–5pm. Me-guru sightseeing bus: Toyota Commemorative Museum of Industry and Technology (Sangyo Gijutsu Kinenkan; 1 min.). Train: Meitetsu Line to Sako (3 min.). Subway: Kamejima (10 min.). Just north of the Noritake Craft Center, about a 25-min. walk from Nagoya Station.

In Nearby Inuyama City

Inuyama City has several worthwhile attractions, so you might want to come for a day of sightseeing and, in summer, top it off with cormorant fishing (see below). The **Inuyama Tourist Information Center,** in Inuyama Station (② **0568/61-6000;** www.city.inuyama.aichi.jp), is open daily 9am to 5pm. To reach Inuyama, take the Meitetsu rapid limited express from Meitetsu Nagoya Station (beside Nagoya Station) 25 minutes to either Inuyama Station (fare: ¥540) or one stop farther to Inuyama Yuen Station (fare: ¥590).

Japanese cities do not give exact street addresses. However, everyone will know where these attractions are.

Inuyama Castle ★   Constructed in 1537 atop a bluff overlooking the Kiso River, this four-story *donjon*—much smaller than most of Japan's castles—is Japan's oldest and is a designated National Treasure. It miraculously survived centuries of earthquakes (part of it was damaged by an 1891 earthquake but then repaired) and wars, including in 1584 when Toyotomi Hideyoshi and his 120,000 retainers used it to stage war against Tokugawa Ieyasu, whose forces were spread over Komaki Mountain. Owned by the same family from 1618 to 2004 (it's now under management of a foundation), it displays a few samurai outfits and offers a nice, expansive view over the river that's especially worth a look if you intend to join the nearby cormorant fishing. The castle is so diminutive you can see everything in 15 minutes.

(*) **0568/61-1711.** Admission ¥500 adults, ¥100 children. Daily 9am–5pm. Station: Inuyama (15 min.).

Museum Meiji Mura ★★★   Inuyama City's most important attraction is one of my favorite museums in Japan. In fact, it may well be the best reason for a Nagoya stopover. A 100-hectare (250-acre) open-air architectural museum, it features more than 65 buildings and structures dating from the Meiji Period (1868–1912), all beautifully situated on landscaped grounds on the shores of a lake. Before Japan opened its doors in the mid-1800s, unpainted wooden structures dominated Japanese architecture; after Western influences began infiltrating Japan, however, stone, brick, painted wood, towers, turrets, and Victorian features came into play. Unfortunately, earthquakes, war, fire, and developer greed have destroyed most of Japan's Meiji-Era buildings, making this a priceless collection.

On the grounds are Western homes that once belonged to foreigners living in Nagasaki and Kobe, official government buildings and schools, two churches and a cathedral, a post office, a bathhouse, a *kabuki* theater, a brewery, bridges, Japanese-style homes (including one that belonged to Japanese novelists Mori Ogai and Natsume Soseki), a martial-arts hall, an assembly hall used by Japanese immigrants in Hilo, Hawaii, and even a prison. Don't miss the front facade and lobby of the original Imperial Hotel in Tokyo, designed by Frank Lloyd Wright and containing some of the hotel's original Wright-designed furniture. In fact, most of the buildings display furniture and other items related to the building in which they're housed. You can mail a postcard from the post office, buy candy at the old candy shop, have coffee or tea in the Imperial Hotel sitting on original Wright-designed chairs, or stop for a drink at the brewery. Plan on spending at least 3 hours here.

(*) **0568/67-0314.** www.meijimura.com. Admission ¥1,600 adults, ¥1,200 seniors, ¥1,000 high-school students, ¥600 junior-high and elementary students. Daily 9:30am–5pm (to 4pm Nov–Feb; closed Mon Dec–Feb). Station: Inuyama, then bus from platform no. 2; 20 min. to Meiji Mura (¥410 one-way).

WATCHING CORMORANT FISHING ★★★

There are two places near Nagoya where you can watch **cormorant fishing** every night in summer (except during a full moon or the 2 or 3 days following a heavy rain). In this ancient, 1,300-year-old Japanese fishing method, trained *ukai* (seabirds) dive into the water in search of *ayu*, a small Japanese trout. At nightfall, wooden fires are lit in suspended cages at the fronts of long wooden boats to attract the ayu, whereupon leashed cormorants are released into the water. To ensure that the cormorants don't swallow the fish, the birds are fitted with neck rings.

In **Inuyama,** cormorant fishing takes place on the Kiso River from June to mid-October. Spectators can board wooden boats departing from 6 to 8pm June to August, or 5:30 to 7:45pm September and October to observe the spectacle firsthand. While waiting for the full darkness that must descend before the fishing takes place, you can dine on *obento* box meals for ¥2,500 or ¥3,500, which you must order at least 2 days in advance, or you can bring your own food and drink onboard with you (beer and soft drinks are also sold before boarding). In any case, the actual fishing itself occupies only 20 minutes, so board one of the earlier boats to make it worthwhile. Call **Kigo Gawa Kanko** (© **0568/61-0057**) to make reservations and then pick up your tickets at its ticket office near the bridge (located about a 5-minute walk from Inuyama Yuen Station). Tickets for boarding the boats and watching the fishing cost ¥2,500 for adults and ¥1,250 for children in June and September to mid-October, ¥2,800 and ¥1,400 respectively in July and August. Alternatively, though it's not traditional, you can also watch cormorant fishing during the day, on Tuesday, Thursday, and Saturday, with boats departing from 11:30am to 1:45pm and costing ¥3,800 for adults and ¥2,900 for children, including lunch.

The city of **Gifu** features cormorant fishing from mid-May to mid-October on the Nagaragawa River, where you can view the entire spectacle aboard a small wooden boat. To reach Gifu, take either the Meitetsu train or the JR train from Nagoya to Gifu Station (20 min.; ¥540). From there, take a bus (¥200) 16 minutes to Nagara-bashi, where you'll see the ticket office for the **Gifu City Cormorant Fishing Viewing Boat Office** (**Gifu-shi Ukai Kanransen Jimusho;** © **058/262-0104**). To be assured a place, reservations should be made in advance. Tickets cost ¥3,300 for adults and ¥2,900 for children for the 6:15pm boarding every day and weekend boardings at 6:45pm and 7:15pm. On weekdays, the 6:45 and 7:15pm are ¥3,000 for adults and ¥2,600 for children. Note that you are advised to bring your own snacks or meal and drinks, as there is no place to purchase them at the boat office. Cormorant fishing begins around 7:45pm. For more information, go to **www.gifucvb.or.jp.**

WHERE TO STAY
Expensive

In addition to the hotels listed below, the **Nagoya Hilton,** 1–3–3 Sakae, Naka-ku, Nagoya 460-0008 (© **800/445-8667** in the U.S. and Canada, or 052/212-1111; www.hilton.com), offers 438 units to mostly foreign business travelers.

Nagoya Marriott Associa Hotel ★★ A location right over Nagoya Station makes this Nagoya's most convenient hotel. Occupying the 15th to 52nd floors of Nagoya's tallest building, it offers the city's best views (ask for a room facing the castle and downtown; higher floors cost more), not to mention quick access to the many restaurants and shops on the lower floors of this "vertical city." Despite its central location, it doesn't skimp on facilities, offering a health club; good-size, up-to-date guest rooms; and a wide range of in-house dining possibilities (to eat at French restaurant Mikuni, considered Nagoya's top restaurant, make reservations months in advance). Don't miss having a drink at the 52nd-floor Sky Lounge Zenith (daily 11:30am–midnight; ¥1,000 music charge in the evening)—but all this is assuming you can even find the hotel. Guests arriving by train not only have to search for the obscure ground-floor entryway, but have to battle the crowds taking elevators to the many restaurants (reception is on the 15th floor). Luckily, it's worth it.

(Tips) A Double or a Twin?

For the sake of convenience, the price for two people in a room is listed as a "double" in this book. Japanese hotels, however, differentiate between rooms with a double bed or two twin beds, usually with different prices. Although most hotels charge more for a twin room, sometimes the opposite is true; if you're looking for a bargain, therefore, be sure to inquire about prices for both. Note, too, that hotels usually have more twin rooms than doubles, for the simple reason that Japanese couples, used to their own futon, traditionally prefer twin beds.

1-1-4 Meieki, Nakamura-ku, Nagoya 450-6002. ✆ **800/228-9290** in the U.S. and Canada, or 052/584-1113. Fax 052/584-1112. www.associa.com/nma. 774 units. ¥24,000–¥36,000 single; ¥32,000–¥44,000 double; from ¥40,000 executive-floor double. AE, DC, MC, V. Station: Nagoya (below the hotel). **Amenities:** 6 restaurants, including Mikuni (p. 369), 2 bars; 2 lounges; concierge; executive-level rooms; 20m (66-ft.) 4-lane pool, Jacuzzi, and fitness gym (fee: ¥3,150); room service; smoke-free rooms. *In room:* A/C, TV, hair dryer, Internet (fee: ¥1,575 per day), minibar, trouser press.

Sofitel The Cypress Nagoya ★★ With a contemporary, boutiquelike atmosphere, this hotel has a great location near Nagoya Station and friendly multilingual service. Standard rooms are fairly small but comfortable, and because some face other buildings, ask for a room on a higher floor, where you might have an urban view (ones facing the station are my favorite). Deluxe rooms add space, larger windows, and sink and vanity areas separate from the bathrooms. In short, you won't go wrong staying here, especially if you're looking for a small, personable hotel near the station.

2-43-6 Meieki, Nakamura-ku, Nagoya 450-0002. ✆ **052/571-0111.** Fax 052/569-1717. www.sofitelthe cypress.com. 115 units. ¥20,000–¥23,000 single; ¥25,000–¥32,000 double. AE, DC, MC, V. Station: Nagoya (5 min.). Turn left out of the Sakura Dori/Central exit and then the 1st right just before the post office. **Amenities:** 2 restaurants; bar; room service; smoke-free rooms. *In room:* A/C, TV, hair dryer, Internet (fee: ¥1,050 per day), minibar.

Westin Nagoya Castle ★★ Situated just west of Nagoya Castle, about 2.5km (1½ miles) from Nagoya Station and Sakae, the chief attraction of this 30-some-year-old hotel—a local favorite for special occasions and meetings—is the wonderful views of the moat and castle from its rooms, especially at night when the castle is illuminated. Rooms are spacious enough and feature Heavenly Beds, but it's worth staying here only if you get a room with a view (and for most room types, you won't pay more for that view). Otherwise, the location is rather inconvenient, though courtesy shuttle buses to Nagoya Station once an hour are a big plus, and joggers might like the proximity of the castle grounds and an adjacent park; ask the concierge for its map of a 3.6km (2.2-mile) suggested jogging route.

3-19 Hinokuchi-cho, Nishi-ku, Nagoya 451-8551. ✆ **800/937-8461** in the U.S. and Canada, or 052/521-2121. Fax 052/531-3313. www.castle.co.jp/wnc. 195 units. ¥26,000 single; ¥34,000–¥43,000 double; from ¥26,000 executive single; from ¥34,000 executive double. AE, DC, MC, V. Subway: Tsurumai Line to Sengencho (10 min.). Bus: Free shuttle from Nagoya Station every hour on the hour 10am–8pm (15-min. ride). **Amenities:** 5 restaurants; bar; lounge; babysitting; concierge; executive-level rooms; indoor 5-lane 25m (80-ft.) pool and Jacuzzi (fee: ¥1,575) w/exercise room and sauna; room service; smoke-free rooms. *In room:* A/C, TV, hair dryer, minibar, Wi-Fi.

the b nagoya ★   Japanese business hotels used to be dingy, depressing affairs, but this stylish chain illustrates how far they've come. Known for its contemporary, upbeat decor, reasonable rates, and good downtown locations, the b offers smallish, spotless rooms with focused bed lights and deep tubs (two features I especially appreciate), free coffee in the lobby, and a convenience store on-site. Sakae, with its shops, restaurants, and nightlife, is a few minutes' walk away.

4-15-23 Sakae, Naka-ku, Nagoya 460-0008. ⓒ **052/241-1500.** Fax 052/264-1732. www.ishinhotels. com/theb-nagoya/en. 219 units. ¥8,800–¥10,000 single; ¥12,000–¥16,000 double. AE, DC, MC, V. Station: Sakae (exit 13, 3 min.). On Hisaya Odori, facing the park. **Amenities:** Restaurant; lobby computer w/free Internet; smoke-free rooms. *In room:* A/C, TV, fridge, hair dryer, Internet.

Ekimae MontBlanc Hotel (**Value**   There isn't a lot to say about this simple hotel except that it's close to the station and offers mostly single functional rooms at reasonable rates. The cheapest singles are minuscule, and though double rooms are adequate in size, there are only 13 of them. The hotel's corner location frees it from proximity to taller buildings, which means you can actually look outside rather than face another building (ask for a room on a higher floor). Otherwise, there's not much to crow about; this is strictly a sleeping machine with a fancy name.

3-14-1 Meieki, Nakamura-ku, Nagoya 450-0002. ⓒ **052/541-1121.** Fax 052/541-1140. www.montblanc-hotel.jp. 277 units. ¥7,600–¥8,800 single; ¥12,200–¥13,300 double. AE, DC, MC, V. Station: Nagoya (2 min.). Turn left out of the Sakura Dori/Central exit and then the 1st right just before the post office. **Amenities:** 2 restaurants. *In room:* A/C, TV, fridge, hair dryer, Wi-Fi (in half the rooms).

Tokyo Dai-Ichi Hotel Nishiki ★★ (**Finds**   This smart-looking hotel is my top pick among Nagoya's moderately priced finds in the city center. Located in the heart of Nagoya's nightlife and business district on Nishiki Dori, it has prices comparable to those of a business hotel but with a much classier atmosphere and decor. Targeting business-people as well as female travelers (some may find the flower-patterned bedspreads too feminine), it offers smartly decorated rooms with large desks and larger-than-usual bath towels. There's only one double, but some of the standard twins have two sinks (good for two people trying to get ready at the same time), while deluxe twins are separated into living and sleeping areas and even have two TVs. Rooms facing another building have glazed windows, so if seeing out is important to you, be sure to say so.

3-18-21 Nishiki, Naka-ku, Nagoya 460-0003. ⓒ **052/955-1001.** Fax 052/953-6783. www.tdh-nishiki. co.jp. 233 units. ¥9,240–¥11,500 single; ¥15,015–¥25,410 double. AE, DC, MC, V. Station: Sakae (exit 1, 3 min.). **Amenities:** 3 restaurants; concierge; smoke-free rooms. *In room:* A/C, TV, fridge, hair dryer, Internet.

Inexpensive

In addition to the choices here, Toyoko Inn has several properties in Nagoya. Most convenient to Nagoya Station is **Toyoko Inn Nagoya-eki Sakuradori-guchi Honkan,** 3–16–1 Meieki (ⓒ **052/571-1045;** www.toyoko-inn.com), with an annex catty-corner across the street. Rates start at ¥6,195 for one person and ¥8,715 for two, including Japanese breakfast, free in-room Internet and free use of lobby computers. From Nagoya Station's Central Exit, walk straight on Sakura-dori and turn left at the Junkudo bookstore.

Meiryu Ryokan   A Japanese Inn Group member and family-owned for more than 60 years, this is a no-nonsense place. Customers are a mix of travelers (including families), students, and during the week, Japanese businessmen. *Tatami* rooms are spotless and cozy, with more space and features than most other hotel rooms in this price category, including a closet, but have glazed windows beyond the *shoji* screens. The men's public bathroom has a sauna, but the female bath doesn't and is smaller (female guests are fewer). The owners' son, who often clerks the front desk and is the third-generation innkeeper, speaks English well and is very helpful.

2-4-21 Kamimaezu, Naka-ku, Nagoya 463-0013. ✆ **052/331-8686.** Fax 052/321-6119. www.japan-net. ne.jp/~meiryu. 22 units, none with bathroom. ¥5,250 single; ¥8,400 double; ¥11,025 triple. Japanese breakfast ¥630 extra; Japanese dinner ¥2,310 extra (advance dinner reservations required; not available Sun). AE, MC, V. Station: Kamimaezu (exit 3, 4 min.). Walk straight out of the station 1 block and turn left; it's on the 2nd block, on the left. **Amenities:** Lobby computer w/free Internet. *In room:* A/C, TV, Internet.

Petit Ryokan Ichifuji ★ This Japanese Inn Group *ryokan* is way out there in Ozone (pronounced *ozon-ay*)—so be sure to get directions before heading out. Ishida Tomiyasu, who speaks a little English, inherited the 50-year-old ryokan from his father and grandfather, and together with his wife, Yoko, has created a restful Japanese interior with wood floors and wainscoting, calligraphy, and a cypress public bath (daily 24 hr.). All except one of the rooms is tatami, with rates that vary depending on the season and room size.

1-7 Saikobashi-dori, Kita-ku, Nagoya 462-0818. ✆ **052/914-2867.** Fax 052/981-6836. www.jin.ne.jp/ ichifuji. 10 units, none with bathroom. ¥6,300–¥8,000 single; ¥10,000–¥14,000 double; ¥16,500–¥20,400 triple. Rates include continental breakfast. Rates 10% higher on nights before holidays and in peak season. AE, MC, V. Station: Heiandori (exit 2, 3 min.); Ozone (10 min.). **Amenities:** Restaurant (w/computer and free Internet until noon). *In room:* A/C, TV, Wi-Fi (in some), no phone.

WHERE TO DINE

One of Nagoya's specialties is **kishimen,** fettuccine-like broad and flat white noodles usually served in a soup stock with soy sauce, tofu, dried bonito shavings, and chopped green onions. Nagoya is also famous for **miso nikomi udon**—udon noodles served in a bean-paste soup and flavored with such ingredients as chicken and green onions. **Cochin** (free-range) chicken and **tonkatsu** (breaded pork cutlets) with a red miso sauce are also Nagoya favorites.

Around Nagoya Station

The best place for one-stop dining is Nagoya Station itself, on the 12th and 13th floors of one of the twin towers atop the station. Called **Towers Plaza,** it offers about 40 food-and-beverage outlets (in addition to Farmer's Restaurant Moku Moku; see below) serving noodles, sushi, tempura, tofu dishes, grilled eel, *shabu-shabu,* steaks, Chinese food, Indian curries, Italian fare, and more, most with plastic-food displays.

If you reserve early enough (at least 2 months in advance), you might also get one of the coveted tables at French restaurant **Mikuni** on the 52nd floor of the Nagoya Marriott Associa Hotel (✆ **052/584-1111**). Decorated in Art Nouveau style and considered by some to be the city's finest restaurant due to its celebrated chef Kiyomi Mikuni (who has restaurants also in Tokyo and Sapporo) and healthy *cuisine naturelle,* it offers set lunches for ¥6,800 to ¥9,000 from 11:30am to 1:30pm and set dinners for ¥14,000 to ¥17,000 from 5:30 to 9pm (last order), with a menu that changes monthly.

Farmer's Restaurant Moku Moku ★ VARIED JAPANESE Boasting its own farm in Mie Prefecture, where it grows its own organic produce and raises cows, pigs, and chickens, as well as its butcher shop, this buffet restaurant offers lots of choices, including soups, vegetables, fish, breads (from its own bakery), sausages, desserts, and vegetable juices. To find Moku Moku in the "city" that Nagoya Station has become, take an escalator to the second floor and then transfer to an elevator for the 13th floor. There's a branch

> **(Tips) A Note on Japanese Characters**
>
> Many establishments and attractions in Japan do not have signs in Roman (English-language) letters. Those that don't are indicated in this guide with an oval with a number that corresponds to a number in chapter 17 showing the Japanese equivalent. Thus, to find the Japanese for, say, **Soramame** (see below), refer to no. 108 in chapter 17.

downtown, on the seventh floor of La Chic shopping complex, 3–6–1 Sakae (✆ **052/241-0909**).

13th floor, Towers Plaza, Nagoya Station, 1-1-4 Meieki, Nakamura-ku. ✆ **052/587-0909.** Lunch buffet ¥1,850; dinner buffet ¥2,800. AE, DC, MC, V. Daily 11am–3pm and 5–9:30pm (last order).

(108) **Soramame** ★ (**Finds**) VARIED JAPANESE   This former bathhouse, built about 90 years ago, has found a second life as an airy restaurant with split-level dining. Primarily a drinking establishment popular with a young crowd, it offers a wide variety of choices, including avocado gratin, grilled chicken, and lots of vegetable dishes, from radishes to leeks to potatoes. Unfortunately, there's no English-language menu, but the Japanese menu does have hand-drawn pictures of some of its vegetables.

3–17–28 Meieki, Nakamura-ku. ✆ **052/566-5550.** Dishes ¥550–¥1,000. AE, DC, MC, V. Mon–Sat 5pm–midnight (last order). Station: Nagoya: (4 min.). From the Central Exit, walk straight down Sakura-dori and turn left at Junkudo bookstore; it's across the street from Toyoko Inn annex, to the right.

(109) **Yamamoto-ya Honten** UDON NOODLES   This chain noodle shop, a 2-minute walk from Nagoya Station, specializes in *miso nikomi udon*. Its noodles, all handmade, are thick, hard, and chewy and are served in a type of bean paste that's special to Nagoya. You can order it plain or with additions like tofu, cochin chicken, or pork (an English-language menu with explanations makes ordering easy), and if you like your noodles spicy, add spices to your food from the large bamboo container on your table. A small dish of vegetables (cabbage, shaved onion, cucumber) is brought to your table as soon as you're seated and is replenished free of charge.

25–9 Meieki, basement of the Horiuchi Building, Sakura Dori, Nakamura-ku. ✆ **052/565-0278.** Udon dishes ¥1,050–¥1,942. AE, DC, MC, V. Daily 11am–10pm. Station: Nagoya (exit 6, 2 min.); on Sakura Dori's north side, below Junkudo bookstore, in an area called "Gourmet Avenue."

In Sakae

If you are collecting T-shirts or are hungry for a burger, there's a **Hard Rock Cafe** on Hirokoji Street not far from the Hilton, at 1–4–5 Sakae, Naka-ku (✆ **052/218-3220;** Sun–Thurs 11:30am–11pm, Fri 11:30am–midnight, Sat 11:30am–3am). In addition, **Farmer's Restaurant Moku Moku** (see above) has a branch in Sakae.

The 59's Café & Diner INTERNATIONAL   This place is a hoot. It's worth coming to this small basement bar just to see the waitresses wearing cowboy hats or to gaze at the lava lamps and Spam containers on the counter along with the whiskey. But it serves decent food as well, including a pretty good burger, fish and chips, and other bar fare, and the music is mostly '50s and '60s rock 'n' roll. Wednesday and Friday are Ladies' Nights, when females can drink as much as they can for 100 minutes for ¥1,500, after which those cowboy hats might start looking quite fashionable.

3-15-10 Nishiki, Naka-ku. (© **052/971-0566.** Main dishes ¥600–¥1,300. No credit cards. Mon–Sat 6pm–4am; Sun 6pm–midnight. Station: Sakae or Hisaya-odori (3 min.); on Hisaya Odori, west of the TV tower.

Hourai-ken Matsuzakaya EEL   This eel restaurant is a branch of two famous restaurants near Atsuta Shrine. There's no English-language menu, but you can't go wrong ordering one of the various *unagi donburi* (rice casserole with eel on top). Most famous is the Hitsumabushi, a set meal for ¥2,730 that includes *unagi donburi,* various condiments, miso soup, and Japanese pickles. Eating it is a ritual: First, dish out some of the eel casserole into the smaller wooden bowl and eat it plain. For the next course, try it with some of the seaweed and green onions that come with it. Finally, add some of the soup and wasabi to the last mixture you tried.

The other, more elegant branches are both south of Atsuta Shrine at 2–10–26 Jingu, Atsuta-ku (© **052/682-5598;** Wed–Mon 11:30am–2:30pm and 4:30–8:30pm); and at 503 Goudo-cho, Atsuta-ku (© **052/671-8686;** Tues–Sun 11:30am–2pm and 4:30–8:30pm).

In the south building of Matsuzakaya department store, in the back on the 10th floor (look for the sign that says UNAGI HORAIKEN), 3-16-1 Sakae, Naka-ku. © **052/264-3825.** Unagi teishoku (set meal) ¥1,575–¥3,780. AE, MC, V. Daily 11am–9pm (last order). Station: Yabacho (1 min.).

Tiger Cafe FRENCH   With its antique-looking advertisements for Pernod, tiled walls and floor, small tables, and rattan chairs facing the open facade, this coffee shop is the closest thing in Nagoya to a Parisian cafe. Stop for a drink, a snack of quiche, or dine on more substantial fare such as the fish or meat dish of the day and be glad you're not part of the traffic whizzing by.

A branch, with the same hours and menu, is at 1–8–26 Nishiki (© **052/220-0031;** station: Fushimi), across from the Hilton Hotel and down a side street with a Starbucks on the corner.

1-9-22 Higashi-sakura, Higashi-ku. © **052/971-1031.** Main dishes ¥1,600–¥2,000. No credit cards. Mon–Sat 11am–2:30am; Sun 11am–midnight. Station: Sakae (6 min.); north of Oasis 21 on a side street, across from the NHK Building (both of which you can't miss).

(110) **Torigin Honten** ★ COCHIN CHICKEN   In the heart of Nagoya, this 37-year-old casual restaurant with counter, tatami, or table seating is known for its *Nagoya cochin* (free-range chicken). Although it serves *yakitori,* this is not your usual yakitori restaurant; rather, dining here should be considered a culinary adventure of the chicken, with parts of the bird served in ways you've never imagined. All set meals include raw cochin with real gold flakes, though you're allowed to substitute a cooked dish if you like. The popular Gourmet yakitori (¥1,950) comes with eight different skewers, which may include *tsukune* (meatballs), chicken skin, and breast meat with miso paste. An amiable staff makes it diner-friendly; a black-and-white *kura*-style facade makes it easy to identify. If this main shop (Honten) is full, you may be led to one of three nearby branches, one of which offers tatami rooms with a view of the garden, but I prefer the liveliness of the main restaurant.

3-14-22 Nishiki, Naka-ku. © **052/973-3000.** Cochin main dishes ¥750–¥1,950; set meals ¥2,900–¥5,200. Snack charge ¥300 per person in main shop, ¥500 in its branches. AE, DC, MC, V. Daily 5–11pm (last order). Station: Sakae (exit 1, 2 min.).

(111) **Yabaton** ★★ (Finds) TONKATSU   You'll recognize this Everyman's eatery in Nagoya's downtown district immediately by its curtains displaying comical pigs dressed like sumo wrestlers. In operation since 1947, its interior is all about pigs and sumo (I'll let you draw your own conclusions about the connection). It's famous for its *tonkatsu*

(pork cutlet), and you'll be asked whether you want yours with its homemade sauce *(sa-u-zu)* or red *miso;* the former is thicker and sweeter, but the latter is the specialty here (if you don't specify, you'll be served the miso, but if you can't decide, ask for a little of both). *Donburi,* a breaded and fried pork cutlet on rice, is the cheapest, but recommended is *hire,* a tender cut with less fat. Main dishes all come with cabbage; rice or miso soup costs extra. Deep-fried vegetables and seafood (scallops, oysters) are also available. And in case you're interested, Yabaton souvenirs—T-shirts, key chains, towels—are for sale, all adorned with comical pigs dressed like sumo wrestlers and baseball players. There's a branch in nearby La Chic shopping complex, on the seventh floor (© **052/269-7070;** daily 11am–11pm).

3-6-23 Osu. © **052/241-2409.** Main dishes ¥735–¥1,470; set meals ¥995–¥1,680. AE, DC, MC, V. Tues–Sun 11am–9pm. Station: Yabacho (exit 4, 3 min.). Turn right at the overpass; it's on the southwest corner of Wakamiya-Otsu Dori intersection.

2 ISE-SHIMA NATIONAL PARK ★★

465km (289 miles) W of Tokyo; 100km (60 miles) S of Nagoya

Blessed with subtropical vegetation, small islands dotting its shoreline, and the most revered Shinto shrine in Japan, **Ise-Shima National Park** merits a 1- or 2-night stopover if you're anywhere near Nagoya. Located on and around Shima Peninsula and covering 518 sq. km (200 sq. miles), this national park has bays and inlets that make up the home of the Mikimoto pearl and thousands of pearl-cultivating rafts. Although you could conceivably cover the major attractions on a day's outing from Nagoya, I've recommended accommodations in case you'd like to take in the sights at a more leisurely pace.

Ise-Shima's major attractions are concentrated in the small towns of Ise, Futami, Toba, and Kashikojima, all in Mie Prefecture. **Ise** (also called Ise-Shi, which translates as Ise City) is where you'll find the Ise Grand Shrines. **Futami** is famous for a theme park based on Japan's history from 1477 to 1598 and a majestic traditional inn, now a museum. **Toba** contains Mikimoto Pearl Island, which offers a pearl museum and demonstrations by its famous women divers, as well as the Toba Aquarium. In **Kashikojima,** there's an amusement park with a Spanish theme and boat trips around Ago Bay that, with its islets and pearl-cultivating oyster rafts, is one of the most scenic spots in the park.

ESSENTIALS

GETTING THERE   By Train   The easiest way to get to Ise-Shima is from Nagoya on the private Kintetsu Railway's **Ise Shima Liner** (© **052/561-1604;** www.kintetsu.co.jp), which departs every 30 minutes or so from Kintetsu Station, next to the JR Nagoya Station. It takes about 1 hour and 30 minutes via limited express to reach Ise (with stops at both Ise-Shi and Ujiyamada stations), about 1 hour and 45 minutes to reach Toba, and 2 hours and 10 minutes to reach Kashikojima (*note:* only JR trains go to Futami; see below). A ticket from Nagoya to the end of the line in Kashikojima costs ¥3,480 one-way. There are also Kintetsu trains to Shima Peninsula from Kyoto (2¼ hr. to Toba; fare: ¥3,780) and from Osaka's Uehonmachi Station (2 hr. to Toba; fare: ¥3,550 and ¥3,450). Most economical, however, is to purchase a Kintetsu Rail Pass *before* arriving in Japan, which costs ¥3,500, is valid for 5 days (but only three journeys can be aboard a limited express train), and includes travel to and from Nagoya, Osaka/Kyoto, and Ise (see "Getting Around Japan," in chapter 3, for more information).

If you're traveling on a **Japan Rail Pass,** you can also reach Ise-Shima by **JR Mie Kaisoku** (rapid express) trains, which depart hourly from Nagoya Station, but you'll be charged an extra ¥490. JR trains stop at Ise-Shi and Futami-no-ura before terminating at Toba, where, if you're heading to Kashikojima, you'll have to transfer to the Kintetsu Line (fare from Toba to Kashikojima: ¥460).

By Bus   Buses depart nightly from Tokyo's Ikebukuro Station's east exit at 10:20 and 11:20pm, arriving at Ise-Shi Station at 7:10 and 8:10am respectively and Toba 30 minutes later. The fare to Ise-Shi Station is ¥8,200 one-way. From Kyoto Station, buses depart four times a day for the Ise Grand Shrines and Ise-Shi Station for ¥3,000.

VISITOR INFORMATION   Be sure to drop by the Tourist Information Centers in Tokyo or the international airports at Narita or Osaka to pick up the free leaflet, "Ise-Shima," which lists train schedules from Osaka, Kyoto, and Nagoya and gives information on the park's main attractions (you can also download it from the Japan National Tourist Organization's website at www.jnto.go.jp by looking under "Browse by Destinations"). Otherwise, drop by the **Ise City Tourist Information Offices** located in front of the Outer Shrine Gate (✆ **0596/28-3705**), open daily 8:30am to 5pm, and at Kintetsu Ujiyamada Station in Ise City (✆ **0596/23-9655**) open daily 9 to 5:30pm; or check its website at www.ise-kanko.jp. The **Toba Tourist Office** at exit 1 of Toba Station (✆ **0599/25-2844;** www.toba.gr.jp) is open daily 9am to 5:30pm. More information on the area is available at www.iseshima-kanko.jp.

GETTING AROUND   Transportation within Ise-Shima National Park is either by train or by bus. **Trains** are convenient if your destinations are Ise City, Toba, Futami, and Kashikojima (see "Getting There," above). Some major sites, however, including the Ise Grand Shrines and Ise Azuchi Momoyama Bunkamura, are best reached by bus. For sightseers, there's the **CAN-Bus,** which you can board in front of the JR stations in Ise City and Toba. Buses, departing about once an hour on weekdays and twice an hour on weekends, travel from Ujiyamada and Ise-Shi stations to both Outer and Inner Shrines of the Ise Grand Shrines and Ise Azuchi Momoyama Bunkamura before continuing onward to Toba. One-day passes for ¥1,000 and 2-day passes for ¥1,600 can be bought aboard the buses (unfortunately, the bus timetable is in Japanese only). There are also local buses that run between the Outer and Inner Shrine of the Ise Grand Shrines; you must also take a bus for Parque España.

In Ise, it makes sense to rent a **bicycle,** available at Ujiyamada Station (¥500 for 4 hr.). Ise-Shi and Ujiyamada stations are a 7-minute walk apart. There are luggage storage facilities at Ujiyamada, Toba, and Ise-Shi stations, as well as at the entrance to the Inner Shrine in Ise.

EXPLORING ISE-SHIMA NATIONAL PARK

The easiest way to see the park's sights is to start in Ise City, the northern gateway to Ise-Shima National Park, and work your way down the peninsula to Kashikojima.

Ise City (Ise-Shi)

The Ise Grand Shrines (Ise Jingu) ★★   Tied historically to the imperial family and considered the spiritual home of the Japanese people, Japan's most venerable Shinto shrines, the Ise Grand Shrines (✆ **0596/24-111**), consist of an Outer Shrine and an Inner Shrine, plus more than 100 minor shrines spread through a dense forest of Japanese cypress. As the Outer and Inner shrines are about 6.5km (4 miles) apart, your best bet is to first visit the Outer Shrine, which is a 5-minute walk from Ise-Shi Station, and then

either cycle or take a bus to the Inner Shrine. In addition to the CAN-Bus (described above in "Getting Around"), a local bus runs between the two shrines every 10 to 15 minutes (fare: ¥410). Because of the distance between the shrines and their large grounds, plan on spending at least 2 hours exploring Ise.

The **Outer Shrine (Geku)** was founded in 478 and is dedicated to the Shinto goddess of industry, agriculture, clothing, and housing. The **Inner Shrine (Naiku)** was founded a few centuries earlier and is dedicated to Amaterasu, the sun goddess. Both are among the few Shinto shrines in Japan without any Chinese Buddhist influences and are therefore thought to be the purest style of Shinto architecture. Constructed of plain cypress wood with thick thatched roofs in the oldest style of architecture in Japan, they're starkly simple and have no ornamentation except for gold and copper facing on beams and doors. In fact, if you've come all the way to Shima Peninsula just to see the shrines, you may be disappointed—there's nothing much to see (and no photos are allowed). The shrines are so sacred that no one is allowed near them except members of the imperial family and high-ranking Shinto priests. Both shrines are surrounded by four wooden fences, and lesser mortals are allowed only as far as the third gate.

The fences don't allow you to see much, but that doesn't stop the estimated seven million Japanese who come here annually. They come because of what the shrines represent, which is an embodiment of Japanese Shinto itself. The Inner Shrine is by far the more important because it's dedicated to the sun goddess, considered to be the legendary ancestress of the imperial family. It contains the *Yata-no-Kagami* (Sacred Mirror), one of the Three Sacred Treasures of the emperor.

According to legend, the sun goddess sent her grandson to Japan so that he and his descendants could rule over the country. Before he left, she gave him three insignia—a mirror, a sword, and a set of jewels. As she handed him the mirror, she is said to have remarked, "When you look upon this mirror, let it be as if you look upon me." The mirror, therefore, is said to embody the sun goddess herself and is regarded as the most sacred object in the Shinto religion. It's kept in the deep recesses of the Inner Shrine in a special casket and is never shown to the public. (The sword is in the Atsuta Shrine in Nagoya, and the jewels are in the Imperial Palace in Tokyo.)

Perhaps the most amazing thing about the Outer and Inner shrines is that, even though they were founded centuries ago, the buildings themselves have never been more than 20 years old; for more than 1,300 years, they have been completely torn down and rebuilt exactly as they were on neighboring sites every 20 years. Not only does the practice ensure that the shrines don't deteriorate but also that ancient building techniques are passed down through the generations. The 62nd rebuilding will take place in the fall of 2013.

Even though you can't see much of the shrines, they're still the most important stops in Ise-Shima. The Inner Shrine, considered the more sacred of the two, is approached by crossing the Isuzu River via the elegant Uji Bridge (also rebuilt every 20 years), passing through a manicured garden, and then entering a dark forest of 800-year-old cypress trees. Watch how Japanese stop after crossing the second small bridge on the approach to the shrine to wash and purify their hands and mouths with water from the Isuzu River. Its source lies on the Inner Shrine, and it's considered sacred.

ISE'S HISTORIC DISTRICTS ★★★   After visiting the Inner Shrine (a 45-min. walk round-trip), turn right after recrossing Uji Bridge for the nearby historic district of **Oharai-machi,** whose 800m-long (½-mile) main street is lined with beautiful wooden buildings and *kura* (storehouses), some dating from the Edo and Meiji periods and others newly constructed but faithful to traditional architecture. This once served as the main pilgrimage road leading to Ise Jingu. During the Edo Period, when travel was strictly controlled, joining a mass pilgrimage to Ise was for many Japanese a once-in-a-lifetime opportunity to venture beyond their homes; it's estimated a fifth of the population joined pilgrimages to Ise during that time. Today it's an interesting area for a stroll, shopping, or a meal.

About halfway down is **Okage Yokocho** (𝄐 **0596/23-8828**) a re-created Meiji Era village with teahouses, restaurants, and shops selling Japanese candies, traditional toys, and folk crafts. If you have time, stop by ⑪⑫ **Okageza** ★ (𝄐 **0596/23-8844;** daily 10am–5:30pm, to 4:30pm in winter), a museum housed in an authentic Edo-Era building that captures the spirit of Oharai-machi during the Edo Period; dioramas of half-scale models and lively street scenes vividly convey what life was like for both the residents and the pilgrims passing through. On a bridge overlooking a model of the city and its shrines, take note of the small man: He's not half-scale; the average Edo man measured 4 feet, 11 inches. Admission is ¥300 for adults and ¥100 for children. You'll spend about 20 minutes here.

Off the beaten tourist track is **Kawasaki,** which served as Ise City's business district during the Edo Period, when boats traversing the Setagawa River delivered goods to storehouses along the river. A grass-roots movement has restored four of these storehouses along with an Edo-Era house, grouped together in the ⑪⑬ **Merchant's House Museum (Ise-Kawasaki Shonin-Kan),** 32–25–3 Kawasaki (𝄐 **0596/22-4810;** Wed–Mon 9:30am–5pm), which you can tour for ¥300. In addition to a high-class teahouse, displays include Ise's own paper money, the first paper money in Japan and developed to lessen the load of pilgrims who might otherwise be forced to carry heavy pieces of gold or silver. Surrounding buildings now house restaurants and shops selling crafts, food, and antiques (ask for a map of the area at the museum). In a country where old neighborhoods are disappearing by the minute, the local people who fought to preserve this historic district deserve medals. It's a 15-minute walk north from Ujiyamada Station or northeast from Ise-shi Station.

Futami

Edo Wonderland Ise (Ise Azuchi Momoyama Bunkamura) ★★ (Kids) The

castle you see on the hill from Futami-no-ura Station is not the former residence of a famous shogun but a replica of Azuchi Castle in Edo Wonderland Ise, one of Japan's many theme parks. If you have youngsters in tow or if you haven't seen one of these period theme parks elsewhere in Japan, go to one—they're fun! This one is among my favorites because, rather than try to re-create a village in Holland or Spain, it's centered on a specific time in Japan's history, the Age of the Warring States—the Sengoku Era (1477–1573), when local warlords struggled for supremacy, and the Azuchi-Momoyama Era (1573–98), when Oda Nobunaga gained control of the land and finally put an end to civil war. In keeping with the theme of this Japanese equivalent of Dodge City, all the staff are dressed in 16th-century costumes, and attractions reflect the pre–Edo Era; visually, it looks just like a movie set. You can watch period dramas such as the action-charged antics of a ninja troupe, be spooked at haunted houses, try to negotiate 11 challenging obstacles in the Ninja Labyrinth, or try your hand at throwing ninja weapons at a target. There are no thrill rides here, but there are old-fashioned game centers, including shooting ranges using bows and arrows and other weaponry of the era. That gold-roofed castle is dedicated to Nobunaga, who built Azuchi Castle; its top-floor, lined with real gold, has a great views. You'll spend 2 to 3 hours here.

ℂ **0596/43-2300.** www.ise-bunkamura.co.jp. Admission ¥3,900 adults, ¥2,500 junior-high and high-school students, ¥900 children. Daily 9am–5pm (9:30am–4pm mid-Nov to mid-Mar). Station: Futami-no-ura (15 min.). CAN-Bus: to the front entrance.

Hinjitsukan   I used to recommend overnighting at this majestic inn until it sadly closed in 1999, so I'm thrilled it has now reopened as a museum rather than being demolished. Built in 1887 as an inn for important visitors to Ise Grand Shrines, including the imperial family, it faces Futami-ga-ura Beach (popular during the Edo Period as a place for pilgrims to wash and purify themselves before visiting the shrines) and is surrounded by a serene garden. After entering a side entrance (the grand main entryway is reserved for the imperial family), you'll find yourself in a traditional inn consisting of winding corridors leading to tatami rooms. Most impressive are the Grand Hall with its 120 tatami mats and the elaborate Goten, where VIPs of yore stayed. Beyond Hinjitsukan along the beach is Okitama Shrine and one of the region's most famous sites: A large rock and small rock jutting offshore, joined by a huge sacred rope. Called Meotoiwa, or Wedded Rocks, they're considered a symbol of a good and harmonious marriage. The most auspicious time to view them is in summer at sunrise, when the sun rises between them. But you have to get up as early as 4am, so that's one spectacle I haven't seen.

566–2 Chaya Futami-cho. ℂ **0596/43-2003.** Admission ¥300 adults, ¥150 children. Wed–Mon 9am–5pm. Station: Futami-no-ura (12 min.). CAN-Bus: Futami-ga-ura Omotesando (10 min.).

Toba

Mikimoto Pearl Island ★★   Toba's best-known attraction, located on a small island connected to the mainland by a pedestrian bridge and consisting of several buildings, is touristy but still quite enjoyable, especially if you have a weakness for pearls or have ever wondered how they're cultivated.

To learn about the man who toiled through years of adversity to produce the world's first cultured pearl, visit **Kokichi Mikimoto Memorial Hall,** built in 1993 to commemorate the 100th anniversary of Mikimoto's success. Born in Toba in 1858 as the eldest son of a noodle-shop owner, Kokichi Mikimoto went to Yokohama as a young man and was surprised to see stalls selling pearls with great success. He reasoned that if oysters produced pearls as the result of an irritant inside the shell, why couldn't humans introduce the irritant themselves and induce oysters to make pearls? It turned out to be harder than it sounded. It wasn't until 5 years after he started his research that Mikimoto finally succeeded in cultivating his first pearl, here on what is today called Mikimoto Pearl Island. In 1905, Mikimoto cultivated his first perfectly round pearl, after which he built what is probably the most successful pearl empire in the world.

The **Pearl Museum** tells all you'd probably ever want to know about the creation of pearls, with English-language videos showing the insertion of the round nucleus into the shell and the harvesting of the pearls 2 years later, as well as explanations of the process of making a pearl necklace by hand, from the selection and sorting of pearls to the drilling and stringing. You can learn about the criteria used for pricing pearls (luster is the most important) and color selection. The museum also contains some of Mikimoto's earliest jewelry and models made with pearls, many of which were only recently reacquired by Mikimoto & Co. Ltd. through auctions. My favorite is the brooch made for the 1937 Paris International Exhibition, which can be worn a dozen different ways by employing various clasps. The five-story Pearl Pagoda has 12,760 Mikimoto pearls and took 750 artisans 6 months to complete, after which it was exhibited at the Philadelphia

World Exhibition in 1926. The Liberty Bell, a third the size of the original, has 12,250 pearls and was displayed at the New York World's Fair in 1939.

In addition, *ama* (**women divers**) in traditional white outfits demonstrate how women of the Shima Peninsula have dived through the ages in search of abalone, seaweed, and other edibles. They were also essential to the pearl industry, diving to collect the oysters and then returning them to the seabed following insertion of the nuclei. At one time, there were thousands of ama, known for their skill in diving to great depths for extended periods. It is said that there are still more than 1,000 of these women divers left in Mie Prefecture, but I've seen them only at demonstrations given for tourists. If you happen to see ama working in earnest (diving for abalone and other food, not pearls), consider yourself lucky. Here you can watch them from the air-conditioned comfort of a viewing room built especially for overseas guests.

Of course, there's also a shop selling Mikimoto pearl jewelry and a restaurant. You can easily spend 1½ hours on Pearl Island.

1-7-1 Toba. ℭ **0599/25-2028.** www.mikimoto-pearl-museum.co.jp. Admission ¥1,500 adults, ¥750 children 7–15. Jan–Nov daily 8:30am–5pm; Dec daily 9am–4:30pm. Closed 2nd Tues–Thurs of Dec. Station: Toba (3 min.)

Toba Aquarium ★ Kids   Next to Pearl Island is one of Japan's largest aquariums, containing more than 850 species of animals and some 20,000 creatures. Various zones and themes make it easy to navigate. The display of marine animals around Ise-Shima and Japan includes giant spider crabs and the finless porpoise, the world's smallest whale. The exhibit of "living fossils"—creatures that have remained relatively unchanged since ancient times—includes sharks, horseshoe crabs, and the nautilus (which are bred here; babies are often on display), while the marine mammal kingdom includes Commerson's dolphins, Russian walruses, Baikal seals, and sea lions, with sea-lion shows several times a day. The aquarium also boasts exotic and rare creatures such as dugongs, African manatees, and Amazonian turtles and frogs. My only complaint is that some tanks look rather bare and outdated in today's world of ever-more-sophisticated aquariums; maybe the animals don't mind, but spectators sure do. Though it's not as sophisticated or complete as the Osaka Aquarium, you can spend 90 minutes here, longer if you have kids.

3-3-6 Toba. ℭ **0599/25-2555.** www.aquarium.co.jp/english. Admission ¥2,400 adults, ¥1,200 junior-high and elementary students, ¥600 children. Nov to mid-Mar daily 9am–4:30pm; mid-Mar to mid-July and Sept–Oct daily 9am–5pm; mid-July to Aug daily 8:30am–5:30pm. Station: Toba (10 min.).

Kashikojima

At the southern end of the Shima Peninsula, the last stop on the Kintetsu Line is Kashikojima, where one of the main attractions for Japanese is a 50-minute **boat cruise of Ago Bay.** Vessels, built to resemble Spanish galleons or with other Spanish-based themes, depart from the town's boat dock, about a 2-minute walk from the tiny train station, every half-hour or so between 9:30am and 4:30pm (until 3:30pm in winter), weather permitting, and cost ¥1,500 for adults, half-price for children. You'll pass pearl-cultivating rafts, fishing boats, and many small islands along the way. For more information call the **Shima Marine Leisure Co.** (ℭ **0599/43-1023**).

Parque España (Shima Spain Mura) ★★ Kids   You may wonder what this Spanish village is doing in southern Ise Shima. Mie Prefecture has a sister relationship with Valencia in Spain, a relationship that is exploited to the hilt in this ambitious theme park. A huge facility that employs about 40 Spanish-speaking natives, the amusement park includes a shopping area specializing in products from Spain; a plaza that stages dances, festivals, and other outdoor entertainment; a coliseum that features folk dancing and singing; a 360-degree cinema; a clown circus; and amusement rides that range from an adventure lagoon ride through a world of fantasy to the fastest roller coaster I'll ever care to ride (and one of the longest, lasting more than 3 hair-raising min.). Although the park opened to much fanfare in 1994, it has suffered declining attendance ever since, which is bad for business but means there's virtually no waiting time for rides, except during school holidays.

Most educational is the Museo Castillo de Xavier, a reproduction of the castle where Francis Xavier was born (Xavier later brought Christianity to Japan); it presents a brief overlook of highlights in Spanish history, though in Japanese. Still, there's no mistaking the replica of prehistoric drawings from the Altamira caves, the model of the *Santa Maria* that Columbus sailed to America, and a replica of the entrance to the Prado Museum. A film introduces Spain's greatest artists, including Goya, Velázquez, and El Greco. There are amusements geared to all ages, as well as numerous restaurants. Plan to spend about 3 hours here.

$\copyright$ **0599/57-3333.** Passport admission to most attractions ¥4,800 adults, ¥3,800 seniors and children 12–17, ¥3,200 children 4–11; extra charges for gaming houses and flamenco show. Admission only, which includes the museum and most shows but no rides (which you can purchase separately for ¥200–¥600 per ride), ¥2,800, ¥1,800, and ¥1,200 respectively. Hours vary, but generally Mon–Fri 9:30am–5pm, Sat–Sun and holidays 9:30am–6pm (check with the tourist office). Closed last 2 weeks of Feb. Station: Ugata (Kintetsu Line), then a bus that runs 2 or 3 times per hour; or Kashikojima Station, then a bus that runs once an hour. Both buses cost ¥360 for the 15-min. ride.

WHERE TO STAY

Kashikojima is the best place to go if you want to escape the crowds and relax in a rural setting, while Toba and Ise have the greatest number of attractions.

Ise

(114) **Asakichi** ★ Because a pilgrimage to Ise Jingu during the Edo Period was often the only trip a commoner might make in his lifetime, he often lived it up to the hilt in Furuichi, Ise's former red-light district. Located between the Inner and Outer shrines, it was filled with many *ryokan,* brothels, and restaurants. Now only Asakichi remains, founded more than 200 years ago by the present owner's family, on an impossibly narrow street. In any case, the ramshackle ryokan seems little changed since then, built on a slope (and containing steep stairs) and even containing a museum of sorts filled with dusty, Edo-Era family memorabilia which you can request to see. The tatami rooms are simple. Meals are served on request in the privacy of your room or in a dining hall with a view over the rooftops. Western breakfasts are available. The proprietor doesn't speak much English but understands the basics.

109 Nakanocho, Ise-Shi, Mie 516-0034. $\copyright$ **0596/22-4101.** Fax 0596/22-4102. 10 units (3 with bathroom). ¥12,600 per person. Rates include 2 meals. No credit cards. Station: Ise-Shi, then bus no. 01 or 02 from platform 7 another 9 min. to the Nakanocho stop (1 min.). **Amenities:** Communal fridge; museum. *In room:* A/C, TV, no phone.

(115) **Hoshidekan** ★★ (Finds) Catering to the health conscious, this inexpensive 87-year-old wooden Japanese Inn Group *ryokan* has several tatami rooms with windows framed with gnarled roots and bamboo (they simply don't make windows like this anymore) encircling an inner courtyard. It's nothing fancy, but it's run by a friendly, spry 80-something woman (assisted by her son and his wife) who is a strong advocate of macrobiotic vegetarian meals, which are served in your simple tatami room and the

adjoining restaurant. Both Japanese and Western meals are available, but we prefer the **379** ¥1,300 *Genmai teishoku* vegetarian course for dinner. The food, however, is only one of the reasons to stay here. We also like the rental bicycles, perfect for visiting Ise Jingu and nearby Kawasaki historic district.

2–15–2 Kawasaki, Ise-Shi, Mie 516-0009. ℂ **0596/28-2377.** Fax 0596/27-2830. www.hoshidekan.jp. 10 units (none with bathroom). ¥5,800 single; ¥10,200 double; ¥15,300 triple. Breakfast ¥900 extra; dinner from ¥1,300 extra. AE, MC, V. Station: Ise-Shi, then a 7-min. walk in the opposite direction from the shrine; look for the sign on the right that says HOSHIDE. **Amenities:** Macrobiotic restaurant (reservations required); rental bikes (¥300 per day); smoke-free rooms. *In room:* A/C, TV, no phone.

Toba

Thalassa Shima Hotel & Resort ★★   Although the approach to this luxury hotel doesn't seem to promise much, inside it's another story. Everything about this sophisticated seaside hotel is focused on its stunningly beautiful setting on the sea, with nary another building in sight (a public beach, open July–Aug, is a short walk away). It exudes a soothing, subdued atmosphere, fitting for a resort dedicated to healing. Thalassa Shima offers thalassotherapy, which uses seawater, seaweed, and sea-mud treatments to combat stress, fatigue, and excess weight, as well as aromatherapy, reflexology, and other treatments. My coauthor was skeptical that a 1-night stay involving a seaweed bath, an underwater-jet treatment, a massage bath, and pressure therapy could make much difference, but she had to admit she left the hotel much more relaxed and feeling beautiful! Rooms, bathed in cool, crisp whites, have small balconies. Due to the hotel's isolation, you'll want to take your meals here, either at **Lumiere** with its nouvelle French cuisine or the classic Japanese restaurant, both with views of the sea.

Please leave both url and email; no English version of site.

1826–1 Shirahama, Uramura-cho, Toba-shi, Mie 517-0025. ℂ **0599/32-1111.** Fax 0599/32-1109. www. thalasso.co.jp. reservation@thalasso.co.jp. 112 units. ¥25,000–¥40,400 single or double; ¥21,500–¥28,500 per person including 2 meals. Rates higher in peak season. Thalassotherapy treatment from ¥19,000. AE, DC, MC, V. Free 25-min. shuttle bus every hour from JR or Kintetsu Toba Station. **Amenities:** 2 restaurants; bar; exercise room; spa w/glass-enclosed seawater pool and outdoor Jacuzzi overlooking the bay, French thalassotherapy, and other therapies; room service; smoke-free rooms. *In room:* A/C, TV w/free videos/ DVDs and players on request, hair dryer, minibar.

Kashikojima

116 **Ishiyama-So** ★ (Finds)   If you're looking for an inexpensive, unusual place to stay, a good choice is this family-run *minshuku* located on a small island just a stone's throw from the Kashikojima pier. It can be reached only via the hotel's private boat—call to let them know you've arrived at Kashikojima; the boat will arrive shortly, and you'll be delivered right to the front door. Its location on the water, with a lobby done up in Southeast Asian decor and floor-to-ceiling windows overlooking the water, gives it a slightly exotic atmosphere, right up to the small crabs scurrying through the front door. There's a sun deck overlooking the bay, you can swim off the dock (because of boat traffic, though, you shouldn't go farther than the dock), and footpaths crisscross the small island. Two rooms are Western style and all face the bay. Note that only Japanese meals are served and must be paid for in cash.

Yokoyama-jima, Kashikojima, Ago-cho, Mie 517-0502. ℂ **0599/52-1527.** Fax 0599/52-1240. 6 units (3 with bathroom, 3 with sink and toilet only). ¥4,500–¥6,000 per person including breakfast; ¥9,000– ¥10,000 per person with 2 meals. MC, V. A 2-min. walk from the station to Kashikojima pier, then a 2-min. boat trip. *In room:* A/C, TV, no phone.

Shima Kanko Hotel Bay Suites ★★★ On a promontory above Ago Bay, this deluxe newcomer offers more luxury and pampering than sister property the Classic (see below). In fact, you'd be hard-pressed to find more exclusive (and more expensive) digs anywhere else in Japan. An all-suite hotel, it offers individual pickup from the station, a hushed environment that makes it seem more like a high-class inn rather than a hotel (no children 11 and younger allowed), and a rooftop garden with 360-degree views. Rooms, most with balconies, provide the ultimate in comfort and decor, including to-die-for bathrooms with heated stone floors and tubs overlooking the bay. Because of its isolation, hotel guests generally dine in either the Japanese restaurant (where *kaiseki* meals start at ¥15,000) or the French restaurant (set dinners begin at ¥24,000). The rates below reflect the seasons.

Kashikojima, Ago-cho, Shima, Mie 517-0593. ✆ **0599/43-2111.** www.miyakohotels.ne.jp/shima. 50 units. ¥69,000–¥95,000 double; ¥48,000–¥60,000 per person including 2 meals. AE, DC, MC, V. Station: Kashikojima (free pickup from the station). **Amenities:** 2 restaurants; lounge; smoke-free rooms; spa. *In room:* A/C, TV and DVD library, hair dryer, Internet, minibar, MP3 docking station.

Shima Kanko Hotel The Classic ★★★ Sitting on a hill above Ago Bay, this is a resort hotel in the old tradition, established in 1951 and boasting impeccable service and great views (though the Bay Suites, above, has robbed some of its views). The hotel boasts its own garden (cared for by three gardeners), at the edge of which is the lovely outdoor pool, free for hotel guests. I especially like the pathway leading down to a private dock where you can sit and watch pearl cultivators at work on their rafts. On the hotel's roof is an observatory, great for watching the beautiful sunsets. In addition, most rooms have views of the bay and are spacious, and despite periodic updating, they retain a pleasant old-fashioned, '50s atmosphere with their shoji screens and wooden furniture. French restaurant La Mer is famous for its abalone and Mie beef; it's pricey, but there's no other choice in the area.

Kashikojima, Ago-cho, Shima, Mie 517-0593. ✆ **0599/43-1211.** Fax 0599/43-3538. www.miyakohotels.ne.jp/shima. 117 units. ¥19,058–¥32,918 single; ¥20,790–¥34,650 double. Peak season (Aug and New Year's) ¥5,775 extra; Sat and evenings before holidays ¥3,465 extra. AE, DC, MC, V. Station: Kashikojima (then free shuttle to hotel or a 5-min. walk). **Amenities:** Restaurant; lounge; concierge; outdoor pool w/ children's slides; room service; smoke-free rooms; free Wi-Fi in lobby. *In room:* A/C, TV, hair dryer, Internet (in some), minibar.

WHERE TO DINE

Ise

Bon Vivant ★★ **Finds** FRENCH Occupying a former post office built in the early 1900s near the Outer Shrine, this delightful choice is divided into two parts: an informal brasserie with tall ceilings and antiques (my preference), and a more elegant restaurant. Both feature the creations of owner-chef Kawase-san, made from locally grown products. For lunch, the brasserie is slightly cheaper, with my ¥2,100 set meal including an appetizer of ham, sliced abalone, Matsuzaka beef, and corn mousse; a main course of baked chicken with potato gratin and vegetables; and a dessert. The dinner menu is the same for both the restaurant and brasserie. Or, for a light snack, there's Café de Bon Vivant across the street, open Monday to Saturday 10am to 7pm and Sunday 10am to 5pm.

20–24 Honmachi, Ise. ✆ **0596/26-3131.** Reservations required. Set dinners ¥5,000–¥10,000; set lunches ¥2,100–¥5,700 in the restaurant, ¥890–¥2,830 in the brasserie. MC, V. Restaurant Tues–Sun noon–1:30pm; Wed–Sun 5:30–7:30pm (last order). Brasserie Tues–Sun 11:30am–2pm; Wed–Sun 5:30–8pm (last order). Station: Ise-Shi (5 min.). From the JR Ise-Shi Station, take the main exit and walk straight on Geku Sando; it's on a side street to the left (look for a white building with a red roof), just before the Outer Shrine.

(117) **Sushi Kyu** ★★ (Kids) SUSHI/LOCAL SPECIALTIES Located on the main street of Oharai-machi (near the Inner Shrine) in a 130-year-old former *ryokan,* this traditional restaurant offers tatami seating at low tables with a view out over the river. Waitresses in traditional Japanese worker clothes serve sushi and local cuisine from a Japanese-language menu. Try the *tekone sushi* (raw bonito marinated with soy sauce and mixed with vinegared rice) served in a wooden tub, or the obento of various delicacies.

20 Uji Nakanokiri-machi, Ise. (C) **0596/27-0229.** Set meals ¥1,050–¥2,500. No credit cards. Wed–Mon 11am–8pm; Tues 11am–5pm (on the 1st and last day of every month it closes at 7pm). Station: Ise-Shi, then local bus or the CAN-Bus to the Inner Shrine stop, from which it's a 5-min. walk to Oharai-machi historic district.

Toba

(118) **Oosakaya** SUSHI Located 2 blocks inland from Mikimoto Pearl Island on the other side of the train tracks, this simple local eatery with tatami, table, and counter seating was opened in 1950 by the present owner's grandmother. It offers assorted *nigiri-zushi* (sushi platters) and *maki-sushi* (sushi rolls), but the specialty is *ebi* fry—humungous shrimp deep-fried in batter. The ebi-fry *teishoku,* which includes miso soup, rice, and pickled vegetables, costs ¥1,600 with two ebi fries and ¥2,000 for three ebi fries. Those with voracious appetites can order one of the ¥3,600 set courses, which come with sushi or sashimi in addition to ebi fries and other dishes.

1-4-64 Toba. (C) **0599/25-2336.** Set meals ¥1,600–¥3,600. AE, DC, MC, V. Fri–Wed 11am–2pm and 4–8:30pm (last order). Station: Toba. Walking in the direction of Mikimoto Pearl Island, turn right under the tracks and take the 2nd street left; Oosakaya will be on the right.

3 MORE OF OLD JAPAN: KANAZAWA ★★

622km (386 miles) W of Tokyo; 224km (140 miles) NE of Kyoto

Near the northwest coast of Honshu on the Sea of Japan, Kanazawa is the gateway to the rugged, sea-swept Noto Peninsula. It was the second-largest city (after Kyoto) to escape bombing during World War II, and some of the old city has been left intact, including a district of former samurai mansions, old geisha quarters, Edo-Era canals, and tiny narrow streets that run crookedly without rhyme or reason (apparently to confuse any enemies foolish enough to attack). Kanazawa is most famous for its **Kenrokuen Garden,** one of the most celebrated gardens in all of Japan (and one of my favorites). It's the main reason people come here, though several fine museums are worth a visit, too. Kanazawa is also renowned for its crafts.

Kanazawa first gained notoriety about 500 years ago, when a militant Buddhist sect joined with peasant fanatics to overthrow the feudal lord and establish its own autonomous government, an event unprecedented in Japanese history. The independent republic survived almost 100 years before it was attacked by an army of Oda Nobunaga, who was trying to unite Japan at a time when civil wars wracked the nation. Kanazawa was subsequently granted to one of Nobunaga's retainers, Maeda Toshiie, who constructed a castle and transformed the small community into a thriving castle town. The Maeda clan continued to rule over Kanazawa for the next 300 years, amassing wealth in the form of land and rice and encouraging development of the arts. Throughout the Tokugawa shogunate, the Maedas remained the second-most powerful family in Japan and controlled the largest domain in the country. The arts of Kutani ware, Yuzen silk dyeing, lacquerware, and *noh* theater flourished—and enjoy popularity in Kanazawa even today. Japan's fourth-largest city at the end of the Feudal Era, Kanazawa now has a population of 460,000 and is capital of Ishikawa Prefecture. With about 178 rainy days a year, it has a local proverb you'd be wise to heed: "Even if you forget your packed lunch, don't forget your umbrella."

ESSENTIALS

GETTING THERE   By Train   Direct **JR trains** from Osaka (via Kyoto) depart hourly; the ride takes less than 3 hours and costs ¥6,930 for an unreserved seat. From Nagoya, direct trains depart for Kanazawa every hour and take about 3 hours; the cost is ¥6,620. From Tokyo, take the Joetsu Shinkansen to Echigo-Yuzawa and switch there for a limited express train to Kanazawa; the trip takes about 4½ hours and costs ¥11,840. In 2014, the Shinkansen will extend from Tokyo all the way to Kanazawa, cutting travel time to 2½ hours.

By Bus   JR Highway buses (℃ **03/3844-1950;** www.jrbuskanto.co.jp) depart six times daily from Shinjuku Station's New South Exit in Tokyo (with a stop also at Ikebukuro Station's east exit), arrive at Kanazawa Station 8 hours later, and cost ¥7,840. There are also night buses, departing from both Tokyo Station's Yaesu South Exit and Shibuya's Mark City and arriving the next morning, for the same price. Buses also depart 10 times daily from Nagoya (¥4,060 for the 4-hr. trip) and twice a day from Osaka's Umeda Station (¥4,300, with trips taking 4 hr. and 40 min.). There are also two buses a day from Takayama (with a stop in Shirakawa-go), which take 2¼ hours and cost ¥3,300.

VISITOR INFORMATION   Be sure to pick up the flyer "Kanazawa" at the Tourist Information Centers in Tokyo, at the Narita or Kansai international airports (you can also download it from the Japan National Tourist Organization's website at www.jnto. go.jp by looking under "Browse by Destinations"). In Kanazawa, the **Tourist Information Center** (℃ **076/232-3993**) can book hotel rooms and distributes maps, brochures, and the very useful *Eye on Kanazawa* with tips on sightseeing. To find the center, open daily 9am to 7pm (with English-speaking volunteers on duty 10am–6pm), turn right after passing through the wicket (you'll be heading toward the East Gate exit); it will soon be on your left beside a shopping arcade. For more information, see **www.kanazawatourism.com** and **www4.city.kanazawa.lg.jp**.

INTERNET ACCESS   The **Ishikawa Foundation for International Exchange,** a 5-minute walk from the east exit of Kanazawa Station (on the road running btw. the Miyako and Nikko hotels), on the third floor of the Rifare building at 1–5–3 Honmachi (℃ **076/262-5931**), has four computers you can use free of charge for 30 minutes daily 8:30am to 5:15pm.

GETTING AROUND   Kanazawa's attractions spread south and southeast from the station (take the East Gate exit). Katamachi, 3km (2 miles) southeast of the station, is Kanazawa's downtown. Sights are too far-flung to see everything on foot, so the easiest way to get around Kanazawa is by **bus.** All major lines depart from Kanazawa Station, and as many as 15 lines pass Kenrokuen Garden, including the Kenrokuen Shuttle, which departs from platform 6 at Kanazawa Station. Take a ticket when boarding the bus and pay when you get off; the fare is ¥200 to most sights.

Easiest for tourists, however, is the **Kanazawa Loop Bus (Shu-yu Bus),** which departs from platform 3 at Kanazawa Station's east exit every 12 minutes and travels to all the tourist sights, making 19 stops in a circular route. Stops are announced in English and displayed on a digital board at the front of the bus. A single ride costs ¥200 and a 1-day pass, which also allows rides on city buses, costs ¥500. The bus runs daily from 8:36am to 6pm.

Kanazawa is fairly flat, making **cycling** a reasonable alternative. **JR Rental Cycle** (*©* **076/261-1721;** daily 8am–8pm), at the west exit of Kanazawa Station, rents bicycles for ¥1,200 per day.

EXPLORING KANAZAWA

Much of Kanazawa's charm lies in the atmosphere of its old neighborhoods. Be sure to wear your good walking shoes, as the best way to explore various parts of the city is via your own two feet. One suggested itinerary for tackling the city's sights is to take the Loop Bus to the Higashi Chaya district, then another Loop bus onward to Kenrokuen and the sights in its vicinity, and then walk the 15 minutes to the Naga-machi Samurai district. Directional English-language signs to major sights are posted throughout the city. Or, if you wish, call the Tourist Information Center (see above) at least 2 weeks in advance of your visit to request a Goodwill Guide to show you the city; the service is free, but you're expected to pay for the guide's entrance fees, transportation, and lunch.

In addition to the sights below, you should also check out cultural events and classes offered at the **Ishikawa International Lounge,** 1–8–10 Hirosaka (*©* **076/260-9901;** www.ifie.or.jp/english/facilities/lounge; Loop Bus: Hirosaka), including those that cover origami, calligraphy, the tea ceremony, Japanese flower arranging, Japanese folk dancing, Japanese cooking, and even Japanese language classes. Classes are free, but you are required to make a reservation and pay for material costs (flower arranging, for example, costs ¥800). The Ishikawa International Lounge, open Monday to Friday 9am to 5pm and Saturday 9am to 4pm, can also answer questions or concerns (such as legal matters) regarding staying or living in Japan.

The Top Attraction

Kenrokuen Garden ★★★   At one time, Kanazawa possessed an impressive castle belonging to the powerful Maeda clan, but it was destroyed by fire several times, the last time in 1881. Kanazawa's main attraction, the 10-hectare (25-acre) **Kenrokuen Garden,** once served as the castle's outer garden. The largest of what are considered to be the three best landscape gardens in Japan—the other two are Kairakuen Garden in Mito and Korakuen Garden in Okayama—it's considered by some to be the grandest. Its name can be translated as "a refined garden incorporating six attributes"—spaciousness, careful arrangement, seclusion, antiquity, elaborate use of water, and scenic charm. Ponds, trees, winding streams, rocks, mounds, and footpaths have all been combined so aesthetically that the effect is spellbinding. Best of all, unlike most other gardens in Japan, there are no surrounding skyscrapers to detract from splendid views, making this one of my personal favorites.

Altogether, it took about 150 years to complete the garden. The fifth Maeda lord started construction in the 1670s, and successive lords added to it according to their individual tastes. The garden as you now see it was finished by the 13th Maeda lord in 1837; only after the Meiji Restoration was it opened to the public. In addition to pines, cherry trees, irises, ponds, and other elements of natural beauty, there are several historic structures, including a tea-ceremony house dating from 1774 and, most important, Seisonkaku Villa (see below). Plan on 1½ hours of blissful wanderings. *Tip:* You may want to arrive early in the morning or near the end of the day, as Kenrokuen Garden is a favorite destination of Japanese tour groups, led by flag-carrying guides who explain everything in detail—through loudspeakers.

Moments Tea for the Soul

Just a few minutes' walk from Kenrokuen is a much smaller garden, the **Gyoku-sen-en,** 8–3 Kosho-Machi (✆ **076/221-0181;** Thurs–Tues 9am–4pm). Built during the Edo Period and utilizing water from Kenrokuen, it contains waterfalls, a pond shaped in the *kanji* symbol for water, a stone lantern with a hidden statue of the Virgin Mary (Christianity was banned during the Edo Period), and Kanazawa's old-est teahouse, but what makes this place special in my book is the 1-hour formal tea ceremony (make reservations 2 days in advance), led by women in kimono who explain the history and the process of the ceremony in English. As Nishida Junko, whose husband is the garden's fifth generation of owners, explained: "The tea ceremony is not a show but rather the chance to share our one moment together"; the poignancy of her words brought tears to my eyes and made this my best tea-ceremony experience ever. Admission to the garden is ¥500, with the tea ceremony costing ¥1,000 more.

1–4 Kenroku-machi. ✆ **076/234-3800.** Admission ¥300 adults, free for seniors, ¥100 children. Mar to mid-Oct daily 7am–6pm; mid-Oct to Feb daily 8am–5pm. Loop Bus: Kenrokuen-shita (3 min.).

In the Vicinity of Kenrokuen Garden

The sights here are listed in the order you'll reach them on foot from Kenrokuen. Kanazawa Castle Park and Gyokusen-en should be seen *before* entering Kenrokuen.

Kanazawa Castle Park   Ishikawa Gate (Ishikawamon), visible from the northwest corner of Kenrokuen and reached via bridge over a busy thoroughfare, served as the south entrance to the castle and is the castle's only remaining original structure. Observing how big and grand the gate is, you can appreciate the magnitude of the original Maeda castle. Remarkably, its roof tiles are actually lead, in case emergency dictated they be melted down for musket balls. The area just beyond the gate is the newly created Kanazawa Castle Park, which contains a botanical garden with a contemporary layout and recon-structed fortifications (the Hishi Yagura and Hashizume-mon Tsuzuki Yagura watchtow-ers, and, linking them, the Gojikken Nagaya storehouse) built in 2001 using traditional Japanese construction techniques; an English-language pamphlet and audio buttons make this a fascinating must for architecture buffs, but you can skip these empty build-ings if time is of the essence.

Kenroku-machi. ✆ **076/234-3800.** Free admission to Castle Park; castle reconstruction ¥300 adults, ¥100 children. Park Mar to mid-Oct daily 7am–6pm, mid-Oct to Feb daily 8am–5pm; castle reconstruc-tion daily 9am–4pm. Loop Bus: Kenrokuen-shita (5 min.).

Ishikawa Prefectural Museum for Traditional Products and Crafts (Ishikawa Kenritsu Dento Sangyo Kogeikan) ★★★   If I had time to visit only one museum in Kanazawa, this would be my choice. It's by far the best place in town to view and learn about all the beautiful handcrafted items for which Kanazawa has long been famous (the Maeda lords promoted crafts over warfare). There are English-language explanations, a detailed English-language pamphlet, and a free audio guide that describes how the crafts are made. You can see the famous Kutani pottery, first produced under the patronage of the Maeda clan in the 1600s and known for its hues of green, red, purple, navy blue, and yellow, as well as displays of Kaga Yuzen dyeing and hand-painting on silk, Kanazawa lacquerware (which uses raised lacquer painting), paulownia woodcrafts, metalwork, family Buddhist altars, Kanazawa gold leaf, *taiko* drums, *koto* and *shamisen* stringed instruments, lion masks, bambooware, fishing lures (using feathers of wild birds) and rods, folk toys, *washi* (Japanese paper), umbrellas, and even fireworks. Schedule about an hour to appreciate everything.

1–1 Kenroku-machi. ℂ 076/262-2020. Admission ¥250 adults, ¥200 seniors, ¥100 children. Daily 9am–5pm (closed 3rd Thurs of every month Apr–Nov and every Thurs Dec–Mar). Loop Bus: Hirosaka (6 min.). Next to Seisonkaku Villa; you can also enter the museum directly from Kenrokuen.

⑲ **Seisonkaku Villa** ★★ (Finds)   Just outside the Kodatsuno (southeast) exit of Kenrokuen Garden is this must-see villa, built in 1863 by the 13th Maeda lord as a retirement home for his widowed mother. Elegant and graceful, it has a distinctly feminine atmosphere with delicately carved, brightly painted wood transoms and painted shoji screens decorated with seashells, butterflies, flowers, and other motifs. The bedroom is decorated with tortoises painted on the shoji wainscoting; tortoises were associated with long life, and it must have worked—the mother lived to be 84. Expect to linger about 20 minutes here.

1–2 Kenroku-machi. ℂ 076/221-0580. www.seisonkaku.com. Admission ¥700 adults, ¥300 junior-high and high-school students, ¥250 children. Thurs–Tues 9am–5pm. Loop Bus: Hirosaka (5 min.). Next to the Ishikawa Prefectural Museum for Traditional Products and Crafts.

Ishikawa Prefectural Art Museum (Ishikawa Kenritsu Bijutsukan) ★   One of the Maeda clan's lasting contributions was its encouragement of the arts, in full evidence here. After seeing how crafts are made at the Ishikawa Prefectural Museum for Traditional Products and Crafts (see above), stop here to see changing exhibits of Ishikawa Prefecture's most important cultural assets, including Kutani ware, Kaga Yuzen silk, lacquerware, and items such as samurai gear that belonged to the Maeda family, as well as contemporary oil paintings and decorative art by artists who were born in Ishikawa, lived here, or had some connection to the prefecture (artists to look for include Nakagawa Kazumasa, Takamitsu Kazuya, and Miyamoto Saburo). One room is reserved solely for the museum's most valuable treasures, a pair of pheasant-shaped incense burners (by a 17th-c. Kyoto potter). Be sure to take advantage of the English-spoken audio guides included in the admission fee, which provide commentary on individual works of art and their significance. You'll need 45 minutes here.

2–1 Dewa-machi. ℂ 076/231-7580. www.ishibi.pref.ishikawa.jp/english/index.html. Admission ¥350 adults, ¥280 seniors and university students, free for children. Daily 9:30am–5pm. Closed 3–4 days monthly during exhibit changes. Loop Bus: Hirosaka (4 min.). Just south of Kenrokuen Park, not far from Ishikawa Prefectural Museum for Traditional Products and Crafts (discussed above).

21st Century Museum of Contemporary Art ★★   In a word, this museum is fun! Centrally located between Kenrokuen Garden and the Katamachi shopping district, Kanazawa's newest museum, with the aim of revitalizing the arts in Kanazawa and attracting young visitors, is ensconced in a striking circular building that has no front or back, allowing visitors to explore it from all directions (and, from time to time, lose themselves in it). Galleries, which range from bright spaces with sunlight pouring through glass ceilings to darkened rooms with no natural light, display a collection that concentrates on works of the past 15 years, particularly of Japanese artists born after 1965, along with contemporary works from around the world shown in changing exhibitions. My favorite: Leandro Erlich's outdoor "swimming pool" topped with a roof of glass and shallow water; look in, and you might see people who, having entered through a subterranean tunnel, look like they're walking underwater.

1–2–1 Hirosaka. ☏ **076/220-2800.** www.kanazawa21.jp. Admission ¥350 adults, ¥280 seniors and university students, free for children 17 and under. Special exhibits ¥1,000, ¥800, and ¥400 respectively. Sun and Tues–Thurs 10am–6pm; Fri–Sat 10am–8pm. Loop Bus: Hirosaka (2 min.).

The Naga-machi Samurai (Buke Yashiki) District

About a 15-minute walk west of Kenrokuen Garden and just a couple minutes' walk west of Katamachi (Kanazawa's main shopping district), the Naga-machi Samurai District is basically a few streets lined with beautiful wooden homes hidden behind gold-colored mud walls (higher-ranked samurai had higher walls; the lowest rank had only hedges) and bordered by canals left over from the Edo Period. An unhurried stroll in the neighborhood will give you an idea of what a feudal castle town might have looked like. But only fleetingly: Lord Maeda had as many as 8,000 samurai retainers, who in turn had their own retainers, making the samurai population here very large indeed. To see how those in the lowest military class lived, stop by the ⑫⓪ **Kanazawa Ashigaru Hakubutsukan,** consisting of two homes open free to the public daily 9am to 5pm. In addition, the **Kanazawa Shinise Memorial Hall** (☏ **076/220-2524;** daily 9:30am–5pm), a former Chinese pharmacy established in 1579, displays the old store and family residence and, upstairs, exhibits Kanazawa crafts and products from some 60 local stores for ¥100 (children are free).

To reach the Naga-machi Samurai District from Katamachi, take the side street to the right of the Excel Hotel Tokyu.

⑫① **Nomura Samurai House (Buke Yashiki Ato Nomura Ke)** ★   Stop 20 minutes here to see how higher-ranking samurai lived back in the Edo Period. Occupied by 11 generations of the Nomura family for 400 years, this traditional Japanese home boasts a drawing room made of Japanese cypress, with elaborate designs in rosewood and shoji screens painted with landscapes, and a tea-ceremony room upstairs (tea costs ¥300). Rooms overlook a small, charming garden with a miniature waterfall, a winding stream, huge carp, and stone lanterns (many people come just for the garden). Personal effects of the Nomura family and objects from the Edo Period are on display, including a samurai outfit, swords, lacquerware, the family altar, and a box for bush warblers (deliberately dark so the birds would sing).

1–3–32 Naga-machi. ☏ **076/221-3553.** Admission ¥500 adults, ¥400 high-school students, ¥250 children. Apr–Sept daily 8:30am–5:30pm; Oct–Mar daily 8:30am–4:30pm. Loop Bus: Korinbo (5 min.). Take the side street to the right of the Excel Hotel Tokyu, turn right at the T, and then turn left.

Other Sights

Higashi Chaya District   There are approximately 50 geisha practicing their trade in three old entertainment quarters in Kanazawa, including this one. A walk here reveals rather solemn-looking, wood-slatted facades of geisha houses dating from the 1820s, where men of means have long come to be entertained with music, dancing, songs, the tea ceremony, poem recitals, and other pleasurable pursuits. Geisha still perform at seven houses in the Higashi Chaya District, but most of the other former geisha homes have been turned into shops, inns, and restaurants. For an inside peek at the geisha world, visit the 190-year-old ⑫② **Shima Geisha House,** 1–13–21 Higashiyama (☏ **076/252-5675;** daily 9am–6pm), a former tearoom where merchants as well as men of letters came to watch geisha perform. Inside, you'll find rooms that were allotted to personal use, as well as to performing, along with displays of ordinary artifacts from combs, hair ornaments, pipes, and game boards to cooking utensils. Architectural details worth noting include several stairways (so that customers could come and go without being seen); a small Shinto shrine at the entrance to the home; a more elaborate family Buddhist altar in a place of honor in a front room; the gleaming wood-lacquered surfaces of furniture; and the cloisonné door pulls on sliding doors. Admission is ¥400 for adults, ¥300 for children; but you'll probably also want to enjoy tea in the new addition facing a garden, which, depending on the accompanying sweet, costs ¥500 to ¥700. It takes 10 minutes or so to tour the house.

(123) **Myoryuji Temple** ★★ Myoryuji Temple (1–2–12 Nomachi; ✆ 076/241-**0888**) is popularly known as Ninja-dera (Temple of the Secret Agents) because of its secret chambers, hidden stairways, tunnels, and trick doors. Built by the Maeda clan for family prayer in 1643, it looks small from the outside, just two stories high to comply with height restrictions during the Edo Period. Inside, four stories are evident, but even this is false: Three more levels are concealed. The fortresslike structure contains an amazing 29 stairways and a labyrinth of corridors, along with such trick devices as pitfalls to trap unsuspecting intruders, slatted stairs where lances could stab at passing legs, escape hatches, secret stairways, and rooms that could be opened only from the outside—just one more example of how deep paranoia ran during the Edo Period. Although rumor has it that a tunnel once connected the temple to the castle to serve as an escape route for the feudal lord in case of attack, a river running between them makes it unlikely. Unfortunately, photography is not allowed.

You must phone ahead for a reservation; chances are good that you'll be able to see it the same day you call. To ensure that you don't get lost (which would be quite easy because of all the trick doors), you must join a guided tour. Unfortunately, tours are in Japanese only, but there's an English-language booklet that lets you follow along, and demonstrations of the various trick devices are fairly self-explanatory. Tours, given daily from 9am to 4:30pm (to 4pm in winter), last 30 to 40 minutes and cost ¥800 for adults, ¥600 for children (however, the temple does not recommend tours for children of any age, due to their tendency to talk and make noise, and children 5 and younger are not admitted). To reach it, take the Loop Bus to Jusangenmachi, cross the bridge you see straight ahead of you over the river, take the second left (Teramachi), and then the first right. It will be on your right.

SHOPPING

Kanazawa's most famous products are its **Kutani pottery,** with its bright five-color overglaze patterns, and its hand-painted **Yuzen silk.** Kanazawa also produces *maki-e* lacquerware, sweets, toys, wooden products, and almost all of Japan's gold leaf. For convenient shopping for these and other souvenirs, try the **Omiyage Kan shopping arcade** right in Kanazawa Station, open daily 8:30am to 7pm.

For department stores, boutiques, and contemporary shops, visit the **Katamachi and Tatemachi shopping streets,** within walking distance of Kenrokuen Garden and the Naga-machi Samurai district. **Omi-cho Market,** just off Hyakumangoku Dori between the station and Kenrokuen Garden, was established 280 years ago as the "kitchen of Kanazawa" and today is a vibrant city market with more than 170 stalls selling seafood, vegetables, fruit, and more. It's open Monday to Saturday from 10am to 6pm.

Ishikawa Prefectural Products Center (Kanko Bussankan) Located just north of Kenrokuen Garden, this is the place to come for one-stop shopping of all the products Ishikawa Prefecture is famous for. The ground floor sells crafts ranging from lacquerware and pottery to glassware, foodstuff, and toys, while the second floor houses more crafts and a sushi restaurant. Open daily 10am to 6pm (upstairs closes at 4pm; closed some Tues Nov–Mar). 2–20 Kenroku-machi. ☎ **076/222-7788.** Loop Bus: Kenroku-en-shita (2 min.). Backtrack to Hyakumangoku Dori and turn right.

(124) **Kaga Yuzen Traditional Industry Center (Kaga Yuzen Dento Sangyo Kaikan)** Yuzen dying was brought from Kyoto to Kanazawa in 1712, where a new technique emerged that uses just five colors—indigo, crimson, ocher, green, and purple. A 13-minute English-language video describes the painstaking process of hand-drawing the pattern and its colors and the role Yuzen cloth dying played in Kanazawa history (admission: ¥300). Otherwise, take the stairs to the left of the entryway to the basement shop, where you can purchase scarves, purses, fans, ties, clothing, *furoshiki* (traditionally used for wrapping presents), and other items made from hand-dyed Yuzen cloth, which borrows heavily from nature for its designs—mainly flowers and landscapes. Open Thursday to Tuesday 9am to 5pm. 8–8 Kosho-machi. ☎ **076/224-5511.** www.kagayuzen.or.jp. Loop Bus: Kenroku-en-shita (2 min.). Cross Hyakumangoku Dori, turn right, and then left after the parking lot.

Kanazawa Crafts Hirosaka Finely crafted glassware, embroidery, fans, jewelry, pottery, umbrellas, and other items by local artisans are sold here. Open Tuesday to Sunday 10am to 6pm. 1–2–25 Hirosaka. ☎ **076/265-3320.** Loop Bus: Hirosaka (1 min.). Beside Kanazawa Noh Museum, near the 21st Century Museum of Contemporary Art.

(125) **Kutani Kosen Pottery Kiln (Kutani Kosengama)** ★ If your interest lies in pottery, it's worth a visit to this Kutani-ware kiln and shop, open since 1870 and about a 10-minute walk from Myoryuji Temple. In addition to browsing its showroom, you can also take a 15-minute tour, led by a guide who speaks some English, to see the entire process of producing handmade Kutani ware, including the potters' wheels, the hand painting of designs, and the kilns. It takes 3 months to produce each piece, sold only here. Open daily 9am to noon and 1 to 5pm. 5–3–3 Nomachi. ☎ **076/241-0902.** City Bus No. 1 or 2: 20 min. from Kanazawa Station from platform 8 to the Nomachi Eki stop (3 min.). Walk back toward the city center and take the 1st left (beside a small canal); it's almost immediately on the left.

(126) **Sakuda** Thinking about wallpapering a room in gold leaf? Then you'll want to pay a visit to Sakuda, located in a modern building in the Higashi Chaya District. (As much as 98% of Japan's entire national output of gold leaf is produced in Kanazawa.) You can watch artisans at work, pounding the gold leaf and spreading it until it's paper-thin and translucent; it's the equivalent of pounding a ¥10 coin into the size of a tatami mat. But most people come here to shop for gold-leafed vases, boxes, chopsticks, bowls, trays, screens, furniture, and—this being Japan—golf balls and clubs. You can even buy gold flakes to add to your coffee or sake. Don't miss the second-floor bathrooms; the women's is done entirely in gold leaf, the men's in platinum. The staff was serving complimentary tea spiked with gold leaf to everyone who dropped by during my last visit. Open daily 9am to 6pm. 1–3–27 Higashiyama. ☎ **076/251-6777.** www.goldleaf-sakuda.jp. Loop Bus: Hashibacho (4 min.).

(127) **Shamisen no Fukushima** (Finds) There used to be other makers of the three-stringed *shamisen* instrument in Kanazawa to keep the geisha supplied with one of the tools of their trade, but this fourth-generation-owned shop, in the Higashi Chaya District, is the only one remaining. While you may not be in the market for a *shamisen*, from 10am to 4pm you can have a short lesson in English (¥300) and then play as long as you

wish, followed by a cup of tea. An upstairs showroom shows how these instruments are made, including the cat and dog skin used to cover the sound box (cat skin is more expensive). Open Monday to Saturday 10am to 5:30pm; closed holidays, the second and fourth Saturdays of the month, and mid-August. 1–1–8 Higashiyama. (C) **076/252-3703.** Loop Bus: Hashibacho (2 min.). On Kannon-machi St.

(128) **Tawaraya Ame** (Kids) They've been selling Japanese confectionery from this traditional wood-slatted building since 1830. Tawaraya makes candy from rice and barley, using malt instead of sugar, and now touts the candy as health food. One of the candies, *Jiro Ame,* is soft like honey, purportedly developed for babies who, for one reason or another, could not be breast-fed. *Okoshi Ame* is hard and comes in a wooden bucket; the staff recommends breaking the hard candy with a hammer (kids love this) and putting it in a refrigerator. Soft lollipops and hard candy (true jawbreakers!) and candy flavored with Japanese apricot, ginger, mulberry, and other flavors are also available. Open Monday to Saturday 9am to 6pm; Sunday 9am to 5pm. 2–4 Kobashi-machi. (C) **076/252-2079.** Loop Bus: Kobashi (2 min.). Cross the bridge and turn left.

WHERE TO STAY

Keep in mind that some accommodations may add a surcharge to the prices below during peak season—New Year's, Golden Week (Apr 29–May 5), and mid-July through mid-November.

Directions are from Kanazawa Station; minutes in parentheses indicate the walking time required from the bus stop.

Expensive

Hotel Nikko Kanazawa ★★★ Kanazawa's tallest building was designed by a Japanese-French team, who succeeded in giving it a boutique-hotel ambience despite its size. Its lobby exudes a French-colonial drawing room atmosphere, adorned with a bubbling fountain, rattan chairs stuffed with pillows, fake trees, antiques, and Asian decorative art ranging from ginger jars to Japanese lacquered boxes. The English-speaking concierge staff receives high marks, and its location in front of the station can't be beat for convenience. Rooms are spacious, all with double-size or larger beds and decent-size bathrooms, and are decorated with items made with Yuzen cloth, gold leaf, and other Kanazawa handicrafts. Rooms on higher floors offer great views of either mountains or the Japan Sea in the distance.

2–15–1 Hon-machi, Kanazawa, Ishikawa 920-0853. (C) **800/645-5687** in the U.S. and Canada, or 076/234-1111. Fax 076/234-8802. www.hnkanazawa.co.jp. 254 units. ¥28,000–¥68,000 single or double. AE, DC, MC, V. Station: Kanazawa (east exit, 1 min.). **Amenities:** 5 restaurants, including Le Grand Chariot (p. 392); bar; lounge; babysitting; concierge; access to next-door health club and spa w/indoor pool (fee: ¥2,100); lobby computer w/free Internet; room service; smoke-free rooms. *In room:* A/C, TV, hair dryer, Internet, minibar.

Kanazawa Miyako Hotel Although the hotel's cheerless exterior could use an update and the lobby is purely functional, all of the rooms are nicely done and its twin rooms (there are only five doubles) are among the largest for their price in Kanazawa. Add to that the Miyako name (synonymous with service), smoke-free restaurants, and a convenient location (across the street from and linked to the station via an underground passage), and you'll see why I like this lodging. There are even rooms for ladies with a vanity, a bigger bed than the standard singles (don't ask me why), and a toiletry bag that includes bath gel and other female-oriented amenities. I also like rooms facing the station's bus terminal; when a Loop Bus pulls out, I know I have 12 minutes to make the next one.

(**Moments**) **Live Like a Local**

For a unique experience, consider spending the night in your own *machiya,* a traditional wooden town house common during the Edo Period. You'll have the entire home, complete with kitchen, futon, and bathroom, plus extras like Japanese umbrellas and *yukata* (not to mention TVs and Internet connection). Homes rent for ¥54,000 for two to three people and ¥72,000 for four to five, including breakfast. Contact **Kikunoya Machiya Kanazawa,** 3–22 Kazue-machi ((**076/287-0834**; www.machiya-kanazawa.jp).

6–10 Konohanacho, Kanazawa, Ishikawa 920-0852. (**076/261-2111.** Fax 076/261-2113. www.miyako hotels.ne.jp/kanazawa. 193 units. ¥11,550–¥13,860 single; ¥20,790–¥32,340 double. AE, DC, MC, V. Station: Kanazawa (east exit, 1 min.). **Amenities:** 2 restaurants; bar/lounge; room service; smoke-free rooms. *In room:* A/C, TV, fridge (in some), hair dryer, Internet (in some).

Moderate

APA Hotel Kanazawa-Ekimae   Although just a business hotel, this place does have a special feature that sets it apart: large public baths complete with sauna and open-air bath, all free to hotel guests. Other pluses include a convenient location just steps away from Kanazawa Station; bold use of bright colors that are a welcome relief from the usual bland white of most business hotels; and a Seattle's Best Coffee (with free Wi-Fi). If you're not a fan of public baths, however, you might choose to stay elsewhere; the hotel is not geared toward tourists, little English is spoken, and rooms are so minuscule that if you open your luggage you may have to leap to reach your bed. Even the deluxe corner rooms would be considered small in a regular hotel.

If you'd rather be in the heart of the city, the **APA Hotel Kanazawa-Chuo,** 1–5–24 Katamachi ((**076/235-2111**), offers similar-size rooms at similar rates and a Seattle's Best Coffee with Wi-Fi, but the water tapped for its indoor and outdoor baths is from hot springs.

1–9–28 Hirooka, Kanazawa, Ishikawa 920-0031. (**076/231-8111.** Fax 076/231-8112. www.apahotel. com. 456 units. ¥8,000–¥9,000 single; ¥11,000–¥18,000 double. AE, MC, V. Station: Kanazawa (west exit, 2 min.). **Amenities:** 3 restaurants; bar; hot-spring baths w/sauna; lobby computer w/Internet (¥100 for 10 min.); smoke-free rooms. *In room:* A/C, TV, fridge, hair dryer, Internet.

Kanazawa Manten ★ (**Value**)   A fountain at the entrance, a front desk backed by trees, jazz playing in the hotel restaurant, indoor/outdoor baths, and attentive service all conspire to make this business hotel (located on the opposite side of the station from where the buses depart) seem like it's more expensive than it is. Alas, the overwhelmingly single rooms (there are only 72 twin rooms and 10 doubles) are no different or larger than those of any other business hotel, with semi-double-size beds that take up most of the floor space. On the bright side, the windows can be opened or covered by panels for complete darkness, and on each floor there's a convenience corner with a microwave, trouser press, and vending machines. In short, the cramped quarters and self-serve philosophy of the upper floors reinforce the business-hotel status, but at least in the lobby and the baths you can feel grand.

1–6–1 Kita-yasue, Kanazawa, Ishikawa 920-0022. (**076/265-0100.** Fax 076/265-0120. 551 units. ¥6,800 single; ¥12,600 double. AE, DC, MC, V. Station: Kanazawa (west exit, 3 min.). Turn right out of the station and continue along the tracks, past the car park. **Amenities:** Restaurant; lounge; public baths w/Jacuzzi, sauna (men only), and steam room (women only); lounge computer w/free Internet. *In room:* A/C, TV, fridge, hair dryer, Internet.

Inexpensive

In addition to the recommendations here, there's the **Toyoko Inn Kanazawa Korinbo,** 2–4–28 Korinbo (⟁ **076/232-1045;** www.toyoko-inn.com), offering singles from ¥4,700 and doubles from ¥7,560, including breakfast. See the description of the Toyoko Inn in Kobe (p. 425) for more on this chain.

Ryokan Murataya   This Japanese Inn Group *ryokan* is in the heart of Kanazawa, not far from Katamachi and Tatemachi shopping streets and within walking distance of Kenrokuen. It's modern and rather uninteresting from the outside but comfortable and pleasant inside. Note the old-fashioned 50-some-year-old telephone in the reception used to connect Murataya with the outside world; but LAN cables at the Hibachi allow you to hook up your computer. All rooms are clean and are Japanese style with tatami, with extralong futons for tall foreigners. A plus is the inn's own map of the Katamachi area, showing the locations of banks, post offices, stores, and restaurants.

1–5–2 Katamachi, Kanazawa, Ishikawa 920-0981. ⟁ **076/263-0455.** Fax 076/263-0456. www.muratayaryokan.com/e. 11 units, none with bathroom. ¥4,700 single; ¥9,000 double; ¥12,600 triple. Continental breakfast ¥500 extra; Japanese breakfast ¥800 extra. AE, DC, MC, V. Loop Bus: Katamachi (3 min.). Take the small pedestrian lane on the right side of the APA Hotel and then turn left. **Amenities:** Lobby computer w/free Internet. *In room:* A/C, TV.

Via Inn Kanazawa ★   This business hotel, located inside Kanazawa Station with reception on the third floor, offers all of life's basic necessities, including decent-size rooms and a microwave on each floor (there's a grocery store below the hotel). There are only four twin rooms and no doubles, but two people can stay in a single room for the lowest price below if they don't mind forced togetherness.

Kanazawa Station, Kanazawa, Ishikawa 920-0858. ⟁ **076/222-5489.** Fax 076/222-5485. 206 units. ¥5,800 single; ¥7,000–¥11,000 double. AE, DC, MC, V. Station: Kanazawa (inside the station). **Amenities:** Lobby computer w/free Internet. *In room:* A/C, TV, fridge, hair dryer, Internet.

Yogetsu ★★ ⟨Finds⟩   Geisha used to live in this 190-year-old *machiya* (traditional wooden home) located on the main street of the Higashi Chaya District, but now it's a charming inn with just a handful of tatami rooms. Remarkably, most of the house retains its original character. Note the entryway door, with a small door built into the larger one; other unique characteristics include an old-style metal tub and a breakfast room overlooking a courtyard garden. Unlike most inns, you have to pay extra for use of a *yukata* (¥200) or a towel (¥100).

1–13–22 Higashiyama, Kanazawa, Ishikawa 920-0831. ⟁ **076/252-0497.** 4 units, none with bathroom. ¥4,500 per person. Breakfast ¥500 extra. No credit cards. Loop Bus: Hashibacho (4 min.). On the main street of Higashi Chaya District. *In room:* A/C, no phone.

WHERE TO DINE

Kanazawa's local specialties, known collectively as **Kaga Ryori,** consist of seafood, such as tiny shrimp and winter crabs, as well as freshwater fish, duck, and mountain vegetables. Popular in winter is *jibuni,* a duck-and-vegetable stew.

All directions are from Kanazawa Station.

Forus, a shopping center located next to Kanazawa Station (look for *Aeon* on its facade), has a slew of restaurants on its sixth floor, including Mori Mori Sushi and Budoonoki (see below), as well as those serving noodles, *tonkatsu,* and Indian and Korean fare. Most are open daily from 11am to 11pm.

Le Grand Chariot ★★ FRENCH   The highest spot in Kanazawa, this combination lounge and restaurant offers a gorgeous setting and great views, particularly at sunset, making this a good romantic splurge. The sophisticated lounge occupies the center of the room, while dining tables line windows at either side with the best ringside views; from the west windows you can even see the Japan Sea on the horizon. Only changing set meals are available, but they offer a choice of a main dish, artfully presented, along with a buffet of appetizers and desserts. Live music serenades you from 8:30 to 11pm, but the cover charge (¥854 on weekdays and ¥1,365 weekends) is waived for diners.

Hotel Nikko Kanazawa, 30th floor, 2-15-1 Hon-machi. 𝄐 **076/234-1111.** Set lunches ¥1,900–¥2,500; set dinners ¥5,000. AE, DC, MC, V. Daily 11:30am–2pm and 5:30–9:30pm (last order). Station: Kanazawa (east exit, 1 min.).

⑫⑨ **Mori Mori Sushi** ⟮**Value**⟯ SUSHI   This conveyor-belt sushi restaurant has colored plates, each signifying a specific price, but there's also a menu with photos so you can order what you want if it doesn't float past. There are spigots for hot water at the counter; serve yourself and add powdered tea. There's a more colorful branch at Omi-cho Market (𝄐 **076/262-7477**), open Monday to Saturday from 10am to 5pm.

Forus, 6th floor. 𝄐 **076/265-3510.** Sushi platters ¥120–¥360. No credit cards. Daily 11am–10pm (last order). Station: Kanazawa (east exit, 1 min.). Turn left out of the station.

Around Kenrokuen Garden

⑬⓪ **Miyoshian** ★★ ⟮**Finds**⟯ KAGA KAISEKI   A great place to try the local Kaga cuisine right in Kenrokuen Garden, this 100-year-old restaurant consists of three separate wooden buildings, the best of which is a traditional room extending over a large pond. This is where you'll probably dine, seated on tatami with a view of an ancient pond (giant carp swim in the murky waters). Only set meals of Kaga cuisine are served, all featuring *jibuni.* The more expensive the meal, the more dishes it adds. The ¥1,575 *yugao* meal includes soup, jibuni, sashimi, a seasonal dish such as eel on rice, and pickles. The ¥3,150 *chakaisekifu* meal adds such dishes as salmon, crab, tofu, and various small delicacies. Lunch is served from 11am to 2pm, but you can also come just for green tea and sweets for ¥525.

Kenrokuen Garden, 1–11 Kenrokumachi. 𝄐 **076/221-0127.** Kaga teishoku ¥1,575–¥3,150. DC, MC, V. Thurs–Tues 9am–4pm. Loop Bus: Kenrokuen-shita (5 min.). Turn right after entering the park.

Katamachi

Radiating from Katamachi Shopping Street and Saigawa Odori (called Chuo Dori by the locals) is an area full of restaurants and drinking establishments.

Budoonoki ITALIAN   An informal eatery with a high ceiling and an open facade facing a courtyard, this pleasant restaurant offers salads, pizzas, and pastas, including versions you've probably never thought of, like lotus root salad, pizza with laver seaweed and leek, or spaghetti with duck and horseradish in a thick sauce. Other choices include the fish of the day, fried Iberico pork cutlet, or rice omelet with a sauce of beef and red wine. After 6pm you can nibble on tapas (¥714 for three tapas). Finish it all off with

Japanese green-tea parfait. There's a branch on the sixth floor of Forum next to Kanazawa Station (☎ **076/265-3521**), open daily 11am to 11pm.

1-3-21 Katamachi. ☎ **076/232-7878.** Main dishes ¥880–¥1,650; set lunches ¥880–¥1,800. MC, V. Thurs–Tues 11am–9:30pm (last order). Loop Bus: Katamachi (2 min.). In a small alley off Katamachi St. called Prego.

Kincharyo VARIED JAPANESE   This, without a doubt, is Katamachi's easiest restaurant to find: It's located on the third floor of the very visible Excel Hotel Tokyu. Sister restaurant to a famous 90-year-old restaurant in the Teramachi Temple district (near Myoryuji Temple), it offers tempura, *Kaga kaiseki,* sushi, and steak, but most popular are the obento with a variety of dishes for ¥1,732 to ¥3,465.

Excel Hotel Tokyu, 2-1-1 Korinbo. ☎ **076/263-5511.** Set dinners ¥3,550–¥9,240; set lunches ¥1,732–¥3,465. AE, DC, MC, V. Daily 11:30am–2pm and 5–9pm (last order). Loop Bus: Korinbo (1 min.).

⑬ **Kitama** ★ VARIED JAPANESE/KAGA   Sitting on tatami mats, you'll have a pleasant view of moss-covered greenery at this modern restaurant with a 150-year-old history. The *Kojitsu obento* (¥2,100), served in an upright lunch box, features sashimi, small pieces of pork and fish, fried shrimp, a soybean patty, and various seasonal vegetables. The *jibuni teishoku* (¥1,890), with duck stew, clear soup, pickled vegetables, rice, and hors d'oeuvres, is also quite satisfying. The restaurant is also known for its tempura and kaiseki (artfully prepared multicourse meals) starting at ¥4,200.

2-3-3 Katamachi. ☎ **076/261-7176.** Set meals ¥1,050–¥4,200. AE, MC, V. Daily 11:30am–8:30pm (last order). Closed irregularly. Loop Bus: Katamachi (2 min.). From the intersection of Katamachi and Chuo, walk 1 block west on Chuo Dori and turn right; the restaurant will be on your left with a display case and bamboo fence at its entrance.

Higashi Chaya District

Bistro Todoroki-Tei ★ FRENCH   This former bank dating from the Taisho Period (1912–26) has been turned into an attractive restaurant boasting tall ceilings, gleaming dark wood, and period light fixtures. Big-band jazz and swing music playing in the background add to its nostalgic atmosphere. For dinner you might opt for the Caesar salad, prepared tableside and large enough for two to share, followed by confit of duck, grilled beef with a lemon soy sauce, or fish of the day.

1-2-1 Higashiyama. ☎ **076/252-5755.** Main courses ¥2,000–¥3,500; set lunches ¥1,200–¥3,500. AE, DC, MC, V. Daily 11:30am–2:30pm (to 3:30pm Sat–Sun and holidays) and 6–10:30pm. Loop Bus: Hashibacho (1 min.) Beside the bus stop and *Koban* (police box).

⑬ **Jugetsuya** ★ (Finds) KAISEKI/KAGA   Dining in this former teahouse means sitting at a huge wooden slab of a counter, with leg wells for those errant appendages and a view of a small garden. At lunch four meals are offered, which change with the seasons. Summer may feature cold *udon* noodles with sesame sauce, while winter might bring steaming bowls of *jibuni.* Dinners feature kaiseki with local *Kaga* dishes.

1-26-16 Higashiyama. ☎ **076/253-3321.** Reservations recommended. Set lunches ¥1,050–¥2,750; set dinners ¥6,300–¥8,400. AE, DC, MC, V. Tues–Sun 11:30am–3pm and 6–9pm. Loop Bus: Hashibacho (4 min.). On the main street of Higashi Chaya District.

Elsewhere

⑬ **Kotobuki-Ya** ★★★ (Finds) VEGETARIAN   Specializing in *shojin ryori* (Buddhist vegetarian cooking), Kotobuki-ya is in a beautiful 165-year-old merchant's house with a two-story airy entryway. Dining here, on beautiful lacquer and pottery tableware while seated at tables or on tatami, is a wonderful experience—not surprisingly, they have had many fine reviews. For lunch, you can dine for ¥2,625 on the *shojin ryori obento* or splurge on kaiseki for ¥5,500. Kaiseki dinners are vegetarian or with fish. If you order kaiseki you'll be seated in your own private room (or, if you order the obento lunch, you can have your own room for ¥350 extra per person). Two of the rooms have views of the garden.

2-4-13 Owari-cho. ℂ **076/231-6245.** Reservations required by 4:30pm for dinner. Set lunches ¥2,625–¥5,500; kaiseki dinners ¥8,400–¥15,000. AE, DC, MC, V. Daily 11:30am–1:30pm and 5–7:30pm (last order). Loop Bus: Musashigatsuji (3 min.). North of Hyakumangoku Dori, on a side street btw. 2 small parking lots.

4 OSAKA

553km (343 miles) W of Tokyo; 42km (26 miles) SW of Kyoto; 339km (212 miles) E of Hiroshima

Although its history stretches back almost 1,500 years, Osaka first gained prominence when Hideyoshi Toyotomi, the most powerful lord in the land, built Japan's most magnificent castle here in the 16th century. To develop resources for his castle town, he persuaded merchants from other parts of the nation to resettle in Osaka. During the Edo Period, the city became an important distribution center as feudal lords from the surrounding region sent their rice to merchants in Osaka, who in turn sent the rice onward to Tokyo and other cities. As the merchants prospered, the town grew and such arts as *kabuki* and *bunraku* flourished. With money and leisure to spare, the merchants also developed a refined taste for food.

Today, with the legacy of the city's commercial beginnings still present, Osaka is known throughout Japan as an international and progressive business center and is the mover and the shaker of the Kansai region. Capital of Osaka Prefecture and with a population of about 2.6 million, it's the third-most populated city in Japan (after Tokyo and Yokohama). Osakans are usually characterized as being outgoing and clever at money affairs. (One Osakan greeting is "Are you making any money?") It's also known for its food, castle, port, underground shopping arcades, and *bunraku* puppet theater, and boasts the oldest state temple in Japan, one of the nation's best aquariums, and the only Universal Studios outside the United States. Because of its international airport, it also serves as a major gateway to the rest of Japan. Indeed, some travelers base themselves in Osaka, taking day trips to Kyoto, Nara, Kobe, and Mount Koya.

ESSENTIALS
Getting There
BY PLANE　Osaka's **Kansai International Airport** (**KIX**; ℂ **072/455-2500**; www.kansai-airport.or.jp) receives both domestic and international flights. The two major domestic airlines that fly into KIX are **Japan Airlines** (JAL; www.jal.com) and **All Nippon Airways** (ANA; www.ana.co.jp). From Tokyo's Haneda and Narita airports, flight time is about 1¼ hours. A **JAL** fare is ¥23,600 one-way, though discount fares go as low as ¥11,100.

ARRIVING AT KIX　Arriving at KIX, you experience Japan at its modern best. Constructed on a huge man-made island 5km (3 miles) off the mainland in Osaka Bay and connected to the city by a six-lane highway and two-rail line bridge, this 24-hour airport boasts the latest in technology—glass elevators ferry passengers to the four floors of the complex in an atrium setting, dozens of computers spread throughout the terminal provide Internet access for ¥100 per 10 minutes, and touch screens provide information in many languages. And, like the city itself, it's traveler-friendly: Signs are clear and abundant, and facilities—which range from restaurants and shops to a **post office** (second floor south; Mon–Sat 8am–7pm, Sun 8am–5pm), **ATMs** that accept foreign credit cards, a children's **playroom** in the international departure area (free of charge), **cellphone** rental counters, and **dental and medical clinics**—are seemingly endless.

GETTING FROM KIX TO OSAKA   Taxis are prohibitively expensive: Expect to spend at least ¥17,000 for an hour's cab ride to the city center. Easiest, especially if you have luggage, is the **Kansai Airport Transportation Enterprise** (© 072/461-1374; www. kate.co.jp), which provides bus service to major stations and a few hotels in Osaka (and even stations in Kyoto and Kobe). Most fares cost ¥1,500, and tickets can be purchased at counters in the arrival lobby. Another bus service, the **OCAT Shuttle** (© 06/6635-3000; www.ocat.co.jp), travels from KIX to the Osaka City Air Terminal (a downtown bus station for shuttle buses going to the airport), next to JR Namba Station (the major train station in Namba) in the heart of Osaka; buses depart every 30 minutes for the 48-minute ride and cost ¥1,000.

If you want to take the **train** into Osaka or even farther to Kyoto, simply walk through KIX's second-floor connecting concourse (baggage carts are designed to go on escalators and as far as train ticket gates). The **JR Airport Express Haruka,** which travels to Tennoji and Shin-Osaka stations before continuing to Kyoto, departs about twice an hour; the fare to Shin-Osaka is ¥2,470 for the 50-minute trip. Slower is the **JR Rapid Service (JR Kanku Kaisoku),** which travels from the airport to Tennoji and Osaka stations. The 70-minute trip to Osaka Station costs ¥1,320. *Note:* When returning to the airport from Osaka, make sure you're in a compartment that goes all the way to KIX; not all of them do. If you a have a **Japan Rail Pass,** you can ride these trains for free. Exchange your voucher at the Kansai Airport (rail) Station on the third floor (daily 6am–11:30pm).

Next to the JR trains in the same station at the airport is the private **Nankai Line,** which has three types of trains to Namba Nankai Station. The sleek **rapi:t a** (pronounced "rapito alpha") train reaches Namba in 35 minutes. There's one train an hour, and ordinary reserved seats cost ¥1,390. The **rapi:t b** ("rapito beta") at the same price stops at more stations, including Sakai, and takes 39 minutes. You can also take an ordinary **Nankai Express Line** for ¥890 and reach Namba in 43 minutes.

ITAMI AIRPORT   If you're arriving on a domestic flight, chances are you'll arrive at Itami Airport (ITM; © 06/6856-6781), north of the city. Buses connect to various parts of Osaka; to Osaka Station, the ride takes 25 minutes and costs ¥620.

BY TRAIN   Osaka is 3 hours from Tokyo by Shinkansen bullet train; tickets are ¥13,240 for an unreserved seat (the Nozomi Shinkansen, which is not valid with a Japan Rail Pass, is faster and more expensive). All Shinkansen bullet trains arrive at **Shin-Osaka Station** at the city's northern edge. To get from Shin-Osaka Station to Osaka Station and other points south, use the most convenient public transportation, the **Midosuji Line** subway; the subway stop at Osaka Station is called **Umeda Station. JR trains** also make runs between Shin-Osaka and Osaka stations.

If you haven't turned in your voucher for your **Japan Rail Pass** yet, you can do so at Osaka Station's or Shin-Osaka Station's Green Windows (daily 5:30am–11pm).

If you're arriving in Osaka from Kobe or Kyoto, the commuter lines, which will deliver you directly to Osaka Station in the heart of the city, are more convenient than the Shinkansen, which will deposit you at out-of-the-way Shin-Osaka Station.

OSAKA THE REST OF WESTERN HONSHU

10

ATTRACTIONS ●
Floating Garden Observatory **1**
Museum of Oriental Ceramics **22**
National Bunraku Theater **41**
Osaka Castle **18**
Osaka International
  Peace Center **19**
Osaka Museum of History **20**
Osaka Shochikuza **35**
Sega Amusement Theme Park
  (Umeda Joypolis) **11**
Shitennoji Temple **44**
Spa World **45**

NIGHTLIFE ◆
Billboard Live **6**
Cinquecento **29**
Murphy's **28**
Rug Time Osaka **33**
Sam & Dave **14, 30**

Railway
Subway
ⓘ Tourist Info

0   1/4 mi
0   0.25 km

YODOGAWA
RIVERSIDE
PARK

HANSHIN RWY MAIN LINE

JR LOOP LINE

Fukushima

Osaka Visitors'
Information
Center Umeda

Umeda

Umeda

Nishi-Umeda

Higashiumeda

Nakazakicho

KITA-KU
(NORTH WARD)

Temma

Sakuranomiya

O-Kawa River

OGIMACHI
PARK

Ogimachi

Minamimorimachi

MINAMI-TEMMA
PARK

Aqua Bus
Port

Temmabashi

TANIMACHI LINE

Tanimachi-4-Chome

Remains of
Naniwa Palace

Morinomiya

HIGASHI (EAST)

OSAKA
CASTLE
PARK

NISHINOMARU
GARDEN

Osakajo-Koen

Kyobashi

Katamachi

Neya River

Osaka
JR Osaka
Station

Watanabebashi

Nakanoshima

Higobashi

Hommachi

UTSUBO
PARK

Awaza

NISHI (WEST)

KEIHAN NAKANOSHIMA LINE

Dojima River

Tosabori River

Tosabori Dori

Chuo Odori

Naniwa Suji

Aqua Bus
Port

Yodoya-bashi

Oebashi

NAKANOSHIMA
PARK

Naniwabashi

Kitahama

Kusuri-Tokyogai
(wholesale street)

Midosuji Dori
MIDOSUJI LINE

Yotsubashisuji Dori
YOTSUBASHI LINE

SAKAISUJI LINE

Sakaisuji
Hommachi

Shinsaibashi Suji

Hommachi Dori

Macchamachisuji Dori
Hanshin Expressway Loop Route

CHUO LINE

Oimatsucho Dori

ACCOMMODATIONS
Family Inn Fifty's Edobori **24**
Hearton Hotel Nishi Umeda **3**
Hotel Dormy-Inn **32**
Hotel Granvia Osaka **8**
Hotel. Il Monte **12**
Hotel International House Osaka **42**
Hotel Metro The **21 34**
Hotel Nikko Osaka **26**
Imperial Hotel Osaka **15**
New Otani Osaka **17**
Rihga Royal Hotel **23**
Second Inn Umeda **4**
Sheraton Miyako Hotel **43**
Swissôtel Nankai Osaka **38**
The Ritz-Carlton Osaka **5**
Toyoko Inn Osaka Namba **40**
Weekly Mansion Otemae **21**

DINING
Bar Tachibana **10, 35**
Capricciosa **9, 37**
Enoteca **7**
Fugetsu **31**
Honfukuzushi **27**
Japanese Organic Café **39**
Kani Doraku **36**
Namaste **13, 25**
Okonomiyaki Kiji **2**
Panorama Sky Restaurant Asahi **16**
Sh'un Kushiage and Wine **38**

BY BUS   JR **"Dream" night buses** depart from both Tokyo Station's Yaesu exit and Shinjuku Station's New South exit several times nightly (including a bus just for women), arriving at Osaka Station about 9 hours later and costing ¥5,000. Cheaper still is a nightly **JR Seisyun Eco Dream bus** from both Tokyo Station (at 11pm) and Shinjuku Station (at 9:50pm) for ¥4,300, arriving at Osaka Station at 7:03am and 6:13am respectively. There are also many **JR day buses** from Tokyo Station to Osaka Station costing ¥6,000. Tickets for most buses can be bought at any major JR station, JR bus terminal, or at a travel agency; for inquiries, call ℃ **03/3516-1950** (℃ **03/3844-0489** for reservations) or check www.jrbuskanto.co.jp. In addition, **Willer Express** (℃ **050/5805-0383;** http://travel.willer.co.jp) buses depart Tokyo and Shinjuku stations several times nightly, arriving at Osaka Station the next morning. The cost of these range from ¥4,200 to ¥8,600, depending on the date and type of seat (reclining seats cost more); only online reservations are accepted.

Visitor Information

AT THE AIRPORT   The **Kansai Tourist Information Center** (℃ **072/456-6025;** daily 9am–9pm Nov–Mar, 8:30am–8:30pm Apr–Oct) counters are near both the south and north end of the International Arrivals Lobby. The multilingual staff can help with general travel information about Japan, book hotels, and provide brochures and maps of the larger Kansai area, including Kyoto and Kobe.

IN TOWN   At **Osaka Station,** the **Visitors Information Center Umeda** (℃ **06/6345-2189;** daily 8am–8pm) is at the east (Midosuji) exit of JR Osaka Station in a kiosk; the English-speaking staff gives out good maps of the city and can assist in securing a hotel room. Another center is located in **Shin-Osaka Station** on the third floor (℃ **06/6305-3311;** daily 9am–6pm). Note that if you're arriving by Shinkansen, you'll be up on the fourth floor, so simply go down one flight to the tourist office. At **JR Namba Station,** you'll find the **Visitors Information Center Namba** (℃ **06/6631-9100;** daily 9am–8pm) in the Nankai Namba Station across from Takashimaya Department Store. Another Tourist Information Center is in **JR Tennoji Station** (℃ **06/6774-3077;** daily 9am–6pm).

To find out what's going on in Osaka, *Kansai Scene* (www.kansaiscene.com) is a free bilingual monthly magazine with articles, reviews, listings, and information on the Kansai area. *Meet Osaka,* a quarterly pamphlet available free at tourist offices and many hotels, has maps and information on sightseeing, *bunraku,* festivals, concerts, and special exhibits and events. Look, too, for the free *Osaka Guide,* published every 2 months by the Osaka Convention and Tourism Bureau with information on special events, museum exhibitions, concert information, and even which nearby beaches are open in summer.

Finally, information on Osaka city is available on the Web at **www.osaka-info.jp**, and **www.kansai.gr.jp** gives information on the Kansai region.

CONSULATES   Several embassies maintain consulates in Osaka, including **Australia** (℃ **06/6941-9448**); **Great Britain** (℃ **06/6120-5600**); **New Zealand** (℃ **06/6373-4583**); and the **United States** (℃ **06/6315-5900**).

INTERNET ACCESS   Near the Midosuji exit of Osaka Station is an area called Float Court, where you'll find **New Square** (℃ **06/6341-7870**), open daily 8am to 10pm and charging ¥262 for 30 minutes of computer use.

MAIL   The Central Post Office, or Osaka Chuo Yubinkyoku, is in the Osaka Ekimae No. 1 Building, 1–3–1 Umeda, Kita-ku (℃ **06/6347-8112**), a 5-minute walk south of Osaka Station. It's open for mail Monday to Friday 9am to 6pm; its ATM service for

Tips A Note on Directions

For all the attractions, accommodations, and restaurants listed below, I've included the nearest subway or JR station followed by the walking time to the establishment once you reach the indicated station (in parentheses).

international credit cards is available 24 hours Monday to Saturday and from 12:05am to 8pm Sunday and holidays.

Orientation

Osaka is divided into various wards, or *ku,* the most important of which for visitors are Kita-ku (North Ward), which encompasses the area around Osaka Station; and Chuo-ku (Central Ward), where you'll find Osaka Castle and Namba, the heart of the city. Some city maps divide Osaka by location: Kita (North), around Osaka Station; Minami (South), around Namba and Shinsaibashi; Higashi (East), around Osaka Castle; and Nishi (West) which is Osaka's bay area. Shin-Osaka Station, three subway stations north of Osaka (Umeda) Station, is a tourist wasteland with a few hotels.

AROUND OSAKA STATION   **Kita-ku** embraces the area around Osaka and Umeda stations and includes many of the city's top hotels, the city's tallest buildings, lots of restaurants, and several shopping complexes, mostly underground.

AROUND OSAKA CASTLE   Osaka Castle, which lies to the east, is the historic center of the city. It's in **Chuo-ku,** which stretches through the city center.

MINAMI/NAMBA   Four subway stops south of Umeda Station is Namba (also referred to as **Minami,** or South Osaka), with a cluster of stations serving subways, JR trains, and Kintetsu and Nankai lines, all of which are connected to one another via underground passageways. This is the heart of the city, bustling with the spirit of old Osaka, where you'll find more hotels, Osaka's liveliest eating and entertainment district centered on a narrow street called **Dotombori** (also written Dotonbori), and major shopping areas such as the enclosed pedestrian streets **Shinsaibashi-Suji** and **America-Mura** with imported goods from America. Farther south is **Den Den Town,** Osaka's electronics district; and **Dogayasuji,** famous for cooking supplies. Connecting Kita-ku with Namba is Osaka's main street, **Midosuji Dori,** a wide boulevard lined with gingko trees and name-brand shops.

AROUND TENNOJI PARK   At the south end of the JR Loop Line is **Tennoji-ku,** which was once a thriving temple town with **Shitennoji Temple** at its center. In addition to a park with a zoo, it boasts **Spa World,** one of Japan's biggest and most luxurious public bathhouses.

OSAKA BAY & PORT   West of the city around Osaka Bay is where you will find **Universal Studios Japan** and Universal CityWalk shopping and dining complex; **Tempozan Harbour Village** with its first-class aquarium, shopping complex, and Suntory Museum; and domestic and international ferry terminals.

Getting Around

Despite its size, I find Osaka easier to get around than other large Japanese cities because there are lots of English-language signs and information. The exception is Osaka Station, used for JR trains, and its adjoining Umeda Station, used by subway lines and private railway lines Hankyu and Hanshin. Underground passages and shopping arcades complicate navigation; there's no escaping—you will get lost.

When exploring by foot, it helps to know that most roads running east and west end in *"dori,"* while roads running north and south end in *"suji,"* which means "avenue."

BY SUBWAY   Osaka's user-friendly subway network is easy to use because all lines are color-coded and the station names are in English (even English-language announcements are on many lines). Lines run from about 5am to midnight. The red **Midosuji Line** is the most important one for visitors; it passes through Shin-Osaka Station and on to Umeda (the subway station next to Osaka Station), Shinsaibashi, Namba, and Tennoji. Fares begin at ¥200 and increase according to the distance traveled; or, purchase a pre-paid **Rainbow Card** for ¥500 to ¥3,000 to prevent having to buy an individual ticket each time. For more information, stop by the **Osaka Municipal Transportation Access** office at Namba Station (© **06/6211-9503**), open Monday to Friday 9am to 7pm and weekends and holidays 10am to 7pm, or check the website www.kotsu.city.osaka.jp.

Transportation Passes: If you think you'll be traveling a lot by subway on a given day, consider purchasing a **1-Day Pass (Ichinichi-Joshaken)** for ¥850, which allows unlimited rides on subways and buses all day. On the 20th of each month (or on the following day if the 20th falls on a Sun or holiday) and every Friday, this pass (nicknamed No-My-Car-Day) costs just ¥600 and offers slight discounts to several attractions.

For sightseeing, there's the **Osaka Unlimited 1-Day Pass,** which costs ¥2,000 and allows unlimited rides on subways, city buses, and private railways in Osaka plus free entrance to 25 attractions, including Osaka Castle, Floating Garden Observatory, Shitennoji Temple, Museum of Oriental Ceramics, and Osaka International Peace Center. If you're a visitor to Japan, you're also entitled to the **Osaka Unlimited 2-Day Pass** for ¥2,700, valid for travel on subways and buses and providing the same free admission as the 1-Day pass but for 2 days; for this you must show your passport. Passes are available at the Osaka Visitors' Information Centers and at the Osaka Municipal Transportation Access office in Namba (see above).

For trips outside Osaka, the **Kansai Thru Pass** (**Surutto Kansai;** www.surutto.com) allows foreigners (you must show your passport) to ride subways, private railways (no JR trains), and buses throughout Kansai, including Osaka, Kyoto, Kobe, Nara, and Mount Koya, with a 2-day pass costing ¥3,800 and a 3-day pass costing ¥5,000. It's available at the KIX Travel Desk (first floor international arrivals) or at the Visitor Information Centers in Osaka, but you'd have to do quite a bit of traveling to make this worthwhile.

BY JR TRAIN   A Japan Railways train called the Osaka Kanjo Line, or **JR Loop Line,** passes through Osaka Station and makes a loop around the central part of the city (similar to the Yamanote Line in Tokyo); take it to visit Osaka Castle. Fares begin at ¥120.

SEEING THE SIGHTS
Near Osaka Station
Floating Garden Observatory (Kuchu Teien Tenbodai)   This futuristic observatory 167m (557 ft.) high looks like a space ship floating between the two towers of the Umeda Sky Building. Take the superfast glass elevator from the East Tower building's third floor; you'll then take a glass-enclosed escalator that also bridges the two towers before depositing you on the 39th floor. I'm not afraid of heights, but taking an escalator over thin air in an earthquake-plagued nation certainly caught my attention; it made the "floating" observatory feel safe in comparison. From here, you have an unparalleled view

of Osaka, making it a popular nightspot for couples on dates. My own interest in the place, however, has waned since the female attendants stopped wearing cone-shaped hats.

Umeda Sky Building, 1–1–88 Oyodo-naka, Kita-ku. (C) **06/6440-3901.** www.kuchu-teien.com. Admission ¥700 adults, ¥500 junior-high and high-school students, ¥300 children. Daily 10am–10:30pm. Station: JR Osaka or Umeda (Central North exit of JR Osaka Station, 9 min.).

Museum of Oriental Ceramics (Toyotoji Bijutsukan) ★★★ (Finds) This modern facility, about a 15-minute walk south of Osaka Station on Nakanoshima Island in the Dojima River, is my favorite museum in Osaka. Indeed, its 2,700-piece collection of Chinese, Korean, and Japanese ceramics—of which 300 are on display at any one time on a rotating basis—ranks as one of the finest in the world. Built specifically for the collection, the museum does a superb job showcasing the exquisite pieces as the masterpieces they truly are, in darkened rooms that utilize natural light and computerized natural-light simulation. Korean celadon, Chinese ceramics from the Song and Ming dynasties, Arita ware from the Edo Period, and much more are on display. Even if you've never given ceramics more than a passing glance, you're likely to come away with a heightened sense of appreciation. You'll want to spend 30 minutes or more here.

1–1–26 Nakanoshima, Kita-ku. (C) **06/6223-0055.** www.moco.or.jp. Admission ¥500 adults, ¥300 students, free for children. Tues–Sun 9:30am–5pm. Closed during exhibition changes. Station: Naniwabashi on the Keihan Nakanoshima Line (exit 1, 1 min.) or Yodoyabashi (exit 1, 1 min.).

Sega Amusement Theme Park (Umeda Joypolis) ★ (Kids) I suppose it could be argued that you haven't experienced today's Japan unless you've visited at least one Joypolis, the reigning king of amusement arcades. This one, on the eighth and ninth floors of a shopping arcade complete with a Ferris wheel on top, overloads the senses with lots of flashing lights, bells and whistles, and throngs of squealing kids and teenagers. In addition to arcade games, virtual rides simulate gliding through the air or shooting the rapids of a wild river. *Note:* Children 15 and under aren't allowed here after 7pm, those 17 and under aren't allowed after 10pm and some "rides" carry height restrictions, with rules enforced by what—the joy police?

HEP FIVE, Umeda Kita-ku. (C) **06/6366-3647.** Free admission; attractions ¥600. Daily 11am–11pm (you must enter by 10:15pm). Station: JR Osaka or Umeda (5 min.).

Around Osaka Castle

Osaka Castle (Osaka-jo) ★★ First built in the 1580s on the order of Toyotomi Hideyoshi, Osaka Castle was the largest castle in Japan, a magnificent structure used by Toyotomi as a military stronghold from which to wage war against rebellious feudal lords in far-flung provinces. By the time he died in 1598, Toyotomi had accomplished what no man had done before: crushed his enemies and unified all of Japan under his command.

After Toyotomi's death, Tokugawa Ieyasu seized power and established his shogunate government in Edo. But Toyotomi's heirs had ideas of their own: Considering Osaka Castle impregnable, they plotted to overthrow the Tokugawa government. In 1615, Tokugawa sent troops to Osaka where they not only annihilated the Toyotomi insurrectionists but destroyed Osaka Castle. The Tokugawas rebuilt the castle in 1629, but the main tower was destroyed by lightning 36 years later, and the rest burned in 1868 as the shogunate made their last stand against imperial forces in what later became known as the Meiji Restoration.

The present Osaka Castle dates from 1931 and was extensively renovated in 1997. Built of ferroconcrete, it's not as massive as the original but is still one of Japan's most famous castles and is impressive with its massive stone walls, black and gold-leaf trim, and copper roof. Its eight-story *donjon* (keep) rises 39m (130 ft.), with a top-floor observatory offering bird's-eye views of the city. The rest of the donjon houses a museum that uses videos, holograms, models, and artifacts to describe the life and times of Toyotomi Hideyoshi and history of the castle. Unfortunately, most explanations are in Japanese only, but there's plenty to see, including a folding screen with scenes of the intense fighting that took place between Toyotomi and Tokugawa forces, samurai armor and gear, a full-scale reproduction of Toyotomi's Gold Tea Room, and a model of Osaka Castle during the Toyotomi Era. If you want, you can have your photo taken in period clothing for ¥300. Plan on about 45 minutes here.

1–1 Osakajo, Chuo-ku. © **06/6941-3044.** www.osakacastle.net. Admission ¥600 adults, free for children 15 and under. Daily 9am–5pm. Station: Osakajo-Koen on the JR Loop Line or Morinomiya (15 min.); or Temmabashi or Osaka Business Park (10 min.).

Osaka International Peace Center ★

Located on the southern edge of Osaka Castle Park, this museum strives for global peace by educating present and future generations about the horrors of war, related by those who survived it. Unlike other museums in Japan dedicated to peace—including those in Hiroshima and Nagasaki—this one does not shy away from Japan's role in the Asian conflict, including its war campaign in China, the abduction of Koreans to work in dangerous areas, and massacres committed by Japanese in Singapore, Malaysia, and elsewhere. But its main focus is on wartime death and destruction, with personal testimonies of air raid survivors (15,000 people died during World War II air raids on Osaka), displays centering on suicide attacks by *kamikaze* pilots at the end of the war, graphic photographs of Hiroshima and Nagasaki after the atomic bombs were dropped, and a section devoted to the horrors of the Auschwitz concentration camp. You'll probably spend 30 sobering minutes here.

2–1 Osakajo, Chuo-ku. © **06/6947-7208.** www.peace-osaka.or.jp. Admission ¥250 adults, ¥150 high-school students, free for children. Tues–Sun 9:30am–5pm. Closed on days following national holidays and last day of each month. Station: Morinomiya (3 min.) or Osakajo-Koen (8 min.).

Osaka Museum of History ★ (Kids)

Your visit to this museum, located in a modern building on the site of former Naniwa Palace (built in 645 by Emperor Kotoku), begins on the 10th floor with a life-size re-creation of the palace and continues as you descend floors, with hands-on exhibits, videos, and archaeological displays highlighting Osaka's history as a major distribution center and its growth into a metropolis (a bonus: pausing on each floor for stunning views of Osaka Castle and its park). With the help of volunteer guides and printed information, you can dig for artifacts and piece them together, or become a banker, weighing and exchanging Osaka money for currency from other areas of Japan. A personal favorite is the realistic reproduction of Dotombori from a century ago. In the basement are archaeological remains of Naniwa Palace, while a reconstruction of a 5th-century warehouse is on museum grounds. Plan on at least an hour here.

4–1–32 Otemae, Chuo-ku. © **06/6946-5728.** www.mus-his.city.osaka.jp. Admission ¥600 adults, ¥360 high-school and university students, free for junior-high school students and children. Wed–Mon 9:30am–5pm (Fri to 8pm). Station: Tanimachi 4-chome (3 min.).

Around Tennoji

Shitennoji Temple   Founded over 1,400 years ago as the first—and therefore oldest—officially established temple in Japan, Shitennoji Temple is the spiritual heart of Osaka. It was constructed in 593 by Prince Shotoku, who is credited with introducing Buddhism to Japan. However, like most wooden structures in Japan, its buildings have been destroyed repeatedly through the centuries by fire and war, including the 1615

Tokugawa raid on Osaka Castle and World War II. And through the centuries, the buildings have been faithfully reconstructed exactly as they were in the 6th century, with the Main Gate, the five-story Buddhist Pagoda, the Main Golden Hall, and the Lecture Hall all on a north-south axis. Japanese flock to Shitennoji to pay respects to Prince Shotoku, who remains a revered, popular figure even today. There's also a turtle sanctuary. But the best thing to do here is wander the temple's newly restored Japanese Landscape Garden, first laid out during the Tokugawa regime and a lovely oasis with its manicured bushes, meandering streams, and waterfall.

1-11-18 Shitennoji, Tennoji-ku. *C* **06/6771-0066.** Admission to temple buildings ¥300; garden admission ¥200. Daily 8:30am–4:30pm (garden daily 10am–4pm). Station: Shitennoji-mae Yuhigaoka (exit 4, 5 min.); or JR Tennoji (north exit, 10 min.).

Spa World ★ (Kids) This is one of the most luxurious and ambitious bathhouses I've seen. Accommodating up to 5,000 people, it draws upon hot springs 890m (2,970 ft.) below the earth's surface. On its roof, in a large hangarlike room, is a covered swimming complex that includes a pool, various water slides, a kids' pool with aquatic activities, and a sunning terrace with Jacuzzi. You wear your swimming suits here (rental suits available). For a more grown-up experience, the rest of the large complex is divided into themed, geographical bathing zones, which are rotated between the sexes (no suits allowed) and include luxurious locker rooms. At the Asian Zone, for example, Middle Eastern music and tiled mosaics set the tone for the Turkish bath, while China is represented by a medicinal bath. Massage, sauna, mud baths, and hot stone and moxibustion treatments are available. If you're timid about going to a public bath, this one will convert you. If you're already a fan, you'll want to move in. But sorry, people with tattoos—associated with the Japanese mafia—aren't allowed.

3-2-24 Ebisu-higashi, Naniwa-ku. *C* **06/6631-0001.** www.spaworld.co.jp/english. Admission weekdays: ¥2,400 adults, ¥1,300 children for 3 hr.; ¥2,700 adults, ¥1,500 children for all day. Weekends: ¥2,700 adults, ¥1,500 children for 3 hr.; ¥3,000 adults, ¥1,700 children for all day. Daily 24 hr. (maintenance takes place in some areas from 8:45–10am). Station: Shin-Imamiya or Dobutsuenmae (2 min.).

Osaka Bay Area

Osaka's well-developed waterfront offers a quick getaway for Osakans wishing to escape urban life. In addition to shopping malls, an aquarium, and other attractions, it boasts **Universal Studios Japan,** one of Japan's major draws.

Osaka Aquarium (Kaiyukan) ★★★ (Kids) Of all the aquariums in Japan, this is probably my favorite. One of the world's largest—encompassing 26,570 sq. m (286,000 sq. ft.) and containing 2.9 million gallons of water—it's constructed around the theme "Ring of Fire," which refers to the volcanic perimeter encircling the Pacific Ocean. Tours begin through a tunnel filled with reef fish, followed by an escalator ride to the eighth floor; from there, you'll pass through 15 different habitats ranging from arctic to tropical as you follow a spiraling corridor back to the ground floor, starting with the daylight world—a Japanese forest—above the ocean's surface and proceeding past Antarctica, Monterey Bay, the Great Barrier Reef, and other ecosystems as you travel to the depths of the ocean floor. The walls of the aquarium tank are constructed of huge acrylic glass sheets, making you feel as if you're immersed in the ocean. You'll see 30,000 specimens representing 580 species; stars of the show include whale sharks (the largest fish in captivity), Antarctic penguins, the odd-looking ocean sunfish (which has the circumference of a truck tire but is as flat as a pancake), and the Japan giant spider crab with its incredible

> **Tips** **Mutineers Need Not Apply**
>
> The quickest and most scenic way to travel between Suntory Museum/aquarium and Universal Studios is via the ***Captain Line*** shuttle boat (📞 **06/6573-8222**) with its all-female crew, which departs every 30 minutes and charges ¥600 for the 10-minute ride. A bonus: The boat ticket includes a ¥300 discount for the aquarium.

3m (9¾-ft.) span. English-spoken audio guides are available for rent for ¥300. Allow about 1½ hours to tour the aquarium, avoiding weekends.

1-1-10 Kaigan-dori, Minato-ku. 📞 **06/6576-5501.** www.kaiyukan.com. Admission ¥2,000 adults, ¥900 children 7–15, ¥400 children 4–6, free for children 5 and under. Daily 10am–8pm. Closed 7 days a year (in June and in winter). Station: Osakako (5 min.).

Suntory Museum ★   The Suntory Museum, which you can tour in about 30 minutes, is that fantastically modern-looking structure you see near the aquarium, designed by well-known architect Tadao Ando. It stages changing exhibitions in airy rooms against a dramatic background of the sea beyond its glass walls. Past exhibits have included posters by Toulouse-Lautrec, paintings by German expressionists, and glass by Emile Gallé. There's also a 3-D IMAX theater with scenes so real you'll think you are part of the film, a good museum shop, the Sky Lounge (perfect for taking a break), and a restaurant, Café Solare (p. 414).

1-5-10 Kaigan-dori, Minato-ku. 📞 **06/6577-0001.** www.suntory.com/culture-sports/smt. Admission varies; check the website or *Meet Osaka* quarterly for current information. Museum Tues–Sun 10:30am–8pm; IMAX Tues–Sun 11am–7pm (last show). Station: Osakako (5 min.).

Universal Studios Japan ★★★ **(Kids)**   Following the tradition of Universal's Hollywood and Orlando theme parks, this park takes guests on a fantasy trip through the world of American blockbuster movies, with thrill rides, live entertainment, back-lot streets, restaurants, shops, and other attractions based on actual movies. Board a boat for a harrowing encounter with a great white straight out of *Jaws,* escape a T-Rex as you roller-coaster your way through a setting of *Jurassic Park,* dream your way through the mega-coaster *Hollywood Dream,* fly and leap at high speed among skyscrapers in the *Amazing Adventures of Spider Man—The Ride,* and see, feel, and smell *Sesame Street 4-D Movie Magic* or *Shrek's 4-D Adventure* (4-D in movie lingo means there are smells and other sensations). Unfortunately, most of the attractions have been dubbed into Japanese (I wonder why the original English isn't available on audio guide), so it helps to know the movies beforehand. Plan for an entire day here, but note that it is immensely popular: Avoid weekends, arrive early, and buy a Universal Express Pass Booklet, which allows priority entry into designated rides (the price of these varies by type, age, and advance purchase, so check the website).

2-1-33 Sakurajima, Konohana. 📞 **06/6465-3000.** www.usj.co.jp. Studio Pass to all attractions ¥5,800 adults, ¥5,100 seniors, ¥3,900 children 4–11. Hours vary according to the season; generally daily 10am–5pm in winter, 9am–8:30 or 9pm in summer, and 9 or 10am–7pm the rest of the year. Station: Universal City (5 min.).

Northwest of Osaka, the town of Takarazuka (in Hyogo Prefecture) is synonymous with the all-female **Takarazuka Troupe.** Founded in 1914 to attract vacationers to Takarazuka, the troupe proved instantly popular with the general public, whose taste turned from traditional Japanese drama to lively Western musicals and entertainment. Performances are held at the **Takarazuka Grand Theatre** (📞 **0570/00-5100;** www.kageki.hankyu.co.jp/english) most days throughout the year (closed Wed), usually at 1pm on weekdays and at 11am and 3pm on weekends and holidays. Tickets range from about ¥3,500 to ¥11,000. For more information on the troupe, see "Takarazuka Kagekidan" on p. 221.

SHOPPING

Osaka is famous in Japan for shopping, in no small part because of the discerning nature of the Osakans themselves. Osaka, after all, developed as a commercial town of merchants—and who knows merchandise better than the merchants themselves?

Osaka must rank as one of the world's leading cities in underground shopping arcades. Enter the vast underground arcades in Umeda (where the JR, Hanshin, subway, and Hankyu train lines intersect) with such names as **Whity Umeda, Hankyu Sanbangai, Diamor Osaka,** and **Dojima Underground Shopping Center,** and you may never emerge in this lifetime. **Crysta Nagahori,** connecting Nagahoribashi Station to Yotsubashi-suji, has a glass atrium ceiling, flowing streams of water, and 100 shops, making it one of the largest—if not the largest—shopping malls in Japan. Nearby are **Namba Walk, Nan-nan Town,** and **Namba City,** all interconnected by underground passageways.

There are plenty of aboveground shopping options as well. **Den Den Town** (Station: Nipponbashi or Ebisucho) is Osaka's electronics shopping region (*Den* is short for "electric"), similar to Tokyo's Akihabara and just as good. Some 200 open-fronted shops here deal in electrical and electronic equipment, from rice cookers and refrigerators to DVD players, MP3 players, calculators, cameras, and computers. As in Tokyo, shops specializing in *manga, anime,* and costumes have also moved in, especially on Sakai Suji. **Animate,** 4–10–6 Nipponbashi (📞 **06/6636-0628**), offers two floors of the latest manga and anime books and goods. Like most shops here, Animate is open daily 10am to 8pm.

Running north to south and a few blocks east of Nankai Namba Station is **Sennichimae Doguya-suji,** a covered shopping lane with about 45 open-fronted shops selling all the pots, pans, dishes, and implements you'd ever need to prepare and serve Japanese food. Chopsticks, chopstick rests, pottery, lacquerware, frying pans, trays, kitchen knives, rice bowls, plastic food, and lots of gift ideas are here at very inexpensive prices—not surprising, as Osaka is known as "the nation's kitchen." Just east of Sakasuji Avenue is **Kuromon Ichiba,** a covered market where professional chefs shop. It's worth a stroll for local color and a look at seafood, fruit, vegetables, pickles, and other edibles (many you may not recognize). Food stalls along the market offer opportunities for snacks and picnic supplies.

Midosuji Dori, a wide boulevard lined with gingko trees running north and south in the heart of the city, is the city's calling card for name-brand boutiques. Just to the east is **Shinsaibashi-suji,** a covered promenade with many long-established shops, some dating back to the Edo Period. On the other side of Midosuji Dori is **America-Mura,** a popular spot for young Japanese shopping for T-shirts, Hawaiian shirts, ripped jeans, and other American fashions at inflated prices; its biggest marketplace is **Big Step.** Teens also flock to **Marui 0101,** a seven-story department store on the corner of Shinsaibashi-suji and Nankai Dori, and to **HEP FIVE,** a huge shopping complex near Umeda with a Joypolis amusement arcade and a Ferris wheel on top.

Universal CityWalk, near Universal Studios, offers everything from Hello Kitty goods to Italian imports. In Rinkan Town near KIX airport is **Rinku Premium Outlets,** one of the largest outlet malls in Japan, with some 150 shops.

WHERE TO STAY

Many Osaka hotels are clustered around Osaka Station. In the listings below, the nearest subway or JR station is indicated followed by the number of minutes it takes to walk from the station to the hotel (in parentheses). In addition to the choices below, the **Toyoko Inn** chain (www.toyoko-inn.com) has some 25 properties in Osaka offering accommodations starting at ¥5,670 for a single room with in-room and lobby Internet access, free 3-minute local calls, a coin laundromat, and breakfast.

Around Osaka & Shin-Osaka Stations
Very Expensive

The Ritz-Carlton, Osaka ★★★   Opened in 1997, the Ritz-Carlton's first Japanese venture rejected the grandiose marble lobbies popular in Japan at the time, choosing instead a small and intimate one, done in old-world style with overstuffed sofas, 100-year-old Persian carpets, Italian marble fireplaces, stunning flower arrangements, crystal chandeliers, antiques, and museum-grade landscape paintings and portraits from the 18th and 19th centuries. Unique standouts include the Bar with its 110 kinds of whiskey, 50 kinds of cigars, and live music nightly; La Baie, rated by many as Osaka's best French restaurant; a very popular afternoon tea served in the lobby lounge with live classical music; and a health club free to hotel guests. Stylish rooms—located from the 24th through 37th floors and among the largest in the city—offer panoramic views, especially from deluxe corner rooms.

2–5–25 Umeda, Kita-ku, Osaka 530-0001. (℃) **800/241-3333** in the U.S. and Canada, or 06/6343-7000. Fax 06/6343-7001. www.ritzcarlton.com. 292 units. ¥46,273–¥61,698 single; ¥58,138–¥75,564 double. Club floors ¥61,698–¥68,817 single, ¥73,563–¥83,055 double. ¥5,000 extra on Sat and holiday evenings. AE, DC, MC, V. Station: Osaka, Umeda, or Nishi-Umeda (7 min.). **Amenities:** 4 restaurants; 2 bars; lounge; concierge; executive-level rooms; health club w/gym, 20m (66-ft.) indoor lap pool, and indoor/outdoor whirlpools; room service; smoke-free rooms; spa w/dry and wet saunas and baths (fee: ¥1,000). *In room:* A/C, TV/DVD player, Internet, minibar, MP3 docking station.

Expensive

Rihga Royal Hotel ★   Osaka's oldest and largest hotel, opened in 1935 and later joining the Rihga chain, is located on Nakanoshima, an island in the middle of the Dojima River in the heart of Osaka (a 10-min. ride from Osaka Station). It enjoys a good reputation among Japanese and a high occupancy rate on weekends, due in no small part to the convention center next door. Its wide-ranging facilities include a 60-store shopping arcade, a deli with health-conscious choices, and—at the other end of the extreme—the best-stocked hotel gourmet foods shop I've seen, with hundreds of eye-popping pastries and delicacies. It also has one of my favorite lobby lounges in the city—a restful oasis where you can sip your drink and watch a cascading waterfall against a backdrop of cliffs and foliage. Comfortable guest rooms have a range of rates and interior designs, from modern to classical drawing-room style. In short, you could do much worse than this hotel, despite the crowds, but for a more intimate experience, go elsewhere.

5–3–68 Nakanoshima, Kita-ku, Osaka 530-0005. (℃) **06/6448-1121.** Fax 06/6448-4414. www.rihga.com. 974 units. ¥19,635–¥53,130 single; ¥32,340–¥56,595 double. Presidential Towers executive floor from

¥54,285 double. AE, DC, MC, V. Station: Nakanoshima (1 min.); or JR Osaka Station west exit, free shuttle
every 6–15 min. **Amenities:** 18 restaurants; 3 bars; 2 lounges; concierge; executive-level rooms; indoor
circular "shape-up" pool, 25m (82-ft.) lap pool, Jacuzzi, and sauna (fee: ¥2,000); room service; smoke-free
rooms. *In room:* A/C, TV, hair dryer, Internet, minibar.

Moderate

Hearton Hotel Nishi Umeda ★★ (Value) Newly opened west of JR Osaka Station,
the Hearton (pronounced "heart on") is convenient to shops, clubs, and restaurants
around the station, as well as to the Airport Limousine Bus and the subway. Catering to
business travelers, it offers simple, well-lit, spotless rooms, facing the railroad tracks but
with double-paned windows that block out noise. In addition to the rates below, couples
on a budget can stay in a single with a semi-double-size bed for ¥11,800.

3-3-55 Umeda, Kita-ku, Osaka 530-0001. © **06/6342-1111.** Fax 06/6342-1122. www.hearton.co.jp. 471
units. ¥10,600–¥10,800 single; ¥17,000–¥18,500 double; ¥21,600 triple. AE, DC, MC, V. Station: JR Osaka
(Sakuradori exit, 3 min.). Walk through the Umesankoji covered arcade and follow the tracks; it will be on
your left. **Amenities:** Restaurant; coffee shop; rental bikes (¥1,000 per day); lobby computer w/free Internet; smoke-free rooms. *In room:* A/C, TV, fridge, hair dryer, Internet.

Hotel Granvia Osaka (Kids) You can't get any closer to Osaka Station than this hotel,
with discounts for holders of Japan Rail Passes making it even more attractive for train
travelers. Parents might also rejoice at discounts offered for Universal Studios. But there
are prices to pay: a ground-floor lobby that's hard to find in the maze that is Osaka Station, and elevators that are crowded with hungry masses on their way to the hotel's many
19th-floor restaurants. Rooms, on floors 22 to 26, are cramped except those on deluxe
floors. Families may want to opt for one of the huge "Corner Family" rooms (though
they're a steep ¥56,595 or more), while those in search of R & R might find relaxation
in the 24th-floor Freja rooms, designed with unique Scandinavian furnishings and aromatherapy amenities.

3-1-1 Umeda, Kita-ku, Osaka 530-0001. © **06/6344-1235.** Fax 06/6344-1130. www.granvia-osaka.jp.
650 units. ¥16,170–¥27,720 single; ¥24,255–¥48,500 double. Discounts available for holders of Japan Rail
Pass. AE, DC, MC, V. Station: Osaka or Umeda (1 min.; above the station). **Amenities:** 7 restaurants; bar; 2
lounges; room service; smoke-free rooms. *In room:* A/C, TV, hair dryer, Internet, minibar.

Hotel Il Monte ★ (Finds) This smart-looking hotel has a convenient location that
brings in both business and leisure travelers and is my top choice for budget accommodations near the station. A small reception on the third floor has a helpful staff. Breakfast
is the only meal available, and in the lobby you'll find free coffee and tea and computers
with Internet connections. Simple, modern rooms have a 200-channel music system and
double-paned windows to shut out noise; two people can stay in the largest single room
for ¥13,000.

7-13 Doyama-cho, Kita-ku, Osaka 530-0027. © **06/6361-2828.** Fax 06/6361-3525. www.ilmonte.co.jp.
122 units. ¥8,000–¥9,000 single; ¥15,000–¥20,000 double. AE, DC, MC, V. Station: Osaka, Umeda, or
Higasahi Umeda (10 min.). From JR Osaka Station's Central Exit, turn left and walk past Hankyu Department Store, HEP FIVE and HEP NAVIO to Shin-Midosuji Ave.; it's beside the Hankyu-Higashi Dori shopping
street. **Amenities:** Lobby computer w/free Internet; smoke-free rooms. *In room:* A/C, TV, hair dryer, Internet, minibar.

Hotel Laforet Shin-Osaka I can't think of any reason to stay near Shin-Osaka Sta-
tion except for the sheer convenience of nearby bullet trains, as there are no attractions here
and the rest of Osaka is just a short subway ride away. If you're unconvinced, this modern
hotel is your best bet, just a minute's walk from the station and offering comfortable rooms
with contemporary decor. Deluxe rooms are swankier, with massage chairs and round desks.

1–2–70 Miyahara, Yodogawa-ku, Osaka 532-0003. ☎ **06/6350-4444.** Fax 06/6350-4460. www.laforet hotels.com/shinosaka. 332 units. ¥15,000–¥17,000 single; ¥18,000–¥22,000 double. AE, DC, MC, V. Station: Shin-Osaka (1 min.). Take the west exit and turn right. **Amenities:** 2 restaurants; bar; lobby computer w/Internet (¥100 for 5 min.); room service; smoke-free rooms. *In room:* A/C, TV, hair dryer, Internet (fee: ¥500 per stay), minibar.

Inexpensive
Family Inn Fifty's Edobori ★ Ⓥalue This motel-like facility, south of Nakanoshima island, offers low prices and no-nonsense small but clean rooms, outfitted with double bed, sofa bed, wall-mounted TV, and tiled bathroom (but no closet). Check-in is automated, but humans behind the front desk can help with the process (you'll need a credit card). You pay extra for toothbrushes and slippers here. The catch is that the place is a bit of a chore to reach from Osaka Station (because it's across a footbridge south of the Rihga Royal Hotel's back parking lot, some travelers have been known to use the luxury hotel's shuttle bus). Once you're settled in, you'll find its location fine.

2–6–18 Edobori, Nishi-ku, Osaka 550-0002. ☎ **06/6225-2636.** www.fiftys.com. 80 units. ¥5,250 single; ¥8,400 double; ¥9,450 triple. Smoking rooms ¥1,050 extra. Higher rates summer and weekends. Rates include continental breakfast. AE, MC, V. Station: Nakanoshima (exit 2, 5 min.); walk past the conference center Grand Cube and cross Tosabori-bashi bridge, continue 1 block, turn left and then right. **Amenities:** Coffee shop; lobby computer w/free Internet; smoke-free rooms; Wi-Fi in coffee shop. *In room:* A/C, TV.

Second Inn Umeda Ⓥalue This business hotel, next to the Ritz-Carlton, is convenient to the station and offers sparse rooms that meet all basic needs, including refrigerators in all except the cheapest singles and showers instead of tubs. Determined couples can save money by sharing a semi-double-size bed for ¥7,200.

2–5–16 Umeda, Kita-ku, Osaka 530-0001. ☎ **06/6346-1177.** Fax 06/6346-3006. 128 units. ¥5,800–¥6,200 single; ¥8,400–¥9,000 double. AE, MC, V. Station: Osaka (7 min.) or Nishi-Umeda (exit 10, 4 min.). **Amenities:** Smoke-free rooms. *In room:* A/C, TV, fridge (in most), Internet.

Around Osaka Castle
Expensive
Imperial Hotel Osaka (Teikoku Hotel) ★★★ One of Osaka's top luxury hotels, the Imperial is situated north of Osaka Castle on the cherry tree–lined Okawa River in a relaxing, resortlike setting, next to a large office complex containing shops and restaurants. It provides free shuttle ride service to Osaka Station and complimentary bikes to explore the area (it's a 10-min. ride to Osaka Castle). Like its Tokyo namesake, its bold interior designs show the same Frank Lloyd Wright inspirations, including an Old Imperial Bar that pays homage to the American architect. The hotel's fitness center is the largest and best equipped in the city, while restaurants take advantage of the river and city views. The high-ceilinged, spacious rooms offer large windows with remote-control drapes and great views (request rooms facing the river), good working desks, down pillows and comforters, fluffy bathrobes, aromatherapy amenities, and marble bathrooms with magnifying mirrors and vanity stools at sinks.

1–8–50 Temmabashi, Kita-ku, Osaka 530-0042. ☎ **800/223-6800** in the U.S. and Canada, or 06/6881-1111. Fax 06/6881-1200. 390 units. www.imperialhotel.co.jp. ¥29,400–¥49,350 single; ¥34,650–¥54,600 double; from ¥48,300 Imperial executive floor double. ¥3,465 more Sat and nights before holidays. Rates exclude service charge. AE, DC, MC, V. Station: JR Sakuranomiya west exit (5 min. to the hotel's riverside entrance); or Osaka Station west exit, free shuttle every 20 min. (more on weekends). **Amenities:** 6 restaurants; bar; 2 lounges; bikes (free for hotel guests); children's day-care center (from ¥1,323 per 30 min.); concierge; executive-level rooms; golf driving range (fee: ¥5,250); Osaka's largest state-of-the-art health club w/3 lit outdoor tennis courts, 25m (82-ft.) indoor pool, spa, Jacuzzi, and sauna (fee: ¥2,100 morning, ¥5,250 afternoon); medical clinic; room service; smoke-free rooms. *In room:* A/C, TV, fax, hair dryer, Internet, minibar.

New Otani Osaka ★ In a business park that's home to corporate headquarters for KDDI, NEC, Panasonic, and other giants, this Leading Hotel of the World member attracts both business and tourist clientele. Its proximity to Osaka Castle Park, popular with joggers, families, and young Japanese, and its varied public facilities, ranging from a multitude of restaurants to a fitness club, give the property something of an "urban resort" atmosphere. Everything about the hotel's public spaces is visually pleasing, from the airy, four-story atrium lobby with a sunken lounge in its center to the indoor pool with its glass-vaulted ceiling. Rooms, however, are rather standard, with rates based on size, height, and view. The best rooms provide the city's most dramatic views of Osaka Castle, which is lit at night, but at fairly hefty prices.

1-4-1 Shiromi, Chuo-ku, Osaka 540-8578. ℂ 800/223-6800 in the U.S. and Canada, or 06/6941-1111. Fax 06/6941-9769. www.osaka.newotani.co.jp. 525 units. ¥22,050–¥27,300 single; ¥39,900–¥45,150 double. ¥3,150 extra Sat and nights before holidays. Rates exclude service charge. AE, DC, MC, V. Station: JR Loop Line to Osakajo-Koen (3 min.) or Osaka Business Park Station (3 min.). Across the moat from Osaka Castle. **Amenities:** 10 restaurants; 2 bars; lounge; children's day-care center (¥7,875 for 3 hr.); concierge; executive-level rooms; fitness club w/indoor and outdoor pools and sauna (fee: ¥2,625); room service; 2 outdoor tennis courts; smoke-free rooms. *In room:* A/C, TV, hair dryer, Internet (fee: ¥840 for 24 hr.); minibar.

Inexpensive
Weekly Mansion Otemae (Kids) West of Osaka Castle, this property is a good choice for groups, families, and long-staying guests. Accommodations, which range from studio apartments to three-bedroom units, come with kitchenettes, allowing guests to save money and to experience shopping at Osaka's famous food markets. The helpful English-speaking staff is happy to provide directions to local shops, restaurants, and tourist attractions. Housekeeping service is available for an extra fee.

1-3-2 Tokuicho, Chuo-ku, Osaka 540-0025. ℂ 06/6949-4471. www.wmt-osaka.jp. 111 units. ¥7,000–¥11,000 single; ¥9,000–¥13,000 double; ¥15,000–¥24,000 triple. Discounts for stays of 7 or more nights. AE, MC, V. Station: Tanimachi 4 chome (exit 4, 5 min.). Head east and turn right at the 2nd stoplight; it's on your right). **Amenities:** Rental bikes (fee: ¥1,050 per week); lobby computer (¥100 for 10 min.). *In room:* A/C, TV, hair dryer, Internet, kitchenette.

Namba & Shinsaibashi
Expensive
Hotel Nikko Osaka ★ A white monolith soaring 32 stories aboveground (and with four stories of shopping and parking underground), the Nikko has a great location above a subway station right on Osaka's most fashionable boulevard, Midosuji Dori, making its lobby lounge a popular spot for locals meeting friends. In fact, location is mainly what you're paying for here: There is no health club, and guests are overwhelmingly business travelers. Rooms have a pleasing, clean modern design, with indirect lighting, focused bedside lights, and air purification/ionization machines, and because there are no high buildings to obstruct views, city panoramas are a plus from most floors. Still, you'll pay more for rooms on higher floors and for more space. This is a good choice if you want to be in the midst of Osaka's shopping and nightlife.

1-3-3 Nishi-Shinsaibashi, Chuo-ku, Osaka 542-0086. ℂ 06/6244-1111. Fax 06/6245-2432. www.hno.co.jp. 642 units. ¥21,367–¥23,677 single; ¥32,917–¥43,890 double; Nikko executive floors from ¥35,805 double. AE, DC, MC, V. Station: Shinsaibashi (exit 8 underneath the hotel, 1 min.). **Amenities:** 5 restaurants; bar; 2 lounges; executive-level rooms; room service, smoke-free rooms. *In room:* A/C, TV, hair dryer, Internet (in most rooms), minibar.

Swissôtel Nankai Osaka ★★★   This 36-story hotel exudes luxury, from its sophisticated, four-story lobby to its spacious, well-appointed rooms. Located in the vibrant Namba area and connected to Nankai Namba Station, which offers the most rapid service to KIX airport as well as tourist destinations such as Kyoto and Mount Koya, the Swissôtel could well be the most conveniently located hotel in Osaka. Not surprisingly, guests include international flight crews in addition to tourists and business executives. Upon arrival at Nankai Namba Station, all guests have to do is use the hotel courtesy phone on platform 9 to alert staff to help with luggage, and the helpful concierge offers a handy guide telling how to reach many tourist sights and nearby cities. Spacious rooms have wide windows providing city views. For business travelers, Business Advantage rooms offer ergonomic chairs, larger desks, office supplies, and espresso machines, with the best exuding a Japanese atmosphere with a low bed on a raised tatami floor.

5–1–60 Namba, Chuo-ku, Osaka 542-0076. ✆ **800/637-9477** in the U.S. and Canada, or 06/6646-1111. Fax 06/6648-0331. www.swissotel.com. 548 units. ¥34,650–¥70,075 single; ¥40,425–¥84,315 double; Swiss Executive Club from ¥76,230 double. Sat and nights before holidays ¥3,465–¥5,775 extra. AE, DC, MC, V. Station: Nankai Namba (1 min.). **Amenities:** 8 restaurants, including Sh'un Kushiage (p. 413); bar; lounge; concierge; executive-level rooms; health club w/gym, sauna, and atrium lap pool (fee: ¥2,000 for each); room service; smoke-free rooms; spa. *In room:* A/C, TV, hair dryer, Internet (¥1,680 per 24 hr.), minibar.

Inexpensive

There are more than a dozen **Toyoko Inn** hotels in Osaka, including Toyoko Inn Osaka Namba, 2–8–7 Motomachi (✆ **06/4397-1045;** www.toyoko-inn.com; station: Namba), offering singles for ¥6,720 and doubles starting at ¥7,770, including Japanese breakfast. Check the website for more information and other locations.

Hotel Dormy-Inn   One of the few inexpensive hotels in the shopping and nightlife area of Shinsaibashi, and the only one in America-mura, this chain entry offers standard business-type rooms, spotlessly clean with two kinds of pillows and sliding window panels to cut out light and highway noises, as well as 10 combination rooms with tatami areas and twin beds. Public baths made of cedar are a plus, but alas, little English is spoken.

2–17–3 Nishishinsaibashi, Chuo-ku, Osaka 542-0086. ✆ **06/6211-5767.** Fax 06/6211-5773. 134 units. ¥7,000–¥10,000 single; ¥11,000–¥18,000 double. Rates include breakfast. AE, DC, MC, V. Station: Yotsubashi (exit 5, 5 min.) or Shinsaibashi (exit 7, 7 min.). 1 block south of Europa Dori and 3 blocks west of Midosuji Dori. **Amenities:** Restaurant (breakfast only); smoke-free rooms. *In room:* A/C, TV, fridge, hair dryer, Internet.

Hotel Metro The 21 Ⓥ**alue**   This hotel has a great location for night owls, just a few minutes' walk from Dotombori, Osaka's main nightlife district. Its mostly single rooms, along with 100 twins and doubles, are very small but clean and modern, with higher rates charged for higher floors. There's also a ladies' floor for extra security, decorated with a more feminine touch and adding women's toiletries. Stock your empty fridge with purchases from the ground-floor 7-Eleven.

2–13 Soemon-cho, Chuo-ku, Osaka 542-0084. ✆ **06/6211-3555.** Fax 06/6211-3586. www.metro.21.co.jp/e. 339 units. ¥9,975 single; ¥14,700–¥21,000 double. AE, DC, MC, V. Station: Nipponbashi (exit 2, 5 min.); cross Dotombori canal and turn left. Or Namba (exit 14, 10 min.); cross Dotombori Canal and turn right. **Amenities:** 2 restaurants; bar; room service; smoke-free rooms. *In room:* A/C, TV, fridge, hair dryer, Internet.

Elsewhere in the City
Moderate

Sheraton Miyako Hotel ★★   A multilingual staff providing excellent service, easy access to both Itami and Kansai airports, and good dining choices make this hotel popular, especially for business travelers. It's also well located for sightseeing, with the Osaka Museum of History, Osaka Castle, and Namba with its many bars and restaurants all 1.5km (1 mile) away. Spacious and comfortable rooms offer city views (there are no other high buildings near the hotel), bedside controls for lighting and other functions, down quilts, and a choice of pillows. The atrium swimming pool, with a sliding roof, is a great place to relax, but families will be disappointed to learn that it is not open to children 11 and under.

6-1-55 Uehonmachi, Tenoji-ku, Osaka 553-0001. © **800/325-3535** in the U.S. and Canada, or 06/6773-1111. Fax 06/6773-3322. www.sheraton.com/miyakoosaka. 575 units. ¥17,325–¥21,945 single; ¥27,720–¥39,270 double. Premium Sheraton rooms from ¥39,270 double. AE, DC, MC, V. Station: Uehonmachi (2 min.). **Amenities:** 6 restaurants; 2 bars; child-care center (¥5,250 for 2 hr.); executive-level rooms; health club w/Jacuzzi, steam and dry sauna (fee: ¥3,450); 25m (82-ft.) atrium pool (fee: ¥1,050); racquetball and tennis courts; room service; smoke-free rooms. *In room:* A/C, TV, hair dryer, Internet, minibar.

Inexpensive

Hotel International House Osaka (Value) The International House, providing information and counseling services for foreigners living in Kansai, is a modern facility used also for international seminars, conventions, and meetings. It also includes this hotel, used mainly by those attending seminars but open to the public; try to book well in advance. Rooms are spartan with about as much personality as those in a business hotel, but they have everything you need, including tiny tiled bathrooms, *yukata,* and a small desk. Some 40 of the 50 rooms are singles, making this a great choice for the single traveler, but note that they don't have closets and are fairly small. The twins, however, are of adequate size; there are also two triples.

8-2-6 Uehommachi, Tennoji-ku, Osaka 543-0001. © **06/6773-8181.** Fax 06/6773-0777. 50 units. ¥6,800 single; ¥13,000 double; ¥16,000 triple. Rates include breakfast. AE, DC, MC, V. Station: Uehommachi (5 min.), Tanimachi 9-chome (8 min.), or Shitennoji-mae (5 min.). **Amenities:** 2 restaurants. *In room:* A/C, TV, fridge, hair dryer, Internet.

WHERE TO DINE

There's a saying among Japanese that whereas a Kyotoite will spend his last yen on a fine kimono, an Osakan will spend it on food. You don't have to spend a lot of money, however, to enjoy good food in Osaka. Local specialties include **Oshi-zushi** (pressed square-shaped sushi), **udon** noodles with white soy sauce, and **takoyaki** (wheat-flour dumplings with octopus).

Osaka is probably best known, however, for **okonomiyaki,** which literally means "as you like it." Its origins date from about 1700, when a type of thin flour pancake cooked on a hot plate and filled with miso paste was served during Buddhist ceremonies. It wasn't until the 20th century that it became popular, primarily during food shortages, and gradually, other ingredients such as pork, egg, and cabbage were added. Today, Osaka is riddled with inexpensive okonomiyaki restaurants—more than 4,000 of them.

Around Osaka Station

In addition to the choices below, two good restaurants, **Bar Tachibana** and **Namaste,** listed in the Namba section, have branches near Osaka Station.

Moderate

Enoteca ★ CONTINENTAL   Shelves filled with wine bottles line the walls of this upscale shop, in the back of which is a casual restaurant specializing in meals that complement our favorite form of the grape. The relaxed ambience and reasonably priced food drew us in (okay, so the wine had something to do with it), but what better way to imbibe a celebratory glass or two than with selections of cheese, smoked salmon, a classic beef stew, or the day's lunch? The menu is limited, but the fun part is selecting a bottle from the shop (corkage fee is ¥1,000) to accompany your meal.

Herbis Plaza, 2nd floor, 2–5–25 Umeda. ☎ **06/6343-7175.** Main dishes ¥1,000–¥1,800; set lunch ¥880–¥950. AE, DC, MC, V. Daily 11am–9:30pm (last order). Station: Nishi-Umeda (3 min.). South of Osaka Station in the Herbis Plaza complex adjacent to the Ritz-Carlton.

Inexpensive

Capricciosa Kids PIZZA/PASTA   This chain restaurant is very popular with students and families for its pizza and pasta, available in regular size (good for one person) or large size for hearty appetites or two diners. The English-language menu lists everything from pizza *capricciosa* (with bacon, salami, onion, and more) to spaghetti with eggplant and spinach in meat sauce. The salads are big enough for two to share. While the cheesy decor and fake plants just don't do it for me, a walk through Yodobashi Camera shop with its endless stock is a trip.

There's a branch in the Namba Oriental Hotel Building, 2–8–17 Sennichimae (☎ **06/6644-8330;** station: Midosuji), open daily 11am to 10:30pm.

Yodobashi Camera, 8th floor, 1–1 Obukacho. ☎ **06/6488-2271.** Pizza and pasta ¥910–¥1,010 for small sizes, ¥1,250–¥1,920 for large sizes. AE, DC, MC, V. Daily 11am–10pm. Station: JR Osaka or Umeda (1 min.). Just north of the station.

(134) **Okonomiyaki Kiji** OKONOMIYAKI   Takimikoji Village, located in the basement of the same building as the Floating Garden Observatory (p. 400), is a fun place for a meal. It's a re-created Showa-Era 1920s and 1930s Japanese village, boasting everything from an old-fashioned sweets shop and a barbershop to a post office and a miniature shrine. There are also about a dozen restaurants here, including this one, serving what some Osakans swear is the best *okonomiyaki* in town. Queues of people waiting to get in are common, but your order is taken while you wait so when you finally sit down your order arrives quickly. Until then you can gaze upon customer photos and *meishi* (business cards) that paper the walls and ceiling. Other restaurants here—some of them branches of well-known Osaka establishments—serve *kushikatsu, teppanyaki,* noodles, *yakitori,* and more.

Umeda Sky Building basement, 1–1–90 Oyodo-naka. ☎ **06/6440-5970.** Okonomiyaki ¥600–¥900. No credit cards. Fri–Wed 11:30am–9:30pm. Station: JR Osaka (west exit, 15 min.).

Around Osaka Castle

Inexpensive

Panorama Sky Restaurant Asahi Value VARIED WESTERN   Views and the beer are the best reasons to pay a visit to this Asahi beer hall, which does provide panoramic city views but none of the nearby castle. Popular with area office workers, it offers pizza, pasta, beefsteak, scallops, and rather mundane choices from an English-language menu. The set lunches are a bargain and come with salad, rice, vegetables, and all-you-can-drink tea, coffee, or juice. Or, come for a snack and wash it down with a mug or two of Asahi beer.

IMP Building, 26th floor, 1–3–7 Shiromi Chuo-ku. ☎ **06/6946-2595.** Main dishes ¥850–¥2,800; set lunches ¥880–¥1,200 weekdays, ¥900–¥1,500 weekends and holidays. AE, DC, MC, V. Mon–Fri 11:30am–2pm and 4:30–10pm; Sat–Sun and holidays 11:30am–10pm. Subway: Osaka Business Park (1 min.). JR train: Osakajo-Koen (4 min.). In Osaka Business Park, across from the New Otani Hotel.

Namba

Dotombori (or Dotonbori), a narrow pedestrian lane just off Midosuji Dori that flanks the south bank of the Dotombori River Walk, is the center of Osaka's most famous nightlife district, which radiates from Dotombori on both sides of the canal; you'll find lots of restaurants and bars in this area.

Expensive

Sh'un Kushiage and Wine ★★ KUSHIAGE/FRENCH/FUSION   Osakans claim southern Osaka as the birthplace of *kushiage* (breaded and deep-fried meat, seafood, and vegetables), but this restaurant offers its own sophisticated version by combining kushiage and French cuisine and utilizing organic and seasonal vegetables. In addition, some 500 international wines, including some exclusive to the restaurant, are offered to complement kushiage, along with 10 different kinds of mineral water. Don't be put off by the terms "breaded and deep-fried," which here translate into surprisingly light and delicate fare, available in two set meals that change every 2 weeks. Alternatively, there's the French six-course meal, which may include an *amuse bouche,* scallops in tomato with tofu mouse, potage, bass with mustard spinach sauce, pan-seared veal, dessert, and coffee. Like most kushiage restaurants, seating is at a wooden counter with an open kitchen, but the setting, dimly lit with glass walls revealing stored wine and water bottles, is much classier.

Swissôtel, 5-1-60 Namba, Chuo-ku. ✆ **06/6646-1111.** Set dinners ¥9,124–¥10,279. AE, DC, MC, V. Wed–Sun 5–9:30pm (last order). Station: Nankai Namba (1 min.).

Moderate

(135) **Kani Doraku** CRAB   Specializing in *kani* (crab), this restaurant is difficult to miss: It has a huge model crab on its facade, moving its legs and claws. Part of a chain originating in Osaka 20 years ago, this is the main shop of more than 50 locations throughout Japan, including another one just down the street at 1–6–2 Dotonbori (✆ **06/6211-1633**). Dishes range from *kani-suki, ckani-chiri* (a kind of crab sukiyaki), and fried crab dishes to crab croquette, roasted crab with salt, crab salad, crab sushi, and boiled king crab. The easiest thing to do, however, is to order a set meal from the display case outside or from the menu with its photos. This main location occupies several floors, with some tables offering a view of the water.

1-6-18 Dotonbori. ✆ **06/6211-8975.** Set dinners ¥3,990–¥5,985; set lunches ¥1,995–¥3,990. AE, DC, MC, V. Daily 11am–11pm. Station: Namba (exit 14, 2 min.). On Dotombori beside the Ebisu-bashi Bridge.

Inexpensive

A healthy choice in Namba Station (just outside the south exit near Namba Park) is **Japanese Organic Café** (✆ **06/6644-2782**), serving inexpensive soups, brown rice balls, curry, and organically grown coffee, with main dishes priced below ¥780. It's open Monday to Friday 8am to 9:30pm and Saturday and Sunday 9am to 9:30pm.

(136) **Bar Tachibana** TOFU/VARIED JAPANESE   Whether you're sightseeing in Dotombori or here for *kabuki,* this restaurant, in a lovely, typical Japanese setting in the basement of the Shochikuza Theater, is a good pick. A microbrewery (¥450 for a glass of light or dark beer), Tachibana specializes in tofu (only in Japan!), with tofu included in most of the set meals. There's no English-language menu, but a changing daily lunch and the *tofu teishoku* (¥2,600) are affordable and delicious. You can see famous kabuki actors dining here, but how could you recognize them without their makeup?

Another Tachibana (✆ **06/4796-5770**) is located in the basement of the Hilton Hotel in Umeda, open Monday through Friday 11am to 3pm and 5 to 11pm and Saturday 11am to 11pm.

Osaka Shochikuza Theater, 2nd basement, 1-9-19 Dotonbori. ✆ **06/6212-6074.** Main dishes ¥680–¥1,700; set dinners ¥2,600–¥5,800; set lunches ¥850–¥3,800. AE, DC, MC, V. Daily 11:30am–11pm. Station: Namba (exit 14, 2 min.). Look for its improbable entrance, on Dotombori near the bridge.

THE REST OF WESTERN HONSHU

10

OSAKA

(137) **Fugetsu** OKONOMIYAKI Big Step is the biggest shopping complex in America-Mura, young Osakans' favorite place to shop for American clothing. As such, this branch of a famous *okonomiyaki* restaurant appeals to young diners with its hip, modern interior, pop music, and individual booths for dining. I recommend the squid, octopus, and *yakisoba* (pork-fried noodles) or the *butatama,* an okonomiyaki with pork and egg from the English-language menu.

Big Step, 3rd floor, 1–6–14 Nishi Shinsaibashi. 🕾 **06/6258-5189.** Okonomiyaki ¥600–¥1,100; yakisoba ¥650–¥1,200. No credit cards. Thurs–Tues 11am–8:30pm. Station: Shinsaibashi (2 min.).

(138) **Honfukuzushi** SUSHI ★★ (Finds) More than just a place to dine, this sushi shop, in operation for more than 180 years, is part of the Osaka experience. Back in the old days, sushi shops were strictly takeout operations, with customers bringing in their own dishes, making their orders, and then returning home to wait for *geta*-clad deliverers. Nowadays you eat your sushi here; best are the counter seats, where you can watch sushi being pressed in wooden molds, Osaka style. A Japanese-language menu with photos, a display case at the entryway, and a friendly staff can help with ordering. Or, if you just want to try *oshi-zushi* (Osakan sushi), order the *hakozushi,* which comes with six pieces for ¥590. Tokyo-style *nigiri* and *maki*-sushi are also available.

1–4–19 Nishi Shinsaibashi-suji. 🕾 **06/6271-3344.** Sushi sets ¥1,200–¥3,300; set lunches ¥800–¥1,050. AE, MC, V. Daily 11am–9:30pm (last order). Station: Shinsaibashi (2 min.). Inside the Shinsaibashi covered shopping arcade, behind Daimaru department store; look for the huge wooden sushi mold above the door.

Namaste ★★ INDIAN This is a good place for hot and spicy Indian food, including tandoori and chicken, mutton, prawn, fish, and vegetable curries. The owner, who will wait on you, is so friendly and happy you might think he's reached nirvana. You can reach yours by telling him how hot to make your food. The set lunches are a particularly great deal.

A second Namaste, located in Umeda in the basement of the Ekimae Dai 4 building, 1–11–4 Umeda (🕾 **06/6345-7774**), has the same great food and same great owner.

Rose Building, 3–7–28 Minami Semba. 🕾 **06/6241-6515.** Main dishes ¥750–¥1,500; set dinners ¥1,980–¥4,300; set lunches ¥785–¥1,980. AE, DC, MC, V. Daily 11:30am–3pm and 5:30–11pm. Station: Shinsaibashi (exit 1, 3 min.). 3 blocks north of the Sony Tower Building; walk north on Midosuji Dori, turn east (right) at the Rolex shop and walk past the Shinsaibashi-Suji covered pedestrian shopping street; it will be on the right.

Osaka Bay Area

In addition to the choice below, Universal CityWalk has lots of restaurants, most of which are open daily from 11am to 9 or 10pm, including **Bubba Gump's** (🕾 06/4804-3880) for shrimp; **Hard Rock Cafe** (🕾 06/4804-3870) with its T-shirts for sale and a menu of burgers, steaks, sandwiches, and barbecued ribs; the inexpensive, conveyor-belt **Daisuki Sushi** (🕾 06/6467-1122), which serves two pieces of sushi for ¥105 to ¥210; and a branch of **Fugetsu** (p. 414) serving *okonomiyaki.*

Inexpensive

Café Solare PASTA This casual, airy, and down-to-earth restaurant, with some tables offering a view of the harbor, is convenient if you're visiting the Suntory Museum or nearby Osaka Aquarium (you don't have to buy museum admission to eat here). The pasta is freshly made, and there are also salads, soups, and other items at the self-service counter. Alternatively (or after your meal), you might want to retire to the museum's ninth-floor Sky Lounge (Tues–Sun 11:30am–8:30pm), offering cocktails and other 415 drinks, a limited menu and daily set lunches (¥1,030), and views of the harbor and port.

Suntory Museum, Tempozan Harbour Village, 1-5-10 Kaigandori. ℂ **06/5577-0009.** Main dishes ¥730– ¥850. AE, DC, MC, V. Tues–Sun 11am–9pm. Closed when the museum is closed. Station: Osakako (5 min.).

OSAKA AFTER DARK
Performing Arts

BUNRAKU   The **National Bunraku Theater,** 1–12–10 Nipponbashi, Chuo-ku (ℂ **06/6212-2531** for information, or 0570/07-9900 for reservations; www.ntj.jac. go.jp/english), was completed in 1984 as the only theater in Japan dedicated to Japanese traditional puppet theater. Productions are staged five times a year, with most productions running for 2 weeks at a time and held daily at 11am for Part 1 and at 4pm for Part 2. When *bunraku* is not being performed, other traditional performing arts are often shown, including classical Japanese music. English-language programs are available. To find out whether a performance is being held, check the website above or *Meet Osaka,* or contact one of the visitor information centers (see "Essentials" on p. 394). Tickets usually run ¥2,300 to ¥5,800. The National Bunraku Theater is located east of Namba and the Dotombori entertainment district, a 1-minute walk from exit 7 of Nipponbashi Station.

KABUKI   The **Osaka Shochikuza,** 1–9–19 Dotombori, Chuo-ku (ℂ **06/6214-2211;** station: Namba), was built more than 50 years ago but was remodeled in 1997 as part of a revival of interest in *kabuki.* Traditional kabuki is performed in January, July, and some other months of the year (the schedule changes yearly), and performances start usually at 11am and 4:30pm, with tickets ranging from ¥4,200 to ¥13,650 for major performances. Performance information is also listed in *Meet Osaka.* The theater is located on Dotombori, just west of the Ebisu-bashi Bridge.

LIVE MUSIC   **Billboard Live Osaka,** Basement 2 of the Herbis Plaza ENT Building, 2–2–22 Umeda (ℂ **06/6342-7722,** reservations required; station: Nishi-Umeda), offers live music ranging from jazz and R&B to funk, reggae, and bossa nova, with a great sound system and several levels surrounding the stage providing good views. Steely Dan, Sa-Ra, Rickie Lee Jones, Sean Lennon, and George Benson have played here. Tickets average ¥5,900 to ¥8,000 for most acts, with popular artists costing up to ¥21,000. Smaller, less high-tech and more affordable is **Rug Time Osaka,** on the fourth floor of the Across Building, 2–6–14 Shinsaibashi Suji (ℂ **06/6214-5306;** station: Namba or Shinsaibashi), which offers a wide range of live jazz bands in three nightly sets, with cover charge ranging from ¥1,500 to ¥3,000. It's open daily 5pm to 3am.

The Bar Scene

Osaka's liveliest—and most economical—nightlife district radiates from a narrow pedestrian lane called **Dotombori** (or Dotonbori), which flanks the south bank of the Dotombori Canal. About a 2-minute walk from exit 14 of Namba Station or less than a 10-minute walk from Shinsaibashi Station, it's lined with restaurants and drinking establishments and is good for a lively evening stroll even if you don't wish to stop anywhere.

Cinquecento   This bar is a cut above the rest with its sophisticated decor, pasta, burgers, and other Western fare, not to mention that all food and drink are priced at only ¥500. Of note is the red Wall of Shame, where gold plaques identify those crazy enough to have consumed 100 shots in one sitting. Weekdays 7:30pm to 5am, weekends 8pm to 5am. Matsumiya Building, 10–1–2 Higashishinsaibashi. ℂ **06/6213-6788.** Station: Nigahoribashi or Nipponbashi (5 min.). Off Sakai Suji Dori.

THE REST OF WESTERN HONSHU

10

OSAKA

Murphy's Of Osaka's several Irish pubs, this is probably the most popular (and my favorite), drawing a mixed crowd of both Japanese and foreigners and offering live Irish music most Wednesdays. Fish and chips or shepherd's pie are reasonable and surprisingly good, but you can also make a meal of the Guinness or Kilkenny Ale. Monday through Thursday 5pm to 1am; Friday to Saturday 5pm to about 3am. Lead Plaza Building, 6th floor, 1–6–31 Higashi Shinsaibashi. © 06/6282-0677. Station: Nagahoribashi (1 min.) or Shinsaibashi (4 min.). On Suzuki St. (1 block north of Europa Dori/Shimizu Dori), the road to the south of the Daimaru department store, several blocks east of the Shinsaibashi-suji covered arcade, on the right in a small building with lots of tiny bars.

Sam & Dave Four With exposed, wrapped pipes and fluorescent lighting, this bar with a dance floor and pool table stages events several times a month, including salsa lessons every Tuesday until 8:30pm (followed by salsa music and dancing until midnight). Thursday is reggae nights. Happy hour is until 9pm. It attracts both a Japanese and *gaijin* (foreign) crowd, catering to different tastes in music through its special events.

Attracting a larger foreign clientele is **Sam & Dave Five** in Nagahoribashi, across from the post office (© 06/6251-5333), which has a bigger dance floor and holds salsa nights on Thursdays. It's open Wednesday to Friday 7pm to 5am and Saturday 10pm to 8am. **Sam & Dave Two Shinsaibashi,** 1 block east of Midosuji Street near Softbank (© 06/6243-6848), has a Japanese clientele and is the hot spot for hip-hop, soul, and R&B. Hours are Tuesday through Sunday 7pm to 4am, Friday to Saturday 7pm to 5am. Plaza Umeshin Building, 4–15–19 Nishi-tenma. © 06/6365-1688. Fri–Sat ¥1,080–¥2,000 cover, which includes 1 drink. Station: JR Kitashinchi (2 min.), Umeda (5 min.), Osaka (7 min.). Southeast of Osaka Station on a triangle-shaped parcel of land where Midosuji Dori curves southward before crossing the river and Nakanoshima Island.

5 KOBE

589km (366 miles) W of Tokyo; 75km (47 miles) W of Kyoto; 31km (19 miles) W of Osaka

In January 1995, the world was riveted by news of one of the worst natural disasters of that decade: the Great Hanshin Earthquake that struck Kobe, killing more than 6,400 people and destroying much of the city. In the years since, Kobe has risen from the ashes with more attractions, hotels, and urban redevelopment than ever before and with only a few telltale signs of the city's grimmest hours. Indeed, if it weren't for several earthquake memorials and a museum dedicated to the event, visitors would never guess at the devastation of just 15 years ago.

Blessed with the calm waters of the Seto Inland Sea, Kobe (the capital of Hyogo Prefecture) has served Japan as an important port town for centuries. Even today its port is the heart of the city, its raison d'être. I find Kobe's port fascinating; unlike many harbor cities where the port is located far from the center of town, Kobe's is right there, demanding attention and getting it. One of the first ports to begin accepting foreign traders in 1868 following Japan's 2 centuries of isolation, this vibrant city of 1.5 million inhabitants is quite multicultural, with foreigners from more than 120 different nations residing here. Each group of immigrants has brought with it a rich heritage, and there are a number of fine restaurants serving every kind of cuisine—including Western, Chinese, Korean, and Indian—as well as many steakhouses offering that famous local delicacy, Kobe beef.

Equally famous is Kobe's wonderful nightlife, crammed into a small, navigable, and rather intimate quarter of neon lights, cozy bars, lively pubs, and sophisticated night-clubs. As one resident of Kobe told me, "We don't have a lot of tourist sights in Kobe, so we make up for it in nightlife." Yet the attractions Kobe does offer are unique to Japan, including a neighborhood of Western-style residences built around the turn of the 20th century and museums devoted to fashion and to the city's 1995 earthquake. Kobe is also one of Japan's major sake-producing regions.

ESSENTIALS

GETTING THERE   By Plane If you're arriving at Kansai International Airport (KIX; see "Getting There," under Osaka, on p. 394), there are a couple options for travel onward to Kobe. Easiest are the **Airport Limousine Buses** operated by Kansai Airport Transportation Enterprise (✆ 072/461-1374; www.kate.co.jp), departing KIX every 20 minutes for Sannomiya Station, costing ¥1,900 one-way, and taking about 75 minutes. If you want to use your **Japan Rail Pass,** take a *kaisoku* (rapid train making only major stops) to Osaka Station and change there for the JR Kobe Line's 20-minute ride to Sannomiya Station (considered the heart of the city). If you're staying in a hotel closer to Shin-Kobe Station, take the JR Airport Express Haruka train from the airport to Shin-Osaka Station and transfer there for a speedy Shinkansen connection to Shin-Kobe Station (see p. 395 in the Osaka section for information).

If you're arriving at Kobe Airport (UKB; ✆ **078/304-7777;** www.kairport.co.jp), which opened in 2006 on Port Island to serve domestic flights, you can take the **Portliner Monorail** to Sannomiya Station in 16 minutes for ¥320.

By Train The **Shinkansen** bullet train takes 3¼ hours from Tokyo, 31 minutes from Kyoto, and about 14 minutes from Osaka; the fare from Tokyo for an unreserved seat is ¥13,760. All Shinkansen trains arrive at **Shin-Kobe Station,** which is linked to **Sannomiya Station** (considered the heart of the city) via a 3-minute subway ride (or a 20-min. walk). If you're arriving from nearby Osaka, Kyoto, Himeji, or Okayama, it may be easiest to take a JR express train stopping at Sannomiya Station if you're staying in one of the area's hotels.

By Bus **JR Highway Buses** (✆ **03/3515-1950;** www.jrbuskanto.co.jp) depart from Tokyo Station's Yaesu south exit for Kobe four times nightly (two of the buses make stops also at Shinjuku Station's new South Exit), with the 10:30pm bus arriving at Sannomiya Bus Terminal (near Sannomiya Station) at 7:46am. Fares range from ¥5,000 to ¥8,690, depending on the bus and the season.

VISITOR INFORMATION There are tourist information offices at **Shin-Kobe Station** (✆ **078/241-9550;** daily 9am–6pm) and outside the west exit of **Sannomiya Station** on Flower Road in the Kotsu Center Building (✆ **078/322-0220;** daily 9am–7pm). The English-speaking staff can provide maps and sightseeing information and make hotel reservations. Ask here for your **Kobe Welcome Coupon,** available only to foreigners and containing 16 coupons offering slight discounts to more than 70 sights and facilities, including the City Loop Line and most museums. More tourist information is available online at **www.feel-kobe.jp/english.**

INTERNET ACCESS The **Litz Comic Café,** on the sixth floor of the Tatsumi Building at 5–3–2 Asahi Dori (✆ **078/241-8815**), is open 24 hours and charges ¥480 for the first hour and then ¥50 for each subsequent 10 minutes. It's a 2-minute walk southeast of

Sannomiya Station, down a small street parallel to the tracks (there's a Starbucks on the corner), on the sixth floor above a pachinko parlor.

ORIENTATION & GETTING AROUND   Squeezed between Mount Rokko rising in the north and the shores of the Seto Inland Sea to the south, Kobe stretches some 29km (18 miles) along the coastline but in many places is less than 3km (2 miles) wide. It's made up of many *ku* (wards) such as Nada-ku, Chuo-ku, and Hyogo-ku. The heart of the city lies around Sannomiya, Motomachi, and Kobe stations in the **Chuo-ku (Central Ward).** It's here you'll find the city's nightlife, its port, many restaurants and shopping centers, and most of its hotels. Unlike most other Japanese cities, many of the major streets in Kobe have names with English-language signs posted, so it's easier to get around here than elsewhere. Additionally, the various maps provided by the tourist office are good.

Because the city isn't very wide, you can walk to most points north and south of Sannomiya Station. South of Sannomiya Station is the **Sannomiya Center Gai** covered-arcade shopping street, beyond which lies Kobe's business and administrative district. North of Sannomiya Station are bars and restaurants clustered around narrow streets such as **Higashimon Street.** Kitano-zaka leads uphill to **Kitano-cho** (usually shortened to Kitano) with its Western-style houses, about a 15-minute walk north of Sannomiya Station. **Shin-Kobe Station** is a 20-minute walk north of Sannomiya. Running from Shin-Kobe Station south through Sannomiya all the way to the port is a flower-lined road—called, appropriately enough, **Flower Road.**

About a 10-minute walk west of Sannomiya Station is **Motomachi Station,** south of which lies the fashionable Motomachi covered-arcade shopping street, **Chinatown,** and **Meriken Park,** established to commemorate the birthplace of Kobe's port. The next stop on the JR line from Motomachi Station is **Kobe Station,** just south of which is **Harborland,** a waterfront development with hotels, restaurants, and the colorful Mosaic outdoor restaurant and shopping complex.

Two train stops east of Sannomiya Station is one of the city's most ambitious urban renewal projects, **HAT Kobe** (an abbreviation of Happy Active Town), a mixed-use neighborhood of apartment complexes, research facilities, schools, and museums, including the Disaster Reduction Museum, which chronicles the Great Hanshin Earthquake. Nearby **Nada Ward** is home of several renowned breweries.

Because of restricted space, Kobe has also constructed two artificial islands in its harbor, Port Island (home of Kobe Airport) and Rokko Island. Farther afield, on Mount Rokko, is the Arima Onsen Spa.

A 13km (8-mile) **City Loop** bus, distinguished by its old-fashioned appearance, passes all major attractions, including Kitano, Chinatown, Meriken Park, and Harborland. Buses run three to four times an hour from about 9:30am to 5:30pm, with the route marked on the map distributed by the tourist office. It costs ¥250 for adults and ¥130 for children per ride. Or, a 1-day pass, allowing you to get off and reboard as often as you like and offering slight discounts to attractions mainly in Kitano, costs ¥650 for adults and ¥330 for children.

You can also use the **JR Local Commuter train,** which stops at Sannomiya, Motomachi, and Kobe stations, if you don't mind walking to destinations north and south of these stations (the City Loop Line buses will get you closer to major attractions). The subway is useful only for transportation between Shin-Kobe and Sannomiya stations. The **Portliner Monorail** connects Sannomiya with Port Island, while the Rokko Liner travels between JR Sumiyoshi Station and Rokko Island.

In addition to the sights below, you might wish to drop by **City Hall** on Flower Road, where on the 24th floor there's an **observatory** (© **078/331-8181**) open free to the public Monday to Friday 8:15am to 9pm, Saturday 10am to 10pm, and Sunday and holidays 10am to 9pm.

Evidence of the damage wrought by Kobe's horrific earthquake can be found at **Meriken Park,** a 10-minute walk south of Motomachi Station or a minute's walk from the Meriken Park stop on the City Loop bus. On its eastern edge is the **Port of Kobe Earthquake Memorial,** dedicated to the thousands of people who lost their lives in the tragic 1995 earthquake. Established with the intent of preserving some of the quake's horrific force (240,000 buildings and homes were destroyed), it shows unrepaired damage, including tilted lampposts and a submerged and broken pier.

Kitano

When Kobe was chosen as one of five international ports following the Meiji Restoration, foreign traders and diplomats who settled here built homes in much the same style as those they left behind in their native lands. Approximately 30 of these Western-style homes, called *ijinkan,* remain on a hill north of Sannomiya Station called Kitano-cho, along with a surprising number of churches, synagogues, and other religious centers to serve Kobe's international community. Because the area seems so exotic to young Japanese, this is the number-one draw for domestic visitors, who come also to shop the area's many boutiques, including its many bridal stores (there are also many wedding venues in Kitano).

Approximately 20 Victorian- and Gothic-style homes are open to the public, many with lovely views of the sea from verandas and bay windows. Although you may not be interested in visiting most of them, Kitano is very pleasant for an hour's stroll. It's located about a 15-minute walk north of Sannomiya Station (via Kitano-zaka) or a 10-minute walk west of Shin-Kobe Station. Or take the City Loop bus to Kitano Ijinkan. For orientation purposes, there's the **Kitano Tourist Information Center,** across from the Weathercock House (© **078/251-8360;** daily 9am–6pm), with maps of the area.

Two of the more interesting homes open to the public are the **Moegi no Yakata,** 3–10–11 Kitano-cho (© **078/222-3310**), a pale-green, 107-year-old home built for a former American consul general, Hunter Sharp, and filled with antiques; and **Kasamidori-no-Yakata** ★, 3–13–3 Kitano-cho (© **078/242-3223**), popularly referred to as the Weathercock House because of its rooster weather vane. This 1909 brick residence was built by a German merchant and is probably Kobe's most famous home if not its most elaborate. Admission to either home, located across from one another, is ¥300, or purchase a combination ticket for ¥500. Children enter free. They're open daily April to November from 9am to 6pm and December to March from 9am to 5pm (Weathercock House closed the first Tues in June and Feb).

Another home of note (because it contains porcelain, glass, and art, not because of its historical value) is **Uroko no Ie,** 2–20–4 Kitano-cho (© **078/242-6530;** daily 9am–6pm in summer, to 5pm in winter), which has a castlelike exterior and is nicknamed the Fish-Scale House because of its slate walls. It contains lovely antiques, including Meissen porcelain and Tiffany glass, as well as a small private museum of Western 18th- to 20th-century art, with a few works by Andrew Wyeth, Utrillo, and others. Admission is ¥1,000 for adults, ¥300 for children.

420

THE REST OF WESTERN HONSHU

10

KOBE

> ## Moments   Ships Ahoy
>
> What better way to see this port town than by sea? A variety of sightseeing boats depart from Naka Pier Central Terminal, between Meriken Park and Kobe Harborland (take the City Loop bus to Nakatottei Pier). They range from **Luminous Kobe 2** (✆ **078/333-8414**), known for its French cuisine and departing three times daily for 2-hour cruises costing ¥2,100 (not including food), to **Villaggio Italia** (✆ **078/367-2651**), mock pirate boats that depart hourly and cost ¥1,000. Children pay half fare.

A GARDEN RETREAT   If you're a gardener, want a respite from city life, or simply want to spend an hour in a cooler climate, take the Shin-Kobe ropeway located next to Shin-Kobe Station for a 10-minute ride to the **Nunobiki Herb Garden** ★ (✆ **078/271-1160**), with its lovely, meandering, fragrant gardens planted with various flowering shrubs and herbs and offering great views over Kobe. Be sure to take the ropeway to the end (don't get off at the first stop) and then walk downhill past gardens planted with sage, mint, lavender, roses, seasonal herbs, Japanese plants, and a greenhouse. The garden opens daily at 10am, closing at 5pm on weekdays and 8:30pm on weekends, holidays, and peak season (mid-July to Aug). From December to March it closes daily at 5pm. It's closed for 2 weeks in January. Admission, including round-trip by ropeway, is ¥1,200 for adults, half-price for children.

Chinatown ★

Like the Kitano-cho area, **Chinatown** (called Nankin-machi), a 3-minute walk south of Motomachi Station (or to the Sakaemachi 1-chome stop on the City Loop bus), is worth a walk-through for its lively street scene, with sidewalk vendors selling snacks and with open-fronted souvenir shops and produce stands. If the sidewalk vendors tempt you, eat your snack in the central square called **Nankin Park,** adorned with statues representing the animals of the 12-year Chinese astrological calendar. Chinatown's public restroom, called **Garyoden,** which means "palace of a secluded wise man," is certainly one of Japan's most colorful—its outer wall is decorated with five-clawed dragons and is based on a famous Chinese epic about a dragonlike hero; it's located a block off the main street. You may also want to come to Chinatown for a meal in one of its many restaurants.

Kobe Harborland

Kobe Harborland is a leisure center that's fun to stroll and browse. It's a few minutes' walk from either Kobe Station or Meriken Park, or you can take the City Loop bus to Harborland. For shopping, stop by Kobe Hankyu department store or Promena Kobe mall, but best is **Mosaic,** a restaurant and shopping complex designed to resemble a Mediterranean village. Through the use of varying architectural and color schemes, it avoids the generic mall atmosphere, and with a diversity of ethnic goods and foods, it mirrors Kobe's international roots. Shops here are open daily from 11am to 8pm.

Beside it is **Mosaic Garden,** a small amusement park for younger children complete with kiddie rides, carousel, roller coaster, enclosed Ferris wheel, and games arcade. It's open daily from 11am to 10pm, with rides costing ¥300 to ¥600. For older kids, there's the Museum games arcade inside Mosaic.

If you're on your way to the Disaster Reduction Museum, below, it might be worthwhile to check out what's being shown at the **Hyogo Prefectural Museum of Art** practically next door (℗ **078/262-0901;** www.artm.pref.hyogo.jp). Designed by renowned Japanese architect Tadao Ando, it displays contemporary art, prints, sculpture, and other works produced by artists with connections to Hyogo Prefecture, as well as temporary exhibits from around the world. It's open Tuesday through Sunday from 10am to 6pm and charges ¥500 for adults, ¥400 for high-school and college students, and ¥250 for children; special exhibits cost more.

Disaster Reduction Museum ★★★   Despite its rather official-sounding name, this facility gives a human dimension to the Great Hanshin Earthquake, which measured 7.3 on the Richter scale. Sheathed in glass and built to withstand both vertical and horizontal earthquakes, it vividly conveys what happened during the first moments of the earthquake and the weeks, months, and years that followed. English-speaking volunteers are on hand to help explain some of the museum's more technical displays; audio guides are also available.

A visit to the museum begins with a powerful 7-minute film that re-creates the exact moment the earthquake struck, with computer-generated scenes that show buildings imploding or bursting into flames and highways collapsing (the graphics might be too much for young children). From the movie theater, visitors emerge into a life-size diorama depicting a typical Kobe neighborhood destroyed by the quake. They then enter another movie theater where a 15-minute documentary shows actual footage shot shortly after the quake and during the weeks that followed, presented through the eyes of a teenage survivor. Other displays in the museum concentrate on the individual experiences of survivors, emergency relief, and reconstruction. A hands-on section helps visitors learn how construction techniques can minimize and even prevent earthquake damage and dispenses information on disaster management. There is no other facility in Japan quite like this one; you can easily spend an hour here.

1-5-2 Wakinohama Kaigan-Dori, Chuo-ku. ℗ **078/262-5050.** www.dri.ne.jp/english. Admission ¥500 adults, ¥400 high-school and college students, ¥250 children. Tues–Sun 9:30am–5:30pm (to 7pm Fri–Sat; to 6pm July–Sept). You must enter 1 hr. before closing. Station: JR Nada (12 min. south, toward the harbor).

Hakutsuru Sake Brewery Museum ★   Everything you ever wanted to know about sake production is available at this former brewery, with English-language videos and pamphlets describing the various painstaking steps and comparing the old techniques to those used today. Hakutsuru, established in 1743, is one of many sake breweries in this part of Kobe; its actual brewery is now across the street (closed to the public). Plan on spending 30 minutes on your self-guided tour, which ends with hints on how to enjoy sake and—what would a brewery tour be without this?—free tastings.

4-5-5 Sumiyoshi-minami-machi, Higashinada-ku. ℗ **078/822-8907.** www.hakutsuru-sake.com. Free admission. Tues–Sun 9:30am–4:30pm. Station: Hanshin Sumiyoshi (5 min.); JR Sumiyoshi (15 min.).

Kobe Fashion Museum ★ (Finds)   Located on artificial Rokko Island, this is Japan's first museum devoted to fashion, housed in a contemporary, sophisticated setting that does justice to the highbrow costumes it contains. Temporary displays devoted to individual designers (there was a great show by John Galliano on one of my visits, in a setting designed by Japanese architect Tadao Ando) allow closer inspection than you could ever get at a fashion show. Other displays, which are imaginative tableaux complete with visual images, music, and lighting, may feature anything from 20th-century gowns by

> **(Finds) Silver & Gold**
>
> On the opposite side of Mount Rokko is **Arima Onsen,** one of Japan's oldest hot-spring spas. Two public baths here are the ⑬⑨ **Kin-no-Yu** (📞 **078/904-0680**), or Gold Spring, with copper-colored waters that have twice the salinity and iron of seawater; and the ⑭⓪ **Gin-no-Yu** (📞 **078/904-0256**), or Silver Spring, with transparent water rich in carbonic acid. It's said that if you bathe in both these waters and drink carbonated water, you'll be cured of all ailments. The Kin-no-Yu, open daily 8am to 10pm (closed the second and fourth Tues of every month), charges ¥650, while the Gin-no-Yu, open daily 9am to 9pm (closed the first and third Tues of every month), charges ¥550. A combination ticket to both is ¥1,000. Buses from Sannomiya Station reach Arima Onsen in 40 minutes and cost ¥680 one-way. You can also travel by train to Rokko Station, followed by a trip via cable car, bus, and ropeway. For more information, contact the Kobe Tourist Information office or the Arima Onsen Tourist Information Office (📞 **078/904-0708; www.arima-onsen.com**).

Christian Dior to extravagant *kabuki* costumes or ethnic clothing worn by indigenous peoples from around the world. Displays change four or five times a year, rotating the many costumes owned by the museum. In all, a very entertaining, unique museum, and a must-see for fashionistas with an hour to spare.

2–9 Koyocho-naka, Rokko Island. 📞 **078/858-0050.** Admission ¥500 adults, ¥250 children and seniors. Thurs–Tues 10am–6pm. Closed 1 week during exhibit changes. Take the local JR train to Sumiyoshi Station, transferring there for the Rokkoliner monorail to Island Center.

WHERE TO STAY

Some hotels charge more for Saturday nights and nights before holidays, as well as during peak season (Golden Week, summer holidays, and New Year's).

Expensive

Crowne Plaza Hotel   This hotel is directly connected by covered walkway to Shin-Kobe Station—very convenient if you're arriving by Shinkansen train. Rising 37 stories, with rooms on the 14th to 33rd floors, it offers impressive views of Kobe and the bay or the mountains from some of its restaurants and most of its fully equipped rooms. Rates are based on room size and height, with top floors commanding the grandest views at the highest prices (all singles face the wooded mountains). A plus is the large mall occupying the first four floors, with many additional choices in dining.

1 Kitano-cho, Chuo-ku, Kobe 650-0002. 📞 **887/227-6963** in the U.S., or 078/291-1121. Fax 078/291-1151. www.anacrowneplaza-kobe.jp. 592 units. ¥15,015 single; ¥21,945–¥38,115 double; from ¥34,650 Crowne Plaza Club double. AE, DC, MC, V. Station: Shin-Kobe (1 min.). **Amenities:** 6 restaurants; 2 bars; lounge; concierge; executive-level rooms; health club w/gym and indoor pool (fee: ¥1,050); lobby computer (¥100 for 10 min.); room service; smoke-free rooms; spa. *In room:* A/C, TV, fridge, hair dryer, Internet.

Hotel Monterey Amalie ★   Taking its name from a long-ago Dutch sailing vessel and decorated in a nautical theme, this property is part of a smart chain of boutique hotels that targets mostly female Japanese travelers with old-world European decor and atmosphere. From its ivy-covered facade to whitewashed walls (some of which could use a fresh coat) and heavy-beamed ceilings, it looks much older than its 1992 construction date. Wood-floored guest rooms feature natural wooden furniture, sheer curtains and heavy wooden shutters, tiled bathrooms, and free-standing wardrobes. Ask for a room overlooking Ikuta Shrine, but because occupancy is enviably high, book early. Otherwise, try nearby sister hotel Monterey Kobe (© **078/392-7111**), with slightly cheaper prices and a medieval cloister–like atmosphere.

2-2-28 Nakayamate Dori, Chuo-ku, Kobe 650-0004. © **078/334-1711.** Fax 078/334-1788. www.hotel monterey.co.jp/kobe. 69 units. ¥17,000 single; ¥30,000–¥40,000 double. AE, DC, MC, V. Station: Sannomiya (10 min.). Just west of Ikuta Shrine. **Amenities:** Restaurant; smoke-free rooms. *In room:* A/C, TV, hair dryer, Internet, minibar.

Hotel Okura Kobe ★★ **Kids**   This majestic 35-story hotel has the prestige of the Okura name, as well as a grand location right beside Meriken Park, within easy walking distance of the Motomachi covered shopping arcade and Chinatown. Its inviting lobby has views of a small garden (the only hotel garden in downtown Kobe) against a backdrop formed by the port. Each elegantly appointed room has all the comforts you'd expect, plus the bonus of great views from its more expensive rooms, which are on higher floors facing either the harbor or the city with Mount Rokko rising behind it (standard rooms provide only city views). In short, this hotel appeals to everyone from businessmen on weekdays to tourists on weekends. Even the imperial family makes this their home base when in Kobe. *Tip:* Upon check-in, ask for immediate free membership in the Okura Club International, which allows late checkout, discounts to its health club, free use of the outdoor pool, and other privileges.

2-1 Hatoba-cho, Chuo-ku, Kobe 650-8560. © **800/526-2281** in the U.S. and Canada, or 078/333-0111. Fax 078/333-6673. www.kobe.hotelokura.co.jp. 475 units. ¥16,800–¥23,100 single; ¥22,050–¥47,250 double. Rates exclude service charge. AE, DC, MC, V. Station: Motomachi (10 min. south). City Loop bus: Meriken Park (1 min.). Free shuttle service from Sannomiya Station daily and Shin-Osaka Station (weekends and holidays only) 2–3 times an hour. **Amenities:** 5 restaurants; 2 bars; babysitting; children's day-care center (fee: ¥5,250 for 2 hr.; reservations required 2 days in advance); concierge; health club w/gym, sauna, and heated indoor lap pool (fee: ¥4,200); outdoor pool (fee: ¥1,260; free w/membership); room service; free shuttle service; smoke-free rooms; 2 lit outdoor tennis courts. *In room:* A/C, TV, hair dryer, Internet, minibar.

Kobe Meriken Park Oriental Hotel ★★   An outstanding location on a spit of land jutting seaward from the edge of Meriken Park (it's practically on the water and surrounded by a park) makes this Kobe's best hotel with a view—which it capitalizes on by providing each room with a balcony with views of Kobe's harbor and of the city as it rises up the hills. Popular with couples (weddings are big here), the hotel looks like one of the many cruise ships that dock nearby, rising 14 stories in a lopsided half circle. Its center is hollow, an airy atrium filled with palm trees and bubbling fountains. In addition to standard rooms, there are more expensive Com'fill rooms (designed to "fill you with comfort" with higher-quality beds and aromatherapy) and Sea'fill rooms (where earth tones are fused with red and blue, meant to relay sea sunsets) on higher floors, with corner rooms providing views even from their bathrooms. A free shuttle provides service from Sannomiya Station every 20 to 30 minutes.

5-6 Hatoba-cho, Chuo-ku, Kobe 650-0042. © **078/325-8111.** Fax 078/325-8106. www.kobe-orientalhotel. co.jp. 331 units. ¥16,800–¥21,000 single; ¥24,150–¥36,750 double. Rates exclude service charge. Rates ¥5,250 higher on Sat and days before holidays. AE, DC, MC, V. Free shuttle service every 20–30 min. from Sannomiya Station. Loop Line bus: Nakatottei Pier (5 min.). **Amenities:** 5 restaurants; bar; children's day-care center (¥5,250 for 2 hr.); indoor pool w/sun deck and sauna (fee: ¥1,050); room service; free shuttle service; smoke-free rooms. *In room:* A/C, TV, hair dryer, minibar, Wi-Fi.

the b kobe ★★ (Finds) Located just minutes from Sannomiya Station, this hotel wins hands-down as Kobe's most chic moderately priced hotel, offering mostly twin rooms smartly but sparingly done up in brown and red color tones. Reception is on the second floor, where you'll also find a machine dispensing free coffee and a computer you can use for free. In short, a stylish retreat with a convenient location make this a popular business hotel.

2–1–5 Shimoyamatedori, Chuo-ku, Kobe 650-0011. ☎ **078/333-4880.** Fax 078/333-4876. www.ishinhotels. com. 158 units. ¥8,400–¥9,450 single; ¥13,650–¥19,950 double. AE, DC, MC, V. Station: Sannomiya (3 min. south). On Ikuta Shinmichi St. **Amenities:** Lobby computer w/free Internet; smoke-free rooms. *In room:* A/C, TV fridge, hair dryer, Internet.

Holiday Inn Express Shin-Kobe (Kids) This is a good choice if you want to be near Shin-Kobe Station but don't want to spend a lot of money. Although it doesn't offer much in the way of facilities, there's a playground nearby, making it good for families, as do the two double-size beds in the twin rooms. Shoji screens (and window panels that close for complete darkness) and small rooms are reminders you're in Japan.

6–4–14 Hatazuka-dori, Chuo-ku, Kobe 651-0068. ☎ **078/222-1212.** Fax 078/222-1222. www.holidayinn-kobe.com. 95 units. ¥8,316–¥9,240 single; ¥13,860–¥18,480 double. Rates include continental breakfast. AE, DC, MC, V. Station: Shin-Kobe (5 min.). Take the south exit, head east over the Ikuta River, and turn right; it's on a side street to the left, just before the playground. **Amenities:** Restaurant; lobby computer (¥100 for 10 min.); smoke-free rooms. *In room:* A/C, TV, fridge, hair dryer, Wi-Fi.

Hotel Tor Road ★ Knickknacks on the piano, antiques, and dark-wood wainscoting lend an English country atmosphere to this tourist hotel's lobby. The decent-size rooms are clean and tastefully decorated with double-size beds (except in the singles) and larger-than-usual bathrooms, with twins and doubles even providing a separate sink area. Each of the so-called "Concept Rooms" on the ninth floor is designed around a different theme. The "cat" room, for example, has the logo of a cat repeated on the drapes, pillows, sheets, and elsewhere, but I fail to see why anyone would pay more for it (except that it does have a king-size bed, a rarity in moderately priced hotels, making it a good choice for couples). At the other extreme are the single rooms with semi-double-size beds, where budget-conscious couples can cuddle for ¥10,000.

3–1–19 Nakayamate Dori, Chuo-ku, Kobe 650-0004. ☎ **078/391-6691.** Fax 078/391-6570. htorroad@ oak.ocn.ne.jp. 76 units. ¥8,000 single; ¥13,000–¥18,000 double. Rates ¥2,000 more in the single room and ¥3,000 more in double rooms on Sat and day before holidays. AE, DC, MC, V. Station: Sannomiya or Motomachi (10 min.). On Tor Rd. just north of Ikuta Shinmichi Dori. **Amenities:** Restaurant; smoke-free rooms. *In room:* A/C, TV, hair dryer, Internet, minibar.

Inexpensive

Green Hill Hotel Urban Between Sannomiya and Shin-Kobe stations, this simple business hotel with mostly single rooms in a dormitory-like setting is primarily a place to park your head at night (I'd try the other recommendations first). Rather shabby rooms are about as small as they come, most without closets and with glazed windows and minuscule plastic-unit bathrooms. Best are the Japanese rooms. Free tea is dispensed from machines on each floor. Don't confuse this with the older Green Hill Hotel around the corner.

2–5–16 Kano-cho, Chuo-ku, Kobe 650-0001. ☎ **078/222-1221.** Fax 078/242-1194. 102 units. ¥4,900 single; ¥9,500–¥10,500 double; ¥12,000 Japanese room double. Rates ¥1,000 more per person in high season. AE, DC, MC, V. Station: Shin-Kobe or Sannomiya (10 min.); btw. the stations, on Flower Rd. **Amenities:** Coffee

Toyoko Inn Kobe-Sannomiya II (Value) One of Japan's fastest-growing business hotel chains surpasses others for such perks as computers in the lobby guests can use for free, free Wi-Fi in the lobby, semi-double-size beds in singles, free domestic phone calls (for calls up to 3 min.), and free Japanese breakfasts. Rooms are small but clean, and female travelers even get a cosmetic set geared just for them. If this one's full, Toyoko Inn Kobe-Sannomiya I, 2–2–2 Gokodori (© **078/271-1045**), is only 5 minutes away and about ¥500 cheaper.

5-2-2 Kumoi Dori, Chuo-ku, Kobe 651-0096. © **078/232-1045**. Fax 078/232-1046. www.toyoko-inn. com. 334 units. ¥5,985–¥6,300 single; ¥7,350–¥8,400 double. Rates include Japanese breakfast. MC, V. Station: Sannomiya (east exit, 2 min.). Behind Daiei department store; turn left onto the busy thoroughfare in front of JR Sannomiya Station and then another left. **Amenities:** Lobby computer w/free Internet; smoke-free rooms. *In room:* A/C, TV, fridge, hair dryer, Internet.

Super Hotel Kobe This chain comes close to Toyoko Inn's cheap price and ever-expanding network of hotels, but it falls short of its competitor when it comes to atmosphere and amenities. You have to ring the doorbell to gain admission, and rooms—all singles—are minuscule with just the basics.

2-1–11 Kano-cho, Chuo-ku, Kobe 650-0001. © **078/261-9000**. Fax 078/231-9090. www.superhotel. co.jp. 87 units. ¥5,460 single. Rates include breakfast. AE, MC, V. Station: Shin-Kobe or Sannomiya (10 min.); btw. the stations, on the west side of Flower Rd. (its entry is on a side street). **Amenities:** Smoke-free rooms. *In room:* A/C, TV, fridge, hair dryer, Internet, no phone.

WHERE TO DINE

With its sizable foreign population, Kobe is a good place to dine on international cuisine, including French, Indian, and Chinese food. The greatest concentration of Chinese restaurants is along a pedestrian lane in Chinatown, called **Nankin-machi** by the locals, just a 2-minute walk south of Motomachi Station. If you're on a budget, you may just want to wander through and buy sticky buns or other inexpensive fare from the many street stalls. In the center of Nankin-machi is a plaza, good for people-watching.

Very Expensive

Alain Chapel ★★★ FRENCH For elegant dining and contemporary French cuisine, Alain Chapel is one of the city's top choices. In a stately drawing-room setting with great panoramic views of either Kobe city or the sea, it is under the helm of Philippe Jousse, who achieved two Michelin stars at the original Alain Chapel in France. The changing menu may include the likes of pigeon breast with black truffles or roast lamb in pistachio crumbs. Good for a romantic splurge.

Kobe Portopia Hotel, 31st floor, 6–10–2 Minatojima, Port Island. © **078/303-5201**. www.portopia.co.jp. Reservations recommended. Main dishes ¥3,696–¥10,395; set dinners ¥11,550–¥18,480; set lunches ¥5,544–¥6,930. AE, DC, MC, V. Daily 11:30am–2pm and 5:30–9pm (last order). Portliner Monorail from Sannomiya Station to Shimin Hiroba Station (2 min.); or free shuttle service every 20 min. from Sannomiya and Shin-Kobe stations.

Expensive

Kitano Club ★ FRENCH Located in Kitano on a hill overlooking the city, this well-known, upscale restaurant has been offering meals with a view for more than 50 years. Join the well-heeled who come to soak in the fabulous vistas, listen to live jazz or popular music, and dine on selections that change monthly, with choices that may range from

Kobe beef and fresh catch of the day to roast lamb with eggplant cake. Afterward, retire to the bar or adjacent lounge (until midnight). Be sure to call to make sure it's open, as this is a popular wedding venue.

1–5–7 Kitano-cho. © **078/222-5123.** Reservations recommended. Main dishes ¥4,000–¥6,205; set dinners ¥8,400–¥15,750. AE, DC, MC, V. Daily 5:30–10:30pm (last order). Station: Shin-Kobe (7 min.). Go west on Kitano Rd. from Crowne Plaza Hotel, taking the 1st street on the right (look for the Kitano Chapel on your left); it will be on your left in the 2nd building.

Wakkoqu ★ TEPPANYAKI STEAKS   This tiny, second-floor restaurant has room for only 30 diners at two counters, where expert chefs cook sirloin, tenderloin, or other cuts of tender Kobe beef on the grill in front of them. Fixed-course meals come with such side dishes as soup and fried vegetables. This is a good place to try Kobe's most famous product.

Hillside Terrace, 1–22–13 Nakayamate Dori. © **078/222-0678.** Reservations recommended. Set dinners ¥7,500–¥11,000; set lunches ¥2,940–¥5,040. AE, DC, MC, V. Daily noon–9:30pm (last order). Station: Sannomiya (7 min.). On Pearl St. just east of Kitano-zaka, in a brick building.

Moderate

Bistro Café de Paris ★ FRENCH   A little bit of Paris in the heart of Kobe is offered by this popular and lively bistro, complete with sidewalk seating and *chansons* in the background. Lunch features set meals that come with soup, salad, a choice of main dish, bread, and coffee or tea, as well as sandwich and pizza sets. Dinner is more substantial, with main dishes ranging from roast lamb with mustard to beef bourguignon. Or, come for the afternoon cake set for ¥1,050, which gives you a choice of 10 different desserts (think tarts, tiramisu, or the mousse of the day) plus coffee, and sit and watch the world parade by.

1–7–21 Yamamoto Dori. © **078/241-9448.** Main dishes ¥1,680–¥1,998; set dinners ¥2,940–¥5,250; set lunches ¥1,050–¥2,415. AE, MC, V. Daily 10am–10pm (last order). Station: Sannomiya (10 min.). On the east side of Kitano-zaka, north of Pearl St.

Ganesha Ghar (Value NORTHERN INDIAN   This fourth-floor, one-room walk-up is owned by a kind owner/chef, who has made this his cozy home-away-from-home, right down to live Indian broadcasts or movies on the television and a clock set to Indian time. Worth seeking out for its authentic, delicious tandoori and curry at unbeatable prices, it offers a weekday lunch for ¥1,000, for example, consisting of salad, tandoori, vegetable curry, chicken curry, nan, and saffron rice. By the way, Ganesha Ghar means home of Ganesh (the elephant god of prosperity), but once you've eaten here, you might want to move in, too.

Louvre Bldg. 4F, 1–6–21 Nakayamate Dori. © **078/391-9060.** Curries ¥1,000–¥1,500; set dinners ¥2,000–¥7,000; set lunches ¥1,000–¥1,500. No credit cards. Daily 11am–3pm and 5–11pm. Station: Sannomiya (4 min.). From the intersection of Kitano-zaka and Ikuta Shinmichi St., walk west past 2 small alleys and turn right at the first real street; it will be on the left.

(141) **Steakland Kobe** STEAKS   If you want to eat *teppanyaki* steak but can't afford the high prices of Kobe beef, one of the cheapest places to go is Steakland Kobe, which is used to tourists and offers an English-language menu. Lunch specials, served from 11am to 3pm, feature steak, miso soup, rice, Japanese pickles, a salad, and coffee. More expensive Kobe beef is also available, with the least expensive fixed-price dinner offering Kobe sirloin costing ¥4,480. Set dinners come with soup, fried vegetables, rice or bread, and coffee or tea. You'll sit at a counter, behind which young chefs cook your meal.

1–8–2 Kitanagasa Dori. © **078/332-1653.** Steaks ¥1,980–¥5,280; set steak dinners ¥2,680–¥7,480; set lunches ¥980–¥2,980. AE, DC, MC, V. Daily 11am–10pm (last order). Station: Sannomiya (2 min.). On the

Inexpensive

In addition to the choices here, Mosaic (p. 420) has a variety of restaurants, including **Fisherman's Market** (📞 **078/360-3695**) offering buffets of grilled and steamed seafood, rotisserie chicken, pastas, curry, paella, pizza, and other fare. All-you-can-eat buffets cost ¥1,782 for lunch and ¥2,380 for dinner; on weekends it's ¥2,097 and ¥2,709 respectively. It's open daily 11am to 9:30pm (last order).

⑭ **Hyotan** (Value GYOZA   Roll up your sleeves and join the working class at this greasy hole-in-the-wall eatery underneath the tracks of Hanshin Sannomiya Station. It must be doing something right, as it's been selling nothing but *gyoza*—favored for the light texture of its dumpling skin and stuffed with minced pork, leek, and cabbage—for more than 40 years. Gyoza come seven to a serving. At your table will be soy sauce, vinegar, and chili sauce, which you should mix in the little bowl provided; some regulars also mix chili sauce and miso paste. Avoid the noontime rush, when this tiny place is like an assembly line for speed eating.

1-31-37 Kitanagasa Dori. 📞 **078/331-1354.** 7-gyoza serving ¥370. No credit cards. Mon–Fri 11:30am–2:30pm and 5–10:30pm; Sat–Sun 11:30am–10:30pm. Closed the 2nd and 4th Mon of each month. Station: Sannomiya (2 min.). Underneath the tracks of Hankyu Sannomiya Station in a small passageway called Sun West, at the west end near Ikutasuji; look for its red curtains and phone number.

Nishimura COFFEE SHOP   In business some 60 years, Nishimura is a Kobe landmark, but if you can't find it just follow your nose; the smell of roasting coffee broadcasts its location. Some 20 types of coffee are available, as well as snacks, sandwich sets, and desserts. The second floor is nonsmoking.

1-26-1 Nakayamate Dori. 📞 **078/221-1872.** Coffee from ¥500. No credit cards. Daily 8:30am–11pm. Station: Sannomiya (9 min.). On the north side of Yamate Kansen Dori (also called Nakayamate Dori), across from Higashimon St. in a mock German half-timbered building.

Pinocchio PIZZA/PASTA   This small and cozy corner establishment opened in 1962 and proudly claims to have never fallen victim to the many fads that have come and gone since then. Instead, it still produces handmade pizza, which you can order from the menu or create yourself by ordering the basic pizza for ¥945 and adding ingredients such as garlic, asparagus, mushroom, chicken, or bacon, all priced at ¥105 each. Salads, pasta, pilaf, and gratin are also available from an English-language menu with photos. If the place is full, add your name to the list and wait outside.

2-3-13 Nakayamate Dori. 📞 **078/331-3330.** Pizza and pasta ¥1,260–¥1,680; set lunches ¥1,310. AE, DC, MC, V. Daily 11:30am–midnight. Station: Sannomiya (12 min.). On the south side of Yamate Kansen Dori (also called Nakayamate Dori), west of Ikuta Shrine and 1 block east of Tor Rd.

KOBE AFTER DARK

Kobe has a wide selection of English-style pubs, bars, expatriate hangouts, and nightclubs. All the establishments below are easily accessible to foreigners, and most are within walking distance of Sannomiya Station.

The Club & Music Scene

Garage Paradise   Candlelight, gauzy curtains draped from the high ceiling, Roman statues, a copper-and-stone bar, and stone walls set the scene at this basement with five sets of good, live music nightly. The interesting setting attracts the local foreigner clientele.

Open daily 7pm to 3am (Sun to 2am). Kobe Yamashita Building, basement, 1–13–7 Nakayamate Dori. ✆ **078/391-6640.** Cover Sun–Thurs ¥520; Fri–Sat ¥520 for women, ¥720 for men. Station: Sannomiya (9 min.). On Yamate Kansen Dori east of Higashimon, catty-corner from Nishimura coffee shop.

Satin Doll   This traditional jazz club first opened in 1972 and remains one of the city's top venues. Its sophisticated interior offers table and bar seating with some city views. There are three live music sets nightly (7, 8:30, and 10pm) of mostly Japanese talents; an English-language menu offers mainly snacks. Open Tuesday to Sunday 6pm to midnight. Bacchus Building, 1–26–1 Nakayamate Dori. ✆ **078/242-0100.** Cover from ¥500, more for international acts, plus ¥500 table charge. Station: Sannomiya (9 min.). On Yamate Kansen Dori opposite Higashimon Dori.

Sone   Kobe's oldest and best-known jazz club has changed little since its 1969 opening, offering the same traditional jazz, including Dixieland ensembles and piano-vocalist duos, in a clubby, dated atmosphere. There are four stages nightly, and most of its older crowd come to eat; the Japanese-language menu lists pasta, pizza, fish, and Kobe steaks, with set meals starting at ¥2,100. Open daily 5pm to 12:30am (Sun to midnight). 1–24–10 Nakayamate Dori. ✆ **078/221-2055.** Cover usually ¥900. Station: Sannomiya (5 min.). North of the station on the left side of Kitano-zaka.

The Bar Scene

Hobgoblin Kobe   This popular British import (there are three branches in Tokyo alone) prides itself on its ales (including its own Hobgoblin brand) and lagers, as well as its British pub decor. It offers a pretty decent menu as well, from sandwiches to tortilla wraps to a homemade pie of the day, bangers and mash, and beer-battered fish and chips. Big screens show major sporting events, but live, free music takes over Friday and Saturday at 9:30pm. Open Monday to Saturday from 5pm and Sunday from 3pm to the wee hours. Kondo Building, 7th floor, 4–3–2 Kano-cho. ✆ **078/325-0830.** www.hobgoblin.jp. Station: Sannomiya (1 min.). Across from the station to the north, at the juncture of Ikuta Shinmichi and Flower Rd., above a McDonald's.

Second Chance   This all-nighter, in business an astonishing 35 years (which makes it older than virtually all of its customers), is a small, one-room bar favored by night owls who don't mind the rather sparse furnishings. This is where people congregate when the other bars have had the good sense to close down for the night. The last Saturday of every month features live music (usually hip-hop or reggae), with a cover charge of ¥3,500 for guys and ¥2,500 for gals, including all you care to drink for both men and women. Open daily 6pm to 5am. Takashima, 2nd floor, 2–1–12 Nakayamate Dori. ✆ **078/391-3544.** Station: Sannomiya (10 min.). On Yamate Kansen Dori west of Higashimon and catty-corner from Nishimura coffee shop.

6 THE TEMPLES OF MOUNT KOYA ★★★

748km (465 miles) W of Tokyo; 199km (124 miles) S of Osaka

If you've harbored visions of wooden temples nestled in among trees whenever you've thought of Japan, the sacred mountain of **Mount Koya** is the place to go. It's all here—head-shaven monks, religious chanting at the crack of dawn, the wafting of incense, temples, towering cypress trees, tombs, and early morning mist rising above the treetops. Mount Koya—called Koyasan by Japanese—is one of Japan's most sacred places and the mecca of the Shingon Esoteric sect of Buddhism. Standing almost 900m (3,000 ft.) above the world, the top of Mount Koya is home to more than 115 Shingon Buddhist temples scattered through the mountain forests. Some 50 of these temples offer accommodations, making this one of the best places in Japan to observe temple life firsthand.

A World Heritage Site, Koyasan first became a place of meditation and religious learning almost 1,200 ago when Kukai, known posthumously as Kobo Daishi, was granted the mountaintop by the imperial court in 816 as a place to establish his Shingon sect of Buddhism. Kobo Daishi was a charismatic priest who had spent 2 years in China studying esoteric Buddhism before returning to his native land to spread his teachings among Japanese. Revered for his excellent calligraphy, his humanitarianism, and his teachings, Kobo Daishi remains one of the most beloved figures in Japanese Buddhist history. When he died in the 9th century, he was laid to rest in a mausoleum on Mount Koya. His followers believe Kobo Daishi is not dead but simply in a deep state of meditation, awaiting the arrival of the last bodhisattva (Buddha messiah). According to popular belief, priests opening his mausoleum decades after his death found his body still warm.

Through the centuries, many of Kobo Daishi's followers, wishing to be close at hand when the great priest awakens, have had huge tombs or tablets constructed close to Kobo Daishi's mausoleum, and many have had their ashes interred here. Pilgrims over the last thousand years have included emperors, feudal lords, samurai, and common people, all climbing to the top of the mountain to pay their respects. Women, however, were barred from entering the sacred grounds of Koyasan until 1872.

ESSENTIALS

GETTING THERE   The easiest way to get to Koyasan is from Osaka. **Nankai Railway's** ordinary express *(kyuko)* **Koya Line** trains depart from Osaka's Namba Station every half-hour or hour bound for Gokurakubashi, and the trip south takes about 1 hour and 40 minutes. If you want to ride in luxury, Nankai limited-express trains with reserved seating depart five times daily and arrive in Gokurakubashi about 1 hour and 15 minutes later. After arriving at the last stop, Gokurakubashi, you continue your trip to the top of Mount Koya via a 5-minute ride in a cable car. The entire journey from Namba Station to Mount Koya costs ¥1,230 one-way, including the cable car; if you take the faster limited express, it'll cost ¥760 extra. You'll save money, however, with Nankai's **discount ticket** called **Koyasan World Heritage Ticket** (available at Namba Station), which includes round-trip travel from Namba Station and the cable car, plus unlimited rides on Koya's buses for 2 days and a 20% discount to the attractions listed below. The cost is ¥2,780 if you travel by ordinary express and ¥3,310 by limited-express. Children pay half fare. For more information on travel to and around Koyasan, go to **www.nankaikoya.jp**.

VISITOR INFORMATION   At the top of Mount Koya is Koyasan Station, where you'll find a booth of the local tourist office, the main office of which is located approximately in the center of Koyasan village near Kongobuji Temple. You can pick up a map of Koyasan and book a room in a temple at either office, but it is recommended that you fax ahead for a reservation (see "Where to Stay & Dine," below). Both offices are open daily from 8:30am to 4:30pm in winter (Nov–Feb), to 5pm the rest of the year. The main office has a computer with Internet access you can use for free, as well as a 90-minute rental audio guide for ¥500 that's highly useful for learning more about what you're seeing throughout Koyasan, including the location of famous mausoleums and tombstones in Okunoin. For more information, contact the **Koyasan Tourist Association** (*C* **0736/56-2616**) or check the websites **www.koya.org/eng** and **www.shukubo.jp/eng**.

GETTING AROUND Outside the cable car station, you must board a **bus** that travels 2km (1¼ miles) along a narrow, winding road to the village of Koyasan and then continues along the main street all the way through town to the Okunoin-guchi and Okunoin-mae bus stops, the location of Kobo Daishi's mausoleum. The bus passes almost all the sights along the way, as well as most temples accommodating visitors and the Koyasan Tourist Association's main office. Buses depart every 30 or 40 minutes between 6:29am and 7pm; the trip to Okunoin-mae takes 20 minutes and costs ¥400. Otherwise, once you're settled in at your temple accommodations, you can probably walk to Okunoin and other locations mentioned below.

EXPLORING MOUNT KOYA

THE TOP ATTRACTION The most awe-inspiring and magnificent of Koyasan's many structures and temples, **Okunoin** ★★★ contains the mausoleum of Kobo Daishi. The most dramatic way to approach Okunoin is from the Okunoin-guchi bus stop, where a pathway leads 1.5km (1 mile) to the mausoleum. Swathed in a respectful darkness of huge cypress trees forming a canopy overhead are monument after monument, tomb after tomb—approximately 200,000 of them, all belonging to faithful followers from past centuries. The audio guide from the tourist office (see "Visitor Information," above) will guide you to the most famous tombstones, including those of the Toyotomi, Shimadzu, Maeda, Asano, and Matsudaira clans.

I don't know whether being here will affect you the same way, but I am always awestruck by the sheer density of tombstones, the iridescent green moss, the shafts of light streaking through the treetops, the stone lanterns, and the gnarled bark of the old cypress trees. Together, they present a dramatic picture representing more than a thousand years of Japanese Buddhist history. If you're lucky, you won't meet many people along this pathway. Tour buses fortunately park at a newer entrance to the mausoleum at the bus stop called Okunoin-mae. I absolutely forbid you to take this newer and shorter route; its crowds lessen the impact of this place considerably. Rather, make sure you take the path farthest to the left, which begins near the Okunoin-guchi/Ichinohashi stops. Much less traveled, it's also much more impressive and is one of the main reasons for coming to Koyasan in the first place. And be sure to return to the mausoleum at night; the stone lanterns (now lit electrically) create a mysterious and powerful effect.

At the end of the pathway, about a 30-minute walk away, is the **Lantern Hall,** or Torodo, which houses about 21,000 lanterns, donated by prime ministers, emperors, and others. Two sacred fires, which reportedly have been burning since the 11th century, are kept safely inside. The mausoleum itself is behind the Lantern Hall. Buy a white candle, light it, and wish for anything you want. Then sit back and watch respectfully as Buddhists come to chant and pay respects to one of Japan's greatest Buddhist leaders. Many who have successfully completed the pilgrimage to Shikoku Island's 88 Buddhist temples, often dressed in white and carrying a staff, conclude their journey here.

MORE TO SEE & DO ⑭ **Kongobuji Temple** ★★, located near the main Koyasan Tourist Association office in the center of town (ⓒ **0736/56-2011**), is the central monastery headquarters of the Shingon sect in Japan. Although Kongobuji was originally built in the 16th century by Toyotomi Hideyoshi to commemorate his mother's death, the present building is 150 years old, reconstructed following a fire. Pictures by famous artists from long ago decorate the rooms, including those depicting Kobo Daishi's trip to China, and the huge kitchen, big enough to feed multitudes of monks, is also on view. The most important thing to see, however, is the temple's magnificent rock garden,

reputedly the largest in Japan and said to represent a pair of dragons in a sea of clouds.
If it's raining, consider yourself lucky—the wetness adds sheen and color to the rocks.
Admission is ¥500 for adults, ¥200 for children.

Another important site is the **Garan ★** (© **0736/56-3215**), the first buildings constructed on Koyasan and still considered the center of religious life in the community. It's
an impressive sight with a huge *kondo* (main hall), first built in 819 by Kobo Daishi; a
large vermilion-colored *daito* (pagoda), which many consider to be Koyasan's most magnificent structure and which is very much worth entering (¥200 each for the kondo and
daito); and the oldest building on Mount Koya, the Fudodo, which was built in 1197.
Next to the complex is the ⑭ **Reihokan Museum** (© **0736/56-2254**), displaying
wooden Buddha sculptures, scrolls, art, and other Koyasan treasures spread through two
buildings, with exhibitions changed four times a year. Admission here is ¥600 for adults,
¥350 for students, and ¥250 for children.

All of the sites above are open daily: 8:30am to 4:30pm November to April, and
8:30am to 5 or 5:30pm May to October.

WHERE TO STAY & DINE

Although this community of 4,000 residents has the usual stores, schools, and offices of
any small town, there are no hotels here. The only place you can stay is at a temple, and
I strongly urge you to do so.

Japanese who come here have almost always made reservations beforehand, and you
should do the same. You can make reservations by calling the temple directly or through
travel agencies such as the **Japan Travel Bureau** (© **03/5796-5454;** www.jtb-sunrise
tours.jp). You can also make reservations upon arrival in Koyasan at either Tourist Association office before 4pm (see "Essentials," above), but I suggest faxing a minimum of 7
days in advance to be sure you can get a space (fax **0736/56-2889**), especially during
peak travel seasons; include your name, address, phone and fax numbers, e-mail address,
dates of stay, and number of people.

WHAT IT'S LIKE TO STAY AT A KOYASAN TEMPLE Prices for an overnight stay in
one of the temples, including two vegetarian meals, range from ¥10,000 to ¥15,000 per
person, depending on the temple and room. You may need to supply your own towel and
toiletries. Check-in is around 3pm (5pm at the latest) and checkout is at 9am.

Your room will be tatami and may include a nice view of a garden. Both baths and
toilets are communal. High-school and college students attending Koyasan's Buddhist
university live at the temple; they'll bring your meals to your room, make up your futon,
and clean your room. The *shojin ryori* (Buddhist vegetarian meals) are generally quite
good, and because Buddhist monks are vegetarians but not teetotalers (beer and sake are
made of rice and grain), alcoholic drinks are readily available at the temples for an extra
charge. Meals are at set times. Dinner is at 5:30pm, and because the students must leave
for school, breakfast is usually served by 7:30am. The morning religious service is at 6 or
6:30am; you don't have to attend, but I strongly recommend that you do. There's something uplifting about early morning meditative chanting, even for nonbelievers; some
temples include sacred fire ceremonies as well.

Below are just a few of the dozens of area temples open to overnight guests (rates are
based on two people to a room). They're all located very near the indicated bus stop. All
of them have public baths, but none offer rooms with bathrooms.

⑭ **Ekoin ★** This 100-year-old temple, with origins stretching back almost 1,100
years when Kukai was said to have erected a stupa on this site, has nice grounds and is

THE REST OF WESTERN HONSHU

THE TEMPLES OF MOUNT KOYA

nestled in a wooded slope an easy walk from Okunoin. For centuries it enjoyed support of the Shimadzu clan of southern Kyushu. It's known for its excellent Buddhist cuisine, and the master priest will give *zazen* meditation lessons if his schedule permits. Every morning there's both a chanting service and a fire ceremony. Most rooms have nice sitting alcoves, and towels and *yukata* are provided. Reservations should be made in advance, especially for peak season; there's always someone here who speaks a little English.

497 Koyasan, Koya-cho, Ito-gun, Wakayama-ken 648-0211. ℂ 0736/56-2514. Fax 0736/56-2891. ekoin@ mbox.co.jp. 36 units, none with bathroom. ¥10,000–¥15,000 per person. Rates include 2 meals. AE, MC, V. Bus: Karukayado-mae. **Amenities:** Computer w/free Internet access. *In room:* TV (most rooms), no phone (in some).

(146) **Rengejoin Temple** ★★   This temple's head priest speaks English, so a lot of foreigners are directed here; it's a good place to meet people and to find out about Buddhism. It's also one of the few temples that may take you in without a reservation. Established 900 years ago, it was rebuilt 150 years ago after a fire. Rooms have views of a nice garden with a pond; pluses are the English-language videos placed in some rooms that explore the history and significance of Mount Koya and Kongobuji Temple, as well as both evening and morning services conducted in both Japanese and English. The disadvantage is that it's on the opposite end of town from Okunoin, about a 40-minute walk away.

700 Koyasan, Koya-cho, Ito-gun, Wakayama-ken 648-0211. ℂ 0736/56-2233. Fax 0736/56-4743. 48 units, none with bathroom. ¥11,550–¥15,750. Rates include 2 meals. No credit cards. Bus: Ishinguchi stop. *In room:* TV, no phone.

(147) **Shojoshinin** ★★★   Of all Koyasan's temples, this one has the most curb appeal. Originating as a thatched hut built by Kukai more than 1,150 years ago and once the second-largest temple in Koyasan after Kongobuji, today it boasts attractive 150-year-old buildings against a wooded backdrop, including a large wooden structure with rooms overlooking a small garden and pond. Towels and *yukata* are provided. It's usually full in August and peak seasons, so make reservations early. It has a great location at the beginning of the tomb-lined pathway to Okunoin, making it convenient for your late-night stroll to the mausoleum.

566 Koyasan, Koya-cho, Ito-gun, Wakayama-ken 648-0211. ℂ 0736/56-2006. Fax 0736/56-4770. 30 units, none with bathroom. ¥9,600–¥15,000 per person. Rates include 2 meals. No credit cards. Bus: Okunoin-guchi. *In room:* TV (most rooms), no phone (in most rooms).

(148) **Tentokuin**   The rooms of this temple, which dates from 1622, are located in a new annex. Most look out onto the garden, which in the 1930s was described as one of the most beautiful places in Japan. With a natural mountain background, the garden is of the "borrowed landscaping" style and retains its layout design dating from the Momoyama Period. Rates depend on room size and garden view.

370 Koyasan, Koya-cho, Ito-gun, Wakayama-ken 648-0211. ℂ 0736/56-2714. Fax 0736/56-4725. 55 units, none with bathroom. ¥9,500–¥15,000 per person. Rates include 2 meals. AE, V. Bus: Senjuin-bashi. *In room:* TV, no phone.

7 HIMEJI, A CASTLE TOWN ★

640km (400 miles) W of Tokyo; 130km (81 miles) W of Kyoto; 87km (54 miles) E of Okayama

The main reason tourists come to Himeji, in Hyogo Prefecture, is to see its 400-year-old beautiful **castle,** which embodies better than any other castle the best in Japan's military architecture. If you were to see only one castle in Japan, this is my pick.

Because of the castle's proximity to Himeji Station on the Shinkansen line, many tourists stop only long enough to see the castle and a few other sites before continuing onward. I've included a few recommendations, however, for those wishing to make an overnight stop.

ESSENTIALS

GETTING THERE   A stop on the **Tokaido/Sanyo Shinkansen** bullet train, which runs between Tokyo and Kyushu, Himeji is about 3½ hours from Tokyo, 1 hour from Kyoto, and less than a half-hour from Okayama. The fare from Tokyo is ¥14,700 for a nonreserved seat.

VISITOR INFORMATION   The **Himeji Kanko Navi Port** Tourist Information Center (© **079/287-0003**) is located at the central exit of the station's north (castle) side, to the right after you exit from the ticket gate. Open daily from 9am to 5pm, the staff can answer questions and make hotel reservations. You can also use a bike from here free of charge (see below). For online information see **www.himeji-kanko.jp/en**; some information is also provided at **www.city.himeji.lg.jp/en**.

There are coin lockers at the station for those stopping in Himeji only for a few hours to see the castle.

INTERNET ACCESS   **Jyukukan Himeji,** beside the Himeji Washington Hotel Plaza, 98 Higashi Ekimai-cho (© **079/286-6006**), is open 24 hours and charges ¥290 for the first 30 minutes and then ¥100 for each subsequent 15 minutes.

ORIENTATION & GETTING AROUND   You can **walk** to Himeji's attractions. The main road in town is Otemae Dori, a wide boulevard that stretches from Himeji Station north to Himeji Castle (you can walk the distance in about 15 min.). To the east (right) of Otemae Dori are two parallel streets, Miyukidori and Omizusuji, both covered shopping arcades. If you want, you can use a **bicycle** free of charge from 9am to 6pm by filling out an application form (before 4pm) at the Himeji Kanko Navi Port, where you'll be given a ticket and told where to go to pick up the bicycle. Finally, the red-painted, retro-looking **Himeji Castle Loop Bus** makes runs daily from 9am to 5pm (only on weekends and holidays Dec–Feb) every half-hour or so from Himeji Station to the castle and beyond. It costs ¥100 per ride or ¥300 all day.

SEEING THE SIGHTS

Himeji Castle ★★★   As soon as you exit from Himeji Station, you'll see Himeji Castle straight ahead at the end of a wide boulevard called Otemae Dori. Perhaps the most beautiful castle in all of Japan, Himeji Castle is nicknamed "White Heron Castle" in reference to its white walls, which stretch out on either side of the main *donjon* and resemble a white heron poised in flight over the plain. Whether it looks to you like a heron or a castle, the view of the white five-story donjon under a blue sky is striking, especially when the area's 1,000 cherry trees are in bloom. This is also one of the few castles in Japan that has remained virtually as it was since its completion in 1618, surviving even the World War II bombings that laid Himeji city in ruins. From 1956 to 1964, the castle underwent massive restoration, during which parts were totally disassembled and then rebuilt using traditional methods. In 1993, the castle, along with Horyuji Temple in Nara, became Japan's first UNESCO's World Heritage Sites.

Originating as a fort in the 14th century, Himeji Castle took a more majestic form in 1581 when a three-story donjon was built by Toyotomi Hideyoshi during one of his military campaigns in the district. In the early 1600s, the castle became the residence of

Ikeda Terumasa, one of Hideyoshi's generals and a son-in-law of Tokugawa Ieyasu. He remodeled the castle into its present five-story structure. With its extensive gates, three moats, turrets, and a secret entrance, it had one of the most sophisticated defense systems in Japan. The maze of passageways leading to the donjon was so complicated that intruders would find themselves trapped in dead ends. The castle walls were constructed with square or circular holes through which gun muzzles could poke; the rectangular holes were for archers. There were also drop chutes where stones or boiling water could be dumped on enemies trying to scale the walls.

On weekends (and sometimes weekdays), volunteers hang around the castle ticket office and are willing to guide tours of the castle for free. It gives them an opportunity to practice their English while you learn about the history of the castle and even old castle gossip. But even if you go on your own, you won't have any problems learning about the history of the castle, as there are good English-language explanations throughout the castle grounds. With or without a guide, you'll spend at least 2 hours here. But beware, there are lots of stairs. *Tip:* A combination ticket, allowing discounted admission to both the castle and Koko-en (see below), is available at either entrance. *Note:* Himeji Castle is under renovation until March 2014, during which parts of the castle may be restricted to visitors. An observation area, however, will allow visitors to observe the repair process utilizing traditional techniques.

68 Honmachi. ℂ 079/285-1146. www.himeji-castle.gr.jp. Admission ¥600 adults, ¥200 children. Combination ticket to both Himeji Castle and Koko-en ¥720 adults, ¥280 children. June–Aug daily 9am–6pm; Sept–Apr daily 9am–5pm. You must enter 1 hr. before closing time. A 15-min. walk straight north of Himeji Station via Otemae Dori.

(149) **Koko-en** ★★★ (Finds)   Although laid out only in 1992, this is a wonderful garden, occupying land where samurai mansions once stood at the base of Himeji Castle, about a 5-minute walk away. Actually it's composed of nine separate small gardens, each one different and enclosed by traditional walls, with lots of rest areas to soak in the wonderful views. The gardens, typical of those in the Edo Period, include a garden of deciduous trees, a garden of pine trees, a garden of flowers popular during the Edo Period, tea-ceremony gardens, and traditional Japanese gardens with ponds, waterfalls, and running streams. If you wish, relax at the Souju-an teahouse in the Cha-no-niwa (tea-ceremony garden) with tea and a sweet (¥500; daily 10am–4pm) or dine at a restaurant overlooking a carp pond (see "Where to Dine," below). In any case, I wouldn't miss this special place. If you don't stop (but how could you resist?), you can stroll through all the gardens in about 45 minutes.

68 Honmachi. ℂ **079/289-4120.** Admission ¥300 adults, ¥150 children. Combination ticket to both Himeji Castle and Koko-en ¥720 adults, ¥280 children. Daily 9am–5pm (to 6pm May–Aug). A 15-min. walk north of Himeji Station; turn left in front of Himeji Castle (the entrance will be on your right).

A PILGRIMAGE TO MOUNT SHOSHA & ENGYOJI TEMPLE

If you're staying overnight, you might consider a half-day trip to **Mount Shosha** (called Shoshazan in Japanese; ℂ **079/266-3327**), the 360m-high (1,200-ft.) mountain retreat of Engyoji Temple, founded more than 1,000 years ago by a holy man who received enlightenment from the God of Wisdom and Intellect. Since then, Japanese have flocked to the mountain to seek purification of both body and spirit. Many make it a fun day's outing as well, bringing obento lunch boxes with them to enjoy under the wooded trees (you'd be wise to do the same, as there are no dining facilities on temple grounds). No doubt, the fact that scenes from *The Last Samurai* starring Tom Cruise were shot here

boosted its popularity. But I like this 3- to 4-hour excursion mainly for the lovely hike.
The temple buildings spread along the mountaintop are a bonus.

To reach Shoshazan, take bus no. 8 from in front of Himeji Station or Himeji Castle 25 minutes to the last stop (fare: ¥260). From there, board a ropeway (cable car) that departs every 15 minutes and costs ¥900 round-trip (half-price for children). Be sure to check when the last ropeway departs the mountain (5pm in winter; 6 or 7pm in summer).

After paying an admission of ¥300 for admission to temple grounds (children get in free), you'll walk 20 minutes to reach the Maniden, the main temple building. An impressive, cliff-side wooden structure dedicated to the Goddess of Mercy, it was first constructed in 970, burned to the ground almost 1,000 years later, and was reconstructed in 1932. Other highlights among the many other structures spread along the mountaintop are the Jikido, a former dormitory for priests-in-training (this, together with Jogyodo and Daikodo, make up the Three Temples, where *The Last Samurai* was filmed) and the five mausoleums of the Honda clan, rulers of Himeji Castle in the 17th century.

WHERE TO STAY

Expensive

Hotel Nikko Himeji ★★   The Nikko is Himeji's most luxurious hotel. Its location only a 1-minute walk from Himeji Station's Shinkansen side is a definite plus, as are its dining options, its top-floor lounge with a view of the castle, and its health club. For castle views in the distance, ask for a room on a higher floor facing north (single rooms, however, do not offer castle views). Rooms are comfortable with large windows.

100 Minami-ekimai-cho, Himeji 670-0962. © **079/222-2231.** Fax 079/224-3731. www.hotelnikkohimeji. co.jp. 257 units. ¥10,925–¥11,200 single; ¥20,700–¥32,000 double. AE, DC, MC, V. A 1-min. walk from the south (Shinkansen) exit of Himeji Station. **Amenities:** 4 restaurants; bar; lounge; health club w/20m (66-ft.) indoor lane pool, sauna, whirlpool, and exercise room (fee: ¥1,500); smoke-free rooms. *In room:* A/C, TV, hair dryer, Internet, minibar.

Moderate

Claire Higasa   This family-owned hotel is a good bet. Although distinctly a business hotel with its 50 single rooms, coin-operated fax and photocopy machine in the lobby, and soda and noodle vending machines, several pluses—such as soothing music and flower arrangements in the lobby and an accommodating, English-speaking staff—take it out of the ordinary. Rooms on the fifth floor offer Internet connection if you have your own computer; or, ask for a room with castle view on the sixth or seventh floor. The bathrooms are tiny and the shower/sink combination faucet a bit mind-boggling for the technically challenged, but who cares when the large seventh-floor public baths with Jacuzzi jets have castle views?

22 Junishomae-cho, Himeji 670-0911. © **079/224-3421.** Fax 079/289-3729. www.hotel-higasa.com. 60 units. ¥7,350 single; ¥13,650–¥14,700 double; ¥12,600 Japanese-style double. MC, V. Station: Himeji (north exit, 5 min.). Walk north on Otemae-Dori toward the castle and after the Shirogane intersection (the one with a large, one-way street named Junishomae Dori and a traffic light) take the next left; it's 4 short blocks farther, on the left across from a small park. **Amenities:** Japanese-style pub (3-min. walk from hotel); lobby computer w/free Internet; smoke free rooms. *In room:* A/C, TV, fridge, hair dryer, Internet (in some).

Himeji Washington Hotel Plaza   Some of the staff at this business hotel speak a little English, and everyone is extremely helpful. Rooms are tiny but cheerful (the cheapest doubles couldn't get much tinier), with windows that open (though some face another building), panels that close for complete darkness, and slippers that, so the hotel claims, are washed after every guests' use (my goodness, what do the other hotels do?). The lobby is on the second floor, above an Internet cafe.

98 Higashi Ekimae-cho, Himeji 670-0926. ℂ **079/225-0111.** Fax 079/225-0133. 149 units. ¥5,800–¥6,500 single; ¥11,000–¥12,000 double. AE, DC, MC, V. Station: Himeji (north exit, 5 min.). Walk north on Otemae Dori toward the castle; turn right at the 1st large intersection, Shirogane, on a street called Junishomae (a one-way street with a traffic light) and walk past 2 covered shopping arcades and Starbucks; it will be on the left. **Amenities:** Restaurant; Internet cafe; smoke-free rooms. *In room:* A/C, TV, hair dryer, Internet, minibar.

Inexpensive

Toyoko Inn Himeji-eki Shinkansen Minami-guchi ★ (Value) This budget chain beats all the rest with free use of computers in the lobby with Internet access (and free Wi-Fi in the lobby for those traveling with laptops) and free domestic phone calls from lobby phones. Next to Himeji Station's south (Shinkansen) exit, it offers tiny rooms, with singles from the ninth floor boasting views of the castle in the distance.

97 Minami-ekimae-cho, Himeji 670-0962. ℂ **079/284-1045.** Fax 079/284-1046. www.toyoko-inn.com. 210 units. ¥5,880 single; ¥7,980 double. Rates include free Japanese breakfast. AE, DC, MC, V. A 1-min. walk from the south (Shinkansen) exit of Himeji Station, to the left. **Amenities:** Lobby computer w/free Internet; smoke-free rooms. *In room:* A/C, TV, fridge, hair dryer, Internet.

WHERE TO DINE

Just east of Otemae Dori, the main drag from Himeji Station to the castle, is a parallel street called **Miyukidori,** a covered shopping arcade with lots of restaurants and coffee shops.

In the listings below, directions are from Himeji Station.

(150) **Asaka Sushi** SUSHI   This is sushi Himeji style; you order by the plate, and then, using cups of sauce and brushes at your table, you brush on your sauce yourself. There's no menu at this small neighborhood eatery, very much a local place with room for only 10 patrons, but there's a display case outside. The *nigiri* will give you one sushi each of octopus, squid, shrimp, tuna, and whitefish; the *anago* is four pieces of grilled conger eel on rice; the *tekka* is eight pieces of tuna and rice rolled in nori seaweed. Each plate costs ¥400 to ¥500.

106 Shiroganemachi. ℂ **079/222-3835.** Sushi ¥400–¥500 a plate. No credit cards. Mon–Sat 10:30am–6pm. Walk north on Otemae Dori toward the castle until you come to the 1st one-way street with a traffic light (Junishomae Dori; the intersection is called Shirogane); turn left and then right. It'll be on your left (3 min.).

(151) **Kassui-ken ★** EEL/NOODLES   This charmless restaurant would not have much to recommend it except for one overwhelming feature: It overlooks a waterfall and koi pond in lovely Koko-en Garden. It's certainly the most picturesque place in town to try Himeji's specialty, conger eel. If that's too exotic, however, it also serves a few noodle dishes, spaghetti, and fried rice. Or you can stop just for dessert or a refreshing drink of beer, soda, or coffee; but avoid the busy lunchtime crowd.

Koko-en, 68 Honmachi. ℂ **079/289-4131.** Main dishes ¥840–¥1,050; set meals ¥1,575–¥2,940. No credit cards. Daily 9:30am–4:30pm (9:30am–5:30pm Apr 25–Aug). Inside Koko-en.

Sainte Vierge ★★ FRENCH   This is Himeji's fanciest place for French cuisine, with an elegant drawing-room ambience and white table-clothed tables spaced far apart for privacy. Only set meals are served, giving choices of fish, meat, or both as main courses, along with side dishes. Because this is a popular wedding venue, especially on weekends, be sure to call first to see whether it's open to the public. Otherwise, the owner also has

a casual, less expensive French-Italian bistro-style restaurant called **Angelot,** 23 Tatemachi (© **079/226-1113**), on the same street but 2 blocks west of Otemae Dori. It's open
Wednesday to Monday from 11:30am to 2pm and 6 to 10pm.

Konyamachi 23. © **079/223-1122.** Set dinners ¥2,310–¥10,500; set lunches ¥1,575–¥1,890. AE, DC, MC,
V. Wed–Mon noon–2pm and 6–8pm (last order). Walk north on Otemae Dori toward the castle and take
the 2nd right after the Shirogane intersection (there's a bank here); it's past the 2 covered shopping
arcades, on the right.

8 OKAYAMA: GATEWAY TO SHIKOKU

733km (455 miles) W of Tokyo; 218km (136 miles) W of Kyoto; 160km (100 miles) E of Hiroshima

Okayama is a major gateway to the island of Shikoku (see chapter 11), thanks to the Seto
Ohashi Bridge, which measures almost 9.5km (6 miles) in length and connects Okayama
Prefecture on Honshu island with Sakaide on Shikoku. Before the bridge was built in
1988, it took an hour by ferry to reach Shikoku, whereas traveling by train or car along
the double-decker bridge cuts travel time down to just 15 minutes. Now there are two
other bridges linking Honshu with Shikoku (one near Kobe and the other in Hiroshima
Prefecture), but they're for vehicular travel only (no train service).

For those of you less interested in bridges, Okayama and its environs are important for
other reasons, too. Okayama city, capital of Okayama Prefecture with a population of
700,000, boasts one of the most beautiful gardens in Japan. In nearby Kurashiki (see
"Kurashiki, Market Town of Many Charms," beginning on p. 445), a historic quarter
ranks as one of the most picturesque neighborhoods in Japan. And scattered through
Okayama Prefecture are a couple so-called **International Villas,** accommodations
located primarily in rural areas with amazingly low rates.

ESSENTIALS

GETTING THERE   Okayama is a major stop on the **Shinkansen** Tokaido/Sanyo Line,
about 4 hours from Tokyo (fare: ¥15,850 for an unreserved seat), 1 hour and 20 minutes
from Kyoto (fare: ¥6,820), and 45 minutes from Hiroshima (fare: ¥5,350).

Buses depart nightly from Shinjuku Station's west exit in Tokyo: at 9:30pm (Shi-
moden Bus Co.; © **03/5438-8511**) and at 9:45pm (Ryobi Bus Co.; © **03/3928-6011**),
both arriving at Okayama Station the next day at 7:50am and costing ¥9,800 one-way.
From Tokyo Station, JR buses (© **03/3844-0489**) depart from the Yaesu south exit at
8:40pm and arrive in Okayama at 7:18am for ¥10,000.

Flights from Tokyo to Okayama Airport (© **086/294-5201;** www.okayama-airport.
org) take about 1 hour and 15 minutes and cost ¥30,200, though JAL bargain fares, with
restrictions, go for as low as ¥11,100. An Airport Limousine Bus shuttles passengers to
Okayama Station in about 30 minutes for ¥740.

VISITOR INFORMATION   Before departing Tokyo or Narita or Kansai airports, stop
by the Tourist Information Center for the leaflet "Okayama, Kurashiki and Seto Ohashi
Bridge," which contains useful information on train transportation to Okayama and
important sights in the prefecture (you can also download it from the Japan National
Tourist Organization's website at www.jnto.go.jp by looking under "Browse by Destinations"). In Okayama, the **Okayama City Tourist Information Office** (© **086/222-
2912;** daily 9am–6pm) is inside Okayama Station near the central exit of the east side

(look for the sign displaying a question mark). The office is well prepared for foreign visitors, supplying English-language maps and brochures.

Just a 5-minute walk from Okayama Station is the **Okayama International Center,** 2–2–1 Hokancho, Kita-ku, where at the first-floor Information Counter (© **086/256-2914;** Mon–Sat 9am–5pm) you can also obtain tourist information, get maps, and access the Internet. To find the center, take the west exit of the station's central gate and turn right (north) onto the main street running in front of the station until you come to a 7-Eleven, where you should turn left; the center is the big building on your right. More information on Okayama is available on the Internet at **www.pref.okayama.jp** and **www.city.okayama.jp.**

INTERNET ACCESS   You can access the Internet at the Okayama International Center free of charge, but you're limited to 30 minutes of usage and because there are only two computers, you may have to wait. Otherwise, head to Club Mont Blanc on the sixth floor of the OPA building across from Okayama Station's east exit, 6–3 Honmachi (© **086/224-7050**), open 24 hours and charging ¥290 for 30 minutes.

GETTING AROUND   Okayama's sights are all clustered within walking distance of each other, due east of Okayama Station. You can walk from Okayama Station to Okayama Castle in about 30 minutes via Momotaro Odori. Otherwise, board a **streetcar** from Okayama Station's east side bound for Higashiyama (platform 1) and disembark about 6 minutes later at the Shiroshita streetcar stop (the third stop; to your right will be the very noticeable Okayama Symphony Hall building). Pay the ¥100 fare when you get off. From here you can continue walking straight ahead (east) 15 minutes to Okayama Castle and then visit nearby Korakuen Garden and Yumeji Art Museum.

SEEING THE SIGHTS

Korakuen Garden ★★★   Okayama's claim to fame is this garden, considered one of Japan's three most beautiful landscaped gardens (the other two are in Kanazawa and Mito). Completed in 1700 by the Ikeda ruling clan after 14 years of work, its 11 hectares (28 acres) are graced with a pond, running streams, pine trees, plum and cherry trees, flowering bushes such as azaleas and hydrangeas, bamboo groves, teahouses, and tea plantations. The surrounding hills, as well as Okayama's famous black castle, are incorporated into the garden's design (luckily, laws limiting the size of surrounding buildings protect the views). Its name, Korakuen, means "the garden for taking pleasure later," which has its origins in an old saying: "Bear sorrow before the people; take pleasure after them." This garden differs from most Japanese gardens in that it has large expanses of grassy open areas—the first Japanese garden to do so and still a rarity in crowded Japan. Other unusual features worth seeking out are the Ryuten, a wooden pavilion that straddles a stream where you can soak your feet, and an enclosure of red-crested cranes. You can easily spend an hour here.

(**Tips**) **When You're Done Sightseeing**

The fastest way to return to Okayama Station is by bus no. 1 from the Korakuen-mae bus stop, located outside Korakuen Garden just before the bridge to Yumeji Art Museum.

Kids Joypolis

If you have children in tow, you might want to temper Okayama's cultural offerings with some good old-fashioned fun at **Joypolis,** 2–10–1 Shimoishii (*(C* **086/232-8790;** daily 10am–midnight), a chain of Japan's most sophisticated and largest video-game arcades. In addition to a toddler's play area, pachinko, slot machines, video games, virtual horse races, and simulators (how good are you at skateboarding or racing cars?), there are 3-D motion rides and other amusements. Entry is free, with most attractions individually priced between ¥300 and ¥600. With or without kids, it's worth visiting one of these eye-opening arcades at least once while you're in Japan. To reach it, take the east exit from Okayama Station and turn right (south) onto Shiyakusho Suji Street. *Note:* You must be 17 or older to stay after 6pm and 19 or older to stay after 10pm.

1–5 Korakuen. *(C* **086/272-1148.** Admission ¥350 adults, ¥140 children, free for seniors. Combination ticket to Okayama Castle and Korakuen Garden ¥520 adults, ¥260 children. Apr–Sept daily 7:30am–6pm; Oct–Mar daily 8am–5pm. Streetcar stop: Shiroshita (20 min.). Continue walking straight east and then turn left for the footbridge.

Okayama Castle (Overrated) Originally built in the 16th century, Okayamajo was destroyed in World War II and rebuilt in 1966. Thanks to its black exterior, it has earned the nickname "Crow Castle"; it was painted black to contrast with neighboring Himeji's famous White Heron castle. Unlike castles of yore, an elevator whisks you up to the fourth floor of the *donjon.* The top floor affords a good view of the park and the city beyond, while the other floors contain a few swords, samurai outfits, lacquerware, and other Edo-Period items, most identified in Japanese only and quickly seen in 15 minutes or so. There's also a children's play area with old-fashioned toys, but probably the most rewarding thing to do here is to try on a kimono and have someone snap a picture of you with your own camera. Donning costumes is free, but only five participants are accepted at 10 and 11am, and 1, 2, and 3pm. Frankly, if you've seen other Japanese castles, you might just want to photograph this one from the outside and move on. For a fairy-tale fantasy indulgence, you can rent swan-shaped paddle boats on the river below the castle (just be glad your neighbors aren't here to see you).

2–3–1 Marunouchi. *(C* **086/225-2096.** Admission ¥300 adults, ¥120 children. Combination ticket to Okayama Castle and Korakuen Garden ¥520 adults, ¥260 children. Daily 9am–5pm. Streetcar: Shiroshita stop (15 min.). Continue walking east; it will be on your right.

(152) **Yumeji Art Museum (Yumeji-Kyodo Bijutsukan)** This museum, in a brick building topped by a cock weather vane just a few minutes' walk north of Korakuen, is dedicated to the works of Yumeji Takehisa. Born in Okayama Prefecture in 1884, Yumeji is sometimes referred to as Japan's Toulouse-Lautrec and is credited with developing the *fin de siècle* Art Nouveau movement in Japan. This collection includes some of his most famous works (beautiful women were his favorite subjects), mostly in the sparse, Nihonga style of painting. The small three-room exhibition, with displays changed every 2 months, can be toured in about 15 minutes.

2–1–32 Hama. *(C* **086/271-1000.** www.yumeji-art-museum.com. Admission ¥700 adults; ¥400 junior-high, high-school, and college students; ¥300 children. Tues–Sun 9am–5pm. Streetcar: Shiroshita stop (23 min.). Just north of Korakuen Garden, a short walk across Horai-bashi Bridge.

A CYCLING EXCURSION

For some rural R & R, head west from Okayama city to the historic Kibiji District, once home to the ancient Kibi kingdom and known today for its huge burial mounds, temples, shrines, and five-story pagoda, all connected via a marked biking path that traverses this pastoral landscape. It's fun to cycle from one historic destination to the next, but what I like most about this ride is its rural setting, through villages, past peach groves, and along paddies (much of the bike path is actually on the same raised walkways farmers use to separate and dam their paddies and to get to their fields).

Rental bikes (✆ 0866/92-0233) are available daily 9am to 6pm to the right outside Soja Station, which you can reach in 34 minutes by JR train from Okayama Station (fare: ¥400), with trains running two to three times an hour. Bikes rent for ¥400 for 2 hours, plus ¥200 each additional hour. Although you can return bikes to Soja Station, I suggest forking out an additional ¥600 drop-off fee and cycling the bike path's entire 15km (10 miles) to Ichinomiya Station, where you can ditch the bike and hop on a train for an 11-minute ride back to Okayama Station (fare: ¥200). It takes 3 to 4 hours to bike the entire path and stop at sights along the way. *Caveat:* Although the bike path is well marked most of the way, with signs in English saying KIBIJI DISTRICT with a picture of a bike, I got lost trying to find Ichinomiya Station. Villagers are apparently used to lost cyclers and soon had me merrily on my way. Be sure to pick up a cycling map when you rent your bike; the Okayama International Center also has information on the Kibiji District (see "Visitor Information," above).

SHOPPING

You can choose from a sampling of products and crafts made in Okayama Prefecture at the ⑮ **Okayama Prefectural Local Products Center (Harenokuni Okayamakan),** 1–1–22 Omotecho (✆ 086/234-2270; Wed–Mon 10am–7pm), conveniently located beside (south of) the Shiroshita streetcar stop. Bizen pottery (unglazed pottery with a history stretching back 1,000 years), *igusa* (rush-grass mats), wooden trays, bambooware, papier-mâché toys, sake, and more are all for sale here.

For general shopping, there's a large underground shopping arcade called **Ichibangai** at Okayama Station, with boutiques selling clothing, shoes, and accessories. Across from the station and connected to Ichibangai is **Takashimaya** department store. In the heart of the city, just south of Shiroshita streetcar stop, is the 1km (half-mile) **Omotecho** covered shopping arcade, where you'll find **Tenmaya,** Okayama's largest department store.

WHERE TO STAY
Expensive
Hotel Granvia Okayama ★★   Owned by the West JR Railway Group and offering a discount for holders of a Japan Rail Pass, this hotel boasts a great location just east of Okayama Station (although connected to the station via a second-floor walkway, it might be easier to find if you go out the east central exit and look for it on your right). Rooms, on the 8th to 18th floors, with the best city views offered by more expensive twins and doubles on higher floors (most singles face another building), have blackout curtains and good bedside reading lamps. Among the hotel's several food-and-beverage outlets, best are those on the 19th floor with great views; among these, Applause, a classy cocktail lounge with a curved window facade, is a favorite for drinks (but note that there's a ¥1,050 music charge after 8pm).

1–5 Ekimoto-cho, Okayama 700-8515. ✆ **086/234-7000.** Fax 086/234-7099. www.granvia-oka.co.jp. 328 units. ¥13,860–¥15,939 single; ¥25,410–¥36,960 double. 10% discount for JR Pass holders. AE, DC, MC, V.

Connected to Okayama Station's east side by direct walkway (1 min.). **Amenities:** 5 restaurants; bar; 2
lounges; computer w/free Internet (in business center); concierge; 20m (66-ft.) indoor pool, sauna, and
Jacuzzi (fee: ¥1,200); room service; smoke-free rooms. *In room:* A/C, TV, hair dryer, Internet, minibar.

Hotel Okura Okayama ★★   This Western-style hotel joined the Okura family in
2007 but has been a local favorite since its 1973 opening. Located on a hill above the city
and surrounded by greenery, it has a resortlike holiday atmosphere. The lobby, with a
restful view of wooded hills and a waterfall, boasts an impressive four-story wall made of
Bizen-yaki ceramic tiles, for which Okayama Prefecture is famous. Comfortable, larger-
than-average rooms face either the city or woods. City views are more dramatic; these
rooms come with a map to help you pick out the speck of the castle, which you can just
barely see if you squint No matter—the night views are even better. Restaurants also take
advantage of the hotel's location with views of either greenery or great city panoramas.
In summer there's a beer garden and barbecue restaurant on the terrace. The main drawback to staying here is one of access—there are free shuttle buses from the Higashiyama
streetcar stop (last stop from Okayama Station), but only in the mornings and evenings
(every 30 min. 7:30–9am and 6–9:30pm), and the public bus from Okayama Station's
no. 9 platform departs for the hotel only eight times a day.

4–1–16 Kadota Honmachi, Okayama 703-8274. ✆ **086/273-7311.** Fax 086/271-0292. www.okura.com.
175 units. ¥10,000 single; ¥18,000–¥22,000 double. Rates exclude tax and service charge. AE, DC, MC, V.
Taxi: 15 min. **Amenities:** 4 restaurants; bar; lobby computer w/free Internet; room service; smoke-free
rooms. *In room:* A/C, TV, fridge, hair dryer, Internet (in some).

Moderate

Kooraku Hotel   This business hotel has a convenient location about halfway between
Okayama Station and the Shiroshita streetcar stop (considered the heart of the city), on
a street lined with cherry and willow trees beside the small Nishigawa River. Rooms range
from tiny singles, the smallest of which is only 14 sq. m. (150 sq. ft.), to deluxe 36-sq.-m.
(387-sq.-ft.) corner twins with lots of light and big bathrooms. Couples who want to stay
very close can sleep in a single room for ¥8,000. Ask for a room facing the front. Pluses
include a post office and pharmacy next door and a bar in the basement.

5–1 Heiwa-cho, Okayama 700-0827. ✆ **086/221-7111.** Fax 086/221-0007. www.hotel.kooraku.co.jp. 211
units. ¥6,750–¥7,700 single; ¥11,000–¥20,000 double. AE, DC, MC, V. A 7-min. walk east of Okayama Station. Take the central (east) exit, walk straight ahead on Momotaro Odori, and turn right on Nishigawa
Ryokudo Koen Suji. **Amenities:** Restaurant; bar; lobby computer w/free Internet; smoke-free rooms.
In room: A/C, TV, fridge, hair dryer, Internet.

Mitsui Garden Hotel Okayama ★   This smart-looking business hotel near
Okayama Station distinguishes itself from most in this category with handsome public
baths and rooms that are small but with an upbeat color scheme and modern decor.
There are mostly singles and a few twins and doubles; because most face another building
and are dark, you might want to request one that doesn't. Best are the superior doubles,
with sofas and air purifiers. There's a coin-operated fax, copy machine, and computer
with free Internet connections off the lobby.

1–7 Ekimoto-cho, Okayama 70-0024. ✆ **086/235-1131.** Fax 086/225-8831. www.gardenhotels.co.jp. 352
units. ¥7,800–¥9,300 single; ¥16,000–¥16,800 double. AE, DC, MC, V. A 2-min. walk southeast of Okayama
Station. Take the central (east exit) and turn right; it's behind Hotel Granvia. **Amenities:** Buffet restaurant
open only for breakfast (Japanese/Western); computer w/free Internet; smoke-free rooms. *In room:* A/C,
TV, fridge, hair dryer, Internet.

Comfort Hotel (Value)   This hotel has a great location for sightseeing, across from the Shiroshita streetcar stop and halfway between Okayama Station and the castle, a 15-minute walk from each. Spotlessly clean and opened in 2005, it offers small but modern mostly double rooms (a rarity in Japan, as most Japanese couples prefer twin beds), along with such perks as free rental bikes, free breakfasts, and free coffee in the lobby from 3pm to midnight.

1–1–13 Marunouchi, Okayama 700-0823. (©) **877/424-6423** in the U.S. and Canada, or 086/801-9411. Fax 086/801-9495. www.comfortinn.com. 208 units. ¥5,800 single; ¥8,500–¥12,000 double. Rates include continental breakfast. AE, DC, MC, V. Streetcar: Shiroshita (1 min.; across the intersection to the right). **Amenities:** Free rental bikes; lobby computers w/free Internet; smoke-free rooms. *In room:* A/C, TV, fridge, hair dryer, Wi-Fi.

(154) **Matsunoki Ryokan** ★★ (Finds)   This family-owned enterprise welcomes foreigners and gives them (to my mind) special treatment. Although it offers rooms with and without bathrooms in a cluster of three buildings, foreigners are automatically given rooms in the newer, main building, all with bathrooms at a price normally given to bathroomless units (only if accommodations in the main building are full, which rarely happens, are foreigners shunted to the older buildings). Spotless rooms are mostly Japanese style, though three Western-style rooms are available, with glazed windows that open. The owners speak some English and offer a small gift to those who make reservations through Matsunoki's Web home page. Meals are served in a cheerful communal dining hall (Western breakfasts are available), but even better is the *ryokan's* nearby Matsunoki-Tei (see "Where to Dine," below). You'll like this place, especially because they will do your laundry for free.

19–1 Ekimoto-machi, Okayama 700-0024. (©) **086/253-4111.** Fax 086/253-4110. www.matunoki.com. 58 units, 23 with bathroom. ¥5,250 single with bathroom; ¥8,400 double with bathroom (foreigners are only put in rooms with bathrooms). Breakfast ¥600 extra; dinner ¥1,300 extra. V (5% extra if paying by credit card). Station: Okayama (west exit, 2 min.). Walk west on the street to the north of NHK; it's just past the New Station Hotel, on the right. **Amenities:** Restaurant; lobby computers w/free Internet; room service. *In room:* A/C, TV w/free videos, hair dryer.

WHERE TO DINE

Okayama's most famous dish is Okayama *barazushi,* which features Seto Inland Sea delicacies and fresh mountain vegetables. Traditionally served during festive occasions, it consists of a rice casserole laced with shredded ginger and cooked egg yolk and is topped with a variety of goodies, including conger eel, shrimp, fish, lotus root, and bamboo.

Expensive

Kuriya Sen ★★ KAISEKI/TEPPANYAKI   For a memorable meal with a view, head to this 20th-floor restaurant with sweeping views over the city, located in the ANA Hotel across from Okayama's west exit. With a modern, minimalist design, it offers changing kaiseki meals for lunch and dinner, along with grilled steaks and seafood prepared at a 12-seat *teppanyaki* counter. A stylish bar on the same floor offers cocktails with the same mesmerizing views.

ANA Hotel Okayama, 20th floor, 15–1 Ekimoto-machi. (©) **086/898-2284.** Reservations recommended. Set lunches ¥2,100–¥8,000; set dinners ¥4,100–¥17,325. AE, DC, MC, V. Daily 11:30am–2pm (to 3pm Sat–Sun) and 5:30–10pm. Okayama Station (west exit, 1 min.).

Value **Countryside Delights: Okayama International Villa Group**

If you're not on a tight schedule and you don't mind roughing it a bit, you might consider treating yourself to a few days in the countryside of Okayama Prefecture in one of two **International Villas**. Established in 1988 by the Okayama Prefectural Government to provide international guests the opportunity to experience rural Japan, the two villas are now managed by the local municipalities. Meals are not provided, so guests are expected to either dine out or cook and clean up after themselves.

In Hattoji, a village reached in about an hour via train and then bus or taxi, there's the **Hattoji Villa**, a 19th-century renovated thatched farmhouse with four Japanese-style rooms. Shiraishi Island in the Seto Inland Sea, which features beaches, shrines, and hiking trails, is home to the **Shiraishi Villa**, an airy glass-and-wooden building with four twin rooms and one Japanese-style room and with great views of the Seto Inland Sea. To reach Shiraishi from Okayama requires a 45-minute train ride, a 7-minute walk to the port, and a 22- to 50-minute ride on a ferry.

If these villas were privately owned, you'd easily pay more than twice what you'll be charged: ¥3,500 per person (¥4,000 for single travelers). Rooms, all without private bathroom, are rented individually, or you can rent the entire villa. Note, however, that only non-Japanese visitors and their Japanese guests are allowed to stay at Shiraishi Villa, while Hattoji Villa is open to both non-Japanese and Japanese guests. The maximum length of stay is 7 nights. For more information about the villas, their location, and rates, contact the Okayama International Villa Reservation Desk at ☏ **086/256-2535** Monday through Saturday 9am to noon and 1 to 5pm; you can also fax the center at 086/256-2576. More information is also available at **www.harenet.ne.jp/villa.**

Moderate

(155) **Matsunoki-Tei** ★★ **Value** KAISEKI/SHABU-SHABU The family that has long run the inexpensive Matsunoki *ryokan* (see "Where to Stay," above) also owns this very refined Japanese restaurant, located in an older house in a beautiful traditional setting. Dining here is a luxurious experience, as you sit in a private tatami room (some with leg wells under the table) and enjoy well-prepared dishes brought by an efficient and courteous staff. Although kaiseki is one of the most expensive meals you can have in Japan, it's quite reasonable here, and the all-you-can-eat *shabu-shabu* has a 2-hour time limit (indicate whether you want kaiseki or shabu-shabu when making your reservation). Even more economical are the obento lunch boxes for ¥1,700 and more elaborate mini-kaiseki lunches.

20–1 Ekimotomachi. ☏ **086/253-5410.** Reservations required by noon for evening meals. Kaiseki ¥3,700–¥10,000; all-you-can-eat shabu-shabu ¥3,400; set lunches ¥1,700–¥4,500. No credit cards. Daily 11am–2pm and 5–10pm. See Matsunoki (under "Where to Stay," above) for directions.

Petite Mariée ★ FRENCH   Brick walls, a beamed ceiling, French music, a large bouquet of flowers, and numerous European knickknacks set the mood at the tiny (non-smoking) Petite Mariée, which serves inexpensive yet good French food. The set meals change every 3 days, but my ¥1,250 set lunch consisted of creamy mushroom potage, bread, seafood soufflé, vegetables, and coffee or tea. A glass of wine with lunch costs only ¥150 extra. Unfortunately, set meals are written in Japanese only (though the main dishes of set meals are displayed outside), while the a la carte menu, which may include roast lamb or scallops, is in French. Nevertheless, this is a civilized place for a meal.

1–3–8 Yanagimachi. © **086/222-9066.** Main dishes ¥1,950–¥5,550; set lunches ¥1,250–¥2,300; set dinners ¥2,950–¥9,850. MC, V. Thurs–Tues 11:30am–2pm and 5–9pm (last order). Closed 3rd Tues of every month. Station: Okayama (8-min. walk southeast). Take the central (east) exit, turning right (south) onto Shiyakusho-suji; go 1 block past the gas station (it will be on your right) and turn left onto Akura Dori. It's 2 blocks farther on your right.

Inexpensive

In addition to the choices below, there are some inexpensive, rustic snack houses along the moat that separates Okayama Castle and Korakuen Garden, at Tsukimi Bridge, where you can order a drink, noodles, or ice cream and relax with a view of the castle. Most are open daily 8:30am to 5pm (to 4:30pm in winter).

(156) **Okabe** (Finds) TOFU   This informal eatery in the heart of Okayama is a local institution, popular for its specialty, homemade tofu. There's no problem ordering, as it serves only two *teishoku* (set meals), both with soup, rice, and pickled vegetables: the Okabe teishoku with two kinds of tofu, the other a *donburi* (rice bowl) topped with *namayuba*, a kind of tofu. Seating is along one long counter, behind which an army of women scurry to get out orders. It's simple but atmospheric.

1–10–1 Omotecho. © **086/222-1404.** Okabe teishoku ¥800; donburi ¥850. No credit cards. Mon–Sat 11:30am–2pm. Closed national holidays. Streetcar: Shiroshita (2 min.). Walk south through the Omotecho covered shopping arcade 2 min. to the stoplight and turn right (west); it's on the left, on a corner. You'll see Okabe's open-fronted tofu shop; the restaurant is around the corner.

(157) **Shikisai** VARIED JAPANESE   Located just outside the entrance to Korakuen Garden (its name translates as "Four Seasons of Color"), this modern restaurant is decorated with Bizen pottery and Japanese *ikebana* and is a good place to try Okayama specialties for lunch, including *barazushi* (¥1,575) and seasonal dishes such as *nabe* (a one-pot stew eaten in winter), *anago* (sea eel), and mini-kaiseki meals, as well as *soba* and *udon* noodles. The menu is written in Japanese only, so look at what others are eating. Top it off with Doppo, a locally brewed beer.

1–5 Korakuen-gaien. © **086/273-3221.** Set lunches ¥1,260–¥2,100. No credit cards. Daily 11am–3pm. Streetcar: Shiroshita (11 min.). Located just north of the main entrance gate, next to a souvenir shop.

(158) **Yamadome** ★ KUSHIKATSU   This 40-year-old restaurant has been renovated and now sports a classy modern interior, classical music, and local artists' work on the walls. It serves fried foods on sticks, from beef to fish to vegetables. The menu is in Japanese only, but the owner speaks English. A 10-stick *kushikatsu* course costs ¥1,350.

1–22 Tenjincho. © **086/224-6886.** Kushikatsu sticks ¥120–¥170; set lunches ¥630–¥1,270; kushikatsu sets ¥1,350–¥2,290. No credit cards. Mon–Sat 11am–2:30pm and 5–9:30pm. Closed 1 week in mid-Aug. Streetcar: Shiroshita (1 min.). Just north of the streetcar stop, on a side street across from a gas station (which you can see from the stop).

9 KURASHIKI, MARKET TOWN OF MANY CHARMS ★★★

26km (16 miles) W of Okayama

If I were to select the most picturesque town in Japan, **Kurashiki** would certainly be a top contender. Here, in the heart of the city, clustered around a willow-fringed canal, is a delightful historic district of old buildings and *ryokan* perfect for camera buffs.

As an administrative center of the shogunate in the 17th century, Kurashiki blossomed into a prosperous market town where rice, sake, and cotton were collected from the surrounding region and shipped off to Osaka and beyond. Back in those days, wealth was measured in rice; large granaries were built to store the mountains of granules passing through the town, and canals were dug so that barges laden with grain could work their way to ships anchored in the Seto Inland Sea. Kurashiki, in fact, means "Warehouse Village."

It's these warehouses, still standing, that give Kurashiki its distinctive charm. Kurashiki is also known throughout Japan for its art museums, including the prestigious Ohara Museum of Art with its collection of European and Japanese art. For these reasons, Kurashiki is hardly undiscovered, and Japanese flock here in droves, especially in summer months. Yet despite its overcrowdedness, Kurashiki still rates high on my list of places to see in Japan.

ESSENTIALS

GETTING THERE **By Train** If you're arriving in Kurashiki by **Shinkansen** (which takes about 4½ hr. from Tokyo, excluding transfers, and almost 2 hr. from Kyoto), you'll arrive at **Shin-Kurashiki Station,** about 9.5km (6 miles) west of **Kurashiki Station** and the heart of the city; the **local train** that runs between the two stations departs about every 15 minutes and takes 9 minutes. Note, however, that not all Shinkansen trains stop at Shin-Kurashiki, and if you're arriving from Tokyo, you'll have to change trains in Okayama. In addition, because Shin-Kurashiki Station is not in the center of town, if you're coming from the east (like from Tokyo), you'll probably find it much more convenient to transfer from the Shinkansen in Okayama to the local Sanyo train, which will take you in 13 minutes directly to Kurashiki Station (fare: ¥320).

By Bus The same buses that depart from Tokyo's Shinjuku station for Okayama (see "Okayama: Gateway to Shikoku," earlier in this chapter) continue onward to Kurashiki, arriving in Kurashiki about 40 minutes after their Okayama stop and costing ¥10,000 one-way.

VISITOR INFORMATION There's a tourist information office outside the south (main) exit of **Kurashiki Station** (✆ 086/424-1220), on the second floor of the Terminal Hotel to the right, open daily 9am to 7pm. Another information office, called the **Kurashiki-Kan** (✆ 086/422-0542), is right on the canal in the historic district and has a rest area with tables and vending machines; open daily 9am to 6pm (to 5:15pm in winter), it was built in 1916 and is ironically the only Western-looking wooden building in the area. Both offices distribute maps and brochures, including the useful "Walking Map of Kurashiki." More information online is at **www.city.kurashiki.okayama.jp/kankou**.

ORIENTATION The willow-lined canal, called the **Bikan Historical Quarter,** is only a 10-minute walk from Kurashiki Station; take the south exit and walk south on Chuo Dori, turning left just before the Kurashiki Kokusai Hotel. In fact, you can walk virtually everywhere of interest in Kurashiki; the Bikan Historical Quarter is zoned mostly for pedestrians.

EXPLORING THE BIKAN HISTORICAL QUARTER & ENVIRONS

Kurashiki's **historic old town** is centered on a canal lined with graceful willows and 200-year-old granaries made of black-tile walls topped with white mortar. Many of the granaries have been turned into museums, *ryokan,* restaurants, and boutiques selling handblown glass, Bizen pottery, papier-mâché toys, women's ethnic clothing imported from Bali and India, and mats and handbags made of *igusa* (rush grass), a local specialty. Street vendors sell jewelry, their wares laid out beside the canal, and healthy young boys stand ready to give visitors rides in rickshaws.

A resident advised me that because of the crowds that descend upon Kurashiki during the day (about four million tourists come here a year), I should get up early in the morning before the shops and museums open and explore this tiny area while it's still under the magic spell of the early morning glow. "Real lovers of Kurashiki come on Monday," he added. "Because that's when most everything is closed, and there are fewer people." I've found that early evening is also a magical time to walk the streets, especially after sunset when many buildings along the canal are illuminated.

Do try to avoid weekends, but no matter when you come, you're likely to fall under the city's spell. One of the most rewarding things to do in Kurashiki is simply explore (don't neglect the side streets btw. the canal and Achi Shrine on Tsurugatayama Park; even rain only enhances the contrasting black and white of the buildings).

THE MAIN SIGHTS

Japan Rural Toy Museum (Nihon Kyodogangu-Kan) ★★ (Kids) Almost next to the Folkcraft Museum is this museum with its delightful and colorful display of traditional and antique Japanese toys from every prefecture. Opened in 1967, it has thousands upon thousands of items crammed into four rooms, including kites (200 of them!), miniature floats, antique Japanese dolls, masks, and spinning tops. Incidentally, the huge top in the corner helped the owner of the museum, Ohga Hiroyuki, gain entry into the *Guinness World Book of Records* in 1983—by spinning 1 hour, 8 minutes, and 57 seconds. You can tour the museum in much less time than that—30 or 40 minutes. A large store at the entrance sells great traditional Japanese toys.

1-4-16 Chuo. ℂ **086/422-8058.** Admission ¥400 adults, ¥300 junior-high and high-school students, ¥200 children. Daily 9am–5pm. On the canal.

Kurashiki Folkcraft Museum (Kurashiki Mingei-Kan) Under the slogan USABILITY EQUALS BEAUTY, this museum contains folk crafts not only from Japan but from various other countries as well, giving unique insight into their cultural similarities and differences as reflected in the items they make and use in daily life. Spread through three old rice granaries, displays change three times a year and may include baskets, ceramics, glass, textiles, and woodwork. Unfortunately not all items are identified in English, but you'll appreciate their beauty. Plan on 30 minutes here.

1-4-11 Chuo. ℂ **086/422-1637.** Admission ¥700 adults, ¥400 university and high-school students, ¥300 children. Tues–Sun 9am–5pm (to 4:15pm Dec–Feb). On the canal, beside the Kurashiki-Kan tourist office.

Ohara Museum of Art (Ohara Bijutsukan) ★★★ This is by far Kurashiki's most impressive museum, a must-see even on a short list of sightseeing. Ohara Magosaburo, who believed that even people in remote Kurashiki should have the opportunity to view great works of art (that's his beautiful mansion across the canal from the museum), founded it in 1930 as Japan's first museum of Western art. The main building, a two-story stone structure resembling a Greek temple, is small but manages to contain the works of such greats as Picasso, Matisse, Vlaminck, Chagall, Manet, Monet, Degas, Pissarro, Sisley, Toulouse-Lautrec, Gauguin, Cézanne, El Greco, Renoir, Miró, Kandinsky, Klee, Pollack, Jasper Johns, Oldenburg, Frank Stella, Rothko, De Kooning, Warhol, and Hundertwasser. The museum has expanded so much since its founding that several annexes have been added over the years. A crafts gallery housed in a renovated granary contains works by some of my favorites, including ceramics by Hamada Shoji, Bernard Leach, and Kawai Kanjiro; and woodblock prints by Munakata Shiko, who lived in Kurashiki 3 years. An annex is devoted to Japanese artists painting in the Western style and to contemporary Japanese artists, which makes for a fascinating comparison. Yet another building displays ancient Chinese art, primarily from prehistoric times to the Tang Dynasty (A.D. 618–907). Allow 1½ hours to see everything, but because your ticket is good all day, you don't have to see it all at once. An audio guide, which will direct you to the most important works in the main gallery, is available for ¥500.

1-1-15 Chuo. ℂ **086/422-0005.** www.ohara.or.jp. Admission ¥1,000 adults, ¥600 university and senior-high students, and ¥500 children. Tues–Sun 9am–5pm. On the canal.

(159) **Ohashi House (Ohashi-tei)** Built in 1796 by a wealthy rice merchant, this traditional mansion is typical of the era, with front rooms used for entertaining guests and for business (the doorsill leading to the warehouse can be removed for easy transport), and the rear used as family living quarters. A front gate, usually allowed only the samurai class, is proof how important the Ohashi family was; another unique feature is a guesthouse, rare in merchant's homes. Once much larger (a hotel occupies the former garden), the home's 20 remaining rooms contain family heirlooms but are otherwise fairly empty. It's the only merchant's house open to the public, so come for a 15-minute spin through if you've never seen the inside of a traditional Japanese home.

3-21-31 Achi. ℂ **086/422-0007.** Admission ¥500 adults, ¥300 seniors and children. Tues–Sun 9am–5pm. Across Chuo Dori from the Bikan Historical Quarter, behind the Nikko Hotel.

IVY SQUARE

A 1-minute walk from the canal and museums is a complex called **Kurashiki Ivy Square,** 7–1 Honmachi. Built as a cotton mill by a local spinning company in 1889, this handsome redbrick complex shrouded in ivy has been renovated into a hotel, restaurants, museums, and a few boutiques and galleries selling crafts. It's especially romantic in the evening when, from mid-July to the end of August, there's a beer garden in the inner courtyard (daily 6–9:30pm) and classical music wafts from loudspeakers built into the courtyard's brick floors.

Museums at Ivy Square include **Kojima Torajiro Memorial Hall** (ℂ **086/422-0010**), named for and displaying paintings by the local artist who went to Europe to purchase most of the pieces in the Ohara museum (he died, however, before completion of the museum). It's open Tuesday to Sunday from 9am to 5pm. Most unique, however, in my opinion, is the (160) **Orgel Musée** (ℂ **086/427-3904**), where 30-minute concerts on 30 antique organs, player pianos, and music boxes from Europe, the United States, and Japan take place. You must enter on the hour, at 10am, 11am, 1pm, 2pm, 3pm, 4pm, and 5pm. Admission for both museums is ¥500 for adults and ¥300 for children.

Expensive

(161) **Ryokan Kurashiki** ★★★ (Finds) The best place to stay to get a feeling for old Kurashiki is right in the heart of it—in one of the old warehouses on Kurashiki's picturesque willow-lined canal. This venerable *ryokan* consists of an old mansion and three converted rice-and-sugar warehouses more than 250 years old, all interconnected in its own little compound. Filled with antiques and curios, it has long, narrow corridors, nooks and crannies, and the peaceful sanctuary of an inner garden. There's no other ryokan in Japan quite like this one. Its five rooms, which are actually two- and three-room suites consisting of a tatami living room and sleeping quarters with Western-style beds, are simply elegant, with antiques placed here and there, two TVs, and Jacuzzi tubs. Two are big enough for up to six people. Guests can elect to eat in their room, in a tatami room overlooking the canal, or in a delightful terrace tea lounge overlooking a small garden (Western-style breakfasts are available).

4–1 Honmachi, Kurashiki 710-0054. ℂ **086/422-0730.** Fax 086/422-0990. www.ryokan-kurashiki.jp. 5 units. ¥28,000–¥48,000 per person. Rates include 2 meals but exclude service charge. Rates ¥1,000 higher in peak season. AE, DC, MC, V. In the Bikan Historical Quarter, on the canal. **Amenities:** Restaurant; tea lounge. *In room:* A/C, TV, fridge.

(162) **Tsurugata** ★★ Rustic furniture, gleaming wood, and high ceilings are trademarks of this *ryokan*, on the canal in the Bikan Historical Quarter's oldest building, constructed in 1744. It was once a merchant's house and shop selling rice, cotton, seafood, and cooking oil. The most expensive rooms have a view of the garden with its 400-year-old pine trees and stone lanterns, while the least expensive, rather ordinary rooms are on the second floor without a view. All rooms have private toilets and there are public baths. Its meals are memorable. This ryokan is owned by the Kurashiki Kokusai Hotel, which has long been the most popular hotel for foreign visitors (see below).

1–3–15 Chuo, Kurashiki 710-0046. ℂ **086/424-1635.** Fax 086/424-1650. 11 units, all with toilet, 3 with bathroom. ¥13,800–¥33,600 per person. Rates include 2 meals. Rates ¥1,050 higher in peak season. AE, DC, MC, V. In the Bikan Historical Quarter, on the canal. **Amenities:** Restaurant; smoke-free rooms. *In room:* A/C, TV.

Moderate

Hotel Kurashiki If you prefer a hotel near Kurashiki Station, you can't get any closer than this Japan Railways Group combination business-tourist hotel above the station (holders of the Japan Rail Pass can get a discount). Its rooms are spotless and pleasantly decorated, with double-paned windows to shut out noise and nicely tiled bathrooms instead of the usual one-unit cubbyholes of most business hotels. The most expensive singles have double-size beds and sofas, making them quite roomy for Japan, though the cheapest rooms in all categories are quite small. Personally, I think it's a shame to come all this way and miss out staying in the Bikan Historical Quarter, but if it's convenience you want, this is your best bet. The rates below reflect both room types and the seasons.

1–1–1 Achi, Kurashiki 710-0055. ℂ **086/426-6111.** Fax 086/426-6163. www.hotels.westjr.co.jp. 133 units. ¥8,400–¥9,450 single; ¥15,750–¥33,600 double. 10% discount for holders of Japan Rail Pass. AE, DC, MC, V. Above Kurashiki Station's south exit. **Amenities:** 2 restaurants; smoke-free rooms. *In room:* A/C, TV, hair dryer, Internet, minibar.

Kurashiki Ivy Square Hotel ★ An interesting place to stay and a good choice in this price category, this hotel occupies a brick converted cotton mill on Ivy Square. Much of the architectural style of the old mill has been left intact, and rooms have a rural, simple atmosphere. Some rooms face a tiny expanse of green grass and an ivy-covered wall or a canal with koi fish (much better than those facing a parking lot). Deluxe rooms are actually two-room suites. The Bikan Historical Quarter is just a minute's walk away, but the train station is a 25-minute hike away.

7–2 Honmachi, Kurashiki 710-0054. © 086/422-0011. Fax 086/424-0515. www.ivysquare.co.jp. 161 units, all with toilet, 67 with bathroom. ¥7,875 single with toilet, ¥10,500 single with bathroom; ¥13,125 twin with toilet; ¥16,800–¥28,350 twin/double with bathroom. ¥1,050 extra per person in peak season. AE, DC, MC, V. A minute's walk south of the Bikan Historical Quarter. **Amenities:** Restaurant; bar; summer beer garden; access to nearby sports club w/gym and pool (fee: ¥800); smoke-free rooms. In room: A/C, TV, fridge, hair dryer.

Kurashiki Kokusai Hotel ★★ This has long been Kurashiki's most popular Western-style hotel—and it's easy to see why. This delightful hotel, built in 1963, blends into its surroundings with black-tile walls set in white mortar. Its atmosphere is decidedly old-fashioned, which only adds to the charm. Look for the two huge woodblock prints in the lobby, *Great Barriers of the Universe,* by Japanese artist Munakata Shiko (you can see more of his work at the Ohara Museum). Rooms have nice touches of locally made crafts that lift them out of the ordinary, including woven place mats, Kurashiki glass lampshades, and woodblock prints by a local artist. Female travelers receive a flower in their room. A newer annex offers slightly larger (mostly) twin rooms with larger bathrooms, but I prefer the smaller (and cheaper) rooms in the old building facing the back with a pleasant view of the Ohara Museum, garden greenery, and the black-tile roofs of the old granaries.

1–1–44 Chuo, Kurashiki 710-0046. © 086/422-5141. Fax 086/422-5192. www.kurashiki-kokusai-hotel. co.jp. 106 units. ¥9,000 single; ¥14,000–¥20,000 double. Rates exclude tax and service charge and are ¥1,050 higher per person in peak season. AE, DC, V. A 10-min. walk south of Kurashiki Station, on Chuo Dori next to the Bikan Historical Quarter. **Amenities:** Restaurant; bar; lounge; summer beer garden; computer in business center w/free Internet; smoke-free rooms. In room: A/C, TV, hair dryer, Internet, minibar.

Inexpensive

Toyoko Inn Kurashikieki Minamiguchi (Value) This inexpensive business hotel has a good location between Kurashiki Station and the Bikan Historical Quarter, above a convenience store. It also tries harder than most business hotels to draw in customers, offering free Internet access from two computers in the lobby, free domestic calls from lobby phones, free Wi-Fi in the lobby, and free breakfast. Rooms are tiny, with most of the room taken up by double- or queen-size beds, but the price is right. Ask for a room on a top floor for unobstructed city views.

2–10–20 Achi, Kurashiki 710-0055. © 086/430-1045. Fax 086/430-1046. www.toyoko-inn.co.jp. 154 units. ¥5,250 single; ¥6,300–¥7,350 double. Rates include continental breakfast. MC, V. A 3-min. walk south of Kurashiki Station, on Chuo Dori on the left side. **Amenities:** Lobby computer w/free Internet; smoke-free rooms. In room: A/C, TV w/free movies, fridge, hair dryer, Internet.

Young Inn Kurashiki For inexpensive rooms close to the station, you might try this rather different kind of place (at least for Japan). A redbrick building, it has an informal youth-hostel feel and seems more European than Japanese. Painted in bright colors, it looks as though it might have been rather chic at one time but has faded over the years. It caters mainly to young people and has two to three beds per room (all with sink); the beds are arranged on different levels in bunk-bed style. In fact, the three-bed rooms on the fifth floor have to be seen to be believed—the third bed (which is actually a semi-double-size, so four can stay here) is about 3m (10 ft.) off the floor, and you have to climb a ladder to reach it. Definitely for the nimble who are unafraid of heights. The 10 nonsmoking rooms all have private bathrooms, and four rooms have free Wi-Fi (make requests when making reservations). Cinderella wannabes take note: There's a midnight curfew.

1–14–8 Achi, Kurashiki 710-0055. ✆ **086/425-3411.** Fax 086/427-8388. www.kurashiki.jp/english.htm. 37 units, 4 with bathroom. ¥4,000 single without bathroom; ¥7,000 single with bathroom; ¥7,000 double without bathroom; ¥11,000 double with bathroom; ¥12,000 triple without bathroom; ¥14,000 quad without bathroom. Rates exclude tax. No credit cards. A 2-min. walk from Kurashiki Station to the right (west) behind the Terminal Hotel. **Amenities:** Coffee shop; smoke-free rooms; Wi-Fi in coffee shop. *In room:* A/C, coin-op TV, Wi-Fi (in some), no phone (in some).

WHERE TO DINE

If you're here in summer, you might wish to take advantage of an evening beer garden. You'll find them atop the Hotel Kurashiki, in the courtyard of Ivy Square, and on the lawn of the Kokusai Hotel. The first two offer only all-you-can-eat-and-drink sets for around ¥3,500, while the last option has an a la carte menu as well.

Moderate

Hachikengura ★★ FRENCH   Occupying a converted rice granary that once belonged to the Ohashi family (described above in the Ohashi House review), this is my top pick for an atmospheric meal, boasting a soaring wood-beamed ceiling, tiled walls, a worn wooden floor, and a window with views of the Ohashi mansion kitchen. Traditional French cuisine, such as duck confit or quail stuffed with foie gras, is served in a nouvelle style. You can eat here more economically if you come for lunch.

Hotel Nikko Kurashiki, 3–21–19 Achi. ✆ **086/423-2400.** Main dishes ¥2,000–¥4,800; set lunches ¥1,600–¥5,000; set dinners ¥5,000–¥15,000. AE, DC, MC, V. Daily 11:30am–3pm and 5:30–10pm. Across from the Bikan Historical Quarter.

Inexpensive

El Greco Coffeehouse COFFEE SHOP   El Greco is Kurashiki's most famous coffee shop, open since 1959 and simply decorated with a wooden floor, wooden tables and benches, vases of fresh flowers, and El Greco prints. It serves coffee, fruit juice, milkshakes, ice cream, and cake from an English-language menu.

1–1–11 Chuo. ✆ **086/422-0297.** Coffee ¥500. No credit cards. Tues–Sun 10am–5pm. Next door to the Ohara Museum in an ivy-covered stone building.

⑯③ **Kamoi ★** SUSHI   This sushi restaurant, occupying a 200-year-old rice granary on Kurashiki's willow-fringed canal, is simply decorated with stark-white walls, dark wooden beams, and a collection of cast-iron teapots. Because the menu is in Japanese, select from the plastic-food display outside the front door or from the pictures from the menu. In addition to sushi set meals, other set meals include a *tempura teishoku,* the *Kamoi Teishoku* (featuring sashimi and *barazushi*—a rice dish covered with vegetables and seafood and commonly served during festivals), and—my favorite—the *Kurashiki Obento* with tempura, vegetables, rice, and soup.

1–3–17 Chuo. ✆ **086/422-0606.** Set meals ¥1,365–¥3,100. No credit cards. Thurs–Tues 10am–6pm (closed 2nd Mon of each month). Catty-corner across the canal from the Ohara Museum of Art.

⑯④ **Kanaizumi** UDON   Kanaizumi, housed in a warehouse-style building with tall ceilings, is easy to spot: Just look for its chef rolling out *udon* behind a large window open to the street (though he's on duty only from 11am–1pm daily). In addition to the thick, handmade wheat udon noodles, tempura, sashimi, and local cuisine is served, but all fixed-price meals come with udon. As the menu is in Japanese only, make your selection from the display case or from pictures in the menu.

Kiyutei STEAKS Enter through the front gate just off the canal, pass through the small courtyard, and go into a small room dominated by a counter with cooks grilling steaks, the specialty of the house. There's an English-language menu; you're probably best off ordering one of the set meals, which offer also grilled salmon, the day's fish, and other choices in addition to steak.

1–2–20 Chuo. ☎ **086/422-5140.** Set dinners ¥1,300–¥5,000; set lunches ¥1,000–¥4,200. AE, DC, MC, V. Tues–Sun 11am–9pm (Dec–Feb Tues–Sun 11:30am–8:30pm). On the canal, across from the main entrance of the Ohara Museum of Art.

Kuku CURRIES A cute little shop with just a counter and three tables and jazz background music, this is an inexpensive alternative if you're searching for something different. Its curries on the English-language menu run the gamut from Thai green or red curry to curries with eggplant, chicken, or pork, and there's an assortment of Asian beers, from Thailand, the Philippines, Indonesia, and India. It's near the Bikan Historical District, on a picturesque lane (if it weren't for those darn overhead electric/telephone lines), but ask the tourist office for directions.

11–19 Honmachi. ☎ **086/424-3075.** Curries ¥750–¥900; set lunches ¥980–¥1,200. No credit cards. Thurs–Tues 11:30am–8pm. A 4-min. walk northeast of the historic district.

Ristorante Rentenchi PIZZA/PASTA This cozy, tiny restaurant (with an English-language menu), run by a kind husband-and-wife team, is a good choice for inexpensive dining between Kurashiki Station and the Bikan Historical Quarter. Neapolitan-style, thick-crusted pizza from a wood-burning oven is the specialty, most with one or two toppings, though several more can be added upon request.

2–19–18 Achi. ☎ **086/421-7858.** Reservations recommended. Pizza and pasta ¥950–¥1,800; set lunches ¥1,050–¥2,800. AE, DC, MC, V. Wed–Mon 11:45am–2pm and 6–10pm. An 8-min. walk south of Kurashiki Station on Chuo Dori, on the left side (look for the Italian flag).

10 OFF THE BEATEN PATH: MATSUE ★

724km (450 miles) SW of Tokyo; 186km (116 miles) NW of Okayama; 402km (251 miles) NE of Hakata (Fukuoka)

Capital of Shimane Prefecture and with a population of about 194,000, **Matsue** lies near the northern coast of western Honshu. It's off the beaten track for most foreign tourists, who tend to keep to a southerly route in their travels toward Hiroshima and Kyushu. Japanese, however, are quite fond of Matsue, and a fair number of them choose to spend their summer vacation in and around this pleasant town, visiting its castle and other sights, including a nearby museum highlighting contemporary Japanese art in a fantastic garden setting. Hugging the shores of Lake Shinji and Nakaumi Lagoon, cut in half by the Ohashi River, and crisscrossed by a network of canals, Matsue is a pretty castle town blessed with Edo-Era architecture, particularly along the castle moat where many samurai settled. All these things conspire to make a trip to Matsue—despite its out-of-the-way location—very worthwhile.

ESSENTIALS

GETTING THERE **By Train** The easiest way to reach Matsue is from Okayama via the 2½-hour **JR limited express Yakumo train** ride that costs ¥5,670 for an unreserved seat.

BY BUS   A bus departs from Tokyo's Shibuya Station (in front of Mark City) nightly at 8pm, arriving at Matsue Station at 6:26am and costing ¥11,550 one-way. From Hiroshima, 14 buses depart daily, taking 3½ hours and costing ¥4,000 one-way.

VISITOR INFORMATION   At the Tokyo or Narita or Kansai airport Tourist Information Centers, pick up the leaflet "Matsue and Izumo Taisha Shrine" (you can also download it from the Japan National Tourist Organization's website at **www.jnto.go.jp** by looking under "Browse by Destinations"). Upon arrival at **Matsue Station,** stop at the **Matsue International Tourist Information Office** (✆ **0852/21-4034;** daily 9am–6pm), located in a contemporary-looking kiosk in front of the station's north exit, where you can pick up English-language brochures on Matsue and Shimane Prefecture and a good map of the city. Be sure, also to ask for a brochure listing discounts (up to 50%) available to international visitors for nine tourists sights in and around Matsue, including Matsue Castle and Adachi Museum of Art (you'll have to show your passport at each sight for the discount). Go to **www.city.matsue.shimane.jp** and **www.kankou-shimane.com/en** for more information on Matsue online.

INTERNET ACCESS   On the third floor of **Town Plaza Shimane,** 8–3 Tonomachi (✆ **0852-31-5056;** Lake Line stop: Town Plaza Shimane), computers are available with free Internet connection. It's open Monday to Friday from 9am to 7pm and Sunday from 9am to 5pm.

MAIL   The main post office is a 5-minute walk from the north exit of Matsue Station, on the street that runs in front of the station to your right (east). Its ATM facilities are open Monday to Friday 7am to 11pm, Saturday 9am to 9pm, and Sunday and holidays 9am to 7pm.

ORIENTATION & GETTING AROUND   Matsue's attractions lie to the northwest of the station and across the Ohashi River, and although buses run virtually everywhere, you can easily cover most distances **on foot.** Matsue Castle is about a 30-minute walk from Matsue Station, with most attractions located just north of the castle along a picturesque moat on a street called Shiomi Nawate. To the west of Matsue Station, about a 10-minute walk away, is Lake Shinji, famous for its sunsets.

If you prefer to ride, ¥500 buys you an all-day pass for the **Lake Line,** which features red, old-fashioned buses running every 20 minutes in a 50-minute loop through the city beginning at Matsue Station and stopping at most tourist sights daily between 8:40am and 6:56pm (8:20am–6:11pm Dec–Feb). Single trips cost ¥200.

GOODWILL GUIDES   Although Matsue's sights are concentrated in one area of town and are easy to find on your own, you may want a "goodwill guide" to show you around, especially if you're going to Izumo Taisha Shrine. Established by the Japan National Tourist Organization, the goodwill guide network is composed of volunteers with foreign-language abilities who act as guides in their city. All you have to do is pay their transportation costs and entrance fees into museums and sights—and it's nice if you buy them lunch, too. If you wish to have a guide, apply at the tourist information office 2 or 3 days in advance (by phone ✆ **0852/21-4035;** by fax 0852/27-2598).

SEEING THE SIGHTS

International visitors are entitled to 50% discounts at Matsue Castle, Buke Yashiki, Lafcadio Hearn Memorial Museum, Adachi Museum of Art, and a few other attractions by showing their passport at attraction entrances. The prices below are the regular fare, without the discount.

Matsue Castle ★★ First built in 1611 and partly reconstructed in 1642 and again in the 1950s, Matsue Castle is the only castle along this northern stretch of coast built for warfare as opposed to serving merely as a residence. It's also one of Japan's few remaining original castles—that is, it's not a ferroconcrete reconstruction. Rising up from a hill about 1.5km (1 mile) northwest of Matsue Station with a good view of the city, the five-story *donjon* (which actually conceals six floors to give its warriors a fighting advantage) houses the usual *daimyo* and samurai gear, including armor, swords, helmets, and lacquerware that belonged to the Matsudaira clan, who ruled for 10 generations.

Lafcadio Hearn (a European who lived in Matsue in the 1890s, adopted Japanese citizenship, and wrote extensively about Japan and Japanese) said of Matsue Castle: "Crested at its summit, like a feudal helmet . . . the creation is a veritable architectural dragon, made up of magnificent monstrosities." As you walk through the castle up to the top floor, notice the staircase. Although it looks sturdy, it's light enough to be pulled up to halt enemy intrusions. Concealed holes on the second floor could serve as drop chutes for raining stones down on invaders. The top floor, with windows on all four sides from which the feudal lord could command his army, is one of the few watchtowers remaining in Japan. And to think the castle almost met its demise during the Meiji Restoration when the ministry of armed forces auctioned it off, hoping to rid the city of its Feudal-Era landmark. Luckily, former vassals of the clan pooled their resources and bought the castle. In 1927, the grounds were donated to the city.

Also on castle grounds is the **Matsue Kyodo Kan,** a Western-style, Meiji-Era building built in 1903 to accommodate Emperor Meiji should he ever turn up (he never did). Today it houses the Matsue Historical Museum, with free admission to its changing exhibits. You can tour this and the castle in less than an hour.

1–5 Tonomachi. ☎ **0852/21-4030.** Admission ¥550 adults, ¥280 children. Daily 8:30am–5pm (to 6:30pm Apr–Sept). Lake Line bus: stop no. 7, Matsue-jo Otemae (1 min.). Or a 30-min. walk northwest of Matsue Station.

Attractions near the Castle

Most of these attractions are located on Shiomi Nawate, a small, picturesque street beside the castle's north moat. I've listed them in geographic order, walking from east to west.

⑯ **Teahouse Meimei-an** This is one of Japan's most renowned and well-preserved thatch-roofed teahouses, built in 1779 upon orders of a 29-year-old lord of the Matsudaira clan. It's located at the top of a flight of stairs, from which you have a good view of Matsue Castle (read: photo op). Note the waiting room (and its ancient toilet), for guests awaiting a summons to the teahouse. A separate building offers bitter Japanese green tea and sweets for an additional ¥400, which you might find refreshing before you move on to your next destination.

278 Kitahori-cho. ☎ **0852/21-9863.** Admission ¥400 adults, ¥300 students, free for children. Daily 9am–5pm (green tea served until 4:15pm). Lake Line bus: stop no. 9, Shiomi Nawate (4 min.). Or a 5-min. walk northeast of Matsue Castle, back from Shiomi Nawate on a small side street and up a flight of stairs to the left.

⑯ **Buke Yashiki** ★ This ancient samurai house, facing the castle moat, was built in 1730 and belonged to the Shiomi family, one of the chief retainers of the Matsudaira feudal clan residing in the castle. High-ranking samurai, the Shiomi family lived pretty much like kings themselves, having separate servants' quarters, a tearoom, and even a shed for their palanquin. Compared with samurai residences in wealthier regions of Japan, however, this samurai house is considered rather austere. As you walk around it, peering into rooms with their wooden walls slid open to the outside breeze, you'll see furniture and objects used in daily life by samurai during the Edo Period. You can see it all in 10 minutes.

305 Kitahori-cho. ℂ **0852/22-2243.** Admission ¥300 adults, ¥150 children. Daily 8:30am–5pm (to 6:30pm Apr–Sept). Lake Line bus: stop no. 10, Koizumi Yakumo Kinenkan-mae (3 min.). Northeast of Matsue Castle across the moat, on Shiomi Nawate.

Lafcadio Hearn Memorial Museum (Koizumi Yakumo Kinenkan) Here you'll find memorabilia of writer Lafcadio Hearn (1850–1904) including his desk, manuscripts, photographs, and smoking pipes. Japanese are fascinated with this man who married the daughter of a Matsue high-ranking samurai, became a Japanese citizen, and adopted the name Koizumi Yakumo. He was one of the first writers to give Japanese the chance to see themselves through the eyes of a foreigner and to describe Japan to the outside world. His books still provide insight into Japanese life at the turn of the 20th century and are available at all bookstores in Japan with an English-language section.

Because most Japanese will assume it's out of respect for Hearn that you've come to Matsue, you may want to read one of his books before coming here. His volume *Glimpses of Unfamiliar Japan* contains an essay called "In a Japanese Garden," in which he gives his impressions of Matsue, where he lived for 15 months before moving to Kumamoto to teach English.

For die-hard Hearn fans, next to the memorial is **Lafcadio Hearn's Old Residence** (ℂ **0852/23-0714**), a Japanese-style house (and former samurai mansion) where Hearn lived in 1891. It has a pleasant, small garden immortalized in Hearn's essay "In a Japanese Garden." Admission here is ¥350 for adults, ¥180 for children. It's open daily 9am to 5pm (10am–4:40pm Dec–Feb). You can tour both the museum and the residence in 30 minutes.

322 Okudani-cho. ℂ **0852/21-2147.** Admission ¥300 adults, ¥150 children. Daily 8:30am–5pm (to 6:30pm Apr–Sept). Lake Line bus: stop no. 10, Koizumi Yakumo Kinenkan-mae (1 min.). On Shiome Nawate north of Matsue Castle.

⑯⑦ **Gesshoji Temple** ★ This is the family temple and burial ground of the Matsudaira clan, feudal lords of Matsue and the surrounding region. It was established back in 1664 by Matsudaira Naomasa, whose grandfather was the powerful Tokugawa Ieyasu. Nine generations of the Matsudaira clan are buried here, each in his own small compound spread throughout the solemn grounds; Naomasa's grave, the grandest and largest, is the one at the far left (allow 20 min. to see all of them). What I like most about this cemetery is that it seems ancient and forgotten; you might find yourself the only living soul here. At the grave of the sixth lord is a stone turtle (described by Hearn as "the monster tortoise") famous for midnight strolls that terrorized residents; if you rub its head, you'll have good luck. Stop for ceremonial green tea (¥400) in a room of a modern building facing a great little garden. And in June, temple grounds are famous for stunning hydrangeas—don't miss it.

Sotonakabara-cho. ℂ **0852/21-6056.** Admission ¥500 adults, ¥300 high-school students, ¥150 junior-high school and children. Daily 8:30am–5:30pm (to 5pm Nov–Mar). Lake Line bus: stop no. 15, Gesshoji-mae (4 min.). A 15-min. walk west of Matsue Castle.

A MUSEUM ON THE SHORES OF LAKE SHINJI

Shimane Art Museum (Kenritsu Bijutsukan) This modern museum with huge glass windows overlooking Lake Shinji showcases works by artists of Shimane Prefecture, as well as art that employs water as a theme. Most of the permanent collection consists of works by Japanese artists, though there are also a few pieces by Monet, Courbet, and Rodin. In addition to its many paintings, woodblock prints, photography, crafts, and

ceramics, there's a rooftop terrace and an outdoor sculpture garden (free of charge) along
Lake Shinji, perfect for a sunset stroll. In fact, the museum is so attuned to sunsets that
in summer it remains open 30 minutes past sunset. You can see the permanent exhibit
in about 30 minutes.

1–5 Sodeshi-cho. ✆ 0852/55-4700. Admission ¥300 adults, free for children. Special exhibitions cost
¥1,000 adults, ¥600 university and high-school students, ¥300 junior-high school students and children.
Wed–Mon 10am–6:30pm (Mar–Sept closes 30 min. after sunset). Lake Line bus: stop no. 27, Kenritsu
Bijitsukan (in front of the museum). Or a 15-min. walk west of Matsue Station.

BOAT TRIPS

The **Horikawa Pleasure Boat Tour** (**Horikawa Meguri;** ✆ 0852/27-0417) is a tour of
the castle moat aboard flat-bottom boats (take off your shoes and sit on tatami) with a
rooftop canopy that lowers for tight squeezes under bridges. It's a picturesque, relaxing
way to see the city, with trips around the castle lasting about an hour. In winter, you can
keep warm huddled under a *kotatsu* (a kind of heated blanket). Note, however, that commentary is in Japanese only. Boarding spots are at Karakoro Hiroba near the Kyobashi
Bridge (Lake Line Bus stop no. 6) and Otemae near Matsue Castle (Lake Line Bus stop
no. 8). Boats run every 15 minutes daily from 9am to 5pm (to 6pm in summer) March
through October and in November from 9am to 4pm; every 20 minutes daily from 9am
to 4pm December through February. An all-day ticket allowing you to disembark and
embark as much as you like costs ¥1,200 for adults and half-price for children, but foreigners can ride for ¥800 by showing their passport.

SHOPPING

For one-stop shopping for locally crafted goods, visit the **Shimane Prefectural Products
and Tourist Center (Shimane-ken Bussankanko-kan),** 191 Tonomachi (✆ 0852/22-
5758; daily 9am–6pm), just southeast of Matsue Castle (Lake Line bus to stop no. 8 to
Otemae, and then a 1-min. walk). In a modern building that resembles the black-and-
white structures typical of the region, the center sells the many agricultural and fishing
products of the region on its ground floor, while the second floor sells everything from
ceramics and abacuses (one of the few prefectures in Japan that still produces them) to
toys, lacquerware, and jewelry, all products of Shimane Prefecture.

Another interesting place to shop is the **Karakoro Art Studio,** Kyomise Karakoro
Hiroba Square (✆ 0852/20-7000; Wed–Mon 9:30am–6:30pm), a handsome, century-
old former bank renovated into studios and shops selling locally made sweets, tea, jewelry, glassware, woodworking, and other crafts. Changing exhibitions are held in the
basement vaults. It's located south of the castle on the moat; both the Lake Line bus and
Horikawa Pleasure Boat Tour stop here.

EASY SIDE TRIPS

IZUMO TAISHA GRAND SHRINE (IZUMO TAISHA) (Overrated) The most important
religious structure in the vicinity of Matsue is easy to see on a half-day side trip, but come
only if you have extra time. **Izumo Taisha,** 195 Kizuki Higashi, Taisha-cho, Izumo-shi
(✆ 0853/53-3100; daily sunrise–sunset), is considered one of Japan's holiest shrines
because, according to popular lore, all the gods in the Shinto pantheon gather here for 1
month every autumn to determine the world's fate for the upcoming year. In Izumo this
month is called the "Month with the Gods." Everywhere else in Japan, it's referred to as
the "Month without Gods," because they're all away performing their duty here, housed
in those long buildings flanking both sides of the main shrine. Otherwise, like the Ise

THE REST OF WESTERN HONSHU

OFF THE BEATEN PATH: MATSUE

Grand Shrines, the main shrine here, reconstructed in 1744, is considered too sacred for mere mortals and is hidden away from close inspection. You'll have to content yourself with a picture showing how it looked 1,000 years ago, when it was reputedly 24m (79 ft.) higher to heaven on top of huge pilings. This makes it the oldest site of a Shinto Grand Shrine displaying the Taisha style of architecture. It's dedicated to Okuninushi-no-mikoto, the Shinto deity responsible for medicine, farming, and happiness. To the left of the main shrine is the marriage shrine, where you'll see people throwing coins up into the bristled ends of thick, twisted rice ropes adorning the entrance; legend has it that if a coin gets stuck in the bushy end, the thrower will have good luck in marriage.

It's a 30- to 40-minute JR train ride from Matsue Station to Izumoshi Station (¥570), followed by a 30-minute bus ride (¥510) bound for Izumo Taisha ("Taisha-yuki"; get off at the last stop). Or, for a more atmospheric journey, you can also reach Izumo Taisha Grand Shrine by taking the private Ichibata Railway from Matsue Shinjiko Onsen Station (departures are once or twice an hour) 55 minutes to Izumo Taisha-mae Station (¥790). Note, however, that you'll probably have to change trains at Kawato Station, as there's only one direct train on weekends and holidays. Still, it's an interesting ride, with the train stopping at stations no larger than American closets. From Izumo Taisha-mae Station it's a 3-minute walk to the shrine entrance. Admission to the shrine is free.

ADACHI MUSEUM ★★★ (Finds) I was blown away the first time I laid eyes on the Adachi Museum, 320 Furukawa-cho, Yasugi (© **0854/28-7111;** www.adachi-museum.or.jp/e; daily 9am–5:30pm, to 5pm Oct–Mar), which houses one of Japan's premier collections of Japanese modern art (from the Meiji, Taisho, and Showa periods) amid the meticulously sculpted garden that I consider one of Japan's finest. Exhibitions in the main building, which are changed four times a year to reflect the seasons, are comprised of some 200 early modern Japanese works and include the largest collection of distinguished painter Yokoyama Taikan, with at least 20 of his 130 works here always on display. Also on display are Japanese *douga*, or illustrations from children's books and magazines, as well as pottery by Kawai Kanjiro and Kitaoji Rosanjin. An annex, opening in November 2010 to commemorate the museum's 40th anniversary, will display another 120 paintings of late-modern Japanese artists.

But what makes this museum truly unique is its perfectly landscaped **Adachi Museum Garden** ★★★, crafted to complement Taikan's masterpieces and continually visible through cleverly designed windows to incorporate it into the museum's artwork. The effect is surreal, as though the garden is a still picture, a scroll, a Taikan painting. There are several outdoor viewing spots, as well as a coffee shop overlooking a koi pond and two teahouses serving traditional cakes and powdered green tea (one with a nice view of a moss garden). You'll want to spend at least 2 hours here, more if you opt for the ¥500 audio guide describing more than 100 works of art or the ¥300 audio guide that provides highlights of the gardens and exhibits.

Admission to the museum is ¥2,200 for adults, ¥1,700 for university students, ¥900 for high-school students, and ¥400 for children, but foreigners can get a 50% discount by showing their passport. To get there, take the JR train from Matsue Station 20 minutes to Yasugi, and then board one of the free shuttle buses that depart nine times a day for the 20-minute ride to the museum. (At last check, buses departed for Adachi at 9am, 10am, 11am, and 11:55am; and at 1pm, 2pm, 2:25pm, 3pm, and 4:15pm, but you'd be wise to verify this.) There are also city buses directly from Matsue, but they're infrequent, so check with the tourist office for a schedule. Alternatively, the Yakumo limited express train traveling between Okayama and Matsue also stops at Yasugi Station, so you could disembark here and deposit your luggage in one of the station's 12 coin lockers before visiting the museum and then traveling onward.

WHERE TO STAY

Directions for listings below start from Matsue Station.

Expensive

⟨168⟩ **Minami-Kan** ★★ (**Finds**) You'll be treated like royalty at this *ryokan,* located right beside Lake Shinji. Although parts of the ryokan, including its lobby and rooms with private bathroom, are modern, the original building stems from 1888 and boasts several great tatami rooms with nice wood detailing (these have private toilets but no tubs). Most rooms have views of the lake, but if you really want to feel special, stay in the two-room garden cottage right beside the lake with views of the lake and a garden. Minami-Kan is also renowned for its restaurant, open to the public daily from 11:30am to 2:30pm and 5:30 to 9:30pm, with set meals costing ¥1,575 to ¥6,300. It's a good place to try *taimeshi,* a local specialty of steamed rice and freshwater fish.

14 Suetsugu Honmachi, Matsue, Shimane-ken 690-0843. ✆ **0852/21-5131.** Fax 0852/26-0351. 7 units, 5 with bathroom, 2 with toilet only; 1 cottage with bathroom. ¥23,250–¥30,180 per person, including 2 meals. Rates exclude service charge. ¥4,620 extra on Sat and nights before holidays. AE, DC, MC, V. Taxi: 8 min. Lake Line bus: stop no. 6, Kyobashi (2 min.). Off the Kyomise covered shopping arcade in the heart of Matsue. **Amenities:** Restaurant; hot-spring baths. *In room:* A/C, TV, minibar.

Moderate

Hotel Ichibata ★ Matsue's best-known tourist hotel is the Hotel Ichibata, which first opened its doors more than 40 years ago in a part of town called Matsue Shinjiko Onsen, a hot-spring spa. Pluses include the hotel's indoor and outdoor hot-spring public baths with views over Lake Shinji and a nearby jogging path that hugs the shores of the lake. Just behind the hotel is the private Ichibata Line train to Izumo Taisha. None of the singles or doubles have a view of the lake, but the more expensive twins and all the Japanese-style rooms do, including some combination-style rooms with both beds and tatami area.

30 Chidori-cho, Matsue, Shimane-ken 690-0852. ✆ **0852/22-0188.** Fax 0852/22-0230. www.ichibata. co.jp/hotel. 142 units. ¥9,390 single; ¥17,100–¥27,600 double; from ¥23,400 Japanese style for 2. ¥2,100 extra Sat and nights before holidays. AE, DC, MC, V. Lake Line bus: stop no. 18, Chidori Minami Koen (1 min., in front of the hotel). **Amenities:** 4 restaurants; bar; lounge; outdoor beer garden (summer only); indoor/outdoor hot-spring baths; room service. *In room:* A/C, TV, fridge, hair dryer, Internet.

Tokyu Inn Part of a national business hotel chain, the Tokyu Inn is a good choice for travelers who want to spend the night close to Matsue Station. Rooms are small and generic but have everything you need, including Tempur-Pedic Comfort Pillows that mold to your head; bathrooms are a bit larger than in most business hotels. Paying slightly higher rates in each category will get you a larger bed in single rooms and a larger room in double and twin rooms. There are also women's rooms equipped with humidifiers, irons, and female-oriented toiletries.

590 Asahimachi, Matsue, Shimane-ken 690-0003. ✆ **0852/27-0109.** Fax 0852/25-1327. www.tokyu hotels.co.jp. 181 units. ¥8,200–¥10,500 single; ¥15,300–¥31,500 double. AE, DC, MC, V. Across the street from Matsue Station's north exit to the right. **Amenities:** Restaurant; lounge; smoke-free rooms. *In room:* A/C, TV, hair dryer, Internet, minibar.

Inexpensive

Matsue New Urban Hotel Although it's a business hotel with the usual vending machines in the lobby, this property near Lake Shinji and within walking distance of

Matsue Castle and other tourist sights offers large hot-spring baths and rooms with great views of the lake. Rooms facing away from the lake are slightly cheaper, though some of these on higher floors do have views of Matsue Castle in the distance. If you let them know of your arrival, they will pick you up at the station. By the way, this is the newest of four Urban hotels in Matsue. The original hotel, next door, and the two you can see from the station's north exit are more worn, with fewer amenities, but they are less expensive.

40–1 Nishi-chamachi, Matsue, Shimane-ken 690-0845. © 0852/23-0003. Fax 0852/23-0018. 76 units. ¥6,300–¥7,140 single; ¥9,450–¥12,600 double. AE, DC, MC, V. Free shuttle bus from Matsue Station every 30 min. 7–9am. Lake Line bus: stop no. 23, Suetsugu Jinja-mae (3 min.). **Amenities:** Restaurant; rooftop beer garden (summer only); rental bikes (free 1st hr., ¥315 next 4 hr.); hot-spring baths; lobby computer w/free Internet. *In room:* A/C, TV, fridge, hair dryer, Wi-Fi.

(169) **Ryokan Terazuya** ★★★ (**Value**) Terazuya offers good value for your money, but it also offers something money can't buy: true hospitality. This Japanese inn has been in business since 1893, owned by the Terazu family, who has shown so much kindness to foreigners that many consider their stay here a highlight of their trip. The Terazus treat guests like family, teaching them the tea ceremony in the tearoom, showing them how to make sushi in the communal dining hall, giving calligraphy lessons, and singing traditional *noh* songs in the tatami party room. They've even been known to escort guests to the *onsen*. The postwar building, while nothing special on the outside, is spotless and colorfully decorated inside. Located across from a small shrine, it's also near the Shimane Art Museum and Lake Shinji, making it convenient for watching those famous sunsets. And although it's only a 7-minute walk from Matsue Station (head west along the north side of the railroad tracks), the Terazus will pick you up if you call ahead. *Note:* If faxing, please do so during Japanese business hours so as not to wake them.

60–3 Tenjin-machi, Matsue, Shimane-ken 690-0064. © **0852/21-3480.** Fax 0852/21-3422. www.mable. ne.jp/~terazuya/english. 9 units, none with bathroom. ¥4,500 per person with coffee and bread; ¥5,000 per person with breakfast; ¥7,000 per person with breakfast and dinner. No credit cards. Lake Line bus: stop no. 27, Kenritsu Bijutsukan (3 min.). **Amenities:** Restaurant. *In room:* A/C, TV, Wi-Fi.

Toyoko Inn Matsue Ekimae This budget chain offers tiny rooms with all the basics, along with free Internet access at lobby computers (and free Wi-Fi in the lobby for those traveling with laptops), and free domestic calls from lobby phones. A good choice if you don't need much personal attention.

498–10 Asahimachi, Matsue, Shimane-ken 690-0003. © **0852/60-1045.** Fax 0852/60-1046. www. toyoko-inn.com. 190 units. ¥4,935–¥5,960 single; ¥6,510–¥7,770 double. Rates include Japanese breakfast. AE, DC, MC, V. From Matsue Station's north exit, walk past the buses to the main road and turn left (3 min.). **Amenities:** Lobby computer w/free Internet; smoke-free rooms; Wi-Fi. *In room:* A/C, TV, fridge, hair dryer, Internet.

WHERE TO DINE

Much of Matsue's regional cuisine comes from Lake Shinji, including sea bass, smelt, carp, freshwater eel, and a small black clam (*shijimi*, popular in soups). *Warigo soba*, which comes with stacked layers of noodles, to which you add grated *daikon* radish, yam, fish flakes, seaweed, and other condiments, is also popular.

Moderate

Ji Beer Kan GRILLED MEAT In a large, airy setting beside the castle moat west of the Hearn Memorial Museum, this is Matsue's microbrewery/restaurant (every town seems to have one now). You'll find it on the second floor above a souvenir shop. Three different kinds of beer are brewed: a pilsner, a fruity pale ale, and an herb-flavored ale; a sampler of all three costs ¥950. Daily 11am to 4pm, set lunches, including those with grilled meats, as well as lighter fare like *udon* and *soba*, are available. Or, for gluttonous abandon, come for dinner from 5 to 9pm for the all-you-can-eat-in-90-minutes option for ¥2,500. It includes vegetables, appetizers, and strips of beef and pork you cook yourself at a grill at your table. For an additional ¥1,500 for women and ¥2,500 for men, it's all-you-can-drink in 90 minutes as well. Or, if all you want is a beer, buy one from a counter in the souvenir shop and take it outside to enjoy at the tables beside the moat.

509–1 Kuroda-cho. ☎ **0852/55-8877.** All-you-can-eat dinner ¥2,500; set lunches ¥900–¥2,800. AE, MC, V. Daily 11am–9pm. Lake Line bus: stop no. 11, Horikawa Yuransen Noribo (1 min.).

(170) **Kyoragi** ★★ LOCAL SPECIALTIES Located across from Ji Beer Kan (see above), this modern restaurant with a wood interior, lots of windows, and both tatami and table seating specializes in dishes based on original Izumo recipes, using organic meats and vegetables whenever possible. There are pictures of some of the set meals offered on the Japanese-language menu, including the very tasty *Hanagoromo* set lunch for ¥1,680 with lots of local delicacies. The *kokoro* set meal, served only for dinner (¥2,625), allows you to choose from almost a dozen different kinds of fresh fish for your main course, along with side dishes that change weekly. From Tuesday to Friday, there's a daily set lunch for only ¥735.

512–5 Kuroda-cho. ☎ **0852/25-2233.** Set dinners ¥2,625; set lunches ¥1,260–¥2,100; kaiseki from ¥4,200. DC, MC, V. Tues–Sun 11am–2pm and 5–10pm (open on holiday Mon, closing Tues instead). Lake Line bus: stop no. 11, Horikawa Yuransen Noribo (1 min.).

River View ★ Value CONTINENTAL Decorated in white, with a large wooden terrace (open only in summer) overlooking a river and soft rock or jazz background music, this restaurant turns out very good dishes that might include mustard steak, grilled fish, vegetable risotto, shoulder pork roast, or grilled chicken. Portions are small, so order several dishes if you're hungry, or go for one of the set meals such as the one for ¥3,150, which offers five dishes. This is one of the few options for late, late dining in Matsue.

562–1 Otesemba-cho. ☎ **0852/60-6122.** Main dishes ¥980–¥1,830; set dinners ¥3,150–¥5,250. AE, MC, V. Daily 5:30pm–midnight. A 3-min. walk north of Matsue Station, 2 blocks behind Tokyu Inn.

Inexpensive

(171) **Bankichi** ★ Finds YAKITORI Bankichi is a lively, friendly place, presided over by the grinning, English-speaking owner/cook. Customers seem to be content, too, as they crowd into this small restaurant with counter and booth seating. A branch of an Osaka *yakitori-ya*, Bankichi offers an English-language menu of various yakitori, including chicken, minced chicken meatballs, and chicken with leek or green pepper (which come with two sticks per dish), as well as its own brand of sake and wine. There's a ¥200 snack charge.

491–1 Asahimachi. ☎ **0852/31-8308.** Yakitori ¥200–¥300. MC, V. Daily 5pm–1am. From Matsue Station's north exit, turn left out of the station's north exit on the main street; it will be on your right, before Toyoko Inn (2 min.).

(172) **Kaneyasu** ★ Value FISH/VARIED JAPANESE This modest one-counter place with tatami rooms upstairs has good food and is run by grandmotherly, bustling women. It has been around for more than 50 years, and most of its customers are local working people, so avoid the noontime rush. It has a great lunch *teishoku*, which includes a piece of *yakizakana* (grilled fish), vegetable, soup, tofu, rice, and tea. In the evening, such dishes as grilled fish, yam, bamboo, seasonal dishes, and various vegetables are available,

but it's probably easier to order one of the two set meals, both of which feature locally caught seafood.

569-3 Otesemba-cho. ☎ **0852/21-0550.** Set dinners ¥1,500–¥2,000; lunch teishoku ¥650–¥900. No credit cards. Mon–Fri 11am–2pm; Mon–Sat 5–9pm. Closed holidays. 1 block north of the main street that runs in front of Matsue Station's north exit.

(173) **Yakumoan** ★★ (Finds) SOBA NOODLES A wonderful place to stop off for lunch if you're sightseeing along Shiomi Nawate north of Matsue Castle, this lovely *soba* shop with a teahouselike atmosphere is surrounded by a stone wall with a large wooden entryway, a grove of bamboo, bonsai, a Japanese garden, and a pond full of prize carp. Part of the restaurant, a former samurai residence, dates from 200 years ago. Its specialty is noodles, all handmade, including the local specialty Warigo *soba* and *udon*. You'll find a plastic-food display case to the left as you step through the entryway. Seating is at either tables or tatami.

308 Kitabori-cho. ☎ **0852/22-2400.** Noodles ¥650–¥900; set meals ¥1,100–¥1,320. No credit cards. Daily 11am–3pm (last order). Lake Line bus: stop no. 10, Koizumi Yakumo Kinenkan-mae (1 min.). On Shiomi Nawate St., near the Buke Yashiki samurai house.

11 HIROSHIMA ★★

894km (554 miles) W of Tokyo; 376km (235 miles) W of Kyoto; 279km (174 miles) E of Hakata/Fukuoka

With a population of more than one million, Hiroshima looks just like any other up-and-coming city in Japan. With modern buildings and an industry that includes the manufacture of cars and ships, it's a city full of vitality and purpose with a steady flow of both Japanese and foreign business executives in and out.

But unlike other cities, Hiroshima's past is clouded: It has the unfortunate distinction of being the first city ever destroyed by an atomic bomb. (The second city—and it is hoped the last—was Nagasaki, on Kyushu island.)

It happened one clear summer morning, August 6, 1945, at 8:15am, when a B-29 approached Hiroshima from the northeast, passed over the central part of the city, dropped the bomb, and then took off at full speed. The bomb exploded 43 seconds later at an altitude of 600m (1,980 ft.) in a huge fireball, followed by a mushroom cloud of smoke that rose 8,910m (29,700 ft.) in the air.

There were approximately 350,000 people living in Hiroshima at the time of the bombing, and almost a third lost their lives on that day. The heat from the blast was so intense that it seared people's skin, while the pressure caused by the explosion tore clothes off bodies and caused the rupture and explosion of internal organs. Flying glass tore through flesh like bullets, and fires broke out all over the city. But that wasn't the end of it: Victims who survived the blast were subsequently exposed to huge doses of radioactive particles. Even people who showed no outward signs of sickness suddenly died, creating panic and helplessness among the survivors. In the years that followed, blast survivors continued to suffer from the effects of the bomb, with a high incidence of cancer, disfigurement, scars, and keloid skin tissue.

Ironically, Hiroshima's tragedy is now the city's largest tourist draw, and visitors from around the world come to see Peace Memorial Park with its haunting museum. But Hiroshima, laced with rivers and wide, tree-lined boulevards, boasts other worthwhile attractions as well, including several excellent museums. Hiroshima is also the most

ATTRACTIONS ●
Hiroshima Castle **1**
Hiroshima Museum
    of Art **7**
Hiroshima Prefectural
    Art Museum **2**
Peace Memorial
    Museum **18**
Peace Memorial Park **13**
Shukkei-en Garden **3**

DINING ◆
Anderson Kitchen **14**
Atago **22**
Kanawa **20**
Kissui **21**
Kushinobo **15**
No-no-Budou **9**
Okonomi-Mura **17**
Ristorante Mario **19**
Sushi Tei **10**

ACCOMMODATIONS ■
Hotel Granvia Hiroshima **5**
Mitsui Garden Hotel Hiroshima **23**
Regalo **11**
Rihga Royal Hiroshima **8**
Sansui Ryokan **12**
Hotel Sunroute **21**
Toyoko Inn Hiroshima-Eki
    Minamiguchi-Migi **6**
Toyoko Inn Hiroshima-Eki
    Shinkansen-Guchi **4**
Toyoko Inn Hiroshima Heiwa-Odori **16**

popular gateway for trips to nearby Miyajima, a jewel of an island considered to be one of Japan's most scenic spots, covered later in this chapter.

ESSENTIALS

GETTING THERE   By Plane   Flights from Tokyo's Haneda Airport to Hiroshima take about 1½ hours and cost ¥30,900 on JAL, though advance purchase fares can be as low as ¥14,100. **Hiroshima Airport** (HIJ; ℂ **0848/86-8151;** www.hij.airport.jp/english) is also served by flights from Seoul, Beijing, Shanghai, and Taipei. Limousine Buses connect the airport with Hiroshima Station's Shinkansen (north) exit in 48 minutes, costing ¥1,300 one-way.

By Train   Hiroshima is about 6 hours from Tokyo by **Shinkansen** bullet train (you have to change trains in Okayama or Shin-Osaka if you have a Japan Rail Pass, because only the Nozomi, which is not covered by the pass, covers the entire distance in 4 hr.), 3 hours from Kyoto, and 1 hour and 10 minutes from Hakata Station on Kyushu. The fare from Tokyo is ¥17,540 for an unreserved seat; ¥10,280 from Kyoto.

By Bus   Buses depart from Tokyo Station every night at 8 and 9pm, both reaching Hiroshima Station at 8am the next morning. The one-way fare is ¥12,060. From Osaka, buses depart six times a day, taking 5 hours to reach Hiroshima and costing ¥5,000.

By Boat   You can also reach Hiroshima by **high-speed boat** from Matsuyama on Shikoku in 1 hour and 10 minutes for ¥6,900, but slower ferries, which cover the distance in 2 hours and 30 minutes, are cheaper (¥3,500) and provide better views of the Seto Inland Sea. Hiroshima Port, in Ujina, is connected to Hiroshima Station by streetcar in 43 minutes.

VISITOR INFORMATION   Before leaving Tokyo or the Narita or Kansai airports, pick up a copy of the leaflet "Hiroshima and Miyajima," at the Tourist Information Center. (You can also download it from the Japan National Tourist Organization's website at www.jnto.go.jp by looking under "Browse by Destinations.")

In Hiroshima, you'll find two local tourist offices at **Hiroshima Station.** One, at the north exit where Shinkansen bullet trains arrive, is open daily from 9am to 12:30pm and 1:30 to 5:30pm. The main tourist office (ℂ **082/261-1877**), at the station's south exit, is open daily April through September from 9:30am to 6pm (until 7pm Aug) and October through March from 8:30am to 5pm. A third tourist office is located in the center of **Peace Memorial Park** in the Rest House (ℂ **082/247-6738;** daily 9:30am–6pm Apr–Sept, 8:30am–5pm Oct–Mar). All three facilities have English-language brochures of Hiroshima and Miyajima with maps. Online information on Hiroshima is available at **www.hcvb.city.hiroshima.jp.**

INTERNET ACCESS   Media Café Popeye, located in the Hondori covered shopping arcade (ℂ **082/545-0369**) above a shop called Beams, is open 24 hours and charges ¥250 for the first 30 minutes, and then ¥60 for each subsequent 10 minutes.

MAIL   Hiroshima's main post office, 2–62 Matsubara-cho (ℂ **082/261-6401**), is located to the right after exiting from Hiroshima Station's south side. Its ATM services are available Monday to Saturday 12:05am to 11:55pm and Sunday 12:05am to 8pm.

ORIENTATION & GETTING AROUND   One legacy of Hiroshima's total destruction was its rebirth into one of Japan's most navigable cities, with wide, open boulevards instead of the usual cramped streets. Hiroshima's main attractions, including Peace Memorial Park, Hiroshima Castle, Shukkei-en Garden, Hiroshima Prefectural Art Museum, and Hiroshima Museum of Art, lie to the west and southwest of Hiroshima only ¥150 one-way; children pay half fare. If you need to transfer to another line, ask the driver for a *norikae* (transfer) card, which you then pass through the card machine upon alighting from the first streetcar and again when boarding the second streetcar. When you arrive at your destination, return the card to the streetcar driver. A 1-day pass, which you can buy from the conductor, costs ¥600. Be sure to pick up a streetcar map from the tourist office.

It's probably easiest to make the circuit to Hiroshima's centrally located attractions **on foot.** From Hiroshima Station, you can walk to Shukkei-en Garden and the Prefectural Art Museum in about 15 minutes, from which it's another 10-minute walk to Hiroshima Castle. You can walk onward to Peace Memorial Park in about 15 minutes, passing the Hiroshima Museum of Art and the A-Bomb Dome on the way. Just east of Peace Park is the **Hondori** covered shopping arcade and its neighboring streets, considered the heart of the city with its many department stores, shops, and restaurants.

SEEING THE SIGHTS

As you walk around Hiroshima today, you'll find it hard to imagine that the city was the scene of such widespread horror and destruction just 65 years ago. On the other hand, Hiroshima doesn't have the old buildings, temples, and historic structures that other cities have, yet it draws a steady flow of travelers who come to see Peace Memorial Park, the city's best-known landmark (Hiroshima draws 9.4 million tourists a year, 217,000 of them from other countries). Dedicated to peace, the city also seems committed to art: In addition to its fine art museums, you'll find statues, stone lanterns, memorials, and sculptures lining the streets.

PEACE MEMORIAL PARK & ENVIRONS

Peace Memorial Park (Heiwa Koen) ★★★ lies in the center of the city. English-language signs all over the city indicate how to reach it. From Hiroshima Station, take streetcar no. 2 or 6 to the Genbaku-Domu-mae (in front of the Atom Bomb Dome, which is just north of the park) stop. The first structure you'll see as you alight from the streetcar is the **A-Bomb Dome (Genbaku Domu),** the skeletal ruins of the former Industrial Promotion Hall, left as a visual reminder of the death and destruction caused by the atomic bomb and now on the World Heritage List. Across the river is the park; it takes about 10 minutes to walk from its northern end to the museum.

Along the way you'll see the park's most touching statue, the **Children's Peace Monument,** dedicated to the war's most innocent victims, not only those who died instantly in the blast but also those who died afterward from the effects of radiation. It's a statue of a girl with outstretched arms, and rising above her is a crane, a symbol of happiness and longevity in Japan. The statue is based on the true story of a young girl, Sadako, who suffered from the effects of radiation. She believed that if she could fold 1,000 paper cranes she would become well again. However, even though she folded more than 1,000 cranes, she still died of leukemia. Today, all Japanese children are familiar with her story, and around the memorial are streamers of paper cranes donated by schoolchildren from all over Japan. To the east of the statue is the **Rest House,** where you'll find a branch of the Hiroshima Tourist Office.

Also in Peace Memorial Park is a **Cenotaph for Korean Victims.** It's a little-publicized fact that 20,000 Koreans were killed that fateful summer day, most of them brought to Japan as forced laborers. The monument reads: "The Korean victims were given no funerals or memorial services and their spirits hovered for years unable to pass on to heaven." It's significant to note that for 29 years, the cenotaph remained outside the park. In 1999, Hiroshima's mayor, calling for an end to prejudice against Korean residents in Japan, gave the memorial a new home within the park.

Between the statue and the museum is the **Memorial Cenotaph,** designed by Japan's famous architect Kenzo Tange (who also designed the Tokyo Metropolitan Government offices in Shinjuku; see p. 195). Shaped like a figurine clay saddle found in ancient tombs, it shelters a stone chest, which in turn holds the names of all of those killed by the bomb. An epitaph, written in Japanese, carries the hopeful phrase, "Let all the souls here rest in peace, for we shall not repeat the evil." If you stand in front of the cenotaph, you'll have a view through the hollow arch of the Peace Flame and the A-Bomb Dome. It is said that the **Peace Flame** will continue to burn until all atomic weapons vanish from the face of the earth and nuclear war is no longer a threat to humanity.

East of the Peace Flame is the **Hiroshima National Peace Memorial Hall for the Atomic Bomb Victims** (© 082/543-6271). Its Hall of Remembrance, a 360-degree panorama re-creating the bombed city as seen from the hypocenter, is made of 140,000 tiles, the number of people estimated to have died by the end of 1945. The rest of the memorial is a vast, computerized audiovisual library with information on victims, their histories, and photos. The English-language leaflet not only provides excellent information but also gives access to the large-screen computers (insert it to activate them). Admission is free and it's open the same hours as the Peace Memorial Museum.

Just beyond is the main focus of the park, the **Peace Memorial Museum (Heiwa Kinen Shiryokan)** ★★★, 1–2 Nakajima-cho, Naku-ku (© 082/241-4004; www.pcf.city.hiroshima.jp; daily 8:30am–6pm Mar–Nov [until 7pm in Aug], daily 8:30am–5pm Dec–Feb). It comprises two buildings: the East Building, which tells of Hiroshima before the bomb fell and what happened to the city in the following months and years, and the West Building, which concentrates on that fateful August day. Entrance to the museum is in the East Building; admission is ¥50. Although an audio guide is available for an additional ¥300, you can learn just as much by reading the excellent English-language descriptions throughout the museum. You must enter 30 minutes before closing time, but you'll need at least 1 hour here to do the museum justice.

The newer East Building addresses Hiroshima's militaristic past, challenging the city's former self-characterization as a blameless victim. In great detail, it explains why Hiroshima was selected as the blast site: As Imperial Headquarters, Hiroshima was home to Japan's military command center as well as a military supply base (Mitsubishi, which produced warships, was based here). It also gives food for thought as to why the bomb was dropped, suggesting that the high cost to develop the bomb (called the Manhattan Project), coupled with the desire to establish U.S. supremacy over the Soviet Union and facilitate defeat in Japan, all played a role. TV screens show actual footage of the bomb being dropped and its aftermath. A 360-degree photograph shows Hiroshima's utter destruction. The museum also documents Hiroshima's current dedication to the abolition of nuclear weapons; a globe of the world provides a chilling map of nuclear proliferation. On the ground floor is the Video Theatre, where two English-language documentaries are shown throughout the day. One is an appeal for peace from a mother's point of view, with footage of the bombing, while the second film takes a more scientific look at the atomic bombs in both Hiroshima and Nagasaki.

The West Building concentrates on the suffering caused by the atomic bomb, beginning with panoramas of scorched earth and seared victims and photographs of the atomic bomb that destroyed the city and the intensity of the blast's epicenter. It then shows in graphic detail the effects of the blast on bodies, buildings, and materials. Most of the photographs in the exhibit are of burned and seared skin, charred remains of bodies, and people with open wounds, while displays explain the effects of radiation, including hair loss, keloid scars, leukemia, and cancer. There's a bronze Buddha that was half-melted in the blast and melted glass and ceramics. Tattered clothing and other personal effects are accompanied by short biographies of their owners, many of them children and teenagers and many of whom died in the blast.

Needless to say, visiting Peace Memorial Park is a sobering and depressing experience but perhaps a necessary one. And to think that what was dropped on Hiroshima is small compared to the bombs of today; as early as 1961, the Soviet Union had tested a hydrogen bomb 3,300 times more powerful than the atomic bomb dropped on Hiroshima. From the museum, the closest streetcar stop is Fukuro-machi, where you can catch streetcar no. 1 for Hiroshima Station.

MORE SIGHTS & ATTRACTIONS

Hiroshima Castle ★★   Completed in 1591 but destroyed in the atomic blast, Hiroshima Castle was reconstructed in 1958. Its five-story wooden *donjon* is a faithful reproduction of the original, but the main reason to come here is the very good museum housed in the castle's modern interior, which can be toured in about 30 minutes. The museum is devoted to Hiroshima's history as a flourishing castle town, with good English-language presentations. It also gives the best description I've seen on castles in Japan, including differences in architecture between those built on hills (for defense) and those built on plains (mainly administrative). Videos (with English translations via earphones) describe Hiroshima's founding and the construction of Hiroshima Castle, while displays explain the differences in lifestyle between samurai and townspeople, the hierarchy of the feudal administration system, and other aspects of Edo life. There's also samurai gear, models of old Hiroshima and the castle, and, for children, a kimono and samurai outfit they can try on. The top of the donjon provides a panoramic view of the city.

21–1 Moto-machi, Naka-ku. ℂ 082/221-7512. Admission ¥360 adults, ¥180 children. Daily 9am–6pm (to 5pm on weekdays Dec–Feb, 6pm weekends). A 15-min. walk north of Peace Memorial Park, or a 25-min. walk west of Hiroshima Station. Streetcar: 1, 2, or 6 to Kamiya-cho (10 min.).

Hiroshima Museum of Art (Hiroshima Bijutsukan) ★★ (Finds   This gem of a private museum, housed in a modern round building in a park in the heart of the city, has a permanent collection of some 200 paintings, half by French painters from Romanticism to Ecole de Paris and presented in chronological order in four rooms. Though small, virtually every piece is by a well-known artist, including Delacroix, Courbet, Corot, Manet, Monet, Renoir, Degas, Toulouse-Lautrec, Rousseau, Cézanne, Gauguin, van Gogh, Matisse, Picasso, Braque, Utrillo, Chagall, and Modigliani. Also on display are about 90 works by Japanese artists in the Western style from the Meiji Era to the present, including works by Kuroda Seiki and Kishida Ryusei. You'll spend an hour here.

3–2 Motomachi, Naka-ku ℂ 082/223-2530. www.hiroshima-museum.jp. Admission ¥1,000 adults, ¥500 university and high-school students, ¥200 junior-high and elementary students. Special exhibits cost more. Daily 9am–5pm. Streetcar: 1, 2, or 6 to Kamiya-cho (Kencho-mae exit, 3 min.). In Chuo Park, across from the Rihga Royal Hotel (Hiroshima's tallest building).

Hiroshima Prefectural Art Museum (Hiroshima Kenritsu Bijutsukan)   The main focus of this museum is art created by artists who have some kind of relationship to Hiroshima Prefecture, including Aimitsu (look for his self-portrait), Minami Kunzo, Kobayashi Senko, and Hirayama Ikuo (famous for his paintings of Hiroshima after the atomic bomb, especially *The Holocaust of Hiroshima*), as well as works from the 1920s and 1930s by non-Japanese artists who have influenced contemporary art in Japan such as Salvador Dalí, Lyonel Feininger, Picasso, and Thomas Hart Benton. Asian decorative arts, including ceramics and lacquerware, round out the permanent collection. If you purchase a combination ticket to Shukkei-en Garden, you can enter the garden directly from the museum. Plan on about 30 minutes here.

2–22 Kaminobori-cho, Naka-ku. © **082/221-6246.** www1.hpam-unet.ocn.ne.jp. Admission ¥500 adults, ¥300 university students, free for children. Combination ticket for museum and Shukkei-en Garden ¥600 adults and ¥340 students. Tues–Fri and Sun 9am–5pm; Sat 9am–7pm. Streetcar: 9 to Shukkeien-mae (1 min.). Adjacent to Shukkei-en Garden; a 15-min. walk from Hiroshima Station.

Shukkei-en Garden Shukkei-en Garden, which means "landscape garden in minia-ture," was first laid out in 1620 by a master of the tea ceremony, with a pond constructed in imitation of famous Lake Xi Hu in Hangzhou, China. Using streams, ponds, islets, and bridges, it was designed to appear much larger than it actually is and is best viewed on a 30-minute circular stroll. Like everything else in Hiroshima, it was destroyed in 1945, but amazingly, it looks like it's been here forever. Unfortunately, like most gardens in Japan, tall neighboring buildings detract from the garden's beauty (there ought to be a law), but it's still a pleasant respite from city traffic.

2–11 Kaminobori-cho, Naka-ku. © **082/221-3620.** Admission ¥250 adults, ¥150 university and high-school students, ¥100 children. Combination ticket for Hiroshima Prefectural Art Museum and the gar-den ¥600 adults and ¥340 students. Daily 9am–6pm (to 5pm Oct–Mar). Adjacent to Hiroshima Prefectural Art Museum.

EXPLORING SIGHTS OF THE SETO INLAND SEA

BY BOAT Stretching between Honshu and the islands of Shikoku and Kyushu, the Inland Sea is dotted with more than 3,000 pine-covered islands and islets, part of which is protected as Seto-Naikai (Seto Inland Sea) National Park. Hiroshima Prefecture serves as a departure point for boats traveling to islands throughout the Seto Inland Sea and to Shikoku. For an interesting day's excursion, I suggest taking the Shinkansen 30 minutes to Mihara (fare: ¥2,220), from which you can take a **high-speed boat** operated by Mihara-Setoda Kyodo Line (© **0848/64-0564**) 30 minutes to Setoda on Ikuchijima island. Ferries depart approximately once an hour, with one-way fares costing ¥800.

From Setoda's ferry pier, it's about a 10-minute walk to **Choseizan Kosanji Temple** ★★, at 553–2 Setoda (© **0845/27-0800;** www.kousanji.or.jp). This place is like no other, a re-creation of famous historic buildings from throughout Japan, erected by a former business-man-turned-Buddhist-priest over a 30-year period beginning in 1936 in honor of his mother. Occupying a picturesque hillside setting with many flowering trees, the grounds contain remakes of Byodoin Temple outside Kyoto, Nikko's Yomeimon Gate, Horyuji's Hall of Visions in Nara, and other important buildings, all expertly crafted. Be sure to tour **Choseikaku Villa,** built in 1927 as the home of the priest's beloved mother and employing an amazing variety of woods for its intricately carved transoms, paneling, and other tradi-tional features. Another highlight is the **grotto cave** (beside Byodoin Temple). Stretching 350m (1,155 ft.), it depicts unfortunate souls in hell being burned, chopped to pieces, eaten by animals, and suffering other gruesome forms of torture, for crimes ranging from murder and thievery to drinking too much or having sex with a nun. After passing through caves and Buddhist statues, you then emerge to see a 15m (50-ft.) statue of the Goddess of Mercy, hoping by now that she is, indeed, merciful. On the crest of the hill is the Heights of Eternal Hope for the Future, a huge white-marble installation by a Hiroshima sculptor; its jagged edges resemble a glacier and there's a coffee shop here in what looks like an igloo.

Other things to see include museums showcasing art relating to Buddhism, the tea cere-

Admission to Kosanji Temple, open daily 9am to 5pm, is ¥1,200 for adults, ¥700 for high-school students, and free for children. By the way, near the front gate to Kosanji is a branch of a famous ice-cream shop, (174) **Dolce,** Kosanji-mae Ten (✆ **0845/26-4036**), renowned for its *Hakata-no-shio,* an ice cream that contains salt obtained from seawater (and tastes much better than it sounds). Ikuchijima is also known for its many outdoor sculptures placed around the island and for its 800m (2,640-ft.) Sunset Beach, a popular swimming destination.

BY BICYCLE   A more active way to see the Seto Inland Sea is to cycle across on the **Shimanami Kaido** (also referred to as the Nishi Seto Expressway and the Setouchi Shimanami Seaway), a 70km (43-mile) route between Onomichi in Hiroshima Prefecture and Imabari on Shikoku Island. The route travels over six islands connected by seven bridges, with numerous temples (including the Choseizan Kosanji Temple, above), sightseeing spots, restaurants, and inns along the way. Rental bikes are available at (175) **Onomichi Ekimae Kowan Chushajo,** 9 Higashi Goshocho, Onomichi City (✆ **0848/22-5332**), open daily 7am to 6pm. Bikes cost ¥500 for a day, plus a deposit of ¥1,000. If you wish to make a one-way trip and leave your bike in Imabari or at one of the 13 cycle-rental stops along the way, you forfeit your deposit. The bridges along the route charge a toll, which you deposit into a box on the honor system, for a total of ¥500 if you go all the way to Shikoku (you can buy prepaid toll tickets at the Onomichi cycling shop so you don't have to fish for change). To reach Onomichi from Hiroshima, take the JR Sanyo Honsen line 1½ hours to Onomichi Station (fare: ¥1,450), from which it's a 3-minute walk to the port where the cycling company is located. If you have a Japan Rail Pass, it's quicker to take the Shinkansen 30 minutes to Mihara, followed by a 10-minute local train (fare: ¥230) to Onomichi Station.

If you wish to cycle but have no interest in going all the way to Shikoku (truth be told, the beginning of the biking trail, from Onomichi, is not that interesting), I suggest taking the ferry from Mihara to Setoda (described above) and renting a bike at the **Setoda-cho Kanko Annaisho** (in front of the Hirayama Ikuo Museum; ✆ **0845/27-0051;** daily 9am–5pm). You can cycle around Ikuchijima in a couple of hours. Or, you can bike from Kosanji over the Tatara Ohashi bridge to Oyamazumi Shrine (with a fantastic collection of samurai weaponry; see p. 492), on Omishima island, in about 2 hours. You can drop off your bike at the Shimanami-no-eki Mishima rental shop there, take a bus 9 minutes to Inokuchi-ko (buses depart approximately twice an hour; fare: ¥200), and from there take a high-speed boat for ¥1,250 back to Mihara for the Shinkansen to Hiroshima (at last check, afternoon boat departures were at 3:36 and 4:55pm but you should confirm this).

For more information on cycling the Shimanami Kaido, see the section on Matsuyama in chapter 11.

WHERE TO STAY
Expensive
Rihga Royal Hotel Hiroshima ★★★   The 33-story Rihga Royal stands out as Hiroshima's tallest hotel and has a convenient location in the heart of the city between Hiroshima Castle and Peace Park. It's connected to a large complex called Motomachi CRED, which includes the Pacela shopping mall and Sogo department store. A sophisticated, European atmosphere and polished service make it a favorite among foreign travelers; even the lobby lounge—with its tall ceiling and circular glass facade—makes

for a cheerful meeting place. Large rooms with luxurious furnishings come with plenty of features, including semi-double-size beds in the singles and twins, and magnifying mirrors and lots of counter space in the bathrooms. Rates are based on floor height and room size, but even some of the cheapest twins have views of the castle or Peace Park. The best views, however, are from top floors with panoramas of the Seto Inland Sea (you can even see Miyajima). A nice touch are the pictorial maps in each room describing the view, but the best view of all is afforded from the 33rd-floor Rihga Top lounge.

6–78 Motomachi, Naka-ku, Hiroshima 730-0011. ℂ **082/502-1121.** Fax 082/228-5415. www.rihga.com. 490 units. ¥16,170–¥18,480 single; ¥23,100–¥35,805 double; from ¥40,425 executive double. AE, DC, MC, V. Streetcar: 1, 2, or 6 to Kamiya-cho (1 min.). **Amenities:** 7 restaurants; 2 bars; lounge; babysitting; concierge; executive-level rooms; health club w/gym, atrium-style 25m (82-ft.) pool, Jacuzzi, and sauna (fee: ¥3,150 for pool and sauna; ¥6,300 for everything); health and dental clinic; room service; smoke-free rooms. *In room:* A/C, TV, hair dryer, Internet (fee: ¥1,050 per 24 hr.), minibar.

Moderate

Hotel Granvia Hiroshima ★   Owned by JR West (and offering discounts to holders of the Japan Rail Pass), this hotel is convenient for short stays because it's connected to the Shinkansen (north) side of the station. Inconvenient, however, is that to get to Hiroshima's sights and streetcars, which are on the other side of the station, you have to navigate a confusing underground passage (if you have a rail pass, you can pass through the station, which is much quicker). Rooms are comfortable but are small and have no view, unless you count views of the Shinkansen pulling into the station. A plus are the hotel's many dining options, including one serving Hiroshima-style *okonomiyaki*.

1–5 Matsubara-cho, Minami-ku, Hiroshima 732-0822. ℂ **082/262-1111.** Fax 082/262-4050. www.hgh. co.jp. 410 units. ¥11,319–¥15,939 single; ¥15,592–¥34,650 double. 20% discount for holders of Japan Rail Pass. AE, DC, MC, V. Attached to Hiroshima Station. **Amenities:** 9 restaurants; 2 bars; lounge; outdoor beer terrace (summer only); concierge; access to health club in Hiroshima Station w/gym, indoor pool, and sauna (discount ticket at concierge desk ¥2,000); room service; smoke-free rooms. *In room:* A/C, TV, Internet, minibar.

Hotel Sunroute ★★   Although most hotels in this chain are strictly business hotels, this hotel's excellent location, next to the river and catty-corner from the museum in Peace Memorial Park, plus two very good restaurants with great views, makes it a popular choice for tourists as well. The highest-priced rooms have the additional advantage of views of the park and river; the cheapest rooms, however, are on low floors and have no views whatsoever. Nice touches are bedside reading lights that can be dimmed and chilled glasses in the fridge.

3–3–1 Otemachi, Naka-ku, Hiroshima 730-0051. ℂ **082/249-3600.** Fax 082/249-3677. www.sunroute.jp. 284 units. ¥8,925–¥9,975 single; ¥15,750–¥26,250 double. AE, DC, MC, V. Streetcar: 1 to Chuden-mae (3 min.). Backtrack north to Heiwa Odori and turn left; it's on your left before the river. **Amenities:** 2 restaurants, including Kissui (p. 470); bar; smoke-free rooms. *In room:* A/C, TV, hair dryer, Internet, minibar.

Mitsui Garden Hotel Hiroshima ★   Located on Heiwa Odori (Peace Blvd.), about an 8-minute walk east of Peace Memorial Park, this is a smart-looking business hotel. Although not as convenient as the Sunroute (see above), it's classier, with a chic lobby outfitted in warm, dark browns and small rooms with a contemporary edge, sufficient desk space and individual reading lights. I especially like the rooms on the Ladies' Floor, which are cheerfully done in yellow instead of the usual white. Room air conditioners can be set for either Celsius or Fahrenheit, taking away the guessing for most of us.

9–12 Naka-machi, Naka-ku, Hiroshima 730-0037. ℂ **082/240-1131.** Fax 082/242-3001. www.garden hotels.co.jp/eng. 280 units. ¥9,800–¥10,500 single; ¥15,000–¥18,000 double; from ¥24,000 executive double. AE, DC, MC, V. Streetcar: 1 to Fukuro-machi (5 min.). Walk south (the same direction as your streetcar) on Rijo Dori to Heiwa Odori (there's a small shrine on the corner) and turn left; it will be on your left. **Amenities:** 3 restaurants; bar; executive-level rooms; smoke-free rooms. *In room:* A/C, TV, fridge, hair dryer, Internet.

Inexpensive

Regalo ★★ (**Finds**)   Located on one of Hiroshima's many rivers, about halfway between Hiroshima Station and downtown, this small hotel offers great value and has some English-speaking staff. The cheapest rooms have glazed windows facing the back, while rooms only slightly more expensive have refreshing views of the river. A very atmospheric Italian restaurant also capitalizes on the river view, while across the street, right beside the river, is the hotel's open-air pavilion cafe. In the lobby are telephones with free domestic calls to land lines (in-room phones are only for receiving calls, not for making calls). In short, this establishment is a pleasant surprise compared to most inexpensive lodgings and has more personality than the Toyoko Inn chain.

9–2 Hashimoto-cho, Naka-ku, Hiroshima 730-0015. ✆ 082/224-6300. Fax 082/224-6301. www.regalo-h. com/hiroshima. info@regalo-h.com. 63 units. ¥6,500–¥7,000 single; ¥9,500–¥10,000 double; ¥12,000 triple. Rates include breakfast. AE, DC, MC, V. Streetcar: 1, 2, or 6 to Kanayama-cho (2 min.). Walk back toward the bridge but don't cross it; turn left at the river. Or a 13-min. walk from Hiroshima Station. **Amenities:** Restaurant; cafe; tea lounge; lobby computer w/free Internet; smoke-free rooms. *In room:* A/C, TV, fridge, hair dryer, no phone.

Sansui Ryokan ★   This is a good choice for travelers who like meeting locals rather than staying in impersonal hotels. It's run by the motherly and very hospitable Katou-san, who cheerfully oversees operations, has kimono you can try on for free, and can even arrange lessons in calligraphy or the tea ceremony (¥1,500 each) if you make reservations 3 weeks in advance. It has a cozy communal room offering free coffee and tea, but note that tatami rooms on the second floor are reached by steep stairs. Best of all, it's only a few minutes' walk west of Peace Memorial Park.

4–16 Koami-cho, Naka-ku, Hiroshima 730-0855. ✆ 082/293-9051. Fax 082/233-2377. www.sansui-ryokan.com. 6 units, none with bathroom. ¥4,200 single; ¥7,500 double; ¥10,500 triple. Breakfast ¥600 extra. MC, V. Streetcar: 2 or 3 to Kaomi-cho (1 min.). Walk toward the river, turn left, and then left again. **Amenities:** Rental bikes (¥300 per day); free coffee. *In room:* A/C, TV, no phone.

Toyoko Inn Hiroshima-Eki Shinkansen-Guchi (**Value**)   This business chain has the usual two computers in the lobby with free Internet access (and free Wi-Fi in the lobby for travelers with laptops), free domestic calls from lobby phones, and tiny rooms with all the basics. There are other branches: Hiroshima-Eki Minamiguchi-Migi, 1–26 Nodori-cho (✆ 082/502-1045), but it's a 9-minute walk southwest of the station; and Toyoko Inn Hiroshima Heiwa-Odori, 5–15 Tanaka-machi (✆ 082/504-1045), which is closer to downtown, but it's a 7-minute walk from the nearest streetcar station, past the nightlife district.

2–6–25 Hikari-machi, Higashi-ku, Hiroshima 732-0052. ✆ 082/506-1045. Fax 082/506-1052. www. toyoko-inn.com. 190 units. ¥6,300 single; ¥8,400 double. Rates include Japanese breakfast. AE, DC, MC, V. A 3-min. walk from Hiroshima Station's North Shinkansen exit, straight ahead. **Amenities:** Lobby computer w/free Internet; smoke-free rooms. *In room:* A/C, TV, fridge, hair dryer, Internet.

WHERE TO DINE
Expensive

Atago ★★ TEPPANYAKI   This *teppanyaki* steak restaurant, on the ground floor of an office building on Heiwa (Peace) Odori just east of Rijo Dori, is good and convenient if you're visiting the Peace Memorial Museum just across the river. It's strikingly modern with its marble tables and geometric lines, and chefs prepare steak or seafood before your eyes. The ¥2,900 set steak lunch from the English-language menu includes salad, steak, a vegetable, miso soup, rice, and dessert.

7-20 Nakamachi. ⓒ 082/241-9129. Reservations recommended. Set dinners ¥8,000–¥20,000; set lunches ¥2,900–¥8,000. AE, DC, MC, V. Tues–Sun 11:30am–2pm and 5–9:30pm (last order). Streetcar: 1 to Fukuro-machi (2 min.). Btw. tiny Shirakami-sha Shrine and ANA Hotel on Heiwa (Peace) Odori.

(176) **Kanawa** ★★ (Finds) OYSTERS   There are 10,000 rafts cultivating oysters in Hiroshima Bay, with a yearly output of 30,000 tons of shelled oysters. Needless to say, oysters are a Hiroshima specialty, and this houseboat, moored east of Peace Memorial Park on the Motoyasu River at the Heiwa Odori Bridge, is one of the best places to enjoy them. Although winter is the optimal time for fresh oysters, the owner has his own oyster rafts and can harvest them also in summer, as well as freeze his best stock in January so he's able to serve excellent oysters year-round. This floating restaurant has been here more than 45 years, and dining is in tatami rooms with views of the river. The English-language menu lists set meals that feature oysters prepared various ways, including in the shell, fried, baked, steamed in soy broth, and marinated in vinegar. In addition to oysters, flounder, eel, and a few other dishes are available.

On the Motoyasu River, at Heiwa-Ohashi Bridge. ⓒ 082/241-7416. Reservations recommended. Main dishes ¥1,000–¥2,750; set dinners ¥5,500–¥11,000; set lunches ¥3,300–¥7,150. AE, DC, MC, V. Daily 11am–2pm; Mon–Sat 5–9pm; Sun and holidays 5–8:30pm (last order). Streetcar: 1 to Chuden-mae (3 min.). Backtrack north to Heiwa Odori and turn left; it's just past the Sunroute Hotel.

Moderate

Kissui ★★ KAISEKI   Convenient to Peace Memorial Park, great 15th-floor views, and beautifully prepared kaiseki meals make this an optimal choice for tourists. Choose from the various seasonal kaiseki and *shabu-shabu* set meals from the English-language menu according to your budget. No matter what you choose, you can't go wrong here.

Hotel Sunroute, 15th floor, 3-3-1 Otemachi. ⓒ 082/249-5657. Kaiseki set meals ¥5,775–¥9,975; shabu-shabu set meals ¥5,040–¥8,190; set lunches ¥2,100–¥7,875. AE, DC, MC, V. Daily 11:30am–2pm and 5–8:30pm (last order). Streetcar: 1 to Chuden-mae (see directions to hotel in review of Hotel Sunroute).

Inexpensive

In addition to the choices here, the Pacela building, part of the fancy Motomachi CRED (pronounced "ku-re-do" in Japanese) complex next to the Rihga Royal hotel, offers several ethnic choices, including restaurants serving Vietnamese, Korean, Chinese, Italian, and Indian cuisine.

Anderson Kitchen INTERNATIONAL   Occupying an old, renovated bank building in the Hondori covered shopping arcade, this popular place not far from Peace Memorial Park has a gourmet food department on its ground floor offering baked goods, wine, and imported delicacies, while the second floor has a cafeteria with various counters specializing in different types of food—salads, sandwiches, pizza, pasta, steaks, Chinese dishes, desserts, or drinks. Just pick up a tray and select the items you want. You pay at the end of each counter.

7-1 Hondori. ⓒ 082/247-2403. Dishes ¥735–¥2,360. No credit cards. Thurs–Tues 10am–9:30pm (last order). Streetcar: 1 to Hondori (1 min.); in the Hondori covered shopping arcade 1 block to the east.

(177) **Kushinobo** ★★ KUSHIYAKI   This is a friendly, rub-elbows-with-the-locals kind of place, lively and crowded and decorated with Japanese knickknacks. It's located

due east of the Hondori covered shopping arcade. Although kushiyaki connoisseurs like ordering skewers a la carte, you'll probably be better off ordering from the English-language menu listing only set meals. I always enjoy the Kushinobo-gozen with 10 skewers of vegetables, meat, and seafood plus fresh vegetables, rice, soup, and dessert, but what I like most is watching skewers being prepared behind the counter and the friendly interactions between customers. The chef is a serious fellow, but he speaks English and somehow manages to keep all the orders straight.

Parco-mae, 7–4 Horikawa-cho. © **082/245-9300.** Reservations recommended. Set dinners ¥2,350–¥3,200; set lunches ¥1,200–¥1,500. AE, DC, MC, V. Daily 11:30am–1:30pm and 5–9:30pm (last order). Streetcar: 1, 2, or 6 to Hatchobori (2 min.). Walk south on Chuo Dori 2 blocks to Parco department store and turn right into a covered shopping arcade; take the 1st left and then the 1st right. Look for its Chinese-style red facade.

(178) **No-no-Budou** ★ (Value) JAPANESE BUFFET   This popular buffet restaurant in the Pacela shopping complex specializes in healthy, organic foods, with some 50 choices that change daily but always include choices of Chinese and Japanese dishes, from noodles and fried vegetables to soups and salads. Some seats beside windows provide city views, but avoid the lunchtime rush.

Motomachi CRED complex, 7th floor of Pacela, 78–6 Motomachi. © **082/502-3340.** Buffet lunch ¥1,575; buffet dinner ¥1,890. AE, DC, MC, V. Daily 11am–4pm and 5–10pm. Streetcar: 1, 2, or 6 to Kamiya-cho (1 min.); follow the underground signs for the Astram Line and take the exit on your left.

(179) **Okonomi-Mura** ★★ (Finds) OKONOMIYAKI   Although the people of Osaka claim to have made *okonomiyaki* popular among the masses, the people of Hiroshima claim to have made it an art. Okonomiyaki is a kind of Japanese pancake filled with cabbage, meat, and other fillings. Whereas in Osaka the ingredients are mixed together, in Hiroshima each layer is prepared separately, which means the chefs have to be quite skilled at keeping the entire thing together. This is the best place in town to witness these short-order cooks at their trade, although the building doesn't look as though it contains restaurants. Its name means "okonomiyaki village," and that's what it is—floors of individual stalls, dishing out okonomiyaki (the food still remains a dish for the masses). All offer basically the same menu—sit down at one of the counters and watch how the chef first spreads pancake mix on a hot griddle; follows it with a layer of cabbage, bean sprouts, and bacon; and then adds an egg on top. If you want, you can have yours with *udon* (thick wheat noodles) or *soba* (thin buckwheat noodles). The portions are enormous; this is one of Hiroshima's most beloved establishments. I suggest wandering through and stopping at one that catches your fancy. Or, for a specific recommendation, try (180) **Chii-chan** (© **082/249-8102**) on the second floor, offering food from an English-language menu until 1am (closed on Tues); Chii-chan and his female staff sell 200 to 500 okonomiyaki a day.

5–13 Shintenchi. © **082/241-2210.** Set meals ¥730–¥1,365. No credit cards. Daily 11am–9pm, but some stalls stay open later. Streetcar: 1, 2, or 6 to Hatchobori (2 min.). Walk south on Chuo Dori 4 blocks (you'll see Yamada on the corner) and turn right.

Ristorante Mario ★★ (Value) ITALIAN   Located south across Heiwa Odori from the Peace Memorial Museum, this casual restaurant beckons with a cozy, terra-cotta-hued interior, a glass facade open wide in nice weather, and a kind, welcoming staff. The food is good, too, with about a dozen kinds of pasta on the English-language menu, such as spinach and sweet-potato gnocchi with a cheese sauce. There are also a few main dishes of the day.

4–11 Nakashima-cho. ⓒ **082/248-4956.** Reservations recommended. Pasta ¥1,050–¥1,480; set dinner ¥5,500; set lunches ¥1,180–¥2,280. AE, DC, MC, V. Daily 11:30am–2:30pm; Mon–Fri 5–11pm; Sat–Sun 4–11pm. Streetcar: 1 to Chuden-mae (4 min.). Backtrack north to Heiwa Odori and turn left; it's beyond the river to the left.

(181) **Sushi Tei** ★ (**Value** SUSHI   Excellent sushi at reasonable prices is the reason this establishment is so popular. You'll be seated at the counters, as cooks shout greetings and orders back and forth. Ordering is made easy by an English-language menu. There are many other Sushi Tei restaurants in town, but this is perhaps the most convenient, as it is near the A-Bomb Dome, 1 block south of Aioi Dori, between the Kamiyacho and Genbaku-Dome-mae stops.

1–4–31 Otemachi. ⓒ **082/545-1333.** Sushi sets ¥840–¥2,100. AE, MC, V. Mon–Sat 5pm–midnight; Sun and holidays noon–10pm. Streetcar: 1, 2, or 6 to Kamiyacho (1 min.).

12 MIYAJIMA, SCENIC ISLAND IN THE SETO SEA ★★★

13km (8 miles) SW of Hiroshima

Easily reached in about 30 minutes from Hiroshima, **Miyajima** is a treasure of an island only 2km (1¼ miles) off the mainland in the Seto Inland Sea. No doubt you've seen pictures of its most famous landmark: a huge red *torii*, or shrine gate, rising out of the water. Erected in 1875 and made of camphor wood, it's one of the largest *torii* in Japan, measuring more than 16m (53 ft.) tall. It guards Miyajima's main attraction, Itsukushima Shrine, designated a World Heritage Site in 1996.

With the Japanese penchant for categorizing the "three best" of virtually everything in their country—the three best gardens, the three best waterfalls, and so on—it's no surprise that Miyajima is ranked as one of the three most scenic spots in Japan (the other two are Matsushima in Tohoku; and Amanohashidate, a remote sand spit, on the Japan Sea coast). Only 31 sq. km (12 sq. miles) in area and consisting mostly of steep, wooded hills, it's an exceptionally beautiful island, part of the Seto-Naikai (Inland Sea) National Park that is mostly water, islands, and islets. Of course, this distinction means it can be quite crowded with visitors, particularly in summer.

Miyajima has been held sacred since ancient times. In the olden days, no one was allowed to do anything so human as to give birth or die on the island, so both the pregnant and the ill were quickly ferried across to the mainland. Even today there's no cemetery on Miyajima. Covered with cherry trees that illuminate the island with snowy petals in spring, and with maple trees that emblazon it in reds and golds in autumn, Miyajima is home to tame deer that roam freely through the village, and to monkeys that swing through the woods. It's a delightful island for strolls and hikes—but avoid coming on a weekend.

ESSENTIALS

GETTING THERE   The easiest way to reach Miyajima is from Hiroshima. You can travel from Hiroshima by JR train, streetcar, bus, or boat, but the fastest and most reliable method is the **train,** which departs from Hiroshima Station approximately every 5 to 15 minutes, depending on the time of the day, and costs ¥400 (free for JR Rail Pass holders) for the 26-minute ride to Miyajimaguchi (if you're downtown or in Peace Memorial Park, you might find it easier to catch the train at Nishi-Hiroshima Station).

Otherwise, a **streetcar** takes about an hour from Hiroshima Station to Hiroden Miya-jimaguchi, the last stop, and costs ¥270. All modes of transportation deposit you at Miyajimaguchi, from which it's just a 2-minute walk to the **ferry** bound for Miyajima. There are two ferry companies offering the 10-minute ride to Miyajima for ¥170, but if you have a **Japan Rail Pass,** you can ride on the JR ferry for free.

Alternatively, boats travel from downtown Hiroshima directly to Miyajima in about 45 minutes. Operated by **Aqua Net Hiroshima** (© 082/240-5955; www.aqua-net-h.co.jp), boats depart from Motoyasu-bashi Bridge, near the A-Bomb Dome, 11 to 12 times daily. Fare is ¥1,900 one-way; children pay half fare. Note that service is suspended during inclement weather and when the tide is low.

VISITOR INFORMATION On Miyajima island, stop off at the **Tourist Information Office** (© 0829/44-2011), located in the Miyajima ferry terminal and open daily 9am to 6pm. It has an English-language flyer with a map, and the helpful staff can show where restaurants and accommodations are on the map or even make accommodations reservations for you. For ¥300 you can rent an English-spoken audio guide that describes the 20 places of interest noted on a companion map with a recommended walking tour—a great convenience. For more information, visit **www.miyajima.or.jp** and **www.miyajima-wch.jp**.

GETTING AROUND You can **walk** to all the sights, accommodations, and restaurants listed below. If you wish to visit one of the island's beaches or explore more of the island, rental **bicycles** are available daily 8am to 5pm at the JR ferry pier (last checkout is 3pm) costing ¥320 for 2 hours or ¥1,050 for the entire day. Inquire at the JR ticket window. Otherwise, shuttle **buses** travel to the beaches year-round and twice an hour in July and every 15 minutes in August for ¥300. Ask the Tourist Information Office for a schedule.

EXPLORING THE ISLAND
Seeing the Sights

Miyajima's major attraction, **Itsukushima Shrine ★★**, 1–1 Miyajima-cho (© 0829/44-2020), is less than a 10-minute walk from the ferry pier (turn right from the terminal), at the end of a long narrow pedestrian street called Omotesando Dori that is lined with souvenir shops and restaurants. Founded in 593 to honor three female deities, the wooden shrine is built over the water so that, when the tide is in, it appears as though the shrine is floating. A brilliant vermilion, it contrasts starkly with the wooded hills in the background and the blue of the sky above, casting its reflection in the waters below. If you do happen to see Itsukushima Shrine when the tide is in and it's seemingly floating on water, you should consider yourself very lucky indeed—most of the time the lovely shrine floats above a surface that's only a little more glamorous than mud. That's when imagination comes in handy (the Hiroshima tourist offices may have a tide calendar).

The majority of the shrine buildings are thought to date from the 16th century, preserving the original style of 12th-century architecture, but they have been repaired repeatedly through the centuries. Most of the shrine buildings are closed, but from sunrise to sunset daily (usually 6:30am–6pm in summer, to 5 or 5:30pm in winter), you can walk along the 230m (770-ft.) covered **dock,** which threads its way past the outer part of the main shrine and the oldest *noh* stage in Japan. From the shrine, you'll have a good view of the red *torii* standing in the water. **Bugaku** (festival dances) are staged here 10 times a year (expect those days to be crowded with tour groups). An ancient dance performed to the accompaniment of court music, Bugaku was introduced to Japan centuries ago from India through China and Korea. The performer's costume is orange, matching the shrine around him. Admission to the shrine is ¥300 for adults, ¥200 for high-school students, ¥100 for children.

Turn right upon exiting the shrine. After a few minutes, you'll come to the island's most interesting museum, the **History and Folklore Museum (Rekishi Minzoku Shiryokan)** ★★, 57 Miyajima-cho (✆ **0829/44-2019;** Tues–Sun 8:30am–5pm). It has a colorful, English-language brochure to guide you through the 170-year-old house (which once belonged to a wealthy soy-sauce merchant and is built around a small Japanese garden), as well as through several other buildings. Packed with items donated by the people of Miyajima, the museum is a window into commoners' daily lives in ages past, with farm tools, water jars, cooking objects, carved-wood boxes, furniture, lacquerware, combs, and much more. Be sure to see the narrow, three-room dwelling in the back of the museum complex, typical of the island. Admission is ¥300 for adults, ¥170 for high-school students, and ¥150 for junior-high and elementary students. It will take about 30 minutes to see everything.

Another sight worth exploring is **Daisho-in Temple,** on the slope of Mount Misen, 210 Miyajima-cho (✆ **0829/44-0111;** daily 8am–5pm). One of the most famous Shingon temples in western Japan, it has numerous worthwhile sights spread on its leafy grounds, including a mandala made of colored sand that was created by Tibetan priests, a main hall where worshipers pray for health and contentment, and a hall dedicated to Kobo Daishi, founder of the Shingon sect (his remains are interred on Mount Koya). In Henshokutsu Cave are Buddhist icons and sand gathered from all 88 pilgrimage temples on Shikoku; making a round here is considered as auspicious as visiting the temples themselves. Other halls contain deities thought to bring good health and to save humans from earthly sexual desires. Every year there are fire-walking festivals here, in which worshipers walk over hot coals. An excellent brochure at the entrance describes the various sights, free to the public.

Enjoying Miyajima's Natural World

The other popular thing to do on Miyajima is to visit its highest peak, 525m (1,750-ft.) **Mount Misen.** Signs direct you to Momijidani Park, a pleasant hillside park covered with maple trees (spectacular in autumn) and cherry trees (heavenly in spring) and marked by a picturesque stream. From here, you can take the **Miyajima Ropeway** (✆ 0829;44-0880; www.miyajima-ropeway.info) to Mount Misen; round-trip tickets cost ¥1,800 for adults and ¥900 for children. However, you might wish to enjoy some of the scenery by walking back down (it takes about an hour), in which case one-way tickets cost ¥1,000 and ¥500 respectively. In any case, the summit of Mount Misen, a 30-minute walk from the cable car station, offers splendid views of the Seto-Naikai (Inland Sea) National Park, and Mount Misen itself is home to much of the island's wild monkey population. But it is best known for Kobo Daishi's visit in 806, when he spent a 100-day retreat here and is said to have lit the Eternal Fire, which has reputedly been burning for more than 1,200 years and was used to light the Peace Flame in Hiroshima's Peace Memorial Park.

Miyajima is also known for its beaches. If you're looking to swim, there are two beaches west of the town and shrine: **Suginoura** and **Tsutsumigaura Natural Park** (you can also camp here). Ask at the tourist office for a schedule of shuttle buses that will bring you to the beaches.

WHERE TO STAY

You can see Miyajima easily on a day's trip from Hiroshima, but because it's such a beautiful respite from city life and because most tourists are day-trippers, you'll enjoy the island much more if you stay behind after the last ferry leaves. An added benefit of a longer stay: Itsukushima Shrine is illuminated at night, a gorgeous sight overnighters should not miss. I've therefore included a few recommendations on where to stay, but avoid Golden Week and weekends in July, August, October, and November (when maple leaves are in full color), because accommodations are usually full.

(182) **Guest House Kikugawa** ★ Located in a quiet residential neighborhood an easy walk from the ferry pier, this guesthouse is modern yet adheres to traditional Japanese design with its whitewashed walls, dark timber framing, white paper lanterns, and simple elegance. The owner, Kikugawa-san, speaks English and is an accomplished chef, serving Japanese food in his pleasant restaurant with a restful view of a maple tree (advance reservations required). Six of the guest rooms are Western style and are rather ordinary, reflected in the cheaper room rates below. The two other more expensive rooms face the front; the smaller is a tatami room, while the larger has a tatami area and a loft with Western-style beds. Because this place is small, make reservations 6 months in advance if you want to stay here in July, August, October, or November.

66615–796 Miyajima-cho, Hatsukaichi-shi, Hiroshima-ken 739-0511. © **0829/44-0039.** Fax 0829/44-2773. www.kikugawa.ne.jp. 8 units. ¥7,140 single; ¥12,600–¥17,850 double. ¥1,050 more per person in peak season. Breakfast ¥1,050 extra; dinner ¥3,675 and ¥5,250 extra. MC, V. A 3-min. walk from the ferry terminal; walk through the short tunnel in front of the terminal toward the right and then turn right. **Amenities:** Restaurant; Wi-Fi in lobby. *In room:* A/C, TV, hair dryer.

(183) **Iwaso Ryokan** ★★★ (Finds) This is the most famous *ryokan* on the island, and with a history spanning more than 150 years, it was also the first ryokan to open on Miyajima, which explains its idyllic location in Momijidani Park. It's highly recommended for a splurge, with the price dependent on the room, its view, and the meals you select (when booking your room, be sure to specify any dietary needs such as vegetarian food only, whether you want a Western breakfast, or whether there are Japanese foods you cannot eat). The newest part of the ryokan was built in 1981, and though some of its newer rooms have very peaceful and relaxing views of a stream and woods and even Itsukushima Shrine, I prefer the rooms dating from about 80 years ago; they have more individuality. If you really want to go all out and live like a feudal lord, there are also a couple of separate *hanare* (cottages) that are more than 80 years old, all exquisitely decorated. Open your shoji screens to see maples, a gurgling brook, and woods, all in utter privacy. You'll be treated like royalty here, but of course you have to pay for it. Dinner is served in your room, while breakfast is served in its restaurant (open also for lunch to the public).

Momijidani, 345 Miyajima-cho, Hatsukaichi-shi, Hiroshima-ken 739-0522. © **0829/44-2233.** Fax 0829/44-2230. www.iwaso.com. 38 units, 7 without bathroom. ¥19,950–¥42,000 per person. Cottages ¥36,900–¥42,150 per person. Rates are higher during peak season and nights before holidays. Rates include 2 meals. AE, V. A 15-min. walk from the ferry pier in Momijidani Park. Pickup service available. **Amenities:** Restaurant; hot-spring baths; lobby computer (¥150 for 15 min.). *In room:* A/C, TV, minibar, hair dryer.

(184) **Miyajima Morinoyado** ★★ (Value) You're forgiven if you pass this place by, thinking it must be an exclusive *ryokan*. Indeed, if it weren't a municipally owned People's Lodge (Kokumin Shukusha), rates here would easily be three times as much as they are. Though modern, it has a lovely Japanese design with a lobby overlooking a carp pond. On the other hand, the many school groups and families staying here leave no doubt that it's a public lodge, and it's quite a hike from the ferry pier. Both tatami rooms and Western-style twins—simple but spacious and spotless—are available, some with views of the bay. The public baths look onto rock gardens. Reservations should be made

11 months in advance, especially for August, but sometimes there are cancellations; when I dropped by on a weekday in June, rooms were available. Both Western and Japanese breakfasts, served in a restaurant, are available; dinners are Japanese and are served in your room.

Miyajima-cho, Hatsukaichi-shi, Hiroshima-ken 739-0588. ℂ **0829/44-0430.** Fax 0829/44-2248. www. morinoyado.jp/english. 30 units, 26 with bathroom, 4 with toilet only. ¥5,040–¥5,775 per person room only; ¥9,555–¥11,865 per person with 2 meals. ¥735 more per person on Sat, nights before holidays, and during peak season (New Year's and mid-July to Aug). Discounts given for children. No credit cards. A 25-min. walk from the ferry pier, across from the aquarium and just before the tunnel. **Amenities:** Restaurant. *In room:* A/C, TV.

Momiji-so ★★ This small, Japanese-style house has a great location in Momijidani Park, not far from the ropeway to Mount Misen, and has been in business for 90 years. Tatami rooms vary in size, though all have artwork, flowers, and views of the surrounding park; the best looks out over a koi pond. A plus is the nice outdoor Japanese restaurant serving noodles, barbecued conger eel on rice, and other dishes—weather permitting, you'll dine outside. Not much English is spoken, but they're used to foreigners and are very kind. Note that during Golden Week and October through November, you must take both of your meals here.

Momijidani-koennai, Miyajima-cho, Hatsukaichi-shi, Hiroshima-ken 739-0500. ℂ **0829/44-0077.** Fax 0829/44-0076. www.gambo-ad.com. 7 units, 4 with bathroom. ¥8,400 per person without meals; ¥10,500 per person with breakfast; ¥16,800 per person with 2 meals. No credit cards. A 25-min. walk from the ferry pier in Momijidani Park. Pickup service available. *In room:* A/C, TV, minibar, no phone.

⑱⑤ **Ryoso Kawaguchi ★★** This 300-year-old home, with whitewashed walls, wood floors, and exposed beams, has a traditional atmosphere, and modern updates like Wi-Fi and two private-use baths make it comfortable. Tatami accommodations include two airy rooms with lofts for sleeping and a two-room suite good for families. The dining room and bar overlook a garden courtyard, while the third-floor lounge has a view of the five-storied pagoda. The ninth-generation innkeepers speak English and are gracious and welcoming.

469 Miyajima-cho, Hatsukaichi-shi, Hiroshima-ken 739-0554. ℂ **0829/44-0018.** Fax 0829/44-2361. www.gambo-ad.com. 10 units, all with toilet, none with bathroom. ¥7,000 single; ¥13,000–¥14,000 double; ¥19,500–¥21,000 triple. Breakfast ¥1,050 extra; dinner ¥3,675 extra. No credit cards. A 10-min. walk from the ferry pier. **Amenities:** Restaurant; karaoke bar; lobby computer (¥100 for 15 min.). *In room:* A/C, TV, Wi-Fi.

WHERE TO DINE

There are no addresses in this section, because the village is small, and the address would only be meaningful to the postman.

⑱⑥ **Fujitaya ★★ (Finds** ANAGOMESHI Although the building itself is not old, this pleasant restaurant has a history of more than 80 years and preserves a traditional atmosphere with its wooden ceiling, shoji lamps, and a back courtyard with a maple tree, moss-covered rocks, and water running from a bamboo pipe into a pool carved into a flat rock. Fujitaya serves only *anagomeshi* (barbecued conger eel on rice), which comes with side dishes (such as pickled vegetables), soup, and tea. It closes when it runs out of *anago.*

ℂ **0829/44-0151.** Anagomeshi meal ¥2,300. No credit cards. Daily 11am–4pm. A 20-min. walk from the ferry pier, on the right side of the road leading toward Daishoin after exiting from Itsukushima Shrine. Look for its name written on an oversize paddle on its facade.

(187) **Koumitei** ★ OKONOMIYAKI   Convenient to the ferry pier, this simple restaurant with counter, table, and tatami dining stays open later than most restaurants on the island and is one of the cleanest *okonomiyaki* restaurants we've seen. Both Hiroshima-style (which is prepared for you) and Kansai-style (which you prepare yourself) okonomiyaki are available from the English-language menu.

(C) **0829/44-0177.** Okonomiyaki ¥780–¥1,300; set meals ¥1,000–¥1,300. No credit cards. Thurs–Tues 11am–2:30pm and 5–9pm. A 1-min. walk from the ferry pier, catty-corner to the right.

(188) **Tonookajaya** NOODLES   Dine inside or out at this tiny teahouselike shop next to the five-story pagoda. The shop serves mostly *udon* (thick wheat noodles), including udon with tempura, but it also offers a few other choices on its English-language menu, including *amazake* (a sweet rice porridge; served Oct–May). What makes this place especially interesting is the 200-year-old pine tree out front that has been guided through the centuries to attain its unique, horizontal shape. You can also come here just for drinks.

(C) **0829/44-2455.** Main dishes ¥650–¥750. No credit cards. Daily 10am–5pm. A 10-min. walk from the ferry pier on the hill with the 5-story pagoda, down steps leading toward the bay.

Shikoku

The smallest of Japan's four main islands, Shikoku is also the one least visited by foreigners. That's surprising considering the natural beauty of its rugged mountains, its mild climate, and its most famous monuments—88 sacred Buddhist temples. Many Japanese wish to make a pilgrimage to all 88 temples at least once in their lifetime as a tribute to the great Buddhist priest Kobo Daishi, who was born on Shikoku in 774 and who founded the Shingon sect of Buddhism.

This pilgrimage has been popular since the Edo Period, as many believe that a successful completion of the tour exonerates Buddhist followers from rebirth. It used to take almost 2 months to visit all 88 temples on foot. Even today, you can see pilgrims making their rounds dressed in white—only now they're more likely to go by organized tour buses, which cut travel time down to 2 weeks.

GETTING TO SHIKOKU For centuries, the only way to reach Shikoku was by boat. However, the 1988 completion of the Seto Ohashi Bridge, which links Shikoku with Okayama Prefecture and accommodates both cars and trains, changed Shikoku forever. In 1999, the completion of a series of bridges spanning six scenic islands in the Seto Inland Sea connected Shikoku with Hiroshima Prefecture (complete with cycling paths offering scenic views and now one of Shikoku's hottest attractions), followed by a third bridge, for cars only, linking Shikoku with Kobe.

In any case, Shikoku is no longer as far off the beaten track as it used to be, because access is now so easy. Shinkansen travelers can simply transfer in Okayama to trains bound for either Takamatsu or Matsuyama. The energetic can even cycle from Honshu to Shikoku on the Shimanami Kaido, the bike path stretching from Hiroshima Prefecture to Ehime Prefecture.

---

1 TAKAMATSU ★

805km (500 miles) W of Tokyo; 71km (44 miles) S of Okayama

The second-largest town on Shikoku, with a population of 427,000, Takamatsu, the capital of Kagawa Prefecture, is on the northeastern coast of the island, overlooking the Seto Inland Sea. Takamatsu means "high pine," and the city served as the feudal capital of the powerful Matsudaira clan from 1642 until the Meiji Restoration in 1868. The Matsudairas are responsible for Takamatsu's most famous site, Ritsurin Garden, one of the most outstanding gardens in Japan. Takamatsu also boasts more bonsai nurseries than anywhere else in Japan, while nearby is Kotohiragu Shrine, a popular mountaintop destination that requires a real workout just to see.

ESSENTIALS

GETTING THERE **By Plane** JAL flies from Tokyo's Haneda Airport (¥29,500 for a regular one-way ticket; as low as ¥12,100 if purchased in advance) in 1 hour and 20 minutes. There is also air service from Kagoshima and Okinawa. An airport bus delivers passengers downtown in about 45 minutes for ¥740.

By Train   **JR's Marine Liner** trains depart from Okayama Station approximately twice an hour, reaching Takamatsu in an hour; the fare is ¥1,470. From Matsuyama, trains take about 2½ hours and cost ¥5,500.

By Bus   JR buses (© 03/3844-1950; www.jrbuskanto.co.jp) depart Tokyo Station's Yaesu south exit nightly at 8:20 and 8:50pm (the latter bus also picks up passengers at Shinjuku Station at 9:30pm), reaching Takamatsu at 5:48am and 7:04am respectively the next day. The one-way fare is ¥10,000.

VISITOR INFORMATION   The **Takamatsu Information Plaza** (© 087/851-2009; daily 9am–6pm), located outside the main exit of the train station in a small building on the left side of the circular plaza, offers an English-language map of the city. You can also pick up the Shikoku Passport; although in Japanese only, it gives slight discounts to some of the listings below, including Ritsurin Garden, Shikoku Mura, ANA Hotel Clement, and Royal Park Hotel Annex in addition to others. In addition, the Kagawa Welcome Card gives discounts to foreigners; you must download it at **www.21kagawa.com/visitor**.

Information is available online at **www.city.takamatsu.kagawa.jp/kankou**.

If you crave a bit of news from home or plan to remain in the area, head for **I-Pal Kagawa,** 1–11–63 Bancho (© 087/837-5908; www.i-pal.or.jp/en; Tues–Sun 9am–6pm), located about a 15-minute walk south of Takamatsu Station on Chuo Dori in the northwest corner of Central (Chuo) Park. Here you'll find magazines and newspapers in many languages, CNN on the tube, and three computers you can use free of charge for 30 minutes. This is also a good place to find out what's going on in the area.

INTERNET ACCESS   In addition to I-Pal Kagawa, **E-Topia Kagawa** (© 087/822-0111), on the fourth and fifth floors of the Symbol Tower next to Takamatsu Station, has some 20 computers you can use for 1 hour for free (be sure to bring your passport with you for identification). It's open Tuesday to Sunday from 10am to 8pm.

ORIENTATION & GETTING AROUND   Takamatsu Station, Takamatsu Port, and the local streetcar terminus are clustered at the north edge of the city on the coast of the Seto Inland Sea, in a new urban development called Sunport Takamatsu, which also includes the 30-story Takamatsu Symbol Tower, convention halls, exhibition and concert facilities, restaurants, shops, and offices. Office workers take respite along the Waterfront Harbor Walk and Tamamo Park, site of Takamatsu Castle's remains.

Most of the hotels and restaurants listed below, as well as Ritsurin Garden, are located south and southeast of Sunport Takamatsu. **Chuo Dori** is the town's main avenue, running south from Sunport to Ritsurin Garden and beyond. Bisecting Chuo Dori and paralleling it to the east are shopping arcades. In fact, a total of 4km (2½ miles) of covered shopping arcades make Takamatsu's the longest in Japan.

Although the main attractions of Takamatsu are spread out, they're easily reached from Takamatsu Station by **JR train** or by a commuter streetcar called the **Kotoden Line.** The Kotoden streetcar terminus, called **Kotoden Chikko Station,** is a 2-minute walk from Takamatsu Station's main exit, past the ANA hotel and to the right. Fares start at ¥180. Two stops south on the Kotoden streetcar (or a 25-min. walk from Takamatsu Station) is **Kawaramachi Station,** the heart of the city where you'll find many department stores, restaurants, and nightspots.

SEEING THE SIGHTS
Ritsurin Garden ★★★   Ritsurin Garden was once the summer retreat of the Matsudaira family. Work on the park began in the 1600s and took about 100 years to complete.

Using the backdrop of adjacent Mount Shiun in a principle known as "borrowed landscaping," the 75-hectare (185-acre) park, Japan's largest Cultural Heritage Garden, incorporates the pine-clad mountain into its overall visual design. Basically, the garden, arranged around six spring-fed ponds and 13 scenic mounds, can be divided into two parts: a traditional, classical, southern garden; and a modern, northern garden, once a lord's private hunting grounds and with wide grassy lawns and huge lotus ponds. No matter the season, something is always in bloom, from plum and cherry trees in spring to camellias in winter (a bulletin board at the entrance identifies what's in bloom). English-speaking volunteers are on hand most days to provide free tours if you wish.

The **southern garden** is the more interesting one, representing what's called a strolling garden, in which each bend of the footpath brings another perspective into view, another combination of rock, tree, and mountain. The garden is absolutely exquisite, and what sets it apart are its twisted, contorted pines. On one of my visits, a mist was rolling off Mount Shiun, lending mystery to the landscape; what better fits the image of traditional Japan than mist and pine trees? Altogether, there are some 1,400 pine trees and 350 cherry trees in Ritsurin Garden, which you should tour in a counterclockwise fashion to fully appreciate the changing views. Although I consider this garden just as beautiful as those in Okayama and Kanazawa, tall buildings on its eastern periphery detract from its overall effect; without them I would give this garden top rating.

There are a couple of things you can stop and see during your tour of the park. In the northern garden are the **Sanuki Folk Art Museum (Sanuki Mingei Kan),** which is included in the park's admission fee and displays local folk art and handicrafts such as ceramics, lacquerware, furniture, and items used in daily Edo life (regrettably, there are no English-language descriptions); and the **Commerce and Industry Hall (Shoko-shoreikan),** which sells local products, including kites, masks, woodcarvings, umbrellas, fans, and food items and sponsors craft-making demonstrations on weekends and holidays. But my favorite thing to do is drop by **Scooping the Moon House (Kikugetsu-tei)** in the southern garden, with its teahouse dating from feudal days overlooking a pond. Powdered tea, used in tea ceremonies, costs ¥710 for adults and ¥550 for children. It takes about an hour to see the southern garden; add another half-hour if you also take in the northern garden.

1-20-16 Ritsurin-cho. ℭ **087/833-7411.** www.pref.kagawa.jp/ritsurin. Admission ¥400 adults, ¥170 children. Daily sunrise–sunset (approx. 7am–5pm in winter, 5:30am–7pm June–Aug). Kotoden streetcar: Ritsurin-koen Station (10 min.). JR train: If you have a Japan Rail Pass, go by JR train toward Tokushima; get off at Ritsurin-koen Kita Guchi, turn right out of the station, follow the tracks to the 1st street, and turn right (4 min.).

Shikoku Mura Village ★★   On the northeastern edge of town, this open-air museum boasts more than 30 traditional houses, sheds, and storehouses dating from the Edo Period and collected from all over Shikoku. The structures, picturesquely situated on the wooded slope of Yashima Hill, include thatch-roofed homes of farmers and fishermen, century-old cottages used by lighthouse keepers, a rustic tea-ceremony house, a 250-year-old rural *kabuki* stage, rice and soy-sauce storehouses, and sheds for pressing sugar and for producing paper out of mulberry bark. There's also a suspended bridge made of vines, once a familiar sight in Shikoku as a means for crossing the island's many gorges and ravines; if you look closely, however, you'll see that this one is reinforced by cables. It takes at least 1½ hours to stroll through the village (and there are lots of stairs). I heartily recommend a visit if you haven't had the opportunity to see similar villages in

(Finds)   Bonsai Is Big in Kinashi

If you've long admired the art of **bonsai**—the crafting of miniature pines and other trees through skillful manipulation—you might wish to take a stroll through **Kinashi,** a western suburb of Takamatsu. With more than 80 nurseries, half of them cultivating bonsai, Kinashi has been a center of bonsai since the Edo Period and remains the largest bonsai-growing region in Japan. To reach it, take a local JR train from Takamatsu Station two stations to Kinashi, walk north a few minutes, and then turn right into Bonsai Street. One of the largest nurseries, (189) **Nakanishi Chinshouen** ((*C*) **087/882-0526;** www.kinashi-bonsai.com/chinshouen), across the street from the station, is owned by a fifth-generation bonsai cultivator; some of the larger pines here were started by his ancestors. You're welcome to walk through this and other nearby nurseries. This is the only place I've ever seen bonsai groves, with hundreds of tiny pine trees planted in rows. On the 5th, 15th, and 20th of each month from 9am to 5pm, there's a Bonsai Auction on Bonsai Street, where serious bidding takes place.

Takayama or Shirakawago, as they convey, better than anything else, rural life in Japan in centuries past.

91 Yashima-naka-machi. (*C*) **087/843-3111.** Admission ¥800 adults, ¥500 high-school students, ¥300 children. Daily 8:30am–6pm (Nov–Mar to 5:30pm). Kotoden streetcar: Kotoden Yashima Station (about a 20-min. ride) and then a 5-min. walk. JR train: Take a JR train bound for Tokushima and get off at Yashima Station (15 min.).

EASY SIDE TRIPS FROM TAKAMATSU

If you're spending more than a day in Takamatsu, these major attractions are worth the trek.

KOTOHIRA ★★   If you have 4 hours to spare, one of the best historical side trips you can take is to Kotohira, home of Japan's oldest kabuki theater and of **Kotohiragu Shrine** ★★, 892 Kotohira-cho ((*C*) **0877/75-2121**), one of Japan's oldest and most popular shrines (also known as Kompira Shrine). It takes about an hour to reach Kotohira by JR train from Takamatsu, but that isn't the end of it—the shrine itself is at the top of 785 granite steps, which on average take 40 minutes to ascend. If that's too much for you, you can hire one of the porters who wait at the bottom of the steps, but they'll take you only to the *omon* (main gate), which is reached after climbing 365 steps. It costs ¥5,300 one-way and ¥6,800 round-trip to ride in these palanquins. What decadence.

Otherwise, begin the long trek up to Kotohiragu Shrine by taking the JR Kotohira Station's only exit. Walk straight past a small park (with a wooden tower lighthouse that served as a beacon for traveling pilgrims in the Edo Period), and pass the Kotoden Station. (You can also travel from Takamatsu in 1 hr. by Kotoden streetcar.) Turn left at the T-junction with a post office. You'll soon see, to the right, a sloping, narrow street lined with souvenir shops (though I wouldn't buy anything on the way up). Eventually, you'll reach the first flight of stairs. If you're making a detour to the kabuki theater (described below), turn left after the 22nd step, from which the theater is only a 3-minute walk uphill on the right.

At about the 475th step (in case you're counting), just past the stables to the right, you'll find **Shoin,** built in 1659 to receive important visitors. Its doors and alcoves contain paintings by Maruyama Okyo, a famous 18th-century landscape artist, making the building an Important Cultural Property. Especially famous is the painting of two tigers drinking from a stream. It's open daily from 8:30am to 4:30pm; admission is ¥500 for adults, ¥200 for students, and free for children. After another 15-minute workout, you'll reach **Hongu,** the main shrine, where you'll be rewarded with a sweeping view of the surrounding countryside as well as of the shrine itself. Popularly known as Kompira-San, Kotohiragu Shrine was originally founded in the 11th century but has been rebuilt many times, with the main shrine buildings re-erected about 100 years ago. It's dedicated to the Shinto god of seafarers and voyagers (look for the Votive Picture Pavilion with photos of ships and other vessels that have asked for blessings) and, in recent years, has even become revered as the protector of foreign travelers. For my part, I was just thankful for having successfully traveled the stairs to the shrine. And to be honest, the shrine itself is not the main draw; most of the three million annual hikers, it seems, come for the hike itself and the comradeship it inspires. If you're still game (and want to say you went the entire distance), you can continue another 583 steps to **Okunoyashiro.** You can say your prayers here, but the inner shrine is closed to the public. Kotohiragu Shrine is open daily from sunrise to sunset (7pm in summer; 5pm in winter).

Because you're in the vicinity, you should make every effort to see the highly recommended ⑲ **Kompira Grand Playhouse** (**Komnpira O-Shibai** or Kanamaruza) ★, 241 Otsu, Kotohira-cho (© **0877/73-3846**), which was built to entertain the masses flocking to Kotohiragu Shrine. Located about 300m (985 ft.) to the left of the 22nd step as you ascend, and then up the hill on the right, it's the oldest existing kabuki stage in Japan, stunning in its simplicity and delightful in its construction. As there was no electricity when it was built in 1835, the sides of the hall are rows of *shoji* screens and wooden coverings, which can be opened and closed to control the amount of light reaching the stage. Notice the check-in counter at the entrance for *geta* (wooden sandals), *tatami* seating, paper lanterns, and revolving stage, which was turned by four men in the basement (be sure to check out the basement). You can also tour the various makeup and dressing rooms behind the stage and watch a video in Japanese. It's open daily from 9am to 5pm (except for 16 days in Apr when kabuki is performed to sellout crowds) and charges an admission of ¥500 for adults, ¥300 for junior-high and high-school students, and ¥200 for children (the Shikoku Passport offers a discount). Ask for the English-language handout.

BENESSE ART SITE NAOSHIMA ★★★ Naoshima, a small island in the Seto Inland Sea, is devoted to contemporary art in a big way, with two striking museums,

⒡Fun Facts Doggedly Faithful

In the olden days, faithful who could not manage a trip to Kotohiragu Shrine in person would set a barrel adrift at sea, along with an offering and a plea for passing fishermen to take the offering to the shrine on their next pilgrimage. The more resourceful would even send dogs on the pilgrimage, with a tag that read "Kotohira Pilgrimage" and a pouch of money around their necks. Travelers who encountered the dogs used the money to buy the animals food and passage on boats until the dogs reached their destination.

interactive installations housed in traditional buildings, and outdoor sculptures spread throughout the island, making it the nation's major destination for cutting-edge art in Japan. But more than that, Naoshima is a place of discovery, with a unique symbiotic relationship between natural scenic beauty and art. Plan on at least 6 hours for the experience, including the 50-minute ferry from Takamatsu. Note that for art venues closed on Monday, if Monday is a national holiday, they stay open but will close the next day, on Tuesday, instead.

Shikoku Kisen ferries (© 087/821-6798) depart Takamatsu Port five times daily (¥970 for a round-trip ticket) for Miyanoura Port on Naoshima (you can also reach Naoshima from Uno in Okayama Prefecture's in 20 min.; one-way fare: ¥280). At Miyanoura there's a **Tourist Information Center** (Umino-eki Naoshima), open daily 8:30am to 6pm and offering an English-language map of the island, rental bikes (¥500 for the day), and schedules for buses that travel to all art sites (bus fare: ¥100 per ride).

From Miyanoura Port, you can take the bus 5 minutes (stop: Nokyo-mae, in front of JA Bank) or walk 30 minutes to Honmura, where you'll find a handful of **Art House Projects** ★★★, old buildings that have been remodeled by artists into interactive art installations. At Kadoya (by Miyajima Tatsuo), you'll see a 200-year-old farmhouse that contains a darkened room with a shallow pool of water and submerged colored numbers that blink on and off at varying frequencies, with the speed of each number controlled by an islander and each number representing a human life. Go'o Jinja is an Edo-Era shrine that has been transformed by Sugimoto Hiroshi, with glass stairs, white rocks, and a narrow underground passageway that leads to a tomblike space. Ishibashi is a restored family home of a salt-producing family now housing paintings by Senji Hiroshi, while Gokaisho, where residents once gathered to play the Japanese game *go,* contains Suda Yoshiro's *Camelia* artwork. Haisha is a transformed dental clinic now housing sculptures and graphic art, but my favorite is Minamidera, a stark wooden building designed by famed architect Tadao Ando, with an installation by James Turrell called *Backside of the Moon.* After being led into a pitch-black room by staff, you wait about 10 minutes until your eyes adjust, when you see a faint glow ahead. You're told you can walk to the light to touch it, only to find . . . well, you'll have to "see" for yourself. Art House Projects are open Tuesday to Sunday 10am to 4:30pm and cost ¥1,000 for a combination ticket for all six (children 14 and younger get in free to all of Naoshima's art museums). Buy your ticket at the tourist office above, at Ueda's Tobacconist (across from Nokyo-mae bus stop), or the Honmura Lounge & Archive beside the bus stop.

From Honmura, it's a 10-minute bus ride and a walk uphill to **Benesse House** ★★★, a museum designed by Tadao Ando and containing an expensive hotel (© 087/892-3223; rates begin at ¥34,650 for a twin), cafe, restaurant, and art by Jasper Johns, Robert Rauschenberg, Frank Stella, Jackson Pollock, Andy Warhol, and others who created site-specific art that takes Ando's architecture and Naoshima's natural beauty into consideration. It's open daily 8am to 9pm, with admission costing ¥1,000.

The nearby **Chichu Art Museum** ★★ (© 087/892-3755; www.chichu.jp), 3 minutes away by bus (there's a free shuttle bus btw. the two museums weekends and holidays) or a 30-minute walk, was also designed by Ando. It's a striking concrete structure with sharp angles, contemplative spaces, and only a few works of art, including a room of Monet paintings, light installations by James Turrell, and a room by Walter De Maria containing a huge granite ball and gold-leaf-covered bars. This museum is open Tuesday to Sunday 10am to 6pm (to 5pm Oct–Feb) and costs ¥2,000. From here, the bus back to Miyanoura Port takes 20 minutes.

Information on Benesse Art Site Naoshima is available at © 087/892-2887 or **www.naoshima-is.co.jp**. General information on Naoshima is available from the Naoshima Tourism Association at © 087/892-2299 or **www.naoshima.net**.

WHERE TO STAY

Expensive

ANA Hotel Clement Takamatsu ★★ In Sunport across from Takamatsu Station (and offering a discount to holders of a Japan Rail Pass), the city's most expensive hotel is also its most conspicuous: sleek, 21 stories high, cutting across the landscape like a white sail, and by far the best place in town. It's designed with an aquatic theme, with a cascading fountain in the sunlit lobby lounge, carpets and chandeliers with wavy patterns, bubbled or crackled glass in public places, and curving, seductive lines everywhere, even in corridors. It's the kind of place sightseers happily return to after a hard day's work. Room rates are based on size, floor, view, and amenities, with the best twin and double rooms offering views of the sea or nearby Tamamo Park, even from windows in the bathroom. But the least expensive rooms are also recommendable—spacious and chic with contemporary furnishings and good bedside reading lamps. Ask for a room on the highest available floor. Note that the cheapest double has only a semi-double bed.

1–1 Hamano-cho, Takamatsu 760-0011. © **877/424-2449** in the U.S. and Canada or 087/811-1111. Fax 087/811-1100. www.ichotelsgroup.com. 300 units. ¥12,470–¥18,480 single; ¥20,790–¥40,425 double. 10% discount with Japan Rail Pass, Kagawa Welcome Card, or Shikoku Passport. AE, DC, MC, V. Station: Takamatsu (1 min.). **Amenities:** 4 restaurants; bar; lounge; beer garden (summer only); concierge; room service; smoke-free rooms. *In room:* A/C, TV, hair dryer, Internet, minibar.

Moderate

Rihga Hotel Zest This beige-brick hotel, consisting of a main building and newer annex, appeals to both business and leisure travelers with its convenient location on Chuo Dori next to Hyogomachi shopping arcade. It has an accommodating staff and offers a variety of rooms at different price ranges. The cheapest rooms, including all singles, are located in the main building and are narrow with tiny bathrooms. More expensive and spacious annex rooms sport shoji screens and window panels that close for complete darkness. There are also four combination rooms with both tatami areas and beds.

9–1 Furujinmachi, Takamatsu 760-0025. © **087/822-3555.** Fax 087/822-7516. www.rihga.com. 122 units. ¥7,855–¥9,470 single; ¥15,015–¥28,875 double. 10% discounts with the Kagawa Welcome Card; be sure to mention the card when making your reservation and show it when you check in. AE, DC, MC, V. Station: Takamatsu (a 10-min. walk south of the station, on Chuo Dori just past Hyogomachi arcade). **Amenities:** 4 restaurants; lounge; rooftop beer garden (summer only); lobby computer w/free Internet; smoke-free rooms. *In room:* A/C, TV, hair dryer, minibar.

Royal Park Hotel Annex This business hotel, with imitation Art Deco decor in its lobby and hallways, offers mostly single rooms in a convenient location near Kawaramachi Station in the heart of the city's shopping and nightlife district. Rooms, though small, are pleasantly decorated, but it's been awhile since I've seen pink-tiled bathrooms like those here. The cheapest singles are on lower floors where traffic is noisiest. The hotel's seven twins are all corner rooms, bright and large for the price with vanity/sink separate from the—you guessed it—pink bathrooms (which also have a sink).

11–1 Fukudamachi, Takamatsu 760-0048. © **087/823-1111.** Fax 087/823-1123. 117 units. ¥5,500–¥7,850 single; ¥13,860–¥16,200 double. AE, DC, MC, V. Kotoden streetcar: Kawaramachi (5 min.). Take the west exit (in the direction of the bus stop) and walk north on Ferry Dori, turning right at the 1st traffic signal and crossing the tracks; you'll see the hotel on the left. **Amenities:** 2 free rental bikes; lobby computers w/free Internet; smoke-free rooms. *In room:* A/C, TV, hair dryer, Internet, minibar.

> **(Tips)   A Double or a Twin?**
>
> For the sake of convenience, the price for two people in a room is listed as a "double" in this book. Japanese hotels, however, differentiate between rooms with a double bed or two twin beds, usually with different prices. Although most hotels charge more for a twin room, sometimes the opposite is true; if you're looking for a bargain, therefore, be sure to inquire about prices for both. Note, too, that hotels usually have more twin rooms than doubles, for the simple reason that Japanese couples, used to their own futon, traditionally prefer twin beds.

Inexpensive

In addition to the choice here, there's the **Toyoko Inn Takamatsu Hyogomachi,** 3–1 Hyogomachi (✆ **087/821-1045;** www.toyoko-inn.com), an 8-minute walk southeast of Takamatsu Station on Chuo Dori beside the Hyogomachi arcade. It offers the usual freebies for which this chain is known, including lobby computers with Internet access; Wi-Fi in the lobby, domestic phone calls from lobby phones, nightly in-house movies, and Internet access in rooms. Singles go for ¥6,090 and twins/doubles for ¥8,190, including breakfast.

Business Hotel Parkside Takamatsu ★ (Value)   Although a business hotel, this small, boutique-like hotel has a great location across from Ritsurin Garden. Rooms are small, but who cares when you can open the window and look out over the fabled garden? Some rooms have only a partial view or none at all, so be sure to request a ringside seat on an upper floor (note that smoke-free rooms, unfortunately, are on the third floor). A bonus: The hotel provides discount tickets to Ritsurin Garden.

1–3–1 Ritsurin-cho, Takamatsu 760-0073. ✆ **087/837-5555.** Fax 087/837-3000. 116 units. ¥4,950–¥5,400 single; ¥7,950–¥8,400 double; ¥11,900 triple. AE, DC, MC, V. Kotoden streetcar: Ritsurin Koen (10 min.). Walk straight from the west exit and turn right on Chuo Dori; the hotel will be on the right. **Amenities:** Restaurant; free rental bikes; lobby computers w/free Internet. *In room:* A/C, TV, fridge, hair dryer, Internet.

WHERE TO DINE

Takamatsu is known throughout Japan for its *sanuki udon*—thick white noodles made from wheat flour. Takamatsu also has a fresh supply of fish from the Seto Inland Sea.

Expensive

Szechwan ★★★ CHINESE   Classic standards, such as bird's-nest soup, sweet-and-sour pork, and chicken with cashew nuts, receive innovative makeovers at this elegant 29th-floor restaurant with white tablecloths and background jazz music. Add panoramic views of the Seto Inland Sea and excellent service, and you're in for a memorable dining experience.

29th floor, Takamatsu Symbol Tower, 2 1 Sunport. ✆ **087/811-0477.** Main dishes ¥1,800–¥3,500; set lunches ¥1,500–¥3,500; set dinners ¥5,250–¥10,500. AE, DC, MC, V. Daily 11am–3pm and 5–10pm. Station: Takamatsu (1 min.).

Moderate

(191) **Tenkatsu** TEMPURA/SUSHI   This well-known tempura and sushi restaurant is in a modern-looking building with a plastic-food display case and a window where passersby can

SHIKOKU

11

TAKAMATSU

> **Tips**   **A Note on Japanese Characters**
>
> Many hotels, restaurants, attractions, and other establishments in Japan do not
> have signs giving their names in Roman (English-language) letters. Chapter 17
> lists the Japanese equivalents for all such places described in this guide. Thus, to
> find the Japanese characters for, say, Tenkatsu (see below) refer to no. 191 in
> chapter 17.

watch a chef prepare sushi. Inside the restaurant are tatami mats and tables, but I suggest
sitting at the counter, which encircles a large pool filled with fish. As customers order, fish
are swept out of the tanks with nets—they certainly couldn't be fresher. A photo menu
(along with prices for fish in the tanks) and a display case help you choose. For a splurge,
order a *kaiseki* course, beginning at ¥5,250.

7–8 Hyogomachi. ℂ 087/821-5380. Reservations required for kaiseki. Set lunches ¥840–¥2,100; set
dinners ¥1,575–¥3,675. AE, DC, MC, V. Mon–Fri 11am–2pm and 4–10pm; Sat–Sun 11am–9pm. Station:
Takamatsu (a 5-min. walk south from the station). Walk south on Chuo Dori until it intersects with a large
covered pedestrian shopping arcade called Hyogomachi. Turn right and walk all the way through the
arcade; upon emerging, you'll find the restaurant on your left.

(192) **Tokiwa Saryo** ★★ (Finds) VARIED JAPANESE   This restaurant, easily spotted
with its castlelike roof, occupies what was once a traditional Japanese inn and retains
many of its original traditional features, including a delightful inner courtyard complete
with a pond, dwarf pine trees, carp, and some lanterns (take off your shoes at the
entrance and deposit them into a locker). You'll probably want to order one of the set
meals, such as *obento* lunch boxes or tempura and sashimi *teishoku*, made easy to choose
from by photos in the Japanese-language menu. At any rate, the food is delicious and
very reasonably priced; you can't go wrong.

1–8–2 Tokiwa-cho. ℂ 087/861-5577. Set dinners ¥2,000–¥4,000; set lunches ¥1,050–¥3,000. AE, DC, MC,
V. Daily 11am–2:30pm and 5–9:30pm (last order). Kotoden streetcar: Kawaramachi Station (2 min.). From
the west exit (with its BUS STOP sign), take the side street south (to the left) parallel to Tokiwa-cho (a covered arcade); the restaurant will be on your right, on the corner.

Inexpensive

(193) **Kanaizumi** SANUKI UDON   This modern cafeteria is about as casual as you
can get—your noodles (available in three sizes, warm or cold) are scooped for you as you
go through the line and you choose your ingredients and side dishes, including tempura
and sushi (¥80–¥180). Be prepared for slippery noodles and the good-natured slurping
sounds of a noodle shop.

9–3 Konyamachi. ℂ 087/822-0123. Sanuki udon ¥160–¥330. No credit cards. Daily 9:30am–5pm. Station: Takamatsu (15 min.). Walk south of the station; the restaurant is off Chuo Dori to the right just before
the city art museum.

(194) **Maruichi** ★ YAKITORI   Although a cozy and friendly drinking establishment,
this is also a great place for an inexpensive meal. An English-language menu lists sashimi,
kimchi (Korean spiced cabbage), fried chicken, tempura, shrimp dumplings, and, of
course, a variety of *yakitori* costing ¥150 to ¥240 per skewer. An evening of eating, drinking, and merriment here should cost about ¥2,500 per person, including the obligatory
¥280 snack charge.

1-4-13 Tokiwa-cho. ✆ **087/861-7623.** Main dishes ¥550–¥900. AE, DC, MC, V. Mon–Sat 5pm–1am.
Kotoden streetcar: Kawaramachi Station (1 min.). Take the west exit (with the BUS STOP signs), use the
upper promenade deck to cross the street, take the elevator to street level; turn right to take the small
alleyway. Maruichi is on the left, with white lanterns and a red, yellow, and green sign with a red circle.

Milano No Okazuyasan ★ NORTHERN ITALIAN   Beneath an Italian flag is the
recessed entrance to this cozy second-floor restaurant. Hospitable chef-owner Mr. Takeda
serves mainly homemade pastas, from the usual spaghetti Bolognese with meat sauce to
spinach fettuccine with cream sauce or veal ragout with white fettuccine, as well as a
handful of pizzas and main dishes that might include seafood saffron risotto. Set lunches
include all the salad and fresh-baked bread you can eat, plus a choice of soup, dessert, or
coffee. Don't miss the homemade bread, and top it all off with a cappuccino and dessert.

Egou Building, 11–14 Kamei-cho. ✆ **087/837-1782.** Main dishes and pasta ¥840–¥1,280; set lunches
¥840–¥945; set dinners ¥1,880–¥4,680. MC, V. Daily 11am–10pm. Kotoden streetcar: Kawaramachi (4
min.). Take the west exit (with the BUS STOP sign) and walk through the covered walking arcade (Tokiwa-
cho) until the awning ends; continue straight and then start looking carefully for Milano on your left.

(195) **Shabutei Maru** ⓥ**alue** SHABU-SHABU   This casual, small, second-floor eatery
has inexpensive lunches of chicken, pork, and beef, with second helpings of rice and
vegetables included in the price. From 5pm, it offers all-you-can-eat *shabu-shabu* (and in
winter, sukiyaki) with a 90-minute time limit—kind of like an "on-your-mark, get-set,
go" spree of uninhibited gorging. Ditto with all the beer, sake, or soft drinks you can
drink if you pay ¥1,200 more. Various grades of meat are available, from beef and pork
(the cheapest) to top-grade *wagyu* beef. Seating is at counters or tables and, as you might
have guessed, the place is usually very crowded.

8-8 Kamei-cho. ✆ **087/835-9842.** Set lunches ¥499–¥3,200; all-you-can-eat shabu-shabu dinners
¥1,800–¥3,500 for men, ¥1,700–¥3,300 for women. DC, MC, V. Daily 11:30am–2pm and 5–10pm (last
order). Kotoden streetcar: Kawaramachi (5 min.). Take the west exit and walk through the Tokiwa-cho
covered arcade; it's catty-corner from the southeast corner of Chuo Park, just off Chuo Dori on Kikuchi-
kan-dori.

2 MATSUYAMA CASTLE & DOGO SPA ★★

947km (588 miles) W of Tokyo; 192km (120 miles) E of Takamatsu; 211km (132 miles) SW of Okayama

Although Matsuyama is Shikoku's largest town and the capital of Ehime Prefecture with
a population of more than 515,000, it has the relaxed atmosphere of a small town.
Located on the island's northwest coast, Matsuyama features one of Japan's best-preserved
feudal castles and what I consider to be the most delightful, historic public bathhouse in
the country, located in Dogo Onsen. The nearby Shimanami Kaido, a series of bridges
connecting Ehime and Hiroshima prefectures, has a dedicated cycling lane, with fantastic
views of the Seto Inland Sea.

ESSENTIALS

GETTING THERE   By Plane   Flights connect Matsuyama with Tokyo, Osaka,
Nagoya, Fukuoka, Sapporo, Kumamoto, Kagoshima, and Okinawa. The flight from
Tokyo takes 1 hour and 25 minutes and costs ¥32,000 for a one-way ticket, though
tickets purchased for certain flights at least 28 days in advance can run as low as ¥13,300.
Buses connect the airport to downtown in 30 minutes for ¥400.

By Train   The easiest way to reach Matsuyama is by **JR train** from Okayama (on Honshu island), with 15 departures daily; the trip takes 2 hours and 40 minutes, and the fare is ¥6,120. There are also hourly departures from Takamatsu, taking about 2½ hours and costing ¥5,500.

By Bus   A **JR bus** (© 03/3844-1950; www.jrbuskanto.co.jp) departs nightly from Tokyo Station at 8:20pm and a **Nishi Tokyo Bus** (© 03/5376-2222) departs nightly from Shinjuku Station at 7:10pm; they arrive respectively at Matsuyama Station the next day at 8:36am and at Matsuyama Shieki (City Station) at 7:10am. One-way fare for either is ¥12,000.

By Boat   Matsuyama is also linked by ferry to several ports on Honshu and Kyushu islands, including Osaka (overnight: 8⅔ hr.), Oita (near Beppu; 3¾ hr.), and Hiroshima (70 min. by high-speed boat). The fare to Matsuyama is ¥6,300 from Osaka, ¥6,900 from Hiroshima and ¥3,200 from Beppu. Boats dock at **Matsuyama Port (Matsuyama Kanko Ko),** where buses transport passengers to Matsuyama Station in about 20 minutes for ¥45.

VISITOR INFORMATION   The **Matsuyama City Tourist Information Office** (© 089/931-3914; daily 8:30am–8:30pm) is inside JR Matsuyama Station to the left as you exit the wicket. Be sure to pick up the booklet "Shikoku Passport"; although in Japanese only, it provides many discounts on attractions, hotels, and restaurants. The **Dogo Tourist Information Center** (© 089/943-8342; daily 8am–8pm) is across the street from the Dogo Onsen streetcar stop. The **Ehime Prefectural International Center (EPIC),** located between Matsuyama Castle and Dogo Onsen (© 089/917-5678; www.epic.or.jp; Mon–Sat 8:30am–5pm), provides information on Ehime Prefecture, including Uchiko, Tobe, and the Shimanami Kaido cycling path. You'll also find English-language newspapers and three computers you can use for free. To reach EPIC, take streetcar no. 3, 5, or 6 heading toward Dogo Onsen to the Minami-machi stop. Backtrack and look to the right for the INFORMATION sign with a question mark; the office is in a barrack partially hidden behind another building. More information is available online at **www.city.matsuyama.ehime.jp** and at **www.mcvb.jp/convention**, the latter also with good city maps.

INTERNET ACCESS   In addition to EPIC, above, you can also check e-mail at **COMS,** on the second floor at 6–4–20 Sanbancho (© 089/943-5776; Tues–Sat 9am–8:30pm and Sun/holidays 9am–5pm) for ¥100 an hour. It's a 7-minute walk from either Matsuyama Station or Matsuyama Shieki; or take the streetcar to the Minami-horibata-cho stop. By the way, in the same building is the Matsuyama International Center (© 089/943-2025), which also offers information about the area.

ORIENTATION & GETTING AROUND   **JR Matsuyama Station,** which serves long-distance trains, is on the west edge of town, with most attractions, hotels, shopping, and restaurants spreading to the east. **Matsuyama Castle** lies less than 2.5km (1½ miles) due east of the station. Just southwest of the castle is the **Okaido** shopping arcade, a covered pedestrian passageway lined with restaurants and shops and considered to be the heart of the city. **Dogo Onsen,** Japan's oldest hot-spring spa, is on the eastern edge of the city.

The easiest and most convenient form of transportation in Matsuyama is **streetcar.** The no. 5 line runs from Matsuyama Station to the Okaido arcade, Matsuyama Castle, and Dogo Onsen. The fare is ¥150 per trip or ¥400 for a **1-day pass (Ichinichi Joshaken).** An old-fashioned locomotive-style streetcar nicknamed "Botchan" (after a novel by Natsume Soseki set in Matsuyama) runs between Matsuyama Station and Dogo

Onsen. This costs ¥300 per ride, but if you have the 1-day pass you're entitled to one ride for only ¥100.

SEEING THE SIGHTS

The Shikoku Passport gives discounts for both Matsuyama Castle and Dogo Onsen.

Matsuyama Castle ★★   Right in the heart of the city, Matsuyama Castle crowns the top of a 131m (435-ft.) hill, commanding an impressive view. It was built by feudal lord Kato Yoshiakira more than 400 years ago, later falling into the hands of the powerful Matsudaira family that ruled the surrounding region from here during the Edo Period. Like most structures in Japan, Matsuyama Castle has suffered fire and destruction through the ages, but unlike many other castles (such as those in Osaka and Nagoya), this one was renovated with original materials in the 1850s. There's only one entrance, a pathway leading through a series of gates that could be swung shut to trap attacking enemies. A secret gate allowed a surprise rear attack, while drop chutes could be used to rain stones onto the enemy. Drums were used to communicate, whether it was to warn of invaders or simply give the time. The granary could store enough rice to feed 2,000 people for a year. The three-story *donjon* houses some samurai gear, swords, screens, and scrolls from the Matsudaira family, as well as photographs of Japan's other castles. Allow yourself 30 minutes to tour the inside.

Surrounding the castle is a park; if you're feeling energetic, you can walk uphill through the park to the castle in about 15 minutes. Otherwise, the easiest way to reach the castle is to take the streetcar to the Okaido stop, walk 5 minutes north on the street next to Starbucks, and then, from the east side of Katsuyama Hill, take a cable car or chairlift (more fun) from the modern cable station on the left side of the street (there's also a walking path to the castle from here). A round-trip ticket for either the cable car or the chairlift, and including admission to the castle, costs ¥1,000 for adults and ¥400 for children.

(C) **089/921-4873.** Admission ¥500 adults, ¥150 children. Daily 9am–5pm (to 4:30pm Dec–Jan and 5:30pm in Aug.). Streetcar: Okaido stop, then chairlift.

DOGO ONSEN ★★★

Dogo Onsen boasts a 3,000-year history and claims to be the oldest hot-spring spa in Japan. According to legend, the hot springs were discovered after a white heron healed an injured leg by soaking it in the thermal mineral waters. Located in the city's northeast, about a 20-minute streetcar ride from Matsuyama Station (take streetcar no. 5 to Dogo Onsen, the last stop), Dogo Spa can accommodate about 7,000 people in 34 hotels and *ryokan,* which means the narrow streets resound at night with the slap of thonged slippers and the occasional clatter of *geta* (wooden platform sandals) as vacationers go to the various bathhouses dressed in *yukata* (cotton robes). Friendly conversations start as tourists gather on the hour to see the Bochan clock (across from the historic Dogo Onsen streetcar station, built in 1895), an animated clock featuring characters from Natsume Soseki's novel, and soak their feet in the nearby foot bath, one of 10 foot baths scattered through Dogo Onsen. Be sure to stop at the Dogo Onsen Tourist Information Center, located at the entrance to the shopping arcade, on the right.

Most of the hotels and ryokan in Dogo have their own onsen, but I suggest that no matter where you stay, you make at least one trip to **Dogo Onsen Honkan ★★★**, 5–6 Yunomachi, Dogo ((C) **089/921-5141**), a wonderful three-story public bathhouse built in 1894. A wooden structure with shoji screens, tatami rooms, creaking wooden stairways, and the legendary white heron topping the crest of its castlelike roof, this Momoyama-style building is as much a social institution as it is a place to soak and scrub. On busy days, as many as 4,000 people pass through its front doors. The water here is transparent, colorless, tasteless, and alkaline, helpful for rheumatism and neuralgia. At the very least, it makes your skin feel soft and smooth. The hottest spring water coming into the spa is 120°F (49°C); the coolest, 70°F (21°C). But don't worry—the waters are mixed to achieve a comfortable 108°F (42°C).

Bathing in the ground-floor granite bath, however, is just a small part of the experience here. Most people come to relax, socialize, and while away an hour or more, and I suggest you do the same. Although you can bathe for as little as ¥400 for adults and ¥150 for children 2 to 11, it's worth it to pay extra for the privilege of relaxing on tatami mats in a communal room on the second floor, dressed in a rented *yukata,* drinking tea from a lacquered tea set, and eating Japanese rice crackers. If the weather is fine, all the shoji screens are pushed open to let in a breeze, and as you sprawl on the tatami, drinking your tea and listening to the clang of the streetcar and voices of people coming and going, you can imagine that you've landed in ancient Japan. To my mind, the entire scene resembles an old woodblock print suddenly come to life. Be sure to take a peak inside the Botchan Room, said to be the favorite room of novelist Natsume Soseki.

The cost of the bath, yukata, crackers, and tea for 1 hour is ¥800. Use of a smaller, more private bath and lounging area for an hour where tea and crackers are also served costs ¥1,200 and includes a visit to Yushinden (see below). And if you really want to splurge for 1 hour and 20 minutes, you can rent a private tatami room on the third floor, which also comes with tea, sweets, and yukata, for ¥1,500. Children 2 to 11 years old pay half-price for all these fares. This differentiation in luxury probably dates from the early days when there were separate baths for the upper class, priests, commoners, and even animals.

While at the spa, be sure to see the **Yushinden,** special rooms built for the imperial family in 1899 for their visits to the spa and last used in 1952. You can take a tour of its rooms for ¥250 for adults and ¥120 for children.

The spa is open daily 6am until 11pm, but you must enter by 10:30pm. You must enter the second and third floors, both of which close at 10pm, by 9 and 8:40pm respectively; you must enter the Yushinden by 9pm.

A NEARBY TEMPLE   After your bath, you may want to visit **Ishiteji Temple ★**, 2–9–21 Ishite (*C* **089/977-0870**), about a 15-minute walk east of Dogo Onsen Station; from the station, walk under the neon archway and keep going straight east. Established in 728, it's the 51st of Shikoku's 88 sacred temples. Its main Nio-mon Gate, built in 1318 with a blend of Chinese and Japanese styles, is a good example of architecture of the Kamakura Period. You'll see statues of Kobo Daishi, as well as an old-fashioned arcade of stalls that seems little changed over the decades. Notice the huge straw sandals at the main gate; those with feet or leg ailments are thought to regain their health by touching them. You'll also see regular-size sandals at the temple, donated by older Japanese in hopes of regaining new strength in their legs (who knows, maybe they've been walking the pilgrimage). Behind the main temple is a tunnel containing stone statues representing the 88 temples of Shikoku; pausing in front of each statue is considered a short circuit to the actual pilgrimage, convenient for those who don't have time for the real thing but still hope for the pilgrimage's blessings. And by the way, all those paper cranes you see in front of the main hall were folded in prayer for world peace, a practice that started with the American invasion of Iraq. The temple is open 24 hours.

If you have time for a side trip around Ehime Prefecture, I strongly recommend an excursion to the village of Uchiko, which has some fine old homes and buildings dating back to the Edo Period and the turn of the 20th century. Whereas about 70% of Matsuyama was destroyed during World War II, Uchiko was left intact, and a tiny part of the old historic district is a living memorial to the days of yore, when it prospered as a production center for wax. Even the 25-minute express train ride from JR Matsuyama Station (departing every hour or so; fare: ¥1,250) is enjoyable as you weave through valleys of wooded hills past grape, *mikan* orange, persimmon, rice, and tobacco farms. At Uchiko Station, ask for the "Visitors' Guide" at the train station ticket window; it contains a map showing the 5-minute walk to Yokaichi, the historic part of town. There are also signs in English pointing the way. Because addresses in this village of 11,600 souls are only for postmen, I've omitted them. All sights listed below are open daily 9am to 4:30pm.

Your first stop from the station is ⑲⑥ **Uchiko-za** (*C* **0893/44-2840**), a kabuki theater built in 1916 (look for the signpost on the left after you pass the creek). Though not as grand as the one near Takamatsu (p. 481), it's a good example of how townspeople used to enjoy themselves years ago. It features a revolving stage, windows that can be opened and closed to control the amount of light reaching the stage, and a small display of memorabilia (note the ultimate platform shoes, *geta,* used by *bunraku* puppeteers). Admission is ¥300 for adults, half-price for children. You're better off, however, with a combination ticket for ¥390 and ¥200 respectively that allows admission to the theater, Museum of Commercial and Domestic Life, and the wax museum of the Kami-Haga Residence listed below. Cheaper admission is also offered through the Shikoku Passport at each attraction.

A 5-minute walk farther along the main street, on the right, is the **Museum of Commercial and Domestic Life (Akinai to Kurashi Hakubutsukan; *C* 0893/44-5220)**. This museum—once housing a pharmacy and built in typical Uchiko style—uses life-size figures, recordings (alas, in Japanese only), and authentic artifacts in its dioramas depicting the daily lives of a merchant and a druggist's family. One of the dioramas, for example, is of a Taisho-Era pharmacy, with two figures kneeling on a tatami floor as they discuss the business at hand, while another shows a family eating, the servant seated on a step below to show a lower status. But my favorite is of the woman in the kitchen, complaining about all the work she has to do. Admission here is ¥200 for adults, half-price for children.

As you continue your walk along Yokaichi's quaint main street, you'll pass galleries and shops, some offering bambooware, peaches, and other products from shelves on the sidewalk (payment is on the honor system; deposit your money in the proffered bamboo shaft). You might want to stop by the **Machi-ya Shiryokan** (*C* **0893/44-5212**), a restored home open free to the public (as an empty house, it wouldn't be of much interest if it weren't free), but don't miss the **Kami-Haga Residence ★** (*C* **0893/44-2771**), which I consider the highlight of a trip to Uchiko. Unfortunately, the residence is closed for renovation until April 2011, though you can still visit its museum. In any case, Kami-Haga Residence, built in 1894 without the use of nails, is especially grand, containing four toilets (two for the family, one for children, and one for guests) and even a room used only for giving birth. It belonged to a merchant who made his fortune exporting wax. During the Edo and Meiji periods, Uchiko gained fame as a center of candle-making and wax production, producing about 30% of the country's wax, used for lighting, umbrellas, and for the styling of elaborate Feudal-Era hairdos. You can see the traditional methods for wax production in the "wax museum" out back for ¥100.

Today, only one person carries on the wax-making tradition—a man named ⑲ **Omori,** who represents the sixth generation of candle-makers. Following the same techniques as those developed by his ancestors 200 years ago, he collects his own haze berries (a kind of sumac) and makes his candles by hand. You can observe him at his workshop, located on the right as you head back to the train station (✆ **0893/43-0385;** Tues–Thurs and Sat–Sun 9am–5pm).

WHERE TO DINE   A 10-minute walk east of Yokaichi (or a 15-min. walk from the train station), across the Oda River, is the Uchiko Fresh Foods Market, famous in Japan as one of the few co-ops where farmers can sell produce directly to consumers. Here, too, is **Karari** (✆ **0893/43-1122**), a restaurant offering both Western and Japanese dishes featuring local ingredients. Nestled among trees beside the river and with large windows that almost make you feel like you're dining in a treehouse, it offers a weekend buffet for ¥1,575 with 50 choices of dishes, while weekdays set meals go for ¥1,200 to ¥2,000. It's open daily 11am to 8pm (last order). No credit cards are accepted.

CYCLING THE SHIMANAMI KAIDO ★★★

If you're a bicyclist—and even if you're not—you owe it to yourself to ride one of Japan's most rewarding cycling routes: a dedicated biking and pedestrian lane that connects Ehime Prefecture on Shikoku with Onomichi in Hiroshima Prefecture on Honshu (Japan's main island). Part of the Shimanami Kaido route (also called the Setouchi Shimanami Sea Route), which is actually a series of seven bridges that hopscotch across the Seto Inland Sea via six islands, the cycling path runs beside vehicular traffic on the bridges but often diverges from the highway on the islands. Needless to say, views of the sea and surrounding countryside are great, even from the bridges, and the pathway, clearly marked in green, is easy to follow (though steep in some areas). If you want, you can cycle the entire 70km (43-mile) distance between Shikoku and Honshu in less than 7 hours, whereupon you could either return to Shikoku by bus or continue your travels onward (send your luggage beforehand to your next hotel by *takkyu-bin;* see p. 630). Or, you may wish to simply cycle for a few hours and then head back; or, you can go as far as you wish, leave your rental bike at one of 13 bike drop-off sites along the cycling path, and then catch a bus back (check bus schedules beforehand, as buses do not go to all drop-off sites). In my opinion, of the entire cycling path, the stretch from Shikoku is more scenic and easier to follow than the stretch closer to Hiroshima (for information on cycling the Shimanami Kaido from Hiroshima Prefecture, see p. 467). Note that the Shikoku Passport gives discounts at Shiyoden Treasure Museum and for bike rentals and accommodations at Sunrise Itoyama.

If you're not going the distance, for a fun day's outing I suggest bicycling to Omishima, an island you'll reach in about 2 hours, where another 30 minutes of cycling will bring you to **Oyamazumi Shrine,** guarded by a 2,600-year-old tree. Worshiped through the years by samurai, the shrine is home to the **Shiyoden Treasure Museum ★★** (✆ **0897/82-0032**), with an astounding collection of helmets, armor, and swords, all donated to the shrine by warriors who wished to express thanks for victories in battle. The museum contains about 80% of Japan's samurai gear designated National Treasures (eight items; look for the red mark) or National Important Cultural Assets, including items once worn by Minamoto Yoshitsune and Minamoto Yoritomo (who donated his sword and outfit just before establishing his Kamakura shogunate in 1192). The museum is open daily 8:30am to 5pm; admission is ¥1,000 for adults, ¥800 for university and high-school students, and ¥400 for children. By the way, there's a bike drop-off center, called Shimanami-no-eki Mishima, just before the shrine, where you can leave your bike and catch a bus to Imabari (check bus schedules beforehand).

Rental bikes are available at the foot of the first bridge (the Kurushima Kaikyo Bridge) at **Sunrise Itoyama** (✆ **0898/41-3196;** www.sunrise-itoyama.jp), which also offers a restaurant, showers, and rooms without private bathrooms beginning at ¥4,200 for a single and ¥6,300 for a twin (no credit cards accepted). Bikes rent for ¥500 a day, plus a ¥1,000 deposit which you forfeit if you decide to ditch your bike at one of the drop-off sites; be sure to ask the folks at Sunrise Itoyama for a bus schedule back. You'll also have the annoyance of bridge toll fees at varying distances, which you deposit into boxes on the honor system (or, you can purchase a coupon for ¥500 covering all the tolls at Sunrise Itoyama). There are also power-assisted bikes for ¥800; I've rented one (in the interest of research, of course—twice) and found it helpful on the circular ramp that climbs 65m (213 ft.) just to meet the first bridge. However, power-assisted bikes must be returned to Sunrise Itoyama, and they have only enough juice to run about 4 hours or so. Sunrise Itoyama is open for bike rentals daily 8am to 8pm (to 5pm Oct–Mar).

To reach Sunrise Itoyama, take an express train from Matsuyama Station 30 minutes to Imabari, from where there are only three to five buses a day to Sunrise Itoyama. You'll probably find it easier, therefore, to take a local train 5 minutes onward from Imabari to Hashihama Station, from which the cycling center is a 20-minute walk; or, if you notify Sunrise Itoyama in advance, they offer pickup and drop-off service at Hashihama Station.

WHERE TO STAY

Your Shikoku Passport provides a discount on rates for the ANA Hotel, Hotel Patio Dogo, and for some single rooms of the Toyoko Inn Matsuyama Ichibancho (except during such peak times as Golden Week or New Year's); mention the discount when making your reservation and show it upon check-in.

Very Expensive

(198) **Yamatoya Besso** ★★★ The ultimate *ryokan* experience awaits you at this famous ryokan in Dogo Onsen. It's the little things that make it special: the rustle of kimono as you're met by bowing, smiling women in the front courtyard; pillars of salt at the front door in good Shinto fashion; lit shoji lanterns guiding the way through hushed hallways; scrolls of haiku poems, in beautiful calligraphy, decorating all the rooms and changed seven times a year to fit the season. With a history dating back 140 years—it was rebuilt in 1988 as a refined, luxurious inn—it offers rooms that preserve the integrity of the past with TVs hidden behind shoji screens and old-fashioned cypress tubs that use water from the hot springs. For a real splurge, there are even four rooms with their own open-air tubs. Lavish kaiseki meals feature seafood of the Seto Inland Sea. The only thing lacking at this superb ryokan is the requisite garden.

2-27 Dogo Sagidani-cho, Matsuyama 790-0836. ✆ **089/931-7771.** Fax 089/931-7775. 19 units. ¥46,350–¥81,000 per person. Rates include 2 meals. Weekday and off-season discount available. AE, DC, MC, V. Streetcar: Dogo Onsen (5 min.). **Amenities:** Indoor/outdoor hot-spring baths. *In room:* A/C, TV, hair dryer.

Expensive

ANA Hotel ★ Matsuyama's premier hotel (called Zenniku Hotel in Japanese) has a great location in the heart of the city, just a few minutes' walk to the Matsuyama Castle ropeway and the Okaido covered shopping arcade; streetcars heading for Dogo Onsen pass right in front of the hotel. Built in 1979 but constantly updated, it offers business hotel-like inexpensive singles (the cheapest listed here), as well as larger and well-appointed singles, twins, and doubles; ask for a double or twin with a castle view.

3-2-1 Ichiban-cho, Matsuyama 790-8520. ℂ **800/993-3563** in the U.S. and Canada, or 089/933-5511. Fax 089/921-6053. www.ichotelsgroup.com. 327 units. ¥6,930–¥20,559 single; ¥19,635–¥40,425 double; ¥21,368–¥32,340 twin. AE, DC, MC, V. Streetcar: Okaido (1 min.). **Amenities:** 3 restaurants; bar; tea lounge; rooftop beer garden (summer only); room service; smoke-free rooms. *In room:* A/C, TV, hair dryer, Internet, minibar.

Moderate

Hotel Patio Dogo ★   With a great location just across the street from the delightful Dogo Onsen Honkan spa, this comfortable, medium-class hotel offers semi-double beds in singles, and queens in the more expensive double rooms. Ah, space at last! Best are rooms on the second through fourth floors whose windows overlook the historic spa. The most expensive accommodations in each category are larger, corner rooms. In the evening, be sure to join all the other tourists staying in Dogo and wear your *yukata* across the street for a nighttime soak in the historic spa.

20-12 Yuno-machi, Dogo, Matsuyama 790-0842. ℂ **089/941-4128.** Fax 089/941-4129. www.patio-dogo.co.jp. 101 units. ¥7,665–¥9,135 single; ¥11,550–¥24,825 double. AE, DC, MC, V. Streetcar: Dogo Onsen (5 min.). Walk though the covered shopping arcade and turn left. **Amenities:** Restaurant (a branch of Sushimaru; see "Where to Dine," below); lobby computer w/free Internet; smoke-free rooms (singles only). *In room:* A/C, TV, fridge, hair dryer, Wi-Fi.

Old England Dogo Yamanote Hotel ★★   An outdoor terrace cafe; a lobby decorated in old-world style with wainscoting, chandeliers, and antique-filled cabinets; and classical music playing in the background transport a touch of England to the heart of Dogo Onsen. A sign outside declaring SINCE 1886 refers to a *ryokan* that once stood here, but the owner tore it down and opened this hotel in 2003. Still, this is a classy choice if you prefer a bed to a futon, with rooms sporting brocade bedspreads and curtains, wood floors, and roomy bathrooms (but note that the cheapest doubles are with semi-double-size beds). Although most people staying here pay rates that include meals in the hotel's good French restaurant, my rates below are for rooms only. The hotel doesn't offer much in the way of services, but it does have both indoor and outdoor public baths.

1-13 Dogosagidani-cho, Dogo, Matsuyama 790-0836. ℂ **089/998-2111.** Fax 089/998-2112. 70 units. ¥10,700–¥19,050 single; ¥15,100–¥38,100 double. Rates ¥2,100 higher per person on nights before holidays. AE, MC, V. Streetcar: Dogo Onsen (10 min.). Walk though the covered shopping arcade; it's behind Dogo Onsen Honkan. **Amenities:** Restaurant; coffee shop; indoor/outdoor hot-spring baths. *In room:* A/C, TV, hair dryer, minibar.

Inexpensive

(199) **Minshuku Miyoshi**   This simple establishment is located in Dogo Onsen near Ishiteji Temple but it's hard to spot; if you call ahead, someone may be able to pick you up at the Dogo Onsen streetcar stop (or meet you in front of Ishiteji Temple). Although not much English is spoken, they're used to foreigners here. Clean but simple tatami rooms, all with sink and toilet, make it a good choice for young budget travelers, especially because they'll even wash and dry your clothes for free if you have a lot of laundry.

3-7-23 Ishite, Matsuyama 790-0852. ℂ/fax **089/977-2581.** 6 units, none with bathroom, all with toilet. ¥4,000 without meals; ¥5,000 with breakfast; ¥7,350 with breakfast and dinner. All rates are per person. No credit cards. Streetcar: Dogo Onsen (10 min.). Bus: 52 to Ishiteji. Across from Ishiteji Temple, painted green and set back from the road to the left of the store selling tombstones. *In room:* A/C, TV, no phone.

Toyoko Inn Matsuyama Ichibancho (Value) It's hard to beat this chain business hotel for its handy location in front of Katsuyama-cho streetcar stop near the castle and nightlife area and its long list of freebies, including free domestic calls from lobby phones, two free TV movies nightly, free rental bikes, and even free curry-rice dinners from 6 to 7:30pm to the first 30 people who show up. Of course, rooms are cookie-cutter identical and tiny, but otherwise provide all you need for a night's rest.

1–10–8 Ichiban-cho, Matsuyama 790-0001. ℂ **089/941-1045.** Fax 089/941-2046. www.toyoko-inn.com. 216 units. ¥5,460–¥6,090 single; ¥8,190 double. Rates include Japanese breakfast. AE, DC, MC, V. Streetcar: Katsuyama-cho (1 min.). **Amenities:** Free rental bikes; lobby computer w/free Internet; smoke-free rooms. *In room:* A/C, TV, fridge, hair dryer, Internet.

WHERE TO DINE
Expensive
Kadota ★ FRENCH Chef Kadota, a gold medalist in the Culinary Olympics, worked at both the Okura Hotel and ANA Hotel Matsuyama before opening his own restaurant here in 1993. Small and cozy, with classical music playing in the background, flowers on every table, and French cuisine served on elegant tableware, it offers homemade appetizers, organic vegetables whenever possible, and—the house specialty—steaks and seafood in season. Your dinner may start with yellowtail sashimi in mandarin orange sauce or fish bouillabaisse, followed by Seto Inland Sea bream served in a white-wine sauce or steak in red-wine sauce with sweet-potato gratin.

3–4–25 Sanban-cho. ℂ **089/931-3511.** Reservations recommended. Main dishes ¥1,365–¥2,625; set dinners ¥5,250–¥15,750; set lunches ¥2,100–¥3,150. AE, DC, MC, V. Daily 11am–2pm and 5–9pm (last order). Closed 2 days in Aug. Streetcar: Kencho-mae (5 min.). Take the side road to the east of the ANA hotel, continue straight 7 blocks, and then turn right where you'll see the restaurant with a tree lit in tiny white lights.

Moderate
(200) **Kushihide** (Finds) YAKITORI/CHICKEN Behind the counter of this 50-year-old eatery are some 400 individual sake cups inscribed with the names of regular customers; the cook joked that this way, the cups didn't have to be washed. Washed or unwashed, they're testimony to the popularity of this simple eating and drinking venue. As soon as you sit down, a large bowl of cabbage with a dip and an appetizer will be placed in front of you. The restaurant is famous for its fried chicken leg and thigh for ¥945, included in some of the set meals, but it also offers other chicken dishes as well, including chicken sukiyaki, chicken burgers, *senzanki* (fried chicken), and even chicken sashimi (the restaurant claims to be one of the few places you can eat it safely, as the restaurant raises its own chickens and serves them the day of their demise). In fact, chicken or chicken broth is a part of virtually every dish offered here—even in its ice cream.

3–2–8 Nibancho. ℂ **089/921-1587.** Yakitori ¥210–¥265; set meals ¥1,890–¥4,725. AE, MC, V. Daily 4:30–11pm. Streetcar: Okaido (2 min.). Walk down Okaido Arcade and take the 1st right after the stoplights; it's 1 block farther on your left.

(201) **Sushimaru** SUSHI Located just east of the Okaido shopping arcade, Sushimaru has Japanese *noren* (shop curtains), a display case outside, and old fashioned architecture. A *higawari* (today's lunch) consisting of sushi, *nigiri* sushi (sushi rolls), salad, and soup for ¥800, is available most days, but even more popular is the changing *tsukigawari* (monthly lunch), served daily until 2pm and including various dishes in addition to sushi. A Japanese-language menu with photos shows other set meals. In the evening, kaiseki featuring sashimi are also available.

Another Sushimaru with much the same menu and same hours is located across the street from Dogo Onsen in the Hotel Patio Dogo at 20–12 Yunomachi (② **089/932-6157**).

2-3-2 Nibancho. ② **089/941-0447.** Set meals ¥1,050–¥3,700; kaiseki ¥3,700–¥10,000. AE, DC, MC, V. Mon–Fri 11am–2pm and 4:30–10:30pm; Sat–Sun and holidays 11am–10:30pm. Streetcar: Okaido (4 min.). Walk south along the Okaido shopping arcade. After you cross Nichiban-cho (the 1st light), take the 1st small street on your left; it will be on your right a few shops down.

Inexpensive

Dogo Beer Bakushukan (Finds If you agree that "One gulp of beer taken just after a bath is the time when you feel most refreshed," as proclaimed in this microbrewery's pamphlet, then after bathing at Dogo Onsen Honkan head straight across the street for some sake or beer. (The parent company has been a sake producer for more than a century; they opened a brewery in 1996 following deregulation, which had long assured a beer monopoly by the major players.) An upbeat establishment with an eclectic decor mixing the traditional (bamboo ceilings) and the modern (artwork), it offers German-style beers (Cologne-style Kolsch, alt, and stout), along with typical Japanese pub grub, including boiled *edamame* (soybeans), *yakitori,* sashimi, and fried chicken, but it's most famous for its deep-fried *jyakoten* (fish paste).

20–13 Yuno-machi, Dogo. ② **089/945-6866.** Main dishes ¥370–¥2,000. No credit cards. Daily 11am–10pm. Streetcar: Dogo Onsen. To the left of Dogo Onsen Honkan.

Kyushu

The southernmost of Japan's four main islands, Kyushu offers a mild climate, famous hot-spring spas, beautiful countryside, national parks, and warm, friendly people. It also boasts a couple of high-tech theme parks that make it Japan's number-one destination for visitors from Korea, Taiwan, Hong Kong, and other places in Asia.

Historians believe that Japan's earliest inhabitants lived on Kyushu before gradually pushing northward. According to Japanese legend, it was from Kyushu that the first emperor, Jimmu, began his campaign to unify Japan. Kyushu is therefore considered to be the cradle of Japanese civilization. And because Kyushu is the island closest to Korea and China, it has served through the centuries as a point of influx for both people and ideas from abroad, including those from the West.

---

1 FUKUOKA

1,174km (730 miles) W of Tokyo; 450km (281 miles) W of Hiroshima

With a population of 1.4 million, Fukuoka is Kyushu's largest city and serves as a major international and domestic gateway to the island. On the northern coast of Kyushu, it lies closer to Seoul, Korea, than to Tokyo.

During Japan's feudal days, Fukuoka was divided into two distinct towns separated by the Nakagawa River. Fukuoka was where the samurai lived since it was the castle town of the local feudal lord. Merchants lived across the river in Hakata, the commercial center of the area. Both cities were joined in 1889 under the common name of Fukuoka. Fukuoka's main train station, however, is in Hakata and is therefore called Hakata Station. Hakata Station serves as the terminus of the Tokaido-Sanyo Shinkansen Line from Tokyo (though only Nozomi bullet trains, which aren't covered in the Japan Rail Pass, travel the entire distance; Hikari bullet trains require a transfer).

In the 13th century, Fukuoka was selected by Mongol forces under Kublai Khan as the best place to invade Japan. The first attack came in 1274, but Japanese were able to repel the invasion. Convinced the Mongols would attack again, Japanese built a 3m-high (10-ft.) stone wall along the coast. The second invasion came in 1281. Not only did the Mongols find the wall impossible to scale, but a typhoon blew in and destroyed the entire Mongol fleet. Japanese called this gift from heaven "divine wind," or *kamikaze,* a word that took on a different meaning during World War II when young Japanese pilots crashed their planes into American ships in a last-ditch attempt to win the war.

Today, Fukuoka is a modern, internationally oriented commercial and business center with a highly developed port and coastal area. Although it's not a must-see tourist destination, there are some interesting museums, shrines, and a temple worth seeing if you've arrived in Fukuoka on the Shinkansen.

GETTING THERE   By Plane   Direct flights connect **Fukuoka Airport (FUK;** ℂ **092/621-6059;** www.fuk-ab.co.jp) to a variety of international cities, including Beijing, Shanghai, Hong Kong, Seoul, and Bangkok, as well as numerous domestic cities. Flying time from Tokyo's Haneda Airport is 1½ hours; the regular, one-way fare costs ¥36,800 on Japan Airlines. However, because of fierce competition on the Fukuoka-Haneda route, bargains do exist. **Skymark** ((ℂ 03/3433-7670 in Tokyo, or 092/736-3131 in Fukuoka; www.skymark.co.jp), a small airline serving Fukuoka, offers 10 flights daily from Haneda to Fukuoka for as low as ¥16,800 one-way. Even JAL offers advance-purchase fares as low as ¥16,800 depending on the time of day and season. To get into town, there's a subway station located directly under the domestic terminal of **Fukuoka Airport** (if you've arrived at the international terminal, take the free shuttle bus to the domestic terminal). The trip to Hakata Station takes only 5 minutes and to Tenjin, 11 minutes; the fare is ¥250, or you can purchase a 1-day subway pass for ¥600 if you plan to sightsee the same day. Alternatively, there's Nishitetsu bus service directly from the domestic terminal every 20 to 30 minutes to Hakata Station's bus terminal; the cost is ¥250.

By Train   Fukuoka's **Hakata Station** is the last stop on the Nozomi Shinkansen bullet train from Tokyo, with the trip taking approximately 5 hours and costing ¥21,210 for an unreserved seat. If you have a Japan Rail Pass, which doesn't cover Nozomi trains, you'll have to take the Hikari Shinkansen and change trains in Osaka or Okayama; the trip takes almost 6 hours, not including transfers. Hiroshima is 1 hour and 10 minutes away; Kyoto is 2 hours and 45 minutes away.

By Bus   A Nishitetsu "Hakata" bus ((ℂ **0120/489-939;** www.nishitetsu.co.jp/bus/ highway/gb) departs from Tokyo's Shinjuku Station nightly at 9pm, arriving at Hakata Station at 11:10am the next morning. The fare is ¥15,000 one-way.

VISITOR INFORMATION   You can pick up the leaflet "Fukuoka" at the Tourist Information Centers in Tokyo or Narita or Kansai airports or download it from JNTO's website at www.jnto.go.jp by looking under "Browse by Destinations."

  Fukuoka Tourist Information Office ((ℂ **092/431-3003;** daily 8am–7pm) is in Hakata Station near the East Gate. It has maps and sightseeing pamphlets. Ask for **Rainbow,** a free monthly with concert, exhibition, events, and festival information; and **Fukuoka Now,** good for restaurant and nightlife listings. Be sure to pick up the free **Welcome Card** and accompanying guide, which gives overseas visitors discounts for selected hotels, restaurants, attractions, and shops (the card must be presented at check-in to receive hotel discount). More information by phone is available at the Tourist Information Call Center for Foreign Travelers at ℂ **092/751-6904**. On the Internet, sightseeing information is available at **www.yokanavi.com** and **www.city.fukuoka.jp**. Other useful sites include **www.fukuoka-now.com** (good for restaurants, exhibitions, events, and nightlife) and **www.fukuoka-tourism.net**, with information on Fukuoka Prefecture, including Fukuoka City, Dazaifu, and Space World.

INTERNET ACCESS   You can check e-mail 24 hours a day at **Media Café Popeye,** located on the eighth floor of the Kotsu Center, next to Hakata Station ((ℂ **092/432-8788**). It charges ¥390 for 1 hour.

MAIL & ATM   An international post office, with a counter for stamps and mail that is open 24 hours, as well as an ATM that accepts international credit cards, is located next to the Hakata (west) exit of Hakata Station.

Iki Island
Gonoura
To Kami-Tsushima
To Pusan
Kitakyushu
INLAND SEA NATIONAL PARK
Genkai Sea
Kokura
To Kobe, Osaka and Tokyo
Inland Sea
Nogata
Fukuoka (Hakata)
Dazaifu
Nakatsu
Karatsu
Hirado
Hirado Island
Yamamoto
Taku
Tosu
Yabakei
Bungo-Takada
Imari
Sasebo
Saga
Kurume
Hita
Beppu
To Osaka, Shikoku
Sagonoseki
Arita
Yanagawa
Ariake Sea
Yamaga
Oita
Usuki
Omura Bay
Isahaya
Arao
ASO-KUJU NAT'L PARK
▲ Mt. Kuju
Unzen Spa
Shimabara
Saiki
Nagasaki
Obama
Mt.Unzen
Kumamoto
▲ Mt. Aso
▲ Mt. Sobo
UNZEN-AMAKUSA NAT'L PARK
Shiranui
Takachino
Kami Island
Yatsushiro
Shimo Island Hondo
Gokase River
Nobeoka
Amakusa Islands
Itsuki
Yatsushiro Bay
Hyuga
Ushibuka
Kuma
Minamata
Hitoyoshi
Nagashima Island
Okuchi
Kobayashi
Takanabe
Kami-Koshiki Island
Akune
Mt. Kirishima ▲
Miyazaki
To Osaka
Sendai
Mt. Takachiho-no-mine ▲
Oyodo River
Kushikino
Hayato
KIRISHIMA-YAKU NAT'L PARK
Miyakonojo
To Osaka & Tokyo
Shimo-Koshiki Island
Shinkansen
Kagoshima
▲ Mt. Sakurajima
Nichinan
PACIFIC OCEAN
Chiran
Kagoshima Bay
Tarumizu
Makurazaki
Kanoya
Shibushi Bay
JAPAN
Ibusuki
KIRISHIMA-YAKU NAT'L PARK
Cape Toi
Tokyo
Ferry Routes
Railways
Sata
Map area
0   25 mi
0   25 km
Cape Sata
Osumi Straits

ORIENTATION   Although Hakata Station is the terminus for the Shinkansen bullet train and trains departing for the rest of Kyushu, with most of Fukuoka's hotels clustered nearby, the heart and business center of Fukuoka is an area to the west called **Tenjin.** It's home to several department stores, its own train station and bus center, a large underground shopping arcade, and restaurants. Just a few minutes' walk from Tenjin is **Nakasu,** one of Japan's most famous nightlife districts, with more than 2,000 bars, restaurants, and small clubs clustered on what's actually an islet bounded by the Nakagawa River.

Across the river from Nakasu (and a 10-min. walk west of Hakata Station) is **Canal City Hakata,** an intriguingly designed (by award-winning American architect Jon Jerde)

Tips **A Note on Japanese Characters**

Many establishments and attractions in Japan do not have signs in Roman (English-language) letters. Those that don't are indicated in this guide with an oval with a number that corresponds to a number in chapter 17 showing the Japanese equivalent. Thus, to find the Japanese for, say, the **Tochoji Temple** (see below), refer to no. 202 in chapter 17.

entertainment, hotel, and shopping complex with 125 shops and restaurants. Also nearby and within walking distance are Tochoji Temple, Hakata Machiya Folk Museum, Kushida Shrine, and the Fukuoka Asian Art Museum.

GETTING AROUND You can **walk** from Hakata Station to most of the attractions recommended below.

By Subway Fukuoka City Subway (☏ **092/471-8111;** http://subway.city.fukuoka.lg.jp) is the easiest method of transportation because there are only three major lines. One line connects Hakata Station to Tenjin (the third stop), passing Nakasu-Kawabata on the way—the stop for the Nakasu nightlife district. This same line will also take you to Fukuoka Airport. Stops are announced in English. Fares start at ¥200, but if you think you'll be riding a lot, a 1-day subway pass for ¥600 allows unlimited rides.

By Train Whereas Hakata Station serves as the terminus for the Shinkansen and Japan Railways trains departing for the rest of Kyushu, Tenjin has its own station, called **Nishitetsu Fukuoka Station,** located inside the Mitsukoshi department store building and useful for trips to Dazaifu.

By Bus The city's two bus terminals are located near Hakata Station at the Kotsu Center and in Tenjin near Nishitetsu Fukuoka Station and Mitsukoshi department store; both are clearly marked in English. Buses running inside the central Hakata-Tenjin District charge a flat fare of ¥100. Most useful for tourists is the so-called "¥100 Bus," which sports a big ¥100 coin on its side and travels a circular route going both directions from Haktaka Station to 18 stops in the downtown area, including Tenjin, Canal City, and the Hakata Riverain shopping/cultural complex.

EXPLORING THE CITY

About an 8-minute walk northwest of Hakata Station and located on the right side of Taihaku-Dori is ⑳ **Tochoji Temple,** 2–4 Gokushomachi (☏ **092/291-4459;** daily 9am–5pm; subway: one stop from Hakata Station to Gion, exit 1, 1 min.; ¥100 Bus: Gionmachi, stop no. 16; look for a picture of a Buddha at the front gate). This modern reconstruction of a long-established temple, established by Kobo Daishi, may not look like much, but up on the second floor is Japan's largest seated wooden Buddha, measuring 10m (33 ft.) tall and carved in 1988. Admission is free, but you are asked to refrain from taking photographs. Particularly interesting is the trip through the Hells of Buddhism, upon which you can embark by entering the small room to the left of the Buddha. After viewing colored reliefs of unfortunate souls burning in hell, being boiled alive, and suffering other tortures, enter the darkened, twisting passageway and walk through it guided by a rail, whereupon you'll reach the end—enlightenment! It's fun for older kids.

On the other side of Taihaku-Dori, down the side street with a 7-Eleven and marked by a large cement *torii,* is the ㉒ **Hakata Machiya Folk Museum (Hakata Machiya Furusato-Kan)** ★, 6–10 Reisen-machi (© **092/281-7761;** www.hakatamachiya.com; daily 10am–6pm; subway: Gion, exit 2, 4 min.; ¥100 Bus: Gion-machi, stop no. 16). This museum celebrates the history and cultural heritage of Hakata, the old merchants' town, concentrating primarily on the Meiji and Taisho eras. It occupies three buildings, two of which are Meiji-Era replicas; the third is an authentic, 150-year-old house of a weaver. On display are items used in everyday life, as well as dioramas depicting festivals, everyday street scenes, and a home typical of a Hakata merchant family. On a telephone, you can listen to *Hakata-ben,* the local dialect, which is quite difficult even for native Japanese speakers to understand. You can also watch artisans at work on Hakata's most famous wares, including the highly refined Hakata dolls, tops, wooden containers, and *Hakata-ori* cloth, used for *obi* sashes and famous for loincloths worn by sumo wrestlers. Be sure to see the 22-minute film of the Yamakasa Festival, Fukuoka's most famous festival, featuring races of men carrying enormous floats. Add another 30 minutes to see the museum itself and its crafts shop. Admission is ¥200 for adults and free for children.

Beyond the Hakata Machiya Folk Museum is **Kushida Shrine,** 1 Kamikawabata-machi (© **092/291-2951;** shrine grounds daily 24 hr.), Fukuoka's oldest shrine. Site of the Yamakasa Festival, it has long been the shrine for merchants praying for good health and prosperity. Most interesting is a tall, towering float on view (except in June when it is being rebuilt) that is used in the Yamakasa Festival held in mid-July and decorated with dolls made by Hakata doll makers. Incredibly, the elaborate floats are made anew every year.

If you're ready for dining or shopping, retrace your steps through Kawabata-dori arcade and take the escalator leading to **Canal City Hakata,** a virtual city-within-a-city complete with hotels, shops, restaurants, the Club Sega amusement arcade, and a 177m-long (590-ft.) canal that runs through its center.

EASY SIDE TRIPS FROM FUKUOKA
Dazaifu

If you have 4 or more hours to spare, I heartily recommend taking a side trip to **Dazaifu,** a pleasant village that is home to a shrine that is immensely popular with Japanese, and the Kyushu National Museum. Dazaifu has a festive atmosphere, and one of the main reasons to visit, in my opinion, is to see everyone else.

The best way to reach Dazaifu is from Nishitetsu Fukuoka Station in Tenjin (in the Mitsukoshi department store). Take a *tokkyu* (limited express) of the Nishitetsu Tenjin Omuta Line (there are departures every 30 min.) 12 minutes to Futsukaichi (the second stop); transfer there (across the platform) for the 8-minute train ride on the Nishitetsu Dazaifu Line (two stops) to Dazaifu Station, the last stop (though there are a few trains that go directly from Fukuoka Station to Dazaifu). If you don't catch a limited express, the trip to Dazaifu can take about 50 minutes. In any case, the fare is ¥390 one-way. The **Dazaifu City Tourist Information Desk** (© **092/925-1880;** daily 9am–5:30pm), located inside Dazaifu Station, has an English-language pamphlet.

Dazaifu Tenmangu Shrine ★★★, 4–7–1 Saifu Dazaifu (© **092/922-8225;** www.dazaifutenmangu.or.jp), is a 5-minute walk from the station, reached by taking a right onto a pedestrian lane lined with shops selling souvenirs, sweets, and crafts, followed by three bridges (representing the past, present, and future) spanning a turtle-filled pond shaped in the kanji for "heart." The shrine itself was established in 903, soon after the death of Michizane Sugawara, who was demoted from his position as Minister of the

Right in Kyoto and exiled to Dazaifu, where he continued his scholarly studies despite extreme hardship. Today, Michizane is deified as the god of literature and calligraphy, which explains why this shrine is so popular. As the head office of 12,000 Tenmangu shrines spread throughout Japan and presided over by the 39th-generation Michizane descendant, it draws six million visitors a year, many of them high-school students praying to pass tough entrance exams into universities. Behind the main hall, which dates from 1591, hang wooden tablets, written with the wishes of visitors—mostly for successful examination scores. Also behind the main hall is an extensive plum grove with 6,000 trees; the plum blossom, in bloom from late January to March, is considered the symbol of scholarship.

Whatever you do, a must-see is **Komyozenji Temple** ★ (© 092/922-4053), just a 2-minute walk from the shrine. This Zen temple, built in 1275, boasts Kyushu's sole rock garden, arranged to form the Chinese character for "light." In the back is also a combination moss-rock garden, representing the sea and land and shaded by maple trees. It's a glorious sight and is almost never crowded, except in autumn when changing maple leaves make it even more spectacular. To see it, take your shoes off, throw ¥200 into the donation box, and walk to the wooden veranda in back where you can sit and meditate. It's open daily from 8am to 5pm.

Behind Dazaifu Tenmangu Shrine, to the right, is an escalator that will take you to the **Kyushu National Museum,** 4–7–2 Ishizaka (© 092/918-2807; www.kyuhaku.jp), which in 2005 opened as Japan's first new national museum in 100 years. Perched on a hillside, it's a strikingly modern structure that undulates down the slope in mimicry of the hills around it, with surrounding woods reflected on its glass facade. Through permanent and special exhibits, it focuses on Japan's cultural heritage, how that heritage has been influenced by other Asian cultures through the ages, and the role Kyushu has played

Take Me Out to the Ballgame

If you're in town March through September, consider seeing the **Fukuoka Softbank Hawks** baseball team play one of its 70-some home games in Fukuoka Yahoo! Japan Dome (© 092/847-1006), the first retractable-roof stadium in Japan. Tickets start at ¥1,500 for an unreserved seat in the outfield and are available at major convenience stores or at the box office. Personally, I find watching the spectators as much fun as watching the game, with their coordinated cheering, flag waving, trumpet blowing, and more. Oddly enough, the roof is kept closed (in case it rains and so that players aren't distracted by their shadows), but when the Hawks win, they open the roof and celebrate with eight specialty fireworks. And this being Japan, the dome is part of a larger **Hawks Town** complex (www.hawkstown.com) with a hotel, restaurants, and other amusements. To reach Hawks Town, take the subway to the Tojinmachi stop, from which it's about a 15-minute walk. Or take bus no. 39 or 306 from gate 5 of the Kotsu Bus Center in front of Hakata Station to the Fukuoka-Dome Mae. On game days, there are also special shuttle buses departing from the bus centers in Tenjin and Kotsu Center near Hakata Station.

in cultural exchange. Religious objects, musical instruments, ceramics, lacquerware, art, and other items from ancient to modern times from a number of nations are on display in permanent and special exhibits, including goods that reached Japan via the Silk Road and European trading ships. It's open Tuesday to Sunday from 9:30am to 5pm and costs ¥420 for adults, ¥130 for university and high-school students, and free for children. Special exhibits cost more.

Space World

Space World, 4–1–1 Higashida (© **093/672-3600;** www.spaceworld.co.jp), in the town of Kitakyushu, is a space travel–theme amusement park with thrill rides, including roller coasters, water rides, a 100m-high (330-ft.) Ferris wheel, a movie theater with seats that move in sync with the action, an IMAX theater, kiddie rides, and Space Dome, in which visitors take a "shuttle" to a space station and then, from there, embark on roller-coaster journeys around the solar system or through a black hole. You'll probably spend a minimum of 4 hours here. An all-inclusive pass costs ¥4,200 for adults (12 and older), ¥3,150 for children ages 6 to 11, ¥2,100 for seniors (proof of age required), ¥1,050 for children ages 4 and 5, and free for children 3 and younger. It's open daily 10am to 5pm, with extended hours holidays and weekends. It's closed the first 3 weeks of December and the last 3 weeks of January, except on weekends. To reach Space World, take a JR Kaisoku (express) train from Fukuoka's Hakata Station directly to Space World Station. The trip time is about 60 minutes, and the park is a 5-minute walk from the station. If you have a JR Rail Pass, it's quicker to take the Shinkansen bullet train 20 minutes from Hakata Station to Kokura Station, transferring there to a local line for the 10-minute ride to Space World. Likewise, if you're coming from Honshu via Shinkansen, transfer in Kokura. If you have luggage to stow, there are lockers at Kokura Station and at Space World's entrance.

WHERE TO STAY
Expensive

Grand Hyatt Fukuoka ★★★   Fukuoka's top hotel commands a grand setting in the innovative Canal City Hakata, with easy pedestrian access to the city's main sights. Its black-marbled lobby has a curved facade that overlooks the shopping complex, but for guests who desire solitude, the hotel also has its private roof garden. Service throughout the hotel is superb—along the order of "Your wish is our command." Small but stylish rooms provide views of the private garden or the river and its night scenes. Besides all the luxury, a stay at the Grand Hyatt is fun, with Canal City's many shops and restaurants right outside the door.

1–2–82 Sumiyoshi, Hakata-ku, Fukuoka 812-0018. © **888/591-1234** in the U.S., or 092/282-1234. Fax 092/282-2817. www.fukuoka.grand.hyatt.com. 370 units. ¥28,000–¥37,000 single; ¥34,000–¥43,000 double; from ¥43,000 Grand Club double. Welcome Card discounts available. AE, DC, MC, V. Station: Hakata (12 min.). ¥100 Bus: Canal City Hakata-mae (stop no. 4; 2 min.). **Amenities:** 3 restaurants, including Aroma's (p. 506); 2 bars; lounge; concierge; executive-level rooms; fitness center and spa w/25m (82-ft.) indoor pool (fee: ¥2,100); room service; smoke-free rooms. *In room:* A/C, TV, hair dryer, Internet, minibar.

Hakata Miyako Hotel ★   Near Hakata station's east (Shinkansen) exit, this attractive property with the famous Miyako name offers a convenient connection to Fukuoka Airport (just 5 min. via subway) and is close to shops and restaurant complexes. Spacious rooms have floor-to-ceiling windows that let in plenty of light, though city views are not

Tips **A Double or a Twin?**

For the sake of convenience, the price for two people in a room is listed as a "double" in this book. Japanese hotels, however, differentiate between rooms with a double bed or two twin beds, usually with different prices. Although most hotels charge more for a twin room, sometimes the opposite is true; if you're looking for a bargain, therefore, be sure to inquire about prices for both. Note, too, that hotels usually have more twin rooms than doubles, for the simple reason that Japanese couples, used to their own futon, traditionally prefer twin beds.

spectacular. The one disadvantage: Tourist sights are on the west side of the station, so you have to go through the station concourse to reach them.

2-1-1 Hakataeki-higashi, Hakata-ku, Fukuoka 812-0013. © 092/441-3111. Fax 092/481-1306. www.miyakohotels.ne.jp/hakata/english. 266 units. ¥12,474–¥19,635 single; ¥21,945–¥25,410 double. Welcome Card discounts available. AE, DC, MC, V. Station: Hakata (1 min.). **Amenities:** 2 restaurants; bar/lounge; concierge; room service; smoke-free rooms. *In room:* A/C, TV, hair dryer, Internet, minibar.

Moderate

Canal City Fukuoka Washington Hotel (**Value**) Though part of a nationwide business-hotel chain, this Washington has more style: it's located in Canal City Hakata, Fukuoka's number-one shopping-and-entertainment complex, offering convenience right outside the front door. The cheapest singles face the Grand Hyatt above the Canal City complex, while higher-priced, larger singles and all twins and triples have views outward toward the city. The downside: Its good location makes it popular; you'll find the lobby crowded at check-in and checkout times.

1-2-20 Sumiyoshi, Hakata-ku, Fukuoka 812-0018. © **092/282-8800.** Fax 092/282-0757. www.wh-rsv.com/english. 423 units. ¥7,800–¥11,400 single; ¥15,000–¥20,500 double. Welcome Card discounts available. AE, DC, MC, V. Station: Hakata (10 min.). ¥100 Bus: Canal City Hakata-mae (stop no. 4; 1 min.). **Amenities:** Coffee shop; lobby computer (¥100 for 10 min.); smoke-free rooms. *In room:* A/C, TV, hair dryer, Internet, minibar.

Dukes Hotel Hakata ★ Flower boxes, plants, and evergreens outside the entrance hint that this is no ordinary hotel. Indeed, it's a reasonably priced hotel with class, with a small but very civilized lobby that exudes charm and invites you to linger among its Chinese vases, palm trees, antiques, and classical music. Most of the rooms, tiny but comfy with a simple decor that suggests an English-style countryside manor, are singles, with only nine twins and nine doubles. In the world of cloned business hotels, this establishment, a short walk from Hakata Station in the direction of Canal City, is a welcome relief. Farther from the station but in the heart of the city (4 min. from the Nakasu-kawabata subway stop or Higashi-Nakasu/stop no. 11 of the ¥100 Bus), **Dukes Hotel Nakasu,** 1–1 Nakasunakashima-machi, Hakataku (© **092/283-2800**), offers the same amenities and style at a cheaper price.

2-3-9 Hakataeki-mae, Hakata-ku, Fukuoka 812-0011. © **092/472-1800.** Fax 092/472-1900. www.dukes-hotel.com. info@dukes-hotel.com. 153 units. ¥8,190–¥9,450 single; ¥12,600–¥13,650 double. AE, DC, MC, V. Station: Hakata (2 min.). From the west (Hakata) exit, take the road straight ahead (the one btw. Fukuoka City Bank and the red stone Center Building); it's down this street on your right in the 2nd block. **Amenities:** Cafe; smoke-free rooms. *In room:* A/C, TV, fridge, hair dryer, Internet (8th floor only).

JR Kyushu Hotel Fukuoka   One block east of Hakata Station, this hotel offers a convenient location, rooms that are larger than those in most business hotels, and discounts to those with Japan Rail Passes. Though there are no doubles per se, two can tough it out in a single room with a semi-double-size bed for ¥13,800. A ladies' floor offers specialized amenities.

2-2-4 Hakataeki-Higashi, Hakata-ku, Fukuoka 812-0013. ℂ **092/413-8787.** Fax 092/413-9746. www. jrhotelgroup.com. 90 units. ¥7,500–¥8,800 single; ¥14,600 double. 10% discount with Japan Rail Pass. AE, DC, MC, V. Station: Hakata (a 2-min. walk from the east Shinkansen exit). **Amenities:** Restaurant. *In room:* A/C, TV, fridge, hair dryer.

Inexpensive

In addition to the choices here, Toyoko Inn (www.toyoko-inn.com) has four locations within walking distance of Hakata Station. **Toyoko Inn Hakataguchi Ekimae,** 1–15–5 Hakataekimae (ℂ **092/451-1045**), and **Toyoko Inn Hakataguchi Ekimae2,** 1–16–6 Hakataekimae (ℂ **092/437-1045**), both a 2-minute walk northwest of the station, have doubles starting at ¥7,140 and ¥8,190 respectively. **Toyoko Inn Hakata Gion,** 1–38 Gion-cho (ℂ **092/281-1045**), a 5-minute walk northwest of the station, and **Toyoko Inn Hakata-eki Minami,** 2–10–23 Hakataeki-minami (ℂ **092/475-1045**), a 13-minute walk southeast of the station, offer similar rates. As with most Toyoko Inns, they all offer computers in the lobby providing free Internet access, complimentary breakfast, free Internet in the rooms, and free Wi-Fi in the lobby.

Hakata JBB Hotel   In the heart of the city, beside the Hakata Machiya Folk Museum and within easy walking distance of Canal City Hakata, the Asian Art Museum, and other attractions, this is a simple but well-managed establishment, offering free coffee every morning in the lobby. Open-air passageways lead to tiny but well-kept rooms complete with toothbrush, shampoo, and pajamas. Beds are semi-double-size and are for single use, but married couples or two women can room together for ¥6,000. You won't find anything in the city center cheaper than this.

6-5-1 Reisen-machi, Hakata-ku, Fukuoka 812-0039. ℂ **092/263-8300.** Fax 092/263-8301. www.jbb hotel.com. 59 units. ¥4,500 single; ¥6,000 double. No credit cards. Station: Hakata (10 min.). Subway: Gion (exit 2, 4 min.). ¥100 Bus: Okunodo (stop no. 15; 3 min.). *In room:* A/C, TV, fridge, hair dryer, no phone.

Wafu Ryokan Kashima Honkan ★ (Finds)   It comes as something of a surprise to find a traditional Japanese inn in the heart of Kyushu's largest city, and an inexpensive one to boot. Housed in a 100-year-old building with a homey atmosphere, an enclosed garden, and rambling hallways leading to simple *tatami* rooms, each one different, it's a good choice for budget-seeking traditionalists. Its convenient location, down the street from the Hakata Machiya Folk Museum, is another plus.

3-11 Reisen-machi, Hakata-ku, Fukuoka 812-0039. ℂ **092/291-0746.** Fax 092/271-7995. kashima-co@ mx7.tiki.ne.jp. 27 units, none with bathroom. ¥4,725 single; ¥8,400 double; ¥1,050 more per person Sat and nights before holidays. Japanese breakfast ¥1,050 or Western breakfast ¥735 extra; dinner ¥3,675 extra. MC, V. Station: Hakata (10 min.). Subway: Gion (exit 2; 3 min.). ¥100 Bus: Okunodo (stop no. 15; 2 min.). **Amenities:** Lobby computers w/free Internet; Wi-Fi (in lobby). *In room:* A/C, TV, fridge.

WHERE TO DINE

For one-stop dining, head to **Canal City Hakata** (ℂ **092/282-2525**), a 10-minute walk west of Hakata Station or a 1-minute walk from Canal City Hakata-mae bus stop no. 4. You'll find dozens of restaurants in this shopping complex, situated around a canal and water fountains and offering everything from Chinese, Italian, and Japanese cuisine to fast food and bar snacks. On the fifth floor is **Ramen Stadium 2,** with eight ramen shops offering noodles, *gyoza* (dumplings), and other fare from different regions of Japan, including Tokyo, Sapporo, Kanagawa, Kyoto, Miyazaki, and Fukuoka. Pick your meal from the ticket vending machine outside each shop; there are photos of most selections, priced from ¥600 to ¥1,050. Like most restaurants in Canal City, they're open daily from 11am to 11:30pm.

For a bit more local flavor, head to one of Fukuoka's famous 200 *yatai* **stalls**★ (street-side food stalls). Most are located in Tenjin and along the Nakagawa River, on Nakasu Island south of Kokutai-Doro Avenue. Most stalls sell ramen, though some also serve *oden, yakitori,* tempura, and other simple fare. They're open daily from about 6pm to 2am. Many nighttime revelers stop here before or after a spin through the Nakasu entertainment district. Choose a stall and sit down, and you'll be served a steaming bowl of ramen, most of which average about ¥700.

Aroma's EUROPEAN   Located in the Grand Hyatt, with its great location in Canal City, this upbeat, modern restaurant has a great lunch buffet serving mostly Mediterranean-inspired cuisine, including salads, soup, and many fish, meat, and vegetable choices. In the evening, you can dine a la carte on dishes like grilled beef tenderloin steak filet, sautéed Nagasaki sea bream on asparagus risotto, or *suteki don buri* (steak on a bed of steamed rice), or opt for the set meal (available Mon–Thurs nights) or the weekend dinner buffet.

Grand Hyatt Fukuoka, 1–2–82 Sumiyoshi. ✆ **092/282-1234.** Set dinner (Mon–Thurs) or buffet dinner (Fri–Sun) ¥3,500; buffet lunch Mon–Fri ¥2,100, weekends and holidays ¥2,300. AE, DC, MC, V. Daily 11:30am–2:30pm and 5:30–10pm. Station: Hakata (12 min.). ¥100 Bus: Canal City Hakata-mae (stop no. 4; 2 min.).

(204) **Kazaguruma** LOCAL SPECIALTIES   In a relocated 200-year-old farmhouse accented with heavy wooden beams, this lively *izakaya* specializes in locally brewed *shochu* (an *izakaya* is a Japanese bar with beer, sake, and Japanese food, generally open only from 5 or 6pm). It offers a fish of the day (because the description is in Japanese only, you might try asking a neighboring diner for help with translations; this is a friendly place), *yakitori,* sashimi, and other local favorites. Or order one of the set meals (for which you must make a reservation the day before).

Dangam Building 1F, 1–13–1 Hakata-eki Higashi. ✆ **092/481-3456.** Main dishes ¥420–¥1,000; set lunch ¥680; set dinners ¥2,500 and ¥4,000. AE, DC, MC, V. Mon–Fri 11:30am–1:30pm and 5pm–3am; Sat 5pm–midnight. Station: Hakata (1-min. walk from the east exit). Walk straight ahead, cross the main street, and take the 1st alley left.

(205) **Shinshusoba Murata** NOODLES   Across from Hakata Machiya, this traditional eatery specializes in homemade buckwheat noodles, served by a friendly staff to customers sitting at counters made of wood slabs or on *tatami*. Although traditional soba is usually made with 80% buckwheat and 20% wheat, the tasty *kikouchi* offered here is 100% buckwheat and is served cold with vegetables. The most expensive dishes include tempura.

2–9–1 Reisen-machi. ✆ **092/291-0894.** Soba ¥600–¥1,750. MC, V. Daily 11:30am–8:30pm (closed 2nd Sun of each month). Subway: Nakasu-Kawabata (2 min.); ¥100 Bus: Gion-machi (stop no. 16; 1 min.).

(206) **Ume no Hana** VEGETARIAN/TOFU   Located along the Naka River on Nakasu island, this restful and low-key chain is known for its appetizing low-calorie, light vegetarian cuisine. It offers a variety of meals centered on tofu and vegetables, though some set meals may include fish and seafood. It's simply decorated in that sparse yet elegant Japanese way, with seating at low tables with leg wells. There's a branch nearby in the second basement of the ACROS building, 1–1–1 Tenjin (✆ **0120-20-9022**).

2 NAGASAKI ★★

1,329km (826 miles) SW of Tokyo; 152km (95 miles) SW of Fukuoka

Unlike Kumamoto, Kagoshima, Beppu, and other well-known Kyushu destinations, Nagasaki doesn't have a castle, a famous landscaped garden, or hot-spring spas. Rather, its charm is much more subtle. Many people in Japan—including foreign residents—consider this city one of the country's most beautiful. It's a place of hills rising from the deep, U-shaped harbor with boats and ferries chugging back and forth, of houses perched on terraced slopes, of small streets and distinctive neighborhoods, and of people extremely proud of their hometown. Without a doubt, Nagasaki is one of Japan's most livable cities, despite its population of 448,000 residents. It's also perhaps Japan's most cosmopolitan city, with a unique blend of outside cultures interwoven into its history, architecture, food, and festivals.

Nagasaki, capital of Nagasaki Prefecture and located on the northwest coast of Kyushu, opened its harbor to European vessels in 1571 and became a port of call for Portuguese and Dutch ships; Chinese merchants soon followed and set up their own community. Along with traders came St. Francis Xavier and other Christian missionaries, primarily from Portugal and Spain, who found many converts among the local Japanese. During Japan's more than 200 years of isolation, only Nagasaki was allowed to conduct trade with outsiders and thus served as the nation's window on the rest of the world. Even today, Japanese come to Nagasaki for a dose of the city's intermingled cultures. Its harbor remains one of Japan's most active.

All the city's major attractions are connected to its diversified, and sometimes tragic, past. Nagasaki is best known as the second city to be destroyed by an atomic bomb.

ESSENTIALS

GETTING THERE **By Plane** **JAL** and **ANA** serve Nagasaki Airport (NGS; © **0957/52-5555;** www.nabic.co.jp/english) from Tokyo's Haneda Airport. Flight time is 1 hour and 50 minutes, and the regular one-way JAL fare is around ¥39,000, though tickets purchased 28 days in advance can cost more than half that on certain flights. **Skynet Asia Airways** (SNA; © **0120/737-283** toll-free in Japan; www.skynetasia.co.jp), a local airline connecting a few cities in Kyushu with Tokyo, offers a regular one-way Nagasaki-Tokyo fare of ¥31,600, with cheaper fares if you book 2 months in advance for selected flights. Airport **buses** travel to Nagasaki Station in about 45 minutes for ¥800.

By Train Trains depart Hakata Station in **Fukuoka** approximately twice an hour, arriving at Nagasaki Station about 2 hours later at a cost of ¥4,410 for an unreserved seat. From **Tokyo,** take the Nozomi Shinkansen bullet train to Hakata Station and transfer there for a train to Nagasaki; travel time is about 7½ hours, depending on connections, and the fare is ¥23,420 for an unreserved seat.

VISITOR INFORMATION Pick up the leaflet "Nagasaki, Unzen, Goto Islands, Iki and Tsushima" from the Tourist Information Center in Tokyo or Kansai or Narita international airports, or download it from JNTO's website at www.jnto.go.jp by looking under "Browse by Destinations." In Nagasaki, the **Nagasaki City Tourist Information Office**

(© 095/823-3631; daily 8am–8pm) is located just outside the main ticket gates of Nagasaki Station, to the right in the Seattle's Best coffee shop. Information on Nagasaki is also available online at **www.at-nagasaki.jp**. See **www.nagasaki-tabinet.com** for information on Nagasaki Prefecture, including Unzen.

INTERNET ACCESS   Located in the Hamano-machi covered shopping arcade in the heart of downtown Nagasaki, **Internet Café Cybac,** 2–46 Aburaya-machi (© **095/818-8050**), open 24 hours, charges a one-time ¥300 fee and then ¥300 for the first 30 minutes, plus ¥100 for each additional 15 minutes.

ORIENTATION   Along with Kobe and Sapporo, Nagasaki is one of Japan's most navigable cities, with lots of English-language signs pointing the way to attractions. City layout follows natural boundaries set by the Urakami River, the long and narrow Nagasaki Bay, and the many steep-sloped hills. **Nagasaki Station,** along with AMU Plaza next door offering shopping and dining options, isn't located in the downtown part of the city; rather, most nightspots, shops, and restaurants are located southeast of the station, clustered around an area that contains **Shianbashi Dori** and **Kanko Dori streets,** the **Hamano-machi** covered shopping arcade, and a newly developed waterfront area called **Dejima Wharf** that includes restaurants, the Nagasaki Prefectural Art Museum with Spanish art and art related to Nagasaki, and Seaside Park. Nearby is **Chinatown,** with Chinese restaurants and shops selling Chinese-made souvenirs and clothing. Farther south is **Glover Garden,** where many foreigners settled in the 19th century. Nearby is **Hollanders Slope (Oranda-zaka,** also referred to as Dutch Slope), undoubtedly Nagasaki's prettiest street, a cobbled lane lined with wooden houses built by former European residents (a century ago, the people of Nagasaki referred to all Europeans as Hollanders). **Peace Park** and its atomic-bomb museum are located north of Nagasaki Station on the other end of town.

GETTING AROUND   **By Streetcar**   Streetcars have been hauling passengers in Nagasaki since 1915 and have changed little in the ensuing years; they're still the easiest—and most charming—way to get around. Four lines run through the heart of the city, with stops written in English. Because streetcars have their own lanes of traffic here, during rush hour they're usually the fastest on the road. It costs a mere ¥120 (half-price for children) to ride one no matter how far you go; pay at the front when you get off. You are allowed to transfer to another line only at **Tsukimachi Station** (ask the driver for a transfer ticket, a *norisugi,* when you disembark from the first streetcar); otherwise, you must pay each time you disembark. If you think you'll be riding more than five times in 1 day, you can save a few yen with a ¥500 **pass,** sold at the tourist office and at many hotels, which allows unlimited rides for 1 day. Streetcars run from about 6:15am to 11:30pm.

On Foot   With the exception of Peace Park, you can also get around Nagasaki easily on foot, which is certainly the most intimate way to experience the city and its atmosphere. You can walk from the Hamano-machi downtown shopping district to Glover Garden, for example, in 20 minutes, passing Chinatown, Dejima, and the Dutch Slope on the way.

By Bus   Destinations are in Japanese only—stick to the streetcars.

EXPLORING THE CITY
Nishizaka Hill
After Nagasaki opened its port to European vessels, missionaries came to the city to convert Japanese to Christianity. Gradually, however, the Japanese rulers began to fear that these Christian missionaries would try to exert political and financial influence

KYUSHU

12

NAGASAKI

Church Shrine
Post Office ⓘ Tourist Info
━━ Railway

0   1/10 mile
0   100 meters

Honrenji Temple

NAGASAKI PARK

Ken-ei Bus Station

Nagasaki Station

Central Post Office

Nishi Nakamachi
Umamachi Dori
City Hall
Chamber of Commerce
Imauomachi Dori
Nagasaki River

GOTO MACHI

Fukuromachi Dori

Kofukuji Temple

KOZEN MACHI

City Hall Street

Manzaimachi Dori

Megane-bashi

Nagaski Port Terminal

Ohato Dori

Prefecture

Nakajima Gowa

Kanko Dori

Teramachi Dori

Hamanomachi Arcade

Dejima Wharf

DEJIMA MACHI

CHINA TOWN

Nagasaki Bus Station

Sofukuji Temple

Nagasaki Prefectural Art Museum

Nagasaki Harbor

MOTOKAGO MACHI

Oura Gawa

ATTRACTIONS ●
Confucius Shrine and
  Historical Museum of
  China **30**
Dejima **18**
Glover Garden **33**
Hollanders Slope **27**
Nagasaki Atomic
  Bomb Museum **2**
Nagasaki Museum of
  History and Culture **10**
Nagasaki Ropeway to
  Mt. Inasa **6**
Nishizaka Hill **3**
Peace Park
  (Hirano-machi) **2**
Sofukuji Temple **21**
Spectacles Bridge **16**
Suwa Shrine **11**

ACCOMMODATIONS ■
Best Western Premier
  Hotel Nagasaki **1**
Chisun Grand Nagasaki **14**
Hotel Majestic **32**
Hotel New Nagasaki **9**
Hotel Wingport Nagasaki **5**
JR Kyushu Hotel Nagasaki **7**
Nagasaki International
  Hostel Akari **15**
Nagasaki Hotel Monterey **28**
Nishikiso Bekkan **26**
Sakamoto-ya **12**
Toyoko Inn Nagasaki
  Ekimae **13**
Victoria Inn Nagasaki **20**

DINING ◆
Dai-ichi-no Taberu **8**
Gohan **23**
Harbin **17**
Hortensia **4**
Kagetsu **24**
Obinata **25**
Red Lantern **19**
Shikairo **31**
Shippoku
  Hamakatsu **22**
Tia **20**
Tokiwa **29**

through their converts. Who was to say that conversion to Christianity wasn't the first step toward colonization? So in 1587, Toyotomi Hideyoshi, ruler of Japan, officially banned Christianity. In 1597, 26 male Christians (20 Japanese and 6 foreigners) were arrested in Kyoto and Osaka, marched 30 days through the snow to Nagasaki, and crucified on **Nishizaka Hill** as examples of what would happen to offenders. Through the ensuing decades, there were more than 600 documented cases of Japanese, Portuguese, and Spanish Christians being put to death in the Nishizaka area. In 1862, the 26 martyrs were canonized by the pope.

Today, on Nishizaka Hill, about a 4-minute walk north of Nagasaki Station up a steep slope, there's the Monument to the 26 Saints, with statues of the martyrs carved in stone relief. Immediately striking is that three of them look very young; indeed, the youngest was only 12. Behind the relief is the small **Twenty-Six Martyrs Museum** (© **095/822-6000;** www.26martyrs.com; daily 9am–5pm) housing artifacts relating to the history of Christianity in Japan, including paintings and drawings of the 26 saints, reward notices for those turning in Christians to authorities, and religious objects, as well as remains of Japanese martyrs returned to Nagasaki in 1995 after more than 380 years of interment in Macau. Perhaps most amazing about the history of Christianity in Japan is that the religion was practiced secretly by the faithful throughout Japan's isolation policy, surviving more than 200 years underground without the benefits of a church or clergy. Admission to the museum, which can be toured in 15 minutes, is ¥250 for adults, ¥150 for junior-high and high-school students, and ¥100 for children.

Peace Park (Hirano-machi) ★★

On August 9, 1945, at 11:02am, American forces dropped an atomic bomb over Nagasaki, 3 days after they had dropped one on Hiroshima. The bomb, which exploded 480m (1,600 ft.) aboveground, destroyed about a third of the city, killed an estimated 74,000 people, and injured 75,000 more. Today, Peace Park, located north of Nagasaki Station, serves as a reminder of that day of destruction with a museum, memorials, and statues. Nagasaki's citizens are among the most vigorous peace activists in the world; a peace demonstration is held in Peace Park every year on the anniversary of the bombing, along with a declaration for peace by the city mayor.

Near the Nagasaki Atomic Bomb Museum (see below), a black pillar marks the exact epicenter of the atomic blast; a black casket contains names of the bomb's victims. Ironically, the bomb exploded almost directly over the Urakami Catholic Church, built after centuries of persecution in Japan and of which only a fragmented wall remains. A few minutes' walk farther north, separated by several streets, is the largest part of Peace Park (the nearest streetcar station to this section is Matsuyama). It occupies the site of a former prison; all 134 inmates died in the blast. A fountain is dedicated to the wounded who begged for water; many of them died thirsty. Statues donated by countries from around the world line a pathway leading to Peace Statue, a 9m-high (30-ft.) statue of a male deity. One hand points to the sky from where the bomb came (meant as a warning?), and the other hand points to the horizon (representing hope? the future?).

Nagasaki Atomic Bomb Museum ★★★   Visiting this museum, with English-language displays, is by far the most important thing to do in Peace Park. Upon entering, guests circle an empty, glass-dome foyer via a spiraling ramp—bringing to mind, perhaps, the atomic mushroom cloud? This is followed by photographs of the city as it looked before the bomb, accompanied by the ominous, loud ticking of a clock. Displays illustrate events leading up to the bombing, the devastation afterward, Nagasaki's postwar restoration, the history of nuclear weapons, and the subsequent peace movement. Objects, photos, and artifacts graphically depict the bomb's devastation, including a clock stopped precisely at 11:02am, personal belongings ranging from mangled spectacles to a student's singed trousers, hand bones encased in a clump of melted glass, and photographs of victims, including a dead mother and her baby and a 14-year-old whose face has been hideously burned. On video, survivors describe their personal experiences on that fateful day. The adjoining Peace Memorial Hall for Atomic Bomb Victims contains a Remembrance Hall, with portraits of those who lost their lives. The museum is by no means pleasant, but something every concerned individual should see. Plan on at least an hour here, more if you opt for the ¥150 audio guide. (If you've already seen the far more comprehensive Peace Memorial Museum in Hiroshima, this one will be largely repetitive.)

7–8 Hirano-machi. ⓒ **095/844-1231.** www1.city.nagasaki.nagasaki.jp/peace. Admission ¥200 adults, ¥100 children. Daily 8:30am–5:30pm (until 6:30pm May–Aug). Streetcar: 1 or 3 to Hamaguchi-machi (5 min.).

Dejima

When the Tokugawa shogunate adopted a national policy of isolation in the 1630s, only Nagasaki was allowed to remain open as a port of trade with foreigners. Because the Portuguese and Spaniards were associated with the outlawed Christian religion, they were expelled in 1639; only the Dutch and the Chinese were allowed to remain and continue trading. In 1641, all the Dutch were confined to a tiny, fan-shaped artificial island called Dejima, where they remained for 218 years (at any given time, about 15 Dutchmen were in residence; no wives were allowed). This was Japan's only official contact with the outside world; the director of Dejima was required to travel to Edo every 1 to 4 years to report to the shogun. Otherwise, the only people allowed to cross the bridge into the Dutch community were Japanese prostitutes and traders.

Today, after having become part of the mainland through land reclamation and decades of languishing as little more than a streetcar stop, Dejima has been reborn through an ambitious project to re-create the island as it was in the early 19th century, with more than a dozen structures resurrected. After you alight at the Dejima streetcar stop and pay the admission of ¥500 for adults, ¥200 for high-school students, or ¥100 for children, go to the **Deputy Chief Factor's Quarters** (6–3 Dejima-machi; ⓒ **095/821-7200;** www1.city.nagasaki.nagasaki.jp/dejima) for a map and information in English. From there you'll be directed to a re-created kitchen, the First Ship Captain's Quarters with furnishings of the period, the Chief Factor's Residence, and the Head Clerk's Quarters with examples of equipment and knowledge brought to Japan from Europe. The No. 1 Warehouse documents the painstaking restoration of Dejima's historic buildings, while the No. 2 Warehouse describes Dejima's role in the introduction of Western science and culture to Japan. At the Dejima Theatre, a 12-minute video (English-language audio phones available) recaptures daily life in a former Dejima Dutch factory. The most important thing to see in Dejima is the **Dejima Museum of History,** which is housed in a blue, colonial-style wooden building constructed in 1877 as Japan's first Protestant seminary. It gives an excellent account of the historical development of the island, what life was like for the Dutch who lived here, and how the trading system worked. Nearby, in a replica of an old stone warehouse, is the museum's annex with folk objects from Holland and artifacts unearthed during Dejima excavations. Dejima is open daily 8am to 6pm; you'll probably spend 45 minutes here.

Nagasaki Museum of History and Culture ★★   The most fun way to gain an understanding of Nagasaki's unique and important role in Japan's exchange of culture, trade, and ideas with the outside world is to visit this museum. With the help of English-language explanations and a free audio guide, you'll learn about the introduction of Western languages, medicine, astronomy, and other sciences via Nagasaki's contact with the Dutch; Japan's cultural exchanges with China and Korea; Christianity in Japan; and Nagasaki's role as a trading port. Our favorite: displays of Nagasaki arts and crafts, including local artwork influenced by Western and Chinese styles popular at the time and ranging from porcelain and lacquerware to glass and tortoiseshell objects. The adjoining *Bugyosho* (Magistrate's Office), faithfully reconstructed based on historical records and archaeological digs, is a fine example of mid-1600 Japanese architecture (note the *shoji* panels that slide around corners to be stored away, thereby opening completely the interior to the exterior). In addition to viewing a short 3-D movie (with an English-language written explanation) recounting a year in the life of the magistrate, you'll see rooms where smugglers were interrogated and brought to trial (there are also periodic live reenactments of trials; contact the tourist office for details). Plan on spending an hour here (more if there is a reenactment).

1–1–1 Tateyama. 📞 **095/818-8366.** www.nmhc.jp. Admission ¥600 adults, ¥400 high-school students, ¥300 children. Daily 8:30am–7pm. Closed 3rd Tues of the month. Streetcar: 3 to Sakura-machi (5 min.).

Glover Garden ★★   After Japan opened its doors to the rest of the world and established Nagasaki as one of a handful of international ports, Nagasaki emerged as one of the most progressive cities in the country, with many foreign residents. A number of Western-style houses were built during the Meiji Period (1868–1912), many of them on a hill overlooking Nagasaki and the harbor. Today, that hill has been developed into Glover Garden, which showcases nine Meiji-Era buildings and homes on lushly land-scaped grounds. Some of the structures stand on their original site; others have been moved here. The stone-and-clapboard houses have sweeping verandas, Western parlors, the most modern conveniences of the time, and Japanese-style roofs. Most famous is **Glover Mansion,** Japan's oldest Western-style house, built in this location in 1863 and romanticized as the home of Madame Butterfly, the fictitious, tragic heroine of Puccini's opera. Married to a Japanese woman (and much more faithful than his Puccini counterpart), Thomas Glover was a remarkable Scotsman who, among other things, financially backed and managed ship-repair yards in Nagasaki, brought the first steam locomotive to Japan, sold guns and ships, and exported tea. The **Ringer House,** dating from the early Meiji Period, contains a display of photos, clothes, and artifacts of Kiba Teiko, a Japanese opera singer who played Madame Butterfly.

Among other buildings, a former boys' academy houses photographs of old Nagasaki, including portraits of foreigners who used to live here. The Mitsubishi Dock House, built in 1896 to serve as a rest house for ship crews, offers great views of the harbor. One of Nagasaki's first Western restaurants is now a quaint cafe. And don't miss the **Nagasaki Traditional Performing Arts Museum,** which displays floats and dragons used in Nagasaki's most famous festival, the Okunchi Festival, held in October. The museum's highlight is an excellent film of the colorful parade, featuring massive ships deftly maneuvered on wheels and Chinese dragon dances. At any rate, views from Glover Garden of the harbor are among the best in the city. Plan on spending about 1 hour here.

8–1 Minami Yamate-machi. 📞 **095/822-8223.** www.glover-garden.jp. Admission ¥600 adults, ¥300 high-school students, ¥180 children. Daily 8am–6pm (to 9:30pm Golden Week and mid-July to mid-Oct).

> ## ⓂMoments   A View from the Top
>
> The best panoramic view of Nagasaki is from atop 330m (1,090-ft.) Mount Inasa, which you can reach in 7 minutes from Nagasaki Station by taking bus no. 3 or 4 to the Ropeway-mae stop (fare: ¥150). A 2-minute walk from the bus stop is Fuchi Shrine, where believers come to pray for a good marriage, safe childbirth, and academic success. Beside the shrine is the Nagasaki Ropeway (✆ **095/861-3640;** daily 9am–10pm), which delivers you to the top of Mount Inasa in 5 minutes (round-trip fare: ¥1,200 adults, ¥900 junior-high and high-school students, ¥600 children). A hilltop observation deck provides 360-degree panoramic views; we recommend you arrive before sunset and stay for the zillion twinkling lights. You might also consider dining here at **Hikari** (✆ **095/862-1050**), a restaurant with great views and delectable local dishes, including *champon* (for a discussion of this cuisine, see "Where to Dine," later in this section).

Streetcar: Oura Tenshudoshita (7 min.); cross the bridge, turn left after the ANA Hotel Nagasaki Glover Hill, and walk uphill, following the signs.

Temples, Shrines, Views & Bridges
Confucius Shrine (Koushi-byo) and Historical Museum of China ★   Chinese residents living in Nagasaki built this colorful, red-and-yellow shrine in 1893, aided by the Ch'ing Dynasty in China. This is the only Confucian mausoleum outside China built by the Chinese. In fact, the land upon which it stands belongs to China and is administered by the Chinese embassy in Tokyo. The main hall contains a statue of Confucius, attended by courtyard statues representing his 72 disciples. More fascinating, however, is the small Historical Museum of China located behind the main hall with bronze jars, ceramics, jade carvings, painted enamel vases, and other treasures on loan from Beijing's National Museum of Chinese History and Beijing Palace's Museum of Historical Treasures. You can see everything in a half-hour.

10–36 Oura-machi. ✆ **095/824-4022.** Admission ¥600 adults, ¥400 high-school students, ¥300 children. Daily 8:30am–5pm. Streetcar: Oura Tenshudoshita (3 min.). Walk inland (continuing in the same direction of your streetcar if you're coming from downtown), and turn left when you reach a small playground on your right near the Dutch Slope.

Sofukuji Temple ★   Sofukuji is Nagasaki's most famous temple. Distinctly Chinese with its Ming architecture, it dates back to 1629, when it was founded by Chinese residents. Its Buddha Hall, painted a brilliant red and decorated with Chinese lanterns, was designed and cut in China before transportation to Nagasaki. Erected in 1646, it's the oldest building in Nagasaki and is a National Treasure. Another National Treasure is the temple's beautiful gate, which employs a complex jointing system and features brightly painted detailing. But most fascinating, in my opinion, is the temple's gigantic cauldron, built by a priest during a terrible famine in the 1680s to cook enough porridge to feed more than 3,000 people a day.

7–8 Kayjiya-machi. ✆ **095/823-2645.** Admission ¥300 adults, ¥200 junior-high and high-school students, ¥100 children. Daily 8am–5pm. A 7-min. walk from the Hamano-machi downtown shopping district. Streetcar: Shokakuji-shita (4 min.); head back toward the bay, turning right at Sofukuji St.

KYUSHU   12   NAGASAKI

Spectacles Bridge (Megane-bashi)   In addition to the temples described above, the Chinese also left their mark on Nagasaki with several bridges. Most famous is the so-called Spectacles Bridge, built in 1634 by a Chinese Zen priest. One of Nagasaki's most photographed objects, it's the oldest stone-arched bridge in Japan and is named after the reflection its two arches cast in the water (although I wouldn't know, because I've never seen the Nakashima River larger than a trickle except once, after a heavy rain). There's a promenade along the river, complete with benches and children's playgrounds. It's a 5-minute walk from the Hamano-machi shopping arcade.

Streetcar: Nigiwai-bashi or Kokaidomae.

Suwa Shrine   Although Nagasaki's famous Okunchi Festival has Chinese roots, it's celebrated at this Shinto shrine, built to promote Shintoism at a time when the feudal government was trying to stamp out Christianity. Today, with a good location on top of a hill with views over the city, the shrine symbolizes better than anything else the spiritual heart of the Japanese community. When Japanese women turn 33 and men turn 40, they come here to pray for good health and a long life. Newborns are brought 30 days after their birth to receive special blessings and then again for their 3rd, 5th, and 7th birthdays. On New Year's, the grounds are packed with those seeking good fortune in the coming year. People also visit to ask the shrine's many deities for favors—good marriage, safe childbirth, good health, and more. You can even have your automobile blessed here. The shrine sells English-language fortunes. If you're satisfied with your fortune, keep it; if not, tie it to the branch of a tree and the fortune is conveniently negated.

18–15 Kami-Nishiyama-machi. ✆ **095/824-0445.** Free admission. Daily 24 hr. Streetcar: Suwa Jinja-mae (4 min.); take the underground passage and follow the signs up many stone stairs.

A SIDE TRIP TO HUIS TEN BOSCH ★★★

If you're ready for some R & R from your travels in Japan but have only 1 day to spare, perhaps **Huis Ten Bosch,** in Sasebo (✆ **0956/27-0001;** www.huistenbosch.co.jp), will do the trick. This replica of a 17th-century Dutch village boasts tree-lined canals, brick houses, city squares, brick-paved roads, churches, museums, shops, restaurants, hotels, and even stately private homes—proof at how adept Japanese are at imitation. Most of the buildings are faithful reproductions of originals back in the Netherlands; even the bricks were imported from Holland. Although I was a bit skeptical about visiting an imitation Dutch village in Japan, I must admit that the grounds and craftsmanship are beautifully done (Huis Ten Bosch is also environmentally conscious, with its own desalination and sewage treatment plants; it also generates much of its own energy). Even Holland itself isn't this pristine. In fact, I consider this the country's premier theme park designed for adults. But although there are some rides and attractions, this is not an amusement park in disguise.

Highlights include **Palace Huis Ten Bosch,** a replica of the formal residence of Queen Beatrix of the Netherlands, which contains an art gallery and period rooms showing how upper-class Dutch lived; baroque and flower **gardens;** a mirror maze; children's indoor playground; **museums** with collections of porcelain, ornamental glass, teddy bears, carillons, and music boxes; and **theaters** that re-create the flooding of a Dutch town, introduce M. C. Escher's works with a 3-D film, and show a movie in which the audience is the cast (each visitor's face is scanned and instantly digitalized using computer processing). There are also solar-powered cruises of Omura Bay and the village's canals; parades, dances, concerts, and other events daily; more than 50 shops; and more than 40 restaurants (including open-air beer and wine gardens). The park is so vast that there are shuttle buses and other forms of transportation, but to really feel like you're in Holland, rent one of the park's bicycles.

A 1-day Passport Ticket to Huis Ten Bosch and its attractions costs ¥5,600 for adults, ¥4,400 for children 12 to 17, and ¥3,400 for children 4 to 11 (3 and under are free). The best time to visit is spring, during—what else?—tulip season. Open March through Christmas, daily 9am to 9:30pm (last entrance 8pm); December 26 through February, 9am to 8:30pm (last entrance 7pm).

To reach Huis Ten Bosch, take the **JR Sea Side Liner Express** from Nagasaki Station to Huis Ten Bosch Station (1 hr. and 20 min.); the train departs approximately every hour and costs ¥1,430 one-way. *Tip:* The *nimai kippu* for ¥2,600, available at Nagasaki Station's JR ticket window, is valid for one round-trip or as a one-way ticket for two people. Also available is an Admission and Round-trip fare ticket for ¥4,800, but a Passport Ticket for ¥6,700 is an even better deal, as it includes the round-trip fare, admission, and entrance to all attractions.

WHERE TO STAY

Nagasaki has reasonably priced hotels, but keep in mind that some accommodations may raise their rates during peak times, which are Golden Week (Apr 29–May 5), Obon (mid-Aug), and the Okunchi Festival (Oct 7–9).

Expensive

Best Western Premier Hotel Nagasaki ★★★ One of Nagasaki's finest hotels, the Best Western's marbled lobby, decorated with large Oriental vases, has a distinct Asian flair. Rooms, which combine colonial-style decor with Chinese accents, offer the usual comforts, with one floor reserved for women and offering amenities geared toward female travelers. There are only three single rooms in the hotel, though discounts are given for single use of twins and doubles. Rooms on the 14th Sky Floor, with so-called Hollywood twins (two singles pushed together) or double beds, have the best views; otherwise, visit the 15th-floor buffet restaurant or bar for panoramic vistas.

2–26 Takara-machi, Nagasaki 850-0045. (✆) **800/528-1234** in the U.S. and Canada, or 095/821-1111. Fax 095/823-4309. www.bestwestern.co.jp/nagasaki. 183 units. ¥15,000–¥17,000 single; ¥22,526–¥31,767 double. Rates include breakfast. AE, DC, MC, V. Streetcar: Takara-machi (1 min.). Station: Nagasaki (8 min.); walk north in the direction of Peace Park. **Amenities:** 4 restaurants; bar; lounge; beer hall (summer only); babysitting; concierge; Japanese roof garden; room service; smoke-free rooms. *In room:* A/C, TV, hair dryer, Internet, minibar.

Hotel Majestic ★★ The Majestic is a small, charming, quiet hotel. The beautifully appointed rooms are decorated in one of several themes; the country-living theme, for example, sports wooden floors, light-oak furnishings, and claw-foot bathtubs. All rooms have small balconies and larger-than-average bathrooms. There are no singles, the cheapest twins offer no views, and even more expensive rooms overlook a parking lot toward views of the harbor, glimpsed between buildings (best views are from the fourth floor). No matter. The best things about this getaway are its small size—which means no tour-bus groups in the lobby—and its great location near Glover Garden. Its cozy, European-style restaurant/bar will make you feel at home.

2–28 Minami Yamate-machi, Nagasaki 850-0931. (✆) **095/827-7777.** Fax 095/827-6112. 23 units. ¥21,945–¥31,185 double. AE, DC, MC, V. Streetcar: 1 to Tsuki-machi, then 5 to Oura Tenshudoshita (2 min.); cross the bridge and walk straight past the ANA Hotel Nagasaki Glover Hill. **Amenities:** Restaurant; bar; smoke-free rooms. *In room:* A/C, TV, minibar.

Hotel New Nagasaki ★★   One of Nagasaki's deluxe hotels, the Hotel New Naga-saki beats Best Western in location, right next to the train station. Its rooms, with TVs providing 40 channels for music and radio, are among the city's largest, with some even offering a view of Nagasaki's busy port. Add the hotel's wide range of facilities (including a fitness club), and you have what amounts to one of Nagasaki's best choices. The huge, marbled lobby, however, can be crowded and noisy.

14–5 Daikoku-machi, Nagasaki 850-0057. ℂ **095/826-8000.** Fax 095/823-2000. www.newnaga.com. 130 units. ¥25,200–¥47,250 double; ¥27,300 executive double. Rates exclude service charge. AE, DC, MC, V. Station: Nagasaki (1 min., to the right). **Amenities:** 3 restaurants; bar; lounge; concierge; executive-level rooms; well-equipped fitness club w/indoor lap pool (and retractable roof) and sauna (fee: ¥5,250 for everything); room service; smoke-free rooms. *In room:* A/C, TV, hair dryer, Internet, minibar.

207 Sakamoto-ya ★★★ (Finds   This beautiful 114-year-old *ryokan* (Nagasaki's old-est) right in the heart of the city is a wonderful place, especially when you consider how rare traditional ryokan are nowadays in major Japanese cities. Most of the rooms, which are named after plants, flowers, and trees, have a Japanese-style bathtub made of wood, as well as traditional artwork on the walls. The best room is *Matsu No Ma* (Pine Room), which even has its own miniature garden with a tiny shrine. Rates vary according to the room and the meals served; you may opt for the *shippoku* dinner, a Nagasaki specialty consisting of a variety of dishes showing European and Chinese influences. Western breakfasts are also served on request.

2–13 Kanaya-machi, Nagasaki 850-0037. ℂ **095/826-8211.** Fax 095/825-5944. 10 units. ¥15,750–¥30,500 per person. Rates include breakfast and dinner. AE, DC, MC, V. Station: Nagasaki (10 min.). Take the streetcar or turn right out of the station and follow the streetcar tracks south to the 1st streetcar stop (Goto-machi); turn left on the street btw. Shinwa Bank and a travel agency, and walk up a slight incline to an old building, where you turn right. *In room:* A/C, TV, minibar.

Moderate

Chisun Grand Nagasaki   Close to the station, this combination tourist/business hotel with a sleek Italianate design and handicap-accessible public places evokes the atmosphere of a boutique hotel away from the crowds. We also like the hotel's discount ticket to the next-door hot springs and health club. Rooms are stylish yet practical, with comfortable beds sporting fluffy quilts with earth-tone runners, throw pillows, and recessed headboard shelves with controls. Rooms above the 10th floor have views of the city and harbor, while Grand Floor rooms on the 14th floor add MP3 docks, humidifi-ers/air purifiers, bathrobes, and other amenities. Unfortunately there are no closets, just wall-pegs with hangers. Note, too, that there are no singles.

5–35 Goto-machi, Nagasaki 850-0036. ℂ **095/826-1211.** Fax 095/826-1238. www.solarehotels.com. 153 units. ¥12,000–¥18,000 double; Chisun Grand floor from ¥15,000 double. AE, DC, MC, V. A 6-min. walk south of the station. **Amenities:** Restaurant; executive-level rooms; next-door health club and onsen (fee: ¥1,000); smoke-free rooms. *In room:* A/C, TV, fridge, hair dryer, Internet, MP3 docking station.

JR Kyushu Hotel Nagasaki   You can't get closer to Nagasaki Station than this busi-ness hotel on the station's second floor; those traveling with a Japan Rail Pass will also profit from a discount. Otherwise, rooms are your basic boxes, with alcoves serving as closets, small bathrooms, and no views. Those wishing to avoid any quality time in their rooms might take advantage of adjoining Amu Plaza's many shops and restaurants (the hotel's Royal Host coffee shop is also a good bet for breakfast).

1–1 Onoue-machi, Nagasaki 850-0058. ℂ **095/832-8000.** Fax 095/832-8001. www.jrhotelgroup.com. 144 units. ¥6,900 single; ¥12,600 double. 10% discount with Japan Rail Pass. AE, DC, MC, V. **Amenities:** Coffee shop; smoke-free rooms. *In room:* A/C, TV, fridge, hair dryer.

Nagasaki Hotel Monterey ★ Step into old Portugal in this whimsical place complete with whitewashed walls, imported tiles, a small chapel with decorations imported from Portugal, and hand-painted furnishings. There's even a kerosene lamp museum on hotel premises, free to hotel guests. Popular with young women, the hotel fits the historic past of Nagasaki and is conveniently located at the bottom of Hollander Slope. Rooms, too, give hints of Portugal with their terra-cotta-colored floor tiles, dark-wood or painted furniture, and shuttered windows.

1–22 Oura-machi, Nagasaki 850-0918. ℂ **095/827-7111.** Fax 095/820-7017. 123 units. ¥12,000–¥12,500 single; ¥16,500–¥37,500 double. AE, DC, MC, V. Streetcar: 1 to Tsuki-machi, then 5 to Oura Kaigan Dori (1 min.); walk inland. **Amenities:** 2 restaurants, smoke-free rooms. In room: A/C, TV, fridge, hair dryer, Internet.

Inexpensive

In addition to the choices below, the **Toyoko Inn Nagasaki Ekimae,** 5–45 Goto-machi (ℂ **095/825-1045;** www.toyoko-inn.com), is a 5-minute walk south of Nagasaki station. It offers small singles starting at ¥5,460 and doubles at ¥7,560, plus lobby computers with free Internet access and free Japanese breakfast.

Hotel Wingport Nagasaki This business hotel is closer to Nagasaki Station than Toyoko Inn but can't compete when it comes to services and amenities. Still, you might find a room here if other places are full. It offers mostly singles that couldn't get much smaller. However, the fact that they're spotless, with white walls and cheerful bedspreads, helps alleviate claustrophobia, as do good bed lights and windows that can be opened. Panels close for complete darkness; note that some rooms face another building. The deluxe twins are actually quite roomy for a business hotel, with a sofa, a semi-double-size bed, and a single bed.

9–2 Daikoku-machi, Nagasaki 850-0057. ℂ **095/833-2800.** Fax 095/833-2801. 200 units. ¥5,800 single; ¥8,000–¥12,000 double. AE, DC, MC, V. Station: Nagasaki (2 min.). Cross both sets of streetcar tracks in front of the station and take the small side street beside Family Mart. **Amenities:** Lobby computer w/free Internet. In room: A/C, TV, hair dryer, Internet.

Nagasaki International Hostel Akari ★ (Value) With the best prices in central Nagasaki, this family-owned, nonsmoking establishment is run by a friendly, English-speaking young couple, who provide more than just a bed, including a warm welcome, their own guide map, and even free "Short Walks with Nagasaki Locals" program, daily guided walks led by locals. Rooms (doubles, twins, and triples) have *tatami* floors but are outfitted with Western beds. In addition, there are two bathless dormitory-style rooms, one with bunk beds sleeping four people and the other sleeping eight.

2–2 Kojiyamachi, Nagasaki 850-0871. ℂ **095/801-7900.** www.nagasaki-hostel.com. 11 units (9 with bathroom). ¥5,600–¥6,000 double; ¥8,400 triple; ¥2,500 per person in dormitory. MC, V. Streetcar: 3 to Kokaido-mae (2 min.). **Amenities:** Lobby computer w/free Internet; kitchen; library. In room: A/C.

Nishikiso Bekkan This Japanese inn has a comfortable, lived-in atmosphere and friendly owners. Its simple *tatami* rooms vary in price depending on size and view, with the best views over rooftops from the *ryokan*'s hilltop location. It's located near the Hamano-machi shopping arcade in the heart of the city.

1–2–7 Nishikoshima, Nagasaki 850-0837. ℂ **095/826-6371.** Fax 095/828-0782. 11 units, 6 with bathroom. ¥4,200–¥5,250 per person. Breakfast ¥750 extra; dinner ¥3,675 extra. AE, DC, MC, V. Streetcar: 1 to Tsuki-machi, then 4 to Shianbashi. Head under the neon arch on the right onto Shianbashi Dori, turn right at the cute *koban* police box, walk 1 block past Maruyama Park and turn left; it will be on your right up the hill. In room: A/C, TV, minibar.

Victoria Inn Nagasaki ★★ 〔**Value**〕 Right in the heart of the city, this small hotel has an intimate lobby that resembles a rich merchant's home in old Nagasaki rather than a place to check in. Beds are at least double-size (some are even queen-size or king-size), but note that the cheapest singles face a wall 3m (1 ft.) away; if you're claustrophobic, specify a room with an outdoor view. One of the best things about this hotel is its convenient location, near Chinatown and just a stone's throw from the Hamano-machi shopping arcade and the city's nightlife. You can walk to most sites, including Glover Mansion and Sofukuji and Kofukuji temples. We also like its buffet restaurant specializing in seasonal organic dishes.

6–24 Doza-machi, Nagasaki 850-0841. 〔C〕 **095/828-1234.** Fax 095/828-0178. 87 units. ¥7,000–¥12,127 single; ¥7,700–¥23,100 double. AE, DC, MC, V. Streetcar: 1 to Kanko Dori (1 min.). The hotel is across from the streetcar stop, behind a building; look for its sign. **Amenities:** Restaurant (Tia, p. 521); bar; concierge; room service; smoke-free rooms. *In room:* A/C, TV, hair dryer, Internet, minibar.

WHERE TO DINE

Nagasaki's most famous food, called *shippoku,* is actually an entire meal of various courses with Chinese, European, and Japanese influences. It's a feast generally shared by a group of four or more and includes such dishes as fish soup, sashimi, and fried, boiled, and seasonal delicacies from land and sea. Another Nagasaki specialty is *champon,* a Chinese noodle usually served in soup with meat, seafood, and vegetables.

Nagasaki's nightlife district centers on a small area south of Hamano-machi known as **Shianbashi,** which begins just off the streetcar stop of the same name and is easily recognizable by the neon arch that stretches over the entrance of a street called Shianbashi Dori. Shianbashi shimmers with the lights of various drinking establishments and *yakitori-ya,* which are often the cheapest places to go for a light dinner. Another good hunting ground for restaurants is **China Town.**

Expensive

〔208〕**Kagetsu** ★★★ 〔**Finds**〕 SHIPPOKU/KAISEKI This traditional restaurant is the ultimate Japanese dining experience, an oasis of dignified old Japan, where kimono-clad waitresses shuffle down wooden corridors and serve guests constantly changing exquisite dishes in *tatami* rooms. First established in 1642 and formerly a geisha house, Kagetsu is one of Japan's longest-running restaurants; the oldest part of the present wooden building is about 360 years old. Display cases exhibit treasures related to Kagetsu's history. Behind the restaurant, which is set back from the road, is a beautiful 300-year-old garden. I'll never forget my evening stroll here as a half-moon rose above gnarled, stunted pines. The back of the restaurant, consisting mainly of glass, was lit up, so I could see into a multitude of private tatami rooms all on different levels. It was like a woodblock print suddenly sprung to life. There must be at least two of you if you want to feast on *shippoku* or *kaiseki.*

2–1 Maruyama-machi. 〔C〕 **095/822-0191.** Reservations required at least a day (a week is better) in advance. Lunch obento (available only weekdays) ¥5,200; shippoku set lunch ¥10,080; shippoku or kaiseki set meals ¥13,860–¥18,900. AE, DC, MC, V. Daily noon–3pm and 6–10pm (last order). Closed irregularly. Streetcar: Shianbashi (3 min.). Head under the neon arch of a bridge onto Shianbashi Dori, continue straight, and then take the road btw. the cute *koban* police box and the small park; it's straight ahead where the street ends, with the traditional gate.

Moderate

〔209〕**Gohan** ★★ ORIGINAL JAPANESE English-speaking owner-chef Tsunehiro Yoshimura is a musician, so you'll hear interesting music as you dine on creative, original meals here. The interior of this restaurant is authentically old; salvaged beams and pieces from five different houses were given new lives here. The handwritten menu changes daily, but the set dinner more than satisfies. Included may be sashimi, new potato with sesame seed, whole snapper, crayfish, tofu, soup, and rice. The dishes themselves are by Iwata Keisuke, a talented local potter of some renown, while hip waiters deliver food from an open kitchen. The entire experience is very highly recommended.

2–32 Aburayamachi. (C) **095/825-3600.** Set lunches ¥840–¥1,575; set dinners ¥3,150–¥6,300. AE, MC, V. Mon–Sat 11:30am–2pm and 5pm–midnight (last order 10pm). Streetcar: Shokakujishita (1 min.). Walk 1 block down Sofukuji-dori toward the temple and take the 1st left; it's the 2nd building on your right with the name on the *noren* (short curtains hung outside a shop or restaurant to signify it is open)—look carefully, it's easy to miss.

Harbin ★★ FRENCH/RUSSIAN Established in 1959, Harbin is a Nagasaki tradition, one of those places you don't want to miss. Its owner was born in Manchuria and named his restaurant after Harbin, a town close to his birthplace that was once an international city of Russian, Chinese, and Japanese residents. His family-run restaurant serves a unique blend of French and Russian cuisine; in recent years, his French-trained chef son has brought his own interpretations to the menu. A small, unpretentious-looking establishment, it offers a changing menu, written in Japanese, English, and Russian, which may include fried chicken Kiev style, Georgian spicy lamb pot, and roasted French duck in a red currant sauce, along with homemade sausages and bread. The *coulibiac* (traditional Russian salmon pie), when available, is perhaps the best thing on the menu. The ¥997 set lunch consists of *borsch* (beet soup), three kinds of *piroshki* (stuffed, savory pastries), salad, and coffee or tea.

Kanko Dori covered shopping arcade (which bisects Hamano-machi). (C) **095/824-6650.** Main dishes ¥1,575–¥3,625; set meals ¥3,675–¥6,300; set lunches ¥997–¥2,940. No credit cards. Daily 11:30am–2:30pm and 5–10pm (last order). Closed every other Wed. Streetcar: Kanko Dori. Walk straight through the covered shopping arcade to the 3rd block; it's on the left, above a Doutour coffee shop.

Hortensia INTERNATIONAL This buffet restaurant is located on the second floor of the Park Side Hotel in the leafy green area of Peace Park, next to the Atomic Bomb Museum, making it a good choice if you're in the area. Lunch (available until 2pm) features an all-you-can-eat buffet of Chinese, Western, and Japanese fare, as well as set meals. In the evenings, both set meals and a buffet are offered, except during the summer months (June–Aug) when the restaurant transforms itself into a beer garden (in spirit only, as it's indoors), with all you can eat and drink for ¥3,500 within a 2-hour time limit.

Park Side Hotel, 14–1 Heiwa-machi. (C) **095/845-3191.** Buffet lunch ¥1,400; buffet dinner ¥3,500; set meals ¥3,150–¥6,300. AE, DC, MC, V. Daily 11:30am–2pm and 5–9pm (last order). Streetcar: Hamaguchi-machi (3 min.).

Obinata ★★ (Finds) ITALIAN One of my favorite restaurants, Obinata is an oasis of old Europe in the heart of Kyushu. The place has a warm, earthy feel to it, due perhaps to its heavy wooden beams, large bouquets of flowers, oil wick lamps on each table, scattered antiques, and classical music playing softly in the background. The atmosphere is cozy and the service is a delight. The menu, in Italian, lists such dishes as beef filet grilled with crushed black pepper with cream sauce; veal and ham served with wine sauce; risotto; spaghetti; lasagna; and pizza, all served with fresh, homemade bread. Dishes are creative and fun, and there's a wide selection of Bordeaux, Moselle, and Rhine wines—the owner is a wine buff.

3–19 Funadaiku-machi. (C) **095/826-1437.** Main dishes ¥2,000–¥6,000; pizza and pasta ¥1,200–¥2,200. AE. Mon–Sat 6–11pm (last order). Streetcar: Shianbashi (3 min.). Walk under the neon-lit arch onto Shianbashi

Dori and go along the right side of the Fukusaya castella cake shop (an old traditional building); it will be almost immediately on your left—look for the sign.

(210) **Shikairo** ★★ CHAMPON   If you're interested in eating *champon* (a thick Chinese noodle usually served in soup with meat, seafood, and vegetables), this is the Chinese restaurant that claims to have invented it. First opened in 1899, it occupies a five-story modern building, with two red pillars and other hints of Chinese-influenced architecture, not far from Glover Garden. Unless you've made a reservation for a private room, take the elevator to the fifth floor, where you'll be treated to great harbor views and delicious food (be sure to dine at off-peak hours to snag a table with the best views). The English-language menu, complete with pictures, offers several champon set meals, including one for ¥1,470 that also includes *gyoza* (dumplings), rice, and pickled vegetables, available all day. After eating, be sure to see the restaurant's free museum on the second floor, where displays depict the history of the restaurant and objects relating to champon.

4–5 Matsugae-machi. ✆ 095/822-1296. Main dishes ¥997–¥1,985; set meals ¥1,470–¥3,150. AE, DC, MC, V. Daily 11:30am–3pm and 5–8pm (last order). Streetcar: Oura Tenshudoshita (1 min.).

(211) **Shippoku Hamakatsu** SHIPPOKU   This modern restaurant, just a minute's walk from the Hamano-machi covered shopping arcade (and behind Internet Café Cybac) is one of Nagasaki's best-known *shippoku* restaurants. The ground floor, with Western-style table seating, is made private with alcoves and bamboo screens; upstairs is a large *tatami* room with individual low tables and seat cushions. It offers shippoku set meals for lone diners for both lunch and dinner (¥2,940), making it a good place to try this unique cuisine if you're alone. More extensive set meals are for parties of two or more.

6–50 Kajiya-machi. ✆ 095/826-8321. Set lunches ¥1,000–¥2,940; dinner shippoku set meals ¥2,940–¥10,500. AE, DC, MC, V. Daily 11:30am–8:30pm (last order). Streetcar: Shianbashi (4 min.). Walk under the arch with the clock and take the 2nd right; it's in the middle of the block on the left (look for a black facade and a lattice door).

Tokiwa SASHIMI/TEMPURA/KAISEKI   Raw fish doesn't come any fresher than at this conveniently located restaurant between Hamano-machi and Glover Garden. Tokiwa features a wooden counter surrounding a large pool filled with live fish; when its number is up, the fish is scooped out of the water and then prepared right before your very eyes. Sometimes the fish is gutted and filleted with only the head, heart, and skeleton left intact, so that the sashimi can be arranged around the alive and still-quivering creature and be delivered to your table. Too fresh? Opt for one of the lunch *teishoku* (set meals), which range from sashimi to tempura.

Loisir Hotel, 2–33 Oura-machi. ✆ 095/824-2211. Set lunches ¥980–¥2,500; set dinners ¥2,100–¥8,400. AE, DC, MC, V. Daily 11:30am–2pm and 5–9:30pm (last order). Streetcar: Ourakaigan Dori (1 min.); across the street from the stop.

Inexpensive

(212) **Dai-ichi-no Taberu** INTERNATIONAL   Organic veggies, fish, stir fries, soups, noodles, and other healthy dishes are the focus of this all-you-can-eat buffet restaurant next to Nagasaki Station in Amu Plaza (which has many other restaurants; look for the sign THANKS GIVING! WE LOVE NATURE). Avoid the noontime rush, as hungry crowds make it a challenge to reach the food. Fortunately, dishes are replenished quickly, and something new is added frequently, making a second perusal of offerings almost mandatory. For ¥1,000 extra, you can add all the beer you can drink in 90 minutes.

5th floor, Amu Plaza, 1–1 Onoue-machi. ✆ 095/8182388. Buffet lunch ¥1,300 weekdays, ¥1,500 weekends; buffet dinner ¥1,600. No credit cards. Daily 11am–3pm and 5–11pm. Beside Nagasaki Station, in Amu Plaza.

Red Lantern LOCAL/NOODLES <u>Value</u>   On a fine summer's evening, one of the most picturesque places for a meal is at an outside table at Dejima Wharf, a complex of restaurants, bars, and shops strung along a boardwalk near the Dejima historic district. Red Lantern, with its delicious local fare, generous servings and reasonable prices, is a popular choice for locals and tourists alike. The ¥700 weekday lunch special—with a main dish plus rice, soup, and pickles—is a great deal.

Dejima Wharf, 1–1 Dejima. *©* **095/829-0475.** Main dishes ¥300–¥1,800; set lunches ¥800–¥850. AE, MC, V. Tues–Sun 11:30am–2:30pm and 5:30pm–midnight. Streetcar: Dejima (2 min.).

Tia ★ ORGANIC JAPANESE BUFFET   This restaurant's name ("aunt" in Spanish) reflects the homey atmosphere and home-cooked food your aunt might serve. With about 30 different organic dishes, from fish and pork to tofu and vegetables, there's enough variety to please everyone. In a rustic room with wooden tables, this restaurant has a diverse clientele and is very popular for lunch; if you're into speed eating, you can opt for a 30-minute buffet time limit for ¥800.

Victoria Inn, 6–24 Doza-machi. *©* **095/828-1234.** Obento lunch box ¥650; lunch buffet ¥1,300; set dinner ¥1,500; dinner buffet and all you can drink ¥3,500. AE, DC, MC, V. Daily 11:30am–3pm and 6–9pm. Streetcar: 1 to Kanko Dori (1 min.).

3 UNZEN SPA & ITS HELLS ★★

66km (41 miles) SE of Nagasaki

Unzen Spa is a small hot-spring resort town located about 700m (2,300 ft.) above sea level in the pine-covered hills of the Shimabara Peninsula. Thanks to its high altitude, cool mountain air, great scenery, and hot sulfur springs, Unzen became popular in the 1890s as a summer resort for American and European visitors, who came from as far away as Shanghai, Hong Kong, Harbin, and Singapore to escape the oppressively humid summers. They arrived in Unzen by bamboo palanquin from Obama, 11km (6¾ miles) away. In 1911, Unzen became the first prefectural park in Japan. In 1934, the area became **Unzen-Amakusa National Park** ★★, one of the nation's first national parks; it covers 282 sq. km (113 sq. miles).

I like Unzen Spa because it's small and navigable. It consists basically of just a few streets with hotels and *ryokan* spread along them, a welcome relief if you've been spending hectic weeks rushing through big cities and catching buses and trains. Hiking paths wind into the tree-covered hills, and dense clouds of steam arise from solfataras (vents) and fumaroles, evidence of volcanic activity. For visitors, the best result of all that thermal activity is the abundance of hot springs: Unzen's name derives from *"Onsen,"* meaning "hot spring."

ESSENTIALS

GETTING THERE   The only way to get to Unzen via public transportation is by bus. From Nagasaki, buses depart three times a day from the Ken-ei Bus Terminal (*©* **095/826-6221**) across the street from Nagasaki Station (sit on the right side of the bus for the most panoramic views). The ride takes about 1 hour and 40 minutes and costs ¥1,900 one-way. If you have a rail pass, take the train from Nagasaki to Isahaya Station, go straight out of the station and take the stairs on the right-hand side to cross the street, and then walk down the stairs to the Shimatetsu Bus Center (*©* **0957/22-4091**), where you can catch one of 10 buses a day to Unzen at a cost of ¥1,300 for the 75-minute trip.

Ask for bus and train schedules at the tourist information counter at Nagasaki Station. And by the way, both these buses pass through Obama, which sports flags with "I heart Obama" and a cartoon drawing of the U.S. president.

You can also reach Unzen from Kumamoto. From Kumamoto Port (which you can reach in 25 min. by bus from Kumamoto Station for ¥420), take the Kumamoto Ferry (✆ **096/356-2755;** 1 hr.) for ¥680 or the faster 30-minute Ocean Arrow for ¥800 to Shimabara Port, where you can catch a bus bound for Unzen, which takes an additional 40 minutes and costs ¥730 one-way.

VISITOR INFORMATION   Pick up the free leaflet "Nagasaki, Unzen, Goto Islands, Iki and Tsushima" from the Tourist Information Center in Tokyo or Kansai or Narita international airports, or download it from JNTO's website at www.jnto.go.jp by looking under "Browse by Destinations."

In Unzen, the **Tourist Information Center** (✆ **0957/73-3434;** www.unzen.org; daily 9am–5pm), is located in the heart of Unzen Spa next to the Unzen Spa House and across from the police station (btw. the Nishi-Iriguchi and Oyama-no-Johokan bus stops). Not much English is spoken, but it has a good English-language map of Unzen and the surrounding area, a hiking map, and an English-language audio guide for ¥200 per day that provides information on sights and history. Nearby is the park's **Mount Unzen Visitor Center** (✆ **0957/73-3636;** Fri–Wed 9am–6pm, to 5pm Nov–Mar), with displays and information on the entire national park and a knowledgeable park ranger who can provide hiking information.

GETTING AROUND   Buses from Nagasaki make four stops in Unzen Spa, terminating at Unzen's Shimatetsu Bus Center (✆ **0957/73-3366**). I've provided the bus-stop name for accommodations so you can alight at the nearest stop. Otherwise, Unzen is so small you can walk from one end to the other in about 20 minutes.

WHAT TO SEE & DO

When the area around Unzen Spa was designated a national park in 1934, it was named after what was thought to be an extinct volcanic chain, collectively called Mount Unzen. In 1990, however, a peak in Mount Unzen—Mount Fugen—erupted for the first time in almost 200 years, killing several dozen people on its eastern slope and leaving behind a huge lava dome. Unzen Spa, on the opposite side, was untouched and remains the area's most popular resort town.

THE HELLS (JIGOKU)   Unzen Spa literally bubbles with activity, as sulfurous hot springs erupt into surface cauldrons of scalding water in an area known as the Hells (Jigoku). Indeed, in the 1600s, these cauldrons were used for hellish punishment, as some 30 Christians were boiled alive here after Christianity was outlawed in Japan. Today, Unzen Spa has more than 30 solfataras and fumaroles, with the Hells providing the greatest show of geothermal activity, making this spot Unzen's number-one attraction. It's a favorite hangout of huge black ravens, and the barren land has been baked a chalky white through the centuries. Pathways lead through the hot-spring Hells, where sulfur vapors rise thickly to veil pine trees on surrounding hills. A simple cross erected on stones serves as a memorial to the Christians killed here.

PANORAMIC VIEWS ★   If you feel like taking an excursion, head for Mount Fugen, Unzen's most popular destination outside Unzen Spa. To reach it, make reservations for a shared taxi with Heisei Kanko Taxi (✆ **0975/73-2010**), which departs three times a day from the Visitor's Center to **Nita Pass,** about a 23-minute ride (round-trip fare:

ⓜ Moments **Fertile Grounds**

I was looking for an easy hike, somewhere quiet to write in my journal, and settled for Konohanasakuya-Hime Jinja, a hillside shrine established 300 years ago above the Gensei-Numa Marsh on the edge of Unzen Spa. Unknowingly, I had picked a shrine dedicated to the deity of flowers, where people come to pray for fertility, safe childbirth, and family harmony. So imagine my delight when I reached the shrine's small clearing to discover two unmistakable statues of— well, you'll just have to see for yourself. Benches provide views over Unzen to Mount Myoken and the ropeway.

¥860). From Nita Pass, board the 3-minute ropeway for ¥1,220 round-trip to go up higher to **Mount Myoken,** which at 1,333m (4,399 ft.) offers spectacular panoramic views. If you're ready for some real climbing, however, continue for another hour or so along a marked path leading starkly uphill to the summit of **Mount Fugen,** once Unzen's highest peak at 1,359m (4,485 ft.) above sea level—this is the peak that erupted in 1990. On a clear day, you'll be rewarded with splendid views of other volcanic peaks as far away as Mount Aso in the middle of Kyushu, as well as Mount Heisei Shinzan (a lava dome), born during Mount Fugen's last eruption and now Unzen's loftiest peak at 1,483m (4,894 ft.). Allow at least 2½ hours for the hike to Mount Fugen and back.

TAKING THE WATERS On the main street of Unzen are a finger spa and two foot spas, where you can soak the appropriate appendages in outdoor baths for free. If you'd like to get more than your feet wet (though all accommodations below offer hot-spring baths), the **Unzen Spa House,** across from the Unzen Kanko Hotel (© **0957/73-3131**), is open Monday to Saturday 10am to 6pm; on Sundays and holidays (including summer school vacation from mid-July through Aug), it's open to 7pm. Indoor cypress baths and *rotenburo* (outdoor hot-spring baths) cost ¥800. In the Spa House is also the **Vidro Museum** (daily 9am–6pm), with Edo-Era Nagasaki glass and Bohemian, Italian, French, and other glassware. Admission here is ¥700; or, buy a ticket for the spa and museum for ¥1,100.

WHERE TO STAY

Keep in mind that, as with most resort areas in Japan, Unzen tends to be crowded and sometimes even fully booked during Golden Week and New Year's, and from mid-July to August. The best times of year are late April to June, when Unzen's famous azalea bushes are in glorious bloom, and late October and early November, when the maple leaves turn brilliant reds.

With the exception of one inexpensive lodging at the end of this section, all the *ryokan* and hotels listed here are within an easy walk of bus stops along the route traversed by the bus from Nagasaki, so I've included the bus stops for each establishment below. You can also tell the bus driver where you're staying, and he'll drop you off at the nearest stop (if you're arriving from Kumamoto, buses go only to the bus terminal).

Expensive

Kyushu Hotel ★★★ Despite its name, the Kyushu Hotel, built in 1917, is a lovely, old-style *ryokan* in an updated building with a view of a lovely traditional garden from its luxurious lobby. Pluses include a gracious and accommodating staff (the third-generation owners speak English) and fusion cuisine served in the dining hall that successfully blends Western and Japanese styles, but you can also opt for Japanese meals served in your room. Best of all, the Kyushu Hotel offers some of the most scenic views in town; many of its rooms boast great views of the hills as well as the Hells. *Tatami* rooms feature alcoves with Western-style chairs next to large windows, affording relaxing places to take in the view. There are also five Western-style rooms and five combination rooms with tatami areas and beds. The communal baths are spacious and inviting with both indoor and outdoor bathing, but if you don't care to bathe with everyone, reserve the private family bath, also with outdoor bath, for ¥2,100 (there's a 40-min. time limit).

Obamacho, Unzen-shi 320, Nagasaki-ken 854-0697. ☎ **0957/73-3234.** Fax 0957/73-3733. qshuyyk@alpha.ocn.ne.jp. 90 units. ¥16,800–¥42,000 per person. Rates include breakfast and dinner. AE, DC, MC, V. Bus: Oyama-no-Johokan (1 min.). **Amenities:** Restaurant; bar; lounge; indoor/outdoor hot-spring baths. *In room:* A/C, TV, fridge, hair dryer.

(213) **Miyazaki Ryokan** ★★   One of the largest Japanese inns in Unzen, this modern *ryokan* first opened 75 years ago and overlooks a beautiful, gracefully manicured garden with hills and sulfur vapors rising in the background—absolutely exquisite when the azaleas are in bloom. Upon arrival, you'll be served green tea and sweets by graceful women in kimono. Afterward, you'll want to ease into the large, marble hot-spring bath overlooking a rock-lined outdoor bath, separated for men and women. Or, if you're shy about bathing with others or want to make it a family affair, make a reservation, at no extra charge, for the private family bath. Although breakfast (Western style, if desired) is served in a communal dining area, an excellent *kaiseki* dinner is served in your guest room in true ryokan fashion. In addition to Japanese-style *tatami* rooms, there are combination rooms with twin beds and a separate tatami area. Because rates are the same regardless of which direction the rooms face, I advise securing one that looks out over the garden or, barring that, the Hells (views from here are not as good, however, as from the Kyushu Hotel, above).

Obamacho, Unzen-shi 320, Nagasaki-ken 854-0692. ☎ **0957/73-3331.** Fax 0957/73-2313. www.miyazaki-ryokan.co.jp. 96 units. ¥16,800–¥42,000 per person. ¥2,000 extra per person Sat, nights before holidays, and ¥3,000 extra per person peak season. Rates include breakfast and dinner. AE, DC, MC, V. Bus: Oyama-no-Johokan (2 min.). **Amenities:** Lounge; indoor/outdoor hot-spring baths; sauna. *In room:* A/C, TV, hair dryer.

Moderate

Unzen Kanko Hotel ★★★ (Finds)   If you're the least bit romantic, you won't be able to resist staying at this old-fashioned mountain lodge, built in 1935 of stone and wood, covered in ivy, and resembling a Swiss chalet. No wonder it's been designated an Important Tangible Cultural Heritage Site. The lobby, main dining hall, and public spaces have changed little over the decades, with whitewashed walls, dark-beamed ceilings, and inviting sofas and chairs. The rooms are rustic and old-fashioned, too, with heavy ceiling-to-floor curtains tied back to reveal a balcony (ask for a room facing the front), brass doorsills, a high ceiling, and wooden beams, along with modern additions such as duvet-covered beds.

Obamacho, Unzen-shi 320, Nagasaki-ken 854-0621. ☎ **0957/73-3263.** Fax 0957/73-3419. www.unzenkankohotel.com. 48 units. ¥13,860 single; ¥23,100 double. AE, DC, MC, V. Bus: Nishi-Iriguchi (1 min.). **Amenities:** Restaurant; bar; lounge; billiard room; hot-spring baths (including a family bath; get the key at reception); library. *In room:* A/C, TV, hair dryer.

⑭**Kaseya Ryokan**   Located on the main street through town not far from the bus center (the last stop on buses into town from Nagasaki), this economically priced *ryokan* dates from 1909. The kind owners are fond of children; they have three of their own and remembered my cowriter's daughter many years later. All of the rooms are Japanese style, simply decorated but with high ceilings and flower arrangements. Ask for a room in the back—they're quieter. A small shop in the lobby sells handmade crafts, while a massage chair is available free of charge. Coffee is free in the mornings, and Western-style breakfasts are available.

Obamacho, Unzen-shi 315, Nagasaki-ken 854-0621. ✆ **0957/73-3321.** Fax 0957/73-3322. info@kaseya. jp. 13 units, none with bathroom. ¥8,550 per person. Rates higher during Golden Week and New Year's. Rates include breakfast and dinner. AE, MC, V. Bus: Jinja-mae (2 min.). **Amenities:** Hot-spring baths (including a private one for families); lobby computer w/free Internet. *In room:* A/C, TV.

⑮ **Seiunso Kokumin Shukusha** ⓥ**alue**   Formerly a youth hostel, this updated public lodging offers as much comfort and as many facilities as a moderately priced resort hotel. Rooms are pleasant, Japanese style (you lay out your own futon here); most have a small balcony offering views of the surrounding woods, and all have sinks and toilets. There are also three combination rooms with both beds and *tatami* areas that are quite spacious, are accessible to travelers with disabilities, and have the best views; you can stay in these rooms for the same charge if they're not booked. In addition to public baths, there are two private family baths (¥1,050 for 50 min.). Reserve early to stay here. The main disadvantage is that the location is outside Unzen, about a 30-minute walk from the Hells, and check-in isn't until 4pm.

Obamacho, Unzen-shi 500–1, Nagasaki-ken 854-0621. ✆ **0957/73-3273.** Fax 0957/73-2698. 63 units (without bathroom but with toilets). ¥7,920 per person with 2 meals. No credit cards. Bus: Nishi-Iriguchi (20 min.). Pickup service available from Shimatetsu Bus Center. **Amenities:** Restaurant; indoor/outdoor hot-spring baths w/relaxation room; playground. *In room:* A/C, TV.

WHERE TO DINE

Even if you don't stay at the **Unzen Kanko Hotel,** you may want to come here for lunch. Its old-fashioned dining hall is large with a high ceiling, wainscoting, wooden floors, white tablecloths, and flowers on each table. It serves both Japanese and Western selections, with two set lunches for ¥3,000 and ¥3,800 and set dinners for ¥9,800, along with a la carte items such as beef curry and pasta. The dining hall is open for lunch from noon to 2pm and for dinner starting at 6pm, with last orders taken at 8pm.

Hyaku-nen JAPANESE FUSION   The best views in town, a photo menu, an English-speaking staff, and delicious food make this a solid choice for lunch. The *Okami Nabe* lunch for ¥1,600 may include sashimi, boiled vegetables, and flavored steamed rice, along with mushrooms, pork, vegetables, egg and rice cake that you cook at your table for the *nabe* (stew cooked at your table), followed by dessert and tea.

In the Kyushu Hotel. ✆ **0957/73-3234.** Set meals ¥1,600–¥3,000. AE, MC, V. Daily 11am–4pm. Bus: Nishi-Iriguchi (1 min.).

Spa House Restaurant LOCAL DISHES   The most popular dish in this simple restaurant is *Shimabara nabe,* a soup with rice cake, chicken, and vegetables. Other types of soups, stews, and eel are also served.

In the Spa House. ✆ **0957/73-3131.** Main dishes ¥850–¥1,200. AE, MC, V. Daily 11am–4pm. Bus: Nishi-Iriguchi (1 min.).

4 KUMAMOTO ★

1,293km (804 miles) SW of Tokyo; 189km (118 miles) S of Fukuoka

Located roughly halfway down Kyushu's western side, Kumamoto boasts a fine castle and a landscaped garden, both with origins stretching from the first half of the 17th century. Once one of Japan's most important castle towns, Kumamoto today is the progressive capital of Kumamoto Prefecture, with a population of 670,000. Yet it retains a small-town atmosphere, which is precisely why I like it.

ESSENTIALS

Getting There   By Plane   JAL and **ANA** fly to Kumamoto Airport (KMJ; ✆ **096/ 232-2810;** www.kmj-ab.co.jp) from Tokyo in 1 hour and 40 minutes, with one-way fares ranging from ¥14,600 for a 28-day advance purchase on certain flights to ¥36,800 for a regular ticket. Local airline **Skynet Asia Airways** (✆ **0120/737-283** toll-free; www. skynetasia.co.jp) offers a regular one-way ticket for ¥28,600, but advance-purchase tickets can go as low a ¥11,600. Airport shuttle buses operate from the airport to Kumamoto Station and the Kumamoto Kotsu (bus) Center downtown, taking about 54 minutes and costing ¥670.

By Train   It takes about 9 hours to reach Kumamoto from **Tokyo,** not including transfers, at a cost of ¥22,340 for an unreserved seat. From **Fukuoka's Hakata Station** (terminus of the bullet train from Tokyo), limited express trains depart three times an hour, reaching Kumamoto in about 1½ hours and costing ¥3,740 for a reserved seat. (In 2011, a new bullet train will connect Kumamoto and Fukuoka in 35 min.) There are also four express trains daily from **Beppu,** reaching Kumamoto in 3 hours.

VISITOR INFORMATION   The leaflet "Kumamoto and Mount Aso," distributed by the Tourist Information Centers in Tokyo and in Narita and Kansai international airports, contains information on how to get to Kumamoto and places of interest in the city (you can also download it from JNTO's website at www.jnto.go.jp by going to "Browse by Destinations"). In Kumamoto, here's a **Kumamoto Tourist Office** inside Kumamoto Station near the ticket gate (✆ **096/352-3743;** daily 8:30am–7pm). It has an English-language map and brochure and is staffed by helpful English speakers who can make lodging reservations. In the city center, there's another Kumamoto Tourist Information kiosk at Ninomaru parking lot west of the Hohoate gate of Kumamoto Castle (✆ **096/322-5060;** daily 9am–5:30pm, to 5pm Nov–Mar). If you're coming by plane, stop by the **Kumamoto Airport Information Office** (✆ **096/232-2810;** daily 6:50am– 9:30pm).

More information is available on the city's website at **www.city.kumamoto.kumamoto. jp** and Kumamoto Prefecture's website at **www.visitkumamoto.com**.

INTERNET ACCESS   The **Kumamoto City International Center,** 4–8 Hanabata-cho (✆ **096/359–2121;** streetcar: Kumamotojo-mae), offers three computers with free Internet access on the second floor Monday to Friday 9am to 8pm and weekends 9am to 7pm (closed the second and fourth Mon of every month). Otherwise, **Media Café Popeye,** located on the Kamitori covered shopping street (✆ **096/326-6767;** streetcar: Torichosuji), is open 24 hours and charges ¥420 for an hour's use of its computers.

MAIL & ATMS   There's a convenient post office, with ATMs that accept international credit cards, at Kumamoto Station's north side; it's open Monday to Friday 8am to 7pm

> **Tips** **Bus & Ferry from Unzen Spa**
>
> From Unzen Spa, the fastest way to reach Kumamoto is to take a bus (there are nine daily departures) 40 minutes to Shimabara Port (fare: ¥730), where you can then board a 1-hour ferry (fare: ¥680) or a 30-minute Ocean Arrow (fare: ¥800) to Kumamoto Port. Buses connect Kumamoto Port with Kumamoto Station in 25 minutes for ¥420.

and weekends 9am to 7pm. Kumamoto's main post office, located in front of the Senba-bashi streetcar stop, has longer hours: Monday to Friday 7am to 11pm, Saturday 9am to 9pm, and Sunday and holidays 9am to 7pm.

ORIENTATION & GETTING AROUND **Kumamoto Station** lies far south of the city's downtown area, but transportation between the two is easy via streetcar no. 2, which departs from in front of the station and reaches the downtown area in about 10 minutes. **Downtown** centers on three covered shopping streets called Shimotori, Kamitori, and Sunroad Shinshigai, with many department stores, shops, hotels, bars, pachinko parlors, and restaurants in the area. Here, too, is the city's bus station, the **Kumamoto Kotsu Center,** from which all buses in the city depart. Just north of downtown, within walking distance, rises **Kumamoto Castle,** which is surrounded by moats, turrets, and expansive greenery, on the edge of which are several museums and historic sites. **Suizenji Garden** lies far to the east.

Getting around Kumamoto via old-fashioned **streetcar** is easy because there are only two lines. Streetcar no. 2 is most convenient for tourists; the only one departing from Kumamoto Station, it passes through downtown and near Kumamoto Castle (stop: Kumamotojo-mae) before going onward to Suizenji Garden (stop: Suizenji-Koen-mae). Streetcar fare is a flat rate of ¥150; pay when you get off.

Because the grounds surrounding Kumamoto Castle encompass 97 hectares (242 acres), with a circumference of 9km (5½ miles), many visitors opt to see sights via the **Kumamoto Castle Loop Bus** (Shiromegulin), which departs every 30 minutes from Kumamoto Station, operates daily from 8:30am to 5pm, and stops at Kumoto Castle, Hosokawa Mansion, and other places of interest. This bus costs ¥130 for a single journey or ¥300 for the entire day along with discounts to attractions on its route.

If you plan on taking public transportation at least four times in 1 day, you can save money by purchasing a **1-day pass,** which allows unlimited travel on streetcars and all city buses (but irritatingly, not the Kumamoto Castle Loop Bus) for ¥500. It includes a 20% discount to six sights, including Kumamoto Castle.

THE TOP ATTRACTIONS

Kumamoto Castle ★★   Completed in 1607, Kumamoto Castle is massive. It took 7 years to build, under the direction of Kato Kiyomasa, a great warrior who fought alongside Tokugawa Ieyasu in battle and was rewarded for his loyalty with land. The castle was built atop a hill and had two main towers, 49 turrets, 29 gates, and 18 two-story gatehouses; to make the walls impossible for enemies to scale, they were built with curves at the bottom and nearly vertical at the top and were crowned with an overhang. More than 100 wells ensured water even during a siege, while camphor and gingko trees were planted for firewood and edible nuts. The castle passed into the possession of the Hosokawa family in 1632 and remained an important stronghold for the Tokugawa shogunate throughout its 250 years of rule, particularly in campaigns against the powerful and independent-minded lords of southern Kyushu. During that time, 11 generations of the Hosokawa clan ruled over Kumamoto.

Much of the castle was destroyed in 1877 during the Seinan Rebellion led by Saigo Takamori, a samurai who was unhappy with the new policies of the Meiji government in which ancient samurai rights were rescinded. Saigo led a troop of samurai in an attack on the castle and its imperial troops, who remained under siege for 53 days before government reinforcements finally arrived and quelled the rebellion. When the smoke cleared, most of the castle lay in smoldering ruins.

The castle was reconstructed in 1960 of ferroconcrete, and although it's not nearly as massive as before, it's still quite impressive and remains Kumamoto's star attraction (famous Japanese director Kurosawa Akira used it for his epic drama *Ran*). The interior houses a museum with elaborately decorated palanquins, models of Kumamoto and the castle during the Edo Period, armor, swords, former possessions of both Kato Kiyomasa and the Hosokawa family, and rifles and other artifacts from the Seinan Rebellion. Beside the castle is a replica of Honmaru Goten Palace, a 17th-century palace that was destroyed in the Seinan Rebellion but has been painstakingly reconstructed using traditional methods. Behind the castle is one of 11 remaining turrets, which is three tiered and five stories. Because the castle grounds are large, you'll probably spend more than an hour here. If you intend to visit Hosokawa Mansion (see "More to See & Do," below), buy a joint ticket for entrance to both sights (¥640 for adults and ¥240 for children).

1–1 Honmaru. ℂ 096/352-5900. Admission ¥500 adults, ¥200 children. Apr–Oct daily 8:30am–5:30pm; Nov–Mar daily 8:30am–4:30pm. Kumamoto Castle Loop Bus: stop 5 (5 min.). Streetcar: Kumamotojo-mae (10 min.) or Shiyakusho-mae (6 min.).

Suizenji Garden (Suizenji Jojuen) ★   Laid out in the 1630s by Hosokawa Tadatoshi as a retreat for the tea ceremony and as the grounds of a nearby temple, Suizenji Garden took about 80 years to complete. The garden wraps itself around a cold spring-fed lake (considered particularly good for making tea). But what makes the place especially interesting is that its design incorporates famous scenes in miniature from the 53 stages of the ancient **Tokaido Highway,** which connected Kyoto and Tokyo. (The 53 stages were also immortalized in Hiroshige's famous woodblock prints.) Most recognizable are cone-shaped Mount Fuji and Lake Biwa; near the garden's entrance is Nihon Bashi (Bridge of Japan), Edo's starting point on the Tokaido Road. The park is small—almost disappointingly so—and for the life of me, I can't figure out more than a handful of the 53 stages. Maybe you'll have better luck. Pastoral views are also marred by—my pet peeve—surrounding buildings. Take solace by sipping tea in a traditional thatched-roof teahouse with views of the pond (under renovation until autumn of 2010). Also on garden grounds is **Izumi Shrine,** built in 1878 and dedicated to the Hosokawa lords, as well as a *noh* theater, where noh is performed in spring and fall ceremonies. A stroll of the garden takes about 30 minutes.

8–1 Suizenji Koen. ℂ 096/383-0074. Admission ¥400 adults, ¥200 children. Mar–Nov daily 7:30am–6pm; Dec–Feb daily 8:30am–5pm. Streetcar: 2 from Kumamoto Station or the downtown area to Suizenji-Koen-mae (about a 20-min. ride), followed by a 3-min. walk (back the way you've come, take the 1st right and the next right along a narrow shop-lined street).

Contemporary Art Museum, Kumamoto ★ (Finds) Because it's free (except during special exhibitions) and centrally located in downtown Kumamoto, consider taking a 30-minute jaunt through this forerunner in contemporary art, in which art is treated as an experience rather than something to be viewed passively by the viewer. Showcasing works by local talent Ide Nobumichi, as well as commissioned installations by Kusama Yayoi (look for her *Infinity Mirrored Room*) and Miyajima Tatsuo (with a pillar of flashing diodes) and special exhibits, it seems more like a community center than a museum, with a children's play corner and a Ping-Pong table designed by Ishii Hiroshi that responds digitally to the ball. My favorite is the library, with art, books, and comfortable sofas (a favorite place, apparently, for dozing off), where there's a free jam session the second and fourth Friday of every month at 6:30pm, as well as nightly piano music from 7 to 7:30pm, followed by 10 minutes of darkness in which a ceiling light installation, by James Turrell, slowly transforms from blue to red.

2-3 Kamitori-cho. © **096/278-7500.** www.camk.or.jp. Free admission, except for some special exhibits. Wed–Mon 10am–8pm (you must enter by 7:30pm). Streetcar: Toricho-suji (1 min.).

Hosokawa Mansion (Kyu-Hosokawa Gyobutei) ★ A 10-minute walk north of Kumamoto Castle, this 300-year-old samurai mansion was built by a subsidiary member of the Hosokawa clan, Lord Gyobu, and was enlarged in the 1800s. Guided tours (often available in English) lasting 15 minutes take visitors through 24 rooms, including the lord's study and reception room, teahouse, kitchen, and servants' quarters. You'll see Edo-Era furnishings and personal items including an Edo clock, a suitcase, clothing, games, a woman's cosmetic case, lacquerware, a kimono chest, and more, giving you a good idea of how feudal lords lived during the Edo Period.

3-1 Furukyo-machi. © **096/352-6522.** Admission ¥300 adults, ¥100 children. Combination ticket for Hosokawa Mansion and Kumamoto Castle ¥640 adults, ¥240 children. Apr–Oct daily 8:30am–5:30pm; Nov–Mar daily 8:30am–4:30pm. Kumamoto Castle Loop Bus: stop 7 (1 min.).

SHOOTING THE KUMAGAWA RAPIDS ★★

If you've had enough of shrines, castles, and gardens, consider shooting the **Kumagawa Rapids.** Compared to wild rivers in the United States, the Kumagawa seems pretty tame; people do the trip not so much for the thrill of the ride but for the scenery of a narrow river valley bordered by wooded hills and for the camaraderie afforded by sitting on *tatami* in a traditional wooden boat steered by boatmen fore and aft. You can also ride a modern raft guided by a staff of young professionals that goes through slightly rougher water. Reservations are a must for all rides.

The **Kumagawa Kudari Kabushiki Company,** Shimoshin-machi 333–1 (a 20-min. walk from Hitoyoshi Station; walk straight ahead to the third stoplight and turn left), Hitoyoshi City (© **0966/22-5555**), offers two different 90-minute routes in its wooden boats. The **Calm Course (Seiryu Course)** covers 8km (5 miles) of a gentle stretch of the river beginning in Hitoyoshi and ending in Watari. It's offered year-round; December through February, the boats have *kotatsu* (small, quilt-covered tables with heaters). The cost is ¥2,835 for adults and ¥1,890 for children; winter trips with kotatsu cost ¥3,675 and ¥2,835, respectively.

The **Rapids Course (Kyuryu Course)** covers 10km (6¼ miles), beginning downriver in Watari (a 5-min. walk from Watari Station; turn left out of the station and left again over the tracks) and ending in Kyusendo, and is more exciting and requires more skillful maneuvering, though the river is still only a grade 2. It's offered April through October and costs ¥3,675 for adults and ¥2,100 for children. During rainy season (mid-June to mid-July), this trip is sometimes canceled due to swollen rivers or high winds.

Kumagawa Kudari Kabushiki also offers rafting. The **Fighting Course** (90 min.) for ¥6,300 begins at Watari Station; from there you'll be taken to Ishochi, where you will put in and raft to Kyusendo. The **All Around** rafting course (3 hr.) runs from Watari to Kyusendo and costs ¥7,875. Both of these run April through October, include a post-trip soak in an *onsen* in Kumagawa-sou, and conclude with a return trip via minibus to Watari. Note, however, that children 10 and under and adults 60 and over are not allowed on rafting trips.

You can reach **Hitoyoshi** by bus from Kumamoto Kotsu Center in about 1½ hours, with fares costing ¥2,300 one-way. There are also six trains a day from Kumamoto Station to Hitoyoshi; the express train takes 1½ hours and costs ¥1,774. Trains and buses connect Watari and Kyusendo with Kumamoto. If you're going onward to **Kagoshima,** you can return to Hitoyoshi by local train for a bus that will deliver you to Kagoshima Chuo Station in 2 hours for ¥2,070. There is also a retrofitted scenic sightseeing train, the **Isaburo-Shinpei,** which travels between Hitoyoshi and Yoshimatsu twice a day in a little over an hour, including switchbacks along the way and stops at scenic overlooks. The fare is ¥720, with a surcharge of ¥500 added during peak season (free for holders of Japan Rail Pass). From Yoshimatsu, it then takes 1 hour and 40 minutes by train onward to Kagoshima Chuo Station (fare: ¥1,430). For timetables, contact the JR information office in Kumamoto Station.

SHOPPING

One of Kumamoto's most famous products is its Higo Inlay or **damascene,** in which gold, silver, and copper are inlaid on an iron plate to form patterns of flowers, bamboo, and other designs. Originally used to adorn sword guards and armor, damascene today is used on such accessories as paperweights, jewelry, and tie clasps. Another Kumamoto product is the **Yamaga lantern,** made of gold paper and used during the Yamaga Lantern Festival held in August. Other local products include Amakusa pearls, pottery, knives, toys, and bamboo items.

One place to shop for Higo Inlay, pottery, tea, *shochu,* sake, and confections is the ㉖ **Display Hall of Kumamoto Products (Kumamoto-ken Bussankan),** located on the ground floor of the NTT Building at 3–1 Sakura-machi (✆ **096/353-1168;** daily 10am–6:30pm). It's a 1-minute walk west of the Kumamotojo-mae streetcar stop.

The **Prefectural Traditional Crafts Center,** near Kumamoto Castle at 3–35 Chibajo-machi (✆ **096/324-4930;** Tues–Sun 9am–5pm) offers a wider selection of traditional crafts from throughout the prefecture, including Yamaga paper lanterns, Amakusa pearls, bamboo-ware, ceramics, woodworks, toys, musical instruments, and more. It's a 5-minute walk from the Skiyakusho-mae streetcar stop or take Kumamoto Castle Loop Bus to Stop 8.

WHERE TO STAY

Expensive

Hotel New Otani Kumamoto ★★ (Value) A convenient location next to the station, the respected New Otani name, a perceptive staff, a unique design, and reasonable rates are reasons to stay here. Rooms are comfortable, with queen-size beds in both single and double rooms, and come with individual reading lights with dimmer switches, windows with blinds to block light and double-paned glass to block noise, massage shower heads, and such extras as hangers with nonslip pads and bathroom phones.

1–13–1 Kasuga, Kumamoto 860-0047. ℂ **800/421-8795** in the U.S. and Canada, or 096/326-1111. Fax
096/326-0800. www.newotani.co.jp. 130 units. ¥12,705 single; ¥20,790–¥36,960 double. AE, DC, MC, V.
Station: Kumamoto (1 min., to the left). **Amenities:** 4 restaurants, including Fontana di Otani (p. 533); 2
bars (1 w/live piano music); men's sauna (fee: ¥1,050); lobby computer (¥100 for 10 min.); room service;
smoke-free rooms. *In room:* A/C, TV, hair dryer, Internet, minibar.

Hotel Nikko Kumamoto ★★★   In the same building as the Contemporary Art
Museum and an adjoining shopping complex in the heart of downtown, this 14-story
hotel with upbeat modern decor is the most luxurious in Kumamoto. Large, comfortable
rooms, with views of either Kumamoto Castle or Mount Aso in the distance, offer sitting
areas, closets that light up as soon as you open them, focused bedside reading lights so
your partner can sleep, blackout curtains for total darkness, and excellent insulation from
traffic noise. Singles sport double-size beds, doubles have queen-size beds, and twins have
large bathrooms with separate tub/shower/toilet areas.

2–1 Kamitori-cho, Kumamoto 860-8536. ℂ **800/645-5687** in the U.S. and Canada, or 096/211-1111. Fax
096/211-1175. www.nikko-kumamoto.co.jp. 191 units. ¥17,325 single; ¥31,185–¥43,890 double. AE, DC,
MC, V. Streetcar: Toricho-suji (1 min.). **Amenities:** 4 restaurants, including Tao-Li (p. 533); lounge; concierge; room service; smoke-free rooms. *In room:* A/C, TV, hair dryer, Internet, minibar.

Moderate

JR Kyushu Hotel Kumamoto ★ (Value   This business hotel right next to Kumamoto Station offers convenience, reasonable prices, and 10% discounts for holders of the
Japan Rail Pass. As a whopping 140 of its 150 rooms are singles, make reservations in
advance for its one double or eight twin rooms. (It also has one room for those with
limited mobility.) Singles are small but have surprisingly roomy bathrooms, while twins
are corner rooms with windows on two sides and a sofa.

3–15–15 Kasuga, Kumamoto 860-0047. ℂ **096/354-8000.** Fax 096/354-8012. www.jrhotelgroup.com.
150 units. ¥6,900 single; ¥12,600 double. AE, DC, MC, V. Station: Kumamoto (1 min., to the right). **Amenities:** Restaurant; smoke-free rooms. *In room:* A/C, TV, fridge, hair dryer, Internet.

KKR Hotel Kumamoto ★ (Finds   Located north of Kumamoto Castle across the
street, this trendy hotel buzzes with activity as a popular wedding and banquet venue
(weekdays are quieter and also cheaper). The best reason to stay here is its up-close view
of the castle, with the absolute best views provided by twin and triple rooms above the
hotel's rooftop garden (visible also from the hotel's Japanese restaurant). Unfortunately,
none of the hotel's 11 single rooms have castle views (solo travelers can stay in a castle-
view twin for ¥10,000), and there are no double rooms.

3–31 Chibajo-machi, Kumamoto 860-0001. ℂ **096/355-0121.** Fax 096/355-7955. 54 units. ¥8,000 single;
¥14,500–¥16,000 double. ¥1,000 extra per person on nights before holidays. AE, DC, MC, V. Kumamoto
Castle Loop Bus: Kumamoto Prefectural Traditional Crafts Center (2 min.) Streetcar: Shyakusho-mae (10
min., follow the streetcar tracks north and then take the 1st left over the bridge; the hotel is straight
ahead.) **Amenities:** 2 restaurants; free rental bicycles. *In room:* A/C, TV, fridge, hair dryer, Internet.

Kumamoto Hotel Castle   This tall brick hotel is just east of Kumamoto Castle, with
good views of the castle from some of its more expensive twin rooms. A subdued and
conservative hotel that's been a city mainstay for more than 45 years, it's popular with
middle-aged Japanese, including locals who come for receptions or to dine in one of its
restaurants. Rooms are rather standard, with the cheapest singles no larger than those at
the Toyoko Inn (see below), though deluxe doubles and twins face the castle in a more
spacious setting with windows that open.

4–2 Joto-machi, Kumamoto 860-8565. ℂ **096/326-3311.** Fax 096/326-3324. www.hotel-castle.co.jp. 185 units. ¥10,279–¥16,747 single; ¥18,480–¥28,875 double. AE, DC, MC, V. Streetcar: Shiyakusho-mae (2 min.). **Amenities:** 3 restaurants; bar; room service; smoke-free rooms. *In room:* A/C, TV, hair dryer, Internet, minibar.

Inexpensive

Kajita Stuffed birds, a mongoose, and a cobra greet you at this friendly, family-run establishment; a stay here certainly won't be your cookie-cutter hotel experience. A member of the Japanese Inn Group, it has a central location, just a 10-minute walk to the castle grounds and a 2-minute walk to the streetcar that will take you onward to Suizenji Garden. *Tatami* rooms, named after flowers, are simple but clean. If you call, you'll most likely be picked up at the station. A cupboard in the hall has self-service coffee and tea free of charge.

1–2–7 Shinmachi, Kumamoto 860-0004. ℂ **096/353-1546.** Fax 096/353-1546. higoshiro@yahoo.co.jp. 10 units, none with bathroom. ¥4,000 single; ¥7,200 double; ¥10,500 triple. Breakfast ¥700 extra; dinner ¥2,000 extra. AE, MC, V. Bus: 1 from Kumamoto Station to Shinmachi stop (2 min.). Take the narrow road btw. a bank and a big brick health center and then take the 1st left. It's on the left, on the corner. *In room:* A/C, TV, no phone.

Toyoko Inn Kumamoto Shinshigai (Value) Right in the middle of downtown near department stores and shopping, this business chain offers the usual tiny rooms and free perks that make it the number-one choice for budget travelers, including free domestic calls from lobby phones, free Wi-Fi in the lobby, and free nightly in-room movies (sometimes in English). Just a 2-minute walk away is Toyoko Inn Kumamoto Karashima Koen, 1–24 Koyaimamachi (ℂ **096/322-1045**), but most convenient is the Toyoko Inn Kumamoto Ekimae, just a 2-minute walk from the station at 2–8–10 Kasuga (ℂ **096/351-1045**), both with similar low prices and the same amenities.

3–25 Shinshigai, Kumamoto 860-0803. ℂ **096/324-1045.** Fax 096/324-1046. www.toyoko-inn.com. 221 units. ¥5,775 single; ¥8,085 double. Rates include Japanese breakfast. AE, DC, MC, V. Streetcar: Karashimacho (1 min.). Walk down Sunroad Shinshigai covered shopping arcade and take the 2nd left onto Sakae Dori. **Amenities:** Lobby computers w/free Internet; smoke-free rooms. *In room:* A/C, TV w/free movies, fridge, hair dryer, Internet.

WHERE TO DINE

Kumamoto's specialties include *dengaku* (tofu, and sometimes taro and fish, coated with bean paste and grilled on a fire), *karashi renkon* (lotus root that has been boiled, filled with a mixture of bean paste and mustard, and then deep-fried), and *basashi* (raw horse meat sliced thin and then dipped in soy sauce flavored with ginger or garlic).

Expensive

(217) **Senri** ★★ LOCAL SPECIALTIES/VARIED JAPANESE You can try Kumamoto's local dishes at this restaurant right in Suizenji Garden, available from a Japanese menu featuring set meals. For lunch, you can choose main dishes such as eel, river fish, or tempura, served with side dishes of vegetable, soup, rice, and tea. Or order the *kyodo-ryori* course, which includes local specialties such as fried lotus, *basashi,* and *dengaku.* In the evening, only *kaiseki* cuisine is available and it must be ordered at least 1 day in advance. Dining is in small *tatami* rooms; choice rooms face the garden.

Suizenji Garden. ℂ **096/381-1415.** Reservations recommended, a must for kaiseki. Kaiseki set dinners from ¥5,250; set lunches ¥2,100–¥3,150. No credit cards. Daily 11am–2pm and 5–9pm. Streetcar: Suizenji-Koen-mae; Senri has its own entrance to the right of Suizenji Garden's main gate and also an entrance in Suizenji Garden.

Tao-Li ★ NOUVELLE CANTONESE   This sophisticated contemporary restaurant in the heart of downtown serves Cantonese cuisine, though with a nouvelle twist to such standards as sweet-and-sour pork and Peking duck. Set meals are the way to go with the English-language menu; the *Yamucha* (dim sum) set lunch, for example, offers an appetizer, soup, sautéed vegetables, rice or noodles, and a dessert along with fried, steamed, and crispy-fried dumplings. There must be a minimum of two persons, however, for the set dinners.

Hotel Nikko Kumamoto, 2–1 Kamitori-cho. ✆ **096/211-1662.** Set lunches ¥1,600–¥3,100; set dinners ¥5,775–¥12,000. AE, DC, MC, V. Daily 11:30am–2:30pm and 5–9:30pm (last order). Streetcar: Toricho-suji (1 min.).

Moderate

⑱ **Aoyagi** ★ LOCAL SPECIALTIES   Everyone in Kumamoto knows this restaurant, located in the downtown area just off the Shimotori covered shopping arcade. The modern building offers seating on *tatami,* at the counter, or at low tables with leg wells. There are photos outside the front door and in the menu showing dishes of *basashi,* eel, *kamameshi* (rice casseroles), and other local specialties. A tasty vegetarian set meal for ¥2,000 includes *dengaku* and *renkon,* while three types of set dinners for ¥5,250 include all the local favorites. Set lunches center on kamameshi and sushi, such as the Ladies' Sushi Set for ¥1,600.

1-2-10 Shimotori. ✆ **096/353-0311.** Set lunches ¥1,000–¥3,150; set dinners ¥1,580–¥5,250. AE, MC, V. Daily 11:30am–10pm. Streetcar: Toricho-suji (2 min.). Walk down Shimotori shopping arcade 2 blocks to Sannenzakadori (just past Daiei) and turn right; it's in the 2nd block on the right.

Fontana di Otani ITALIAN/CONTINENTAL   For dining near Kumamoto Station, this casual restaurant in one of Kumamoto's most well-known hotels is a good bet. Its menu features lighter fare such as spaghetti, curry, and sandwiches, available all day, as well as a very reasonably priced set lunch (served until 2pm) that includes a trip through a salad bar. The set dinner (available 5–9pm) offers a choice of main dish, such as sea bream and clams in a Marsala sauce, along with side dishes.

Hotel New Otani Kumamoto, 1-13-1 Kasuga. ✆ **096/326-1111.** Main dishes ¥1,260–¥1,680; set dinners ¥3,000; set lunches ¥1,300–¥1,500. AE, DC, MC, V. Daily 11:30am–10pm. Station: Kumamoto (1 min., to the left).

Inexpensive

⑲ **Higo Fukunoya** ★ **Finds** ORGANIC JAPANESE   Although its location is not convenient to either Kagoshima Station or downtown (it lies on the streetcar route btw. them), people who like healthy, organic meals go out of their way to dine at this restaurant, simply decorated with rough wooden floors, contemporary Japanese background music, and tables overlooking a canal. It's located at the back of a complex of Edo-Era buildings, which also contain an organic health-food store and shops selling natural, environmentally friendly products. For lunch there's a vegetarian set lunch, two *obento* choices, and a *kaiseki* meal, while dinner features three kaiseki meals.

15 Nakatoji-machi. ✆ **096/323-1552.** Reservations required for dinner. Set lunches ¥1,260–¥3,150; set dinners ¥3,150–¥7,350. AE, MC, V. Thurs–Tues 11:30am–2pm and 6–9:30pm (last order; last order Sun 8:30pm). Streetcar: Gofukumachi (1 min.). Head straight ahead (instead of turning like the tracks); turn right at the 1st light; it will be on your left.

⑳ **Kokutei** **Value** NOODLES   Located in a simple black-and-white building, this famous ramen restaurant has been serving homemade noodles since 1959. Its name means "in the black" house—they must have known they'd be a success. Popular with locals from office workers to grandmothers, it can get quite crowded (avoid the lunch rush). Prices depend on the number of pork slices you choose to eat with your ramen or whether you add an egg or vegetables. Don't eat noodles? Ask for *me iranai* and you'll have a steaming bowl of soup.

1-2-29 Nihongi. ℂ **096/352-1648.** Noodles ¥590–¥820. No credit cards. Daily 10:30am–8:30pm (closed 1st and 3rd Thurs of every month). Kumamoto Station (5 min.) Turn right out of the station and left at the Nihongi-guchi streetcar stop; it's up ahead, on the right on the corner.

(221) **Tateki** ★ KUSHIAGE   Located on a street filled with striptease clubs (be sure to match the *kanji* in chapter 17 with the sign outside the door—otherwise you'll get more than skewered food), this 30-year-old restaurant serves *kushiage*, or skewered meats and vegetables. Although kushiage isn't unusual in Japan, Tateki's method of cooking and serving it is: Instead of counter seating, behind which the cook prepares your food, here you sit on *tatami* while a waiter in a beret kneels at your personal hibachi and grills your meal in front of you. The least-expensive set dinner comes with 10 sticks of meat and vegetables plus appetizer, salad, and *soba*, while the set lunch consists of seven sticks, two sauces, rice, soup, appetizer, and salad.

Kaishika Building, 1–11–8 Shimotori. ℂ **096/325-4989.** Set lunch ¥1,050; set dinners ¥2,100–¥4,200. No credit cards. Daily 11:30am–11pm. Streetcar: Kumamotojo-mae (5 min.). Walk east on Ginza Dori 3 blocks, turn right into the Shimotori shopping arcade, and after 1 block turn right onto an unmarked street called Korinjidori; Tateki will be on the left toward the back of the 2nd (brick) building with a statue of a dog outside.

5 KAGOSHIMA ★

1,483km (927 miles) SW of Tokyo; 315km (197 miles) S of Fukuoka; 197km (123 miles) S of Kumamoto; 343km (214 miles) SW of Beppu

With a population of 600,000 residents and as capital of Kagoshima Prefecture, Kagoshima is a city of palm trees, flowering trees and bushes, wide avenues, and people who are like the weather—warm, mild-tempered, and easygoing. The city spreads along Kinko Bay and boasts one of the most unusual bay vistas in the world: Sakurajima, an active volcano, rising from the waters. During summer vacation (July 21–Aug), there are nightly fireworks displays over the bay (with a huge one held the end of Aug). Kagoshima is also home to Sengan-en Garden, one of my favorite gardens in Japan.

Because of its relative isolation at the southern tip of Japan, far away from the capitals of Kyoto and Tokyo, Kagoshima has developed an independent spirit through the centuries that has fostered a number of great men and accomplishments. Foremost is the Shimazu clan (also spelled Shimazu), a remarkable family that for 29 generations (almost 700 years) ruled over Kagoshima and its vicinity before the Meiji Restoration in 1868. Much of Japan's early contact with the outside world was via Kagoshima, first with China and then with the Western world. Japan's first contact with Christianity occurred in Kagoshima when St. Francis Xavier landed here in 1549; although he stayed only 10 months, he converted more than 600 Japanese to Christianity. Kagoshima is also where firearms were introduced to Japan.

By the mid–19th century, as the Tokugawa shogunate began losing strength and the confidence of the people, the Shimazu family was already looking toward the future and the modernization of Japan. In the mid-1850s, the Shimazu family built the first Western-style factory in the country, employing 200 men to make cannons, glass, ceramics, land mines, ships, and farming tools. In 1865, while Japan's doors were still officially closed to the outside world and all contact with foreigners was forbidden, the Shimadzu family smuggled 19 young men to Britain so they could learn foreign languages and technology. After these men returned to Japan, they became a driving force in the Meiji Restoration and Japan's modernization.

Another historical figure who played a major role during the Meiji Restoration was Saigo Takamori, who was born in Kagoshima Prefecture. A philosopher, scholar, educator, and poet, he helped restore Emperor Meiji to power, but because he was also a samurai, he subsequently became disillusioned when the ancient rights of the samurai class were rescinded and the wearing of swords was forbidden. He led a force of samurai against the government in what is called the Seinan Rebellion but was defeated. He then withdrew to Shiroyama in Kagoshima, where he committed suicide in 1877. Today, Saigo has many fans among Japanese, who still visit the cave on Shiroyama Hill where he committed suicide.

ESSENTIALS

GETTING THERE   By Plane   You can reach Kagoshima Airport (KOJ; www.koj-ab. co.jp) from Tokyo (flight time: 1 hr. 45 min.), Osaka (1 hr. 10 min.), and Sapporo (2 hr. 35 min.) in addition to several other cities in Japan. JAL one-way fares range from ¥14,600 for a 28-day advance purchase to ¥39,000 for a regular ticket. Skynet Asia Airways (toll-free © 0120/737-283; www.skynetasia.co.jp), offers four flights daily from Tokyo's Haneda Airport for ¥31,600 one-way (and as low as ¥12,600 for an advance-purchase ticket for certain flights). The airport is linked to Kagoshima Chuo Station in 1 hour by **limousine bus,** which departs every 10 to 15 minutes and costs ¥1,200.

By JR Train   Thanks to the Kyushu Shinkansen Tsubame, which presently links Kagoshima with Shin-Yatsushiro but will stretch the entire length between Kagoshima and Fukuoka by 2011, travel time is approximately 8½ hours from Tokyo (if you have a Rail Pass, travel time will be slower because you can't take the Nozomi), 5 hours from Osaka, 2 hours and 12 minutes from Fukuoka, and 1 hour from Kumamoto. Tickets from Tokyo cost ¥26,980 for an unreserved seat, ¥8,920 from Fukuoka, and ¥5,850 from Kumamoto. All trains travel to Kagoshima Chuo (Central) Station.

By Bus   Buses connect Kyushu's cities more cheaply than the train. From Fukuoka's Tenjin Station, 24 buses depart daily and cost ¥5,300 one-way for the 4-hour trip.

VISITOR INFORMATION   Stop by the Tourist Information Centers in Tokyo or Narita or Kansai international airports to pick up the leaflet called "Kagoshima and Vicinity," which includes information on Ibusuki and Chiran, or download it from JNTO's website at www.jnto.go.jp by looking under "Browse by Destinations."

In Kagoshima, there's a Tourist Information Center at **Kagoshima Chuo Station** (© **099/253-2500;** daily 8:30am–7pm) near the East Exit, as well as at the airport (© **0995/58-4686;** daily 7am–9:15pm). They have good English-language maps and a hefty guide that covers everything from public transportation to recommended sightseeing itineraries.

The **Kagoshima Prefectural Visitors Bureau** is located on the first floor of the Sangyo Kaikan Building, 9–1 Meizan-cho (© **099/223-5771;** Mon–Fri 8:30am–5:15pm), where you can obtain information on the city as well as the prefecture, including Ibusuki and Chiran. To find the office, take the streetcar to the Asahi-Dori stop and then walk southeast (toward the bay); the Sangyo Kaikan Building is on your left in the second block. More information is available at **www.kagoshima-kankou.com/for.**

INTERNET ACCESS **Comic Buster,** 3–1 Chuo-cho (© **099/250-6369**), is about a 1-minute walk to the left after exiting from Kagoshima Chuo Station's east exit, on the fourth floor next to Sunkus convenience store. Open 24 hours, it charges ¥120 for 30 minutes.

MAIL & ATMS Kagoshima's main post office (© **099/252-4188**), where you can send letters and packages and obtain cash through ATMs, is located just north of Kagoshima Chuo Station, past the Amu Plaza. Its ATMs are open Monday to Friday 7am to 11pm, Saturday 9am to 9pm, and Sunday 9am to 7pm.

ORIENTATION & GETTING AROUND Downtown Kagoshima lies between Kagoshima Chuo Station with its adjacent Amu Plaza (a shopping, restaurant, and recreation complex—you'll see the Ferris wheel on top) and Kinko Bay, northeast of the station, with **Tenmonkan-Dori** (a covered shopping street) serving as the heart of the city.

You can walk from the station to downtown in about 20 minutes, but the city is also easy to get around by **streetcar** and **bus.** There are two streetcar lines (fare: ¥160), as well as two types of buses—City View buses and Kagoshima City buses. The **Kagoshima City buses** are regular buses used as commuter transportation by the people living here, while the **City View buses** are geared toward tourists. Running every 30 minutes from 9am to 5pm daily (to 5:30pm daily mid-July through Aug), City View buses look like old-time streetcars, have English-language announcements, and travel a 14km (9-mile) circuit through the city, beginning at Kagoshima Chuo Station (with departures on the hour and half-hour). They stop at all tourist sights, including Sengan-en, Sakurajima Ferry Terminal and Kagoshima Aquarium, and Tenmonkan covered shopping street. The fare is ¥180, half fare for children, and you pay when you get off. There is also a Night City View bus that operates to popular viewing spots around the city.

If you think you'll be doing a lot of traveling by streetcar and bus (including City View buses), invest in a 1-day pass for ¥600, half fare for children, allowing unlimited travel on Kagoshima's streetcars and on City View and Kagoshima City buses, plus slight discounts to the top attractions, including the ferry to Sakurajima and Sengan-en. Passes can be purchased at the Tourist Information Center in Kagoshima Chuo Station and aboard buses and streetcars.

WHAT TO SEE & DO
The Top Attractions
MOUNT SAKURAJIMA ★ With ties to Naples, Italy, as its sister city, Kagoshima bills itself the "Naples of the Orient." That's perhaps stretching things a bit, but Kagoshima is balmy most of the year and even has its own Mount Vesuvius: Mount Sakurajima, an active volcano across Kinko Bay that has erupted 30 times through recorded history and

---

Moments **Evening Cruises**

One of the most popular ways to enjoy summer nights in Kagoshima is on a boat cruise of Kinko Bay, offered mid-July through August every evening from 7 to 9pm (except for a few days during Obon in mid-Aug), the highlight of which are fireworks over the water. Boats depart from the Kagoshima side of the Sakurajima Ferry Terminal and charge ¥1,000 for adults, half fare for children. Call © **099/293-2525** for more information.

continues to puff steam into the sky and occasionally cover the city with fine soot and ash. In 1914, Sakurajima had a whopper of an eruption and belched up 3 billion tons of lava. When the eruption was over, the townspeople were surprised to discover that the flow was so great it now blocked the 500m-wide (1,700-ft.) channel separating the volcano from a neighboring peninsula; Sakurajima, which had once been an island, was now part of the mainland.

Magnificent from far away and impressive if you're near the top, Sakurajima can be visited by **ferry,** which departs from the Sakurajima Ferry Terminal. The terminal is about an 8-minute walk from downtown Kagoshima or the Shiyakusho-mae streetcar stop, or a 2-minute walk from the Kagoshima Suizokukan-mae/Sakurajima-sanbashi City View bus stop. Ferries run 24 hours, departing every 10 to 15 minutes during the day and about once an hour through the night. The 15-minute trip to Sakurajima costs ¥150 for adults, ¥80 for children. Upon reaching Sakurajima, stop off at the small **tourist counter** (© 099/293-4333; daily 8:30am–5pm) in the ferry terminal for a map of the island and information about buses to Furusato Onsen and beyond.

There are lava fields with walking paths near Sakurajima's ferry pier. The **Nagisa Lava Trail** is a 3km (1¼-mile) trail that starts near the pier and travels past huge lava boulders and pine trees (many, unfortunately, dying of disease). From the nearby **Sakurajima Visitor Center** (© 099/293-2443), with displays relating the history and natural history of Sakurajima, longer trails lead to the **Karasujima Observation Point.**

Another fun thing to do on Sakurajima is visit **Furusato Onsen ★★**, at the Furusato Kanko Hotel (© 099/221-3111), with open-air hot-spring baths set amid lava rocks right beside the sea. It has an indoor 25m (82-ft.) lap pool heated with hot-spring water, and indoor hot-spring baths with windows overlooking the bay. You wear your swimsuit in the pools but should completely disrobe and wear only the provided white cotton *yukata* when using the outdoor bath (an English-language handout provides guidelines). Furosato Onsen is open to visitors daily 8am to 8pm. Note, however, that various parts of the *onsen* are closed for cleaning on different days of the week: The outdoor bath is closed Monday and Thursday until 3pm; the indoor hot-spring bath is closed Wednesday until 2pm; and the indoor hot-spring pool is closed Wednesday and Thursday until noon. Admission is ¥1,050 including yukata; bring your own towel or buy one for another ¥210. You can reach Furusato Onsen by taking the free **Furusato Kanko Hotel shuttle bus** departing daily from the Sakurajima Ferry Terminal every 30 minutes from 8:45am to 5pm (no service 12:20–2:20pm). Otherwise, take the **Kagoshima Kotsu Bus** that departs daily once an hour from the ferry terminal, costing ¥290 for the 15-minute trip. For more information on the Furusato Kanko Hotel, see "Where to Stay," below.

GUIDED TOURS OF SAKURAJIMA   Because Sakurajima is sparsely populated with only limited public transportation, you might want to join one of two tours operating daily that visit lava fields, lookout points (including the Yunohira lookout point halfway up the volcano), a shrine half-buried in lava, and other sights. The JR Kyushu Bus 6-hour tour for ¥4,000 combines city sights and Sakurajima (© 099/247-5244), while the 3½-hour Sakurajima Nature Sightseeing Tour costs ¥2,200 (© 099/257-2111). Buses depart from Kagoshima Chuo Station East 9 and East 8 platforms, respectively. Children pay half fare.

SENGAN-EN GARDEN ★★★   Whereas Sakurajima, rising dramatically out of the bay, is Kagoshima's best-known landmark, Sengan-en, 9700–1 Yoshino-cho (© 099/247-1551), is its most widely visited attraction. The grounds of a countryside villa, it's a garden laid out more than 300 years ago by the Shimadzu clan, incorporating Sakurajima

(Fun Facts) **Mount Sakurajima's Produce**

Mount Sakurajima's rich soil grows the world's largest radishes, averaging about 17 kilograms (37 lb.) but sometimes weighing in at as much as 36 kilograms (80 lb.), and the world's smallest oranges, only 3 centimeters (1¼ in.) in diameter.

and Kinko Bay into its design scheme in a principle known as borrowed landscape. There's a lovely grove of bamboo, a waterfall located a 30-minute walk up a nature trail with good views over the bay, and the requisite pond, but my favorite is a particularly idyllic spot where the 21st lord of the Shimadzu family held famous poem-composing garden parties. Guests seated themselves on stones beside a gently meandering rivulet and were requested to have completed a poem by the time a cup filled with sake came drifting by on the tiny brook. Ah, those were the days! Today it remains Japan's only garden with its original *kyokusui* (poem-composing garden) still intact.

The good life is also apparent in the **Iso Residence,** which was built as a villa by the Shimadzu clan about 350 years ago and became the family's main residence when the Meiji Restoration made feudal lords obsolete. Now only one-third its original size, the stately manor can be viewed by joining a tour conducted every 20 minutes and given in Japanese only (but with an English-language information sheet). You'll see 11 of the villa's 25 rooms, including a bedroom, a bathroom, a dressing room, living quarters, and reception rooms; throughout are furnishings and artifacts that once belonged to the Shimadzu clan. Ceremonial green tea and a sweet are included with the tour, served in a room with a view of an inner pond and garden. The 32nd generation of the Shimadzu family, incidentally, now resides in Kagoshima.

A must after visiting the garden, and included in the admission price to Sengan-en, is the **Shoko Shuseikan Museum,** located next to the garden. Built in the mid-1850s as Japan's first industrial factory, it houses items relating to the almost 700-year history of the Shimadzu clan, including family heirlooms ranging from lacquerware to tea-ceremony objects, palanquins used to carry Shimadzu lords back and forth to Edo (present-day Tokyo; the trip from Kagoshima took 40–60 days), everyday items used by the family, and photographs. An exhibit explores southern Kyushu's role in maritime trade and the scope of the Shuseikan Project in its manufacture of cannons, textiles, and other products. In all, you'll probably spend at least 2 hours seeing everything, especially if you stop off at souvenir shops selling Satsuma glassware, pongee silk, and other Kagoshima products.

Sengan-en and the Shoko Shuseikan Museum are open daily from 8:30am to 5:30pm (to 5:20pm in winter); Iso Residence is open daily from 9am to 4:40pm (last tour). Admission to Sengan-en and Shoko Shuseikan Museum is ¥1,000 for adults and ¥500 for children. Tours of the residence are an extra ¥500 for adults and ¥250 for children. To reach Sengan-en, which is on the edge of town to the north, take a City View bus (30 min. from Kagoshima Chuo Station) to the Sengan-en-mae bus stop.

MORE TO SEE & DO

KAGOSHIMA CITY AQUARIUM (SUIZOKU-KAN IOWORLD) This aquarium, within walking distance of downtown and located beside the Sakurajima Ferry Terminal at 3–1 Honko-Shinmachi (© **099/226-2233;** daily 9:30am–6pm; you must enter by

5pm; closed first Mon in Dec and the following 4 days), concentrates on sea life from waters surrounding Kagoshima Prefecture. The largest tank is home to stingrays, bluefin tuna, Japanese anchovy, a whale shark, and other creatures from the Kuroshio (Black Current), which flows from the East China Sea past Kagoshima to the Pacific Ocean. Another tank contains squid, octopuses, the Japanese giant crab (the world's largest crab), and fish that inhabit the Kagoshima seas. Other highlights include the world's only display of tube worms (which inhabit the deep sea by hydrothermal vents), a 3-D movie of the surrounding seas, the world's largest eel, and a children's touch pool. Dolphins, which have access to open waters, are used only for educational shows (conducted in Japanese only). Expect to spend at least an hour here, more if you have kids. Admission is ¥1,500 for adults, ¥750 for junior-high and high-school students, and ¥350 for children. It's an 8-minute walk from the Suizokukan-guchi streetcar stop, or take a City View bus to the Kagoshima City Aquarium bus stop.

MUSEUMS   For an overview of Japanese history in general and Kagoshima Prefecture in particular, visit the ⑫ **Kagoshima Prefectural Museum of Culture (Reimeikan),** 7–2 Shiroyama-cho (🕿 **099/222-5100;** Tues–Sun 9am–5pm; closed 25th of each month unless it falls on Sat or Sun). It occupies the former site of Tsurumaru Castle, of which only the stone ramparts and moat remain. Upon entering the museum, you'll walk over a glass floor above a map of Kagoshima Prefecture (much of it is islands). The museum then traces the history of the people of Kagoshima over the last 30,000 years, including the rise of the Shimadzu clan in the 11th century and Kagoshima's preeminence as a pottery center after Korean potters were brought here in the late 1500s. There are models of an 18th-century samurai settlement, Tsurumaru Castle, and, best of all, Tenmonkan-Dori as it might have looked 80 years ago. The second floor is devoted to folklore and everyday life with bambooware, festival objects, and farming and fishing implements. The third floor shows Satsuma swords, pottery, scrolls, and paintings and has a hands-on learning room for children with old-fashioned toys and samurai outfits that can be tried on. You'll spend about an hour here. Admission is ¥300 for adults, ¥190 for college and high-school students, and ¥120 for children. To reach it, take a City View bus to the Satsuma Retainers Memorial stop or take a streetcar to Shiyakusho-mae stop; it's a 4-minute walk inland.

Only a few minutes' walk away from the Prefectural Museum is the **Kagoshima City Museum of Art (Kagoshima Shiritsu Bijutsukan),** 4–36 Shiroyma-cho (🕿 **099/224-3400;** Tues–Sun 9:30am–6pm), which has a collection of Western-style works by artists from Kagoshima Prefecture. Look for the portrait of Saigo Takamori, painted by Masayoshi Tokonomi, to the left upon entering the permanent gallery. A small selection of paintings by Western artists is also displayed (Pissarro, Monet, Renoir, Matisse, Kandinsky, Picasso, Warhol), as well as decorative art including the famous Satsuma pottery and cut glass. You can see everything in about 20 minutes. Admission is ¥200 for adults, ¥150 for college and high-school students, and ¥100 for children. To reach the museum, take a City View bus to Statue of Saigo Takamori stop; the museum is a minute's walk away to the right of the statue. Or take the streetcar to Asahi-Dori and take the street beside the Minami-Nippon bank; it's a 5-minute walk ahead.

Although it's not as conveniently located, the **Nagashima Museum** ★★★, 3–42–18 Take (🕿 **099/250-5400;** daily 9am–5pm), is a very worthwhile private museum on a hill high atop the city with great views of Sakurajima and Kagoshima. While its focus is mostly works by such Kagoshima artists as Kuroda Seiki, it also contains some works by well-known Western artists such as Picasso, Braque, Kandinsky, Renoir, and Chagall, as well as pottery from South America. But most impressive, in my opinion, is an outstanding collection of mainly 19th-century white Satsuma pottery, including many pieces that were originally imported to London, Paris, and New York, and the more utilitarian 17th- to 20th-century black Satsuma pottery. An hour is enough time to see everything, but try to time your visit so you can eat lunch in the museum's French restaurant, **Camellia** (open daily 11am–3pm with set meals starting at ¥1,800 weekdays and ¥2,000 weekends), which has great views over the city. Admission to the museum is ¥1,000 for adults, ¥800 for college and high-school students, and ¥400 for children. You'll have to take a taxi to get here; it's about a 7-minute ride from Kagoshima Chuo Station.

A SIDE TRIP TO THE GARDENS OF CHIRAN

If you have an extra morning or afternoon, I suggest taking an excursion to **Chiran ★★**, a small village 31km (19 miles) south of Kagoshima. Surrounded by wooded hills and rows of neatly cultivated tea plantations, it's one of 102 castle towns that once bordered the Shimadzu kingdom during the Edo Period. Although the castle is no longer standing, seven old gardens and samurai houses have been carefully preserved.

Apparently, the village headman of Chiran had the opportunity to travel with his lord Shimadzu in the mid-1700s to Kyoto and Edo, taking with him some of his local samurai as retainers. The headman and his retainers were so impressed with the sophisticated culture of Kyoto and Edo that they invited gardeners to Chiran to construct a series of modestly sized gardens on the samurai estates surrounding the castle.

Some of these gardens remain and are located on a delightful road nicknamed **Samurai Lane,** which is lined with moss-covered stone walls and hedges. As descendants of the samurai are still living in the houses, only the gardens are open to the public. There are two types of gardens represented: One, belonging to the Mori family, is of the miniature artificial-hill style, in which a central pond symbolizes the sea, and rocks represent the mountains; the others are "dry" gardens, in which the sea is symbolized not by water but by white sand that is raked to give it the effect of rippling water. The gardens are masterful demonstrations of the borrowed-landscape technique, in which surrounding mountains and scenery are incorporated into the general garden design. Although the gardens are small, they are exquisite and charming. Notice, for example, how the tops of hedges are cut to resemble rolling hills, blending with the shapes of mountains in the background.

The seven gardens open to the public are indicated by a white marker in front of each entry gate. All seven can be visited for ¥500 for adults, ¥300 for children, and they're open daily from 9am to 5pm. Plan on about an hour to see them. For more information on the samurai gardens, call ☎ **0993/58-7878.**

I also recommend a visit to Chiran's **Peace Museum for Kamikaze Pilots (Heiwa Kaikan; ☎ 0993/83-2525;** daily 9am–5pm), dedicated to the mostly young pilots who trained in Chiran for World War II suicide missions, steering bomb-laden planes into Allied warships and other targets. In addition to *kamikaze* aircraft and uniforms, it displays photographs of 1,036 pilots just before their departures, along with farewell letters and personal memorabilia. A film shows actual footage of the kamikaze pilots in action. Although there isn't much in English, there's an English-language pamphlet, and volunteers are sometimes on hand to explain the museum (to be sure a guide is available, call for a reservation). You'll spend about an hour here. Admission is ¥500 for adults, ¥300 for children.

Chiran's samurai gardens can be reached in about 1½ hours by a bus that departs across the street from Kagoshima Chuo Station at stop no. 16 East (the tourist office in the station has a timetable and a map showing bus departures). There are eight buses a day, including departures at 9:07, 10:17, and 11:17am; the ride costs ¥850 to the Bukeyashiki-Iriguchi bus stop. The same bus then travels onward to the Peace Museum (bus stop: Tokkokannon-Iriguchi) in 7 minutes. There are also three buses a day between the samurai gardens and Ibusuki (see section 6, later in this chapter), with the fare costing ¥940.

SHOPPING

Local Kagoshima products include *oshima tsumugi,* beautiful silk made into such items as clothing, handbags, and wallets; *shochu,* an alcoholic drink made from such ingredients as sweet potatoes and drunk on the rocks or mixed with hot or cold water; furniture, statues, and chests made from **yaku cedar;** and **Satsuma pottery**—probably Kagoshima's most famous product. It has been produced in the Kagoshima area for more than 380 years. Satsuma pottery comes in two styles: black and white. White Satsuma pottery is more elegant, thus it was used by former lords; the black pottery was used by the townspeople in everyday life.

A good place to shop for local items is the **Kagoshima Brands Shop,** downtown in the Sangyo Kaikan Building (the same building housing the Kagoshima Prefectural Visitors Bureau) at 9–1 Meizan-cho (ⓒ **099/225-6120;** daily 9am–6pm, closed the first and third Sun of the month). This one-room shop offers tinware, handmade knives, Satsuma pottery, glassware, *oshima tsumugi,* yaku cedar, *shochu,* and other locally made items. To reach it, take the streetcar to the Asahi-Dori stop, from which the shop is a 1-minute walk away toward the bay.

The most famous cake of Kagoshima (the one all Japanese tourists must buy before returning home) is *karukan,* a delicious spongy white cake made from rice, with Chinese and Korean origins. The most famous maker of karukan today is ㉓ **Akashiya,** 4–16 Kinseicho (ⓒ **099/226-0431;** daily 9am–7pm), which began selling the cakes 160 years ago. It has the solemnity of a first-rate jewelry store and is just as refined. It's located on the side street to the right of Yamakataya department store, a 1-minute walk from the Asahi-Dori streetcar stop. Although cakes are now available made with an *anko* (sweet red-bean paste) center, old-timers insist that only the plain white square ones (¥ 189 for a small, good snack) are the real thing.

WHERE TO STAY

Expensive

Castle Park Hotel (Shiroyama Kanko Hotel) ★★   Kagoshima's foremost hotel sits 106m (353 ft.) high atop the wood-covered Shiroyama Hill and commands a great view of the city below and Sakurajima across the bay. Opened more than 40 years ago, it offers updated, comfortable rooms, the most recommended (and more expensive) of which face the volcano and city with the best views in town. Other pluses include hot-spring (including open-air) baths with views of Kinko Bay, a free English-language movie shown nightly on a screen off the lobby, and good restaurants that take advantage of the hotel's views and gardenlike setting (I especially like the buffet restaurant with its outdoor terrace and the microbrewery with its summer beer garden). In short, this is a great respite from city life, and to offset the hotel's main drawback—an isolated location away from the city center—it offers free shuttle buses to Tenmonkan-Dori in the heart of the city and Kagoshima Chuo Station every hour or more frequently (it's also served by both daytime and the night City View buses).

41-1 Shinshoin-cho, Kagoshima 890-8586. ⓒ **099/224-2211.** Fax 099/224-2222. www.shiroyama-g. co.jp. 365 units. ¥12,000–¥22,000 single; ¥22,000–¥49,000 double. ¥1,000 extra per person Fri; ¥2,000 extra per person Sat and holidays. AE, DC, MC, V. Taxi or free shuttle bus 12 min. from Kagoshima Chuo

> **(Tips)   A Note on Japanese Characters**
>
> Many establishments and attractions in Japan do not have signs in Roman (Eng-
> lish-language) letters. Those that don't are indicated in this guide with an oval
> with a number that corresponds to a number in chapter 17 showing the Japa-
> nese equivalent. Thus, to find the Japanese characters for, say, Furusato Kanko
> Hotel (see below), refer to no. 224 in chapter 17.

Station. City View Bus: Shiroyama (1 min.). **Amenities:** 5 restaurants; lounge; 2 bars; outdoor/indoor hot-spring baths; room service; sauna; smoke-free rooms. *In room:* A/C, TV, hair dryer, Internet, minibar.

(224) Furusato Kanko Hotel ★★ (Finds)   Although this *ryokan* on Sakurajima is inconvenient for sightseeing, it's great for relaxation. It boasts open-air hot-spring baths set amid rocks right beside the sea, an indoor 25m (82-ft.) lap pool heated with hot springs, and indoor hot-spring baths overlooking the sea (see "What to See & Do," ear-lier in this chapter; hotel guests are charged a one-time rental fee of ¥210 for the bathing *yukata*). Afterward, retire to the shrinelike Meditation Room for spiritual cleansing as well. Rooms are all Japanese style, most with balconies overlooking great sea views. Some even boast views from their bathrooms, while the very best (and most expensive) have private terraces with outdoor hot-spring baths. Breakfast features *kamameshi* (rice casse-roles) made with hot-spring water; dinner consists mainly of seafood, *tonkotsu* (slowly stewed pork), and other local specialties. Movies (sometimes English-language) are shown nightly in a small theater. This is a great getaway.

1076 Furusato-cho, Kagoshima 891-1592. (℘) **099/221-3111.** Fax 099/221-2345. info@furukan.co.jp. 42 units. ¥14,150–¥22,150 per person. ¥2,100 extra per person weekends and holidays. Rates include break-fast and dinner. AE, DC, MC, V. For directions to Furusato Kanko Hotel, see Mount Sakurajima, earlier in this chapter. **Amenities:** Restaurant (serving lunch only); indoor pool; great indoor/outdoor hot-spring baths. *In room:* A/C, TV, hair dryer, minibar.

Moderate

JR Kyushu Hotel Kagoshima   Convenient to Kagoshima Chuo Station (you can enter it right from the station), this business hotel offers clean, mostly single rooms, devoid of character but equipped with the basics, including larger-than-usual desks. A new annex scheduled to open spring 2010 adds 273 higher-priced rooms (from ¥7,300 for a single and ¥ 12,800 for a double). The biggest plus besides convenience: Japan Rail Pass holders receive a 10% discount.

1–1–2 Take, Kagoshima 890-0045. (℘) **099/213-8000.** Fax 099/213-8029. www.jrhotelgroup.com. 138 units. ¥6,900 single; ¥12,600 twin. AE, DC, MC, V. Station: Kagoshima Chuo Station (west exit, 1 min.). **Amenities:** Lobby computer w/free Internet. *In room:* A/C, TV, fridge, hair dryer, Internet.

Kagoshima Tokyu Hotel (Kids)   This medium-priced hotel is in a newer area of Kagoshima, smack-dab on the waterfront with a good view of the volcano, even from its lobby lounge. Its twins and doubles face the water with balconies—great for watching the sunrise over Sakurajima. Note that singles, however, all face inland. All feature Tempur-Pedic pillows and focused bed lights, making for comfy in-bed reading. Out-door pools, including a children's pool, and connecting rooms make this a good bet for families, and the outdoor hot-spring pool and Jacuzzi (you wear your bathing suit here) are open year-round free to hotel guests. In summer, take advantage of the outdoor, seaside beer terrace with its good view. The main disadvantage, however, is that it's a 15-minute bus ride from the station and downtown.

22–1 Kamoike Shinmachi, Kagoshima 890-0064. (*C*) **099/257-2411.** Fax 099/257-6083. www.tokyuhotels japan.com/en. 206 units. ¥10,279–¥12,705 single; ¥18,480–¥31,185 double. AE, DC, MC, V. Bus: 27 from platform 15 of Kagoshima Chuo Station to Nokyo-kaikan-mae (2 min.). **Amenities:** 2 restaurants; bar; summer beer garden; outdoor pools; outdoor hot-spring bath; Jacuzzi; room service; smoke-free rooms. *In room:* A/C, TV, fridge, hair dryer, Internet.

Richmond Hotel Kagoshima Kinseicho This business hotel is located in the heart of downtown, with easy access from Kagoshima Chuo Station via streetcar passing right outside the front door. Check-in and checkout is accomplished via automatic machines, though humans are on hand to help guide you through the process. Note that rates below are for Richmond Hotel members, which requires a ¥500 one-time membership fee, thereby shaving up to ¥2,700 off the price of a single room per night and ¥3,500 off the price of a double. Otherwise, this is your standard business hotel with small rooms, though there are special single rooms for ladies (reservations required) featuring Tempur-Pedic pillows, free bottled water, terry-cloth robes, and female-oriented toiletries. Note that the cheapest singles and doubles are actually the same room, fine for one person but cramped for two.

5–3 Kinseicho, Kagoshima 890-0828. (*C*) **099/219-6655.** Fax 099/219-6668. www.richmondhotel.jp. 220 units. ¥9,000 single; ¥12,800–¥13,000 double. AE, DC, MC, V. Streetcar: Asahi Dori (1 min.). **Amenities:** Restaurant; lobby computer w/free Internet. *In room:* A/C, TV, fridge, hair dryer, Internet.

Inexpensive

In addition to the choices here, there are two Toyoko Inns near the Tenmonkan Dori covered shopping street and two near Kagoshima Chuo Station. **Toyoko Inn Kagoshima Tenmonkan No. 2,** 1–43 Higashi Sengoku-cho ((*C*) **099/224-1045;** www.toyoko-inn. com), offers the usual lobby computers with free Internet access, free Wi-Fi in the lobby, and free domestic calls from lobby phones, charging ¥5,460 for a single and ¥8,190 double, including a Japanese breakfast. Other Toyoko Inns, with cheaper prices, are the nearby (and older) **Toyoko Inn Kagoshima Tenmonkan No. 1,** 3–6 Yamanokuchi-cho ((*C*) **099/219-1045); Toyoko Inn Kagoshima Chu-eko Higashi-guchi,** 26–25 Chuo-cho ((*C*) **099/813-1045),** a 4-minute walk east of the station; and the newest property, **Toyoko Inn Kagoshima Chuo-eki Nishi-guchi,** 2–28–10 Nishida ((*C*) **099/814-1045),** a 3-minute walk west of the station.

Gasthof Hotel ★ After traveling to Europe, the owner of this inexpensive, 40-year-old hotel decided to re-create the coziness of a German bed-and-breakfast with a cafe in the lobby, antiques in the hallway, and rooms that vary in decor, furniture, and bedspreads, including four-poster beds in some. Although it falls short, the Gasthof has a lot more character than a regular business hotel and has a convenient location near Kagoshima Chuo Station. If you are lucky, the owner may even take you on a personal tour of his private Asian art museum, overflowing with priceless treasures from pottery to Buddha statues. Another plus is the Japanese restaurant and two *izakaya* (Japanese pub) in the same building.

7–1 Chuo-cho, Kagoshima 890-0053. (*C*) **099/252-1401.** Fax 099/252-1405. info@gasthof.jp. 48 units. ¥5,250–¥5,565 single; ¥8,925 double; ¥12,600 triple. Breakfast ¥525 extra. AE, DC, MC, V. Station: Kagoshima Chuo (3 min.). Take the underground passageway to wide, tree-lined Napoli Dori (beside Daiei department store), walk 3 blocks, and turn left at the Mobil gas station; it's at the end of the street on the left. **Amenities:** 4 restaurants/bars; lobby computer w/free Internet. *In room:* A/C, TV, fridge.

Nakazono Ryokan   A member of the Japanese Inn Group, this simple, laid-back *ryokan* with Japanese-style rooms is located near Kagoshima Station (not to be confused with Kagoshima Chuo Station), about a 10-minute walk from the Tenmonkan-Dori covered shopping street and a 3-minute walk from the Sakurajima ferry pier. Its English-speaking owner is knowledgeable about area sightseeing and has even prepared handouts on how to get to Ibusuki and Chiran. No meals are served, but there's a communal refrigerator, and the owner will direct you to nearby restaurants or, if you wish, help you order delivery pizza or sushi.

1–18 Yasui-cho, Kagoshima 892-0815. (C) **099/226-5125.** Fax 099/226-5126. www.satsuma.ne.jp/myhome/shindon. 10 units, none with bathroom. ¥4,200 single; ¥8,400 double; ¥11,970 triple. AE, V. Streetcar: Shiyakusho-mae (3 min.). Take the small alley that runs on the south side of a temple with a big bell and then the 1st left. *In room:* A/C, coin-op TV.

WHERE TO DINE

While in Kagoshima, be sure to try its local dishes, known as ***Satsuma ryori*** (Satsuma was the original name of the Kagoshima area). This style of cooking supposedly has its origins in food cooked on battlefields centuries ago; if that's the case, it certainly has improved greatly since then. Popular Satsuma specialties include ***Satsuma-age*** (ground fish mixed with tofu and sake and then deep-fried), ***tonkotsu*** (black pork that has been boiled for several hours in miso, *shochu,* and brown sugar—absolutely delicious), ***sake-zushi*** (a rice dish flavored with sake and mixed with vegetables and seafood), and ***Sat-suma-jiru*** (miso soup with chicken and locally grown vegetables including Sakurajima radishes). ***Kibinago*** is a small fish belonging to the herring family that can be caught in the waters around Kagoshima; a silver color with brown stripes, it's often eaten raw and arranged on a dish to resemble a chrysanthemum.

Expensive
Iso Kuwahara-kan CONTINENTAL   If you are sightseeing at Sengan-en, have lunch in this pleasant, historic building constructed in a Western style and dating from 1904. Built for the Shimadzu clan to serve as an assay office, today it houses a Western restaurant specializing in set meals, with offerings that generally give a choice of a main dish—such as seafood risotto, steak, and beef stew—along with side dishes.

9688–1 Yoshinocho. (C) **099/248-5883.** Set dinners ¥4,200–¥10,000; set lunches ¥1,890–¥5,250. No credit cards. Daily 11am–2:30pm and 5:30–9pm (last order). City View Bus: Sengan-en-mae stop (1 min.).

Kumasotei ★★ SATSUMA RYORI   Located in the city center, this restaurant specializes in local Satsuma dishes but carries them one step further by featuring them as part of *kaiseki* set meals. It reminds me more of a private home or *ryokan* because dining is in individual *tatami* rooms. If there isn't a crowd, you'll probably have your own private room; otherwise, you'll share. The main menu is in Japanese, but there's a smaller English-language menu with photos of the various set meals, which may include such local dishes as *Satsuma-age, tonkotsu, Satsuma-jiru, kibinago,* or *sakezushi,* as well as *shabu-shabu.*

6–10 Higashi Sengoku-cho. (C) **099/222-6356.** Set dinners ¥3,360–¥10,500; set lunches ¥2,100–¥5,250. AE, DC, MC, V. Daily 11am–2:30pm and 5–9:30pm (last order). Streetcar: Tenmonkan-Dori (4 min.). Walk through the Tenmonkan-Dori covered shopping street 4 blocks and turn left; it will be on your right.

Moderate
(225) **Ajimori** ★ BLACK PORK   This 30-year-old establishment specializes in pork from small black pigs, which the locals claim is more tender and succulent than regular

pork. The restaurant is divided into two parts: the upper floors, with both table seating and private *tatami* rooms, serve *Satsuma Kuroshabu,* a Kagoshima specialty of black-pork *shabu-shabu;* the first floor is a casual dining room specializing in *tonkatsu,* breaded black-pork cutlet. If you order the Kuroshabu, you'll eat it just like the more common beef shabu-shabu, cooking it yourself at your table by dipping it into a boiling broth and then in raw egg or sauce. Portions are generous, but if you wish, you can also order tonkatsu as a side dish. Otherwise, go to the first floor for perhaps the lightest, best-tasting tonkatsu you'll ever have; the set lunches, available every day except Sundays and holidays, are a bargain.

13–21 Sennichi-cho. ⓒ **099/224-7634.** Shabu-shabu set dinners ¥4,200–¥8,400, set lunch ¥3,150; tonkatsu set lunch ¥680. AE, DC, MC, V (only for meals costing more than ¥10,000). Thurs–Tues 11:30am–2:15pm (1:30pm last order for shabu-shabu) and 5:30–8:45pm (8pm last order for shabu-shabu). Streetcar: Tenmonkan-Dori (3 min.). Walk all the way through Tenmonkan-Dori and keep going past the *koban* police box onto Ginza St.; it's on the left just before the next arch with the eyeglasses motif.

226 **Arahobana** ★★★ (Finds AMAMI-OSHIMA CUISINE Amami-Oshima, a tropical isle in Kagoshima Prefecture 380km (236 miles) south of Kagoshima City, has its own distinct local cuisine and culture. You can learn about some of that island culture here, where there's live music and dancing in the evening; the Amami musicians and waiters will even teach you their dance and let you try your hand at playing their own version of the *shamisen* (traditionally covered with snake skin) and drums. The healthy cuisine, utilizing guava, mango, sugar cane, and spices and featuring dishes like free-range chicken and sweet potato, has a unique flavor very different from Japanese cuisine. The owner, a native of Amami-Oshima, is active in the slow food movement (as opposed to fast food). It's located in Dolphin Port shopping/dining complex, near the aquarium and Sakurajima ferry pier.

Dolphin Port 2F, 5–4 Honko-Shinmachi. ⓒ **099/219-8670.** Set dinners ¥1,480–¥4,200; daily lunch ¥1,580. AE, MC, V. Daily 11am–11:30pm. Streetcar: Shiyakusho-mae (8 min.). Waterfront City View Bus: Kagoshima Suizokukan-mae/Sakurajima-sanbashi (3 min.).

Inexpensive

227 **Noboruya** (Finds RAMEN This popular, inexpensive restaurant in the center of town is Kagoshima's best-known *ramen* (noodle) shop, in business for more than 60 years. It's a simple place, occupying one room of a small, wooden home with one counter and an open kitchen. As only one dish is served, there's no problem ordering. A big bowl of ramen comes with noodles (made fresh every day) and slices of pork, all seasoned with garlic (you can add extra garlic if you want). You also get as much pickled radish as you want (supposedly good for the stomach) and tea. As you eat your ramen at the counter, you can watch an army of women peeling garlic and cooking huge pots of noodles over gas flames—it's a great place to soak up local atmosphere.

2–15 Horie-cho. ⓒ **099/226-6695.** Ramen ¥1,000. No credit cards. Mon–Sat 11am–7pm. Streetcar: Izuro-Dori (1 min.). Walk down the wide street (Miami Dori) marked by stone lanterns on each side and take the 1st right; Noboruya is at the end of the 2nd block on the left, with its entrance around the corner.

228 **No-no-Budou** (Value JAPANESE BUFFET Of the dozen or so restaurants located on the fifth and sixth floors of Amu Plaza adjoining Kagoshima Chuo Station, this is one of the more interesting, featuring 70 dishes that change every few months, with various offerings of tempura, soups, salads, fish, noodles, vegetables, and much, much more. Evening buffets also include sashimi and sushi. There's a large nonsmoking

section. Other choices in Amu Plaza run the gamut from pork *shabu-shabu* and *tonkatsu* to Italian and Chinese fare.

Amu Plaza, 5th floor, 1–1 Chuo-cho. © **099/206-7585.** Dinner buffet ¥2,880; lunch buffet ¥1,480. AE, MC, V. Daily 11am–2:30pm and 5–9:30pm (last order). Beside Kagoshima Chuo Station.

6 SOUTHERN KYUSHU'S TOP SPA: IBUSUKI ★

50km (31 miles) S of Kagoshima

At the southern tip of Satsuma Peninsula, Ibusuki is southern Kyushu's most famous hot-spring resort and is home to 47,500 residents. With a pleasant average temperature of 66°F (19°C) throughout the year due to warm ocean currents, it's a region of lush vegetation, flowers, and palm trees. It also boasts Japan's best natural hot-sand bath and a good public beach, making it a fine choice for a low-key vacation.

ESSENTIALS

GETTING THERE Ibusuki is approximately an hour from Kagoshima Chuo Station by **JR train,** with the fare costing ¥970 one-way. **Buses** depart from Kagoshima's Yamagataya Bus Center in the heart of the city (near the Asahi Dori streetcar stop) seven times a day (some make stops at Kagoshima Chuo Station before traveling onward), reaching Ibusuki's train station 1½ hours later and costing ¥930 one-way.

VISITOR INFORMATION **Ibusuki Tourist Information** (© **0993/22-4114;** daily 9am–6pm) is located in Ibusuki Station. For online information, go to www.city.ibusuki. lg.jp and www.kagoshima-kankou.com/for.

GETTING AROUND The small town of Ibusuki is spread along the coast, and public **buses** run along the main streets. **Taxis** are also readily available. However, probably the easiest way to get around is by **rental bike,** available 8am to 5pm daily at the car-rental office in the Ibusuki Station building for ¥500 for 2 hours or ¥1,500 all day. With a Japan Rail Pass, rates are ¥300 and ¥900 respectively. By bike it takes about 7 minutes to the Natural Sand Bath and about 25 minutes to public swimming beaches and Chiringashima.

WHAT TO SEE & DO

TAKING A HOT-SAND BATH The most popular thing to do in Ibusuki is to have yourself buried up to your neck in black sand at Yunohama Beach, heated naturally by hot springs that surface close to the ground before running into the sea. To take part, head to the Natural Sand Bath (**Suna Mushi Kaikan**) ★★★ (© **0993/23-3900;** daily 8:30am–noon and 1–9pm), a modern facility nicknamed **Saraku** by the locals (*saraku* has two meanings: to walk around, and to enjoy the sand). Take the elevator up to the reception, pay ¥900 for the baths and rental *yukata* (add another ¥200 if you didn't bring a towel), change into the yukata in the dressing room, and then head down to the beach. One of the women there will dig you a shallow pit. Lie down, arrange your yukata so no vulnerable areas are exposed, and then lie still while she piles sand on top of you. It's quite a funny sight, actually, to see nothing but heads sticking out of the ground. The water, a hot 185°F (85°C), contains sodium chloride and is considered beneficial in alleviating rheumatism, arthritis, gastrointestinal troubles, neuralgia, and female disorders. It is also valued as a beauty treatment for the skin. After your 15-minute sand bath, go indoors for a relaxing hot-spring bath and the sauna. The Natural Sand Bath is a 20-minute walk or 7-minute bike ride from Ibusuki Station; from the main exit, head straight down Chuo Dori to the beach and turn right. You can also take a bus to the Suna Mushi Kaikan stop.

(229) **SATSUMA DENSHOKAN** ★★★ You'd expect to find this world-class private gallery in a big city like Tokyo, but Satsuma Denshokan, located in Hakusuikan Ryokan (see below; daily 8:30am–5pm), is at home instead in this small resort town, thanks to the *ryokan*'s owners who have spent the last 60 years amassing this amazing 3,000-piece collection. Housed in a restful, Kyoto-style building set within a reflective pond, it shows some 380 pieces on a rotating basis, including artifacts dating from the Meiji Restoration, Satsuma ceramics created especially for export and made popular by the 1867 Paris Exposition, and Chinese ceramics and porcelain spanning 8 centuries, including rare finds with Imperial stamps. Admission is ¥1,500 for adults, ¥1,200 for university students, ¥600 for high-school students, and ¥300 for children. You can easily spend an hour or more here, aided by an audio guide. There's no public transportation here, so you'll have to take a taxi 5 minutes from Ibusuki Station.

SWIMMING & HIKING Also on the beach, but on the opposite edge of town from the sand baths, is Ibusuki's popular public beach, Sun-Beach Ibusuki, as well as Chiringashima, a small, uninhabited island and national park. During low tide, you can walk to the island via sand-bridge in about 10 minutes. Be sure to inquire beforehand what time the tide comes in, however, so you don't get stranded.

WHERE TO STAY
Expensive

(230) **Hakusuikan Ryokan** ★★★ (Finds) A driveway lined with pine trees sets the mood for this modern, elegant, and resortlike *ryokan* right on the beach with landscaped lawns and one of the most impressive hot-spring baths I've ever seen. Established in 1960 and expanded over the years, the ryokan seems like a village, with several buildings connected by corridors. The public bath—a reproduction of an Edo-Era hot-spring spa—is classy and refined, also designed like a small village with a large bathing area made of cypress wood and stone with pools of varying temperatures, a huge *rotenburo* (outdoor hot-spring pool), a sand bath, a steam room, and a replica Edo-Era sauna with a round dome. Even the dressing rooms are faithfully styled after the Edo Period, though naturally with all the latest conveniences. Another plus: the ryokan's own museum, Satsuma Denshokan (see above).

Several room types are available. Least expensive are the 30 Western-style twins, all of which face inland and are rather ordinary looking. Better are the Japanese-style *tatami* rooms facing the sea, as well as the ryokan's 115 combination rooms, spacious with both beds and separate tatami areas and available in various price categories. Meals are served in a choice of restaurants. This place is the perfect getaway; you'll want to change into your *yukata* as soon as you arrive. No wonder former Prime Minister Koizumi chose this ryokan for a summit meeting with Korea.

Chirin-no-Sato, Ibusuki, Kagoshima-ken 891-0404. © **0993/22-3131.** Fax 0993/23-3860. www.hakusuikan. co.jp/en. 205 units. ¥15,900–¥36,900 per person. ¥1,050–¥2,100 extra on weekends. Rates include breakfast and dinner. AE, DC, MC, V. Taxi: 5 min. from Ibusuki Station. (No public transportation.) **Amenities:** 5 restaurants; coffee shop; 2 bars (including a shochu tasting bar); 2 lounges; nightclub; lobby computer w/free Internet; fantastic indoor/outdoor hot-spring and sand bath; museum; outdoor swimming pool. *In room:* A/C, TV w/pay movies, hair dryer, Internet, minibar.

Ibusuki Iwasaki Hotel ★ (**Kids**) This is Ibusuki's best-known spa hotel, a self-contained resort on 50 hectares (125 acres) of lush tropical grounds with pleasant walking trails throughout. It's very popular with Japanese tour groups for its facilities, including huge public baths, outdoor swimming pools kids love (they like the amusement hall with table tennis, 10-pin bowling, and video games, too), a beach, and the Ibusuki Golf Club (hotel guests get discounts; or ask about golf packages). During the off season, however, you have the hotel seemingly to yourself. Another plus is the resort's private, eclectic museum featuring Japanese artists painting in the Western style, some Western artists (Gauguin), crafts from Papua New Guinea, and Satsuma pottery. All rooms have either a full or partial view of the sea and a balcony; the best rooms also have views of the wonderful grounds, one of the resort's best features and well worth a stroll. Nights here are nice, with the sound of waves and frogs croaking in the lotus pond.

3755 Juni-cho, Ibusuki, Kagoshima-ken 891-0493. ℂ **0993/22-2131.** Fax 0993/24-3215. http://ibusuki. iwasakihotels.com/en. 285 units. ¥15,015–¥25,410 double. AE, DC, MC, V. Taxi: 5 min. from Ibusuki Station; bus (7 times daily) to Ibusuki Iwasaki Hotel stop (bus does not have a number). **Amenities:** 4 restaurants; coffee shop; rental bikes (¥525 for 2 hr.); bowling arcade; fitness room (fee: ¥500); indoor/outdoor hot-spring baths overlooking the sea; hot-sand baths (fee: ¥1,050); Ibusuki Golf Club; Jacuzzi; minigolf (fee: ¥1,050 for 2 hr.); museum and craft gallery (admission: ¥600); elaborate outdoor pool w/waterslide and children's pool; room service; soccer field; outdoor lighted tennis courts. *In room:* A/C, TV, fridge, hair dryer.

Moderate

(**231**) **Kyuka-Mura Ibusuki** (**Value**) This government-owned lodge is located right at the water's edge near the public beach (but a bit far from town) and offers reasonably priced, basic accommodations, making it a popular choice with Japanese families. During summer vacation months, on New Year's, in March during spring vacation, and in May during school trips, you should reserve 6 months in advance. At other times, it's relatively easy to get a room here. The cheapest rooms are the eight Western-style rooms, which face inland and have toilets but no bathrooms, but I prefer the Japanese-style rooms for the same price (also with toilet only) that are the size of 7½ *tatami* mats and have glass sliding doors opening seaside. Most expensive are roomy, 10-mat Japanese-style rooms facing the sea with bathroom (you can even see the water from the tub); some even have a balcony with chairs.

10445 Higashikata, Ibusuki, Kagoshima-ken 891-0404. ℂ **0993/22-3211.** Fax 0993/22-3213. www. qkamura.or.jp. 65 units (7 with bathroom, 58 with toilet only). ¥4,800–¥6,400 per person. Buffet breakfast ¥1,300 extra. Japanese dinner ¥2,100–¥5,250 extra. MC, V. Free shuttle buses depart from in front of Ibusuki Station 3 times a day; look for a bus with QKAMURA written on it. **Amenities:** Restaurant; lounge; rental bikes (¥200 per 30 min.); indoor/outdoor hot-spring baths; Ping-Pong; sand baths (fee: ¥945). *In room:* A/C, TV, fridge.

Inexpensive

(**232**) **Marutomi** ★ Just a minute's walk from the Natural Sand Bath at Yunohama Beach, this inexpensive inn is a family-run affair. Following the *ryokan* tradition of naming rooms instead of assigning numbers, rooms are named after fish (the owner was a fisherman); you can even stay in the Tuna Room! All the rooms are Japanese style, clean and with more character than many in this price range. Meals, which include fresh seafood, are served communally at low tables on *tatami*. Several blocks north is an annex, Marutomi2, with hot-spring baths, a communal kitchen, and three additional rooms. Guests can use facilities at both inns. If you call from the station, the owner may be able to pick you up.

5–24–15 Yunohama, Ibusuki, Kagoshima-ken 891-0406. ✆ **0993/22-5579.** Fax 0993/22-3993. 7 units, none with bathroom. ¥4,200 per person without meals; ¥5,000 per person with breakfast; ¥7,500 per person with dinner and breakfast. No credit cards. Station: Ibusuki (20 min.). From the main exit, walk straight on Chuo Dori to the beach and turn right; just past the Natural Sand Bath turn right again. It's on the right. Bus: Going in the direction of the Ibusuki Iwasaki Hotel (ask for the Ibusuki Iwasaki Hotel *yuki* bus; the bus does not have a number), get off at the Suna Mushi Kaikan stop and walk inland. **Amenities:** Small hot-spring bath. *In room:* A/C, TV, no phone.

WHERE TO DINE

Aoba VARIED JAPANESE   This simple restaurant near Ibusuki Station offers a variety of *teishoku* set meals from its Japanese menu, including those featuring tempura, sashimi, sushi, *hirekatsu* (pork filet), and grilled eel, available all day. Another good choice is its Satsume Teishoku, featuring Kagoshima specialties such as *Satsuma-age, tonkotsu,* chicken sashimi, and *kibinago* (see the dining section in the Kagoshima section earlier for a description of local cuisine). Full *kaiseki* courses are also available.

1–2–11 Minato. ✆ **0993/22-3356.** Teishoku set meals ¥980–¥1,680; kaiseki ¥2,000–¥4,000. No credit cards. Thurs–Tues 11am–3pm and 5:30–10pm. Station: Ibusuki (1 min.). Turn left out of the station; it's on the main road to the left.

(233) **Chozjuan** ★★ (Finds) SOMEN   If you're adventurous, try this fun, open-air restaurant specializing in *somen* (cold noodles) in the countryside near Mount Kaimon. Seating is under a pavilion beside a man-made waterfall, so you eat to the accompaniment of running water with Japanese traditional music playing in the background. In the middle of your table will be a large round container with water swirling in a circle; when you get your basket of noodles, dump them into the cold water, fish them out with your chopsticks, dip them in soy sauce, and enjoy. Probably best is to order one of five set meals, which in addition to noodles come with such main dishes as grilled trout or carp sashimi, along with vegetables and soup. Hot noodles are available in winter, when you can also dine indoors.

Although not as atmospheric, there's another Chozjuan across from the west exit of Ibusuki Station, 2167–1 Omase Jyuni-cho (✆ **0993/22-5272**). In addition to somen, it serves local specialties like black pork over rice and is open daily from 11am to 3pm and 5 to 10pm (last order; sooner if they run out of noodles).

Kaimon-cho, Tosenkyo. ✆ **0993/32-3155.** Somen ¥530; set meals ¥1,300–¥2,600. No credit cards. May–Sept daily 10am–8pm; Oct–Apr daily 10am–5pm. Bus: 7 departures weekdays from Ibusuki Station (a 30-min. ride); 4 weekend departures. From the bus stop, the restaurant is ahead to the left and down the stairs (there are photos of food at its entrance).

7 BEPPU, KING OF THE HOT-SPRING SPAS ★★

1,228km (763 miles) SW of Tokyo; 186km (116 miles) SE of Fukuoka

Beppu gushes forth more hot-spring water than anywhere else in Japan. With approximately 2,832 hot springs spewing forth 130,000 kiloliters (34 million gal.) of water daily, it has long been one of the country's best-known spa resorts. Some 11.5 million people come to Beppu every year to relax and rejuvenate themselves in one of the city's 85 public bathhouses, and they do so in a number of unique ways: They sit in mud baths up to their necks, they bury themselves in hot black sand, they soak in hot springs, and on New

KYUSHU

12

BEPPU, KING OF THE HOT-SPRING SPAS

Year's they bathe in water filled with floating orange peels. They even drink hot-spring water and eat food cooked by its steam.

Bathing reigns supreme here—and I suggest you join in the fun. After all, visiting Beppu without enjoying the baths would be like going to a world-class restaurant with your own TV dinner.

Not a very large town, with a population of 121,300, Beppu is situated on Kyushu's eastern coast in a curve of Beppu Bay, bounded on one side by the sea and on the other by steep hills and mountains. On cold days, steam rises everywhere throughout the city, escaping from springs and pipes and giving the town an otherworldly appearance. Indeed, nine of the hot springs look so much like hell that that's what they're called—Jigoku, the Hells. But, rather than a place most people try to avoid, the Hells are a major tourist attraction. In fact, everything in Beppu is geared toward tourism, and if you're interested in rubbing elbows with Japanese on vacation—particularly the older generation—this is one of the best places to do so.

ESSENTIALS

GETTING THERE By Plane The nearest airport is Oita Airport (OIT; www.oita-airport.jp), a 45-minute bus ride away (bus fare: ¥1,450). **JAL** flights from Tokyo's Haneda airport take about 1½ hours and cost ¥35,700 one-way, though 28-day advance-purchase fares dip as low as ¥14,600 for certain flights.

By Train From Tokyo, take the Shinkansen to Kokura and transfer there to a limited express bound for Beppu; the trip takes nearly 8 hours (not including transfers) and costs ¥22,420 for unreserved seats. There are also direct trains daily from Hakata Station in Fukuoka (trip time: 2 hr.) and Kumamoto (3 hr.).

By Ferry Ferries make nightly runs to Beppu from Osaka, with fares beginning at ¥8,800; at last check, a ferry departs Osaka's South Pier at 6:50pm and arrives the next morning. Contact tourist offices in Osaka (see chapter 10) or the **Ferry Sunflower** in Osaka (© 06/6572-5181) for more information.

From Shikoku, the most practical ferry is from Yahatahama, running six times daily and costing ¥3,020 one-way for the almost 3-hour trip; contact the **Uwajima Unyu Co.** for information (© 0894/23-2536).

VISITOR INFORMATION Before leaving Tokyo or the Narita or Kansai airports, pick up a copy of the leaflet "Beppu and Vicinity" at the Tourist Information Center, or download it at www.jnto.go.jp by looking under "Browse by Destinations." The **Beppu Tourist Information Office** (© 0977/21-6220; daily 9am–5pm) is located in Beppu Station at the east (main) exit. A second tourist office (© 0977/23-1119; daily 10am–5pm) is in Sol Paseo, an international shopping arcade, a 5-minute walk due east of the main exit. Here you will find computers with free Internet access. More information is available at **www.beppu-navi.jp** and **www.we-love-oita.or.jp**.

ORIENTATION & GETTING AROUND **Beppu Station** is located near the center of the city. Its main exit is to the east and the sea, while to the west lie the Hells and the majority of hot-spring baths. Because most destinations are not within walking distance, the easiest ways to get around Beppu are by bus and by taxi. Of the two bus companies serving Beppu, the **Kamenoi Bus Company** (© 0977/23-0141) is the largest and serves most of the city. Bus fares begin at ¥140 and increase according to the distance, but if you plan on doing a lot of sightseeing, there's a 1-day pass called **My Beppu Free**—which nonetheless costs ¥900 for adults, half-price for children 11 and under. It allows unlimited travel on Kamenoi

TAKING THE WATERS

Beppu is divided into eight hot-spring areas, each with its own mineral content and natural characteristics. Although any hot-spring bath can help stimulate metabolism and blood circulation and create a general feeling of well-being, there are specific springs with various mineral contents that Japanese believe help relieve ailments ranging from rheumatism and diabetes to skin disease. The tourist office has a pamphlet so you can select the baths that will benefit you the most. And whatever you do, don't rinse off with plain water after taking your bath because this will wash away all those helpful minerals. You should bring your own towel and, for some places, a *yukata* (cotton kimono), though the latter is also available for sale or for rent.

Hot-Spring Baths

SUGINOI PALACE   A 15-minute bus ride from Beppu Station, **Suginoi Palace** ★★ (✆ **0977/24-1141;** www.suginoi-hotel.com; daily 9am–11pm) is an amusement center with one of the best-known baths in all of Japan. Called **Tanayu** and built of natural woods and glass, it's refined and spacious, with different kinds of baths both inside and out that take advantage of its hillside perch with great views out over the town toward the sea. In addition to an indoor bath, Jacuzzi, and sauna with panoramic views, there are outdoor cypress tubs, waterfall massages (great for shoulders and backs), and even shallow pools with headrests so you can recline to gaze upon the view. Admission costs ¥1,000 for adults and ¥600 for children on weekdays, ¥1,500 and ¥900 respectively on weekends, and ¥2,000 and ¥1,200 respectively on holidays. If, however, you're staying at the Suginoi Hotel (p. 554), you can use the baths for free.

If you're shy about disrobing in front of strangers or have kids in tow, you might want to visit Suginoi's **Aqua-Beat.** It's a water park with water slides (great fun!), children's pools, a simulated wave pool, an artificial beach, outdoor hot springs, and a Jacuzzi. A bar-coded locker key on a wristband allows you to lock up your valuables, wear your bathing suit (rental suits available), and dine without having to worry about carrying money; upon exiting, you'll simply feed it into a machine to get your bill. Admission is ¥2,800 for adults, ¥1,600 for junior-high and high-school students, and 1,000 for children 4 to 12. In the off season (Sept–June), it costs only ¥1,500, ¥1,000, and ¥500 respectively. Guests staying at the Suginoi Hotel can go for free. It's open Monday to Friday 10am to 6pm and Saturday, Sunday, and holidays from 10am to 8pm, with extended hours during major holidays (closed for maintenance early May to June and Nov 24–Dec 4). To reach Suginoi Palace, take the hotel's free shuttle from Beppu Station (daily 10am–4pm). By the way, much of the energy to run the vast complex, including the hotel, is steam generated.

TERMAS SPA (KITAHAMA ONSEN)   A hot-spring public spa beside the sea, Termas Spa, 11–1 Kyomachi (✆ **0977/24-4126;** Fri–Wed 10am–10pm), offers indoor baths and a sauna, as well as a large outdoor hot-spring pool and Jacuzzi for both sexes overlooking the sea (you wear your swimsuit here). Admission is ¥500 for adults, half-price for children. It's a 20-minute walk from Beppu Station (take the east exit and turn left when you reach the sea; it will be on the right); or take bus no. 20, 21, 23, 25, or 26 to Matogahama Koen stop.

One of the unique things you can do in Beppu is take a bath in hot sand, considered useful for treating muscle pain, arthritis, and indigestion. Although several public baths offer hot-sand baths, one of the most atmospheric places is the **Takegawara Bathhouse ★★★**, 16–23 Motomachi, Beppu 874 (© **0977/23-1585;** daily 8am–10:30pm, closed third Wed of each month). Built in 1879 in traditional, Meiji-Era architecture, this beautiful wooden structure is one of the oldest public baths in the city and has an interior that resembles an ancient gymnasium, dominated by a pit filled with black sand. The attendants are used to foreigners here; they'll instruct you to change into the provided *yukata* and lie down in a hollow they've dug in the sand. An attendant will then shovel sand on top of you and pack you in until only your head and feet are sticking out. I personally didn't find the sand all that hot, but it is relaxing as the heat soaks into your body. You stay buried for 10 minutes, contemplating the wooden ceiling high above and hoping you don't get an itch somewhere. When the time is up, the attendant will tell you to stand up, shower off the sand, and then jump into a bath of hot water. The cost is ¥1,000. To reach the bathhouse, take the main (east) exit from Beppu Station and walk toward the sea, turning right at the street just before the big intersection (across from Tokiwa). The bathhouse is a couple of blocks down this street on the right, with its entrance around the corner.

MORE TO SEE & DO

THE HELLS (JIGOKU)   You might as well join everyone else and go to the Hells, boiling ponds created by volcanic activity. Their Japanese name, Jigoku, refers to the burning hell of Buddhist sutras. Seven of the nine Hells are clustered close together in the Kannawa hot-spring area, within walking distance of each other, and they can be toured in about 90 minutes or so. Each hell has its own attraction, but because a few are kind of hokey, you might just want to visit a couple. **Umi Jigoku,** or Sea Hell, has a nice garden setting (spectacular in spring when azaleas are in bloom), a cobalt-blue pond, a greenhouse with giant lotus plants, and a foot bath where you can soak your feet in hot springs. **Oniishibozu Jigoku** features bubbling mud, a foot bath, and its own hot-spring baths (extra admission charged for the baths); **Kamado Jigoku,** the Oven Hell, was used for cooking and has a statue of a red devil (read: photo op); **Chinoike Jigoku,** the Blood-Pond Hell, is blood red in color because of the red clay dissolved in the hot water; **Tatsumaki Jigoku,** or Waterspout Hell, has one of the largest geysers in Japan. Skip **Yama Jigoku,** featuring animals living in deplorable conditions, and **Oniyama Jigoku,** featuring much of the same for crocodiles. To reach Kannawa, take bus no. 2 from Beppu Station's west exit 25 minutes to Umijigoku-mae bus stop. After walking to the seven Hells, you can then take bus no. 16 from the Kannawa bus stop onward to the other two Hells.

The Hells are open daily 8am to 5pm. A combination ticket, costing ¥2,000 for adults, ¥1,300 for high-school students, ¥1,000 for junior-high students, and ¥900 for children, allows entrance to eight Hells. Separate entrance fee to each one is ¥400. A ninth Hell, the **Kinryu Golden Dragon Jigoku** costs ¥200; I like its sign, which announces matter-of-factly, IF YOU FALL IN THE POND, YOU WILL BE BOILED. For more information, contact the **Beppu Tourist Information Office** (see above).

BEPPU CITY TRADITIONAL BAMBOO CRAFTS CENTER   Beppu is famous for its bamboo crafts, and the best place to shop for bambooware and to learn more about this amazingly durable material is this museum, the Beppu-shi Takezaiku Dento Sangyo Kaikan, 8–3 Higashisoen (© **0977/23-1072;** Tues–Sun 8:30am–5pm). Exhibits explain how bamboo grows, the different varieties of bamboo (620 kinds are found in Japan;

(Finds) **On the Road to Hell**

Smack-dab in the midst of the Hells, across from Oniyama Jigoku, is the **Beppu Utamaro Gallery (Minzoku Shiryokan),** 338–3 Kannawa Shibuya ((℃ **0977/66-8790;** daily 9:30am–5pm), a museum devoted to sex. Fertility gods, erotic statues, pictures of zebras and lions in the act, replicas of penises from the animal kingdom ranging from tiny to humongous, Edo-Era erotic woodblock prints by Utamaro, kinky dioramas (including an adult version of Snow White and her seven little men), and a small theater with porn films are just some of the things on display here. Think of those unsuspecting visitors hoping to see a gallery devoted to famed Ukiyo-e artist Utamaro's work! Admission is ¥700.

1,250 grow worldwide), and the role bamboo has played in daily Japanese life, with displays that include palanquins, fish traps, lunch boxes, toys, fans, hats, bows, and arrows, and a beautiful 1920s stationery box by National Living Treasure Sato Chiyota. Even Edison's electric light bulb used a bamboo filament. You can see it in 15 minutes, but with your new appreciation for bamboo, you'll easily spend an additional 15 minutes in its shop. Admission is ¥300 for adults and high-school students, ¥100 for children. To reach it, take bus no. 1 from Beppu Station's east exit to the Minabaru stop (fare: ¥230), backtrack to the traffic light, and walk 3 minutes on the downhill street on the right.

MONKEYS & AN AQUARIUM On Beppu's southern border rises **Mount Takasaki,** home to some 1,200 wild monkeys and one of Japan's largest monkey habitats ((℃ 097/532-5010; daily 8:30am–5pm). At the base of the mountain where they're fed, however (to keep them from raiding farmers' fields), it's nothing but concrete and they don't seem particularly wild or concerned about the humans walking among them. Admission is ¥500 for adults (half-price for children). Come here only if you have children, combining it with a trip to **Umitamago,** Kaigan, Takasakiyama-shita ((℃ **097/534-1010;** daily 9am–6pm), across the highway via pedestrian bridge. This aquarium, opened in 2004, features an 8m-high (26-ft.) circular tank with 3,000 fish and sea creatures, as well as seals, sea lions, dolphins, sea otters, sea turtles, a touch pool with harmless sharks and rays, a discovery room for small children, and shows. Admission is ¥1,890 for adults, ¥950 for junior-high and elementary students, and ¥630 for children (free for children 3 and younger). To reach Mount Takasaki and the aquarium, take an Oita Kotsu bus that departs from Beppu Station four times an hour (there is no bus number) for 10 minutes to Takasakiyama stop; unfortunately, your My Beppu Free pass isn't accepted on this bus, so you'll have to pay ¥230.

WHERE TO STAY

As with most hot-spring spas, Beppu levies a hot-springs tax: ¥150 per person, per night. In addition, some places raise their rates for New Year's, Golden Week (Apr 29–May 5), Obon (mid-Aug), Saturdays, and evenings before holidays.

Expensive

(234) **Sennari Inn** ★★★ (Finds) This 70-year-old inn was originally built as a vacation villa and still serves as a serene haven from the outside world with its traditional architecture and beautiful garden views from every room. It's also known for its elaborate

meals that may include specialties like *fugu* (blowfish), though the second-generation owner will accommodate personal tastes and allergies if given advance notice. Dinner is served true *ryokan* style in the comfort of your room, while breakfast is offered in a communal *tatami* room.

2–18 Noguchimoto-machi, Beppu 874-0933. **℃ 0977/21-1550.** Fax 0977/21-1542. 8 units. ¥15,750–¥25,000 per person including 2 meals; ¥8,400 per person without meals off season, ¥10,500 per person without meals in high season. AE, MC, V. Station: Beppu (3-min. walk northeast). **Amenities:** Indoor/outdoor hot-spring baths; Internet (in lobby). *In room:* A/C, TV, fridge.

Suginoi Hotel ★★ **Kids** One of the best-known hotels in Beppu, Suginoi is famous for its adjoining Suginoi Palace with its hot-spring baths and a water park, both free to hotel guests (p. 551). Situated on a wooded hill with a sweeping view of the city and sea below, it's a lively and noisy hotel, filled with good-natured vacationers; if you like being in the middle of the action, this is the place for you. This is actually two hotels in one, each with its own check-in counter and both offering Japanese-style, Western-style (with beds), and combination (with both beds and *tatami* area) rooms. Rates are based on season, room type, and view; those facing inland are slightly cheaper. The older main building (Hon-Kan) is larger, catering primarily to families and groups (its Western-style rooms face only inland), though it does offer the Ceada Spa and luxurious Ceada Floor rooms with a modern twist on traditional Japanese design complete with open-air baths. The so-called Good Time Floor is geared toward families (meals are served in-room here) and even offers a private hot-spring tub big enough for the entire family (you can reserve it for free). The newer Hana-kan is smaller and has mostly Western-style rooms, including those facing the sea. With all the kiddie diversions—water park, game room, and cheap eats in Suginoi Palace (even a McDonald's)—this is a perfect choice for families. The downside is that the place is so vast you have to hike to its various facilities, and it's inconvenient to the rest of Beppu.

Kankaiji, Beppu 874-0822. **℃ 0977/24-1141.** Fax 0977/21-0010. www.suginoi-hotel.com. 562 units. ¥15,900–¥40,050 per person, including 2 meals. Rates higher in peak season. AE, DC, MC, V. Free hotel shuttle bus every hour (daily 10am–4pm). Taxi: 8 min. **Amenities:** 6 restaurants; bar; 2 lounges; Suginoi Palace with hot-spring baths and Aqua-Beat (see "Taking the Waters," above); two 24-hr. hot-spring baths for hotel guests only; lobby computer (¥100 for 10 min.); spa w/hot sand baths; smoke-free rooms, water park. *In room:* A/C, TV, hair dryer, minibar.

Moderate

Hotel Arthur I like the location of this hotel, just a 3-minute walk from Beppu Station but tucked away on a side street near restaurants and bars. A warmly decorated lobby sporting a medieval suit of armor leads to the usual small rooms, which have shades in addition to curtains for extra darkness. Some single rooms from the seventh floor have views of the sea at no extra charge. Other extras include a 10th-floor restaurant with good views from three sides and decent Western food, plus two small hot-spring baths, one with a sauna (and the first I've ever seen with a TV in it), with alternating hours for men and women. The hotel does a good job explaining all its services in English.

1–2–5 Kitahama, Beppu 874-920. **℃ 0977/25-2611.** Fax 0977/24-0073. www.hotel-arthur.co.jp. 123 units. ¥5,500–¥7,500 single; ¥9,500–¥14,000 double. Rates higher on Sat and holidays for double occupancy. AE, DC, MC, V. Station: Beppu (3 min. from east exit); turn right just past the Ekimae Onsen. **Amenities:** Restaurant; indoor hot-spring bath; lobby computer w/free Internet; sauna; smoke-free rooms. *In room:* A/C, TV, fridge, hair dryer, Internet.

235 Sakaeya ★★ **Finds** The oldest *minshuku* (family-run inn) in the city, this is one of the best places to stay near the Hells. There are several interesting features here that have utilized the hot springs for decades, including old radiators heated naturally from hot springs and a *jigokugama* (stone oven) in the courtyard that uses steam from hot springs for cooking (many older homes in Beppu still use such ovens). Use of the oven is free in case you want to cook your own meals, but there's also a modern kitchen you can use. I recommend, however, that you opt for rates that include meals. Most of your dinner will be steamed using the hot springs and then served in a Japanese dining room with whitewashed walls and a heavy timbered ceiling. In winter, the *kotatsu* (a table with a heating element and covered with a blanket to keep legs warm) in the dining room is steam heated. All rooms are Japanese style, the oldest of which don't have bathrooms but are very nice and date from the Meiji Period (1868–1912), while those with private bathroom are in a newer addition that nonetheless maintains a traditional atmosphere with sitting alcoves.

Ida, Kannawa, Beppu 874-0043. ✆ **0977/66-6234.** Fax 0977/66-6235. 12 units, 7 with bathroom. Rates per person ¥3,675–¥5,250 without meals; ¥13,650–¥21,000 with 2 meals. Rates exclude service charge. Rates higher on weekends and holidays. No credit cards. Bus: Jigokubara (2 min.); take the 1st left. **Amenities:** Indoor hot-spring baths. *In room:* A/C, TV, fridge.

Inexpensive

Kokage   This 40-year-old *minshuku* offers simply furnished Japanese and twin rooms. Those with bathrooms have hot-spring water, while one room for three people has only a sink and toilet. There's also a public, rock-lined, hot-spring bath, and meals are served in a homey dining room with a cluttered but interesting collection of antique lamps, clocks, and other items. If you like, the owners will fit you out in a wedding kimono and take your picture with your camera. Note, however, that there's a midnight curfew and the inn is lax about answering faxes. If you don't get an answer by e-mail, try reserving by phone.

8–9 Ekimaecho, Beppu 874-0935. ✆ **0977/23-1753.** Fax 0977/23-3895. kokage@mx6.tiki.ne.jp. 11 units (10 with bathroom, 1 with toilet only). ¥4,350 single with bathroom; ¥7,650 double with bathroom; ¥9,900 triple with toilet only, ¥11,475 triple with bathroom. AE, MC, V. Station: Beppu (2 min.). From the station's main east exit, walk straight ahead for 2 blocks to a stoplight just past Ekimae Onsen, turn right, and then turn immediately right again into a small alley (it's easy to miss). **Amenities:** Lobby computer w/free Internet. *In room:* A/C, TV.

(236) Yokoso ★ (Value   Housed in a beige-colored, two-story building on Ideyuzaka, the main road between the group of Hells, Yokoso offers what are probably the cheapest rooms in all of Beppu. Run by kind, English-speaking, third-generation innkeepers, it has simple, clean Japanese-style rooms. Air-conditioning in summer is coin-operated, but steam heating is free. No meals are served, but a communal open-air kitchen is available, complete with a hot-springs-powered oven and suggestions for how long to cook food in bamboo steamers (there's a grocery store across the street). Four public baths boast water from hot springs. In an annex are 25 more rooms, a *rotenburo* (outdoor bath; you wear your swimming suit here), and a carp pond in a garden. It also has one of the most interesting saunas I've ever seen, so tiny you have to crawl inside; heated naturally with hot springs, it even has a grass floor, as in the days of yore. Note that there's an 11pm curfew here.

Ida 3 Kumi, Kannawa, Beppu 874-0043. ✆ **0977/66-0440.** Fax 0977/66-0440. www.coara.or. jp/~hideharu. 35 units. ¥3,400 per person. No credit cards. Bus: Jigokubara (3 min.); take the 1st left, around the corner from Sakaeya, above. **Amenities:** Lobby computer (¥100 per 30 min.). *In room:* Coin-op A/C, coin-op TV, no phone.

(237) **Biliken** VARIED JAPANESE   It is easy to spot this casual restaurant, popular with shoppers, businessmen, and family and on the main street halfway between the station and the sea, because of the gold statue to the left of the doorway of Biliken—a curious-looking, bald-headed, round-tummied god who is said to bring good luck. A display case outside and a picture menu make ordering easy for Japanese set meals that include tempura, broiled eel, sashimi, *tonkatsu,* and more, with seating on *tatami* or at dark lacquered tables.

2-1-18 Kitahama. (C) **0977/21-2088.** Set meals ¥750–¥2,100; set lunch ¥600. No credit cards. Fri–Wed 11:30am–9:30pm. Station: Beppu (4 min.), on the left side of the main road leading to the sea.

(238) **Mitsu Boshi** ★★ FRENCH KAISEKI   This small, cozy restaurant on the main road leading south of the seven cluster of Hells serves French cuisine with a Japanese twist, presented in a *kaiseki* style with set meals consisting of many small dishes expertly executed by the owner-chef. Seasonal seafood, steaks with one of four sauces, and original creations round out the menu, with vegetarian meals available on request.

284 Kannawa. (C) **0977/67-3536.** Main dishes ¥945–¥2,100; set dinners ¥2,520–¥6,300; set lunches ¥1,000–¥5,250. AE, MC, V. No credit cards. Wed–Mon 11am–3pm and 5–9pm. Bus: Kamenoi Bus 5, 41, or 43 from Beppu Station's west exit 16 min. to Kannawa (1 min.). In front of the bus stop, on Miyuki Zaka.

Okinawa

Okinawa Prefecture, an archipelago of 160 islands between Kyushu and Taiwan, seems like its own country. Maybe that's because once upon a time, it *was* its own kingdom—the Ryukyu Kingdom—with dynasties and castles (constructed mostly btw. the 14th–18th c.), as well as its own languages, culture, and cuisine. Although it was invaded by Satsuma (in what is now Kagoshima in southern Kyushu) in the early 1600s, the Ryukyu Kingdom retained domestic autonomy, trading freely with China and elsewhere, until it was annexed to Japan after the 1868 Meiji Restoration; in 1879 it was renamed Okinawa Prefecture.

You might know Okinawa as a site of brutal combat during World War II (several sites and memorials recount the horrific battle and massive casualties). If you're a diver, you might know Okinawa as one of the best diving spots in the world. But what I've always liked about Okinawa—apart from its unique museums, historic sites, tropical weather, and the finest beaches I've seen in Japan—is its laid-back, rural atmosphere. In fact, parts of Okinawa are so off the beaten path, they seem like they're caught in a time warp of a few decades past.

Of Okinawa's 160 islands (part of the Ryukyu Island chain), only 40 some are inhabited. The largest, **Okinawa Island** (Okinawa-honto), is home to Naha, capital of Okinawa Prefecture and gateway to the rest of the islands by sea and by air. After visiting Okinawa Island's many attractions, you might wish to fly or take a ferry onward to one or more of my other favorites, like **Kume Island,** renowned for its beaches, sugar cane fields, and historic sites relating to the Ryukyu Kingdom. **Iriomote** is famous for its vast pristine wilderness and for scuba diving.

Information on Okinawa is available at **www.pref.okinawa.jp** and **www.ocvb.or.jp**.

1 OKINAWA ISLAND ★

1,539km (956 miles) SW of Tokyo

On April 1, 1945, Allied forces landed on Okinawa Island in an attempt to seize control of the island and use it as a base for an invasion of mainland Japan. The Battle of Okinawa, the only land battle on Japanese territory, raged for the next 82 days, with many Japanese troops and drafted Okinawans, including high-school students, ensconced in the island's many caves. By the time the horrific fighting was over, more than 200,000 people had lost their lives. Just a few weeks later, after atomic bombs were dropped on Hiroshima and Nagasaki, the Japanese surrendered.

Okinawa was then placed under control of the U.S. government until 1972, when sovereignty reverted back to Japan. Remaining, however, are American military bases, which were greatly expanded during the Korean War and that occupy land that had belonged to Okinawans for generations (75% of American bases in Japan are in Okinawa). Many protests have been lodged against the U.S. presence, especially following rapes of local women and girls by U.S. servicemen; as part of ongoing negotiations, some 8,000 troops will transfer from Okinawa to Guam in 2014.

Tips **Island Hopping on a Discount**

If you plan to visit at least two Okinawan islands in addition to Okinawa Island, you can save money by purchasing an Okinawa Island Pass, valid on five specific routes within the Okinawan island chain, including flights from Naha to Kume or Ishigaki, on Japan Transocean Air (a subsidiary of JAL). A minimum of two flights, at ¥9,000 each, is required. *Note:* Tickets must be purchased from JAL before arriving in Japan.

Okinawa Island has a number of sites and attractions that make a 2- or 3-day stay particularly worthwhile, including nine castle sites dating from the Ryukyu Kingdom era that are on the UNESCO World Heritage list, a world-class aquarium, a theme park containing Japan's second-longest limestone cave and exhibits related to Okinawa history and culture, and several memorials for victims of the Battle of Okinawa. There are also more lighthearted pursuits, including shopping and dining in downtown Naha, sunning and swimming on the island's many white sandy beaches, and snorkeling and scuba diving among the island's surrounding coral reefs.

ESSENTIALS

GETTING THERE **By Plane** JAL flights from Tokyo's Haneda Airport take 2 hours and 50 minutes and cost ¥40,900 for a regular one-way flight to Naha Airport (OKA; ℂ 098/840-1151), though tickets bought 28 days in advance can fall as low as ¥16,300 for selected flights. Flights from Osaka's Kansai Airport take 1½ hours and cost ¥34,200 one-way; from Fukuoka it takes 1¾ hours and costs ¥27,500 one-way. After stopping by the **Visitor Information Center** in either the international terminal (ℂ 098/859-0742; daily 10:30am–7:30pm) or the domestic terminal (ℂ 098/857-6884; daily 9am–9pm), head to Naha Kuko Station in the domestic terminal, where the Yui Rail monorail delivers you to Kencho-mae Station in downtown Naha in 12 minutes for ¥230. There are also Airport Limousine Buses that travel to major resorts throughout the island; it costs ¥1,860 and takes 2 hours to travel to Busena on the northwest coast.

By Ferry Ferries travel to Naha from various ports on Honshu and Kyushu, including Tokyo, Osaka, and Kagoshima. Most frequent are those from Kagoshima, which depart every day or two and take about 25 hours, with prices starting at ¥13,200 for the cheapest class.

VISITOR INFORMATION In addition to the Visitor Information Centers at the airport, you'll find the **Naha Tourism Information Center** on Okiei Street, just off Kokusai Dori, at 2–1–4 Makishi (ℂ 098/868-4887; www.naha-navi.or.jp; Mon–Fri 8:30am–8pm; Sat–Sun 10am–8pm), where you can pick up city maps and brochures. Be sure, too, to get the free **Okinawa Island Guide,** with information on sightseeing, marine sports, dining, accommodations, events, and more, along with maps.

ORIENTATION & GETTING AROUND **Naha,** in the south part of Okinawa Island, is home to Naha Airport and the island's major attraction, Shurijo Castle. Its most famous downtown boulevard is **Kokusai Dori** (Yui Rail stop: Kencho-mae or Makishi), lined with souvenir shops, department stores, hotels, restaurants, and bars.

OKINAWA

13

OKINAWA ISLAND

ATTRACTIONS ●
Emerald Beach **1**
The Former Japanese Navy
  Underground Headquarters **9**
Himeyuri Peace Museum **10**
Nakijin Castle **2**
Naminoue Beach **8**
Native Okinawan Village **1**
Ocean Expo Park **1**
Oceanic Culture Museum **1**
Okinawa Churaumi Aquarium **1**
Okinawa Prefectural Museum
  & Art Museum **8**
Okinawa Prefectural Peace
  Memorial Museum **11**
Okinawa World **12**
Shuri Castle Park **7**

ACCOMMODATIONS ■
The Busena Terrace
  Beach Resort **3**
Hotel Jal City Naha **8**
Lohas Villa **8**
Rizzan Sea-Park Hotel **4**
Sora House **8**
Tokyo Dai-ichi Hotel Okinawa
  Grand Mer Resort **5**

DINING ◆
Ashibiuna **7**
Herb **2**
Ino Ocean View **1**
Ishigakijima Kitchen Bin **6**
Makishi Public Market **8**
Sam's Maui **8**
Suitenrou **8**

For the Okinawa Prefectural Museum and Shurijo Castle, you'll have to take the **Yui Rail** monorail. It runs from Naha Airport through downtown Naha to Shuri Station, the last stop, in 27 minutes for ¥290. In operation daily 6am to 11:30pm, trains depart every 6 to 15 minutes and start at ¥200. One-day passes with unlimited rides cost ¥600; children pay half fare.

Also in the southern part of Okinawa are sites relating to World War II, as well as Okinawa World, a theme park with a cave and restored Okinawan homes housing galleries and exhibitions. U.S. military bases are located mostly in central Okinawa Island, where you'll also find Okinawa City, the island's second-largest town, and Chatan, both with many establishments, shops, and services geared toward military personnel and their families. Chatan is especially trendy, with its American Village shopping mall, dive and surf shops, international restaurants, beaches, and other amusements. North Okinawa Island, the least populated, is a hilly region with resorts, golf courses, beaches, snorkeling and diving spots, and Okinawa Churaumi Aquarium.

For destinations outside Naha, you'll have to take a **bus** from the Naha Bus Terminal (© 098/867-7386; Yui Rail stop: Asahibashi). The Tourist Information Centers have pamphlets with bus information (those with numbers 20 and higher service outlying areas). Take a ticket upon boarding (fares, which increase with the distance covered, are posted up front) and pay when you get off.

If you have an international driver's license, you might wish to **rent a car.** There are many rental agencies, with locations at the airport, in Naha, at hotels and other locations. Prices start at ¥2,800 for 24 hours in a subcompact, plus ¥1,575 per day for insurance and an extra ¥1,050 in high season. For more information contact **ABC-Rent-A-Car** (© 0120/703-701; www.abc-car.net/en), **Budget Rent A Car** (© 0120/130 543); or **Okinawa Tourist Rent-A-Car** (© 0120/34-3732).

Otherwise, you can hire a **taxi** (© 098/831-9007) for ¥3,150 per hour or ¥21,300 for the whole day. Mr. Takara is an English-speaking driver who knows the island well; make a reservation and negotiate the fare at © 098/868-7508.

WHAT TO SEE & DO
In Naha
Okinawa Prefectural Museum & Art Museum (Okinawa Kenritsu Hakubutsukan & Bijutsukan) ★ Kids Make these two museums under one roof your first stop. While the art museum is interesting for its changing exhibitions of contemporary art, including works by artists with a connection to Okinawa, the Prefectural Museum is a must if you wish to learn more about Okinawa's history, culture, and natural history and therefore gain a better understanding for what you'll see elsewhere. You'll learn about the formation of the Ryukyu archipelago; the rise and fall of the mighty Ryukyu Kingdom with its extensive trade routes to China, Japan, and Southeast Asia; the Battle of Okinawa and subsequent U.S. occupation; and Okinawan folklore, crafts, and culture. A discovery room for children is equipped with traditional toys, clothing, musical instruments, and more. Be sure to ask for the free audio guides to both museums, where you'll spend at least 1½ hours to see both.

Omoromachi 3-1-1, Naha. © 098/941-8200. www.museums.pref.okinawa.jp. Admission to Prefectural Museum ¥400 adults, ¥250 university and high-school students, ¥150 children; art museum ¥300, ¥200, and ¥100 respectively (special exhibits cost more). Daily 9am–6pm (Fri–Sat to 8pm). Yui Rail: Omoromachi Station (10 min.). West of the station toward the port.

Shuri Castle Park (Shurijo Koen) ★★★   Naha's top attraction was first constructed between the 13th and 14th centuries and served as the epicenter of the Ryukyu Kingdom for about 500 years, until the establishment of Okinawa Prefecture in 1897. Serving as both a residence for the king and an administrative and religious center, it shows architectural influences from both China and Japan but is uniquely Ryukyuan in style. Unfortunately, the original structures were destroyed in the Battle of Okinawa, but as a reflection of the site's importance, this partial re-creation, along with eight other historic properties in Okinawa Prefecture, has been designated as a World Heritage "Gusuku Sites and Related Properties of the Ryukyu Kingdom." Lots of information and pamphlets in English explain the significance of what you're seeing; you'll probably spend about an hour here, longer if you catch one of the 40-minute traditional court dances (performed, at last check, on Wed, Fri–Sun, and holidays at 11am, 2pm, and 4pm).

1–2 Kinjocho, Shuri, Naha. ✆ **098/886-2020.** www.oki-park.jp/shurijo-park. Admission ¥800 adults, ¥600 high-school students, ¥300 children. July–Sept daily 8:30am–8:30pm; Apr–June and Oct–Nov daily 8:30am–7:30pm; Dec–Mar daily 8:30am–6:30pm. Yui Rail: Shurijo Station, then a 15-min. walk or bus 8 to Shurijo-mae stop.

In South Okinawa Island

Buses for the following destinations depart from Naha Bus Terminal.

The Former Japanese Navy Underground Headquarters (Kyukaigun Shireigo) ★   This is where the Japanese Navy, under Rear Admiral Ota, took its last stand in the Battle of Okinawa. A system of underground tunnels stretching 450m (1,475 ft.) and built by civilians using shovels and pickaxes, it remains almost exactly as it was, including the operations room and where Ota killed himself with a grenade. Rather than surrender, many of his staff also committed suicide; 2,400 bodies were eventually recovered after the war. Before touring the tunnels, which are rather bare but convey what it must have been like to live here (audio explanations throughout the tunnels are available in English, but you have to request them to be turned on), first tour the one-room museum. Most poignant are farewell letters written to family members.

236 Aza Tomishiro. ✆ **098/850-4055.** Admission ¥420 adults, ¥210 children. Daily 8:30am–5pm. Bus: 33, 46, or 101 to Tomigusuku Park-mae, then a 10-min. walk.

⑱ **Himeyuri Peace Museum (Himeyuri Heiwa Kinen Shiryokan)** ★★★   Of all the war memorials, this one affects me the most, perhaps because it gives a personal dimension to the tragedy of war. It tells the story of 240 girls and teachers who in March 1945 were assigned to serve as nurse assistants in an army hospital buried inside a series of caves, where they were faced with indescribably filthy conditions and duties, including disposal of amputated limbs and burying the dead. As U.S. forces approached, the girls were thrown out of the caves to fend for themselves, where they were killed in battle or, fearing rape, took their lives. In all, 226 perished; this museum, filled with portraits and personal accounts, was founded by the survivors. You'll spend about 40 minutes here, but note that it also takes time to get here.

671–1 Aza-Ihara, Itoman. ✆ **098/997-2100.** Admission ¥300 adults, ¥200 high-school students, ¥100 children. Daily 9am–5pm. Bus: 34 or 89 to Itoman Bus Terminal (40 min.), then bus 82, 107, or 108 15 min. to Himeyuri Memorial Tower in front of the museum.

Okinawa Prefectural Peace Memorial Museum (Heiwa Kinen Shiryokan) ★★★
Through dioramas, video screens, photographs, testimonials, and a free audio guide

OKINAWA

13

OKINAWA ISLAND

in English, this museum vividly conveys the impact of the Battle of Okinawa on the Okinawan people, from their forced mobilization to the last days of battle, when many died in caves from artillery fire, flamethrowers, or starvation; at the hands of Japanese soldiers; or from forced suicide. But it doesn't stop there: the museum also describes Okinawan life before and after the war, from forced assimilation under the Japanese to postwar protests over the vast seizure of land for U.S. occupation. An hour and 30 minutes at this must-see will make you reflect not only on the human cost of war, but also on what Okinawans have endured for more than a century.

614-1 Aza-Mabuni, Itoman. © **098/997-3844.** www.peace-museum.pref.okinawa.jp. Admission ¥300 adults, ¥150 children. Daily 9am–5pm. Bus: 89 to Itoman Bus Terminal (40 min.), then 82 to Heiwa-kinendo-iriguchi.

Okinawa World ★★ **Kids** Okinawa's largest theme park promotes the region's history, culture, and natural sciences with a variety of attractions, including Gyokusendo Cave, which you can walk through in about 30 minutes along an 890m (2,900-ft.) walkway suspended above water and filled with impressive stalagmite and stalactite formations; a museum devoted to the *habu*, Okinawa's indigenous poisonous snake; an orchard of 450 tropical fruit trees; an outdoor plaza for performances of the local Eisa dance; and workshops for potters, glass blowers, weavers, and other artisans housed in restored century-old Okinawan homes. Plan on 3 hours to see everything.

1336 Maekawa, Tamagusuku, Nanjo. © **098/949-7421.** Open Pass to everything ¥1,600 adults, ¥600 children. Apr–Oct daily 9am–6:30pm; Nov–Mar daily 9am–6pm. Bus: 54 or 83 to Gyokusendo-mae.

In North Okinawa Island

OCEAN EXPO PARK (KAIYOHAKU KINEN KOEN) ★★ **Kids** This expansive park on the northwestern coast, site of the 1975 International Ocean Expo, contains several attractions, most important of which is the **Okinawa Churaumi Aquarium** ★★ (© 098/48-3740; www.kaiyouhaku.com; daily Mar–Sept 8:30am–8pm, Oct–Feb 8:30–6:30pm), which concentrates on the oceans and currents surrounding the Ryukyu Islands, from coral reef habitats to the deep sea. Highlights include huge whale sharks and manta rays, dolphin shows, a touch pond for kids, a movie theater, and a close look at the colorful tropical fish that call the surrounding waters home. Admission is ¥1,800 for adults, ¥1,200 for high-school students, and ¥600 for children. Plan on 1½ hours here.

I also recommend strolling through the park's free **Native Okinawan Village (Okinawa Kyoudo Mura),** featuring more than a dozen sites modeled after a village from the Ryukyu Kingdom period, including thatch-roofed houses and storehouses, grand homes where the manor lord and priestess lived, and an *utaki* (sacred forest). Nearby, the **Oceanic Culture Museum (Kaiyo Bunka-kan;** © **098/48-2741;** daily May–Aug 8:30am–7pm, Sept–Apr 8:30am–5:30pm), displays items relating to oceanic people from Asia through the South Pacific, including replica boats and canoes, fishing gear, money (like the Yap's stone currency), clothing, and more. Admission is ¥170 for adults, ¥50 for children. There's also **Emerald Beach,** where you can swim free (open only Mar–Oct).

To reach Ocean Expo Park, take express bus no. 111 from Naha Bus Terminal 105 minutes to Nago Bus Terminal, followed by a 55-minute ride on bus no. 65, 66, or 70.

Marine Sports

BEACHES Okinawa, with a swimming season that runs from about March through October, has a huge variety of white sandy beaches, most with gentle slopes. Most accessible is **Naminoue Beach,** located right in Naha (bus no. 5 or 15 to Seibumon stop), but there are prettier beaches outside the city, especially to the north. Some are public beaches and some are resort beaches open to the public; many also have coral reefs popular with snorkelers. Some charge small fees. Favorites include **Okuma Beach, Emerald Beach** (in Ocean Expo Park, above), **Manza Beach, White Beach, Ikei Beach** (on Ikei Island), **Busena Beach** (popular for its watersports like windsurfing) and beaches on outlying islands like **Ie Island, Minna Island, Izena Island,** and **Iheya Island.** Ask the tourist office for bus and ferry information.

DIVING & SNORKELING   Due to its crystal-clear waters and coral reefs teeming with marine life, Okinawa is a diving mecca year-round, with Maeda Point the most popular dive spot on Okinawa Island. There are numerous dive shops offering instruction in English for everything from certification courses to *taiken* diving (experience dives for uncertified divers) to guided dives for those already certified. **Dive Okinawa** has seven shops, including one in Naha at 2–3–13 Minato-machi (© **0120/10-2743;** www.dive-okinawa.com), and offers a variety of options, including an all-day trip to the Kerama Islands, considered one of the premier dive spots in the world. Snorkeling trips start at ¥7,350 and two dives cost ¥16,800. **Reef Encounters International,** 1–273 Miyagi, in Chatan (© **098/936-8539;** www.reefencounters.org) offers diving around Okinawa Island, to the Kerama Islands, and to islands farther afield, as well as night diving. A half-day of beach diving or snorkeling costs ¥9,800. ***Note:*** Dangerous sea creatures include the box jellyfish, lionfish, the crown-of-thorns starfish, and the Erabu black-banded sea krait.

SHOPPING

Okinawa is famous for a variety of crafts, including *bingata* (stencil-dyed fabric with bright tropical motifs made into clothing and accessories), pottery, Ryukuan lacquer-ware, Ryukyuan glassware, *kariyushi* shirts (the Okinawan version of the Hawaiian Aloha shirts), *Shisha* (lion dogs, used to ward off evil spirits), *shuri-ori* weaving, and *awamori* (a potent spirit made from Thai rice and black-*koji* mold). There are many souvenir shops along the 1.5km (1 mile) **Kokusai Dori,** but for one-stop shopping, be sure to visit **Tenbusu Naha,** in the Naha-shi Dento Kogei-kan building on Kokusai Dori at 3–2–10 Makishi (© **098/868-7866**), with the Naha Municipal Arts and Crafts Museum with English-language descriptions of Okinawa's various crafts (open daily 9am–6pm; admission ¥300 adults, ¥200 students, ¥100 children); the Traditional Arts & Crafts Center where you can try your hand at Bingata stencil dying and other crafts; a shop selling local crafts; and a theater with performance art three times daily Monday to Friday.

Just a few minutes' walk south of Kokusai Dori via the covered Heiwa Dori shopping arcade is **Makishi Public Market (Makishi Kousetsu Ichiba)** with food items unique to Okinawa (including pig's face, feet, and stomach), while another 7-minutes' walk farther south on Heiwa Dori brings you to **Tsuboya Yachimun Dori** with its 20-some ceramic-art workshops and galleries, definitely worth the stroll.

WHERE TO STAY

Most hotels charge extra during peak season (New Year's, Golden Week, and summer school vacation), with discounts in the off season. Directions are from Naha Airport.

Expensive

The Busena Terrace Beach Resort ★★ **Kids**   Located on the northern tip of Okinawa Island and surrounded on three sides by water, this resort with an elegant yet tropical atmosphere is the ultimate getaway. In addition to many on-site facilities, including a spa and indoor and outdoor pools, Busena Beach and Busena Marine Park with an underwater observatory and glass-bottom boats are just a short walk or free shuttle ride away. The resort also offers a wide range of activities, from a kids' club to sunset cruising and fishing, along with rentals for beach umbrellas, sea kayaks, and windsurfing. Rooms range from standard ones facing inland toward a distant cape to more expensive rooms facing the ocean with balconies, but for true luxury there are "cottage" suites (from ¥103,950) with huge balconies and views from both bedroom and living room. Restaurants also take advantage of the beautiful views, making this a good choice for a romantic retreat.

1808 Kise, Nago City, Okinawa 905-0026. ☎ 098/51-1333. Fax 098/51-1331. www.terrace.co.jp. 410 units. ¥42,735–¥56,595 double; club floor from ¥72,765 double. Rates ¥11,550 higher in peak season. AE, DC, MC, V. 120 min. via Airport Limousine from the airport. **Amenities:** 6 restaurants; lounge; 2 bars; rental bikes (¥2,625 for 3 hr.); children's center (¥7,350 per day); executive-level rooms; gym; indoor/outdoor pools; smoke-free rooms; spa. *In room:* A/C, TV, hair dryer, Internet, minibar.

Rizzan Sea-Park Hotel (Kids)   This behemoth (it claims to have more rooms than any other hotel in Okinawa) has a great location on an 800m (½-mile) white sandy beach about halfway up the western coast. It offers lots of activities for the entire family, including marine sports, but it's too big for my tastes (just the distance from your room to the elevator can be quite a trek). Rooms (twins, suites, and family rooms) have balconies but are rather standard; it's worth splurging for a view of the ocean.

1496 Aza Tancha, Onna Village, Kunigami-gun, Okinawa 904-1496. ☎ 098/964-6611. Fax 098/964-6660. www.rizzan.co.jp/english. 558 units. ¥17,000–¥19,000 per person, including 2 meals. Rates higher in peak season; off-season discounts available. AE, DC, MC, V. 70 min. via Airport Limousine from the airport. **Amenities:** 9 restaurants; lounge; 2 bars; children's center (fee charged); concierge; computer corner w/free Internet; minigolf; indoor/outdoor pools; smoke-free rooms; spa; tennis courts. *In room:* A/C, TV, fridge, hair dryer.

Moderate

Hotel Jal City Naha   It seems a shame to come all this way just to spend the night in Naha, but this is a good choice if you're in transit to another island or prefer this hotel's location right on Kokusai Dori. Rooms are small but stylish, with good views out over the city from its higher floors.

1-3-70 Makishi, Naha, Okinawa 900-0013. ☎ 098/866-2580. Fax 098/867-8491. www.naha.jalcity.co.jp. 304 units. ¥15,015–¥16,745 single; ¥18,480–¥30,030 double. Rates higher in peak season; off-season discounts available. AE, DC, MC, V. Yui Rail: Makishi Station (8 min.). **Amenities:** Restaurant; smoke-free rooms. *In room:* A/C, TV, fridge, hair dryer, Internet.

Tokyo Dai-ichi Hotel Okinawa Grand Mer Resort ★★ (Finds)   It isn't on the coast, but this family hotel on top of a hill outside Okinawa City has lots of pluses, including free shuttle service from the airport (you can also take it to the airport and then board the monorail for Naha), a multilingual staff, a summer beer garden on a grassy lawn, and shuttle services to Araha and Sunset beaches July through September (and even free use of beach gear). All rooms have balconies; best are studio rooms for two people, complete with kitchenette.

1205-2 Yogi, Okinawa City, Okinawa 904-2174. ☎ 098/931-1500. Fax 098/931-1509. www.daiichihotel-okinawa.com. 297 units. ¥16,000–¥19,000 double. Rates higher in peak season; off-season discounts available. AE, DC, MC, V. 50 min. via free shuttle from Naha Airport (reservations required). **Amenities:** 2 restaurants; lounge; children's day-care center (¥1,050–¥2,100 per hour); 24-hr. fitness center; computer corner w/free Internet; concierge; indoor pool w/children's pool; sauna; spa; smoke-free rooms. *In room:* A/C, TV, fridge, hair dryer, Internet.

Inexpensive

Of four Toyoko Inns (www.toyoko-inn.com) in Naha, most centrally located are **Toyoko Inn Naha Asahibashi Ekimae,** 2–1–20 Kume (© **098/951-1045;** Yui Rail: Asahibashi Station), with doubles starting at ¥8,190, and **Toyoko Inn Naha Miebashi-eki,** 1–20–1 Makishi (© **098/867-1045;** Yui Rail: Miebashi), with doubles for ¥5,985. Both rates include Japanese breakfast.

Lohas Villa ★   With an easy-to-find convenient location on Okiei Dori, near the tourist office and a stone's throw from Kokusai Dori, this nonsmoking guesthouse attracts a backpacking crowd and exudes a laid-back Southeast Asian atmosphere with a third-floor reception filled with fake plants and wooden furniture. There's a communal fridge and microwave. Each room is slightly different, with a double bed, futon, or bunk beds; seven dormitory rooms stack 'em three deep.

2-1-6 Makishi, Naha, Okinawa 900-0013. © **098/867-7757.** www.lohas-cg.com. 35 units (none with bathroom). ¥4,500 single; ¥6,300 double; ¥1,500 dormitory bed. Off-season and 1-week discounts available. No credit cards. Yui Rail: Miebashi (5 min.). **Amenities:** Lobby computer w/free Internet. *In room:* Coin-op A/C, TV, no phone.

Sora House ★★ (Finds)   The building is old, but this fifth-floor walk-up is grand, with a friendly proprietor and a large, comfy communal room with a kitchen, dining area, sofas, and free use of computers, as well as a rooftop courtyard. It's the kind of place where you don't mind hanging out. There are four dormitory rooms sleeping six to eight people each, along with four simple but bright and cheerful rooms with bunk beds (which you can also book as a single).

2-24-15 Kumoji, Naha, Okinawa 900-0015. © **098/861-9939.** www.mco.ne.jp/~sora39. 8 units (none with bathroom). ¥3,500 single; ¥5,000 double; ¥1,700 dormitory bed. No credit cards. Yui Rail: Miebashi (1 min. from the north exit). **Amenities:** Rental bikes (¥500 per day); lobby computer w/free Internet; communal kitchen. *In room:* A/C, no phone.

WHERE TO DINE

Okinawan cuisine is big on pork, including *tebichi* (pigs' feet), simmered for hours in soy sauce and sake to make it soft and glutinous, and *rafute,* pork belly simmered in fish broth and *awamori* liquor. Other favorites include Okinawa *soba,* made with white flour instead of the mainland's usual buckwheat; and dishes made with *goya* (bittermelon), like stir-fried *goya champuru* containing tofu, pork, egg, and other ingredients. Champuru means to "mix together" in Okinawan dialect, with the ultimate example being taco rice, an adaptation of Mexican tacos (introduced by Americans stationed here) served with rice instead of tortillas. *Kyutei* cuisine, blending Chinese and Okinawan flavors and ingredients, originated with the Ryukyuan royal court.

Pair it with the local Orion Beer or awamori, Japan's oldest distilled liquor, introduced to the Ryukyu Kingdom from Siam (present-day Thailand) in the early 15th century and made with Thai rice. By the way, Okinawan food and drink must be healthy—Okinawans live longer than those anywhere else in the world.

In addition to the choices below, other good bets include **Makishi Public Market,** where food vendors sell local specialties on the second floor, and **Ino Ocean View Restaurant** in the Okinawa Churaumi Aquarium (© **098/48-2745**), offering a buffet of Okinawan specialties daily 11:30am to 3pm for ¥1,260, along with panoramic views.

(240) **Ashibiuna** ★ OKINAWAN DISHES   Located south of the Shurijo Castle exit, this quaint restaurant occupies a wooden house with a red-tiled roof, a reconstructed

home of a high-ranking official of the Ryukyu Kingdom. Its English-language lunch menu offers set meals of all the local favorites, including tebichi, Okinawa noodles, and goya champuru, all served with white rice or *jyushi* (rice with pork and vegetables). The dinner menu, in Japanese only, offers set courses that include sashimi, grilled fish, and other fare, along with local specialties.

2–13 Tounokura Shuri, Naha. ℭ 098/884-0035. Set dinners ¥3,150–¥5,250; set lunches ¥800–¥900. AE, MC, V. Daily 11:30am–3pm and 5:30pm–midnight. Yui Rail: Shurijo (15 min.). Turn right out of the south exit, cross the intersection, and continue straight on Ryutan Dori until you see Family Mart on the right, where you should turn left; it will be almost immediately on the right, behind a stone wall and entryway covered with bougainvillea.

Herb VEGETARIAN ★ (Finds) This cute restaurant, perched on a hill with great views over treetops toward the sea, is a destination in itself, which is good because it takes some effort to get here. Located in north Okinawa Island across from Nakajinjo Castle (on the World Heritage list and worth a visit for its rock-strewn ruins and visitor center), it offers two set meals of mostly raw seasonal fruit and vegetables (like dragon fruit, aloe, or *goya*), herbs from its own garden, and whole-grain bread and brown rice, as well as a daily pasta with salad (the menu is in Japanese only, but there are photos). Drinks include soybean milk and juice made from apples, oranges, carrots, or aloe and lemon. You must make reservations by 9am the day of your visit.

1471 Imadomari Nakajin-son. ℭ 098/56-5681. Set meals ¥1,200–¥2,000. No credit cards. Sun–Thurs 11am–5pm. From Hwy. 515, across from Nakajin Castle, 1.5km (almost 1 mile) on a winding road.

Ishigakijima Kitchen Bin HAMBURGERS (Value) This burger joint in Chatan offers large and regular-size burgers made with local Ishigaki beef and topped with choices like avocado, cream cheese, or bacon and cheese. Or, you might opt for taco rice or pork bowl with *kimchi* and mayonnaise. Instead of fries, try the *goya* chips.

1–11–1 Chatan. ℭ 098/936-7587. Dishes ¥640–¥1,480. AE, MC, V. Daily 11am–10pm. Bus: 20, 28, 29, or 120 to Chatan (5 min.). On one of Chatan's main streets, in a bright yellow building.

Sam's Maui TEPPANYAKI With Polynesian decor complete with Tiki torches and Hawaiian music, this restaurant is popular with tourists and locals alike. Set meals from the English-language menu offer steak, prawns, scallops, and other entrees, cooked on a *teppanyaki* grill in front of you, along with seasonal vegetables (like green papaya *kimchi*), soup (including an East Indian curry soup), salad, and potatoes or rice.

1–3–53 Makishi, Naha. ℭ 098/861-9595. www.sams-okinawa.jp/maui. Set dinners ¥2,850–¥5,500. AE, DC, MC, V. Daily 5pm–midnight. Yui Rail: Makishi (8 min.). On Kokusai Dori, across from OPA.

(241) **Suitenrou** KYUTEI ★ A dramatic stone entryway and an interior reminiscent of the days of the Ryukyu Kingdom set the tone for the elaborate meals served here. Set meals containing famous Okinawan dishes and photographs make ordering easy. The ¥5,250 dinner is a 12-course meal that may include pork ear salad, fermented tofu, sesame-flavored pork, duck, and fish wrapped in kelp, but the highlight is a nightly performance (at 7 and 8pm) on the second floor, of folk dancing and court dances once performed for Chinese envoys visiting Shurijo Castle.

1–3–60 Makishi, Naha. ℭ 098/863-4091. Reservations required. Set dinners ¥3,150–¥10,500; set lunches ¥2,100–¥3,150. AE, DC, MC, V. Daily 11am–11pm (last order). Yui Rail: Makishi (8 min.). On Kokusai Dori, near Hotel Jal City.

94km (58 miles) W of Okinawa Island

I first visited **Kume Island (Kumejima)** in the mid-1980s, when it was still considered rather remote, but I have to say that with the exception of more attractions, it hasn't changed much since then. What always comes to mind whenever I picture the island is its natural beauty, its rows of sugar cane accented against red-colored earth, majestic Ryukyu pines, white sandy beaches, and azure seas. A port of call for trade between China and the Ryukyu Kingdom in Naha, Kume Island still displays traces of Chinese influence, from graves and buildings that follow the principles of *feng shui* (geomancy) to guardian dogs placed virtually everywhere. It's the perfect destination if you want to get away from the hustle and bustle of everyday life, though sights and activities like castle ruins, the historic Uezu Residence, an outlying island popular for snorkeling, a public bath boasting deep-sea mineral water, and a facility dedicated to local weaving would make it hard to remain idle for long. I think the most telling testimony to the down-to-earth, unpretentious nature of the island's 9,300 residents is the products they're known for: deep-sea salt, handmade textiles, their own miso paste and *awamori*, and—unsurprising for an island that's been inhabited for more than 1,000 years—mineral water. If you want, there's a "school" where you can learn more about the island from islanders themselves.

ESSENTIALS

GETTING THERE & GETTING AROUND   Flights from Naha take 30 minutes and cost ¥11,800 one-way, though flights go as low as ¥8,600 for advance purchases (July–Sept, there are also direct flights from Tokyo). From Naha's Tomari Port, **Kume Line Ferries** (© 098/868-2686) arrive at Kanegusuku Terminal about 4 hours later and cost ¥3,000 one-way or ¥5,700 round-trip.

Kume Airport is located on the north end of the island, the ferry terminal is on the west side, and Kume Town and Eef Beach on the southeast end. An infrequent **bus,** with a schedule that coincides with flights to and from the airport, travels from the airport and Kanegusuku Terminal to various locations on the island, including Eef Beach Hotel, the Bade Haus, and Kume Town, with a ride all the way to the last stop costing ¥390. Another bus circles part of the island four or five times a day, but only on certain days. Otherwise, **taxis** start at ¥450; a taxi from the airport to Eef Beach will cost about ¥2,200. Most convenient is to rent a car. **Japaren Rent-A-Car** (© 0120/41-3900 toll-free) offers its cheapest subcompact for ¥4,725 for 24 hours, plus ¥1,050 for insurance, with free pickup at the airport.

VISITOR INFORMATION   The Kumejima Town Tourist Association (© 098/985-7115; bus stop: Eef Beach Hotel-mae; Mon–Fri 8:30am–5:30pm) is located on the main road of Kume Town.

WHAT TO SEE & DO

It's probably safe to say most tourists come to Kume Island for its **beaches.** Most famous is **Eef Beach** (bus stop: Eef Beach Hotel-mae) on its southeast end, the island's largest beach at 2km (1¼ miles) long and certainly one of Japan's best. Most people make a point, too, of taking a boat to **Hate-no-Hama,** a treeless sandy island surrounded by

> **(Moments)** **Going to School**
>
> You can mingle with the islanders at **Shimanogakko** (© **098/985-3551**), which offers excursions and classes for everything from trekking and sea kayaking to trying your hand at *tsumugi* weaving or playing the *sanshin* (a three-string instrument). Three-hour kayaking costs ¥6,300, while the 2-hour sanshin lesson costs ¥3,150. Your teacher may not speak English, but you could find the experience priceless.

crystal-clear, aquamarine water just 7km (4 miles) east of Kume Town (bus stop: Tomari Fisherina). You can rent snorkeling equipment here for ¥1,500 from May through October, but there isn't much else to do (pack a picnic lunch). Hate-no-Hama Kanko Service (© 090/8292-8854) is one of several boat companies that will take you round-trip for ¥3,500 on a flexible schedule.

Just off the eastern coast is another island, **Oujima,** connected to Kume Island by bridge and home to several sites (bus stop: Nishi-oujima). **Bade Haus Kume-Island** ★ (© 098/985-8600; daily 10am–10pm) has the distinction of being the only bathing facility in the world that uses 100% deep-ocean water (from depths of 612m/2,020 ft.). Its main pool opens toward a white sandy beach with outdoor deck chairs and open-air Jacuzzi; there's also a steam room, dry sauna, a spa with indoor and outdoor baths, and a treatment room for oil body massages, hot-stone therapy, and other treatments. Admission is ¥2,000; add ¥500 for the spa. Free shuttles run from several resorts, including Cypress Hotel and Eef Beach Hotel. Next to the Bade Haus is the **Sea Turtle Museum (Kumejima Umigame Kan)** (© 098/985-7513; Wed–Mon 9am–5pm), with tanks of baby and adult loggerhead, green, and hawksbill sea turtles. Explanations are in Japanese only, but a 10-minute film shows Kume Island as a major breeding ground. Admission is ¥300 for adults, ¥200 for children. Nearby on the beach is a natural phenomenon, the **"Tatami Ishi,"** a field of hardened lava divided into distinct pentagonal and hexangular shapes.

My favorite attraction is the **Yuima-ru Pavilion (Yuima-ru-kan)** ★★ north of Kume Town (© 098/985-8333; bus stop: Maja; daily 9am–5pm), where you can observe women engaged in making *tsumugi,* a type of silk textile. Of about 250 Okinawan artisans engaged in the craft, 150 of them live on Kume Island. A 30-minute film shows the painstaking steps of collecting the silk and forming the thread, making the dyes from vegetation found on the island, dying each string according to the selected pattern, and then weaving them together on a loom. Remarkably, the women here are engaged in every step, right down to the cultivation of silk worms. You can watch them at work; a shop sells their products.

If you have a car, be sure to stop by the **Uezu Residence (Uezuke)** on Hwy. 242 (daily 8am–6pm; to 5pm in winter), built in the 1720s as the home of an important lord during the Ryukyu Kingdom and noted for its tiled roof and—to protect it from typhoons—limestone wall and *fukugi* trees. Admission is ¥300 for adults, ¥200 for junior-high students, and ¥100 for children. The Gushikawa and Uegusuku castle ruins are also worth a stop.

WHERE TO STAY

You'll pay more in peak season, generally from about June through October, Golden Week, and New Year's.

Cypress Resort Near the airport, this is about as upscale as it gets on Kumejima. In addition to lazing by the pool or walking to the beach, you can sign up for activities, including snorkeling trips to Hate-no-Hama, scuba diving, and free shuttle service and discount tickets to Bade Haus. All rooms are with balcony facing the sea.

803–1 Ohara, Kumejima, Okinawa 901-3132. ✆ **098/985-3700.** Fax 098/985-3701. info.kumejima@ urhm-inc.jp. 84 units. Peak season ¥27,500–¥35,500 single, ¥34,000–¥47,000 double; low season ¥10,500–¥18,500 single, ¥17,000–¥30,000 double. Rates include breakfast. AE, DC, MC, V. Bus stop: Cypress Resort, or a 3-min. taxi ride or 15-min. walk from the airport. **Amenities:** Restaurant; rental bikes (¥3,000 per day in peak season, ¥2,000 in low season); fitness room; outdoor pool; spa. *In room:* A/C, TV, hair dryer, Internet.

Eef Beach Hotel (Kids) This is Kume Island's oldest hotel, with a great location right on Eef Beach. It offers trips to Hama-no-Hata and shuttles to Bade Haus, while a sports club rents beach chairs, snorkeling gear, and other equipment. Most rooms are ocean views with balconies, but the so-called "garden-view" rooms are cheaper. A good, solid choice for families.

548 Janado, Aza, Kumejima Town, Okinawa 901-3107. ✆ **098/985-7111.** Fax 098/985-7111. 80 units. Peak season ¥29,850 single, ¥37,400–¥40,800 double; low season ¥18,480 single, ¥25,410–¥28,875 double. Rates include breakfast. AE, DC, MC, V. Bus stop: Eef Beach Hotel-mae. **Amenities:** Restaurant; rental bikes (¥1,000 for 2 hr.); computer and Wi-Fi free in lobby; 2 outdoor pools; outdoor tennis courts. *In room:* A/C, TV, hair dryer, fridge.

(242) **Nankurunaisa** It's name translates as "everything's going to be all right," which pretty much sums up this laid-back *minshuku* just a block from the tourist office and Eef Beach (though the water is pretty shallow here). A modern building, it has a pleasant covered terrace where breakfast is served and both Japanese and Western-style rooms.

160–68 Aza, Higa, Kumejima Town, Okinawa 901-310. ✆/fax **098/985-7973.** 9 units. ¥5,500 per person peak season, ¥5,000 low season. No credit cards. Bus stop: Eef Beach Hotel-mae. *In room:* A/C, TV, hair dryer.

WHERE TO DINE

(243) **Kameyoshi** VARIED JAPANESE There's table and *tatami* seating at this local restaurant that seems to offer a bit of everything, including sushi, *katsudon* (fried pork), *unagi-shu* (eel on rice), *gyoza*, pizza, and Okinawan specialties like *rafute*, all from a Japanese-language menu with photos. Ordering is easiest with one of the set meals, like the ramen and gyoza set, the Okinawa set with sashimi, or the sushi set.

160–39 Aza, Higa, Kumejima Town. ✆ **098/985-8703.** Set meals ¥800–¥2,300; set lunches ¥700. No credit cards. Wed–Mon 11:30am–9:30pm (last order). Bus stop: Eef Beach Hotel-mae. Beside the tourist office.

3 THE YAEYAMA ISLANDS—ISHIGAKI & IRIOMOTE ★★

450km (279 miles) SW of Okinawa Island; 2,000km (1,240 miles) SW of Tokyo

The **Yaeyama archipelago,** closer to Taiwan than to Okinawa Island, is a chain of 19 islands, most of them small. **Ishigaki Island,** with 80% of the Yaeyama Islands' population, serves as the area's gateway and administrative center. Most famous of the Yaeyama Islands is **Iriomote** ★★★, a rather mysterious island covered mostly with subtropical primeval forests preserved in a national park that you can explore by kayak and on foot.

At about the same latitude as the Bahamas, the Yaeyama Islands are also blessed with beautiful beaches and coral reefs. Come here to commune with nature.

ESSENTIALS

GETTING THERE & GETTING AROUND   Two **flights** daily from Tokyo's Haneda airport land at Ishigaki Airport 3½ hours later and start at ¥59,400 one-way (as low as ¥21,100 for tickets purchased 28 days in advance). Otherwise, planes depart Naha every hour or less and cost ¥24,100 (¥7,600 for 28-day advance purchase fares on some flights) for the 65-minute trip. A bus travels from the airport to the bus terminal (in downtown Ishigaki near the port) in 15 minutes for ¥200.

VISITOR INFORMATION   The **Ishigaki Tourist Office,** located across from Shinei Park about a 5-minute walk from the bus terminal and Outer Islands Ferry Terminal (© **0980/82-2809;** www.city.ishigaki.okinawa.jp/International/tourist.html; Mon–Fri 8:30am–5:30pm), has maps and information in English and can help with bus schedules around Ishigaki and ferry schedules to Iriomote.

WHAT TO SEE & DO

ISHIGAKI   **Ishigaki City,** on the south end of the island and where most of the island's 48,000 residents live, has an interesting **public market** just a few blocks inland from the bus terminal and ferry terminal. Of the island's many beaches, **Maezato Beach,** in front of the ANA Hotel (bus stop: ANA Hotel & Resort), is closest to the city center, but other popular destinations include **Sukuji Beach** with its long, sandy shoreline (bus stop: Seamen's Club); **Kabira Bay,** famous for its black pearl cultivation (bus stop: Kabira), and the **Yonehara Coast,** with its beach, campground, and grove of Yaeyama Palm Trees, found only on these islands (bus stop: Yonehara Palm Grove). Buses are infrequent, so check schedules beforehand; 5-day bus passes range from ¥1,000 to ¥2,000 depending on the route.

Ishigaki is also famous for its corals, many manta rays, and drop-offs. The **Umicoza Diving School,** 827–15 Kabira (© **0980/88-2434;** www.umicoza.com) offers diving excursions for the novice and expert alike. Its two-tank dive trip to "manta ray point" costs ¥12,600, including lunch.

IRIOMOTE   Your main reason for coming this far is **Iriomote Island (Iriomotejima),** which at 289 sq. km (115 sq. miles) is the second-largest Okinawan island but is almost entirely covered by a dense subtropical forest laced by rivers that drain into Japan's largest mangrove swamp. Its most famous resident is the Iriomote cat, a shy, nocturnal wildcat found only here, but your only chance of seeing one of the 100 or so remaining animals is only a picture of it on many road signs. There are, however, many crabs, birds, butterflies, and other things to see in what is sometimes called "Asia's Amazon."

You can reach Iriomote by ferry ride from the Outer Islands Ferry Terminal in Ishigaki City, with boats departing two to four times an hour for the 40-minute trip. Operated by three different ferry companies, boats travel to Ohara Port on the east coast for ¥1,770 one-way and, less frequently, to Uehara Port on the west coast for ¥2,300. The Iriomote-jima Kotsu Bus travels approximately six times a day between the two ports for ¥680; or, purchase a 3-day pass for ¥1,000. Otherwise, each of the ferry companies operates its own buses on Iriomote, which you can ride free only if you purchased their ferry ticket (some drivers, however, don't seem to care).

In any case, because Iriomote is not easy to navigate on your own, this is one of the few times I recommend an organized tour. **Hirata Tourism Company,** 2 Misaki-cho in

Ishigaki City (✆ **0980/82-6711;** www.hirata-group.co.jp/english), offers several guided tours in English into Iriomote's remote wilderness that involve hiking and boat trips. The Sangara Falls Tour, for example, available year-round, includes a 30-minute kayak ride along a river beside a mangrove forest followed by a hike over rough terrain to a waterfall, where you have the chance to swim and eat a sack lunch before heading back. Departing at Ishigaki at 8:40am and returning at 4:10pm, it costs ¥14,500 for adults and ¥11,00 for children, including the ferry and lunch.

Although tours provide an up-close view of Iriomote's wilderness, you might want to stay another day or two to enjoy the island's beaches. **Hoshizuma no Hama,** located north of Uehara Port, is known for its coral and star-shaped sand. **Pension Hoshino-suna,** a pension/restaurant on the beach (see below) rents snorkeling equipment for ¥1,050 for 3 hours, plus a ¥1,000 deposit, and offers diving trips, like a two-tank boat dive for ¥11,000.

WHERE TO STAY

Guest House Rakutenya (Value) Located inland about a 6-minute walk from the Outer Islands Ferry Terminal, this comfortable inn occupies two buildings, one of which is a rare, two-story wooden dwelling that belonged to the English-speaking owner's grandparents and the other a typical Okinawan home with a red-tiled roof. Both are filled with quirky collectibles and antiques. Two of the rooms are twins, while the rest are *tatami*.

291 Okawa, Ishigaki City, Okinawa 907-0022. ✆/fax **0980/83-8713.** www3.big.or.jp/~erm8p3gi/english/english.html. 10 units (none with bathroom). ¥3,000 per person. ¥500 extra per person in peak season. No credit cards. Bus stop: Ishigaki Bus Terminal (6 min.); walk inland a few short blocks; it's past busy Yui Road, on the other side of a parking lot behind a rock wall. **Amenities:** Free computer and Wi-Fi in lobby. *In room:* Coin-op A/C, TV, no phone.

Hotel East China Sea Near the bus terminal, Outer Islands Ferry Terminal, and downtown Ishigaki City, this convenient choice offers rooms with rattan furniture that impart a slight South Seas look, as well as Japanese-style rooms. But the best feature, in my opinion, is the balconies from all rooms facing the busy port with its fleet of ferries, fishing boats, and pleasure boats.

2–8 Misakicho, Ishigaki City, Okinawa 907-0012. ✆ **0980/88-1155.** Fax 098/88-1156. www.eastchinasea.jp. 99 units. ¥17,000 single; ¥24,000–¥52,000 double. Rates ¥1,000–¥2,000 higher per person in peak season; off-season discounts available. Rates include breakfast buffet. AE, DC, MC, V. Bus stop: Ishigaki Bus Terminal, then a 2-min. walk east. **Amenities:** Restaurant. *In room:* A/C, TV, hair dryer.

Pension Hoshinosuna ★ (Finds) On a hill, above the famous Hoshizuma no Hama beach with its pretty islet-studded bay and sand shaped like stars, this pension is popular for its dive shop, rental snorkeling equipment, and restaurant with an outdoor terrace facing the sea offering Okinawan specialties. It has Western- and Japanese-style rooms with dreamy views of the ocean. A great, inexpensive getaway.

289–1 Uehara, Iriomote, Okinawa 907-1541. ✆ **0980/85-6448.** hoshizuna@lime.ocn.ne.jp. 10 units. ¥7,500–¥10,000 per person, including 2 meals. AE, MC, V. Pickup available from Uehara Port. **Amenities:** Restaurant. *In room:* TV, fridge.

WHERE TO DINE

Hitoshi VARIED JAPANESE This *izakaya* (Japanese drinking establishment) is well known among the locals; anyone can point you in the right direction. It specializes in *maguro* (tuna) served as sushi and sashimi but also offers Okinawan specialties like *guru-kan* (deep-fried local fish), *shima rakkyo* (pickled Okinawan scallion), *jimami* (peanuts) tofu, *ikka sumi yakisoba* (squid black-ink fried noodles), and *fu* (wheat gluten) *champuru* from a Japanese menu. Seating is at the counter or at tables with leg wells.

197–1 Okawa, Ishigaki City. ℂ **0980/88-5807.** Main dishes ¥450–¥800. No credit cards. Mon–Sat 5–10pm (last order). Bus stop: Bus Terminal (5 min.). On the road west of the post office, past Yui Road on the left.

Northeastern Honshu: Tohoku

Because so many of Japan's historic events took place in Kyoto, Tokyo, and other cities in southern Honshu, most visitors to Japan never venture farther north than Tokyo. True, northeastern Honshu (called the Tohoku District) does not have the famous temples, shrines, gardens, and castles of southern Japan, but it does have spectacular mountain scenery, national parks, hot springs in abundance, excellent ski resorts, and many hiking trails. Its rugged, mountainous terrain, coupled with cold, snowy winters, has also helped preserve the region's traditions. You won't find any of Tokyo's edgy flashiness here, but rather a down-to-earth practicality, warm hospitality, and a way of life that harks back generations.

Matsushima, about 3 hours north of Tokyo, is considered one of Japan's most scenic spots, with pine-covered islets dotting its bay. Farther north, near the middle of Tohoku, is the pleasant village of **Kakunodate,** once a thriving castle town and famous for its remaining samurai houses and cherry trees. Occupying 862 sq. km (333 sq. miles) of northern Tohoku is the resplendent **Towada-Hachimantai National Park,** best visited for its scenic lakes; rustic hot-spring spas that seem little changed over the decades; skiing; and hiking, including a trail that flanks the picture-perfect Oirase Stream. And after a day of trekking or skiing, what could be better than a soothing hot-spring soak?

TOHOKU ESSENTIALS

Getting There & Getting Around Northern Tohoku's major airports are in Aomori and Akita. The regular one-way JAL fares from Tokyo's Haneda Airport are ¥30,200 to Aomori Airport (AOJ) and ¥24,700 to Akita (AXT). You can also travel to Tohoku via **Shinkansen** bullet train from Ueno or Tokyo Station in Tokyo to Akita (¥16,470 for a reserved seat), with stops at Kakunodate and Tazawako, a convenient springboard for travel onward to Towada-Hachimantai National Park.

Although there is bus service in the national park, buses to some of the more remote areas are infrequent or nonexistent. For that reason, Tohoku is one of the few regions in Japan where **rental cars** are a great convenience, if not a necessity. In addition to car-rental agencies at both Aomori and Akita airports, there are JR Eki Rent-A-Car offices at train stations throughout Japan, including Aomori, Morioka, Kakunodate, and Tazawako stations, which offer 20% discounts for train fares booked in conjunction with car rentals. You'll also find Toyota Rent-A-Car (www.toyotarentacar.net) offices virtually everywhere. If you want to keep your driving to a minimum, I suggest taking a Shinkansen as far as Tazawako or Kakunodate and then, after seeing the sights there, drive to Nyuto Onsen for the night before continuing northward to Lake Towada. A 2-day rental of a subcompact car costs about ¥14,700, including mileage and insurance. Drop-off fees can add ¥4,000 to ¥9,000, depending on the distance. Keep in mind that Tohoku's winter season, from November to March, can bring below-freezing temperatures and up

Tips **Touring Northern Japan**

Depending on your destinations, it might make sense to visit cities in Tohoku and Hokkaido in reverse from what I've laid down here due to more convenient bus connections. See chapter 4 for a recommended itinerary.

to a foot of snowfall virtually overnight. Some mountain passes are occasionally closed due to snowfall, though access to major ski resorts is generally open. See "Getting Around Japan," in chapter 3, for information on renting a car. Contact information for rental agencies in Tohoku is provided under destination listings below.

1 THE PINE-CLAD ISLANDS OF MATSUSHIMA ★

375km (234 miles) NE of Tokyo

Because the trip to northern Tohoku or onward to Hokkaido is such a long one, the most pleasant way to travel is to break up the journey with an overnight stay in **Matsushima ★**. Matsushima means "Pine-Clad Islands"—and that's exactly what this region is. More than 260 pine-covered islets and islands dot Matsushima Bay, giving it the appearance of a giant pond in a Japanese landscape garden where twisted and gnarled pines sweep upward from volcanic tuff and white sandstone, creating bizarre and beautiful shapes.

Matsushima is so dear to Japanese hearts that it's considered one of the three most scenic spots in Japan (the other two are Miyajima in Hiroshima Bay and Amanohashidate on the north coast of Honshu)—and was so designated about 270 years ago in a book written by a Confucian philosopher of the Edo government. Basho (1644–94), the famous Japanese haiku poet, was so struck by Matsushima's beauty that it's almost as though he were at a loss for words when he wrote: "Matsushima, Ah! Matsushima! Matsushima!"

Unfortunately, motorboats have been invented since Basho's time, detracting from the beauty that evoked such ecstasy in him long ago.

ESSENTIALS

GETTING THERE From Tokyo, take the **Tohoku Shinkansen** train from Ueno or Tokyo Station to Sendai, which costs ¥10,080 for an unreserved seat and will take from 1½ to 2¼ hours, depending on the number of stops. In Sendai (there's a tourist office in Sendai Station, open daily 8:30–8pm, where you can pick up a map of Matsushima and boat and train schedules), change to the **JR Senseki Line**—it's well marked in English and trains depart approximately every half-hour. From Sendai, the trip to **Matsushima Kaigan Station** takes about 25 minutes by express train and costs ¥400.

A more picturesque way to get to Matsushima, however, is to take the Senseki Line from Sendai only as far as **Hon-Shiogama** (about 18 min. by express), where you can catch a **sightseeing boat** operated by the Marubun Matsushima Kisen Co. (② **022/365-3611;** www.marubun-kisen.com/english) for a 50-minute trip to **Matsushima Kaigan Pier;** tickets cost ¥1,400 for adults, ¥1,260 for children. You'll pass the unsightly Tohoku power station, which, it is said, was built in such a way "as not to distract from Matsushima Bay's

beauty, but rather harmonize with it." I don't even have to tell you my thoughts on this. Otherwise, it's a pleasant trip, despite the nonstop commentary in Japanese. Boats depart from both Hon-Shiogama and Matsushima Kaigan piers in both directions daily every half-hour from 9am to 3:30pm but only once an hour from 9am to 3pm December through March. From Hon-Shiogama Station, it's a 10-minute walk to the boat pier; take a right out of the station, cross the street, turn right at the first red light (crossing under the tracks), and continue straight on.

VISITOR INFORMATION   Upon your arrival in Matsushima, stop off at one of the two **Matsushima Tourist Association offices,** where you can pick up an English-language map with information on major sites and get directions to your hotel. One is located to the right after you exit **Matsushima Kaigan Station** (© **022/354-2263;** weekdays 9:30am–4:30pm, weekends and holidays 9am–5pm). Adjoining the tourist office is a hotel-reservation counter where you can book rooms for free; you can also leave your luggage here (¥200–¥300 per bag), useful if you're making a quick stopover (there are also lockers in Sendai Station).

If you're arriving in Matsushima by boat, you'll find another information office in the modern building to the left of **Matsushima Kaigan Pier** (© **022/354-2618;** daily 8:30am–5pm, to 4:30pm in winter).

Information is available also on the at www.matsushima-kanko.com.

ORIENTATION & GETTING AROUND   **Matsushima Kaigan Station** lies to the west of the boat pier and Matsushima's main attractions; the train station and pier are about a 6-minute walk apart. All of Matsushima's major attractions are within walking distance of both the station and the pier (though the pier is more centrally located); you can cover the entire area on foot in a half-day of sightseeing. Otherwise, a Loop Line Bus that passes many sights and most hotels runs daily twice an hour (7:44am–6:14pm from Matsushima Kaigan Station) and costs ¥100.

SEEING THE SIGHTS

CRUISING THE BAY   Arriving in Matsushima by **sightseeing boat** is a good introduction to the bay because you'll pass pine-covered islands and oyster rafts along the way. Board the boat in Hon-Shiogama for the 50-minute trip to Matsushima Kaigan Pier (see "Getting There," above).

If you come by train or even if you arrive by boat, you might want to take a **boat trip** in the bay. Regular sightseeing boats depart from the pier once an hour between 9am and 4pm, making 50-minute trips around the bay; they charge ¥1,400 for adults, half-price for children.

 Tips   A Note on Japanese Characters

Many hotels, restaurants, attractions, and other establishments in Japan do not have signs giving their names in Roman (English-language) letters. Chapter 17 lists the Japanese equivalents for all such places described in this guide. Each set of characters representing an establishment name has a number that corresponds to the number that appears inside the oval before the establishment's name in the text. Thus, to find the Japanese for, say, **Zuiganji Temple** (see below), refer to no. 244 in chapter 17.

(244) **Zuiganji Temple** ★★★ Matsushima's best-known structure is the most famous Zen temple in northern Japan. Located just a couple minutes' walk from Matsushima Kaigan Pier and 10 minutes from the train station, its entrance is shaded by tall cedar trees. On the right side of the pathway leading to the temple are caves and grottoes dug out by priests long ago; adorned with Buddhist statues and memorial tablets, they were used for practicing *zazen* (sitting meditation) and are an impressive sight. Here, too, you'll find what is probably Japan's only monument to . . . eels!

Now a National Treasure and the highlight of a stay in Matsushima, Zuiganji Temple was originally founded in the Heian Period (828) as a Tendai temple but became a Zen temple in the 13th century. After a period of decline, it was remodeled in 1604 by order of Date Masamune, the most powerful and important lord of northern Honshu (more on him below). Unifying the region known as Tohoku, Date built his castle in nearby Sendai, and today almost all sites in and around Sendai and Matsushima are tied to the Date family. It took hundreds of workers 5 years to build the impressive main hall, a large wooden structure that was constructed in the *shoin-zukuri* style typical of the Momoyama Period and served as the Date family temple. But it's the temple's interior that impresses, especially the wood-carved transoms and brilliantly painted, gold-plated *fusuma* (sliding doors). A room at the back is dedicated to the samurai who were laid to rest here, having followed their Date lord into death by committing ritualistic suicide. On temple grounds is the **Zuiganji Art Museum (Seiryuden),** which houses temple and Date family treasures displayed on a rotating basis, including painted sliding doors, portraits and statues of the Date clan, teacups, scrolls, calligraphy, and woodblock prints, many of Matsushima as it looked in former times. In all, you'll probably spend an hour at Zuiganji Temple.

Under the supervision of Zuiganji Temple is **Godaido,** a small wooden worship hall on a tiny island not far from the pier. Connected to the mainland by a short bridge, its grounds are open night and day and are free, but there's not much to see other than the bay. Nevertheless, Godaido is often featured in brochures of Matsushima, making this delicate wooden temple one of the town's best-known landmarks.

91 Aza-chonai. ✆ **022/354-2023.** Admission for both Seiryuden and Zuiganji Temple ¥700 adults, ¥400 children. Daily 8am–3:30pm Dec–Jan, to 4pm Nov and Feb, to 4:30pm Oct and Mar, to 5pm Apr–Sept.

(245) **Entsuin** ★★ (Finds) This lesser-known temple was also built in the early Edo Period, more than 360 years ago by the Date clan. It features a small rock garden (with seven rocks representing the Seven Deities of Good Fortune), a moss garden with six different types of moss, a lovely rose garden, an Edo-Period garden with a pond and "borrowed landscaping," and a small temple housing an elaborate statue of Lord Date Mitsumune, grandson of Lord Date Masamune, who founded the Sendai fief. Depicted here on a white steed, Mitsumune was reportedly poisoned by the Tokugawa shogunate and died at the tender age of 19 in Edo Castle. The seven statues surrounding him represent retainers who committed ritual suicide to follow their master into death. The interior walls are all covered with an overlay of gold. The painting of an occidental rose on the right-hand door is thought to be the first in Japan (hence the rose garden); other Western flowers include narcissus and corona. Be on the lookout for "hidden" joined crosses above the door that are slanted; because Christianity was banned in Edo Japan, the Date clan used crosses as a symbol for silent revolt. Expect to spend about 45 minutes here, enjoying the serenity (this temple doesn't get near the crowds of Zuiganji) and views of the wonderful gardens.

67 Aza-chonai. ✆ **022/354-3206.** Admission ¥300 adults, ¥150 high-school students, ¥100 children. Daily 8:30am–5pm (to 4pm in winter). Next to Zuiganji Temple (to the left as you face it).

Kanrantei   Another famous structure is Kanrantei, the "Water-Viewing Pavilion," just a 1-minute walk from the pier. A simple wooden teahouse, it was used by generations of the Date family for such aesthetic pursuits as viewing the moon and watching the ripples on the tide. Originally it belonged to warlord Toyotomi Hideyoshi as part of his estate at Fushimi Castle near Kyoto, but he presented it to the Date family at the end of the 16th century; it was moved here in 1645, where it remains one of the largest teahouses in Japan. For an additional ¥300 or more (depending on the accompanying sweet), you can drink ceremonial green tea while sitting on *tatami* and contemplating the bay, its islands, and the boats carving ribbons through the water. After tea, wander through the small museum containing samurai armor, ceramics, lacquerware, and tea-ceremony utensils belonging to the Date family.

56–1 Aza-chonai. ℂ 022/353-3355. Admission ¥200 adults, ¥150 university and high-school students, ¥100 children. Daily 8:30am–5pm (to 4:30pm Nov–Mar).

Museums

Belgium Orgel Museum ★★
This museum displays the entire Belgium National Music Box Museum, which was bought and shipped lock, stock, and barrel from Bruges, Belgium. The 100 or so music boxes, dating from 1860 to 1950, are priceless. Some were owned by kings, while others were designed for theaters, exhibitions, dance halls, cafes, or train stations; they are quite huge and elaborate. The largest in the collection (and one of the largest in the world) boasts 619 wooden pipes, drums, trumpets, and xylophones. There are also phonographs, player pianos, harmoniums, and other early inventions (including a 1900 Ediphone). Best of all, some of the music boxes (including the largest one) are played on request. You can easily spend 45 pleasurable minutes here.

33–3 Funendo. ℂ 022/353-3600. Admission ¥800 adults, ¥400 children. Daily 9am–5:30pm. Station: Matsushima Kaigan (15 min.). On the main road, an 8-min. walk from the pier.

⑳ Michinoku Date Masamune Historical Museum (Michinoku Date Masamune Rekishikan) ★
This wax museum details the life and times of Date Masamune (1567–1636) through 25 life-size, audiovisual diorama displays. Showing everything from how he lost sight in one of his eyes at age 5 to his marriage at age 13 to his victories in battle (he fought his first battle at age 15), the dioramas bring to life what might otherwise be dull history. At the very least, you get to see how people dressed back then and learn why Date Masamune was nicknamed the One-Eyed Dragon. Of less interest are wax figures of early-19th- and 20th-century personalities of northern Japan; be sure to ask for the English-language pamphlet, since—with the exception, perhaps, of former prime minister Koizumi and New York Yankees (now Los Angeles Angels) baseball star Hideki Matsui—you otherwise won't know who the heck they are. Plan on spending 30 minutes here.

Matsushima Kaigan. ℂ 022/354-4131. www.date-masamune.jp. Admission ¥1,000 adults, ¥600 junior-high and high-school students, ¥500 children. Daily 8:30am–5pm (9am–4:30pm in winter). Across from Godaido Temple, set back from the main street.

Islands

On the southern edge of Matsushima, about an 8-minute walk from Matsushima Kaigan Station, is **Oshima,** a small island once used as a retreat by priests. Long ago there were more than 100 hand-dug caves carved with scriptures, Buddhist images, and sutras, but today the island and its remaining 50 caves and stone images are rather neglected. There's no fee, there's no gate, and the island never closes. Connected to the mainland by bridge, it's a nice quiet spot in which to sit and view the harbor; you can walk around the entire island in about 20 minutes. Because it was a Buddhist retreat, women were forbidden on the island until after the Meiji Restoration in 1868.

At the other end of Matsushima, about a 10-minute walk from the boat pier, is **Fukurajima,** another island connected to the mainland, this time by a long red concrete bridge with orange-colored railings. It's a botanical garden of sorts, with several hundred labeled plants and trees, but mostly it's unkempt and overgrown—which comes as a surprise in cultivated Japan. It will take you less than an hour to circle the island, and there are many resting spots along the way, including a snack shop selling ice cream and drinks. The island gate is open daily 8am to 5pm (4:30pm in winter) and admission is ¥200 or adults, half-price for children.

WHERE TO STAY

Because this is a popular tourist destination, accommodations in Matsushima are not cheap, especially during the peak months of May through November. For the Tanabata Festival (Aug 6–8 in Sendai) and the Toronagashi Festival (Aug 15–16 in Matsushima), rooms may be fully booked 6 months in advance and rates are at their highest. Rates are generally lower during the off-season months (Dec–Apr).

Directions are given from the boat pier or train station, whichever is closer. The pier and station are about a 6-minute walk apart.

Expensive

(247) **Hotel Ichinobo** ★★ Despite its large size, modern facilities, and the word "hotel" in its name, this property has the atmosphere of a traditional *ryokan* (albeit a rather large, modern one) and offers mostly Japanese-style rooms. It's surrounded by pine trees and boasts lovely landscaped grounds and ponds, with views of the sea and islands from all its rooms and the wonderful public baths, including outdoor baths. It also offers 26 aesthetically furnished Matsushima Club twin rooms that include DVD players (and free DVD rentals) and use of a private lounge; some of these boast glassed-in, private whirlpool baths off private balconies. Dinners are served in one of two restaurants, one featuring a pond where hapless fish await their fate and the other offering Italian cuisine. Glass buffs should not miss the hotel's Kyohei Fujita Museum of Glass, dedicated to the only glass artist designated a National Living Treasure until his death. Although Ichinobo's location on the northern edge of Matsushima—about a 20-minute walk from the pier—is inconvenient, staff will fetch you upon arrival, and the Loop Line Bus also stops here.

1–4 Takagi Azahama, Matsushima-cho, Miyagi-gun 981-0215. © **022/353-3333.** Fax 022/353-3339. www.ichinobo.com/matsushima. 126 units. ¥23,000–¥30,000 per person. Rates include 2 meals. AE, DC, MC, V. Free shuttle bus from pier or train station. Loop Line Bus: Hotel Ichinobo. **Amenities:** 2 restaurants; bar; tea lounge; outdoor pool; glass museum; sauna; smoke-free rooms. *In room:* A/C, TV, DVD players (in some), hair dryer, minibar.

Moderate

Matsushima Century Hotel ★ This gleaming white hotel, near Fukuurajima island, is popular with families. I recommend taking a Japanese-style room or a combination room with both *tatami* area and beds, as these all face the bay with a balcony and chairs. Otherwise, if you're on a budget, the cheapest Western-style rooms, though sunny and cheerful, face inland, are small with unit baths, and have no balconies. Public baths have views of the bay. Meals are served in a restaurant; breakfast is an all-you-can-eat buffet.

8 Aza Senzui, Matsushima-cho, Miyagi-gun 981-0213. ℂ **022/354-4111.** Fax 022/354-4191. www.century hotel.co.jp. 135 units. ¥12,600–¥24,150 per person, including 2 meals. ¥3,000 extra Sat and nights before a holiday. AE, DC, MC, V. A 5-min. walk east of the pier. Call for a pickup from the station. Loop Line: Century Hotel. **Amenities:** Restaurant; coffee shop; lobby computer w/free Internet; outdoor pool w/ children's pool; sauna overlooking the bay; smoke-free rooms. *In room:* A/C, TV, fridge, hair dryer.

(248) **Taikanso** ★★ ⟮**Value**⟯ Able to accommodate 1,100 guests, Matsushima's largest hotel sprawls atop a plateau surrounded by pine-covered hills and offers the best views in town, including views of the island-studded bay from its indoor and outdoor public baths. Although it's a bit of a hike from attractions, it is served by the Loop Line Bus. Both Western- and Japanese-style rooms are available, though the cheapest rooms (singles and twins) face inland. All the Japanese-style rooms face the sea (though views are marred for some by a bus parking lot), including wonderful combination rooms (the most expensive) that offer the best of both worlds with *tatami* areas and beds. A plus here is that you can choose from several restaurants to dine in (including one that offers a crab dinner), with rates dependent on the meal and restaurant. One of the least expensive is one of my favorites: Shiosai (see below), which has the best view in town of both Matsushima Bay and the surrounding hills. The front desk is very helpful with English-language sightseeing information.

10–76 Aza Inuta, Matsushima-cho, Miyagi-gun 981-0215. ℂ **022/354-2161.** Fax 022/353-3431. www. taikanso.co.jp. 256 units. ¥10,500–¥21,000 per person. ¥2,000–¥4,000 extra weekends and peak season. Rates include 2 meals. AE, DC, MC, V. Station: Matsushima Kaigan (15 min.). Loop Line Bus: Taikanso. **Amenities:** 4 restaurants, including Shiosai; bar; 2 lounges; outdoor pool; room service; smoke-free rooms. *In room:* A/C, TV, hair dryer, minibar.

Inexpensive

Hotel Daimatsuso An older, worn hotel, with a lobby crowded by a souvenir shop and vending machines (and with free coffee in the morning), it's homey nonetheless and close to the train station. The cheapest rooms (both Japanese and Western style) have no bathrooms and look unceremoniously onto another building; this is where you'll probably end up if you opt for a room without meals. Otherwise, best are Japanese-style rooms with balconies on the fifth floor facing the sea, some of which are combination rooms with beds and *tatami* areas. Rooms come with the basics, though some of the bathrooms are so small you have to wonder how some people fit into them. Dinner is served in your room, while breakfast is in the dining room.

25 Azachonai Matsushima, Matsushima-cho, Miyagi-gun 981-0213. ℂ **022/354-3601.** Fax 022/354-6154. 41 units, 3 with toilet only, 29 with bathroom. ¥6,300–¥7,350 per person without meals; ¥10,500–¥12,600 per person with 2 meals. AE, DC, MC, V. Station: Matsushima Kaigan (1 min.). Walk straight out of the station; the hotel will be on your left. *In room:* A/C, TV, minibar.

Resort Inn Matsushima ⟮**Value**⟯ This modern, simple budget hotel with Western-style rooms is located on a steep hill above the train station and has a nice outdoor terrace where you can have breakfast. Catering mostly to couples and families, it offers only twins (though solo travelers can stay in a twin room) and larger family rooms with two twin beds and two sofa beds, most with views of the sea. Higher rates below are for peak season and weekends.

17 Sanjukari, Matsushima Aza, Matsushima-cho, Miyagi-gun 981-0213. ℂ **022/355-0888.** Fax 022/355-0889. 29 units. ¥8,000–¥10,000 single; ¥14,000–¥18,000 twin; ¥18,000–¥24,000 triple; ¥20,000–¥28,000 quad. Rates include breakfast. Dinner ¥2,000 extra. AE, DC, MC, V. Station: Matsushima Kaigan (10 min.). Take a right out of the station, then another right under the tracks, and continue straight up the hill; the hotel will be on your left. Free shuttle from the station daily 3–6pm. *In room:* A/C, TV, fridge, hair dryer.

In summer, stalls up and down the main street of Matsushima sell grilled octopus, corn on the cob, and crab.

(249) **Donjiki Chaya** NOODLES/ODANGO This rustic noodle shop with an English-language menu is a convenient place for an inexpensive lunch if you're visiting Zuiganji and Entsuin temples. Built about 400 years ago, it's easy to spot because of its thatched roof, with sliding doors pushed wide-open in summer and *tatami* seating. In addition to buckwheat noodles, it also serves *odango*, pounded rice balls covered with sesame, red-bean, or soy sauce (¥480 for five pieces). Or, stop by for a refreshing plum vinegar drink—it's much better than it sounds.

89 Chonai, Matsushima. ☎ 022/354-5855. Noodles ¥380–¥580. No credit cards. Apr–Nov daily 9am–5pm; Dec–Mar Sat–Sun and holidays 9am–4pm. In front of Entsuin Temple, a 5-min. walk from Matsushima Kaigan Station or the pier; across from Entsuin Temple.

Shiosai ★★ (Value) FRENCH Located atop a hill, this restaurant has the best view in town. Book a table at sunset close to the floor-to-ceiling windows overlooking Matsushima, where you can watch the day fade and lights in the town below begin to glimmer. Only set meals are available, but they're very good and surprisingly inexpensive. My ¥2,940 dinner consisted of pumpkin soup, seafood cocktail and steak, salad, bread, dessert, and coffee or tea. It's a good place for a romantic meal. Or, from 3 to 5pm, come for teatime and enjoy the view.

Taikanso Hotel, 7th floor, 10–76 Aza Inuta. ☎ 022/354-2161. Set lunches ¥1,260–¥2,835; set dinners ¥2,415–¥4,095. AE, DC, MC, V. Daily 11:30am–3pm and 5:30–8:30pm (last order). For directions, see "Where to Stay," above.

Ungai ★ (Finds) BUDDHIST VEGETARIAN Located on the grounds of Entsuin Temple (dining here gets you free admission to the temple), this is a great place for a peaceful meal, as you dine in a modern *tatami* room and look out over a garden. It serves three set meals typical of Buddhist vegetarian cuisine (which features many small dishes with vegetables and tofu that change with the seasons); let your budget be your guide. Although reservations should be made 1 day in advance, your hotel may be able to reserve on the same day.

Entsuin Temple, 67 Aza-chonai. ☎ 022/353-2626. Reservations required. Set meals ¥4,040, ¥5,775, and ¥8,085. No credit cards. Daily 11:30am–2pm (last order). To the right just past Entsuin's entrance.

2 KAKUNODATE, TOWN OF SAMURAI HOMES ★

Kakunodate was founded in 1620 by feudal lord Ashina Yoshikatsu, who chose the site for its river and easily defended mountain. His samurai retainers settled just south of his hilltop castle, in modest thatched-roof homes behind wooden fences along wide, fine streets, which they lined with weeping cherry trees imported from Kyoto. To help support themselves, the samurai engaged in cottage industry, crafting beautiful products made from cherry bark. Meanwhile, merchants settled in their own district, in narrow, cramped quarters. Many of the town's 13,000 residents are direct descendants of the town's original samurai and merchants.

Although the castle is long gone, Kakunodate's castle-town architectural layout remains remarkably intact, with one of the country's best-preserved (though regrettably small) samurai districts in Japan. It's also famous for its cherry trees, not only in the samurai district but also along the banks of the Hinokinai River, and for its crafts produced from local cherry bark. Yet Kakunodate is an unpretentious village, with only a few of the souvenir and tourist shops that plague other picturesque towns. ***Note:*** Technically speaking, Kakunodate merged with the town of Tazawako and another village to form a new administrative city called Semboku in 2005, but for clarity's sake I refer to them here by their historic and popular names.

ESSENTIALS

GETTING THERE   From Tokyo, take the **Tohoku Shinkansen** train from Ueno or Tokyo Station to Morioka and then the **Akita Shinkansen** to Kakunodate. (You can travel via most Shinkansen the entire distance from Tokyo without having to transfer.) The trip takes about 3½ hours and costs ¥15,850 for a reserved seat (some trains require reservations). Kakunodate is just one stop after Tazawako. (See "Towada-Hachimantai National Park," below.)

VISITOR INFORMATION   After you exit Kakunodate Station, look for the **Kakunodate Tourist Information Center** to the right, housed in a replica of a traditional warehouse (© **0187/52-1170;** daily 9am–6pm), where you can pick up an English-language map from the helpful, English-speaking staff and reserve a hotel room. More information is available at **www.city.semboku.akita.jp**.

ORIENTATION & GETTING AROUND   You can walk to all the sights and lodging and dining recommendations below (though you might opt for a short taxi ride to your accommodations if you're weighed down by luggage). To reach the samurai district, about a 15- to 20-minute walk from the station, walk straight out of the station and continue until it ends at a T-intersection (you'll see a post office across the street; this is the former merchant district and the heart of the city). Here, you turn right. Or, you might wish to tour by **rental bike,** available in a shop on the plaza in front of the train station next to the police *koban* for ¥300 for 1 hour or ¥1,500 for 5 hours.

CAR RENTALS   If you've rented a car through **JR Eki Rent-A-Car** (© **0187/53-2070**), you can pick it up at Folkloro Kakunodate, a JR-owned hotel beside the train station to the left. For **Toyota Rent-A-Car** in Kakunodate, call © **0187/55-2100.**

SEEING THE SIGHTS

Kakunodate is at its most glorious (and crowded) in late April, when its hundreds of cherry trees are in full bloom. The most popular viewing spot is along the Hinokinai River, where two rows of some 400 cherry trees form a shimmering tunnel of blossoms for 2km (1¼ miles). They were planted in 1933 to commemorate the birth of the present emperor, Akihito.

THE SAMURAI DISTRICT (BUKEYASHIKI) ★★   Of Kakunodate's 80-some samurai mansions built during the Edo Period, only seven remain. Still, the district retains its feudal atmosphere to an amazing degree, thanks to its wide streets flanked by weeping cherry trees and dark wooden fences. These fences and traditional entry gates are employed even today to conceal more-modern homes, giving a clean, crisp line of vision throughout the district. It's a strong contrast to the jumble of most Japanese cities, and even to the merchant district that's just a short walk away.

If you're walking from the station, you'll pass several samurai houses on Bukeyashiki Dori that are open free to the public (though admittance inside is restricted), including the **Odano Samurai House** to the right, the **Kawarada Samurai House** next door, the

Matsumoto Samurai House across the street (where you can usually see craftsmen at work), and the city-owned Iwahashi Samurai House on the right, which has appeared in movies.

But the first major place of interest will be the ②⑤⓪ Aoyagi Samurai Manor (Kakunodate Rekishi-mura Aoyagi) ★★★, 26 Higashi Katuraku-cho (✆ 0187/54-3257), to the right through an impressive entry gate that serves as testimony to the Aoyagi family's high samurai status. This is more than a mere manor, however, as it's actually a compound of several traditional buildings spread throughout an unkempt garden, each filled with a wealth of eclectic treasures from the 17th to 20th centuries, collected through the ages by the Aoyagi family and well documented in English. As you wander through the buildings, you'll see samurai armor, rifles, swords, dolls, kimono, sake cups, *ukiyo-e* (woodblock prints), scrolls and screens, Meiji-Era uniforms and medals, farm tools, antique phonographs, and cameras. Other buildings hold shops, a teahouse, and a restaurant. You'll want to spend at least an hour exploring here. Open daily 9am to 5pm (to 4pm in winter). Admission is ¥500 for adults, ¥300 for junior-high and high-school students, and ¥200 for children.

Next door is the Ishiguro Samurai House ★★, Omotemachi (✆ 0187/55-1496). In contrast to the Aoyagi Samurai Manor, this thatched-roof home remains almost exactly as it might have looked when it was constructed 200 years ago by the Ishiguro samurai family. After the Meiji Restoration, the family became landlords and collected rice as rent. Today, English-speaking, 12th-generation Ishiguro Naotsugi continues to live here; he has opened five simple but elegant rooms to the public in the main house. Family heirlooms, including samurai gear, winter *geta* (fur-lined and with spikes), scales for weighing rice, and old maps of Kakunodate are on display in a former warehouse. The medical illustrations (copies), by the way, are from Japan's first book on anatomy, copied from a Dutch book in 1774 by Kakunodate samurai Odano Naotake. You can see everything in less than 30 minutes, though if Ishiguro-san is on hand to answer questions, you might linger longer. Open daily 9am to 5pm. Admission is ¥300 for adults and ¥150 for children.

SHOPPING

Kakunodate has been famous for its cherry-bark crafts since the Edo Period. You can observe this painstaking craft by watching artisans at work at the ②⑤① Kakunodate-machi Denshokan, 10–1 Omotemachi Shimocho (✆ 0187/54-1700), just a couple minutes' walk from the samurai houses on Bukeyashiki Street on the left. In addition to seeing how strips of cherry bark are applied to tea canisters, boxes, vases, and other goods in live demonstrations by local craftsmen, you can tour a museum devoted to the craft along with displays of samurai outfits and items that once belonged to the Kakunodate feudal lord, as well as everyday items used by common people such as straw raingear and *geta* ice skates, and wonderful photos of days long past. And of course, you can also browse for cherry-bark products in its large shop. Admission to the *denshokan* is ¥300 for adults and ¥150 for children. It's open daily 9am to 5pm (to 4:30pm in winter).

WHERE TO STAY

Although you can easily tour Kakunodate's sights in a day, I've included a few accommodations in case you're arriving from Tokyo or seeking respite in a small town. Keep in mind that you should book well ahead if you hope to stay here during peak seasons: cherry-blossom season (roughly late Apr through early May) and summer holidays (mid-July through Aug).

Folkloro Kakunodate   No English is spoken at this JR-affiliated hotel, but its location next to Kakunodate Station and its simple but clean, modern, and inexpensive Western-style rooms make it a logical choice for a 1-night stopover, especially if you have a Japan Rail Pass, which gives a 10% discount. Only two types of rooms are available: 11 twins and 15 deluxe twin family rooms that sleep up to four. Note, however, that the family rooms, with twin beds and two sleeper sofas, seem cramped for four but are roomy for two. Higher rates below are for peak season.

14 Nakasuga-sawa, Kakunodate, Senboku-shi, Akita. ℗ 0187-53-2070. Fax 0187-53-2118. 26 units. ¥7,350–¥9,450 single; ¥12,600–¥16,800 twin; ¥17,850–¥24,300 triple; ¥21,000–¥27,720 quad. Rates include breakfast buffet. AE, DC, MC, V. To the left after you exit the train station. **Amenities:** Restaurant; car-rental agency; smoke-free rooms. *In room:* A/C, TV, fridge, hair dryer.

㉕②**Ishikawa Ryokan**   One of Kakunodate's oldest *ryokan*, open since the Edo Period and now in its fifth generation of innkeepers, it now occupies a dated building constructed in 1920. Although corridors suggest the ordinary, the Japanese-style rooms are fine, simple but with nice wood details. And the elderly owners are every bit as self-effacing and hospitable to guests as their ancestors must have been to traveling samurai and other high officials. Though they don't speak English, they make your stay here a real treat. Meals, should you opt for them, are served in your room. Prices remain the same here all year.

32 Iwasemachi, Kakunodate, Senboku-shi, Akita. ℗ **0187-54-2030.** Fax 0187-54-2031. 11 units (2 with bathroom, 1 with toilet only). ¥6,500 per person without meals; ¥13,500 per person with 2 meals. No credit cards. Station: Kakunodate (12 min.). Walk straight out of the train station and turn left when you reach the covered benches (1 block before the T intersection); the ryokan will be on your right. *In room:* A/C, TV.

㉕③ **Tamachi Bukeyashiki Hotel ★★** (Finds)   This delightful hotel is deceiving—it looks as though it has been here since the Edo Period, with its whitewashed walls, open wooden beams, and rustic ambience, but it was built in 1999. It combines tradition with modern comfort, with gleaming wood floors, contemporary Japanese art, and Japanese- and Western-style rooms that exude class, from sensuously curving paper lampshades to ceramic tissue holders. Breakfast (Western breakfast is available) is served in a restaurant with dark-wood tables overlooking a garden. This small, intimate establishment is a perfect choice for experiencing Kakunodate's relaxed, small-town charm.

23 Tamachi Shimocho, Kakunodate, Senboku-shi, Akita. ℗ **0187-52-1700.** Fax 0187-52-1701. 12 units. ¥17,850–¥21,999 per person with 2 meals; ¥12,600–¥15,750 per person with breakfast only. AE, DC, MC, V. Station: Kakunodate (12 min.). Walk straight out of the train station and turn left at the 3rd street; the hotel will be 2 blocks down, on your right. **Amenities:** Restaurant. *In room:* A/C, fridge, hair dryer, Internet.

WHERE TO DINE

In addition to the choices here, a simple dining room at the Aoyagi Samurai Manor, called **Inaniwa Korai Udon** (℗ **0187-52-8015**), offers noodle dishes, including tempura *soba* (¥1,260) and *inaniwa udon* (noodles with mountain vegetables, ¥900). Open daily 10am to 4pm (but only on weekends in winter), it has an English-language menu. Likewise, the **Folkloro Kakunodate** next to the train station (see above) has a simple restaurant open daily from 11am to 9pm offering set meals for ¥790 to ¥1,500 from its English-language menu, including those with *inaniwa udon, oyakodon* (rice topped with chicken and egg), and *gyudon* (rice topped with beef).

㉕④ **Nishinomiyake ★** VARIED JAPANESE   This pleasant and inexpensive restaurant is located in the family compound of the Nishinomiya clan, a samurai family that later became merchants and built the main house and five warehouses that are on display today. The restaurant is in a warehouse dating from 1919 and offers a limited menu of

fried seafood, noodles, beef hash with rice, hamburger steak, *ebi* (shrimp) fry, and other
dishes. Best, perhaps, is to order one of the *obento* lunch boxes. After your meal, be sure
to wander through the other warehouses, including a small museum housing family
treasures and a crafts shop.

11–1 Tamachi Kami-cho. ✆ **0187/52-2438.** Obento ¥1,500–¥2,000. No credit cards. Daily 10am–5:30pm
(last order; 4:30pm in winter). Station: Kakunodate (8 min.). Walk straight out of the train station and turn
left at the 3rd street; the restaurant will be almost immediately on your right.

(255) **Shichibe** ★ LOCAL SPECIALTIES Take your shoes off at the entrance and
then head for one of the tables with chairs or *tatami* seating with leg wells towards the
back, where you'll have a view of a small garden. Traditionally decorated with white walls,
wood crossbeams, and *shoji*, it serves most of Kakunodate's local specialties, including
inaniwa udon, oyakodon, and *kiritampo nabe* (a one-pot stew consisting of newly harvested rice pounded into a paste and then charcoal grilled before simmering in chicken
broth with vegetables), along with *tonkatsu* and a tofu set meal. The menu is in Japanese
only, but there are pictures.

15 Yokomachi. ✆ **0187/54-3295.** Main dishes ¥1,200–¥2,000; set lunch ¥900; set meals ¥1,600–¥3,000. No
credit cards. Mon–Sat 11am–7pm; Sun 11am–5pm. Station: Kakunodate (9 min.). Just before the Samurai
District to the right, catty-corner from the City Office marked on the map; look for the bamboo gate.

3 TOWADA-HACHIMANTAI NATIONAL PARK

Towada-Hachimantai National Park, spreading 862 sq. km (333 sq. miles) through north-
central Tohoku and shared by three prefectures, is blessed with mountain ranges, lakes,
streams, and hot-spring spas. It's perfect for the outdoor enthusiast, offering hiking in summer and skiing in winter. Most easily accessible from Tokyo is **Lake Tazawa** at the southern
end of the park, with its nearby ski lifts, hot-springs, and biking and hiking opportunities.
Far to the north, and a good choice if you're heading onward to Hokkaido, are the pristine
Lake Towada and delightful **Oirase Stream** with its riverbank hiking trail.

Unfortunately, bus service through the national park is either infrequent or nonexistent. There's a bus, for example, that travels from Lake Towada south to Tazawako Station, but not vice versa. The easiest way to get around is by rental car.

LAKE TAZAWA, NYUTO ONSEN & MOUNT KOMAGATAKE

Lake Tazawa (Tazawako) has the distinction of being the deepest lake in Japan, 423m
(1,387 ft.) deep. Crystal clear, the caldera offers swimming as well as cycling along its
rim. Nearby are several ski resorts, as well as the Nyuto Onsen rustic hot-spring spas at
the base of Mount Nyuto, which make good bases for exploring the area. Mount Komagatake is a popular destination for trekkers.

Essentials
GETTING THERE From Tokyo, take the **Tohoku Shinkansen train** from Ueno or
Tokyo Station to Morioka and then the **Akita Shinkansen** to Tazawako Station. (You
can travel via some Shinkansen the entire distance from Tokyo without having to transfer.) The trip takes about 3 hours and costs ¥15,240 for a reserved seat. Tazawako is one
stop before Kakunodate (see the "Kakunodate, Town of Samurai Homes" section earlier).
You can also reach Tazawako Station by Towada Taxi sightseeing bus (✆ **0186/35-2111**)

from Yasumiya on Lake Towada (information on Lake Towada below) from mid-April to October for ¥6,000. Buses depart Yasumiya at 9am and reach Tazawako Station at 4pm, with stops at scenic spots along the way; reservations are required. From Tazawako Station you must then board a bus to all the recommendations below, including Nyuto Onsen.

VISITOR INFORMATION For information on Lake Tazawa and vicinity, including skiing and bus schedules throughout the region, or for hotel reservations, stop by the **Tazawako Tourist Information Center** inside Tazawako Station (℃ **0187/43-2111;** daily 8:30am–6:30pm). They also offer one computer with free Internet access and a topographical model of the area. More information is available at **www.city.semboku.akita.jp**. For information on Nyuto Onsen, see its website at **www.nyuto-onsenkyo.com**.

ORIENTATION & GETTING AROUND The town of Tazawako, in Akita Prefecture, is the transportation launching pad for visiting the southern region of Towada-Hachimantai National Park. **Buses** depart from the Tazawako Bus Terminal across from Tazawako Station for Lake Tazawa, area ski resorts, Mount Komagatake, and Nyuto Onsen hot-spring spas. Ask for bus schedules at the Tazawako Tourist Information Center.

Lake Tazawa is just a 15-minute bus ride from Tazawako Station; note that some buses stopping here go onward to Tazawako Skijo ski resort, Kogen Onsen, and Nyuto Onsen, all of which lie northeast of the lake. Otherwise, a bus departs Tazawako Station approximately every hour for Tazawako Skijo (a 30-min. ride), Kogen Onsen (37 min.), and Nyuto Onsen (45 min.). In Nyuto Onsen, there's a bus that runs between the seven hot-spring spas; after purchasing the Yumeguri-cho ticket book for ¥1,500 at your inn, you can make reservations for the bus and enter all seven hot-spring baths at no extra charge.

CAR RENTALS Tazawako is a good starting point for driving excursions through Towado-Hachimantai National Park. **JR Eki Rent-A-Car** (℃ **0187/43-1081**) is located beside Tazawako Station. For **Toyota Rent-A-Car** in Tazawako, call ℃ **0187/43-2100**.

What to See & Do

SWIMMING & CYCLING AT LAKE TAZAWA Just 20km (13 miles) in circumference, Lake Tazawa is popular for its small swimming beach a couple minutes' walk from Tazawakokohan bus stop. Outside the swimming season—mid-July through August—you'll find nary a soul there. You can rent bicycles here for ¥400 for the first hour and ¥300 for every additional hour; mountain bikes run ¥600 per hour. It takes about 2 hours to ride around the lake; unfortunately, you have to share the road with vehicular traffic, but because this is a popular cycling route, motorists know to keep a lookout. (Still, it may be prudent to avoid weekends and the mid-July and Aug vacation crunch.) Except for one small stretch, the road is mostly flat and is pleasantly wooded and relatively unspoiled; circle the lake counterclockwise in the left lane, which puts you on the inside track closer to the lake. Along the way you'll pass a nice restaurant (see "Where to Dine," below) and a golden statue of the legendary Princess Tatsuko, a nymphlike beauty just off the shoreline. According to myth, the princess drank from Lake Tazawa hoping for eternal beauty; instead, she was turned into a dragonlike serpent as punishment for her vanity.

Sightseeing boats, some of which make stops to explore the surrounding woods, operate on Lake Tazawa from late April to early November; a 40-minute trip costs ¥1,170.

Laka Tazawa is a 15-minute bus ride from Tazawako Station. All buses going to Nyuto Onsen stop here—the name of the bus stop at the Lake is called Tazawakohan—and the fare is ¥350.

SKIING Of several area ski resorts, largest is **Tazawako Skijo** (✆ **0187/46-2011**), with nine lifts. A 1-day lift ticket costs ¥3,800 and ski-equipment rental costs ¥6,000 for everything; snowboarding is also available. Buses from Tazawako Station (traveling in the direction of Nyuto Onsen) reach Tazawako Skijo in about 30 minutes and cost ¥510.

CLIMBING MOUNT KOMAGATAKE Visible from Lake Tazawa, Akita Prefecture's tallest mountain is actually a 1,637m-high (5,402-ft.) dormant volcano. It's a popular destination for hikers, though a bus that deposits hikers at the 8th Station makes it a fairly quick hike—you can reach the top in about 1½ hours. At the peak, you're rewarded with grand vistas of the surrounding mountains, as well as more hiking trails. It's also said to be the best in northern Japan for alpine plants. Because the path is steep at times, wear nonslip soles. (All Japanese you see will be outfitted head to toe in hiking regalia.) From Tazawako Station, six buses a day make the 1-hour trip directly to Mount Komagatake's 8th Station for ¥810. Or, take a more frequent bus 37 minutes to Kogen Onsen (¥580) and transfer there for a 25-minute ride to the 8th station (¥410). Buses run daily July and August but only on weekends June, September, and October.

Where to Stay

(256) Qkamura National Park Resort Village (Kyukamura Tazawako-Kogen) (Value)
This government-owned public lodging offers the convenience of being on Nyuto Onsen's main road (buses from Tazawako Station stop right outside). While it lacks the wonderful ambience of the other rustic inns in the area and has about as much charm as a dormitory, it offers both indoor and outdoor hot-spring baths (daily 24 hr.) and nearby hiking paths. In addition, it's the only place to stay if you prefer Western-style rooms, though Japanese *tatami* rooms are also available (you'll lay out the futon yourself). Rooms are simple but clean and pleasant, with sinks and toilets (three Western-style rooms have bathrooms), and buffet-style meals are served in the dining room. If you stay here, you can still sample the other *ryokan*'s hot-spring baths for a modest fee.

2-1 Komagatake, Tazawako-machi, Senboku-shi, Akita 014-1201. ✆ **0187/46-2244.** Fax 0187/46-2700. www.qkamura.or.jp. 38 units (all with toilet, 3 with bathroom). ¥11,340 single with toilet only, ¥11,865 single with bathroom; ¥10,500 per person double with toilet only, ¥10,965 per person double with bathroom. Rates include 2 meals. AE, MC, V. Bus: From Tazawako Station, 50 min. to Qkamura-mae stop (look for the sign that reads NATIONAL PARK RESORT VILLAGE). **Amenities:** Indoor/outdoor hot-spring baths; smoke-free rooms. *In room:* A/C, TV, fridge, hair dryer.

(257) Taenoyu ★★ A relative newcomer in Nyuto Onsen (it opened in 1952), this inn merges old-fashioned comfort (updated *tatami* rooms, polished wood floors, antiques) with classy elegance, making it a good choice for those who find the Qkamura too pedestrian and the Tsuru-no-yu too rustic. Located on the main road, across from a river, it offers both indoor and outdoor baths, including a private family outdoor bath available 1 hour for free and a mixed-sex bath (shy females can wrap a towel around them, but men are supposed to bathe in the buff). Meals, which include Akita Prefecture specialties and edible wild plants gathered from around the hotel, are served communally in a tatami room with a view of the river or in a cozy lounge with tables, antiques, and a fireplace. Best are rooms with a view of the river.

2-1 Komagatake, Tazawako-machi, Senboku-shi, Akita 014-1201. ✆ **0187/46-2740.** Fax 0187/46 2207. http://taenoyu.com/web-english.html. 17 units, 10 with toilet, none with bathroom. ¥11,000–¥18,000 per person including 2 meals. Rates exclude tax and service charge and are ¥1,000 higher on weekends and in peak season. AE, DC, MC, V. Bus: From Tazawako Station, 53 min. to Taeno-onsen stop. **Amenities:** Indoor/outdoor hot-spring baths. *In room:* A/C, no phone.

258 Tsuru-no-yu Onsen ★★★ Finds By far, this is the best place to stay in Nyuto Onsen, if not in all of Tohoku. Contrary to what you might think, however, it's not refined or elegant; it's not even expensive. Rather, nestled in a wooded valley more than 2.5km (1½ miles) off the already isolated main Nyuto Onsen road, this is about as remote as you can get in Japan. And with its thatched-roof row house of tiny *tatami* rooms lit by oil lamps, complemented by the sound of rushing water and steam rising from the outdoor baths, it seems positively ancient. I've never seen anything like it.

Tsuru-no-yu opened as an *onsen* (hot-spring spa) 350 years ago; its oldest building—the thatched row house of connected rooms with blackened walls—is 100 years old. Your dinner will be cooked on your *irori* (open-hearth fireplace); breakfast is served in a tatami dining hall, with all the guests dressed in *yukata* (cotton kimono). Additions that ramble along the hillside were constructed over the years, along a rushing stream that serenades you to sleep. If you're on a budget, however, you can stay in the self-cooking wing, which offers simple tatami rooms and allows you to cook your own meals in a communal kitchen. Outdoor sulfurous baths are separated for men and women, but there is one mixed bath where you can wrap a towel around you. Unfortunately, day-trippers spoil some of the fun of staying here (baths are open to the public daily 10am–3pm for ¥500). Evenings, however, are magical. *Caveat:* Avoid the modern annex Yama no Yado about 10 minutes down the road. Its indoor baths are unspectacular (and its outdoor bath is for both sexes); if you've come this far, stay in the real thing.

50 Kokuyurin, Tazawako-machi, Senboku-shi, Akita 014-1204. ☎ **0187/46-2139.** Fax 0187/46-2761. www.tsurunoyu.com. 35 units (14 with toilet, none with bathroom). ¥9,600–¥15,900 per person including 2 meals. ¥2,780 per person in the self-cooking wing, plus ¥200 for kitchen use and ¥735 futon charge. Winter heating charge ¥1,050 extra. MC, V. Pickup available from Arupa Komakusa bus stop. **Amenities:** Indoor/outdoor hot-spring baths. *In room:* No phone (in most).

Where to Dine

Orae ★ WESTERN/VARIED JAPANESE Located beside Lake Tazawa, a 15-minute walk counterclockwise from the bus stop or a short bike ride, this casual restaurant is my top pick for lunch, due in no small part to its on-site Tazawako microbrewery (the *dunkel* beer is very good) and views of the lake from both its airy, glass-enclosed dining room and outdoor terrace. The menu, in Japanese only, offers a limited selection of Western dishes, including pizza, pasta, salads, hamburger steak, and baked chicken, along with Japanese dishes. *Croques* are a specialty, changing with the season, from those filled with *edamame* (soybean) in summer to taro in autumn.

37–5 Haruyama, Tazawako. ☎ **0187/58-0608.** Main dishes ¥800–¥1,230; set meals ¥1,210–¥1,360. AE, DC, MC, V. Daily 11:30am–8:30pm (last order). Bus: Tawazakohan (15 min.). Walk around the lake to the right.

LAKE TOWADA & OIRASE STREAM ★★

Located at the northern end of Towada-Hachimantai National Park on the border between Aomori and Akita prefectures, **Lake Towada** (Towadako in Japanese) is considered one of the park's top scenic gems. It's certainly one of Japan's least spoiled lakes, with only two small villages on its perimeter and encircled by wooded cliffs and mountains. Best, however, is **Oirase Stream,** the only river flowing out of Lake Towada. A shaded mountain stream that courses over boulders and down waterfalls, it is flanked by a hiking trail offering one of the prettiest walks in Tohoku. In autumn, leaves of gold and red render the scenery truly spectacular.

Essentials

GETTING THERE   As Lake Towada does not lie close to a train station, your final journey to the lake must be by **bus** to Yasumiya, a small village on Lake Towada with a tourist office and a few accommodations. The bus rides are through scenic, mountainous terrain (you might want to pack some Dramamine). The name of the bus stop in Yasumiya is Towadako.

From Tokyo, take the 3-hour **Shinkansen train** to Hachinohe (fare: ¥15,350), and then board a **JR bus** to Yasumiya, which takes about 2¼ hours and costs ¥2,600. If you're arriving from Hokkaido, take the train to Aomori. Outside Aomori Station, to the left, you can board a **JR bus** from platform no. 8 bound for Lake Towada, with the last stop at Yasumiya 4 hours later and costing ¥3,000. If you have a JR Rail Pass, you can ride both these buses for free (but not with a JR East Pass). Note also that both these buses travel on the road beside the hiking trail along Oirase Stream (see below) and make several stops there, with about five or six runs daily (less frequently in winter). You must make a reservation for the JR bus in advance at a major JR train station or travel agency. For more information, contact the **JR bus** company in Aomori at ✆ **017/723-1621** or visit **www.jrbustohoku.co.jp.**

CAR RENTALS   **JR Eki Rent-A-Car** has offices at Aomori Station (✆ **017/722-3930**) and Morioka Station (✆ **019/624-5212**). **Toyota Rent-A-Car** also has offices in Aomori Station (✆ **017/739-0115**) and near Morioka Station (✆ **019/622-0100**).

VISITOR INFORMATION   Before leaving Tokyo or the Narita or Kansai airports, pick up the "Towada-Hachimantai National Park" leaflet at the Tourist Information Center, or download it from JNTO's website at www.jnto.go.jp by looking under "Browse by Destinations." In Yasumiya, the **Lake Towada Information Center** (✆ **0176/75-2425;** daily 8am–5pm) is located next to the JR Bus Center (to the right after you exit the bus terminal's main door).

ORIENTATION & GETTING AROUND   Yasumiya, a village on the southwestern shore of Lake Towada, has a bus terminal, a tourist office, and a handful of accommodations and restaurants. On the eastern side of the lake is Nenokuchi, trail head for hikes along Oirase Stream. The **JR buses** that run between Yasumiya and Aomori or Hachinohe also stop at Nenokuchi and several locations along the Oirase hiking trail (including Oirase Keiryu Grand Hotel), making approximately a dozen runs a day from April to early November. Otherwise, your best bet for travel between Yasumiya and Nenokuchi is via **sightseeing boat** (see below).

Seeing the Sights

In Yasumiya, the major point of interest is **Towada Jinja Shrine,** surrounded by giant cedars and boasting marvelous woodcarvings of animals. A curious custom here is to buy a fortune, put money or rice inside, twist it into the shape of a missile, and then hike up the steep flight of wooden steps beside the shrine 20 minutes to a scenic spot (the last part of the hike is down metal ladders—only for the adventurous on a rainy day) where you then throw your missile into the lake. If it sinks, your wish will come true. Near Towada Jinja Shrine, look for the sculpture of two young women. Unlike the golden nymph at Lake Tazawa, these broad-shouldered, wide-hipped young ladies were sculpted just after the war, when such proportions were thought necessary to rebuild the nation. My Japanese friends, however, think they're very unflattering.

SIGHTSEEING BOATS ON LAKE TOWADA   The best way to enjoy the pristine beauty of crystal-clear **Lake Towada (Towadako),** a double caldera formed some 20,000 years ago by a volcanic eruption, is aboard excursion boats that cruise the waters. About 44km (27 miles) of undulating coastline marked by capes, inlets, cliffs, and trees that put on a spectacular autumn show make this one of Towada-Hachimantai National Park's major draws. Two cruises are available: a 50-minute cruise that travels between Yasumiya and Nenokuchi (available only Apr to early Nov), and a 45-minute cruise that begins and ends at Yasumiya (available year-round). Many visitors take the boat to Nenokuchi (Oirase Stream trail head), send their luggage onward (see below), and begin hiking. The cost of either cruise is ¥1,400. A surcharge of ¥500 is levied if you wish to sit in the top lounge. Children pay half fare.

HIKING OIRASE STREAM ★★   To my mind, hiking along the Oirase Stream is the major draw for a trip to Lake Towada. A clear-running, gurgling stream that runs 67km (42 miles) on its way from the lake to the Pacific Ocean, it's at its picture-perfect best in **Oirase Gorge,** where hikers are treated to a myriad of waterfalls, rapids coursing over moss-covered boulders, and a dense wood of ferns, Japanese beech, oaks, and other broad-leaved trees, particularly stunning in autumn. A trail runs beside the stream from Nenokuchi on the lakeshore 14km (8¾ miles) to Yakeyama. Most hikers, however, go only as far as Ishigedo, hiking the 9km (5½ miles) in about 2 hours (there are kilometer markers along the path in English). Disappointingly, a road runs through the gorge beside the stream, but the pathway often diverges from the road, and the roar of the swift-running river and the 13 waterfalls masks the sound of vehicles. The hike upstream (toward Nenokuchi) is considered the most picturesque, as it affords a full view of the cascading rapids.

There are nine bus stops on the road beside Oirase Stream, including Nenokuchi, Ishigedo, and Yakeyama. Because buses run only once an hour or so, you might consider taking a bus first and then hiking back. For hikers traveling onward, there's luggage transfer service between the JR bus stop in Nenokuchi and the Keiryu Tourist Center (just west of Oirase Keiryu Grand Hotel in Yakeyama). You could, for example, drop off your luggage at the JR bus station at Nenokuchi, hike, and then pick it up at the Keiryu Tourist Center (or vice versa) and then catch the bus back to Hachinohe or Aomori. There are transfers in both directions three to four times a day from Golden Week (Apr 29–May 5) to early November; the cost is ¥400 per bag. For more information, contact the **Keiryu Tourist Center** at ⓒ **0176/74-1121.**

Where to Stay

Peak season is August and October; book far in advance for these months.

259 **Himemasu Sanso** ⓥⓐⓛⓤⓔ   This simple *minshuku* in Yasumiya offers clean *tatami* rooms, with views of the surrounding wooded hills. Meals are served communally and usually feature trout from Lake Towada and local wild mountain vegetables; Western-style breakfasts are available on request. The owners will pick you up when you arrive by bus, but because they don't speak much English, you should go to the Lake Towada Information Center (see above) and have someone from there place the call.

16–15 Towada Kohan Yasumiya, Oaza Okuse, Towada-shi, Kamikita-gun, Aomori 018-5501. ⓒ **0176/75-2717.** Fax 0176/75-2717. 8 units, none with bathroom. ¥6,500 per person, including 2 meals. No credit cards. Bus: Towadako in Yasumiya (15 min., inland from the JR bus station). **Amenities:** Hot-spring bath. *In room:* TV, no phone.

Oirase Keiryu Grand Hotel   The main reason for staying in this large, rather ordinary hotel is its location on Oirase Stream, making it an easy base for hiking the trail.
Buses that traverse the Oirase Stream stop here, including those that travel to or from
Aomori and Hachinohe stations, but the hotel also offers its own free shuttle bus
approximately three times a day from Hachinohe Station (inquire about departure times
when making reservations). The hotel is divided into two sections: the older, rustic Dai-
ichi (first) Wing with 105 rooms, and the newer Daini (second) Wing with 85 (more
expensive) rooms. I prefer the Daini with its lobby overlooking the stream and maple
trees and its hard-to-overlook giant fireplace sculpture by eccentric Okamoto Taro. It
offers both Japanese *tatami* and twin rooms, about half with views of Oirase Stream.
Public hot-spring baths also take advantage of river views. Meals are served communally
in a dining room. Rates vary according to the season, whether it's a tatami or twin room
(twins are less expensive), and whether it's a weekday, Friday, or night before a holiday.
The rates below reflect the full price range.

231 Aza Tochikubo, Oaza Okuse, Towada-shi, Aomori 034-0398. © **0176/74-2121.** Fax 0176/74-2128.
190 units. ¥8,810–¥19,050 per person without meals; ¥13,380–¥27,450 per person including 2 meals. AE,
DC, MC, V. Bus: Yakeyama (1 min.). **Amenities:** 6 restaurants; 5 bars and lounges; indoor and outdoor
hot-spring baths. *In room:* A/C, TV, fridge, hair dryer.

Towada Hotel ★★★   This imposing, elegant hotel is my top choice for a splurge on
Lake Towada. Secluded on a wooded hill overlooking the lake (and practical only if you
have your own car), it was built in 1938 using huge cedar logs in a mix of Western-lodge-
meets-Japanese-temple style, with a modern addition built years later. Former U.S.
ambassador Edwin Reischauer and Emperor Showa have stayed here; nowadays most
American guests are high-ranking officers from a nearby U.S. military base. Although all
rooms face the lake, best are the Japanese rooms, all in the older part of the hotel and
elegant with great views. Western-style rooms, though spacious and beautifully designed,
do not have as good a view; be sure to ask for a room on the top floor and be sure, too,
to wander over to the older wing for a look at its beautiful wood details in the old lobby
(crafted by shrine and temple carpenters). Unfortunately, the public baths do not have
hot-spring waters (instead, it's heated water from a mountain stream), but they do have
lakeside views and outdoor tubs. Meals, served in a communal dining room with a mix
of Japanese and Western dishes, are substantial. Western-style breakfasts are available.

Kosaka-machi, Towadako Nishi-kohan, Akita 018-5511. © **0176/75-1122.** Fax 0176/75-1313. 50 units, 8
with toilet, 42 with bathroom. Peak season ¥18,900–¥24,150 per person; regular season ¥15,750–
¥18,900. Off-season discounts available. Rates include 2 meals. AE, DC, MC, V. Pickup service available
from JR bus terminal in Yasumiya. **Amenities:** Restaurant and lounge; indoor/outdoor public baths;
sauna. *In room:* A/C, TV, hair dryer, minibar.

Tsuta Onsen ★   This classic, north-country inn dates from 1909 and is one of
Tohoku's most famous traditional *ryokan*. *Tsuta* means "ivy" in Japanese, a theme carried
out not only in pillars, transoms, and other architectural details but also in the dense,
surrounding beech forest. Rooms in the oldest wooden structure (built in 1918) and an
annex (built in 1960), both up a long flight of stairs, have beautiful wood-carved details
and good views but are without bathrooms (they're also cheaper), while the west wing
1988 addition, with gleaming wood floors salvaged from an old ryokan, has an elevator
and the convenience of toilets (a few have bathrooms), but its rooms lack the character
of the older rooms. For the best views, be sure to request a room facing away from the
street. For those who don't like sleeping on futons, three combination units offer *tatami*

areas, beds, and bathrooms. The hot-spring baths are new but preserve traditional bath-house architecture, with high ceilings and cypress walls; they're considered beneficial for healing scars and other skin problems. Breakfast is served in a dining room, while dinner is served your room. Although not on the Oirase Stream and not as conveniently located as, say, the Oirase Keiryu Hotel (see above), the Tsuta is one of a kind and is served by the same JR bus that travels between Aomori and Lake Towada (it's about a 15-min. bus ride to Yakeyama). It also has its own 1-hour hiking trail to a nearby lake.

Okuse, Aza Tsutanoyu, Towada-shi, Aomori 034-0301. ☎ **0176/74-2311.** Fax 0176/74-2244. info@thuta. co.jp. 50 units (4 with bathroom, 20 with toilet only). ¥10,650–¥26,400 per person, including 2 meals. AE, DC, MC, V. Bus: From Aomori Station, a 2-hr. JR bus ride to Tsuta Onsen stop (1 min.). **Amenities:** Hot-spring indoor bath. *In room:* TV.

Where to Dine

Most accommodations serve breakfast and dinner. For an inexpensive meal on the Oirase Gorge trail, a small snack bar at Ishigedo sells ramen noodles, tempura *soba,* ice cream, and drinks.

Shinshuya LOCAL SPECIALTIES   There's nothing unique about this restaurant, but it does have an English-language menu, views of Lake Towada, and a convenient location near the path to Towada Jinja Shrine. *Inaniwa udon* (noodles with mountain vegetables), *kiritampo nabe* (a one-pot stew consisting of newly harvested rice pounded into a paste and then charcoal grilled before simmering in chicken broth with vegetables), Towada beefsteaks, and fish are just some of the local specialties. Once you've decided on your meal, purchase tickets at the counter.

16–11 Yasumiya. ☎ **0176/75-3131.** Main dishes ¥1,000–¥3,150. No credit cards. Daily 8am–6pm (10am–4pm in winter). Bus: Towadako (3 min.). On the 2nd floor above a souvenir shop beside the lake.

Hokkaido

Hokkaido, the northernmost of Japan's four main islands, has a landscape strikingly different from that of any other place in Japan. With more than 83,000 sq. km (32,000 sq. miles) and accounting for 22% of Japan's total landmass, it has only 4.5% of its population. In other words, Hokkaido has what the rest of Japan doesn't: space. The least developed of Japan's four islands, it's your best bet for avoiding the crowds that plague Japan's more well-known playgrounds during peak travel season.

Hokkaido didn't open up to development until after the Meiji Restoration in 1868, when the government began encouraging Japanese to migrate to the island (at the expense of Hokkaido's indigenous people, the Ainu). Even today, Hokkaido has a frontier feel to it, and many young Japanese come here to backpack, ski, camp, and tour the countryside on motorcycles or bicycles. There are dairy farms, silos, and broad, flat fields of wheat, corn, and potatoes. Where the fields end the land puckers up, becoming craggy with bare volcanoes, deep gorges, and hills densely covered with virgin forests and dotted with clear spring lakes, mountains,

rugged wilderness, wild animals, bubbling hot springs, and rare plants. The people of Hokkaido are as open and hearty as the wide expanses of land around them.

Much of Hokkaido's wilderness has been set aside as national and prefectural parkland. Of these areas, Shikotsu-Toya, Daisetsuzan, and Akan national parks are among the best known, offering a wide range of activities from hiking and skiing to bathing at *onsen*, or hot-spring spas.

Hokkaido's main tourist season is in July, when days are cool and pleasant with an average temperature of 70°F (21°C). While the rest of the nation is afflicted by the rainy season, Hokkaido's summers are usually bright and clear. Winters are long and severe; still, ski enthusiasts flock to slopes near Sapporo and to resorts such as Niseko and Daisetsuzan National Park. February marks the annual Sapporo Snow Festival, featuring huge ice and snow sculptures.

With its New Chitose Airport, the city of Sapporo—Japan's largest city north of Tokyo—serves as a springboard to Hokkaido's national parks and lakes. Yet despite all the island has to offer, Hokkaido remains virtually undiscovered.

1 ESSENTIALS

GETTING THERE & GETTING AROUND The fastest way to reach Hokkaido is to fly. Flights from Tokyo's Haneda Airport to Sapporo's **New Chitose Airport** take about 1½ hours. JAL's regular one-way airfare from Tokyo costs ¥33,600 to Sapporo, ¥31,500 to **Hakodate** on the western side of the island and ¥39,000 to **Kushiro** on the eastern side. JAL also flies from Osaka to Sapporo for ¥41,300. All airfares go up by about ¥2,000 in peak season, but there are discounts for advance purchase. Another option is renegade airline **Air Do** (© **0120-057-333** toll-free), which offers one-way tickets from Tokyo to Sapporo for ¥26,000 or less. Better yet, buy domestic tickets from JAL or ANA in conjunction with international flights to Japan, which must be purchased outside Japan and range from ¥10,000 to ¥13,650 per flight (see chapter 3 for details).

For centuries, the only way to travel overland between Honshu and Hokkaido was via a 4-hour ferry ride, but the opening of the Seikan Tunnel in 1988 allowed the entire trip between the islands to be made by train in little more than 2 hours—more than a fourth of which is in the 55km (34-mile) tunnel. Today, travel to Hokkaido by land is generally via the **Tohoku Shinkansen** bullet train from Ueno or Tokyo Station in Tokyo to Hachinohe in Tohoku, followed by the **limited express Hakucho train** from Hachinohe all the way to Hakodate on Hokkaido. The entire trip from Tokyo to Hakodate via train takes about 6 hours and costs ¥18,750 for a reserved seat one-way. The trip from Tokyo to Sapporo takes about 9 hours (not including transfers) and costs ¥22,780 for reserved seating. Your **JR Rail Pass** is good for all trains. *Note:* By 2011, the Tohoku Shinkansen will extend farther north all the way to Shin-Aomori (in addition, faster bullet trains will shave about 50 min. off the trip to Hakodate), with future plans calling for a new Hokkaido Shinkansen to extend all the way to Sapporo by 2013.

Public transportation around Hokkaido is by train and bus. In addition to regular bus lines, sightseeing buses link the national parks and major attractions. Although they're more expensive than trains and regular buses, and although commentaries are in Japanese only, they offer unparalleled views of the countryside and usually stop at scenic wonders, albeit sometimes only long enough for the obligatory photo. Keep in mind that bus schedules fluctuate with the seasons and can be infrequent; some lines don't run during snowy winter months. Try to get bus and train schedules before setting out on each leg of your journey. In small towns, everyone knows the local bus schedules, even clerks at front desks. Otherwise, you might find yourself waiting to make a transfer.

JR HOKKAIDO PASSES   If you plan to travel a lot in Hokkaido and don't have a Japan Rail Pass (see chapter 3 for information on rail passes), consider purchasing one of several special passes issued by Japan Railways that allows unlimited travel on JR trains and buses in Hokkaido. The **Hokkaido Rail Pass,** for example, works just like the Japan Rail Pass (valid for travel throughout Hokkaido, but you must be a foreign tourist visiting Japan). The ordinary pass, which can be purchased abroad (at JTB and other authorized travel agencies) or at train stations in Hakodate, Sapporo, Kushiro, and a few other cities in Hokkaido, costs ¥15,000 for 3 days and ¥19,500 for either 5 consecutive days or a 4-day Flexible pass you can use any 4 days within a 10-day period. Alternatively, the **JR Hokkaido Round Tour Pass (Hokkaido Furii Pasu)** can be used by anyone (including Japanese and foreigners living in Japan) and can be purchased at any JR rail station. Allowing unlimited travel in Hokkaido, the 7-day pass costs ¥25,500, but note that it's not valid on certain dates at the beginning of May, in mid-August, and over New Year's. For more information visit **www2.jrhokkaido.co.jp/global**.

RENTING A CAR   Because distances are long and traffic is rather light, Hokkaido is one of the few places in Japan where driving your own car is actually recommended. Because it's expensive, however, it's economical only if there are several of you. Rates for a 1-day rental of a compact car in July or August with unlimited mileage and insurance begin at ¥9,975 per day, with each additional day costing ¥7,350; rates run about ¥3,000 cheaper the rest of the year. Car-rental agencies are found throughout Hokkaido, often near train stations as well as at Chitose Airport outside Sapporo and at Kushiro Airport in Kushiro. In Sapporo, **Toyota Rent-A-Car** (© 011/281-0100; www.toyotorentacar.net)

is located east of Sapporo Station. **JR Eki Rent-A-Car Hokkaido** (© **011/241-0931**), near the east exit of Sapporo Station (their offices are always near a JR station), offers 20% discounts for train fares booked in conjunction with car rentals. For routes and road conditions, go to **www.northern-road.jp/navi/eng.**

A GOOD STRATEGY FOR SEEING HOKKAIDO If you're traveling from Tokyo, your first destination in Hokkaido should be **Hakodate,** an interesting and convenient 1-night stopover. From there you can board a local train bound for **Sapporo,** stopping off at **Shikotsu-Toya National Park** along the way. From Sapporo, two worthwhile destinations are **Sounkyo Onsen** in **Daisetsuzan National Park** and **Akan National Park.** To follow this plan, you'll need at least a week. You can also do this tour in reverse by flying into eastern Hokkaido (such as Kushiro) and taking the train back to Tokyo; see chapter 4 for a sample itinerary.

INFORMATION Additional information on Hokkaido is available online at **www. visit-hokkaido.jp.**

2 HAKODATE, SOUTHERN GATEWAY TO HOKKAIDO ★

888km (549 miles) NE of Tokyo; 283km (177 miles) SW of Sapporo

Hakodate, the southern gateway to Hokkaido (and Hokkaido's third-largest city with a population of 285,000), is about as far as you may care to get in a day if you arrive in Hokkaido from Tokyo by train. Hakodate makes a good 1-night stopover because it has a famous nighttime attraction and one early morning attraction, which means you can easily see a little of the city before setting out for your next destination. For those who want to linger longer, it also boasts quaint historic districts of renovated warehouses (now housing restaurants and shops) and century-old Western-style homes, churches, and administrative buildings. Founded during the Feudal Era, Hakodate was one of Japan's first ports opened to international trade following the Meiji Restoration. With its clanking streetcars, sloping streets lined with historic buildings, and port, it retains the atmosphere of a provincial outpost even today.

ESSENTIALS

GETTING THERE   By JR Train   From Tokyo, take the **Shinkansen** bullet train to Hachinohe (3 hr.), and then transfer to a direct train for Hakodate (about 3 hr.). The total fare for a reserved seat is ¥18,750. There's also a night train (the *Hokutosei*) that departs Tokyo Station at 6:50pm, arriving in Hakodate the next morning at 6:34am and costing ¥26,420; if you have a JR Rail Pass, you pay only the ¥12,430 sleeping-car surcharge. Hakodate is about 3½ hours from Sapporo.

By Plane   JAL flies from Tokyo's Haneda Airport to Hakodate Airport (HKD) in 1¼ hours for ¥31,500 (one-way), though 7-day advance-purchase fares can go for as low as ¥16,600 on certain flights. Limousine buses travel to JR Hakodate Station in 20 minutes for ¥400.

GETTING AROUND   With the exception of Mount Hakodate, the most pleasant way to see Hakodate is on foot. The city is easy to navigate, and there are many English-language signs. Otherwise, streetcars are the major form of transportation (stops are announced in English), with fares starting at ¥200; take a ticket upon entering the back door and pay when you get off. There's also a 1-day streetcar pass for ¥600.

VISITOR INFORMATION   The **Tourist Information Centers** located in Tokyo and at Tokyo and Osaka international airports have a leaflet called "Hakodate and Vicinity." (You can also download it from JNTO's website at www.jnto.go.jp by looking under "Browse by Destinations.") Otherwise, the **Hakodate Tourist Office** (✆ **0138/23-5440;** daily 9am–7pm, to 5pm Nov–Mar) is inside the station to your left as you exit the wicket. It has an excellent English-language map and brochure of Hakodate and can help with accommodations. Check **www.hakodate-kankou.com** for more information.

INTERNET ACCESS   Check e-mail at **HotWeb Café,** 18–1 Wakamatsucho (✆ **0138/ 26-3591;** Wed–Mon 10am–8pm), a 3-minute walk from Hakodate Station (on the left side of the road that runs btw. stores Wako and Boni Moriya). It charges ¥400 for 1 hour with the purchase of a drink.

In addition to the sights here, you might wish to soak away the aches of travel in one of Hakodate's hot-spring spas. Yunokawa Spa is Hokkaido's oldest, but it's 25 minutes away by streetcar (ask the tourist office for a map and list of baths). More accessible is **Yachi-gashira Public Hot-Springs Bath,** located at the foot of Mount Hakodate (✆ **0138/22-8371;** daily 6am–9:30pm; closed second and fourth Tues of every month; streetcar: Yachigashira). It's famous for its rust-colored waters, but what strikes me most is its size, capable of accommodating—I shudder at the thought—more than 500 bathers.

HISTORIC HAKODATE   You can take the streetcar to the Jujigai or Suehiro-cho stops to explore Hakodate's historic districts, but more fun is to walk 12 minutes from the station (past the morning market and continuing along the seaside promenade) to the renovated **waterfront warehouse district** with its shops and restaurants and the nearby **Meijikan** (✆ **0138/27-7070**), a former 1911 brick post office now housing glassware boutiques. A few minutes' walk inland is historic **Motomachi,** a picturesque neighborhood of steep slopes and turn-of-the-20th-century Western-style clapboard homes, consulates, churches, and other buildings; most impressive is the **Old Branch Office of the Hokkaido Government** in Motomachi Park, which contains a Tourist Information Center (✆ **0138/27-3333;** daily 9am–7pm, to 5pm in winter).

MOUNT HAKODATE AFTER DARK   Hakodate is probably most famous for its night view from atop Mount Hakodate, which rises 330m (1,100 ft.) about 3km (1¾ miles) southwest of Hakodate Station, so you should time your visit just at sunset (though note that it can be chilly up there, even in Aug). Few vacationing Japanese spend the night in Hakodate without taking the cable car to the top of this lava cone, which was formed by the eruption of an undersea volcano. From the peak, the lights of Hakodate shimmer and glitter like jewels on black velvet. I wouldn't miss it, not only for the view, but for the camaraderie shared by everyone making the pilgrimage. There's an informal restaurant here (where you can indulge in a drink or a snack while admiring the spectacular view) as well as the usual souvenir shops.

You can reach the foot of Mount Hakodate via a 5-minute streetcar ride from Hakodate Station to the Jujigai stop. From there, walk about 6 minutes to the ropeway that will take you to the top. The round-trip costs ¥1,160 for adults and ¥590 for children. Ropeway hours are daily 10am to 10pm early May through October (from 9am during Golden Week and July 25–Aug 20), and 10am to 9pm November through April. From April 20 to November you can also reach the top of Mount Hakodate directly by bus from Hakodate Station; the 30-minute trip costs ¥360 for adults and half-price for children.

THE MORNING MARKET   The other must-do is a visit to Hakodate's morning market, which is spread out just south of the train station daily from about 5am to noon. Walk around and look at the variety of foods for sale from about 300 vendors, especially the hairy crabs for which Hokkaido is famous. You can make an unusual breakfast of fruit, raw sea urchin, or grilled crab from the stalls here.

WHERE TO STAY
Hakodate's peak tourist season is in July and August. Accordingly, some hotels raise their rates during this time.

> ### (Tips) A Double or a Twin?
>
> For the sake of convenience, the price for two people in a room is listed as a "double" in this book. Japanese hotels, however, differentiate between rooms with a double bed or two twin beds, usually with different prices. Although most hotels charge more for a twin room, sometimes the opposite is true; if you're looking for a bargain, therefore, be sure to inquire about prices for both. Note, too, that hotels usually have more twin rooms than doubles, for the simple reason that Japanese couples, used to their own futon, traditionally prefer twin beds.

Expensive

Hakodate Danshaku Club Hotel & Resorts ★★ (Kids With a convenient location near Hakodate Station and the morning market, this locally owned hotel is named after a Hokkaido potato; a 1902 horseless carriage that once belonged to the farmer/shipbuilder who developed the *danshaku* gracing the modern lobby. Standard rooms would qualify as suites elsewhere, with one or two bedrooms (sleeping up to four persons) that can be closed off from the living area by shojilike doors, as well as a fully stocked kitchen, a balcony facing Mount Hakodate, and spacious bathrooms complete with generous tubs and windows also providing views.

22–10 Otemachi, Hakodate, Hokkaido, 040-0064. © **0138/21-1111.** Fax 0138/21-1212. www.danshaku-club. com. 52 units. ¥22,000–¥38,000 double. Winter discounts available. AE, DC, MC, V. Station: Hakodate (3 min., past the morning market). **Amenities:** Restaurant; cafe; lobby computer w/free Internet access; smoke-free rooms. *In room:* A/C, TV, hair dryer, Internet, kitchen.

Moderate

B&B Pension Hakodate-Mura This immaculate, mostly Western-style Japanese Inn Group member, decorated with whitewashed walls, wood furniture, and fresh and dried flowers, is built around a courtyard where you can eat breakfast. In addition to spotless Western-style rooms with wood floors (including a triple and a quad with a loft bed), there are three *tatami* rooms; only one double has a bathroom. Rules are similar to a youth hostel's (check-in at 3pm, checkout at 10am, and the door locks at 11pm), but what I like is its location near the waterfront warehouse district and Motomachi, only a 15-minute walk from Hakodate Station.

16–12 Suehiro-cho, Hakodate, Hokkaido, 040-0053. © **0138/22-8105.** Fax 0138/22-8925. www. bb-hakodatemura.com. 16 units (1 with bathroom). ¥6,280 single; ¥10,540–¥12,960 double. Western breakfast ¥800 extra. AE, MC, V. Streetcar: Jujigai (2 min.); follow the streetcar tracks for 1 block, turn right, and then turn left. **Amenities:** Lobby computer w/free Internet access; smoke-free rooms. *In room:* TV.

(260) Hotel Route Inn Grantia Hakodate Ekimae ★ (Value Despite a no-flair atmosphere and small rooms, this hotel rises above the ordinary with a convenient location near the station, reasonable prices, good views (reserve a room above the fourth floor for the best harbor views; the top floor is nonsmoking), and large hot-spring baths on the 13th floor (the women's bath looks out on the station; I can't vouch for the view from the men's bath). Family rooms have one king-size bed (and not much else) that you are welcome to put the entire family in. In-room pluses include Washlet toilets with English-language instructions, good bedside reading lamps, and cards sold in vending machines

> **(Tips) A Note on Japanese Characters**
>
> Many establishments and attractions in Japan do not have signs in Roman (English-language) letters. Those that don't are indicated in this guide with an oval with a number that corresponds to a number showing the Japanese equivalent. Thus, to find the Japanese for, say, **Hotel Route Inn Grantia Hakodate Ekimae** (see below), refer to no. 260 in chapter 17.

for ¥1,000 that allow you to watch movies (including Hollywood releases in English) all night long.

21–3 Wakamatsu-cho, Hakodate, Hokkaido, 040-0063. (𝐶 **0138/21-4100.** Fax 0138/21-4101. www.route-inn.co.jp 286 units. ¥6,900 single; ¥12,500 double; ¥14,500 family room. Off-season discounts available. AE, DC, MC, V. Station: Hakodate (1 min. from main exit, to the left). **Amenities:** Restaurant; coffee shop; lobby computers w/free Internet access; smoke-free rooms. *In room:* A/C, TV, hair dryer, Internet, minibar.

Inexpensive

In addition to the choice here, there's a 260-room **Toyoko Inn Hakodate Ekimae Asaichi** just a couple minutes' walk from Hakodate Station at 22–7 Otemachi (𝐶 **0138/23-1045;** www.toyoko-inn.com), and the slightly newer **Toyoko Inn Hakodate Daimon** (𝐶 **0138/24-1045**) a 4-minute walk from the station, both with the usual freebies for which this chain is famous, including lobby computers with free Internet access and free in-room Internet access. Double rooms at both start at ¥7,980, including Japanese breakfast. Winter discounts (Oct–May) are available.

Niceday Inn (Value) Mrs. Saito, a kind and generous woman, gives a warm welcome, making you feel right at home; staying here is like living in a Japanese home. Although Mrs. Saito's English is limited, she offers tourist information and a map, and tries to help with whatever you need. The inn is very simple but offers clean Japanese- and Western-style rooms. No meals are served, but free instant coffee, a refrigerator, a TV, and a public phone are available in the small communal entry room.

9–11 Otemachi, Hakodate 040-0064. (𝐶 **0138/22-5919.** 4 units, none with bathroom. ¥3,500 per person. No credit cards. Station: Hakodate (8 min.). Take the west exit out of the station and walk straight past the morning market; after crossing the wide, tree-lined avenue, take the 3rd left (across from the Kokusai Hotel entrance). The inn is a white, 2-story building on your right. *In room:* A/C or fan, no phone.

WHERE TO DINE

Several of Hakodate's harborfront warehouses have been renovated into smart-looking shopping and dining complexes. They're about a 12-minute walk from Hakodate Station; you can reach the complexes by walking past the morning market and continuing along the seaside promenade.

Hakodate Beer ★ BAR FOOD/SEAFOOD In a brick building about halfway between the waterfront warehouse district and the station, this beer hall has four kinds of beer brewed in the large copper vats you can see as you dine on such fare as boiled shrimp, squid (Hakodate is famous for squid), fish and chips, sirloin steak, sausages by Carl Raymon (a famous Hakodate sausage maker), the day's pasta, Japanese-style fried chicken, or a "steamboat"—seafood, sliced meat, vegetables, and dumplings cooked in boiling broth at your table and dipped in chili sauce (¥3,130 for three or four people), all listed on an English-language menu with photos. There's live piano music in the evenings, and in summer there are tables outside. A local institution.

5–22 Ohtemachi. ☏ **0138/23-8000.** Main dishes ¥720–¥1,580. AE, DC, MC, V. Daily 11am–10pm. Station: Hakodate (6 min.).

Hakodate Kaisen Club SEAFOOD   Located in the waterfront warehouse district, this casual, lively seafood restaurant, on the second floor of a wooden building above an enormous supermarket selling seafood and other Hakodate food products, has a high, airy ceiling, wood tables set up on wood floors, and sweeping harbor views. Managed by local fishmongers, it offers a range of fresh seafood, including king crab, fried fish, squid, and *kaisen-don,* a bowl of rice topped with seafood, as well as Hakodate Beer. The menu is in Japanese, but there are pictures. There's an outdoor terrace only for drinks.

Hakodate Nishi Hatoba 2F, 22–6 Suehirocho. ☏ **0138/24-8107.** Main dishes ¥1,000–¥2,000. AE, DC, MC, V. Daily 11am–9pm. Streetcar: Jujigai (5 min.). Walk toward the harbor and turn left at the waterfront. Look for the sign that says SEA FRESH MARKET.

(261) **Shinmura** SUSHI   Two things make this conveyor-belt sushi bar in the morning market unusual: The sushi chefs are all women (women's hands are said to be too hot to make sushi), and you can choose your fish or seafood from tanks out front and have it diced into sashimi right before your eyes. Otherwise, prices are determined by the color of the plate on the belt.

22–2 Otemachi. ☏ **0138/27-7885.** 2 pieces of sushi ¥125–¥525. No credit cards. Daily 9:30am–9:30pm (10am–8pm in winter). Hakodate Station (2 min.). From the west exit, walk past the morning market; Shinmura is past the 1st small intersection on the right-hand side (look for the tanks out front).

Tao Tao ASIAN FUSION   This eclectic cafe in a bright yellow building in the Motomachi District offers interesting Asian food, including *obachahan* (Manila-style pork fried rice), tacos with rice, and pad Thai (rice noodles Thai style). The tofu salad is very good, with lots of greens and a spicy dressing. There's an outdoor patio out back, open in summer.

15–19 Motomachi. ☏ **0138/22-0002.** Main dishes ¥800–¥1,000. No credit cards. Tues–Fri 6–11pm; Sat–Sun and holidays noon–11pm. Streetcar: Suehiro-cho (3 min.); walk 2 blocks up Hachimanzaka and turn left. It's just below the Roman Catholic church (the one with a rooster on top).

3 SAPPORO

1,200km (746 miles) NE of Tokyo; 283km (177 miles) NE of Hakodate

Sapporo is one of Japan's newest cities. About 140 years ago, it was nothing more than a scattering of huts belonging to Ainu and Japanese families. With the dawning of the Meiji Period, however, the government decided to colonize the island, and in 1869 it established the Colonization Commission. The area of Sapporo (the name comes from the Ainu word meaning "big, dry river") was chosen as the new capital site, and in 1871, construction of the city began.

During the Meiji Period, Japan looked eagerly toward the West for technology, ideas, and education, and Hokkaido was no exception. Between 1871 and 1884, 76 foreign technicians and experts (including 46 Americans) who had colonization experience were brought to this Japanese wilderness to aid in the island's development. Sapporo was laid out in a grid pattern of uniform blocks similar to that of an American city. In 1876, the

HOKKAIDO

15

SAPPORO

ACCOMMODATIONS ■
Hotel Gracery Sapporo **6**
Hotel Monterey Edelhof **13**
JR Tower Hotel Nikko Sapporo **5**
Nada **21**
Nakamuraya Ryokan **10**
Sapporo Aspen Hotel **2**
Sapporo Grand Hotel **15**
Toyoko Inn Sapporo
   Nishi-Guchi-Hokudai-mae **1**
Toyoko Inn Sapporo-eki Kita-Guchi **3**
Toyoko Inn Sapporo-eki Minami-Guchi **12**
Toyoko Inn Sapporo Susukino Minami **26**
Toyoko Inn Sapporo Susukino Kosaten **23**

DINING ◆
Hyosetsu-no-Mon **24**
Kita-no-Fuji **27**
Komugi-no-le La Pausa **17**
Mikuni Sapporo **5**
Palace Toriyoshi **22**
Ramen Yokocho **25**
Sapporo Bier Garten **4**
Sky J **5**
Taj Mahal **11**

ATTRACTIONS ●
Ainu Museum **7**
Aurora Town **19**
Botanic Garden **9**
Clock Tower (Tokeidai) **18**
Natural Science Museum **8**
Odori Koen (Park)
   Promenade **16**
Pole Town **20**
Sapporo Factory **14**

Sapporo Agricultural College was founded to train youth in skills useful to Hokkaido's colonization and development.

The Sapporo of today, capital of Hokkaido Prefecture, has grown to 1.9 million residents, making it the largest city north of Tokyo (and the fifth largest in Japan). In 1972, it was introduced to the world when the Winter Olympics were held here, and its many fine ski slopes continue to attract winter vacationers, as does the Snow Festival, held every February (see the "Japan Calendar of Events," in chapter 3). In August, when the rest of Japan is sweltering under uncomfortably high temperatures and humidity, Sapporo stays pleasantly cool.

ESSENTIALS

GETTING THERE   By Plane   Flights take 1½ hours from Tokyo's Haneda Airport, 2 hours from Hiroshima, and 2¼ hours from Fukuoka. See "Getting There & Getting Around," under "Essentials," earlier in this chapter, for flight details from Tokyo. Sapporo's **New Chitose Airport** (© **0123/23-0111;** www.new-chitose-airport.jp), located about 43km (27 miles) southeast of the capital, is connected to downtown by either **Airport Limousine Bus,** which delivers passengers to a few major hotels in about 70 minutes for ¥1,000; or by **JR trains** that operate every 15 minutes between Chitose Airport Station and Sapporo Station, with the 36-minute trip costing ¥1,040.

By JR Train   Trains from Tohoku and other regions on Honshu arrive in Hakodate, where you'll transfer to a train departing every hour or so for Sapporo. The fare from Tokyo to Sapporo costs ¥22,780, with trips averaging 10 hours including transfers. Trains from Hakodate take about 3½ hours and cost ¥8,590 for a reserved seat (the LEX Hokuto and Super Hokuto have only reserved seats). Otherwise, overnight trains also depart from Ueno Station in Tokyo and arrive in Sapporo the next morning, taking about 16 hours and costing from ¥25,270. In addition, an overnight train from Osaka departs around noon and arrives in Sapporo the next day at 9:52am, with fares starting at ¥25,620.

VISITOR INFORMATION   Be sure to pick up the useful leaflet "Sapporo and Shikotsu-Toya National Park" at a **Tourist Information Center** in Tokyo or international airports in Tokyo or Osaka (or download it at www.jnto.go.jp). In JR Sapporo Station, the excellent **Hokkaido-Sapporo Tourist Information Center** (© **011/213-5088;** daily 8:30am–8pm), located opposite the west ticket gate, offers a wealth of information not only on Sapporo but all of Hokkaido, making it a must stop for travelers to other destinations on the island. Here, too, is a JR information counter (daily 8:30am–7pm), where you can pick up JR train and bus schedules or get rail passes validated. Additionally, the **Sapporo International Communications Plaza,** on the third floor of the MN Building across from the Clock Tower (see "A Stroll Around Sapporo," below) at N1 W3, Chuo-ku (© **011/211-3678;** Mon–Sat 9am–5:30pm; closed holidays), provides maps and information on tourist attractions, daily life, and transportation. Online, you can check **www.welcome.city.sapporo.jp** or **www.sta.or.jp**.

INTERNET ACCESS   Inside the Hokkaido-Sapporo Tourist Information Center (see above) is Café Norte, open daily 8:30am to 8pm with five coin-operated computers (¥100 per 10 min.). Also, on the first floor of the Century Royal Hotel (1 min. west of Sapporo station's south exit), **i-café** (© **011/221-3440**) charges ¥180 for 30 minutes and is open 24 hours a day.

2 blocks east of Sapporo Station, has a 24-hour window for stamps and mail and ATMs for international credit cards (weekdays 7am–11pm; Sat 9am–9pm; Sun and holidays 9am–7pm). Otherwise, there's a smaller post office in the east end of Sapporo Station's Paseo shopping mall, also with ATMs.

ORIENTATION & GETTING AROUND   After the jumble of most Japanese cities with their incomprehensible address systems, Sapporo will come as a welcome surprise. Its streets are laid out in a grid pattern, making the city easy to navigate. Addresses in Sapporo refer to blocks that follow one another in logical, numerical order.

Sapporo Station lies at the north end of the city, with downtown and many of its attractions, hotels, and restaurants spreading to the south. The center of Sapporo is **Odori (Main St.),** a tree-lined avenue south of Sapporo Station that runs east and west and bisects the city into north and south sections. **North 1st Street,** therefore, refers to the street 1 block north of Odori. The other determinant landmark is the **Soseigawa River,** which marks addresses east and west. **West 1st Street** runs along the west bank of the Soseigawa River, while **East 1st Street** runs along the east bank.

Addresses in Sapporo are generally given by block. **N1 W4,** for example, the address for the Sapporo Grand Hotel, means it's located in the first block north of Odori and 4 blocks west of West 1st Street. If you want to be more technical about it, the entire, formal address of the hotel would read N1-jo W4-chome. "Jo" refers to blocks north and south of Odori, while "chome" refers to blocks east and west of the river. Better yet, street signs in Sapporo are in English.

Central Sapporo is easy to cover on foot. You can walk south from Sapporo Station to **Odori Park** in less than 10 minutes (an underground passage btw. the two will open in 2011) and on to **Susukino,** Sapporo's nightlife district, in another 7 or 8 minutes. For longer distances, transportation in Sapporo is via **bus,** three **subway** lines (which interchange at **Odori Station**), and one **streetcar** line. Fares begin at ¥200 for buses and subways and ¥170 for streetcars, but easier are prepaid cards available in denominations beginning at ¥1,000 and valid for all conveyances. **One-day cards,** allowing unlimited rides on all modes of transport in 1 day, are also available for ¥1,000. A 1-day card for subways only costs ¥800, except on weekends and holidays when they're discounted to ¥500. Children pay half fare. Cards can be purchased at subway stations and on buses and streetcars.

Finally, the white-colored **Sapporo Stroll Bus** (Burari Sapporo Kanko Bus), operating early May to early November, and the blue- or orange-colored **Sapporo Walk Bus** (operating year-round) are **tourist buses** that travel in a loop to tourist sites around the city (unfortunately, neither goes to Nopporo Forest Park). Single fares are ¥200 for adults, half-price for children. A 1-day pass (available only when the Sapporo Stroll Bus is in operation), ¥750 for adults and ¥380 for children, allows you to get on and off as many times as you want between 9am and 7pm. Stops are announced in English and bus stops are clearly marked. Pick up a map showing stops and routes at the Tourist Information Center.

A STROLL AROUND SAPPORO

One of the first things you should do in Sapporo is walk around. Starting from **Sapporo Station** (which contains a chic shopping and restaurant complex) take the road leading directly south called **Eki-mae Dori** (which is also West 4th). This is one of Sapporo's main thoroughfares, taking you south through the heart of the city.

YOUR FIRST STOP   Four blocks south of the station, turn left on N1; after a block, you'll find Sapporo's most famous landmark, the **Clock Tower (Tokeidai),** N1 W2, Chuo-ku (© **011/231-0838**). This Western-style wooden building was built in 1878 as a drill hall for the Sapporo Agricultural College (now Hokkaido University). The large clock at the top was made in Boston and was installed in 1881. In summer, it attracts tourists even at night; they hang around the outside gates just to listen to the clock strike the hour. Inside the tower is a local-history museum, not worth the price of admission. By the way, across the street is **Sapporo International Communications Plaza,** where you can obtain information on Sapporo (see "Visitor Information," above).

ON TO ODORI PARK   If you continue walking 1 block south of the Clock Tower, you'll reach **Odori Koen Promenade,** a 103m-wide (344-ft.) boulevard stretching almost 1.6km (1 mile) from east to west. In the middle of the boulevard is a wide median strip that has been turned into a park with trees, flower beds, and fountains. This is where much of the **Sapporo Snow Festival** is held in early February, when ice and packed snow are carved to form statues, palaces, and fantasies. Begun in 1950 to add a bit of spice and life to the cold winter days, the Snow Festival now features some 240 snow and ice sculptures and draws about 2.1 million visitors a year. One snow structure may require as much as 300 6-ton truckloads of snow, brought in from the surrounding mountains. The snow and ice carvings are done with so much attention to detail that it seems a crime they're doomed to melt (see "Japan Calendar of Events," in chapter 3).

Odori Park is also the scene of the **Sapporo Summer Festival,** celebrated with beer gardens set up the length of the park from late July to mid-August and open every day from noon. Various Japanese beer companies set up their own booths and tables under the trees, while vendors put up stalls selling fried noodles, corn on the cob, and other goodies. Live bands serenade the beer drinkers under the stars. It all resembles the cheerful confusion of a German beer garden, which isn't surprising considering Munich is one of Sapporo's sister cities (Portland, Oregon, is another one). Some of the other festivals held in Odori Park are the **Lilac Festival** in late May heralding the arrival of summer, and **Bon-Odori** in mid-August with traditional dances to appease the souls of the dead.

THE UNDERGROUND SHOPPING ARCADES   From Odori Park, you can continue your walk either above or below ground. Appreciated especially during inclement weather and during Hokkaido's long, cold winters are two underground shopping arcades, known collectively as Sapporo Chikagai, with about 140 shops open daily 10am to 8pm. Underneath Odori Park, from the Odori Station all the way to the TV tower in the east, is **Aurora Town,** with boutiques and restaurants. Even longer is the 390m (1,300-ft.) **Pole Town,** which extends from the Odori Station south all the way to **Susukino,** Sapporo's nightlife amusement center, where you'll find many restaurants and pubs (see "Where to Dine," later in this chapter). Before reaching Susukino, however, you may want to emerge at **Sanchome** (you'll see escalators going up), where you'll find more shopping at the 1km-long (½-mile) **Tanuki-koji** covered shopping arcade's 200 boutiques, traditional specialty shops, and restaurants.

THE BOTANIC GARDEN ★   Backtracking now toward the station, you should stop at the 13-hectare (32-acre) **Shokubutsu-en;** its entrance is at N3 W8 (© **011/221-0066**). It contains some virgin forest and more than 4,000 varieties of plants gathered from all over Hokkaido, arranged in marshland, herb, alpine, and other gardens. Of greater interest, perhaps, is the section devoted to plants used by the Ainu, whose extensive knowledge of plants covered not only edible ones but also those with medicinal use and other properties, including organic poison used for arrows to kill bears and other game. Unfortunately, there's no English-language explanation of plant usage. Still, with lots of trees and grassy lawns, it's a good place for a summer picnic.

Worth visiting on garden grounds is Japan's oldest **natural science museum,** founded in 1882 to document the wildlife of Hokkaido and housed in a turn-of-the-20th-century, Western-style building. Be sure, too, to visit the small, one-room **Ainu Museum,** which displays some fine examples of Ainu artifacts, including traditional clothing, jewelry, farming tools, hunting traps, harpoons, a canoe, and bamboo mouth harps (played by women and children). A 13-minute video, filmed in 1935, shows the ritualistic killing of a brown bear, a ceremony to give thanks and send the bear's soul to the afterlife, and the skinning. In any case, you'll probably want to spend an hour touring the garden and its museums.

The Botanic Garden and its museums are open April 29 to September 30, Tuesday through Sunday 9am to 4pm (Oct–Nov 3, 9am–3:30pm). Admission, including museums, is ¥400, ¥280 for children. From November 4 to April 28, only the garden and greenhouse are open (Mon–Fri 10am–3pm; Sat 10am–noon); admission then is ¥110 for everyone.

NOPPORO FOREST PARK (NOPPORO SHINRIN KOEN)

If you have an extra half-day or more, I heartily recommend this park on the outskirts for its two very worthwhile attractions. To reach the park, fastest is to take a **JR train** 10 minutes to Shin-Sapporo Station (¥260), and then transfer to **JR bus** no. 22 for a 15-minute ride to the last stop, Kaitaku-no Mura (¥200). You can also take the **Tozai subway line** 20 minutes to Shin-Sapporo Station, and then get on the same bus. Or, there are three **JR buses** a day from Sapporo Station (departing btw. 9–10am) directly to the park in 68 minutes (¥230; free with the Japan Rail Pass), but quicker is to take a local JR train to Shinrin Koen Station and then transfer to a JR bus to Kaitaku-no Mura, which cuts travel time to about 30 minutes. Before setting out, get bus and train schedules at the tourist office in Sapporo Station. All buses stop first at the Historical Museum of Hokkaido (Kinenkan Iriguchi) before stopping at the Kaitaku-no Mura. It's about a 10-minute walk between the two attractions.

Historical Museum of Hokkaido (Kaitaku Kinenkan) ★ This museum does a great job detailing Hokkaido's development from prehistoric to modern times, with lots of information in English, including an audio guide (¥130 extra). The section on the indigenous Ainu is especially good, with displays of clothing, a house, items used for trade with the Japanese and other artifacts, along with descriptions of their forced assimilation into Japanese culture (after the Meiji Restoration, Ainu were restricted from hunting and fishing on land they had used for generations and tattoos and earrings were prohibited). You'll also learn about Hokkaido's early contacts with Russia, the lives of 19th-century Japanese pioneers (including former samurai who had lost their land and stipends with the Meiji Restoration), the opening of Hakodate Port, the establishment of Sapporo Agricultural College, and more. The Living Experience Room provides hands-on experience with tools, including a hand loom, and interactive displays. If history's your thing, you can easily spend 2 hours here.

Konopporo, Atsubetsu-cho. ✆ **011/898-0456.** www.hmh.pref.hokkaido.jp. Admission ¥500 adults, ¥170 university and high-school students, free for seniors and children. Tues–Sun 9:30am–4:30pm. Closed some national holidays.

Historical Village of Hokkaido (Kaitaku-no Mura) ★★ (Kids) This open-air museum of more than 50 historical Japanese- and Western-style buildings, dating mostly from the Meiji and Taisho eras and brought here from around Hokkaido, includes homes, farmhouses, a shrine, a church, a newspaper office, a post office, a police box (manned by a sword-wielding police officer), and many small businesses, including a blacksmith, brewery, barbershop, grocery, inn, and sleigh factory—all how they would have looked in the past. Highlights include the Matsuhashi Family Residence, Hokkaido Middle School, the Aoyama fisherman's family complex, and the Hokuseikan Silkworm house. In summer, staff members dressed in Meiji-Era clothing are on hand to answer questions. Kids like being able to run and explore; there's an old-fashioned playground with a seesaw, and other traditional play equipment; nearby is the Traditional Activities Room, where children can make crafts and play games at no extra charge. There are horse-drawn carriage rides in summer and horse-drawn sleighs in winter (extra fee charged). You can easily spend 2 hours here, wandering through a fishing village, farm village, mountain village, and town. *Tip:* Wear slip-on shoes, as they must be removed to enter many of the structures.

Konopporo 50–1, Atsubetsu-cho. © 011/898-2692. www.kaitaku.or.jp. Admission Apr–Nov ¥830 adults, ¥610 university and high-school students; Dec–Mar ¥680 and ¥550, respectively. Free for children and seniors; free also for high-school students on Sat. May–Sept daily 9am–5pm; Oct–Apr Tues–Sun 9am–4:30pm. Bus: Kaitaku-no-Mura (1 min.).

HITTING THE SLOPES

Skiing is big in Sapporo, site of the 1972 Winter Olympics and easily accessible by plane from many cities in Japan—there are slopes within city limits and more than a dozen skiing areas less than 2 hours away, most open from early December to late April. On the west edge of town are Okurayama Jump Hill and Miyanomori Jump Hill, both sites of the 1972 Winter Olympics. Here, too, is the **Sapporo Bankei Ski Area** (© 011/641-0071), just 20 minutes from downtown Sapporo and popular for after-work and night skiing (it stays open to 10pm). You can reach them by subway to Maruyama Koen Station, followed by a 15-minute bus ride. Just 2.5km (1½ miles) south of Sapporo Station is **Nakajima Park** (Station: Nakajima Koen), with free use of cross-country skis in winter.

Farther afield to the west, the **Sapporo Teine** ski areas (© 011/682-6000) were the sites of the alpine, bobsled, and toboggan events for the Olympics. A lift joins the two areas, creating Hokkaido's longest run (6km/3¾ miles). A 4-hour, 6-hour, or 1-day lift pass costs ¥3,500, ¥3,900, or ¥4,800 respectively; ski-rental equipment is available from ¥4,950 in the day and ¥3,000 at night. Snowboarding gear costs ¥4,950 per day. Keep in mind that gear sizes are generally smaller than in the West (ski boots up to 30cm, size 12 in the U.S., and snowboard boots up to 28.5cm, size 10½ in the U.S.). Take the JR Ishikari Liner train from Sapporo Station 20 minutes to Teine Station and then take JR bus no. 70 another 19 minutes to Teine Olympia-mae.

Niseko (www.niseko.ne.jp and www.niseko.gr.jp), 90km (56 miles) and a 3½-hour bus ride west of Sapporo, is considered by our skiing and snowboarding friends as the best ski resort in Hokkaido for its fine powder, extensive night skiing, and hot-spring spas (it's also very popular with Aussies wishing to ski in their off season). Three skiing regions (An'nupuri, Niseko Village, and Grand Hirafu/Hanazono), joined by a network of some 60 runs, 38 gondolas and lifts, and shuttle buses that provide easy exploration of the different areas, offer a variety for skiers of all levels. An 8-hour lift ticket costs ¥4,900, with rental prices comparable to those at Teine. To get there, reserve a seat with Chuo

(☏ **011/231-0500**) or Donan (☏ **011/865-5511** or 0123/46-5701) bus company; both go to Niseko from either Chitose Airport or Sapporo Station and cost ¥3,850. Alternatively, you can also go by JR Niseko Express train (operating daily from mid-Dec through mid-Feb) from Sapporo Station to Niseko in about 2 hours, followed by a shuttle bus. JR offers a great "Tebura Skip" Niseko package, costing ¥5,500 for the Niseko Express train or ¥4,500 for a local train (available mid-Feb to mid-Mar) that includes the round-trip train and shuttle bus from Sapporo, an 8-hour lift ticket, and ski or snowboard rental with boots. For more information on skiing around Sapporo, stop by the Hokkaido-Sapporo Tourist Information Center in Sapporo Station or go to **www.snowjapan.com**.

WHERE TO STAY

Sapporo has a large selection of fine hotels in various price categories. The busiest tourist seasons are summer and early February during the annual Snow Festival. If you plan to attend the festival, book your room at least 6 months in advance. At other times you should have no problem finding a room, but it's always wise to make a reservation in advance. In winter (excluding festival time), some upper- and medium-priced hotels lower their room rates, sometimes by as much as 40%; be sure to ask for a discount.

Expensive

Hotel Monterey Edelhof ★★ Although opened in 2000, this elegant hotel embraces the architectural exuberance of early 1900s Vienna, with lots of marble, stained-glass windows, Art Deco embellishments, and Otto Wagner–inspired designs. Even the elevators have old-fashioned floor dials, classical music plays in public spaces, and function rooms carry such names as Belvedere. Forgive me a sudden craving for Sacher torte. Located in downtown Sapporo, on the upper floors of an office building, the hotel offers small but smartly decorated rooms with a slight Art Deco motif. The hotel spa, which uses hot springs tapped deep below ground, is a huge (though pricey) plus.

N2 W1, Chuo-ku, Sapporo 060-0002. ☏ **011/242-7111**. Fax 011/232-1212. www.hotelmonterey.co.jp/eng. 181 units. ¥17,325 single; ¥32,340–¥43,890 double. AE, DC, MC, V. Station: Sapporo (8 min.). **Amenities:** 2 restaurants; bar; lounge; hot-spring spa w/sauna and Jacuzzi (fee: ¥1,515); lobby computer w/free Internet; room service; smoke-free rooms. *In room:* A/C, TV, hair dryer, Internet, minibar.

JR Tower Hotel Nikko Sapporo ★★★ Elegance and convenience—not to mention top-class restaurants, a deluxe spa (offering everything from reflexology to indoor/outdoor hot-spring baths), and spectacular views from all rooms—make this the best place to stay in Sapporo. Located above Sapporo Station and presided over by a walkie-talkie-toting staff who makes sure everything runs smoothly, it offers rooms (23rd–34th floors) with all the latest in hotel design, including desks with flip tops so they can double as mirrored vanities, separate tub/shower areas, and towels embroidered with different-colored insignia to take out the guessing game of which towel belongs to whom. *A caveat:* Train passengers are forced to undergo a roundabout hike to reach hotel elevators, though strategically placed signs help assure them they're on the right track.

JR Tower, W2 N5, Chuo-ku, Sapporo 060-0005. ☏ **011/251-2222**. Fax 011/251-6370. www.jrhotels.co.jp/tower/english. 350 units. ¥18,000–¥20,000 single; ¥26,000–¥44,000 double. 10% discount for holders of Japan Rail Pass. AE, DC, MC, V. Above Sapporo Station. **Amenities:** 4 restaurants, including Sky J (p. 610); hot-spring spa w/sauna, Jacuzzi (¥1,500); room service; smoke-free rooms. *In room:* A/C, TV, hair dryer, Internet, minibar.

Sapporo Grand Hotel ★ This dignified hotel, open since 1934 and one of Sapporo's old-timers, has a good downtown location near the Botanic Garden and Odori Park.

An appealing choice of dining and drinking outlets (including those serving Hokkaido specialties) and a helpful English-speaking staff help make your stay enjoyable. The hotel occupies three buildings constructed at various times: Business travelers take advantage of the mostly singles in the annex, company executives generally stay in the main building, and everyone from families to the well-heeled heads to the east building for its family rooms (with four beds) and so-called Comfort Rooms on top floors that offer the extra advantages of humidifiers, duvet-covered beds, and big-screen TVs. Most rooms are fairly large and nicely furnished but—a sign of the hotel's age—have small windows and small bathrooms. Note, too, that some of the cheapest rooms face another building.

N1 W4, Chuo-ku, Sapporo 060-0001. (C) **011/261-3311.** Fax 011/231-0388. www.grand1934.com. 562 units. ¥18,480 single; ¥27,145–¥63,525 double. AE, DC, MC, V. Station: Sapporo (8 min.). **Amenities:** 5 restaurants; 2 bars; lounge; business corner w/pay computers; room service; smoke-free rooms; spa. *In room:* A/C, TV, hair dryer, Internet, minibar.

Moderate

Hotel Gracery Sapporo (formerly Sapporo Washington Hotel) ★   With a great location across from Sapporo Station's south side, this 2006 property is a manifestation of the Washington chain's plan to establish reasonably priced hotels in convenient urban centers. Its seventh-floor lobby, with massage chairs and free coffee, overlooks the station, with guest rooms rising above to the 16th floor. A no-contact key card allows you to enter your room with a simple wave, check out on departure day at lobby kiosks, and even buy beer. Rooms are small but stylish, especially the executive singles with TVs that double as computers at no extra charge or the Ladies Rooms with special amenities such as humidifiers, window panels that close for complete darkness, and a feminine decor. Add the 150 movies-on-demand, and this hotel succeeds as an urban getaway at an affordable price. The range of rates reflects the seasons.

N4 W4-1, Chuo-ku, Sapporo 060-0004. (C) **011/251-3211.** Fax 011/241-8238. www.wh-rsv.com. 440 units. ¥8,500–¥12,000 single; ¥14,000–¥21,000 twin; Snow Festival ¥14,000–¥14,500 single, ¥26,000 twin. AE, DC, MC, V. Station: Sapporo (1-min. south of the station, across the street to the right). **Amenities:** Restaurant; lobby computers w/free Internet; smoke-free rooms. *In room:* A/C, TV, fridge, hair dryer, Internet.

(262) **Nakamuraya Ryokan** ★   If you want to stay in a *ryokan*, this modern and comfortable Japanese inn, just a stone's throw from the Botanic Garden, is a good choice. First opened more than 110 years ago but now occupying a nondescript 50-year-old building, it offers pleasant Japanese-style *tatami* rooms, some with a sitting area near the window. The hallways with eaves and slatted wooden doors to each room are a nice touch. Although rooms have their own tub, you might want to take advantage of the public baths here. If you order dinner, it will be served ryokan style in your room by kimono-clad women. To receive the low rates listed below, you must book in advance and mention the Japanese Inn Group.

N3 W7, Chuo-ku, Sapporo 060-0003. (C) **011/241-2111.** Fax 011/241-2118. www.nakamura-ya.com. 26 units. Rates for foreign guests ¥7,350 single; ¥13,650 double. Snow Festival rates ¥8,400 single; ¥15,750 double. Breakfast ¥1,500 extra; dinner ¥2,100–¥5,000 extra. AE, MC, V. Located btw. the Botanic Garden and Old Government Building. Station: Sapporo (10 min.). **Amenities:** Restaurant. *In room:* A/C, TV, fridge.

Sapporo Aspen Hotel (Kids)   Built in 1996, this hotel has an English-speaking staff and a convenient location just north of Sapporo Station (its brochure says 100 steps, but I didn't count them). Otherwise, rooms are rather small for the price but are comfortable enough, with windows that open, heavy curtains to block light, sitting areas and desks, and plenty of counter space in bathrooms. Families take note: 14 so-called "quartet" rooms have four twin beds and roomy bathrooms with two sinks and separate rooms for the toilet and tub. The best views are from the west side overlooking Hokkaido University and a distant forest.

N8 W4-5, Kita-ku, Sapporo 060-0808. (C) **011/700-2111.** Fax 011/700-2002. www.aspen-hotel.co.jp/english/frame.htm. ¥9,500–¥14,500 single, ¥17,500–¥21,000 twin, ¥39,000 quad; June–Sept and Snow Festival ¥11,500–¥17,500 single, ¥21,500–¥28,000 twin, ¥53,000 quad. AE, DC, MC, V. Station: Sapporo (a 2-min. walk straight north of the station, on the left). **Amenities:** Restaurant; coffee shop; rental bicycles (fee: ¥1,500 per day); concierge; smoke-free rooms (reserve in advance). *In room:* A/C, TV, fridge, hair dryer, Internet.

Inexpensive

Nada (Value) A bit of a hike from the station (a 30-min. walk southwest), this little family inn has friendly hosts who offer Japanese-style rooms (some up a steep flight of stairs), all nonsmoking and including dormitory-style rooms with futons at cheaper prices if you're willing to share with strangers. The communal kitchen has a cozy, wooden dining area. There is no curfew. Backpackers from all over the world have found their way here.

S5 W9 Chuo-ku, Sapporo 064-0805. (C) **011/551-5882.** Fax 011/551-0303. www.sapporonada.com. 10 units, none with bathroom. ¥3,000 per person; ¥2,500 per person in dormitory. Winter heating charge ¥200 extra. Breakfast ¥500 extra. MC, V (5% extra if you pay by credit card). Taxi: ¥1,000 Subway: Susukino (10 min.). Walk west on South 4 (Rte. 36) 5 blocks to West 9 (there's a gas station on the corner), turn left, and then right on the 4th street. **Amenities:** Rental bikes (fee: ¥500 per day); communal kitchen; smoke-free rooms. *In room:* TV, no phone.

(263) **Toyoko Inn Sapporo Nishi-Guchi Hokudai-mae** ★ (Finds) This inexpensive business-hotel chain offers free TV movies, free use of lobby computers (plus free high-speed Internet in rooms and free Wi-Fi in the lobby), free domestic calls from lobby phones, and little extras such as semi-double- or double-size beds in the mostly single rooms (rooms are so small, a sign suggests stowing luggage under the bed). The twins are great for friends traveling together (or couples who wish they weren't)—the bathroom splits the room in halves, each containing its own bed, TV, mirror, hair dryer, and more. The staff is friendly. Because the hotel is located across from Hokkaido University, rooms are hard to come by during February entrance exams, but there are two other properties within walking distance of Sapporo Station, **Toyoko Inn Sapporo-eki Kita-Guchi,** a 2-minute walk northeast at N6 W1 ((C) **011/728-1045**), and **Toyoko Inn Sapporo-eki Minami-Guchi,** a 5-minute walk southeast at N3 W1 ((C) **011/222-1045**), as well as two properties in the Susukino nightlife district, the **Toyoko Inn Sapporo Susukino Minami** ((C) **011/551-1045**) and the **Toyoko Inn Sapporo Susukino Kosaten** ((C) **011/207-1045**).

N8 W4-22-7, Kita-ku, Sapporo 060-0808. (C) **011/717-1045.** Fax 011/717-1046. www.toyoko-inn.com. 180 units. June–Sept and Snow Festival ¥5,985–¥6,300 single, ¥8,400 double; Oct–May ¥4,410–¥4,725 single, ¥6,825 double. Rates include Japanese breakfast. AE, DC, MC, V. Station: Sapporo (3 min.). Walk straight north, turn left at the gas station, and then turn right; the hotel will be on the right. **Amenities:** Lobby computer w/free Internet; smoke-free rooms. *In room:* A/C, TV w/free movies, fridge, hair dryer, Internet.

WHERE TO DINE

Hokkaido's specialties include crab, corn on the cob, potatoes, *Jingisukan* (Genghis Khan—a dish of mutton and vegetables that you grill yourself), salmon, and *Ishikari nabe* (a stew of salmon and other Hokkaido vegetables, also cooked at your table).

Sapporo is also famous for its ramen, and the most popular place to eat them is on a tiny, narrow street in Susukino popularly known as **Ramen Yokocho.** Located just 1 short block east of the Susukino Station, it's an alleyway of noodle shop after noodle shop. It doesn't matter which one you choose—just look for an empty seat. Each very small shop consists of a counter and some chairs, with photos of various dishes outside the front door. Most are open daily from 11:30am to 3am. Ramen generally begin at ¥800 for a steaming bowlful.

Very Expensive

Mikuni Sapporo ★★ FRENCH   Mikuni Kiyomi has a reputation as *the* Japanese authority on French food. Hokkaido-born and the proprietor/chef of several Mikuni restaurants in Tokyo and elsewhere, Mikuni has brought his expertise home to triumphant reviews. Located on the ninth floor of Stellar Place in Sapporo Station in a setting that is less than stellar (and accessed by an elevator that is hard to find), the restaurant overcomes its disappointing decor with great cuisine, available only as set meals. A seasonal, autumn lunch, for example, may include cappuccino-style autumn mushrooms and chestnuts, either pan-fried codfish with potatoes and lentils or braised pork garnished with French beans and sweet-potato purée, plus dessert and coffee. There are an extensive wine list and knowledgeable sommeliers to advise you.

Stellar Place 9F, W2 N5. (C) **011/251-0392.** Reservations strongly suggested. Set dinners ¥8,000–¥17,000; set lunches ¥3,200–¥10,000. AE, DC, MC, V. Daily 11:30am–2:30pm and 5:30–9pm (last order). In Sapporo Station.

Expensive

Hyosetsu-no-Mon KING CRAB   This well-known restaurant, in business more than 40 years in Sapporo's Susukino nightlife district, specializes in giant king crab caught in the Japan Sea north of Hokkaido. Its menu (in Japanese but with photos) is easy enough—it consists almost entirely of king crab dishes. Set courses include a cooked crab, sashimi, crab soup, crab tempura, and vegetables. Although set dinners are expensive, there are usually seasonal specials for ¥3,500 available all day.

S5 W2 (next to Sluggers Batting Stadium). (C) **011/521-3046.** Set dinners ¥3,500–¥13,860; set lunches ¥1,980–¥4,000. AE, DC, MC, V. Daily 11am–10pm (last order). Subway: Susukino (2 min.).

Sky J ★★★ INTERNATIONAL   Breathtaking views, reasonable prices, and a wide array of tempting dishes make this sleek restaurant a popular place to dine. The lunch buffet gets top ratings, with a wide range of Western and Asian dishes, all identified in English and utilizing lots of organic veggies, along with nine kinds of bread and a huge dessert table. For dinner, served until 9pm, both set meals and an a la carte menu are available, with an example of the former including Hokkaido specialties such as salmon and seasonal ravioli with caviar as a starter, followed by steak with a cumin flavor and eggplant fondue. From 8pm, the Sky J morphs into a classy cocktail lounge, with live music (and a ¥750 cover charge unless you dine before 8pm). But it's the views that set this place apart.

35th floor, JR Tower Hotel Nikko Sapporo, W2 N5. (C) **011/251-6377.** Lunch buffet ¥2,200; set dinners ¥5,200–¥8,000; main dishes ¥1,600–¥3,600. AE, DC, MC, V. Daily 11:30am–2:30pm and 5:30pm–midnight. Station: Sapporo.

Moderate

(264) **Kita-no-fuji** (Finds) CHANKO NABE   Located in the heart of the Susukino nightlife district and named after a famous sumo wrestler born in Hokkaido, this restaurant, decorated with sumo memorabilia, specializes in the famous hearty stews favored by

sumo wrestlers, *chanko nabe,* which you'll cook at your table. There's a picture menu in Japanese only, with more expensive nabe featuring crab, but you can also tell them how much you want to spend per person. Unfortunately, the staff in this busy nightspot has no time for cordiality, but this is definitely a unique place to dine.

Susukino Plaza, S7 W4. *©* **011/512-5484,** or 512-1339 for reservations. Reservations recommended. Chanko nabe ¥2,300–¥3,200. AE, DC, MC, V. Daily 4–11pm. Subway: Susukino (7 min.). To the left of a building with a Maya-like facade; look for flags and pictures of sumo wrestlers.

(265) **Palace Toriyoshi** ★★ (Finds) YAKITORI/VARIED   In a building filled with restaurants and bars in the Susukino nightlife district, this tiny restaurant serves *yakitori* with a twist, including many original creations by owner/chef Mr. Okuyama, who opened for business in 1980. How about cherry tomatoes covered in cheese; lotus root; a small onion filled with minced chicken; tofu salad; savory custard topped with a rose you can eat; or eggplant with minced meat? Because the menu is in Japanese, the best strategy is to tell the waiter what you like to eat and how much you want to spend; Mr. Okuyama will fix a meal to suit your budget.

Japanland Building, 2F (2nd floor), S5 W5. *©* **011/521-2002.** Reservations recommended. Yakitori ¥157–¥273; set meals ¥2,625–¥6,300. AE, DC, MC, V. Mon-Sat 5–11pm (to 10pm national holidays). Subway: Susukino (3 min.).

Inexpensive

Komugi-no-ie La Pausa (Value) ITALIAN   Right across the street from the Clock Tower, this light and airy restaurant serves Neapolitan pizza baked in a stone kiln, as well as homemade pasta and cakes. Set lunches, with a choice of pasta or pizza and more side dishes added the more expensive they get, are a great deal. Pizzas come with a variety of toppings; my sausage pizza came with lots of cheese, eggplant, tomatoes, and capers. *Komugi-no-ie,* by the way, means "Wheat House."

N1 W3. *©* **011/252-2231.** Pasta and pizza ¥980–¥1,660; set dinners ¥1,765–¥2,480; set lunches ¥780–¥920. AE, DC, MC, V. Daily 11am–11:30pm. Subway: Odori (1 min.). In the same building as International Communications Plaza, marked on maps.

Sapporo Bier Garten ★ JINGISUKAN   If you think of beer when you hear the word "Sapporo," then a trip here is a must. Famous throughout the world, Sapporo beer was brewed in the handsome, ivy-covered brick buildings here from 1890 to 2003. Today they hold restaurants, shops, and the Sapporo Beer Museum (*©* **011/731-4368;** daily 9am–6pm), with displays unfortunately in Japanese only, but admission is free and samples cost only ¥20. There used to be a beer garden as well, but now it exists in name only. Still, this is a good destination for beer and a meal, especially in the historic, cavernous Kessel Hall, where you dine underneath a huge 1912 mash tub. The specialty here is *Jingisukan,* which you cook yourself on a hot skillet at your table. The best deal in the house is the appropriately named King Viking, which for ¥3,670 gives you as much Jingisukan and draft beer as you can consume in 100 minutes. Otherwise, for all you timid drinkers, draft beer starts at ¥430 for a small and ¥530 for a half liter, with the all-you-can-eat Jingisukan without drinks starting at ¥2,620. By the way, a 12-minute walk away (or a short ride on the Sapporo Walk Bus) is **Sapporo Factory,** N2 E4, Chuo-ku (*©* **011/207-5000**), a complex centered on another old Sapporo Beer brick building housing more restaurants and 160 shops (daily 11am–8pm).

N7 E9. *©* **011/742-1531.** www.sapporo-bier-garten.jp. All-you-can-eat *Jingisukan* ¥2,620–¥3,670. AE, DC, MC, V. Kessel Hall daily 11:30am–10pm. Bus: Chuo Bus no. 188 from platform 2 (north of Sapporo Station) or Sapporo Walk. Bus: Sapporo Biiruen (1 min.).

Taj Mahal (Value) INDIAN   This second-floor Indian restaurant tries too hard with its Indian mirrored fabrics, brass lamps, and Indian music, as the food alone is reason enough to come here. The service is friendly and the choices are varied—in addition to tandoori and kabobs, they serve chicken, lamb, seafood, and vegetable curries (but no pork or beef). You choose how spicy you want it, from very mild to very, very hot. Tasty lunch specials are served until 3pm, but not on Sundays or holidays. There's a branch in Sapporo Factory (see above; (C) **011/207-0765**), open daily 11am to 9:30pm.

N2 W3. (C) **011/231-8850.** www.tajmahalgroup.com. Curries ¥1,350–¥1,750; set dinners ¥1,600–¥2,580; set lunches ¥680–¥1,650. AE, DC, MC, V. Mon–Fri 11am–3pm and 5–10pm (last order); Sat–Sun 11am–10pm. Station: Sapporo (6 min.). Walk south on the left side of Eki-mae Dori and when you come to JTB, turn left; it will be on the right.

4 NOBORIBETSU SPA & SHIKOTSU-TOYA NATIONAL PARK

If you have only a couple days to spare to visit one of Hokkaido's national parks, head to **Shikotsu-Toya National Park** ★★, the closest to Sapporo and the first national park you'll reach if you enter Hokkaido via train to Hakodate. This 987-sq.-km (381-sq.-mile) national park encompasses lakes, volcanoes, and the famous hot-spring resort of **Noboribetsu Onsen** ★★, home to 800 people.

Famous for the variety of its hot-water springs ever since the first public bathhouse opened here in 1858, Noboribetsu Spa is one of Japan's best-known spa resorts and is the most popular of Hokkaido's many spa towns. It boasts 11 different types of hot water, each with a different mineral content, and gushes 10,000 tons a day. With temperatures ranging between 113°F (45°C) and 197°F (92°C), the waters contain all kinds of minerals, including sulfur, salt, iron, and gypsum, and are thought to help relieve such disorders as high blood pressure, poor blood circulation, rheumatism, arthritis, eczema, and even constipation.

Also known for its seasonal beauty, Noboribetsu is an impressive sight in spring, when 2,000 cherry trees lining the road into the *onsen* are in full bloom. In autumn, thousands of Japanese maples burst into flame. In the nearby village of **Shiraoi** on Lake Poroto, a museum and village commemorate the native Ainu and their culture.

ESSENTIALS

GETTING THERE   Noboribetsu Onsen is accessible only by **bus.** The nearest train station is **Noboribetsu Station** in the town of Noboribetsu, which lies on the main **JR train** line that runs between Hakodate and Sapporo, a little more than 2 hours from Hakodate and 1 hour and 10 minutes from Sapporo. Fares for a reserved seat are ¥4,360 from Sapporo, ¥6,700 from Hakodate. From Noboribetsu Station it's only a 10- to 15-minute bus ride to the last stop of Noboribetsu Onsen (¥330; departures two or more times an hour).

There is also one direct bus, the **Kosoku Onsen-go,** from Sapporo Station to Noboribetsu Onsen costing ¥1,900 for the 1¾-hour trip. Contact **Donan Bus** ((C) **011/865-5511**) for more information.

VISITOR INFORMATION & GETTING AROUND   The **Noboribetsu Tourist Association** ((C) **0143/84-3311;** daily 9am–6pm) is on Noboribetsu Onsen's main street, just a minute's walk north of the bus depot (continue up the hill; it will be on your left side

Tips   **Un-Bearable Park**

As you wander around Noboribetsu Onsen, you'll see advertisements for a bear park and an Ainu village attraction. The best thing about this place is the trip via ropeway—the bear park occupies one of the tallest hills around. The 135 or so bears, however, are crowded together in concrete pens in one of the saddest sights I've ever seen, and the Ainu "village" is just a few huts. Although the bears, many of them rescued from extermination or brought here as orphaned cubs, are luckier than some of their peers (government policy advocated the extermination of Hokkaido brown bears in the 1950s and still allows some of the remaining wild bears to be hunted and culled annually), the admission (including ropeway) of ¥2,520 is too high a price for this joyless place. Skip it—you're better off spending your money elsewhere. Or donate money for a cause: Dedicated employees bent on saving brown bears here have begun a nonprofit organization in hopes of moving the bears off the mountain to a place where there's more room.

with a clock above the door). In addition to a map, ask for the useful pamphlet "A Guide to Walking Trails in Noboribetsu Onsen." You may not encounter anyone who speaks English, but luckily the town is so small you shouldn't have any problem getting around. For more information, go to **www.noboribetsu-spa.jp/nobo**.

WHAT TO SEE & DO
Enjoying Noboribetsu's Natural Wonders

TAKING THE LOCAL WATERS   Although all the spa hotels and *ryokan* have their own taps into the spring water, almost everyone who comes to Noboribetsu Onsen makes a point of going to the most famous hotel bath in town, **Dai-ichi Takimotokan** ★★ (☎ **0143/84-2111;** www.takimotokan.co.jp), one of the first bathhouses to open at the hot springs. Now a huge, modern bathing hall with some 30 tubs and pools containing different mineral contents at various temperatures, it's an elaborate affair with hot-spring baths and Jacuzzis both indoors and out, saunas, steam rooms, and waterfall massage (this is one of my favorites—you sit under the shooting water and let it pummel your neck and shoulders). Although the baths are separate for men and women, there's an indoor swimming pool for families with a slide and play area for children, so be sure to bring your swimsuit. If you're staying at the Dai-ichi Takimotokan or Takimoto Inn (see "Where to Stay," below), you can use the baths for free at any time—in the evenings, don't miss bathing in the outdoor baths, where you can order beer, soft drinks, or sake and enjoy the nice mountain scenery. Otherwise, Dai-ichi Takimotokan is open to the public daily from 9am to 6pm (you must enter by 5pm); the charge is ¥2,000 for adults, half-price for children 3 to 12.

HELL VALLEY (JIGOKUDANI) ★   To get an idea of what all this hot water looks like, visit Hell Valley at the north edge of town past the Dai-ichi Takimotokan hotel (see "Where to Stay," below). This volcanic crater 446m (1,485 ft.) in diameter has a huge depression full of bubbling, boiling water and rock formations of orange and brown. As you walk the concrete path that winds along the left side of the crater (called Hell Valley Promenade), keep an eye down below to the right for a tiny shrine dedicated to the deity

Another Island, Another People: The Ainu of Hokkaido

Hokkaido is home to the Ainu, the native inhabitants of Japan's northernmost island. Not much is known about their origins; it's not even clear whether they're Asian or Caucasian, but they are of different racial stock than the Japanese. They're round-eyed and light-skinned, and Ainu males can grow thick beards and mustaches.

The Ainu arrived in Hokkaido approximately 800 years ago. Living in a harsh environment with few resources, they were skilled at using the plants and animals around them for everything from medicine to utensils. With no metal at their disposal, they carved arrows with wooden "knives" and then dipped them in poison to increase their efficiency. Clothes were fashioned from bark, wild rye, or even salmon skin. Traditionally, they lived as hunters and fishermen, using dogs to help in the hunt and setting up trip traps with arrows to catch wild animals. Animistic, they had gods for every object and phenomenon, whether sun, thunder, fire, or animals. Most important to Ainu culture were bear cubs, kept in captivity before being killed, with elaborate ceremonies held to send the cub's spirit to the next life.

After Hokkaido was opened for development in the late 1800s, the Ainu were forcibly assimilated into Japanese society, and many died with the spread of smallpox, measles, cholera, and other newly introduced diseases. Like Native Americans, they were often discriminated against, and their culture was largely destroyed. Hunting and fishing were prohibited, and male Ainu were taken from their families for forced labor. Eventually, the Ainu took Japanese names and adopted the Japanese language and clothing. Today, there are an estimated 23,000 Ainu still living in Hokkaido, some of whom earn their living from tourism, selling Ainu woodcarvings and other crafts, or performing traditional dances and songs.

that protects eyes (those most in need are apt to miss it); local lore says that if you rub some of the protective water over ailing eyes, they'll be cured. Farther along, you'll soon reach a sign for OYUNUMA and a path leading uphill to the left through lush woods; if you follow it for about 10 minutes, you'll come to a lookout point over a large pond of hot bubbling water called Oyunuma (the lookout is across the road; it's another 5-min. walk to the pond). Return to the road and turn right (west) and then right again on the road leading downhill, where you will soon see a hiking path on the left that runs alongside the steaming Oyunuma River; halfway down is a natural foot bath. If you want to take a different route back, return to the road and the Oyunuma path but look for the Funamiyama (Mount Funami) Promenade to the right. It traces the backbone of several ridges, passing a number of small stone guardians before ending up back at Hell Valley.

Especially for Kids

Noboribetsu Date Jidai Mura ★★ (Kids)   A visit to this reproduction of a Feudal-Era village is the closest you can get to taking a time machine back to the last days of the

Edo Period. Shops, restaurants, theaters, the downtown, and a samurai district are built as they were of yore, staffed by people dressed in period clothing. See ninja warriors fighting in a trick mansion or outdoor theater, local merchants hawking their wares, Edo-Era tenements with life-size models (I especially like the one of the boy in the outhouse), a ninja museum showing tricks of the trade, and courtesans performing in this Disney-esque re-creation of how Japan might have looked when the shogun reigned. Although shows are in Japanese (the ninja shows are probably the only ones that would interest children), the various attractions are fun for the entire family, and if you haven't seen another historical theme village elsewhere in Japan, this rather small one is worth a 2-hour visit (an English-language pamphlet gives showtimes). To commemorate the day forever, you can don a kimono, samurai, or ninja outfit and have your photo taken in front of a traditional backdrop for ¥3,500. Lockers are available on-site.

53–1 Naka-Noboribetsu-cho, Noboribetsu-shi. 🕿 **0143/83-3311.** www.edo-trip.jp. Admission ¥2,900 adults, ¥2,100 seniors, ¥1,500 children. Apr–Oct daily 9am–5pm; Nov–Mar Thurs–Tues 9am–4pm. You must enter 1 hr. before closing. Bus: From Noboribetsu Onsen or JR Noboribetsu Station to Jidai Mura (fare: ¥330). Located halfway btw. Noboribetsu Onsen and Noboribetsu city.

Noboribetsu Marine Park Nixe ★ Kids Small children love this combination Danish theme park and aquarium, located near Noboribetsu Station. (If you're traveling with luggage, lockers are available both here and at the station.) The aquarium, one of the largest in northern Japan, is in Castle Nixe, modeled after a Danish castle (and visible from the station), where you'll see sharks (from an underwater tunnel), morays, salmon, sturgeon, king crab, giant octopus, and other sea creatures. More attractions include a touch pool with small sharks, rays, and horseshoe crabs; a reptile house with snakes, turtles and lizards; dolphin and sea lion shows; a king penguin parade; a game arcade; the ubiquitous souvenir shops (selling Danish and aquarium-related gifts); and a handful of kiddie rides (¥200–¥300 extra). You can see everything in about 2 hours.

1–22 Noboribetsu Higashi-machi, Noboribetsu-shi. 🕿 **0143/83-3800.** www.nixe.co.jp. Admission ¥2,400 adults, ¥1,200 children. Daily 9am–5pm. Closed 5 days in early Dec. Station: Noboribetsu (7 min.). Walk straight out the exit and turn right after 1 block.

Learning About the Ainu in Nearby Shiraoi

Poroto Kotan and the Ainu Museum ★★ Shiraoi (an Ainu word meaning "Place of Many Horseflies") was settled by the Ainu long before Japanese arrived; today, it's a small town of some 22,000 inhabitants, including Ainu. Poroto Kotan ("Big Lake Village" in Ainu), nestled on the shores of Lake Poroto, is a mock village of native houses made entirely from wood and reeds, a native plant garden, a dance area, probably the most important Ainu museum anywhere, and a research center dedicated to preserving Ainu culture. If you're lucky, your visit will coincide with two annual festivals: one, in the spring, to pray for life's necessities; the other in the fall to give thanks for the harvests (call for festival dates).

After passing, regrettably, through a huge souvenir hall, you'll find yourself surrounded by traditionally built houses, where there are demonstrations of Ainu weaving techniques, woodworking, and other crafts, and where native dances and performances of the *mukkur* (Ainu mouth harp) are performed by Ainu in traditional costume. Unfortunately, bears (and dogs) are kept in captivity here in filthy metal cages, but even this is an Ainu tradition—in spring, when the mother bear left her cave in search of food, Ainu fetched the cubs to keep in a wooden cage in the village until they were old enough for slaughter. Bears were revered as gifts from the gods. The most important thing to see, however, is the excellent museum, with English-language descriptions of Ainu history, culture, society, and traditions, a video (Japanese-language only) and displays of utensils, clothing (such as salmon-skin boots), fish hooks (the Ainu excelled at fishing), jewelry, and other everyday artifacts.

If you wish, you can lunch on dried salmon, potato cakes, *ohau* (a stew of mountain vegetables, meat, and fish), and herb tea bought from one of the stalls. Although the village is small and can be toured in about an hour, it's an important stop for those wishing to learn about Ainu culture and the indigenous people who have little left of what was once a rich heritage.

2–3–4 Wakakusa-cho, Shiraoi-cho, Hokkaido 059-0902. $\mathcal{C}$ **0144/82-3914.** www.ainu-museum.or.jp. Admission ¥750 adults, ¥550 high-school students, ¥450 junior-high students, ¥300 children. Daily 8:45am–5pm. Closed 1 week for New Year's. Train: 13 min. by JR express train or 25 min. by local train from JR Noboribetsu Station to JR Shiraoi Station, and then a 10-min. walk. Turn left out of the station, take the stairs over the track, turn right and then right again at Koen Dori; keep walking straight and look for the sign AINU MUSEUM. **Note:** Only 5 express trains running btw. Hakodate and Sapporo daily (with stops at Noboribetsu Station) stop at Shiraoi, so make sure yours does; otherwise, local trains are more frequent.

WHERE TO STAY

The busiest tourist seasons are July through September and during New Year's, which are when hotel rates are at their highest, particularly on weekends (avoid Golden Week, Obon in mid-Aug, and New Year's). October, when the leaves are changing, is also popular. All places below charge a daily ¥150 hot-springs tax.

Expensive

(266) **Oyado Kiyomizu-ya ★★**   You'll be royally welcome at this elegantly modern *ryokan* with traditional touches, one of our favorites in Hokkaido. You'll be ushered down a long corridor decorated with plants, stones, and paper lanterns to the elevator that will whisk you up to your room. Least expensive are average-looking Western-style rooms, making the simple but pleasant Japanese *tatami* rooms a better choice. For a splurge, combination rooms are actually two-room suites with a tatami room where you'll dine and a separate bedroom.

The ryokan is beside a roaring river, the sounds of which will sing you to sleep as you snuggle against fur-lined futons and down covers. But it's the delicious seasonal *kaiseki* meals that assure the ryokan many repeat guests; the parade of beautifully prepared dishes includes local specialties. Service is impeccable, and the second-generation owner, Mr. Iwai, speaks excellent English; he can answer your questions regarding Noboribetsu and the surrounding area. (A sake connoisseur, he can also recommend which of the 14 different kinds of sake he keeps on hand might go best with your meal.) If you're looking for a place far from tour groups, souvenir shops, and impersonal service, you'll be happy here.

173 Noboribetsu Onsen-machi, Noboribetsu-shi, Hokkaido 059-0551. $\mathcal{C}$ **0143/84-2145.** Fax 0143/84-2146. www.kiyomizuya.co.jp. 43 units. ¥10,000 single; ¥16,000 double. Rates exclude tax. Breakfast ¥2,000 extra; dinner ¥5,000–¥10,000 extra. Rates including 2 meals and tax ¥13,800–¥21,150 (rates ¥2,100 higher on nights before holidays). AE, DC, MC, V. The staff will pick you up at the station if you tell them your arrival time in advance; otherwise, it's above Noboribetsu Onsen's main street, a 10-min. walk from the bus terminal. **Amenities:** Coffee shop; karaoke bar; indoor/outdoor hot-spring baths (the outdoor bath alternates days for men and women); Wi-Fi (in the lobby). *In room:* TV.

Moderate

Dai-ichi Takimotokan ★ This is Noboribetsu Onsen's best-known *ryokan,* thanks to its long history (opened in 1858) and its gigantic public baths. Today, however, it's a large, modern facility with little personality and lots of noisy tour groups. The most compelling reasons to stay here are its location near Hell Valley and its famous hot-spring baths, which hotel guests are entitled to use free anytime, night or day. Another plus: free shuttle bus service November through March from Chitose Airport in Sapporo and throughout the year from downtown Sapporo (call the hotel for reservations). Most rooms are simple *tatami,* spread throughout four buildings. Oldest and cheapest are those in the East Building, without tubs or air-conditioning (but some with views of an enclosed garden), while rooms in the West Wing are a step up with private bathroom. The South Building has Japanese-style rooms and eight Western-style rooms, but it's a hike to the hot-spring baths. Most luxurious are rooms in the Main Building, with top floors offering the best views. Guests staying in the East and West buildings or Western-style rooms dine in a buffet restaurant offering Japanese, Chinese, and Western food (or can pay more for a traditional Japanese meal), while those staying in tatami rooms in the South and Main building can opt for a Japanese dinner served in their rooms.

55 Noboribetsu Onsen-machi, Noboribetsu-shi, Hokkaido 059-0595. ✆ **0143/84-3322.** Fax 0143/84-2202. www.takimotokan.co.jp. 399 units, 342 with bathroom, 57 with toilet only. ¥9,150–¥16,150 per person off season; ¥13,275–¥23,715 per person peak season. Sat and holidays ¥2,100 extra per person. Rates include 2 meals. AE, DC, MC, V. A 5-min. walk uphill from the bus station, beside Hell Valley. **Amenities:** 3 restaurants; lounge; 2 bars; coin-op lobby computers; indoor pool; 24-hr. indoor/outdoor hot-spring baths. *In room:* A/C (in some), TV, minibar.

267 **Kashoutei Hanaya ★** This is a modern *ryokan* but with such traditional touches as a small Japanese garden off the lobby, flower arrangements, bamboo, decorative floors, and Japanese music playing softly in public areas. Most rooms are Japanese style, with or without bathroom, while the three Western-style rooms are without bathroom (all rooms, however, have toilet and sink). Meals are served in your room. The owner speaks English. The ryokan is on the edge of town, about a 5-minute walk from the bus terminal.

134 Noboribetsu Onsen-machi, Noboribetsu-shi, Hokkaido 059-0551. ✆ **0143/84-2521.** Fax 0143/84-2240. www.kashoutei-hanaya.co.jp. 21 units (5 with bathroom, 16 with toilet only). ¥12,750–¥26,400 per person. Rates include 2 meals. AE, MC, V. Bus: From Noboribetsu Station to Byoin-mae/Kashotei Hanaya-mae (if you're arriving by bus, you'll get off before reaching the terminal—ask the bus driver to let you know where—the ryokan will be close behind you, across the road). Pickup service also available from Noboribetsu Onsen bus terminal. **Amenities:** Coffee shop; indoor/outdoor hot-spring baths (open 24 hr.). *In room:* A/C, TV, minibar.

Inexpensive

Takimoto Inn If you prefer a hotel with beds to a *ryokan* with futons, this quiet and moderately priced hotel has the additional advantage of allowing guests to use Dai-chi Takimotokan's airport shuttle and famous baths across the street 24 hours for free. All rooms are twins (but can be used as singles or triples) and spartan, with metal doors that clang shut with the finality of a prison and minuscule bathrooms. There's no view, but windows do open. Buffet meals offer a mix of Japanese and Western food.

76 Noboribetsu Onsen-machi, Noboribetsu-shi 059-0551. ✆ **0143/84-2205.** Fax 0143/84-2645. www.takimotoinn.co.jp. 47 units. ¥7,350 per person, including 2 meals. Sat ¥1,200 extra (rates higher New Year's, Golden Week, Obon). AE, DC, V. A 5-min. walk uphill from the bus station, across the street from Dai-ichi Takimotokan. **Amenities:** Restaurant; hot-spring bath (guests can also use Dai-ichi Takimoto-kan's baths free). *In room:* TV, fridge.

NOBORIBETSU SPA & SHIKOTSU-TOYA

(268) **Fukuan** SOBA   This small, traditional *soba* shop (take your shoes off at the entrance) serves its own buckwheat noodles. Because the menu is in Japanese only, I recommend ordering the *tenseiro,* a tempura soba with shrimp and vegetables; or the *Ebi-tenoroshi soba,* a summertime meal of cold soba, shrimp tempura, seaweed, dried fish flakes, and Japanese daikon radish. Or look around at what others are eating.

30 Noboribetsu Onsen-machi. (2) **0143/84/2758.** Soba ¥680–¥1,400. No credit cards. Daily 11:30am–2pm and 6–10:30pm (closed irregularly 1 day a month). A 1-min. walk from the bus terminal, on the main street across from the tourist information office.

Poplar Restaurant WESTERN   If you find yourself looking for a place for lunch, a draft beer, or coffee, try this restaurant, which serves inexpensive Western dishes from a limited English-language menu with pictures. While they may not win any culinary awards, items include beefsteak, hamburger steak, fried shrimp, grilled salmon, and pork cutlet. There's a monthly special set for ¥1,000.

Takimoto Inn. (2) **0143/84-2205.** Main dishes ¥700–¥2,500. AE, DC, MC, V. Daily 11am–2pm (last order). A 5-min. walk from the bus terminal, near Hell Valley and across from Dai-ichi Takimotokan.

5 SOUNKYO SPA & DAISETSUZAN NATIONAL PARK

Although I find it difficult to rank nature in terms of beauty, there are some who maintain that **Daisetsuzan National Park** ★★★ is the most spectacular of Hokkaido's parks. With its tall mountains covered with fir and birch trees and sprinkled with wildflowers, its river gorge laced with waterfalls, and hiking trails, Daisetsuzan National Park is the perfect place to come if you've been itching to get some exercise in relatively unspoiled countryside. Lying in the center of Hokkaido (east of Sapporo), this national park—Japan's largest—contains three volcanic mountain groups, including the highest mountain in Hokkaido, Mount Asahi, 2,254m (7,513 ft.) high. Hiking in summer and skiing in winter are the primary pursuits of the park's visitors.

Nestled at the very edge of Sounkyo Gorge, Daisetsuzan's most famous natural attraction, is **Sounkyo Onsen** ★, the perfect base for exploring the national park. Once rather unattractive with a hodgepodge of ugly cement buildings, Sounkyo has reinvented itself with attractive and compatible alpine-style buildings and stone and wood paths that do justice to the magnificent scenic backdrop and its soothing hot springs. Yet it remains a mountain village, home to 600 residents and only a dozen or so accommodations, most of them small affairs. More important, Sounkyo Spa serves as the starting point for the cable-car trip to the top of a neighboring peak with its hiking trails and easy ski slope. From late January to mid-March, the spa is the scene of the Ice Falls Festival, a winter fantasyland with giant ice castles, frozen waterfalls lit with colored lights, and weekend fireworks.

ESSENTIALS

GETTING THERE   The only way to reach Sounkyo Onsen by public transportation is by **bus.** If you're coming from Sapporo, take the **JR train** 2½ hours to Kamikawa (four departures daily; ¥6,180 one-way), transferring there for the 30-minute bus ride (¥800) directly to Sounkyo Onsen. Buses depart about 11 times a day and generally connect with train arrivals, but it's always wise to check ahead with the JR counter in Sapporo

Station's Hokkaido-Sapporo Tourist Information Center (or, have a Japanese call the Kamikawa bus terminal at ☎ **01658/2-1316**).

There are two buses a day—called the Sunrise Asahikawa-Kushiro-go—connecting Sounkyo Onsen with Akanko Onsen in Akan National Park (see the next section for more on Akan), with the one-way fare costing ¥3,260 for the 3½-hour trip. Reservations are required; call ☎ **01658/5-3321** in Sounkyo, or 0154/67-2205 in Akan; or drop by the bus terminal in either town. All bus fares are half-price for children.

VISITOR INFORMATION & ORIENTATION The **tourist information office** (☎ **01658/5-3350;** daily 10:30am–5pm) is located in front of the bus stop, next to the post office. The staff's English is limited but they have maps and can point you in the direction of your lodging or even make reservations for you. In any case, the village is so tiny that you won't have any difficulty getting around; it's basically two streets leading up to the ropeway, and a pedestrian lane, called Canyon Mall Street, that wanders through the center of town.

EXPLORING SOUNKYO ONSEN

Before exploring the environs, you might want to pop into Sounkyo's **Daisetsuzan National Park Visitor Center,** located across from the ropeway (☎ **01658/9-4400;** June–Oct daily 8am–5:30pm, Nov–May Tues–Sun 9am–5pm), with displays on the park's animals, plants, and geological wonders. Unfortunately, displays are in Japanese, though an English-language handout offers rudimentary explanations, a topographical map shows the layout of Daisetsuzan National Park, and a TV shows the park's changes through the seasons. If you plan on hiking, you might ask the staff for recommended trails, as well as a rundown on places where brown bears are often spotted. Entrance to the center is free.

SOUNKYO GORGE The Sounkyo Gorge is a river valley hemmed in on both sides by rock walls rising almost 150m (500 ft.) and extending some 19km (12 miles). Unfortunately, a major rock slide has closed most of the gorge to sightseers (you used to be able to cycle much of the gorge), but you can still see a small portion by walking 3km (2 miles) from Sounkyo Spa (walk down to the highway and turn right) and keeping to the right when the highway disappears into a tunnel. This will bring you to a parking lot beside the roaring river and a view of two famous waterfalls side by side: the Ginga no Taki (Silver River Falls) and the Ryuusei no Taki (Shooting Star Falls). At the far end of the parking lot is a fence, beyond which you can see the gorge. Bring some drinks or a picnic lunch. There are also buses that travel here from Sounkyo Spa, but they're infrequent (ask the tourist office for a schedule).

GOING TO THE TOP OF MOUNT KURODAKE ★ Take the **cable car** directly from Sounkyo Onsen to Mount Kurodake, where you'll be rewarded with sweeping views. The tops of the mountains are really beautiful here, covered with wildflowers and alpine plant life. It would be a shame to come to Sounkyo and not spend a few hours amid its lofty peaks. The trip by cable car takes 7 minutes, with round-trip tickets costing ¥1,850 for adults and ¥950 for children. From the cable-car station, walk a few minutes farther up the mountain, where you'll come to a chairlift. The chairlift ride (my favorite part) takes 15 minutes, swinging you past lush forests of fir and birch. Round-trip fare here is ¥600 for adults and ¥400 for children. Ropeway and lift operating hours vary; in the summer the ropeway runs daily 6am to 7pm, in winter it's 9am to 4pm (call ☎ **01658/5-3031** for more information).

DAY HIKES   You can forgo the cable car and chairlift up **Mount Kurodake** and hike instead; plan on the entire day up and back. Or, for a short hike, forgo the chairlift on Mount Kurodake and hike about 1 hour from the fifth stage (where the chairlift begins) to the seventh stage (where the chairlift ends). If you're prepared to exert yourself climbing over boulders, however, the most rewarding journey is the 1½-hour hike from the seventh stage onward to the peak of Kurodake, 1,950m (6,500 ft.) high. There, if the weather is clear, you'll be greeted with views of the surrounding mountain ranges. If you feel like taking a day hike, there's a circular path along the top of mountain ridges that you can hike in about 8 hours. Be sure to note lift operating hours before setting out. *Note:* If you plan on hiking past the seventh stage, you must first check in at the hut to the left of where the chairlift ends, where you sign your name and give your route so that tabs can be kept on you while on the mountain (hiking from here is recommended only in July–Aug, as snow can cover the ground other months of the year). Hiking boots are recommended, but you can also rent rubber boots here for ¥500, a must if you don't have hiking boots because trails are slippery and wet (small streams from winter snows cascade down the trail even in July). Note, however, that rental sizes only go up to 28 centimeters (12 in.).

As for other hiking possibilities, across the highway and river from Sounkyo Spa is the **Panoramadai** hiking course, where you can hike to a panoramic lookout in about an hour. Past the Taisetsu Hotel above Sounkyo Spa is the Momidijani Course, which takes about 1-hour round-trip and follows a mountain stream to a waterfall.

For more information on these and other hiking trips, stop by the **Daisetsuzan National Park Visitor Center.**

SKIING   From November to March, **Mount Kurodake** becomes a skier's haven, with beginner-to-intermediate slopes. Although you can rent skis up on the mountain at the cable-car station, keep in mind that your feet may be too big (at last check, boots went up to 28cm/12 in.). Skis and boots rent for ¥3,000, while a 1-day cable-car and chairlift ticket goes for ¥3,700.

TAKING THE WATERS   In the village Community Center, you'll find **Kurodake-no-yu** (*©* 01658/5-3333), a public hot-spring bath with large, spotless, and attractive indoor and outdoor baths plus a sauna. The spa charges ¥600 for adults (half-price for children) and is open daily 10am to 9pm (closed Wed Nov–Apr, except during Ice Festival). Buy your tickets at the entrance's vending machine.

WHERE TO STAY

There are plenty of inexpensive pensions and hotels in Sounkyo. The army of college-age Japanese you see working in the area comes from other parts of Japan to work for the summer. They may not know a lot about the area, but most of them speak some English. If you want to stay here in July, August, or September, be sure to make advance reservations. Rates below include the ¥150 *onsen* tax.

Moderate

Taisetsu Hotel ★★ (Value)   This hotel's ridge-top location above town gives it good views of the surrounding gorge and mountains from some rooms. What makes this a top pick, however, are its three gorgeous baths, two of which are open 24 hours; best are the seventh-floor indoor and outdoor baths with great views and the newer outdoor baths overlooking expansive greenery. Most rooms are Japanese style, spread in a west wing (ask for a room on a top floor facing the front toward the gorge) and an east wing (request a room facing the back toward the hills, as those facing the front overlook a characterless *ryokan*). Best of all are the 10 *Yukihana* two-room suites on the sixth floor, complete with a huge bathroom with a hot-spring bath affording panoramic views. Guests staying here dine in private rooms in an exclusive Japanese restaurant. Otherwise, rates are based on meals, with the cheapest served buffet style in a characterless dining hall and the more expensive in Top of the Canyon, which serves a mix of Japanese and Western dishes. You can also choose to dine in your room for ¥2,000 more.

Sounkyo Onsen, Kamikawacho, Kamikawa-gun 078-1701. ✆ **01658/5-3211.** Fax 01658/5-3420. www. taisetsu-g.com. 216 units. ¥15,000–¥32,000 per person. Rates include 2 meals. AE, DC, MC, V. An 8-min. walk from the bus terminal. **Amenities:** 4 restaurants; Japanese-style pub; indoor/outdoor hot-spring baths; sauna; whirlpool baths. *In room:* TV, fridge, hair dryer.

Inexpensive

Onsen Pension Ginga ★ (Value)   This cute lodge is bright and airy, with a glass-enclosed communal dining room decorated in European drawing-room style and both Japanese- and Western-style rooms, most with large windows providing great panoramic views (best are the corner rooms, and room no. 208). Rooms without bathrooms do have sinks. Japanese meals, served in the dining room, feature local fish and seasonal home-grown vegetables. Unfortunately, the hot-spring bath here is small.

Sounkyo Onsen, Kamikawacho, Kamikawa-gun 078-1701. ✆ **01658/5-3775.** 17 units (5 with bathroom). ¥7,500 per person without bathroom, ¥8,865 per person with bathroom. Rates include 2 meals. No credit cards. A 2-min. walk from the bus terminal. **Amenities:** Small indoor hot-spring bath. *In room:* TV, no phone.

(269) **Resort Pension Yama-no-ue**   This pension offers simple *tatami* rooms with just the basics. There are communal toilets, sinks, and showers; but for a real hot-spring bath, guests staying here are entitled to use the Spa Kurodake in the adjoining building for free. In summer, the small dining room serves ample meals of Hokkaido cuisine. If you stay more than 1 night or in winter, you'll dine at Beergrill Canyon (see below). Breakfast is Western style. Because the owner is an avid photographer and butterfly collector, you'll see gorgeous shots of the area and captured butterflies on the walls. In autumn, you can even make arrangements to go salmon fishing with him.

Sounkyo Onsen, Kamikawacho, Kamikawa-gun 078-1701. ✆ **01658/5-3206.** Fax 01658/5-3207. www. p-yamanoue.com. 14 units, none with bathroom, 1 with toilet. ¥8,800–¥12,600 per person. Rates include 2 meals. No credit cards. A 2-min. walk from the bus terminal. *In room:* TV, no phone.

WHERE TO DINE

Beergrill Canyon ITALIAN   Located in the same building as Spa Kurodake (identified as "Community Center" on some English-language maps), this casual restaurant serves various pizzas, pastas, and other fare from its English-language menu (in winter it also serves Japanese food). Choices include pizza with mushrooms and bacon, spaghetti with rainbow trout and mushrooms, spicy curry chicken, grilled venison, and Hokkaido sirloin steak. For a complete meal, add a minisalad, bread, or rice to your entree by paying ¥250 extra. Wash it all down with beer. There are two computers you can use for free if you order something.

Sounkyo. ✆ **01658/5-3361.** Main dishes ¥650–¥2,500; set dinners ¥2,500–¥7,000; set lunches ¥1,500 ¥2,300. No credit cards. Daily 11:30am–3:30pm and 5:30–9pm (last order); longer hours on weekends in summer (9:30am–9pm). Closed Wed Nov–Jan and Mar–Apr.

(270) **Ramen House Tozanken** RAMEN   For an inexpensive, quick meal, stop by this ramen house located at the bottom of the pedestrian slope (look for its red *noren*).

Its English-language menu with pictures lists nine different kinds of ramen, such as the deep-fried chicken ramen or Asahikawa ramen (with handmade miso soup, vegetables, and roast pork), as well as rice bowls and *gyoza*. In nice weather you can sit at the outdoor tables.

Sounkyo. ℂ **01658/5-3005.** Main dishes ¥650–¥1,000. No credit cards. Daily 10am–10pm. Closed Nov–Mar.

6 AKANKO SPA & AKAN NATIONAL PARK

Spreading through the eastern end of Hokkaido, **Akan National Park** ★★ features volcanic mountains, dense forests of subarctic primeval trees, and three caldera lakes, including Lake Akan. The best place to stay in the park is **Akanko Onsen,** a small hot-spring resort on the edge of Lake Akan and home to some 2,000 residents. It makes a good base for active vacations ranging from fishing to hiking and from which to explore both Akan National Park and nearby Kushiro Marshland National Park, famous for its red-crested cranes. It also has a re-created Ainu village, with one of the best music and dance performances I've seen.

ESSENTIALS
GETTING THERE **By JR Train & Bus** Because there's no train station at Akanko Onsen itself, transportation to the resort town is by train to Kushiro or Kitami and then by bus to Akanko. Kushiro is about 4 hours from Sapporo by JR train (¥8,610 for an unreserved seat); Kitami is 4½ hours away (¥8,290 for an unreserved seat). From **JR Kushiro Station,** buses depart two to five times a day for Akanko; the 2-hour trip costs ¥2,650 one-way. From **Kitami,** buses depart twice a day (at last check at 9:30am and 3pm), and the 70-minute trip costs ¥1,800. You must make a reservation for this bus by calling ℂ **0157/23-2181** in Kitami or ℂ **0154/67-2205** in Akanko.

Two Sunrise buses a day depart Sounkyo Onsen for Akanko Onsen (at last check at 9:27am and 4:57pm), with the one-way fare costing ¥3,260 for the 3½-hour trip. Reservations are required; call ℂ **01658/5-3321** in Sounkyo, or 0154/67-2205 in Akan, or drop by the bus terminal in either town. All bus fares are half-price for children.

By Plane Because Akan National Park lies at the eastern extremity of Hokkaido, you may wish to fly at least one-way between here and Tokyo. The closest airport to Akanko Onsen is **Kushiro Airport** (KUH), with the flight from Tokyo taking about 1½ hours and costing ¥39,000 for a regular one-way fare, though tickets purchased 28 days in advance can run as low as ¥13,900 on selected flights. From Kushiro Airport, buses travel to Akanko in about 1 hour and 20 minutes for ¥2,090.

VISITOR INFORMATION **Akanko Onsen's Tourist Association** (ℂ **0154/67-2254;** daily 9am–6pm) is located just a 2-minute walk from the Akanko Onsen bus terminal, in the direction of the lake and on the main street through town. (Turn left out of the bus terminal and take the first right and then the next left; it will soon be on your left next to the post office and across from the New Akan Hotel Shangri-La.) Occasionally there's an English-speaker here, and in any case you can pick up an English-language pamphlet about Akan National Park with a map of the town and two foldouts on hiking. The staff will also make reservations for hotels and *ryokan*. More information is available at **www.lake-akan.com.**

For information on the park and its natural wonders, drop by the **Akankohan Eco Museum Center** (ℂ **0154/67-2785;** Wed–Mon 9am–5pm), located beside the lake about a 7-minute walk from the bus terminal. Displays, in Japanese only, show off native flora and fauna, including the Hokkaido brown bear and sika deer (both stuffed), *marimo* (duckweed), and live freshwater fish such as white-spotted char and kokanee salmon. Admission is free.

GETTING AROUND Akanko Onsen is small, and walking is the best way to get around. It consists primarily of one main street that snakes along the lake, with *ryokan* and souvenir shops lining both sides.

WHAT TO SEE & DO
Seeing the Sights
SIGHTSEEING BUS TOURS OF AKAN NATIONAL PARK If you're not renting a car, the best way to see Akan National Park's most important natural wonders is aboard a sightseeing bus. The **Akan Panorama bus** departs Lake Akan daily February to early October, making stops at several scenic spots along the way, including Mashu and Kussharo lakes. **Mashu,** a crater lake that is considered one of Japan's most beautiful lakes, was called "lake of the devil" by the Ainu because no water flows either into it or out of it. Surely Mashu is one of Japan's least-spoiled lakes: Because of the steep, 200m-high (660-ft.) rock walls ringing it, the lake has remained inaccessible to humans (the bus stops at an observation platform high above the water). **Kussharo** is one of Japan's largest mountain lakes, but what makes it particularly interesting is its hot-spring waters right on the beach; in summer, you can see people digging holes to sit in the hot springs. The bus also stops at the foot of Mount Iou with its sulfurous caldrons and at Bihoro Pass (a scenic overlook) before reaching Bihoro Station north of the park (where you can catch the train to Sapporo). *Note:* Frequent fog often eliminates scenic views, there are tacky souvenir shops at every stop, and tours are in Japanese.

Sightseeing buses, costing ¥3,760 to Bihoro Station, depart Akan at 8 or 9:25am, depending on the season, and arrive at Bihoro Station about 5 hours later (be sure to check departure times beforehand, as bus schedules change throughout the season). You can also do this tour in reverse; called the **Kuroyuri-go** tour, buses depart Bihoro Station at around 10:40am and arrive in Akan at around 4pm (this same bus returns to Bihoro after a 2-hr. stay in Akan). Finally, you can also tour Akan National Park from Kushiro May through October by boarding the **White Pirica** bus outside Kushiro Station at 8:30am, arriving at Akan around 2:10pm (cost of this tour is ¥3,200). Children pay half fare for all tours. For more information, call **Akan Bus Company** at ✆ **0154/37-2221.**

RED-CRESTED CRANES & BUS TOURS OF KUSHIRO MARSHLAND NATIONAL PARK Red-crested cranes, the official birds of Hokkaido, are regarded as both a good omen and a national symbol of Japan. Because they mate for life, they're also considered a symbol for love. Once threatened with extinction, these graceful and beautiful creatures now lead protected lives in and around **Kushiro Marshland National Park (Kushiro Shitsugen),** Japan's largest marshland. If you don't have a car, the best way to see the marshlands and catch a glimpse of the cranes in their natural habitat is via sightseeing bus. Tours are conducted in Japanese only but traverse the marshland and make stops at observatories and Tancho-Tsuru Koen (see below). The **Akan Bus Company** (✆ **0154/37-2221**) offers tours of the marshland that begin and end at Kushiro Station once or twice a day (8:25am and/or 2pm) from May to October; the 4¾-hour tours cost ¥2,870 for adults and ¥1,330 for children. From July to September 20, there's a daily 4¾-hour **bus and train tour** (aboard the Norokko-go steam locomotive), departing Kushiro Station at 8:25am and costing ¥3,500 for adults and ¥1,440 for children. For more information, contact the Kushiro Tourism Association (© **0154/31-1993;** www. kushiro-kankou.or.jp/english).

If you prefer sightseeing on your own, the best place to learn about cranes is at the excellent **Akan Kokusai Tsuru Center (Akan International Crane Center)** ★, 23–40 Akan (© **0154/66-4011;** daily 9am–5pm). In addition to a film showing their beautiful courtship dance and nesting habits, it has fun, interactive displays with lots of English-language explanations. You'll learn just about everything you'd ever want to know about red-crested cranes here, from why they fly to how much an egg weighs. Best of all, however, is adjacent **Tancho-no-Sato,** an excellent observatory on private land where 200 red-crested cranes live, court, and mate November through March. This is a great place to photograph the birds in action, and you'll be surprised at how large they actually are. Admission to both the International Crane Center and Tancho-no-Sato is ¥400 for adults, half-price for children. Plan on staying at least an hour in winter, less in summer when the birds have returned to their native marshlands. The International Crane Center is some 40 minutes from Akanko Onsen by bus; get off at the Tancho-no-Sato stop (fare: ¥1,570). Incidentally, the bus that stops here is the same one that goes from Akanko Onsen to Kushiro Airport and Kushiro Station, so it's possible to stop here, visit, and then catch the next bus (buses are infrequent, however, so get the schedule beforehand).

In summer, your best bet for observing cranes outside the marshland is the **Japanese Crane Reserve (Tancho-Tsuru Koen),** Kushiro-cho (© **0154/56-2219;** daily 9am–6pm, to 4pm in winter), a marshy area set aside in 1958 for breeding and raising cranes. It now has some 20 cranes—some of them second and third generation—living in natural habitats behind high meshed fences. They are fed three times a day, at 9:30am and 1 and 4pm. Admission is ¥400 for adults and ¥100 for children. Also on the way to Kushiro airport and station, it's located 1 hour by bus from the Akanko Onsen bus terminal; get off at the Tsuru-koen stop. If all you want is a quick look, note that one bus a day en route to the airport makes a 15-minute stop at this park, which is enough time to see some of the birds before you continue on.

ATTRACTIONS IN AKANKO ONSEN ★   Although the Ainu originally lived near Kushiro, not Akan, they have built the **Ainu Kotan Village** in Akanko Onsen (© **0154/ 67-2727**) and now number about 130 individuals, making this area Hokkaido's largest Ainu community. Although the Ainu Kotan Village itself is just one street lined with souvenir shops (selling mostly woodcarvings), it leads to a thatched-roof lodge, where you can see Ainu performing traditional dances and playing bamboo mouth harps. This is the most professional Ainu production I've seen, and because the dances aren't the same as those performed at Poroto Kotan in Shiraoi (see "Noboribetsu Spa & Shikotsu-Toya National Park," earlier in this chapter), these are highly recommended even if you've already been to Poroto Kotan. Thirty-minute shows are performed five times a day in summer (including evenings), less frequently in winter. Admission is ¥1,000 for adults, half-price for children. Alongside the performance lodge is the **Seikatsu Kinen Kan** (May–Oct, daily 10am–10pm), an Ainu home and outbuildings that display various Ainu utensils and crafts. Admission here is ¥300 for adults and ¥100 for children (skip it if you've been to Poroto Kotan).

Enjoying the Outdoors

BOATING   For Japanese visitors, one of the most popular activities in Akanko Onsen is a **boat cruise of Lake Akan,** which provides a close-up view of the mountains, islands, and shoreline, all stunningly beautiful. Lake Akan is famous for its very rare spherical green algae, a spongelike ball of duckweed called *marimo* that's been designated a Special Natural Monument. Found in only a few places in the world, marimo is formed when many separate and stringy pieces of algae at the bottom of the 43m-deep (144-ft.) lake roll around and eventually come together to form a ball, gradually growing larger and larger. It takes 150 to 200 years for marimo to grow to the size of a baseball; some in Lake Akan are as much as 29 centimeters (12 in.) in diameter—meaning they are very old indeed. Supposedly, when the sun shines, the marimo rise to the surface of the water, giving Lake Akan a wonderful green shimmer. On the **Marimo Discovery Cruise** you'll make a 15-minute stop at Churui Islet to see the **Marimo Exhibition Center** with a few tanks of marimo. One-hour cruises operate from May to mid-November and cost ¥1,750 for adults and ¥920 for children, including the exhibition center. Boats depart every hour or so, with the last boat departing at 5:30pm in summer. Less frequent is the 45-minute **Akan's Scenic Cruise,** which departs three times a day and travels through more scenic narrow passages between islands and into islets (but not to the Marimo Exhibition Center). This costs ¥1,350 for adults and ¥680 for children. If you want to see both the Marimo Exhibition Center and the narrow passages, there's the 35-minute **High Speed Cruise,** which costs ¥3,500.

I hope you'll boycott the motorboats, which disturb the peace and quiet of this nature's wonderland—but maybe the price alone will deter you: ¥1,000 for 5 minutes.

CANOEING   To get a real feel for Akan Lake at duck and goose level, take a canoe trip in a two-person Canadian canoe, available May to October. For beginners, a 45-minute trip costs ¥2,100 for adults and ¥1,600 for children. There's also a 90-minute Adventure Course for ¥5,300 for adults and ¥3,700 for children that goes farther afield, while the 2½-hour Yaitai island course includes a trip to uninhabited Yaitai island in the lake. You may see carp spawning, deer, or—if you are really lucky—bear. Make canoe reservations at the **Akan Nature Center** (✆ 0154/67-2801), shown on the English-language map.

FISHING ★★   Lake Akan is one of Japan's most famous fishing lakes. In addition to kokanee salmon, said to have originated in the lake, sport fish include rainbow trout, steelhead trout, and white spotted char, a native fish. If you want to fish, contact **Fishing Land** (✆ 0154/67-2057), located beside the New Akan Hotel Shangri-La. A fishing permit costs ¥1,500 per day and includes fishing in Akan River and Hiotan Pond, as well as the lake. A rental rod and lures cost ¥1,000. Add ¥3,000 if you want to be dropped off at a fishing spot by boat. Fly-fishing season is from May to the end of November, except from mid-July to mid-August when it's too hot. From January to March, you can ice fish.

HIKING   Akanko Onsen's easiest walk begins and ends right in town. Start at the **Akankohan Eco Museum Center** at the east end of town, where to the left you'll find an easy, 30-minute footpath leading through a primeval forest of pines and ferns, past *bokke* (volcanic, bubbling mud), and along the lakeshore. It ends at the boat dock with cruises of Lake Akan (see above). If you want to make this an hour's hike, take the steps to the right of the Eco Museum Center leading uphill at the orange *torii* gate to the Inari Shinto Shrine and follow the path through woodlands along a ridge before descending to the lake and joining the path described above. Both paths are shown on the English-language pamphlet describing the Akankohan Eco Museum Center.

For more serious hiking, while out on your boat trip you'll see two cone-shaped volcanoes: **Mount Oakan (Oakandake)** to the east and **Mount Meakan (Meakandake)** to the south. Both are surrounded by virgin forests and are popular daylong destinations for hikers. **Mount Oakan** (called "male mountain" by the Ainu for its supposed manly features) is dormant, with a summit about a 4½-hour hike from Akanko Onsen. You can reach the trail entrance, Takiguchi, in 5 minutes via one of the buses going in the direction of Kushiro (get off at the Takiguchi stop). Plan about 6 hours for the ascent and descent. **Mount Meakan** (which the Ainu called "female mountain") is an active volcano, so check before you go. It's the highest mountain in the Akan area at 1,500m (4,900 ft.) above sea level and is covered with primeval forests of spruce and fir. There are three hiking trails up Mount Meakan. If you're hiking the entire distance, the trail access closest to Akanko is located at the west end of town, where you can follow the Furebetsu Woodland Road, a former transport road, to an old sulfur mine for 3 hours to get to the trail entrance, from which it's another 3 hours to the peak where you'll be rewarded with panoramic views of the surrounding area. Otherwise, there is bus service from Akan Onsen to beautiful Lake Onneto July through September, from which it's about 2½ hours to the summit. Pick up English-language alpine guides with maps to Mount Oakan and Mount Meakan at the tourist association.

A shorter hike follows a trail to **Mount Hakuto-zan,** from which you also have a good view of the town and lake. It takes about 20 minutes to reach Akan's skiing area and another 50 minutes to reach Mount Hakuto-zan observatory, a grassy and moss-covered knobby hill that remains slightly warm throughout the year because of thermal activity just below the surface. The woods of birch and pine here are beautiful, and what's more, you'll probably find yourself all alone. Stop at the local tourist office for directions to the trail head and a map in Japanese.

WINTER ACTIVITIES In winter, Lake Akan freezes over and becomes a playland for winter sports. International marathon ice-skating races—200km (125 miles)—have brought attention to the area's natural riches. **Cross-country skiing** (rental equipment ¥1,000 for 2 hr.), **ice-skating** (¥1,000 for 1 hr.), and **ice fishing** (¥1,500 a day) are popular sports. For downhill skiers, the **Kokusetsu Akan-kohan ski ground** (© 0154/ 67-2881) is blessed with a magnificent view of Mount Oakan rising behind Lake Akan. The F.I.S.-certified slalom course attracts ski teams and individuals in training, while the intermediate and beginner slopes are popular with less demanding skiers. A day pass for lifts costs ¥2,500; ski-rental equipment costs ¥3,000 per day.

In February, illuminated ice sculptures, traditional dance, nightly fireworks over the frozen lake, and stalls selling food make for a fun midwinter festival. Contact the tourist office for more details.

WHERE TO STAY
Expensive

271 **Yuku-no-Sato Tsuruga** ★★★ (Finds Cranes are the main motif throughout, but what makes this hotel a standout are its beautiful and fantasy-provoking hot-spring baths. One is designed as a village, spread on several levels and including a cavelike room and an outdoor bath beautifully landscaped with stones and pines overlooking the lake. The other includes a rooftop hot-spring bath with 360-degree panoramic views. Even if you don't stay here, you can visit the baths from noon to 5pm for ¥1,470.

The rest of the hotel, with natural woods throughout and well-appointed guest rooms, do not disappoint. Most rooms are Japanese style, the best (and most expensive) of which have lakeside views, large bathrooms (some with open-air tubs), bar areas for entertaining, and seating around an indoor hearth. There are also more than 50 combination rooms with *tatami* area and beds.

4–6–10 Akanko Onsen, Akancho, Kushiro-shi 085-0467. ☏ **0154/67-2531.** Fax 0154/67-2754. www. tsuruga-g.com. 233 units. ¥19,950–¥39,375 per person, including 2 meals. Off-season discounts available. AE, DC, MC, V. A 10-min. walk from the bus terminal; turn left out of the terminal, take the 1st right to the main street, and turn left. There are also free shuttle buses operating from Kushiro and Kitami stations (reservations required). **Amenities:** 3 restaurants; bars; lounge; beautiful indoor/outdoor hot-spring baths. *In room:* A/C, TV, hair dryer, Internet, minibar.

Inexpensive

㉒ **Onsen Minshuku Kiri**   Located above a souvenir shop on the main street (look for a wooden, roofed sign with black lettering on white), these simple accommodations include clean Japanese-style rooms and a small cypress hot-spring bath.

4–3–26 Akanko Onsen, Akancho, Kushiro-shi 085-0467. ☏ **0154/67-2755.** Fax 0154/67-2755. 7 units (none with bathroom). ¥3,500 per person. Breakfast from ¥500 extra. AE, MC, V. A 9-min. walk from the bus terminal; turn left out of the terminal, take the 1st right to the main street, and turn left on the main street. **Amenities:** Indoor hot-spring bath. *In room:* TV.

WHERE TO DINE

㉓ **Porono**AINU   For a different kind of lunch, head to the Ainu Kotan Village and look for a souvenir shop called Mingei Kissa with a sign reading HANDMADE FOLKCRAFT AND AINU TRADITIONAL FOOD. In the back you'll find two tables, a counter, and funky decor and music. The menu lists *rataskepu,* a cold vegetable dish with beans, corn, and pumpkin; *pochimo,* a fried potato cake (a bit hard); Ainu curry with venison and local vegetables; pumpkin cakes; and drinks such as *shikerebe* (bark tea). Or order the Ainu *teishoku* set meal (rice with red beans and deer soup last time I was there). I did not love the food, but I found it interesting to eat items gleaned from the natural surroundings.

Ainu Kotan Village, Akanko Onsen. ☏ **0154/67-2159.** Dishes ¥400–¥500; Ainu teishoku ¥850. No credit cards. Daily noon–11pm (noon–9:30pm winter).

HOKKAIDO

15

AKANKO SPA & AKAN NATIONAL PARK

Fast Facts

1 FAST FACTS: JAPAN

AMERICAN EXPRESS There are no American Express customer-service offices in Japan.

AREA CODES All telephone area codes for Japanese cities begin with a zero (03 for Tokyo, 06 for Osaka, 075 for Kyoto), but drop the first zero if calling Japan from abroad.

BUSINESS HOURS Government offices and private companies are generally open Monday through Friday 9am to 5pm. Banks are open Monday through Friday 9am to 3pm (but usually will not exchange money until 10:30 or 11am, after that day's currency exchange rates come in). Neighborhood post offices are open Monday through Friday 9am to 5pm. Major post offices, however (usually located near major train stations), have longer hours and may be open weekends as well. (Some central post offices, such as those in Tokyo and Osaka, are open 24 hr. for mail.)

Department stores are open from about 10am to 8pm. Most are open daily but may close irregularly (always the same day of the week). Smaller stores are generally open from 10am to 8pm, closed 1 day a week. Convenience stores such as 7-Eleven and Family Mart are open 24 hours.

Keep in mind that museums, gardens, and attractions stop selling admission tickets at least 30 minutes before the actual closing time. Similarly, restaurants take their last orders at least 30 minutes before the posted closing time (even earlier for *kaiseki* restaurants). Most national, prefectural, and city museums are closed on Monday; if Monday is a national holiday,

however, they'll remain open and close on the following day, Tuesday, instead. Privately owned museums, however, are usually closed on holidays.

DRINKING LAWS The legal drinking age is 20. Beer, wine, and spirits are readily available in grocery stores, some convenience stores, and liquor stores. Many bars, especially in nightlife districts such as Shinjuku and Roppongi, are open until dawn. If you intend to drive in Japan, you are not allowed even one drink.

DRUGSTOREs Drugstores, called *kusuri-ya,* are found readily in Japan. Note, however, that you cannot have a foreign prescription filled in Japan without first consulting a doctor in Japan, so it's best to bring an adequate supply of important medicines with you. No drugstores in Japan stay open 24 hours. However, ubiquitous convenience stores like 7-Eleven, Lawson, and Family Mart, open day and night throughout Japan, carry such nonprescription items as aspirin.

EARTHQUAKES Kobe's tragic 1995 earthquake brought attention to the fact that Japan is earthquake-prone, but in reality, most earthquakes are too small to detect (of the more than 100,000 earthquakes annually in Japan, only 1% are big enough to feel). However, in case of an earthquake you can feel, there are a few precautions you should take. If you're indoors, take cover under a doorway or against a wall and do not go outdoors. If you're outdoors, stay away from trees, power lines, and the sides of buildings; if you're surrounded by tall buildings, seek cover in a doorway. If you're near a beach or the bay, evacuate to higher ground in case of a tsunami. Never use elevators during a quake. Other precautions include noting emergency exits wherever you stay; all hotels supply flashlights, usually found attached to your bedside table. More information on earthquakes is provided by the Japan Meteorological Agency at www.jma.go.jp.

ELECTRICITY The electricity throughout Japan is 100 volts AC, but there are two different cycles in use. In Tokyo and in regions northeast of the capital, it's 50 cycles, while in Nagoya, Kyoto, Osaka, and all points to the southwest, it's 60 cycles. Leading hotels in Tokyo often have two outlets, one for 100 volts and one for 220 volts; almost all have hair dryers in the rooms. You can use many American appliances in Japan because the American standard is 110 volts and 60 cycles, but they may run a little slowly. Note, too, that the flat, two-legged prongs used in Japan are the same size and fit as in North America, but three-pronged appliances are not accepted.

EMBASSIES & CONSULATES Most embassies are located in Tokyo (see "Fast Facts: Tokyo" in chapter 5). There are, however, U.S., British, New Zealand, and Australian consulates in Osaka (see "Osaka" in chapter 10). For the location of other consulates, inquire at the respective embassies.

EMERGENCIES The national emergency numbers are ℂ **110** for **police** and ℂ **119** for **ambulance** and **fire** (ambulances are free in Japan unless you request a specific hospital). You do not need to insert any money into public telephones to call these numbers. However, if you use a green public telephone, it's necessary to push a red button before dialing. If you call from a gray public telephone or one that accepts only prepaid cards, you won't

see a red button; in that case simply lift the receiver and dial. Be sure to speak slowly and precisely.

HOLIDAYS See "When to Go" in chapter 3.

INTERNET ACCESS See "Staying Connected" in chapter 3.

LANGUAGE English is widely understood in major hotels, restaurants, and shops, but it's hit-or-miss elsewhere. Be sure to pick up the free "Tourist's Language Handbook," at the Tourist Information Center. Also, see "Dealing with the Language Barrier," in chapter 2 and the glossary in chapter 16.

LAUNDRY & DRY CLEANING All upper- and most midrange hotels offer laundry and dry-cleaning services (but it's expensive, with a laundered shirt costing about ¥400). For same-day service, it's usually necessary to turn in your laundry by 10am; many hotels do not offer laundry service on Sundays and holidays. Budget accommodations sometimes have coin-operated machines. Otherwise, coin-laundries (as they're known in Japan) are abundant, and many hotel guest rooms have a pullout laundry line over the tub for hand washables.

LEGAL AID Contact your embassy if you find yourself in legal trouble. The **Legal Counseling Center,** 1–4 Yotsuya, Shinjuku (ℂ **03/5367-5280;** www.horitsu-sodan.jp; station: Yotsuya), is operated by three bar associations and provides legal counseling with English interpreters Monday to Friday from 1 to 4pm.

LOST & FOUND If you've forgotten something on a subway, in a taxi, or on a park bench, don't assume it's gone forever; if you're willing to trace it, you'll probably get it back. If you can remember where you last saw it, the first thing to do is telephone the establishment or return to where you left it, as there's a good chance it will still be sitting there. If you've lost something on the street, go to the nearest *koban* (police box); items found in the neighborhood will stay there for 3 days or longer.

Be sure to notify all your credit card companies the minute you discover your wallet has been lost or stolen. **Visa**'s emergency number in Japan is ℂ **00531/11-15555. American Express** cardholders can call ℂ **03/3220-6220** and for traveler's checks it's ℂ **0120/779-656. MasterCard** holders should call ℂ **00531/11-3886** and **Diners Club** holders should call ℂ **0120/074-024** in Japan.

LUGGAGE & LOCKERS Storage space on Shinkansen bullet trains is limited, so travel with the smallest bag you can get away with. Coin-operated lockers are located at major train stations as well as at most subway stations, but most lockers are generally not large enough to store huge pieces of luggage (and those that do are often taken). Lockers generally cost ¥300 to ¥800 depending on the size. Some major stations also have check-in rooms for luggage, though these are rare. If your bag becomes too much to handle, you can have it sent ahead via *takkyu-bin*, an efficient forwarding service available at upper-range hotels and all convenience stores in Japan. At Narita and Kansai international airports, service counters will send luggage to your hotel the next day (or vice versa) for about ¥2,000 per bag.

MAIL If your hotel cannot mail letters for you, ask the concierge for the location of the nearest post office, recognizable by the red logo of a capital T with a horizontal line over it. Mailboxes are bright orange-red. It costs ¥110 to airmail letters weighing up to 25 grams and ¥70 for postcards to Australia, North America, and Europe. Domestic mail costs ¥80 for letters up to 25 grams, and ¥50 for postcards. Post offices throughout Japan are also convenient for their ATMs, which accept international bank cards operating on the PLUS and Cirrus systems, as well as MasterCard and Visa.

Although all **post offices** are open Monday through Friday from 9am to 5pm, international post offices (often located close to the central train station) have longer hours, often until 7pm or later on weekdays and with open hours also on weekends (in Tokyo and Osaka, counters are open 24 hr.). If your hotel does not have a shipping service, it is only at these larger post offices that you can mail packages abroad. Conveniently, they sell cardboard boxes in several sizes with the necessary tape. Packages sent via surface mail cannot weigh more than 20 kilograms (about 44 lb.) and take about a month to reach North America, with a package weighing 10 kilograms (about 22 lb.) costing ¥6,750. Express packages, which take 3 days to North America and can weigh up to 30 kilograms (66 lb.), cost ¥12,550 for 10 kilograms (22 lb.). For more information, visit **www.post.japanpost.jp**.

MEASUREMENTS Before the metric system came into use in Japan, the country had its own standards for measuring length and weight. Rooms are still measured by the number of *tatami* straw mats that will fit in them. A six-tatami room, for example, is the size of six tatami mats, with a tatami roughly .9m (3 ft.) wide and 1.8m (6 ft.) long.

NEWSPAPERS & MAGAZINES Three English-language newspapers are published daily in Japan: the *Japan Times* and the *Daily Yomiuri* (the former with a weekly supplement from *The Observer* and the latter with a weekly supplement from the *Washington Post*), as well as the *International Herald Tribune/Asahi Shimbun.* Major bookstores carry the international editions of such newsmagazines as *Time* and *Newsweek*. You can also read the *Japan Times* online at www.japantimes.co.jp and the *Daily Yomiuri* at www.yomiuri.co.jp/dy.

PASSPORTS For information on obtaining passports, contact the following agencies:

For Residents of Australia: Contact the **Australian Passport Information Service** at ✆ **131-232,** or visit the government website at www.passports.gov.au.

For Residents of Canada: Contact the central **Passport Office,** Department of Foreign Affairs and International Trade, Ottawa, ON K1A 0G3 (✆ **800/567-6868;** www.ppt.gc.ca).

For Residents of Ireland: Contact the **Passport Office,** Setanta Centre, Molesworth Street, Dublin 2 (✆ **01/671-1633;** www.irlgov.ie/iveagh).

For Residents of New Zealand: Contact the **Passports Office** at ✆ **0800/225-050** in New Zealand or 04/474-8100, or visit www.passports.govt.nz.

For Residents of the United Kingdom: Visit your nearest passport office, major post office, or travel agency or contact the **United Kingdom Passport Service** at ✆ **0870/521-0410** or visit www.ukpa.gov.uk.

For Residents of the United States: To find your regional passport office, check the U.S. State Department website (www.state.gov) or call the **National Passport Information Center** toll-free number (✆ **877/487-2778**) for automated information.

POLICE The national emergency number for police is ✆ **110.**

SMOKING You must be 20 years old to smoke in Japan. Smoking is banned in most public areas, including train and subway stations and office buildings. In many cities, ordinances also ban smoking on sidewalks but allow it in marked areas, usually near train stations. Many restaurants have nonsmoking sections, though bars do not. Most hotels have designated nonsmoking floors nowadays, though Japanese-style inns, because of their small size, usually do not; some business hotels also don't. If you want to sit in the non-smoking car of the Shinkansen bullet train, ask for the *kinensha* (some lines are completely smoke-free); during peak times, be sure to reserve a seat in the non-smoking car in advance.

TAXES A 5% consumption tax is imposed on goods and services in Japan, including hotel rates and restaurant meals. Although hotels and restaurants are required to include the tax in their published rates, a few have yet to comply (especially on English-language menus). In Tokyo, hotels also levy a separate accommodations tax of ¥100 to ¥200 per person per night. In hot-spring resort areas, a ¥150 *onsen* tax is added for every night of your stay.

In addition to these taxes, a 10% to 15% **service charge** will be added to your bill in lieu of tipping at most of the fancier restaurants and at moderately priced and upper-end hotels; in *ryokan,* service charge can be as high as 20%. Business hotels, *minshuku,* youth hostels, and inexpensive restaurants do not impose a service charge.

As for **shopping,** a 5% consumption tax is also included in the price of most goods. (Some of the smaller vendors are not required to levy tax.) Travelers from abroad, however, are eligible for an exemption on goods taken out of the country, although only the larger department stores and specialty shops seem equipped to deal with the procedures. In any case, most department stores grant a refund on the consumption tax only when the total amount of purchases for the day at their store exceeds ¥10,000. You can obtain a refund immediately by having a sales clerk fill out a list of your purchases and then presenting the list to the tax-exemption counter of the department store; *you will need to show your passport.* Note that no refunds for consumption tax are given for food, drinks, tobacco, cosmetics, film, and batteries.

TELEPHONES For information on how to make calls or where to rent mobile phones in Japan, see "Staying Connected" in chapter 3.

TELEVISION If you enjoy watching television, you've come to the wrong country. Almost nothing is broadcast in English; even foreign films are dubbed in Japanese. Most upper-range hotels, however, offer **bilingual televisions,** whereby you can switch from Japanese to English if the program or movie was originally in English, though only a few (and fairly dated) English movies and sitcoms are broadcast each week. The plus of bilingual TVs is that you can listen to the nightly national news broadcast by NHK at 7 and 9pm. Otherwise, major hotels in larger cities have cable or satellite TV with English-language programs including CNN broadcasts (sometimes in Japanese only) and BBC World as well as in-house pay movies. But even if you don't understand Japanese, I suggest that you watch TV at least once; maybe you'll catch a samurai series or a sumo match. Commercials are also worth watching. *Note:* Japan switches from analog to digital broadcasting in July 2011. Many hotels have already replaced older TV sets with new equipment.

A word on those **pay video programs** offered by hotels and many resort *ryokan:* Upper-range hotels usually have a few choices in English, and these are charged automatically to your bill. Most business hotels, however, usually offer only one kind of pay movie—generally "adult entertainment." If you're traveling with children, you'll want to be extremely careful about selecting your TV programs. Many adult video pay channels appear with a simple push of the channel-selector button, and they can be difficult to get rid of. In budget accommodations, you may come across televisions with coin boxes attached to their sides, or, more common nowadays, vending machines offering pre-paid cards. These are also for special adult entertainment videos. Now you know.

TIME Japan is 9 hours ahead of Greenwich Mean Time, 14 hours ahead of New York, 15 hours ahead of Chicago, and 17 hours ahead of Los Angeles. Because Japan does not go on daylight saving time, subtract 1 hour from the above times in the summer when calling from countries that have daylight saving time such as the United States.

Because Japan is on the other side of the international date line, you lose a day when traveling from the United States to Asia. (If you depart the United States on Tues, you'll arrive on Wed.) Returning to North America, however, you gain a day, which means that you arrive on the same day you left. (In fact, it can happen that you arrive in the States at an earlier hour than you departed from Japan.)

TIPPING One of the delights of being in Japan is that there's no tipping—not even to waitresses, taxi drivers, or bellhops. If you try to tip them, they'll probably be confused or embarrassed. Instead, you'll have a 10% to 15% service charge added to your bill at higher-priced accommodations and restaurants. That being said, you might want to tip, say, your room attendant at a high-class *ryokan* if you've made special requests or meals are served in your room; in that case, place crisp, clean bills (¥3,000–¥5,000) in a white envelope on the table of your room at the beginning of your stay; but it's perfectly fine if you choose not to tip.

TOILETS If you need a restroom, your best bets are at train and subway stations (though these can be dirty), big hotels, department stores, and fast-food restaurants. Use of restrooms is free in Japan, and though many public facilities supply toilet paper, it's a good idea to **carry a packet of tissues,** because many others do not.

In parks and some restaurants, especially in rural areas, don't be surprised if you go into some restrooms and find men's urinals and private stalls in the same room. Women are supposed to walk right past the urinals without noticing them.

Many toilets in Japan, especially those at train stations, are **Japanese-style toilets:** They're holes in the ground over which you squat facing forward toward the end with a raised hood. Men stand and aim for the hole. Although Japanese lavatories may seem uncomfortable at first, they're actually more sanitary because no part of your body touches anything.

Western-style toilets in Japan are usually very high-tech. Called **Washlets,** these combination bidet toilets have heated toilet seats, buttons and knobs directing sprays of water of various intensities to various body parts, and even lids that raise when you open the stall. But alas, instructions are usually in Japanese only. Listen to the voice of experience: Don't stand up until you've figured out how to turn the darn spray off.

VISITOR INFORMATION The **Japan National Tourist Organization (JNTO)** publishes a wealth of free, colorful brochures and maps. Be sure to get "The Tourist's Language Handbook," a phrase booklet to help foreign visitors communicate with Japanese. Other useful JNTO publications include the free "Tourist Map of Japan," showing the four major islands and major highway and railway lines, with maps of major cities on the reverse side; a "Directory of Welcome Inns," which lists inexpensive accommodations throughout Japan, with a free reservation system; and the invaluable "Railway Timetable," which contains timetables for Shinkansen trains and major train lines throughout Japan.

JNTO Online: You can reach JNTO via the Internet at **www.jnto.go.jp** (and at **www.japantravelinfo.com** for North American travelers; **www.seejapan.co.uk** for British travelers; and **www.jnto.org.au** for Australian travelers), where you can read up on what's new, view maps, get the latest weather report, find links to online hotel reservation companies and tour companies, and browse through information ranging from hints on budget travel to regional events. JNTO also showcases local's tourism attractions, Japanese cuisine, and other topics on YouTube at www.youtube.com/visitjapan.

JNTO Overseas: If you'd like information on Japan before leaving home, contact one of the following JNTO offices:

In the **United States:** 11 W. 42nd St., 19th floor, New York, NY 10036 (✆ **212/757-5640;** visitjapan@jntonyc.org); and Little Tokyo Plaza 340 E. 2nd St., Ste. 302, Los Angeles, CA 90012 (✆ **213/623-1952;** info@jnto-lax.org).

In **Canada:** 481 University Ave., Ste. 306, Toronto, ON M5G 2E9, Canada (✆ **416/366-7140;** info@jntoyyz.com).

In the **United Kingdom:** Fifth Floor, 12 Nicholas Lane, London EC4N 7BN, England (✆ **020/7398-5678;** info@jnto.co.uk).

In **Australia:** Level 7, 36–38 Clarence St., Sydney NSW 2000, Australia (no phone; travelinfo@jnto.org.au).

JNTO in Japan: Your best bet for general or specific information on Japan is at one of JNTO's three excellent **Tourist Information Centers (TICs).** They're located in downtown Tokyo, at Narita Airport outside Tokyo, and at Kansai International Airport outside Osaka (see chapters 5 and 10 for locations and open hours). All distribute leaflets on destinations throughout Japan and can provide train, bus, and ferry schedules and leaflets on major attractions and sights—for example, Japanese gardens, hot springs, museums, and art galleries. They also carry information on hotels and *ryokan* and will book accommodations for you for free.

Local Information: You'll also find locally run tourist offices in nearly every city and town throughout Japan, most of them conveniently located at or near the main train station. Look for the logo of a red question mark with the word INFORMATION written below. Although the staff at a particular tourist office may not speak English (many do), they can point you in the direction of your hotel, perhaps provide you with an English-language map (usually free), and, in many cases, even make hotel bookings for you. Note, however, that they're not equipped to provide you with information on other regions of Japan (for that, go to a TIC). I've included information on local tourist offices throughout this book (see "Visitor Information," in the regional chapters), including how to reach them after you disembark from the train and their open hours.

WATER The water is safe to drink anywhere in Japan, although some people claim it's too highly chlorinated. Bottled water is also readily available.

WEATHER Everything from daily forecasts to estimated dates for the cherry blossom or rainy season, along with other fun data, is available from the Japan Meteorological Agency at www.jma.go.jp.

2 AIRLINE & HOTEL WEBSITES

AIRLINES

Aeroméxico
www.aeromexico.com

Air Canada
www.aircanada.com

Air France
www.airfrance.com

Air India
www.airindia.com

Air New Zealand
www.airnewzealand.com

Alitalia
www.alitalia.com

American Airlines
www.aa.com

British Airways
www.british-airways.com

Cathay Pacific
www.cathaypacific.com

China Airlines
www.china-airlines.com

Continental Airlines
www.continental.com

Delta Air Lines
www.delta.com

Japan Airlines
www.jal.com

Jetstar Airways
www.jetstar.com

KLM Royal Dutch Airlines
www.klm.com

Korean Air
www.koreanair.com

Lufthansa
www.lufthansa.com

Northwest Airlines
www.nwa.com

Philippine Airlines
www.philippineairlines.com

Qantas Airways
www.qantas.com

Singapore Airlines
www.singaporeair.com

Skymark
www.skymark.co.jp

Skynet Asia Airways
www.skynetasia.co.jp

Swiss Air
www.swiss.com

Thai Airways International
www.thaiair.com

Turkish Airlines
www.thy.com

United Airlines
www.united.com

US Airways
www.usairways.com

Virgin Atlantic Airways
www.virgin-atlantic.com

MAJOR HOTEL CHAINS

Best Western International
www.bestwestern.com

Courtyard by Marriott
www.marriott.com/courtyard

Crowne Plaza Hotels
www.ichotelsgroup.com/crowneplaza

Four Seasons
www.fourseasons.com

Hilton Hotels
www.hilton.com

Holiday Inn
www.holidayinn.com

Hyatt
www.hyatt.com

InterContinental Hotels & Resorts
www.ichotelsgroup.com

Ishin Hotels Group
www.ishinhotels.com

JAL/Nikko
www.jalhotels.com

JR Hotel Group
www.jrhotelgroup.com

Marriott
www.marriott.com

New Otani
www.radisson.com

Prince
www.princejapan.com

Radisson Hotels & Resorts
www.newotani.co.jp

Ritz-Carlton
www.ritzcarlton.com

Sheraton Hotels & Resorts
www.starwoodhotels.com/sheraton

Sunroute
www.sunroute.jp/WelcomeSV

Super Hotel
www.superhotel.co.jp

Toyoko Inn
www.toyoko-inn.com

Tokyu
www.tokyuhotels.japan.com

Washington Hotels
www.wh-rsv.com

Westin Hotels & Resorts
www.starwoodhotels.com/westin

FAST FACTS

16

AIRLINE & HOTEL WEBSITES

17

A Japanese-Character Index of Establishment Names

A JAPANESE-CHARACTER INDEX

17

A Glossary of Useful Japanese Terms

PRONUNCIATION

In pronouncing the following vocabulary, keep in mind that there's very little stress on individual syllables. Here's an approximation of some of the sounds of Japanese:

a   *as in* father

aa *held slightly longer than* a

e   *as in* pen

i   *as in* pick

ii *held slightly longer than* i

o   *as in* oh

oo *held slightly longer than* o

u   *as in* boo

uu *held slightly longer than* u

g   *as in gift at the beginning of words; like* ng *in* sing *in the middle or at the end of words*

Vowel sounds are almost always short unless they are pronounced doubled, in which case you hold the vowel a bit longer. Similarly, double consonants are given more emphasis than only one consonant by itself.

USEFUL WORDS & PHRASES

Basic Terms

Yes   **Hai**

No   **Iie**

Good morning   **Ohayo gozaimasu**

Good afternoon   **Konnichiwa**

Good evening   **Konbanwa**

Good night   **Oyasuminasai**

Hello   **Haro** (or **Konnichiwa**)

How are you?   **Ogenki desu ka?**

How do you do?   **Hajimemashite?**

Goodbye   **Sayonara** (or **Bye-Bye**)

Excuse me/Pardon me/I'm sorry   **Sumimasen**

Please (when offering something)   **Doozo**

Please (when requesting something)   **Kudasai**

Thank you   **Domo arigato**

You're welcome   **Doo-itashimashite**

I'm American   **Amerikajin desu**

I'm Canadian   **Canadajin desu**

I'm English   **Igirisujin desu**

Sorry, I don't speak Japanese   **Sumimasen, Nihongo wa hanasemasen**

Do you understand English?   **Eigo wa wakarimasu ka?**

Where is the toilet?   **Toire wa, doko desu ka?**

My name is . . .   [Your name] **to mooshimasu**

What is your name?   **O-namae wa, nan desu ka?**

What time do you open/close?   **Nanji ni akimasuka? Nanjini shimarimasuka?**

This one   **Kore**

That one   **Are**

Travel Terms

Train station   **Eki**

Airport   **Kuukoo**

Subway   **Chika-tetsu**

Bus   **Basu**

Taxi   **Takushii**

Airplane   **Hikooki**

Train   **Densha**

Ticket   **Kippu**

One-way ticket   **Katamichi-kippu** (or **katamichiken**)

Round-trip ticket   **Oofuku-kippu** (or **oofukuken**)

I would like to buy a ticket.   **Kippu ichimai o kaitai no desu kedo.**

Tourist Information Office   **Kanko annaijo** (or **kanko kyookai**)

Police   **Keisatsu**

Police box   **Koban**

Post office   **Yuubin-kyoku**

I'd like to buy a stamp.   **Kitte o kaitai no desu kedo.**

Bank   **Ginkoo**

Hospital   **Byooin**

Drugstore   **Yakkyoku**

Convenience store   **Konbiniensu stoaa**

Lodging Terms

Hotel   **Hoteru**

Japanese-style inn   **Ryokan**

Japanese-style lodging in a family home   **Minshuku**

Youth hostel   **Yuusu hosuteru**

Cotton kimono   **Yukata**

Room   **Heya**

Do you have a room available?   **Heya ga arimasu ka?**

I'd like a private bathroom.   **Basu toile tsuki no heya o onegaishimasu.**

Dining Terms & Phrases

Restaurant **Resutoran** (serves Western-style food)

Dining hall **Shokudoo** (usually serves Japanese food)

Coffee shop **Kissaten**

Japanese pub **Izakaya** or **Nomiya**

Breakfast **Chooshoku**

Lunch **Ohiru/lanchi**

Dinner **Yuushoku**

Japanese green tea **Ocha**

Black (Indian) tea **Koocha**

Coffee **Koohi**

Water **Mizu**

I would like a fork, please. **Fooku o kudasai.**

I would like a spoon, please. **Supuun o kudasai.**

I would like a knife, please. **Naifu o kudasai.**

Numbers

1	**Ichi**	20	**Nijuu**
2	**Ni**	30	**Sanjuu**
3	**San**	40	**Shijuu** (or **yonjuu**)
4	**Shi**	50	**Gojuu**
5	**Go**	60	**Rokujuu**
6	**Roku**	70	**Nanajuu**
7	**Shichi** (or **nana**)	80	**Hachijuu**
8	**Hachi**	90	**Kyuuju**
9	**Kyuu**	100	**Hyaku**
10	**Juu**	1,000	**Sen**
11	**Juuichi**	10,000	**Ichiman**
12	**Juuni**		

INDEX